Contents

The contents of this publication are believed correct at the time of printing, but the current position may be checked through the AA. While every effort is made to ensure that information appearing in advertisements is correct, no responsibility can be accepted by the AA for inaccuracies.

Produced by the Publications Division of the Automobile Association, Fanum House, Basingstoke, Hampshire RG21 2EA.
Editor: *Patricia Kelly*　　　　　　　　Designer: *Howard Aldridge*
Compiled by: *Publications Research Unit*　　Maps by: *Cartographic Unit*
Advertising: *Peter Whitworth*　Tel Basingstoke 20123
Cover transparencies by courtesy of Picturepoint Ltd.
We acknowledge the kind help of all the tourist offices, boards and departments for the countries covered, who supplied photographs.
Photo-typeset and printed in Great Britain by Petty & Sons Ltd, Leeds.
© The Automobile Association 1978
ISBN 0 09 131981　　　　　　　　　　　　　　　　　　　55615

Fore-warned is fore-armed

Welcome to the 1978 edition of the *AA Guide to Motoring on the Continent* – we hope you will find it both useful and interesting to read, and an important addition to your holiday planning.

A topic covered by many of the leading newspapers this year has been 'overloading the car'. In this introduction we would like to stress the dangers of loading your car to the gunwales.

Obviously, when going on holiday, it is easy to take with you 'everything but the kitchen sink', and consequently to overload your vehicle. This can create safety risks, however, and in most countries committing such an offence can involve on-the-spot fines. It would also be a great inconvenience if your car was stopped because of overloading – you would not be allowed to proceed until the load had been reduced. The maximum loaded weight, and its distribution between front and rear axles is decided by the vehicle manufacturer and if your owner's handbook does not give these facts you should seek the advice of the manufacturer direct. There is a public weighbridge in all districts and when the car is fully loaded (not forgetting the passengers, of course) use this to check that the vehicle is within the limits.

Sensible roof-rack loading is a wise move as it can greatly affect petrol consumption and speed. On an average family saloon, a badly-packed roof-rack can reduce maximum speed by as much as 15mph. Petrol consumption can increase from about 15% at 40mph to as much as 27% at 70mph. This will mean a considerable increase in petrol bills on a long journey where high average speeds can be maintained. On the other hand a well-packed roof-rack will increase consumption by only 12% at 40mph or 15% at 70mph.

Select the cases most suited to the shape and size of the roof-rack, keeping the heaviest items in the boot if possible. Arrange the largest at the bottom and pile the smaller cases in order of size. This provides the smallest frontal area and is the most aerodynamic layout. Having found the most suitable pieces of luggage, there will be even less wind resistance if you cover them. Use a piece of canvas or leathercloth wide enough to cover the sides of the stacked cases and long enough to cover the bottom of the rack and be folded back over the cases on the roof. Lash the cover down tightly with rope or an elastic 'spider'.

After travelling about 10 miles, stop and check the tightness of the securing clamps or ties. The roof-rack will usually have settled under its laden weight and can be tightened down slightly. An unstable roof-rack is a potential danger.

Any warnings relating to Continental touring are worth listening to. As Marcus Jacobson, AA Chief Engineer, discovered to his cost on a recent trip. Having been previously warned of impending bad weather, he chose to ignore the pessimistic forecast and ultimately became trapped in a snowdrift which lifted his car 8ft off the road. Always obtain up-to-the-minute road and weather conditions before you set off on any journey – this way any possible disasters can be avoided.

In fact, the majority of problems that beset tourists can be avoided. Motorists often unwittingly contravene minor motoring regulations, *eg* crossing white lines (Spain); ignoring traffic lights and signs; not wearing seat belts (compulsory in most countries); allowing a child to sit on the front seat; drinking and driving (which incurs heavy penalties), and exceeding speed limits, which all attract on-the-spot fines.

Please turn to the relevant pages within the Guide for further information on each of the above points. With the full facts at your disposal, you will not, hopefully, fall foul of the law abroad. Remember, fore-warned is fore-armed.

Continental motoring – no problem!

by **Marcus Jacobson, AA Chief Engineer.**

Over the years I must have motored about $\frac{1}{4}$ million miles on the Continent, yet I have never tired of it for I continue to discover new and interesting places, routes which I meant to explore but previously missed.

If you have to spend many hours behind the wheel, you might as well make yourself comfortable and gain the maximum enjoyment out of it, rather than clock up miles and speed records. I have recently returned from a 6,500-mile excursion all over Europe in a 'shopping basket on wheels'. Having a small car has its compensations, such as the startled looks of a group of tourists who had freely quenched their thirst with the local vino, when they saw my little Fiesta emerging in a cloud of dust apparently right out of the crater of Vesuvius and charging down the slope straight at them. It is a brake fade test I do not recommend to the layman.

After leaving speed-restricted Britain it may be tempting to let the car zip along at high speed – but fewer and fewer countries will allow you to do that. Even in Germany the police can take a far from lenient view if you recklessly ignore the posted 130km/h (81mph) recommended speed limit on some Autobahnen, thus constituting a 'potential hazard', and woe betide you if you get involved in an accident while speeding.

For quite a few GB-plated vehicles the journey comes to an abrupt halt within the first or last hour on foreign soil. Driving on the 'wrong side of the road' does not come naturally to many, particularly at roundabouts, and you have to allow for the fact that it is customary for cars, trucks or mopeds to suddenly emerge from the right and dart in front of you. You may not approve, and talk about major and minor roads, but it is *their* country after all. The considerable amount of construction work, with inevitable congestion and road re-routing, going on in and around most Continental ports, tends to make a mockery of any tight timetable. So it is as well to relax and allow an extra hour or so at either end of the trip to get used to your vehicle's handling with a full load, the traffic manners of the 'natives' and road repairs and temporary traffic lights as well. 80% of all serious accidents or body-crunching crashes involving GB cars and caravans occur within a radius of about 80km of the port of landing or re-embarkation.

Flashing of headlights can be a polite warning that you are speeding right into a police trap, a not uncommon affair in parts of France. This is usually a fairly painless business involving a substantial on-the-spot fine. The excuse that you thought the 60 signs meant 60mph won't get you anywhere – except into an argument and possibly an additional fine.

Do not be put off if you find that while your map shows a road as the N1 Calais to Paris, signs indicate the D901 instead – it is the same road. With the creation of an extensive network of motorways France has undertaken a regrading of large sections of the old National routes to mere local feeder ones. They can therefore be quite narrow in sections and far removed from the long, straight, fast and almost empty roads of the pioneering days of Continental motoring. Equally surprising can be the fact that large sections of German Autobahnen are just ribbons of tail-to-tail, heavy trucks and tour coaches, jam-packed with private cars on the outer lane. Since heavy trucks are banned from using them on Saturdays and Sundays, and private motorists are anxious to make an early long-weekend start on Friday, avoid getting caught up in a frustrating stop-go rush to beat the clock. You are often much better off on the quite extensive non-motorway network of the Bundesstrassen – the A roads of Germany.

Most Continental countries are active in extending and improving their motorways and principal trunk roads – but few are three-lane in both directions, except when there are crawler lanes for the lumbering trucks with their trailers. Sitting in the fast, outer lane is not to be recommended. It can be quite frightening when someone overtakes you at speed on the allegedly slower lane. If you cause a blockage it is quite legal. So get used to their lane discipline of moving over quickly after overtaking, and always use your mirror. Since motorists are creatures of habit, sticking to familiar routes, it pays to take to the newer and less familiar fast roads or motorways which are running more or less parallel with the old network, but at a distance of 20 to 100 miles from it. Though it may add a bit on total mileage it saves time, temper and above all fuel.

It is tedious to pre-plan everything, as if it were a military exercise. However, it pays to have a last-minute look at those traffic regulations which you are likely to encounter: unfamiliarity with road signs, speed and parking regulations, opening hours of Customs posts, National Public Holidays and Saints' Days, as well as early closing hours, can play havoc with any motoring trip. Not only will shops and banks be closed, but those welcome frontier *bureau de change* offices may be securely barred too.

Changing dollars or sterling, travellers' cheques or notes into foreign currency could involve you in a small, double banking charge carried out by a bank or *bureau de change* in a third country – for they go through the motion of changing it into local currency first and then into the currency you asked for in the first place. But this small loss may be preferable to accepting the terms of an eager 'open-at-all-times' *bureau de change* at some Italian port – for these money-changers frequently make you pay dearly for not studying the banking hours.

I found recently in the border areas of Germany, Holland, Luxembourg, Belgium and France that it is all too easy to be confronted by closed shops and cafés everywhere, depending on the local agreements of traders. Many shops and restaurants were closed on either Monday or Tuesday; Wednesday afternoon was early closing day somewhere else, and to top it all, the French petrol pump attendant five miles from the frontier only accepted French currency. If this sounds unreasonable, you try to obtain goods or service in a provincial town in England, offering Scottish or Irish £ notes, or after hours on an early closing day.

When it comes to maps, the golden rule is to get the most up-to-date ones and forget about those you found useful five years ago. Traffic-free zones, one-way systems, express ways, fly-overs and underpasses seem to sprout vigorously in many European towns, but are none too clearly signposted. Be warned, do not attempt to brave them at peak traffic times. The locals may not be very tolerant of 'imbecile foreigners' trying to find a particular spot or a café on the corner.

Nationalism expresses itself in many ways and is not confined to the Welsh insisting on putting their inscrutable placenames on signposts. One of Europe's main trunk routes, the E5, passes through a politically sensitive zone, so don't be confused when you cross from Germany and are confronted by huge signs to Lüttich. Suddenly all signs to Lüttich will cease, and only signs to Luik will be found. Finally that name will disappear too, and instead you will be given the distance to Liège. Don't worry, you haven't gone off course, all the names are for the same place. Similar confusion occurs on the Italian borders with Switzerland, Austria and France. For good measure you are supposed not only to be literate but also to know several languages as well, for many road signs, whilst basically international, carry a vital message in the national language (in the case of multi-lingual countries, the regionally preferred one).

You sometimes get the impression on French, Italian and Swiss motorways in mountainous areas, that you are about to drive into a mountain that suddenly looms ahead. Instead, you find yourself driving along a tunnel motorway. These can have a marked rise and fall plus a few fast long bends. Overtaking inside them is quite common and encouraged to speed traffic along, so lane discipline is vital. Likewise one must be prepared for dramatic and irritating changes in light intensity. While the tunnels may be fairly well lit for night conditions, there is such a contrast between the long, dim caverns and the brilliant outside, particularly when mountain slopes are covered by snow, that photochromatic-type sunglasses cannot adjust quickly enough to allow drivers to see far ahead. Quite a few serious accidents occur annually when unsuspecting foreigners pile their cars into guard rails, which are found on the sweeping bends leading into or out of a rapid succession of tunnels.

Customs posts are not always manned – nor always open. Some countries take drastic steps against night-time 'freebooting'. When it gets dark the single stout pole comes down. On a recent trip I arrived at a Customs post to find the pole padlocked in position and the guardian of the key nowhere to be found. The Ardennes have a number of such local crossings, for it is quite easy to follow country roads which wind their way in and out of France, Belgium and Luxembourg. This situation of ill-defined borders, ideal for a bit of smuggling, promotes occasional attempts by the authorities to curb it. My car was recently checked three times by German frontier police, for I crossed in all innocence close to a spot where they had had a shoot-out with a terrorist gang 24 hours previously.

The Continent is riddled with automatic barrier level crossings – and they still have a variety of trains using them at odd times. There are quite a few single pole barriers to be found on other routes as well. They bar access to private roads, military training areas, swamps and forests. Just as we have our Irish border problems, so there are the lonelier stretches of the old Basque areas of the Pyrenees and the Italian-Austrian border zones of South Tirol that are best avoided at night, for they can have their own terrorist and sabotage problems.

In Austria and Switzerland the local gendarmes lower single pole barriers on mountain routes when there is likely to be an avalanche, deep snow drift, rock slide or similar risk. It is foolhardy to try to wriggle your car past the poles. There is nothing for it but to turn around and try another route. From about March to May the Alps can turn nasty very quickly and engulf the unwary traveller. Huge snow masses may be poised to rush down with the speed of an express train. It always pays to ask the local police for the latest road and weather information both sides of a pass. Ignoring their pessimistic forecast, I once found my car and occupants being lifted 8ft off the road by a mild snowslide. I had to dig away the snow with numbed hands to get a proper hold for the tyres, fearful of a cracking exhaust setting off *another* snowslide.

Don't be fooled by all those glossy posters. In Alpine countries you can get both brilliant sunshine and lovely white snowscapes but around Eastertime you are as likely to get a fair bit of poor visibility, fog, hail, and snow turning into sleet and rain. Such conditions call for extra care, for the roads will be near freezing, at least on the shaded sections of hairpin bends. There is only one way to tackle such routes — gentle throttle in 2nd gear (or first if they are steep) and the minimum of abrupt steering correction or brake application.

The friendly advice to lower tyre pressures to get a better grip in soft snow or on a sandy beach is not only outdated — it is *wrong*. On modern radial tyres an increase of about 20% will minimise tread blocking tendencies. Check tyres before you set off, and since you are likely to want to do a bit of fast, long-distance motoring, increase tyre pressure to the handbook setting for high-speed motoring with a full load.

There are three basic rules which I found helpful:

1 Make sure your car has had its check and major service a week before you set out. Having the car properly serviced is always a good idea, for the facilities for having it done abroad are limited and usually two or three times as expensive as back home.

When one trundles along the principal holiday routes and finds a bonnet-up car, it is odds on that it will be a UK-registered one. Continentals seem to have learned that it rarely pays to skimp on maintenance if you want to cover long distances.

2 Have a good look round the tyres and check tyre pressures. If they tend to lose a little air in the course of a few days, get a tyre specialist firm or garage to take them off the rim, fit a new valve, permanently repair the slow puncture or replace them if they are down to 2mm depth of tread.

3 Stow luggage securely and arrange it so that the emergency triangle, torch, spares and overnight bags are within easy reach.

There are ways to economise and make up for the slightly higher cost of fuel — quite apart from buying the special Italian petrol coupons at the frontier for foreign currency, or preferably for £ sterling in England. For instance, resist the temptation to speed and check whether using a motorway is necessary. Many motorways on the Continent are toll roads and tolls are substantial. In Italy you are supposed to get a concessionary rate on several of them, if you have a non-Italian registration number plate — but many of the toll booth operators conveniently forget to give you that privilege.

It would be easy to fill a page or two with names and addresses of hotels and restaurants which I found good value — though not necessarily cheap. I'll mention a few which I have found outstanding in their respective class and country.

In Spain there is a state-run *parador* not far from Bilbao, overlooking the Basque countryside, where they serve superb meals in flamboyant Spanish style and make one feel like a count. The Palacia de Setais in Sintra, the old capital of the Moors, in Portugal, offered seafood and wine to tempt the most discerning palate; in Clères, near Rouen, I treated myself to traditional French cuisine and also visited the local motor museum, and saw a fine collection of wildfowl in the grounds of the Châteaux opposite.

Italian cooking can be as predictably uniform as a selection from any Chinese restaurant menu but I enjoyed the local flavour of the small restaurants in the old towns of Bergamo and St Mignano which do not display the fixed price tourist menu.

The Belgians are especially fond of their stomachs and many *auberges* in the Ardennes can provide a spread befitting any gourmet.

In Gröningen I saw a delightful wedding procession of horse-drawn carriages from the steps of one of the town square restaurants, whilst tucking into a solid Dutch meal; in the Fränkischer Hof Hotel in Dinkelsbühl the night-watchman greeted me with a blast of his postillion's horn and a medieval ditty. He was in good tune and the local wine and roe deer steak were excellent.

But for oldtime charm nothing can surpass the Hotel Schupfen am Rhein, Diessenhofen, near Schaffhausen with its 16th-century four-poster beds and excellent river fishing.

The places I most enjoyed are undiscovered, as yet, little fishing hamlets which are blessed by steep, badly surfaced, access roads. They are a rarity along the Mediterranean shores. The placenames? I am keeping them to myself, for I want to return before the locals discover that fishing is less profitable than catering for mass tourism.

'Self-help' or plain pilfering is not uncommon in Italy from about Rome southwards and in central Milan (that nightmare of one-way streets, trams and roadworks); car radios and cameras are the major targets.

While in Switzerland it is generally safe to leave the car unattended overnight in sleepy streets, I would not recommend doing so in many capital cities, nor in England for that matter. On one of Italy's busiest Autostrada the manager of a motel near Naples insisted on my taking every movable article out of the car before I had a meal and sent a porter to help me perform the tedious but essential task.

Italy recently introduced stringent currency control regulations. When they are being enforced they can delay you considerably at frontier check points. It is not unusual for those who plan to take in the southern slopes of the Alps to find themselves crossing backwards and forwards in and out of Italian enclaves, so be prepared for delays.

You may find too, that here the Swiss Customs men, like their Italian counterparts, speak one language only — Italian. Many Swiss are far from multi-lingual, particularly so in French or Italian-speaking cantons. In many parts of the Continent, especially in Italy and Spain, the locals do not speak anything but their own language, so do not expect too much by way of being given directions or helpful advice.

Some local advice is best ignored altogether. Foreigners are fair game so don't be tempted by the man who knows just where to get a real bargain, whether it be a Swiss watch, a brooch, a coral necklace, or a piece of antique furniture. Italy and Portugal have many local workshops producing deceptively genuine-looking articles and the squares of main cities are plagued with the hard-luck merchant who is looking for a sucker — *you*. Not far from Pompeii I was offered such 'genuine' antiques. A flashlight revealed their true origin — a half-obliterated consignment number.

If it is sea, sun and beach you want, make sure that motorway traffic and express trains do not roar past your site, for this added 'attraction' is a quite common and little advertised feature of some Italian and French campsites. If it is medieval or historical places, or French châteaux, that interest you, why go for the ones in which camera-happy tourist parties almost fall over one another? Just as there is more to England than the Tower of London and Windsor Castle, so you'll find all over the Continent little gems to take in at your leisure, rather than merely filing past 'Crown Jewels' in bullet-proof glass cages. There are still a fair number of sights which the tour operators' coaches have missed!

IN ADVANCE...

Accommodation

Hotels and motels   The lists of hotels and motels for each country have been compiled from information given by members, by the motoring organisations and tourist offices of the countries concerned, and from many other sources. The establishments shown in italics indicate that particulars have not been confirmed by the management.

Your comments concerning the whole range of hotel information — whether included in this Guide or not, and whether in praise or in criticism — will always be most welcome; a special form will be found on page 350, and all such information will be treated in the strictest confidence.

Complaints   *You are advised to bring any criticism to the notice of the hotel management immediately. This will enable the matter to be dealt with promptly to the advantage of all concerned.* If a personal approach fails, members should inform the AA. You are asked to state whether or not your name may be disclosed in any enquiries we may make.

Classification   Although the system of classification on the Continent is similar to the AA system in this country, the variations in the traditions and customs of hotel-keeping abroad often made identical grading difficult.

Hotels and motels are classified by stars. The definitions are intended to indicate the type of hotel rather than the degree of merit. Meals, service, and hours of service should be in keeping with the classification, and all establishments with restaurants must serve meals to non-residents and are expected to give good value for money.

★ Hotels simply furnished but clean and well kept; all bedrooms with hot and cold running water; adequate bath and lavatory facilities.
★★ Hotels offering a higher standard of accommodation; adequate bath and lavatory facilities on all main floors and some private bathrooms and/or showers.
★★★ Well-appointed hotels; at least 40 per cent of bedrooms with private bathrooms and bidets.
★★★★ Exceptionally well-appointed hotels offering a very high standard of comfort and cuisine, room and night service; at least 80 per cent of bedrooms with private bathrooms; suites available on request.
★★★★★ Luxury hotels offering the highest standard of accommodation, service, and comfort.

Motels, etc   Motels, motor hotels and some purpose-built hotels are indicated by white stars *(eg ☆☆)*.

These establishments conform to the major requirements of their star classification but their facilities are designed to cater particularly for overnight stays. In some cases, porterage and room service may be rather restricted for the classification but this is offset by studio-type bedrooms, a higher proportion of private bathrooms to bedrooms, extended meal hours, and more parking space.

A list of motels, published by the European Motel Federation, is obtainable by AA members from Hotel and Information Services, AA, Basingstoke, Hants RG21 2EA.

Charges   The two charges shown against B are the minimum for a single room and the maximum for a double, including breakfast. The figures against Pn are the minimum and maximum charges for full board, per person, per day. **Pn** indicates that full board terms only are available. LD in the gazetteer indicates that *demi-pension* terms only are available — which means that in addition to the charge for rooms, guests are expected to pay for one main meal whether it is taken or not.

Hotels are not required by law to exchange travellers' cheques for guests, and many small hotels are unable to do so. You must expect to pay a higher rate of commission for this service at a hotel than you would at a bank.

Every effort is made to get up-to-the-minute prices, but tariffs may be increased due to changes in taxes or economic circumstances and during public holidays, festivals, etc. You are advised to confirm prices when making reservations.

Reservations   The practice is the same on the Continent as it is in this country; rooms are booked subject to their still being available when confirmation is received. It is therefore most important that confirmation should be sent to the hotel as soon as possible after the rooms have been offered. Unfortunately, many hotels will not accept bookings for one or two nights only. Sometimes a deposit is required which can be arranged through your bank. Many hotels do not hold reservations after 19.00hrs, and you should advise hotels if you anticipate a late arrival or if you are unable to take up your booking for any reason. Unwanted rooms can then often be relet and you will be saved the expense of paying for them, as a confirmed booking represents a legal contract.

Hotel telephone numbers are given in the gazetteer.

The AA regrets that it cannot make reservations on your behalf, except in conjunction with one of the holiday schemes, details of which are available from any AA travel agency.

When writing direct, it is advisable to enclose an international reply coupon; these are available from any post office.

When reservations are made on the spot, it is the custom on the Continent to inspect the rooms offered and to ask for the price before accepting them. No embarrassment is caused by this practice, and British visitors are urged to adopt it in their own interests.

Double rooms may not be reduced in price when let to one person; however, a double room is generally cheaper than two single rooms. Accommodation in an annexe may be of a different standard from rooms in the main hotel building; it is advisable to check the exact nature of the accommodation at the time of reservation.

AA signs   The AA issues signs on request to hotels listed in this Guide. You are advised, however, not to rely solely on the sign, but to check that the establishment still appears in this edition.

Villas and chalets   Full details of this AA service can be obtained from any AA travel agency.

Camping and caravanning   Information is given separately in the AA *Guide to Camping and Caravanning on the Continent.*

Currency

As all countries (including the United Kingdom) have regulations controlling the import and export of currency, you are advised to consult your bank for full information before making final arrangements.

Documents required

You should ensure that any documents you are carrying are secure, but readily available if demanded. Amongst these would be your passport, driving licence, and registration and insurance papers. Inconvenience is caused if any of these are lost or not immediately available for inspection.

European Economic Community regulations   For vehicles equipped to carry ten or more passengers, including the driver (these include minibuses which are classed as coaches), there are regulations which require a special record of man-hours to be maintained, and which lay down the minimum age for driving such vehicles. At the time of going to press these regulations are being reviewed and if you plan to tour with a vehicle in the category described you should contact the nearest Traffic Area Office of the Department of Transport or, if in Northern Ireland, the Ministry of Development, Belfast.

International Driving Permit (IDP)   This document allows any person of 18 years of age or over, and who holds a valid United Kingdom or Republic of Ireland driving licence (not provisional), to drive in countries where the national licence is not acceptable.

The AA is empowered to issue these documents on behalf of Goverment departments in the United Kingdom and Ireland. For licences issued outside the British Isles, you should apply to a motoring organisation – or if there is none, to the licensing authority – in the country where the national licence was issued.

When applying for an International Driving Permit a photograph of passport size will be required before issue. Of the countries in the Guide the following require an IDP: *Spain; Austria* – for holders of Irish Republic licences only.

National driving licence Providing that you are over the minimum age limit, you may drive in all the countries covered by this Guide – except those listed above – on a valid British driving licence (not provisional).

Italy The licence must be supported by an official translation which is available from the AA.

Austria It is advisable that a German translation of the British driving licence should also be carried and this is available from any frontier office or office of the Austrian motoring club (ÖAMTC).

The recommendations of a new International Convention on Road Traffic may have some effect on the recognition of national driving licences but at the time of going to press it was not possible to state the full effect of any new regulations. However, the AA will give publicity to any changes should they arise.

Insurance With the exception of Portugal, motor insurance is compulsory by law in all the countries covered in this Guide, but you are strongly advised to ensure that you are adequately covered for all countries in which you will travel. It is best to seek the advice of your insurance company regarding the extent of cover and full terms of your existing policy. Not all insurers will be willing to offer cover in the countries that you intend to visit and it may be necessary to seek a new, special policy for the trip from another company. Should you have any difficulty, AA Insurance Services will be pleased to help you.

An International Green Card of Insurance is recognised in most countries as evidence that you are covered to the minimum extent demanded by law. It will be issued by your own insurers but since its provisions are an extension to an existing policy, an additional premium will be charged. It will name all the countries for which it is valid and should be specially endorsed for a caravan or trailer if one is to be towed. The document will not be accepted until you have signed it.

Green Cards and the Common Market (EEC) In accordance with a Common Market Directive, the production and inspection of Green Cards at the frontiers of Common Market countries is no longer a legal requirement and the principle has been accepted by other European countries who are not members of the EEC. The Community countries concerned are Belgium, Denmark, France, West Germany, Republic of Ireland, Luxembourg, and the Netherlands. The non-EEC countries also subscribing to the Directive are Austria, Czechoslovakia, the German Democratic Republic, Finland, Hungary, Norway, Sweden and Switzerland. Italy, although a member of the EEC, prefers tourists to be able to produce a Green Card if required. You are advised to consult your insurer regarding this matter.

The fact that Green Cards will not be inspected does not remove the necessity of having insurance cover as required by law in the countries concerned. All private car policies issued by British insurance companies should now provide cover for the minimum legal requirement in the countries mentioned. This does not mean that the full extent of your cover at home is automatically extended, however, and in some circumstances you may find yourself without adequate cover. You are therefore strongly advised to contact your insurers in good time prior to any trip abroad to ensure that the cover you have is satisfactory.

The fact that Green Cards are not legally required in EEC countries or those listed above, and that they may not be inspected at the frontiers of those countries, does not mean that they have been abolished altogether. They will still be required for other countries in Europe (*eg* Spain) and for such countries as Turkey, Israel, Morocco and Tunisia. In addition, they may prove more effectively than an Insurance Certificate that the minimum insurance requirements operative in the country visited have been met. They are internationally recognised by police and other authorities and may save a great deal of inconvenience in the case of an accident.

Spain Extra insurance is recommended in the form of a Bail Bond (see Insurance in the country section).

Nationality plate A nationality plate of the approved pattern, oval with black letters on a white background, and size (GB at least 6.9in by 4.5in), must be displayed on a vertical or near vertical surface at the rear of your vehicle (and caravan or trailer if you are towing one). On the Continent checks are made to ensure that a vehicle's nationality plate is in order. In some countries fines are imposed for failing to display a nationality plate, or for not displaying the correct nationality plate. Up to two (British or Irish) are issued free to anyone who takes AA *5-Star Vehicle Security*. A list of international distinguishing signs appears on pages 23 and 24.

Passports and visas

Every person in the vehicle must hold an up-to-date passport valid for all countries through which it is intended to travel.

There are various types of passport, including a limited British visitor's passport available from main post offices, depending upon the user's requirements. Further information can be obtained from any of the passport offices listed below. Applications in the United Kingdom should be made to your nearest passport office allowing four weeks for passport formalities to be completed and should be accompanied by two identical passport photographs.

Channel Islands

Guernsey	White Rock, St Peter Port
Jersey	Victoria Chambers, St Helier

England

Liverpool	Passport Office, 5th Floor, India Buildings, Water Street, L2 0QZ, *tel* 051-227 3461
London	Passport Office, Clive House, 70 Petty France, SW1H 9HD *tel* 01-222 8010
Peterborough	Passport Office, 55 Westfield Road, PE3 6TG *tel* 0733 263636

Isle of Man

Isle of Man	Government Office, Douglas

Northern Ireland

Belfast 1	F & C Office, Passport Agency, Marlborough House, 30 Victoria Street, BT1 3LY *tel* 32371

Scotland

Glasgow	Passport Office, 1st Floor, Empire House, 131 West Nile Street, G1 2RY *tel* 041-332 0271

Wales

Newport	Passport Office, Olympia House, Upper Dock Street, NPT 1XA, Gwent (Mon) *tel* 0633 52431

Irish Passport

Irish citizens resident in the Dublin Metropolitan Area or in Northern Ireland should apply direct to the Passport Office, 39 Dawson Street, Dublin 2. If resident elsewhere in Ireland, application should be made through the nearest Garda Station. Irish citizens resident in Britain should apply to the Irish Embassy, 17 Grosvenor Place, London SW1X 7HR.

Visas

Holders of a British passport bearing on the cover the name of a colony, protectorate, trust territory, or showing the national status as 'British Protected Person' should consult the embassy or consulate of the countries to be visited.

Vehicle Registration Document

The vehicle registration document of the car should be carried and should show that the vehicle is registered in your name. If the document cannot be carried or is not in your name, contact either the AA or the Department of Transport.

Temporary Importation

A motor vehicle, caravan, boat, or any other type of trailer is subject to strict control on entering a country and attracts Customs duty and a variety of taxes, but much depends upon the circumstances and the period of the import and also upon the status of the importer. A person entering a country in which he has no residence, with a private vehicle for holiday or recreation purposes and intending to export the vehicle within a short period enjoys special privileges and the normal formalities are reduced to an absolute minimum in the interests of tourism. Importers of any type of commercial vehicle or one to be used to support commercial enterprises do not have the same tolerance.

A person entering a country with a motor vehicle for a period of generally more than three months or to take up residence, employment, or with the intention of disposing of the vehicle should seek advice concerning his position well in advance of his departure. Any AA service centre will be pleased to help.

A temporarily imported vehicle should not:
    be left in the country after the importer has left;
    be put at the disposal of a resident of the country;
    be retained in the country longer than the permitted period;
    be lent, sold, hired, given away, exchanged or otherwise disposed of.

A bona fide tourist will generally be allowed to import anything considered in use or in keeping with his status, but such articles, where not consumable, must be exported when the importer leaves the country. In the case of some portable items of high value *ie* a portable television set, the Customs may make a note in the importer's passport and in his own interest he should ensure the entry is cancelled when exporting the item.

Carnet de Passages en Douane This is a valuable document which enables a motorist to temporarily import certain vehicles into another country without having to deposit duty. The cost of this document, which can be issued by the AA, depends on the number of countries to be visited which require a *Carnet de Passages en Douane.* Generally the document is not required for motor vehicles temporarily imported into European countries for periods not exceeding six months by bona fide tourists. Any other category of person should refer to the AA to ascertain if a Carnet can be issued.

Belgium a Carnet is required for towed pleasure craft over 18ft (5.5 metres) long, motor boats, and outboard motors without boats.

France a Carnet is required for outboard engines exceeding 92cc (5cv as applied to marine engines) with or without boats.

Luxembourg a Carnet is required for all towed pleasure craft.

If you are issued with a *Carnet de Passages en Douane,* you must ensure that it is properly discharged as you cross each frontier in order to avoid inconvenience and expense, possibly including payment of Customs charges, at a later date.

Medical treatment

The National Health Service is available in the United Kingdom only and medical expenses incurred overseas cannot be reimbursed by the United Kingdom Government. However, there are reciprocal health agreements with some of the countries covered by this Guide (see below).

You are strongly advised to take out comprehensive and adequate insurance cover before leaving the United Kingdom. AA members should see the AA brochure *5-Star Travel* for details of medical benefits available under Personal Security.

Reciprocal Health Agreements If you are visiting any of the European Community countries, the EEC Social Security Regulations will probably entitle you to receive treatment on the same basis as insured people in that country. However, not everyone is covered. A Form E111, certificate of entitlement, is usually required in order to benefit from these arrangements. Further details and the application form for Form E111 are contained in leaflet SA28. Leaflet SA30 lists all of the countries, in addition to the EEC countries, with which the UK has health agreements and states what documents must be carried in order to receive urgent medical treatment free or at a reduced cost. Leaflets SA28 and SA30 are available from local offices of the Department of Health and Social Security or from travel agents.

Further information about health care arrangements overseas is obtainable from the Department of Health and Social Security, Alexander Fleming House, Elephant and Castle, London SE1 6BY, *tel* 01-407 5522 ext 6641 (non-EEC countries), ext 6681 (EEC countries).

Vaccination requirements and medical advice for travel abroad Guidance about international vaccination requirements and other medical advice is given in the leaflet *Notice to Travellers* obtainable from the Department of Health and Social Security at the above address and telephone number, ext 6749/6711.

Preparing your vehicle for a holiday abroad

We know as well as anyone how expensive mechanical repairs and replacement parts can be on the Continent. A vast number of the breakdowns we have dealt with have occurred simply because people did not take enough trouble to prepare their cars before setting off. Remember that a holiday abroad is not just another day trip, but often involves many miles of hard driving over roads completely new to you, perhaps without the facilities you have come to take for granted in this country. Many people think that it can never happen to them — it can and will if the car is not properly prepared or if it is overloaded.

We recommend that a major service be carried out shortly before your holiday or tour abroad. In addition it is advisable to have a general check of the car to see that there are no other visible or audible defects. It is impracticable for us to provide you with an itemised check list in view of the differences that exist between the various makes and types of car but using the manufacturer's handbook for your particular car, it should be possible to ensure that no obvious faults are missed. If AA members would like a thorough check of their car made by one of the AA's experienced engineers, any service centre can arrange this at a few days' notice. Our engineer will then submit a written report complete with a list of the repairs required. There is a fee for this service; for more detailed information please ask for our leaflet *Tech 8.*

The following tips should prove useful:

Tyres   Inspect your tyres carefully; if you think they are likely to be more than three-quarters worn before you get back, it is better to replace them before you start out. Expert advice should be sought, if you notice uneven wear, scuffed treads, or damaged walls, on whether the tyres are suitable for further use. In some Continental countries, drivers can be fined if tyres are badly worn.

When checking tyre pressures, remember that if the car is heavily loaded the recommended pressures may have to be raised a few pounds per square inch above normal. This should also be done for high-speed driving. Check the recommendations in your handbook. Don't check the pressure immediately after a run, as the tyres will still be hot and pressure will have increased quite a lot, even after a short trip. Don't forget about your spare. Many unfortunates know how embarrassing it is to have a blowout miles from anywhere, only to find that the spare, which they last pumped up a year ago, is flat!

Tubeless tyres   In some countries, tubeless tyres are not in general use. It is a good idea to take an inner tube of the correct size and type so that this can be fitted if all else fails. When the tube is inserted it is advisable to put this wheel on the rear axle, in case a blowout should occur. Moderate speeds only should be used until the tyre has been properly repaired.

Warm–climate touring   In hot weather and at high altitudes, excessive heat in the engine compartment can cause carburation problems. It is advisable, if you are towing a caravan, to consult the manufacturers about the limitations of the cooling system, and the operating temperature of the gearbox fluid if automatic transmission is fitted.

Cold–weather touring   If you are planning a winter tour to the Continent, make sure that you fit a high-temperature (winter) thermostat and make sure that the strength of your anti-freeze mixture is correct for the low temperatures likely to be encountered.

If you are likely to be passing through snow-bound regions, it is important to remember that for many resorts and passes the authorities insist on wheel chains, spiked or studded tyres, or snow tyres. In some countries, such as Austria and Germany, however, the use of spiked or studded tyres is banned. See Road and winter conditions page 40.

Note: The above comments do not apply where severe winter conditions prevail. It is doubtful whether the cost of preparing a car, normally used in the UK, would be justified for a short period. However, the AA's Technical Services Department will be pleased to advise on specific enquiries.

Brakes   The brakes are one of the really vital parts of the car and yet they are very often neglected. Like other mechanical parts, brakes become worn with use and unless they are regularly checked and maintained, worn linings and pads, or hydraulic fluid leaking from faulty cylinders or perished hoses could prove lethal.

If you are about to start a long Continental trip and the brake linings of your vehicle are more than half worn, it is in your interests – and other people's – to change them before you leave. It is also advisable to have your brake fluid changed if it is more than two years old. Fluid that has absorbed moisture can lead to brake failure in arduous conditions, such as descending long mountain passes.

Engine and mechanical   Consult your vehicle handbook for servicing intervals. Unless the engine oil has been changed recently, drain and refill with fresh oil and fit a new filter. Deal with any significant leaks by tightening up loose nuts and bolts and renewing faulty joints or seals.

If you suspect that there is anything wrong with the engine, however insignificant it may seem, it should be dealt with straight away. Even if everything seems in order, don't neglect such commonsense precautions as checking valve clearances, sparking plugs, and contact breaker points, and make sure that the distributor cap is sound. The fan belt should be checked for fraying and slackness. If any of the items mentioned previously are showing signs of wear but are still serviceable, it is a good idea to replace them and take the displaced parts with you as spares.

Any obvious mechanical defects should be attended to at once. Look particularly for play in steering connections and wheel bearings and, where applicable, ensure that they are adequately greased. A car that has covered a high mileage will have absorbed a certain amount of dirt into the fuel system and as breakdowns are often caused by dirt, it is essential that all filters (petrol and air) should be cleaned.

The cooling system should be checked for leaks and any perished hoses or suspect parts replaced.

"Parlez~vous Lucas?"

Motoring on the continent, you may find other problems besides language. To make sure your holiday remains enjoyable, Lucas Service has established a European network of 2,500 distributors and sub-distributors who will be pleased to help you on any electrical service you may need. Simply ring any main Lucas Service distributor and he will direct you to the nearest sub-distributor who will give you prompt and courteous attention.

Before you leave the U.K., write for a full list of Lucas Service distributors in continental Europe.

Address your letter to:

Miss M. King
Lucas Service Overseas Limited
Windmill Road, Haddenham   Aylesbury Bucks HP17 8JB

Lucas Service

Electrical Don't begin a journey without first making a check of the electrics. This applies particularly if the car is not so new and perhaps a light or a switch is not working. Any malfunction can very easily go unnoticed until the battery is run flat or even a fire occurs, so it is very important to trace any small fault.

Check that all the connections are sound and that the wiring is in good condition. Should any problems arise with the charging system, it is essential to obtain the services of a qualified auto-electrician.

Lighting adjustments Left dipping headlights are not permitted. However, there are several adaptors which can be used, but owing to the variety both of bulbs and headlamps, manufacturers should be consulted for the best method of adapting either of these for Continental use. In France, yellow headlights are used.

Remember to have the lamps set to compensate for the load being carried.

Spares The problem of what spares to carry is a difficult one; it depends on how long you are likely to be away. It is possible to hire an AA Spares Kit; full information about this service is available from any AA service centre.

In addition to the items contained in the spares kit, the following would also prove useful:
a pair of windscreen wiper blades;
a length of electrical cable;
an inner tube of the correct type;
a roll of insulating or adhesive tape.

a torch;
a fire extinguisher;
a tow rope;

It is compulsory in some countries to carry a set of spare bulbs. Remember that when ordering spare parts for dispatch abroad you must be able to identify them as clearly as possible and by the manufacturer's part numbers if known. When ordering spares, always quote the engine and chassis numbers of your car.

General Make sure that you have clear all-round vision. See that your seat belts are securely mounted and not damaged, and remember that in most Continental countries their use is compulsory.

If you are carrying skis, remember that they should point to the rear. You must be sure that your vehicle complies with the regulations concerning dimensions for all the countries you intend to pass through (see country sections). This is particularly necessary if you are towing a trailer of any sort. If you are planning to tow a caravan, you will find advice and information in the AA's *Guide to Camping and Caravanning on the Continent.*

Mileages The following is a list of mileages to selected points on the Continent from representative Belgian and French ports. This is **not** intended to be a complete mileage chart.

	OSTEND	DIEPPE	CALAIS	LE HAVRE			OSTEND	DIEPPE	CALAIS	LE HAVRE
AMSTERDAM	172	297	223	364		LISBON	1299	1170	1296	1157
AVIGNON	612	543	609	548		LYON	472	403	469	408
BARCELONA	869	800	865	805		MADRID	975	846	972	833
BASLE	433	492	480	434		MARSEILLE	667	598	664	603
BERLIN	523	648	574	705		MILAN	668	639	700	644
BILBAO	742	613	738	600		NAPLES	1159	1129	1184	1134
BORDEAUX	540	491	535	398		NICE	764	696	761	701
BRUSSELS	71	195	122	244		PARIS	185	120	182	125
COLOGNE	202	306	253	355		ROME	1028	998	1053	1003
FLORENCE	856	826	881	831		SALZBURG	649	679	700	733
FRANKFURT	320	424	371	473		STRASBOURG	336	371	389	425
GENEVA	509	440	506	445		TOULOUSE	624	523	621	517
GENOA	753	689	754	694		TRIESTE	833	894	884	899
HAMBURG	424	549	475	617		VENICE	832	803	857	808
INNSBRUCK	628	665	679	670		VIENNA	769	863	820	917

Planning your route

The AA European Route Planning Service, available only to AA members, consists of a series of throughroute maps, planning maps and town plan books for which a small charge is made.

Throughroute maps: (scale approximately 33 miles to 1 inch)

A series of six maps each based on a different main European cross-Channel port: Boulogne, Calais, Cherbourg, Dieppe, Le Havre and Ostend/Zeebrugge. These maps are not ordinary road maps but are designed to give guidance on straightforward journeys by indicating the easiest and quickest AA-recommended route plus the mileage from each port to a large number of destinations in Western Europe.

European Route Planning map: (scale approximately 33 miles to 1 inch)

Suitable for general planning purposes, this map covers Western Europe excluding Scandinavia. It shows motorways, main roads, distances and road numbers and includes an index of placenames.

Area Route Planning maps: (scale approximately 16 miles to 1 inch, except Finland, north of Trondheim in Norway and north of Östersund in Sweden)

These maps are designed for planning a tour in a particular area or a general tour of a country. They include town plans of ports, mileage charts, mountain pass and tunnel information, road conditions and other touring information.

A suggested route will be marked on the European or Area Route Planning maps by our route specialists on request.

Town Plan books
Four books each containing 24 throughway town plans that have been drawn with the intention of helping members to find their way through or around a town with the minimum of inconvenience.

Book 1 contains plans of the larger towns along the main routes of Western France, Spain and Portugal.

Book 2 contains plans of the larger towns along the main routes of Eastern France, Switzerland and Italy.

Book 3 contains plans of the larger towns along the main routes of Belgium, South Germany and Austria.

Book 4 contains plans of the larger towns along the main routes of Belgium, Netherlands, North Germany and Denmark.

To obtain the service, complete the application form on pages 19 and 20 and post it to the Automobile Association, Fanum House, Basingstoke, Hants RG21 2EA, enclosing your remittance.

PLEASE MENTION THIS GUIDE WHEN YOU BOOK

Stop the miseries of Travel Sickness

Travel Sickness: what makes it even more sickening is that if one member of your holiday party suffers from it, then everybody suffers!

Whether you go by car, coach, plane, boat or hovercraft – take SEA-LEGS.

Pleasant to take, virtually tasteless, and suitable for all the family, SEA-LEGS stays effective long enough for you to take it on the night before you set out!

As soon as you've seen your travel agent, see your chemist about SEA-LEGS.

If you can't take the ups and downs of travel, take

sea-legs

and settle down to a good journey.

Application form for Route Planning Maps

The Route Book Service has been replaced by a special range of maps to assist you in planning your tour. Three different types of maps and four town plan books are available as described below. If required, a suggested route can be marked on the European or Area Route Planning maps by our route specialists. To obtain this service please complete the application form below and send it direct to The Automobile Association, Fanum House, Basingstoke, Hants RG21 2EA, with the appropriate remittance.

Please complete in BLOCK CAPITALS

Mr/Mrs/Miss   Initials   Surname

Address to which route maps should be sent:

County/Postcode

Date of application	Telephone numbers: Home Business
Membership number	Continental port of landing

1 European Throughroute Maps

A series of maps (scale approx 33 miles to 1 inch) based on the principal cross-Channel ports. Each map indicates the AA-recommended throughroutes from the port to all destinations in Western Europe – as far north as Copenhagen and eastwards as far as Berlin; Prague, Budapest, Bucharest, Athens and Istanbul. Specially suitable for journeys using main routes.

EUROPEAN THROUGHROUTE MAPS

Please tick box(es) of map(s) required.		Sale price per map	Total price of maps
Boulogne			£ : p
Calais			
Cherbourg		40p each	
Dieppe			..........:..........
Le Havre			
Ostende/ Zeebrugge			

2 European Route Planning Map

Suitable for general planning purposes (scale approx 33 miles to 1 inch). Covers the same area as European throughroute maps described above. Shows motorways, main roads, distances and road numbers. Includes an index of placenames.

European Route Planning Map		40p each	.........:.........

3 Area Route Planning Maps

A series of maps (scale approx 16 miles to 1 inch, except Finland, north of Trondheim in Norway and north of Östersund in Sweden) with town plans of ports, connected with GB, and touring information including road conditions, ferries, mileage charts, mountain passes and tunnels etc. See sketch map for area covered by each map. Designed for planning a tour in a particular area or a general tour of a country.

continued overleaf

19

	Please tick box(es) of map(s) required.	Sale price per map	Total price of maps
			£ : p

AREA ROUTE PLANNING MAPS

Map	Box	Price
1 Western France	☐	
2 Eastern Spain	☐	
3 Western Spain and Portugal	☐	
4 Belgium, Eastern France and Switzerland	☐	40p each
5 South Germany, Austria and North Italy	☐	....:....
6 Southern Italy	☐	
7 Belgium, Netherlands and North Germany	☐	
8 Southern Scandinavia	☐	
9 Northern Scandinavia	☐	

4 Town Plan Books

Book 1 *France* Arras Avignon Bordeaux Chartres Clermont-Ferrand Le Mans Lyon Paris-Ring-Road Rouen Toulouse Tours Versailles *Spain* Barcelona Burgos Cordoba Granada Madrid Malaga Seville Toledo Valencia Zaragoza *Portugal* Lisbon Porto

Book 2 *France* Arras Avignon Cannes Dijon Lille Lyon Marseille Monte-Carlo Paris-Ring-Road Reims Strasbourg *Belgium* Brussels *Luxembourg Switzerland* Basle Bern Geneva Lausanne Zürich *Italy* Florence Genoa Milan Naples Pisa Rome

Book 3 *France* Arras Lille Reims Strasbourg *Netherlands* Hook of Holland Rotterdam The Hague *Belgium* Antwerp Bruges Brussels Gent *Luxembourg Switzerland* Basle Schaffhausen Zürich *Germany* Bonn Cologne Frankfurt Freiburg Munich Stuttgart *Austria* Innsbruck Salzburg Vienna

Book 4 *France* Arras Lille *Netherlands* Amsterdam Arnhem Hook of Holland Rotterdam The Hague Utrecht *Belgium* Antwerp Bruges Brussels Gent Liège *Germany* Aachen Berlin Bonn Bremen Cologne Düsseldorf Hamburg Hannover *Denmark* Copenhagen Odense *Sweden* Malmö

	Book 1	☐	
Remittance should be by crossed cheque or postal order, payable to The Automobile Association.	Book 2	☐	40p each
	Book 3	☐	....:....
	Book 4	☐	
	Total remittance enclosed		£ : p

5 If you require us to suggest a route and indicate it on the map(s), please list the placenames (in BLOCK CAPITALS) in the order in which they will be visited. If you require route information for countries other than those listed above, please give details here.

Please tick (√) this box if a caravan is being towed ☐

Date of departure	For office use only: A/C No. 7710/672

20

ON THE WAY...

Emergency

Accidents

The country sections give individual country regulations and information on summoning the fire, police and ambulance services. The international regulations are similar to those in the UK; the following recommendations are usually advisable.

If you are involved in an accident you must stop. A warning triangle should be placed on the road at a suitable distance to warn following traffic of the obstruction. The use of hazard warning lights in no way affects the regulations governing the use of warning triangles. Medical assistance should be obtained for persons injured in the accident. If the accident necessitates calling the police, leave the vehicle in the position in which it comes to rest; should it seriously obstruct other traffic, mark the position of the vehicle on the road and get the details confirmed by independent witnesses before moving it.

The accident must be reported to the police if it is required by law (see country sections); if the accident has caused death or bodily injury; or if an unoccupied vehicle or property has been damaged and there is no one present to represent the interests of the party suffering damage. Notify your insurance company by letter if possible, within 24 hours of the accident; see the conditions of your policy. If a third party is injured, the insurance company or bureau, whose address is given on the back of your Green Card or frontier insurance certificate, should be notified; the company or bureau will, if necessary, pay compensation to the injured party.

Make sure that all essential particulars are noted, especially details concerning third parties. This record will be useful when completing the insurance company's accident form.

First aid

Expert assistance should be summoned immediately. Unless you have a knowledge of first aid you should be extremely cautious about attending anyone injured in an accident. The following notes may be useful.

Bleeding and wounds To stop bleeding apply pressure to the sides of the wound. Cleanse around and away from the wound, taking care not to disturb any blood clot. Apply and maintain pressure to the bleeding part with dressing, cover with pad, and bandage firmly.

Broken bones Fractures should be moved as little as possible. Support the injured part at once.

Poison If the patient is unconscious do not attempt to treat except with artificial respiration, if needed. Conscious casualties of corrosive poisons which destroy tissue (eg acids) should be given large quantities of milk to drink. With narcotics (eg sleeping pills) the casualty should be made to vomit, by giving him two tablespoons of salt in a glass of warm water to drink.

Shock Loosen any tight clothing, wrap the casualty in a blanket or coat and lay him down at absolute rest.

Fainting Lay patient down and raise lower limbs, **EXCEPT IN CASE OF FRACTURE.** Loosen tight clothing about neck, waist, and chest, and ensure fresh air.

Asphyxia The exhaled air (mouth to mouth, or mouth to nose) method of artificial respiration is strongly recommended and should be learned by everyone.

Exhaled air resuscitation Lay patient on his back. Tilt the head and chin away from the chest to clear airway, making sure that it is not obstructed by the tongue or foreign matter. Open your mouth and take a deep breath. Pinch the casualty's nostrils together, then seal your lips around the mouth. Blow into his lungs until the chest rises, then remove your mouth and watch the chest deflate. Repeat giving the first four inflations as rapidly as possible. Lung inflation can also be carried out through the nose. The casualty's mouth should be sealed with the thumb holding the lower jaw.

First-aid kit It is always advisable to carry a first-aid kit.

Breakdown and general assistance

In order to obtain free roadside assistance from the main European motoring clubs which are affiliated to the Alliance Internationale de Tourisme (AIT), it is necessary to be an AA member and to possess AA travel insurance – 5-Star Service.

The AA *5-Star Service* provides a wide range of service, insurance and credit facilities within certain specified limits and is divided into three parts:

1 *Vehicle Security* includes vehicle recovery, the location and delivery of spare parts, free roadside assistance from AIT patrols*, the use of the AA Continental Emergency Centre based at Boulogne, AIT credit vouchers*, legal assistance*, financial assistance toward the turnout of a breakdown vehicle and towage, comprehensive service booklet, emergency repatriation voucher, and chauffeur service following illness.

2 *Touring Security* includes cover for car hire, travel and accommodation expenses following the loss of the use of a vehicle due to breakdown, accident or theft.

3 *Personal Security* includes cover for luggage, medical expenses, loss of deposits, loss of money and personal accident.

Items starred are available to full members only.

If an AA member has not taken 5-Star Service and he requires the vehicle recovery and/or spare parts service, the AA will help but assistance cannot be provided until a deposit to cover service fees and all estimated costs has been made. In addition a charge is made for arranging emergency medical assistance.

AA Reservation Service

The AA network of Service Centres, Travel Agencies and Regional Offices throughout the United Kingdom offers a first-rate booking service for car-ferry, hovercraft and motorail services. Write, telephone or make a personal visit for your reservations.

For instant confirmation of ferry reservations on many services, ring one of the numbers listed below (Monday to Friday 09.00–17.00):

The South-East	01-977 0177
The West and Wales	Bristol 24417
The Midlands	021-550 7648
The North	061-486 0777
Scotland	041-812 2888
Northern Ireland	Belfast 26242
Republic of Ireland	Dublin 777004

Garages

The garages listed in the gazetteer for each country are those which are most likely to be of help to members on tour, because of their situation and the services they have stated they can provide. Although the AA cannot accept responsibility for difficulties over repairs to members' cars, any unsatisfactory cases will be noted for amendment in later editions of the *Guide to Motoring on the Continent.*

It cannot be emphasised too strongly that disputes with garages on the Continent must be settled on the spot. It has been the AA's experience that subsequent negotiations can seldom be brought to a satisfactory conclusion.

In selecting garages, preference has been given to those which provide a breakdown service (see below), good garaging space in major cities and in the Channel ports and those accepting AIT Credit Vouchers. The number of garages holding each agency reflects, as far as possible, the relative popularity of the various makes of cars. Although firms normally specialise in the makes for which they are accredited agents, they do not necessarily hold stocks of spare parts. Certain garages will repair only the make of car for which they are official agents as indicated in the text.

A complete list of service agencies for your own make of car is generally available through your own dealer. It has been found on occasion that some garages on the Continent make extremely high charges for repairing tourists' cars; always ask for an estimate before authorising a repair.

France All prices must be displayed on the premises so that they are clearly visible and legible. When you have had a repair carried out, you should receive an invoice stating the labour charge, *ie* the hourly rate (displayed) multiplied by the time spent or the time shown on the time schedule for each operation, and not just a lump sum. The price of supplies and spares, shown separately. Parts which have been replaced must be returned to you, unless it is a routine replacement or the repair is carried out free during the guarantee period.

Spain Garages are officially classified. Blue signs displayed outside garages indicate the classification I to III as well as the type of work that can be dealt with, by means of symbols. There must be set prices for common repair jobs and these must be available to customers so that they may authorise repairs. A complaints book must also be available and this is inspected during official visits by representatives of the local authority.

Breakdowns   An explanation of the breakdown service symbols is given on page 2. *Breakdown services operated by Continental garages have no connection with the AA Continental Breakdown Service.*

Details of services operated by clubs affiliated to the AA are given under the Motoring Club section in the countries concerned.

Hours of opening   In most Continental countries normal business hours are 08.00–18.00hrs; these times may be altered on Sundays and public holidays, when repairs, breakdown service, and petrol are often unobtainable. An indication of service outside normal business hours is given by abbreviations (see page 2).

In many countries, especially France, it may be difficult to get a car repaired during August because many garages close down for annual holidays.

International distinguishing signs

(Established by international conventions and/or as notified to the United Nations)

During the validity of this book it is possible that the distinguishing signs may be standardised. The suggested new signs, which are given in parentheses, will be used on a national basis *ie* for aircraft, radio, and boats, etc.

A	(AT)	Austria
ADN	(YD)	Democratic Yemen (formerly Aden)*
AFG	(AF)	Afghanistan[1]
AL		Albania
AND	(AD)	Andorra
AUS	(AU)	Australia*
B	(BE)	Belgium
BDS	(BB)	Barbados*
BG		Bulgaria
BH	(BZ)	Belize (formerly British Honduras)
BR		Brazil
BRN	(BH)	Bahrain
BRU	(BN)	Brunei*
BS		Bahamas*
BUR	(BU)	Burma
C	(CU)	Cuba[1]
CDN	(CA)	Canada
CH		Switzerland
CI		Ivory Coast
CL	(LK)	Sri Lanka (formerly Ceylon)*
CO		Colombia[1]
CR		Costa Rica
CS		Czechoslovakia
CY		Cyprus*
D	(DE)	German Federal Republic[1]

DDR	(DD)	German Democratic Republic
DK		Denmark
DOM	(DO)	Dominican Republic
DY		Benin (formerly Dahomey)
DZ		Algeria
E	(ES)	Spain (including African localities and provinces)
EAK	(KE)	Kenya*
EAT	(TZ)	Tanzania (formerly Tanganyika)*
EAU	(UG)	Uganda*
EC		Ecuador
ET	(EG)	Arab Republic of Egypt
F	(FR)	France (including overseas departments and territories)
FJI	(FJ)	Fiji*
FL	(LI)	Liechtenstein[1]
GB		United Kingdom of Great Britain & Northern Ireland*
GBA		Alderney*
GBG		Guernsey*	Channel Islands
GBJ		Jersey*
GBM		Isle of Man*[1]
GBZ	(GI)	Gibraltar
GCA	(GT)	Guatemala
GH		Ghana
GR		Greece

GUY	(GY)	Guyana* (formerly British Guiana)
H	(HU)	Hungary
HK		Hong Kong*
HKJ	(JO)	Jordan
I	(IT)	Italy
IL		Israel
IND	(IN)	India*
IR		Iran[1]
IRL	(IE)	Ireland*
IRQ	(IQ)	Iraq[1]
IS		Iceland
J	(JP)	Japan*
JA	(JM)	Jamaica*
K	(KH)	Khmer Republic (formerly Cambodia)
KWT	(KW)	Kuwait[1]
L	(LU)	Luxembourg
LAO	(LA)	Laos
LAR	(LY)	Libya[1]
LB	(LR)	Liberia[1]
LS		Lesotho (formerly Basutoland)*
M	(MT)	Malta*
MA		Morocco
MAL	(MY)	Malaysia*
MC		Monaco
MEX	(MX)	Mexico
MS	(MU)	Mauritius*
MW		Malawi*
N	(NO)	Norway
NA	(AN)	Netherlands Antilles
NIC	(NI)	Nicaragua
NL		Netherlands
NZ		New Zealand*
P	(PT)	Portugal
P	(AO)	Angola
P	(CV)	Cape Verde Islands
P	(MZ)	Mozambique*
P	(GN)	Guinea
P	(ST)	São Tomé and Principe
PA		Panama[1]
PAK	(PK)	Pakistan*
PE		Peru
PL		Poland
PY		Paraguay
R	(RO)	Romania
RA	(AR)	Argentina
RB	(BW)	Botswana (formerly Bechuanaland)*

RC	(TW)	Taiwan (Formosa)
RCA	(CF)	Central African Republic
RCB	(CG)	Congo
RCH	(CL)	Chile
RH	(HT)	Haiti
RI	(ID)	Indonesia*
RIM	(MR)	Mauritania[1]
RL	(LB)	Lebanon
RM	(MG)	Malagasy Republic (formerly Madagascar)
RMM	(ML)	Mali
ROK	(KP)	Korea (Republic of)
RP	(PH)	Philippines
RSM	(SM)	San Marino
RSR	(RH)	Rhodesia (formerly Southern Rhodesia)*
RU	(BI)	Burundi[1]
RWA	(RW)	Rwanda
S	(SE)	Sweden
SD	(SZ)	Swaziland*
SF	(FI)	Finland
SGP	(SG)	Singapore*
SME	(SR)	Surinam (Dutch Guiana)*
SN		Senegal
SU		Union of Soviet Socialist Republics
SY	(SC)	Seychelles*
SYR	(SY)	Syria
T	(TH)	Thailand*
TG		Togo
TN		Tunisia
TR		Turkey
TT		Trinidad and Tobago*
U	(UY)	Uruguay
USA	(US)	United States of America
V	(VA)	Holy See (Vatican City)
VN	(VD)	Republic of Vietnam
WAG	(GM)	Gambia
WAL	(SL)	Sierra Leone
WAN	(NG)	Nigeria
WD	(DM)	Dominica* } Windward Islands
WG	(GD)	Grenada*
WL	(LC)	St Lucia*
WS		Western Samoa*
WV	(VC)	St Vincent (Windward Islands)*
YU		Yugoslavia
YV	(VE)	Venezuela
Z	(ZM)	Zambia*[1]
ZA		South Africa*
ZR		Zaire (formerly Congo Kinshasha)

*In countries marked with an asterisk the rule of the road is drive on the left; otherwise drive on the right.

Notes
[1] Not included in the United Nations list of signs established according to the 1949 Convention on Road Traffic.

International time

All Continental countries are ahead of GMT as follows:

Country	Hours ahead of GMT Winter	Summer	Country	Hours ahead of GMT Winter	Summer
United Kingdom	**0**	**1**	Luxembourg	1	2
Austria	1	1	Netherlands	1	2
Belgium	1		Portugal	0	1
France and			Spain and		
Monaco	1	2	Andorra	1	2
Germany	1	1	Switzerland		
Italy and			and		
San Marino	1	2	Liechtenstein	1	1

Journey times

It is not difficult, other than in extremely heavy traffic or adverse weather conditions, to maintain a steady average speed on Continental motorways. The table below is a guide to journey times at average speeds expressed in kilometres.

Distance in kilometres	Average speed in mph									
	30		40		50		60		70	
	hrs	mins	hrs	mins	hrs	mins	hrs	mins	hrs	mins
20		25		19		15		13		11
30		37		28		22		19		16
40		50		37		30		25		21
50	1	2		47		37		31		27
60	1	15		56		45		38		32
70	1	25	1	5		52		43		36
80	1	39	1	15	1	0		50		42
90	1	52	1	24	1	7		56		48
100	2	4	1	33	1	15	1	2		53
150	3	6	2	20	1	52	1	33	1	20
200	4	8	3	6	2	30	2	4	1	46
250	5	10	3	53	3	7	2	35	2	13
300	6	12	4	40	3	44	3	6	2	40
350	7	14	5	27	4	21	3	37	3	7
400	8	16	6	12	5	0	4	8	3	32
450	9	18	6	59	5	37	4	39	3	59
500	10	20	7	46	6	14	5	10	4	26

Motoring advice to drivers visiting the Continent

Motoring laws in Europe are just as wide and complicated as those in the UK but they should cause little difficulty to the average British motorist who is usually well trained. He should, however, take more care and extend greater courtesy than he would normally do at home, and bear in mind the essentials of good motoring — avoiding any behaviour likely to obstruct traffic, to endanger persons or cause damage to property. It is also important to remember that when travelling in a country the tourist is subject to the laws of that country.

Road signs are mainly international and should be familiar to the British motorist but in every country there are a few exceptions. He should particularly watch for signs indicating crossings and speed limits. Probably the most unusual aspect of motoring abroad to the British motorist is the universal and firm rule of giving priority to traffic coming from the right and unless this rule is varied by signs, it must be strictly observed.

The following information will be common to the countries covered in this Guide but any national variations will be indicated in the country sections.

Caravan and luggage trailers   Carry a list of contents, as this may be required at a frontier.

Common law claims   In Spain, particularly and, to a lesser extent, in some other countries common law claims *ie* claims to be made against other parties following, for example, a road accident — not to be confused with claims made under the benefits of 5-Star Travel Service — are frequently not recoverable in full. Claims for vehicle hiring charges are invariably reduced, and, in certain cases, may not be admissible at all.

If an accident occurs in Spain and your vehicle is repaired in the United Kingdom you are generally only entitled to recover, subject to liability, an amount equal to the cost of repairing the vehicle in Spain which is usually considerably less than the UK cost. AA members may contact the Association's Legal Services, Head Office, for advice on such matters.

Crash helmets   All riders of motorcycles, irrespective of the capacity of their machine, should wear crash helmets.

Dimensions and weight restrictions   Although there are no dimension restrictions for the ordinary private car, there may be some for other types of vehicles. If in doubt, please consult a local AA service centre. Also, see the Major road tunnels section pages 36–37, as some vehicle dimensions are restricted because of the shape of the tunnels. For weight restrictions, see the Introduction page 4.

Drinking and driving   There is only one safe rule — if you drink, don't drive. The laws are strict and penalties severe.

Hazard warning lights   Although four flashing indicators are allowed in the countries covered in this Guide, they in no way affect the regulations governing the use of warning triangles.

Level crossings   Practically all level crossings are indicated by international signs. Most guarded ones are the lifting barrier type, sometimes with bells or flashing lights to give warning of an approaching train.

Lights   For driving abroad, lights must be adjusted so that they do not dip to the left. The easiest way to do this is to use an adapter (see page 16).

Dipped headlights should be used when passing through a tunnel, irrespective of its length and its lighting. In some countries, the police will wait at the end of the tunnel, checking emerging vehicles for this requirement.

Minibus   A minibus, equipped to carry ten or more passengers (including the driver) is classed as a commercial vehicle (passenger-carrying) and, as such, attracts special regulations and possibly heavy taxes and tolls (see page 10).

Mountain passes   Always engage a low gear before either ascending or descending steep gradients, keep well to the right side of the road and avoid cutting corners. Avoid excessive use of the brake. If the engine is overheating, pull off the road, making sure you do not cause an obstruction, leave the engine idling, and put the heater controls, including the fan, into the maximum heat position. Under no circumstances remove the radiator cap until the engine has cooled down. Do not fill the coolant system of a hot engine with cold water.

Give way to vehicles proceeding up a gradient. Priority must always be given to postal coaches travelling in either direction. Their route is usually signposted.

Overtaking   When overtaking on roads with two lanes or more in each direction, always signal your intention in good time, and after the manoeuvre, signal and return to the inside lane. Do not remain in any other lane.

Parking   In most Continental countries the police are extremely strict with parking offenders. Before parking a vehicle you are advised to find out from the local authorities about any rules which apply. It is usually obligatory to park facing the direction in which the traffic is flowing.

Priority   The general rule is to give way to traffic coming from the right which is sometimes varied at roundabouts. This is the one aspect of Continental driving which may cause the British driver the most confusion because his whole training and experience makes it unnatural. Road signs indicate priority or loss of priority and tourists are well advised to make sure that they understand such signs.

Great care should be taken at intersections and tourists should never rely on receiving the right of way, particularly in small towns and villages where local traffic, often slow moving, will assume right of way regardless of oncoming traffic.

Always give way to public service and military vehicles. Blind or disabled people, funerals and marching columns must always be allowed right of way.

Road signs   Most road signs throughout Europe are internationally agreed and the majority would be familiar to the British motorist. Please refer to the insert for signs relating to the countries covered by this guide.

Roundabouts   Priority at roundabouts is given to vehicles entering the roundabout unless signposted to the contrary. This is a complete reversal to the United Kingdom rule, and particular care should be exercised when manoeuvring while circulating in an anti-clockwise direction on a roundabout. It is advisable to keep to the outside lane on a roundabout if possible, to make your exit easier.

Rule of the road   In all European countries, drive on the right and overtake on the left.

Signals   Signals of a driver's intentions must be given clearly, within a reasonable distance, and in good time. In built-up areas, the general rule is not to use horns unless safety demands it; in many large towns and resorts, as well as in areas indicated by the international sign, the use of the horn is totally prohibited.

Speed limits   **Note** It is important to adhere to speed limits at all times. Offenders may be fined and driving licences impounded on the spot, thus causing great inconvenience and possible expense.

Traffic lights   In principal cities and towns these operate in a way similar to those in the United Kingdom, although they are sometimes suspended overhead. The density of the light may be so poor that lights could be missed. There is usually only one set on the right-hand side of the road some distance before the road junction, and if you stop too close to the corner the lights will not be visible.

Trams   Trams take priority over other vehicles. Always give way to passengers boarding and alighting. Never position a vehicle so that it impedes the free flow of a tram. Trams must be overtaken on the right except in one-way streets.

Valuables   Tourists should pay particular attention to the security of their money and items of value while touring. Whenever possible excess cash and travellers' cheques should be left with the hotel management **against a receipt.** In some areas, children and youths cause a diversion to attract tourists' attention while pickpockets operate in organised gangs. Unusual incidents, which are more likely to occur in crowded markets or shopping centres, should be avoided.

It cannot be stressed too strongly that all valuables should be removed from a parked car even if it is parked in a supervised car park or lock-up garage.

Warning triangles   It is advisable to carry a warning triangle even in countries where their use has not been made compulsory. They are placed on the road to warn traffic approaching from the rear that a vehicle has stopped or broken down and is causing an obstruction. Where triangles are required by law, the appropriate country section will give the regulations covering their use. Warning triangles can be purchased from the AA. They come complete with a functional case and can be unpacked and ready for use in seconds.

Passes and tunnels
Principal mountain passes

It is best not to attempt to cross mountain passes at night, and daily schedules should make allowance for the comparatively slow speeds inevitable in mountainous areas.

Gravel surfaces (such as grit and stone chips) vary considerably; they are dusty when dry, slippery when wet. Where known to exist, this type of surface has been noted. Road repairs can be carried out only during the summer, and may interrupt traffic. Precipitous sides are rarely, if ever, totally unguarded; on the older roads stone pillars are placed at close intervals. Gradient figures take the mean on hairpin bends, and may be steeper on the insides of the curves, particularly on older roads.

Before attempting late-evening or early-morning journeys across frontier passes, check the times of opening of the Customs offices. A number of offices close at night *eg* the Timmelsjoch border crossing is closed between 20.00 and 07.00hrs.

Caravans Passes suitable for caravans are shown. Those shown to be *negotiable* by caravans are best used only by experienced drivers driving cars with ample power. The remainder are probably best avoided. A correct power-to-load is always essential.

Conditions in winter Winter conditions are given in italics in the last column. *UO* means usually open, although a severe fall of snow may temporarily obstruct the road for 24–48 hours, and wheel chains are often necessary; *OC* means occasionally closed between the dates stated; *UC* usually closed between the dates stated. Dates for opening and closing the passes are approximate only. Warning notices are usually posted at the foot of a pass if it is closed, or if chains or snow tyres should or must be used. Wheel chains may be needed early and late in the season, and between short spells (a few hours) of obstruction. At these times conditions are usually more difficult for caravans.

In fair weather, wheel chains or snow tyres are only necessary on the higher passes, but in severe weather you will probably need them (as a rough guide) at altitudes exceeding 2,000ft. (See also Road and winter conditions page 40).

Pass and height	From To	Distances from summit and max gradient		Min width of road	Conditions
*Albula 7,595ft Switzerland *(Map 12 C1)*	Tiefencastel (2,821ft) La Punt (5,546ft)	31km 9km	1 in 10 1 in 10	12ft	*UC Nov–late May.* An inferior alternative to the Julier; tar and gravel; fine scenery. Alternative rail tunnel (see page 37).
Allos 7,382ft France *(Map 28 C2)*	Barcelonnette (3,740ft) Colmars (4,085ft)	20km 24km	1 in 10 1 in 12	13ft	*UC early Nov–late May.* Very winding, narrow, partially unguarded but not difficult otherwise; passing bays on southern slope, good surface.
Aprica 3,875ft Italy *(Map 29 A4)*	Tresenda (1,220ft) Edolo (2,264ft)	14km 15km	1 in 11 1 in 16	13ft	*UO.* Fine scenery; good surface, well graded; *suitable for caravans.*
Aravis 4,915ft France *(Map 28 C4)*	La Clusaz (3,412ft) Flumet (3,008ft)	8km 12km	1 in 11 1 in 11	13ft	*OC Dec–late Mar.* Outstanding scenery, and a fairly easy road.
Arlberg 5,912ft Austria *(Map 12 C1/2)*	Bludenz (1,905ft) Landeck (2,677ft)	33km 35km	1 in 8 1 in 7½	20ft	*OC Nov–Apr.* Modern road; short, steep stretch from west, easing towards the summit; heavy traffic; *negotiable by caravans;* rail alternative. (see page 38).
Aubisque 5,610ft France *(Map 20 C3)*	Eaux Bonnes (2,461ft) Argelès-Gazost (1,519ft)	11km 32km	1 in 10 1 in 10	11ft	*UC early Nov–June.* A very winding road; continuous but easy ascent; the descent incorporates the Col de Soulor (4,757ft); 8km of very narrow, rough, unguarded road, with a steep drop.

*Permitted maximum width of vehicles 7ft 6in
†Permitted maximum width of vehicles 8ft 2½in

Pass and height	From To	Distances from summit and max gradient		Min width of road	Conditions
Ballon d'Alsace 3,865ft France *(Map 11 A2)*	Giromagny (1,830ft)	17km	1 in 9	13ft	*UO.* A fairly straightforward ascent and descent, but numerous bends; *negotiable by caravans.*
	St-Maurice-sur-Moselle (1,800ft)	9km	1 in 9		
Bayard 4,094ft France *(Map 28 C3)*	Chauffayer (2,988ft)	18km	1 in 12	20ft	*UO.* Part of the Route Napoléon. Fairly easy, steepest on the southern side; *negotiable by caravans from north to south.*
	Gap (2,382ft)	8km	1 in 7		
***Bernina** 7,644ft Switzerland *(Map 12 C1)*	Pontresina (5,915ft)	15.5km	1 in 10	16ft	*OC Nov–late Apr* during the day, but closed at night. A good road on both sides; *negotiable by caravans.*
	Poschiavo (3,317ft)	17km	1 in 8		
Bonaigua 6,797ft Spain *(Map 22 C4)*	Viella (3,150ft)	23km	1 in 12	14ft	*UC Nov–Apr.* A sinuous and narrow road with many hairpin bends and some precipitous drops; the alternative route to Lérida through the Viella tunnel is open in winter.
	Esterri del Aneu (3,185ft)	16km	1 in 12		
Bracco 2,018ft Italy *(Map 29 A2)*	Riva Trigoso (141ft)	15km	1 in 7	16ft	*UO.* A two-lane road with continuous bends; passing usually difficult; *negotiable by caravans;* alternative toll motorway available.
	Borghetto di Vara (318ft)	18km	1 in 7		
Brenner 4,495ft Austria-Italy *(Map 13 A1)*	Innsbruck (1,885ft)	39km	1 in 12	20ft	*UO.* Parallel toll motorway open; heavy traffic may delay at Customs; *suitable for caravans;* Resia Pass and Felbertauern Tunnel possible alternatives.
	Vipiteno (3,115ft)	14.5km	1 in 7		
†Brünig 3,304ft Switzerland *(Map 11 B1)*	Brienzwiler Station (1,886ft)	6km	1 in 12	20ft	*UO.* An easy but winding road; heavy traffic at weekends; *suitable for caravans.*
	Giswil (1,601ft)	13km	1 in 12		
Bussang 2,365ft France *(Map 11 A2)*	Thann (1,115ft)	22km	1 in 10	13ft	*UO.* A very easy road over the Vosges; beautiful scenery; *suitable for caravans.*
	St-Maurice-sur-Moselle (1,800ft)	8km	1 in 14		
Campolongo 6,152ft Italy *(Map 13 A1)*	Corvara (5,145ft)	6km	1 in 8	16ft	*UO.* A winding but easy ascent; long level stretch on summit followed by easy descent; good surface; *suitable for caravans.*
	Arabba (5,253ft)	4km	1 in 8		
Cayolle 7,631ft France *(Map 28 C2)*	Barcelonnette (3,740ft)	32km	1 in 10	13ft	*UC early Nov–May.* Narrow and winding road with blind bends.
	Guillaumes (2,687ft)	33km	1 in 10		
Costalunga (Karer) 5,752ft Italy *(Map 13 A1)*	Cardano (925ft)	23km	1 in 8	16ft	*UO.* A good, well-engineered road; *caravans prohibited.*
	Pozza (4,232ft)	10km	1 in 7		
Croix-Haute 3,858ft France *(Map 27 B3)*	Monestier-de-Clermont (2,776ft)	36km	1 in 14	18ft	*UO.* Well engineered; several hairpin bends on the north side; *suitable for caravans.*
	Aspres-sur-Buech (2,497ft)	28km	1 in 14		
Envalira 7,897ft Andorra *(Map 22 C4)*	Pas de la Casa (6,851ft)	6km	1 in 12	20ft	*OC Nov–Apr.* A good two-lane road with wide bends on ascent and descent; fine views; *negotiable by caravans.*
	Andorra (3,375ft)	30km	1 in 10		
Falzarego 6,945ft Italy *(Map 13 A1)*	Cortina d'Ampezzo (3,958ft)	17km	1 in 12	16ft	*OC Nov–Mar.* Well-engineered; bitumen surface; many hairpin bends on both sides; *negotiable by caravans.*
	Andraz (4,622ft)	9km	1 in 12		
Faucille 4,331ft France *(Map 10 D1)*	Gex (1,985ft)	11km	1 in 10	13ft	*UO.* Fairly wide, winding road across the Jura mountains; *negotiable by caravans* but it is probably better to follow La Cure–St-Cergue–Nyon.
	Morez (2,247ft)	28km	1 in 12		

*Permitted maximum width of vehicles 7ft 6in
†Permitted maximum width of vehicles 8ft 2½in

See page 28 for other abbreviations

Pass and height	From To	Distances from summit and max gradient		Min width of road	Conditions
Fern 3,969ft Austria *(Map 12 D2)*	Nassereith (2,742ft) Lermoos (3,244ft)	9km 10km	1 in 10 1 in 10	20ft	*UO*. An easy pass but slippery when wet; *suitable for caravans*.
*****Fluela** 7,818ft Switzerland *(Map 12 C1)*	Davos-Dorf (5,174ft) Susch (4,659ft)	13km 13km	1 in 10 1 in 8	16ft	*OC Nov–May*. Tolls levied in winter to pay for snow clearance (Nov16–May15); 5 Swiss Francs per car. Easy ascent from Davos; some acute hairpin bends on the eastern side; bitumen surface; *negotiable by caravans*.
†**Forclaz** 5,010ft Switzerland France *(Map 28 C4)*	Martigny (1,562ft) Argentière (4,111ft)	13km 19km	1 in 12 1 in 12	16ft	*UO Forclaz; Montets OC Nov–early Apr*. A good road over the pass and to the frontier; in France narrow and rough over Col des Montets (4,793ft); *negotiable by caravans*.
Fugazze 3,802ft Italy *(Map 29 B4)*	Rovereto (660ft) Valli del Pasubio (1,148ft)	27km 12km	1 in 8 1 in 8	10ft	*UO*. Bitumen surface; several hairpin bends, narrow on northern side.
*****Furka** 7,972ft Switzerland *(Map 11 B1)*	Gletsch (5,777ft) Realp (5,066ft)	10km 13km	1 in 10 1 in 10	13ft	*UC Oct–Jun*. A well-graded modern road, but with narrow sections and several sharp hairpin bends on both ascent and descent. Fine views of the Rhône Glacier.
Galibier 8,385ft France *(Map 28 C3)*	Lautaret Pass (6,751ft) St-Michel-de-Maurienne (2,336ft)	7km 34km	1 in 14 1 in 8	10ft	*UC Oct–Jun*. Mainly wide, well-surfaced but unguarded. Ten hairpin bends on descent then 5km narrow and rough. Rise over the Col du Télégraphe (5,249ft), then eleven more hairpin bends. (In 1976 tunnel under Galibier summit caved in; new, longer road over summit rises to 8,678ft).
Gardena (Grödner-Joch) 6,959ft Italy *(Map 13 A1)*	Val Gardena (6,109ft) Corvara (5,145ft)	6km 10km	1 in 8 1 in 8	16ft	*OC Nov–late May*. A well-engineered road, very winding on descent.
Gavia 8,604ft Italy *(Map 12 D1)*	Bormio (4,019ft) Ponte di Legno (4,140ft)	25km 16km	1 in 5½ 1 in 5½	10ft	*UC mid Oct–late Jun*. Steep and narrow but with frequent passing bays; many hairpin bends and a gravel surface; not for the faint-hearted; extra care necessary.
Gerlos 5,341ft Austria *(Map 13 A2)*	Zell am Ziller (1,886ft) Wald (2,890ft)	29km 15km	1 in 12 1 in 11	14ft	*UO*. Hairpin ascent out of Zell to modern toll road; the old, steep, narrow, and winding route with passing bays and 1-in-7 gradient is not recommended, but is *negotiable with care*.
†**Grand St Bernard** 8,114ft Switzerland–Italy *(Map 28 C4)*	Martigny (1,562ft) Aosta (1,913ft)	44km 33km	1 in 9 1 in 9	13ft	*UC late Oct–early Jun*. Modern road to entrance of road tunnel (usually open) see page 36; then narrow but bitumen surface over summit to frontier; also good in Italy; *suitable for caravans, using tunnel*.
*****Grimsel** 7,100ft Switzerland *(Map 11 B1)*	Innertkirchen (2,067ft) Gletsch (5,777ft)	25km 6km	1 in 10 1 in 10	16ft	*UC late Oct–Jun*. A fairly easy, modern road, but heavy traffic at weekends. A long ascent, finally hairpin bends; then a terraced descent with six hairpins into the Rhône valley.
Grossglockner 8,212ft Austria *(Map 13 B2)*	Bruck an der Glocknerstrasse (2,480ft) Heiligenblut (4,268ft)	33km 15km	1 in 8 1 in 8	16ft	*UC late Oct–Jun*. Numerous well-engineered hairpin bends; moderate but very long ascents; toll road; very fine scenery; heavy tourist traffic; *negotiable preferably from south to north, by caravans*.

*Permitted maximum width of vehicles 7ft 6in
†Permitted maximum width of vehicles 8ft 2½in

See page 28 for other abbreviations

Pass and height	From To	Distances from summit and max gradient		Min width of road	Conditions
Hochtannberg 5,510ft Austria *(Map 12 C2)*	Schröcken (4,163ft) Warth (near Lech) (4,921ft)	6km 4km	1 in 7 1 in 11	13ft	*OC Jan–May.* A reconstructed modern road.
Iseran 9,088ft France *(Map 28 C4)*	Bourg-St-Maurice (2,756ft) Lanslebourg (4,587ft)	49km 33km	1 in 12 1 in 9	13ft	*UC mid Oct–mid Jun.* The second highest pass in the Alps. Well-graded with reasonable bends, average surface; several unlit tunnels on northern approach.
Izoard 7,743ft France *(Map 28 C3)*	Guillestre (3,248ft) Briançon (4,396ft)	32km 20km	1 in 8 1 in 10	16ft	*UC late Oct–mid Jun.* A fairly easy but winding road with many hairpin bends.
*****Jaun** 4,948ft Switzerland *(Map 11 B1)*	Broc (2,378ft) Reidenbach (2,759ft)	25km 8km	1 in 10 1 in 10	13ft	*UO.* A modernised but generally narrow road; some poor sections on ascent, and several hairpin bends on descent; *negotiable by caravans.*
†Julier 7,493ft Switzerland *(Map 12 C1)*	Tiefencastel (2,821ft) Silvaplana (5,958ft)	36km 7km	1 in 10 1 in 7½	13ft	*UO.* Well-engineered road approached from Chur by Lenzerheide Pass (5,098ft); *suitable for caravans.*
Katschberg 5,384ft Austria *(Map 13 B2)*	Spittal (1,818ft) St Michael (3,504ft)	35km 6km	1 in 5½ 1 in 6	20ft	*UO.* Steep though not particularly difficult; parallel toll motorway, including tunnel, now open; *negotiable by light caravans,* using tunnel
*****Klausen** 6,404ft Switzerland *(Map 12 C1)*	Altdorf (1,512ft) Linthal (2,165ft)	25km 23km	1 in 11 1 in 11	16ft	*UC early Nov–mid May.* Easy in spite of a number of sharp bends; *no through route for caravans as they are prohibited on part of road in Canton of Glarus.*
Larche (della Maddalena) 6,545ft France–Italy *(Map 28 C3)*	Condamine (4,291ft) Vinadio (2,986ft)	19km 32km	1 in 12 1 in 12	10ft	*OC Nov–Mar.* An easy, well-graded road; narrow and rough on ascent, wider with better surface on descent; *suitable for caravans.*
Lautaret 6,752ft France *(Map 28 C3)*	Le Bourg-d'Oisans (2,359ft) Briançon (4,396ft)	38km 28km	1 in 8 1 in 10	14ft	*OC Dec–Apr* during the day, but closed between 19.00–07.00hrs Nov–Apr. Modern, evenly graded, but winding, and unguarded in places; very fine scenery; *suitable for caravans.*
Loibl (Ljubelj) 3,500ft Austria–Yugoslavia *(Map 14 C1)*	Unterloibl (1,699ft) Kranj (1,263ft)	10km 29km	1 in 5½ 1 in 8	20ft	*UO.* Steep rise and fall over Little Loibl Pass to tunnel under summit; from south to north just *negotiable by experienced drivers with light caravans.* The old road over the summit is closed to through traffic.
*****Lukmanier (Lucomagno)** 6,289ft Switzerland *(Map 12 C1)*	Olivone (2,945ft) Disentis (3,772ft)	18km 22km	1 in 11 1 in 11	16ft	*UC early Nov–mid May.* Rebuilt, modern road; *suitable for caravans.*
†Maloja 5,960ft Switzerland *(Map 12 C1)*	Silvaplana (5,958ft) Chiavenna (1,083ft)	11km 32km	level 1 in 11	13ft	*UO.* Escarpment facing south; fairly easy but many hairpin bends on descent; *negotiable by caravans,* possibly difficult on ascent.
Mauria 4,258ft Italy *(Map 13 B1)*	Lozzo Cadore (2,470ft) Ampezzo (1,837ft)	14km 31km	1 in 14 1 in 14	16ft	*UO.* A well-designed road with easy, winding ascent and descent; *suitable for caravans.*
Mendola 4,475ft Italy *(Map 12 D1)*	Appiano (1,365ft) Sarnonico (3,208ft)	15km 8km	1 in 8 1 in 10	16ft	*UO.* A fairly straightforward, but winding road; well guarded; *suitable for caravans.*
Mont Cenis 6,834ft France–Italy *(Map 28 C3)*	Lanslebourg (4,587ft) Susa (1,624ft)	11km 28km	1 in 10 1 in 8	16ft	*UC Nov–May.* Approach by industrial valley. An easy, broad highway but with poor surface in places; *suitable for caravans;* alternative rail tunnel (see page 37).

*Permitted maximum width of vehicles 7ft 6in
†Permitted maximum width of vehicles 8ft 2½in

See page 28 for other abbreviations

Pass and height	From To	Distances from summit and max gradient		Min width of road	Conditions
Monte Croce di Comélico (Kreuzberg) 5,368ft Italy *(Map 13 A/B1)*	San Candido (3,847ft)	15km	1 in 12	16ft	*UO.* A winding road with moderate gradients; beautiful scenery; *suitable for caravans.*
	Santo Stefano di Cadore (2,978ft)	22km	1 in 12		
Montgenèvre 6,100ft France—Italy *(Map 28 C3)*	Briançon (4,396ft)	11km	1 in 14	16ft	*UO.* An easy, modern road; *suitable for caravans.*
	Cesana Torinese (4,429ft)	8km	1 in 11		
Monte Giovo (Jaufen) 6,869ft Italy *(Map 12 D1)*	Merano (1,063ft)	41km	1 in 8	13ft	*UC Nov—early May.* Many well-engineered hairpin bends; *caravans prohibited.*
	Vipiteno (3,115ft)	19km	1 in 11		
***Mosses** 4,740ft Switzerland *(Map 11 A1)*	Aigle (1,378ft)	18km	1 in 12	13ft	*UO.* A modern road; *suitable for caravans.*
	Château-d'Oex (3,153ft)	15km	1 in 12		
Nassfeld (Pramollo) 5,092ft Austria—Italy *(Map 13 B1)*	Tröpolach (1,972ft)	10km	1 in 5	13ft	*UO.* An alternative to the Plöcken Pass, which is often closed for long periods during the winter. The Austrian section is mostly narrow and winding, with tight, blind bends; the winding descent in Italy has been improved.
	Pontebba (1,841ft)	12km	1 in 10		
Nufenen 8,130ft Switzerland *(Map 11 B1)*	Ulrichen (4,416ft)	13km	1 in 10	13ft	*UC mid Oct—mid Jun.* The approach roads are narrow, with tight bends, but the road over the pass is good; *negotiable by light caravans (limit 1.5 tons).*
	Airolo (3,745ft)	24km	1 in 10		
***Oberalp** 6,709ft Switzerland *(Map 12 C1)*	Andermatt (4,737ft)	10km	1 in 10	16ft	*UC early Nov—mid May.* A much improved and widened road with a modern surface; many hairpin bends but long level stretch on summit; *negotiable by caravans.*
	Disentis (3,772ft)	22km	1 in 10		
***Ofen (Fuorn)** 7,070ft Switzerland *(Map 12 D1)*	Zernez (4,836ft)	22km	1 in 10	12ft	*OC Nov—Mar.* Good, fairly easy road through the Swiss National Park; *suitable for caravans.*
	Santa Maria im Münstertal (4,547ft)	14km	1 in 8		
Petit St Bernard 7,178ft France—Italy *(Map 28 C4)*	Bourg-St-Maurice (2,756ft)	31km	1 in 20	16ft	*UC late Oct—Jun.* Outstanding scenery; a fairly easy approach but poor surface and unguarded broken edges near the summit; good on the descent in Italy; *negotiable by light caravans.*
	Pré St-Didier (3,335ft)	23km	1 in 12		
Peyresourde 5,128ft France *(Map 20 D3)*	Arreau (2,310ft)	18km	1 in 10	13ft	*OC late Nov—early Apr.* Somewhat narrow with several hairpin bends, though not difficult.
	Luchon (2,067ft)	14km	1 in 10		
***Pillon** 5,070ft Switzerland *(Map 11 B1)*	Le Sépey (3,212ft)	14km	1 in 11	13ft	*UO.* A comparatively easy modern road; *suitable for caravans.*
	Gsteig (2,911ft)	7km	1 in 11		
Plöcken (Monte Croce-Carnico) 4,468ft Austria—Italy *(Map 13 B1)*	Kötschach (2,316ft)	14km	1 in 7	16ft	*OC Dec—Apr;* Nassfeld Pass possible alternative. A modern road with long reconstructed sections; heavy traffic at summer weekends; delay likely at the frontier; *negotiable by caravans;* to avoid congestion *caravans are prohibited at summer weekends.*
	Paluzza (1,968ft)	16km	1 in 14		
Pordoi 7,346ft Italy *(Map 13 A1)*	Arabba (5,253ft)	9km	1 in 10	16ft	*OC Nov—May.* An excellent modern road with numerous hairpin bends; *negotiable by caravans.*
	Canazei (4,806ft)	12km	1 in 10		
Port 4,098ft France *(Map 22 C4)*	Tarascon (1,555ft)	18km	1 in 10	14ft	*OC Nov—Apr.* A fairly easy road but narrow on some bends; *negotiable by caravans.*
	Massat (2,133ft)	13km	1 in 10		

*Permitted maximum width of vehicles 7ft 6in

See page 28 for other abbreviations

Pass and height	From To	Distances from summit and max gradient		Min width of road	Conditions
Portet-d'Aspet 3,507ft France *(Map 20 D3)*	Audressein (1,625ft) Fronsac (1,548ft)	19km 38km	1 in 7 1 in 7	11ft	*UO.* Approached from the west by the easy Col des Ares (2,611ft) and Col de Buret (1,975ft); well-engineered road, but calls for particular care on hairpin bends; rather narrow.
Pötschen 3,221ft Austria *(Map 13 B2)*	Bad Ischl (1,535ft) Bad Aussee (2,133ft)	17km 8km	1 in 11 1 in 11	23ft	*UO.* A modern road; *suitable for caravans.*
Pourtalet 5,879ft France–Spain *(Map 20 C3)*	Eaux-Chaudes (2,152ft) Biescas (2,821ft)	23km 34km	1 in 10 1 in 10	11ft	*UC Nov–May.* A fairly easy, unguarded road, but narrow in places; poor but being rebuilt on Spanish side.
Puymorens 6,281ft France *(Map 22 C4)*	Ax-les-Thermes (2,362ft) Bourg-Madame (3,707ft)	29km 27km	1 in 10 1 in 10	18ft	*OC Nov–Apr.* A generally easy modern tarmac road, but narrow, winding, and with a poor surface in places; not suitable for night driving; *suitable for caravans.* Alternative rail service available between Ax-les-Thermes and La Tour-de-Carol.
Quillane 5,623ft France *(Map 22 C4)*	Quillan (955ft) Mont-Louis (5,135ft)	63km 5km	1 in 12 1 in 12	16ft	*OC Nov–Mar.* An easy, straightforward ascent and descent; *suitable for caravans.*
Radstädter-Tauern 5,702ft Austria *(Map 13 B2)*	Radstadt (2,808ft) St Michael (3,504ft)	21km 26km	1 in 6 1 in 7	16ft	*OC Nov–Apr.* Northern ascent steep but not difficult otherwise; parallel toll motorway including tunnel now open; *negotiable by light caravans, using tunnel.*
Resia (Reeschen-Scheideck) 4,954ft Italy–Austria *(Map 12 D1)*	Spondigna (2,903ft) Prutz (2,841ft)	30km 35km	1 in 10 1 in 10	20ft	*UO.* A good straightforward alternative to the Brenner; *suitable for caravans.*
Restefond (La Bonette) 9,193ft France *(Map 28 C2/3)*	Jausiers (near Barcelonnette) (3,986ft) St-Etienne-de-Tinée (3,766ft)	23km 27km	1 in 9 1 in 9	10ft	*UC early Oct–late Jun.* The highest pass in the Alps, completed in 1962. Narrow, rough, unguarded ascent with many blind bends, and nine hairpins. Descent easier; winding with twelve hairpin bends.
Rolle 6,463ft Italy *(Map 13 A1)*	Predazzo (3,337ft) Mezzano (2,126ft)	21km 25km	1 in 11 1 in 14	16ft	*OC Nov–Mar.* Very beautiful scenery; bitumen surface; a well-engineered road; *negotiable by caravans.*
Rombo (see Timmelsjoch)					
Roncesvalles (Ibañeta) 3,468ft France–Spain *(Map 20 A/B2)*	St-Jean-Pied-de-Port (584ft) Pamplona (1,380ft)	26km 53km	1 in 10 1 in 10	13ft	*UO.* A slow and winding, scenic route; *negotiable by caravans.*
Route des Crêtes 4,210ft France *(Map 11 A/B2)*	St-Dié (1,125ft) Cernay (902ft)	— —	1 in 8 1 in 8	13ft	*UC Nov–Apr.* A renowned scenic route crossing seven ridges, with the highest point at Hôtel du Grand Ballon.
†St Gotthard 6,860ft Switzerland *(Map 11 B1)*	Göschenen (3,704ft) Airolo (3,745ft)	19km 15km	1 in 10 1 in 10	20ft	*UC Nov–mid May.* Modern, fairly easy; a new road avoids top twenty-five hairpin bends of the famous terraced descent of thirty-seven bends. Heavy traffic; *negotiable by caravans* (max height vehicles 11ft 9in). Alternative rail tunnel (see page 37).
*San Bernardino 6,778ft Switzerland *(Map 12 C1)*	Mesocco (2,549ft) Hinterrhein (5,328ft)	22km 8km	1 in 10 1 in 10	13ft	*UC Nov–mid June.* Easy, modern roads on northern and southern approaches to tunnel (see page 36); narrow and winding over summit; via tunnel *suitable for caravans.*

*Permitted maximum width of vehicles 7ft 6in
†Permitted maximum width of vehicles 8ft 2½in

See page 28 for other abbreviations

Pass and height	From To	Distances from summit and max gradient		Min width of road	Conditions
Seeberg (Jezersko) 3,990ft Austria–Yugoslavia *(Map 14 C1)*	Eisenkappel (1,821ft) Kranj (1,263ft)	14km 33km	1 in 8 1 in 10	16ft	*UO*. An alternative to the steeper Loibl and Wurzen passes; moderate climb with winding, hairpin ascent and descent.
Sella 7,264ft Italy *(Map 13 A1)*	Plan (5,269ft) Canazei (4,806ft)	9km 9km	1 in 9 1 in 9	16ft	*OC Nov–May*. A finely engineered, winding road; exceptional views of the Dolomites.
Semmering 3,215ft Austria *(Map 14 D2)*	Mürzzuschlag im Mürztal (2,205ft) Gloggnitz (1,427ft)	13km 16km	1 in 16 1 in 16	20ft	*UO*. A fine, well-engineered highway; *suitable for caravans.*
Sestriere 6,660ft Italy *(Map 28 C3)*	Cesana Torinese (4,429ft) Pinerolo (1,234ft)	12km 55km	1 in 10 1 in 10	16ft	*UO*. Mostly bitumen surface; *negotiable by caravans.*
Silvretta (Bielerhöhe) 6,666ft Austria *(Map 12 C1)*	Partenen (3,451ft) Galtür (5,195ft)	15km 10km	1 in 9 1 in 9	16ft	*UC late Oct–late May*. For the most part reconstructed; thirty-two easy hairpin bends on western ascent; eastern side more straightforward. Toll road; *caravans prohibited.*
†Simplon 6,578ft Switzerland–Italy *(Map 28 D4)*	Brig (2,231ft) Domodóssola (919ft)	22km 41km	1 in 9 1 in 11	23ft	*OC Nov–Apr*. An easy, reconstructed modern road, but 13 miles long, continuous ascent to summit; *suitable for caravans.* Alternative rail tunnel (see page 37).
Somport 5,350ft France–Spain *(Map 20 C3)*	Bedous (1,365ft) Jaca (2,687ft)	31km 30km	1 in 10 1 in 10	12ft	*UO*. A favoured, old established route; generally easy; but in parts narrow and unguarded; fairly good-surfaced road; *suitable for caravans.*
*Splügen 6,930ft Switzerland–Italy *(Map 12 C1)*	Splügen (4,790ft) Chiavenna (1,083ft)	9km 30km	1 in 9 1 in 7½	10ft	*UC Nov–May*. Mostly narrow and winding, with many hairpin bends, and not well guarded; care also required at many tunnels and galleries.
††Stelvio 9,080ft Italy *(Map 12 D1)*	Bormio (4,019ft) Spondigna (2,903ft)	22km 28km	1 in 8 1 in 8	13ft	*UC Oct–Jun*. The third highest pass in the Alps; the number of acute hairpin bends, all well-engineered, is exceptional – from forty to fifty on either side; the surface is good, the traffic heavy. Hairpin bends are too acute for long vehicles.
†Susten 7,300ft Switzerland *(Map 11 B1)*	Innertkirchen (2,067ft) Wassen (3,018ft)	28km 19km	1 in 11 1 in 11	20ft	*UC Nov–Jun*. A very scenic route and a good example of modern road engineering; easy gradients and turns; heavy traffic at weekends; *negotiable by caravans.*
Tenda (Tende) 4,331ft Italy–France *(Map 28 C2)*	Borgo S Dalmazzo (2,103ft) La Giandola (1,059ft)	24km 29km	1 in 11 1 in 11	18ft	*UO*. Well guarded, modern road with several hairpin bends; road tunnel at summit; suitable for caravans; *but prohibited during the winter.*
Thurn 4,177ft Austria *(Map 13 A/B2)*	Kitzbühel (2,502ft) Mittersill (2,588ft)	19km 11km	1 in 12 1 in 16	16ft	*UO*. A good road with narrow stretches; northern approach rebuilt; *suitable for caravans.*
Timmelsjoch (Rombo) 8,232ft Austria–Italy *(Map 12 D1)*	Obergurgl (6,322ft) Moso (3,304ft)	14km 23km	1 in 7 1 in 8	12ft	*UC mid Oct–late June*. Roadworks on Italian side still in progress. The pass is open to private cars (without trailers) only as some tunnels on the Italian side are too narrow for larger vehicles; toll road.

*Permitted maximum width of vehicles 7ft 6in   ††Maximum length of vehicle 30ft
†Permitted maximum width of vehicles 8ft 2½in   See page 28 for other abbreviations

34

Pass and height	From To	Distances from summit and max gradient		Min width of road	Conditions
Tonale 6,181ft Italy *(Map 12 D1)*	Edolo (2,264ft) Dimaro (2,513ft)	30km 27km	1 in 14 1 in 8	16ft	*UO*. A relatively easy road; *suitable for caravans.*
Tosas 5,905ft Spain *(Map 22 C4)*	Puigcerdá (3,708ft) Ribas de Freser (3,018ft)	25km 25km	1 in 10 1 in 10	16ft	*UO*. Now a fairly straightforward, but continuously winding two-lane road with many sharp bends; some unguarded edges; *negotiable by caravans.*
Tourmalet 6,936ft France *(Map 20 D3)*	Luz (2,333ft) Ste-Marie-de-Campan (2,811ft)	19km 16km	1 in 8 1 in 8	14ft	*UC Nov–late Jun.* The highest of the French Pyrenees routes; the approaches are good though winding and exacting over summit; sufficiently guarded.
Tre Croci 5,935ft Italy *(Map 13 A1)*	Cortina d'Ampezzo (3,983ft) Pelos (2,427ft)	7km 48km	1 in 9 1 in 9	16ft	*UO*. An easy pass; very fine scenery; *suitable for caravans.*
Turracher Höhe 5,784ft Austria *(Map 13 B1)*	Predlitz (3,024ft) Reichenau (3,281ft)	20km 8km	1 in 5½ 1 in 4½	13ft	*OC Nov–Apr.* Formerly one of the steepest mountain roads in Austria, now much improved; steep, fairly straightforward ascent, followed by a very steep descent; good surface and mainly two-lane width; fine scenery.
***Umbrail** 8,205ft Switzerland– Italy *(Map 12 D1)*	Santa Maria im Münstertal (4,547ft) Bormio (4,019ft)	13km 19km	1 in 11 1 in 11	14ft	*UC early Nov–late May.* Highest of the Swiss passes; narrow; mostly gravel surfaced with thirty-four hairpin bends but not too difficult
Vars 6,919ft France *(Map 28 C3)*	St-Paul-sur-Ubaye (4,823ft) Guillestre (3,248ft)	8km 20km	1 in 10 1 in 10	16ft	*OC late Nov–late Apr.* Easy winding ascent with seven hairpin bends; gradual winding descent with another seven hairpin bends; good surface; *negotiable by caravans.*
Wurzen (Koren) 3,520ft Austria– Yugoslavia *(Map 13 B1)*	Riegersdorf (1,752ft) Kranjska Gora (2,657ft)	7km 6km	1 in 5½ 1 in 5½	13ft	*UO*. A steep two-lane road which otherwise is not particularly difficult; *caravans prohibited.*
Zirler Berg 3,310ft Austria *(Map 12 D2)*	Seefeld (3,870ft) Zirl (2,041ft)	7km 5km	1 in 7 1 in 6½	20ft	*UO*. An escarpment facing south, part of the route from Garmisch to Innsbruck; a good modern road but heavy tourist traffic and a long steep descent, with one hairpin bend, into the Inn Valley. Steepest section from the hairpin bend down to Zirl.

*Permitted maximum width of vehicles 7ft 6in   See page 28 for other abbreviations

Major road tunnels

All charges listed below should be used as a guide only.

In addition to the seven road tunnels below, more are being planned. The Arlberg road tunnel in Austria (14km long) may open in 1979. The Frejus road tunnel between France and Italy (12.7km long) and the St Gotthard road tunnel in Switzerland (16.3km long) may now not open until 1980.

Pyrenees
France—Spain
Map 21 B4

This new trans-Pyrenean tunnel is now open. The tunnel is 3km (2 miles) long, and runs nearly 6,000ft above sea level between Aragnouet and Bielsa. It is probable that there will be a toll.

Grand St Bernard
Switzerland—Italy
Map 28 C4

The tunnel is over 6,000ft above sea level; although there are covered approaches, wheel chains may be needed to reach it in winter. The Customs, passport control, and toll offices are at the entrance. The tunnel is 5.9km (3½ miles) long. The permitted maximum dimensions of vehicles are – *height* 4m (13ft 1in) *width* 2.5m (8ft 2in).

The minimum speed is 40kph (24mph) and the maximum 80kph (49mph). Do not stop or overtake. There are breakdown bays with telephones on either side.

Charges

The toll charges are calculated according to the wheelbase.

(in Swiss francs or Italian lire)	Fr	L
motorcycles	4	1,400
cars: wheelbase up to 6ft 10in	12	4,150
wheelbase from 6ft 10in to 10ft 6in	18	6,200
wheelbase over 10ft 6in	27	9,350
with caravan	27	9,350
minibuses	27	9,350
coaches	54–90	18,700–31,800

Mont Blanc
Chamonix
(France)—
Courmayeur (Italy)
Map 28 C4

The tunnel is over 4,000ft above sea level. It is 11.6km (7 miles) long. Customs and passport control are at the Italian end. The permitted maximum dimensions of vehicles are: *height* 4.15m (13ft 7in); *length* 18m (59ft); *width* 2.5m (8ft 2in). *Total weight* 35 metric tons (34 tons 9cwt); *axle weight* 13 metric tons (12 tons 16cwt). The minimum speed is 50kph (31mph) and the maximum 80kph (50mph). Do not stop or overtake. Keep 100m (110 yd) between vehicles. Turn side and rear lights on, but not headlights. There are breakdown bays with telephones.

Charges

The tolls are calculated according to the wheelbase (in French francs).

		Fr
cars:	wheelbase up to 2.3m (7ft 6½in)	28
	wheelbase from 2.3m to 2.63m (7ft 6½in to 8ft 7½in)	43
	wheelbase from 2.64m to 3.3m (8ft 7½in to 10ft 10in) and cars with caravans	57
	wheelbase over 3.3m (10ft 10in)	130
vehicles:	with three axles	200
	with four, or more axles	260

San Bernardino
Switzerland
Map 12 C1

This tunnel is over 5,000ft above sea level. It is 6.6km (4 miles) long, 4.8m (15ft 9in) high, and the carriageway is 7m (23ft) wide.

Do not stop or overtake in the tunnel. Keep 100m (110yd) between vehicles. Switch on side and rear lights, but not headlights.

There are breakdown bays with telephones.
No tolls are charged.

Felbertauern
Austria
Map 13 B2

This tunnel is over 5,000ft above sea level; it runs between Mittersill and Matrei, to the west of and parallel to the Grossglockner Pass.

36

The tunnel is 5.2km (3¼ miles) long, 4.5m (15ft) high, and the two-lane carriageway is 7m (23ft) wide.

From November to April wheel chains are usually needed on the approach to the tunnel.

Charges
(in Austrian schillings)

	Single Sch	Return Sch
cars	180	310
caravans	90	150
motorcycles	45	80
coaches	540–1080	920–1840

Return tickets are issued. Those for cars are interchangeable between the Grossglockner Hochalpenstrasse and Felbertauern Strasse.

Katschberg
Austria
Map 13 B2

This tunnel is 3,642ft above sea level, and forms an important part of the Tauern autobahn between Salzburg and Carinthia. The tunnel is 5.4km (3½ miles) long, 4.50m (15ft) high, and the two-lane carriageway is 7.50m (25ft) wide. For charges see Tauern autobahn page 54.

Radstädter Tauern
Austria
Map 13 B2

This tunnel is 4,396ft above sea level. It is 6.4km (4 miles) long, and runs to the east of and parallel to the Tauern railway tunnel. With the Katschberg Tunnel (see above) it forms an important part of the Tauern autobahn between Salzburg and Carinthia. For charges see Tauern autobahn page 54.

Rail tunnels

Vehicles are conveyed throughout the year through the St Gotthard Tunnel (Göschenen-Airolo), the Simplon Tunnel (Brig-Iselle) and the Lotschberg Tunnel (Kandersteg-Goppenstein-Brig). Services are frequent and no advance booking is necessary and although the actual transit time is 15/20 minutes, some time may be taken by the loading and unloading formalities.

The operating company issues a full timetable and tariff list which is available from the AA, the Swiss National Tourist Office or at most Swiss frontier crossings.

Albula Tunnel
Map 12 C1

Thusis (2,372ft)/Tiefencastel (2,821ft)-Samedan (5,650ft) 5.9km (3½ miles) long.

Motor vehicles can be conveyed through this tunnel, but you are recommended to give notice. Thusis *tel* (081) 811113, Tiefencastel (081) 711112, Samedan (082) 65404.

Services

Five daily in each direction from 20 December to 31 March.

Charges

These are given in Swiss francs and are likely to increase.

	1st class	2nd class
		Fr
cars (up to eight passengers)		62 (including driver)
motorcycles		14.00 per 100kg
caravan		52
passengers	21	13.60

**France–Italy
The Mont Cenis Tunnel
(Fréjus Tunnel)**
Italy Map 28 C3

Modane (3,524ft) France–Bardonecchia (4,305ft) 13.6km (8½ miles) long.

Booking

Advance booking is unnecessary, but motorists should report at least 15 minutes before the train is due to start.

All Customs formalities are carried out at Modane, but there is passport control at both stations.

The driver must drive his vehicle on and off the wagon. Trailer caravans and baggage trailers are accepted only if accompanied by a towing vehicle.

Maximum dimensions	The maximum overall length permitted is 10m (32ft 10in); the maximum permitted height decreases as the width increases, according to the dimensions, shown below:

Width	6ft 7in	6ft 11in	7ft 2in	7ft 6in	7ft 10in	8ft 2in
Height	9ft 1in	9ft 0in	8ft 11in	8ft 9in	8ft 8in	8ft 7in

Services

There are trains from both stations all the year round hourly between 07.00 and 21.00hrs.

Charges
(in French francs or Italian lire)

The rates quoted are payable at Modane for journeys in either direction; they cannot be paid in advance in sterling.

	Fr	L
cars		
up to 12ft (3.80m)	30	5,600
up to 14ft (4.42m)	36	6,700
over 14ft (4.42m)	42	7,800
caravan trailers*	30	5,600
luggage trailers*	20	3,700
motorcycles, solo and scooters	13	2,400
with sidecar	20	3,700

Passengers: fares are included in the freight rates up to a maximum of eight including the driver.
*Accepted only if accompanied by towing vehicle.

Austria

Motor vehicles can be conveyed through the following tunnels:

Arlberg Tunnel Langen (3,990ft)–St Anton (4,222ft) Map 12 C1/2.
Tauern Tunnel Böckstein (3,711ft) (near Bad Gastein)–Mallnitz Map 13 B1/2.

Karawanken Tunnel Rosenbach-Jesenice (Yugoslavia) Map 34 A4.
Arlberg Tunnel 10.2km (6½ miles) long.

Booking

Advance booking is unnecessary (except for request trains), but motorists must report at least 30 minutes before the train is due to start. The driver must drive his vehicle on and off the wagon.

Maximum dimensions
They are: height 11ft
width 10ft 4in

Services

From November to March, when the Arlberg Pass is closed, trains operate in each direction every two hours between 08.00 and 21.00hrs. When the pass is open, there are three trains daily from Langen to St Anton, plus two trains operating on request only.

From St Anton to Langen there are three scheduled trains per day, operating on a request basis.

The minimum trainload acceptable is Sch 1,200 and any surcharge necessary to make up this sum is shared. It is very rare that these request services are used by a sufficient number of vehicles to make up the minimum surcharge of Sch 1,200.
Duration 15 minutes.

None of the rates given can be paid in advance in sterling.

Charges	Single Sch	Return Sch
cars (including passengers)	160	240
motorcycles (with or without sidecar)	30	
*caravans	100	140
*boat trailers	100	140
per passenger	11	

*These are not accepted without a towing vehicle.

Tauern Tunnel	8.5km (5½ miles) long.

Booking	As for the Arlberg Tunnel

Maximum dimensions	For caravans and trailers these are: height 8ft 10½in width 8ft 2½in

38

Services   In summer, trains run approximately every half-hour in both directions, 07.40–23.00hrs; and every hour during the night providing there is sufficient traffic; additional trains are run during the day when necessary. In winter, there is a service approximately every hour 04.45–22.05hrs. *Duration* 10 minutes.

Charges   As for the Arlberg Tunnel.

Karawanken Tunnel   8.5km (5½ miles) long.
Since the opening of the Loibl Tunnel, see page 31, assuring an all-year-round link between Klagenfurt and Ljubljana, the use of the Karawanken Tunnel by motorists is not an economic proposition.

Petrol information

Owing to the fluctuation of currencies, the price of petrol per litre in the country sections is given in the currency of the country and should be used as a guide only. The minimum amount of petrol which may be purchased is usually five litres (just over one gallon). It is advisable to keep the petrol tank topped up, particularly in remote areas or if wishing to make an early start when garages may be closed. Some garages may close between 12.00 and 15.00hrs for lunch.

Cars hired in countries where petrol coupons are available will not be entitled to coupons.

Remember that the fuel which is contained in the tank may be temporarily imported duty free, but that duty may have to be paid on any carried in cans. On sea and air ferries and Continental car-sleeper trains operators insist that spare cans must be empty. *Note:* a roof rack laden with luggage increases petrol consumption, which should be taken into consideration when calculating mileage per gallon.

You are strongly advised to secure your petrol with a locking filler cap.

Report forms
(accommodation, garages, roads)

We would appreciate your comments on accommodation, garages and roads to help us to prepare future publications. Please list your comments on the report forms provided at the back of the Guide. The accommodation report form is for your comments on hotels and motels which you have visited, whether they are listed in the handbook or not.

Similarly, the garage report form can be used for your reports on garages which you have visited. The road report form can be used for particularly bad stretches and road works.

Road and winter conditions

Main roads are usually in good condition but often not finished to our standards. The camber is often steeper than that usually found in the United Kingdom, and edges may be badly corrugated and surfaces allowed to wear beyond the customary limits before being repaired. In France such stretches are sometimes signposted *Chaussee déformée*. However, there are extensive motorway systems in Germany and Italy, and many miles of such roads in other countries. When roads under repair are closed, you must follow diversion signs – often inadequate – such as *Déviation* and *Umleitung*. To avoid damage to windscreens or paintwork, drive slowly over loose grit and take care when overtaking. Further information on roads is also given under country sections.

Motoring on the Continent during the winter months is restricted because of the vast mountain ranges – the Alps sweeping in an arc from the French Riviera, through Switzerland, northern Italy, and Austria to the borders of Yugoslavia, the Pyrenees which divide France and Spain – as well as extensive areas of Spain, France and Germany which are at an altitude of well over 1,000ft. However, matters have been eased with improved communications and modern snow-clearing apparatus.

Where comment is warranted, details are given under the Roads section of each country. Details of road and rail tunnels which can be used to pass under the mountains are given on pages 36–39, and the periods when the most important mountain passes are usually closed are given on pages 28–35. If you want a conventional seaside holiday between

October and March, you will probably have to travel at least as far south as Lisbon, Valencia, or Naples to be reasonably certain of fine weather. In Scandinavia winter motoring is possible, except that certain mountain roads in Norway are closed, and conditions in the far north are likely to be extreme.

Wheel chains, spiked or studded tyres and snow tyres

Wheel chains

These are chains which fit over the tyres to enable the wheels to grip on snow or icy surfaces. Wheel chains are sometimes called snow chains or anti-skid chains. Full-length chains which fit right round a tyre are the most satisfactory, but they must be fitted correctly. Check that the chains do not foul your vehicle bodywork; if your vehicle has front-wheel-drive put the steering on full lock while checking. If your vehicle has radial tyres it is essential that you contact the manufacturers of your vehicle and tyres for their recommendations in order to avoid damage to your tyres. Chains should only be used when compulsory or necessary as prolonged use on hard surfaces will damage the tyres.

Spiked or studded tyres

These are tyres with rugged treads onto which spikes or studs have been fitted. For the best grip they should be fitted to all wheels. Spiked or studded tyres are sometimes called snow tyres.

Snow tyres

These are usually heavy-duty tyres with rugged treads. Snow tyres (preferably fitted to all wheels) are suitable for some level surfaces and some very gradual slopes. Of the devices mentioned above, they are the least effective. In fair weather, wheel chains, spiked or studded tyres, or snow tyres are only necessary on the higher passes, but in severe weather you will probably need them (as a rough guide) at altitudes exceeding 2,000ft.

If you think you will need any of these devices, it is better to take them with you from home, but this is not always practicable.

Information on hiring and buying wheel chains in the countries where they are most needed is given under the heading Tyres in the country sections.

Wheel chains and spiked or studded tyres damage the road surface if it is free of snow or ice; there are definite periods when these may be used and in certain countries the use of spiked or studded tyres is illegal.

If wheel chains, spiked or studded tyres, or snow tyres are compulsory, this is usually signposted.

See also Cold-weather touring, page 14.

Winter-sports centres

You can usually reach these, as at least one main approach road is swept, but you may need wheel chains, spiked or studded tyres, or snow tyres.

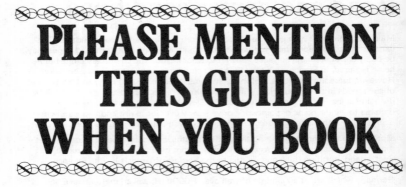

PLEASE MENTION THIS GUIDE WHEN YOU BOOK

ON ARRIVAL...

Weather information

Any AA service centre can give general information about winter weather conditions on the Continent, but detailed information about conditions on mountain passes and main roads is available from the AA London Operational Centre, Stanmore, *tel* 01-954 7373. Information is received from the European Road Information Centre, which gets daily reports from all associated motoring clubs. You can also get information about current Continental conditions from the weather centres of the Meteorological Offices in:

London	01-836 4311
Manchester	061-832 6701
Newcastle upon Tyne	Newcastle upon Tyne 26453
Southampton	Southampton 28844
Glasgow	041-248 3451
Watnall, Nottingham	Hucknall 3311

If you want more detailed information when planning your holiday, contact the World Climatology Branch of the Meteorological Office at Bracknell, Berkshire, *tel* 20242. For detailed information a charge is made, the amount depending on the work involved in answering the specific enquiry.

When you are abroad, you should contact the nearest office of the appropriate national motoring club.

Customs concessions

Visitors to the countries listed in this Guide which are not members of the EEC may assume as a general guide that they may temporarily import personal articles duty free, providing the following conditions are met:

1 that they are for personal use and are not to be sold;
2 that they may be considered as being in use and in keeping with your personal status;
3 that they are taken out when you leave;
4 that you stay less than 6 months in any 12-month period, unless otherwise stated.

Customs officers may withhold concessions at any time and may ask the traveller to deposit enough money to cover possible duty. Concessions may not apply if the traveller enters the country more than once a month, or if he is under 17 years of age (an alternative age may apply in some countries). Should you be taking a large number of personal effects with you, it would be a wise measure to prepare in advance an inventory to present to the Customs authorities on demand. All dutiable articles must be declared when you enter a country, otherwise you will be liable to penalties. It is generally accepted that the following quantities can be taken into most European countries (with the exception of the EEC countries), without payment of duty or purchase tax:

1 **Tobacco** 200 cigarettes or 250 grammes of other manufactured tobaccos;
2 **Wine** 1 litre of wine with the exception of *Austria* and *Switzerland* (2 litres).
3 **Spirits** 1 litre of spirits with the exception of *Portugal* (half a litre);
4 **Toilet water** 0.25 litre.
5 **Cameras** 1 camera, 1 cine-camera.

Customs concessions for the United Kingdom

Returning to the United Kingdom When returning to the United Kingdom you must declare everything (purchases or gifts) in excess of the duty-free allowances (set out below) which you have obtained abroad or on the journey, or free of duty or tax in this country. You must also declare any alterations or additions which have been made to your motor car while abroad.

41

Prohibitions and restrictions

The importation of certain goods into the United Kingdom is prohibited or restricted. These include controlled drugs, counterfeit coins, firearms (including gas pistols), ammunition, explosives, gold coins, medals, medallions and similar gold pieces, horror comics, indecent and obscene books, magazines, films and other articles, live animals and birds, derivatives of rare species including certain fur skins, and garments thereof, and plumage, meat and poultry (not fully cooked), plants, potatoes, bulbs, trees and certain vegetables and fruit, radio transmitters (including walkie-talkies), radio microphones and microbugs.

Duty and tax-free allowances

You are entitled to the allowances in either column 1 or column 2. The countries of the EEC (Common Market) are Belgium, Denmark, France, West Germany, the Irish Republic, Italy, Luxembourg, the Netherlands and the United Kingdom (but not the Channel Islands).

Goods obtained duty and tax-paid in the EEC.

Goods obtained outside the EEC, or duty or tax-free in the EEC.

Tobacco goods

Cigarettes	300	200	
or			
Cigarillos	150	100	double if you live outside Europe
or			
Cigars	75	50	
or			
Tobacco	400 grammes	250 grammes	

Alcoholic drinks

Over 38.8° proof (22° Gay Lussac)	1½ litres	1 litre
or		
not over 38.8° proof or fortified or sparkling wine	3 litres	2 litres
plus		
still table wine	3 litres	2 litres

Persons under 17 are not entitled to tobacco and drinks allowances.

Perfume	75 grammes (3 fl oz or 90cc)	50 grammes (2 fl oz or 60cc)
Toilet water	375cc (13 fl oz)	250cc (9 fl oz)
Other goods	£50 worth	£10 worth

Please note

1 The allowances apply only to goods carried in baggage which is cleared by you at the time of your arrival. Goods obtained duty and tax-paid may not be mixed with goods obtained duty and tax-free to obtain the higher allowances.

2 None of the allowances apply to goods brought in for sale or other commercial purposes.

3 Reduced allowances apply to certain persons crossing the land frontier from the Republic of Ireland, and to seamen and aircrew members.

4 Whisky, gin, rum, brandy, vodka, and most liqueurs normally exceed 38.8° proof, but advocaat, cassis, fraise, and suze may be less.

Fortified wines include port, sherry, vermouth, madeira, and aperitifs.

Sparkling wines include champagne, perelada, spumante, and semi-sparkling wines.

Still table wines include claret, sauterne, graves, chianti.

Other wine: Burgundy, chablis, hock, and moselle may be either sparkling or still, depending on manufacture.

When duty is payable

1 Spirits, wine, tobacco, lighters and perfume are charged according to quantity and kind. The Customs charges are likely to be substantially more than the price you paid and will be chargeable on the amount you have in excess of the duty-free allowances.

2 Other goods: duty and VAT will be charged at the appropriate rate on articles which are not wholly admissible free under the duty-free allowance.

Customs offices

Many Customs offices at the main frontier crossings are open 24 hours daily to deal with touring documents.

Those with restricted opening times are listed below. The hours shown are for the handling of tourist documents. At all frontier crossings, other transactions, such as the payment of duty, can be carried out during normal business hours only.

The table can be read in either direction; *eg* for France—Belgium read from left to right, for Belgium—France read from right to left.

Nearest town	Map ref	Road number	Frontier post	Opening times		Frontier post	Road number	Map ref	Nearest town
France						**Belgium/Luxembourg**			
Dunkirk	3 A1	N16A	Oost-Capel	06.00-22.00		Kapelhoek (Stavele)	9	3 A1	Ypres
Lille	3 B1	N41	Baisieux	08.00-12.00 14.00-18.00 Mon-Fri		Hertain	8	3 B1	Tournai
Valenciennes	3 B1	N45	Maulde	06.00-22.00		Bléharies	71	3 B1	Tournai
Maubeuge	3 B1	N49	Cousolre	07.00-21.00		Leugnies	36	3 B1	Beaumont
Avesnes	3 B1	N362	Hestrud	07.00-22.00		Grandrieu	21	3 B1	Beaumont
Rocroi	10 C4	D949	Givet	08.00-21.00		Petit Doische	N46	10 C4	Philippeville
Rocroi	10 C4	D949	Givet	08.00-21.00		Dion	N46	10 C4	Beauraing
France						**Germany**			
Metz	11 A3	D954	Villing	06.00-22.00 (1 Oct-31 Mar)	04.00-23.00 (1 Apr-30 Sep)	Ittersdorf Villinger Strasse	269	11 A3	Saarlouis
France						**Italy**			
Bourge St-Maurice	28 C4	N90	Col du Petit St-Bernard	Always (when pass is open)		Col du Petit St-Bernard	26	28 C4	Aosta
St Michel de-Maurienne	28 C3	N6	Grand-Croix	Always (when pass is open)		Molaretto	25	28 C3	Susa
France						**Spain**			
Biarritz	19 B3	N10	Béhobie	Always 07.00-24.00	15 Jun-30 Sep 1 Oct-14 Jun	Béhobia	N1	19 B3	San Sebastián
Bayonne	20 C3	D20	Ainhoa	1 May-30 Sep 1 Oct-30 Apr	07.00-24.00 07.00-22.00	Dancharinea	N121	20 C3	Pamplona
St-Jean-Pied-de-Port	20 C3	D933	Arnéguy	as above		Valcarlos	C135	20 C3	Pamplona
Oloron-Ste-Marie	20 C3	N134	Urdos	May-Oct 07.00-24.00 Nov-Apr 09.00-21.00	16 Jun-30 Sep 07.00-24.00 1 Oct-15 Jun 08.00-21.00	Canfranc	N330	20 C3	Jaca
Pau	20 C3	N134 bis	Eaux-Chaudes	1 Jun-31 Oct 1 Nov-31 May	07.00-24.00 08.00-21.00	Sallent-de-Gallego	C136	20 C3	Huesca
Montrejeau	20 D3	D125	Bagnères de Luchon	08.00-22.00		Bosost-El Portillón	D27	20 D3	Viella
St-Béat	20 D3	N618C	Fos	As above	1 May-30 Sep Always 31 Oct-30 Apr 08.00-21.00 *Hols & Hol eves* 08.00-24.00	Lés	N230	20 D3	Viella
Amélie-les-Bains	22 D4	D115	Prats-de-Mollo	1 Jun-30 Sep 08.00-24.00 1 Oct-31 May 08.00-20.00		Camprodón	C151	22 D4	Ripoll
Belgium						**Netherlands**			
Maldegem	3 B2	68	Stroobrugge	Summer: 07.00-24.00 Winter: 07.00-21.00		Eede	N97	3 B2	Breskens
Gent	3 B2	56	Watervliet	07.00-19.00		Veldzigt	Unclass	3 B2	Breskens
Gent	3 B2	58b	Zelzate	06.00-21.00		Sas van Gent	Unclass	3 B2	Terneuzen
Antwerp	4 C2	Unclass	Putte	06.00-24.00		Putte	Unclass	4 C2	Bergen-op Zoom
Turnhout	4 C2	20	Weelde	07.00-24.00		Baarle-Nassau	Unclass	4 C2	Breda

43

Nearest town	Map ref	Road number	Frontier post	Opening times	Frontier post	Road number	Map ref	Nearest town

Netherlands / Germany

Nearest town	Map ref	Road number	Frontier post	Opening times	Frontier post	Road number	Map ref	Nearest town
Emmen	4 D3	N92	Coevorden	06.00-24.00	Escherbrügge	403	4 D3	Nordhorn
Zutphen	4 D2	Unclass	's-Heerenberg	06.00-24.00	Heerenbergerbrücke	E36	4 D2	Emmerich
Venlo	4 D2	Unclass	Herungerweg	06.00-22.00	Niederdorf	60	4 D2	Moers

Italy / Switzerland

Nearest town	Map ref	Road number	Frontier post	Opening times	Frontier post	Road number	Map ref	Nearest town
Aosta	28 C4	27	Grand St Bernard Pass / Tunnel	Always (when pass is open) / Always	Grand St Bernard Pass / Tunnel	21	28 C4	Martigny
Domodóssola	28 D4	337	Ponte Ribellasca	05.00-24.00/01.00	Camedo	69	28 D4	Locarno
Luino	28 D4	394	Zenna	06.00-23.00 Hols 06.00-24.00	Dirinella	Unclass	28 D4	Locarno
Luino	28 D4	Unclass	Fornasette	Weekdays–06.00-23.00 Holidays–06.00-24.00	Fornasette	Unclass	28 D4	Lugano
Porlezza	28 A4	340	Valsolda	05.00-02.00 (Oct-Mar 05.30-01.00)	Gandria	Unclass	28 A4	Lugano
Chiavenna	12 C1	36	Montespluga	05.00-01.00 (when pass is open)	Splügen Pass	64	12 C1	Thusis
Tirano	29 A4	38	Piattamala	1 May-30 Sep 05.00-02.00 / 1 Oct-30 Apr 05.00-01.00	Campocologno	29 via Bernina Pass	29 A4	Pontresina
Bormio	12 D1	38	Giogo di Maria (Stelvio)	05.00-24.00 (when pass is open)	Umbrail Pass	28	12 D1	Sta Maria
Glorenza	12 D1	41	Tubre	04.00-24.00	Mustair	28	12 D1	Sta Maria

Switzerland / Austria

Nearest town	Map ref	Road number	Frontier post	Opening times	Frontier post	Road number	Map ref	Nearest town
Zernez	12 D1	27	Martina	04.00-24.00	Nauders (Zolhaus)	185	12 D1	Nauders

Italy / Austria

Nearest town	Map ref	Road number	Frontier post	Opening times	Frontier post	Road number	Map ref	Nearest town
Merano	12 D1	448	Passo del Rombo	07.00-20.00 (when pass is open)	Timmelsjoch	186	12 D1	Sölden
Tolmezzo	13 B1	52 bis	Timau (Monte Croce Carnico)	Always May-Sep; Oct 08.00-20.00; Nov-Apr 08.00-18.00 (when pass is open)	Mauthen via Plöcken Pass	110	13 B1	Ober-Drauburg
Pontebba	13 B1	Unclass	Passo di Pramollo	Always (when pass is open)	Nassfeld	Unclass	13 B1	Hermagor

Portugal / Spain

Nearest town	Map ref	Road number	Frontier post	Opening times	Opening times	Frontier post	Road number	Map ref	Nearest town
Oporto	17 A3	N13	Valenca do Minho	1 Apr-31 Oct 07.00-01.00 / 1 Nov-31 Mar 08.00-24.00		Tuy	550	17 A3	Vigo
Vila Real	17 B3	N2	Vila Verde da Raia	1 Nov-31 Mar 08.00-21.00 / 1 Apr-31 Oct 07.00-24.00	May-Oct 07.00-24.00 / Nov-Apr 09.00-21.00	Feces Verin	N525	17 B3	Orense
Bragança	18 C2	N218-1	Quintanilha	Apr-Oct 07.00-24.00 / Nov-Mar 08.00-21.00	Nov-Apr 09.00-21.00	San Martin del Pedroso/Alcañtara	N122	18 C2	Zamora
Guarda	17 B1	N16	Vilar Formoso	Apr-Oct 07.00-01.00 / Nov-Mar 08.00-24.00		Fuentes de Oñoro	N620	17 B1	Salamanca
Castelo Branco	23 B4	N355	Segura	Apr-Oct 07.00-24.00 / Nov-Mar 08.00-21.00	1 May-1 Oct 07.00-24.00 / 2 Oct-30 Apr 09.00-21.00	Piedras Albas	C525	23 B4	Caceres
Santarém	23 B4	N246-1	Galegos	As above	1 Apr-31 Oct 07.00-24.00 / 1 Nov-31 Mar 09.00-21.00	Valencia de Alcántara	N521	23 B4	Caceres
Elvas	23 B3	N4	Caia	Apr-Oct 07.00-01.00 / Nov-Mar 08.00-24.00	07.00-24.00	Badajoz	N5	23 B3	Mérida

Nearest town	Map ref	Road number	Frontier post	Opening times		Frontier post	Road number	Map ref	Nearest town
Mourão	23 B3	N256	Sã Leonardo	Apr-Oct 07.00-24.00 Nov-Mar 08.00-21.00	1 Apr-31 Oct 07.00-24.00 1 Nov-31 Mar 08.30-21.00	Villanueva del Fresno	C436	23 B3	**Olivenza**
Beja	23 B3	N260	Vila Verde de Ficalho	Apr-Oct 07.00-24.00 Nov-Mar 08.00-21.00	1 Apr-30 Sep 07.00-24.00 1 Oct-31 Mar 08.00-21.00	Rosal de la Frontera	N433	23 B3	**Seville**
Faro	23 B2	N125	Vila Real de Santo Antonio	08.00-23.30	1 May-31 Oct 08.00-24.00 1 Nov-30 Apr 09.00-21.00	Ayamonte	N431	23 B2	**Huelva**

Denmark / Germany

Nearest town	Map ref	Road number	Frontier post	Opening times	Frontier post	Road number	Map ref	Nearest town
Abenrå	1 A1	A10 (E3)	Kruså	Always	Kupfer-mühle	76(E3)	1 A1	**Flensburg**
			Padborg	06.00-24.00	Harrislee			

Electrical information

The public electricity supply in Europe is predominantly AC (alternating current) of 220 volts (50 cycles) but can be as low as 110 volts. In some isolated areas low voltage DC (direct current) is provided. European circular two-pin plugs and screw-type bulbs are usually the rule.

However, before connecting any appliances, it is advisable to consult the hotel or campsite proprietor, or check the voltage stamp on a light bulb.

Useful electrical adaptors (not voltage transformers) which can be used in Continental shaver points and light bulb sockets are available in the United Kingdom. Members can consult an AA service centre for the address of the suppliers if they are unable to obtain one from an electrical retailer.

Photography

Photography in European countries is generally allowed without restriction, with the exception of photographs taken within the vicinity of military or government establishments. This especially applies in the case of Balkan states, where penalties can include the confiscation of film or, in an extreme case, arrest.

Religious services

Refer to your religious organisation in the British Isles. A directory of British Protestant churches in Europe, North Africa, and the Middle East, entitled *English Speaking Churches,* can be purchased from The Commonwealth and Continental Church Society, 175 Tower Bridge Road, London SE1 2AQ *tel* 01-407 4588.

Use your headlights when visibility is poor

France: take a tip from us . . .

It is still possible for those who prefer the freedom of using their own transport, rather than embarking on a package tour, to undertake a motoring holiday on the Continent and stay in reasonably comfortable hotels, without sacrificing holidays in following years in order to pay for it.

Two of the AA's route planners have recently returned from a route inspection trip to France, their task being to check town plans, recommended routes, signposting, road and traffic conditions, for the benefit of members using the Overseas Route Service. In addition, they were asked to discover and suggest economies that could be made to reduce the overall cost of the holiday without depriving the motorist and his family of enjoyment through too spartan an existence. This article is intended to pass on some of the hints and facts that emerged from their experiences during the summer of 1977.

Factual information on the Driveaway scheme, however, has been brought up to date to include 1978 details.

Be prepared When planning any holiday, and especially with Continental travel in mind, the first two questions to be answered are, of course, 'when?' and 'how?'. No matter what country you live in, the months of July and August are inevitably the peak season, when you can expect to pay high season prices for your ferry crossing.

For the budget-conscious, the shortest crossing is the obvious choice. Another factor, however, to bear in mind, is the ultimate destination once you have made your crossing. If you are forced to travel in the peak period then it would be wise, if not essential, to book early for the ferry, and when abroad, choose accommodation a little inland from the coast or outside large towns.

Driveaway European Hotel Voucher Scheme 1978

To assist with the problem of finding hotel accommodation and to help the holiday budget, the **Driveaway European Hotel Voucher Scheme** with the Inter-Hotel Group which includes Inter-France, Inter-Switzerland and Union Hotels, Italy and also the hotel chains of Ring-Hotels, Germany and Agip motels, Italy, offers a choice of over 250 hotels throughout France, Italy, Germany and Switzerland. Hotels were selected because of their character and charm, and a high level of service and attention to guests' needs. They range from small, 2-star hotels to large, modern 4-star hotels in some of Europe's major cities.

Château de la Motte Fénelon, Cambrai – Inter-Hotel chain.

Inter-Hotels vouchers cost from £7.50 per person per night and entitle you to a double-bedded or twin-bedded room with bath or shower in a 2-star hotel. Continental breakfast and taxes are also included in the cost of the voucher. If there is no room available with a bath or shower, a refund of 15 French francs per person or equivalent in local currency will be given.

46

A child over three but under 14 years qualifies for a special rate of £5.00 per voucher but children must share the parents' room. For a child under three years, a free cot will usually be provided in the parents' room, subject to availability. Single room vouchers are £11.50 per person.

A supplementary charge of approximately £2 per person per night for accommodation in 3-star and £4.00 per person per night in 4-star hotels is payable on arrival at the hotel.

You simply purchase the number of vouchers you require before leaving for your holiday and then each hotel you stay in will make a reservation, on your behalf, for the next night's hotel. Please remember to check in by 6.00pm, or if you are going to be delayed, to telephone ahead.

If you have travelled on the Continent before, your own experience will no doubt tell you that it is advisable to commence looking for the night's accommodation no later than 4.00pm. These vouchers relieve you entirely of the anxiety caused by searching for adequate accommodation, particularly during peak times. They therefore allow you greater freedom – more chance to sightsee, by travelling greater distances, or alternatively, to spend longer over a meal or visit to a place of interest. You are also ensured of a consistent standard in each of the hotels.

The main advantages of using the scheme are:

1 the cost of your holiday can be budgeted far more accurately;

2 by purchasing the vouchers prior to departure, in sterling, you are protected against a drop in exchange rates whilst you're abroad;

3 you do not have to carry such large sums of money, because your accommodation is paid for;

4 the scheme includes a booking service which provides you with the security of your next hotel accommodation, booked in advance of your arrival.

For full details of the Driveaway European Hotel Voucher Scheme, see the brochure ARGOSY *Driveaway Holidays in Europe,* available from any AA travel agency.

Settle for a snack   Although food will always feature strongly in anyone's holiday budget, when on a motoring holiday, many find the need of three meals a day unnecessary. The midday break, for instance, could easily be dispensed with, without causing too much hardship. Why not settle for a snack instead and save yourself time and money?

Throughout all of France there are numerous supermarkets and hypermarkets which carry large stocks of beers, lemonade and extremely palatable wines from about 60p per bottle. Cheese, too, is a very good buy and fresh fruit from farm shop or local market, along with a freshly-baked French loaf will ensure a most agreeable lunch that will not break the bank.

47

On the other hand, should you tire of a daily diet of bread and cheese, ham, paté etc, then many large shopping complexes and hypermarkets include a cafeteria where hot snacks can be obtained. The hypermarkets sampled by our route planners were clean, efficient and provided satisfactory meals reasonably cheaply compared to restaurant prices.

Whatever your preference, most food shops open between 7.00am and 7.30pm and remain open on Sunday mornings, and like department stores, close on Mondays (all or half-day). Some local grocers and hypermarkets stay open longer. **Remember:** lunchtimes usually last for up to two hours.

Don't forget to fill up with petrol when visiting hypermarkets. Our route planners found that petrol costs on average were *essence* (2-star) 2.09 francs* compared with 2.14 francs per litre and *super* (4-star) was 2.25 francs against 2.31 francs* per litre at normal filling stations.

Le bon répas   After a long day's travelling, you may wish to look no further than your hotel for the evening meal. It was found, however, that local restaurant prices compared favourably with those of hotels, and, in any case, the natural atmosphere of an intimate French restaurant added immeasureably to the enjoyment of the meal.

A typical menu *table d'hôte* or menu *touristique,* on average, offer set meals for between 20 and 35 francs* and generally include service and sometimes even wine. When not included, wine can be bought by the carafe at moderate cost. Children are welcome in restaurants. Many will share a menu between two children.

Know your facts   On entering any resort or major town, it is recommended that you visit the local tourist office, known as the *Office de Tourisme* or *Syndicate d'Initiative,* who usually have English-speaking staff and can give advice on local events, amenities, hotels, restaurants and excursions to vineyards, châteaux etc. Do ask about local markets and regional crafts which could just produce that small gift or souvenir at a mere fraction of the price you would pay in souvenir shops.

Sign language   With petrol costs at approximately £1.25 per gallon*, it is obviously of paramount importance that the holiday route is well planned and prepared. Inaccurate navigation or ignorance of the conditions likely to be encountered could prove costly in terms of petrol, time and inconvenience. For example, it is essential that you are aware of Continental signposting. From the Channel ports the newcomer will soon see direction signs *poids lourds* or *toutes directions* which are easily explained. In France diversions and bypasses marked *poids lourds* are intended for heavy traffic, lorries etc and signs marked *toutes directions* are used to direct 'all traffic' along the same road or route through towns. Signs with the words *péage* or *par péage* lead to toll roads.

Tolls versus time   Tolls are charged on most motorways (autoroutes) in France which you may feel are expensive, especially over long distances *eg* Calais-Nice, and return, amount to £34 in tolls.

It is purely a matter of personal choice to compare the cost and time saved against the expenditure on overnight accommodation. The autoroutes, as well as being built to the highest standard, also offer every facility for the motorist. There are frequent service areas and also laybys with picnic areas. Many of which also include toilets. The cost of refreshments in service areas may be considered to be a little costly, however.

You may feel, though, that you would be missing too much of the country by this means of travel. If so, then you will find the signposting between major towns and along main roads is generally efficient, but on secondary roads and in open country, there are not always advance direction signs, and some confusion may arise.

The **AA Overseas Route Service,** available to AA members, can help you plan your holiday. For full details of the Route Planning Service and application form, please see pages 17–20.

*Prices correct as at July 1977. These are subject to alteration.

AUSTRIA

Population 7,460,000 **Area** 32,376 sq miles **Maps** 12, 13 & 14

How to get there The usual approach from Calais, Ostende, and Zeebrugge is via Belgium to Aachen to join the German *Autobahn* network, then onwards via Cologne to Frankfurt; here the routes branch southwards via Karlsruhe and Stuttgart for Innsbruck and the Tirol, or eastwards via Nürnberg and Munich to Salzburg for central Austria. The distance to Salzburg is just over 700 miles and usually requires two night stops. Vienna, the capital, is a further 200 miles east. Travelling via Holland is a straightforward run joining the German *Autobahn* system near Arnhem. Alternatively, Austria can be reached via northern France to Strasbourg and Stuttgart, or via Basle and northern Switzerland. This is also the route if travelling from Dieppe, Le Havre, and Cherbourg.

Travel information

Accidents **Fire** ☎122 **police** ☎133 **ambulance** ☎144
A driver who is involved in an accident must stop and exchange particulars with the other party. If personal injury is sustained it is obligatory that you obtain medical assistance for the injured persons, and immediately report the incident to the police. All persons who arrive at the scene of an accident are obliged to render assistance, unless it is obvious that everything necessary has already been done.

Accommodation The official hotel guide is available from the Tourist Office in London. Additional information on accommodation at small inns, in private homes, and at farmhouses may be obtained from local and regional tourist information offices. Hotels are officially classified from A1 (luxury) to D (simple hotels). Room, pension, service, and heating charges are exhibited in bedrooms.

Breakdowns (ÖAMTC) If your car breaks down, try to move it to the side of the road so that it obstructs the traffic flow as little as possible, and place a warning triangle on the road 50 metres from the rear of the vehicle. If you require assistance you should telephone the nearest centre of the ÖAMTC who will help you but they will charge for their services. Roadside service is available to AA members upon production of their *5-Star Travel Booklet*. The ÖAMTC

49

Austria

usually operate between 07.00 and 19.00hrs with the exception of Vienna which operates 24 hours and Graz, between 07.00 and 24.00hrs. The telephone number of the breakdown service in Vienna is 0222/9540.

Patrol service
(Strassenwacht)
This operates around Vienna and on the south and west motorways when the volume of traffic demands it. The patrols are in radio contact with the ÖAMTC offices.

Note: The ARBÖ, known also by other names eg Automobile Club of Vienna, is not recognised by AIT or FIA, and AA members using their assistance will almost certainly be charged and no reimbursement can be claimed under 5-Star Service.

British
Consulates
6020 Innsbruck, Erlerstrasse 17/1 ☎28320
1030 Vienna, Reinestrasse 40 ☎731575

Currency and
banking
The unit of currency is the Austrian schilling, divided into 100 groschen. There is no restriction on the amount of foreign or Austrian money that a bona fide tourist may import into the country. The only export restriction is on Austrian currency. No one may take more than Sch15,000 out of the country.

Banking hours
Monday, Tuesday, Wednesday and Friday 08.00–12.30hrs, 13.30–15.00hrs; Thursday 08.00–12.30hrs, 13.30–17.30hrs. The bank counter at the ÖAMTC head office (Schubertring 1, Vienna 1) is open on Monday–Friday 08.00–17.00hrs, Saturdays 08.00–12.00hrs; exchange offices at some main railway stations are open on Saturdays, Sundays, and public holidays.

Dimensions and
weight restrictions
Vehicles must not exceed:
height 4 metres;
width 2.5 metres;
length vehicle/trailer combination 18 metres; weight trailers without brakes may weigh up to 750kg and may have a total weight up to 50% of the towing vehicle.

Drinking and driving
A driver convicted of driving while under the influence of alcohol is severely punished: a minimum fine of Sch5,000 may be imposed, together with either the withdrawal of his licence or one week's imprisonment. Police are entitled to remove the ignition keys from motorists who are apparently under the influence of drink and also from drivers who are showing signs of exhaustion.

Driving licence
Although a valid British licence is accepted in Austria it may present some language difficulty and to overcome this the ÖAMTC will provide a translation into German which is available from any of the Club's frontier or provincial offices. You are recommended to take advantage of this facility which is free. A licence issued in the Republic of Ireland is not accepted and an International Driving Permit is necessary.

First-aid kit
In Austria all motorists are required to carry a first-aid kit by law and visitors are expected to comply. This item will not be checked at the frontier and foreigners will not be penalised if they are not carrying one. However, at the scene of an accident any motorist can be stopped and his first-aid kit demanded and if this is not forthcoming the police may take action.

Hitch-hiking
In Austria, hitch-hiking is generally prohibited on motorways and highways. There are special provisions in Styria and Vorarlberg; in both Federal Lands hitch-hiking is prohibited for boys under the age of 16 and for girls under the age of 18.

Holidays and events
Holidays based on religious festivals are not always fixed on the calendar but any current diary will give actual dates. The Whit period (a religious holiday) should not be confused with the British Spring Holiday.

Fixed holidays

1 January	New Year's Day
6 January	Epiphany
1 May	Public holiday – Labour Day
15 August	Assumption Day
26 October	National Holiday
1 November	All Saints' Day
8 December	Immaculate Conception
24, 25, 26 December	Christmas

Austria

Moveable holidays	Good Friday Easter Saturday Easter Monday Ascension Day (early May) Whit Saturday Whit Monday Corpus Christi (early June, always a Thursday).

Annual events		
	January	**Innsbruck** International Ski Jumping **Salzburg** Mozart Week **Imst** Tobogganing Competition **Kitzbühel** International Hahnenkamm Ski-ing Race Winter Sports (January/April)
	February	**Tirol** Processions of Tirolese bands in traditional costumes; Tirolean folklore evenings (all year)
	March	**Vienna** International Spring Fair
	April	**Salzburg** Easter Festival
	May	**Vienna** Vienna Festival **Salzburg** Whitsun Concerts
	June	**Forchtenstein** Castle plays **Baden** Operetta weeks **Ossiach** Carinthian Summer Festival
	July	**Bad Iscki** Operetta weeks **Vienna** Youth Festival **Spittal** Comedy plays **Bregenz** Bregenz Festival (plays on lake) **Salzburg** Salzburg Festival **Marleisch** Lake Festival **Vienna** Musical Summer
	August	**Alpbach** European Forum **Hollabrunn** Folk Festival **Klagenfurt** Timber Fair
	September	**Vienna** Autumn Fair **Innsbruck** Fair **Graz** Autumn Fair
	October	**Graz** Styrian Autumn Festival

The national opera and theatre season lasts from September to June and the concert season from October to June.

A more comprehensive list of annual events can be obtained from the Austrian National Tourist Office (see page 55).

Horn, use of	It is prohibited to use the horn in Vienna unless there is no other way of avoiding an accident.
Insurance	This is compulsory. See page 11.

Frontier insurance Short-term third-party insurance cover cannot be arranged at the frontier. A motorist who does not hold insurance cover will have to take out a Claim Settlement Insurance which costs Sch40. Under this scheme a visiting motorist is not himself insured, but the arrangement authorises the Austrian Bureau of Insurance to deal with any claims resulting from an accident. Damages awarded following a court action are repayable to the Bureau.

Trailers must be covered by a separate policy, not the policy covering the towing vehicle.

Lights Although it is prohibited to drive with undipped headlights in built-up areas, motorists may give warning of approach by flashing their lights. It is prohibited to drive on illuminated urban motorways with sidelights only. In poor visibility motorists may use foglights in conjunction with both

51

Austria

sidelights and dipped headlights. Parking lights are not required if the vehicle can be seen from 50 metres (55yd). Lights on lampposts which are ringed with red do not stay on all night and parking lights will be required.

Medical treatment
In-patient hospital treatment may be free if you produce your UK passport, although a small charge will be made for dependants. Other medical services must be paid for. There is an emergency medical service and if this is required an appeal must be made to the local police.

Motoring club
 The Österreichischer Automobil-Motorrad-und-Touring-Club (ÖAMTC) which has its headquarters at 1/3 Schubertring, 1010 Vienna 1 has offices at the major frontier crossings and is represented in most towns either direct or through provincial motoring clubs. They will assist motoring tourists generally and supply information on touring matters, road and traffic conditions and offer breakdown and technical services. To assist English motorists the frontier offices supply a German translation of the British driving licence which is most useful and helps local police who might otherwise have difficulty if presented with a driving licence only in the English language.

The offices are usually open between 08.00 and 17.00hrs but close at 12.00hrs on Saturdays and are closed on Sundays and public holidays. However, a telephone service (0222/7299) for information is available, including weekends and public holidays, from the Head Office in Vienna between 06.00 and 20.00hrs. The Club's 24-hour breakdown service is available from the Vienna office on telephone number 0222/9540.

Parking
Parking is forbidden on a main road or one carrying fast-moving traffic; on or near tram lines; within 15 metres (16yd) of bus and tram stops; opposite another stationary vehicle, and on the left-hand side of one-way streets with only two driving lanes. In addition, parking is prohibited wherever there is a sign reading *Beschränkung für Halten oder Parken* (restriction for stopping or parking).

On roads which have priority (as a rule Federal Roads), if there is fog or any other impediment to visibility, there is a total ban on stopping.

Motorists who park their car in front of a house or an entry to a property must remain near the vehicle. Cars must be parked facing in the direction of traffic flow.

Vienna
Parking on roads with tram lines is prohibited at all times from 15 December to 31 March; from 1 April to 14 December it is prohibited from 05.00 to 20.00hrs. There is no parking in the centre of the city as it is a pedestrian zone.

In some towns short-term parking is allowed in areas known as Blue Zones where parking is free, except in Vienna where a charge is made for parking tickets available from some banks, tobacco shops and the ÖAMTC. These tickets allow parking for periods of $\frac{1}{2}$, 1, or $1\frac{1}{2}$ hours. Outside Vienna parking for up to $1\frac{1}{2}$ hours in Blue Zones is free. Parking tickets are not used but a parking disc is necessary which is available free of charge from tobacco shops.

In Vienna parked vehicles which obstruct traffic will be towed away and their drivers pay costs arising. A visitor's car will only be towed away if serious obstruction is caused.

Spending the night in a vehicle or trailer on the roadside is not prohibited, except on a priority road.

Passengers
No vehicle may carry more adult passengers than the number for which it was constructed, and passengers must allow the driver free movement. Children under 14 years of age are considered as half persons, and children under 6 years are not counted at all.

Note: Children under 12 years of age must not be transported in the front seats of a vehicle.

Petrol
The approximate price of petrol per litre is: super (octane 97–99) Sch7.30; normal (octane 86–88) Sch6.60.

Police fines
The Austrian police are authorised to impose on-the-spot fines for infringement of minor traffic regulations and once such a fine is paid it is not refunded even if it is established that the fine was unjustified. The policeman is required to issue an official receipt when collecting the fine.

If you refuse to pay the fine then you will be charged to appear in a court which may lead to inconvenience and likely a higher fine. Unless you strongly dispute an on-the-spot fine your best course is to pay and dispose of the matter.

Austria

	Postal and telephone charges		Rates for mail to the UK:		Sch

Postal and telephone charges

Rates for mail to the UK:

Air mail

	Sch
Postcards	4.00
Letters up to 20gm	6.00
20–50gm	10.00
50–100gm	15.00
100–250gm	30.00
250–500gm	55.00

Hours   Post offices are usually open from Monday to Friday 08.00–18.00hrs, with a break between 12.00–14.00hrs.

Telephone rates

A 3-minute call to the UK costs Sch45.00.

Priority   On mountain roads, vehicles travelling uphill have priority. Vehicles which continue straight ahead or make a right-hand turn at a crossroads or intersection have priority over oncoming vehicles turning left, provided that there are no signs to the contrary; in this case, even trams cede priority.

If you wish to turn across the flow of traffic at a junction controlled by a policeman, pass in front of him unless otherwise directed.

Buses must not be prevented from leaving a recognised stopping point.

River Danube   *The following particulars may change:*
Cars are not carried on the pleasure boats passing down the Danube between Passau and Vienna. A car pilot service or transportation by low-loader is in operation between Passau and Linz or Passau and Vienna for the benefit of motorists who want to make the boat journey. The service is operated from Passau by Autovermietung Lermer, Neuburger Strasse 64, Passau 839 and Garage Josefine Graswald, Schmiedgasse 10. Enquiries in Vienna should be made at the Erste Donau-Dampfschiffahrts-Gesellschaft, Zollamts-strasse 1, Vienna 111.

Roads   The motorist crossing into Austria from any frontier enters a network of well-engineered roads. A circular tour taking in the main places of interest can be made in one or two weeks. Old roads have been systematically improved and new ones built. The most famous is the Grossglockner highway (maximum gradient 1 in 8) on which a toll is levied.

The main traffic artery runs from Bregenz, in the west, to Vienna, in the east, via the Arlberg Pass, Innsbruck, Salzburg, and Linz. Long stretches of this road have been duplicated by an *Autobahn* (Motorways; see below). Most of the major Alpine roads are excellent, although some are being reconstructed, and a comprehensive tour can be made through the Tirol, Salzkammergut, and Carinthia without difficulty. Service stations are fairly frequent, even on mountain roads.

Holiday traffic   In July and August, several roads across the frontier become congested, particularly at weekends and on German public holidays (see Germany section); try to cross before 10.00hrs. The points are on the Lindau-Bregenz road; at the Brenner Pass (possible alternative – the Resia Pass); at Kufstein; on Munich-Salzburg *Autobahn* and on the Villach-Tarvisio road. For details of mountain passes, see page 28.

Motorways   About 490 miles of the planned 1,157 miles of the *Autobahnen* (motorways) have now been opened and more stretches are under construction. The only toll levied is on the Brenner and Tauern motorways.

To join a motorway, follow the signposts bearing the motorway symbol. The regulations are usually similar to those in Great Britain. Vehicles unable to travel at a minimum of 40kph (24mph) on the level, and motorcycles under 50cc are prohibited.

For speed limits see Speed, page 55.

Motorway telephones   There are emergency telephone posts sited at 2km ($1\frac{1}{4}$-mile) intervals along the West Autobahn (Salzburg–Vienna). To use the telephone lift the speaking flap and you will be automatically connected to the motorway control. The location of the post is printed inside the speaking flap; read this into the telephone, standing from 6 to 8in away from the microphone. If you ask for help and then find you do not need it, you must tell the motorway control.

Austria

On the Brenner motorway emergency callposts of a different type have been installed. They are coloured red and orange and are furnished with a speaking tube and four levers bearing the symbols for police, Red Cross, repair service, and telephone connection. By pressing the appropriate lever, a motorist will be connected with the required emergency service. When one of the first three levers is used, sufficient indication of what type of help is needed is conveyed to the headquarters in Innsbruck; when the telephone connection lever is used a motorist can talk direct to headquarters, which will send help if required.

At the top of each telephone post there is an orange/yellow light which flashes if there is danger on that stretch of the motorway.

Toll roads   There are about 40 roads throughout Austria on which tolls are charged but these are mainly minor roads and often lead only to beauty spots or places of particular interest. However, the following are important roads on which tolls are charged. The charges, given in Austrian schillings, should be taken as a guide only since they are subject to change.

Salzburg and Carinthia
Felbertauern Tunnel (see page 36)
Grossglockner-High Alpine road
(Grossglockner—Hochalpenstrasse)

	single
car	200
car/caravan combination	300
motorcycle	60
coach	600–1,200

Return tickets for cars are interchangeable between the Grossglockner Hochalpenstrasse and Felbertauern Tunnel.

Tauern Autobahn

	single
car	180
car/caravan combination	270
motorcycle	50
coach	360–720

Salzburg
New Gerlos road

	single
car	60
car and trailer	90
motorcycle	20
coach	300–600

Tirol and Vorarlberg
Silvretta-High Alpine road
(Hochalpenstrasse)
20 per person. If the return journey is made on the same day, the return fare is an extra 8 per person with original ticket.
Group of 26 people: 17 per person; 8 per person for the return journey with original ticket.

Tirol
Brenner Autobahn

	single
car with or without trailer/caravan	120
motorcycle	40
coach	300

Timmelsjoch road	single
car	65
minibus per person 5	40 (minimum fare)
motorcycle per person	10

Only private cars without trailers or minibuses are allowed on the Italian part of the road. All other vehicles and trailers are prohibited.

Winter conditions   *Entry from southern Germany* The main approaches to Innsbruck and to Salzburg and Vienna are not affected.

Entry from Switzerland The approach to Vorarlberg and Tirol is available at all times, as the Arlberg Pass is swept and kept open as much as possible, and there is an alternative rail service.

From Austria into Italy The Resia and Brenner Passes are usually open throughout the year, but snow chains may be necessary in severe weather. The Plocken Pass is occasionally closed in winter, but the Nassfeld Pass is likely to be kept open. Roads entering Italy at Dobbiaco and Tarvisio are usually clear, providing an unobstructed throughroute from Vienna to Venice.

From Austria into Yugoslavia It is best to travel via Travisio (Italy) and Jesenice, via Lavamund and Dravograd, or via Graz and Maribor. Entry via the Wurzen and Seeberg Passes and the Loibl Pass road tunnel is possible but not advised. *Within Austria* In the provinces of Upper Austria and Lower Austria, and in Burgenland, motoring is unaffected by winter conditions; elsewhere, because of the altitude, it is restricted.

When the Grossglockner Pass is closed, Ost Tirol and Carinthia can be reached by either the Felbertauern road tunnels, the Tauern Autobahn, or the Tauern railway tunnel between Bockstein (near Bad Gastein) and Mallnitz (see page 36 and 38).

Winter-sports resorts The main approach roads are swept and are closed only in the most severe weather. Zürs and Lech can be reached via the Arlberg Pass only.

Austria

Wheel/Snow chains
If you plan to motor in areas of high altitude during winter you may find wheel chains are compulsory in certain local conditions. If is probably better to consider purchasing these at home prior to departure, they are stocked by multiple car accessory retailers, and you will have the advantage of ensuring a proper fit and their availability when you want them. Further, they may be useful at home in certain winter conditions. Alternatively they may be hired from the ÖAMTC for a maximum period of 60 days on deposit of between £15 and £30. They are delivered in a packed condition and if they are returned unused then the deposit is returned, less a percentage reduction, according to the length of hire. If the seal is broken and the chains used then 65% of the deposit is retained.

The conditions of hire are fully described in a leaflet issued by the ÖAMTC from any of their offices and also available from the AA upon request.

Seat belts
If your car is fitted with seat belts it is compulsory to wear them. Although it is rare for penalties to be imposed for failing to do so there are laws relating to insurance claims and if it is established that at the time of any accident, front-seat passengers were not wearing seat belts then they are held to have contributed to any injuries sustained.

Shopping hours
Generally these are 08.00–18.00hrs with a 2–4hr break around midday. Saturdays, 08.00–12.00hrs.

Speed
The beginning of a built-up area is indicated by the placename sign and the end by a sign bearing the inscription *Ortsende von* (end of area) followed by the name of the place. In these areas the maximum speed for all vehicles (except mopeds) is 50kph (31mph); mopeds 40kph (24mph). Outside built-up areas, private cars are subject to a speed limit of 100kph (62mph) which is increased to 130kph (80mph) on motorways unless lower speed limits are indicated. Private vehicles towing trailers with a total weight of more than 750kg (1,650lb) are restricted to 60kph (37mph) on roads outside built-up areas except motorways, where the limit is 70kph (43mph). At certain periods during the summer, lower speed restrictions are imposed.

Tourist informaton offices
The Austrian National Tourist organisation maintains two fully-equipped information offices in the UK – in London at 30 St George Street, W1R 9PP and Manchester at 19 Mosley Arcade, Piccadilly Plaza 1. Either of these will be pleased to assist you with any information regarding tourism, whilst in most towns in Austria there will be found a local or regional tourist office who will supply detailed local information.

Traffic lights
A flashing green light indicates that the green phase is about to end.

Tyres
Should show a continuous depth of tread of 1mm. It is an offence to use tyres not up to this standard and Austrian police may carry out a check taking drastic action against offenders which may include halting the vehicle until new tyres are fitted.

Visitors' registration
A visitor staying at a hotel or supervised campsite must sign the guest book. They need not report to the police.

Warning triangles
These are compulsory for all vehicles outside built-up areas. A triangle must be placed on the road behind the vehicle or obstacle, and must be clearly visible from 200 metres (219yd).

Prices are in Austrian schillings

Abbreviations:
pl platz
str strasse

Achenkirch am Achensee Tirol 1,595 (☎05246) Map **13** A2
★★***Achenseehof*** ☎209 rm40 ⇨40 G 15 May–30 Sep Dec–Apr B156–192 Pn287–322 Pool Lake
★**Sporthotel-Imhof** ☎309 rm50 ⇨50 G Lift 15 Dec–20 Oct B215–490 M50–100 Pn220–320 Lake

Admont Steiermark 3,400 (☎03613) Map **14** C2
★★**Post** ☎2416 rm35 ⇨4 ⋒11 G LD B153–446 M55–60 Pn230–300

Alpbach Tirol 1,576 (☎05336) Map **13** A2
★★★★**Böglerhof** Dorfpl ☎227 rm64 ⇨55 ⋒13 G Lift 15 Dec–30 Mar 15 May–30 Sep B250–820 M80–100 Pn260–450 Pool
★★**Alpbacher Hof** ☎237 rm34 (A31) ⇨34 G 18 May–15 Oct 20 Dec–30 Mar B290–650 M90–125 Pn350–490 Pool
★***Gasthof Jakober*** ☎223 rm61 (A) ⇨22 ⋒1 G 20 Dec–1 Oct

Altaussee Steiermark 2,500 (☎06152) Map **13** B2
★★★**Tyrol** ☎7636 rm25 ⇨25 G B230–540 M100–130 Lake
★★**Kitzer** Hauptstr 21 ☎7227 rm21 ⇨6 ⋒6 G B140–410 M70–80 Pn250–400 Lake
24 E Plasonig ☎2747 N☎2458 BL/Maz/Peu/Sim G5

Altmünster Oberösterreich 7,480 (☎07612) Map **13** B2
★★***Alpen*** ☎8377 rm46 ⋒39 Lift Lake
★★**Reiberstorfer** Ebenzweier 27 ☎8105 rm41 ⇨17 ⋒18 G Lift B195–380 M60–90 Pn260–320 Lake
★***Seewies*** ☎8137 rm30 Lake

Amstetten Niederösterreich 21,850 (☎07472) Map **14** C3
★★★**Hofmann** Bahnhofstr 2 ☎2516 tx19212 rm60 (A45) ⇨11 ⋒18 G Lift B185–540 M70–120
24 P Bacher Ardaggerstr 91 ☎2690 N Chy/Ska/Sim G30
24 K Laumer Linzerstr 112 ☎2525 (closed weekends) Peu G15

Anif Salzburg 2,930 (☎06246) Map **13** B2
★★***Friesacher*** ☎2075 rm40 ⇨15 ⋒1
★★***Schlosswirt*** ☎2175 rm36 (A) ⇨24 ⋒5 G Lift 1 Mar–Dec

Arzl im Pitztal Tirol 1,910 (☎05412) Map **12** D2
★★**Post** ☎3111 rm70 ⇨40 ⋒10 G Lift May–Sep 15 Dec–30 Apr B155–460 M60–70 Pn170–300 Pool

Aurach Tirol 830 (☎05356) Map **13** A/B2
★★★***International*** ☎4507 rm20 ⇨15 ⋒5 May–Oct Dec–Apr Pool
★★***Gstrein*** ☎2459 rm20 ⇨20 G Lake

Aussee (Bad) Steiermark 5,200 (☎06152) Map **13** B2
★★**Erzherzog Johann** Kurhauspl 62 ☎2017 rm38 ⇨14 ⋒6 G B190–610 M75–85 Pn245–360
★**Stadt Wien** ☎2068 rm30 (A10) ⇨8 ⋒5 B180–440 M70–90 Pn250–300
H Obermeyr Wiedleithe 100 ☎2413 N M/c Opl/Vau G10

Bad: placenames beginning with Bad are listed under the name which follows it.

Baden bei Wien Niederösterreich 24,300 (☎02252) Map **14** D3
★★★***Herzoghof*** Theresiengasse 5 ☎2117 tx014/480 Alwec rm111 ⇨107 ⋒4 Lift Pool
★★★**Krainerhütte** Helenental ☎4511 tx14303 rm72 ⇨60 ⋒12 G Lift B340–410 Pn550–670 Pool
★★***Sacher*** Helenental ☎2100 rm25 ⇨10 1 May–1 Oct
★★***Wald*** Helenenstr 92 ☎2916 rm30 ⇨3 ⋒12
★**Cholerakapelle** Helenental 40 ☎2850 rm14 (A3) ⋒7 G B185–460 M50–100 Pn190–350
A Gramsel Hotzendorfplatz 2 ☎2989 N Aud/VW

Badgastein Salzburg 5,800 (☎06434) Map **13** B2
★★★★***Elisabethpark*** ☎2551 tx0676613 rm135 ⇨135 G Lift May–Sep Dec–Mar Pool Golf
★★★**Parkhotel Bellevue** ☎2571 tx06776621 rm158 ⇨140 15 Dec–15 Oct B348–708 M120–140 Pn348–688 Pool Golf
★★★**Savoy** ☎2588 tx67/688 rm63 ⇨32 ⋒10 G Lift 15 Dec–20 Oct **Pn**280–540 Pool
★★★***Straubinger*** ☎2012 rm75 ⇨31 ⋒2 Lift Dec–1 Nov
★★**Grüner Baum** ☎2516 tx67-76611 rm97 ⇨61 ⋒2 G 17 Dec–3 Apr 15 May–16 Oct B238–470 M80–120 Pn368–650
★★**Kurhotel Eden** ☎2076 rm36 ⇨11 Lift **Pn**280–380
★**Bristol** (n rest) ☎2219 rm30 ⇨9 ⋒11 G Lift May–Oct Dec–Apr B150–270 M75
24 *F Glawitsch* Böcksteiner Str 347 ☎2084 N☎2907 N Frd/MB

Berwang Tirol 550 (☎05674) Map **12** D2
★★★**Singer** Haus am Sonnenhang ☎8181 rm49 ⇨35 ⋒3 G Lift 20 May–20 Sep 18 Dec–10 Apr B240–860 M80–140 Pn280–540

Bezau Vorarlberg 1,500 (☎05514) Map **12** C2
★★***Gams*** ☎220 rm41 ⇨12 ⋒13
★★**Post** Hauptstr ☎2207 rm38 (A11) ⇨38 G Lift 19 Dec–19 Oct LD B252–375 M100–140 Pn360–480 Pool

Bischofshofen Salzburg 8,900 (☎06462) Map **13** B2
★***Tirolerwirt*** Gasteinerstr 3 ☎2430 rm13 (A) G

Bludenz Vorarlberg 12,000 (☎05552) Map **12** C2
★★**Herzog Friedrich** Mutterstr 6 ☎2703 rm18 ⇨2 ⋒2 G Lift B125-330 Màlc Pn255–350
★★**Schlosshotel Dörflinger** ☎3016 rm32 (A3) ⇨12 ⋒20 G B210–530 M80 Pn350–400
★**Hoher Frassen** (n rest) Obdorfweg 54 ☎2264 rm16 G B120–260
H Zimmermann Brunnenfeld ☎2554 N BL/Chy/Sim G10
Fahrzeug Mäser Austr 4 ☎2764 N Ren

Brand Vorarlberg 550 (☎05559) Map **12** C1
★★★**Scesaplana** ☎221 tx5234121 rm43 ⇨37 Lift 15 Dec–15 Apr 20 May–30 Sep LD B325–780 M70–140 Pool
★★***Hammerle*** ☎213 rm55 (A21) ⇨13 ⋒14 28 May–22 Sep
★***Valbona*** ☎226 rm21 (A11) ⇨2 ⋒6
★**Zimba** ☎219 rm19 ⇨4 ⋒2 G 25May–9 Oct 20 Dec–15 Apr LD B120–300 M60–80 Pn180–250

Braunau am Inn Oberösterreich (☎07722) Map **13** B3
★★***Post*** ☎3492 rm35 ⇨16 ⋒3 G

Bregenz Vorarlberg 23,530 (☎05574) Map **12** C2
★★**Central** (n rest) Kaiserstr 24 ☎22947 tx57779 rm42 ⋒6 B170–550
★★**Weisses Kreuz** Römerstr 5 ☎22488 ta Kreuzhotel tx057/741 rm40 ⇨16 ⋒8 G Lift B190–500

★*Germania* ☎22766 rm15 (A) ⇆2 ⋔5 G

⌷⊅○*Auto-Beck* Arlbergstr 63 ☎22336 Peu/Vau

⌷►24 **Central** Weiherstr 13 ☎22208 N⊛ MB

Bruck an der Glocknerstrasse Salzburg 3,300 (☎06545) Map **13** B2

★★**Lukashansl** ☎rm80 ⇆40 G Lift LD B175–490 M90 Pn180–360

★**Höllern** ☎1240 rm40 (A3) ⇆12 ⋔14 G

Bruck an der Mur Steiermark 17,634 (☎03862) Map **14** C2

★★**Bayer** ☎51218 rm32 ⇆12 ⋔4 B140–480 M50–100 Pn250–440

★★**Schreiner** Bahnhofstr 16 ☎51220 rm60 ⇆6 ⋔6 G

★★**Schwarzen Adler** Mittergasse 23 ☎51331 rm60 ⇆33 ⋔9 B180–560 M70–100 Pn260–340

⌷⊅○**R Reichel** Grazerstr 17 ☎51633 N⊛ Frd/MB

Burgau am Attersee Salzburg 3,000 (☎07663) Map **13** B2

★★**Seehotel Burgau** Salzkammergut ☎266 rm42 (A2) ⇆8 G 1 Apr–31 Oct B120–510 M40–80 Pn200–320 Lake

Dellach am Wörthersee Kärnten 1,300 (☎04274) Map **13** B1

★★★**Gesundheits Centrum Golf Hotel** ☎2511 rm70 ⇆40 G 30 Apr–1 Oct Golf Lake

Dellach Millstättersee See **Millstatt**

Deutschlandsberg Steiermark 5,230 (☎03462) Map **14** B4

★**Rainer** ☎2318 rm28 ⇆6 ⋔3 G B124–288 M30–120 Pn224–244 ⌴

Dienten am Hochkönig Salzburg 820 (☎06416) Map **13** B2

★**Pesentheiner** ☎207 rm25 ⋔11 G 15 Dec–8 Apr 1 Jun–30 Sep B115–150 M120–130 Pn175–235 Pool

Döbriach Kärnten (☎04246) Map **13** B1

⌷►24 **F Burgstaller** Millstättersee ☎7736 Frd

Döllach-Sagritz Kärnten 1,405 (☎04824) Map **13** B1

★★**Post** ☎0428 rm46 (A) ⇆5 ⋔3 G 15 Dec–15 Oct ⌴

★★**Schlosswirt** ☎211 rm30 ⇆13 ⋔4 G 1 Dec–31 Mar 1 Jun–31 Oct B130–340 Pn250–270 ⌴ Pool ◯

Dornbirn Vorarlberg 34,850 (☎05572) Map **12** C2

★★★**Park** Goethestr 6 ☎2691 tx059/109 rm40 ⇆13 ⋔10 G Lift B230–560 M120–140 Pn420–545 ⌴

★★**Zum Hirschen** Marktpl 12 ☎2157 rm34 (A14) ⇆4 ⋔7 G B138–326

⌷⊅○*E Bohle* Schwefel 44 ☎2824 BL/Rov G10

⌷⊅○*R Gerster* Schwefel 41 ☎2886 N⊛ Opl

⌷⊅○**Mäser** Lustenauerstr 97 ☎5601 N⊛ Ren G10

Dürnstein an der Donau Niederösterreich 1,000 (☎02711) Map **14** C3

★★★**Schloss Dürnstein** ☎212 rm35 ⇆29 ⋔4 Lift 15 Mar–30 Nov B320–650 M130–150 Pn520–570 Golf

★★**Richard Löwenherz** ☎222 rm46 ⇆41 ⋔5 5 Mar–20 Nov LD B280–580 Pool

Ehrwald Tirol 2,000 (☎05673) Map **12** D2

★★**Halali** ☎2101 rm12 ⇆2 ⋔10 Jan–Nov G Pn255–295

★★**Schönruh** ☎2322 rm42 (A13) ⇆25 20 May–30 Sep

★★**Sonnenspitze** Kirchpl 14 ☎2208 rm33 ⇆2 ⋔6 G Dec–Apr May–Oct Pn290–370

★★**Spielmann** Wettersteinstr 24 ☎2225 rm40 (A4) ⇆17 ⋔4 G Dec–Oct B177–596 M90 Pn242–418 Pool

★★*Tannenhof* ☎2288 rm15 ⇆15 20 Dec–20 Apr 1 Jun–10 Oct LD B170–320 M80–90 St 5.5%

Eisenstadt Burgenland 10,000 (☎02682) Map **14** D2

★★*Schwechaterhof* F-Lisztgasse 1 ☎2879 tx01/722 rm63 ⇆2 ⋔10 G

★*Eisenstadt* (n rest) Sylvesterstr 5 ☎3350 rm14 ⇆2 ⋔3 G B125–400

⊅○*S Ivanschitz* Rusterstr 24 ☎2752 N⊛ Frd

Engelhartszell Oberösterreich (☎07717) Map **13** B3

★★**Ronthalerhof** ☎8083 rm10 ⇆4 ⋔6 B180–350 Pn215–305

Enns Oberösterreich 9,000 (☎07223) Map **14** C3

★*Drei Mohren* (n rest) Hauptpl 5 ☎351 rm22 G B70

Eugendorf Salzburg (☎06212) Map **13** B2

☆☆*Wallersee* ☎8282 rm12 ⇆2 ⋔10 G B175–450 M50–100

⌷►24 **Wagner** Bundesstr 1 ☎79560 N☎338914 G10

Feld am See Kärnten (☎04246) Map **13** B1

★★**Lindenhof** ☎437 rm27 ⇆5 ⋔14 LD B135–450 M60–70 Pn230–300 Lake

Feldkirch Vorarlberg 22,000 (☎05522) Map **12** C2

★★★*Central-Löwen* ☎22070 tx052/311 rm65 ⇆35 G Lift

★★*Alpenrose* (n rest) Rosengasse 6 ☎22175 rm16 ⇆8 G

★★**Hochhaus** (n rest) ☎22479 rm18 ⇆2 ⋔5 G Lift B140–290

⌷⊅○**P Fehr** Bundesstr ☎23373 N⊛ Frd

Feldkirchen Kärnten 7,770 (☎04276) Map **14** C1

★★**Dauke** ☎2413 rm20 ⇆20 G B180–340 M80 Pn220–240

Ferleiten an der Glocknerstrasse Salzburg 830 (☎06546) Map **13** B2

★★**Lukashansl** ☎220 rm23 (A10) ⇆4 ⋔2 mid May–mid Oct LD B100–240 M60–70 Pn190–210

Fernpass Tirol (☎05265) Map **12** D2

★★**Fernpass** ☎5201 rm23 (A9) ⇆12 ⋔2 G LD B122–344 M50–100 St 10%

Frastanz Vorarlberg 5,000 (☎05525) Map **12** C2

☆☆*Galina* Bundesstr 1 ☎2781 rm30 ⇆30 G Lift 1 Dec–1 Nov

★★**Stern** ☎22717 rm13 ⇆2 ⋔2 G B138–420 M75–85 Pn230–320

Freistadt Oberösterreich 6,000 (☎07942) Map **14** C3

★**Goldener Hirsch** ☎2258 rm30 ⇆10 ⋔6 B135–450 M60–100 Pn200–250

Fügen Tirol (☎05288) Map **13** A2

★**Post** ☎2286 rm60 ⇆26 ⋔8 Lift 15 Dec–31 Oct B200–580 M50–100 Pn280–335 Pool

Fulpmes Tirol 2,500 (☎05225) Map **12** D2

★★*Holzmeister* ☎2260 rm32 ⇆16 ⋔3 1 Jan–15 Oct 1 Dec–31 Dec

Fürstenfeld Steiermark 6,300 (☎03382) Map **14** B4

★★*Hitzl* ☎2144 rm43 ⋔5 G

★*Brauhaus* Grazerpl 2 ☎2429 rm20 ⇆4 ⋔4 ⊅○**M Koller** Fehringerstr 13 ☎2527 N⊛ M/c Frd/MB G10

►24 **H Marth** Ledergasse 27 ☎3298 M/c Cit G20

Fusch an der Grossglocknerstrasse Salzburg 790 (☎06546) Map **13** B2

★★**Post Hofer** ☎226 rm40 ⇆5 ⋔20 G B90–270 M50–80 Pn180–250 ⌴

Austria

★**Lampenhäusl** ☎215 rm32 (A18) ⇌1 G
1 Dec–31 Oct LD B125–250 M50–90
Pn180–215

Fuschl am See Salzburg 700 (☎06226)
Map **13** B2
★★**Seehotel Schlick** ☎237 rm50 ⇌10 ▥10
G LD B120–280 M65–80 Pn230–280 Lake

Galtür Tirol 535 (☎05443) Map **12** C1
★★**Berghaus Franz Lorenz** ☎206 rm23 ⇌17
▥6 G Lift 20 Dec–1 Oct LD B180–500 M110–
140 Pn490–590
★★**Fluchthorn** ☎202 rm50 ⇌23 ▥27 G Lift
1 Jun–30 Sep B260–600 M90–110
Pn320–400
★**Paznaunerhof** ☎234 rm18 ▥6 G Jun–Apr

Gargellen Vorarlberg 600 (☎05557)
Map **12** C1
★★**Alpenrose** ☎314 rm18 ⇌4 ▥7 G
1 Dec–20 Apr 1 Jun–30 Sep B190–300
M80–130 Pn310–410
★★**Feriengut Gargellenhof** ☎274
tx52299 rm34 ⇌7 G Jun–Oct Dec–Apr LD
Pn250–430
★★**Madrisa** Ortsmitte ☎331 tx52269 rm50
⇌22 ▥11 G 16 Jun–20 Sep B140–680
M80–120 Pn240–440 Pool

Gars am Kamp Niederösterreich (☎02985)
Map **14** C3
O Moser J-Staussgasse 307 ☎2259 M/c
Chy/Sim G5

Gaschurn Vorarlberg 1,180 (☎05558)
Map **12** C1
★★★**Epple** ☎251 tx52/389 rm82 ⇌39 ▥25 G
Lift 27 May–30 Jun 3 Dec–8 Apr B380–710
M70–120 Pn620–770 ⚬ Pool

Gerlos Tirol 550 (☎05284) Map **13** A2
★**Kroller** ☎202 rm40 ⇌30 ▥10 G LD
★**Jägerhof** ☎203 rm39 ⇌2 ▥6 B130–300
M45–100 Pn170–240

Gmunden Oberösterreich 12,700 (☎07612)
Map **13** B2
★★★**Post** (n rest) Badgasse 8 ☎3651 rm20
⇌11 ▥9 B170–400
★★**Schwan** Rathauspl 8 ☎3391 rm42 ⇌27
▥4 G Lift B190–550 Pn320–420 Lake
➤**24 J Beham** Georgstr 5 ☎3838 Ren
▨⑤**24 H Klingesberger** Bahnhofstr 22 ☎4382
N⊛ Fia

Golling Salzburg 2,900 (☎06244) Map **13** B2
★**Goldener Stern** Hauptstr ☎220 rm27 ⇌5
▥10 G B120–310 Pn175–230

Götzis Vorarlberg (☎2202) Map **12** C2
▨⑤**Auto Beck** Dr A-Heinzlerstr 61 ☎2203
N⊛ Peu/Vau

Graz Steiermark 252,850 (☎0316) Map **14** B4
★★★**Daniel** Europlatz 1 ☎911080 tx31182
rm94 ⇌36 ▥16 G Lift B215–620 M90–145
Pn385–590
★★★**Park** Leonhardstr 8 ☎33511 tx03/1498
rm63 ⇌48 G Lift B215–650 M90 Pn375–580
★★★**Steirerhof** Jakominipl 12 ☎76356
tx031282 rm98 ⇌95 Lift B550–1100
M55–125 Pn650–920
★★★**Weitzer** Griesgasse 15 ☎913801
tx03-1284 rm177 (A84) ⇌60 ▥38 Lift LD
B195–620 M90–145 Pn385–590
★★★**Wiesler** Grieskai 4 ☎913241 tx3-1130
rm90 ⇌50 ▥6 Lift B160–700 M80 Pn320–560
★★**Mariahilf** Mariahilfer Str ☎913163
tx03-1087 rm45 ⇌10 ▥16 G Lift B150–550
M40–120 Pn300–600
▨⑤*Heidinger* Grieskai 74 ☎912170 N⊛
Frd G25
⑤**J Jacomini** Kärntnerstr 115 ☎22188 N⊛
BL/Jag/Tri
▨⑤**H Krajacic** Idlhofgasse 17 ☎912823 N⊛
BL/Rov G10

➤➤**24 K Repitsch** Liebenauer Hauptstr 79
☎42459 N☎42432 M/c Bed/Maz/Vau
▨⑤**Autozentrale Salis & Braunstein**
Wienerstr 35 ☎911680 N⊛ Opl
Gries am Brenner Tirol 1,300 (☎05274)
Map **13** A1
★*Intertouring* ☎216 rm40 (A20)
10 Dec–6 Oct
★**Weisses Rössl** Hauptstr ☎214 rm30 ⇌30 G
15 Oct–20 Dec B225–480 M70–110

Grieskirchen Oberösterreich (☎07248)
Map **13** B3
▨⑤*Autohaus Doppler* Bahnhofstr 19 ☎784
N⊛ M/c Chy/Sim G25

Gröbming Steiermark 1,920 (☎03685)
Map **13** B2
▨⑤**A Franz** Bundesstr 324 ☎2359 N⊛
Fia/MB G10

Grossglocknerstrasse Kärnten (☎04824)
Map **13** B2
★★**Kaiser-Franz-Josef-Haus** ☎2363 rm70
⇌15 ▥13 May–Oct

Grundlsee Steiermark 1,400 (☎06152)
Map **13** B2
★**Backenstein** ☎8545 rm25 ⇌12 G
B145–510 M60–70 Pn220–340 Lake

Gschnitz Tirol 300 (☎05272) Map **12** D1
★★**Gschnitzer Hof** ☎23113 rm32 ⇌3 ▥6 G
18 Dec–10 Apr 1 Jun–30 Sep Pool

Gstatterboden Steiermark 700 (☎03613)
Map **14** C2
★★**Gesäuse** ☎245519 rm76 ⇌12

Haibach Oberösterreich (☎07713)
Map **13** B3
★★**Donau Faber** ☎8144 rm21 ⇌7 ▥13 G
B115–455 Pn240–325

Haldensee Tirol (☎05675) Map **12** D2
★**Rot-Fluh** ☎465 rm67 ⇌40 ▥6 G Lift
15 Dec–31 Oct B178–730 M65–95
Pn250–430 ⚬ Pool Lake

Hall (Bad) Oberösterreich (☎07258)
Map **14** C3
⑤*G Sommer* Steyrer Str 40 ☎219 N⊛ G6

Hall in Tirol Tirol 11,940 (☎05223)
Map **13** A2
★★★**Park** Kurpark ☎2566 rm45 ⇌17 ▥1 G Lift
★★**Maria Theresia** Reimmichlstr 25 ☎6313
rm25 ▥3 Lift B200–400 (double)
★**Tyrol** ☎6621 tx054223 rm36 ⇌20 ▥14 G
Lift B235–480 Pn305–340 Pool

Hallein Salzburg 14,000 (☎06245)
Map **13** B2
★★**Kurhaus St-Josef** ☎2509 rm90 ⇌7 G
Lift 29 Dec–25 Nov Pool
★**Stern** (n rest) ☎2610 rm35 ⇌2 ▥3 G
1 May–1 Oct B145–410

Hallstatt am See Oberösterreich 1,340
(☎06134) Map **13** B2
★★**Grüner Baum** Marktpl 104 ☎263 rm42
⇌18 ▥2 G 30 Apr–Oct B185–610
M90–210 Pn300–540 Lake

Heiligenblut Kärnten 1,400 (☎04824)
Map **13** B1/2
See also **Grossglocknerstrasse**
★★**Glocknerhof** ☎2244 tx048154 rm69 ⇌40
▥5 G Lift 10 Dec–20 Apr 20 May–10 Oct
Pn250–480 Pool
★★**Rupertihaus** ☎247 rm32 ⇌9 ▥11 G
1 May–15 Oct
★*Post* ☎245 rm36 ⇌13 ▥11 G 20 Dec–15 Oct

Heiterwang Tirol 380 (☎05674) Map **12** D2
★**Fischer am See** ☎29116 rm13 ⇌4 ▥5 G
20 Dec–10 Jan Etr–15 Oct LD B175–460
Màlc Golf Lake

Hinterstoder Oberösterreich 1,000
(☎07564) Map **13** B2
★*Dietlgut* ☎248 rm20 ⇌8 G Pool

Hinterthal am Hochkönig Salzburg
(☎06584) Map **13** B2
★★★*Wachtelhof* ☎288 rm27 (A2) ⊲23 ⋒4
G Dec–30 Apr Jun–30 Sep Pool

Hintertux Tirol 1,400 (☎05287) Map **13** A2
★★*Alpenhof & Haus Berghof* ☎2213
rm64 ⊲28 ⋒2 20 May–15 Oct 20 Dec–30 Apr

Hof bei Salzburg Salzburg 1,240
(☎06229) Map **13** B2
★★★★*Schloss* ☎253 ta Fuschlschloss
tx06/3454 rm69 ⊲45 ⋒1 G Lift Etr–31 Oct ⅌
Pool Golf Lake ◠
★★*Baderluck* ☎216 rm28 (A) ⊲9

Hofgastein (Bad) Salzburg 5,200
(☎06432) Map **13** B2
★★★*Grand Park* Kurgartenstr 26 ☎356
tx67756 rm96 ⊲70 G Lift B385–1300
M110–150 Pn450–700 Pool
★★*Astoria* ☎277 rm55 ⊲10 ⋒15 G Lift
22 Dec–15 Oct Pool
★★*Österreichischer Hof* Kurgartenstr 9
☎216 rm59 ⊲19 ⋒40 G Lift 19 Dec–31 Mar
9 May–30 Oct LD B315–760 M80 Pn390–490
Pool
&🅟 *P Schober* Anger 104 ☎532 Fia/Lnc

Hungerburg See **Innsbruck**

Igls Tirol 1,400 (☎05222) Map **13** A2
★★★*Aegidihof* Bilgeristr 1 ☎7108 rm29 ⊲26
G closed 20 Dec–20 Jan B180–350 M100
Pn235–480
★★★*Iglerhof* Patscherstr 7331 tx53480
rm93 ⊲65 G Lift 15 Dec–15 Mar 15 May–1 Oct
Pool Golf
★★★*Park* ☎7305 tx053576 rm63 ⊲48 G Lift
mid Dec–mid Apr mid May–mid Oct B310–370
M90–110 Pn410–470 Pool
★★★*Sport* ☎7241 tx053314 rm90 ⊲80 G
Lift 15 Dec–1 Oct B325–650 M120–140
Pn380–720 Pool
★★*Alpenhof* ☎7491 rm38 ⊲36 ⋒2 G Lift
20 Dec–30 Mar 15 Apr–30 Sep B215–760
M60–70 Pn270–510
★★*Batzenhäusl* ☎7104 rm25 ⊲17 ⋒4 G
15 Dec–15 Oct
★★*Tiroler Hof* ☎7194 rm50 ⊲8 ⋒2 G
20 May–15 Sep 20 Dec–15 Mar
★★*Waldhotel* ☎7272 rm20 ⊲8 ⋒12 Lift
Dec–Apr May–Oct B320–760 M75–110
Pn330–480 Pool
★*Bon-Alpina* Hilberstr 8 ☎7219 rm52 (A6)
⊲5 15 Dec–15 Oct
★*Gothensitz* (n rest) ☎7211 rm15 (A2) ⊲7
⋒3 G B185–380
★*Oswald* ☎7262 rm13 ⊲3
★*Romedihof* ☎7141 rm22 ⊲11 ⋒6 G
Dec–Apr Jun–Sep B125–200 M60–70 Pn210–
280

Imst Tirol 5,920 (☎05412) Map **12** D2
★★*Linserhof* ☎2415 rm40 ⋒30 G Pool
★★*Post* Postpl 3 ☎2554 rm43 ⊲20 ⋒2 G Lift
15 Dec–15 Oct Pool

Innsbruck Tirol 116,000 (☎05222)
Map **13** A2 **See Plan**
The Herzog-Friedrich Str area is now a
pedestrian precinct and only open to vehicular
traffic at certain times of the day
★★★★*Tyrol* Südtiroler Pl 1 ☎21781
tx53424 Plan **1** rm121 ⊲121 G Lift
20 Dec–6 Jan 1 May–15 Oct B350–1204
Pn480–892
★★★*Europa* Südtiroler Pl 2 ☎35571 tx53424
Plan **2** rm133 ⊲100 ⋒3 G Lift B350–1204
Pn480–892
★★★*Goldener Adler* Herzog-Friedrich Str 6
☎26334 Plan **4** rm37 ⊲15 ⋒21 Lift
B340–880 M100–130

★★*Binder* Dr Glatz Str 20 ☎42236 Plan **5**
rm30 ⊲3 ⋒9 G 1 Dec–15 Oct B130–160 M60
Pn200–250
★★*Central* Erlerstr 11 ☎24866 tx53824
Plan **6** rm62 ⊲12 ⋒35 Lift B245–640
Pn395–790
★★*Goldene Rose* Herzog-Friedrich Str 39
☎22041 Plan **7** rm35 ⊲4
★★*Grauer Bär* Universitätsstr 5 ☎34531
tx053387 Plan **8** rm163 ⊲68 ⋒21 Lift
B300–670 Màlc
★★*Hellenstainer* A-Hofer Str 6 ☎22113
Plan **9** rm48 ⊲13 Lift
★★*Hufeisen* An-der-Lan Str 33 ☎51841
Plan **10** rm28 ⊲20 ⋒8 G Lift
★★*Maria Theresia* M-Theresien Str 31
☎35615 tx05/3300 Plan **12** rm77 ⊲70 ⋒7 G
Lift B360–660 M80 Pn500–660
★★*Schwarzer Adler* Kaiserjägerstr 2 ☎27109
Plan **14** rm22 ⊲16 B200–470 Pn280–630
★*Goldener Stern* Innstr 37 ☎27167 Plan **15**
rm100 ⋒10 Lift B110–160 Pn220–280
★*Greif* Leopoldstr 3 ☎27401 tx53111 Plan **16**
rm58 ⊲14 ⋒29 Lift B190–640 Pn340–485
★*Putzker* (n rest) Höttingerau 41 ☎29163
Plan **17** rm15
★*Touringhaus* (n rest) Brunecker Str 12
☎21781 tx53424 Plan **18** rm35 ⊲1 G Lift
20 Dec–6 Jan & 1 May–15 Oct B270–580
F Hörzinger Rennweg 18 ☎27469 N🅢 Chy
&🅟 *Köllensperger* Kirschentalgasse 10
☎29731 N🅢 Frd
&🅟 *Linser-Auto* Haller Str 119a ☎62421 N🅢
GM G
&🔾 *F Niederkofler* Grassmayrstr 23 ☎25759
N🅢 Dat/Ska
M Steger Haymongasse 9a ☎20377 N🅢
Electrical spares (Lucas Agent)
&🅟 *VOWA* Haller Str 165 ☎62171 Por/VW
At **Hungerburg** (4km N) also funicular from
Innsbruck
★★*Mariabrunn* ☎33161 tx53194 Plan **11**
rm32 ⊲32 G 15 Dec–15 Oct B315–420
M90 Pn390–490
At **Völs** (5km W on No 1A)
🅟▶24 *Meisinger* Innsbruckerstr 57 ☎34516
Peu

Ischgl Tirol 980 (☎05444) Map **12** C1
★*Post* Paznautal ☎233 rm61 ⊲35 ⋒6 G Lift
Dec–May 10 Jun–15 Sep Pool

Ischl (Bad) Oberösterreich 14,000
(☎06132) Map **13** B2
★★*Golf* ☎3590 rm48 ⊲22 ⋒26 G Lift
B390–450 Pn570–700 Pool
★★*Freischütz* Rottenbach 96 ☎3354 rm25
⊲8 G 1 Apr–31 Oct B160–550 M70–100
Pn240–370
★★*Post* Kaiser F-Josef Str 3-5 ☎3441 rm65
⊲32 ⋒3 G Lift 20 Dec–20 Oct B180–580
M65–85 Pn320–610
★*Bayerischer Hof* Schröpferpl 1 ☎3360
ta Bayernhotel rm16 G 1 Mar–10 Dec
B185–370 M40–75 Pn260–300
&🔾 *M Gassner* Grazerstr 9 ☎3321 N🅢 M/c Ren

Itter Tirol (☎0043) Map **13** A2
★★*Schloss Itter* ☎5332 rm25 ⊲11 G Lift
15 Dec–1 Nov Pool

Judenburg Steiermark 11,360 (☎03572)
Map **14** C2
&🔾 *H Fritz* Burggasse 19 ☎2277 N🅢 M/c Opl
▶24 *A Gauper* Hetzendorferstr 53 ☎2430
N🅢 Cit/Peu G3

Kanzelhöhe-Annenheim Kärnten 300
(☎04249) Map **13** B1
★★★*Berghotel & Sonnenhotel* ☎2713 rm60
⊲40 ⋒2 Lift 20 Dec–15 Apr & 1 Jun–15 Oct
Pool Lake

Austria

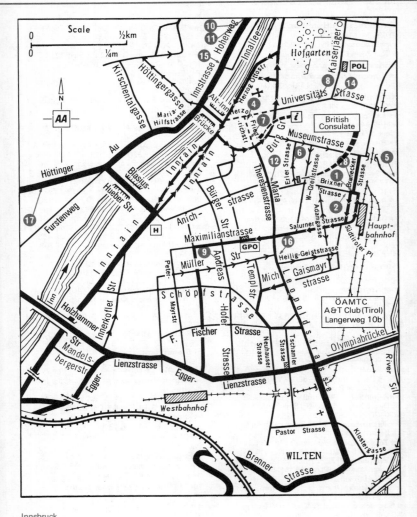

Innsbruck

1	★★★★Tyrol	10	★★Hufeisen
2	★★★Europa	11	★★Mariabrunn
4	★★★Goldener Adler	12	★★Maria Theresia
5	★★Binder	14	★★Schwarzer Adler
6	★★Central	15	★Goldener Stern
7	★★Goldene Rose	16	★Greif
8	★★Grauer Bär	17	★Putzker
9	★★Hellenstainer	18	★Touringhaus

Kirchberg Tirol (☎05357) Map **13** A2
★★*Spertenhof* ☎411 rm11 ⋒7 G B50–145

Kitzbühel Tirol 7,750 (☎05356)
Map **13** A/B2
★★★★**Hirzingerhof** Schwarzseestr 12 ☎3211
tx051/17124 rm27 ⇌27 G Lift May–Sep
B370–700 M85–100 Pn420–460
★★★★**Tennerhof** Griesenauweg ☎3181
tx51/18426 rm47 (A5) ⇌40 ⋒2 17 Dec–2 Apr
1 Jun–10 Oct B220–960 M130–160
Pn360–750 Pool
★★★**Goldener Greif** ☎4311 tx051/17118
rm49 ⇌40 Lift 15 Dec–31 Mar 1 Jun–15 Oct
B200–640 Pn320–810 Pool
★★*Hummer* ☎2813 rm41 ⇌6
★★**Klausner** Bahnhofstr 22 ☎2136 tx18418
rm48 ⇌45 G Lift Dec–mid Apr & Jun–Oct
B400–600(double) M80–95 Pn260–365
★**Pension Erika** J-Pirchlstr 21 ☎4885 rm30
⇌30 20Nov–Apr B350–450 Pn350–450
★★**Schweizerhof** Hahnenkammstr 4 ☎2735
rm36 ⇌40 ⋒14 G 10 Dec–10 Apr
15 May–30 Sep B190–800 M80–110
Pn260–550
★★*Sonnenhof* ☎2721 rm29 ⇌20 ⋒2 G
20 Dec–31 Mar 1 Jun–30 Sep
★★*Zum Jägerwirt* Jochbergstr 12 ☎4281
tx51/17114 rm60 ⇌30 Lift Dec–Mar
⓰&D **Herz** J-Pirchlstr 30 ☎4638 Frd G30

Klagenfurt Kärnten 75,000 (☎04222)
Map **14** C1
★★★**Sandwirt** Pernhartgasse 9 ☎82431
tx42329 rm55 ⇌30 ⋒5 G Lift B190–620 M110
★★**Dermuth** Kohldorferstr 52 ☎21247 rm51
⇌47 ⋒4 B355–650 M90 Pn340–380 Pool
★★**Kur Hotel Carinthia** (n rest) Am Stein 41
☎70883 ta Kurhotel tx42399 rm24 ⇌24 Lift
B336–700
★★**Moser-Verdino** Domgasse 2 ☎83431
tx42467 rm100 ⇌/⋒70 Lift B260–680
M145&àlc Pn480–615
★**Janach** Bahnhofstr 5 ☎85114 rm30 ⇌6
B130–430 M40–70
&D*Kaposi* Pischeldorferstr 219 ☎42200 N&
Frd G30
&D**A Krainer** Rosentaler Str 162 ☎21415 N&
Por G
&D**K Kropiunig** Reinholdweg 7 ☎22796 N&
BL/Rov/Toy G10
⓰&D**24 A Luger** Völkermarkter Str 58 ☎31684
N& BL/Jag/Rov/Tri G14
&D**Mandl** St-Veiter Str 209 ☎43200 N&
Chy/Sim
&D**Sintschnig** Südbahngürtel 8 ☎32144 N&
Frd G10
⓰&D**Wiesner** Rosentaler Str 205 ☎22206
(closed weekends) BL/Rov G50
⓰&D**R Wurm** St-Veiterring 27 ☎80991
Peu/Ren G60

Koflach Stiermark (☎03144) Map **14** C2
&D**J Suppanz** Dillacherstr 4 ☎293 N& M/c
Chy/Sim G40

Kötschach-Mauthen Kärnten 2,830
(☎04715) Map **13** B1
★★*Post* ☎221 rm53 ⇌18 ⋒7 G May–Nov

Krems an der Donau Niederösterreich
22,950 (☎02732) Map **14** C3
★★★**Park** E-Hofbauer Str 19 ☎3266 tx71130
rm70 ⇌50 G Lift B180–480 M85 Pn260–340
★★**Weisse Rose** (n rest) Obere Landstr 19
☎3457 rm31 ⇌12 ⋒6 G B110–420
⓰**J Auer** Wienerstr 82 ☎3501 Bed/Opl
&D**H Starkl** Wienerstr 48 ☎3030 N& M/c
Peu/Ren

Krimml Salzburg 670 (☎06564) Map **13** A2
★★**Klockerhaus** ☎208 rm43 ⇌6 ⋒13
B158–396 M60–80 Pn170–230

Kufstein Tirol 12,000 (☎05372) Map **13** A2
★★*Andreas Hofer* Pirmoserstr 8 ☎3281
rm62 ⇌8 G
★★*Auracher-Löchl* Römergasse 3 ☎2138
rm39 ⇌3 ⋒3 G 20 Dec–30 Sep
★★*Egger* ☎2535 rm52 ⇌3 ⋒3 Lift
★*Post* ☎2024 rm30 (A) ⋒1 1 Dec–31 Oct
&D **H Gaderbauer** Zellerstr 29 ☎2840 N&
Aud/VW
⓰&D**24 Krimbacher** K-Kraftstr 2 ☎2236 N&
Frd/MB G20
⓰&D**A Reibmayr** Fischergries 16 ☎2141 N&
Opl

Kühtai Tirol 50 (☎05229) Map **12** D2
★★★**Astoria** ☎215 rm45 ⇌40 Lift Dec–Apr
Pn490–690 Pool

Landeck Tirol 6,600 (☎05442) Map **12** D2
★★*Post* Malserstr 19 ☎2383 rm79 (A21)
At **Zams** (2km NE)
&D **Plaseller** Buntweg ☎2304 N& Fia/Frd

Langen am Arlberg Vorarlberg 825
(☎05582) Map **12** C1/2
★★*Arlbergerhof* ☎213 rm18 ⇌2 ⋒2 G

Lech am Arlberg Vorarlberg 10,920
(☎05583) Map **12** C2
★★*Arlberg* ☎321 tx052259 rm29 ⇌18 ⋒5
Lift 10 Jun–20 Sep 4 Dec–30 Apr Pool
★★**Schneider** ☎601 rm68 ⇌66 G Lift
26 Nov–9 Apr LD B450–1600 M150–180
Pn950–1300 ⋑ Pool
★★*Tannbergerhof* ☎202 tx52/39117 rm32
⇌26 ⋒6 G Lift 27 Nov–17 Apr
15 Jun–30 Sep LD B290–1320 M140–180

Leibnitz Steiermark (☎03452) Map **14** C1
☆☆**ATS** ☎2163 tx43430 rm55 ⇌5 ⋒50 Lift
B190–380 M38 Pn240–315

Leoben Steiermark 37,800 (☎03842)
Map **14** C2
★★**Baumann** F-Josef Str 10 ☎2565 tx33/402
rm90 ⇌19 ⋒26 G Lift B136–525 M60
⓰&D **Puntinger** Kerpelystr 14 ☎2206 N& M/c
Fia G15
⓰**J Wiedner** Kärntnerstr 130 ☎4896 M/c
Ren/Vlo G10

Leonding See Linz an der Donau

Lermoos Tirol 770 (☎05673) Map **12** D2
★★★**Drei Mohren** ☎2362 tx05558 rm50
⇌36 ⋒5 G Lift 17 Dec–2 Nov LD B335–350
★★**Post** ☎2281 rm66 ⇌22 ⋒7 G
15 Dec–15 Oct LD B184–468 Pn284–424
Pool
★*Loisach* ☎2394 rm44 ⇌14 ⋒7 G Lift
15 Dec–25 Oct

Leutasch Weidach Tirol 1,500 (☎05214)
Map **12** D2
★*Pension Waldheim* ☎288 rm14 ⇌7

Lienz Tirol 12,500 (☎04852) Map **13** B1
★★★**Traube** Hauptpl 14 ☎2551 tx04618
rm50 ⇌50 Lift B350–700 M120–150
Pn510–540 Pool
★★**Glocknerhof** (n rest) Schillerstr 4 ☎2167
rm20 ⇌2 ⋒3 18 Dec–15 Oct B135–370 Pool
★★**Post** Hauptpl 20 ☎2545 rm45 ⇌10 ⋒4 G
B200–460 M90 Pn350–410
★★**Sonne** ☎3311 rm40 ⇌30 ⋒7 G Lift
B180–690 M90–115 Pn360–460
★★**Tyrol** Ober Lienz ☎3482 rm35 ⇌15 ⋒20
G B140–320 M60–80 Pn200–240 Pool
⓰&D**24 E Plössnig** Stadion ☎3110 N& Ren
⓰&D**W Rogen** Kärntnerstr 36 ☎2335 N& Opl
&D**24 J Thum** Industriestr ☎3935 N& ☎3335
N& M/c AR/Chy/Sim G
&D**24 Troger** Dr K-Rennerstr 12 ☎3411
N& ☎3057 N& Frd

Liezen Steiermark 6,110 (☎03612)
Map **14** C2

Austria

★★Karow Bahnhofstr 4 ☎2381 rm35 ⇄9
🛏1 G B135–410 M70–100
🍴🕭24 **A Böhm** Ausseerstr 29 ☎2330 N🚗 M/c
AR/Ren G
🍴🕭24 **T Manner** Salzburgerstr 30 ☎2313
Maz/MB

Linz an der Donau Oberösterreich
206,000 (☎07222) Map **14** C3
☆☆☆**Euro Crest** Wankmüllerhofstr 39 ☎42361
tx02/1795 rm105 ⇄61 🛏44 G Lift B479–752
M95 Pn678
★★Oberdorfer (n rest) Schubertstr 1 ☎27555
rm22 ⇄3
★★Schwechaterhof Landstr 18 ☎72255
rm35 ⇄11 🛏6 G Lift
★★Wolfinger Hauptpl 19 ☎23401 rm25
⇄9 G Lift
🛏**M Eibl** Friedhofstr 30 ☎58300 N🚗 Maz G20
🍴🕭**H Felber** Semmelweiss Str 106 ☎20033
N🚗 BL G20
🍴🕭**H Günther** Hamerlingstr 13 ☎55025 N🚗
M/c Opl
🍴🕭**A Jetzinger** Schiffbaustr 16 ☎78225
(closed weekends) Vau
🍴🕭**H Mayer** Industriezeile 72 ☎79161 N🚗
Aud/VW
🍴🕭**H Stieger** Wiener Str 254 ☎42213 N🚗
BL/Rov
At **Leonding** (5km SW)
🍴🕭**Schoeller** Kremstal Bundesstr ☎55586
N🚗 Ren G100
🍴🕭**Seidl Weibold** Kremstal Bundesstr
☎55360 N🚗 M/c BL/Jag/Tri

Lofer Salzburg 1,500 (☎06248) Map **13** B2
★★Brau ☎207 tx63745 rm25 ⇄6 G
1 May–15 Oct B130–440 M65–70 Pn240–340
★★Post ☎304 tx63745 rm38 ⇄14 🛏9 G
B140–460 M65–70 Pn270–400
★★St-Hubertus rm26 ⇄4 G

Mallnitz Kärnten 1,200 (☎04784)
Map **13** B1
★★Alpen ☎262 rm60 (A25) ⇄26 🛏8 G Lift
20 Dec–Apr 25 May–Oct

Maria Wörth Kärnten 1,000 (☎04273)
Map **14** A4
★★★Linde ☎2278 rm50 ⇄36 🛏11 G Lift
B160–305 Pn385–580 Pool Lake
★★Ebner ☎2283 rm86 ⇄21 🛏12 G Lift
Pn180–350 Pool

Mayrhofen Tirol 2,600 (☎05285)
Map **13** A2
★Strass Hauptstr 198 ☎205 rm66 (A24)
⇄12 🛏3 G Lift

Millstatt Kärnten 1,400 (☎04766)
Map **14** B1
★★Forelle ☎2180 rm54 ⇄34 🛏10 Lift
1 May–15 Oct LD B197–726 M85–150
Pn336–676 Pool Lake
At **Dellach/Millstätter See** (5km SE)
★★Harring ☎507 rm35 (A15) ⇄8 🛏13
Etr–Oct Lake

Mödling Niederösterreich (☎02236)
Map **14** D3
🍴🕭**Mödlinger Autohaus** Haupstr 55 ☎2463
N🚗 Bed/Vau G

Mondsee Oberösterreich 2,100 (☎06224)
Map **13** B2
☆☆☆**Euromotel** Autobahn West ☎(06232)
2876 tx63357 rm46 ⇄46 Lift B325–600
M75 Pn450 Lake
★Leitnerbräu Marktpl 9 ☎2219 rm17 (A10)
⇄1 🛏2 B115–340 M45–100 Pn240–300
🍴🕭24 **W Berger** Poststr 2 ☎2303 N🚗 Opl/Vau
🍴🕭**M Widlroither** Südtirolerstr ☎(06232) 2612
N🚗 M/c BL/Toy

Mutters Tirol 1,350 (☎05222) Map **12** D2
★★Berktold ☎25021 rm21 ⇄9 G
15 Dec–30 Sep

★★Muttererhof ☎27491 rm28 ⇄11 G
18 Dec–10 Apr 10 May–10 Oct LD B250–980
M80–100 Pn300–360

Natters Tirol 1,020 (☎05222) Map **12** D2
★Eichhof ☎266555 rm24 May–Oct
B135–290 M50–60
★Pension Steffi ☎29402 rm12 🛏7 G
1 Dec–20 Sep B150–165 M70

Nauders Tirol 1,200 (☎05473) Map **12** D1
★★Sporthotel ☎236 rm70 ⇄30 🛏5 G Lift
15 Dec–30 Oct Pool
★Hochland ☎272 rm32 (A) ⇄1 🛏14
10 Dec–10 Apr 1 Jun–30 Sep
★Post ☎202 rm42 (A38) ⇄4 🛏11 G
1 Jun–8 Oct LD B125–370 M65–80
Pn200–290
★Verzasca (n rest) ☎237 rm18 🛏6 G
Jun–Sep & 15 Dec–15 Apr B130–170

Neumarkt Steiermark 1,871 (☎03584)
Map **14** C2
★★Gasthof Strimitzhof ☎2106 rm18 ⇄4
G B125–340 (double) M40–60 Pn185–240
🍴🕭24 **J Kaiser** St-Georgen 127 ☎2479 N🚗 G20

Neumarkt am Wallersee Salzburg 1,880
(☎06216) Map **13** B2
★Lauterbacher ☎456 rm12 ⇄6 🛏6 G
B120–220 Pn190–200 Lake
🍴🕭**Poller** Hauptstr 12 ☎207 M/c Fia/Lnc G5

Obergurgl Tirol 300 (☎05256) Map **12** D1
★★★Edelweiss & Gurgl ☎223 rm100 ⇄45
🛏15 G Lift B205–530 M50–100 Pn230–300

Obertauern Salzburg 180 (☎06466)
Map **13** B2
★★★Schütz ☎204 rm37 ⇄4 🛏33 G
15 Dec–15 Apr B320–340 M80–120 Pool
★★Pohl ☎209 rm38 🛏8 26 Nov–23 Apr
17 Jun–17 Sep LD B280–560 M65–90
Pn210–430

Ötz Tirol 1,549 (☎05252) Map **12** D2
★★Alpen ☎232 rm53 ⇄40 🛏8 Lift
15 May–5 Oct B210–500 M60–80
Pn230–300
★★Drei Mohren Hauptstr ☎6301 rm30 ⇄8
🛏12 G B195–420 M80–100 Pn230–336 🏊

Partenen-Bielerhöhe Vorarlberg 610
(☎05558) Map **12** C1
★★★Silvrettasee ☎246 tx052245 VIW
Schruns rm50 ⇄11 🛏20 Lift 18 Dec–15 Oct
B201–258 M76–130 Pn327–442 Pool Lake

Patsch Tirol 670 (☎05222) Map **13** A2
★★Grünwalderhof ☎7304 rm30 ⇄16 G
15 May–30 Sep 15 Dec–15 Mar B200–660
M80–100 Pn320–480 🏊 Pool

Pertisau am Achensee Tirol 1,300
(☎05243) Map **13** A2
★★Kristall ☎34290 tx053440 rm37 ⇄3
🛏11 G Pool
★★Pflander ☎5223 rm53 ⇄40 🛏12 G Lift
Dec–Oct LD B210–270 Pn300–390 Pool Lake

Pfunds-Stuben Tirol 1,852 (☎05474)
Map **12** D1
★★Post ☎202 rm58172 rm100 ⇄100 Lift
15 Jan–15 Dec B230–320 M60–120 Pool

Pichl-Auhof am Mondsee
Oberösterreich 850 (☎06224) Map **13** B2
★★Seehof ☎550 rm35 (A) ⇄10 🛏2 G
1 May–30 Sep Pool Lake

Pörtschach am Wörthersee Kärnten
2,700 (☎04272) Map **14** B/C2
★★★★Park ☎2621 tx042344 rm150 ⇄150
G Lift 1 May–10 Oct 🏊 Lake
★★★Schloss Leonstein ☎2816 tx0442019
rm43 ⇄26 🛏7 G 15 May–30 Sep B230–800
M85–120 Pn390–620 🏊 ♫
★★★Sonnengrund Annastr 9 ☎2343 rm47
⇄18 🛏23 G Lift May–Oct Pool Lake

★★**Schloss Seefels** ☎2377 tx042153 rm74 (A38) ⇌64 ▥6 May–Sep B330–1360 Màlc 🏊 Pool Lake

★★**Werzer Astoria** Bundesstr-1 ☎2231 rm310 (A) ⇌68 ▥4 Etr–Oct 🏊 Pool

Radenthein Kärnten (☎04246) Map **13** B1
★★**Metzgerwirt** ☎252 rm19 ▥19 G
🛏🅖**24 W Flath** Millstatter Str 30 ☎351 N🖚344 N🖚 M/c Opl/Toy G10
🅗🅞**G Tusch** Schattseite 101 ☎389 N🖚 M/c Ren

Radstadt Salzburg 3,500 (☎06465)
Map **13** B2
🅗🅞**W Pfleger** ☎312 N🖚 Frd

Ramsau am Dachstein Steiermark (☎03687) Map **13** B2
🅗🅞**K Knaus** Hauptstr 49 ☎2941 N🖚 BMW/Opl/Vau/Vlo

Rankweil Vorarlberg 8,500 (☎05522)
Map **12** C2
★**Rankweiler Hof** ☎44113 ta 6830 Rankweil rm8 G

Rauris Salzburg (☎06544) Map **13** B2
★★**Rauriserhof** ☎213 rm94 (A90) ⇌23 ▥33 Lift LD **Pn**290–360 Pool

Reutte Tirol 4,500 (☎05672) Map **12** D2
★★**Hahnenkamm** ☎2595 rm25 ⇌20 ▥5 Pool
★**Tirolerhof** Bahnhofstr 16 ☎2557 rm37 ⇌3 ▥8 G B173–276 M80–120 Pn240–320
🛏🅖**24 J Breschjak** Innsbruckerstr 18 ☎2627 N🖚2472 M/c BL/BMW/Cit/Fia/Sab/Ska/Vlo G20
🅗🅞**Schlaffer** Allgäuerstr 68 ☎2622 N🖚 Cit/Frd
🛏🅗🅞**24 K Specht** Innsbruckerstr 12 ☎2457 N🖚 Opl/Ren

Ried Tirol 700 (☎05472) Map **12** D1
★**Post** ☎274 rm14 G 15 May–15 Oct

Saalbach Salzburg 1,800 (☎06586)
Map **13** B2
★★★**Kendler** ☎225 rm43 ⇌15 ▥12 G
1 Jun–18 Sep 18 Dec–Apr LD B160–480 Pn220–310 Pool
★★**Berger's Sport Hotel** ☎577 tx06-68515 rm60 ⇌25 ▥15 G Lift Dec–Apr May–Sep Pool
★★**Reiterhof** ☎257 rm26 ⇌4 ▥5 G 20 Dec–10 Apr
★★**Saalbacherhof** ☎7111 tx66-68513 rm100 ⇌80 ▥20 G Lift 1 Dec–Etr 18 May–30 Sep LD **Pn**260–380 🏊 Pool

Saalfelden Salzburg 10,450 (☎06582)
Map **13** B2
★★**Dick** Bahnhofstr 106 ☎2215 rm30 ⇌12 ▥8 B165–540 M70–90 Pn230–370 Pool
★★**Oberbräu** ☎2442 rm20 (A) ⇌4
🛏🅖**24 J Breitfuss** Leogangerstr 23 ☎2467 Fia G

St Anton am Arlberg Tirol 1,980 (☎05446) Map **12** C2
★★★**Mooserkreuz** ☎2230 rm38 ⇌24 ▥14 G Lift 6 Jun–30 Sep 1 Nov–15 Apr B250–1160 M90–120 Pn370–1480 Pool
★★★**Post & Alte Post** ☎2214 tx05817512 rm108 (A35) ⇌68 ▥40 G Lift 1 Dec–10 Oct LD B170–540 M110–130 Pn350–450
★★**Alpenhof** ☎2495 rm32 ⇌15 ▥2 G 1 Jun–1 Oct 1 Dec–10 Apr
★★**Arlberg** Hauptstr ☎2210 rm60 ⇌45 G Lift 1 Jun–15 Sep B150–510 M90–120 Pn220–350 🏊
★★**Montjola** ☎2302 rm25 (A8) ⇌8 ▥2 20 Jun–25 Aug B195–445 M85 Pn285–350
★**Alpenheim** ☎2389 rm28 ▥14 Dec–Sep
★**Bergheim** (n rest) ☎2255 rm30 ⇌16 ▥1 G 1 Dec–30 Apr 20 Jun–15 Sep B170–260
Tyrol ☎2353 N🖚 BL/Rov G8

St Christoph am Arlberg Tirol (☎05446) Map **12** C1/2
★★★**Hospiz** ☎2611 tx058155 rm100 ⇌100 G Lift

St Gilgen am Wolfgangsee Salzburg 2,620 (☎06227) Map **13** B2
★★★**Park Billroth** ☎217 rm47 (A25) ⇌22 ▥8 15 May–Sep B190–680 M70–110 Pn260–410 St15% 🏊 Lake
★★**Alpenland** (n rest) ☎330 rm16 ⇌1 ▥4 G 1 Jun–15 Sep B95–340 Lake
★★**Hollweger** ☎226 rm31 ⇌17 ▥4 G 15 Dec–30 Oct LD B183–566 M50–100 Pn278–413 Lake
★★**Post** ☎239 rm48 ⇌10 ▥4 G 1 Nov–30 Sep B142.50–582 Pn254–428 Pool Lake
★★**Radetzky** Streicherpl 1 ☎232 rm24 ⇌4 ▥6 G 1 May–1 Oct Lake
★**Mozartblick** (n rest) ☎403 rm23 ⇌2 ▥14 G B95–260 Lake

St Johann im Pongau Salzburg 6,670 (☎06412) Map **14** C2
★**Prem** ☎207 rm52 ⇌14 ▥2 G B135–450 M50–100 Pn185–300

St Johann in Tirol Tirol 5,300 (☎05352) Map **13** A2
★★★**Sporthotel Austria** Speckbacherstr 57 ☎2507 rm50 ⇌40 G Lift 15 Dec–30 Mar 15 May–30 Sep LD **Pn**300–460 Pool
★★**Kaiserhof** ☎2545 rm42 ⇌12 G Lift 15 Dec–30 Sep B195–630 M40–80 Pn250–360
🛏**E Foidl** Pass-Thurnstr 1 ☎2129 N🖚 BL/Dat/Jag/Rov/Tri

St Oswald bei Freistadt Oberösterreich (☎07945) Map **14** C3
🛏🅖**24 H Reindl** ☎225 Bed/Vau G5

St-Polten Niederösterreich 40,000 (☎02742) Map **14** C3
★★**Pittner** Kremsergasse 18 ☎2006 rm100 ⇌14 G Lift
Auto-Dinstl Stifterstr, Mariazellerstr ☎2644 N🖚 Cit G
🛏🅗🅞**O Fuchs** Schuberstr 24 ☎2052 Vau G4
🅗🅞**Huber** Mariazellerstr 85 ☎7566 N🖚 Aud/VW
🛏🅗**F Lutzenberger** Kremser Landstr 8 ☎2475 M/c Dat/Sab/Ska/Toy G30

St Wolfgang am Wolfgangsee Oberösterreich 2,200 (☎06138) Map **13** B2
★★★**Weisses Rössl** ☎358 tx68148 Weiroe A rm63 (A14) ⇌32 ▥8 G Lift Mar–Nov B150–820 M70–100 Pn320–620 🏊 Pool Lake
★★**Appesbach** ☎209 rm16 (A5) ⇌7 ▥3 1 Apr–1 Oct B130–560 M60–90 🏊 Lake
★★**Post & Schloss Eibenstein** ☎346 rm162 ⇌48 ▥23 G Lift Etr–31 Oct B195–285 M70–95 Pn250–325 Pool Lake

Salzburg Salzburg 130,000 (☎06222)
Map **13** B2 See Plan
★★★★★**Gastschloss Mönchstein** Mönchsberg 26 ☎41363 Plan **1** rm13 ⇌13 G Lift Apr–Oct B350–1900 M250 🏊
★★★★**Europa** Rainerstr 31 ☎73391 tx63424 Plan **3** rm104 ⇌52 ▥52 Lift B420–920 M120 Pn640–1140
★★★★**Osterreichischer Hof** Schwarzstr 5 ☎72541 tx63590 Plan **5** rm130 ⇌130 G Lift B375–1300 M200
★★★★**Winkler** F-Josef Str 9 ☎73513 tx06/3961 Plan **6** rm103 ⇌103 Lift B380–585 M125–140 Pn600–885
★★★**Gablerbräu** Linzergasse 9 ☎73441 Plan **7** rm62 ⇌26 Lift B240–700 M80
★★★**Kasererhof** Alpenstr 6 ☎21265 tx063477 Plan **8** rm54 ⇌50 G Lift
★★★**Schlosshotel St-Rupert** Morzger Str 31 ☎43231 Plan **10** rm30 ⇌24 ▥1 G 1 Apr–1 Oct B500–1280 M110–160 Pn710–1700 Pool

Austria

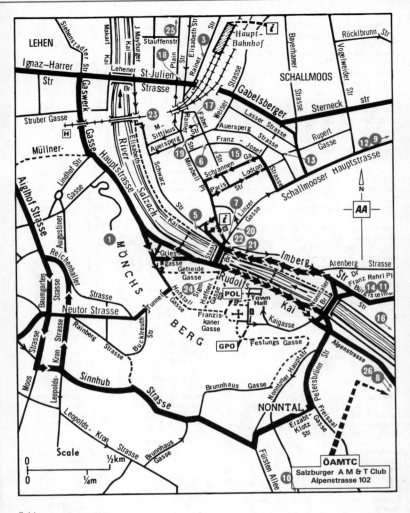

Salzburg

1	★★★★★ Gastschloss Mönchstein		15	★★ Germania
3	★★★★ Europa		16	★★ Gastein
5	★★★★ Österreichischer Hof		17	★★ Markus Sittikus
6	★★★★ Winkler		18	★★ Meran
7	★★★ Gablerbräu		19	★★ Pitter
8	★★★ Kasererhof		20	★★ Schwarzes Rossl
9	★★★ Kobenzl (at Salzburg-Gaisberg)		21	★★ Stein
10	★★★ Schlosshotel St Rupert		22	★★ Traube
11	★★★ Steinlechner		23	★ Carlton
12	★★★ Zistalalm (at Salzburg-Gaisberg)		24	★ Elefant
13	★★ Auersperg		25	★ Plainhof
14	★★ Eden		26	☆ Salzburger

★★★**Steinlechner** Aigner Str 14 ☎20061
Plan **11** rm31 �⊅14 B230–580 M70 Pn340–700
★★**Auersperg** Auerspergstr 61 ☎71757
tx06/3817 Plan **13** rm68 (A18) ⇌20 ⋒23 G
Lift B270–760 M85 Pn760–1020
★★**Eden** Gaisbergstr 38 ☎20118 Plan **14**
(A3) ⇌12 ⋒10 G B300–560
★★**Gastein** (n rest) Ignaz-Rieder-Kai 25
☎22565 Plan **16** rm14 ⇌14 G B300–1200
Màlc
★★*Germania* Faberstr 10 ☎71200 Plan **15**
rm35 ⇌6 Lift
★★**Markus Sittikus** (n rest) M-Sittikus Str 20
☎71121 ta Markushotel Plan **17** rm40 ⇌11 ⋒9
Lift B243–675
★★**Meran** Plainstr 14 ☎72214 Plan **18** rm56
⇌7 Lift
★★**Pitter** Rainerstr 6 ☎78571 tx06/3532
Plan **19** rm210 ⇌90 ⋒40 Lift B260–900
M90–110 Pn430–655
★★**Schwarzes Rössl** Priesterhausgasse 6
☎74426 tx74832 Plan **20** rm55 ⇌7 Lift
1 Jul–30 Sep B215–470 M70 Pn355–495
★★*Stein* Staatsbrücke ☎74346 Plan **21**
rm80 ⇌40 Lift
★★**Traube** Linzer Gasse 4 ☎74062 tx063233
Terra a Plan **22** rm39 ⇌12 ⋒1 G Lift
★ **Carlton** M-Sittikus Str 3 ☎74343 Plan **23**
rm47 ⇌6 ⋒5 G Lift 7 Jan–20 Dec B200–600
M60–85 Pn285–415 Pool
★*Elefant* S-Haffner Gasse 4 ☎43397 Plan **24**
rm39 ⇌12 ⋒3 Lift
★*Plainhof* (n rest) Plainstr 55 ☎72181
Plan **25** rm32 ⇌3 ⋒2 G
☆**Salzburger** (n rest) Alpenstr 48 ☎20871
Plan **26** rm27 ⋒13 G 1 Feb–24 Dec B145–300
⋒&⊙**Austro-Diesel** Innsbrucker-Bundesstr 128
☎44501 N✿ GM
⋒&⊙**Eibl** Linzer Bundesstr 39 ☎78435 N✿
⋒&⊙**Intermotor** Robinigstr 9 ☎77151 N✿
Dat/Sab/Ska
⋒**G Pappas** Siebenstädterstr 46 ☎31531 N✿
MB
⋒&⊙**Pletzer** Schallmooser Hauptstr 52
☎795270 Fia/Ren G20
⋒♦24 **Porsche Interauto** Alpenstr 175
☎20911 Aud/Por/VW G
⋒♦24 **Porsche Interauto** Sterneckstr 17
☎75230 Aud/VW
⋒&⊙**E Scheidinger** Schallmooser Hauptstr 24
☎71176 N✿ Frd G

Salzburg-Gaisberg Salzburg (☎06222)
Map **13** B2
★★★**Kobenzl** ☎21776 tx63833 rm38 ⇌33 G
15 Mar–1 Nov LD B250–1000 Pn350–1500
Pool ∩
★★★**Zistelalm** ☎20104 rm24 ⇌3 ⋒12 G
15 Dec–15 Nov LD B150–550 Màlc
Pn265–350 Pool

Schladming Steiermark 3,300 (☎03687)
Map **13** B2
★★*Alte Post* ☎2571 rm45 ⇌15 ⋒5 G
★★**Grogger** ☎087 rm44 (A) ⇌14 ⋒16 G ✎
Pool

Schönberg/Stubai Tirol 590 (☎05225)
Map **13** A2
★★*Jägerhof* ☎2560 rm90 (A71) ⇌30 ⋒30
G Lift 20 Dec–10 Oct ✎

Schruns Vorarlberg 2,340 (☎05556)
Map **12** C1
&⊙*R Lins* Silvrettastr, Gantschierstr ☎2540
N✿ MB

Schuttdorf See Zell am See

Seeboden Kärnten 3,324 (☎04762)
Map **13** B1
★★★★**Seehof** ☎81714 tx048122 rm95 (A29)
⇌95 G Lift Etr–15 Oct LD B350–1160
M80–120 Pn400–700 ✎ Pool Lake

★★**See Steiner** ☎81713 rm50 G Etr–5 Oct LD
B230–280 M65–90 Pn200–410 Pool Lake

Seefeld Tirol 2,050 (☎05212) Map **12** D2
★★★★**Astoria** ☎2272 tx05-385523 rm60
⇌47 ⋒1 Lift Jun–Sep Dec–Mar B480–740
M120–160 Pool
★★★★*Eden* Münchnerstr 136 ☎2258
tx53885511 rm51 ⇌51 G Lift Dec–Apr
1 May–20 Sep ✎
★★★**Dreitorspitze** Speckbacherstr 182
☎2951 tx05-385525 rm53 ⇌17 ⋒16 Lift G
15 Jun–25 Sep B310–790 Pn310–790 Pool
★★★**Gartenhotel Tümmlerhof** ☎2571 rm74
⇌63 ⋒1 G Lift Dec–Oct LD B230–1000
M125–135 M350–680 Pool
★★★*Karwendelhof* Bahnhofstr ☎2655
tx5385519 rm53 ⇌40 ⋒1 20 Dec–31 Mar
★★★**Klosterbräu** ☎2621 tx5-385517 rm106
(A53) ⇌50 ⋒18 G Lift Dec–Mar Jun–Sep
Pn360–680 Pool
★★★**Philipp** Münchnerstr 68 ☎2301 rm60
⇌15 ⋒45 G Lift Dec–Mar May–Sep
B240–700 M100 Pn300–400
★★★**Schlosshotel** ☎2658 tx5385513 rm21
⇌17 G Lift 19 Dec–1 Apr 1 Jun–1 Oct
★★**Kurhotel** ☎2671 rm54 ⇌35 ⋒12 G Lift
15 Dec–30 Sep LD B200–310 M90–120
Pn340–500 Pool
★★*Regina* Claudiastr 171 ☎2270 rm30 ⇌8
⋒2 10 Jun–30 Sep 20 Dec–10 Apr G
B340–520 (double) M100 Pn240–340

Semmering Niederösterreich 1,400
(☎02664) Map **14** D2
★★★*Silvana* ☎309 rm25 ⇌25 Lift
★★**Südbahn** ☎455 rm114 ⇌30 G Lift ✎ Pool

Serfaus Tirol 800 (☎05476) Map **12** D1
★★**Maximilian** ☎255 rm30 ⇌30 G Lift
11 Jun–30 Sep B130–155 M100
★*Furgler* ☎201 rm40 ⇌31 ⋒9 G Lift
1 Dec–20 Apr 15 May–20 Oct B340–435

Sillian Tirol 2,000 (☎04856) Map **13** B1
★*Post* ☎273 rm60 ⇌10 ⋒10 G

Sölden Tirol 1,900 (☎05254) Map **13** A1
★★**Hochsölden** ☎2229 rm90 ⇌70 G Lift
1 Dec–30 Apr **Pn**340–480

Spittal an der Drau Kärnten 12,300
(☎04762) Map **13** B1
★★★**Salzburg** Tirolerstr 12 ☎3165 rm55
(A26) ⇌16 ⋒11 G LD B170–600 M70
Pn300–400
⋒&⊙**N Nowak** Villacher Str 72 ☎3447
(closed weekends) M/c BMW/Peu/Vlo
♦24 **W Riebler** Koschatstr 13 ☎2561 N✿ Frd G

Steinach am Brenner Tirol 2,560
(☎05272) Map **13** A1/2
★★**Steinacherhof** ☎6241 rm59 ⇌44 G Lift
15 Dec–10 Oct ✎ Pool
★★**Wilder Mann** ☎6210 rm68 (A8) ⇌45
⋒3 G Lift 20 Dec–20 Apr 15 May–5 Oct
B160–260 M70 Pn175–300 Pool
★*Weisses Rössl* ☎6206 rm44 ⇌10 ⋒33 G
Lift LD B150–350 M70 Pn230–270

Steyr Oberösterreich 41,200 (☎07252)
Map **14** C3
★★**Minichmayr** Haratzmüllerstr 1 ☎3419
tx028-134 rm45 ⇌15 ⋒5 B140–400
M25–110&àlc Pn238–325
&⊙**F Hilbert** Madelsederstr 1 ☎63460 N✿ M/c
Frd/Vau G5

Stuben Vorarlberg 700 (☎05582) Map **12** C2
★★*Post* ☎84516 rm55 (A25) ⇌19 ⋒14 G
15 Dec–15 May 1 Jun–30 Aug

Telfs Tirol 5,800 (☎05262) Map **12** D2
★*Hohe Munde* Untermarktstr 17 ☎2408
rm23 ⇌5 ⋒8 G B153–336 M50–80
Pn205–230

Austria

▶24 H Harting Bundesstr 1 ☎2854
Aud/MB/VW G30

Thiersee Tirol 1,800 (☎05376) Map **13** A2
★★**Charlotte** ☎207 rm45 ⇄12 ♏11 G Lift
B200–520 M80–110 Pn335–450 Pool Lake
🅿🛪 **S Mairhofer** ☎255 N🛪 Ren

Thumersbach See **Zell am See**

Traunkirchen am Traunsee
Oberösterreich 1,600 (☎07617) Map **13** B2
★★**Post** ☎307 rm65 ⇄65 Lift Lake

Turracher-Höhe Kärnten (☎04275)
Map **13** B1
★★**Hochschober** ☎8213 tx42152 rm71 (A24)
⇄18 G mid Dec–1st wk after Etr & Jun–mid Oct
Pn308–484 ⏜ Pool Lake

Velden am Wörthersee Kärnten 3,200
(☎04274) Map **14** C1
★★★**Schloss** am Corso 24 ☎2655 rm160
(A60) ⇄100 15 May–30 Sep LD B240–850
M100–120 Pn280–620 ⏜ Pool Lake
★★★**Seehotel Europa** Wrannpark 1 ☎2770
tx04-294522 rm70 (A20) ⇄50 ♏10 G Lift
10 May–Sep LD B260–960 Lake
★★★**Seehotel Veldnerhof-Mösslacher**
am Korso 17 ☎2018 ta Mösslacherhotel rm138
⇄53 ♏41 Lift LD B160–640 M75–95
Pn540–940 ⏜ Lake
★★**Hubertushof** ☎2676 rm55 (A37) ⇄18
♏25 20 Mar–15 Oct B150–370 Pn270–480
Pool Lake
★★**Wrann** Europapl 4 ☎2021 rm48 ⇄4 ♏7
G 15 May–25 Sep Pool
🅿 **O Matschnig** am Korso 18 ☎2067 M/c Ren G

Vienna See **Wien**

Villach Kärnten 34,000 (☎04242)
Map **13** B1
★★★**Park** Moritzschstr 2 ☎23300 tx045582
rm170 ⇄133 G Lift B204–470 M76–110
Pn310–645
★★**Mosser** Bahnhofstr 7 ☎24115 rm50 ⇄15
♏5 B175–480 M65–80 Pn300–430 Pool
★★**Post** Hauptpl 26 ☎26101 tx45723 rm80
⇄31 ♏1 G Lift B195–650 M70 Pn335–930
🅿🛪 **Brodnik** Klagenfurterstr 37 ☎24388 N🛪
Chy/Sim/Ska
🅿🛪24 **V Gram** Tiroler Str 51 ☎24092 Jag/Peu
G60
🅿🛪 **W Lackner** Siedlerstr 25 ☎24825 N🛪
M/c BL/Jag/Rov/Tri G10
🅿🛪 **S Papp** Steinwender Str 15 ☎24826 N🛪
M/c Frd
R Thalmeiner Tirolerstr 19 ☎24590 N🛪 Opl
At **Warmbad** (5km S)
★★★**Josefinenhof** ☎25531 tx045563 rm60
⇄44 ♏5 Lift B310–1000 M85 Pn300–540 ⏜
Pool
★★★**Kurhotel Warmbaderhof** ☎25501
tx045583 rm156 ⇄120 ♏36 G Lift ⏜ Pool

Volders Tirol (☎05224) Map **13** A2
🅿🛪24 **Herman Federer** Fiegerstr 2 ☎2398
Aud/Peu/VW G

Waidhofen-an-der-Ybbs Niederösterreich
(☎07442) Map **14** C2
🅿🛪 **K Plank** Weyrerstr 51a ☎2442 N🛪 M/c Opl
G25

Waidring Tirol (☎05353) Map **13** B2
★★**Tiroler Adler** ☎311 ta Sporthotel rm33
⇄33 G 1 Dec–10 Oct Lift B290–640
M60–100 Pn270–320

Warmbad See **Villach**

Weisskirchen in Steiermark Steiermark
(☎03577) Map **14** C2

▶24 R Kocher Bahnhofstr 21 ☎2567
(closed weekends) Bed/Cit/Vau G

Wels Oberösterreich 48,160 (☎07242)
Map **13** B3
★★★**Greif** Kaiser Josef pl 50 ☎5361
tx025566 rm125 ⇄40 G Lift
★★**Parzer** Kaiser Josef pl 52 ☎6472 rm55 ⇄5
G
🅿🛪24 **K Huber** Hamerlingstr 9 ☎7650 N🛪 Peu/
Tri
🅿🛪 **A & H Markgraf** H-Sachs Str 21 ☎7190
BL/Jag/Rov/Tri

Westendorf Tirol 2,350 (☎05334)
Map **13** A2
★**Jakobwirt** ☎6245 rm60 ⇄44 Lift
20 Dec–30 Mar 10 May–30 Sep LD B150–210
Pn230–330

Wien (Vienna) 1,649,000 Map **14** D3
See Plan

Bold Roman numbers after hotel addresses
are district (Bezirk) numbers. Garages are
listed below under Bezirk headings.

★★★★★**Ambassador** Neuer Markt 5 **I**
☎527511 tx1/1906 Plan **1** rm105 ⇄105 Lift
B620–1420
★★★★★**Bristol** Kärnter Ring 1 **I** ☎529552
tx012474 Plan **2** rm130 ⇄130 G Lift
B656–1860 M195–250 Pn1100–1465
★★★★★**Imperial** Kärntner Ring 16 **I**
☎651765 tx01/2630 Plan **3** rm160 ⇄141
♏10 Lift B600–1700 Màlc
★★★★★**Intercontinental** Johannesgasse 28
III ☎563611 ta Inhotelcor Vienna tx1235
Plan **4** rm500 ⇄500 G Lift B915–1630
M135–165
★★★★★**Sacher** Philharmonikerstr 4 **I**
☎525575 tx012520 Plan **5** rm123 ⇄115 Lift
B390–1800
★★★★**Europa** Neuer Markt 3 **I** ☎521594
tx12292 Plan **6** rm100 ⇄100 Lift B540–970
M160
★★★★**Parkring** Parkring 12 **I** ☎526524
tx13420 Plan **7** rm65 ⇄63 G Lift B450–900
M135 Pn720–830
★★★★**Prinz Eugen** Wiedner-Gürtel 14 **IV**
☎651741 tx012483 Plan **8** rm106 ⇄68 ♏38
Lift B576–985 M160
★★★★**Royal** Singerstr 3 **I** ☎524631
tx01/2870 Plan **9** rm66 ⇄66 Lift B565–870
M100–130 Pn730–950
★★★★**Stephansplatz** Stephanspl 9 **I**
☎635605 tx7/4334 Plan **10** rm68 ⇄49 ♏13
Lift B295–755 Màlc ⏜
★★★**Astoria** Kärntner Str 32 **I** ☎526585
tx12856 Plan **11** rm115 ⇄73 ♏4 Lift B310–
920 M140 Pn590–830
★★★**Bellevue** (n rest) Althanstr 5 **IX**
☎345631 tx7/4906 Plan **12** rm86 ⇄33 ♏17
G Lift B280–690
★★★**Erzherzog Rainer** Wiedner Haupstr 27
IV ☎654646 tx01/2329 Plan **13** rm90 ⇄54
♏10 G Lift B380–1050 M165 Pn690–980
★★★**Kahlenberg** Kahlenberg **XIX** ☎321251
Plan **14** rm33 ⇄14 ♏15 G Lift
★★★**Kaiserhof** Frankenberggasse 10 **IV**
☎651701 tx076872 Plan **15** rm74 ⇄28
♏46 Lift B440–690 M80 Pn470–505
★★★**Kärntnerhof** Grashofgasse 4 **I** ☎521923
tx1-2535 Plan **16** rm43 ⇄20 ♏12 Lift B305–
690
★★★**Palais Schwarzenberg**
Schwarzenbergpl 9 **III** ☎725125 tx07/6124
Plan **17** rm35 ⇄35 Lift ⏜
★★★**Park Schönbrunn** Hietzinger Hauptstr 10
XIII ☎822676 tx01/2513 Plan **18** rm390
⇄320 G Lift B535–1250 M180 Pool
★★★**Römischer Kaiser** (n rest) Annagasse 16
I ☎527751 tx13696 Plan **19** rm26 ⇄16 ♏5

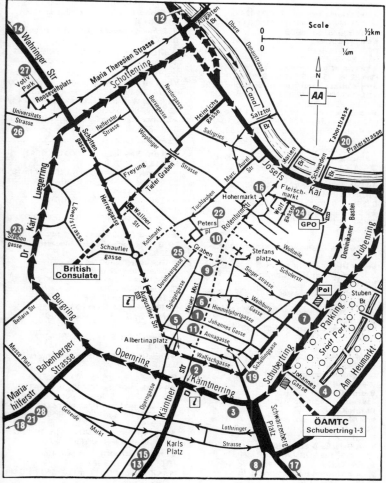

Wien (Vienna)

1	★★★★★Ambassador	15	★★★Kaiserhof
2	★★★★★Bristol	16	★★★Kärntnerhof
3	★★★★★Imperial	17	★★★Palais Schwarzenberg
4	★★★★★Intercontinental	18	★★★Park Schönbrunn
5	★★★★★Sacher	19	★★★Römischer Kaiser
6	★★★★Europa	20	★★★Stefanie
7	★★★★Parkring	21	★★★Tyrol
8	★★★★Prinz Eugen	22	★★★Wandl
9	★★★★Royal	23	★★★Weisser Hahn
10	★★★★Stephansplatz	24	★★Austria
11	★★★Astoria	25	★★Graben
12	★★★Bellevue	26	★★Madeleine
13	★★★Erzherzog Rainer	27	★★Regina
14	★★★Kahlenberg	28	★★Stieglbräu

Austria

Lift B350–950
★★★Stefanie Taborstr 12 **II** ☎242412
tx07/4589 Plan **20** rm160 ⇆100 G Lift
B320–930 M150 Pn600–1490
★★★Tyrol (n rest) Mariahilfer Str 15 **VI**
☎572423 tx01-1885 Plan **21** rm35 ⇆20 ▥15
G Lift B450–750
★★★Wandl (n rest) Peterspl 9 **I** ☎636317
Plan **22** rm135 ⇆45 ▥15 Lift B125–320
★★★Weisser Hahn (n rest) Josefstädter Str 22
VIII ☎423648 tx07/5533 Plan **23** rm68 ⇆24
▥23 Lift B275–800
★★Austria (n rest) Wolfengasse 3 **I** ☎527439
tx12848 Plan **24** rm60 ⇆20 ▥4 Lift B270–790
★★Graben Dorotheergasse 3 **I** ☎521531
tx012870 rm46 Plan **25** ⇆24 Lift B325–760
M70–100 Pn490–750
★★Madeleine (n rest) Geblergasse 21 **XVII**
☎434741 tx075121 Plan **26** rm78 ⇆55 ▥13
G Lift B260–620
★★Regina Rooseveltpl 15 **IX** ☎427681
tx074700 Plan **27** rm127 ⇆63 ▥18 Lift
B285–1120 M100–130 Pn450–810
★★Stieglbräu Mariahilfer Str 156 **XV**
☎833621 Plan **28** rm61 ⇆35 ▥2 Lift
B208–625
Bezirk II
▯☜**P Glaser** Czerningasse 11 ☎243148 N☺
Rov G50
Bezirk III
▯☜**F Eckl** Untere Viaduktgasse 3 ☎738105
N☺ Ren
☜**H Lehmann** Steingasse 14 ☎733787 N☺ BL
Bezirk VI
▯☜**G Wittek** Liniengasse 28 ☎564283 N☺ Frd
Bezirk IX
▯**Votivpark** Universitäts Str ☎423518 N☺
G600
Bezirk X
▯**F M Tarbuk** Davidgasse 90 ☎641631 N☺
Chy/Sab/Sim
▯☜**Teha** Gudrunstr 144 ☎6445080
(closed weekends) M/c AR/Chy/Sim
Bezirk XII
▯☜**Felber** Arndtstr 46 ☎838204 N☺ Opl/Vau
Bezirk XVIII
☜**G Molnar** Thimiggasse 50 ☎474128 N☺
BL G3
Bezirk XX
▯☜**A Geiszler & Söhne** Sachsenpl 10
☎333166 N☺ BL/BMW/Maz/Ren/Vlo
Bezirk XXII
▯☜**Auto Martin** Hirschstettnerstr 92
☎225147 N☺ BL G40

Wörgl Tirol 7,650 (☎05332) Map **13** A2
★★Central Bahnhofstr 27 ☎2459 rm100
⇆14 ▥3 Lift
▯**F Schwarzenauer** Angath Wörgl Haus Nr 47
☎2127 M/c BL G4

Wolfsberg Kärnten (☎04352) Map **14** C1
▯☜**Grohs & Kainbacher** Ritzing ☎2316 N☺
M/c Bed/Vau

Ybbs an der Donau Niederösterreich 6,000
(☎07412) Map **14** C3
★★Royal Weisses Rössel ☎2292 rm32 ⇆7
▥5 Lift 1 Apr–30 Oct
★Steiner ☎2629 rm20 (A10) ⇆14 ▥6 G LD
B110–320 M70–80 Pn210–250

Zams See **Landeck**

Zell am See Salzburg 7,000 (☎06542)
Map **13** B2
★★Berner N-Gassner-Prom 1 ☎2557 rm18 ⇆1
▥2 G Xmas–Etr May–Oct B120–360 M55–75
Pn210–290 Lake
★★Zauner ☎2504 rm35 ⇆10 ▥4 G
1 May–15 Oct Lake
★★Zum Hirschen ☎2447 rm37 ⇆12 G Lift
1 Dec–31 Oct
★Victoria ☎2694 rm33 ⇆1 ▥14 Lift
▯☜**G Altendorfer** Brucker Bundesstr 108
☎3283 Opl
☜**Glockner** ☎2490 N☺ Ren
At **Schuttdorf** (2km S)
▯☜**24 Moser** Brucker Bundesstr 90 ☎2628
Chy/Fia/MB/Sim G14
At **Thumersbach** (2km E)
★★Bellevue ☎3104 rm65 ⇆13 ▥10
20 May–30 Sep B110–460 M65–75
Pn180–300 Lake

Zell am Ziller Tirol 1,750 (☎05282)
Map **13** A2
★Bräu Dorfpl 1 ☎2313 ta Zellerbräu rm37
⇆5 G

Zirl Tirol 4,050 (☎05228) Map **13** A2
★★★Zirler Weinhof ☎2444 rm20 (A13)
⇆9 ▥11 G Lift 15 Dec–15 Nov B300–580
★★Goldener Löwe Hauptpl ☎2330
tx05-3350 rm18 ⇆12 G B170–590 M80–120
Pn260–450
★★Post Meilstr 2 ☎2207 rm41 ⇆19 ▥2 G
Lift B125–340 M50–90 Pn200–280

Zürs am Arlberg Vorarlberg 400
(☎05583) Map **12** C2
★★★Zürserhof ☎513 rm120 ⇆60 ▥5 G Lift
1 Dec–30 Apr

BELGIUM

Population 9,651,000 **Area** 11,775 sq miles **Maps** 3, 4, 10 & 11

How to get there   Many cross-Channel ferries operate direct from Dover and Folkestone to Ostend or from Dover, Felixstowe and Hull to Zeebrugge. Alternatively, it is possible to use the shorter Channel crossings from Dover or Folkestone to France and drive along the coastal road to Belgium. Fast hovercraft services operate from Dover or Ramsgate to Calais and from Dover to Boulogne.

Travel information

AA Port agent   B-8400 Ostende G E Huyghe & Son, 10 Zuidstraat ☎(059)702855

Accidents   **Fire** and **ambulance** ☎900, **police** ☎901 and in large towns ☎906 also

Vehicles must be removed, after the drivers have exchanged particulars, where damage to vehicles only has occurred. The police must be called if an unoccupied stationary vehicle is damaged or if injuries are caused to persons; in the latter case the car must not be moved (see the recommendations on page 21).

Accommodation   There is no official classification, but hotels exhibiting the distinctive sign issued by the National Tourist Office, included in the official hotel guide, must satisfy regulations which lay down standards of comfort and amenities. Room prices are exhibited in hotel reception areas, and full details of all charges including service and taxes are shown in each room. There are few luxury hotels outside Brussels and the major resorts.

Breakdowns   The Belgian motoring club (TCB) maintains an efficient breakdown service known as Touring Secours. Service is available to AA members on production of the *5-Star Travel Booklet.*

Belgium

Patrols
The Touring Secours operates a breakdown service daily between 07.00 and 23.00hrs. If you need help, telephone the number relevant to the zone in which you have broken down (this is indicated on the map on this page) and the Touring Secours will send a patrol to assist you.

The Flemish Automobile Club (VAB-VTB operates only in the Antwerp area) and the Royal Automobile Club of Belgium (RACE) each have patrol cars displaying the signs 'Wacht op de Weg' or (RACE). However, neither is associated with the AA and motorists will have to pay for all services.

British Consulates

2000 Antwerpen, Van Schoonbekeplien 6
☎(031)326940 & 328829
1040 Bruxelles 4, rue Joseph II 28, Britannia House
☎(02)2191165
8400 Oostende, Ijzerstraat 21 ☎(059)701615
9000 Gent, Dok 58 ☎(091)256875
4000 Liege, rue Beeckman 45 ☎(041)235831/2

Currency and banking

The unit of currency is the Belgian franc, divided into 100 centimes. There is no restriction on the amount of currency which may be taken into or out of Belgium, whether in the form of travellers' cheques or Belgian and foreign banknotes. As Belgian currency regulations are subject to change, intending visitors should familiarise themselves with the current exchange regulations before leaving Britain.

Banking hours

Banks are generally open 09.00–15.30hrs from Monday to Friday. With the exception of some banks in Antwerp, all close for lunch. They are closed on Saturdays. Outside banking hours currency can be changed in Brussels at special offices at the Gare du Nord, open 07.00–23.00hrs daily and the Gare du Midi, open 10.00–24.00hrs daily, and at Zaventem Airport, open 07.00–22.00hrs daily.

Dimensions and weight restrictions

Vehicles must not exceed:
height   4 metres;
width   2.5 metres;
length   vehicle/trailer combinations 15 metres.

Belgium

Drinking and driving

A driver with 0.8gr of alcohol per litre of blood is punishable by a fine of between BFr4,000 and BFr40,000 and/or a prison sentence of between 15 days and three months; in addition the driver may be disqualified.

Holidays and events

Holidays based on religious festivals are not always fixed on the calendar but any current diary will give the actual dates. The Whit holiday should not be confused with the British Spring Holiday.

Fixed holidays

1 January	New Year's Day
1 May	Labour Day
21 July	National holiday
15 August	Assumption of the Virgin Mary
1 November	All Saints' Day
11 November	Armistice Day
25 December	Christmas Day

Moveable holidays

Easter Monday
Ascension Day
Whit Monday

Annual events

April

Antwerp, Kortrijk, Tongeren and St Truiden Flanders Spring Festival (April/July)

May

Nationwide May Day celebrations
Ieper Grand Festival of Cats
Bruges Procession of the Holy Blood
Antwerp Fair (May/June)

June

Chimay Music Festival at the castle (June/July)

July

Bruges Son et Lumière (July/September)
Schoten International Festival of Folk Dances
Visé Summer Festival of the Guild of Crossbowmen

August

Bruges, Brussels, and Leuven Flanders Summer Festival (August/September)
Bree Touristic Month (many events)
Overijse Grape and Wine Festival

September

Antwerp Liberation festivities
Wieze Beer Festival

A more comprehensive list of events is obtainable from the Belgium National Tourist Office (see page 74).

Insurance

This is compulsory; make sure your policy gives adequate cover for travel abroad.

Lights

Between dusk and dawn and in all cases where visibility is restricted to 200m, dipped or full-beam headlights must be used. However, headlights must be dipped: where street lighting is continuous permitting clear vision for 100m; at the approach of oncoming traffic (including vehicles on rails); when following another vehicle and, where the road is adjacent to water, at the approach of oncoming craft if the pilot is likely to be dazzled.

Parking lights

Vehicles parked on the public highway must use position lights (parking lights) both day and night if vehicles are not visible from 100 metres.

In built-up areas the position lights may be replaced by a single parking light displayed on the side nearest to the centre of the road providing the vehicle is not more than 6 metres long and 2 metres wide, has no trailer attached to it, its maximum carrying capacity is not more than eight persons excluding the driver.

Belgium

Medical treatment   The provision of medical benefits in Belgium is administered by friendly societies (*Mutualités*) or by regional offices of the Auxiliary Fund for Sickness and Invalidity Insurance (*La Caisse Auxiliaire d'Assurance Maladie – Invalidité*) whose address is 10 boulevard Saint-Lazare, 1030 Brussels, ☎2182300. The address of the nearest local office of the friendly societies may be obtained by local enquiry or from the national federation of friendly societies. You go direct to any doctor or dentist and show him form E111. You will have to pay for treatment and will be given a receipt which will show the service provided (*Attestation de soins donnés*). You can take the doctor's prescription to any chemist, but again you should obtain a receipt for the charge the chemist makes and also make sure he stamps and returns your copy of the doctor's prescription. You will be able to obtain a refund of approximately 75% of the cost on presentation of form E111, together with the receipts from the doctor and chemist, at the nearest office of the insurance societies.

If you or your dependants need hospital treatment, then you should present form E111 to one of the local offices of the friendly societies which will authorise part payment of the cost and advise you where you can obtain the treatment. If you enter hospital urgently and thus are unable to contact the local office beforehand, you should present form E111 to the hospital authorities and ask them to obtain an undertaking to pay part of the cost from the appropriate insurance authority.

Motoring club   The Touring Club Royal de Belgique has its head office at 44 rue de la Loi, 1040 Bruxelles and branch offices in most towns.

Office hours   The Brussels head office is open weekdays 09.00–18.00hrs; Saturday 09.00–12.30hrs. Regional offices are open weekdays 09.00–12.00hrs (Monday from 09.15hrs) and 14.00–18.00hrs; Saturday 09.00–12.00hrs. All offices are closed on Saturday afternoons and Sundays.

Parking   Regulations differentiate between *waiting* (long enough to load or unload goods or for passengers to get in or out) and *parking*. Vehicles must be left on the right-hand side of the road, except in one-way streets when they can be left on either side. Where possible the vehicle must be left on the level shoulder inside built-up areas and on the shoulder, level or otherwise, outside these areas. If the shoulder is used by pedestrians then at least 1 metre must be left for them on the side farthest away from the traffic.

It is illegal to wait or park on: cycle tracks and cycle crossings; level crossings, pedestrian crossings and 5 metres each side of these crossings; a hill, a bend, in tunnels and underpasses; less than 5 metres from an intersection; less than 20 metres on either side of traffic lights and road signals in general except where the vehicle is less than 1.65 metres high and the lower edge of the sign or signal is 2 metres above ground.

Parking is prohibited: at less than 1 metre in front of or behind another stationary vehicle, or in a position where the vehicle causes an obstruction to other vehicles which would prevent their movement; less than 15 metres either side of a bus or tram stop; in front of an entrance to a private or public building; at any place where pedestrians must use the carriageway to avoid an obstacle; if the vehicle would hinder the passage of a vehicle on rails; on roads where there is fast-moving traffic; on a carriageway marked in traffic lanes or where broken yellow lines are painted; opposite another stationary vehicle and on the central reservation of dual carriageways. Parking lights, see page 71.

In many towns and cities there are short-term parking areas known as blue zones where parking discs must be displayed. Outside these areas a parking disc must be used where the parking sign has an additional panel showing a parking disc. In some disc areas parking meters may also be found in which case the parking disc is not valid in the meter bay.

Parking meters   Where these are used the instructions for use will be on the meter.

Passengers   Children under the age of 12 years are not permitted to travel in the front seat of a vehicle.

Belgium

Petrol

The approximate price of petrol per litre is: super (98–100 octane) BFr16.14; normal (90–94 octane) BFr15.62. Most filling stations are closed nightly from 20.00–08.00hrs and all day Sunday.

Police fines

The police are authorised to impose fines, which must be paid within 48 hours with special stamps which are on sale at post offices.

motoring offence	BFr500
motorcycling offence	BFr300
cycling offence	BFr200
pedestrian offence	BFr100

Postal and telephone charges

Surface mail

		BFr
Postcards to France, Germany, Italy, Netherlands and Luxembourg		5.00
other countries		7.00
Letters 20g to those countries listed above		6.50
other countries		14.00
50g		25.00
100g		33.00

Air mail There is an extra charge if the country of destination is outside Europe.

Telephone rate A telephone call to the UK costs BFr22.50 for each minute. In Brussels the *poste restante* address is: Centre Monnaie, 1000 Brussels.

Priority

In built-up areas, a driver must give way – by slowing down or, if need be, by stopping – to bus drivers who have used their direction indicators to show they intend driving away from a bus stop.

Roads

The main roads are generally good. The road numbers of the all-purpose main roads are prefixed 'N'. Motorways (Autoroute/Autosnelweg) are prefixed 'A', or 'E' if the section is part of the European road network. The road system in Brussels is first-class, incorporating underpasses and other modern features, and the signposting for through-traffic is now better. If travelling to Ostende from Louvain (Leuven) or Namur (Namen), you have to follow signs Gent-Gand, as Ostende appears at the exit of the city only.

Motorways

Approximately 687 miles of motorways (*autoroutes*) are open, and more stretches of the planned 1,488-mile network are under construction. Nearly all motorways are part of the European international network.

To join a motorway, follow signposts bearing the motorway symbol; no tolls are charged. Bicycles and motorcycles under 50cc are prohibited but, with certain exceptions, all other vehicles with pneumatic tyres, including those for invalids, are permitted.

Winter conditions

From 1 November to 31 March, motorists may telephone (02)5116667 any time of the day or night for a pre-recorded general report on road conditions, which is constantly brought up to date. They may obtain information concerning a specific section of road in Belgium or a main route abroad by telephoning (02)5127890 between 07.30 and 20.00hrs.

Road signs

Translations of some written signs to be seen on the road are given below:

Passage difficile	Difficult passage
Moeilijke doorgang	
Disque obligatoire	Disc obligatory
Schijf verplicht	
Excepte circulation locale	No entry except for local traffic
Uitgezonderd Plaatselijk Verkeer	

Seat belts

If your vehicle is fitted with seat belts it is compulsory to wear them.

Shopping hours

Shops are usually open 09.00–18.00hrs from Monday to Saturday. Supermarkets are open 09.00–20.00hrs (21.00hrs on Friday).

Speed

In all towns and built-up areas at the beginning of which a sign with the name of the town (white sign with black letters)

73

Belgium

is placed, there is an overall maximum speed limit of 60kph (37mph). Both inside and outside built-up areas, and on motorways, vehicles using makeshift or secondary ropes for towing after breakdowns or accidents are limited to 25kph (15½mph). Outside built-up areas, there is a maximum limit of 90kph (56mph) for private vehicles except on motorways where the speed limit is 120kph (74mph). Mopeds are limited to 40kph (24mph) everywhere. There is a minimum limit of 70kph (43mph) on straight, level stretches of motorway.

Tourist information offices
The Belgian National Tourist Office is at 66 Haymarket, London SW1Y 4RB. Their telephone number is 01-930 9618 and they will be pleased to supply information on all aspects of tourism. In Belgium the National Tourist organisation is supplemented by the Provincial Tourist Federation, whilst in most towns there are local tourist offices. These organisations will help tourists with information and accommodation.

Traffic lights
The three-colour traffic light system operates in Belgium. However, the lights may be replaced by arrows of the individual colours and these have the same meaning as the lights, but only in the direction in which the arrow points.

Tyres
Spiked tyres These are permitted during the winter months. You should enquire the dates when their use is authorised before using these tyres.

They must be fitted to all four wheels and also to a trailer over 500kg and vehicles under 3.5 tonnes. They may not be used on motorways and speed on other roads may not exceed 60kph (37mph). See also Road and winter conditions page 40.

Visitors' registration
All visitors staying for more than three months must obtain a *Permis de séjour* before entering Belgium.

Warning triangles
These are compulsory for all vehicles except two-wheeled vehicles. They must be placed, at least 30m on ordinary roads and 100m on motorways, behind the vehicle to warn following traffic, and they must be visible at a distance of 50m.

Belgium/hotels and garages

Prices are in Belgian francs

St% – Service and tax charge
Supplementary local taxes are payable in addition to the charges shown. These vary from town to town. The VAT rate for accommodation has increased from 8% to 16% since the gazeteer entries were compiled. Allowances should be made when choosing accommodation.

Abbreviations:
av	avenue	r	rue
bd	boulevard	rte	route
pl	place, plein	str	straat

Aalst (Alost) Oost-Vlaanderen 45,250 (☎053) Map **3** B1
★**Bourse van Amsterdam** Grote Markt 26 ☎211581 rm6 ⇆1 B360–765

Aalter Oost-Vlaanderen 10,250 (☎091) Map **3** B2
★**Memling** Markt II ☎741013 rm9 ⇆9 B485–1045 Pn700

Aarlen See**Arlon**

Aartselaar See**Antwerpen (Anvers)**

Albert Plage See**Knokke-Heist**

Alle Namur 850 (☎061) Map **10** D4
★**Charmille** r Liboichant 12 ☎500363 rm11 ⇆5 16 Feb–14 Jan B610–1195

Alost See**Aalst**

Anseremme Namur (☎082) Map **4** C1
★**Lesse** r des Forges 4 ☎222078 rm32 ⇆2 G Apr–Oct LD B485–1210 M325–375&àlc Pn815–835 St8%

Antwerpen (Anvers) Antwerpen 662,350 (☎031) Map **4** C2
★★★★**Century** de Keyserlei 60 ☎331820 tx31509 rm220 ⇆220 G Lift
☆☆☆**EuroCrest** Gerard Legrellelaan 10 ☎372900 tx33843 rm314 ⇆314 G Lift B1110–1595 M300
☆☆☆**Eurotel Antwerpen** Copernicuslaan 2 ☎316780 ta Oteleur tx33965 rm351 ⇆219 ⑂132 G Lift B1250–2300 M450 St8% Pool
☆☆☆**Novotel Antwerpen** Luithagen 6 ☎420320 tx324883 rm121 Lift B120–140 ⏉ Pool
★★★**Plaza** (n rest) Charlotta-lei 43 ☎395970 ta Plahot tx31531 rm80 ⇆75 ⑂5 G Lift B1570–2360
★**Métropole** Handschoenmarkt 5 ☎329248 rm20 ⇆5 ⑂1 10 Jan–20 Dec B485–900 M250–650
🏍**Autostrade-Motors** Boomsesteenweg 441 ☎277910 N☢ Frd
🅿**Centrauto** St-Josefstr 48 ☎301815 N☢ BMW/Jag
🅿**Leyland Motors** Haringrodestr 104 ☎393980 N☢ BL/Jag/Rov/Tri
🏍**J Lins** Grote Tunnelpl 3 ☎339928 N☢ Bed/Tri G
🅿**Servais & Collin** Haringrodestr 54 ☎395990 N☢ AR G
At **Aartselaar** (8km S)
☆☆☆☆**Sofitel Jacques Borel** Boomsesteenweg 15 ☎876850 tx33619 rm125 ⇆125 G Lift B1360–2060 M575 Pool
At **Berchem** (1km S)
🅿**Acker** Uitbreidingstr 92 ☎309999 N☢ Vau
At **Deurne** (4km NE)
★★**Rivierenhof** Turnhoutsebaan 244 ☎242564 rm15 ⇆5 G B400–970 M300 Pn580–650 ⏉ Lake

Arlon (Aarlen) Luxembourg 13,850 (☎063) Map **10** D4
★★★**Arly** av Luxembourg 81 ☎215381 rm27 ⇆27 G Lift 15 Jan–31 Dec B700–1620 M300–850 Pn1200 St% ⏉ Pool
★★**Ecu de Bourgogne** (n rest) pl Leopold 9 ☎211167 rm22 ⇆10 ⑂2 Lift 17 Jan–17 Dec

★★**Nord** r Faubourgs 2 ☎212293 rm26 ⇆8 ⑂2 G 12 Jan–15 Dec B455–1037
🅿**Beau Site** av de Longwy 167 ☎212916 N☢ Frd
🅿**A Clément** r de Bastogne 141 ☎23773 N☢ Jag/Sim
🅿**Lonniaux** av du Luxembourg 100 ☎22345 M/c Opl G

Ath Hainaut 11,262 (☎068) Map **3** B1
🅿**Center** chaussee de Bruxelles 45 ☎224283 N☢ (closed Mon) BL/Rov/Tri G

Bastogne Luxembourg 6,950 (☎062) Map **10** D4
★★**Lebrun** r de Marche 8 ☎211193 rm27 ⇆8 ⑂8 G Etr–Nov LD B320–940 M540
★**Luxembourg** pl Mac-Auliffe 25 ☎211226 rm13 (A) 15 Mar–15 Nov B from 205
🏍**24 F Luc-Nadin** chemin des Scieries 16 ☎211806 G
🅿**Wautelet** r de Marche 50 ☎21061 Ren

Beloeil Hainaut (☎069) Map **3** B1
★★**Couronne** r Durieu 8 ☎679567 rm10 ⇆5 7 Oct–15 Sep

Berchem See**Antwerpen (Anvers)**

Beveren-Waas Oost-Vlaanderen 16,850 (☎031) Map **4** C2
☆☆**Beveren** Grote Baan 280 ☎758623 rm19 ⇆19

Blankenberge West-Vlaanderen 14,325 (☎050) Map **3** B2
★★★**Idéal** Zeedijk 244 ☎411691 rm50 ⇆50 G Lift Etr–15 Sep B790–1540 M340 Pn1152–1272 Pool Sea
★★**Petite Rouge** Zeedijk 127 ☎411032 rm64 ⇆20 ⑂4 Lift 1 Mar–1 Sep (& winter weekends) B550–1480 M400 Pn790–1250 Sea
★**Pacific** J-de Troozlaan 48 ☎411542 rm24 ⑂12 (closed Xmas) B635–1420 M300 Pn625–850
★**Park & Cygne** de Smet de Nayerlaan 133 ☎411811 rm29 20 Mar–20 Oct B395–798 M220 Pn485–1080
★**Suisse** J-de Troozlaan 33 ☎41747 rm30 G Etr–30 Sep

Boom Antwerpen 16,780 (☎03) Map **4** C2
🅿**E Roofthooft** Antwerpsestr 12 ☎880891 (closed weekends) Frd

Bouillon Luxembourg 2,900 (☎061) Map **10** D4
★★**Tyrol** r Haut de la Ville ☎466293 rm12 ⇆10 ⑂2 G Mar–Nov B800–1100 (double) M495 Pn950–1100
★**Semois** r Collège 46 ☎466027 rm45 ⇆12 ⑂2 Lift LD B270–1100 M200–400 Pn750–1030

Bouvignes See**Dinant**

Brasschaat-Polygoon Antwerpen 27,720 (☎031) Map **4** C2
☆☆**Dennenhof** Bredebaan 940 ☎630509 rm25 ⑂20

Bredene West-Vlaanderen 7,292 (☎059) (3km NE of **Ostende**) Map **3** B2
★**Zomerlust** P-Benoitlaan 26 ☎704640 rm20 B310–515 M225

Brugge (Bruges) West-Vlaanderen 119,750 (☎050) Map **4** B2

Belgium

★★★ **Portinari** Garenmarkt 15 ☎331612
rm50 ⇨26 ▥14 Lift B625–1300 M345
★★ *Duc de Bourgogne* Huidenvetterspl 12
☎332038 rm10 ⇨10 1 Feb–30 Jun &
16 Jul–15 Jan
★★ **Europ** (n rest) Augustijnenrei 18 ☎337975
rm28 ⇨6 ▥17 G Lift 1 Mar–1 Dec
B485–1150
★★ **Sablon** Noordzandstr 21 ☎333902 rm48
⇨18 Lift B630–1260 M395 Pn1140–1265
★ **Févéry** (n rest) Collaert Mansionstr 3
☎331269 rm14 ⇨7 ▥7 Lift B400–700
★ **Jacobs** (n rest) Baliestr 1 ☎339831 rm34
⇨17 Lift 15 Mar–30 Sep B535–1025
★ **Londres** 't Zand 11 (off Zuidzandstr)
☎333074 rm25 ⇨1 ▥2 LD B385–960 M300
Pn800–950
★ **Lybeer** (n rest) Korte Vulderssstr 31
(nr cathedral) ☎334355 rm25 1 Mar–5 Nov
B375–650
★ **Pauw** (n rest) St-Gilliskerkhof 8 ☎337118
rm8 ⇨3 B400–750
⬕🅝 **Canada** St-Pieterskaai 36 ☎317370 N🅢 Frd
⬕🅝 **Vandeplas** Komvest 16 ☎332506 N🅢 BL
G10
🅝 *Van Haelewijn* Fort Lapin 31 ☎339877
BL/Rov/Tri
At **Oostkamp** (8km S)
★★★ **Château des Brides** (n rest) Breidels 1
☎822001 rm10 ⇨5 15 Apr–30 Sep
B500–1500

Bruxelles (Brussel) Brabant 1,050,800
(☎02) Map **4** C1 **See Plan**
★★★★★ **Amigo** r de l'Amigo 1 (by town hall)
☎5115910 tx21618 Plan **1** rm183 ⇨172 ▥11
G Lift B1750–2550
★★★★★ **Mac Donald** av Louise 321
☎6498030 tx23322 Plan **2** rm76 ⇨76 G Lift
B2120–2800 M400–600
★★★★★ **Palace** pl Rogier 22 ☎2176200
tx21248 Plan **3** rm356 ⇨356 Lift B1375–2305
M465 Pn2305–3235
★★★★ **Royal Windsor** r Duquesony
☎5114215 tx62905 Plan **4** rm300 ⇨300 G
Lift B2515–3120
★★★★ **Astoria** r Royale 103 ☎2176290
tx25040 Plan **6** rm110 ⇨110 Lift
B1500–1986 M690
★★★★ *Atlanta* bd A-Max 7 ☎2170120
tx21475 Plan **7** rm244 ⇨166 ▥56 G Lift
B1100–1600 M350 Pn1800–1950
★★★ **Bedford** r du Midi 135 ☎5127840
tx24059 Plan **9** rm220 ⇨220 G Lift
B1100–1600 M350 Pn1800–1950
★★★ *Brand Whitlock* (n rest) bd Brand
Whitlock 156 ☎7332966 Plan **10** rm15 ▥12 G
★★★ **Queen Anne** (n rest) bd E-Jacqmain 110
(off pl Brouchère) ☎2171600 Plan **11** rm57
⇨53 ▥53 Lift B650–1125
★★ *Concorde-Louise* (n rest) r de la Concorde
59 ☎128610 Plan **13** rm26 ⇨6 ▥5 Lift
★★ *Noga* (n rest) r du Béguinage 38
☎185032 Plan **14** rm19 ⇨8 ▥8 Lift
★★ *Résidence du Bois* (n rest) av L-Georges
12 (off S end av Louise) ☎470162 Plan **15**
rm15 ⇨4 ▥6 Lift
★★ **Richmond House** (n rest) r de la
Concorde 21 (off av Louise) ☎5124824 Plan **16**
rm27 ⇨17 ▥4 G Lift B275–825
★★ *Scheers* bd A-Max 132 ☎2177761
ta Bruselhotel tx21675 Plan **17** rm62 ⇨44 Lift
★ *Albergo* av de la Toison d'Or 57 ☎5382960
Plan **18** rm70 ⇨60 ▥4 Lift
★ **Astor** r (apt Crespel 9 ☎5116086
Plan **19** rm13 ⇨6 B375–725
★ *Monico Nord* r de Brabant 2 ☎173293
Plan **20** rm26 ⇨10 Lift
Berg chaussée de Waterloo 532 ☎3441546
N🅢 Ren

🅝 **J Decat** chaussée de Louvain 677
☎7339890 N🅢 Maz
⬕🅝 **Leteren Centre** chaussée de Mons 95
☎5222000 N🅢 Aud/VW
⬕🅝 **Leyland Motors** r de Hennin 18–22
☎6492020 N🅢 BL/Rov/Tri
⬕🅝 **P Plasman** chaussée de Waterloo 567
☎3451950 (closed weekends) Frd
⬕🅝 **C F Wismeyer** r Vanderkindere 467
☎3435050 N🅢 Bed/Vau
At **Tervuren** (13km E)
★ *Vignette* chaussée de Louvain 12
☎573056 Plan **22** rm18 ⇨6 ▥1 G
1 Feb–31 Dec

Bruxelles Airport
At **Diegem** (8km NE)
☆☆☆☆ **Sofitel Jacques Borel** Bessenveldstraat
15 ☎7206050 tx26595 Plan **8** rm125 ⇨125
B1440–2330 M250–1000 Pool
☆☆☆ **Novotel Bruxelles Airport** ☎7205830
tx26751 Plan **5** rm162 ⇨162 Lift B869–1014
Pool

Calamine (La) Liège 5,229 (☎087)
Map **4** C/D1
★★ *Sélect* r de Liège 75 (Autorte Melun-
Herbesthal) ☎59005 rm7 ⇨1 G 16 Dec–30 Nov

Casteau Hainaut 2,750 (☎065) Map **3** B1
☆☆ **EuroCrest** chaussée de Bruxelles 38
☎728741 tx57164 rm71 ⇨35 ▥36
B875–1460 M250–1000

Champlon Luxembourg 800 (☎084)
Map **4** C1
★★ **Hostellerie de la Barrière** Barrière 1
☎455155 rm21 ⇨11 ▥2 G LD B590–1170
M340–700 Pn750–850

Charleroi Hainaut 268,650 (☎071)
Map **4** C1 See also **Gosselies**
★★★ **Siebertz** (n rest) quai de Brabant 6
☎314487 tx51200B rm33 ⇨15 ▥9 Lift
B480–1060
⬕🅝 **Leteren** r de Montigny 145 ☎322232 N🅢
Aud/VW G

Chaudfontaine Liège 2,800 (☎041)
Map **4** C1
★★★ *Bains* av Thermes 7 ☎653895 rm35
(A11) ⇨13 Lift

Ciney Namur 7,600 (☎083) Map **4** C1
★★ **Château du Domaine St-Roch**
r Sainfoin 8 ☎21055 rm12 ▥5 G

Coq-sur-Mer (Le) See **Haan (De)**

Courtrai See **Kortrijk**

Coxyde-sur-Mer See **Koksijde**

Dendermonde Oost-Vlaanderen 22,050
(☎052) Map **3** B2
⬕🅝 *Modern* Leopoldlaan 47 ☎212372
Bed/Vau G5

Deurle Oost-Vlaanderen 2,100 (☎091)
Map **3** B1
★★ *Auberge de Pêcheur* Pontstr 42
☎824444 rm15 ⇨11 1 Nov–30 Sep

Deurne See **Antwerpen**

Diegem See **Bruxelles Airport**

Diest Brabant 10,650 (☎013) Map **4** C1
★ **Modern** chaussée de Louvain 4 ☎331066
rm15 ⇨3 ▥8 B425–1000 M250
⬕🅝 **Meelberghs** E-Robeynslaan 10 ☎333388
N🅢 Frd

Dinant Namur 9,850 (☎082) Map **4** C1
★★ **Couronne** r A-Sax 1 ☎222441 rm27 ⇨5
▥2 Lift B368–815 Pn1595
★★ **Gare** r de la Station 39 ☎222056 rm22
⇨6 G Lift 1 Apr–1 Dec LD B300–620
Pn550–650 St16%
★★ **Thermador** r de la Station 3 ☎223135
rm6 ⇨2 B570–1025 Pn865–920

Belgium

Bruxelles (Brussel)
1 ★★★★★Amigo
2 ★★★★★MacDonald
3 ★★★★★Palace
4 ★★★★★Royal Windsor
5 ☆☆☆Novotel Bruxelles Airport
     (at Diegem 8km NE)
6 ★★★★Astoria
7 ★★★★Atlanta
8 ☆☆☆☆Sofitel Jacques Borel
     (at Diegem 8km NE)
9 ★★★Bedford

10 ★★★Brand Whitlock's
11 ★★★Queen Anne
13 ★★Concorde-Louise
14 ★★Noga
15 ★★Résidence du Bois
16 ★★Richmond House
17 ★★Scheers
18 Albergo
19 ★Astor
20 ★Monico-Nord
22 ★Vignette (at Tervuren 13km E)

77

Belgium

★**Banque** pl Gare 49 ☎22020 rm12 ⇌2 G
★**Belle–Vue** r de Philippeville 3 ☎222924
rm7 ⇌5 🎝1 LD B520–720(Double) M200–420
Pn1360–1650
★**Collégiale** r A-Sax 2 ☎22372 rm18
★**Commerce** pl St-Nicolas 12 ☎222744
rm24 Lift 15 Mar–Oct
🏚🅗 **Dinant Motors** r de Bouvignes 53
☎223026 N🅢 Opl G25
🏚🅗**24 Etamenco** r A-Caussin 95 ☎222254
Fia/Lnc
🏚🅗 **M Jaumotte** quai J-B-Culot 18 ☎223007
N🅢 Frd
At **Bouvignes** (2km NW)
★★**Auberge de Bouvignes** r Fétis 2
☎611600 rm5 ⇌3 15 Jan–30 Nov LD
B605–960 M550–920 St15%
At **Payenne-Coustinne** (12km SE)
★**Host Grisons** Gd Route ☎666355 rm14 ⇌8
(closed Feb) LD B900–1650 Pn1250–1450

Dolembreux See **Liège**

Doornik See **Tournai**

Eeklo Oost-Vlaanderen 19,400 (☎091)
Map **3** B2
★**Rembrandt** Koningin Astridplein 2
☎772570 rm7 🎝2
🏚🅗 **B de Baets** Markt 85 ☎771285 N🅢
Aud/VW G10
🏚🅗 **Wolf** Leopoldlaan 4 ☎771440 N🅢 M/c
Frd G

Enghien Hainaut 4,000 (☎02) Map **3** B1
★★**Vieux Cèdre** av Elisabeth 1 ☎3952061
rm6 ⇌2 10 Sep–15 Aug LD B525–1240
M300–750
🅗**Chapelle** r d'Hoves 132 ☎3951509 N🅢
Cit G30

Eupen Liège 15,000 (☎087) Map **4** D1
★★**Bosten** Verviersestr 2 ☎552209 rm14 ⇌6
G B405–910 Màlc Pn905
🏚🅗**O Pierre** rte de Herbestal 120 ☎52331
N🅢52931 Frd

Florenville Luxembourg 2,650 (☎061)
Map **10** D4
★★**France** r Bénéraux Cuvelier 28 ☎311032
rm40 ⇌8 G Lift 16 Feb–30 Dec LD
B440–800 M250–475 Pn735–900
🏚🅗**24 Mauxhin** r de la Station 32c ☎311055
Cit G2

Geel Antwerpen 30,000 (☎014) Map **4** C2
🏚🅗 **Dierckx Puba** Passtr 170 ☎588020 N🅢
BL/Jag/Rov/Tri

Gent (Gand) Oost-Vlaanderen 218,550
(☎091) Map **3** B2
★★★**Europa** Gordunakaai 59 ☎226071
tx11547 rm40 ⇌40 G Lift B850–1225 M320
Pn950–1250
★★**Cour St-Georges** Botermarkt 1 (off
St-Baafsplein) ☎236791 rm70 ⇌40 G Lift
★★**Park** Wilsonplein 1 ☎251781 rm39 ⇌4
🎝18 Lift
★★**Terminus** Kon M–Hendrikplein 6
☎225545 tx11339 rm24 ⇌4 🎝6 Lift
B355–725 Màlc
🏚🅗 **Centre & Docks Motors** Vliegtuiglaan 18
☎510033 N🅢 Bed/Vau G10
🏚🅗 **W Roelens** Doornzelestr 21 ☎232476 N🅢
M/c Toy
🏚🅗 **A Vandersmissen** Fievestr 26 ☎257637
N🅢236723 N🅢 Frd
🏚🅗**24 Leyland Vernaeve** Doornzelestr 31
☎230384 BL/Jag/Rov/Tri G

Gosselies Hainaut 10,700 (☎071)
Map **4** C1
★**John's** pl Station 4 ☎350838 rm17 (A2)
⇌9 🎝17 Lift B415–880 Màlc St16%

Haan (De) (Coq-sur-Mer)
West-Vlaanderen 3099 (☎059) Map **3** B2
(12.5km NE of **Ostende**)
★★**Belle Vue** Koningspl 5 ☎233439 rm51
⇌17 Lift Etr–30 Sep B530–1110 M300–350
Pn800–1000

Halle (Hal) Brabant 20,400 (☎02)
Map **3** B1
★**Eleveurs** Basiliekstr 136 ☎3565309 rm19
⇌7 🎝2 28 Jul–6 Jul

Han-sur-Lesse Namur 800 (☎084)
Map **10** D4
★★**Voyageurs** rte de Rochefort 1 ☎377237
rm45 ⇌15 🎝11 15 Lift 1 Apr–31 Dec LD
B545–1200 M300–650 Pn1100–1300

Hasselt Limburg 40,175 (☎011) Map **4** C1
★**Century** Leopoldpl 1 ☎24799 rm12 ⇌2
6 Jan–22 Dec G
🏚🅗 **Hoffer** Demerstr 66 ☎224911 N🅢 Ren
🏚🅗**Jerrycan** Luikersteenweg 316 ☎278699

Herbesthal Liège (☎087) Map **4** C1
★**Herren** r Mitoyenne 82 ☎80101 rm14 ⇌1

Herentals Antwerpen 18,350 (☎014)
Map **4** C2
🏚🅗**24 Tuerlinx** St-Janstr 116 ☎212312 N🅢
Bed/Opl

Herstal See **Liège**

Hoei See **Huy**

Houffalize Luxembourg 1,325 (☎062)
Map **4** C1
★**Clé des Champs** rte de Libramont 22
☎288044 rm9 🎝4 G Etr–5 Nov B480–765
M250–385 Pn730–850
🏚🅗 **Lambin** Pl du Roi Albert 23 ☎288035 N🅢
BL/Rov/Tri G5

Houyet Namur 1,000 (☎082) Map **4** C1
★**Lesse** de la Gare 12 ☎666402 rm10 LD
B375–650 M240–500 Pn695

Huy (Hoei) Liège 12,750 (☎085)
Map **4** C1
★★★**Aigle Noir** quai Dautrebande 8
☎211064 rm13 ⇌8 🎝2 Lift (closed Aug)
B625–1480 M585–650
★**Wagram** chaussée de Napoléon 2 ☎212679
rm8
🏚🅗**Aunalux** chaussée de Tirlemont 1
☎13840 MB G4

Ieper (Ypres) West-Vlaanderen 21,350
(☎057) Map **3** B1
★**St-Nicholas** G-de Stuerstr 6 ☎200622
rm6 ⇌4
★**Sultan** Grote Markt 33 ☎200193 rm20 ⇌9
G
🏚🅗 **Devos & Dewanckel** Menensteenweg 30
☎200055 G

Kasterlee Antwerpen 6,275 (☎014)
Map **4** C2
★**Dennen** Lichtaartsebaan 89 ☎556107 rm10
⇌5 G

Knokke See **Knokke-Heist**

Knokke-Heist West-Vlaanderen 28,700
(☎050) Map **3** B2
At **Albert Plage**
★★★**Lido** Zwaluwenlaan 16 ☎601925 rm37
⇌14 🎝4 G Lift B400–1120 M300–500
Pn1300–1900
★★★**Résidence Albert** (n rest) Zeedijk 26
☎601041 rm26 ⇌26 G Lift 22 Oct–30 Sep
★★★**Sofitel la Reserve** Elizabethlaan 132
☎600606 tx81657 rm120 B1400–2200
M650 St14% Pool Lake
At **Heist**
★★**Royal** Zeedijk 228 ☎51050 rm49 ⇌9
🎝4 Lift Whi–6 Sep Sea

At Knokke
★★*Cecil* Elizabethlaan 20 ☎601033 rm45
⇋10 Lift Etr–Sep Sea
🛏📞 *SOS* Natienlaan 112 ☎601280 Fia
🛏📞 *Willems* Lippenslaan 121 ☎61071 N📞 Frd
At Zoute (Le)
★★★*Excelsior* Zeedijk 139 ☎602274 rm74
⇋35 🛗1 Lift Etr–Sep Xmas–Jan Sea
★★★*Majestic* Zeedijk 688 ☎601144 rm65
⇋53 G Lift Etr–30 Sep–25 Dec B740–1530
M400 Pn1250–1350
★★*Nouvel* van Bunnenplein 1 ☎601861
tx81272 rm59 ⇋2 🛗21 Lift Etr–30 Sep LD
B620–1540 M375–378 Pn1000–1500 Sea
★*Florida* A–Bréart str 9 ☎601124 rm21 ⇋5
🛗1 Lift B400–800 M195–300 Pn600–720 Sea

Koksijde (Coxyde-sur-Mer)
West-Vlaanderen (☎058) Map **3** B2
★★*Royal* Zeedijk 65 ☎511300 rm30 ⇋7 Lift
Etr–Sep B620–1440 M400–500 Pn825–1170
Sea
🛏📞*M Declerck* Zeelaan 131 ☎51706 N📞 Ren

Kortrijk (Courtrai) West-Vlaanderen
43,400 (☎056) Map **3** B1
★★★*Damier* Grote Markt 41 ☎221547 rm42
⇋19 Lift

La: Each placename beginning with La is listed
under the name which follows it.

Lac de Warfaz See**Spa**

Le: Each placename beginning with Le is listed
under the name which follows it.

Leopoldsburg Limburg (☎011) Map **4** C2
🛏📞24 *Heeren* Diestersteenweg 144
☎341295 Bed/Vau

Leuven (Louvain) Brabant 29,800
(☎016) Map **4** C1
★*Industrie* Martelarenpl 7 ☎221349 rm18
🛗4
🛏*Hergon* Diestsestr 133 ☎223506 N📞 Frd

Leuze Hainaut 7,250 (☎069) Map **3** B1
★*Couronne* pl de la Gare ☎16691 rm10
1 Sep–30 Jul B250–450 M270 Pn500

Libramont Luxembourg 3,350 (☎061)
Map **10** D4
🛏📞*Etienne* av de Bouillon 6 ☎22160 N📞
BL/Rov/Tri G10

Liège (Luik) Liège 432,600 (☎041)
Map **4** C1
★★★★*Couronne* pl des Guillemins 11
☎522168 tx41374 rm79 ⇋46 🛗20 G Lift
☆☆☆☆ *Ramada Inn* av de la Sauvenière 100
☎325919 tx41896 rm105 ⇋105 G Lift
B1270–2040 M250
★★*Angleterre* r des Dominicains 2 (nr pl de
la République Française) ☎234303 rm45
⇋16 Lift
★*Cygne d'Argent* r Beeckman 49 ☎237001
rm20 ⇋10 🛗9 Lift B535–945 M270
Pn1100–1200
📞*Britannique* pl St–Paul 7 ☎322050 N📞 Rov
🛏📞*Brondeel* quai de Coronmeuse 28 ☎271820
N📞 Chy
🛏📞*Renault Belgique Luxembourg* bd de
Laveleye 65 ☎420130 N📞 Ren
🛏📞*Sodia* r L–Boumal 24 ☎526862 N📞 BL/Rov
At Herstal (8km on E5)
★★★*Post House* ☎646400 tx41103 rm100
⇋100 Lift B1175–1520 M300 Sea
☆☆ *Euromotel* r de l'Abbaye 99 ☎644590
tx41459 rm58 (A34) ⇋49 🛗9 B910–1365
M430
🛏📞*Norcia* bd Zénobegramme 50 ☎642450
N📞 Fia

Lier Antwerpen 27,850 (☎031) Map **4** C2
📞*G Guwy* F–van Cauwenbergstr 19
☎800139 N📞 Frd

Ligneuville Liège 1,110 (☎080) Map **4** D1
★★*Moulin* ☎570081 rm18 (A4) ⇋7 G
15 Jan–30 Nov

Lokeren Oost-Vlaanderen 27,150 (☎091)
Map **3** B2
★★*Park* Antwerpsesteenweg 1 ☎482046
rm10 ⇋5 🛗5 G 1 Jan–4 Jul 28 Jul–31 Dec
(closed Mon) LD B650–850 Màlc
🛏📞*Mees* Gentsesteenweg 263 ☎555759
Fia G25
🛏📞24 *Moderne* Weverslaan 14 ☎481400
N📞482174 BMW

Lorce Liège 300 (☎080) Map **4** C1
★*Vallée* ☎85826 rm6 Mar–31 Dec

Louvain See**Leuven**

Louvière (La) Hainaut 22,850 (☎064)
Map **3** B1
🛏📞 24 *J Dupire* r L–Dupuis 10 ☎224031
N📞228653 N📞 BL/Jag/Rov/Tri

Malines See**Mechelen**

Malmédy Liège 6,400 (☎080) Map **4** D1
★★*Bristol* pl Albert-1er 47 ☎777476 rm9
⇋2 🛗6

Marche-en-Famenne Luxembourg 4,950
(☎084) Map **4** C1
★★*Cloche* r Luxembourg 2 ☎311579 rm10
⇋10 G B930–1260 M650 Pn1500 St17% Lake
🛏📞*Leunen* rte de Bastogne 51a ☎311582 N📞
Fia
🛏📞24 *G Thiry* av de France ☎31708 N📞
Aud/VW
🛏📞 *Verhulst* rte de Liège 50 ☎311673 M/c

Mariakerke See**Oostende (Ostende)**

Masnuy-St-Jean Hainaut (☎065)
Map **3** B1
★★★*Amigo* chaussée Brunehault 4 ☎728721
tx57313 rm52 ⇋52 Lift Pool

Mechelen (Malines) Antwerpen 64,650
(☎015) Map **3** B2
★*Memling* Onder de Toren 12 ☎211218
rm10 (A1) ⇋1 🛗1
🍴📞*Festraets* M–Sabbestr 123 ☎202752 N📞
Bed/Vau

Mons (Bergen) Hainaut 61,750 (☎065)
Map **3** B1
🛏📞*Automons* r du chemin de fer 163
☎311126 N📞 Fia
🛏📞*St-Christophe* av Frère-Orban 3 ☎31305
N📞 Chy
🛏📞*A Wattier* r du Grand Jour 3 ☎335173 N📞
Frd
At Boussu (12km W on N22)
🛏📞*Amand* rte de Mons 20 ☎773831 N📞
BL/Jag/Rov/Tri G

Mont Kemmel West-Vlaanderen 1,410
(☎057) Map **3** B1
★★★*Hostellerie Mont Kemmel* Bergstr
339c ☎44145 rm22 (A) ⇋17 G 15 Mar–31 Jan

Nadrin Luxembourg (☎084) Map **4** C1
★★*Ondes* ☎444111 rm15 (A) ⇋7 🛗1 G

Namur (Namen) Namur 31,350 (☎081)
Map **4** C1
🛏📞*Labenne & Franceschini* av F-Golenvaux
23 ☎223000 N📞 GM/Hon G4

Neufchâteau Luxembourg 2,750 (☎061)
Map **10** D4
🛏📞*L Guillaume* av de la Victoire 46 ☎27211
N📞 M/c G
🛏📞*Michaux* av de la Gare 43 ☎27444 N📞 Frd

Neupont Luxembourg 358 (☎084)
Map **10** D4
★★*Baligan* Neupont par Wellin ☎388166
rm11 G Etr–Jan B500–1300 M700–750
Pn1100–1350 St16%

Belgium

★**Ry des Glands** rte de Libin 93 ☎388133
rm12 G 5 Mar–31 Dec LD B500–580 M420
Pn600–660

Nieuwpoort West-Vlaanderen 8,100
(☎058) Map **3** B2
🛏🍴*Omega* Kaai 44 ☎23152 Frd

Nil-St-Vincent Brabant 1,150 (☎010)
Map **4** C1
★*Manoir* chaussée de Namur 18 ☎655325
rm6 30 Sep–31 Aug

Nivelles (Nijvel) Brabant 18,100 (☎067)
Map **4** C1
🛏🍴*F Havaux* pl E-de Lalieux 25 ☎222208
N🍴 BL/Jag/Rov/Tri G80
🛏🍴*C Pardonche* Mont St-Roch 1 ☎222015
AR

Oostende (Ostende) West-Vlaanderen
71,750 (☎059) Map **3** B2 **See Plan**

🅰🅰 agents; see page 69.

★★★★**Impérial** Van Iseghemlaan 74
☎705481 tx81167 Plan **1** rm62 ⇌50 🛁7 G
Lift B820–1510 M420 Pn1195–1375 Sea
★★★*Ambassadeur* Wapenplein 8a ☎700941
Plan **2** rm24 ⇌24 G Lift
★★★**Bellevue-Britannia** prom Albert-1er 55
☎706373 Plan **3** rm58 ⇌49 Lift B705–1770
M535 Pn1185–1595 Sea
★★★**Prado** (n rest) Léopold II Laan 22
☎705306 Plan **4** rm32 ⇌28 Lift LD
B490–1150
★★★**Riff** (n rest) Léopold II Laan 20 ☎707663
Plan **5** rm47 ⇌46 🛁1 Lift B750–1200
★★★**Ter Streep** (n rest) Léopold II Laan 14
☎700911 Plan **6** rm38 ⇌30 🛁8 Lift
B810–1630 Pool
★★★**Westminster** Van Iseghemlaan 22
☎702411 Plan **7** rm60 ⇌60 Lift B880–1160
M300 Pn900
★★*Derby* Van Iseghemlaan 1 ☎72030 Plan **8**
rm20 ⇌3 Lift
★★**Ensor** Kapucijnenstr 27 ☎802857 Plan **9**
rm24 ⇌23 🛁1 G Lift 15 Nov–15 Mar
(weekends only) B600–950 M200 Pn800–875
Sea
★★**Europe** Kapucijnenstr 52 ☎701012 Plan **10**
rm65 ⇌35 G Lift Mar–15 Nov B325–800
M175–220 Pn665–830
★★**Motor Inn** (n rest) Vlisserskaai 7 ☎706362
Plan **11** rm23 🛁7 G Lift 5 Jan–18 Dec Sea
★★**Parc** M-Joséplein 3 ☎701680 Plan **12**
rm52 ⇌11 Lift B505–1040
★**Glenmore** Hofstr 25 ☎702022 Plan **13**
rm50 ⇌14 Lift 2 Apr–1 Oct B340–910 M200
Pn450–575 Sea
★**Nieuwe Sportsman** de Smet de Nayerlaan 9
☎702384 Plan **14** rm10 B300–600 M165
★**Pacific** Hofstr 11 ☎701507 Plan **15** rm50
(A10) ⇌35 G Lift May–15 Oct B400–900
★*Regent* prom Albert-1er 3 ☎703457
Plan **19** rm40 ⇌2 Lift 15 Dec–15 Nov Sea
★**Strand** Vlisserskaai 1 ☎703383 tx81357
Strand B Plan **21** rm21 ⇌18 🛁2 G Lift
15 Dec–3 Nov B850–1200 M350–750
Pn1150–1450
🛏🍴 **Casino Kursaal** Van Iseghemlaan 83
☎703240 N🍴 Peu G50
🛏🍴*Istamboul* Vlisserskaai 8 ☎73849 G40
🛏🍴*Makelberge* Torhoutsteenweg 487
☎75575 N🍴 Bed/Vau
🛏🍴*Ocean* Koningstr 27 ☎702820 N🍴 G200
🛏🍴*Oostende-Motors* Torhoutsteenweg 473
☎704840 N🍴 BL/Jag/Rov/Tri
🛏🍴**24** *Phare* r Longue 91 ☎701364 G70
🛏🍴*F Stoops* chaussée de Torhoutsteen 54
☎702472 N🍴

At **Mariakerke** (1.5km SW on N72)
★**Primula** Raversijdestr 48 ☎705191 Plan **18**
rm15 ⇌2 🛁9 1 Apr–30 Sep B325–700 M125
Pn495–525
At **Raversyde Plage** (4km SW on N318)
★★**Royal Midland** Digue de Mer 354
☎702138 Plan **20** rm34 ⇌8 1 Apr–30 Oct
B435–970 M150 Pn600–650 Sea

Oostkamp See **Brugge (Bruges)**

Panne (De) (La Panne) West-Vlaanderen
7,100 (☎058) Map **3** B2
★★★**Parc** A-Dumontlaan 30 ☎411407 rm48
⇌22 Lift 20 Feb–3 Jan LD B610–1110
M400–600 Pn900–1000 St%
★★**Royal** Zeelaan 178 ☎411116 rm39 ⇌28
G Lift 25 Oct–30 Sep B495–1020 M375
Pn700–850 Sea
★*Mon Bijou* Zeelaan 94 ☎41105 rm35 🛁3 G
Lift
★*Regina Maris* av Bortier 11 ☎411222 rm71
⇌25 🛁25 Lift 5 Feb–5 Jan B485–870
M275–300 Pn650–750 St5% Pool

Payenne-Coustine See **Dinant**

Philippeville Namur 2,400 (☎071)
Map **4** C1
★★**Croisée** r de France 45 ☎666231 rm16
⇌6 G 31 Jan–31 Dec B380–820 M510–875
Pn825–940 St16%
★**Princes de Liège** rte de Givet 1 ☎666104
rm9 ⇌9 G B700–1200 M550–1000
Pn11000–13000
🛏🍴**24** *Michaux* des Quatre-Bras ☎666137 Ren

Profondeville Namur 2,350 (☎081)
Map **4** C1
★**Auberge d'Alsace** av Gl-Gracia Boreuville 42
☎412228 rm6 ⇌6 G LD B500–850
M400–575 Pn3000 St%

Raversyde Plage See **Oostende**

Remouchamps Liège 2,340 (☎041)
Map **4** C1
🛏🚗**24** *J Depreay* rte d'Aywaille 35 ☎844422
M/c Cit G10

Renaix See **Ronse**

Roche-en-Ardenne (La) Luxembourg
1,800 (☎084) Map **4** C1
★★★**Air Pur** rte de Houffalize 11 ☎411223
rm14 ⇌9 Etr–31 Dec LD B860–2300
M800&àlc
★★★**Ardennes** r de Beausaint 2 ☎411112
rm12 ⇌12 G Etr–15 Nov Xmas–1 Jan LD
B720–950 M390–700 Pn970–1040
★★*Belle-Vue* av du Hadja 10 ☎411187 rm25
⇌6
★*Merlettes* r Val du Pierreux 2 ☎411159
rm13 G 1 Apr–10 Sep LD **Pn**1080 Pool
🛏🍴*C Bechet* pl Chanteraine 8 ☎411119
Frd/Toy G2

Rochefort Namur 4,550 (☎084) Map **10** D4
★★**Central** pl Albert-1er 30 ☎211044 rm7
⇌2 1 Nov–30 Sep LD B590–1180
M220–570 St10%
★**Bristol** pl Albert-1er 27 ☎211170 rm7 LD
B570–640 M280–530 Pn700 St10%
★*Fayette* r Jacquet 87 ☎211024 rm17
(A10) ⇌1 🛁3 G 5 Oct–13 Sep

Roeselare (Roulers) West-Vlaanderen
39,850 (☎051) Map **3** B1
🛏🍴*R Vynckier* Westlaan 263 ☎20902 Bed/
Vau

Ronse (Renaix) Oost-Vlaanderen 24,750
(☎055) Map **3** B1
🛏🍴*Bossuyt-Bruyneel* Van Hovestr 14
☎22760 Cit

Roulers See **Roeselare**
St-Nicolas See **Sint Niklaas**

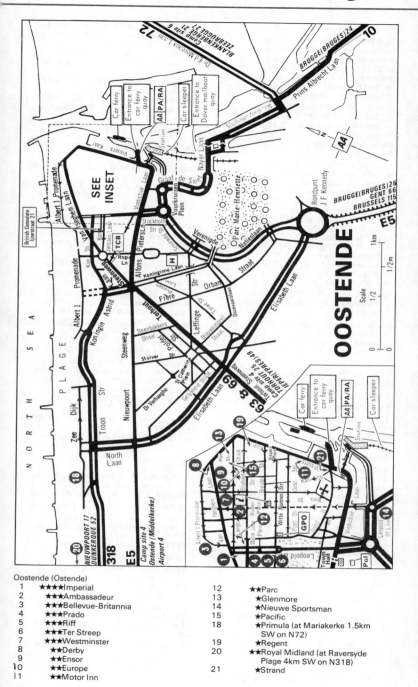

Oostende (Ostende)

No.	Hotel	No.	Hotel
1	★★★★Imperial	12	★★Parc
2	★★★Ambassadeur	13	★Glenmore
3	★★★Bellevue-Britannia	14	★Nieuwe Sportsman
4	★★★Prado	15	★Pacific
5	★★★Riff	18	★Primula (at Mariakerke 1.5km SW on N72)
6	★★★Ter Streep	19	★Regent
7	★★★Westminster	20	★★Royal Midland (at Raversyde Plage 4km SW on N318)
8	★★Derby		
9	★★Ensor		
10	★★Europe	21	★Strand
11	★★Motor Inn		

Belgium

St-Trond See Sint Truiden

Sint Niklaas (St-Nicolas) Oost-Vlaanderen 48,850 (☎031) Map **3** B2
★★★ **Serwir** Koningin Astridlaan 49 ☎765311 tx32422 rm43 ⇆30 ⋒13 Lift B680—1235 St16%
★ **Arend** O-L-Vroupl 8 ☎760126 rm15 ⇆1 ⋒2
圌⚫ **St-Christoffel** Wegvoeringstr 88 ☎761338 N➳ BL/Rov/Tri G

Sint Truiden (St-Trond) Limburg 22,300 (☎011) Map **4** C1
圌⚫ **Celis** Bevingenstweg 1c ☎677951 N➳ BL/Rov/Tri
圌➳24 **Milou** Tiensesteenweg 109 ☎73941 N➳ Ren G100

Spa Liège 9,650 (☎087) Map **4** C1
★★★ **Château Sous-Bois** chemin de la Platte 22 ☎72300 rm20 ⇆20 Lift Etr—Oct
★★★ **Vieille France** rte du Lac 5 ☎771731 rm6 ⇆4 G 1 Jan—1 Sep ✒ Pool Lake
★★ **Grand Cerf** rte Sauvenière 111 ☎772565 rm7 ⇆7 15 Dec—13 Nov LD B1075—1175 (double) M675 St16%
At **Lac de Warfaz** (2.5km NE)
★★ **Lac** ☎771074 rm12 ⇆5 ⋒1 G
At **Tiège-lez-Spa** (5km NE)
★★★ **Charmille** rte de Tiège 38 ☎474313 rm40 ⇆25 G Lift 1 Mar—31 Dec B745—1100 M450 Pn1200—1320 ✒

Spontin Namur 600 (☎083) Map **4** C1
★ **Cheval Blanc** chaussée de Dinant 26 ☎699471 rm12

Stambruges-Grandglise Hainaut 2,450 (☎069) Map **3** B2
★ **Château Vert Gazon** rte de Mons 1 ☎575984 rm7 ⇆6 ⋒1 G 1 Mar—31 Jan LD B588—1196 Màlc

Strombeek See Bruxelles (Brussels)

Tervuren See Bruxelles (Brussels)

Thourout See Torhout

Tiège-lez-Spa See Spa

Tienen (Tirlemont) Brabant 23,950 (☎016) Map **4** C1
圌⚫ **24 Delaisse** Leuvensestr 115 ☎811077 N➳811652 N➳ M/c Toy G6

Tirlemont See Tienen

Tongeren Limburg 20,700 (☎012) Map **4** C1
★ **Lido** Grote Markt 19 ☎231948 rm9 ⇆2 ⋒1 B350—760 M400—650 Pn1000 St16%
圌⚫ **Alberto** Henisstr 121 ☎231291 N➳ G3

Torhout (Thourout) West-Vlaanderen 15,750 (☎050) Map **3** B2
圌⚫ **Deketelaere** Vredelaan 91 ☎212623 N➳ Bed/Vau
At **Wynendaele** (3km)
★ **'t Gravenhof** Oostendestr 335 ☎212314 rm11 ⇆5 ⋒3 G

Tournai (Doornik) Hainaut 33,200 (☎069) Map **3** B1
圌⚫ **American** av Van Cutsem 23 ☎221921 N➳ Frd
圌⚫ **Hautecoeur** quai Staline 11 ☎223721 N➳ Bed/Vau

Turnhout Antwerpen 38,200 (☎014) Map **4** C2
★ **Terminus** Grote Markt 72 ☎42078 rm13 ⇆4 ⋒2 Lift
圌⚫ **Perfect** Nieuwekaai 9 ☎413588 N➳ Ren

Verviers Liège 31,450 (☎087) Map **4** C1
★★★ **Amigo** r Herla 1 ☎221121 tx49128 rm59 ⇆50 ⋒9 G Lift ✒
★★ **Grand** r du Palais 145 ☎223177 rm28 (A13) ⇆7 ⋒2 Lift B390—1130 M375—550 Pn775—1050
⚫ **G Rensonnet** r Jardon 27 ☎34225 N➳ BL/Rov/Tri
圌⚫ **F Spirlet** r S-Lobet 62 ☎223111 N➳ Frd
圌⚫ **Stevens** r de Liège 19 ☎221069 N➳ Lot/Ren G10

Vielsalm Luxembourg 3,700 (☎080) Map **4** C1
圌➳24 **S Graff** r du Vivier 188 ☎216217 N➳ Cit G

Ville-Pommeroeul Hainaut 2,460 (☎065) Map **3** B1
★★ **Relais** rte de Mons 10 ☎620561 rm7 ⇆6 G 1 Mar—31 Jan B700—1400 M500—700 Pn1500—2400

Villers-sur-Lesse Namur 500 (☎084) Map **4** C1
★ **Beau Séjour** r Village 15 ☎377115 rm23 (A5) ⇆9 ⋒10 G 1 Mar—15 Jan LD B515—1055 M500—950 Pn900—1300

Visé Liège 6,750 (☎041) Map **4** C1
圌➳24 **F Heuze** rte de Maestricht 83 ☎792732 Frd

Vresse Namur 500 (☎061) Map **10** D4
★★★ **Eau Vive** r de Petit Fays 52 ☎50047 rm34 (A5) ⇆34 Lift Mar—Dec LD Pool

Wenduine West-Vlaanderen 2,200 (☎050) Map **3** B2
★★ **Mouettes** Zeedijk 7 ☎411514 rm28 ⇆8 ⋒16 Lift 1 Apr—30 Sep B470—1440 M240 Sea

Wepion Namur 4,800 (☎081) Map **4** C1
☆☆☆☆ **Sofitel Jacques Borel** chaussée de Dinant 195 ☎715811 tx59031 rm122 ⇆122 G B1080—1800 M240—320 Pool
★ **Frisia** (n rest) chaussée de Dinant 311 ☎411106 rm9 ⇆2 G

Westende West-Vlaanderen 5,100 (☎059) Map **3** B2
★★ **Rotonde** Zeedijk 400 ☎300495 rm16 ⇆9 Etr—15 Sep Beach Sea

Wevelgem West-Vlaanderen 14,500 (☎056) Map **3** B1
★★★ **Park Cortina** Lauwe str 55 ☎4125222 tx85203 rm36 (A6) ⇆15 ⋒5 G Lift (closed 1—15 Aug) B430—865 M275—650

Wynendaele See Torhout (Thourout)

Xhoffraix Liège (☎080) Map **4** D1
★★ **Trôs Marets** Point de Vue Albert-1er ☎777917 rm7 ⇆3 ⋒4 G 15 Dec—15 Nov LD B370—2270(double) M750—1500

Ypres See Ieper

Yvoir Namur 2,650 (☎082) Map **4** C1
★★ **Vachter** rte de Dinant 22 ☎611314 rm9 ⇆9 G 1 Mar—15 Jan B710—1000 M810—1190 Pn1445—1470 St16%

Zeebrugge West-Vlaanderen (☎050) Map **3** B2
★ **Victoire** P-Trooslaan 5 ☎544025 rm22 ⇆3 Sea

Zolder Limburg 12,000 (☎011) Map **4** C2
★ **Pits** Omloop Terlaemen ☎225520 rm12 ⇆11 ⋒1 B700—1000 M300—800 Pn1250 Pool

Zoute (Le) See Knokke-Le-Zoute

FRANCE & MONACO

Population 52,346,000 **Area** 210,038 sq miles **Maps** 3, 7, 8, 9, 10, 11, 15 & 16

How to get there Motorists can cross the Channel by ship or hovercraft services. Short sea crossings operate from Dover and Folkestone to Boulogne and Calais ($1\frac{1}{2}$–$1\frac{3}{4}$hrs). Longer Channel crossings operate from Dover to Dunkirk ($2\frac{1}{2}$hrs). Newhaven to Dieppe ($3\frac{3}{4}$hrs). Portsmouth to Le Havre ($5\frac{1}{2}$hrs), Cherbourg (4–$6\frac{1}{2}$hrs), or St Malo (8–10hrs). Southampton to Le Havre ($6\frac{1}{2}$–$8\frac{1}{2}$hrs) or Cherbourg (5hrs), Plymouth to Roscoff (7–8hrs) and St Malo (7–9hrs), and Weymouth to Cherbourg (4hrs). Fast hovercraft services operate between Dover and Boulogne or Calais (30–35mins) and between Ramsgate and Calais (40mins).

Travel information

AA Port agents **33076 Bordeaux Cedex** Mory SA Department, Franco Britannique, Zone Portuaire D'Entrepots de Bordeaux-Nord 1 rue Surcouf ☎508400.

62201 Boulogne-sur-Mer G A Gregson & Sons, The Automobile Association, Gare Maritime BP No 152/21 ☎(21) 302222.

62100 Calais G A Gregson & Sons, The Automobile Association, Gare de Transit ☎(21) 344720; ta Gregson-Calais.

50100 Cherbourg Agence Maritime Fougere, Quai de l'Ancien Arsenal ☎532427; Port office (when ferries operating), car ferry terminal ☎532038.

76200 Dieppe G A Gregson & Sons, The Automobile Association, car ferry terminal, Esplanade ☎841941.

76600 Le Havre G A Gregson & Sons, The Automobile Association, 47 boulevard John Kennedy ☎(35) 420566.

13002 Marseille Watson Brown SA, 10 Place de la Joliette ☎903860; ta Energy-Marseille.

AA Continental Emergency Centre Control of AA operations on the Continent is centred at the AA office operated by G A Gregson & Sons, Gare Maritime, Boulogne-sur-Mer 62201 ☎(21) 302222. 24-hour service is available daily (including Sundays) from 1 July to 30 September. During other months, service is available daily (including Sundays but excluding Christmas) from 09.00–18.00hrs and also for scheduled boat sailings.

France

Accidents   **Fire, police, ambulance** Contact the police *(brigade de gendarmerie)*, particularly in cases of injury. Police station telephone numbers are written in each telephone box. In Paris the number is 17. Emergency telephone boxes are stationed every 20km on some roadways and are connected direct to the local police station. In the larger towns emergency help can be obtained from the *police secours* (emergency assistance department).

Motorists involved in an accident must immediately obtain a written report *(procès verbal)* from a bailiff *(huissier)*, a number of whom are usually to be found in towns of any importance. The *procès verbal* should be obtained, if possible, before the vehicle is moved. These reports for the most part constitute *prima facie* evidence in a court of law, or otherwise are valuable in establishing the facts of responsibility in support of claims for damages. The authorised charge for establishing a *procès verbal* is Fr250–300 depending upon the length, and the circumstances of the accident. An official receipt should always be obtained. Motorists are urged to obtain these reports whenever appropriate, especially if they do not consider themselves responsible for the accident. At the discretion of the authorities a sum of money may have to be deposited after the accident to cover court costs or fines. Otherwise the recommendations on page 21 are advisable.

Accommodation   There is a large selection of hotels of all categories. The Commissariat de Tourisme classifies hotels in five categories; one-star to *de luxe.* Local tourist information offices (see page 93) can provide details of hotels and restaurants in the area.

Rates for rooms are usually officially controlled and must be displayed in each room, but the cost of meals is not controlled. Many hotels, particularly along the French Riviera, offer full board terms only, as indicated in the gazetteer LD.

Logis de France These are Government-sponsored tourist inns equivalent to the one-star or two-star categories. They are generally located off the beaten track and offer a high standard for their type and good value for money. There are over 3,000 Logis, some of which are listed in the gazetteer, and they are marked by the symbol **LE**.

The **Logis de France Guide** can be purchased through bookshops.

Relais Routier These are restaurants situated on main roads offering simple accommodation and providing a good meal at a reasonable price. The *Relais Routier Guide* can be purchased through bookshops.

Gites de France This is furnished accommodation in rural France, often at farms, for those who prefer to cater for themselves. There are some 23,000 Gites in 4,000 villages, created with the financial support of the French Government and governed by a charter laid down by the Fédération National de Gites de France.

Personal callers at the office at 178 Piccadilly, London can book a holiday Gite by joining the British section of the Federation, membership costs £3.50, in addition to the booking service, includes a free copy of the *French Farm and Village Guide*. This Guide can also be purchased through bookshops.

Breakdowns   If your car breaks down, try to move it to the verge of the road so that it obstructs the traffic flow as little as possible. Place a warning triangle to the rear of the vehicle to warn following traffic.

On most of the major routes, at intervals of 2–3 miles, signs that say *'Touring Club de France, Secours Automobile, poste d'appel en cas d'urgence'*, outside shops, cafés, garages etc. indicate that a telephone call may be made from there to the nearest garage providing breakdown service. The police will also help by calling assistance.

Touring Secours   This is a radio-controlled breakdown service operated by the Touring Club de France. It is available for 24 hours daily in Paris and from 07.00 to 23.00hrs through a network of regional offices. AA members calling upon the service should produce their *5-Star Travel Booklet*. It is not a free service but AA members may use their credit vouchers.

British Consulates   20000 Ajaccio (Corsica), 2/4 rue Rossi, ☎310598
Biarritz/Bayonne, Societe Basque Automobile, Allées, Paulmy, 64–100 Bayonne ☎(59) 251958
33081 Bordeaux Cedex, 15 cours de Verdun ☎522835/6
62 Boulogne-sur-Mer, c/o British Rail, Gare Maritime ☎(21) 302511
62 Calais, 9–11 rue Felix-Cadras ☎(21) 344548
50 Cherbourg, 8 rue Louis Philippe ☎531446
59 Dunkirk, c/o Jules Roy SA, 6 place de l'Yser ☎667812/3

France

51 Epernay, 37 avenue de Champagne ☎(26) 513102
76 Le Havre, 9 quai George-V ☎422747
59014 Lille Cedex, 11–13, 15 square Dutilleul ☎573549
and 570177
69288 Lyon Cedex, 4th floor, 24 rue Childebert ☎375967/8
13006 Marseille, 24 avenue du Prado ☎534332
57 Metz, 23 rue du XXe Corps Americain ☎683996/8
66000 Perpignan, c/o Raquer France, 1 rue Buffon ☎(69)
349404/345699
75008 Paris 35 rue du Faubourg St-Honore ☎2669142
67001 Strasbourg-Cedex, 10 rue du General Castelnau
☎366491

Crash helmets
It is obligatory for drivers and passengers of all motorised
bicycles over 50cc or motorcycles to wear crash helmets.

Currency
and banking
The unit of currency is the French franc, which is divided into
100 centimes. There is no restriction on the amount of
foreign currency which may be taken into France. Travellers
are, however, restricted to taking Fr5,000 with them when leaving the country, unless,
of course, they imported more currency on entry and completed the appropriate form at
the time.

Banking hours
In most large towns banks are open from Monday to Friday
09.00–16.00hrs; they close on Saturdays and Sundays.
Banks close at midday on the day prior to a national holiday and all day on Monday if the
holiday falls on a Tuesday.
The *Credit Lyonnais* has offices at Le Bourget airport open 24 hours a day and at the
Invalides air terminal in Paris open daily from 07.30hrs until midnight for cashing
travellers' cheques. The *Société Générale* has an office at Orly airport which is open
all night.

Dimensions
Private cars and trailers are restricted to the following
dimensions:
Vehicles height – no restrictions; width – 2.50 metres;
Vehicle trailer combinations total length – 18 metres;
See also Trailers page 93.

Drinking and driving
A driver having 0.8% or more alcohol in his blood is considered
to be under the influence of alcohol and is therefore
automatically subject to a penalty.

Ferries (internal)
All particulars are subject to alteration.

Rhine ferries
See Germany, page 157

Seine ferries
(between Le Havre
and Rouen)
Port Jérôme–Quillebeuf *Map 9 A4*
40.5km (25 miles) from Le Havre ☎ Tancarville (Seine
Maritime) 948911.
The service is liable to interruption at certain tides.
Service Departures from Port Jérôme at 05.40 and 06.10hrs; hourly on the half-hour
between 06.30 and 22.30hrs. Additional services at 10 and 50mins past the hour
during morning, midday and evening peaks.

Departures from Quillebeuf at 05.30hrs; hourly on the hour between 06.00 and 22.00hrs
and at 22.20hrs. Additional services at 20 and 40mins past the hour during morning,
midday and evening peaks.

The following ferries also operate a half-hourly service during the winter months from
06.00 to 21.00hrs, and during the summer, 22.00hrs.

1	**Le Trail–La Maillerave**	*Map 9 A4*
2	**Yainville–Heurteauville**	*Map 9 A4*
3	**Jumieges–Port Jumieges**	*Map 9 A4*
4	**Mesnil–sous–Jumieges**	*Map 9 A4*
5	**Duclar–Berville–sur–Seine**	*Map 9 A4*
6	**Sahurs–La Bouille**	*Map 9 A4*
7	**Le Val–de–la–Have–Grand Couronne**	*Map 9 A4*
8	**Dieppedale–Le Grand Quevilly**	*Map 9 A4*

France

North and West Coast ferries

St-Malo (St-Servan)–Dinard *Map 8 C3*
☎ Dinard 461592
Service It is now usual to cross by the dam of the Rance hydro-electric generating station. There is no toll and the distance is 10km (6 miles).

Quiberon–Le Palais (Belle-Ile-en-Mer) *Map 7 B2* ☎ Quiberon (97) 526013: Le Palais (97) 528001.

Service
From October to March 2–3 daily
From March to May 3–6 daily
June 4–6 daily
From July to August 10 daily
September 3–6 daily
Duration 1 hour
Car space must be booked in advance

La Pallice (La Rochelle 5km)–Sablanceaux (Ile de Re) *Map 8 C1* ☎ La Rochelle 356148

Service From 05.45–23.40hrs approximately every 15 or 20mins. Winter departures 06.15–22.40hrs operating every 30mins.
Duration 15 minutes

Royan–Pointe de Grave (across the Gironde) *Map 15 B3*
☎ Royan 052903; Le Verdon (56) 596084 and 596049
This service may be suspended during adverse weather conditions.

Service From June to September hourly or every 40mins between 07.00–22.20hrs (approx), from Royan; hourly or every 40mins between 06.00–21.20hrs (approx), from Pointe de Grave.
Out of season 8 crossings daily between 08.00–21.00hrs (approx), from Royan; 8 crossings daily between 07.00–22.00hrs (approx) from Pointe de Grave.
Duration 30 minutes

Blaye–Lamarque (across the Gironde) *Map 15 B3* ☎ (56) 420449

Service From morning to evening; from July to mid September 8 sailings daily; from September to June 3–5 sailings daily.
Duration 30 minutes

South Coast ferries Passengers only

To Ile de Port-Cros and **Ile du Levant** *Map 28 C1*
Service Frequent daily services during the summer (limited in winter) from Le Lavandou.
Duration 30–45 minutes
Four sailings daily during the season (limited in winter) from Port d'Hyères.
Duration 1hr to Port Cros; 1hr 15mins to Levant
To Ile de Porquerolles *Map 28 C1*
Service Frequent daily services during the summer (limited in winter) from La Tour-Fondue and from Port d'Hyères.
Duration 20mins from La Tour-Fondue; 30mins from Port d'Hyères
To Iles de Lerins *Map 28 C1*
Service 9 daily services from Cannes during summer months; 5 daily services from Cannes during winter months. Additional services operate on Sundays and public holidays. Full details are available from Compagnie Esterel – Chantéclair, Gare Maritime des Iles, 06400 Port de Cannes ☎ (93) 391182.

Holidays and events

Holidays based on religious festivals are not always fixed on the calendar and any current diary will give actual dates. The Whit period should not be confused with the British Spring Holiday.

Fixed holidays

1 January	New Year's Day
1 May	Labour Day
14 July	Bastille Day
15 August	Assumption
1 November	All Saints' Day
25 December	Christmas

Moveable holidays

Good Friday
Easter Monday
Ascension Day
Whit Monday

France

Annual events		
	January	**Nationwide** Ski-ing events
	February	**Nice** Carnival with dancing, fireworks, and processions (February/March)
		Amelie les Bains Carnival with flower-decked vehicles and the burning of King Carnival
	March	**Vichy** Carnival
	April	**Ajaccio, Bastia, Bonifacio, Sartene** (Corsica) Good Friday processions
		Biarritz Folklore Festival
	May	**Reims** and **Orleans** Festival of Joan of Arc
		Saintes-Maries-de-la-Mer Festival of the Gypsies
		Saint-Tropez 'La Bravade' celebration of 17th-century naval victory
		Cannes Film Festival
	June	**Le Mans** 24-hour Race
		Rouen Joan of Arc Festival
		Brie-Comte-Robert Festival of Roses
		Toulouse Traditional Fair
		Lyon International Music Festival
	July	**Nationwide** Tour de France world-famous cycling race
		Aix-en-Provence Music Festival
		Nationwide Bastille Day
	August	**Aix-les-Bains** Flower Fair
		Biarritz Sea Fair
		Confolens International Folklore Festival
	September	**Dijon** International Folk Festival
		Anduze Assembly of the Desert, Protestant meeting
		Lourdes Festival of the Virgin
	November	**Beaune** etc Burgundy Wine Festival

Further information can be obtained from the French Government Tourist Office (see page 93).

Insurance

This is compulsory; see page 11.

Lights

Headlights should be adapted so that they do not dip to the left (see Preparing your vehicle for a holiday abroad, page 16). Motorists are also advised to comply with the French law which requires all vehicles to be equipped with headlights which emit a yellow beam. This may be accomplished by using amber lens converters.

Alternatively, the outer surface of the headlamp glass can be coated with yellow plastic paint which is removable with a solvent.

Unless street lighting is adequate, cars must have two headlights alight at night whether dipped or otherwise; dipping to one light is not permitted, even for visitor's cars.

In fog, mist, or poor visibility during the day or night, either two foglights or two headlights must be switched on *in addition to* two sidelights. Failure to comply with this regulation will lead to a fine of Fr160–600.

Parking lights must be used in badly lit areas and when visibility is poor.

Medical treatment

The provision of medical benefits in France is administered by local Social Security offices (*Le Caisse Primaire de Securité Sociale*). The address of the local office may be obtained from the Social Service Department of the Town Hall (Hotel de Ville). You may consult any doctor or

France

dentist who will issue a sickness document (*feuille de maladie*) on which he will enter his fee after you have paid him. It should then be taken to the chemist together with the doctor's prescription. After you have paid him, the chemist will enter the cost of the medicines supplied and return the document and prescription to you.

You will be able to obtain a refund or part of the costs of treatment and medicines from the nearest local Social Security Office on presentation of form E111, the receipted sickness document and prescription. On entering hospital, produce form E111 and advise the hospital authorities that you are an insured person. They will carry out the necessary formalities (*prise en charge*) with the Social Security office. A percentage of the cost will be met direct by the local Social Security.

Motoring clubs

Although there are many motoring clubs and organisations in France, the most active as regards to general services to foreign visitors is the TCF (Touring Club de France) whose head office is at 65 avenue de la Grande-Armée, 75782 Paris Cedex 16. They also maintain branch offices in main towns throughout France. They have a wide range of services available to their members but will extend a courtesy service to foreign tourists. When requesting service AA members should produce their *5-Star Travel Booklet.*

Automobile Club du Nord de la France

The Automobile Club du Nord de la France will assist AA members whenever possible. Produce your *5-Star Travel Booklet.*
59 Roubaix (head office) 40—42 rue de Maréchal-Foch
☎ Lille (20)530000. Office hours: 24-hour emergency service.

Automobile Club de l'Ouest

The Automobile Club de l'Ouest will also assist AA members whenever possible. Produce your *5-Star Travel Booklet.*
72 Le Mans (head office) Les Raineries ☎840130. Office hours: weekdays 09.00—12.00hrs, and 14.00—18.00hrs; Saturdays 09.00—12.00hrs.

Parking

As a general rule all prohibitions are indicated by road signs or by red markings on the kerb. It is prohibited to leave a vehicle parked in the same place for more than 24 consecutive hours in Paris and surrounding departments. It is prohibited to park a vehicle on a road with a continuous centre line if the width of the road between the line and a parked vehicle would not allow unimpeded movement of a line of traffic. Parking is forbidden in places where it would obstruct traffic or view.

On some roads in built-up areas, parking is allowed from the 1st to the 15th day of each month on the side of the road where the numbers of the buildings are odd, and from the 16th to the last day of the month on the side of the road with even numbers. This is called alternate unilateral parking.

There are short-term parking areas known as blue zones in most principal towns; in these areas discs must be used (placed against the windscreen) every day, except Sundays and public holidays, between 09.00 and 12.30hrs and 14.30 and 19.00hrs. They permit parking up to one hour. Discs are sold at police stations, but at tourist offices and some clubs and commercial firms they are available free of charge. Due to their size, cars towing trailers may neither circulate nor park in the blue zones between 14.00 and 20.30hrs, except on Sundays and public holidays. There are grey zones where parking meters are in use; in these zones a fee must be paid between 09.00 and 19.00hrs. Motorists using a ticket issued by automatic machines must display the ticket behind the windscreen or nearside front window of their car.

Paris In some parts of the blue zone parking is completely forbidden. It is prohibited to park caravans even for a limited period, not only in the blue zone but in almost all areas of Paris.

Violation of parking regulations Vehicles which are parked contrary to regulations are liable to be removed by the police at the owner's risk and the driver will be liable for any costs incurred. See also Priority on page 89.

Passengers

Children under ten years of age are not allowed to travel in the front seats of a vehicle unless the vehicle does not have rear seats, or if it is impossible to accommodate the children in the rear.

Petrol

The approximate cost of petrol per litre is: super (98 octane) Fr1.97; normal (90 octane) Fr1.82.

France

Police fines

The police usually exercise their extensive powers of levying summary fines on motorists. The officer collecting the fine should issue an official receipt.

A driver may refuse to pay a fine and prefer to go for trial. Unless a motorist strongly disputes the alleged infringement, his best course is to pay the fine, thereby avoiding inconvenience and extra cost. A motorist fined for a serious offence must deposit the money with the police pending proceedings; if he is unable or unwilling to make the deposit, his car may be impounded.

Postal and telephone charges

Rates for foreign postage are:

		Fr
postcards		0.80
letters up to	20gm	1.40
	20–50gm	2.50
	50–100gm	3.20
	100–250gm	6.50

Telephone rates

The charge for a 3-minute call to the UK is about Fr7.50 with a surcharge if the call is made from a hotel. There are very few public telephone boxes. Local calls can be made from a café or restaurant, but for toll or trunk calls you will need to go to a post office. Some public telephones are operated by coins, others by discs called *jetons*. You can buy a *jeton* from the place where you make the call – a café, restaurant, underground or railway station, etc, or from the post office.

To make a call, insert the coins or *jeton* before lifting the receiver, then lift and dial in the normal way; if there is no reply, the coins or *jeton* are returned when you replace the receiver.

Local calls cost 60 centimes from post office call boxes and are untimed. Other calls are based upon time and distance and the time of day that the call is made. If you are not familiar with the system and wish to make a long distance call it is better to do this from a hotel or café where there may be someone on hand to help you.

The address of the Paris post office, which is open 24 hours a day, is 52, rue du Louvre, Paris. For motorway telephones, see page 92.

Priority

Motorists should be extra careful when driving in France. New regulations and signs for priority are being enforced. If there are no priority signs (a blue arrow on a yellow triangle), give way to traffic from the right. Secondary roads are marked with a stop sign or a yellow triangle with a red border. International priority signs will still be in use. On steep gradients, vehicles travelling downhill must give way to vehicles travelling uphill. Give way to street-cleaning vehicles. See also page 27.

Roads

France has a very comprehensive network of roads. They are classified into four main grades – the *autoroutes* (motorways), prefixed A; the *routes nationales* (national roads), prefixed N; *routes départementales* (departmental roads), prefixed D; *chemins vicinaux* (local roads), prefixed V. *Routes nationales* allow high average speeds on long journeys, although a few (eg N1, N6, and parts of N7) carry heavy traffic. Their subsidiary branches are indicated by various references, for example N5bis, N6a, and No 10 ter. Road surfaces are normally good; exceptions are often signposted *chaussée deformée*. The cobble (*pavé*) stretches in the north are gradually being replaced by tarmac. The camber is often severe and the edges rough. It is a widespread practice to surface roads by spreading loose chippings on sprayed tar; too high a speed or careless overtaking can lead to a broken windscreen. The gradients of mountain passes (see page 28) are usually moderate; in some places at high altitudes road edges are not well protected.

Road number changes As part of a decentralisation scheme, many national highways are being transferred to the departments. Some road numbers are simply changed by replacing the prefix N with D, but in some cases the figure 9 is used to precede the last two figures of the old number, eg N315 is now D915, N77 is now D977 and N1 is now D901.

It now appears that many of the local authorities have adopted the recommendation of the Ministry of the Interior to use the figure 9 as the first digit of the new D numbers, but regrettably there are many exceptions where any number between 3 and 9 has been used.

Holiday traffic

Itinéraires bis (Emeraude) and *Itinéraires de delestage*. Special green and yellow signs (arrows) are used to indicate alternative routes to avoid heavy traffic routes and/or traffic hold-ups in towns. The signs

France

on these roads are continuous and when they appear it is usually advantageous to follow them, although you cannot be absolutely sure of gaining time.

Motorways
There are about 2,720 miles of motorway (*autoroute*) open, and 290 miles under construction and due to open in 1978. A total of 3,278 miles of motorways are expected to be in use by the end of 1980. To join a motorway, follow signs with the words *par autoroute* added. Motorcycles of 50cc or less are prohibited; commercial vehicles weighing more than 3 tons are prohibited at weekends. See trailers, page 93. Tolls are charged on most motorways according to the distance travelled. Most cars (including Minis) pay the tolls quoted below if the entire motorway is used. Where only one toll charge is quoted, the same toll applies to all cars with or without caravans.

Toll payment
On the majority of the toll motorways a travel ticket is issued on entry, and toll is paid on leaving the motorway. The travel ticket gives all relevant information about the toll charges, including the toll category of the vehicle. At the exit point, the ticket is handed in. On some motorways the toll collection is automatic; have the correct amount ready to throw into collecting basket.

If change is required use marked, separate lane.

The main toll motorways are:

Autoroute du Nord
A1   *Paris (Porte de la Chapelle)–Roissy-en-France* (**no toll**)
Roissy–Roye–Fresnes (nr Arras)
(**toll:** car Fr21; with caravan Fr30.50)
Fresnes–Lille (**no toll**)
A1/A2   *Roissy-en-France–Cambrai*
(**toll:** car Fr21.50; with caravan Fr32)

Autoroute de l'Est
A4   *Paris–Lagny* (**no toll**)
Lagny–Reims (**toll:** car Fr23; with caravan Fr34.50)
Reims–Metz (**tolls:** car Fr33.50; with caravan Fr50)

Autoroute du Sud (Soleil)
A6   *Paris–Fleury (near Fontainebleau)* (**no toll**)
Fleury (near Fontainebleau)–Lyon (**toll:** car Fr50; with caravan Fr75)
A7   *Lyon–Vienne* (**no toll**)
Vienne–Orange (**toll:** car Fr24; with caravan Fr35)
Vienne–Marseille (**toll:** car Fr35; with caravan Fr49)
A7/A8   *Vienne–Aix-en-Provence*
(**toll:** car Fr35; with caravan Fr49)

Autoroute Esterel–Côte d'Azur (La Provencale)
A8   *Aix-en-Provence–Puget-sur-Argens (Fréjus)*
(**toll:** Car Fr21.50; with caravan Fr33)
Aix-en-Provence–Nice
(**toll:** car Fr32.50; with caravan Fr49)
Nice Ouest–La Paillon (**toll:** car Fr4; with caravan Fr6)
Roquebrune (nr Menton)–Italian frontier (**toll:** car Fr2; with caravan Fr3)

Autoroute Orange–Narbonne (La Languedocienne)
A9   *Orange–Montpellier* (**toll:** car Fr13; with caravan Fr19)
Montpellier–Narbonne (**toll:** car Fr15; with caravan Fr23)

Autoroute La Catalane
B9   *Rivesaltes (Perpignan)–Le Perthus* (**toll:** car Fr7; with caravan Fr10)

Autoroute Paris–Orléans–Tours (L'Aquitaine)
A10/A11   *Paris (Palaiseau)–La Folie Bessin* (**no toll**)
A10   *La Folie Bessin– Orléans Ouest* (**toll:** car Fr16; with caravan Fr24)
Orléans–Tours (**toll:** car Fr19; with caravan Fr28)

Autoroute Paris–Chartres (L'Océane)
A10/A11   *Paris (Palaiseau)–La Folie Bessin* (**no toll**)
A11   *La Folie Bessin–Chartres* (**toll:** car Fr10; with caravan Fr15)
Chartres–La Ferté Bernard Sud (**toll:** car Fr14; with caravan Fr21)

Autoroute de L'Ouest and Normandie
A13   *Paris–Mantes* (**no toll**)
Mantes–Les Essarts (nr Rouen) (**toll:** Fr10)
Mantes–Bourneville (nr Pont Audemer (**toll:** Fr14)
Mantes–Caen (**toll:** Fr26)

France

A26   **Autoroute Calais–Arras**
Lillers–Aix Noulette (**toll:** car Fr4; with caravan Fr6)

A32   **Autoroute Metz–Saarbrücken**
Metz–Freyming (**toll:** Fr5)
Freyming–Saarbrücken (**no toll**)

A34   **Autoroute Freyming–Strasbourg**
Freyming–Strasbourg (**toll:** car Fr17; with caravan Fr25.50)

A36   **Autoroute Beaune–Mulhouse**
Séchin–Montbéliard (**toll:** Fr10)
Montbéliard–Belfort (**no toll**)
Belfort–Mulhouse (**toll:** car Fr5; with caravan Fr7.50)

A37   **Autoroute Dijon–Beaune**
Dijon–Beaune (**toll:** car Fr5; with caravan Fr8)

A41   **Autoroute Grenoble–Annecy**
Annecy–St-Félix (**toll:** car Fr3; with caravan Fr5)
Grenoble–Pontcharra (**toll:** car Fr7.50; with caravan Fr11)

B41   **Autoroute Blanche**
Geneva–Le Fayet (**toll:** car Fr10; with caravan Fr15)

A43   **Autoroute Lyon–Chambéry**
Lyon–Chambéry (**toll:** car Fr24; with caravan Fr36)

A48   **Autoroute Lyon–Grenoble**
Lyon–Grenoble (**toll:** car Fr18; with caravan Fr27)

A/B52   **Autoroute Marseille–Aubagne–Toulon**
Marseille–Aubagne (**no toll**)
Aubagne–Auriol (**toll:** car Fr2; with caravan Fr3)
Aubagne–Toulon (**toll:** car Fr8.50; with caravan Fr13)

A61   **Autoroute des deux Mers**
Bordeaux–La Prade (**no toll**)
La Prade–Langon (**toll:** car Fr4; with caravan Fr6)

A63   **Autoroute de la Côte Basque**
Biarritz–Spanish frontier (**toll:** car Fr6.50; with caravan Fr9.50)

Toll bridges

Tancarville toll bridge *Map 9 A4*
29km (18 miles) from Le Havre
Charges

Vehicles		
cars up to 4cv		Fr4
4–9cv		Fr6.50
over 9cv		Fr9
motorcycles and scooters with or without sidecars		Fr1
coaches up to 29 seats		Fr16
coaches over 29 seats		Fr22
lorries		Fr6.50–23
caravan		Fr2.50
Vehicle passengers		free

Ile d'Oleron toll bridge *Map 15 B3*
Charges (including return)

Vehicles		
cars		Fr18
motorcycles		Fr4
coaches (including passengers)		Fr60
car/caravan combination		Fr36

Ile de Noirmoutier toll bridge *Map 7 B2*
Charges

Vehicles		
cars under 1500kg		Fr8
caravans and cars over 1500kg		Fr10
motorcycles		Fr1

Seudre toll bridge *Map 15 B3*
5km (3 miles) from Marennes
Charges

Vehicles		
car		Fr6
caravan		Fr2
motorcycle		Fr1

91

France

St Nazaire toll bridge Map 7 B2
Charges

Vehicles		
	car	Fr18–23
	car and caravan	Fr31
	motorcycle	Fr5
	moped	Fr1

Motorway telephones

For assistance on a motorway use one of the telephone boxes sited at 2.4km (1½-mile) intervals; they are connected to police stations.

Winter conditions

Although there are five mountain regions – the Vosges, Jura, Central Plateau, Alps and Pyrenees – motoring in winter is not severely restricted. The main channels for south-bound traffic wanting to avoid the Alps and Central Plateau are the N7 (A7) route along the Rhône Valley, the N20 from Limoges to Toulouse, and the highways farther west. Roads into Belgium, Luxembourg and Germany are generally unaffected.

All-the-year-round approaches to Strasbourg and Basle avoiding the Vosges and Jura are routes N4 and N19 respectively. The approach to Switzerland via Pontarlier is very seldom obstructed, and during very severe weather is a better route to Geneva than over the Faucille Pass; alternatively the road via Bourg to Geneva is always open. Italy can be entered via the Mont Blanc tunnel, the Fréjus railway tunnel (avoiding the Mont Cenis Pass), or along the French Riviera via Menton. The main routes to Spain via Biarritz and Perpignan avoid the Pyrenees.

Whenever possible, roads are swept and kept clear.

In certain circumstances of thaw, some barred roads may be used by certain classes of traffic at the driver's risk; passenger vehicles without trailers being used privately may proceed provided they do not exceed 80kph (49mph).

Road signs

Signposting is most efficient, but in open country there are not always advance warning signs. Signs tend to point across the roads they indicate, which is confusing at first. Loopways for heavy vehicles (poids lourds) are often useful for avoiding town centres.

Allumez vos lanternes	Use headlights
Arbres inclinés	Overhanging trees
Arrêt d'autocar présentant un danger particulier	Bus stop causing a particular danger
Barriere de dégel	Thaw barrier
Carriere exploitée a la mine	Mining works
Cassis	150 metres (164yd) from the sign – road deterioration
Chaussée deformée	Bad road surface
Couloir d'avalanches	Avalanche region
Cylindrage	Road roller in use
Fin d'interdiction de stationner	End of no-parking area
Fin ou traversée de piste cyclable	End of crossing of cycle path
Gravillons	Loose chippings
Halte gendarmerie	Halt police
Hauteur limitée a 4m50	Vehicles under 4.5 metres in height only
Interdit aus piétons	Pedestrians prohibited
Passage de hauteur limitée	Restricted passage to vehicles of certain height
Passage protégé	Crossroads protected by stop signs on side roads (proceed with caution)
Priorité a droite	Yield to traffic from the right
Poids lourds	Loopway for heavy vehicles
Poste suivant a 50km	Next callbox 50km away
Route barrée a 300m	Road closed after 300 metres
Route déviée	Diversion
Sens unique	One-way street
Serrez a droite	Keep right
Sortie d'usine	Factory exit
Suppression point noir	Black spots notorious for accidents
Verglas	Glazed frost
Zone a stationnement réglementé	Regulated parking zone

France

Zone bleue   Blue-zone parking
Zone de chute de pierres   Danger from falling rocks

Seat belts   If your vehicle is fitted with seat belts it is compulsory to wear
                        them.

Shopping hours   Department stores are usually open from Monday to Saturday,
                        09.00–18.30hrs. Some foodshops open 07.00 and 20.00hrs
and are open Sunday morning. Most shops are closed on Monday morning and all shops
usually close for two or three hours at lunchtime.

Speed   The beginning of a built-up area is indicated by a sign bearing
                        the placename, and the end by the placename sign with a thin
red line diagonally across it; the limit in these areas, unless otherwise signposted, is
60kph (37mph) for all vehicles except mopeds (vehicles not over 50cc), which are
restricted to 50kph (31mph).

On the approach to a built-up area, the limit is often decreased by stages. In open country,
mopeds are limited to 50kph (31mph).

Outside built-up areas speed limits are:
on normal roads 90kph (56mph)
on dual carriageways and toll-free motorways 110kph (68mph)
on toll motorways 130kph (80mph)

There are no special limits for a private car towing a caravan. All lower speed limits must
be adhered to. Different maximum speed limits can be fixed on a permanent or temporary
basis. Special speed limits are enforced where there are road works; these limits are
indicated by signs. Both French residents and visitors to France, who have held a driving
licence for less than one year, must not exceed 90kph (56mph) – or any lower limit
which is signposted; a plastic disc bearing the figure 90 is displayed at the rear of vehicles
driven by the relevant French residents.

Tourist   The French National Tourist Office maintains a full information
information   service in London at 178 Piccadilly, London W1V OAL
offices   ☎01-493 3171 and will be pleased to answer any
                        enquiries on touring in France.

Once in France you should contact the local tourist office, *Syndicat d'Initiative* which
will be found in all larger towns and resorts. They all have English-speaking staff and
are pleased to give advice on local events, amenities and excursions. They can also
answer specific local queries such as bus timetables and local religious services (all
denominations) not available in the UK.

A further source of information within the country, is the *Accueil de France* (welcome
office) who will also book hotel reservations within their area for the same night, or 24
hours in advance for personal callers only. There are not so many of these offices and
mainly they are located at important stations and airports.

The hours of opening vary considerably depending upon the district and the time of year.
Generally the offices are open between 09.00–12.00hrs and 14.00–18.00hrs from
Monday to Saturday but in popular resort areas *Syndicats d'Initiative* are sometimes
open later and on Sunday mornings.

Traffic lanes   There are special lanes for buses and taxis only in some
(Paris)   streets; they are marked by a continuous yellow line painted
                        one vehicle-width from the kerb. Usually, buses and taxis
in the special lane travel in the opposite direction to other traffic.

Traffic lights   The three-colour system, as in the United Kingdom, is in
                        operation, with the addition of miniatures set at eye-level
and with the posts placed in irregular positions, sometimes overhead and possibly
without a set on the opposite side of the junction. It must be stressed that the lights
themselves are extremely dim, and easily missed.

A flashing amber light is a warning that the intersection or junction is particularly
dangerous. A flashing red light indicates no entry, or may be used to mark obstacles.

Trailers   Only one trailer may be towed. Due to their size, cars towing
                        trailers may neither circulate nor park in the blue zone between
14.00 and 20.30hrs, excluding Sundays and public holidays. If you wish to cross Paris
between these hours when towing a trailer you are recommended to use the boulevard
Périphérique. Vehicles or vehicle-trailer combinations which are longer than 7 metres

France

(23ft), or weight more than 3,500kg (3tons 8cwt 100lb), must stay at least 50 metres (55yd) behind the vehicle in front when driving outside built-up areas. They must also keep to the two right-hand lanes on roads with three lanes or more in each direction.

Tyres   **Spiked or studded tyres** These may be used from 15 November to 15 March provided that a speed of 90kph (56mph) is not exceeded. Vehicles must display at the rear a speed limitation disc bearing the figure 90. The disc can be obtained at road frontier posts.

Wheel chains These can be purchased from vehicle accessory shops in large towns. In other places wheel chains can be purchased, and in some cases hired, from some garages. Establishments have only small supplies. In Paris wheel chains can be hired from:
Paris 4, Etablissements Dethy, 20 place des Vosges; Paris 13, Etablissements Vertadier, 1–3 Rue Paul Bourget. Deposits are about Fr100, and charges are about Fr25–60.

Visitors' registration   A visitors' registration form will be completed by hotel or campsite management. If staying with friends at a private address, the host should notify the authorities.

Warning triangles   It is compulsory to use a warning triangle or the vehicle's flashing hazard warning lights. The triangle must be placed on the road 30 metres (33yd) behind the vehicle or obstacle and must be visible to following traffic from 100 metres (109yd). In certain circumstances, such as electrical failure or accident damage, it may not be possible to use hazard warning lights and a warning triangle is, therefore, recommended.

Monaco

Map 28 C2   The Principality of Monaco has a population of 24,000 and an area of 8 sq miles. The official Monaco Information Centre in the UK is at 34 Sackville Street, London W1X 1DB ☎01-437 3660. Although a sovereign state, it is very much under the influence of France and its laws are similar to those of the major country. Monaco is one large city/state but Monaco Town and Monte Carlo are the two towns of the State.
Motoring regulations are the same as in France but it should be stated that whilst caravans are permitted to pass through the Principality they are not allowed to stop or park.

Prices are in French francs
For additional information on French hotels, see page 84.
The number following the town name is the department number; the department name is in brackets. Towns for which there is a town plan in the *AA Road Book of France* are marked †.

Abbreviations:
av	avenue
bd	boulevard
espl	esplanade
fbg	faubourg
Gl	Général
Ml	Marshal, Maréchal
r	rue
rte	route
sq	square

Abbeville† 80 (Somme) 26,600 (☎22)
Map **3** A1
★★*Relais Vauban* 2 bd Vauban ☎240285
rm22 ⇌22
★*Chalet* 2 av de la Gare ☎242157 rm12 ⇌4
G 15 Jan–15 Dec LD B33–60 M19–35
★*Conde* 14 pl de la Libération ☎240633
rm7 1 Feb–14 Aug 1 Sep–14 Jan LD B34–61
M26–44 & àlc
★*Gare* 13 av de la Gare ☎240409 rm27 ⇌9 G
🅿⛽*Brois* 79 bd de la République ☎240679
N🚗 BL/Tri
🅿⛽*Laffille* 4 bd de la République ☎240248

Aber-Wrac'h (L') 29 (Finistère) (☎98)
Map **7** A3
★★*Baie des Anges* ☎840404 rm17 ⇌14 🏠2

Abrets (Les) 38 (Isère) 2,450 (☎76)
Map **27** B4
★*Belle-Etoile* **LE** pl de la République ☎320497
rm15 ⇌4 🏠2 G 1 Jun–30 Apr B35–105
M20–37
★*Hostellerie Abrésienne* r Gambetta ☎320428
rm22 ⇌1 G LD B35–75 M20–35 Pn50–65

Agay 83 (Var) (☎94) Map **28** C2
★★★*Baumette* ☎440015 rm80 ⇌60 🏠6 G
Lift 15 Mar–3 Oct LD B81–192 M50 Pn130–
185 🏊 Pool Beach Sea
★*Santa Monica* ☎440141 rm17 ⇌5 🏠12
Jun–Sep Sea
At **Camp Long** (1km SW on N98)
★*Beau Site* (n rest) ☎440045 rm23 ⇌4 🏠9
1 Apr–30 Sep B32–78 Sea
At **Dramont** (2km SW)
★★★*Sol et Mar* ☎952560 ta Solemar St
Raphaël rm45 ⇌45 Lift 15 Mar–15 Oct LD
B120–153 M37–47 Pn130–149 Pool Beach
Sea

Agde 34 (Herault) 11,800 (☎67) Map **27** A2
★★*Tamarissiere* ☎942087 rm24 ⇌17 🏠7
15 Mar–15 Dec Sea

Agen† 47 (Lot et Garonne) 35,850 Map **16** C2
★★*Perigord* (n rest) pl XIV-Juillet ☎661004
rm23 ⇌13 G Lift Feb–22 Dec B52–95
🅿⛽*France* 33 cours de Belgique ☎663207
N🚗 Frd
🅿⛽24 *R Lange* 14 bd de la Liberté ☎662084
Chy
🅿⛽*Palissy* 1 r Palissy ☎660239 N🚗 Opl
🅿⛽*F Tastets* 182 bd de la Liberté ☎661068
N🚗 BL/Jag/Rov/Tri

Aigle (L') 61 (Orne) 10,250 (☎34) Map **9** A3
★★★*Dauphin* pl de la Halle ☎241244 rm30
⇌21 🏠1 G LD B40–149 M29–81 Pn107–172

Aiguebelle 83 (Var) 1,170 (☎94) Map **28** C1
See also **Le Lavandou**
★★★★*Roches Fleuries* (4km on N559 to Le
Lavandou) ☎710507 rm50 ⇌42 🏠8 G
25 May–25 Sep LD B106–297 M60–70 Pool
Beach Sea
★★★*Bains* (n rest) (14km NE of Le Lavandou
on N559) ☎Cavalière 149 rm35 ⇌12 🏠18
1 Jun–1 Oct Beach Sea

★★*Plage* (n rest) ☎728074 rm52 (A9) ⇌7
🏠41 15 May–30 Sep Sea

Aiguillon-sur-Mer 85 (Vendée) 2150 (☎51)
★★*Port* 2 r Belle Vue ☎564008 rm33
⇌12 🏠11 25 Mar–30 Sep B41–115 M21–46
Pn66–97 Pool Sea

Ainhoa 64 (Pyrénées Atlantiques) 550 (☎59)
Map **20** C3
★★★*Argi-Eder* ☎299104 rm38 (A4) ⇌38 🏠38
1 Mar–31 Dec B120–145 M38.60–70 Pn185–
195 🏊 Pool
★★*Ithurria* ☎299211 rm30 ⇌20 🏠9 G 25 Dec–
11 Nov B63–115 M40–70 Pn95–110

Aire-sur-l'Adour 40 (Landes) 6,950
(☎57) Map **15** C1
At **Segos** Gers (32) (8km SW on N134)
★★*Domaine du Bassibé* ☎Segos 1 rm12 (A6)
⇌4 🏠12 G Etr–Oct 🏊 Pool

Aire-sur-la-Lys 62 (Pas-de-Calais) 9,700
(☎21) Map **3** A1
★*Europ* (n rest) 14 Grand pl ☎390432 rm16
🏠6 G B28–54
🚗24 H *Delgery* 5 pl J d'Aire ☎390298 Ren
G 12

Aisey-sur-Seine 21 (Côte-d'Or) 160 (☎80)
Map **10** C2
★*Roy* **LE** ☎932163 rm10 ⇌1 🏠5 G
15 Dec–15 Nov LD B42–65 M23–40 Pn70–75
🏊

Aix-en-Provence† 13 (Bouches-du-Rhône)
114,050 (☎91) Map **27** B2
★★★★*Roy René* ☎260301
tx41888 rm66 ⇌47 🏠12 G Lift
★★★*Manoir* (n rest) 8 r Entrecasteaux
☎262720 rm43 ⇌21 🏠22 Lift B67–169
☆☆☆ *Novotel Beaumanoir* Résidence
Beaumanoir A8 (42) 274750 tx400244
rm97 ⇌97 Lift B120–140 Pool
☆☆☆ *Novotel Sud* Arc de Meyran ☎(42)
279049 tx420517 rm80 ⇌80 Lift B120–140
Pool
★★★*Paul Cézanne* (n rest) 40 av V-Hugo
☎263473 rm44 ⇌26 🏠14 Lift B101–212
★★★*PLM Le Pigonnet* av Pigonnet (off road N8
towards Marseille) ☎(42) 590290 tx410629
rm48 ⇌33 🏠15 G Lift B130–225 M75
Pn232–254 Pool
★★*Nègre-Coste* (n rest) 33 cours Mirabeau
☎(42) 277422 rm36 ⇌25 🏠11 G Lift B88–136
M33 Pn110–120
★★*Renaissance* (n rest) 4 bd République
☎260422 rm30 ⇌11 🏠1 11 Feb–31 Dec
B50–95
★★*Rotonde* (n rest) 15 av des Belges
☎262988 rm42 ⇌20 🏠20 G Lift B62–125 Lake
🅿*Azur-Pneu* cours Gambetta 7 ☎262387 N🚗
🅿⛽*Clinque-Auto* 16 r F-Dol ☎262118 Ren G10
🅿⛽*Côte d'Azur* 2 cours Gambetta ☎261960
N🚗 Frd
🅿⛽*Sextius Electric* 50 av P-Brossolette
☎276238 N🚗 Ren
🅿⛽*Verdun-Aix* bd de la République 28
☎279805 N🚗 Ren
At **Celony** (3km SW on N7)
☆☆ *Relais du Soleil* r d'Avignon N7 ☎233309
rm25 ⇌25 G ◖
At **Eguilles** (11km NW)
★★*Belvedere* ☎246292 rm17 (A11) ⇌9 🏠8
LD B72–117 M35 Pn118–122 Pool

Aix-les-Bains† 73 (Savoie) 22,300 (☎79)
Map **27** B4

France

★★★★Albion av d'Albion ☎610244 rm110
⇖85 G Lift May–Sep **Pn**110–220 M50 St15%
Pool Lake
★★★Iles Britanniques pl de l'Etablissement
Thermal ☎350002 rm88 (A8) ⇖43 ⋒20 G Lift
2 May–30 Sep Lake
★★★International 18 av C-de-Gaulle
☎352100 rm62 ⇖57 G Lift B45–140 M35
Pn100–130
★★Parc 28 r de Chambéry ☎612911 rm50
(A8) ⇖14 G Lift Apr–Oct B43–116 M30
Pn90–110 Lake
★★Pavillon pl Gare ☎351904 rm40 ⇖30 ⋒3
G Lift Etr–Oct B38–96 M29 Pn90–150
★Beaulieu 29 av C-de-Gaulle ☎350102
rm31 ⇖15 Lift 1 Apr–1 Oct **Pn**83–100
🛢🏍 **P Seigle** 41 av Marlioz ☎610955 Frd G50

Ajaccio See **Corse (Corsica)**

Albert 80 (Somme) 11,159 (☎22) Map **9** B4
★Basilique 3–5 r Gambetta ☎750471 rm10
⇖6 10 Jan–18 Dec B38–73 M23–52 Pn75–95
★Paix 43 r V-Hugo ☎750164 rm14 (A2) ⇖2 G
B38–66 M23–55&àlc
🛢🏍 **Richard** 39 r A-France ☎750176 Cit

Albertville 73 (Savoie) 17,550 (☎79)
Map **28** C4
★★Million ☎322515 rm30 ⇖26 G Lift
B62–119 M45&àlc Pn150
At **Venthon** (2km NE on N525)
★Chez Teddy (n rest) ☎322383 12 G Lift
B36–51

Albi 81 (Tarn) 49,500 (☎63) Map **16** D1
★★★Grand St-Antoine 17 r St-Antoine
☎540404 ta Hotel Rieux Albi tx520850
rm56 ⇖35 ⋒21 G Lift B85–160 M30–45
Pn140–200
★★Chiffre 50 r Séré de Rivières ☎540460
rm45 ⇖13 ⋒17 G Lift
★★Orléans pl Stalingrad ☎541656 rm68
⋒56 Lift 15 Jan–19 Dec B49–91 M22
Pn100–120
🛢🏍 **Albi** 22 av A-Thomas ☎567903 N🏍 Frd
🛢🏍 **Brison** r de Castres ☎544910 N🏍 BL/Rov/
Tri G5
🛢🏍 **E Puech** 179 av Gambetta ☎541400 Ren G5
At **Fonvialane** (3km N on N606)
★★★Réserve ☎567979 tx520850 rm20
⇖10 ⋒10 Lift 1 Feb–30 Nov LD B101–172
M30–45 Pn160–230 🏊 Pool Lake

Alençon† 61 (Orne) 34,700 (☎33)
Map **8** D3
★★France (n rest) 3 r St-Blaise ☎262636
rm31 ⇖7 ⋒6 B36–78
★★Gare ⎸Ᏼ 50 av Wilson ☎261112 rm22
⇖5 ⋒8 G 2 Jan–25 Dec B47.50–74 M28
Pn122.50
★★Grand Cerf 13 r St-Blaise ☎260051 rm33
⇖17 ⋒1
★Paris (n rest) face de la Gare ☎260524
rm18 ⋒4 G 1 Sep–31 Jul B41–58
🛢🏍 **Guerin** 13 r Demees ☎261328 N🏍 Frd G20
🛢🏍 **B Kosellek** 45 r de Paris ☎264067 N🏍 Lnc
🛢🏍 **Paris** 132 av de Quakenbruck ☎260582
N🏍 Chy/Sim
🛢🏍 **Sodiac** (on N12 3km E of town) ☎260322
N🏍 Ren G30

Alès† 30 (Gard) 45,800 (☎66) Map **27** A2
★★★Christel r E-Quinet ☎522707 rm75 ⇖75
G Lift B95–118 M21–45
★★Grand 1 pl G-Péri ☎861901 rm45 ⇖10
⋒16 G Lift
★Orly (n rest) 10 r Avejan ☎864327 rm44
⎸(A8) ⇖32 ⋒9 G Lift
🛢 **Auto-Service** 914 rte d'Uzés ☎522569 N🏍
BL/Rov/Tri
At **St-Hilaire-de-Brethmas** (2.5km SE)
🛢🏍 **Sud** rte de Nimes ☎864964 N🏍 M/c Ren

Alpe-d'Huez (L') 38 (Isère) 330 (☎76)
Map **28** C3
★★★Chamois d'Or ☎803132 rm40 ⇖24
⋒10 Lift 15 Dec–25 Apr LD B82–210 M50–70
Pn130–195
Altkirch 68 (Haut-Rhin) 6,300 (☎89)
Map **11** B2
★Sundgovienne ⎸Ᏼ (3.5km W on N19)
☎409718 rm31 G Lift 1 Feb–31 Dec
★Terrasse ⎸Ᏼ ☎409802 rm20 ⇖9 ⋒7 G
B27–84 M16.50–40

Alvignac-les-Eaux 46 (Lot) 550 (☎60)
Map **16** C2
★★Palladium av de Padirac ☎386023 rm27
⇖21 ⋒6 G 1 May–30 Sep B61–132 M28–60
Pn98–120 🏊 Pool

Ambert 63 (Puy-de-Dôme) 8,100 (☎73)
Map **27** A4
★★Livradois pl du Livradois ☎821001 rm14
⇖4 ⋒3 G 1 Nov–30 Sep
★Terminus pl de la Gare ☎820803 tx39794
rm12 ⇖2 ⋒6 G 1 Feb–31 Dec
🛢🏍 **24 Mavel** 22 av MI-Foch ☎820050
Chy/Sim G25

Amboise 37 (Indre-et-Loire) 11,150 (☎47)
Map **9** A2
★★★Choiseul 36 quai Violettes ☎572383 rm14
⇖14 G Mar–Nov
★★Bellevue quai C Guinot ☎570226 rm25
⇖10 ⋒15 Mar–31 Dec
★★Château de Pray (2km NE on N751)
☎572367 rm16 ⇖11 ⋒4 G 5 Feb–31 Dec LD
B116–152 M46–52 Sea
★★Lion d'Or 17 quai C-Guinot ☎570023
rm23 ⇖14 G Mar–20 Nov LD B47–105
M36–65 Pn77–100 Sea
★Brèche 26 r J-Ferry ☎570079 rm15 ⇖4
⋒2 G 20 Feb–10 Jan LD B32–86 M22–26
Pn62–84 Sea
★France & Cheval Blanc 6 quai C-de-Gaulle
☎570244 rm21 ⇖8 G 1 Mar–30 Nov LD
B34–94 M22–30 Pn60–83
★Parc 8 r L-de-Vinci ☎570693 rm15 (A1)
⇖8 ⋒5 1 Mar–30 Dec LD B47–121 M28–50
🛢🏍 **SAVEA** rte de Bléré ☎570654 Ren

Amélie-les-Bains 66 (Pyrénées-Orientales)
4,050 (☎69) Map **22** D4
★★★Thermes r des Thermes ☎300100
rm83 ⇖28 ⋒14 G Lift

Amiens† 80 (Somme) 136,800 (☎22)
Map **9** B4
★★★Grand Univers (n rest) 2 r Noyon
☎915251 rm41 ⇖25 ⋒15 Lift B69–117
★★Carlton-Belfort 42 r de Noyon ☎922644
rm41 ⋒8 Lift B75–148 M50–80 Pn175–210
★★Francitel 8 pl A Fiquet ☎913632 tx81962
rm20 ⋒9 G B48–72 M30 Pn110–124 St12%
★★Nord-Sud 11 r Gresset ☎915903 rm26
⇖20 B66–181 M36–52 Pn200
★Normandie (n rest) 1 bis r Lamartine
☎917499 rm23 ⇖2 ⋒8 G B41–83
★Paix (n rest) 8 r de la République ☎913921
rm26 ⇖5 5 Jan–15 Dec B46–78
🏍 **Gueudet** 19 r des Otages ☎920941 N🏍 Ren
🛢🏍 **Leroux** 48 r G-de-Rumilly ☎953720 N🏍
Frd
At **Boves** (7km SE on D334)
☆☆☆ **Novotel Amiens Est** ☎915481 tx140731
rm60 ⇖60 Lift B120–140 Pool
At **Dury** (5km S on N16)
🏍 **Renel** N 16 ☎954242 N🏍 Lnc/Maz/Opl/Vau

Andelys (Les) 27 (Eure) 8,300 (☎32)
Map **9** A4
★Chaine d'Or pl St-Saveur ☎31 rm11 ⇖6
1 Feb–31 Jan

Andlau 67 (Bas-Rhin) 1,900 (☎88)
Map **11** B3

★★Kastelberg LE r du Gl-Köenig ☎089783
rm41 (A10) ⇆30 G LD B54–110 M30–60
Pn94.50–96.50

Andrezieux-Bouthéon See St-Etienne

Angers† **49** (Maine-et-Loire) 143,000 (☎41)
Map **8** C2
★★★Anjou 1 bd Ml-Foch ☎882482 rm50
⇆30 ▥18 G Lift B83–124
★★Boule d'Or 27 bd Carnot ☎437656
tx72930 rm28 ⇆10 G LD B41.50–88
M26.50–68
★★Croix de Guerre 23 r Château-Gontier
☎886659 rm28 ⇆10 ▥4 G B44.50–89
M32.50–64 Pn112.50–176.50
★★France 8 pl de la Gare ☎884942 tx720895
rm62 ⇆17 ▥25 Lift B60–114 M40 Pn98–115
★★Progrès ☎881014 tx720930 rm42 ⇆28
▥14 Lift B74–89
★★Univers (n rest) 16 r de la Gare ☎884358
rm45 ⇆7 ▥14 Lift B35–102.50
▯*Citroën* 3 r Vaucanson St-Serge ☎439852
N▩ Cit
▯▧*GAMA* 17 quai Felix Faure ☎436456 N▩
BMW/Chy/Lnc/Sim
▯▧*Grand Angers* 49 rte de Paris St-Sylvand'Anjou ☎802066 Bed/Dat/Opl G
▯▧*Rallye* 4 bis r St-Maurille ☎880339 N▩
BL/Jag/Rov/Tri

Angerville 91 (Essonne) 2,600 (☎1)
Map **9** B3
★France 2 pl du Marché ☎4952003 rm10 G
15 Feb–15 Jan B40–54 Màlc

Anglet 64 (Pyrénées-Atlantiques) 26,500
(☎59) Map **20** C3
★★Biarritz Golf av Guynemer à la Chambre
d'Amour ☎038302 rm25 ⇆25 G 1 Apr–30 Sep
B41.50–68 M28 Pn65–70 St15% Sea
★Fauvettes 69 r Moulin Barbot à la Chambre
d'Amour ☎037558 rm10 G 1 Apr–30 Sep LD
B38 M24 Sea
▯▧*Aylies* Av d'Espagne ☎039813 N▩ Ren

Angoulême† **16** (Charente) 50,525 (☎45)
Map **15** B3
★★★France 1 pl des Halles ☎954795 rm61
⇆34 ▥13 G Lift B49–128 M33–47 Pn110–165
★★Epi d'Or (n rest) 66 bd R-Chabasse
☎956764 rm30 ⇆30
★★Palais 4 pl F-Louvel ☎954145 rm53 ⇆15
▥12 G
★★Terminus (n rest) av de L-de-Tassigny
☎923900 rm38 Lift B68.50–75(Double)
★Flore 414 rte de Bordeaux ☎950176 rm54
(A12) G
▯▧*H Barbet* 62 r St-Roch ☎951428 Dat
▬▧*24 Boutin* 74 r de Paris ☎950493 G10
▯▧*Richeboeuf* 3 Zone Industrielle, La
Madeleine ☎923788 N▩ Frd
▯▧*Sport* 157 r St-Roch ☎921370 N▩
BL/Jag/Tri
At **Champniers** (7km NE)
☆☆☆*Novotel Angoulême Nord* ☎920040
tx790153F rm100 ⇆100 Lift Bfr120 Pool
☆☆*PM16* LE ☎957377 rm30 ⇆30 B84–110
M22–34 Pn100–128
▯▧*Angoulême Nord* RN10 ☎958139
(closed weekends) Opl

Annecy† **74** (Haute Savoie) 55,000 (☎50)
Map **28** C4
See also: **Duingt
Menthon
Talloires
Veyrier**
★★★★Albigny Sofitel av d'Albigny ☎452010
rm70 ⇆62 ▥8 G Lift
☆☆☆*Mercure* ☎510347 tx300816 rm69 ⇆69
B120–140 Pool

★★★Splendid (n rest) 4 quai E-Chappuis
☎452000 tx30793F rm50 ⇆25 ▥25 Lift
★★Faisan Doré LE 34 av d'Albigny ☎230246
rm42 ⇆26 ▥12 G Lift LD B48–126 M30–42
Pn85–110
★★Jeanne d'Arc (n rest) 26 r Vaugelas
☎455337 rm40 ⇆14 ▥7 Lift B40–86
★★Robinson ☎510943 rm32 ⇆24 G Lift
1 May–1 Oct B53–178 M40 Pn98–159
▰ Pool Lake
▯▧*Ducros* 21 r de l'Isernon ☎454265 N▩
BL/Jag/Rov/Tri
▯▧*Parmelan* av du Petit Port ☎231285 N▩
Opl G10
At **Puya (La)**
★★★★Trésoms & Forêt 3 bd Corniche
☎514384 ta Tresotel tx30754 Chacomin
Anncy Tresotel rm46 ⇆33 ▥1 G Lift 15 Feb–
30 Nov B86–198 M63–90 Pn160–198 Lake

Annemasse 74 (Haute-Savoie) 23,700
(☎50) Map **28** C4
★★National pl J-Deffaugt ☎386022 rm45
⇆27 ▥15 G Lift B63–106 M28–45 Pn110–130
★★Parc 19 r de Genève ☎384460 rm30
⇆6 ▥24 G Lift B74–120
▯▧*SADAL* rte de Taninges Vëtraz-Monthoux
☎374245 N▩ Cit

Anthéor 83 (Var) 200 (☎94) Map **28** C2
★★Réserve d'Anthéor ☎448005 rm12
⇆4 ▥8 1 Feb–30 Sep LD B62.50–84 M22–36
Pn95–101 Beach Sea

Antibes† **06** (Alpes Maritimes) 56,350
(☎93) Map **28** C2
☆☆*Côte-d'Azur* (3km E on N7) ☎342479
rm51 ⇆45 15 Dec–3 Nov Pool
★★Laverne (n rest) av Chênes Antibes
☎615423 rm14 ⇆14 ▥1 Sea
☆☆*Mercator* (n rest) quartier de la Brague
(4km N via N7) ☎335015 rm18 ⇆18
B94–134
At **Cap d'Antibes**
★★★Gardiole chemin de la Garoupe
☎6130503 rm20 ⇆5 Mar–Oct B44–156 M47
★★★Résidence du Cap 161 bd J F Kennedy
☎610944 ta Fay Antibes tx470892 rm40 ⇆40
Lift Mar–Oct B200–350(double) M80–90 St15%
▰ Pool
★★Beau Site bd du Cap ☎615343 rm29 (A9)
⇆8 ▥16 Mar–Oct B52–128 M32 Pn92–116
Sea

Apt 84 (Vaucluse) 11,600 (☎90)
Map **27** B2
▯▧*Germain* 56 av V-Hugo ☎741017 N▩ Frd

Arbois 39 (Jura) 4,250 (☎82) Map **10** D1
★★Messageries LE 2 r Courcelles ☎661545
rm26 ⇆8 ▥4 G B48–95 M35–75
★Paris LE 9 r de l'Hôtel-de-Ville ☎29 rm21
(A8) ⇆8 ▥7 G 15 Mar–15 Nov

Arcachon 33 (Gironde) 14,350 (☎56)
Map **15** B2
See also **Pyla-sur-Mer & Pilat-Plage**
★★★Arc (n rest) 89 bd Plage ☎830629
txOmtarc570503F rm30 ⇆30 Lift B89–198
Pool Sea
★★Maris-Stella (n rest) 8 av Ste-Marie
☎830331 rm14 ⇆7 ▥4 G 1 Mar–1 Nov Sea
▮▧*F Dagut* 19 bd Ml-Leclerc ☎830601 N▩
Cit
▯*Dupin* 61 bd Mestrezat ☎831328 N▩ Aud/
MB/VW
▧*Integral Station* 59 cours Lamarque
☎834096 N▩ Frd

Ardres 62 (Pas-de-Calais) 3,200 (☎21)
Map **3** A1
★★Clément pl du Gl-Leclerc ☎354066 rm19
⇆9 ▥4 G 15 Feb–25 Jan LD B47–117 M38–80
Pn115–145

France

★★**Relais** bd C-Senlecy ☎354200 rm11 (A1)
⇇3 ▥7 1 Feb–6 Jan B42–101 M27–48&àlc
Pn96–110
★*Chaumière* (n rest) ☎354124 rm10 ⇇4 ▥1

Argelès-Gazost 65 (Hautes Pyrénées)
3,700 (☎62) Map **21** B4
★*Bernède* 51 r Foch ☎970664 tx53535
rm35 (A5) ⇇3 ▥6
★**Marie-Bernadette** Ⅼ (n rest) 39 r de l'Arieulat
☎970793 rm18 1 Jun–30 Sep B27–41
★*Mon Cottage* 3 r Yser ☎192 rm16 ⇇8 ▥8 G
Lift

Argelès-sur-Mer 66 (Pyrénées-Orientales)
5,115 (☎68) Map **22** D4
★★**Plage des Pins** ☎360022 rm37 ⇇27 ▥4
G Lift 15 May–30 Sep LD B53–132 M30
Pn87–121 Sea
★**Commerce** 22 La rte de Libramont ☎351017
rm46 ⇇6 ▥14 G Lift 20 Jan–31 Dec LD
B37–68 M21–43 Pn67–77

Argentan 61 (Orne) 17,450 (☎34)
Map **8** D3
★★**Renaissance** Ⅼ av de la 2eD-B ☎671611
rm15 ⇇2 ▥4 G LD B45–85 M40–58&àlc
Pn120–140
🛢🔧*Trois Croix* 50 r de la République ☎143
Opl G

Argentat 19 (Corrèze) 3,750 (☎55)
Map **16** D3
★★**Gilbert** Ⅼ av J-Vachal ☎280162 rm30
⇇11 ▥6 G Lift 1 Nov–1 Oct LD B39–99(double)
M23–65 Pn65–95

Argentière 74 (Haute-Savoie) 102 (☎50)
Map **28** C4
★★*Couronne* ☎2 rm35 ⇇13 ▥7 15 Dec–26 Sep

Argenton-sur-Creuse 36 (Indre) 6,800
(☎54) Map **16** C4
★★**Manoir de Boisvillers** (n rest) 11 r Moulin
de Bord ☎041388 rm20 ⇇6 ▥6 G B52–86
★**France** 8 r J-J-Rousseau ☎040331 rm26
(A10) ⇇3 ▥5 G 15 Dec–15 Nov LD B31–73
M18–30
At **Vivier** (2.5km SE on D48)
★★**Moulin du Vivier** ☎040323 rm15 ⇇3 ▥3
G 21 Feb–31 Dec B50–79 M20–35 Pn75

Arles† **13** Bouches-du-Rhône 50,350 (☎90)
Map **27** B2
★★★★*Jules César* bd des Lices ☎964976
tx49635 rm65 ⇇32 ▥17
☆☆☆**Cantarelles** ☎964410 txChamco Arles
420763 rm35 ⇇34 ▥1 B84–149 M30&àlc
Pn107–128 Pool
★★★**Europa** Pont de Crau ☎961754
tx440096 rm33 (A5) ⇇28 ▥5 G Lift LD
B78–102 M26 Pn100–105 Pool
★★★**Forum** (n rest) 10 pl Forum ☎960024
rm45 ⇇35 ▥3 Lift 20 Jan–20 Dec B50–154
Pool
★★★**Cloitre** 10 r du Cloitre ☎962950 rm35
(A10) ⇇8 ▥16 1 Mar–15 Nov LD B37.50–94
M23
★★*D'Arlatan* (n rest) 26 r Sauvage ☎963675
rm50 (A8) ⇇29 ▥16 G
★★**Mireille** 2 pl St-Pierre ☎964161
tx420763 rm35 (A19) ⇇27 ▥4 Etr–Sep
B48–142 M30 Pn90–131 Pool
★★**Regence** (n rest) 5 r M-Jouveau ☎963985
rm18 ⇇6 ▥2 B44–99(double)
★*Lamartine* 1 r M-Jouveau ☎1383 rm32 ▥7
🛢🔧*24 Comercial-Auto* rte de Tarascon
☎963220 N🛢960815 Cit G50

Arnay-le-Duc 21 (Côte-d'Or) 2,500 (☎80)
Map **10** C2
★*Terminus* Ⅼ r Arquebuse ☎09 rm12 ▥5 G
7 Feb–6 Jan LD B33–61 M24–54

Arras† **62** (Pas-de-Calais) 50,400 (☎21)
Map **3** B1

★★★**Univers** 3 pl Croix Rouge ☎213401
rm38 ⇇17 ▥4 G B58–111 Màlc Pn120–150
★★**Des Grandes Arcades** 8 Grand pl ☎233089
rm22 ⇇8 B37–72 M22–50 Pn60–75
★**Astoria-Carnot** pl de la Gare ☎210814
rm32 ⇇6 ▥8 LD B49–97 M33&àlc
★**Chanzy** Ⅼ 8 r Chanzy ☎210202 rm20 (A8)
⇇6 ▥4 G B36–115 M27
🛢🔧**Central** 183 av Kennedy ☎230824 N🛢
M/c Bed/Opl
🛢🔧**Grands Artois** 40 r Notre-Dame de Lorette
☎230256 N🛢 Ren
🛢🔧**Houviez** 17 r de Lens ☎215441 N🛢 AR/
Hon
🛢🔧**24 Leclercq** 38 bd de Strasbourg ☎216233
N🛢 BL
At **Fresnes-les-Montauban** (13km N)
☆☆☆**Grill** RN 50 ☎216549 tx120945 Abomell
319 rm40 ⇇40 B76.50–117 M30
Pn136.50–150.50
At **Tilloy-les-Nofflaines** (3.5km)
🛢🔧**Nord Service** ☎212474 N🛢 Ren G10

Arreau 65 (Hautes-Pyrénées) 950 (☎62)
Map **21** B4
At **Cadéac** (2km S)
★★**Val d'Aure** ☎063 rm28 (A9) ⇇4 ▥8 G
1 Jun–1 Oct B61–94 M24–67 Pn69–88

Arsy See **Compiègne**

Artemare 01 (Ain) 850 (☎79) Map **27** B4
★*Berrard* Ⅼ ☎873010 rm24 (A16) G B30–44
M16–65 Pn55

Arvert 17 (Charente-Maritime) 2,400 (☎46)
Map **15** B2
★★**Villa Fantaisie** Ⅼ ☎364009 rm23 ⇇7 ▥2
LD B54–122 M32–70 Pn105–125

Ascain 64 (Pyrénées-Atlantiques) 1,900 (☎59) Map **20** C2
★★**Etchola** ☎540008 rm28 (A7) ⇇7 ▥16 G
Jun–Sep B43–126 M46–90 Pn83–155
★★*Rhûne* pl d'Ascain ☎540004 rm33 (A)
⇇23 ▥2 G 1 Apr–15 Oct

Assevillers See **Peronne**

Aubenas 07 (Ardèche) 13,750 (☎75)
Map **27** A3
🛢🔧*R Nave* bd St-Didier ☎352676 AR/BL/MB
G10

Aubusson 23 (Creuse) 6,850 (☎55)
Map **16** D3
★★**France** Ⅼ 6 r Déportés-Politiques ☎661022
rm30 (A4) ⇇9 ▥8 G LD B40–116(double)
M21–80
★**Lion d'Or** 3 pl d'Espagne ☎661388 rm14
⇇3 ▥2 Feb–Dec B35–63 M30 Pn65

Auch† **32** (Gers) 25,100 (☎62) Map **16** C1
★★★**France** pl de la Libération ☎050044
tx520474 rm32 ⇇20 ▥10 G Lift 1 Feb–31 Dec
B60–256 M58–92
★★**Poste** 5 r C Desmoulins ☎050236 rm32
⇇10 ▥15 G B50–99 Pn94–121
🛢🔧*ANAS* 150 rte d'Agen ☎050145 N🛢
Aud/VW G4

Audierne 29 (Finistère) 3,700 (☎98)
Map **7** A3
★★**Cornouaille** (n rest) ☎700913 rm20
(A10) ⇇13 ▥5 G 25 Jun–25 Sep B50–113 Sea

Aulnay-sous-Bois 93 (Seine) 78,210
Map **10** B3
☆☆☆**Novotel** rte de Gonesse (RN 370)
☎9292297 tx691568 rm140 ⇇140 Lift
B120–140 Pool

Aumale 76 (Seine-Maritime) 3,160 (☎35)
Map **9** B4
★*Dauphin* r St-Lazare ☎934192 rm11 ▥2 G
LD B35–51(double) M25–36.50

Aunay-sur-Odon 14 (Calvados) 2,950
(☎31) Map **8** D3

★**St Michel** 6 r Caen ☎776316 rm7 G LD B35–45 M33 ⏴

Auray 56 (Morbihan) 10,400 (☎97) Map **7** B2
⏷▶**Y Guillouet** av du MI-Foch ☎240594 N⏴ Ren G

Aurillac†15 (Cantal) 33,400 (☎71) Map **16** D2
★★**Grand Bordeaux** LE (n rest) 2 av de la République ☎480184 rm50 (A13) ⏴/▥37 G Lift B48–80
⏷▶**R Malroux** 100 av C-de-Gaulle ☎480481 Ren G10
⏷▶**Vidal** 47 av Pupilles-de-la-Nation ☎480151 N⏴ Bed/Opl G20

Auron 06 (Alpes-Maritimes) 1,610 (☎93) Map **28** C2
★★★**Pilon** ☎022015 tx46794F Pilon rm40 ⏴20 ▥10 Lift 15 Dec–10 Apr 1 Jul–31 Aug ⏴ Pool

Autun†71 (Saône-et-Loire) 22,950 (☎85) Map **10** C1
★★**Tête Noire** LE 3 r de l'Arquebuse ☎522539 rm20 ⏴4 ▥9 G LD B50–78.50 M27–48
★**Vieux Moulin** LE Porte d'Arroux ☎521090 rm11 ⏴3 ▥3 G

Auvillers-les-Forges 08 (Ardennes) 800 (☎24) Map **10** C4
★★**Hostellerie Lenoir** LE ☎363011 rm24 ⏴12 ▥6 Lift 10 Feb–2 Jan B83–155 Màlc

Auxerre†89 (Yonne) 40,000 (☎86) Map **10** C2
★★★**Maxime** 2 quai de la Marine ☎521419 rm25 ⏴23 ▥2 G Lift
★★**Cygne** (n rest) 14 r 24 Août ☎522651 rm24 ⏴10 ▥14 G B68–126
★★**Fontaine** 12 pl C Lepère (off r de Paris) ☎524080 rm33 ⏴23 ▥1 G Lift 15 Jan–15 Dec B48–138 M45–60 Pn130–140
★★**Normandie** (n rest) 41 bd Vauban ☎525780 rm44 ⏴13 ▥16 G B59–95
▶**Bourgogne** 38 av de la Tournelle ☎523716 N⏴ N⏴ Ren
⏷**G Lelouche** 46–48 r du 24 Août ☎520836 BL/Tri

Auxonne 21 (Côte-d'Or) 6,950 (☎80) Map **10** D1/2
★**Corbeau** LE 1 r de Berbis ☎363210 rm60 ⏴10 G 5 Feb–5 Jan LD B52–92 M24–50
⏷▶**24 Cone** ☎363220
At **Villers les Pots** (5km NW)
★★**Auberge du Cheval Rouge** LE ☎363411 rm10 ⏴6 ▥4 B41–70 M17–50

Avallon 89 (Yonne) 9,300 (☎86) Map **10** C2
★★★★**Poste** 13 pl Vauban ☎340612 rm30 ⏴25 ▥1 G 15 Feb–15 Nov
★★**Chapeau Rouge** 11 r de Lyon ☎341434 rm40 ⏴30 G
★★**Relais Fleuri** (3.5km E on N6) ☎340285 rm30 ⏴30 B95–119 M40&àlc
⏷▶**Grand de la Porte du Mowan** 2 rte de Paris ☎341303 N⏴ Toy G4
⏷▶**24 M Gueneau** 26 r de Paris ☎341927 M/c Ren G10
At **Cousin Valley** (3km W on D427)
★★**Moulin des Ruats** ☎340714 rm21 ⏴13 1 Mar–1 Nov LD B62–174 Màlc St15%

Avignon†84 (Vaucluse) 93,050 (☎90) Map **27** B2
See also **Villeneuve-les-Avignon**
★★★★**Europe** 12 pl de Crillon ☎814136 ta Horope tx42965 rm65 ⏴46 ▥8 Lift
☆☆☆☆**Holiday Inn** rte Marseille ☎829910 tx431994 rm105 ⏴105 Lift B124–182 M45àlc Pool
☆☆☆**Novotel** N7 ☎826009 tx432878 rm79 ⏴79 Lift B120–140 Pool

★★**Angleterre** (n rest) 29bd de Raspail ☎863431 rm32 ⏴6 ▥13 B28–75
★★**France** 28 pl Clemenceau (off pl de l'Horloge) ☎825886 rm21 ⏴11 ▥7 25 Jan–8 Jun 25 Jun–8 Jan B53–84 M34–52
★★**Midi** (n rest) 53 r de la République ☎810876 tx431074 rm60 ⏴20 ▥20 Lift 15 Jan–15 Dec B50–95
★★**Regina** (n rest) 6 r de la République ☎814245 rm44 ⏴12 ▥6 G Lift
★**Jacquemart** (n rest) 3 r F-David ☎863471 rm20 ⏴2 ▥6 B32–73
★**Mistral** (n rest) bd du Metz ☎822995 tx42033F Reshotel Mistral rm15 ⏴1 ▥8 B61–75(double)
⏷▶**EGSA** 16 rte de Marseille ☎826289 N⏴ Aud/VW G5
Grand Parking 77a av P-Sémard ☎822196 N⏴ BMW G
⏷▶**SARVIA** 124 av P-Semard ☎820180 Opl
At **Avignon Nord Autoroute Junction (A7)** (8km E by D942)
☆☆☆☆**Sofitel Jacques Borel** ☎311643 tx432869 rm100 ⏴100 G Lift B133–215 M40 Pn213 ⏴ Pool

Avranches 50 (Manche) 11,350 (☎33) Map **8** C3
★★**Croix d'Or** 83 r de la Constitution ☎580488 rm26 (A6) ⏴12 ▥5 G B49–148 M30–110
★★**St-Michel** 5 pl Gl-Patton ☎580191 rm26 ⏴11 ▥4 G 1 Apr–31 Oct LD B49–158 M30–100
⏷▶**24 Bretagne** r Nationale ☎580244 G
⏷▶**Poulain** pl Patton ☎580900 N⏴ Ren G2

Ax-les-Thermes 09 (Ariège) 1,600 (☎61) Map **22** C4
★★**Moderne** LE 20 av du Dr-Gomma ☎642024 rm40 (A13) ⏴7 ▥7 G Lift Xmas–31 Oct
★★**Paix** 2 av A-Authie ☎642261 rm47 ⏴15 ▥6 G 22 Mar–31 Oct
★**Roy René** LE ☎642228 rm28 ⏴6 ▥20 G Lift Feb–Oct LD B57–89 M23–49 Pn75–110
★**Lauzeraie** LE prom du Couloubert ☎642070 rm24 ⏴2 ▥5 16 Dec–31 Oct B34–90 M19–42 Pn60–87

Azay-le-Rideau 37 (Indre-et-Loire) 2,755 (☎47) Map **8** D2
★★**Grand Monarque** LE ☎433008 rm30 (A11) ⏴9 ▥6 G 1 Mar–30 Nov LD B43.50–124 M32–70 Pn110–138

Bagnères-de-Bigorre 65 (Hautes-Pyrénées) 10,600 (☎62) Map **21** B4
★★**Vignaux** (n rest) 16 r de la République ☎950341 rm17 ⏴2 May–Oct B36–68.50

Bagnoles-de-l'Orne 61 (Orne) 700 (☎34) Map **8** D3
★★★★**Thermes** ☎371500 rm95 ⏴68 Lift 5 May–20 Sep B87–259 M58 Pn131–205
★★★**Lutetia-Reine Astrid** bd P-Chalvet ☎370311 rm28 (A8) ⏴14 G 15 Apr–Sep B54–129 M50–98 Pn104–143
★★**Bois Joli** av P-du Rozier ☎370933 rm20 ⏴13 ▥2 Etr–20 Sep
★**Ermitage** (n rest) 23 bd A-Christophe ☎371813 rm38 ⏴12 ▥8 G 28 Apr–30 Sep B44–82

Bagnoles-en-Forêt 83 (Var) 560 Map **28** C2
★★**Auberge Bagnolaise** rte Fayence ☎406024 rm12 ⏴2 ▥3 B44–62(double) M25–38 Pn70–80
★**Miresterel** r de l'Ancienne Mairie ☎406049 rm7 ⏴2 ▥1 Feb–Oct LD B36.50–58(double) M21.50–37 Pn65–71

Bagnolet See **Paris**

Bagnols-sur-Cèze 30 (Gard) 17,800 (☎66) Map **27** B2

France

★★Château de Coulorgues rte Avignon
☎895278 rm25 ⇄25 20 Mar–30 Sep
B133–196 M50 Pn200–250 ✒ Pool
⬥⬥*Stolard* rte de Tresques ☎895636 N⬥ Ren

Bains-les-Bains 88 (Vosges) 1,800
(☎29) Map **11** A2
★★Beau-Site 2 pl de la 2e-D-B ☎363174
rm45 ⇄18 May–Sep

Baix 07 (Ardèche) 550 (☎75) Map **27** B3
★★★Cardinale quai du Rhône ☎618807
rm15 ⇄15 Mar–Oct Pool

Bandol 83 (Var) 6,250 (☎94) Map **27** B1
★★★★PLM Ile Rousse bd L-Lumiere
☎294686 tx400372 rm55 ⇄55 G Lift
B188–405 M90 Pn365–700
★★Flots d'Azur 62 av Gl-de-Gaulle
☎294082 tx40383 rm19 ⇄5 ⬥10
1 Mar–30 Sep Sea
★★Golf pl de Renecros ☎294583 tx400383
rm21 ⇄4 ⬥14 Etr–Oct Beach Sea
★★Provencal r Raimu ☎295211 tx400308F
rm22 ⇄11 ⬥11 G B99–123(double) M24–34
Pn119–127
★★Reserve rte de Sanary ☎294271 rm16
⇄12 ⬥11 1 Feb–30 Nov LD B56–97(double)
M50–100 Pn93–112 Sea

Banyuls-sur-Mer 66 (Pyrénées-Orientales)
4,300 (☎68) Map **22** D4
★★★Catalan ☎383244 rm36 ⇄36 G Lift
1 May–10 Oct B109–160 M35–45
Pn100–170 ✒ Pool Sea

Bapaume 62 (Pas-de-Calais) 4,250 (☎21)
Map **9** B4
⬥⬥24 *M Berteaux* 4 r Briquet Tailliandier
☎071364

Bar-le-Duc 55 (Meuse) 20,550 (☎28)
Map **10** D3
⬥⬥*Billet* 83 r Bradfer ☎790130 N⬥ Peu

Barberey See **Troyes Airport**

Barbezieux 16 (Charente) 5,500 (☎45)
Map **15** B3
★★Boule d'Or 11 bd Gambetta ☎780011
rm28 ⇄10 ⬥6 G LD B52.50–64 M25–75
Pn103–115
⬥⬥ *J Gaboriaud* 13 bd Gambetta ☎781213
Opl

Barbizon 77 (Seine-et-Marne) 1,200 (☎1)
Map **9** B3
★★★★Bas-Breau Grande r ☎0664005
ta Babreau tx690953 rm28 ⇄28 G
30 Dec–20 Nov LD B320(double) M130–170
St15%
★★★Pléiades Grande r ☎4374025 rm18
⇄18 G 15 Mar–31 Jan
★★Charmettes Grande r ☎0664021 rm41
⇄32 ⬥9 LD B66–156 Màlc Pn110–140 St15%

Barbotan-les-Thermes 32 (Gers) 450
(☎62) Map **15** A3
★★Château de Bégué (2km SW on N656)
☎095008 rm40 (A7) ⇄14 ⬥5 G 15 Apr–30 Oct
B68.50–107 M45–50&àlc Pn104–150 Lake

Barcelonnette 04 (Alpes de Hautes-
Provence) 2,350 (☎92) Map **28** C3
★★Grand 6 pl Manuel ☎810314 rm30 (A)
⇄21 ⬥2 G

Barfleur 50 (Manche) 750 (☎33) Map **8** C4
★Moderne pl de Gl-de-Gaulle ☎540016
rm20 (A12) ⇄2 B30.50–64.50 M33–45 Pn90
★Phare ⬥ r St-Thomas ☎540207 rm19 (A5)
⇄5 ⬥4 Mar–Nov

Barneville-Carteret 50 (Manche) 2,000
(☎33) Map **8** C4
At **Barneville Plage**
★★Isles ⬥ bd Maritime ☎549076 rm30 ⇄4
⬥11 Mar–15 Sep LD B38–94 M32–43
Pn83–114 Sea

At **Carteret**
★★D'Angleterre 4 r Paris ☎548604 tx17593
rm46 ⇄19 ⬥4 Mar–Oct Sea
★★Marine 2 r de Paris ☎548131 rm29 ⇄16
⬥7 20 Jan–30 Sep Sea
★★Plage et du Cap ⬥ le Cap ☎548696 rm15
(A4) ⇄10 Etr–Nov LD B64–83 M21–50
Pn66–110 ✒ Sea

Bar-sur-Aube 10 (Aube) 7,450 (☎25)
Map **10** C3
★Commerce ⬥ 38 r Nationale ☎270876
rm17 ⇄9 ⬥4 G Feb–Dec LD B53–140
M45–100

Bar-sur-Seine 10 (Aube) 3,450 (☎25)
Map **10** C2
★★Barséquanais 7 av Gl-Leclerc ☎388275
rm24 (A14) ⇄3 ⬥11 20 Jan–20 Dec B35–78
M18–38 Pn50–68

Bastia See **Corse (Corsica)**

Bastide (La) 48 (Lozère) 200 (☎66)
Map **27** A3
★★Pins ☎334007 rm27 ⇄6 ⬥4 15 Mar–31 Oct
⬥⬥24 *Naud Jean-Mar* ☎334018 Ren

Batz-sur-Mer 44 (Loire-Atlantique) 2,250
(☎40) Map **7** B2
★Calme Logis pl du Murier ☎239016 rm22
⇄10 Etr–Oct G

Baugé 49 (Maine-et-Loire) 4,500 (☎41)
Map **8** D2
★Boule d'Or r Cygne ☎891202 rm14 ⇄1 ⬥3
G 15 Mar–15 Feb

Baule (La)† 44 (Loire-Atlantique) 15,200
(☎40) Map **7** B2
★★★Pléiades 28 bd d'Armor ☎602024 rm40
⇄27 ⬥3 G Lift 1 Jun–15 Sep LD B79–166
(double) M35 Pn92–149
★★★Royal espl Casino ☎603306 rm120
⇄60 ⬥25 Lift Etr–Oct Sea
★★Armoric 4 bd d'Armor ☎603683 rm58 (A)
⇄16 ⬥11 Lift May–Oct
★★Bellevue-Plage bd Océan ☎602855
rm34 ⇄29 ⬥5 Lift Mar–Oct Sea
★★Welcome 7 av des Impairs (off allée
Monettes) ☎603025 rm14 ⇄11 Etr–Sep
LD B75–93(double) M36 Pn103–112
★Ar Vro & Terrasse 49 av Gl-de-Gaulle
☎602144 rm44 (A) ⇄8 ⬥8 Jun–20 Sep
★Concorde 1 av de la Concorde ☎602309
rm44 ⇄22 ⬥22 G Etr–30 Sep LD B94–103.50
(double) M36–42 Pn97–122 Sea
⬥⬥*Minot* av du Ml-de-Lattre-de-Tassigny
☎602071 N⬥ Cit G50
At **Baule-les-Pins (La)**
★Villa d'Azur ⬥ 28 av de la Mer ☎601258
rm10 ⬥6 Mar–Nov

Baux-de-Provence (Les) 13 (Bouches-du-
Rhône) 400 (☎90) Map **27** B2
★★★Baumanière ☎973307 tx42203
Baucabro rm25 (A) ⇄19 ⬥6 Lift ✒ ∩ Pool

Bayeux 14 (Calvados) 14,550 (☎31)
Map **8** D4
★★★Lion d'Or ⬥ 71 r St-Jean ☎920690 rm32
⇄12 ⬥11 G 20 Jan–20 Dec LD B64–113
M35–80 Pn105–113
⬥⬥*Gare* 16 bd Sadi-Carnot ☎920070 N⬥ Ren
⬥⬥*St Patrice Automobiles* 54 r St-Patrice
☎920681 N⬥ Cit

Bayonne† 64 (Pyrénées-Atlantiques)
44,750 (☎59) Map **20** C3
★★Capagorry (n rest) 14 r Thiers ☎254822
tx540376 rm48 ⇄25 ⬥20 Lift B97–130
★★Basses-Pyrénées 12 r Tour-de-Sault
☎250029 rm45 (A10) ⇄11 ⬥12 G Lift
B40–87 Mfrom20
⬥⬥*Centre* 19 r D-Etcheverry ☎551334 N⬥
M/c GM

🛏🅿 *Durruty* av de la Légion-Tchèque
☎256025 N🖢 M/c BMW
i➤➤24 *A Marmande* 117 rte de Pau ☎550561
BL/Jag/Rov/Tri

Beaucaire 30 (Gard) 13,000 (☎66)
Map **27** B2
★★**Vignes Blanches** rte de Nimes ☎591312
tx480690 rm55 ⇌45 🏛5 Lift Apr–15 Oct LD
B57–101 Pn109–169 Pool

Beaugency 45 (Loiret) 6,850 (☎38)
Map **9** A2
★★**Ecu Bretagne** I🇪 pl du Martroi ☎445224
rm15 ⇌4 🏛1 G 15 Feb–15 Jan B41–98
M25–70

Beaulieu-sur-Dordogne 19 (Corrèze)
1,715 (☎55) Map **16** C2
★★**Central** ☎910134 rm34 ⇌10 🏛6 G
15 Feb–2 Jan LD B35–91 M20–43 Pn70–85
★★**Turenne** pl Marbot ☎911016 rm21 ⇌5
🏛18 G 1 Apr–30 Sep B60–113 M20–50
Pn105

Beaulieu-sur-Mer 06 (Alpes Maritimes)
4,300 (☎93) Map **28** C2
★★★★★*Réserve* 5 bd Gl-Leclerc ☎010001
tx47301 rm50 (A1) ⇌50 G Lift Pool Sea
★★★★**Métropole** bd Gl-Leclerc ☎010008
tx470304 rm50 ⇌45 🏛5 Lift Dec–Oct LD
Pn255–670 Pool Beach Sea
★★★**Résidence** (n rest) 9 bis av Albert 1er
☎010602 rm21 ⇌21 Lift B122–143 Sea
★★★**Victoria** 47 bd Marinoni ☎010220
tx470303 rm80 ⇌50 🏛20 Lift 19 Dec–15 Oct
LD **Pn**59–97 Sea

Beaumont-sur-Sarthe 72 (Sarthe) 2,250
(☎43) Map **8** D3
★*Barque* ☎970016 rm26 ⇌6 🏛10 G
★**Chemin de Fer** I🇪 ☎970005 rm16 ⇌2 🏛4 G
1 Nov–30 Sep LD B45.50–78(double)
M23–55 Pn55–80

Beaumont-sur-Vesle 51 (Marne) 500
(☎26) Map **10** C3
★**Maison du Champagne** ☎616245 rm10
⇌6 G 15 Feb–15 Jan LD B33–75 M19–42
Pn76–85

Beaune†21 (Côte-d'Or) 20,000 (☎80)
Map **10** C1
★★★**Poste** 3 bd Clémenceau ☎220811
rm27 ⇌17 🏛2 G Lift 20 Mar–18 Nov
★★★**Cep** 27 r Maufoux ☎223548 tx330690
rm20 ⇌18 1 Mar–30 Nov B67–167
☆☆**PLM** Autoroute A6 ☎220301 tx350627
rm120 ⇌20 B108–143 M38
☆☆*Samotel* rte de Chalon-sur-Saône ☎223555
rm34 ⇌34
★*Central* I🇪 2 r V-Millot ☎222423 rm22 ⇌11
🏛11
🛏🅿 **Central** 40 fbg Bretonnière ☎222803 N🖢
Fia G8
🛏🅿**Monnot** 146 rte de Dijon ☎221102 N🖢 Frd
At **Ladoix-Serrigny** (5km NE)
★★**Paulands** ☎214105 ta21550 rm21 ⇌11
B74–113 Màlc

Beaurainville 62 (Pas-de-Calais) 1,950
(☎21) Map **3** A1
★**Val de Canche** I🇪 ☎903222 rm10 ⇌1 G LD
B32–65 M19–50 Pn57–70

Beaurepaire 38 (Isère) 3750 (☎74)
Map **27** B3
★*Fiard* 25 r de la République ☎866202 rm21
(A2) ⇌6 🏛12 31 Oct–30 Sep

Beaurepaire-en-Bresse 71 (Saone-et-Loire) 550 (☎85) Map **10** D1
★★**Croix Blanche** N 78 ☎741322 rm15 ⇌15
G B66–79 M22 Pn90

Beauvais†60 (Oise) 56,750 (☎4)
Map **9** B4

☆☆☆**Mercure** ZAC du Quartier St Lazare
☎4020336 tx150210 rm60 ⇌60 Lift
B120–140 Pool
★**Palais** (n rest) 9 r St-Nicolas ☎4451258
rm14 ⇌3 🏛11 B55–104
i➤➤24 **Beauvais Dépannage** 14 r de Buzenval
☎4450413 Sab/Ska/Vlo
🛏🅿*De la Porte de Paris* 12 bd A-Briand
☎4452326 N🖢 BL/Tri

Beauvallon See **Ste Maxime-sur-Mer**

Beauvezer 04 (Alpes-de-Hautes-Provence)
250 (☎94) Map **28** C2
★★**Alp** ☎1 tx04440 rm65 (A14) ⇌20 G
1 Jun–31 Aug LD B32–68 M25 Pn78–95 🍴

Bedarrides 84 Vaucluse, 2,030 Map **27** B2
☆☆ **7** I🇪 ☎843892 tx42033 F Reshotel rm20
⇌5 🏛2 Pool

Beg-Meil 29 (Finistère) 3,850 (☎98)
Map **7** A3
★★**Bretagne** ☎949804 rm48 (A18) ⇌6 🏛14
Etr–Sep LD B40–117(double) M31–37
Pn69–137
★★*Duchesse Anne* ☎949107 rm30 ⇌9 🏛14
G Etr–Sep
★★**Thalamot** I🇪 Le chemin Creux Fouesnant
☎949738 rm35 🏛8 Etr–20 Sep LD B44–86
M29–52 Pn75–117
★★*Au Bon Accueil* Fouesnant ☎949814 rm14
Etr–20 Sep LD B40–50(double) M19–43
Pn63–76
★*Plage* Fouesnant ☎949806 rm45 (A) ⇌3
🏛4 G Whi–30 Sep

Belfort†90 (Territoire-de-Belfort) 57,350
(☎84) Map **11** A2
★★★**Lion** r G-Clemenceau ☎211700
tx360914 rm82 ⇌44 🏛38 G Lift B89–136
M29–45
★★**Europe** (n rest) ☎216389 rm50 ⇌20 🏛6
Lift B33–100
🛏🅿**Centre** 21 av Wilson ☎214233 N🖢 Opl
At **Danjoutin** (3km S)
☆☆☆**Mercure** ☎215501 tx360801 rm58
⇌58 Lift B120–140 Pool

Belin 33 Gironde, 2,250 (☎56) Map **15** B2
★**Aliénor d'Aquitaine** ☎889111 rm12 ⇌3
🏛9 G LD B67–114(double) M27
★*Hostellerie de Pins* 7 Gimenez ☎23 rm12
G 3 Feb–31 Dec
🛏🅿*Auto* ☎084 Ren G3

Bellême 61 (Orne) 1,850 (☎34) Map **9** A3
★**Relais St-Louis** 1 bd Bansart-de-Bois
☎331221 rm10 ⇌5 🏛2 G 1 Feb–20 Dec
B34–68 M19.50–51 Pn63.50–79.50

Belley 01 Ain 8,250 (☎79) Map **27** B4
★★**Pernollet** 9 pl de la Victoire ☎243 rm26
⇌17 G 15 Dec–15 Nov

Bellevue See **Houches (Les)**

Bénodet 29 (Finistère) 2,100 (☎98)
Map **7** A3
★★★**Gwell-Kaer** av de la Plage ☎910438
rm24 ⇌14 🏛10 G Lift LD B109–193 M40–65
Pn150–175 Sea
★★**Ancre de Marine** I🇪 6 av l'Odet ☎910529
rm25 (A15) ⇌14 1 Mar–31 Oct B55–128
M36–40 Pn90–130 Sea
★★**Grand** 4 av l'Odet ☎910002 rm56 ⇌14
G 5 May–30 Sep
★★**Ker Moor** ☎008 rm70 ⇌30 🏛10 G
Jun–20 Sep 🍴 Pool Sea
★**Bellevue** (n rest) 14 av Plage ☎910423
rm40 (A10) ⇌5 G Etr–Oct B60–100 Sea

Berck-Plage 62 (Pas-de-Calais) 16,500
(☎21) Map **3** A1
🛏🅿*Darets* 1 bd de Paris ☎091199 G20

Bergerac 24 (Dordogne) 28,650 (☎53)
Map **16** C2

France

★★Bordeaux LE 38 pl Gambetta ☎571283
rm45 ⇌22 ▥10 G 1 Feb–30 Dec B50–94
M28–55 Pn90–105
🅿🅰🅳**Bergerac** 109 r Neuve ☎574211
Bergues 59 (Nord) 4,850 (☎20) Map **3** A1
☆☆☆**Novotel Dunkerque** (7km S on D252B)
☎659733 tx820916 rm64 ⇌64 Lift B120–140
Pool
★Tonnelier 4 r du Mont-de-Piété ☎687005
rm10 G B32–45 M25 Pn70–84
Bernay 27 (Eure) 11,300 (☎32)
Map **3** A3
★Angleterre & Cheval Blanc LE 10 r Gl-de-
Gaulle ☎431259 rm23 ⇌1 ▥2 G 1 Mar–28 Jan
LD B39–77 M35–81
★Lion d'Or LE 48 r Thiers ☎431606 rm28 ⇌5
▥9 LD B36–91 M18–55 Pn100–130
🅿🅰🅳**Robillard** rte de Broglie ☎430999 N🆂
BL/Opl G
Besançon†25 (Doubs) 126,200 (☎81)
Map **11** A2
★★★Frantel av E-Droz ☎801444 tx360268
rm96 ⇌96 Lift B126–176
☆☆☆**Novotel** rte de Trey ☎880700 tx360009
rm107 ⇌107 Lift B120–140 Pool
★Gambetta (in rest) 13 r Gambetta ☎820233
rm26 ⇌12 ▥5 B44–76
🅿🅰🅳**Bever** 4 r Pergaud ☎812801 N🆂 Aud/BMW
🅿🅰🅳**Fournier** 81 r de Dôle ☎820522 N🆂
BL/Jag/Rov/Tri
🅿🅰🅳**Hall de l'Automobile** 36 r Mégevand
☎835463 N🆂 Frd
At **Chateaufarine** (6km SW)
☆☆☆**Mercure** Chemin des Essarts l'Amour
☎880040 tx360167 rm59 ⇌59 Lift B120–140
Pool
Besse-en-Chandesse 63 (Puy-de-Dôme)
1,950 (☎73) Map **16** D3
★★Beffroy LE ☎795008 rm17 ⇌8 ▥5 G Xmas
Etr & May–Sep LD B45–108 M35–80 Pn100–
120
Bessines-sur-Gartempe 87 (Haute-Vienne)
3,000 (☎55) Map **16** C3/4
★★Manoir Henri IV ☎760056 rm6 ⇌4 G
☆☆**Toit de Chaume** (5km S on Limoges rd)
☎760102 tx580915 rm20 ⇌20 15 Mar–
15 Nov B89–111 Màlc Pool
★★Vallée N20 ☎760166 rm20 ⇌6 ▥2 G
(closed 8–23 Oct & 11–26 Feb) LD B34–65
M20–31 Pn61–83
Béthune†62 Pas-de-Calais 28,300 (☎21)
Map **3** B1
★★Vieux Beffroi 48 G D Place ☎251500 rm62
(A22) ⇌23 ▥22 Lift B44–98 M28–75
★Bernard & Gare LE 3 pl de la Gare ☎252002
rm34 ⇌20 ▥5 B33.50–82 M26
🅿🅰🅳**Automobiles Bethunoise** 255 bd Thiers
☎252430 N🆂 Ren
🅿🅰🅳**Mizon** av Kennedy ☎251205 N🆂 Peu
Beynac-et-Cazenac 24 (Dordogne) 410
(☎53) Map **16** C2
★★Bonnet LE ☎295001 rm25 (A3) ▥3 G
25 Mar–31 Oct LD B50–107 M38–70
Pn85–110
Béziers†34 (Herault) 85,700 (☎67)
Map **16** D1
★★★Compagnie du Midi 20 bis bd de Verdun
☎287859 ta Mapotel tx51837 Tlse rm35
(A) ⇌18 ▥11 Lift
★★★Imperator (n rest) 28 allées P-Riquet
☎285485 tx490608 rm45 ⇌12 ▥25 G Lift
B58–95
🅿🅰🅳**Chapat** 1 av du Prés Wilson ☎765534 N🆂
Frd G200
🅰🅳**Grand Foch** 117 av Ml-Foch ☎287318 N🆂
BL/Tri
🅿🅰🅳**24 Renault** 121 av du Prés-Wilson
☎760185 N🆂 Ren
Biard See **Poitiers**

Biarritz†64 (Pyrénées-Atlantiques) 27,700
(☎59) Map **20** C3
★★★★★Miramar 13 r des Vagues ☎240440
ta Miramartel rm200 ⇌200 Lift Etr–Oct Sea
★★★★★Palais av de l'Impératrice ☎240940
tx570000 rm150 ⇌130 Lift Etr–Oct B220–440
Màlc Pn280–350 Pool Sea
★★★★Plaza av Edouard-VI ☎240400
tx570048 rm60 ⇌60 Lift B183–214(double)
M40–60 Sea
★★★Regina & Golf 52 av de l'Impératrice
☎240960 rm54 ⇌54 Lift B92–184 M50 Sea
★★★Windsor Grande Plage ☎240852 rm37
⇌27 ▥10 Lift 15 Mar–30 Nov LD B64–122
M25–48 Pn100–130 Sea
★★Beaulieu pl du Port-Vieux ☎242359
rm27 ⇌10 ▥7 G Etr–31 Oct LD B56.50–94
(double) M28 Pn84–100.50 Sea
★★Marbella 11 r Port-Vieux ☎240604 rm40
(A) ⇌21 Lift 1 Apr–1 Oct
★★St-Julien 20 av Carnot ☎242039 rm21
⇌7 ▥2 17 Jan–15 Dec LD B48–84(double)
M24 Pn75–89
★Palacito (n rest) 1 r Gambetta ☎240489
rm26 ⇌10 ▥8
★Washington (n rest) 34 r Mazagran (off pl
G-Clemenceau) ☎241080 rm20 ⇌4 ▥5
1 Apr–15 Oct B41–92
🅰🅳**Central** carrefour Hélianthe ☎240250 N🆂
Ren
🅿🅰🅳**Dart** 20 av de la Marne ☎241476 Chy/Sim
🅿🅰🅳**Eskualduna** 33 av Prés-J-F-Kennedy
☎242010 N🆂 Maz
🅿🅰🅳**Franco-Américain** av Prés-J-F-Kennedy
☎242127 N🆂 M/c
🅿🅰🅳**Paris Biarritz Automobiles** 48 av du
Ml-Foch ☎241945 N🆂 Aud/VW
🅿🅰🅳**Régina** 50 av de l'Impératrice ☎242020
N🆂 MB G50

Bidart 64 (Pyrénées Atlantiques) 3,000 (☎59)
Map **20** C3
★★★Bidartea N10 ☎549468 rm30 ⇌26
▥4 Lift B63–124 M25–35 Pn98–130 Pool Sea

Bitschwiller See **Thann**

Blanc (Le) 36 (Indre) 8,450 (☎54)
Map **9** A1
★Promenade 36 r St-Lazare ☎371007 rm20
⇌1 G 14 Jan–25 Sep 5 Oct–23 Dec

Blangy-sur-Bresle 76 (Seine-Maritime)
3,450 (☎35) Map **9** B4
★Poste 44 Grand r ☎935020 rm14 G
20 Jan–20 Dec B36–58 M27–35
★Ville 2 r N-Dame ☎935157 rm6 2 Sep–12 Aug
LD B42–62 M21.50–80 Pn70–80 St10%

Blaye 33 (Gironde) 4,300 (☎56) Map **15** B3
🅿🅰🅳**Ferandier** rte de Cars ☎420341 N🆂 Peu

Bléré 37 Indre-et-Loire) 4,150 Map **9** A2
★Cher 9 r Pont ☎297515 rm22 (A8)
⇌1 ▥21 B48–75 M30–45

Blériot-Plage 62 (Pas-de-Calais) 74,905
(☎21) Map **3** A1
★Dunes ☎345430 rm12 G 1 Nov–31 Sep

Blois†41 (Loir-et-Cher) 51,977 (☎39)
Map **9** A2
★Bellay (n rest) 12 r Minimes ☎782362
rm12 ⇌5 ▥1
★Cheverny LE ☎780670 rm9 LD B32–44
M20–37 Pn70 Lake
★Gerbe d'Or 1 r Bourg-Neuf ☎780088 rm22
⇌4 ▥8 G
★St Jacques LE pl Gare ☎780415 tx76935
Lect rm28 ⇌2 ▥1 1 Jan–4 Nov 27 Nov–22 Dec
LD B47–74 (double) M25–39
★Viennois LE 5 quai Amédée-Contant ☎741280
rm26 (A15) ⇌8 ▥2 Jan–Nov LD B40–73
M23–45 Sea

🛏🅗🔊**SERVA** 148 av Maunoury ☎784285 N🍴 Ren

🛏🅗🔊**Wilson** 51 av du Prés-Wilson ☎780695 N🍴

Blonville-sur-Mer 14 (Calvados) 800 (☎31) Map **8** D4

★**Mer** (n rest) 🗲 93 av de la Republique ☎879323 rm20 ⊷13 Etr–15 Sep B48–106 Sea

Bollène 84 (Vaucluse) 11,550 (☎90) Map **27** C2

★★**Relais Belle Ecluse** r Suze ☎701514 rm16 ⊷8 ⋔2 Mar–Jan

🛏🚗**24 R Ladame** Sortie de l'Autoroute ☎701046 M/c Peu G30

🅗🔊**Marignan** av M-Coulon ☎701151 G5

Bonneval 28 (Eure-et-Loir) 4,900 (☎37) Map **9** A3

★★**Bois Guibert** N10 ☎982233 rm14 ⊷6 ⋔8 G 5 Jan–25 Dec LD B39–85 M38–50 Pn110–120

Bonny-sur-Loire 45 (Loiret) 1,700 (☎38) Map **9** B2

🛏🅗🔊**Route Bleue** ☎016332 N🍴 Ren

Bordeaux† 33 (Gironde) 226,300 Map **15** B2

| **AA** | agents; see page 83 |

★★★★**Aquitania PLM** Parc des Expositions ☎508380 tx570557 rm210 ⊷210 Lift B105–180 M30–65 ⅋àlc Pool Lake

★★★**Frantel** 5 r R-Lateulade ☎909237 tx540565 rm196 ⊷196 G Lift B143–190 M55

★★★**Normandie** (n rest) 7 cours 30-Juillet ☎521680 tx570481 rm100 ⊷45 ⋔55 Lift B71.50–132

☆☆**Novotel le Lac** Quartier du Lac ☎509970 tx570274 rm173 ⊷173 Lift B120–140 Pool

☆☆**Sofitel Jacques Borel** Quartier le Lac ☎509014 tx540097 rm100 ⊷100 Lift B126.20–189 M40 Pn200–320 ⅋ Pool Lake

★★**Bayonne** (n rest) 15 cours de l'Intendance ☎480088 rm37 ⊷14 ⋔12 Lift B40–97

★★**Francais** (n rest) 12 r Temple (off cours de l'Intendance) ☎481035 rm36 ⊷8 ⋔23 Lift B42–117

☆☆ **Ibis** Quartier du Lac ☎509650 tx550346 rm124 ⊷124 Lift B66–87

★★**Seze** (n rest) 23 allées Tourny ☎526555 rm25 ⊷12 ⋔8 Lift B65–116

★**Etche Ona** (n rest) 11 r Mautrec ☎443649 rm30 ⊷10 ⋔15 4 Jan–20 Dec B52–103

🛏🅗🔊**A Baillac** 31 r Tastet (off cours d'Albert ☎480622 N🍴 Dat

🛏🅗**A Pigeon** 469 rte du Medoc ☎288428 N🍴 GM

🛏🅗🔊**Stewart & Ardern** 126 cours de l'Argonne ☎913104 N🍴 BL/Jag/Rov/Tri

At **Bruges** (5km NW)

🛏🅗🔊**Palau** rte du Médoc 419 ☎288466 N🍴

At **Gradignan** (8km SW on N10)

☆☆☆**EuroCrest** 1 r Prof Villemin ☎891011 tx550922 rm150 ⊷150 Lift B128–159 M50 Pn185 ⅋ Pool

At **Merignac** (4km W on D106E)

☆☆☆**Novotel** av Kennedy ☎474040 tx540320 rm100 ⊷100 Lift B120–140 Pool

Bormes-les-Mimosas 83 (Var) 3,100 (☎94) Map **28** C1

★★**Grand** rm38 ⊷11 ⋔4 Mar–31 Oct G ⅋ Sea
★**Belle Vue** r Gambetta ☎711515 rm15 ⊷2 ⋔11 1 Feb–30 Sep LD B52–74(double) M34 Pn 80–90 Sea

Bossons (Les)
See **Chamonix-Mont-Blanc**

Bouille (La) 76 (Seine Maritime) 700 (☎35) Map **9** A4

★★**Bellevue** quai H-Malot ☎796057 rm20 ⋔2 Feb–Dec

Boulogne-sur-Mer† 62 (Pas-de-Calais) 49,300 (☎21) Map **3** A1 **See Plan**
See also **Portel (Le)**

| **AA** | Continental Emergency Centre; see page 83 |

★★**Alexandra** (n rest) 93 r Thiers ☎313208 Plan **1** rm20 ⊷4 ⋔6 B44–87
★★**Faidherbe** (n rest) 12 r Faidherbe ☎316094 Plan **2** rm35 ⊷10 ⋔10 G Lift Sea
★★**Lorraine** (n rest) 7 pl de Lorraine ☎313478 Plan **3** rm21 ⊷5 ⋔6 B44–74
★★**Marmin** 10 r Monsigny ☎316115 Plan **4** rm24 ⊷12 ⋔8 Lift
★★**Métropole** (n rest) 51 r Thiers ☎315430 Plan **5** rm30 ⊷2 ⋔15 Lift
★**Hamiot** 🗲 1 r Faidherbe ☎314420 Plan **6** rm24 Lift
★**Londres** (n rest) 22 pl de France ☎313563 Plan **7** rm20 ⊷4 ⋔4 Lift B48–66
★**Menestrel** 21 r de Brequerecque ☎316016 Plan **8** rm15 G LD B31–44 M10–34 St12%
🛏🅗🔊**Diderot** bd Diderot ☎313038 BL/MB/Tri
🛏🚗**M Dufour** 12 r C-Butor ☎314335 Ren G100
🛏🅗🔊**Paris** 33 av J-F-Kennedy ☎316508 N🍴 Frd G5
🛏🅗🔊**St-Christophe** bd de la Liane ☎300911 N🍴 AR/GM G

At **Outreuln** (3km SW)

🛏🚗**24 G Goeusser** 8 r du Biez ☎315235

Boulou (Le) 66 (Pyrénées-Orientales) 3,750 (☎68) Map **22** D4

★**Richelieu** (n rest) r Arago ☎374223 rm20 ⊷4 ⋔9 1 Mar–31 Oct B36–68
🚗**24 Carosserie Nouvelle** N 4 av du Gl-de Gaulle ☎374169 G10
🛏🚗**24 R Padrosa** N 13 ☎374229 G30

Bourbon-l'Archambault 03 (Allier) 2,600 (☎70) Map **16** D4

★★**Parc** r du Parc ☎14 rm65 (A) ⊷15 ⋔3 G Lift 25 Apr–10 Oct

Bourg-en-Bresse† 01 (Ain) 45,000 (☎74) Map **27** B4

★★★**Logis de Brou** (n rest) 132 bd Brou ☎221155 rm30 ⊷18 ⋔12 G Lift
🚗**24 Bugey** 28 av de Pont d'Ain ☎215512 Frd G
🛏🅗🔊**DARA** 10 cours de Verdun ☎211555 N🍴 Cit
🛏🅗**24 ARNO** bd E Herriot, zone Industrielle Nord ☎212297 N🍴 Ren

Bourges† 18 (Cher) 80,500 (☎36) Map **9** B1/2

★★★**Angleterre** 1 place 4 Pillers ☎246851 rm32 ⊷12 ⋔9 G Lift 15 Jan–15 Dec B55–102 M28–46 Pn79–134
★★**D'Artagnan** 19 pl Séraucourt ☎246751 rm33 ⊷33 G Lift
★★**Berry** 3 pl du Gl-Leclerc ☎244358 rm54 ⊷15 ⋔6 G Lift B51–125 M29& àlc
★★**Boule d'Or** 13 pl Gordaine ☎705587 rm48 ⊷6 ⋔6 G 20 Jan–20 Dec
★★**Christina** (n rest) 5 r Halle ☎705650 rm38 ⊷4 ⋔33 Lift
★★**Poste** (n rest) 22 r Moyenne ☎700806 rm33 ⊷12 ⋔9 G Lift

Bourget Airport (Le) See **Paris**

Bourg-Madame 66 (Pyrénées-Orientales) 1,200 (☎68) Map **22** C4
🛏🚗**24 Pallarés** ☎5001 G5

Bourgoin-Jallieu 38 (Isère) 22,350 (☎74) Map **27** B4

★**Negociants** 🗲 22 av des Alpes ☎930204 rm17 ⋔4 LD B39–66 M24–45 Pn87–106
🛏🅗🔊**Parenton** 15 r Pontcottier ☎933410 N🍴 Frd

France

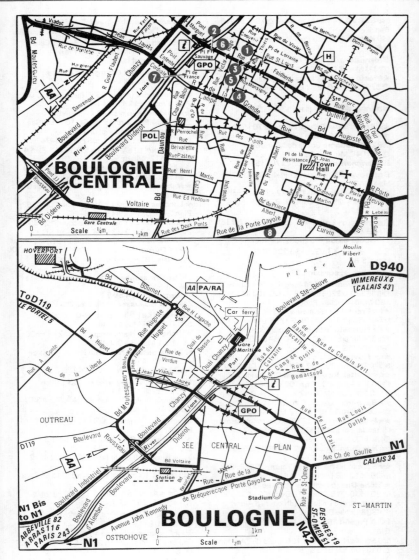

Boulogne

1	★★Alexandra	5	★★Métropole
2	★★Faidherbe	6	★Hamiot
3	★★Lorraine	7	★Londres
4	★★Marmin	8	★Menestrel

🏠🚭24 J B Pellet 5 av Alsace-Lorraine
☎932563 Cit

Bourg-St-Maurice 73 (Savoie) 5,730
(☎79) Map **28** C4
★★**Petit St Bernard** av Stade ☎070432
rm24 ⇆8 🍴4 G Dec–Apr & Jun–Sep B38–101
M25&àlc Pn72–82

Bourgtheroulde 27 (Eure) 1,350 (☎35)
Map **9** A4
★**Corne d'Abondance** pl de la Mairie
☎776008 rm14 ⇆1 G

Boves See Amiens

Brest†29 (Finistère) 172,200 (☎98)
Map **7** A3
☆☆☆**Novotel** N 788 ☎023283 tx940470
rm85 ⇆85 Lift B120–140 Pool
★★★**Voyageurs** 15 av G-Clemenceau
☎802573 rm40 ⇆14 🍴22 Lift B51–123 M30–
70 Sea
🍴🚭24 Brestois 14 r Colbert ☎022020 G100
🏠🚭R Léost 45 r du Moulin à Poudre ☎443324
N🚭 Ren
🚭St-Christophe 132 rte de Gouesnou
☎446980 N🚭 M/c MB/VW

Breviandes See Troyes

Briançon†05 (Hautes-Alpes) 11,500 (☎92)
Map **28** C3
At **Ste-Catherine**
★★★**Mont Brison** (n rest) 1 av de la Gare
☎211455 rm32 ⇆8 🍴20 Lift
★★★**Vauban** av Gl-de-Gaulle ☎211211 rm45
⇆24 🍴14 G Lift LD B62–130 M40 Pn110–140
★★**Moderne** 3 r Alphand ☎555 rm60 ⇆20
🍴20 G Lift

Briare 45 (Loiret) 5,700 (☎38) Map **9** B2
★**Cerf** 22 bd Buyser ☎012038 rm20 ⇆4 🍴4
G 5 Feb–5 Jan

Bricquebec 50 (Manche) 3,200 (☎33)
Map **8** C4
★**Taverne Oudinet** Ⅼ 9 pl Ste-Anne ☎522315
rm10 (A3) G
★**Vieux Château** Ⅼ 4 cour du Château ☎149
rm20 ⇆9 G 15 Feb–30 Sep 15 Oct–3 Jan

Brignogan-Plages 29 (Finistère) 1,050
(☎98) Map **7** A3
★★**Chalet** 44 av Gl-de-Gaulle ☎830624
tx74884 rm40 ⇆10 🍴7 G 1 Jun–15 Sep

Brignoles 83 (Var) 10,500 (☎94) Map **28** C2
★**Univers** Ⅼ pl Caramy ☎691108 rm10 ⇆2 🍴8
G 15 Oct–30 Sep B38–78 M27–34 Pn75–100
🚭M Brun 13 chemin de la Burlière ☎690627
N🚭 Peu
🏠🚭Trans Europe N 7 ☎690737 G23

Brionne 27 (Eure) 4,900 (☎32) Map **9** A4
★**Logis de Brionne** Ⅼ pl St Denis ☎448173
rm15 🍴4 G
★**Vieux Donjon** 19 r de la Soie ☎448062 rm9
⇆1 🍴1 G 15 Oct–25 Sep B38–76 M23–57

Brioude 43 (Haute-Loire) 8,450 (☎71)
Map **27** A3
★★**Le Brivas** rte Puy ☎501049 rm30 ⇆8 🍴22
20 Dec–20 Nov B49–85 M25–70 Pn84–103
★**Moderne** Ⅼ av V-Hugo ☎500730
tx39794 rm21 ⇆4 🍴11 G

Brive-la-Gaillarde†19 (Corrèze) 54,800
(☎55) Map **16** C3
★★**Chapon Fin** 1 pl Ml de Lattre de Tassigny
☎742340 rm30 ⇆15 🍴15 G B50–82 M32
Pn100–113
★★**Crémaillére** Ⅼ 53 av Ml-Staline ☎743247
rm12 ⇆12 28 Feb–Sep 15 Oct–15 Feb
B45–62 M22–55
★★**Quercy** (n rest) 8 bis quai Tourny ☎740926
rm80 ⇆42 🍴38 Lift
★★**Truffe Noir** 22 bd A-France ☎743532
rm31 ⇆28 🍴3 Lift

★**Montauban** Ⅼ 6 av E-Herriot ☎240038
rm21 ⇆2 🍴8 G B37–85 M20–43
🏠🚭G Cremoux 20 av Ml-Bugeaud ☎240913
N🚭 BL/Tri G5
🚭International 23 av des Toulouse
☎742542 N🚭 BMW G15
🏠🚭24 Lavigne 13 av Leon Blum ☎240475
G10
At **Varetz** (14km NW)
★★★**Château de Castel Novel** ☎850001
tx Chamcom 580709 rm38 (A10) ⇆38 Lift
1 May–3 Nov B100–230 Màlc Pn230–260 🏊
Pool

Bron See Lyon

Brou 28 (Eure-et-Loir) 3,650 (☎37) Map **9** A3
★**Plat d'Etain** Ⅼ pl des Halles ☎980398 rm18
⇆5 🍴1 G B33.50–86 M32–46

Bruges See Bordeaux

Bruyères 88 (Vosges) 4,050 (☎29)
Map **11** A3
★**Renaissance** Ⅼ pl Collège ☎575014 rm18
⇆3 🍴3 G

Bugue (Le) 24 (Dordogne) 2,800 (☎53)
Map **16** C2
★★★**Royal Vezere** pl H-de-Ville ☎062001
tx540710 rm52 ⇆41 🍴11 G Lift 1 May–30 Sep
LD B100–161 M37–55 Pn152–210

Bully-les-Mines 62 (Pas-de-Calais)
12,300 (☎21) Map **3** B1
★**Moderne** 84 av Gare ☎291422 rm36
⇆4 🍴5 G LD B29–63 M20–60 Pn60–100

Cabrerets 46 (Lot) 250 (☎65) Map **16** C2
★**Grottes** Ⅼ ☎312702 rm17 (A5) ⇆3 🍴3
1 Apr–1 Nov Pool

Cadéac See Arreau

Caen†14 (Calvados) 122,800 (☎31)
Map **8** D4
★★★★**Relais des Gourmets** 15 r Geole
☎860601 tx170353 rm26 ⇆16 🍴10 Lift
B81–132 M50–100&àlc St15%
★★★**Malherbe** (n rest) pl Ml-Foch ☎844006
tx170555 rm45 ⇆38 Lift B104–173
★★★**Moderne** 116 bd Gl-Leclerc ☎860423
tx170353 rm60 ⇆15 🍴33 G Lift B59–169
M45 Pn140
☆☆☆**Novotel** av de la Côte de Nacre ☎930588
tx170353 rm86 ⇆86 Lift B120–140 Pool
★★**Bristol** (n rest) 31 r du XI-Novembre
(off pl Ml-Foch) ☎845976 rm24 ⇆4 🍴8 Lift
10 Jan–20 Dec B51–94(double)
★★**Metropole** Ⅼ (n rest) 16 pl de la Gare
☎822676 rm38 ⇆11 🍴6 Lift
6 Jan–20 Dec B46–105
★★**Place Royale** (n rest) pl de la République
☎818533 rm42 ⇆9 🍴4 G Lift
★**Bernières** (n rest) 50 r de Bernières
☎815441 rm17 ⇆1 🍴7 B41–76
★**St-Jean** (n rest) 20 r des Martyrs
(off r St-Jean) ☎816873 tx170353 rm15
⇆6 B33.50–69
🏠🚭Chubilleau 43 quai de Juillet ☎845738
N🚭
🏠🚭Eden 24 r du XI-Novembre ☎844032
N🚭 M/c
🚭G Viard 1 av de Paris ☎823090 N🚭 Frd

Cagnes-sur-Mer 06 (Alpes-Maritimes)
29,550 (☎93) Map **28** C2
★★★**Tierce** (n rest) angle bd de la Plage et
Kennedy ☎200209 rm23 ⇆23 G Lift 30 Nov–
30 Oct B95–140 Beach Sea
★★**Cagnard** ☎207321 rm18 ⇆18 G Lift
★★**Savournin** 15 av Renoir ☎206058
tx Chamco-Nice 46041 rm32 ⇆7 🍴11
15 Nov–15 Sep
🚭J Estre 48 bis av de Verdun ☎206155 N🚭
Ren G6

France

At **Cros-de-Cagnes** (2km SE)
☆☆ **Horizon** (n rest) ☎310995 tx46938
Horizon rm43 ⇌22 ▥18 Lift B55–160 Sea
⟊⇗**RNUR** 104 bd de la Plage ☎310831
At **Villeneuve-Loubet** (3km SW)
☆☆ **Mediterranée** (n rest) on N559 ☎200007
rm16 ⇌16 B53–84(double)

Cahors† 46 (Lot) 21,950 (☎65) Map **16** C2
★★**France** (n rest) 252 av J-Jaures ☎351676
tx520394 rm76 ⇌46 ▥30 G Lift B71–124
★**Terminus** Ⅼ (n rest) 5 av C-de Freycinet
☎352450 rm31 ⇌7 ▥18'G Lift B66–114
⟊⟊24 **Recuper-Auto** ☎351516 N☎353503
M/c BL/Dat/Frd/Tri G10
⟊⟊24 **R Noyer** rte de Toulouse ☎351595
N⇗ Ren
⟊⇗ **Grand Garage du Quercy** Pech d'Angély
☎353118 N⇗ Aud/Opl/VW
At **Laroque-des-Arcs** (5km N)
★**Beau Rivage** ☎353058 rm16 ⇌2 ▥14
1 Mar–1 Nov
At **Mercués** (8km NW by N20 & N111)
★★★**Château de Mercués** ☎360001
tx520602 rm48 (A27) ⇌48 Lift 1 Apr–31 Oct
B320–490 Màlc ⇖ Pool

Calais† 62 (Pas-de-Calais) 79,400 Map **3** A1
See Plan
AA agents; see page 83
★★★**Meurice** 5 r E Roche ☎345703 Plan **1**
rm50 ⇌30 ▥12 G Lift B75–118(double) M50
★★**Bellevue** 25 pl d'Armes ☎345375
Plan **2** rm40 ⇌8 ▥8 G Lift B36–82
★★**George-V** r Royale ☎344029 Plan **3**
rm48 ⇌9 ▥8 15 Mar–30 Nov B36–88
★★**Sauvage** 38 r Royale ☎346006 Plan **4**
rm40 ⇌18 B58–101 M26
★**Albion** (n rest) 11 r Vauban ☎343151
Plan **8** rm5
★**Beffroi** (n rest) 10 r A-Gerschel ☎344751
Plan **5** rm16 ▥4 G
★**Richelieu** (n rest) 17 r Richelieu ☎346160
Plan **6** rm14 ▥3 G B38–56
★**Sole Meunière** (n rest) 53 r de la Mer
☎343608 Plan **7** rm14 ▥12 B51–67(double) Sea
⟊⇗ **Calaisienne d'Automobiles** 361 av de St
Exupery ☎347242 N⇗ Peu
⟊⇗ **Commerce** 79–87 quai du Commerce
☎347323 N⇗ Fia G2
⟊⇗ **Minne** 229 bd V-Hugo ☎344408 N⇗
Aud/VW
⇗ **Pierre** 4 r Dolain ☎345894 N⇗ Dat

Calignac 47 (Lot-et-Garonne) (☎58)
Map **15** B2
★**Palmiers** Ⅼ ☎651102 rm15 ⇌3 ▥7 G

Calvi See **Corse (Corsica)**

Cambo-les-Bains 64 (Pyrénées-Atlantiques)
5,150 (☎59) Map **20** C3
★**Bellevue** r des Terrasses ☎257322 rm24
⇌4 ▥10 G B38–61 M20–50 Pn62–70 St10%

Cambrai† 59 (Nord) 41,150 (☎20) Map **3** B1
★★★**Beatus** (n rest) 38 rte de Paris ☎814570
tx82211 rm26 ⇌24 ▥2 G B93.50–120
★★**Motte Fenelon** sq du Château ☎836138
tx120285 rm60 (A30) ⇌54 Lift B46–98
M35 àlc Pn150–160 ⇖ Pool
★★**Mouton Blanc** 33 r Alsace-Lorraine
☎813016 tx820211 rm36 (A6) ⇌14 ▥11 G
Lift 1 Sep–31 Jul B42–82 M47–120 & àlc
Pn110–140
★★**Poste** (n rest) 6 r de Paris ☎813469 rm32
⇌10 ▥19 G Lift B50–124
★**France** (n rest) 37 r Lille ☎813880 rm24
⇌2 ▥5 B41–79
⟊**Beffroi** 8 r XI Novembre ☎812176 N⇗
BL/Tri G5
⟊⇗**Vente** 132 bd Faidherbe ☎815705 N⇗
Opl G5

Camp Long See **Agay**

Cancale 35 (Ille-et-Vilaine) 4,900 (☎99)
Map **8** C3
★★**Continental** Ⅼ au Port ☎586016 rm18 ⇌8
LD B42.50–102(double) M30–65 Pn80–105
Sea

Canet–Plage 66 (Pyrénées-Orientales)
4,360 (☎68) Map **22** D4
★★★**Sables** (n rest) r Vallee du Rhone ☎802363
tx500997 rm41 (A17) ⇌41 Lift B77–142 Pool
★★**Mar-i-Cel** pl Centrale ☎350216 rm60 ⇌57
▥3 Lift LD B48–111 M35 Pn295–350 Sea

Cannes† 06 (Alpes-Maritimes) 71,000 (☎93)
Map **28** C2
★★★★★**Carlton** 60 bd Croisette ☎382190
tx470720 rm330 ⇌330 G Lift B165–420
M85 &àlc Pn150 St15% Beach Sea
★★★★★**Majestic** 163 bd Croisette BP
☎689100 tx470787 rm300 ⇌300 G Lift
B250–420 Màlc St15% Pool Sea
★★★★**Martinez-Concorde** bd Croisette
☎392521 tx470708 rm400 ⇌400 ▥400 G Lift
Jan 15–Oct 31 B100–390 Màlc Pn240–365
Beach Sea
★★★★**Grand** 45 bd Croisette ☎381545
tx470727 rm77 ⇌77 Lift 10 Dec–5 Nov
B190–350 Pn285–460 Pool Beach Sea
★★★★**Méditerranée** 1 bd J-Hibert ☎992275
tx47728 rm125 ⇌125 G Lift Pool Sea
★★★★**Réserve Miramar** 64 bd Croisette
☎382470 tx47767 rm63 (A6) ⇌59 ▥4 Lift
B226–326 Màlc St15%
★★★**Embassy** 8 r de Bone ☎387902
tx47081 rm50 ⇌50 G Lift
★★★**Savoy** r F-Einesy (off bd Croisette)
☎381774 rm55 ⇌35 ▥15 Lift 15 Dec–30 Oct
B125–196 M40–55
★★★**Suisse** r B-Lépine ☎385367 rm73 (A7)
⇌58 Lift 15 Jan–15 Oct
★★**France** (n rest) 85 r d'Antibes ☎392334
tx470749 rm34 ⇌25 ▥8 Lift B75–117
★★**Iles Britanniques** (n rest) 9 bd Alsace
☎390585 rm40 ⇌15 ▥5 Lift
★★**Roches Fleuries** (n rest) 92 r G-
Clemenceau ☎392878 rm24 ⇌8 ▥7 G Lift
15 Dec–15 Nov B36–83 Sea
⇗**Croisette** 30 bd d'Alsace ☎393071 N⇗
Opl
⇗**A Gras** 96 r G-Clemenceau ☎393427
(closed weekends) Aud/Por/VW
⟊⇗**Romeo** 4 bd J-Hibert ☎475541 N⇗ Frd

Capbreton 40 (Landes) 4,600 (☎58)
Map **20** C4
★★**Océan** Ⅼ av de la Plage ☎721022 rm47
(A20) ⇌34 ▥3 Lift 15 Mar–15 Oct B42–84
M20–38 Pn80–93 Sea

Cap Brun See **Toulon**

Cap d'Ail 06 (Alpes-Maritimes) 4,300 (☎93)
Map **28** C2
★★**Cigogne** Ⅼ r de la Gare ☎068257 rm16
⇌8 ▥8 20 Feb–20 Nov LD B99–138 M40&àlc
Pn120–140 Sea
★**Miramar** (n rest) av du 3-Septembre
☎068023 rm27 ▥12 Jan–Nov B34–85 Sea

Cap d'Antibes See **Antibes**

Cap-Ferrat See **St-Jean-Cap-Ferrat**

Cap Martin See **Roquebrune-Cap Martin**

Cap Sardinaux See **Ste-Maxime-sur-Mer**

Carantec 29 (Finistère) 2,600 (☎98)
Map **7** B3
★**Falaise** ☎670053 rm27 ⇌6 G Etr–15 Sep
B29–67 M25–35 Pn65–78 Beach Sea
★**Pors Pol** Ⅼ ☎670052 rm40 ⇌3 ▥21
Etr–25 Sep Sea

Carcassonne† 11 (Aude) 44,650 (☎68)
Map **16** D1

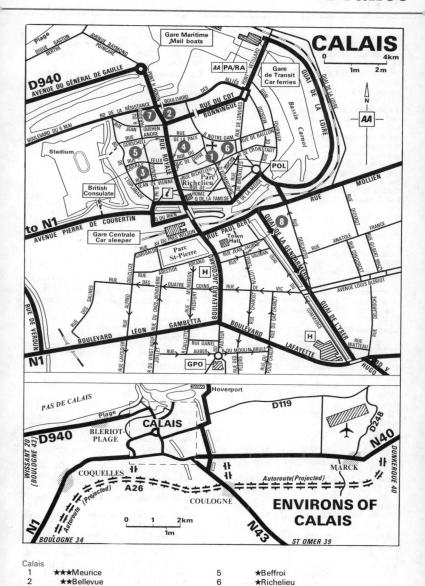

CALAIS

France

★★★***Cité*** (n rest) pl St-Nazaire ☎250334 rm64 ⇌36 ⋔14 G Lift 15 Apr–15 Oct

★★★***Donjon*** (n rest) 2 r Comte Roger ☎251113 rm16 ⇌4 ⋔12 G

★★★**Terminus** 2 av Ml-Joffre ☎252500 tx535135 rm110 ⇌70 ⋔30 G Lift B40–125

☆☆**Croque Sel** rte Narbonne ☎251415 rm11 ⇌11 1 Feb–31 Dec LD B80.50–83 M22–38

★★**Montsegur** 1 av Bunau-Varilla ☎253141 rm21 ⇌6 ⋔15 Lift 15 Jan–15 Dec B61–123 M30

★★***Residence & Auter*** 26 r A-Marty ☎250896 tx Mapotel 51837 rm27 ⇌13 ⋔2 G Lift

★★**Royal** (n rest) 22 bd J-Jaurès ☎251912 rm26 ⇌3 ⋔10 G B40–77

★★**Trencavel** I**E** 286 av Gl-Leclerc ☎251953 rm12 ⇌3 ⋔6 G 1 Mar–20 Jan B75–130(double) M65–110 Pn170–210

i⋑⋑24 Alaux & Gestin av Gl-Leclerc ☎257712 Ren

ⒷⒶⒹ***Audoise*** rte dè Montrial ☎478200 N⋑ Chy/Sim

Ⓑ***Courtade*** 36 av F-Roosevelt ☎250272 N⋑ Frd

ⒷⒶⒹ***Laporta*** 47 av Dr-H-Gout ☎251150 N⋑ BL/Tri

i⋑⋑24 Métropole 42 bd J-Jaurès ☎250401 Tri G20

Carennac 46 (Lot) 400 (☎65) Map **16** C2

★***Fenelon*** I**E** ☎384716 rm24 ⇌8 ⋔4 G Mar–Jan LD B40–71(double) M18–55 Pn55–59

Carentan 50 (Manche) 6,600 (☎33) Map **8** C4

★***Auberge Normande*** I**E** bd Verdun ☎420299 rm13 ⇌6 ⋔2 G LD B35–68 M28

Carhaix 29 (Finistère) 8,950 (☎98) Map **7** B3

★★**France** 14 r des Martyrs ☎930015 rm20 ⇌5 ⋔5 G 20 Jan–20 Dec LD B37–89 M30–54 Pn97–177

ⒷⒶⒹ***Le Saux*** rte de Rostrenen ☎930466 N⋑ Sim G2

Carnac 56 (Morbihan) 3,750 (☎97) Map **7** B2
At **Carnac-Plage**

★★***Armoric*** 53 av de la Poste ☎521347 rm25 ⇌6 ⋔9 Etr–30 Sep LD B57.50–105 M25–42.50 Pn87–100 ⋑

★***Celtique*** 17 av Kermario ☎521149 rm35 ⇌6 ⋔19 Etr–15 Sep LD B50–100 M32 Pn91–110

★***Genêts*** 45 av Kermario ☎521101 rm31 ⇌14 ⋔6 1 Jun–25 Sep B58–103 M38 Pn103–119 Sea

Carquefou See **Nantes**

Carqueiranne 83 (Var) 5,250 (☎94) Map **27** B1

★★**Plein Sud** (n rest) rte Salettes ☎665286 rm17 ⇌5 ⋔12 G 10 Dec–Oct B65–76(double)

Carteret See **Barneville-Carteret**

Cassis 13 (Bouches-du-Rhône) 5,850 (☎91) Map **27** B2

★★★**Plage** pl Bestouan ☎010570 rm29 ⇌13 ⋔16 Lift 15 Mar–Oct LD B60–155 Pn112–133 Sea

★★**Liautaud** av V-Hugo ☎017537 rm32 ⇌14 ⋔15 G Lift 20 Dec–31 Oct LD B51–89 M32–45 Pn77–94 Sea

Casteljaloux 47 (Lot-et-Garonne) 5,450 (☎58) Map **15** B2

★**Grand Cadets de Gascogne** pl Gambetta ☎930059 rm14 ⇌7 ⋔4 G 15 Nov–1 Nov B43–100 M20–80

ⒷⒶⒹ**A Gloriant** N133 ☎930596 Ren G2

Castellane 04 (Alpes-de-Hautes-Provence) 1,300 (☎92) Map **28** C2

★**Ma Petite Auberge** pl M-Sauvaire ☎26 rm18 ⇌4 ⋔15 15 Mar–30 Oct LD B34–64(double) M20–55 Pn75–90

Ⓑ⋑⋑24 **Renault** ☎028 Ren

Castelnaudary 11 (Aude) 10,850 (☎68) Map **16** C1

★★***France & Notre Dame*** 2 av F-Mistra ☎231018 rm32 ⇌10 ⋔7 G

★★***Palmes & Industrie*** I**E** 10 r Ml-Foch ☎230310 tx49935 rm20 ⇌12 ⋔4 G Lift 1 Feb–31 Dec

★***Fourcade*** 14 r des Carmes ☎230208 rm13 ⇌4 ⋔5 G 1 Jun–1 May

Castelsarrasin 82 (Tarn-et-Garonne) 12,250 (☎63) Map **16** C2

★**Moderne** (n rest) 54 r de l'Egalité ☎043010 rm12 ⋔2 G B25.50–43

Castres† **81** (Tarn) 47,550 (☎63) Map **16** D1

★★**Grand** 11 r de la Libération ☎590030 rm35 ⇌15 ⋔11 G Lift 15 Jan–15 Dec B42–115 M27–47

Caudebec-en-Caux 76 (Seine-Maritime) 2,750 (☎35) Map **9** A4

★★**Marine** 18 quai Guilbaud ☎962011 tx770404 rm34 ⇌16 ⋔13 G Lift LD B57–158 M36–72 Pn120–170 ⋑ Pool

★★**Normandie** quai Guilbaud ☎962511 rm11 ⇌2 ⋔3 LD B42–77 M23–50

Caussade 82 (Tarn-et-Garonne) 5,900 (☎63) Map **16** C2

★★**Dupont** 12 r Recollets ☎021202 rm34 (A7) ⇌9 ⋔7 G B45–76 Màlc Pn65–85

★★**Larroque** av de la Gare ☎021014 rm30 ⇌15 ⋔12 G B42–84 M23–42 Pn80–90

ⒷⒶⒹ **Central** 25 bd L-Granié ☎021026 N⋑ Ren

Cauterets 65 (Hautes-Pyrénées) 1,100 (☎62) Map **21** B4

★**Belfort** I**E** r Belfort ☎975018 rm35 ⇌26 ⋔3 Lift Xmas Etr & 1 May–30 Sep B35–69

★★**Mouré** 19 r de Belfort ☎975109 tx530337 rm40 ⇌17 ⋔10 Lift 15 Dec–30 Sep B35–87 M22–40 Pn72–90

At **Pont d'Espagne** (8km SE by N21C)

★***Pont d'Espagne*** ☎300 rm18 Apr–Oct

Cavaillon 84 (Vaucluse) 21,550 (☎90) Map **27** B2

★★★**Christel** Boscodomini ☎710779 tx420547 rm109 ⇌109 Lift B102–115 M25–50 Pn95–105 Pool

Cavalaire-sur-Mer 83 (Var) 2,750 (☎94) Map **28** C1

★★**Bonne Auberge** RN ☎720296 rm35 ⇌13 ⋔10 Etr–Sep LD B69–101 M25 Pn82–100

Cavalière 83 (Var) 850 (☎94) Map **28** C1

★★★***Surplage*** ☎728419 ta Engelfred rm96 (A) ⇌75 ⋔9 Lift 22 Mar–20 Oct Pool Beach Sea

★★**Cap Negre** ☎728046 rm30 ⇌30 Lift Etr–Sep LD B125–141(double) M32àlc Pn134–141 Sea

Celle-Dunoise (La) 23 (Creuse) 750 (☎55) Map **16** C/D4

★**Pascaud** I**E** ☎891066 rm13 ⋔4 G 1 Nov–30 Sep B27.50–49 M17.50–55 Pn65–70

Celony See **Aix-en-Provence**

Cergy See **Pontoise**

Chablis 89 (Yonne) 2,450 (☎86) Map **10** C2

★***Etoile*** 4 r Moulins ☎531050 rm16 ⇌3 ⋔6 G 15 Feb–15 Dec

Ⓑ⋑⋑24 **Terre Route Service** ☎531046 M/c Cit G20

Chagny 71 (Saône-et-Loire) 5,950 (☎85) Map **10** D1

★★**Lameloise** 36 pl d'Armes ☎490210 rm35 ⇌15 ⋔12 G B63–186

★**Capucines** LE rte Chalon ☎490289 rm12
⇌4 ⋔4 2 Jan–30 Nov LD B60–100 M42
★**Paris** 6 r de Beaune ☎490302 rm18 ⇌1 ⋔4
1 Feb–30 Dec LD B45–52 M20–38
⋔⋈*P Peutot* 27 av Gl-Leclerc ☎490073 N⋈

Challans 85 (Vendée) 12,250 (☎51)
Map **8** C1/2
★**Marais** 16 pl Gl-de-Gaulle ☎681513 rm17
⇌4 ⋔13 LD B42–54 M19–65

Challes-les-Eaux 73 (Savoie) 2,600 (☎79)
Map **27** B4
★★★**Château de Challes** r du Château
☎251145 rm70 (A40) ⇌35 ⋔3 G
15 May–25 Sep B43.50–127 M27–50
Pn70–131 Pool

Chàlons-sur-Marne† 51 (Marne) 55,750
(☎26) Map **10** C3
★★**Angleterre** 19 pl Mgr-Tissier ☎682151
rm18 ⇌9 ⋔3 15 Mar–15 Feb LD B46–143
M26–66
★★**Bristol** (n rest) 77 av P-Semard ☎682463
rm24 ⇌11 ⋔13 G B47–84
★★*Mont des Loges* ☎694117 rm23 ⇌1 ⋔22
★★**Pasteur** (n rest) 46 r Pasteur ☎681000
rm27 ⇌9 ⋔8 G B37–82
★**Pot d'Etain** (n rest) 18 pl République
☎680909 rm24 ⇌3 ⋔5 20 Jan–20 Dec
B38.50–89
⋔⋈**Centre** 21 r Thiers ☎644937 N⋈ Frd
⋔⋈*Champagne* 5 av Ampère ☎682910 N⋈
Chy/Sim
⋔⋈*G Poiret* 16 ter r des Martyrs de la Résistance
☎680845 N⋈ BL/Tri
Radiateurs Perret 250 av du Gl-Sarrail
☎681603 radiator repair specialist
⋈24 *Raige* 17 r Clovis Jacquiert ☎681431
G4
⋔⋈**Rennesson de l'Avenue** 133 av de Paris
☎681163 N⋈ Opl
At **Epine (L')** (8.5km E on N3)
★★**Armes de Champagne** ☎681043 rm41
(A12) ⇌9 ⋔20 G 15 Feb–15 Jan B56–116
M26–66

Chalon-sur-Saône 71 (Saone-et-Loire)
60,500 (☎85) Map **10** C1
☆☆☆**Mercure** av de l'Europe ☎465189
tx800132 rm88 ⇌38 ⋔ Lift B120–140 Pool
★★★*Royal* 8 r du Port-Villiers ☎481586 rm54
⇌31 ⋔14 G Lift
★★★**St-Regis** 22 bd de la République
☎480728 rm40 ⇌20 ⋔20 G Lift B60–143
M36–78 Pn126–146
★★**Europe** 11 r du Port-Villiers ☎480386 rm21
⇌5 ⋔3 G B43–96 M30
★★**St-Rémy** (n rest) pl Pont-Paron ☎483804
rm40 ⇌15 ⋔21 G B38–75
★**Laurentides** 28 quai St-Cosme ☎482985
rm33 ⇌13 ⋔13 Lift B48–91 M23–60 &àlc
⋔⋈**Picard** 26 rte d'Oslon ☎488523 N⋈
Aud/VW G30
⋈⋈**Rocade** 91 av de Paris ☎483476 N⋈ Chy/Sim

Chambéry† 73 (Savoie) 58,800 (☎79)
Map **27** B4
★★★★**Grand** 6 pl de la Gare ☎695454
tx320910 rm58 ⇌41 ⋔17 G Lift B112–214
M50–100&àlc
★★★**France** 22 fbg Reclus ☎335118
tx320937 rm48 ⇌42 ⋔6 G Lift B86–160
★★★**Touring** 12 r Sommeiller ☎342781
rm43 ⇌10 ⋔25 G Lift B44–133 M28 Pn90
Actual 381 av du Covet ☎340500 N⋈ BL/Tri
⋈⋈*R Blumet* 1 av de Lyon ☎694473 Lnc/Toy G
⋈⋈*Gauthier & Coudurier* 15 quai de la Rize
☎332809 Peu G20
⋔⋈*Grand Central* 1 r C-Martin ☎343290 N⋈
Cit

Chambon (Lac) 63 (Puy-de-Dôme) 566
(☎73) Map **16** D3
★★**Bellevue** LE ☎886106 rm25 (A) ⋔2 LD
B42–77(double) M26–60 Pn70–84 Lake
★★*Grillon* LE ☎886066 rm18 ⋔7 G Lake

Chambord 41 (Loir-et-Cher) 250 (☎39)
Map **9** A2
★★**St-Michel** LE ☎463131 rm40 ⇌18 ⋔4 G
15 Dec–15 Nov ⋈

Chamonix-Mont-Blanc† 74 (Haute-Savoie)
9,050 (☎50) Map **28** C4
See also **Argentières**
★★★★**Croix Blanche** (n rest) 7 r Vallot
☎530011 tx Mont-Blanc 385614 rm38 ⇌26
⋔10 Lift 1 Jul–31 May B65–130 ⋈ Pool
★★★**Mont-Blanc** pl d'Eglise ☎530564
tx385614 rm59 ⇌53 ⋔2 G Lift 15 Dec–5 Oct
B74–101(double) M45 Pn140–163 ⋈ Pool
★★★**Richemond** r Dr Paccard ☎530885
tx300893 rm54 ⇌38 Lift 20 Dec–17 Apr
17 Jul–17 Sep LD B43.50–127 M37
Pn88–120
★★**Sapinière** r Mummery ☎530763 tx300893
rm35 (A7) ⇌23 ⋔11 G Lift 15 Dec–30 Sep LD
B60–150 M44 Pn115–160
⋔⋈**Bouchet** pl du Mont Blanc ☎530175 Ren
G50
At **Bossons (Les)** (3.5km S)
★★**Aiguille du Midi** ☎530065 rm45 (A) ⇌22
⋔5 G Lift Etr Xmas & 15 May–25 Sep ⋈

Champagnole 39 (Jura) 10,750 (☎82)
Map **10** D1
★★★**Ripotot** 54 r Ml-Foch ☎521545 rm65
⇌40 ⋔3 G Lift 15 May–15 Sep B43–116
M45–65 &àlc Pn90–110

Champillon See **Epernay**

Champniers See **Angoulême**

Champtoceaux 49 (Maine-et-Loire) 1,300
(☎40) Map **8** C2
★**Côte** LE ☎835039 tx720895 rm29 ⇌12 ⋔6
G B42.50–96 M21–38 Pn65–113

Chantemerle 05 Hautes-Alpes 1,500 (☎92)
Map **28** C3
★★*Clos* ☎240013 rm35 ⇌19 ⋔1
15 Jun–20 Sep 20 Dec–20 Apr

Chantilly 60 (Oise) 10,700 (☎4) Map **9** B3/4
★**Angleterre** 5 pl Omer Vallon ☎4570059
rm19 (A4) ⋔4 15 Feb–15 Jan LD B36.50–85
M30 Pn80–100
At **Lys Chantilly** (7km S)
★★★**Lys** Rond Point de la Reine ☎4215019
rm35 (A20) ⇌26 ⋔9 LD B105–149 M47 &àlc
Pn155–170

Chantonnay 85 (Vendee) 7,450 (☎30)
Map **8** C1
★*Chêne Vert* 2 av Mgr-J-Batiot ☎388013
rm20 (A) ⇌2 ⋔2 Mar– 31 Jan
★**Mouton** 31 r Nationale ☎313022 rm12 ⇌2
⋔3 Nov–Sep LD B29–76 M25–38 Pn85–130
⋔**Chauveau-Puaud** 20 av G-Clemenceau
☎313255 N⋈ Cit G9

Chapelle-en-Vercors (La) 26 (Drôme)
850 (☎75) Map **27** B3
★*Bellier* ☎482003 rm13 (A) ⇌7 ⋔1
10 Jun–25 Sep

Charavines 38 (Isère) 1,200 (☎76)
Map **27** B4
★★**Hostellerie Lac Bleu** LE (1.5km N on D50)
☎066048 rm15 ⇌2 ⋔8 Mar–30 Oct
B40–88 M20–50&àlc Pn70–85 Lake

Charbonnières-les-Bains See **Lyon**

Charleville-Mézières† 08 (Ardennes)
63,350 (☎24) Map **10** C4
⋔⋈*C Cailloux* 50 Chaussée de Sedan ☎570101
N⋈ Frd

France

ôᎯᏋ **Central** 20 av J-Jaurès ☎332211 N☸
Chy/Sim
At **Villers-Semeuse** (5km E)
☆☆☆ **Mercure** ☎570529 tx840076 rm67 ➯67
Lift B120–140 Pool

Charmes 88 (Vosges) 6,000 (☎29)
Map **11** A3
★ **Central** Ⓔ 10 r des Capucins ☎380240
rm12 ₥8 G B37–50(double) M20–60
Pn57–64(double)

Charmoy 89 (Yonne) 628 Map **10** C2
★ **Relais de Charmoy** ☎6 rm10 ➯2 ₥4
Feb–Dec LD B33.50–61 M15–42 St15%

Charolles 71 (Saone-et-Loire) 4,350 (☎85)
Map **10** C1
★ **Moderne** Ⓔ 10 av de la Gare ☎240702 rm21
(A7) ➯12 ₥12 G Feb–23 Dec B47–139 M30–70 Pool

Chartres† 28 (Eure-et-Loir) 41,300 (☎37)
Map **9** A3
★★★ **Grand Monarque** 22 pl des Epars
☎210072 rm43 ➯22 ₥8 G Lift
★★ **France** 10 pl des Epars ☎210007 rm40
➯13 G Lift
★★ **Paris** Ⓔ 6 pl de la Gare ☎211013 rm12 ➯1
₥5 16 Feb–20 Aug 6 Sep–31 Jan LD B34–73
M26–44
★★ **Jehan-de-Beauce** 19 av J-de-Beauce
☎210141 rm46 ₥29 Lift
★ **Ouest** (n rest) 3 pl Semard ☎214327 rm26
➯15 B35–80
★ **Poste** 3 r du Gl-König BP152 ☎210427 rm55
➯25 ₥15 G Lift B37–132 M22–40 Pn81–198
ôᎯ **24 Bellenger** 8 av J-de-Beauce ☎213383
Sim
ôᎯᏋ **Paris Brest** 80 r Francois-Lepine ☎211388
N☸ Frd
ôᎯᏋ **Rueller** 104 r fbg la Grappe ☎215119 N☸
Ren
At **Lucé** (SW on N27)
ôᎯᏋ **Sport** r d'Illiers ☎212479 N☸ BL/Jag/Vlo

Chartre-sur-le-Loir (La) 72 (Sarthe)
1,950 (☎43) Map **8** D2
★★ **France** Ⓔ 20 pl de la République ☎444016
ta Pasteau rm32 (A15) ➯11 ₥14 G
1 Mar–31 Jan LD B40–101 M28–65 Pn68–80

Chasseneuil See **Poitiers**

Château-Arnoux 04 (Alpes-de-Hautes-
Provence) 6,250 (☎92) Map **27** B2
★ **Bonne Etape** N85 ☎640009 tx430605 rm18
➯10 ₥8 G 15 Feb–2 Jan LD B105–250(double)
M55–115 Pool Lake
At **St-Auban** (4km SE on N96)
ôᎯ **24 Guillaume** ☎641710 Ren G10

Châteaubriant 44 (Loire-Atlantique)
13,850 (☎40) Map **8** C2
★★ **Ferriere** ☎811012 rm11 ➯6 ₥3 B103–114
M20–45 Pn 115
★ **Armor** (n rest) 19 pl Motte ☎811119 rm20
➯6 ₥7 Lift
★ **Relais Ville en Bois** Ⓔ rte Nantes ☎810144
rm10 (A) ➯3 ₥2

Château Chinon 58 (Nièvre) 2,950 (☎86)
Map **10** C1
★★ **Vieux Morvan** pl Mairie ☎850501 rm23
₥11 1 Jan–15 Dec B34–83 M24–57 Pn59–80

Châteaudun 28 (Eure-et-Loir) 16,150 (☎37)
Map **9** A2
★★ **Beauce** 50 r de Jallans ☎451475 rm22
➯8 ₥8 G 2 Jan–12 Dec LD B46–88
M30–65 Pn105–113
★ **Trois Pastoureaux** 31 r A-Gillet ☎450162
rm10 (A7) ➯2 G (closed Feb) B30–54(double)
M19–26 Pn fr52
ôᎯᏋ **L Touchard** bd du 8 Mai ☎450332 N☸
Aud/VW

Châteaufarine See **Besançon**

Château-Gontier 53 (Mayenne) 8,650
(☎43) Map **8** C2
★★ **Mirwault** (1.5km N by r Basse-du-Rocher)
☎071317 rm10 ₥3 G 1 Feb–24 Dec LD
B39.50–65 M25–65
★ **Anglais** Ⓔ 10 pl Gare ☎071034 rm16 ➯1 ₥1 G
B32.50–51.50 M20 Pn55–60

Château-la-Vallière 37 (Indre-et-Loire)
1,600 (☎47) Map **8** D2
ôᎯᏋ **Esnault** rte Tours ☎24004 N☸ Cit

Châteaulin 29 (Finistère) 5,700 (☎98)
Map **7** A3
At **Port-Launay** (2.5km NE)
★ **Bon Accueil** Ⓔ rte de Brest ☎861577 rm59
➯17 ₥15 G Lift LD B43–91 M25–40
Pn58–120 Lake

Châteauneuf-sur-Loire 45 (Loiret)
5,700 (☎38) Map **9** B2
★ **Nouvel du Loiret** 4 pl A-Briande ☎894228
rm21 ➯4 ₥5 G 3 Jan–18 Dec LD B39–86
M21–38 Pn81–144

Châteauroux† 36 (Indre) 55,650 (☎54)
Map **9** A/B1
★★ **France** 16 r V-Hugo ☎340080 rm44 ➯20
₥10 G Lift
★★ **Résidence** 11 r Marins ☎343630 rm14
➯5
★ **Central** (n rest) 19 av de la Gare ☎340100
rm6 (A)
ôᎯ **Caberry** 124 rte de Blois ☎342362
(closed Sun and Mon) Aud/VW
ôᎯᏋ **Pabanel** 54 av de la Gare ☎340796 N☸ Frd
iᎯ **24 J Sarraf** 34 rte d'Argenton ☎343538
N☸ Ren G5

Château-Salins 57 (Moselle) 2,570 (☎87)
Map **11** A3
★ **Vallet** 50 av Napoleon 1-er ☎051048 rm16
➯16 G Nov–30 Sep

Château-Thierry 02 (Aisne) 13,900 (☎23)
Map **10** C3
★★ **Ile de France** (3km N on N37) ☎831012
rm31 ➯6 ₥16 Lift LD B44–90 M20.50
☆ **Girafe** (n rest) pl A-Briand ☎830206 rm29
(A10) ➯3 ₥9 G B37–81
ôᎯᏋ **Bachelet** 19 quai de la Poterne ☎832178
N☸ M/c Bed/Lnc/Opl G30
ôᎯᏋ **Tourisport** Nogentel ☎831128 BL/Tri G

Châtelaillon-Plage 17 (Charente-Maritime)
5,400 (☎46) Map **15** B4
★★ **Grand** 13 av Gl-Leclerc ☎351239 rm27
➯9 ₥9 Whi–15 Sep
★★ **Hostellerie Select** 1 r G-Musset
☎351059 rm23 ➯6 ₥5 G
★ **Majestic** Ⓔ rte de St-Marsault ☎461014
rm30 ➯9 ₥12 G LD B37–89 M22–50
Pn65–95
ôᎯᏋ **M Aguillon** 25 av des 4 Sergents ☎351449
N☸ Ren

Châtelguyon 63 (Puy-de-Dôme) 3,700
(☎73) Map **16** D3
★★★ **Hermitage** 18 r Brocqueville ☎860034
rm70 (A) ➯35 Lift 5 May–1 Oct
★★★ **International** r A-Punett ☎860672 rm70
➯45 ₥11 Lift 25 Apr–2 Oct B47–118 M32–50
Pn93–155

Châtellerault† 86 (Vienne) 38,300 (☎49)
Map **8** D1
★★★ **Moderne** 74 bd Blossac ☎213011
tx791801 rm38 ➯9 ₥19 G Lift B49–164
M30–80
★★ **Croissant** av J-F-Kennedy ☎210177 rm20
➯8 Lift
★★ **Escale** (n rest) 17 av d'Argenson ☎211350
rm32 ₥15 G Lift
★★ **Univers** 4 av G-Clemenceau ☎212353
rm30 ➯6 ₥12 G Lift LD B44–97 M25–80

France# France

🅱🅳**Burban & Lanoue** L'Oree du Bois RN10
☎213090 Ren G20
🅱🅳**Tardy** bd d'Estriées ☎210185 N🅼 Frd

Châtillon-en-Bazois 58 (Nièvre) 1,120
(☎83) Map **10** C1
★**Poste** Grande r ☎23 rm14 G Lift

Châtillon-sur-Indre 36 (Indre) 3,700 (☎54)
Map **9** A1
★**Auberge de la Tour** LE ☎387217 rm10 🏠2
G 1 Feb–20 Dec LD B40–66 M24–45 Pn78–107
★**Promenade** 88 r Grande ☎387195 rm12
⇆1 G 1 Mar–29 Jan
🅱🅳**Gouillier** 5 rte du Blanc ☎32 N🅼 Ren G4

Châtillon-sur-Seine 21 (Côte-d'Or)
7,950 (☎80) Map **10** C2
★★**Côte d'Or** r C-Ronot ☎041329 rm12 ⇆7
🏠2 G 25 Feb–8 Jan LD B57–137(double)
M39–87 Pn123–192
★★**Sylvia** (n rest) 9 av de la Gare ☎040244
rm20 (A8) ⇆8 🏠4 G B48–103
★**Jura** (n rest) 19 r Dr Robert ☎041402 rm12
⇆1 🏠4 Etr–30 Sep
★**Montagne** pl Joffre rm16 G 1 Jan–8 Dec
🅱🅳**Centre** 3 r Marmot ☎040144 N🅼 Frd G6
🅱🅳**Ferrier** 20 av de la Gare ☎041113 N🅼 Fia G15
🅱🅳**SAGC** 14 bis av E-Herriot ☎041404 Ren

Châtre (La) 36 (Indre) 5,250 (☎54)
Map **16** D4
★**St-Germain** 86 r Nationale ☎15 rm26 ⇆1
🏠1 G

Chaumont 52 (Haute-Marne) 29,350 (☎25)
Map **10** D2
★★★**Terminus–Reine** pl de la Gare ☎032222
tx840920 rm69 ⇆28 🏠20 G Lift B43–120
M28–100
★★**Grand Val** rte de Langres ☎031590 rm64
⇆6 🏠26 G Lift LD B44–89 M18–48
★**France** 25 r Toupot-de-Béveaux ☎030111
rm40 (A5) 🏠6 G B37–74 M20
🅱🅳**G Boni** 11 r P-Burello ☎030455 N🅼 Frd G6
🅱🅳**Diderot** rte de Neuilly ☎032337 N🅼 Opl
🅱🅳**24 François** 11 av de la République
☎030888 M/c Chy/Sim G

Chaumont-sur-Loire† 41 (Loir-et-Cher)
800 (☎39) Map **9** A2
★★★**Château** LE ☎469804 rm20 ⇆20 G
15 Mar–15 Nov LD B114–223 M35–80&àlc
St15%
★**Moutier St-Martin** ☎469813 rm7 ⇆4 🏠3
1 Feb–10 Dec LD B45–64(double) M28–48

Chaunay 86 (Vienne) 1,300 (☎49)
Map **16** C4
★★**Central** ☎492504 rm12 ⇆12 G (closed Feb)
B53–87

Chauvigny 86 (Vienne) 6,850 (☎49)
Map **16** C4
★**Lion d'Or** 8 r Marche ☎463028 rm12 G
15 Jan–15 Dec LD B37–52 M22–35

Chenehutte-les-Tuffeaux See **Saumur**

Chenonceaux 37 (Indre-et-Loire) 350 (☎47)
Map **9** A2
★★★**Ottoni** N76 ☎299009 rm38 (A9) ⇆18
🏠4 G 25 Mar–15 Oct LD B46–132 M44&àlc
★★**Bon Laboureur et Château** N76
☎299002 rm26 (A7) ⇆17 🏠2 G Apr–Oct
LD B50–139 M35–61
★**Roy** r Dr Bretonneau ☎299017 rm26 (A5)
⇆4 🏠5 1 Feb–30 Nov B28.50–63 M17–36.50
Pn68.50–75.50

Cherbourg† 50 (Manche) 34,650 (☎33)
Map **8** C4 **See Plan**

[AA] **agents; see page 83**
★★★**Sofitel Jacques Borel** Gare Maritime
☎533011 tx170613 Plan **1** rm62 ⇆62 G Lift
B97–181 M45 Pn187 Sea

★★**Caligny** (n rest) 41 r Ml-Foch ☎531024
Plan **2** rm47 ⇆7 🏠9 G 5 Jan–20 Dec B28–69
★★**Louvre** (n rest) LE 28 r de la Paix ☎530228
Plan **3** rm41 ⇆7 🏠6 Lift 15 Jan–15 Dec
★**Renaissance** (n rest) 4 r de l'Eglise ☎532306
Plan **4** rm12 🏠10 B36–77 Sea
🅸🅳**Commercial** 103 av Carnot ☎531348 Frd
G15
🅱🅳**24 Ganche** 47 r du Val-de-Saire ☎532868
N🅼537105 Ren
🅱🅳**Poste** 14 bis r de l'Ancien Quai ☎530334
N🅼 Chy/Sim
🅱🅳**Vikings** 10 av de Paris ☎532219 Aud/VW
At **Tourlaville** (4km E)
🅸🅳**Moderne** 13 r P-Després ☎533310 N🅼
M/c G10

Chinon 37 (Indre-et-Loire) 8,350 (☎47)
Map **8** D2
★**Boule d'Or** 66 quai J-d'Arc ☎930313 rm20
⇆2 🏠7 G 1 Feb–15 Dec LD B43–101
M20–50 Pn90–125
★**Gargantua** 73 r Voltaire ☎930471 rm15 (A4)
⇆7 🏠3 G 1 Mar–28 Feb
★**Lion d'Or** 10 pl Jeanne d'Arc ☎930741
rm15 (A5) ⇆2 🏠5 1 Feb–20 Dec B34–90
M18.40–36&àlc Pn67–100
At **Marcay** (7km S on D116)
★★★**Château de Marcay** ☎930347
tx750806 rm26 (A11) ⇆16 🏠10 Lift
1 Mar–31 Dec B114–268 M65&àlc
Pn190–265 ⚓ Pool

Chitenay 41 (Loir-et-Cher) 700 (☎39)
Map **9** A2
★**Clé des Champs** LE rte de Fougères ☎792203
rm10 ⇆1 🏠2 Mar–Feb LD B38–68 M43–60

Cholet 49 (Maine-et-Loire) 54,050 (☎41)
Map **8** C2
★★**Poste** 20 bd Gl-Richard ☎620720 rm65
⇆13 🏠20 G 1 Aug–1 Aug
★**Boule d'Or** 49 r Commerce ☎620178 rm17
⇆3 🏠3 G LD B35–57 M23–80

Ciboure See **St-Jean-de-Luz**

Ciotat (La) 13 (Bouches-du-Rhône)
32,750 (☎91) Map **27** B1
★★★**Rose Thé** (n rest) 4 bd Beau Rivage
☎830923 rm41 (A15) ⇆12 🏠9 G B46–118
Sea
🅳**Electric** rte de Marseille ☎084867 N🅼 Frd

Civrieux-d'Azergues 69 (Rhône) 800
(☎78) Map **27** B4
★★**Roseraie** ☎816178 rm12 ⇆8 🏠4 G
16 Sep–2 Sep LD B45–79 M25–62

Claix See **Grenoble**

Clayette (La) 71 (Saone-et-Loire) 3,000
(☎85) Map **10** C1
★**De la Gare** rm14 🏠3 G

Clécy 14 (Calvados) 1,200 (☎31) Map **8** D3
★★**Site Normand** LE ☎697105 rm10 ⇆5 🏠5
LD B66–136(double) M30–60 Pn90–145

Clelles 38 (Isère) 300 (☎76) Map **27** B3
★★**Ferrat** LE (on N75) ☎9 rm15 ⇆4 🏠1 G
1 Feb–15 Nov LD B58–101(double) M25–40
Pn75–95
🅱🅳**Trieves** N75 ☎26 G10

Clermont 60 (Oise) 7,700 (☎4) Map **9** B4
★**France** ☎4500056 rm16 G

Clermont-Ferrand† 63 (Puy-de-Dôme)
161,250 (☎73) Map **27** A4
★★★**Arverne** 16 pl Delille ☎919206
tx390741 rm57 ⇆48 🏠9 G Lift B75–130
M42 Pn149
★★★**Frantel** bd Gergovia ☎930575 tx470662
F rm124 ⇆124 Lift G B126–176 M52
★★★**Gallieni** 51 r Bonnabaud ☎935969
tx390990 rm80 ⇆56 🏠24 G Lift B66–143
Màlc

111

France

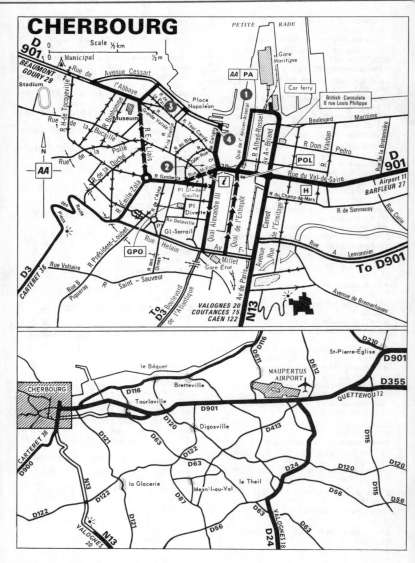

CHERBOURG

Cherbourg
1   ★★★Sofitel Jacques Borel   3   ★★Louvre
2   ★★Caligny   4   ★Renaissance

★★Minimes (n rest) 10 r des Minimes
☎933149 rm30 ⇥7 ⋔6 G B35–82
★Foch (n rest) 22 r Ml-Foch ☎934840 rm15
⇥9 B36–40
★Ravel 8 r de Maringues ☎915133
tx390794 Frantel rm20 ⇥8 LD B52–76(double)
M28–36 Pn75–87
🅱🆇🅾**Auvergne** 17 r Bonnabaud ☎931818
Fia G450
🅱🆇🅾**Beurlat** 13 av Julien ☎939921 N🖏
Bed/Opl
🅱🆇🅾**Domes** 36 bd Pasteur ☎880459 N🖏
AR/Lnc
🅱🆇🅾**Dugat** 23 rte de Lyonn ☎924724 N🖏 Frd
🅱🆇🅾**J Estager** 26 bd C-de-Gaulle ☎934165
BL/Jag/Por/Rov/Tri

Clichy See **Paris**

Cloyes-sur-le-Loir 28 (Eure-et-Loir)
2,600 (☎37) Map **9** A2
★★St-Jacques 35 r N ☎985008 rm21 ⇥12
⋔6 15 Jan–20 Dec B49–108 M35 Pn106–125
🌢 Lake

Cluny 71 (Saone-et-Loire) 4,700 (☎85)
Map **10** C1
★★Bourgogne ⸿E pl de l'Abbaye ☎590058
rm17 ⇥13 ⋔5 G
★★Abbaye ⸿E av de la Gare ☎591114
ta Beaufort rm20 ⇥4 ⋔2 G 2 Feb–15 Dec LD
B31–76 M25–37

Clusaz (La) 74 (Haute-Savoie) 1,700 (☎50)
Map **28** C4
★★★★Beauregard ☎024017 tx30132 rm43
⇥43 Lift 15 Dec–15 Apr 15 Jun–15 Sep Pool

Coaraze 06 (Alpes-Maritimes) 350 (☎93)
Map **28** C2
★★Petite Auberge ☎913091 Bendejun rm7
(A) ⇥7 G 15 Nov–15 Oct

Cognac† 16 (Charente) 22,600 (☎45)
Map **15** B3
★★Auberge 9 r Plumejeau ☎820659 rm27
⇥9 ⋔12 B30–99 Mfrom23 &àlc Pn80–112
★★Moderne ⸿E (n rest) r E-Mousnier ☎821953
rm26 ⇥26 G Lift B54–78
At **St-Laurent-de-Cognac** (6km W)
★★Logis de Beaulieu ⸿E ☎823050 rm21
⋔6 G LD B49–117 Pn100–220

Col de Curebourse See **Vic-sur-Cere**

Collioure 66 (Pyrénées-Orientales) 2,700
(☎68) Map **22** D4
★★Frégate bd C-Pelletan ☎380379 rm30
⇥8 ⋔2
★★Madeloc (n rest) r R-Rolland ☎380469
rm22 ⇥11 ⋔11 1 May–Oct B79–107
★★Méditerranée (n rest) av A-Maillol
☎380533 rm23 ⇥3 ⋔15 G Etr–Oct
★★Terrasses rte Port-Vendres ☎380406
rm20 ⇥2 ⋔4 B46–76 Sea

Colmar† 68 (Haut Rhin) 67,450 (☎89)
Map **11** B2
★★★Champs de Mars 2 av Marne
☎415454 tx880928 rm75 ⇥75 G Lift B120–
145 Mfr40
☆☆☆ **Novotel Colmar** 49 rte de Strasbourg
☎414914 tx880915 rm60 ⇥60 Lift B120–140
Pool
★★★Terminus Bristol 7 pl de la Gare
☎412038 tx87998 Terotel Strasbourg rm95
⇥47 ⋔17 Lift
★★Majestic pl de la Gare ☎414519 rm30
⇥9 ⚘ 3 Lift
🅱🅾**Autotransact** 87 rte de Rouffach ☎413400
N🖏 BL/Tri
🅱🆇🅾**Bolchert** 77 r Morat ☎413125
(closed weekends) Frd

Combeaufontaine 70 (Haute-Saone)
400 (☎84) Map **10** D2

★Balcon ⸿E ☎786234 rm17 ⇥2 ⋔3 G
16 Jan–8 Sep 24 Sep–25 Dec B28–83 M17–52

Combourg 35 (Ile-et-Vilaine) 4,750 (☎99)
Map **8** C3
★Château & Voyageurs ⸿E 1 pl Châteaubriand
☎730030 rm24 (A9) ⇥15 ⋔4 G LD B44.50–
100 M27.50–88 Pn70–90 Lake

Combronde 63 (Puy-de-Dôme) Map **16** D3
★Family ☎971001 rm17 ⋔4 15 Jan–15 Dec
B38–60 M23–38

Commercy 55 (Meuse) Map **10** D3
🅱🆇🅾**Billet** 112 r du 155e ☎910154 Peu

Compiègne† 60 (Oise) 40,750 (☎4)
Map **9** B4
★★Harlay (n rest) 3 r Harlay ☎4403474
rm16 ⇥16 Lift B98–126
★★Résidence de la Forêt 112 r St-Lazare
☎4202286 rm20 ⇥9 ⋔7 G 15 Jan–15 Dec
LD B45–95 M35–45 Pn110–145
🅱🅾**SOVA** 9 r de Soissons ☎4403307
BL/Toy/Vlo G10
At **Arsy** (15km W)
🅱**SCEVI** Autoroute exit (A1) 🖏Arsy 22 M/c G
At **Margny** (2km W on D935)
🅱🅾**Ile-de-France** 36 av O-Butin ☎4404694
N🖏 Frd

Concarneau 29 (Finistère) 19,050 (☎98)
Map **7** A3
★★Grand 1 av P-Guéguen ☎970028 rm33
⇥8 ⋔12 1 May–30 Sep B54–95(double) M33–
50 Pn90–110 Sea
★Sables Blancs ⸿E Plages des Sables
☎970139 rm48 ⇥8 ⋔34 23 Mar–15 Oct
B40–109 M26–52 Pn80–110 Sea
🅱🅾**Lodet** rte Quimper Penenguer ☎971075
N🖏 Ren

Condat 15 (Cantal) 1,730 (☎71) Map **16** D3
★Voyageurs rte de Clermont ☎785115 rm24
G 13 Nov–15 Oct

Condrieu 69 (Rhône) 3,200 (☎74) Map **27** B4
★★★Beau Rivage quai St-Abdon ☎595224
rm27 ⇥23 ⋔4 G 15 Feb–5 Jan LD B139
M100–120 St15% 🌢

Confolens 16 (Charente) 3,200 (☎45)
Map **16** C3
★Auberge Belle Etoile 151 bis rte
Angoulême ☎840235 rm14 ⇥5 ⋔1 G
(closed Oct 1–15) LD B44–69 M22–44
Pn68–85

Conques 12 (Aveyron) 450 (☎65) Map **16** D2
★Ste-Foy ☎698403 rm20 ⇥16 ⋔4 G
15 Mar–3 Nov B49–117 M26–36 Pn100–150

Contrexéville 88 (Vosges) 4,600 (☎29)
Map **10** D2/3
★★★Souveraine ☎080959 rm31 ⇥13 ⋔12
20 May–15 Sep B45–126 M50 Pn91–161 🌢

Coquille (La) 24 (Dordogne) 1,700 (☎53)
Map **16** C3
★Voyageurs ⸿E r de la République, N21
☎558013 rm10 ⇥7 G 20 Mar–31 Oct LD
B42.50–85 M28–75 Pn82–89

Cordes 81 (Tarn) 1,100 (☎63) Map **16** C/D2
★★★Grand Ecuyer ☎560103 rm17 ⇥16 G
B70–172 Màlc 🌢 Pool
★★Vieux Cordes ⸿E ☎12 rm20 (A) ⇥8 ⋔1 G

Corps 38 (Isère) 550 (☎76) Map **27** B3
★★Poste ⸿E pl de la Mairie ☎6 rm15 ⇥5 ⋔4
G B40–79 M25–48 Pn65–80 🌢 Lake
★Roseraie rte du Sautet ☎949111 rm22
⇥12 ⋔5 G 1 Jan–15 Oct 🌢

Corse (Corsica) 20 293,300 (☎95)
Map **28** Inset

Ajaccio Corse du Sud 51,800
★★★★Dolce Vita ⸿E rte des Sanguinaires
☎213520 rm34 ⇥34 Pool Beach Sea

France

★★★★Sofitel Porticcio ☎250034
tx460708 rm100 ⇌100 G Lift B280–435
Pn355–470 ✒ Pool Beach Sea
★★★Continental 22 cours Grandval
☎214116 tx460085 rm80 (A27) ⇌45 ⋒15
G Lift 1 Dec–31 Oct B70–185 M40 Pn100–160
Pool Sea
★★Etrangers 2 r Rossi ☎210126 rm47 (A)
⇌21 ⋒5 G Lift Sea
☆☆Stella di Mare ℡ (7km S on N193)
rte des Sanguinaires ☎213608 rm60 ⇌60
Pool Beach Sea
🛪🅗Citroen 95 cours Napoléon ☎214592 N🏵

Bastia Haute Corse 52,023
★★★Ile de Beauté (n rest) 7 r G-Péri
☎311556 rm55 ⇌55 Lift 1 Mar–31 Oct B100–
140

Calvi Haute Corse 3,700
★★★★Grand bd Wilson ☎650974 rm60
⇌48 ⋒12 1 Apr–30 Sep Beach Sea

Ile-Rousse (L') Haute Corse 2,700
🛪🅗24 Cyrnos av P-Doumer ☎600942
N☎601195 M/c Cit G10

Porto Corse du Sud
★Kalliste ℡ la Marine ☎261031 rm40 ⇌21
⋒19 G 1 Apr–15 Oct Sea

Porto-Vecchio Corse du Sud 7,850
★★★Ziglione (5km on N198) ☎469 rm32
⇌32 15 Mar–15 Oct LD B116–151(double)
Beach Sea

Propriano Corse du Sud 2,950
★★★Arena Bianca rte du Rizzanese
☎20110 rm105 ⇌40 ⋒65 Lift Apr–Oct
Beach Sea
★★★Marinca (5km N on N196) ☎Marinca11
rm58 (A10) ⇌58 Apr–Sep LD B147–169
(double) M50 Beach Sea

St-Florent Haute Corse 1,400
★★★Lauriers Roses ☎370014 rm18 (A)
⇌5 ⋒9 Etr–Oct

Cosne-sur-Loire 58 (Nièvre) 12,350
(☎86) Map **9** B2
★★Grand Cerf 43 r St-Jacques ☎280446
rm20 ⇌6 ⋒6 G 6 Feb–19 Dec
★Vieux Relais ℡ 11 r St-Agnan ☎282021
rm11 ⇌4 ⋒6 G 6 Feb–19 Dec B43–101
M25–95 Pn85–115
🛪🅗R Barre 97 r du Gl-Leclerc ☎281801 Cit

Continière (La) See **Oléron (Ile d')**

Cour-Cheverny 41 (Loir-et-Cher) 1,900
(☎39) Map **9** A2
★★St-Hubert ℡ ☎799660 rm21 ⇌11 ⋒10
Lift 15 Jan–5 Dec LD B40–99 M30–65
Pn100–120
★★Trois Marchands ℡ 3 pl Eglise ☎799644
rm45 (A12) ⇌15 ⋒9 1 Mar–6 Jan B42–86
M35–80 Pn89–103

Courtabeuf See **Orsay**

Cousin Valley See **Avallon**

Cousolre 59 (Nord) Map **3** B1
★★Viennois ℡ rte National ☎642173 rm11
⇌11 G Closed Tue

Coutainville 50 (Manche) (☎33)
Map **8** C4
★Hardy ℡ pl 28 Juillet ☎470411 rm27
(A15) ⇌8 ⋒1 G

Coutances 50 (Manche) 11,950 Map **8** C4
★Moderne bd Alsace-Lorraine ☎451377 rm17
⇌1 15 Jan–30 Sep 15 Oct–15 Dec B32–65
M19–45
★Parvis ☎451355 rm12 ⇌12 LD B41–71
M21&àlc
🛪🅗Bernard rte de Lessay ☎451633 N🏵 BL/Tri
🛪🅗SODIAM rte de St-Lo ☎450255 N🏵 Ren
G50

114

Crèches-sur-Saône See **Mâcon**

Cressensac 46 (Lot) 650 (☎65)
Map **16** C3
★Chez Gilles ℡ N20 ☎377006 rm19 ⇌2 ⋒4
G LD B42–70 M22–60 Pn65–80

Créteil See **Paris**

Creusot (Le) 71 Saône-et-Loire 33,500
(☎85) Map **10** C1
At **Monchanin** (8km E off D28)
☆☆☆Novotel Montchanin-Creusot-Montcea
30 rte du Pont Jeanne-Rose ☎781080
tx800588 rm87 ⇌87 Lift B120–140 Pool

Criel-sur-Mer 75 (Seine-Maritime) (☎35)
Map **9** A4
★★Vielle Ferme ☎867218 rm40 (A22) ⇌30
LD B40–112 M40&àlc Pn68–112 Pool

Croisic (Le) 44 (Loire-Atlantique) 4,350
(☎40) Map **7** B2
★★Océan (1km S) ☎230003 rm24 ⇌13
1 Feb–31 Oct

Croisière (La) See **St Maurice La
Souterraine**

Croix de la Maleyrie (La) See **Donzenac**

Croix-Valmer 83 (Var), 1,900 (☎94)
Map **28** C1
★★★Mer (2.5km SE on N559) ☎976061
rm31 ⇌12 ⋒10 Etr–1 Oct Last dinner 8pm Pool

Cros-de-Cagnes See **Cagnes-sur-Mer**

Crotoy (Le) 80 (Somme) 2,450 Map **3** A1
★Baie quai Léonard ☎278122 rm16 ⇌8 ⋒2
Sea
★Paris 1 pl J-d'Arc ☎278046 rm14 ⇌5 ⋒3
LD B37–90.50 M31–52 Pn80–110 Sea

Crouzille (La) 87 (Haute-Vienne) (☎55)
Map **16** C3
★Lac rm11 ⇌2 1 Apr–1 Oct Lake
At **Nantiat**
☆☆Relais St-Europe ☎399121 rm19 ⇌19
B95 M50 Pn150 Pool

Cuisery 71 (Saône-et-Loire), 1,600 (☎85)
Map **10** C1
★Voyageurs (n rest) r de la Gendarmerie
☎401461 rm9 G 15 Jun–15 Sep B33–50

Dampierre 78 (Yvelines) 750 (☎1) Map **9** B3
★★Château ☎0525289 rm15 ⇌8 ⋒1 G
20 Jan–31 Jul 30 Aug–5 Jan (closed Thu)

Danjoutin See **Belfort**

Dax† 40 (Landes) 20,300 (☎58) Map **15** B1
★★★Parc ℡ 1 pl Thiers ☎741617
tx540481 rm44 ⇌32 ⋒10 G Lift LD B86–105
M40
🛪🅗Landaises av du Sablar ☎740344 N🏵 Ren
At **St-Paul-lès-Dax** (2km W)
🛪🅗24 Duprat-Desclaux rte de Bayonne
N124 ☎743804 BL/Tri
🛪🅗Thermal r Foch ☎(58)742334 N🏵 Frd G8

Deauville† 14 (Calvados) 5,750 (☎31)
Map **8** D4
★★★★★Normandy r J-Mermoz ☎880921
tx170617 rm380 ⇌317 Lift B200–370
M75 Pn230–285 St15% ✒ Pool
★★★★★Royal ☎881641 tx170549 rm350
⇌350 Lift Etr–15 Sep B180–350 M75
Pn300–385 St15% ✒ Pool Golf Sea
🛪🅗Deauville 8 av de la République
☎882134 Ren

Derval 44 (Loire-Atlantique) 2,880
Map **8** C2
★Arnaudière rte Rennes ☎817023 rm10 ⇌2

Deville-les-Rouen See **Rouen**

Dieppe† 76 (Seine-Maritime) 26,150 (☎35)
Map **9** A4 **See Plan**

🄰🄰 agents; see page 83

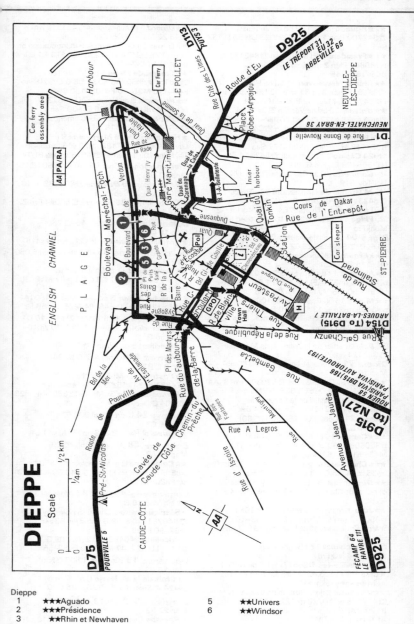

DIEPPE

Scale

Dieppe
1	★★★Aguado	5	★★Univers
2	★★★Présidence	6	★★Windsor
3	★★Rhin et Newhaven		

★★★**Aguado** (n rest) 30 bd de Verdun ☎842700 Plan **1** rm53 ⇨22 ⋒23 Lift B51–132 Sea
★★★**Présidence** bd de Verdun ☎843131 tx180865 Plan **2** rm89 ⇨76 G Lift B65–167 M45
★★**Rhin & Newhaven** 11 bd de Verdun ☎841018 Plan **3** rm31 ⇨9 ⋒2 Lift Feb–Dec LD B47–112 M26–39 Pn65–100 Sea
★★***Univers*** 10 bd de Verdun ☎841255 Plan **5** rm28 ⇨22 ⋒3 Lift 20 Jan–15 Dec Sea
★★**Windsor** 18 bd de Verdun ☎841523 Plan **6** rm46 ⇨40 Lift 19 Dec–18 Nov LD B58–119 M35–40 Pn102–177 Sea
24 Casino 28 r Sygogne ☎842214 N☎855409 BL/Frd G100
Gambetta 10 av Gambetta ☎841374 Opl/Toy G10
24 Grands de Normandie 33 r Thiers ☎842340 N☎842462 Ren G20
Le Prince 2 r Thiers ☎841677 N Cit G2
Plage 4 r Bouzard ☎841036 (closed Sun & Mon) Frd

Digne 04 (Alpes de-Hautes-Provence) 16,600 (☎92) Map **28** C2
★★★***Ermitage Napoleon*** bd Gambetta rm60 (A) ⇨36 ⋒8 G Lift
★★**Aiglon** LE 1 r de Provence ☎310270 tx430605 rm33 (A9) ⇨6 ⋒5 G 1 Feb–30 Nov LD B39.50–95 M21–52 Pn70–105
★★**Mistre** 15 bd Gassendi ☎310016 tx43605 rm36 ⇨12 ⋒9 G 10 Dec–11 Nov B43–132 M35–80 Pn85–120 Pool
★★***Paris*** 2 bd Thiers ☎311115 rm50 ⇨6 G Pool
Balp Quartier de la Tour, rte de Marseille ☎313124 N G10

Digoin 71 (Saone-et-Loire) 11,450 (☎85) Map **10** C1
★**Gare** 79 av Gl-de-Gaulle ☎530304 rm19 (A4) ⇨8 ⋒7 1 Jan–1 Dec LD B38–91 Màlc
★***Moderne*** (n rest) r de la Fayencerie ☎530580 rm12 ⇨1 ⋒1 26 Jan–24 Dec

Dijon† 21 (Côte d'Or) 156,800 (☎80) Map **10** D2
★★★**Central** 10 r Château ☎304400 tx350606 rm90 ⇨30 ⋒40 Lift B60–133 M43 Pn120–152(double)
★★★**Chapeau Rouge** 5 r Michelet ☎302810 rm36 ⇨24 ⋒5 G Lift LD B67–220 Màlc
★★***Ducs*** (n rest) 5 r Lamonnoye (continuation of r Chabot-Charny) ☎326946 rm56 ⇨14 ⋒8 G Lift
★★**Jura** (n rest) 14 av Ml-Foch ☎416112 tx350912 rm75 (A10) ⇨58 Lift B43–101
★***Nord*** 2 r Liberté ☎305520 tx359127 rm27 ⇨6 ⋒3 Lift
Montchapet 12 r Gagnereaux ☎323284 N Frd
At **Hauteville-les-Dijon** (7km NE on D107)
★**Clos** ☎711120 rm14 ⇨5 ⋒6 B36–71 M22
At **Marsanny** (8km SW)
☆☆☆**Novotel Dijon-Sud** rte de Beaune N74 ☎412578 tx350728 rm122 ⇨122 Lift B120–140 Pool
At **Talant** (4km NW)
Vernier 58 bis bd de Troyes ☎415761 Peu

Dinan† 22 (Côtes-du-Nord) 16,400 (☎96) Map **8** C3
★★***Marguerite*** LE 29 pl du-Guesclin ☎392128 tx74884 rm12 ⇨12 Lift
Jago Zone Industrielle ☎390491 Cit
Meyer 21 r des Pivants ☎391272 N Opl/Vau

Dinard 35 (Ille-et-Vilaine) 9,600 (☎99) Map **8** C3
★★★★***Grand*** 46 av George-V ☎461028 rm113 ⇨95 Lift 1 Apr–30 Sep Sea
★★**Bains** 38 av Georges V ☎461371 rm40 ⇨13 ⋒8 Lift B47–108 Pn95–100 Sea
★★***Dinard*** 5 r Levavasseur ☎461310 rm18 ⇨18 20 Mar–15 Oct Sea
★★**Dunes** 5 r G-Clemenceau (continuation of r Prés-Wilson) ☎461272 rm32 ⇨16 ⋒1 LD B44–121 M30–43
★★**Emeraude Plage** 1 bd Albert-1er ☎461579 rm50 (A5) ⇨30 ⋒6 G Etr–20 Sep B48–176 M35–60 Pn100–150 Sea
★★***Printania*** 5 av Georges-V ☎461307 tx74884 rm100 (A) ⇨25 Etr–30 Sep
★★***Roche Corneille*** 4 r G-Clemenceau ☎461447 rm22 ⇨18 ⋒4
★**Hostellerie de la Marjolaine** 9 r Levavasseur ☎461185 rm23 ⇨6 Pn65–80
Parc 10 r Y-Verney ☎461338 N BL/Tri

Divonne-les-Bains 01 (Ain) 4,250 (☎50) Map **10** D1
★★★***Château de Divonne*** ☎500032 rm40 ⇨30 1 Jun–30 Sep Lake
★**Truite** (n rest) 25 Grande r ☎500441 rm22 ⇨8 ⋒4 B40–89

Dolancourt 10 (Aube) 146 (☎25) Map **10** C3
★★***Moulin du Landion*** LE ☎17 rm15 ⇨15

Dol de Bretagne 35 (Ille-et-Vilaine) 5,050 (☎99) Map **8** C3
★★**Bretagne** LE 17 pl Châteaubriand ☎480203 rm30 ⇨1 ⋒8 G B32–62 M18–30 Pn52–62
★**Bresche Arthur** LE bd Deminiac ☎480144 rm25 ⇨2 ⋒9 G LD B48–84 M26.50–58 àlc

Dole† 39 (Jura) 30,500 (☎82) Map **10** D1
★★★***Chandioux*** pl Grévy ☎721757 rm40 ⇨24 ⋒6 G
Morilhat 8 bd Wilson ☎722085

Domfront 61 (Orne) 4,550 (☎34) Map **8** C/D3
★★***Poste*** LE 15 r Ml-Foch ☎385100 tx74884 rm24 ⇨5 ⋒3 G 25 Feb–7 Jan
★***France*** LE r Mont St-Michel ☎385144 rm23 ⇨2 ⋒4 G Dec–Oct

Domme 24 (Dordogne) 900 (☎53) Map **16** C2
★***Nouvel*** pl Halle ☎148 rm15 (A) ⇨1 Lift

Dompaire 88 (Vosges) 950 (☎29) Map **11** A3
★★**Commerce** LE pl Ml-Leclerc ☎365028 tx960573 Dom rm11 ⇨4 G B43.50–85 M20–50 Pn80–101

Domrémy-la-Pucelle 88 (Vosges) 300 (☎29) Map **10** D3
★**Basilique** av Bois-Chenu (S1.5km by D53) ☎940781 rm28 ⋒8 G Feb–Dec B35–63 M32–50 Pn86
★**Pucelle** ☎940460 rm12 (A7) ⋒6 G 1 Jan–31 Oct LD B27–47 M17–30 Pn50–55

Donzenac 19 (Corrèze) 1,800 (☎55) Map **16** C3
At **Croix de la Maleyrie (La)** (5km N)
24 *A Sicard* N20 ☎252235 G20

Donzère 26 (Drôme) 3,400 (☎75) Map **27** B3
★***Roustan*** Centre Ville ☎986127 rm10 ⇨5 ⋒2 G 12 Dec–12 Nov

Douai† 59 (Nord) 47,600 (☎20) Map **3** B1
★**Grand Cerf** 20 r St Jacques ☎887960 rm36 ⇨9 ⋒5 B43–94 M24 & àlc St15%
Faidherbe 47 bd Faidherbe ☎887854 N Bed/Opl G3

Dourdan 91 (Essonne) 7,500 (☎1) Map **9** B3
★★★***Blanche de Castille*** pl des Halles ☎4927548 tx69902 rm40 ⇨40 Lift

Draguignan 83 (Var) 22,450 (☎94) Map **28** C2

★★**Col de L'Ange** ☎682301 rm30 ⇄30
B80–140 M28–38
★★**Parc** 21 bd Liberté ☎680384 rm20 ⇄4
🏠16 10 Jan–22 Dec
🚗**24 Azur** rte de Lorgues ☎681871 M/c Frd

Dramont See **Agay**

Dreux† 28 (Eure-et-Loir) 34,050 (☎37)
Map **9** A3

🏠🚗**Ouest** 51 av des Fenots ☎461145 N🚗
BL/Peu

Dunkerque (Dunkirk)† 59 (Nord)
83,800 (☎20) Map **3** A2

See also **Bergues** and **Malo-les-Bains**

★★★**Europ** 13 r de Leughenaer
☎662907 tx120084 rm73 ⇄73 G Lift
B64–133
★★★**Frantel** r J-Jaurès ☎659722 tx110587
rm126 ⇄126 Lift B117–167
★★**Arcades** (n rest) pl J-Bart ☎665015
tx820093 rm32 ⇄16 🏠6 Lift 2 Jan–30 Nov
B77–145
★★**Borel** (n rest) 6 r Hermite ☎665180
tx820050 rm30 ⇄30 Lift B87–115 St15%
★**Moderne** 2 r Gambetta ☎668024 rm21
⇄2 LD B47–76 Mfr25 Pnfr95
★**Victoria** 5 quai Risban ☎665205 rm27
🏠🚗**Dalinvai** 54 r M-Vincent ☎666830 N🚗
Dat G10
🏠🚗**Flandres** 4 quai des Quatre-Écluses
☎666432 N🚗 Frd
🏠🚗**Gare Auto-Sport** 9 r Belle Vue ☎667105
N🚗 BL/Rov/Tri
🏠🚗**L Patfoort** 9 r du Leughenaer ☎665112
N🚗 Fia

Dury See **Amiens**

Echelles (Les) 73 (Savoie) 1,200 (☎79)
Map **27** B4

★**Commanderie** r de Chambéry ☎366046 rm5
G 16 Oct–6 Oct LD B41–56(double) M25–68
àlc

Ecommoy 72 (Sarthe) 4,100 (☎43)
Map **8** D2

★**Commerce** 🅻🅴 19 pl République ☎271034
rm13 🏠6 G 15 Jan–15 Dec LD B42–77 M20–
28 Pn80–100

Eguilles See **Aix-en-Provence**

Elne 66 (Pyrénées-Orientales) 6,050 (☎69)
Map **22** D4

🚗24 N **Subiros** rte de Perpignan, chemin de las
Trilles ☎372132 Cit

Entraygues-sur-Truyère 12 (Aveyron)
1,600 (☎65) Map **16** D2

★**Truyère** ☎445110 tx53366 Chamcon
Rodez rm20 ⇄15 🏠3 G Lift 15 Mar–15 Nov
B38–111 M28 Pn76–99(double)

Epernay† 51 (Marne) 31,150 (☎26)
Map **10** C3

★★★**Berceaux** 13 r Berceaux ☎512884
rm33 (A9) ⇄17 🏠16 Lift B70.50–106.50
M60–90
★**Europe** 18 r Porte-Lucas ☎512429 rm31
⇄2 🏠15 G
🏠🚗**Citroën** rte de Reims ☎512762
(closed weekends) Cit
🚗**Eur'** 4 Passage Fourché ☎513256 N🚗
AR/BL/Tri
At **Champillon** (6km N on N51)
★★★**Royal Champagne** ☎512506 rm14
⇄14 B139–278 Màlc
At **Vinay** (6km S on N51)
★★★**Briqueterie** rte de Sezanne ☎514712
rm42 ⇄30 🏠12 B71–174 M43–65
Pn165–270

Epinal† 88 (Vosges) 42,850 (☎29)
Map **11** A2

★★**Point Central** 6 quai des Bons Enfants
☎822050 rm12 ⇄5 🏠3
★**Résidence** (n rest) 39 av des Templiers
☎824564 rm18 ⇄10 🏠8 B53–85
★★**Vosges & Terminus** (n rest) pl de la Gare
☎823578 rm48 ⇄6 🏠2 G Lift B28–65
★**Azur** (n rest) 54 quai des Bons-Enfants
☎822915 rm22 ⇄2 🏠2 B22–35
🏠🚗**Epinal** 89 r d'Alsace ☎820594 N🚗 Peu G8
🏠🚗**Spinaliens** 17 r Ml-Lyautey ☎824747 Frd

Epine (L') See **Châlons-sur-Marne**

Erquy-Plage 22 (Côtes-du-Nord) 3,300
(☎96) Map **7** B3

★**Beauregard** 🅻🅴 bd Plage ☎323003 rm17
(A8) Sea

Etaples 62 (Pas-de-Calais) 10,600 (☎21)
Map **3** A1

★**Bellevue** 19 r Herambault ☎096932 rm7
15 Jan–15 Dec Last dinner 9pm
★**Voyageurs** 11 pl Gare ☎946933 rm23 ⇄6
🏠2 G 1 Feb–31 Dec B30.50–69 M42
Pn67–77

Etretat 76 (Seine-Maritime) 1,550 (☎35)
Map **8** D4

★★★**Dormy House** rte Havre ☎270788
rm40 ⇄26 G 10 Mar–14 Nov Golf Sea
★★**Windsor** 9 av George-V ☎270727 rm15
⇄4 🏠3 Etr–Oct

Etsaut 64 (Pyrénées-Atlantiques) (☎59)
Map **21** B4

★**Pyrenees** ☎397862 rm20 (A7) ⇄3 G Xmas
& Etr 1 June–1 Oct B33–52 M22–40 Pn53–68

Evian-les-Bains 74 (Haute-Savoie) 6,200
(☎50) Map **11** A1

★★★★★**Royal** ☎751400 tx380353 rm200
⇄200 G Lift 15 April–Oct B170–540
M75 ᕫ Pool Golf Lake
★★★**Splendide** ☎750485 tx Cachat Evian
34989 rm100 ⇄80 Lift 1 Jun–10 Sep
At **Maxilly-Petite-Rive** (2km E on N5)
★★★**Lumina** ☎752867 tx34748 rm63 ⇄62
G Lift 1 May–15 Sep Pool Lake
At **Verniaz (La)** (3km S)
★★★★★**Verniaz & ses Chalets** ☎750490
tx34069F rm50 (A) ⇄50 G Lift Feb–Dec
ᕫ Pool Lake

Evreux† 27 (Eure) 50,400 (☎32)
Map **9** A3

★★★**Grand Cerf** 🅻🅴 11 r de la Harpe ☎331401
rm26 ⇄4 🏠16 G Lift 1 Mar–31 Jan LD
B67–204 M40 &àlc
★★**Grenoble** (n rest) 17 r St-Pierre ☎330731
rm16 ⇄3 🏠2 G
★★**Normandy** 37 pl Dupont-de-l'Eure
☎331440 rm25 ⇄14 🏠5 G 1 Sep–31 Jul
★★**L'Orme** 🅻🅴 (n rest) 13 r Lombards
☎393412 rm20 ⇄4 🏠6 B53–99
★**Beffroi** (n rest) 2 r Horloge ☎390849 rm16
G
🏠🚗**Hôtel de Ville** 4 r G-Bernard ☎330160
N🚗 Frd
🏠🚗**Vendôme-Auto** 180 rte d'Orléans
☎393810 N🚗 Chy/Sim
🏠🚗**Victor Hugo** 8 bis r V-Hugo ☎392721 N🚗
Fia

Evry 91 (Essonne) 15,600 (☎1) Map **9** B3
☆☆☆**Novotel Paris-Evry** A6 ☎0778270
tx600685 rm180 ⇄180 Lift B120–140 Pool

Eyzies-de-Tayac (Les) 24 (Dordogne) 900
(☎53) Map **16** C2

★★★**Cro-Magnon** ☎069706 rm28 (A12) ⇄21
🏠6 G April–mid Oct LD B76–163 M36–80
Pn95–150 Pool
★★**Centenaire** 🅻🅴 ☎069718 rm30 (A6) ⇄25
🏠5 G 20 Mar–2 Nov LD B84–133 M35–90
Pn115–130

France

★★Glycines ☎069707 rm27 ⇆22 ⋔3 G
1 Apr–10 Oct LD B61.50–127 M32–75
&àlc Pn89–115
★France ☎069723 rm18 (A6) ⇆3 ⋔8 Mar–
15 Oct LD B39–89 M21–60 Pn75–85

Eze-Bord-de-Mer 06 (Alpes-Maritimes)
1,440 (☎93) Map **28** C2
★★★★*Cap Estel* ☎015044 tx47305
Capstel rm44 ⇆44 Lift 1 Feb–Nov Pool
Beach Sea
★★*Bananaraie* (n rest) ☎015139 rm33 (A)
⇆15 ⋔2 Apr–Oct
★★*Cap Roux* ☎015123 rm36 ⇆16 ⋔20
Lift 15 Feb–15 Oct Sea

Falaise 14 (Calvados) 8,650 (☎31)
Map **8** D3
★★Normandie 4 r Al-Courbet ☎901826
rm30 ⇆5 ⋔7 G B34–81 M17 Pn62–73
★★Poste 38 r G-Clemenceau ☎901314 rm24
⇆2 G LD B33–56 M20–34 Pn55–65
★*Belle Epée* 1 r Gambetta ☎900529 rm12
15 Sep–15 Aug
🏠🏵Poste 34 r G-Clemenceau ☎900100

Faouet (Le) 56 (Morbihan) 3,220 Map **7** 83
★Croix d'Or pl Bellanger ☎230733 rm16 G
Lift LD B27–35 M18–60 Pn55

Faverges Haute-Savoie 5,400 Map **28** C4
At **Doussard**
★★Marceau Marceau-Dessus ☎443011 rm27
(A3) ⇆10 G 1 Feb–30 Nov B60–130 M48–100
Pn130–160 ⚓ Lake

Fayl-Billot 52 (Haute Marne) 1,850 (☎27)
Map **10** D2
★Rose des Vents ☎846301 rm11 ⇆1 ⋔6
B35–78 M22 Pn60–75 St12%

Fécamp 76 (Seine-Maritime) 22,250 (☎35)
Map **9** A4
★*Plage* 87 r de la Plage rm17 G 15 Jan–15 Dec
Sea
🚗●24 Rouen pl Bigot ☎281424 M/c Cit G10

Fère-en-Tardenois 02 (Aisne) 2,800 (☎23)
Map **10** C3
★★★Château ☎822113 rm20 ⇆20 1 Mar–
1 Jan B132–239 M100 &àlc St15% ⚓

Fernay-Voltaire See **Geneva Airport**
(Switzerland)

Ferté-Macé (La) 61 (Orne) 7,715 (☎34)
Map **8** D3
★★Grand Turc 12 r St-Denis ☎370044 rm23
⇆2 G Nov–30 Sep

Ferté-St-Aubin (La) 45 (Loiret) 4,300
(☎38) Map **9** B2
★★Perron 9 r du Gl-Leclerc ☎915336 rm33
⇆33 LD B38–93 M21–62 Pn80–96
🏠🏵Gidoin N20 ☎915117 N🏵 Fia G6
🚗●24 Relais de Sologne ☎915711
M/c Ren G10

Figeac 46 (Lot) 10,900 (☎65) Map **16** D2
★★*Carmes* ℄ 18 pl XII-Mai ☎342078
tx51626 Cecilo Cahors rm30 ⇆6 ⋔4 G 15 Jan–
15 Dec

Firminy 42 (Loire) 25,450 (☎77)
Map **27** A4
★★Firm 37 r J-Jaurès ☎560899 rm20 ⇆6
⋔14 G B61–96 M25

Fixin 21 (Côte d'Or) 850 (☎80)
Map **10** C2
★★Chez Jeannette ℄ ☎343108 rm11 (A4)
⋔9 Feb–Dec LD B38–60 M26–60 Pn90–98

Flèche (La) 72 (Sarthe) 16,400 (☎43)
Map **8** D2
🏠🏵Gambetta 41 bd Gambetta ☎940620
N🏵 BL/Tri G4
🏠🏵Welcome 14 av de Verdun ☎940408 N🏵
Frd

Fleurance 32 (Gers) 5,800 (☎62) Map **16** C1
★★Fleurance rte d'Agen ☎061485
tx530416 rm25 ⇆15 ⋔2 B50–120 M28
&àlc Pn99–144

Florac: 48 (Lozère) 2,100 (☎66) Map **27** A3
★Gorges du Tarn ☎450063 rm19 (A8) ⇆8
⋔14 G Etr–15 Oct LD B40–78 M25–35
★Parc ☎450305 rm50 (A26) ⇆12 ⋔23 G
15 Mar–15 Nov LD B38–90 M25–45

Florensac 34 (Herault) 3,050 (☎67)
Map **27** A2
★★Leonce 2 pl de la République ☎770305
rm30 (A10) ⇆5 ⋔10 G Lift 8 Oct–12 Sep
B37–92 M20–50 Pn65–80 St17%

Flotte (La) See **Ré (Ile de)**

Foix 09 (Ariège) 10,250 (☎61) Map **22** C4
★★★Barbacane av de Lerida ☎650044 rm22
⇆19 G 1 Apr–15 Oct LD B53–120 M38
★★★Tourisme ☎650205 rm30 ⇆30 B44–126
M25 Pn107–132

Fontaine See **Grenoble**

Fontainebleau† 77 (Seine-et-Marne) 19,600
(☎1) Map **9** B3
★★★Aigle Noir 27 pl N-Bonaparte ☎4223265
tx60080 rm30 ⇆28 ⋔2 G Lift B160–280
M60 Pn235–280
★★★Napoléon 9 r Grande ☎4222039 rm42
⇆16 ⋔17
★★Londres 1 pl du Gl-de-Gaulle ☎4222021
rm22 ⇆4 ⋔4 1 Mar–31 Jan LD B69–128
M38–75 St15%
★*Forêt* (n rest) av Pres-Roosevelt ☎4223926
rm29 (A4) ⇆5 ⋔8 G B34–84
★*Neuville* 196 r Grande ☎4222339 rm20 (A4)
⇆4 ⋔4 G Feb–Dec
🏠🏵*Aigion* 54 r A-Briand ☎4222843 N🏵 Ren
🏠🏵*François-1 er* 9 r Chancellerie ☎4222034
N🏵 Frd
🚗●24 St-Antoine 97 r de France ☎4223188
N🏵 ☎4222131 BL/Rov
At **Ury** (6km SW on N51)
☆☆☆**Novotel Fontainebleau Ury** N51
N☎4224825 tx600153 rm127 ⇆127 Lift
B120–140 ⚓ Pool ◯

Font Romeu 66 (Pyrénées-Orientales)
3,050 (☎68) Map **22** C4
★★★Bellevue ☎300016 rm70 ⇆30 ⋔20 G
Lift B40–111 M30 Pn75–105
★★Carlit ☎300745 rm37 ⇆4 ⋔19 B58–121
M33–41 Pn80–130
★★Pyrénées (n rest) ☎300149 rm57 (A) ⇆12
Lift 20 Dec–Etr 1 Jul–15 Sep

Fonvialane See **Albi**

Forbach 57 (Moselle) 25,400 (☎87)
Map **11** A3
🏵🏵Guiser 208 r Nationale ☎850806 N🏵
Bed/Opl

Forêt-Fouesnant (La) 29 (Finistère)
2,100 (☎98) Map **7** A3
★Beauséjour ☎560208 rm30 ⋔12
24 Mar–30 Sep B42–69 M24–50 Pn62–70
Sea
★Espérance ℄ ☎560135 rm30 (A19) ⇆16
⋔12 Etr–Oct B37–70 M26–36 Pn65–80 Sea

Fos-sur-Mer 13 (Bouches-du-Rhône)
6,750 (☎91) Map **27** B2
★★★Frantel ☎050057 tx410812 rm146
⇆146 B126–176 M50&àlc Pool ◯ Lake
☆☆☆**Novotel Fos-Camargue** Centre de Vie
La Fossette ☎051210 tx420347 rm93 ⇆93
Lift B120–140 Pool

Foucarmont 76 (Seine-Maritime) 950
(☎35) Map **9** B4
★Normandie ☎12 rm12 ⇆3 ⋔2 1 Mar–31 Jan

Fouesnant 29 (Finistère) 4,900 (☎98)
Map **7** A3
★★ **Pointe Mousterlin** ℝ (at Pointe de
Mousterlin 6km SW by D145 & D134)
☎560412 rm48 ⇆25 ▥10 G 26 May—25 Sep
LD B43—122(double) M38 Pn63—132 Sea
★ **Amorique** ℝ 560019 rm26 (A12) ⇆12
Jun—Sep LD B39—90(double) M25—39
Pn68—95

▥⇗ **M J Bourhis** rte de Quimper ☎560265 Ren

Fougères 35 (Ille-et-Vilaine) 27,700 (☎99)
Map **8** C3
★★ **Voyageurs** (n rest) ☎990820 tx73666
rm38 ⇆8 ▥9 G (closed Xmas & New Year)
B38—87
★ **Moderne** ℝ 15 r Tribunal ☎990024 rm25
⇆1 ▥10 G B40.50—60 M25—30 Pn85—95
▥⇗ **Centre** 12 r J-Ferry ☎990207 N⇗
▥⇗ **L Juban** 60 r Alexandr III ☎990270 N⇗
Ren

Foulain 52 (Haute-Marne) 810 (☎27)
Map **10** D2
★ **Chalet** ☎021111 rm12 ⇆1 ▥3 (Closed Mon)
▥⇗ **Maitre** ☎021016 BL/Tri G5

Frayssinet 46 (Lot) 250 (☎65) Map **16** C2
★ **Bonne Auberge** ℝ ☎2 rm10 (A2) ▥10 G
1 Feb—31 Oct LD B52—84 M25—60
☆ **Escale** ☎310001 rm11 (A3) ▥9 LD
B71.50—124 M25—45 St15%

Fréjus†83 (Var) 30,650 (☎94) Map **28** C2
▥⇗ **Moderne Chiotte** av de Verdun ☎954076
N⇗ Cit
At **Colombier** (3km W)
★★★ **Colombier** rte de Bagnols ☎954592
tx470328 rm60 ⇆40 ▥20 20 Mar—30 Sep
B110—156 M45 Pn138—151 ⇗ Pool

Fresnes-les-Montauban See **Arras**

Fréteval 41 (Loir-et-Cher) 900 (☎39)
Map **9** A2
★ **Chalet du Loir** ☎54 rm11 ▥1 G
1 Mar—31 Jan

Frévent 62 (Pas-de-Calais) 4,450 (☎21)
Map **3** A1
★ **Amiens** ℝ 7 r Doullens ☎042543 rm10 ⇆1
▥3 G

Fumay 08 (Ardennes) 6,150 (☎24)
Map **10** C4
★★ **Roches** 28 av J-Jaurès ☎369012 rm36
⇆8 ▥8 G 1 Mar—31 Jan B42—89 M28—62
Pn82—108

Gacé 61 (Orne) 2,700 (☎34) Map **8** D3
★★★ **Champs** rte d'Alençon ☎355145
rm24 (A10) ⇆14 ▥2 15 Feb—15 Jan LD
B55—140 M35—55 Pool ∩
★ **Etoile d'Or** 60 Grande Rue ☎355003 rm14 G
LD B30—57 M25—35
▥⇗ **C Ducheone** 16 r de Rouen ☎356084 Ren

Gan See **Pau**

Gap†05 (Hautes-Alpes) 29,750 (☎92)
Map **28** C3
★★ **Fons-Régina** 2km S on N85 ☎510253
rm24 ⇆14 15 Dec—30 Oct B49—103 M28
Pn68—85
★★ **Grille** 2 pl F-Euzière ☎511484 rm30 ⇆12
▥18 Lift B76—115(double) M23—42
★ **Poyo** pl F-Euzière ☎510413 rm17 ⇆6 ▥11
G Lift LD B48—81 M22—30
▥⇗ **De Verdun** 4 Rue Paul Bert ☎512618 N⇗ BL
▥⇗ **Gap** 14 av du Cdt-Dumont ☎510561 N⇗
Ren

Garde-St-Cast (La) See **St-Cast**

Gavarnie 65 (Hautes-Pyrénées) 200 (☎62)
Map **21** B4
★ **Voyageurs** ☎974801 rm30 ⇆4 G
1 Apr—30 Oct

Gémenos 13 (Bouches-du-Rhône) 3,050
(☎91) Map **27** B2
★★★ **Relais Magdeleine** ☎822005 rm17
⇆14 ▥3 G 15 Mar—10 Jan Pool

Gennes 49 (Maine-et-Loire) 1,700 (☎41)
Map **8** D2
★★ **Naulets d'Anjou** ☎518188 rm12 ⇆12
15 Mar—15 Jan B53—96 M40—55 Pn106—120
★ **Hostellerie de la Loire** ℝ ☎518103 rm11
⇆4 ▥2 G 12 Feb—31 Dec LD B38.50—90
M21—42 Pn77—90

Gérardmer 88 (Vosges) 10,000 (☎29)
Map **11** A2
★★★ **Beau Rivage** espl du Lac ☎630028
rm56 ⇆39 ▥9 G Lift 10 May—20 Sep
★★ **Parc** av de la Ville-de-Vichy ☎630243 rm24
⇆2 ▥8 G Feb & Etr—Sep LD B44—86 M25—57
Pn62—103 Lake
★ **Echo de Ramberchamp** (n rest) ☎630227
rm17 ⇆11 1 Mar—31 Oct B44—72 Lake
★ **Lac** Bout du lac ☎630421 rm17 (A)
24 Mar—30 Sep
▥⇗24 **Choux** 52 rte de Colmar ☎630088 Sim
At **Saut des Cuves** (3km NE on N417)
★★★ **Saut des Cuves** ☎631024 rm30 ⇆10
▥10 G Lift B74—124 M35—47 Pn100—128

Gex 01 (Ain) 4,400 (☎50) Map **10** D1
★★★ **Mainaz** Cd de la Faucille ☎417717 rm25
▥3 G 15 Dec—6 Jun 27 Jun—10 Nov ⇗ Pool
Lake
★ **Bellevue** av de la Gare ☎415540 rm22 ⇆6
▥6 G 15 Dec—1 Nov Lake
▥⇗ **Modernes** les Verts Campagnes ☎415424
N⇗ Ren
▥⇗ **Prodon** 9 r des Terreaux ☎415517 Cit

Gien 45 (Loiret) 15,350 (☎38) Map **9** B2
★★ **Rivage** 1 quai Nice ☎672053 rm28 ⇆15
▥2 G LD B49—98 M34—59
▥⇗24 **SAGVRA** rte de Bourges ☎670850
Cit G100

Givors 69 (Rhône) 22,000 (☎78) Map **27** B4
At **Grigny** (3km N on D15)
★★ **Manoir** ☎730543 rm11 ⇆7 ▥4
1 Mar—15 Nov

Glénic 23 (Creuse) (☎55) Map **16** D4
★★ **Moulin Noyé** (on N140) ☎520911 rm32
⇆7 ▥6

Gluges See **Martel**

Golfe-Juan 06 (Alpes-Maritimes) 3,236
(☎93) Map **28** C2
★★ **Stellamare** rte Cannes N7 ☎637105
rm21 (A) ⇆6 ▥12 Feb—Oct Sea

Gordes 84 (Vaucluse) 1,600 (☎90)
Map **27** B2
★★ **Mayanelle** r Combe ☎720028 rm10 ⇆6
▥4 5 Feb—5 Jan

Goumois 25 (Doubs) 150 (☎81) Map **11** A2
★★ **Taillard** ℝ ☎442075 rm18 (A1) ⇆8 ▥7 G
10 Feb—31 Oct 10 Dec—10 Jan LD B51—119
(double) M33—56 Pn88—110

Gourdon 46 (Lot) 5,150 (☎65) Map **16** C2
★ **Bouriane** ℝ pl Foirail ☎370637 rm19 ⇆3
▥4 G 1 Mar—30 Jan

Gournay-en-Bray 76 (Seine-Maritime)
6,650 (☎35) Map **9** B4
▥⇗24 **Normandie** 9 bd Montmorency ☎451
N⇗454 N⇗ Peu

Gradignan See **Bordeaux**

Gramat 46 (Lot) 3,550 (☎65) Map **16** C2
★★ **Château de Roumégouse** (4km NW on
N681) ☎386381 rm12 ⇆12 2 Apr—3 Oct
B90—165 M42&àlc
★ **Lion d'Or** ℝ pl République ☎387318 rm18
⇆4 ▥4 15 Jan—15 Dec LD B47—108 M30—75
▥⇗24 **Elias** ☎387106 Ren G10

France

Grande-Motte (La) 34 (Herault) (☎67)
Map **27** A2
★★★*Frantel* r du Pont ☎569081 tx480941
rm135 ⇌135 Lift G B106–212 M59 Pn171–212
🍴 Pool Beach Sea

Grand-Pressigny (Le) 37 (Indre-et-Loire)
1,300 (☎47) Map **9** A1
★*Espérance* L₤ ☎949012 rm10 ⇌2 ⋔1 G
1 Feb–6 Jan

Granville 50 (Manche) 15,200 (☎33)
Map **8** C3
★*Gourmets* 1 r G-Clemenceau ☎501987
rm19 ⇌6 LD B35–65 M32–65 Pn85–100
🛢🔧 *Harel* 5 r C-Desmaisons ☎500104 N🅰
Sim G3

Grasse† 06 (Alpes-Maritime) 35,350 (☎93)
Map **28** C2
★★*Beau Soleil* 12 bd Crouët ☎360170
tx47844 Bosdeil rm50 ⇌40 Lift Pool
🛢🔧 *Imperial* bd du Gl-Leclerc ☎365320 Ren

Gray 70 (Haute-Saône) 9,650 (☎84)
Map **10** D2
★*Château de Rigny* ☎652501 rm25 (A11)
⇌20 G LD B60–220 M55–85 Pn180–200
🛢🔧 *Comtoise* 9 r de Paris ☎652256 Cit

Grenoble† 38 (Isère) 169,750 (☎76)
Map **27** B3
★★★★*Sofitel* 7 av d'Innsbruck ☎095427
tx980470 rm100 ⇌100 G Lift B144–204
M39–61 Pn222 Pool
★★★*Angleterre* (n rest) 5 pl V-Hugo ☎873721
tx320297 rm70 ⇌30 ⋔40 Lift B110–142
★★★*Louvre* (n rest) 3 r Clot-Bey (off bd E-Rey)
☎226944 rm55 ⇌30 ⋔10 Lift
★★★*Savoie* 52 av Alsace-Lorraine ☎440020
rm90 ⇌20 ⋔30 G Lift
★★★*Terminus* (n rest) 10 pl Gare ☎448894
rm50 ⇌12 ⋔12 Lift 23 Aug–Jul B69–160
★★*Alpazur* (n rest) 59 av Alsace-Lorraine
☎444280 rm30 ⇌5 ⋔9 G B40–71
★★*Gallia* (n rest) 7 bd Ml-Joffré ☎873921
tx980882 Code 304 rm36 ⇌16 ⋔12 Lift
B58.50–129
★★*Paris-Nice* (n rest) 61 bd J-Vallier
☎963618 rm29 ⇌5 ⋔13 G B52–86
🛢🔧 *Albertiny* 146 av Leonblum ☎090087
BL/Lnc/Jag G
🛢🔧 *P Rativet* 111 cours J-Jaurès ☎961200
At **Claix** (2.5km W on N75 & D269)
🛢🔧 *Gauduel* 46 av A-Croizat ☎963472 N🅰
Frd
★★★*Oiseaux* ☎980774 tx980718 rm20 ⇌5
⋔10 G 15 Jan–Nov B67–115 M28–45 Pn83–139
Pool
At **Fontaine** (2km NW on D531)
🛢🔧 *Majestic* av G-Péri ☎874971 N🅰 Bed/Opl
At **Pont-de-Claix** (8km S)
★*Globe* 1 cours St-André ☎980929 rm12 (A)
⋔9 G Feb–Dec
At **St Martin d'Hères** (4km SE)
☆☆☆ *Novotel Grenoble-Voreppe* ☎210327
tx320273 rm114 Lift B120–140 Pool
At **Voreppe** (12km NW by A48)

Grigny See **Givors**

Grimaud 83 (Var) 2,450 (☎94) Map **28** C2
★★★*Kilal* ☎432002 tx470230 rm47 ⇌42
⋔5 G Lift 15 Dec–30 Oct B205–410 M75&àlc
Pn345–480

Grisolles 82 (Tarn-et-Garonne) 2,400 (☎63)
Map **16** C1
★★*Garrigues* ☎303159 rm27 ⇌20 G
5 Feb–5 Jan B53–90 M25–35

Gué des Grues 28 (Eure-et-Loir) (☎37)
Map **9** A3
★★*Auberge Gué des Grues* ☎385025 rm5
⇌3 ⋔2 G Lift

Guéret 23 (Creuse) 16,150 (☎55) Map **16** D4
★★*Auclair* 8 pl Bonnyaud ☎520796
rm32 ⇌14 G Lift 16 Feb–14 Jan
★*Auclair* 19 av Senatorerie ☎520126 rm33
(A5) ⇌13 G 1 Feb–8 Jan LD B35–91
M19 Pn59.50–133

Guéthary 64 (Pyrénées-Atlantiques) 1,000
(☎59) Map **20** C3
★★*Gurutzia* ☎265030 rm27 ⇌18 ⋔2 G
15 Dec–31 Oct Sea
★★*Juzan* ☎265009 rm29 ⇌12 ⋔8
Jun–Sep LD B32–80 M23 Pn70–86 Sea
★★*Mariénia* (n rest) ☎265104 rm14 ⇌4 ⋔1
1 Jun–30 Sep B34.50–80.50 Sea

Guilvinec 29 (Finistère) 4,650 (☎98)
Map **7** A3
At **Lechiagat** (1km E)
★★*Port* ☎911010 rm38 ⇌10 ⋔28 Sea

Halles (Les) 69 (Rhône) 250 (☎74)
Map **27** A4
★*Charreton* rte de Bordeaux ☎3 rm11 G
Mar–Dec

Halignicourt See **St-Dizier**

Ham 80 (Somme) 6,275 (☎22) Map **9** B4
★*France* 5 pl Hôtel de Ville ☎810022 rm16
⇌5 ⋔5 G (closed Aug) LD B49–93 M38–75

Hauconcourt See **Metz**

Hauteville-les-Dijon See **Dijon**

Havre (Le) 76 (Seine-Maritime) 219,600
(☎35) Map **8** D4 **See Plan**
🅰🅰 agents; see page 83
★★★*Bordeaux* (n rest) pl Gambetta
☎226944 tx190428 Plan **1** rm31 ⇌20 ⋔11
Lift B103–186
★★★*Marly* (n rest) 121 r de Paris ☎428369
tx190369 Ext103 Plan **5** rm34 ⇌14 ⋔16 Lift
B58–137
★★★*Normandie* (n rest) quai George-V
☎424981 tx19354/121 Plan **2** rm65 ⇌40
⋔15 Lift
★★*France & Bourgogne* 21 cours de la
République ☎212929 Plan **3** rm33 ⇌20 Lift
★★*Ile de France* (n rest) 104 r A-France
☎424929 Plan **4** rm17 ⇌6 ⋔7 B31–76
★★*Monaco* 16 r de Paris ☎422101 Plan **6**
rm11 ⇌3 ⋔2 1 Mar–31 Jan B48–92
M40–100 Sea
★*Petit Vatel* (n rest) 86 r L-Brindeau
☎428510 Plan **7** rm28 ⋔9 B36–54
★*Terminus* 23 cours de la République
☎424275 Plan **8** rm44 ⇌9 ⋔4 Lift
★*Voltaire* (n rest) 14 r Voltaire ☎429521
Plan **9** rm24 ⋔15 B49–64
🛢 *Foch* 30 av Foch ☎425874 N🅰 G200
🛢🅿24 *Normande* 200 bd de Graville
☎482483 N🅰481384 Chy/Sim
▮*Tanguy* 19 r G-Braque ☎423380 Vlo G
🛢🔧 *Le Troadec* 93 r Lesueur N🅰 ☎213303
Aud/VW

Haye-du-Puits (La) 50 (Manche) 1,800
(☎33) Map **8** C4
★*Gare* L₤ ☎460422 rm12 (A1) ⇌1 ⋔1 G
9 Feb–9 Jan B34.50–73 M25–50 Pn70–75

Hayons (Les) See **Neufchâtel-en-Bray**

Hédé 35 (Ille-et-Villaine) 1,500 (☎99)
Map **8** C3
★★*Vieux Moulin* L₤ N137 ☎000414 rm17
⇌11 G 15 Feb–15 Jan LD B78–106 M55–75
Pn90–120

Hendaye-Plage 64 (Pyrénées-Atlantiques)
10,150 (☎59) Map **19** B3
★★*Paris* Rond-Point ☎267561 rm39 ⇌9
⋔24 Lift Etr–1 Oct

Henin Beaumont 62 (Pas-de-Calais) 26,500
(☎21) Map **3** B1

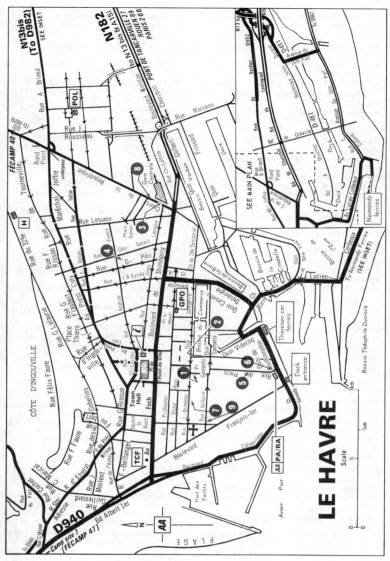

LE HAVRE

Le Havre
1   ★★★Bordeaux
2   ★★★Normandie
3   ★★France et Bourgogne
4   ★★Ile de France
5   ★★★Marly
6   ★★Monaco
7   ★Petit Vatel
8   ★Terminus
9   ★Voltaire

France

At **Noyelles Godault** (3km NE)
☆☆☆ **Novotel Henin Douai** ☎201601
tx110352 rm80 ⇌80 Lift B120–140 Pool

Hohwald (Le) 67 (Bas-Rhin) 500 (☎88)
Map **11** B3
★★★*Grand* ☎083103 rm74 ⇌28 ▥27 G Lift
20 Dec–6 Jan 15 Feb–15 Nov ✒
★*Idoux* ☎083120 rm20 G 15 Dec–15 Nov

Honfleur 14 (Calvados) 9,200 (☎31)
Map **8** D4
★★★ **Ferme St-Siméon** ☎892361 rm8 (A3)
⇌8 G 18 Mar–2 Jan LD B212–282 Màlc
Pn225–240 Sea

Hossegor 40 (Landes) 950 (☎58)
Map **15** A1
★★ **Beauséjour** av Tour-du-Lac ☎720107
rm46 ⇌34 ▥8 G Lift 1 Jun–20 Sep LD
B55.50–136 M45–50 Pn100–150 Pool
★★ **Ermitage** allées des Pins Tranquilles
☎720222 rm12 (A7) ▥12 1 Jun–15 Sep
B85–105 M30 ✒

Houches(Les) 74 (Haute-Savoie) 1,500
(☎50) Map **28** C4
☆☆ **Delta** N506 ☎544503 rm30 ⇌30 G
B96–142
★★ *Piste Bleue* ℡ rte les Chavants ☎544066
rm35 (A) ⇌18 15 Jun–15 Sep 15 Dec–Etr
At **Bellevue**
★*Hutte* ☎St-Gervaise 549 ta Garçon rm25
25 Dec–Etr 1 Jul–31 Aug

Houdement See **Nancy**

Hyères†83 (Var) 39,600 (☎94)
Map **28** C1
★*Central* (n rest) 17 av J-Clotis ☎650345
rm15 ⇌2 ▥6.
🛏🔑 **Sapor** 17 av des Iles d'Or ☎651071 N🅕
Opl/Vau

Ile-Rousse (L') See **Corse (Corsica)**

Illkirch See **Strasbourg**

Inor 55 (Meuse) (☎28) Map **10** D4
★ **Faison Doré** ☎803545 rm15 ▥3 LD
B31.40–48 M20–50 Pn80–85

Isigny-sur-Mer 14 (Calvados) 3,350
(☎31) Map **8** C4
★★ **France** ℡ r Demagny ☎220033 rm20
⇌10 G 1 Feb–10 Dec LD B40–74
M40–55 &àlc Pn75–87

Isle-Adam (L') 95 (Val d'Oise) 10,050
(☎1) Map **9** B3
★★ **Cabouillet** 5 quai de l'Oise ☎4690090
rm9 ⇌6 Lift LD B65–90 M75–120 ✒ Pool
Golf

Issoire 63 (Puy-de-Dome) 15,700 (☎73)
Map **27** A4
★★ **Pariou** ℡ 18 bd Kennedy ☎892211 rm28
⇌10 ▥9 G B45–67 M18–32 Pn65–70
★*Paris* r Espagne ☎892297 rm15 ⇌3 ▥4 G

Issoudun 36 (Indre) 16,550 (☎54)
Map **9** B1
★★ **France & Commerce** 3 r P-Brossolette
☎210065 rm28 ⇌25 ▥3 G 1 Feb–31 Dec
B62–130 M26.50–45

Itxassou 64 (Pyrénées-Atlantiques) 1,250
(☎59) Map **20** C3
★*Arza Mendi* pl Fronton ☎257529 rm13 ⇌1
▥4 Etr–31 Oct LD B38–67 M28–40 Pn70–80

Ivry-la-Bataille 27 (Eure) 2,350 (☎32)
Map **9** A3
★★ **Grand St-Martin** ℡ 9 r Ezy ☎364139
rm10 ⇌4 ▥4 5 Feb–5 Jan LD B61–144
(double) M50–78 Pn100–160
★★ **Moulin** 10 r Henri-IV ☎364051 rm14 ⇌14
1 Mar–31 Jan B88–107 M56 &àlc Pn132

Jard-sur-Mer 85 (Vendée) 1,450 (☎30)
Map **8** C1

★★ **Coquille** Le Port ☎334236 rm10 ⇌2 ▥7
20 Mar–20 Sep LD B47–64 M27–41 Pn83–87
Sea

Joigny 89 (Yonne) 11,950 (☎86)
Map **10** C2
★★ **Moderne** ℡ av R-Petit ☎621628 rm19 ⇌9
▥8 G LD B93.50–123 M64 Pool
★★ **St Jacques** ℡ 14 fbg de Paris ☎620970
rm16 ⇌13 ▥3 G 1 Feb–1 Jan LD B115–210
(double) M120–180
🛏🔑 **Blondeau** 6 fbg de Paris ☎620502 N🅕 GM

Joinville 52 (Haute-Marne) 5,150 (☎27)
Map **10** D3
★★ **Grand Pont** ℡ r A-Briand ☎960986 rm27
(A16) ⇌3 ▥9 G 15 Jan–25 Dec B35–86 M20–
50 Pn60–100
★ **Poste** ℡ pl Grève ☎961263 rm12 ⇌2 ▥2
G 15 Feb–15 Jan LD B38–74 M35
★ **Soleil d'Or** ℡ 9 r Capucins ☎961566
rm11 ⇌1 ▥1 G (closed 2 weeks Feb) LD
B32–54 M18–32
🛏🔑**R Duthoit** av de la Marne ☎961040 M/c
Ren G2

Josselin 56 (Morbihan) 3,000 (☎97)
Map **7** B3
★★*Château* ℡ r Gl-de-Gaulle ☎222011
tx74884 rm41 (A) ⇌10 ▥14 G 1 Mar–31 Jan

Joué-les-Tours 37 (Indre-et-Loire) 6,448
Map **8** D2
★★ **Cèdres** (n rest) Savonière ☎430028 rm35
⇌9 ▥26 G Lift B70–125
★★*Château de Beaulieu* ☎285219 rm17
⇌7 ▥9 15 Jan–15 Dec ✒ Pool

Jougne 25 (Doubs) 900 (☎81) Map **11** A1
★★ **Deux Saisons** ℡ (n rest) ☎891386 rm21
⇌3 ▥7 G 15 Dec–15 Apr 15 Jun–15 Sep
B36–71 M20–35 Pn70–80

Juan-les-Pins 06 (Alpes-Maritimes)
27,400 (☎93) Map **28** C2
★★★★★ **Provençal** bd Littoral ☎611980
tx470756F rm220 ⇌220 G Lift Apr–Oct
B130–390 M80 Pn270–530 ✒ Beach Sea
★★★★ **Belles Rives** bd Littoral ☎610279
tx470984 rm46 (A2) ⇌43 ▥3 Lift Apr–30 Sep
B147–400 Màlc Pn271–370 St15% Beach Sea
★★★ **Astoria** av MI-Joffre ☎612365
tx470800 rm60 ⇌30 ▥20 G Lift B85–165
M36 Pn125–150(double) Sea
★★★ **Helios** 3 av Daucheville ☎615525 rm70
⇌67 ▥3 G Lift Mar–Oct LD B127–394 M70
Pn150–270
★★★*Juana* la Pinède ☎610870 tx47778F rm50
⇌45 G Lift 20 Mar–20 Oct Beach Sea
★★ **Alexandra** r Pauline ☎610136 rm20 ⇌7
▥8 20 Mar–30 Sep Pn85–110
★★ **Cyrano** (n rest) av L-Gallet ☎610483 rm40
⇌12 ▥8 1 Apr–15 Oct B50–120 M30–40 Beach
Sea
★★ **Emeraude** (n rest) av Saramartel
☎610967 rm20 ⇌1 ▥15 1 Apr–30 Sep B41–
104
★★ **Noailles** av G-Gallice ☎611170 rm22 (A6)
⇌4 ▥3 G Jun–Sep B38–141 M24
Pn55–125 St15% Sea
★★*Régence* 2 av Al-Courbet ☎610939 rm20
⇌10 ▥10 22 Mar–1 Oct
★*Midi* bd Poincaré ☎613516 rm17 ⇌2 ▥6
G 15 Dec–15 Oct LD B38.20–73 M25–32
Pn65–85
🛏🔑 **St Charles** 6 r St-Charles ☎610816 N🅕
Cit G80
🛏🔑 **Wilson** 122 bd Wilson ☎342515 N🅕 Opl G1

Jullouville 50 (Manche) 4,000 (☎33)
Map **8** C3
★★ **Casino** ℡ ☎618282 rm58 ⇌17 ▥17
7 Apr–25 Sep LD B37.40–116.50 M31–65
Pn107–128

La Each placename beginning with La is listed under the name which follows it.

Labouheyre 40 (Landes) 2,650 (☎58) Map **15** B2
🏨🛢 **Lafargue** pl du Foirail ☎789111 N🛢 M/c Aud/MB/VW

Ladoix-Serrigny See **Beaune**

Laffrey 38 (Isère) 200 (☎76) Map **27** B3
★★**Grand Lac** ☒ ☎681290 rm20 ⇙20 B48—70 M25—45 Pn71—94 Lake

Lalinde 24 (Dordogne) 3,100 (☎53) Map **16** C2
★★*Château* ☒ r Verdun ☎610182 rm10 ⇙1 🍴1 Nov—Sep
★★*Résidence* ☒ (n rest) 3 r Prof-Testut ☎610181 rm11 ⇙2 🍴6 1 Mar—30 Nov

Lamastre 07 (Ardèche) 3,100 (☎75) Map **27** B3
★★★**Midi** pl Seignobos ☎064150 rm22 ⇙12 🍴2 G 1 Mar—15 Dec LD B42—109 M55—100 Pn100—140
★★**Commerce** ☒ pl Rampon ☎064153 rm23 ⇙5 🍴10 G 1 Mar—1 Dec LD B70—83(double) M26—55 Pn86—100

Lamballe 22 (Côtes-du-Nord) 10,200 (☎96) Map **7** B3
★★**Angleterre** ☒ bd Jobert ☎310621 ta Davidhôtel rm35 (A13) ⇙13 🍴10 G Lift LD B50—115 M30—75
★**Tour d'Argent** ☒ 2 r du Dr Lavergne ☎310137 rm15 ⇙1 🍴5 (closed Oct) LD B32—72 M20—35 Pn62—80

Lanester See **Lorient**

Langeais 37 (Indre-et-Loire) 3,950 (☎47) Map **8** D2
★★*Family & Duchess Anne* ☒ 9 r Tours ☎558203 rm22 ⇙4 🍴4 G 1 Mar—30 Jan
★★**Hosten** 2 r Gambetta ☎558212 rm14 ⇙12 🍴2 G Feb—Dec LD B73—157 M115—175

Langogne 48 (Lozère) 4,350 (☎66) Map **27** A3
★★*Poste* 13 av Foch rm40 ⇙8 🍴8 G 🛥

Langon 33 (Gironde) 6,150 (☎56) Map **15** B2
🏨🛢 **Doux & Trouillot** 45 cours Sadi-Carnot ☎630647 N🛢 M/c Peu G50

Langres 52 (Haute-Marne) 12,500 (☎25) Map **10** D2
★★**Europe** 23 r Diderot ☎851088 rm28 (A9) ⇙8 🍴8 G (closed Oct) LD B36—87 M22—50
★★**Lion d'Or** rte de Vesoul ☎850330 rm18 ⇙4 🍴7 G Mar—Jan LD B46—91 M25—28 Pn80—100 Pool Lake
★★*Amorial* (n rest) 16 r Gambetta ☎850101 rm12 ⇙4 🍴1 G 1 Mar—31 Jan
★**Cheval Blanc** ☎850700 rm20 (A10) ⇙5 🍴6 G 1 Mar—10 Jan LD B35—86 M20—40
🏨🛢 **Europe** rte de Chaumont ☎850378 N🛢 M/c Aud/BMW/VW G2

Langueux See **St-Brieuc**

Lannemezan 65 (Hautes-Pyrénées) 8,500 (☎62) Map **15** B1
🏨🛢 *Pyrénées* 13ter rte de Tarbes ☎989111 Bed/Opl

Lanslebourg 73 (Savoie) 550 (☎79) Map **28** C3
★**Relais Deux Cols** ☒ 73 Val Cenis ☎052341 rm21 G Lift May—30 Sep B37—68 M26—36 Pn75—84 Pool

Lanslevillard 73 (Savoie) 350 (☎79) Map **28** C3
★★**Etoile des Neiges** ☎050041 rm20 (A1) ⇙10 🍴5 G 15 Jun—15 Sep 15 Dec—15 Apr B53—91 M35 Pn 85—95

Laon† **02** (Aisne) 30,200 (☎23) Map **10** C4
★★**Angleterre** 10 bd Lyon ☎230462 rm30 ⇙21 🍴4 G Lift LD B57—113 M28 Pn98—113
★**Bannière de France** 11 r de F Roosevelt ☎232144 rm18 ⇙5 🍴7 G 10 Jan—20 Dec B34—98 M27—70 Pn80—120
★**Commerce** (n rest) 18 pl de la Gare ☎230038 rm21 ⇙21 G B41—69(double)
🏨🛢 **St-Marcel** 45 bd Gras Brancourt ☎232935 N🛢 AR/BL/Lnc/Tri
🏨🛢 **SICB** 121 av de Belgique ☎232067 N🛢 Frd G150

Lapalisse 03 (Allier) 3,800 (☎70) Map **27** A4
★**Galland** 20 pl de la République ☎990721 rm14 ⇙2 🍴1 G 1 Feb—31 Dec B34—77

Laragne 05 (Hautes-Alpes) 3,900 (☎92) Map **27** B2/3
★**Terrasses** av Provence ☎650036 rm17 ⇙3 🍴4 G 1 May—1 Oct B32—63 M22 Pn61—66

Laroque-des-Arcs See **Cahors**

Laumes (Les) 21 (Côte-d'Or) 2,906 (☎80) Map **10** C2
★★**Gare** ☒ ☎960046 rm26 ⇙3 🍴2 G B29—69 M23—39

Laval† **53** (Mayenne) 54,550 (☎43) Map **8** C3
🏨🛢 **Boureau** 9 r Echelle Marteau ☎531314 N🛢 Frd
🏨🛢 **Ouest** 95 quai P-Boudet ☎530969 N🛢 AR/BL/Jag/Tri
🏨🛢 **24 SEGL** 105 r V-Boissel ☎534481 Aud/Lnc/VW

Lavandou (Le) 83 (Var) 3,826 (☎94) Map **28** C1
★★★*Calanque* 62 av Gl-de-Gaulle ☎710046 rm29 ⇙21 🍴8 Lift Sea
★★★**California** ☎710263 rm27 ⇙3 🍴24 20 May—25 Sep LD B69—99 M22 🛥 Pool Beach Golf ∩ Sea
★★★**Résidence-Beach** bd Front-de-Mer ☎710066 rm55 ⇙50 🍴5 Lift 26 May—25 Sep LD B170—230(double) M45 Pn260—320 🛥 Beach Sea
★★**Neptune** (n rest) 26 av Gl-de-Gaulle ☎710101 rm33 ⇙4 🍴18 B39—100 🛥 Pool Golf ∩
★★**Provençale** 11 r Parton Ravello ☎710044 rm13 ⇙3 🍴4 Apr—Sep B53—76(double) M35 Pn90—101.50
★**Petite Bohème** av F-Roosevelt ☎711030 rm16 ⇙6 🍴7 27 Apr—Sep LD B43—90 M32 Pn90—106 Sea
🏨🛢 *M Costa* chemin du Repos ☎710804 N🛢

Lavaur 81 (Tarn) 8,500 (☎63) Map **16** C1
🏨🛢 **SIVA** 1 pl du Pont St-Roch ☎580387
At **St-Lieux-les-Lavaur** (11km NE on D81 & D631)
★★**Chateau** ☎577619 rm17 (A5) ⇙17 B78 (double) Pn85 St12%

Lavoute-sur-Loire 43 (Haute-Loire) (☎71) Map **27** A3
At **Larcenac-St Vincent** (3km N on D103)
★**Relais** ☒ ☎085109 rm10 🍴6 G B32—54 M17.50—34 Pn57—66

Laxou See **Nancy**

Le Each placename beginning with Le is listed under the name which follows it.

Lechiagat See **Guilvinec**

Lecques (Les) 83 (Var) (☎94) Map **27** B1
★**Terrasses** av des Lecques ☎262423 rm14 ⇙10 🍴4 1 Mar—30 Sep B82—109(double) M28 &àlc Pn98—110 Sea

Lens† **62** (Pas-de-Calais) 40,300 (☎21) Map **3** B1

France

🛏🕭 *Thirion* 68 av A-Maès ☎282008 N🗫 Bed/
Opl G10

Les Each placename beginning with Les is
listed under the name which follows it.

Lescar See **Pau**

Lessay 50 (Manche), 1,350 (☎33) Map **8** C4
★**Hostellerie de l'Abbaye** pl St-Cloud
☎463388 rm12 ⇆3 G 1 Nov–30 Sep B32–66
M29–42 Pn58–83
★**Normandie** ⓛ 3 pl Marché ☎464111 rm10
⋔2 G Mar–Oct LD B30–54 M19–40 Pn68–132

Lézignan-Corbières 11 (Aude) 7,450
(☎68) Map **16** D1
🛏🕭 *Lézignan* 63 bd G-Clemenceau ☎270293
N🗫 Ren G10

Libourne†33 (Gironde), 23,000 (☎56)
Map **15** C2
★★*Loubat* 32 r Chanzy ☎511758 rm52 ⇆19
⋔8 G
🛏🕭 *D Agullo* 26 r du President Wilson
☎511460 N🗫 Ren

Lille†59 (Nord) 177,300 (☎20) Map **3** B1
★★★*Bellevue* (n rest) 5 r J-Roisin ☎574586
tx82790 Belvutel rm80 ⇆60 ⋔4 Lift
★★★*Carlton* 3 r de Paris ☎552411 tx110400
rm80 ⇆70 ⋔3 Lift B69–167 M45–60
☆☆☆*Novotel* A1 ☎979225
tx820519 rm92 ⇆92 Lift B120–140 Pool
★★★*Royal Concorde* 2 bd Carnot ☎510511
tx820575 rm111 ⇆65 ⋔22 Lift
🛏🕭 *Delannoy* 208 Faubourg d'Arras ☎961513
N🗫 BL
🛏▶24 *Lilloise Autos* 58 r des Stations
☎571550 N☎549302 Chy/Sim
At **Englos** (7.5km W on D63)
☆☆☆*Motellerie* ☎923015 tx82302F rm100
⇆51 ⋔49 Pool
☆☆☆*Novotel Lille-Lomme* A25 ☎504700
tx120120 rm117 ⇆117 Lift B120–140 Pool
At **Madeleine**
🛏🕭 *Baillet* 201 r du Gl-de-Gaulle ☎515556
N🗫 Jag/Rov/Tri
At **Marcq en Baroeul** (4.5km N on N350)
☆☆☆☆*Holiday Inn* ☎721730 tx120785
rm125 ⇆125 Lift B129–162 M42 Pn211 Pool

Lillers 62 (Pas de Calais) 9,560 Map **3** A1
★*Commerce* 50 pl de la Gare ☎022077
rm10 G 1 Sep–31 Jul LD B27–35 M20–25

Limoges†87 (Haute-Vienne) 147,450 (☎55)
Map **16** C3
★★★★*Frantel* 1 pl République ☎321796
tx580771 rm75 ⇆75 G Lift B126–176 M35
★★★*Luk* 29 pl Jourdan ☎334400 rm55 ⇆55
Lift LD B86–123 M25 Pn120
★★*Jourdan* 2 av du Gl-de-Gaulle ☎774962
rm45 ⇆30 ⋔10 Lift
★*Relais Lamartine* ⓛ (n rest) 10 r des
Coopérateurs ☎775339 rm20 ⇆2 ⋔3 G
🛏🕭 *Bernis* 27 av G-Péri ☎323225 N🗫
🛏🕭 *Colin* 5 cours Gay-Lussac ☎772302 N🗫
BL
🛏🕭 *Generale Automobiles du Limousin SA* rte
de Toulouse ☎304830 N🗫 BL/Jag/Opl/Rov/Tri/
Vau G10
🛏🕭 *Limoges* rte de Toulouse ☎321893 N🗫
G40
▶▶24 *Sports* 12 r de Beaupuy ☎777102 N🗫
M/c G

Lingolsheim See **Strasbourg**

Lion-d'Angers (Le) 49 (Maine-et-Loire)
2,350 (☎41) Map **8** C2
★*Voyageurs* quai Oudon ☎913008 rm13 ⇆4
⋔2 G 8 Feb–15 Nov B39–77 M19–45

Lisieux†14 (Calvados) 26,700 (☎31)
Map **8** D4

★★★**Grand Normandie** ⓛ 11 bis r au Char
☎621605 tx170269 rm83 ⇆17 ⋔14 G Lift
1 May–30 Oct B54–101 M23–54
★★**Lourdes** 4 r au Char ☎311948 rm39 ⇆8
⋔2 G Lift LD B41–65 M33–50 Pn75–85
★★**Regina** 14 r de la Gare ☎311543 txExpolis
170169 rm40 ⇆40 G Lift LD B58–106 M25–60
★**Coupe d'Or** ⓛ 49 r Pont Mortain ☎311684
txExpolis170169 rm16 ⇆2 ⋔5 G B41–103
M28–70 Pn90–108
🛏🕭 *Jonquard* 81 r H-Cheron ☎311217 N🗫
Aud/VW

Loches†37 (Indre-et-Loire) 6,850 (☎47)
Map **9** A2
★*France* 6 r Picois ☎590032 rm23 (A3) ⇆2
⋔6 G 15 Dec–15 Nov LD B34–66 M21–37
At **Bridoré** (14km S on N143)
★★*Barbe Bleue* ☎947269 rm12 ⋔10 1 Mar–
1 Nov B34–78 Màlc pm96–117

Lodève 34 (Herault) 8,200 (☎67) Map **27** A2
★★*Croix Blanche* ☎441087 rm32 (A13) ⇆14
⋔3 G 1 Apr–1 Dec B33–66 M18–37 Pn70–80
★*Nord* 18 bd de la Liberté ☎441008 rm21
⇆2 ⋔2 G Sep–Oct

Longuyon 54 (Meurthe-et-Moselle) 7,500
(☎28) Map **10** D4
🛏🕭 *M R Piquerez* 6 r Mazelle ☎445066 N🗫
Ren G

Lons-le-Saunier†39 (Jura) 23,300 (☎82)
Map **10** D1
★★*Genève* pl XI-Novembre ☎241911 rm41
⇆23 ⋔4 G Lift
🛏🕭 *Sports* 70 r des Salines ☎240321 N🗫 Opl
🛏🕭 *Thévenod* rte de Champagnole ☎244158
N🗫 Aud/MB/VW

Lorient 56 (Morbihan) 71,950 (☎97)
Map **7** B2/3
★★★*Bretagne* 6 pl de la Libération ☎643465
rm34 ⇆29 G Lift B65–140 M40–64
★★★*Richelieu* pl Jules-Ferry ☎213573
tx950810 rm58 ⇆58 Lift B128–171
M35–60 Pn155–200
At **Lanester**
☆☆☆*Novotel Lorient* ☎760216 tx950026
rm60 ⇆60 G Lift B120–140 Pool

Loudéac 22 (Côtes-du-Nord) 10,150 (☎96)
Map **7** B3
★*Voyageurs* ⓛ 10 r Cadélac ☎280047 rm32
⇆3 ⋔15 G Lift 20 Jan–20 Dec

Loudun 86 (Vienne) 8,470 (☎49)
Map **8** D2
★*Roue d'Or* rte Saumur ☎220123 rm16 (A3)
⇆5 ⋔1 G LD B48–84 M26–43

Loué 72 (Sarthe), 1,900 (☎43) Map **8** D2
★★*Ricordeau* 11 r Liberation ☎274003 rm22
(A8) ⇆10 ⋔7 G B63–208 M85

Louhans 71 (Saône-et-Loire) 11,050 (☎85)
Map **10** D1
🛏▶24 *Chevrier,* 11 r du 11 Novembre G5

Lourdes†65 (Hautes-Pyrénées) 18,100
(☎62) Map **15** B1
★★★*Grotte* 66 r de Grotte ☎942887
tx510035 rm83 ⇆83 G Lift Etr–Oct
B100–180 M50 Pn140–200
★★★*Moderne* av B-Soubirous ☎941232
rm105 ⇆42 ⋔15
★★*Provençale* 4 r Baron-Duprat ☎943134
tx48518 rm60 ⇆28 ⋔12 Lift
★★*St-Roch* pl J-d'Arc ☎940214 rm43 (A10)
⇆3 ⋔1 Lift Etr–15 Oct LD B33–63 M20 Pn60–
70
🛏▶24 *Boutes* rte de Tarbes ☎940168
N☎942193 Sim G
🛏🕭 *P Chartier* 14 av A-Marqui ☎942308 N🗫GM
🛏🕭 *Felices* 14 av du Gl-Leclerc ☎943149
N🗫 BL/Tri

Louviers 27 (Eure) 8,900 (☎32) Map **9** A4
At **St-Pierre de Vauvray**
★★★**Hostellerie de St-Pierre** ☎500329
rm16 ⇌12 Lift 1 Jan–30 Jan 1 Mar–30 Nov
B70–200 M50 Pn160–210 ✆
At **Vironvay** (4km SE on N182a)
★★**Saisons** ☎400256 rm14 ⇌9 ▥1 G
10 Feb–10 Jan ✆

Luc (Le) 83 (Var) 5,650 (☎94) Map **28** C2
★**Parc** 1 r J-Jaurès ☎735001 rm10 ⇌2 ▥4
G 15 Dec–15 Nov LD B48–95 M46–80

Lucé See **Chartres**

Luchon 31 (Haute-Garonne) 3,650 (☎61)
Map **21** B4
★★★**Poste & Golf** 29 allées d'Etigny
☎790040 tx520018 rm60 ⇌55 ▥2 Lift
20 Dec–20 Oct B131–222 M42 Pn150–220
✆ Pool
★★**Bains** 75 allées d'Etigny ☎790058
tx530139 rm53 ⇌13 ▥23 Lift
20 Dec–20 Oct B44–119 M37 Pn66–138

Lucon 85 (Vendée) 9,600 (☎30) Map **8** C1
★**Croissant** 1 pl du Acacias ☎561115 rm38
⇌16 ▥16 G (closed Oct) LD B33–71 M20–35
▯☜▯24 **Rallet** 8 r de Fontenay ☎561821 Ren G

Lude (Le) 72 (Sarthe) 4,150 (☎43)
Map **8** D2
★**Maine** LE 24 rte Saumur ☎946054 rm19
⇌2 ▥6 G 8 Sep–10 Jan 10 Feb–1 Aug

Lunel 34 (Herault) 13,600 (☎67) Map **27** A2
★**Palais** 12 av de Lattre-de-Tassigny
☎711139 rm24 ⇌2 ▥4 G 20 Jan–20 Dec

Lunéville† 54 (Meurthe-et-Mosel)
24,727 (☎28) Map **11** A3
★★**Europe** (n rest) 56 r Alsace ☎731617
rm30 ⇌8 ▥10 B48.50–78
▯☜▯ **Nouveau** 70 av de la Libération ☎731181
N☜ Cit
▯☜▯ **R Turck** 95 fbg de Ménil ☎731501 N☜
Ren G20

Lus-la-Croix Haute 26 (Drôme) 500
(☎75) Map **27** B3
★**Touring** LE off N75 ☎585001 rm17 ▥1 G
Apr–1 Oct B28–64 M25–30 Pn60–70

Luxeuil-les-Bains 70 (Haute-Saône) 11,000
(☎84) Map **11** A2
★★**Beau Site** LE 18 r Thermes ☎401467 rm44
(A14) ⇌26 G Lift B41.50–125 M25 Pn143–215

Lyon† 69 (Rhône) 462,850 (☎78) Map **17** B4
See also **Limonest**
★★★★**Grand** 11 r Grolée ☎425621
tx33244 rm143 ⇌90 ▥40 G Lift
★★★★**PLM Terminus** 12 cours de Verdun
☎375811 tx330500 rm139 ⇌79 ▥44 G Lift
B64–169 M39–50
★★★★**Royal Sogetel** 20 pl Bellecour ☎375731
tx310785 rm100 ⇌70 ▥25 G Lift B78–260
M30–60
★★★★**Sofitel** 20 quai Gailleton ☎427250
tx330225 rm196 ⇌196 G Lift B215–331
M83 Pn381 Pool
★★★**Beaux-Arts** (n rest) 75 r Prés-Herriot
☎380950 tx330442 rm80 ⇌50 ▥30 Lift
B126–136
★★★**Carlton Sogetel** (n rest) pl de la
République ☎375731 tx310787 rm90
⇌55 ▥22 G Lift Jan–Jul Sep–Dec B77–192
★★**Continental** 17 pl Carnot ☎381720
rm104 ⇌20 ▥26 Lift B43–90 M23–33
★★**Globe et Cecil** (n rest) 21 r Gaspanin
☎425895 tx310917 rm65 ⇌30 ▥15 Lift B42–
103
▯☜▯**Générale** 32 quai Perrache ☎420705 N☜
Ren
▯☜▯ **Denuzière** 5 r Denuzière ☎376843 G8
▯☜▯ **Dumond** 7 r Duhamel ☎375565 Peu G30

▯☜▯ **A Gacon** 85 r P-Corneille ☎609413 G50
Kennings 70–76 r de Marseille ☎581653
N☜ BL/Jag/Rov/Tri
▯☜▯ **Verdun** 4 cours de Verdun ☎372631 G300
▯☜▯ **Veyet** 82 bd V-Merle ☎602528 N☜ Frd
At **Bron** (10km SE)
☆☆☆**Novotel** 260 av St-Exupery ☎269748
tx340781 rm195 ⇌195 Lift B120–140 Pool
At **Charbonnières-les-Bains** (8km NW by N7)
★★★**Christel** 78 bis rte de Paris ☎344140
tx380768 rm60 ⇌60 B94–122 M30–45
Pn100–125 Pool
At **Dardilly** (10km on N6)
☆☆☆☆**Holiday Inn** Porte de Lyon ☎357020
tx900006 rm204 ⇌204 Lift B116–156
Màlc Pool
☆☆☆**International** Porte de Lyon ☎352805
tx33045 rm200 ⇌200 Lift
☆☆☆**Novotel Lyon Nord** Porte de Lyon
☎351341 tx330962 rm107 ⇌107 Lift
B120–140 Pool
At **La Duchère** (2km NW)
▯☜▯**SATAL** pl du Commerce ☎353560 N☜
Bed/Opl G5
At **St-Priest** (11km SE by D518)
▯☜▯**Kennings** 190 rte de Grenoble ☎908200
N☜ BL/Jag/Rov/Tri

Lyons-la-Forêt 27 (Eure) 900 (☎32)
Map **9** A/B4
★★**Licorne** LE pl Benserade ☎496202 rm24
⇌13 ▥2 G LD B89–177(double) M45–80
Pn100–173

Mâcon† 71 (Saône-et-Loire) 40,500 (☎85)
Map **10** C1
★★★**Frantel** 26 r de Coubertin ☎382806
tx800830 rm61 ▥15 Lift B126–176 M52
☆☆☆**Novotel** A6 ☎370080 tx800869 rm60
⇌60 Lift B120–140 Pool
★★**Bellevue** 36 quai Lamartine ☎380507
tx800837 rm41 ⇌14 ▥14 G Lift LD B53.50–
155.50 M37–82 àlc
★★**Champs-Elysées** 6 r V-Hugo ☎383657
rm52 ⇌16 ▥2 G Lift 15 Dec–31 Oct LD
B47–99 M26–60
★★**Genève** LE 1 r Bigonnet ☎381810 rm62
⇌16 ▥12 Lift Whi–Dec
★★**Terminus** 91 r V-Hugo ☎380102 rm34
⇌18 ▥14 G Lift LD B46–98 M31–55 Pn116–123
★**Charollais** 71 r Rambuteau ☎383623 rm12
▥1 G LD B33–78 M23–50
▯☜▯ **Bois** 39 r Lacretelle ☎384631 N☜ BL/Tri
G10
▯☜▯24 **Chauvot** r J-Mermoz ☎382859 N☜ Opl/
Vlo G25
▯☜▯ **Ferret** 89 rte de Lyon ☎388355 N☜ M/c Cit
▯☜▯ **Renault Macon** Carrefour de l'Europe
☎382550 N☜ Ren
At **Crèches-sur-Saône** (0.5km NW on D89)
★★**Château de la Barge** ☎371204 rm28
⇌17 ▥5 Lift 1 Feb–15 Dec
At **St-Albain** (10km N)
☆☆☆ **Sofitel Jacques Borel** A6 ☎381617
tx800881 rm100 ⇌100 Lift LD B123–196
M48 Pool
At **St-Jean-le-Priche** (7km N on N6)
★★★**Château-St-Jean** ☎370135 rm24
⇌11 1 Mar–31 Oct
At **Sancé-lès-Mâcon** (4km N on N6)
☆☆☆**Vielle Ferme** N6 ☎384693 rm32 ⇌32
LD B111–152 M35–80 Pool

Madeleine See **Lille**

Magescq 40 (Landes) 1,150 (☎58)
Map **15** A1/2
★★**Relais Poste** ☎577025 rm16 ⇌16 G
15 Dec–11 Nov

Maintenon 28 (Eure-et-Loir) 3,350 (☎37)
Map **9** A/B3

France

★***Aqueduc* LE** pl Gare ☎230005 tx720895
rm17 ⇔2 🏠6 G 15 Feb–15 Jan

Malène (La) 48 (Lozère) 250 (☎66)
Map **27** A3
★★★**Château Malène** ☎475112 rm12 ⇔5
🏠7 Lift 1 May–15 Oct B107.50–154.50(double)
M30–80
★***Grand* LE** rm31 ⇔11 🏠3 G 1 May–1 Oct

Malo-les-Bains 59 (Nord) 15,220 (☎20)
Map **3** A2
★***Digue*** 29 Digue de Mer ☎665828 rm21
⇔1 🏠1 Sea

Mamers 72 (Sarthe) 6,800 (☎43) Map **8** D3
★★**Croix Blanche** 5 r Dallieu ☎976263 rm10
⇔2 G (closed Fri) B31–61 M18.50–32

Mandelieu 06 (Alpes-Maritimes) 9,700
(☎93) Map **28** C2
☆**Esterel** ☎389220 rm31 (A6) ⇔24
1 Dec–31 Oct B49–128 M35 Pn85–95
★**Pavillion des Sports** ☎479086 rm14 🏠6
1 Dec–31 Oct LD B54–82 M29–40

Mans (Le)† **72** (Sarthe) 155,250 (☎43)
Map **8** D2
★★★**Concorde** 16 av Gl-Leclerc ☎847170
tx720487 rm64 ⇔32 🏠23 Lift B67–130 Màlc
★★★**Moderne** 14 r Bourg-Belé ☎843640
rm33 (A) ⇔17 🏠11 G
★★**Central** (n rest) 5 bd Rene Levasseur
(off pl de la République) ☎280893 rm50 ⇔10
🏠20 Lift B38–101.50
★**Rennes** (n rest) 43 bd de Gare ☎850070
rm23 ⇔4 🏠9 B46–111.50
🏠**Albion** 108 av F-Geneslay ☎843274 N🏠
BL/Jag/Rov/Tri G10
🏠**Goutard** 20 bis r Barbier ☎283418 N🏠 Vlo
🏠**Leseul** bd P-Lefaucheux ☎846170 N🏠
🏠**Station Bollée** 132 av Bollée ☎844174
N🏠 BL/Jag/Rov/Tri

Marcay See **Chinon**

Margny See **Compiègne**

Margueritttes See **Nimes**

Markstein (Le) 68 (Haut-Rhin) (☎89)
Map **11** A2
★***Belle Vue*** ☎376182 rm18 ⇔3 G 1 Dec–31 Oct

Marlenheim 67 (Bas-Rhin) 1,850 (☎88)
Map **11** B3
★★***Cerf* LE** 179 r Gl-de-Gaulle ☎875006 rm20
(A) ⇔6 🏠4 G 1 Mar–28 Jun 12 Jul–31 Jan
★★**Reeb** N4 ☎875270 rm26 ⇔15 🏠6 G
Feb–15 Jan LD B44–88 M38–100 Pn100

Marmande 47 (Lot-et-Garonne) 17,750
(☎58) Map **15** B2
★***France*** (n rest) pl Couronne ☎642274 rm13
🏠**Aquitaine** 95 rte de Bordeaux ☎640491
N🏠 Frd

Marquise 62 (Pas-de-Calais) 5,050 (☎21)
Map **3** A1
★**Bon Sejour** 80 av Ferber ☎321107 rm8
1 Oct–15 Sep LD B24–35 M20–30
★***Grand Cerf*** 20 av Ferber ☎321039 rm10
⇔3 🏠1 G 15 Jan–15 Dec

Marsanny See **Dijon**

Marseille† **13** (Bouches-du-Rhône) 914,400
(☎91) Map **27** B2

AA agents; see page 83

★★★★**Grand & Noailles** 64 Canebière
☎549148 tx43609 rm180 ⇔180 G Lift
★★★★**Splendide** 31 bd d'Athenes ☎397500
tx41939 rm138 ⇔90 🏠33 G Lift
★★★**Castellane** 31 r du Rouet ☎792754
rm47 ⇔20 🏠20 G Lift B58–108 Màlc
★★★**Royal St George** (n rest) 10 r du Capt
Dessemond ☎525692 rm28 ⇔28 Lift B74–130
Sea
★***Eden Corniche*** (n rest) 156 prom de la

Corniche ☎520189 rm18 (A) ⇔1 🏠3 G Sea
🏠**24 F Bertrand** 243 bd National ☎625473
G10
🏠**Capucines** 59 allée L-Gambetta ☎640057
N🏠 Ren G50
🏠**Garcin** 72 r Monte Cristo ☎340766 N🏠
Chy/Sim G10
🏠**Kennings** 69 bd N-Dame (Angle r Dragon)
☎376505 N🏠 BL/Jag/Rov/Tri
🏠**Major** 20 av R-Schuman ☎201317 G40
At **Penne-St-Menet (La)** (10km E off A52)
☆☆☆**Novotel** ☎439060 tx400667 rm131
⇔131 Lift B120–140 Pool

Marseille Airport
At **Vitrolles** (8km N)
☆☆☆**Novotel Marseilles Aeroport** (A7)
☎899044 tx420670 rm166 ⇔166 Lift
B120–140 Pool

Martel 46 (Lot) 1,600 (☎65) Map **16** C2
At **Gluges** (5km SE on N681)
★★**Falaises** LE ☎373359 rm17 ⇔4
1 Feb–15 Dec LD B35–61 M25–62 Pn59–72

Marvejols 48 (Lozère), 5,950 (☎66) Map **16** D2
★**Paix** LE 2 av de Brazza ☎321017 rm27 (A4)
⇔4 🏠5 G LD B38–86 M17–29 Pn57–71
🏠**24 Mairie** 16 av de Brazza ☎320086 Opl

Massat 09 (Ariège) 750 (☎61) Map **22** C4
★★**Trois Seigneurs** LE av de St-Girons
☎669589 rm25 (A10) 🏠11 4 Mar–31 Oct
B42–87 M28–58 Pn100

Massiac 15 (Cantal) 2,100 (☎71) Map **16** D3
★★**Poste** N9 av de Clermont Ferrand ☎230102
tx39794 rm37 ⇔14 🏠13 Lift 15 Mar–15 Nov

Maubeuge 59 (Nord) 35,500 (☎20)
Map **3** B1
🏠**Pont Rouge Willot** 2 av du Pont Rouge
☎647308 N🏠 Bed/Opl G20

Mauléon-Licharre 64 (Pyrénées-Atlantiques)
4,500 (☎59) Map **20** C3
★★***Bidegain*** 13 r de la Navarre ☎009111
rm30 ⇔10 G 15 Jan–15 Dec

Maxilly-Petite-Rive See **Evian-les-Bains**

Mayenne 53 (Mayenne) 13,500 (☎43)
Map **8** C3
★★**Grand** LE 2 r Ambroise-de-Loré ☎043735
rm29 ⇔9 🏠12 G 22 Jan–24 Dec LD B64–127
(double) M36–110 Pn102–135 Pool
★**Croix Couverte** rte de Paris ☎043248 rm15
🏠4 G B32–54 M24–40
🏠**Bassaler** 26 r P-Lintier ☎041584 N🏠 BMW G
🏠**24 F Blouin** 17 bd Gl-Leclerc ☎041657 G

Mazamet 81 (Tarn) 14,900 (☎63)
Map **16** D1
★★★**Grand Balcon** sq G-Tournier ☎610114
tx520287 rm25 ⇔8 🏠14 Lift 15 Jan–15 Dec
B48.50–116
★**Fabre** 10 r de Verdun ☎610269 rm18 ⇔5 🏠5
B27–51 M20 Pn60–65

Meaux† **77** (Seine-et-Marne) 43,150 (☎1)
Map **9** B3
★★**Sirène** 34 r Gl-Leclerc ☎4340780 rm16
⇔14 G 1 Mar–31 Jan LD B42–128 M33–65
🏠**Brie et Picardie** 32 bd Raoult ☎4340651
N🏠 Frd
🏠**Vance** 37 av F-Roosevelt ☎4332976 N🏠 Ren

Megève 74 (Haute-Savoie) 5,300 (☎50)
Map **28** C4
★★★**Edelweiss** ☎212526 rm36 ⇔26 🏠2 Lift
15 Dec–10 Apr LD B110–224 M50 Pn100–200
★★★**Parc** ☎210574 rm50 ⇔36 Lift
★★★**Beauregard** rte d'Arbois ☎210556 rm20
⇔15 15 Dec–Etr 1 Jul–31 Aug B97–130 M35
Pn127–165
🏠**24 Christomet** r de Praz ☎212139 N🏠
Aud/MB/VW

France

Meillerie 74 (Haute-Savoie) 280 (☎50)
Map **11** A1
★*Terrasses* ☎760406 rm16 G Nov–Sep

Melun†77 (Seine-et-Marne) 39,000 (☎1)
Map **9** B3
★★*Caves de Touraine* 8 quai Ml-Joffre
☎4370348 rm20 ⇌8 ▥3
🅿🆑 *Rolland* 44 av Thiers ☎4393640 N🆁 Frd

Mende 48 (Lozère) 12,000 (☎66) Map **27** A3
★★*France* LE 9 bd L-Arnault ☎650004 rm28
⇌6 ▥5 G 20 Jan–20 Dec
★★*Lion d'Or* 12 bd Britexte ☎650646
tx480302 rm42 ⇌23 ▥19 Lift LD B69–148
M25–48 Pn100–135 Pool
★★*Paris* 2 bd du Soubeyran ☎650003 rm50
⇌5 ▥11 G Lift 1 Mar–1 Dec
🅿⏵24 *Sevene* 19 av Ml-Foch ☎651737
N🆁651620 Frd G5

Menthon-St-Bernard 74 (Haute-Savoie)
850 (☎50) Map **28** C4
★★*Beau Sejour* ☎448204 rm20 ⇌3 ▥15 G
Etr–30 Sep B42.50–95 M32 Pn70–90

Menton†06 (Alpes-Maritimes) 25,300
(☎93) Map **28** C2
★★★*Napoleon* 29 quai Laurenti ☎358950
tx470312 rm40 ⇌40 Lift B125–200 M50
Pn140–205 Pool Sea
★★★*Princes & Richmond* (n rest) 32 av Gl-de-
Gaulle ☎358020 rm45 ⇌39 ▥6 G Lift
20 Dec–3 Nov B70–120 Sea
★★★*Viking* (n rest) 2 av Gl-de-Gaulle ☎358044
rm34 ⇌34 G Lift 20 Dec–15 Oct B90–150
Pool Sea
★★*Aiglon* (n rest) 7 av de la Madone ☎357523
rm30 ⇌24 Lift 19 Dec–31 Oct B50–110 Pool
Sea
★★*Floréal* cours du Centenaire ☎357581
rm62 ⇌40 Lift 20 Nov–20 Sep LD B40–85
M25–30 Pn68–90
★★*Londres* ☎357462 rm26 ⇌5 ▥15 Lift
20 Dec–15 Oct B34–87 M30 Pn68–90
★★*Parc* 11 av Verdun ☎357174 rm75 ⇌62
▥10 Lift 20 Dec–10 Oct B100–170 M45–55
Pn150–180
★★*Prince de Galles* 4 av Gl-de-Gaulle
☎357101 rm60 ⇌31 ▥3 Lift 10 Dec–10 Oct
LD B36.50–117.50 M41 Pn94–118 Sea
★★*Rives d'Azur* prom Ml-Joffre ☎357209
rm37 ⇌16 Lift LD B43–120 M26 Pn72–91 Sea
★*Céline-Rose* 57 av Sospel ☎357469 rm36
⇌3 G Lift LD B37–84 M20 Pn62–72
🅿*Ideal* 1 av Riviera ☎357920 N🆁 Frd

Mercues See **Cahors**

Méréville 54 (Meurthe-et-Moselle) 1,908
Map **9** B3
★★*Maison Carrée* LE rm23 ⇌13 ▥9

Merignac See **Bordeaux**

Metz†57 (Moselle) 117,200 (☎87)
Map **11** A3
★★★★*Royal* 23 av Foch ☎683277 tx860425
rm76 ⇌60 Lift B67–149 M53 Pn175–182
★★*Central* (n rest) 3 bis r Vauban ☎755343
tx930281 rm54 ⇌54 G Lift B82–105
★★*Pergola* (n rest) D103 rte Plappeville
☎302682 rm33 (A8) ⇌7 ▥11 B37–78
🅿⏵24 *Chevalier* 57 bd St-Symphorien
☎687380 N🆁 Ren
🅿🆑 *J M Hubert* 68 r aux Arènes ☎683622
MB
🅿🆑 *RNUR* 50 r Gl-Metman ☎742518 N🆁 Ren
At **Hauconcourt** (9.5km N on A31)
☆☆☆ *Novotel Metz-Hauconcourt*
☎305568 tx860191 rm128 ⇌128 Lift
B120–140 Pool
At **Metz-Borny** (2km E)
🅿🆑 *Europe* N3 ☎741010 N🆁 Opl

Meyrueis 48 (Lozère) 1,100 (☎66)
Map **27** A2
★★*Château d'Ayres* ☎456010 rm20 ⇌8 ▥6
25 Mar–1 Oct
★★*Renaissance* ☎456019 rm30 (A20) ⇌24
LD B75–110(double) M20–75 Pn75–95

Migennes 89 (Yonne) 8,350 (☎86)
Map **10** C2
★★*Paris* 57 av J-Jaurès ☎802322 rm10
⇌2 ▥2 B38–86 M35

Millau†12 (Aveyron) 22,600 (☎65)
Map **16** D2
★★★*International* 1 pl Tine ☎602066 rm100
⇌94 G Lift B65–120 M30–65 Pn100–110
★★*Moderne* 11 av J-Jaurès ☎600123 rm45
⇌16 ▥8 G Lift B48.50–82 M30–65 Pn79–86
★*Causses* LE 26 av J-Jaurès ☎600319 rm24
⇌2 ▥5 G LD B32.50–72 M16.50–38 Pn50–90
🅿⏵24 *P Montagnac* N592, Quartier de Beches
Aud/VW

Milly 37 (Indre-et-Loire) (☎47) Map **8** D1
★*Château de Milly* ☎581456 rm12 ⇌8
Feb–Dec

Mimizan 40 (Landes) 7,700 (☎58)
Map **15** A2
At **Mimizan Plage** (6km on D626)
★★*Côte d'Argent* av M-Martin ☎090708
rm70 (A30) ⇌40 ▥2 Lift Etr–Oct LD B65–140
(double) M45 Sea

Mirail (Le) See **Toulouse**

Miramar 06 (Alpes-Maritimes) (☎93)
Map **28** C2
★★★★*St-Christophe* ☎903136 tx470878
rm40 ⇌22 ▥18 G Lift LD B210–250 St15%
Pool Beach Sea
★★★*Tour de l'Esquillon* Rond-Point de
l'Esquillon ☎903181 rm25 ⇌25 G B132–224
M60–70 Pn200–220 Beach Sea

Mirambeau 17 (Charente-Maritime) 1,409
(☎46) Map **15** B3
★*Union* ☎496164 rm12 (A2) ▥1 G LD
B32.50–51 M21–38 Pn70

Mirepoix 09 (Ariège) 3,900 (☎61) Map **22** C4
★*Commerce* cours du Dr Chabaud ☎681029
rm32 (A7) ⇌7 ▥9 G 21 Oct–30 Sep LD
B39–70.50 M19–70 Pn58.50–90

Modane 73 (Savoie) 5,150 (☎79) Map **28** C3
★*Europe* 35 r J-Ferry ☎050867 rm17 G LD
B27–52 M22–25 Pn60–63 St%

Moissac 82 (Tarn-et-Garonne) 12,150 (☎63)
Map **16** C2
★★★*Moulin* 1 pl du Moulin ☎040355 rm57
⇌45 ▥12 Lift 1 Mar–30 Nov B52–169
M35–70&àlc Pn110–220 Lake
★★*Chapon Fin* pl Recollets ☎040422 rm33
⇌10 ▥19 G 1 Apr–28 Feb
★*Pont Napoleon* ☎040155 rm20 ⇌2 ▥2 G
1 Dec–31 Oct LD B33–53(double) M18–45
Pn51–57

Monestier-de-Clermont 38 (Isère) 850
(☎76) Map **27** B3
★*Major* ☎349111 rm17 (A11) G 15 Nov–20 Oct
LD B29–42 M22–36 Pn60–71
🅿⏵24 *Alpes* ☎15 Peu

Montargis 45 (Loiret) 19,900 (☎38)
Map **9** B2
★★★*Poste* LE 2 pl V-Hugo ☎852277 tx780994
rm35 (A4) ⇌9 ▥12 G LD B50.50–132
M32–90
★*Tour d'Auvergne* 20 r J-Jaurès ☎850116
rm16 ⇌1 ▥6 G Mar–Jan LD B33–55 M30
🅿🆑 *St-Christophe* 46 av d'Antibes Amilly
☎852284 N🆁 Aud/VW

Montauban†82 (Tarn-et-Garonne) 50,450
(☎63) Map **16** C2

★★★**Ingres** 10 av Mayenne ☎633601 tx520319 rm36 ⇌29 ⋒7 G Lift B68–136 M28& àlc
★★**Midi** 12 r Notre Dame ☎631723 tx Chamcom Mtaub 51630 rm62 (A10) ⇌30 ⋒25 C Lift B41–119 M24–60 Pn85–145
★★***Trois Pigeons*** 6 av du II-Régiment-d'Infantrie ☎034530 rm47 ⋒35 G Lift
★**Languedoc** (n rest) 75 fbg Toulousain ☎633215 rm18 (A6) ⋒3 G B28–42
★**Orsay** ☎630057 rm30 ⇌2 ⋒18 G 1 Jul–31 May B34–79 M19–38 Pn60–100
ℹ⚙ ***Montauban Delpoux*** 11 fbg Toulousain ☎630886 N⊛ VW
ℹ⚙ ***Peugeot*** pl Lalaque ☎632426 N⊛ Peu
ℹ⚙ ***SETAM*** rte de Toulouse ☎630483 Frd G
ℹ⚙ **Sport** 646 av J-Moulin ☎032750 N⊛ BL/Tri G8
At **Montbeton** (3km W)
★★★**Coulandrières** rte Castelsarrasin ☎031809 rm22 ⇌21 ⋒1 B70–142 M35–65 Pn104–154 Pool

Montbard 21 (Côte-d'Or) 7,750 (☎80) Map **10** C2
★★**Gare** pl de la Gare ☎920212 rm16 ⋒11 G B33–90 M38–100
★***Ecu*** LE 7 r Auguste Carré ☎921166 rm16 ⇌10 ⋒3 G
ℹ⚙**24 Montbard** 39 r d'Abrantès ☎920623 Ren

Montbazon 37 (Indre-et-Loire) 2,450 (☎47) Map **9** A2
★★★★★***Château d'Artigny*** ☎060177 tx75900 rm55 (A25) ⇌53 G Lift 15 Jan–15 Nov ⛳ Pool
★★★★***Tortinière*** (1.5km N) ☎060019 tx75002 Inftrs 162 rm20 (A) ⇌20 1 Feb–30 Nov Pool

Montbéliard 25 (Doubs) 32,000 (☎81) Map **11** A2
★★**Joffre** (n rest) 35 av Joffre ☎912349 rm30 ⇌11 ⋒19 Lift B71–94

Montceau-les-Mines 71 (Saône-et-Loire) 28,250 (☎85) Map **10** C1
★★***Commerce*** 16 quai J-Chagot ☎093418 rm33 ⇌10 ⋒18 G Lift

Montchanin See **Creusot (Le)**

Mont-de-Marsan† **40** (Landes) 30,200 (☎58) Map **15** B2
★★★**Richelieu** LE 3 r Château-Vieux ☎750016 rm75 ⇌30 ⋒20 G Lift B39.50–93 M26–35
☆☆***Bois Fleuri*** (n rest) rte de St-Sever ☎752468 Pool
ℹ **Continental** 839 av de Ml-Foch ☎750677 N⊛ BL/Tri G10

Mont-Dore (Le) 63 (Puy-de-Dôme) 2,350 (☎73) Map **16** D3
★***Castelet*** av M-Bertrand ☎210529 rm33 ⇌11 Dec–Mar May–Oct
★***Mon Clocher*** LE r M-Sauvagnat ☎210541 tx39794 Amber rm32 ⋒4 15 May–30 Sep Xmas–Etr 20 May–30 Sep
At **Pied du Sancy** (4km S on N683)
★★**Puy Ferrand** ☎210258 rm44 ⇌23 ⋒11 G Lift 15 Dec–20 Sep LD B53–101(double) Pn171–220(double)

Montélimar† **26** (Drôme) 29,150 (☎75) Map **27** B3
★★★**Relais de l'Empereur** pl M-Dormoy ☎012900 tx45537 rm35 (A) ⇌30 ⋒4 G 18 Dec–12 Nov LD B61–226 Màlc
☆☆**Euromotel** rte de Marseille ☎011588 tx345126 rm51 ⇌18 ⋒33 15 Mar–31 Oct B63–141 M30 Pn123–168 Pool
ℹ⚙ ***Gros*** 71 av du Teil ☎010807 N⊛ Bed/Opl
ℹ⚙ **R Magne** 7 fbg St-James ☎012665 N⊛ Cit
ℹ⚙ **Peyrouse** pl d'Aygu ☎010231 N⊛ M/c Frd

Montignac 24 (Dordogne) 3,250 (☎53) Map **16** C3
★***Avenue*** LE av J-Jaurès ☎508281 tx509111 rm16 ⇌2 ⋒6 G 15 Dec–30 Sep
★**Soleil d'Or** LE 16 r IV-Septembre ☎508022 rm24 (A10) ⇌7 ⋒4 G 27 Dec–25 Nov LD B30.50–80 M20–65 Pn63–88

Montigny-sur-Loing 77 (Seine-et-Marne) 2,200 (☎1) Map **9** B3
★★***Vanne Rouge*** r Abbevoire ☎4248210 rm12 ⇌9

Montluçon† **03** (Allier) 58,850 (☎70) Map **16** D4
★★★**Terminus** 47 av M-Dormoy ☎052893 rm45 ⇌8 ⋒25 G Lift B45–105
★★***Univers*** (n rest) 38 av M-Dormoy ☎053347 rm60 ⇌24 ⋒24 G Lift
ℹ⚙**24 Univers** 2 r de Valmy ☎051000 BL/Tri G10

Montmirail 51 (Marne) 3,450 (☎26) Map **10** C3
★**Vert Galant** 2 pl Vert-Galant ☎422017 rm14 ⋒3 G Mar–Jan B31–61 M23–39.50
ℹ⚙**24 J Boussin** 4 pl R-Petit ☎422309 Cit

Montmorillon 86 (Vienne) 7,450 (☎49) Map **16** C4
★★**France Mercier** 2 bd de Strasbourg ☎910051 rm25 ⇌7 ⋒4 G 15 Feb–31 Dec LD B42–96 M40–160

Montoire-sur-le-Loir 41 (Loir-et-Cher) 4,200 (☎39) Map **9** A2
★★**Cheval Rouge** LE pl Ml-Foch ☎820705 rm17 ⇌8 ⋒1 G 1 Nov–30 Sep LD B40–93 M35–80 St12%

Montpellier 34 (Hérault) 195,650 (☎67) Map **27** A2
★★★***Eden*** av de la Pompignane ☎586024 tx48656F rm122 ⇌122 Lift Pool
★★★**Frantel** 218 r du Bastion Le Polygone ☎639063 tx480362 rm116 ⇌116 G Lift B141–181 M52& àlc
★★★***Grand & Midi*** (n rest) 22 bd V-Hugo ☎926961 rm48 ⇌34 ⋒8
ℹ⚙ **Mediterranée** 49 av G-Clemenceau ☎921468 N⊛ BMW
⚙ **Midi** 39 av G-Clemenceau ☎921986 N⊛ BL/Jag/Rov/Tri
At **Perols** (8km S adj to Montpellier Airport)
☆☆☆**Euromotel** rte de Carnon ☎730304 tx480652 rm77 ⇌77 B93.50–128 M40 Pool
At **St-Jean-de-Vedas** (5km W on N113)
ℹ⚙ **Imbert** rte de Sète ☎920297 N⊛ Frd G

Montreuil 62 (Pas-de-Calais) 3,200 (☎21) Map **3** A1
★★★**Château Montreuil** chaussée des Capucins ☎060011 rm15 (A4) ⇌13 ⋒2 G LD B75–123 Màlc ⛳ Pool
★***Chez Edouard*** 7-9 r de Change ☎061033 rm10 ⇌2 ⋒1 G 1 Feb–15 Oct
ℹ⚙ **Damour** av Gl-Leclerc ☎061198 N⊛ Peu

Montrichard 41 (Loir-et-Cher) 3,900 (☎39) Map **9** A2
★★**Bellevue** LE quai du Cher ☎320617 rm30 ⇌27 ⋒3 Lift 15 Dec–15 Nov LD B73–136 M35–75 Pn150
★★***Croix Blanche*** N64 ☎320034 rm19 ⇌3 ⋒3 G LD
★★**Tête-Noire** LE rte de Tours ☎320555 rm42 (A9) ⇌18 ⋒7 1 Feb–2 Jan LD B48–90 M44–57 Pn85–103
ℹ⚙ ***Renault*** 38 rte de Tours ☎320484 Ren G4

Mont-St-Michel (Le) 50 (Manche) 105 (☎33) Map **8** C3
★★**Mère Poulard** ☎601401 rm30 (A14) ⇌14 ⋒8 2 Apr–2 Oct LD B40–124 M50& àlc St15% Sea
★★**Digue** LE ☎601402 rm35 ⇌25 G 15 Feb–31 Dec B84–126 M30–75
★★***Guesclin*** LE ☎601410 rm13 (A) ⇌5 ⋒4 LD 1 Mar–1 Nov Sea

☆☆**K** ☎039111 rm60 ⇌60 Etr–Oct

Morez 39 (Jura) 7,200 (☎82) Map **10** D1
★★**Central Modern** 106 r de la République
☎330307 rm52 (A24) ⇌12 G B40–91
M28–60 Pn92–114
🛏🕭 **Morez Automobiles** 74 r de la République
☎331470 G5

Morgat 29 (Finistère) 7,030 (☎98)
Map **7** A3
★★**Ste-Marine** ☎810801 rm36 ⇌16 📶20
Lift 25 Mar–25 Sep LD B67–114 M35–65
Pn90–115 Sea
★**Julia** ☎810589 rm30 ⇌10 1 Jun–20 Sep

Morlaix† 29 (Finistère) 20,550 (☎98)
Map **7** B3
★★★**Europe** 1 r d'Aiguillon ☎882258 rm60
⇌38 📶5 Lift B46–158 M24–80 Pn75–110
St15%

Mortagne-au-Perche 61 (Orne) 5,150
(☎34) Map **9** A3
★**Tribunal** pl Palais ☎250477 rm15 (A6) ⇌6
📶1 G 1 Feb–30 Dec B32.50–84 M25–42
🛏🕭 **Perche** 58 r de Paris ☎34147 Frd
At **St-Hilaire-le-Chatel** (4km NW on D205)
🛏🕭 **J Poirier** les Gaillons N12 ☎259111 ext 740
N🕭 Bed/Opl

Mortain 50 (Manche) 3,150 (☎33)
Map **8** C3
★**Cascades** 🍺 16 r du Bassin ☎590003 rm15
⇌2 📶1 G 1 Nov–30 Sep LD B31–94 M22–70
Pn80–100

Morzine 74 (Haute-Savoie) 2,657 (☎50)
Map **28** C4
★★**Dahu** ☎457 rm26 ⇌18 📶4 G
18 Dec–15 Apr 1 Jul–31 Aug LD B53–164
M44–51 Pn98–167

Mougins 06 (Alpes-Maritimes) 8,500 (☎93)
Map **28** C2
★★★**Clos des Boyères** ☎900158 rm20 ⇌15
🍴 Pool

Moulins† 03 (Allier) 26,950 (☎70)
Map **9** B1
★★★**Paris** 21 r de Paris ☎440058 tx Cotelex
990512F 202Z rm32 ⇌28 📶4 G Lift
22 Feb–31 Jan LD B65–170 M52–90
Pn150–240
★★**Moderne** 5 pl J Moulin ☎440506 rm44
⇌4 📶19 G Lift B57–112 M30 Pn100–125
★**Parc** 🍺 24 pl République ☎441225 rm25
⇌4 📶18 G Lift B64–107 M28–60
🛈🚩24 **Dubois-Dallois** 27 r des Couteliers
☎442165 Cit

Mouthier 25 (Doubs) 350 (☎81) Map **11** A1
★★**Manoir** 🍺 21 Grande r ☎870637 rm17 ⇌5
G 1 Apr–30 Sep
★**Cascade** 🍺 ☎870635 rm15 ⇌2 📶6 G
20 Dec–3 Nov LD B42.50–77 M27–60
Pn60–74

Mulhouse† 68 (Haut-Rhin) 119,350 (☎89)
Map **11** B2
★★★**Frantel** 4 pl Gl-de-Gaulle ☎429913
tx881807 rm96 ⇌92 📶4 G Lift B126–176
M40–70
★★**Bourse** (n rest) 14 r de la Bourse (off av
Ml-Foch) ☎456685 rm50 ⇌13 📶37 Lift
B93–119
🛈🕭 **Sax** 12 r du Couvent (off av Prés-Kennedy)
☎454654 M/c Frd G200
At **Rixheim** (5km E on N66)
Ott & Wetzel r de Mulhouse ☎440137 N🕭
BL/Jag/Rov/Tri
At **Sausheim** (6km NE on D422)
☆☆☆ **Mercure** ☎445440 tx881757 rm100
⇌100 Lift B120–140 Pool
☆☆☆ **Novotel** r de l'Ile Napoléon ☎444444
tx881673 rm77 ⇌77 Lift B120–140 Pool

Murat 15 (Cantal) 3,050 (☎71) Map **16** D3
★★**Grand & Messageries** 🍺 ☎9 rm30 (A) ⇌11
📶4 G 1 Feb–31 Dec

Muse (La) See **Rozier (Le)**

Najac 12 (Aveyron) 950 (☎65) Map **16** C2
★★**Miquel** ☎457080 rm31 (A7) 📶12 G
1 Dec–31 Jan 1 Mar–31 Oct LD B27.50–51.50
M16.50–31 Pn51–59
★**Belle Rive** 🍺 (2km on D39) ☎457420 rm34
(A4) ⇌13 📶11 G Mar–Oct LD B42–66(double)
M17–29 Pn53–68

Nancy† 54 (Meurthe-et-Mosel) 111,500
(☎28) Map **11** A3
★★★**Frantel** 11 r Raymond Poincare ☎294822
tx960034 rm192 ⇌192 G Lift B147–188
M36–54&àlc
★★★**Grand Concorde** 2 pl Stanislas ☎350301
ta Granotel tx960367 rm60 ⇌34 📶19 Lift
B61–177 M45
☆☆☆**Mercure Nancy Quest** rte de Pons
(4km W) ☎274860
★★★**Palais** 48 r St-Jean ☎243338 tx960525
rm70 ⇌22 📶16 G Lift B54–113 M25 Pn95–130
★★**Albert 1er/Astoria** (n rest) 3 r Armée Patton
☎403124 tx850895 rm141 ⇌65 📶30 G Lift
B55–145 M25–30
★**Americain** 61 r P-Sémard ☎362853 tx Mont
X961052 Poste 189 rm51 ⇌26 📶25 Lift
B55–139.50 rm21–50
★**Poincaré** (n rest) 81 r R-Poincaré ☎532599
rm25 📶8
🛏🕭 **H Gras** 11 r A-Lebrun ☎527087 (closed
weekends) Frd
SOVAN av de Strasbourg ☎528801 (closed
weekends) MB/Opl G30
At **Houdemont** (6km S)
☆☆☆ **Novotel Nancy-Sud** rte d'Espinal
☎551198 tx961124 rm86 ⇌86 Lift B120–140
Pool
At **Laxou** (3km SW)
☆☆☆**Mercure Nancy Quest** 10 r de Saone
☎963710 tx850014 rm100 ⇌100 Lift
B120–140 Pool
☆☆☆ **Novotel Nancy Quest** N4 ☎966746
tx850988 rm120 ⇌120 Lift B120–140 Pool
☆☆☆ **Sofitel Jacques Borel** r de la Saone
☎964221 tx850036 rm100 ⇌100 Lift
B128–194 M32&àlc Pn170–220 Pool
🛏🕭 **Nancéienne** 4 rte de Paris ☎531367
N🕭 Chy

Nans-les-Pins 83 (Var) 1,000 (☎94)
Map **27** B2
★★★**Châteauneuf** 3.5km N ☎789006 rm31
⇌27 📶1 1 Apr–31 Oct B51–212 M40
Pn120–217 🍴 Pool

Nantes† 44 (Loire-Atlantique) 263,700
(☎40) Map **8** C2
★★★**Central** 4 r Couedic ☎717015 tx700666
rm143 ⇌90 📶43 Lift B110–143 M36–62àlc
Pn134–168
★★★**Frantel** 3 r du Dr-Zamenhof, Ile Beaulieu
☎471058 tx711440 rm150 ⇌150 G Lift
B128–151 M52
★★**Bourgogne** (n rest) 9 allée Charcot
☎740334 rm42 ⇌22 📶20 Lift B60–116.50
★★**Graslin** (n rest) 1 r Piron (off pl Graslin)
☎713561 rm46 ⇌8 📶16 Lift B54–88
★**Astoria** (n rest) 11 r de Richebourg ☎743990
rm45 ⇌12 📶32 G Lift B63.50–118
🛏🕭 **Grimaud** rte de Paris ☎495141 N🕭 Hon/
Toy
🕭🚩 **Laizin** 2 bis r Lamoricière ☎717842 (closed
weekends) BL/Rov/Tri G10
🛏🚩24 **RNUR** 68 bd Meusnier-de-Querlon
☎767582
🛏🕭 **Selection** 42 bis r des Hautes-Pavés
☎733314 N🕭 Maz/Vlo G5
At **Carquefou** (4km E on D337, off N23)

France

☆☆☆**Mercure** ☎492924 tx710962 rm78 ⇌78 Lift B120–140 Pool

☆☆☆**Novotel Nantes Carquefou** Allée des Sapins ☎493284 tx711175 rm99 Lift B120–140 Pool

Nantiat See Crouzille (La)

Nantua 01 (Ain) 3,650 (☎74) Map **27** B4

★★★*France* 44 r Dr Mercier ☎765055 rm30 (A14) ⇌12 G 20 Dec–30 Oct

★★**Lac** 15 av de la Gare ☎765012 rm18 ⇌12 ⋔2 G LD B77–99(double) M35–100

★★**Lyon** ⓛ 19 r Dr Mercier ☎765043 rm18 ⇌4 ⋔6 G 1 Nov–26 Sep LD B57–91.50 M23–69

Napoule-Plage (La) 06 (Alpes-Maritimes) 3,000 (☎93) Map **28** C2

★★★★**Ermitage du Riou** bd de Mer ☎389556 tx Ermirio 470072 rm40 ⇌34 ⋔6 Lift B111–324 M51 Pn165–253 Pool Sea

★★★*Beau Rivage* rte Cannes ☎389191 tx Carle 46878 rm40 (A) ⇌38 ⋔8 20 Dec–30 Oct

★★**Belle-Auberge** bd H-Clews ☎389508 rm11 ⇌1 ⋔9 15 Dec–15 Nov B31–77.50 M24.50–35 Pn81.50–84.50 Beach Golf ◠ Sea

★★*Rocomare* ☎389536 rm12 ⋔6 15 Mar–15 Oct Sea

Narbonne†11 (Aude) 40,550 (☎68) Map **22** D4

☆☆☆*Novotel* Quartier Plaisance ☎325481 tx480332 rm96 ⇌96 Lift B120–140 Pool

★★**Dorade** 44 r J-Jaurès ☎326593 tx490604 rm48 ⇌6 ⋔6 G Lift B38.50–89 M25 Pn90–110

★★**Languedoc** 22 av Gambetta ☎322888 tx Tomipy 290987 rm45 ⇌18 ⋔13 Lift B63–126 M30–50

★★**Residence** (n rest) 6 r 1er-Mai ☎321941 rm25 ⇌15 ⋔10 G B92–144

★★**Terminus** (n rest) 2 av P-Sémard ☎320275 rm33 ⇌2 ⋔2

★**Lion d'Or** ⓛ 39 av P-Sémard ☎320692 rm25 ⇌2 ⋔13 G 1 Nov–31 Jan 1 Mar–15 Oct LD B46.50–68.50(double) M21.50–50 Pn65–76.50

⌂⍭⦿ **Fraisse** 36 bd F-Mistral ☎320631 N⊛ BL/Tri

⌂⍭⦿ **J Gabriel** 4 bd du College ☎320246 N⊛ Frd G10

⌂⍭⦿**24** *Languedocienne Distribution Autos* 84 av Carnot ☎322720 Ren G23

At **Narbonne Plage** (15km E on D68 & D168)

★★**Caravelle** ⓛ bd du Front de Mer ☎338038 rm24 ⇌1 Apr–31 Oct LD B42.50–71 Màlc Sea

Nemours 77 (Seine-et-Marne) 11,250 (☎1) Map **9** B3

☆☆☆**Euromotel** (n rest) A6 ☎4281032 tx690243 rm102 ⇌102 B109–144

★★**Ecu de France** 3 r de Paris ☎4281154 rm28 ⇌6 ⋔7 G B42.50–89 M27–95 St15%

★**Roches** av de la Mairie (at St-Pierre) ☎4280143 rm11 (A6) ⇌5 ⋔9 G 1 Nov–30 Sep B34.50–89.50 M26.50–48 Pn101–136.50

★**St-Pierre** (n rest) 10 av Carnot ☎4280157 rm25 ⇌2 ⋔7 G B41.50–69(double)

⌂⍭⦿**24** *Gambetta* 70 av Gambetta ☎4280546 N⊛

Nepoulas par Compreignac 87 (Haute-Vienne) Map **16** C3

☆☆ *Relais St-Eutrope* N20 ☎ 21 La Crouzille rm20 ⇌20 8 Feb–8 Jan

Neuf-Brisach 68 (Haut-Rhin) 2,600 (☎89) Map **11** B2

At **Volgelgrun** (5km E on N415)

☆☆☆**Européen** ☎725157 rm22 ⇌13 ⋔9 LD B61–89 M35–60 Pool

Neufchâtel-en-Bray 76 (Seine-Maritime) 6,150 (☎35) Map **9** B4

★★**Grand Cerf** 9 r Grande ☎930002 rm14 ⇌1 ⋔4 G Jan–Nov LD B47–81 M28–65

★*Mouton d'Or* 21 pl N-Dame ☎931460 rm15 15 Jan–15 Dec

⌂⍭⦿**24** **Lechopier** 31 r St-Pierre ☎930082 N☎930476 Ren

At **Hayons (Les)** (7km W on N28)

★*Escale* ☎Les Hayons 0 rm16 ⋔7 G 15 Jan–15 Dec

Neuville-en-Ferrain See Tourcoing

Nevers†58 (Nièvre) 47,750 (☎86) Map **9** B1

★★★**Magdalena** (n rest) rte de Paris ☎572141 rm40 ⇌30 ⋔10 G Lift B88–126(double)

★★★**St-Louis** 2 pl Mosse ☎572710 rm12 ⇌12 28 Feb–6 Jan

★★*Molière* (n rest) r Molière ☎572996 rm18 ⇌3 ⋔15

★**Ste-Marie** 25 r Petit-Mouesse ☎611002 rm17 (A9) ⋔3 G 1 Mar–15 Jan B48–75 (double) M20–35.50

⌂⍭⦿ **Nandrot & Verma** 4 av Colbert ☎610332 Bed/BMW/Opl G10

⍭⦿ **Tenailles** 16 r Pasteur ☎610674 N⊛ BL

Nice†06 (Alpes-Maritimes) 346,650 (☎93) Map **28** C2 See Plan

★★★★★ **Negresco** 37 prom des Anglais ☎883951 tx46040 Plan **1** rm188 ⇌188 Lift

★★★★*Atlantic* 12 bd V-Hugo ☎884015 tx46840F Plan **2** rm120 ⇌120 Lift

★★★★**Splendid Sofitel** 50 bd V-Hugo ☎886954 tx460938 Plan **3** SofiNce rm130 ⇌130 G Lift B170–210 M48 Pn190–220 Pool

★★★★**Westminster** 27 prom des Anglais ☎882944 tx460872 Plan **4** rm110 ⇌110 Lift B119–218 M45 Pn160–220 Sea

★★★**Brice** 44 r Ml-Joffre ☎881444 tx470658FBriceb Plan **5** rm65 ⇌60 ⋔5 Lift B78–130 M35 Pn115–148

★★★**Frantel** 28 av Notre Dame ☎803024 tx470662 Plan **16** rm201 (A28) ⇌200 ⋔1 G Lift B168–241 M50 Pool

★★★**Gounod** (n rest) 3 r Gounod ☎882620 tx460938 Plan **6** rm45 ⇌35 ⋔10 G Lift 15 Dec–15 Nov B100–140 Pool

☆☆☆**Massenet** 11 r Massenet ☎871131 Plan **7** rm46 ⇌46 G Lift B120–173(double) Màlc

★★★**Napoleon** 6 r Grimaldi ☎877007 tx460949 Plan **8** rm80 ⇌80 Lift B99–167 St17%

★★★**Windsor** (n rest) 11 r Dalpozzo ☎885935 Plan **9** rm60 ⇌33 ⋔22 G Lift B95–128

★★**Albion** 25 bd Dubouchage ☎805733 tx46878 Castriva Plan **10** rm87 ⇌18 ⋔11 G Lift LD

★★*Francia* 9 bd V-Hugo ☎878945 tx46840F Plan **11** rm42 ⇌25 ⋔5 Lift

★★**Locarno** (n rest) 4 av des Baumettes ☎885494 tx46840 Plan **12** rm50 ⇌25 ⋔25 G Lift B67–104

★★**Masséna** (n rest) 58 r Gioffredo ☎854925 tx47192F Plan **13** rm115 ⇌84 ⋔31 Lift B100–200

⌂⍭⦿ **Albert-1er** 2 r Croix-Marbre (off r de France) ☎879948 N⊛ Toy

⌂⍭⦿ **Europ** 5 r Maccarani (off r de France) ☎871181 N⊛ Vlo

⍭⦿ *IMAC* 1 bd de l'Armée-des-Alpes ☎890032 N⊛ AR/Dat/Lnc

⌂⍭⦿ **Kennings** 9 r Veillon ☎805683 N⊛ BL/ Jag/Rov/Tri

⍭⦿ **Michigan** 3 bd de l'Armée-des-Alpes ☎890077 (closed weekends) Opl

⌂⍭⦿ **PCA** 6 bis r Massingy ☎800448 N⊛ Frd

RNUR 2 bd de l'Armée-des-Alpes ☎892757 N⊛ Ren

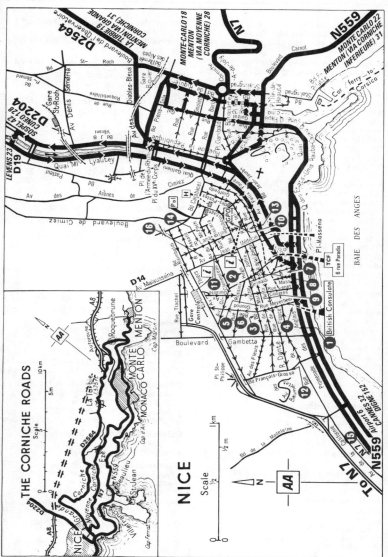

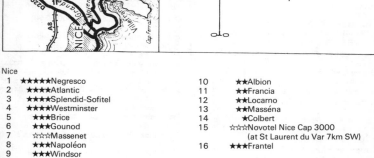

Nice
1 ★★★★★Negresco
2 ★★★★☆Atlantic
3 ★★★★Splendid-Sofitel
4 ★★★★Westminster
5 ★★★Brice
6 ★★★Gounod
7 ☆☆☆Massenet
8 ★★★Napoléon
9 ★★★Windsor

10 ★★Albion
11 ★★Francia
12 ★★Locarno
13 ★★Masséna
14 ★Colbert
15 ☆☆☆Novotel Nice Cap 3000
    (at St Laurent du Var 7km SW)
16 ★★★Frantel

France

At **St-Laurent du Var** (7km SW off N7)
☆☆☆ **Novotel Nice Cap 3000** ☎316115
tx470643 Plan **15** rm101 ⇄101 Lift B120–140
Pool

Nieuil 16 (Charente) 950 (☎45) Map **16** C3
★★★ **Château de Nieuil** ☎713401 rm12 ⇄10
🅟2 G 15 Dec–15 Nov

Nîmes† 30 (Gard) 134,000 (☎66)
Map **27** A2
★★★★ **Imperator** pl A-Briand ☎219030
tx490635 rm64 (A4) ⇄35 🅟29 G Lift 1 Mar–
31 Jan B114–194 M50–80 Pn220–286
★★★ **Cheval Blanc & Arènes** 1 pl des Arènes
☎672003 rm48 ⇄24 🅟15 Lift
☆☆☆ **Novotel Nîmes Ouest** bd Peripherique
☎846020 tx480675 rm96 ⇄96 Lift B120–140
Pool
★★ **Carrière** 6 r Grizot ☎672489 tx49926
Offitour rm55 (A) ⇄15 🅟35 G Lift
🔧 **Automatic** 11 bis bd Talabot ☎676098
(closed weekends) Dat
🔧 **Mediterranée** 64 r de la République
☎840801 (closed weekends) Frd
🔧 **Midi** 186 rte de Montpellier ☎678798 N🛑
🔧🛑 **RNUR** rte de Montpellier ☎846000 N🛑 Ren
🔧🛑 **L Roque** 23 av Carnot ☎672837 N🛑 Por
At **Marguerittes** (7km on N86)
☆☆ **Marguerittes** ☎844071 rm48 ⇄48 LD
B56–71.50

Niort† 79 (Deux-Sèvres) 64,000 (☎48)
Map **15** B4
★★★ **Brèche** 8 av Bujault ☎244178 rm49
⇄19 🅟16 G Lift B45–114 M30–60 Pn95–110
★★ **Grand** (n rest) 32 av Paris ☎242221 rm40
⇄9 🅟31 G Lift B66.50–111
★★ **Terminus** 80 r Gare ☎240038 rm45 ⇄20
🅟15 G Lift
🅸🛑 **Aumonier** 40 rte de Niort, Aiffres ☎244796
BL/Tri
🔧🛑 **Hurtaud** rte de la Rochelle ☎244469 N🛑
Bed/MB/Opl

Nogent-le-Rotrou 28 (Eure-et-Loir)
13,600 (☎37) Map **9** A3
★★ **Dauphin** 39 r Villette-Gate ☎521730
rm26 ⇄6 🅟6 G Mar–25 Jan B49–128
M32–55 Pn115–160

Noirétable 42 (Loire) 2,000 (☎77)
Map **27** A4
★★ **Chaumière** r de la République ☎247300
rm28 (A8) ⇄9 🅟6 Mar–Jan B36–78 M25–75
Pn80–90
🅸🔧 **24 Reparations** ☎247031 Ren G10

Nolay 21 (Côte-d'Or) (☎80) 1,700
Map **28** C1
★ **Ste-Marie** 36 r de la République ☎217319
rm13 (A6) 🅟4 G 2 Feb–2 Jan LD B34–68
M18–45 Pn70–84

Nonancourt 27 (Nonancourt) 1,900 (☎32)
Map **9** A3
★ **Grand Cerf** 17 Grande r ☎581527 rm9 🅟5
G LD B46–50 M21–50
🔧🛑 **Delaunay** rte de Verneuil ☎580136 N🛑 G5

Nontron 24 (Dordogne) 4,100 (☎53)
Map **28** C3
★ **Grand** IE 3 pl Agard ☎560001 rm26 ⇄10
🅟2 Lift 1 Feb–15 Jan B30.50–95 M17.50–70
Pn70–100 St12%

Nouan-le-Fuzelier 41 (Loir-et-Cher) 2,300
(☎39) Map **9** B2
★ **Moulin de Villiers** IE rte Chaon (3km NE by
D44) ☎087227 rm20 ⇄8 🅟5 15 Mar–1 Sep
15 Sep–5 Jan

Nouvion-en-Thiérache (Le) 02 (Aisne)
3,300 (☎23) Map **11** C4
★ **Paix** 37 r V-Vicary ☎970455 rm26 (A2)
⇄5 🅟6 G 15 Dec–15 Jan B36.50–85 M19–35

Noves 13 (Bouches-du-Rhône) 3,600
(☎90) Map **27** B2
★★★ **Petite Auberge** ☎941221 tx43301 rm21
(A6) ⇄19 🅟2 G 8 Feb–Jan Pool

Noyelles-Godault See Henin-Beaumont

Noyon 60 (Oise) 14,050 (☎4) Map **9** B4
★★ **Grillon** 37 r St-Eloi ☎4440087 rm38 (A4)
⇄11 🅟22 G 30 Dec–5 Jul 25 Jul–23 Dec
★ **St-Eloi** 81 bd Carnot ☎4440149 rm24
(A10) ⇄6 G 30 Nov–30 Aug B27–59 M22–35
Pn55–75

Nozay 44 (Loire-Atlantique) 3,250 (☎40)
Map **8** C2
🔧🛑 **J Terrien** 1 rte de Nantes ☎794802 N🛑
Ren

Nyons 26 (Drôme) 5,950 (☎75) Map **27** B3
★★ **Colombet** IE pl de la Libération ☎260366
rm34 ⇄7 🅟9 G Lift 15 Dec–25 Oct
B40.50–127 M32–65 Pn92–125
🔧🛑 **G Mercy** av H-Rochier ☎032 N🛑

Obernai 67 (Bas-Rhin) 8,411 (☎88)
Map **11** B3
★★ **Duc d'Alsace** IE 6 pl de la Gare ☎955534
rm23 ⇄10 🅟1 Lift 15 Mar–15 Jan B34–91.50
M28–52 Pn59.50–76.50

Oléron (Ile d') 17 (Charente-Maritime) (☎46)
Map **15** B3/4

Cotinière (La)
☆☆☆ **Ile de Lumière** (n rest) ☎471080 rm46
⇄20 🅟26 Apr–Oct Pool Beach Sea

Remigeasse (La)
★★★ **Grand Large** ☎470818 rm28 ⇄16 🅟12
25 Mar–30 Oct 🛟 Pool Beach Sea

St-Trojan-les-Bains
☆☆☆ **Novotel Oléron St-Trojan** ☎474246
tx790910 rm80 ⇄80 Lift B120–140 🛟 Pool Sea

Olivet 45 (Loiret) 12,400 (☎38) Map **9** B2
★★★ **Beauvoir** r Beauvoir ☎635757 rm25
⇄9 🅟6 B50–148 M28–80 🛟
★★ **Rivage** IE r R-Blanche ☎660293
tx760926 rm21 ⇄12 🅟4 LD B44–90 M38 Lake

Ollières-sur-Eyrieux 07 (Ardèche) 800
(☎75) Map **27** B3
★ **Vallée** ☎26 rm11

Oloron-Ste-Marie 64 (Pyrénées
Atlantiques) 13,150 (☎59) Map **20** C3
★★ **Béarn Lardonnere** 4 pl de Mairie
☎390099 rm27 (A6) ⇄10 G 1 Mar–31 Jan
B42.50–105 Màlc
🅸 **Haurat** 41 r Carrérot ☎390193 N🛑 Ren

Orange† 84 (Vaucluse) 26,500 (☎90)
Map **27** B2
☆☆☆ **Euromotel Orange** rte de Caderousse
☎342410 tx401550 rm100 ⇄100
B117–149 M40 Pool
★★ **Louvre & Terminus** (n rest) 38 av F-Mistral
☎341008 rm40 ⇄23 🅟17 G Lift 15 Jan–15 Dec
B55–124
★★ **Princes** 7 av l'Arc-de-Triomphe ☎343016
rm47 ⇄11 🅟5 Lift
🅸 **Ameller** rte d'Avignon ☎341234 Opl G
🔧🛑 **Chaix** 20 av Gl-Leclerc ☎345101 N🛑
Toy/Vlo G10
🔧🛑 **Princes** 2–10 av de l'Arc ☎340747 N🛑
BL/Dat
🔧🛑 **SIVA** rte de Lyon (N7) ☎340268 Ren

Orbey 68 (Haut-Rhin) 3,450 (☎89)
Map **11** B2
🅸🔧 **24 A Batot** 39 r Grande ☎472048 G10

Orgeval 78 (Yvelines) 3,300 (☎1)
Map **9** B3
☆☆☆ **Novotel Paris-Orgeval** ☎9759760
tx600174 rm120 ⇄120 Lift B120–140 Pool

★★**Moulin d'Orgeval** ☎975874 rm13 ⇄5
6 Feb–22 Dec LD B67–115(double) Màlc
St15% (rest only) ⚓

Orléans† **45** (Loiret) 110,000 (☎38)
Map 9 B2
★★★★**Sofitel Jacques Borel** 44–46 quai
Barentin ☎621739 tx780073 rm110 ⇄110
G Lift B132–146 M45 Pn219–265 Pool
★★★**Arcades** (n rest) 14 quai Cypierre
☎627410 rm29 ⇄14 ⋒6 Lift B57.50–106
★★★**Cedres** (n rest) 17 r MI-Foch ☎622292
tx760912 F H Cedres rm32 ⇄22 ⋒4 Lift
B59.50–117.50
★★**Grand** 21 r Bannier ☎871979 rm32 ⋒8
Lift
★★**Terminus** (n rest) 40 r de la République
☎872464 rm57 ⇄40 ⋒12 Lift
🚗🚗**F Dailloux** 206 fbg Bannier ☎874825 N⚓
Ren
🚗🚗**Gare** 15 av de Paris ☎872354 N⚓ Frd
🚗🚗**Lion Fort** 44 bd J-Jaurès ☎625829 N⚓
BL/Jag/Tri
At **St Jean-de-Braye** (3km E on N152)
🚗🚗**Orléans Auto-Sport** av L-J-Soulas
☎891547 N⚓ AR/Opl
At **Saran** (2km NW adj to A10 autoroute)
☆☆**Ibis** la Chiperie ☎883993 tx760902
rm108 ⇄108 Lift B66–87 Màlc
At **Source (La)** (10km S off N20)
☆☆☆**Novotel Orléans-Sud** r H-de Balzac
☎630428 tx760619 rm120 ⇄120 Lift
B120–140 Pool

Orsay **91** (Essonne) 19,500 (☎1) Map 9 B3
At **Courtaboeuf** (3km S on D35)
☆☆☆**Mercure** ☎9076396 tx691247 rm114
⇄114 Lift B120–140 Pool
At **Saclay** (7km N on F18)
☆☆☆**Novotel** Christ-de Saclay ☎9418140
tx691856 rm136 Lift B120–140 ⚓ Pool

Outreau See **Boulogne-sur-Mer**

Oyonnax **01** (Ain) 23,350 (☎74) Map 27 B4
★**Nouvel** (n rest) 31 r R-Nicod ☎772811
rm37 ⇄6 ⋒8 G Lift

Pacy-sur-Eure **27** (Eure) 3,600 (☎32)
Map 9 A3
★★**Etape** r Isambard ☎361277 rm10 ⇄6
B40–120 M45

Paimpol **22** (Côtes-du-Nord) 8,500 (☎96)
Map 7 B3
🚗🚗**H Chapalain** quai Duguay Trouin
☎208055 Ren G20

Palaiseau **91** (Essonne) 23,431 (☎1)
Map 9 B3
☆☆☆**Novotel Massy-Palaiseau** la Haute
Garenne ☎9208491 tx691595 rm151 ⇄151
Lift B120–140 Pool

Pamiers **09** (Ariège) 15,200 (☎61)
Map 22 C4
★★**Parc** ☎670258 rm12 ⇄6 ⋒3 G LD
B34–80 M28 Pn60–75
🚗🚗**Pyrénées** 5 rte de Foix ☎671208
Opl

Paramé See **St Malo**

Paray-le-Monial **71** (Saône-et-Loire)
12,150 (☎85) Map 10 C1
★★**Vendanges de Bourgogne** Ⓛ 5 r D-Papin
☎811343 rm15 ⋒10 G 1 Mar–31 Jan B45–82
M24–45 &àlc Pn70
★**Trois Pigeons** 2 r d'Argaud ☎810377
rm33 (A15) ⇄6 ⋒14 G 1 Feb–31 Dec LD B30–
84 M22–55 Pn75–100
🚗🚗**24 P Henry** N79-Les Carres ☎811365 MB
Peu G5

Paris† **75** 2,607,650 (☎1) Map 9 B3
See Plan
See also **Aulnay-sur-Bois, Orsay &
Palaiseau**
*Bold Roman numbers after hotel addresses are
district (Arrondissement) numbers. Garages are
listed below under Arrondissement headings.*
★★★★★**Bristol** 112 fbg St-Honoré **VIII**
☎3592315 tx28961 Plan **15** rm220 ⇄220
★★★★★**George V** 31 av George-V **VIII**
☎7235400 tx650082 Plan **30** rm359 ⇄359
Lift B381–542 Màlc St15%
★★★★★**Meurice** 228 r de Rivoli **I**
☎2603860 tx23673 Plan **45** rm220 ⇄220 Lift
★★★★★**Plaza-Athénée** 25 av Montaigne
VIII ☎3598523 tx650092 Plan **51** rm213
⇄213 Lift B381–842 Màlc St15%
★★★★★**Prince de Galles** 33 av George-V
VIII ☎7235511 tx28027 Plan **52** rm203
⇄203 Lift B299–433 M70 St15%
★★★★★**Raphaël** 17 av Kléber **XVI**
☎5530770 tx610356F Rafotel Plan **53** rm90
⇄90 Lift
★★★★★**Ritz** 15 pl Vendôme **I** ☎2603830
tx220262 Plan **54** rm209 ⇄209 Lift B330–530
M80 &àlc
★★★★★**Royal Monceau** 35 av Hoche **VIII**
☎2277800 tx650361 Plan **57** rm199 ⇄199
Lift
★★★★**Ambassador** 16 bd Haussmann **IX**
☎2469263 tx Ambasado 650912F Plan **3**
rm300 ⇄300 G Lift B190–270 M60
★★★★**Bedford** 17 r de l'Arcade **VIII**
☎2662232 tx290506 Plan **10** rm142 ⇄142
Lift B147–190 M46
★★★★**Castiglione** 40 r du fbg St-Honoré **VIII**
☎2650750 tx210500 Sce 303 Plan **17** rm110
⇄110 Lift B180–251 M50–100 Pn280–324
★★★★**Commodore** 12 bd Haussmann **IX**
☎7709300 tx28601F Plan **20** rm180 ⇄180
Lift
★★★★**Frantel Windsor** 14 r Beaujon **VIII**
☎2277300 tx650902 Plan **29** rm130 ⇄130
Lift B245–439 Màlc
★★★★**Grand** 2 r Scribe **IX** ☎2603350
tx220875 Plan **32** rm600 ⇄600 Lift
B240–360 Màlc
★★★★**Hilton** 18 av Suffren **XV** ☎2739200
tx20955F Plan **34** rm489 ⇄489 G Lift
★★★★**Lancaster** 7 r de Berri **VIII** ☎3599043
tx640991 Loyne Plan **38** rm57 ⇄57 Lift
B340–535 M60 &àlc St15%
★★★★**Lotti** 7 r Castiglione **I** ☎2603734
tx230024 Scribe Plan **40** rm 129 ⇄118 Lift
★★★★**Lutetia** 43 bd Raspail **VI** ☎5484410
tx270424 Plan **42** rm306 ⇄217 ⋒59 Lift
★★★★**Scribe** 1 r Scribe **IX** ☎7420340
tx230024 Plan **58** rm200 ⇄200 Lift B220–
300 Màlc
★★★★**Trémoille** (n rest) 14 r Trémoille **VIII**
☎2256495 Plan **64** rm106 ⇄91 ⋒15
★★★★**Westminster** 13 r de la Paix **II**
☎2615746 tx680035 Plan **68** rm102 ⇄102
G Lift B290–380 Màlc
★★★**Alexander** (n rest) 102 av V-Hugo **XVI**
☎5536465 tx610373 Plan **1** rm62 ⇄51 ⋒11
Lift B178–214
★★★**Astor** 11 r d'Astorg **VIII** ☎2665656
Plan **6** rm141 ⇄94 ⋒30 Lift B137–209 M46
★★★**Atala** 10 r Châteaubriand **VIII**
☎2250162 tx640576 Plan **7** rm50 ⇄35 ⋒15
Lift B115–191 M50
★★★**Balmoral** (n rest) 6 r du GI-Lanrezac
XVII ☎3803050 Plan **8** rm60 ⇄27 ⋒18 Lift
★★★**Baltimore** 88 av Kléber bis **XVI**
☎5538333 Plan **9** rm83 ⇄50 ⋒16 Lift
★★★**Blanche Fontaine** (n rest) 34 r Fontaine
IX ☎5267232 tx260717 Plan **11** rm41 ⇄41
G Lift B118–140

France

France

France

***Bourgogne & Montana** 3 r de Bourgogne **VII** ☎5512022 tx660870 Plan **12** rm35 ⇌28 ⋔6 Lift B116–208 M45–80

***Cambon** (n rest) 3 r Cambon **I** ☎2603809 tx240814 Plan **16** rm44 ⇌21 ⋔21 Lift B170–205

***Castille** 37 r Cambon **I** ☎2615520 Plan **18** rm56 ⇌53 ⋔5 Lift B54–213 M21–29 Pn108–230

***Cayre** (n rest) 4 bd Raspail **VII** ☎5443888 tx270577 Plan **19** rm131 ⇌131 Lift B177–212

***Franklin & Bresil** 19 r Buffault **IX** ☎2802727 tx640988 Plan **28** rm67 ⇌30 ⋔35 Lift B125–158 Pn169–215

***Hélios** (n rest) 75 r de la Victoire **IX** ☎8742864 tx210500 Flash X Paris 327 Plan **33** rm51 ⇌26 ⋔2 Lift B102–130

***Louvre–Concorde** 1 pl Théatre-Français **I** ☎5084300 tx22412 Plan **41** rm238 ⇌124 ⋔92 Lift

***Madison** (n rest) 143 bd St-Germain **VI** ☎3297250 Plan **43** rm57 ⇌43 ⋔11 Lift B62–140

***Massenet** (n rest) 5 bis r Massenet **XVI** ☎2885361 Plan **44** rm41 ⇌33 ⋔2 Lift

***Royal** 33 av de Friedland **VIII** ☎3590814 tx28965 Plan **56** rm57 ⇌47 ⋔8 Lift

***Senat** (n rest) 22 r St-Sulpice **VI** ☎3265348 Plan **59** rm32 ⇌23 ⋔9 G B64–121

***Splendid** 1 bis av Carnot **XVII** ☎3801456 tx280773 Plan **61** rm60 ⇌44 ⋔16 Lift B145–255

***Terminus Nord** (n rest) 12 bd Denain **X** ☎2802000 tx660615 Plan **63** rm230 ⇌72 ⋔85 Lift B125–224

***Victoria Palace** 6 r Blaise-Desgoffe **VI** ☎5443816 tx270557 Holivic Paris Plan **67** rm113 ⇌78 ⋔33 G Lift B180–218 M45

Altona (n rest) r du Fbg Poissonière **X** ☎8786824 Plan **2** rm57 ⇌27 Lift

Angleterre (n rest) 44 r Jacob **VI** ☎2603472 Plan **4** rm30 ⇌30 Lift B120–140

Duminy (n rest) 3 r Mont-Thabor **I** ☎2603280 Plan **21** rm60 ⇌32 Lift B40–116

Elysée (n rest) 12 r Saussaies **VIII** ☎2652925 Plan **22** rm32 ⇌8 ⋔2 Lift B52.50–129.50

Europe (n rest) 15 r de Constantinople **VIII** ☎5228080 Plan **23** rm50 ⇌18 ⋔7 Lift B40–95

Family (n rest) 35 r Cambon **I** ☎2615484 Plan **24** rm24 ⇌16 ⋔4 Lift B69.50–124

Farnese (n rest) 32 r Hamelin **XVI** ☎7205666 tx611732 Plan **25** rm40 ⇌35 ⋔5 Lift B134–169

Florida 12 bd Malesherbes **VIII** ☎2657206 Plan **26** rm47 ⇌27 ⋔6 Lift B64–158 M40

France (n rest) 4 r du Caire **II** ☎2313098 Plan **27** rm55 ⇌12 ⋔3 Lift

Keppler (n rest) 12 r Keppler **XVI** ☎7206505 tx26717F 531 Plan **36** rm54 ⇌17 ⋔10 Lift B56–111

Little Palace (n rest) 4 r Salomon-de-Caus **III** ☎2720815 Plan **39** rm60 ⇌20 ⋔10 Lift

Ministère 31 r Surène **VIII** ☎2662143 Plan **46** rm34 ⇌25 ⋔4 Lift B60–145

Montana-Tuileries (n rest) 12 r St Roch **I** ☎2604510 Plan **47** rm25 ⇌18 ⋔5 Lift

Neva (n rest) 14 r Brey **XVII** ☎3802826 Plan **48** rm33 ⇌14 Lift 1 Sep–31 Jul B54–120

Pacific (n rest) 11 r Fondary **XV** ☎5752049 Plan **50** rm66 ⇌37 ⋔2 Lift B56–104

Rond–Point de Longchamp (n rest) 86 r de Longchamp **XVI** ☎7279627 tx620653 Plan **55** rm33 ⇌25 Lift B71–162

Sevigné (n rest) 6 r de Belloy **XVI** ☎7208890 tx610219 Plan **60** rm30 ⇌30 G Lift B100–155

Splendid (n rest) 29 av de Tourville **VII** ☎5512477 Plan **62** rm45 ⇌10 ⋔8 G Lift B44–152

Vermont (n rest) 11 r Bois de Boulogne **XVI** ☎5000497 Plan **65** rm30 ⇌29 ⋔5 Lift B146–162

*Arts** (n rest) 8 r Coypel **XIII** ☎3312230 Plan **5** rm44 ⇌11 ⋔15 Lift B31–69

*Boursault** (n rest) 15 r Boursault **XVII** ☎5224219 Plan **13** rm13 ⇌5 ⋔2 B40–79

*Brescia** (n rest) 16 r d'Edimbourg **VIII** ☎5221431 Plan **14** rm34 ⇌15 Lift B50–112

*Laffon** (n rest) 25 r Buffault **IX** ☎8784991 Plan **37** rm47 ⇌18 Lift B50–120

*Verniquet** (n rest) 3 r Verniquet **XVII** ☎3802630 Plan **66** rm26 ⇌5 ⋔15 Lift B56–105

Arrondissement V
Latin 196 r St Jacques ☎3261655 BL/Tri

Arrondissement IX
24 Des Ardennes 3 r des Ardennes ☎2033075 BL/Jag/Rov/Tri/Vlo

Coliseum 61 r Rochehouart ☎5268789 N Ren G400

Arrondissement X
Abbeville 5 r d'Abbeville ☎8789837 N Ren G

Arrondissement XI
Como 82 bd Voltaire ☎3553917 BL/MB

Rochebrune 58–60 av Parmentier ☎8052902 Frd

Arrondissement XII
Grand de la Porte Dorée 268 av Daumeshill ☎6281033 Ren G300

Arrondissement XIII (Gare de Lyon, Gobelins, Bois de Vincennes)
P Gesmier 192 r de Tolbiac ☎3310984 N Ren

Gobelins 23 bd Arago ☎7078739 N Cit

Arrondissement XV (Grenelle, Vaugirard, Gare Montparnasse)
Frémicourt 146 bd de Grenelle ☎5756280 N Chy

Arrondissement XVI (Passy, Auteuil, Bois de Boulogne, Chaillot, Porte Maillot)
SIDAT 147 bd Murat ☎5257441 N Toy

Arrondissement XVIII (Montmarte)
Chapelle 20 bd de la Chapelle ☎2061940 Frd G

Grand Pajol 43 r Pajol ☎6071359 Dat G10

Arrondissement XIX (La Villette)
Chambon 88 r de la Villette ☎6070903 Ren G50

At **Bagnolet** (5km E, adj to *bd Périphérique*
☆☆☆**Novotel Paris Bagnolet** 1 av de la Republique ☎8589010 tx670216 Plan **49** rm607 Lift B120–140 Pool

☆☆**Ibis** r J-Jaurès ☎8589026 tx240830 Plan **35** rm414 ⇌414 Lift B97–114 Màlc

At **Clichy** (4km NW)
*Girbal** (n rest) 14 r Dagobert ☎7375424 Plan **31** rm30 ⇌24 ⋔6 G Lift

GPM 10 r de Belfort ☎7399940 N M G

At **Créteil-le-Lac** (12km SE off N5)
☆☆☆**Novotel** rte de Choisy ☎2079102 tx670396 rm110 Lift B120–140 Pool

At **Meudon-la-Forêt** (10km SW)
Royal Chanteclar 29 av de G-de Gaulle ☎6317628 rm15 ⇌15

At **Vincennes** (11km E off N34)
Pacaud 47 r de Strasbourg ☎3287056 N

Paris Airports
Bourget Airport (Le) (14km N off A1)

136

☆☆☆ **Novotel Nord Aeroport** r de Pont Yblon ☎9314888 tx691527 rm140 ⇆140 Lift B120–140 Pool

Charles-de-Gaulle Airport
(22km N off A1)
At **Roissy** (NE via N2)
☆☆☆☆ **Sofitel Jacques Borel** ☎8622323 tx691777 rms352 ⇆352 Lift B144–246 M41 Pn225 🍴 Pool

Orly Airport (16km S by A6)
★★★★ **Air** ☎7260310 ta Sleep-air rm56 ⇆40 🏠16 G Lift

★★★★ **Hilton-Orly** ☎7264000 tx250621 rm388 ⇆388 Lift B187–306.50 Màlc

Pau† 64 (Pyrénées-Atlantiques) 85,900 (☎59) Map 15 B1

★★★ **Continental** 2 r Ml-Foch ☎276931 tx57906 rm110 ⇆70 🏠20 G Lift

★★ **Roncevaux** (n rest) 25 r Louis-Barthou ☎270844 tx CC de Pau 570929 rm45 ⇆18 🏠17 Lift B39–126

★ **Central** (n rest) 15 r L-Daran ☎277275 rm26 ⇆4 🏠9 B35.50–81

📞24 J Broqué rte de Tarbes ☎275971 Ren
🈂️ **Forsans** 55 av de la Résistance ☎324669 N🈂️ bl/Vlo

🈂️ **Lavillauroy** 82 r d'Etigny ☎322476 N🈂️ Frd
🈂️ **Pyrénéenne-Auto** 8 pl Clemenceau ☎270303

At **Gan** (7km S on N134)
★ **Hostide l'Horizon** ☎687272 rm17 (A6) ⇆3 🏠1 1 Dec–31 Oct LD B38.50–82 M24 Pn85–105

At **Lescar** (7.5km NW on D945)
☆☆☆ **Novotel Pau Lescar** N117 ☎321732 tx570939 rm61 ⇆61 Lift B120–140 Pool

Passenans See **Sellières**

Payrac 46 (Lot) 512 (☎60) Map 16 C2
★★ **Hostellerie de la Paix** LE ☎376515 rm26 ⇆9 G 1 Mar–31 Dec B37.50–73 M25–58 Pn55–69

Pen-Guen See **St-Cast**

Penne-St-Menet (La) See **Marseille**

Périgueux† 24 (Dordogne) 37,700 (☎53) Map 16 C3
★★ **Boule d'Or** 8 pl Francheville ☎080251 rm42 ⇆8 🏠12 G B26–89 M28–50 Pn98

★ **Lion d'Or** 17 cours Fénelon ☎534903 rm17
🈂️ **Brout** 18 cours St George ☎082855 Chy/Sim G5

📞 **G Busset** 27 r L-Blanc ☎080808 Frd G30
🈂️ **Cecasmo** 147 rte de Lyon ☎531773 N🈂️ AR
🈂️ **G Lacoste** rte de Bergerac ☎533901 N🈂️ Sim/Vlo
🈂️ **Magot** 192 rte de Lyon ☎536691 MB G10

At **Trelissac** (5km NE on N21)
📞24 **Fournet** rte de Limoges ☎544063 G20

Perols See **Montpellier**

Péronne 80 (Somme) 9,450 (☎22) Map 9 B4
★★ **St-Claude** LE pl L-Daudré ☎840002 rm30 ⇆4 🏠11 1 Mar–31 Jan B48–94 Màlc Pn120–170

★ **Remparts** LE 23 r Beaubois ☎840122 rm16 ⇆5 🏠7 G (closed Aug) LD B48–106 M25–60

At **Assevillers** (adj to *autoroute* A1)
☆☆☆ **Sofitel Jacques Borel** ☎841276 tx14943 rm100 ⇆100 Lift Pool

Pérouges 01 (Ain) 550 (☎74) Map 27 B4
★★★ **Vieux Pérouges** ☎610088 rm22 ⇆18 G

Perpignan† 66 (Pyrénées-Orientales) 108,000 (☎68) Map 22 D4
★★★ **Grand** quai Sadi-Carnot ☎340994 tx50969 rm62 ⇆25 🏠26 Lift

★★★ **Windsor** (n rest) 8 bd Wilson ☎511865 rm57 ⇆26 🏠31 Lift B78–135

★★ **Baléares** 20 av Gl-Guillot ☎503493 rm48 ⇆7 🏠20 Lift B81(double) M25

★★ **Christina** (n rest) 50 cours de Lassus ☎614264 rm35 ⇆20 🏠5 G Lift B52–89

★★ **France** 16 quai Sadi-Carnot ☎349281 txA50950F rm40 ⇆14 Lift

★★ **Nord & Petit Paris** pl de la Cathédral ☎345757 rm70 ⇆14 🏠8 Lift

🈂️ **FA** 4 bd St-Assiscle ☎347050 N🈂️ AR/Frd/Lnc G100

🈂️ **24 Monopole** rte de Narbonne, km 4 ☎612293 N379517 N🈂️ MB

At **Rivesaltes** (5km NW by N9)
☆☆☆ **Novotel-Perpignan** (N9) ☎640222 tx500851 rm85 ⇆85 Lift B120–140 Pool

Perros-Guirec 22 (Côtes-du-Nord) 7,800 (☎96) Map 7 B3
★★★ **Printania** (n rest) r des Bons-Enfants ☎352100 rm65 (A) ⇆38 🏠10 G Lift 15 Apr–15 Sep 🈂️ Sea

★★★ **Trestraou** bd J-le-Bihan (at Trestraou) ☎352405 rm73 (A5) ⇆46 🏠12 Lift B78–137 M40–65 Pn103–149 Pool Sea

★★ **Morgane** LE av Casino ☎352280 rm28 ⇆24 🏠4 Lift 15 May–30 Sep LD B59–128 M40–65 Pn130–160 Pool Sea

★ **Riva-Bella** bd Clemenceau Plage de Trestignel ☎352275 rm28 ⇆10 Etr–20 Sep Sea

📞24 **Côte** 39 r Ml-Joffre ☎352207 Opl G5
At **Ploumanach** (6km W on D788)
★ **Roc'h-Hir** r St-Guirec ☎352324 rm24 🏠5 15 Mar–30 Sep LD 1 Apr–20 Sep

Peyrehorade 40 (Landes) 3,100 (☎57) Map 20 C4
★★ **Central** pl A-Briand ☎730322 rm10 ⇆3 🏠4 G

Pierre-Buffière 87 (Haute-Vienne) 1,250 (☎55) Map 16 C3
★ **Providence** RN ☎006016 tx580091 rm12 ⇆6 🏠2 G B39–83 M25–57

📞24 **Gauthier** ☎006024 Cit

Pierrelatte 26 (Drôme) 10,050 (☎75) Map 27 B3
★★ **Hostellerie Tom** LE 5 av Gl-de-Gaulle N7 ☎040035 rm12 🏠12 G Jan–Oct 1 Dec–30 Dec B46–90 M12–60&àlc

Pilat-Plage 33 (Gironde) 540 (☎56) Map 15 A2
See also **Arcachon & Pyla-sur-Mer**
★★ **Brisants** (n rest) 192 bd de l'Océan ☎227335 tx Bungalotel Pylamer rm18 (A) ⇆8 🏠4 Etr–30 Sep Beach Sea

Pin-au-Haras (Le) 61 (Orne) 500 (☎34) Map 8 D3
★★★ **Tourne-Bride** N24 ☎679202 rm8 ⇆4 🏠1 G 15 Mar–31 Dec

Piriac-sur-Mer 44 (Loire-Atlantique) 1,150 (☎40) Map 7 B2
★ **Plage & Port** LE quai de Verdun ☎435009 rm24 (A14) ⇆6 🏠5 Nov–Sep LD B29.50–75 M20–50 Pn89–122 Sea

Pithiviers 45 (Loiret) 10,450 (☎38) Map 9 B3
★ **Poste** 10 Mail Ouest ☎020014 rm20 ⇆6 G

Ploërmel 56 (Morbihan) 7,050 (☎97) Map 7 B3
★ **Commerce** 70 r de la Gare ☎740532 rm20 ⇆1 🏠4 G

Plombières-les-Bains 88 (Vosges) 3,400 (☎29) Map 11 A2
★ **Abbesses** pl Eglise ☎660040 tx88370 rm44 ⇆21 🏠2 Lift 1 May–30 Sep B48–93 M28–38 Pn74–112

Ploumanach See **Perros-Guirec**

Poitiers† 86 (Vienne) 85,500 (☎49) Map 8 D1

France

★★★**France** 28 r Carnot ☎413201 tx790526
rm86 ⇦46 🛏40 G Lift B53–155 M33
★★★**Royal Poitou** rte de Paris ☎417286
rm32 ⇦30 🛏2 B85–131 M28–52
★★**Europe** (n rest) 39 r Carnot ☎410088
rm44 ⇦7 🛏8 G
🛅🏵 **Poitou-Auto** 99 av de Bordeaux ☎421792
N🏵 Frd
🛅🏵 **SAGAMP** 107 bd du Grand Cerf ☎413452
Bed/Opl G60
At **Biard** (2km W)
🏵 **Barrault** zone Industrielle, de Larney-Nord
☎880294 N🏵 Vlo G10
At **Chasseneuil** (8km N by N21)
☆☆☆ **Relais Poitiers** ☎414141 tx790502
rm100 ⇦44 🛏32 Lift B63–130 M18–50
Pn136 🏊 Pool

Poix-de-Picardie 80 (Somme), 2,200 (☎22)
Map **9** B4
★**Cardinal** pl République ☎900823 rm23 G
(closed 2 Feb–20 Feb) LD B36–53 M23–38
Pn80–85
★**Poste** pl de la République ☎900033 rm19
⇦1 🛏2 G
🛅🏵 **Gressier** r C-Mahaye ☎900044 Peu G3
🛅🏵 **M Miotte** ☎900038 N🏵 G2

Poligny 39 (Jura) 4,900 (☎84) Map **10** D1
★★**Monts de Vaux** ☎123 rm10 ⇦10 G
★★**Paris** lE 7 r Travot ☎371387 rm27 ⇦8 🛏9
G 1 Mar–31 Oct LD B38–95 M24–46 Pn95
★★**Vallée Heureuse** lE ☎179 rm11 ⇦3 🛏2
B48–83 M18–50 Pn80–90

Polisot 10 (Aube) 300 (☎25) Map **10** C2
★**Seine** ☎385109 rm27 ⇦2 🛏7 G

Pons 17 (Charente-Maritime), 5,450 (☎46)
Map **15** B3
★★**Pontoise** r Gambetta ☎940099 rm17 ⇦15
🛏2 G 20 Jan–20 Dec B84 M35–55

Pont-a-Mousson 54 (Meurthe-et-Mosel)
15,100 (☎28) Map **11** A3
★**Européen** (n rest) 158 av Metz ☎810757
rm28 (A6) ⇦7 🛏2 G B55.50–97
★**Poste** 42 bis r V-Hugo ☎810116 rm24 (A8)
⇦2 🛏5 G LD B39–89 M30–70&àlc

Pontanevaux 71 (Saône-et-Loire) Map **27** B4
★★★**Compagnons de Jéhu** ☎372282 rm25
⇦11 Mar–Nov

Pontarlier† 25 (Doubs), 18,850 (☎81)
Map **11** A1
★★**Bon Gite** lE 12 r Salins ☎390872 rm23
🛏2 G 1 Nov–31 Oct B41–60.50 M22
Pn62.50–74.50
★★**Poste** lE 55 r de la République ☎391812
rm55 (A4) ⇦13 🛏8 G 15 Dec–15 Oct LD
B39–104 M25–70 Pn85
★★**Terrasse** 1 r de la République ☎390515
rm32 ⇦7 🛏6 G
🛅🏵 **Belle Rive** 80 r de Besançon ☎391442 N🏵
Sim
🛅🏵 **SAFC** 115 r de Besançon ☎391168 N🏵 Frd

Pontaubault 50 (Manche) 500 (☎33)
Map **8** C3
★**13 Assiettes** lE N176 ☎581403 tx170537
Mt St-Michel rm12 ⇦2 🛏1 1 Mar–31 Nov LD
B34–47 M22–70 Pn75–79

Pont-Audemer 27 (Eure), 10,050 (☎32)
Map **9** A4
★★**Vieux Puits** 6 r N-Dame du Pré ☎410148
rm8 🛏5 15 Jan–15 Dec LD B35–84 Màlc
★**Palais** 8 r S-Dela Quaize ☎410947 rm14
⇦2 LD B33–68 M26–45&àlc
★**Risle** 16 quai R-Leblanc ☎411457 rm18 LD
B34–53.50 M26–30 Pn90

Pont-d'Ain 01 (Ain) 2,300 (☎74) Map **27** B4
★★**Alliés** lE ☎390009 rm18 ⇦6 🛏5 G
B56–96 M33–60

★★**Paris-Nice** lE rte de Lyon ☎390380 rm19
⇦5 🛏2 G 1 Dec–31 Oct

Pont-de-Briques 62 (Pas-de-Calais)
3,475 Map **3** A1
★**Cascade** (n rest) 3 r P-Doumer ☎322125
rm9 G B27–38 St15%

Pont-de-Claix (Le) See **Grenoble**

Pont-de-l'Isère 26 (Drôme) 1,350 (☎75)
Map **27** B3
☆**Portes du Midi** N7 ☎586026 rm18 🛏5
1 Dec–31 Oct B35.50–63

Pont-de-Pany 21 (Côte-d'Or) 190 (☎80)
Map **10** C2
★**Pont-de-Pany** lE ☎346106 rm16 (A8) ⇦3
🛏2 G 1 Feb–15 Nov B37–64 M27–55

Pont d'Espagne See **Cauterets**

Pont-de-Vaux 01 (Ain) 2,150 (☎85)
Map **10** C1
★**Reconnaissance** lE 9 pl Joubert ☎373055
rm12 🛏6 G 6 Feb–1 Jan
🛅🏵**24 C Maingret** 30 pl M-Poisat ☎373126
N🏵 Ren

Pont-du-Gard 30 (Gard) (☎66) Map **27**
A/B2
★★**Pont-du-Gard** ☎870110 rm11 ⇦5 🛏6
1 Mar–20 Dec
★★**Vieux Moulin** Remoulins ☎870135
rm14 ⇦8 🛏4 Mar–Sep LD B85–160(double)
M30–70&àlc Pn220–285

Pontet d'Eyrans (Le) 33 (Gironde) (☎56)
Map **15** B3
🛅🏵**24 Ferandier** ☎427107 Peu

Pont-Evêque See **Vienne**

Pont-l'Evêque 14 (Calvados) 3,800 (☎31)
Map **8** D4
★**Lion d'Or** lE pl Calvaire ☎640038 rm16 ⇦10
LD B45–112 M25–70

Pontoise 95 (Val-d'Oise) (☎1) Map **9** B3
🛅🏵**Filleul** 41 r de Rouen ☎4640962 N🏵
At **Cergy** (4km SW)
☆☆☆ **Novotel** Ville Nouvelle ☎0303947
tx060264 rm196 ⇦196 Lift B120–140 Pool

Pontorson 50 (Manche) 5,550 (☎33)
Map **8** C3
★★**Poste & Croix d'Or** lE 92 r Couesnon
☎600045 rm32 (A16) ⇦6 🛏12 G 2 Feb–31 Dec
★**Bretagne** lE 59 r Couesnon ☎601055 rm29
(A) ⇦29 G 1 Mar–31 Jan
🛅🏵**24 Dore Rent** 43 r de la Libération
☎601110 Chy/Sim

Pont-St-Esprit 30 (Gard) 6,850 (☎66)
Map **27** B2
★**Europe & Poste** 10 bd Gambetta rm23
⇦2 🛏3 G

Pont-Ste-Marie See **Troyes**

Pornic 44 (Loire-Atlantique) 8,200 (☎40)
Map **7** B2
★**Family** r de l'Océan ☎820132 rm18 🛏18
1 Dec–31 Oct Sea

Pornichet 44 (Loire-Atlantique) 5,000
(☎40) Map **7** B2
★**Fleur de Thé** av Sellier ☎610496 rm35
⇦14 G 15 May–16 Sep
★**Sud-Bretagne** lE 42 bd de la République
☎610268 rm35 ⇦28 15 Mar–15 Oct LD
B55–155 M35–75
🛅🏵**24 Cam** 19 bd de la République ☎610410
N🏵

Port-Blanc 22 (Côtes-du-Nord) 2,430
(☎96) Map **7** B3
★**Grand** ☎203702 rm30 ⇦10 🛏10 G
B47.50–70 M25–60 Pn75–90 🏊 Sea

Port-Cros (Ile de) 83 (Var) (☎94)
Map **28** C1

★★**Manoir** ☎719052 rm29 (A1) ⇆8 ▥18
1 May–30 Sep LD B102–224 M60 Pn140–220

Portel (Le) 62 (Pas-de-Calais) 11,500 (☎21)
Map **3** A1
See also **Boulogne-sur-Mer**
★ **Beau Rivage & Armada** bd Pasteur ☎315982
rm12 ⇆5 LD B49–79(double) M20–45
Pn65–75 Sea

Port Grimaud 83 (Var) (☎94) Map **28** C2
★★★**Giraglia** ☎438333 tx47494F rm48
⇆48 G Lift 28 Mar–Oct Pool Beach Golf Sea

Port-Launay See **Châteaulin**

Porto See **Corse (Corsica)**

Port-Vendres 66 (Pyrénées-Orientales)
5,860 (☎69) Map **22** D4
★★★**Compagnie du Midi** quai de la Douane
☎380033 rm60 ⇆30 G Sea
★★**Résidence** rte de Banyuls ☎380069
rm21 ⇆13 ▥2 G Sea

Pouges-les-Eaux 58 (Nièvre) 2,050 (☎86)
Map **9** B2
★**Normandy & St-Léger** N39 ☎688333
rm36 (A) ⇆5 Etr–Oct

Pouilly-sur-Loire 58 (Nièvre) 1,850 (☎86)
Map **9** B2
★**Neuf** (n rest) 44 r W-Rousseau rm10 (A)
⇆3 ▥1 G
★**Relais Fleuri** (0.5km SE on N7) ☎391299
rm10 ⇆8 ▥2 1 Feb–31 Dec B66–101
M23.50–51.50

Pouldu (Le) 29 (Finistère) 600 (☎98)
Map **7** B3
★★**Castel Treaz** ☎969111 rm28 ⇆15 ▥8 Lift
1 Jun–10 Sep B53–122 M35 Pn95–138 Sea
★**Quatre Chemins** ▐E ☎969044 rm35 ⇆6
▥7 1 Jun–15 Sep LD B44–102 M24–42
Pn61–94

Pourville-sur-Mer 76 (Seine-Maritime)
800 (☎35) Map **9** A4
★**Normandy** ☎841805 rm16 ⇆1 ▥2
1 Feb–15 Nov Sea

Pouzauges 85 (Vendée) 5,600 (☎51)
Map **8** C1
★★**Bruyére** r Dr-Barbanneau ☎571346 rm30
⇆12 ▥14 Lift B69–116 M34–55 Pn112–150
Lake

Precy-sous-Thill 21 (Côte-d'Or) 583
Map **10** C2
A Durey N70 N☜ G302

Prémery 58 (Nièvre) 2,800 (☎86) Map **9** B2
★**Poste** 4 Grande r ☎681230 rm16 ⇆1 ▥1 G
1 Mar–31 Jan

Primel-Trégastel 29 (Finistère) 1,521
Map **7** B3
★**Grand** ☎673501 rm36 1 Jul–31 Aug Sea

Privas 07 (Ardéche) 11,250 (☎75)
Map **27** B3
★★**Croix d'Or** 3 cours de l'Esplanade rm14
⇆3 ▥2 G
☖☜**Vacher & Lardon** 10 pl du Foirail ☎643155
N☜ Frd

Propriano See **Corse (Corsica)**

Provins 77 (Seine-et-Marne) 13,118 (☎1)
Map **10** C3
★★**Croix d'Or** 1 r des Capucins ☎4000196
rm7 ⇆4 G
☖☜**Griffon** 21 r E-Nocard ☎4000123 N☜ Frd

Puy (Le)† **43** (Haute-Loire) 29,050 (☎71)
Map **27** A3
★★★**Christel** 15 bd A-Clair ☎094121
ta Ardyprom tx39679 rm30 ⇆30 G Lift
★★**Bristol** av Ml-Foch ☎091338 rm35 (A21)
⇆15 ▥10 G Lift 15 Jan–15 Nov LD B40–83
M19

★★**Lafayette** 17 bd St-Louis ☎093285 rm24
⇆5 ▥1 G Lift 1 Mar–15 Nov
★**Verveine** ▐E 6 pl Cadelade ☎093539 rm31 (A)
⇆2 ▥15 15 Jan–15 Dec

Puya (La) See **Annecy**

Puy Guillaume 63 (Puy-de-Dôme) 2,320
Map **27** A4
★**Larivaut** 1 r E-Vaillant ☎2 rm13 ⇆3 ▥3 G

Pyla-sur-Mer 33 (Gironde) (☎56)
Map **15** A2
See also **Arcachon & Pilat-Plage**
★★★**Guitoune** bd de l'Océan ☎227010
rm21 ⇆15 ▥6 G 15 Jan–15 Nov B57.50–101
M38–75 Pn125–126 Sea
★★**Beau Rivage** 10 bd de l'Océan ☎225241
rm20 (A4) ⇆5 ▥7 1 Jun–10 Sep B42–100
M40 Pn75–113

Quarré-les-Tombes 89 (Yonne) 900
(☎86) Map **10** C2
★**Nord & Poste** ▐E ☎7 rm35 (A24) ⇆4 ▥6
LD B38–88 M26–44 Pn75–90

Quiberon 56 (Morbihan) 4,750 (☎97)
Map **7** B2
★★★**Sofitel Thalassa** Pointe de Goulvas
☎502000 tx730712 rm113 ⇆113 Lift
1 Feb–5 Jan Pool Beach Sea
★★**Beau Rivage** 11 r de Port Maria ☎526088
rm48 ⇆11 ▥23 Lift Etr–Sep LD
Pn116–119 St% Beach Sea
★**Ty Breiz** ▐E (n rest) bd Chanard ☎500990
rm32 ⇆5 ▥20 Etr–Sep B48–130 Sea
At **St-Pierre-Quiberon** (4.5km N on D786)
★★**Plage** ☎522166 tx56510 rm43 (A4)
⇆21 ▥18 Lift Etr–Oct LD B88–116(double)
M38 Pn90–125 Sea

Quillan 11 (Aude) 5,150 (☎68) Map **22** D4
★★**Chaumière** ▐E bd Ch-de-Gaulle ☎200679
rm40 (A) ⇆30 ▥6 G
★**Cartier** 31 bd Ch-de-Gaulle ☎200514
rm30 ⇆11 ▥9 G B40–90 M20–45
⇥24 **Escur** ☎200666 N☎200179 Ren

Quimper† **29** (Finistère) 60,500 (☎98)
Map **7** A3
★★**Celtic** 13 r de Douarnenez ☎950297 rm40
⇆5 ▥3 G
★★**Gradlon** ▐E (n rest) 30 r Brest ☎950439
rm25 ⇆9 ▥8 15 Jan–15 Dec B45–98
★★**Tour d'Auvergne** ▐E 11 r des Réguaires
☎950870 rm45 (A2) ⇆30 ▥11 G Lift
B45–98 M24 Pn97
☖☜**Bozec** pl Locronan ☎950940 N☜ BL/Tri G10
☖☜**Bretagne** rte de Concarneau ☎903200 N☜
Frd
☖⇥24 **Nedelec** 66 rte de Brest ☎954274
N☜954617 N☜ Peu
☖☜**Vigouroux** rte de Benodet ☎951344 N☜
Aud/BMW/VW

Quimperlé 29 (Finistère) 11,750 (☎98)
Map **7** B3
☖☜**Quimperlois** 22 rte de Lorient ☎960456
N☜ Aud/VW

Rabot (Le) 41 (Loir-et-Cher) (☎39) Map **9** B2
☆**Bruyères** ▐E N20 ☎080570 rm38 ⇆28 ▥12
G B56–108 M28–49 Pn75–95 Pool ◯

Raguenès Plage 29 (Finistère) (☎98)
Map **7** A3
★**Chez Pierre** ▐E ☎978106 rm20 ▥4 G
Mar–Sep Sea

Rambouillet 78 (Yvelines) (☎1) Map **9** B3
★**St-Charles** (n rest) 1 r Groussay ☎4830634
rm15 ⇆6 ▥4 1 Jan–20 Dec
☖☜**Gare** 7 r Sadi-Carnot ☎4831151 Ren

Rayol (Le) 83 (Var) 850 (☎94) Map **28** C1
★★★★**Bailli de Suffren** ☎056038 tx420535
rm50 ⇆47 ▥3 Lift May–Sep
Pn264–340 Sea

France

Ré (Ile de) 17 (Charente-Maritime) (☎46)
Map **15** B4

Flotte (La) (1,750)
★★ Richelieu av Plage ☎096070 rm30 ⇄30
1 Feb–2 Jan LD B95–260 M60–100
Pn200–500 ✒ Pool Sea
★ Ilot 10 cours F-Faure ☎090602 rm27 ⇄9
🅿5 Sea

Recologne 25 (Doubs) 260 Map **10** D2
★ Escale LE rm10 (A) G Pool

Reims† 51 (Marne) 183,650 (☎26)
Map **10** C3/4
★★★ Frantel 31 bd P-Doumer ☎885354
rm125 ⇄125 G Lift B122–199 M65
☆☆☆ Mercure RN4 ☎408787 tx830782
rm98 ⇄98 Lift B120–140 Pool
★★★ Paix 25 pl Drouet d'Erlon ☎400408
tx830974 rm100 ⇄100 G Lift B93–159 M37
★★ Crystal (n rest) 86 pl Drouet d'Erlon
☎475988 rm28 ⇄3 🅿8 Lift
★★ Europa (n rest) 8 bd Joffre ☎473329
rm32 ⇄5 🅿16 Lift 6 Jan–21 Dec
★★ Grand du Nord (n rest) 75 pl Drouet d'Erlon
☎473903 rm50 ⇄22 🅿28 Lift B58–89
★★ Univers (n rest) 41 bd Foch ☎475271
rm44 ⇄12 🅿9 Lift B47–92
★ Foch 37 bd Foch ☎474822 rm15 ⇄7
15 Feb–15 Jan
★ Welcome (n rest) 29 r Buirette ☎474114
tx830600 rm70 (A20) ⇄18 🅿32 Lift
15 Jan–20 Dec B31.50–72
🛢🅟 *Champagne* 16 av Brébant ☎401524 N🅖
Peu
🛢🅟 SODIVA N45 ☎478863 (closed weekends)
MB/Por
🛢🅟24 Depann' 40 av d'Epernay ☎080108 G
At **Tinqueux** (4km W off N31)
☆☆☆ Novotel N31 rte de Soissons ☎081161
tx830034 rm125 ⇄125 Lift B120–140 Pool
🛢🅟 Reims Automobiles 2 av R-Salengro
☎082108 N🅖 Opl

Remigeasse (La) See **Oléron (Ile d')**

Remiremont 88 (Vosges) 11,500 (☎29)
Map **11** A2
At **St-Nabord** (5km N on N57)
★★★ Claire Fontaine ☎622396 rm15 ⇄13
🅿2 Lift 15 Mar–31 Oct
★★★ Montiroche (n rest) ☎620659 rm14
⇄13 Mar–Oct B84–110

Renaison 42 (Loire) 2,050 (☎77) Map **27** A4
★ Jacques Coeur rte Vichy ☎044005 rm10
🅿6 Dec–Oct B35–49 M42 B46–85

Rennes† 35 (Ille-et-Vilaine) 205,750 (☎99)
Map **8** C3
★★★ Central (n rest) 6 r Lanjuinais (off quai
Lamennais) ☎302359 tx74728F/Ringren 105
rm43 ⇄19 🅿9 Lift 26 Aug–3 Aug
★★★ Frantel pl du Colombier ☎795454
tx730905 rm140 ⇄140 Lift B126–166
M52
★★★ Guesclin 5 pl de la Gare ☎302801
rm75 ⇄60 G Lift
☆☆☆ Novotel Rennes Alma av du Canada
☎506132 tx740144 rm100 ⇄100 Lift
B120–140 Pool
★★★ Président (n rest) 27 av Janvier
☎309950 tx73004 Ogetel 121 rm34 ⇄26
🅿8 G Lift
★★ Angelina (n rest) 1 quai Lamennais
☎307139 rm25 ⇄6 🅿4 G Lift
★ Angleterre (n rest) 19 r Ml-Joffre ☎307766
rm26 ⇄3 🅿9 B38.50–63
🛢🅟 Mail 30 av du Mail ☎591224 N🅖 Opl
🛢🅟 Ouest 5 r Gutenberg ☎362964 N🅖 Ren
🛢🅟 Ste Rennaise Automobiles rte de Lorient
☎591014 N🅖 Chy

140

Rethel 08 (Ardennes) 9,200 (☎24)
Map **10** C4
★★ Moderne pl Gare ☎390454 rm25 ⇄6 🅿8
G 5 Jan–21 Dec LD B48–96 M35–80
Pn85–130

Rignac See **Granat**

Rilly-sur-Loire 41 (Loire-et-Cher) 400
(☎39) Map **9** A2
★ Château de la Haute-Borde LE ☎469809
rm16 ⇄5 🅿2 G 1 Mar–15 Nov

Riquewihr 68 (Haut-Rhin) 1,200 (☎89)
Map **11** B2
★★ Jules Schmidt ☎479218 rm10 🅿6
1 Mar–31 Dec

Rivesaltes See **Perpignan**

Rixheim See **Mulhouse**

Roanne† 42 (Loire) 56,500 (☎77) Map **27** A4
★★ France (n rest) 19 r A-Roche ☎712117
rm44 ⇄10 🅿15 G 16 Aug–31 Jul
★★ Troisgros 22 cours de la République
☎716697 rm19 ⇄18 🅿1 G 1 Feb–Dec
B76–216 ✒
🛢🅟24 Grand Gobelet 54 av Gambetta
☎712402 Vlo G80
🛢🅟 Lafay 13 pl Diderot ☎710408 Ren
🛢🅟24 Poste 56 r R-Salengro ☎716687 Frd
G80

Rocamadour 46 (Lot) 750 (☎65) Map **16** C2
★★ Beau Site & Notre Dame LE r R-le-Preux
☎386308 tx290987 Paris rm68 (A4) ⇄26 🅿24
G Lift 1 Apr–15 Oct B49–150 M32–70
Pn100–150
★★ Ste-Marie LE r Grand Escalier rm23 (A5)
⇄23 G Etr–15 Oct LD B79(double) M40 Pn120
☆ Château LE rte de Château ☎386222 rm50
(A18) ⇄18 🅿14 20 Mar–5 Nov
★ Lion d'Or LE Porte Figuier ☎386204 rm30
(A7) ⇄3 🅿6 Etr–15 Oct LD B36–71 M24–40

Roche-Chalais (La) 24 (Dordogne)
3,100 (☎53) Map **15** B3
★ Soleil d'Or ☎904237 rm17 ⇄4 🅿3 G
Mar–Sep B37–87(double) M20–50

Rochefort 17 (Charente-Maritime) 32,900
(☎46) Map **15** B3/4
🛢🅟 Central 31 r Lafayette ☎990065 N🅖
BL/Tri G10
🛢🅟 Zanker 76 r Gambetta ☎993733 N🅖 Frd

Rochelle (La)† 17 (Charente-Maritime)
77,500 (☎46) Map **15** B4
★★★ Brises (n rest) Chemin digue Richelieu
☎348937 rm46 ⇄38 🅿8 G Lift B83–170 Sea
★★★ France & Angleterre 22. r Gargouilleau
☎285624 tx79717 rm79 ⇄37 🅿26 G Lift
★★★ Yachtman 23 quai Valin ☎412068
tx790762 rm36 ⇄35 🅿1 G Lift B134–208
M28–85 Pn180–220 Pool
★ Trianon & Plage 6 r de la Monnaie ☎282962
rm18 ⇄5 🅿5 1 Mar–31 Jan
🛢🅟 A Chagneau 124 bd A-Sautel ☎344225
N🅖 Frd

Roche-Posay (La) 86 (Vienne) 1,450
(☎49) Map **9** A1
★ Parc av Fontaines ☎862002 rm80 ⇄25
🅿13 G Lift 5 May–25 Sep

Rodez† 12 (Aveyron) 28,200 (☎65)
Map **16** D2
★★★ Tour Maje (n rest) bd Gally ☎682468
ta 1200 Rodez rm46 ⇄23 🅿19 Lift B59–102
★★ Broussy 1 av V-Hugo ☎681871 tx29987
Paris rm77 ⇄32 🅿15 G Lift
★★ Moderne LE 9 r Abbé-Bessou ☎680310
rm30 ⇄4 🅿15 Lift Sea
★ Poste LE 2 r Béteille ☎680147 tx390794
rm25 ⇄4 🅿10 G Lift 10 Jan–20 Dec
B46–70 M22–55

Roissy See **Paris**

Romans-sur-Isère 26 (Drôme) 34,250 (☎75) Map **27** B3
Standard 1 bd M-Dormoy ☎022955 N Ren G10

Romorantin-Lanthenay 41 (Loir-et-Cher) 17,050 (☎39) Map **9** A/B2
★★**Lion d'Or** 69 r G-Clemenceau ☎760028 rm18 ⇌3 ⋒8 G Mar–Dec LD B65–136 M60–140
★***Orleans*** pl du Gl-de-Gaulle ☎760165 rm10 ⇌5 ⋒1 Mar–Dec

Roquebrune-Cap-Martin 06 (Alpes-Maritimes) 11,250 (☎93) Map **28** C2
★★★***Victoria*** (n rest) 7 prom du Cap-Martin ☎356590 rm32 ⇌32 G Lift 1 Feb–30 Sep Sea
★★★**Vistaëro** Grande Corniche ☎350150 rm27 ⇌27 G Lift B198–340 M75–95 Pn290–345 St15% Pool Sea
★★**Princessias** 15 av G-Drin ☎350342 rm14 ⇌14 G 1 Feb–30 Sep B81–96(double) M35–55 Pn92–110 Sea
★**Westminster** 14 av L-Laurens ☎350068 rm30 (A4) ⇌13 ⋒16 G 1 Feb–10 Oct LD B20–60 M35 Pn85–95 Sea
Quatre Chemins 57 av J-Jaurès ☎350040 N BL G

Roquefort-sur-Soulzon 12 (Aveyron) 950 (☎65) Map **16** A1
★★★***Grand*** av de Lauras ☎609020 rm20 ⇌8 ⋒4 Etr–30 Sep

Roque-Gageac (La) 24 (Dordogne) 400 (☎53) Map **16** C2
★★**Gardette** ☎295158 rm18 (A4) ⇌9 ⋒6 G Mar–Nov B43–101 M24–70&àlc Pn64–95
★**Belle Etoile** ☎295144 rm15 ⇌5 ⋒5 G 15 Mar–18 Oct B41–57 M18–45 Pn75–80

Roscoff 29 (Finistère) 3,750 (☎98) Map **7** B3
★**Bains** 25 pl Lacaze Duthiers ☎697012 rm70 (A40) ⇌1 ⋒12 Lift Mar–Oct LD B38–106 M23–45 Pn60–136 Sea

Rosiers (Les) 49 (Maine-et-Loire) 1,850 (☎41) Map **8** D2
★★**Jeanne de Laval** pl Eglise ☎518017 rm15 (A8) ⇌5 ⋒5 G 20 Dec–12 Nov LD B51–122 M55–90&àlc Pn110–180

Roubaix 59 (Nord) 109,800 (☎20) Map **3** B1
Colisée 27 r de l'Epeule ☎709016 N Opl
Pouthieux av R-Salengro ☎752992 N M/c Hon

Rouen† 76 (Seine-Maritime) 118,350 (☎35) Map **9** A4
★★★**Dieppe** pl B-Tissot ☎719600 tx180413 rm44 ⇌44 Lift LD B89–163 M45 Pn150–185
★★★**Frantel** r Croix de Fer ☎980698 tx180949 rm125 ⇌125 G Lift B138–191 M55
★★★**Poste** 72 r J-d'Arc ☎882088 tx180674 rm85 ⇌55 ⋒8 Lift LD B75–175 Pn142–163
★★***Astrid*** (n rest) 121 r J-d'Arc ☎717588 rm40 ⇌10 ⋒4 Lift
★★**Cardinal** (n rest) 1 pl Cathedral ☎702442 rm21 ⇌4 ⋒16 Lift B46–83
★★**Cathédrale** (n rest) 12 r St-Romain ☎715795 rm25 ⇌23 Lift B40(double)
★★**Europe** (n rest) 87 r aux Ours ☎708330 rm27 ⇌6 ⋒4 Lift B72–80
★★***Nord*** (n rest) 91 r Gros Horloge ☎704141 rm60 ⇌45 Lift
★★**Paris** (n rest) r de la Champmeslé (off quai de la Bourse) ☎700926 rm22 ⇌9 ⋒9 G Lift B44–84
★★**Viking** (n rest) 21 quai du Havre ☎708498 rm37 ⇌16 ⋒11 Lift B47–84
★**Albert-1er** 29 bd des Belges ☎714609 rm13 ⇌3 (closed Sun) LD B26.50–46 M23.50àlc
★**Arcades** (n rest) 52 r des Carmes ☎701030 rm16 ⋒4 B31–48
★**Normandie** (n rest) 19 r du Bec (off r aux Juifs) ☎715577 rm23 ⇌7 ⋒17 Lift B57–100
★**Quebec** (n rest) 18 r Quebec (off r de la République) ☎700938 rm38 ⇌12 G Lift 10 Jan–24 Dec B46–82
★**Vieille Tour** (n rest) 42 pl Haute Vieille Tour ☎700327 rm23 ⇌2 ⋒4 Lift B36–79
C Guez 135 r Lafayette ☎727684 Frd
Omnium d'Autos 31 av de Caen ☎721163 Bed/Opl
At **Déville les Rouen** (3km NW off N13bis)
ANOVA 16 av Carnot ☎741565 N Toy
At **St-Etienne du Rouvray** (2km S off N138)
☆☆☆**Novotel Rouen Sud** le Madrillet ☎665850 tx180215 rm155 ⇌155 Lift B120–140 Pool Golf Lake

Rouffillac See **St-Julien-de-Lampon**

Roussillon 84 (Vaucluse) 1,100 (☎90) Map **27** B2
★★***Rose d'Or*** ☎756021 rm10 ⇌7 ⋒2 15 Dec–5 Nov

Royan† 17 (Charente-Maritime) 18,700 (☎46) Map **15** B3
★★★**Les Embruns** (n rest) 18 bis bd Garnier ☎050217 rm43 (A14) ⇌37 ⋒1 Lift 1 Mar–11 Nov B59–130 Sea
★★**Grand de Pontaillac** (n rest) av de Pontaillac ☎380044 rm55 (A10) ⇌25 ⋒30 G Lift Etr–15 Sep B48–125 Sea
★★***Océanic*** bd F-Garnier ☎051495 rm40 ⇌18 ⋒18 G Lift Sea
Baribeaud 50 bis av de la Grande Conche ☎050462 (closed weekends) AR/Hon
Station Service 75 av de Pontaillac ☎051153 Frd
Thomas rte de Saintes ☎050549 N MB G20

Royat 63 (Puy-de-Dôme) 4,500 (☎73) Map **16** D3
★★★**Métropole** 4 bd Vaquez ☎358018 rm80 ⇌50 ⋒10 Lift 1 May–1 Oct B65–210 M45 Pn120–200

Rozier (Le) 48 (Lozère) 150 (☎65) Map **27** A2
At **Muse (La)** (on D107n)
★★**Rozier & Muse** ☎606001 rm38 ⇌26 ⋒4 G Lift Etr–Sep B45–170

Ruffec 16 (Charente) 4,700 (☎45) Map **15** B4
Lavaud av A-Blanc ☎310145 N Fia G

Rungis 94 (Val-de-Marne) 2,686 (☎1) Map **9** B3
★★★**Frantel** 20 av Ch-Lindbergh ☎6873636 tx260738 rm206 ⇌206 G Lift B167–210 M57&àlc Pool

Sables-d'Olonne (Les)† 85 (Vendée) 18,250 (☎30) Map **8** C1
★★***Beau Rivage*** 40 prom de la Plage ☎320301 rm35 ⇌13 ⋒4 15 Feb–15 Dec Sea
★★***Charmettes*** 22 prom de la Plage ☎320042 rm8 ⇌8 Lift 15 May–30 Sep Beach Sea
★★**Résidence** (n rest) 36 prom Clémenceau ☎320666 rm35 ⇌18 ⋒7 G B52–171
Central 21 pl du Poilu-de-France ☎321477 Ren

Sables-d'Or-les-Pins 22 (Côtes-du-Nord) 1,550 (☎96) Map **7** B3
★★★**Bon Accueil** allée des Acacias ☎414219 rm46 ⇌25 ⋒5 Etr & Whi–Sep LD B36–108 M27–40 Pn75–120 Sea
★★★**Diane** av Brouard ☎414207 rm45 ⇌22 ⋒5 Etr & Whi–Sep LD B36–108 M27–40 Pn75–120 Sea

France

★★Ajoncs d'Or ☎414212 rm80 (A45)
⇄20 ⊫20 Etr & 20 May–20 Sep LD B38–111
M30–50 Pn70–115 Sea
★★Dunes d'Armor ☎414206 rm65 (A18)
⇄38 ⊫4 Whi–20 Sep LD B42–105 M25–57
& àlc Pn80–113 Sea
★Voile d'Or r des Acacias ☎414249 rm16
⇄5 ¹5 Mar–15 Nov B69–85(double) M22–39
Pn95 Sea

Sablé-sur-Sarthe 72 (Sarthe) 11,800
(☎43) Map **8** D2
★ *St-Martin* 3 r Haute St-Martin ☎950003
rm11 ⇄4 ⊫1 Apr–28 Feb

Saclay See **Orsay**

St-Affrique 12 (Aveyron) 9,250 (☎65)
Map **16** D1
★★Moderne av A-Pezet ☎990131 rm37
(A11) ⇄10 ⊫15 G B33–74 M19–55 & àlc
Pn54–73.50

St–Agrève 07 (Ardèche) (☎75) 2,750
Map **27** A3
⊪ *St-Agrève* les Allées ☎72 N⊛ G

St-Aignan 41 (Loir-et-Cher) 3,700 (☎39)
Map **9** A2
★★St-Aignan ⊫ 7–9 quai J-J-Delorme
☎751804 rm23 ⇄2 ⊫12 G 1 Feb–15 Dec LD
B38–114 M28–65

St-Albain See **Mâcon**

St-Amour 39 (Jura) 2,900 (☎82)
Map **10** D1
★Alliance ☎251003 rm16 ⇄10 ⊫4 G
1 Apr–30 Sep LD B64–109(double) M30–58
★Commerce pl Chevalerie ☎251206 rm22
⇄4 ⊫3 1 Feb–31 Dec B39.50–73 M17–52
Pn56–60 Pool

St-Auban See **Châteaux-Arnoux**

St-Aubin-sur-Mer 14 (Calvados) 1,200
(☎31) Map **8** D4
★ *St-Aubin* ⊫ r Verdun ☎973039 rm26 ⇄12
22 Mar–30 Sep Sea

St Avold 57 (Moselle) 18,950 (☎87)
Map **11** A3
☆☆☆ **Novotel-St Avold** RN3A ☎922593
tx860966 rm60 ⇄60 Lift B120–140 Pool Golf

St-Brieuc† 22 (Côtes-du-Nord) 56,300
(☎96) MAP **7** B3
★★★Alexandre 1er 19 pl Diguesclin
☎337945 rm43 ⇄43 G Lift B84–131
★★★Griffon r de Guernesey ☎334003 rm45
⇄33 ⊫12 G Lift LD B70–139 M30–70
Pn223–259
★ *Guesclin* pl du-Guesclin ☎330465 rm30
⇄3 ⊫12
⊪ **Moderne** 44 rue du Dr-Rahuel ☎334015
(closed weekends)
⊪⊛ **Royal** 121 r J-Ferny ☎611091 (closed
weekends)
At **Langueux** (2km SE on D1)
⊪⊳24 *Boschet* r Chaptal ☎333668 N⊛

St-Cast 22 (Côtes-du-Nord) 3,250 (☎96)
Map **8** C3
★★★Royal Bellevue bd de la Mer ☎410004
rm107 (A) ⇄49 ⊫8 Lift 30 Jun–1 Sep
★ *Angleterre & Panorama* ☎410044 rm40
G 6 Jun–7 Sep Sea
At **Garde-St-Cast (La)** (2km SE)
★★★Ar Vro ⊫ ☎410001 rm55 ⇄31 ⊫11 G
Lift 4 Jun–5 Sep LD B82–194 M45–50
Pn150–170 Beach
At **Pen-Guen** (2.5km S)
★★Pins ☎410781 rm38 ⇄7 ⊫5 25 Jun–1 Sep
Sea

St-Céré 46 (Lot) 4,400 (☎60) Map **16** C2
★★Paris & Coq Arlequin ⊫ bd du Dr-Roux
☎380213 rm35 ⇄13 ⊫22 G 3 Mar–3 Jan LD
B55–154 M28–70 Pn100–120

★★Touring 7 pl de la République ☎8
tx51626 CCl Lot Cahor rm31 ⇄6 ⊫1 G
1 Jun–15 Oct

St-Chély-d'Apcher 48 (Lozère) 5,350
(☎66) Map **16** D2
★Lion d'Or 132 r T Roussel ☎310014 rm30
⇄5 ⊫6 G 1 Feb–31 Dec B33–61 M17–28
Pn70–85
⊪⊳24 **Moderne** 42 av de la République
☎310612 N☎310327 N⊛ Ren G10

St-Claude 39 (Jura) 14,100 (☎84)
Map **11** A1
⊪⊳ **Grenard** 23 r Carnot ☎450648 N⊛ Frd

St-Cyprien 24 (Dordogne) 1,800 (☎53)
Map **16** C2
★★Abbaye ⊫ ☎292048 rm18 (A) ⇄7 ⊫10
1 Feb–31 Dec

St-Dié† 88 (Vosges) 26,540 (☎29)
Map **11** A3
★Nouvel 10 r Gambetta ☎562221 rm32
⇄4 ⊫1 B37–86 M35
★ *Vosges* (n rest) 57 r Thiers ☎561621
rm17 ⊫10 G
⊪⊳ **Thouzet** rte de Raon ☎562330 N⊛ Frd
⊪⊳ *Vosges* 51 r d'Alsace ☎562995 N⊛ Cit G

St-Dizier† 52 (Haute-Marne) 39,850 (☎25)
Map **10** C/D3
★★★Gambetta ☎052210 rm33 ⇄30 G Lift
B54.50–151 M26–31
★Soleil d'Or rte de Bar-le-Duc ☎050310
tx840946 rm60 ⇄60 Lift B100–130
M32–42 Pool
⊪⊳ **Clabaut** rte de Bar-le-Duc ☎051512
(closed weekends) Peu
⊪⊳ *Sport-Auto* av Sarrail ☎051050 N⊛ BL/Tri
⊪⊳ *Triangle Motors* rte de Bar-le-Duc
☎052398 Frd
At **Hallignicourt** (4km W on N4)
★Auberge de la Bobotte N4 ☎052075
rm10 ⊫8 G LD B42–74 M23–39 St15%

St-Emilion 33 (Gironde) 3,400 (☎56)
Map **15** B2
★★Hostellerie Plaisance pl Clocher
☎517232 rm12 ⇄12 15 Feb–15 Jan

St-Étienne 42 (Loire) 221,800 (☎77)
Map **27** A4
★★★Christel r Bergson ☎522707 rm107
⇄107 Lift G B109–133 M30–50
★★★Frantel av de Wuppertal ☎252275
tx300050 rm120 ⇄120 G Lift B120–194 M52
★★★Grand (n rest) 10 av Libération ☎329977
tx330811 rm86 ⇄55 ⊫31 Lift B83–166
★★★Terminus du Forez 31 av Denfert-
Rochereau ☎333105 rm66 (A1) ⇄21 G Lift
⊪⊳ **St-Etienne** 50 r D-Claude ☎325025 N⊛
Opl

St Etienne Airport
At **Andrezieux-Boutheon** (17km NW by N82)
☆☆☆ **Novotel St Etienne Aeroport** (RN82)
☎551074 tx900722 rm98 ⇄98 Lift B120–140
Pool

St-Étienne-de-Baigorry 64
(Pyrénées-Atlantiques) 1,800 (☎59)
Map **20** C3
★★Trinquet ☎374014 rm28 ⇄16 ⊫10 G
26 Feb–11 Nov B53–136 M43 Pn75–140 Lake

St-Florent See **Corse (Corsica)**

St-Florentin 89 (Yonne) 7,250 (☎86)
Map **10** C2
★ *Est* 7 r fbg St-Martin ☎351035 rm29 (A6)
G 18 Jan–18 Dec LD B28–54 M17–40

St-Flour 15 (Cantal) 8,800 (☎71) Map **16** D
★★★Europe 12 cours Spy-des-Ternes
☎600364 rm48 ⇄18 ⊫5 Lift 10 Feb–15 Jan
★★Nouvel Bonne Table 16 av République
☎600586 tx990218 rm48 (A30) ⇄40 G Lift
LD B51–95 M21–46 Pn70–86

France

★★St-Jacques 6 pl Liberté ☎600920 rm30
⇄4 🛏15 G
★★Voyageurs 25 r Collège ☎601551
tx990218 Overfel rm39 ⇄16 🛏4 G Lift
1 May–30 Sep LD B50–91 M26–50
Pn80–85
★Parc & Terminus av de la République
☎600829 rm48 ⇄5 🛏5 G Lift Dec–10 Oct LD
B36–53 M17–38
🚗24 Negre ☎600243 N☎600643 Peu G

St-Galmier 42 (Loire) 3,250 (☎77)
Map **27** A4
★★★Christel La Charpinière ☎541020 rm35
⇄35 B126–157 M45 Pool

St-Gaudens 31 (Haute-Garonne) 12,950
(☎61) Map **16** C1
★★Ferrière & France 1 r Gl-Leclerc ☎891457
rm16 ⇄8 🛏5 B34–72 M18&àlc
🚗Midi Pyrénées 52 av du Ml-Joffre
☎891199 N☎ Frd
At **Villeneuve de Rivière** (6km W on N117)
★★Cedres ☎891204 rm20 ⇄8 🛏6
15 Apr–15 Oct

St-Georges d'Aurac 43 (Haute-Loire)
Map **27** A3
🚗24 L Giraud rte de Puy ☎21 Cit G10

St-Georges-de-Didonne 17
(Charente-Maritime) 4,000 (☎46) Map **15** B3
★Bellevue ☎050742 rm19 (A5) ⇄6
Apr–Sep LD B41–75 M25–35 Pn82–95 Sea

St-Germain-de-Joux 01 (Ain) 550 (☎50)
Map **27** B4
★Reygrobellet ☎11 rm20 ⇄13 🛏4 G
15 Nov–25 Sep LD B43–91 M35–70

St-Germain-en-Laye†78 (Yvelines)
42,000 (☎1) Map **9** B3
★★★★Pavillon Henri-IV 21 r Thiers
☎9632066 rm50 ⇄50 G Lift 15 Mar–30 Nov

St-Gervais-les-Bains 74 (Haute-Savoie)
4,800 (☎50) Map **28** C4
★★★Alpenrose ☎782955 tx Sisinger 34414F
rm47 ⇄28 🛏19 Lift 15 Dec–15 Oct Pool
★★Splendid (n rest) ☎782133 rm20 ⇄12
🛏4 Lift 25 Jun–10 Sep 20 Dec–20 Apr
B73–124 Sea

St-Gilles 30 (Gard) 9,800 (☎66) Map **27** A2
At **Saliers** (4km E on N572)
★★★Cabanettes en Camargue ☎873153
tx480451 rm14 ⇄14 G LD B140–185(double)
Pn165–225(double) Pool

St-Gilles-Croix-de-Vie 85 (Vendée)
6,900 (☎30) Map **7** B1
★Embruns 16 bd de la Mer ☎551140 rm23
⇄8 🛏3 LD B53–88 M29 Pn68–90 Sea

St-Girons 09 (Ariège) 8,800 (☎61)
Map **22** C4
★★★Eychenne 8 av P-Laffont ☎662055 rm50
⇄25 🛏15 G B54–129 M27–70 Pn92–125
★★★Truite Dorée 🄻 rte d'Aulus (1km S)
☎661689 rm15 ⇄5 🛏6 Mar–Oct LD B68–116
M28–50 Pn70–100

St-Hilaire-de-Brethmas See **Alès**
St-Hilaire-le-Chatel See
Mortagne-au-Perche

St-Hilaire-du-Harcouet 50 (Manche)
5,750 (☎33) Map **8** C3
★Lion d'Or 🄻 120 r Avranches ☎491082
rm21 ⇄8 🛏10 G B37.50–77 M26.50–36
Pn100–120
★Relais de la Poste 11 r de Mortain ☎491031
rm12 G LD B32.50–41 M17.50–39 Pn62.50

St-Jean-Cap-Ferrat 06 (Alpes-Maritimes)
2,400 (☎93) Map **28** C2

★★★★Grand bd Gl-de-Gaulle ☎010454
tx47184 rm80 ⇄52 🛏12 G Lift Mar–Sep 🏊
Pool Sea
★★★Della Robbia bd Gl-de-Gaulle ☎065269
rm12 ⇄9 🛏3 20 Dec–30 Sep Sea
🚗Toso Le Pont St-Jean ☎010589 N☎ Ren G30
St-Jean-de-Bray See **Orléans**

St-Jean-de-Luz 64 (Pyrénées-Atlantiques)
12,100 (☎59) Map **20** C3
★★★★Chantaco rte d'Ascain ☎261476
rm30 ⇄30 G Etr–Oct B112–228 M60–70
Pn170–215 St15% 🏊 Golf Lake
★★★★Miramar r Ste-Barbe ☎260994 rm25
⇄25 G 15 Dec–15 Nov Sea
★★★★Moderne 43 bd Thiers ☎261461
rm82 ⇄77 Lift 1 Jul–31 Aug B107–200
M45–50 Pn130–180 Sea
☆☆☆Basques Rond-Point Ste-Barbe ☎260424
rm55 ⇄21 🛏15 22 Mar–22 Sep
★★★Poste (n rest) 83 r Gambetta ☎260453
rm35 ⇄19 🛏9 1 Apr–10 Oct B48–102
★★Paris (n rest) 1 bd Passicot ☎260062
rm23 ⇄7 🛏1 1 Mar–1 Dec B42–80 Lake
★★Plage 33 r Garat ☎260646 rm24 ⇄17 🛏5
G 15 Mar–15 Oct LD B52–118 M28
Pn107–127 Sea
★Continental 15 av Verdun ☎260123 rm24
⇄5 🛏15 LD B54–91 M24–32 Pn70–75
🚗Lamerain 4 bd V-Hugo ☎260402 Ren
At **Ciboure** (1km SW off N10)
★Ciboure rte d'Espagne ☎260057 rm22
⇄9 🛏6 B42–74 M28 Pn78–92 Pool

St-Jean-de-Maurienne 73 (Savoie)
10,450 (☎79) Map **28** C3
★★St-Georges (n rest) 344 r République
☎640106 rm24 ⇄16 🛏5 B34–77.50
🚗24 Duverney av du Mt-Cenis ☎641233
Ren G

St-Jean-de-Monts 85 (Vendée) 5,550
(☎30) Map **7** B1
★★Plage espl de la Mer ☎580035 rm56 ⇄22
🛏15 Lift 15 May–15 Sep LD B80–140
Pn110–160
🚗M G Vrignaud ☎586144 Ren

St-Jean-de-Vedas See **Montpellier**
St-Jean-de-Priche See **Mâcon**

St-Jean-le-Thomas 50 (Manche) (☎33)
Map **8** C3
★★Bains 🄻 (opp Post Office) ☎488420
rm28 (A6) ⇄10 🛏5 15 Mar–15 Oct LD
B34–66 M20–36 Pn69–80 Pool

St-Jean-Pied-de-Port 64
(Pyrénées-Atlantiques) 1,900 (☎59) Map **20** C3
★★★Continental (n rest) 3 av Renaud
☎370025 rm19 ⇄19 Lift 1 Apr–5 Nov B94–125
★★Central 1 pl de Gaulle ☎370022 rm14
⇄7 🛏6 Lift B42–117 M20–65 Pn75–132
★★Pyrénées pl Marché ☎370101 rm29
⇄20 🛏3 20 Dec–20 Nov

St-Jorioz 74 (Haute-Savoie) 2,500 (☎50)
Map **28** C4
At **Machevaz**
★★Châtaigniers 🄻 ☎686329 tx300893
rm70 ⇄9 🛏 G May–Sep B44–138 M30–65
Pn87–150 🏊 Pool

St-Julien-de-Lampon 24 (Dordogne)
500 (☎53) Map **16** C2
At **Rouffillac** (N of R Dordogne)
★Cayre 🄻 ☎297024 rm19 (A10) ⇄6 🛏13 G
Nov–10 Oct LD B74–80(double) M23–65
Pn80–85 🏊 Pool

St-Julien-en-Beauchêne 05
(Hautes-Alpes) 150 (☎92) Map **27** B3
★★St-Bermond-Gauthier N75 ☎580352
rm21 ⇄3 🛏3 G 1 Feb–30 Dec B28–55
M20–48 Pn56–66

143

France

St-Julien-en-Genevois 74 (Haute-Savoie)
6,400 (☎50) Map **28** C4
★*Savoyarde* rte de Lyon ☎41 rm10 ➾1

St-Julien-les-Villas See Troyes

St-Lary-Soulan 65 (Hautes-Pyrénées)
750 (☎62) Map **21** B4
★★*Sporting* tx Lourd 51617 rm72 ➾13 ⓜ59
Lift 15 Dec–15 Apr 1 Jul–1 Sep ⚓ Pool

St-Laurent-de-Cognac See Cognac

St-Laurent-du-Var See Nice

St-Lô 50 (Manche) 25,050 (☎33) Map **8** C4
★★*Terminus* **LE** 3 av Briovère ☎571471
rm15 ➾4 ⓜ7 G LD B47–80 M23–34
★★*Univers* **LE** 1 av Briovère ☎571153 rm25
➾10 ⓜ11 LD B40–81 M29
★*Armoric* (n rest) 15 r de la Marne ☎571747
rm20 ➾2 10 Jan–26 Dec B27–57
★*Cremaillère* pl de la Préfecture ☎571468
rm13 ➾1 ⓜ2 B41–77 Màlc
★*Gare* pl Gare ☎571515 rm18 ➾2 ⓜ2 G LD
B31–59 M24–54 Pn76–99
ⓘ➾ *Elisabeth* rte de Coutances ☎571258 N➾
Bed/Opl G
ⓘ➾24 *Legoueix* 2 r Ml-Leclerc ☎571644 Ren G

St-Louis 68 (Haut-Rhin) 18,150 (☎89)
Map **11** B2
★★*Pfiffer* 77 r Mulhouse ☎677444 (rest
closed Sun pm and Mon) rm36 ➾14 ⓜ7 G Lift
6 Jan–3 Aug 18 Aug–21 Dec
ⓘ➾24 *Bader* av Gl-de-Gaulle ☎671565 Ren

St-Malo† 35 (Ille-et-Vilaine) 46,300 (☎99)
Map **8** C3
★★★*Central* 6 Grande r ☎408770 rm47
➾21 ⓜ16 G Lift
★★*Grotte aux Fees* 36 chaussée du Sillon
☎348312 rm42 ➾6 Etr & 1 May–30 Sep Sea
★★*Louvre* 2 r de Marins ☎408662 rm45
➾2 ⓜ16 Lift 1 Apr–30 Sep B52–113 M30
Pn87–103
★*Celtic* (n rest) 25 chaussée du Sillon
☎560948 rm15 ➾2 ⓜ4 1 Jun–15 Sep Sea
★*Noguette* 9 r de la Fosse ☎408357 rm14
➾ⓜ LD B48–104 M20–40 Pn80–90
ⓘ➾ *Corsaires* 2 av L-Martin ☎561866 Frd
ⓘ➾ *Côte d'Emeraude* 131 bd Gambetta
☎560669 Cit
At **Paramé** (1km E)
★★*Rochebonne* 15 bd Châteaubriant
☎560172 rm39 ➾8 ⓜ31 B47–106 M25–32
Pn77–137

St-Marc 44 (Loire-Atlantique) (☎40)
Map **7** B2
★★*Plage* ☎709282 rm40 ➾9 ⓜ15
29 Nov–1 Oct

St-Martin-de-Belleville 74 (Haute-Savoie)
(☎50) Map **28** C4
☆☆☆ *Novotel Val-Thorens* ☎006040
tx980230 rm104 ➾104 Lift B120–140 Pool

St-Martin d'Hères See Grenoble

St-Maurice la Souterraine 23 (Creuse)
(☎55) Map **16** C1
At **La Croisière** (9km W at X-roads N20/N142)
ⓘ➾24 *P Larraud* ☎631503 M/c G

St-Maurice-sur-Moselle 88 (Vosges)
1,900 (☎29) Map **11** A2
★★*Relais des Ballons* **LE** 22 r de la Gare
☎615109 rm19 ➾17 ⓜ1 G 15 Mar–10 Dec
LD B55–110 M46–80 Pn140–170 St15%
★*Bon Sejour* ☎615233 rm18 ➾4 G LD
B37–68 M24–35

St-Maximin-la-Ste Baume 83 (Var)
4,050 (☎94) Map **27** B2
★*Chez Nous* 3 bd J-Jaurès ☎780257
tx83470 rm7 ➾1 G 15 Dec–3 Nov LD B30
M25

Centrauto RN ☎780104 N➾ Ren

St-Michel-de-Maurienne 73 (Savoie)
3,900 (☎79) Map **28** D3
★★*Savoy* **LE** 25 r Gl-Ferrié ☎71 rm24 ➾12 ⓜ2
G 15 Jan–20 Jun Dec 12 Jul–31 Dec B43–110
M32–56 Pn70–95
ⓘ➾ *Baudin* 18 r du Temple ☎15 Sim

St-Michel-en-Grève 22 (Côtes-du-Nord)
400 (☎96) Map **7** B3
★★*Plage* **LE** ☎357443 rm45 ➾5 8 Feb–31 Dec
Sea

St-Nabord See Remiremont

St-Nazaire 44 (Loire-Atlantique) 69,800
(☎40) Map **7** B2
★★*Dauphin* (n rest) 33 J-Jaurès ☎225685
rm20 ➾4 ⓜ12 B49–77
ⓘ➾ *Carnot* 10 bd R-Coty ☎225425 N➾ Frd

St-Omer† 62 (Pas-de-Calais) 18,000 (☎21)
Map **3** A1
ⓘ➾24 *Boulant* 33 bd de Strasbourg ☎382088
N➾ Cit G10
At **Tilques** (3km NW on N43)
★*Vert Mesnil* **LE** ☎381280 rm14 ➾3 ⓜ1 G
B45–80 M19–37&àlc

St-Palais-sur-Mer 17 (Charente-Maritime)
2,250 (☎46) Map **15** B3
★★★*Cordouan* av Pontaillac ☎026051
rm36 ➾10 ⓜ26 5 May–15 Sep LD B125–135
(double) M49 Pn152–157 Sea

St-Paul-de-Loubressac 46 (Lot)
Map **16** C2
★*Relais de la Madeleine* **LE** ☎8 rm20 ➾1 ⓜ6
10 Jan–10 Dec LD B31–59 M20àlc Pn60

St-Paul-lès-Dax See Dax

St-Pée-sur-Nivelle 64
(Pyrénées-Atlantiques) 2,600 (☎59) Map **20** C3
★*Pyrénées-Atlantique* (6km W on N618)
☎540222 rm36 ➾23 ⓜ12 LD **Pn**76–98

St-Pierre-d'Albigny 73 (Savoie) 2,550
(☎79) Map **28** C4
★*Vieux Moulin* ☎22 rm11 ⓜ1

St-Pierre-de-Chartreuse 38 (Isère) 600
(☎76) Map **27** B3
★★*Beau Site* **LE** ☎086134 rm34 ➾19 ⓜ8
G 1 Dec–31 Oct B38–110 M30–80 Pn80–120
Pool

St-Pierre-Quiberon See Quiberon

St-Pol-de-Léon 29 (Finistère) 8,775
(☎98) Map **7** A/B3
★*Voyageurs* 6 pl Evêche ☎690021 rm30
➾2 ⓜ2 G
ⓘ➾ *Charetteur* pl du Créisker ☎690208 N➾
Ren

St-Pol-sur-Ternoise 62 (Pas-de-Calais)
6,550 (☎21) Map **3** A1
★*Lion d'Or* **LE** 74 r Hesdin ☎031044 rm16
➾8 LD B46–73 M26–44 Pn90–100 St12%
ⓘ➾24 *Bailleul* 3E r Bethune ☎030655 Ren G

St-Pons 34 (Hérault) 3,450 (☎67) Map **16** D1
★★*Château de Ponderach* (1.2km S)
☎970257 rm12 ➾9 G Etr–2 Nov ⚓ Pool
ⓘ➾ *J Prax* rte de Castres ☎970142 N➾ Ren

St-Pourcain-sur-Sioule 03 (Allier)
5,600 (☎70) Map **9** B1
★*Chêne Vert* **LE** 35 bd Ledru-Rollin ☎454065
tx390794 rm35 ➾15 ⓜ11 G 15 Feb–4 Jan
B29–84 M25–85&àlc
★*Deux Ponts* **LE** Ilot de Tivoli ☎454114 rm22
➾9 ⓜ4 G 20 Dec–1 Mar 15 Mar–10 Nov LD
B38–93 M29–60 Pn82–106

St-Priest See Lyon

St-Quay-Portrieux 22 (Côtes-du-Nord)
3,600 (☎96) Map **7** B3

144

★★**Bretagne** LE 36 quai de la République ☎324091 rm15 ⋒6 (closed Nov) B43–60 M25–50 Pn75 Sea
★**Gerbot d'Avoine** LE 2 bd Littoral ☎324009 rm26 ⇌2 ⋒8 G (closed 25 Sep–17 Oct) LD B33–104 M25–78 Pn65–98 Sea
★**Plage** ☎324004 rm25 ⇌8 ⋒1 May–Sep B52–70 M21 Pn59–72 Sea
⚐ ***Moderne*** 69 bd Foch ☎324021 G

St-Quentin† **02** (Aisne) 69,200 (☎23) Map **10** C4
★★**Grand** 6 r Dachery ☎626977 tx140225 rm41 ⇌16 ⋒25 B64–114 M52
★★**Paix & Albert-1er** pl de 8 Octobre ☎627762 tx140225 (Hotel de la Paix) rm64 ⇌23 ⋒13 G Lift B46–104 Màlc
⚐ **24 *Centre Technique*** rte d'Amiens ☎627079
⚐ **Danton** 48 r Danton ☎624119 N⚐ G4
⚐ ***J-Jaurès*** r J-Jaurès 66 ☎624423 N⚐ BL/Tri
⚐ **24 Route de Paris** 267 rte de Paris ☎623227 M/c Ren G100

St-Raphaël 83 (Var) 21,400 (☎94) Map **28** C2
★★★***Continental*** (n rest) 25 bd de la Libération ☎950014 rm50 ⇌23 ⋒10 Lift 1 Jan–31 Dec Sea
★★***Beau Séjour*** prom Prés-Coty ☎950375 rm40 ⇌7 ⋒22 Lift 1 Feb–15 Nov Sea
★★**Genève** 18 bd Martin ☎952335 rm30 LD M17 **Pn**70–80
★★***Plage & Mediterranée*** (n rest) 39 bd de la Libération ☎950160 rm50 ⇌27 ⋒12 Lift Apr–31 Oct Sea
★**Au Vieux Port** 108 av Cdt Guildbaud ☎952312 rm15 ⇌4 B37–55 M29–60 Pn90 Sea
⚐ **Bains** r J-Barbier ☎951672 Cit G100
⚐ **Valescure** 142 av de Valescure ☎954278 N⚐ Frd

St-Rémy-de-Provence 13 (Bouches-du-Rhône) 8,000 (☎90) Map **27** B2
★★★**Antiques** av Pasteur ☎920302 rm27 ⇌18 ⋒9 LD B71–116 M40–60 Pn143–179 Pool ∩
★★**Le Castelet des Alpilles** pl Mireille ☎920721 rm19 ⇌13 ⋒4 21 Feb–14 Jan LD B69–152 M27–40 Pn140–180

St-Satur 18 (Cher) 1,760 (☎36) Map **9** B2
★★**Laurier** r du Commerce ☎541720 rm10 ⋒4 G Mar–30 Jan LD B33–65 M24–54

St-Sernin-sur-Rance 12 (Aveyron) 700 (☎65) Map **16** D1
★★**France** ☎996026 ta Place du Fort 12380 rm24 (A4) ⇌4 ⋒6 G B36–71(double) M19–50 Pn59–73

St-Tropez 83 (Var) 5,450 (☎94) Map **28** C1/2
★★★★**Byblos** av P-Signac ☎970004 tx470235 rm59 ⇌59 G Lift 15 Dec–Oct B170–540 Màlc St15% Pool Sea
★★★**Coste** (n rest) bd de la Mer ☎970064 rm35 ⇌25 15 Mar–31 Oct B58–107 Sea
★★★**Ermitage** (n rest) av P-Signac ☎970152 rm29 ⇌5 ⋒24 1 Apr–30 Sep B104–155 Sea
⚐ ***Carnot*** pl Carnot ☎970543 G3

St-Vaast-la-Hougue 50 (Manche) 2,400 (☎33) Map **8** C4
★**France & Fuchsias** LE 18 r Ml-Foch ☎544226 rm16 ⇌3 ⋒7 LD B47–110 M23–60 Pn70–100 ∩

St-Valery-sur-Somme 80 (Somme) 3,150 (☎22) Map **3** A1
★★**Relais Guillaume de Normandy** quai Romerel ☎275236 rm15 ⇌7 Dec–Oct B36–56 M17–48 Pn57–62 Sea
⚐ ***Dereumetz*** rte d'Abbeville ☎255073 G2

St-Vallier-sur-Rhône 26 (Drôme) 5,450 (☎75) Map **27** B3
At **Sarras** (2km W on N86)
★★***Vivarais*** LE av de Vivarais ☎Sarras 25 rm10 ⇌2 ⋒3 G 1 Mar–28 Feb

Ste-Anne-la-Palud 29 (Finistère) (☎98) Map **7** B3
★★★***Plage*** ☎925012 rm35 (A) ⇌30 G 22 Mar–30 Sep Sea

Ste-Catherine See **Briançon**

Ste-Enimie 48 (Lozère) 650 (☎66) Map **27** A3
★***Paris*** LE ☎475002 rm20 (A) ⇌6 ⋒3 1 May–1 Oct

Ste-Marie See **Vars (Col de)**

Ste-Maxime-sur-Mer 83 (Var) 6,650 (☎94) Map **28** C2
★★★**Beau Site** 10 bd des Cystes ☎961963 tx St Maxim970080 rm38 (A26) ⇌20 ⋒16 G Lift 1 Apr–30 Sep LD B105–130 M40 Pn120–165 ⚐ Pool Sea
★★★**Belle Aurore** 3 la Croisette ☎960245 rm20 (A5) ⇌10 ⋒6 1 Feb–15 Oct LD B49–139 M40 Pn100–160 St15% Sea
★★★***Chardon Bleu*** 2 allée du Chardon-Bleu ☎960208 rm30 ⇌15 ⋒7 Apr–Oct Sea
★★***Palmiers*** (n rest) pl 15 Aout ☎960041 rm35 ⇌10 ⋒8 Sea
☆☆**Royal Bon Repos** (n rest) r J-Alcard ☎960874 rm25 ⋒24 7 Apr–15 Oct B89–148 Sea
At **Beauvallon** 4.5km SW by N98
★**Marie Louise** ☎960605 rm14 (A5) ⋒12 1 Mar–Oct B54–115 M35 Sea
At **Cap Sardinaux** (2km NE on N98)
★★***Sardinaux*** ☎961510 rm20 (A) ⋒10 Jun–Sep Beach Sea

Saintes† **17** (Charente-Maritime) 28,450 (☎46) Map **15** B3
★★★***Commerce*** r des Messageries ☎930661 tx Mapotel51837 rm52 ⇌40 ⋒1 G 15 Jan–15 Dec
★★***Nouvel*** (n rest) 1 r Pasteur (off cours National) ☎930172 rm29 ⇌6 ⋒3 G
★★**Terminus** (n rest) espl de la Gare ☎930162 rm40 ⇌10 ⋒2 G B40–83
★**Messageries** (n rest) r des Messageries ☎930127 rm37 ⇌6 ⋒13 G B55–103
⚐ **Savia** rte de Bordeaux ☎934344 N⚐ Frd

Saintes-Maries-de-la-Mer (Les) 13 (Bouches-du-Rhône) 2,245 (☎90) Map **27** A2
★**Mirage** (n rest) r C-Pelletan ☎978043 rm28 ⇌3 ⋒10 1 Apr–4 Nov B40–79 Sea

Salers 15 (Cantal) 550 (☎71) Map **16** D3
★**Beffroi** (n rest) ☎3 rm9 ⇌6 ⋒3 15 Feb–15 Oct B71(double)

Sallanches 74 (Haute-Savoie) 8,450 (☎50) Map **28** C3
☆☆**Ibis** av de Genève ☎581442 tx380271 rm60 ⇌60 Lift B67–96 Màlc

Salon-de-Provence 13 (Bouches-du-Rhône) 35,600 (☎90) Map **27** B2
★**Grand Poste** 1 r Prés-Kennedy ☎560194 rm29 ⇌2 ⋒11 1 Feb–30 Oct B37–71 M19–25 Pn58–66
At **La Barben** (8km SE)
★**Touloubre** ☎562809 rm14 ⇌7 ⋒1 B49–90 M35 Pn85–112
At **Lancon de Provence** (9km SE on A7)
☆☆☆**Sofitel Jacques Borel** (n rest) ☎560715 tx440183 rm100 ⇌100 G B129–195 M46 &àlc

Salses 66 (Pyrénées-Orientales) 2,100 (☎69) Map **22** D4

France

☆☆☆**Euromotel Perpignan** 9 rte Nationale
☎386067 tx500092 rm56 ⇄56 (closed winter)
B90–120 M40

☆☆☆*Roussillon* ☎352467 tx50092 rm56
⇄56 Lift Dec–Oct

Samer 62 (Pas-de-Calais) 2,035 Map **3** A1
⋒⋙**24 Roussel** 21 av C-de Gaulle ☎335144
G4

Sanary-sur-Mer 83 (Var) 10,450 (☎94)
Map **27** B1

★★**Tour** quai Gl-de-Gaulle ☎741010 rm25
⇄10 ⋒6 15 Jan–15 Nov LD B46–90 M25
Pn95–120 Sea

Sancé-les-Mâcon See **Mâcon**

Saran See **Orléans**

Sarlat 24 (Dordogne) 10,900 (☎53)
Map **16** C2

★★★**Host Meysset** ☎590829 rm32 ⇄22 ⋒10
22 Mar–15 Oct LD B111–146 M40–85
Pn110–140

★★★**Madeleine** 1 pl de la Petite Rigaudie
☎591041 rm27 ⇄14 ⋒4 1 Feb–31 Dec LD
B61–97 M45–65 &àlc Pn91–108

★★**St Albert** ⋿ 10 pl Pasteur ☎590109 rm55
(A24) ⇄22 ⋒18 B53–130 M26–100 Pn80–120

★**Lion d'Or** 48 av Gambetta ☎590083 rm26
⇄3 ⋒5 LD

⋒⋙**24 Fournet** rte de Vitrac ☎590523 M/c Frd
G

⋒⋙*Robert* 33 av Thiers/r P-Curie ☎590048 Ren

Sarras See **St-Vallier-sur-Rhône**

Saulieu 21 (Côte-d'Or) 3,200 (☎80)
Map **10** C2

★★★**Poste** (n rest) ⋿ 2 r Grillot ☎640567
tx350540 rm45 ⇄40 G B39–116

★★**Côte d'Or** 2 r Argentine ☎640766 rm22
(A4) ⇄16 ⋒5 G 2 Dec–2 Nov B66–156 Màlc
St15%

★**Aux Quatre Vents** X-rds Nevers-Autun,
47 r J-Ferry ☎640709 rm11 G Feb–Dec LD
B28–43 M19–30 Pn70

⋒⋙*Griesser* pl C-de-Gaulle ☎20 N⋙ Cit

Saumur† **49** (Maine-et-Loire) 34,200
(☎41) Map **8** D2

★★★*Budan* 3 quai Carnot ☎512876 rm80
⇄45 ⋒30 G Lift Sea

★★**Roi René** 94 av Gl-de-Gaulle ☎504503
rm40 ⇄8 ⋒12 G Lift B44–98 M30–50

★**Bretagne** ⋿ 55 r St-Nicholas ☎512638 rm9
G B39–46(double)

★**Croix-Verte** 49 r de Rouen ☎503931 rm18
⇄3 ⋒4 15 Jan–15 Dec B41–70 M19–26
Pn69–79(double)

⋒⋙**M Charbonneau** 103 r du Pont Fouchard
☎501133 N⋙ Ren

At **Chenehutte-les-Tuffeaux** (8km NW)

★★★**Le Prieuré** ☎510101 tx72183 rm38
(A17) ⇄33 ⋒2 1 Mar–1 Jan Pool

Sausheim See **Mulhouse**

Saut-des-Cuves See **Gérardmer**

Saverne 67 (Bas-Rhin) 10,450 (☎88)
Map **11** B3

★★*Geiswiller* ⋿ 17 r Côte ☎911851 rm18
⇄2 ⋒7 1 Feb–15 Jan

★*Boeuf Noir* ⋿ 22 Grande r ☎911053 rm23
⇄7 ⋒6 G 1 Nov–28 Feb 1 Apr–30 Sep LD

★**Chez Jean** ⋿ 3 r de la Gare ☎911019 rm24
⇄20 ⋒4 G Lift LD B42–87 M20–68 Pn100–110

⋒⋙**24 Wallior** 21 r St-Nicolas ☎911752
Cit G

At **Stambach** (4.5km SW)

★★**Fameuse Truite** rte de Lutzelbourg
☎911861 rm32 (A) ⇄6 G

Savignac-les-Eglises 24 (Dordogne) 750
(☎53) Map **16** C3

★★*Parc* ⋿ ☎050012 rm15 (A) ⇄7 ⋒5 G
19 Oct–31 Jan 14 Mar–13 Oct

⋒⋙*M Rousseau* ☎050033 Ren G3

Sées 61 (Orne) 5,250 (☎34) Map **8** D3

★**Cheval Blanc** ⋿ 1 pl St-Pierre ☎278048
rm9 ⋒12 LD B35–50 M19–29

★**Dauphin** 31 pl Halls ☎278007 rm13 (A6)
⇄1 ⋒2 LD B29–52 M22–60 Pn68–85

Segos See **Aire-sur-l'Adour**

Sellières 39 (Jura) 930 Map **10** D1
See also **Poligny**

At **Passenans** (6km SE)

★★**Domaine Turistique du Revermont** ⋿
☎852066 rm28 ⇄24 G Lift 16 Feb–31 Oct
16 Nov–31 Jan Pool

Semur-en-Auxois 21 (Côte-d'Or) 5,400
(☎80) Map **10** C2

★★*Lac* ⋿ (3km S on D1038 at Lac de Pont)
☎971111 rm22 ⇄9 ⋒2 G 1 Feb–15 Dec Lake

★**Côte d'Or** 3 pl G-Gaveau ☎970313 rm15
⇄2 ⋒5 G Feb–Dec LD B28–66 M21–45

★**Gourmets** 4 r Varenne ☎970510 rm15 ⋒3 G
25 Nov–25 Oct LD B28–53 M28–40 &àlc

⋒⋙**J Girard** 21 r du Cours ☎970510 N⋙ Ren
G6

Sénas 13 (Bouches-du-Rhône) 3,300 (☎90)
Map **27** B2

★**Luberon** ⋿ N7 ☎572010 rm7 ⇄1 ⋒3 LD
B32–62(double) M22–60

Senlis 60 (Oise) 14,400 (☎4) Map **8** B4

★★*Nord* ⋿ 66 r République ☎4530116 rm16
⇄3 ⋒5 G 20 Jan–23 Dec

⋒⋙**24 P Delacharlery** rte de Crépy ☎4530818
M/c Ren G50

Senonches 28 (Eure-et-Loir) 3,500 (☎37)
Map **8** A3

★**Forêt** ⋿ pl Champ-de-Foire ☎007850 rm14
⇄3 ⋒3 G 4 Mar–30 Jan LD B27–83
M24–34 Pn80–90

Sens† **89** (Yonne) 27,950 (☎86) Map **10** C3

★★★**Paris & Poste** 97 r de la République
☎651743 rm38 (A4) ⇄22 ⋒6 G
15 Dec–15 Nov LD B60–135 M55

★★*Croix Blanche* 9 r V-Guichard ☎651533
rm25 ⇄2 ⋒6 G

⋒⋙*Senonaise d'Auto* 19 bis r du Gl-Leclerc
☎651033 N⋙ Ren G10

Sept-Saulx 51 (Marne) 350 (☎26)
Map **10** C3

★★**Cheval Blanc** ☎616027 rm26 (A3) ⇄8
⋒14 G 15 Feb–15 Jan LD B52–110 M50–65
Pn160 ⋙

Serres 05 (Hautes-Alpes) 1,400 (☎92)
Map **27** B3

★**Alpes** av Grenoble ☎670018 rm20 (A2) ⇄2
G LD B34–66 M26–39 Pn70–83

⋒⋙**24 M P Reynaud** av de la Gare ☎670011
M/c Ren G3

Serrières 07 (Ardèche) 1,450 (☎75)
Map **27** B3

★**Schaeffer** quai J-Roche ☎340007 rm12
⇄7 Mar–Nov LD B37–55 M25–60

Sète† **34** (Hérault) 40,200 (☎67) Map **27** A2

★★★**Grand** 17 quai Ml-Lattre-de-Tassigny
☎742164 rm51 ⇄24 ⋒19 Lift 4 Jan–24 Dec
B44–168 M30–40

⋒⋙**Cano & Milano** 40 quai du Gl-Durand
☎742944 N⋙ Ren

Sevrier 74 (Haute-Savoie) 2,200 (☎50)
Map **28** C4

At **Machevaz** 2km S by N512

★★**Chataigniers** ⋿ ☎686329 tx300893
rm55 ⇄20 ⋒12 G May–Sep LD B32–87
M20–29 Pn61–112 ⋙ Pool Lake

France

Sezanne 51 (Marne) 6,550 (☎26) Map **10** C3
★★**Croix d'Or** 53 r Notre Dame ☎420127
rm13 ⇄11 ♨2 Lift B39–56 M25–40
★★**France** 25 r J-Jolly ☎420025 rm25 ⇄7
♨10 G 15 Feb–15 Jan B46–95 M40&àlc
♨⥾ **Vissuzaine** 27 r L-Jolly ☎420218 Cit

Siorac-en-Périgord 24 (Dordogne) 800
(☎53) Map **16** C2
★**Scholly** LE r de la Poste ☎296002 rm35
(A5) ⇄20 ♨8 G LD B116–126 M37.50–82
Pn116–127

Sisteron 04 (Alpes-de-Hautes-Provence)
7,450 (☎92) Map **27** B2
★★★**Grand du Cours** av de la Libération
☎610451 rm50 ⇄20 ♨30 G Lift 1 Mar–15 Nov
B74–130 M25–60 Lake
★★**Select** (n rest) pl de la République ☎250
rm14 ⇄3 ♨2 Etr–31 Oct
★★**Touring** 85 av de Libération ☎6 rm30 ⇄2
♨3 G 1 Jan–30 Oct
★**Arcades** pl de la République ☎209 rm10
♨⥾**24 Alpes Automobiles** av de la Libération
☎64464 N⥾ AR/Ren G8

Soissons† **02** (Aisne) 32,150 (☎23)
Map **10** C4
★★**Picardie** 6 r Neuve St-Martin ☎532193
rm33 ⇄6 ♨27 Lift B78–117
★**Rallye** 10 bd de Strasbourg ☎530047
rm12 ⇄1 ♨4 G B47–89
♨⥾**Europ** 55 av de la Gare ☎532149 N⥾ Frd
♨⥾**Jeanne-d'Arc** 96 bd J-d'Arc ☎530414
N⥾ Peu

Souffelweyersheim See **Strasbourg**

Souillac 46 (Lot) 4,400 (☎60) Map **16** C2
★★**Ambassadeurs** LE 12 av Gl-de-Gaulle
☎377836 rm24 (A10) ⇄10 ♨9 G
1 Nov–30 Sep LD B34.50–88 M19–65
Pn60–81
★★**Grand** pl Verninac ☎377830 rm17 ⇄10
G 15 May–30 Sep B38–95 M22–70 Pn96–117
★★**Granges Vieilles** (n rest) rte de Sarlat (1.5km
W on N703) ☎378092 rm10 ⇄10 Apr–Sep
B62–79(double) St12%
★★**Périgord** LE av de Paris ☎377828 rm60
(A30) ⇄20 ♨10 G 1 Mar–31 Oct
★★**Renaissance** LE av J-Jaurè ☎377804
rm30 (A6) ⇄8 ♨22 G Lift 1 Mar–2 Jan
B58–90 M30–70 Pn90–100
★★**Truffière** ☎378895 rm20 ⇄14 ♨6 G
10 Mar–10 Jan
★**Nouvel** LE 21 av Gl-de-Gaulle ☎377958
rm30 ⇄11 ♨11 G
♨⥾**Central** 16 bd L-J-Malvy N⥾ G10
⥾⥾**24 R Fabre** 36 av de Paris ☎377946 N⥾

Souppes 77 (Seine-et-Marne) 4,460
Map **9** B3
★**Mouton** 72 av Gl-Leclerc ☎4297008 rm15
⇄1 ♨1 G

Source (La) See **Orléans**

Sousceyrac 46 (Lot) 1,050 (☎60) Map **16** D2
★**Déjeuner de Sousceyrac** LE ☎380256 rm15
(A4) ⇄2 ♨5 15 Mar–1 Dec LD B29–66 M25–
48 Pn62–65

Soustons 40 (Landes) 5,150 (☎57)
Map **15** A1
★★**Bergerie** av du Lac ☎480143 rm25 (A13)
⇄25 1 May–31 Oct B70–80
♨⥾**Dufour** 40 av Ml-Leclerc ☎22 (closed
weekends) Ren

Stainville 55 (Meuse) 400 (☎28) Map **10** D3
★★★**La Grange** LE ☎786015 rm15 (A7) ⇄10
♨2 G 15 Mar–15 Nov

Stambach See **Saverne**

Strasbourg† **67** (Bas-Rhin) 257,350 (☎88)
Map **11** B3

★★★★**Sofitel** pl St-Pierre-le-Jeune (off r Nuée
Bleue) ☎329930 tx870894 rm180 ⇄180 G
Lift B169–277 M61 Pn291 Pool
★★★★**Terminus-Gruber** 10 pl de la Gare
☎328700 tx87998 rm85 ⇄46 ♨21 Lift
★★★**France** 20 r Jeu des Enfants
☎323712 tx890084 rm70 ⇄10 ♨60 G Lift
B106–160
★★★**Grand** (n rest) 12 pl de la Gare ☎324690
tx870011 rm86 ⇄58 ♨25 Lift B64–137
☆☆☆**Mercure Strasbourg Sud** Autoroute
B35 ☎660300 tx890277 rm98 ⇄98 Lift
B120–140 Pool
★★★**Monopole-Métropole** LE 14 r Kuhn
☎321194 tx893366 rm100 ⇄100 Lift
☆☆☆**PLM-Pont de l'Europe** Parc du Rhin
☎610323 ta PLM tx870833 rm93 ⇄93
B125–150 M30
★★★**Union** (n rest) 8 quai Kellermann (corner
of r Nuée Bleue) ☎327041 rm58 ⇄25 ♨14
Lift
★★**Couronne** (n rest) 26 r du fbg de Saverne
(off bd Prés-Wilson) ☎323545 rm43 ⇄6 ♨13
G B32–62
★★**Rhin** (n rest) 7 pl de la Gare ☎323500
rm63 ⇄10 ♨9 Lift 2 Jan–23Dec B52–92
★★**Vendôme** (n rest) 9 pl de la Gare ☎324523
rm39 ⇄14 ♨21 Lift B44–95
♨**Grand Dierstein** 164a rte de Schirmeck
☎300272 N⥾ BL/Rov/Tri
♨⥾**Nouvelle** 270 rte de Colmar ☎399905 N⥾
Chy/Sim
At **Cronenbourg** (4km NW on D41)
♨⥾**Goetzmann** 60 r du Marché-Gare ☎292000
N⥾ Opl
At **Illkirch** (10km SW)
☆☆☆**Novotel Strasbourg-Sud** rte de Colmar
☎662156 tx890142 rm76 ⇄76 Lift B120–
140 Pool
At **Souffelweyersheim**
♨⥾**Hess** 46 rte de Brumath ☎209090
N⥾ Lnc/Por

Sully-sur-Loire 45 (Loiret) 5,050 (☎38)
Map **9** B3
★★**Poste** 11 r fbg St-Germain ☎010622
rm30 (A10) ⇄8 ♨8 G 8 Mar–25 Jan B35–99
M30 Pn85–110 ♁

Survilliers 95 (Val-d'Oise) 2,750 (☎1)
Map **9** B3
☆☆☆**Mercure** ☎4719203 tx695917 rm118
⇄118 Lift B120–140 Pool
☆☆☆**Novotel** A1/D16 ☎4710652 tx695910
rm79 ⇄79 Lift B120–140 Pool

Talant See **Dijon**

Talloires 74 (Haute-Savoie) 850 (☎50)
Map **28** C4
★★★★**Abbaye** rte Port Talloires ☎447081
rm45 ⇄29 ♨2 G 1 May–30 Sep ♨ Pool Lake
★★★**Cottage** rte G-Bise ☎447110 rm40 (A18)
⇄30 ♨3 G Lift 15 Mar–20 Oct B118–316
M60–155 Pn160–260 St15% Lake
★★**Beau Site** ☎447104 rm38 (A27) ⇄22
♨5 G 15 May–30 Sep ♨ Lake
★★**Vivier** ☎447054 rm43 ⇄21 ♨15 G
1 Apr–15 Oct Lake

Tamnies 24 (Dordogne) 300 (☎53)
Map **16** C2
★**Laborderie** ☎296859 rm18 (A1) ⇄10 ♨6
B38–67 M20–45 Pn50–75 ♨

Tancarville 76 (Seine-Maritime) (☎35)
Map **9** A4
★**Marine** ☎948915 rm16 ⇄4 ♨2 G
15 Feb–15 Jan

Tarare 69 (Rhône) 12,200 (☎74) Map **27** B4
★**Mère Paul** (2km W on N7) ☎631457 rm14
(A4) ⇄7 ♨1 G 15 Oct–20 Sep

France

Tarascon 13 (Bouches-du-Rhône) 10,700
(☎90) Map **27** B2
★★**Terminus** ☎911895 rm27 ⇜3 ▥10
1 Feb–15 Nov B43–91 M27–45 Pn67–110
★**Provençal** ☎911141 rm21 ⇜6 ▥4 G LD
B33–80 M20

Tarascon-sur-Ariège 09 (Ariège) 4,300
(☎61) Map **22** C4
★★**Poste** ㏒ 16 av V-Pilhes ☎646041 rm30
⇜14 ▥4 1 Dec–31 Oct (closed Mon) LD B31–89
M23–65 Pn65–85

Tarbes† **65** (Hautes-Pyrénées) 57,800 (☎62)
Map **15** B1
★★★**Mapotel President** 1 r Gabriel-Faure
☎939840 tx53522 rm57 ⇜45 ▥12 G Lift Pool
★★**Croix Blanche** (n rest) pl Verdun ☎930854
rm30 ⇜5 ▥7 B45–96
★**Royal Henri-IV** (n rest) 7 bd B-Barrère
☎340168 rm22 ⇜10 ▥10 G B44–101
i☎⊘Lafitole & Charrel 1 av B-Barrère
☎340059 N☞ Fia G20

Terrasson-la-Villedieu 24 (Dordogne)
6,250 (☎53) Map **16** C3
★★★★**Rush** av V-Hugo ☎500374 tx57575
rm48 ⇜48 G Lift 1 Mar–1 Jan

Thann 68 (Haut-Rhin) 8,550 (☎89)
Map **11** A2
★**Parc** ㏒ 5 r Kléber ☎371098 rm21 ⇜8 ▥4 G
B33–73 M20–60
At **Bitschwiller** (2km N on N66)
i☎⊘L Klein r du Rhin ☎370134 M/c Ren G10

Théoule 06 (Alpes Maritimes) 800 (☎93)
Map **28** C2
★★**Guerguy la Galère** ☎389671 rm14 ⇜14
G Feb–Oct B180–250 Màlc Sea
★**Hermitage Jules Céser** (n rest) Théoule
Plage ☎389612 rm18 ▥12 1 Feb–Sep Sea

Thiers 63 (Puy-de-Dôme) 17,850 (☎73)
Map **27** A4
★**Centre** (n rest) 10 r Traversière ☎801912
rm12 ⇜1 B33–67
★**Nouvel & Grand** pl Belfort ☎800061 rm22
⇜1 ▥5 G

Thionville 57 (Moselle) 44,200 (☎87)
Map **11** A4
i☎⊘Central 1 rte de la Dique ☎885548 N☞ Frd

Thoissey 01 (Ain) 1,500 (☎74) Map **27** B4
★★**Chapon Fin** ☎040474 rm18 ⇜3 ▥2 G
20 Feb–5 Jan
★**Beau Rivage** av Port ☎040166 rm10 ▥10
15 Mar–30 Oct LD B44–72 M40–53

Thonon-les-Bains 74 (Haute-Savoie)
27,150 (☎50) Map **11** A1
★★**Clos Savoyard** 50 av Genève ☎710391
rm19 (A) ⇜8 ▥8 1 Nov–30 Sep

Thouars 79 (Deux-Sevres) 12,650 (☎48)
Map **8** D2
★**Du Cheval Blanc** 53 r Tremoile ☎660021
rm22 ⇜6 ▥2 G B45–77 M20–40 Pn65–120
i☎⊘Chauvin & Fouchereau r P-Curie
☎662178 N☞ Ren

Thury-Harcourt 14 (Calvados) 1,450
(☎31) Map **8** D3
★**Poste** rte Caen ☎797212 rm11 ⇜5 ▥6 G
25 Feb–15 Jan

Tilloy-les-Nofflaines See **Arras**

Tilques See **St-Omer**

Tinqueux See **Reims**

Tonnay-Boutonne 17 (Charente-Maritime)
1,100 (☎46) Map **8** C1
★**Beau Rivage** r du Passage ☎332001 rm7
G 11 Sep–27 Aug LD B41–51(double)
M22–50 Pn54–60 Lake
i☎⊘A Seureau Grande r ☎332065 N☞ Ren G

Tonnerre 89 (Yonne) 6,550 (☎86)
Map **10** C2
★★**Abbaye St-Michel** ㏒ r St-Michel ☎550599
rm12 ⇜8 ▥11 1 Feb–20 Dec LD B100–190
(double) M56 &àlc ⬗

Toulon† **83** (Var) 185,075 (☎94)
Map **27** B1
★★★**Frantel Tour-Blanche** bd Admiral Vence
☎244157 rm100 ⇜75 ▥25 Lift B106–170
M48 Pn275–318 Pool Sea
☎⊘Azur 5 av F-Cuzin ☎416571 N☞ M/c Frd
☎⊘Carrefour-Auto 49 av du Gl-Pruneau
☎415986 N☞ BL/Jag/Tri
At **Cap Brun** (4km SE on D42)
★★**Résidence du Cap Brun** chemin
P-Guegrand ☎412946 rm23 (A) ⇜11 ▥6
1 Dec–31 Oct Sea

Toulouse† **31** (Haute-Garonne) 383,200
(☎61) Map **16** C1
★★★**Caravelle** (n rest) 62 r Raymond-IV
☎627065 tx530438 rm30 ⇜18 ▥12 G Lift
B110–157
★★★**De la Compagnie du Midi** ☎628493
tx510644 rm65 ⇜33 ▥13 Lift B77–149 M28
★★★**Concorde** 16 bd Bon Repos ☎624860
tx510987 rm97 ⇜70 ▥27 G Lift B130–180
M40 Pn130–210
At **Mirail** (4km SW)
☎⊘24 SMECA 23 r Vauquelin ☎401010
BL/Jag/Tri G

Toulouse Airport
★★★**Frantel Wilson** (n rest) 7 r de Labeda
☎212175 tx530550 rm95 ⇜53 ▥42 G Lift
B132–244
☆☆☆**Novotel Toulouse Purpan** 23 r de
Maubec ☎493410 tx520640 rm124 ⇜124 Lift
B120–140 ⬗ Pool

Touquet-Paris-Plage (Le) 62 (Pas-de-
Calais) 5,600 (☎21) Map **3** A1
★★★★**Mer** 2 r St-Louis (off bd de la Mer)
rm80 ⇜80 Lift Etr & Whi–Sep Sea
★★★**Bristol** 17 Grande rm60 (A) ⇜35 ▥32
Lift Mar–Oct
★★★**Côte d'Opale** bd de la Mer ☎050811
rm28 ⇜20 ▥2 15 Mar–15 Nov LD B69.50–114
M45–150 Pn151.50–185 Sea
★★★**Westminster** av Verger ☎051966
rm145 ⇜145 Lift 20 Feb–6 Jan B150–225
M75 St15%
★★**Plage** (n rest) 13 bd de la Mer ☎050322
rm25 ⇜9 ▥3 1 Mar–3 Nov Sea
★★**St-Christophe** 45 r Bruxelles (off bd de la
Mer) ☎052376 rm22 ⇜9 Etr May–Sep LD
B69–99(double) M28 Pn74–77
★★**Universal** (n rest) 10 r Bruxelles (off bd de la
Mer) ☎051199 rm19 ⇜7 ▥7 Etr–30 Sep
★★**Windsor** 7 r St Georges (off r de la Paix)
☎050544 rm27 ⇜8 ▥4 Lift 1 Apr–1 Oct B43–
97 M40 Pn105
★**Chalet** 15 r de la Paix ☎051299 rm15 ⇜5
▥1 LD B42–93 M29.50 Pn83.50–100 Sea
★**Robert's** 66 r de Londres ☎051198 rm14
⇜3 Apr–Sep LD B35–62 M25–31 Pn63–69
★**Touquet** 18 r de Paris ☎052254 rm19
⇜2 ▥5 LD B33–79
At the **Golf Links** (3km S)
★★★**Manoir** av du Golf ☎052022 rm47 (A10)
⇜45 G Mar–Oct LD B78–152 M50 Pn176 Pool

Tourcoing† **59** (Nord) 102,550 (☎20)
Map **3** B1
☆☆☆**Novotel Neuville-en-Ferrain** ☎940770
tx110656 rm118 ⇜118 Lift B120–140 Pool
☆☆**Ibis** ㏒ ☎768458 tx120695 rm104 ⇜104
Lift B66–87 Màlc
☎⊘Ponthieux 75 r Roubaix ☎746705 M/c Frd

Tournus 71 (Saône-et-Loire) 7,850 (☎85)
Map **10** C1

★★★**Sauvage** pl Champ-de-Mars ☎511445 tx800726 rm30 ⇌25 G Lift 15 Dec–10 Nov LD B66–102 M28 & àlc

★★**Gare** 2 av Gambetta ☎511056 rm15 ⇌3 🍴6 G 1 Jan–20 Nov 20 Dec–31 Dec

★**Terrasses** LE 18 av du 23 Janvier ☎510774 rm12 (A12) ⇌2 🍴2 (closed Nov) LD B37–74 M23–50 Pn75–90

🚗24 *M Pageaud* rte de Paris (N6) ☎510705 N🛏 Ren G4

Tours† **37** (Indre-et-Loire) 145,450 (☎47) Map **9** A2

★★★**Armor** (n rest) LE 26 bis bd Heurteloup ☎052960 tx750008 rm42 ⇌15 🍴16 G Lift B60–139

★★★**Bordeaux** *3* pl du MI-Leclerc ☎054032 rm54 ⇌20 🍴20 Lift B74–138 M26–38 & àlc Pn124–186 St15%

★★★**Central** (n rest) 21 r Berthelot ☎054644 tx750008(central) rm42 ⇌15 🍴16 G Lift B75–151

★★★*Châteaux de la Loire* (n rest) 12 r Gambetta ☎051005 rm32 ⇌10 🍴6 Lift

★★★*Métropole* 14 pl J-Jaurès ☎054051 tx75508 rm80 ⇌40 🍴16 G Lift

★★★**Royal** (n rest) 65 av Grammont ☎050178 tx750008 rm32 ⇌32 G Lift B112–133

★★★**Univers** 5 bd Heurteloup ☎053712 rm76 ⇌60 🍴15 G Lift B57–141 M40

★★**Cygne** (n rest) 6 r du Cygne (off r Colbert) ☎052325 rm20 ⇌3 🍴10 G B32–84

★*Colbert* (n rest) 78 r Colbert ☎052763 rm15 ⇌6 🍴6

★*Foch* (n rest) 20 r MI-Foch (off r Nationale) ☎057059 rm14 ⇌3 🍴5

🛏🚗*Gaillard* 7 r G-Sand ☎206980 N🛏 G10

🛏🚗*Gauron* 33 r Febvotte ☎284345 N🛏 BL/Jag/Rov/Tri

🚗*Grammont* 204 av de Grammont ☎052808 N🛏 G30

🛏🚗*Pont* Menneton ☎202533 N🛏 Frd

🛏🚗*Tourangelle* 20 r d'Entraigues ☎203057 N🛏 Chy G10

Tranche (La) 85 (Vendée) 2,150 (☎30) Map **15** A/B4

★*Ker Paulette* av Plage rm29 (A) ⇌1 🍴6 G Etr & 1 Jun–25 Sep

Trébeurden 22 (Côtes-du-Nord) 2,909 (☎96) Map **7** B3

★★**Family** 22 r des Plages ☎355031 rm27 ⇌15 🍴15 G B40–89 M39–50 Pn75–110 Sea

Tréboul 29 (Finistère) 6,020 (☎98) Map **7** A3

★★**Bains** ☎920221 rm30 (A4) 🍴2 G 1 Jun–20 Sep LD B38–78 M30 Sea

Trégastel-Plage 22 (Côtes-du-Nord) 2,050 (☎96) Map **7** B3

★*Beau Séjour* LE ☎388802 rm25 ⇌10 15 Mar–15 Oct LD B42–134 M30–60 Pn85–140 Sea

★*Belle Vue* LE ☎388818 rm34 ⇌2 🍴28 7 May–30 Sep Sea

★*Mer & Plage* ☎388803 rm40 ⇌20 🍴4 Apr–Sep LD B69–168 M26–95 Pn80–130 Sea

Trelissac See **Perigueux**

Tréport (Le) 76 (Seine-Maritime) 6,900 (☎35) Map **3** A1

🛏🚗24 *Moderne* 8 quai Sadi-Carnot ☎861390 Ren

Trimouille (La) 86 (Vienne) 1,300 (☎49) Map **16** C4

★*Paix* pl Eglise et de la Mairie ☎916050 rm21 ⇌6 🍴11 G 20 Feb–20 Jan B46–96 M19–68 Pn100–110

Trinité-sur-Mer (La) 56 (Morbihan) 1,450 (☎97) Map **7** B2

★★**Le Rouzic** 17 cours des quais ☎527206 rm29 ⇌13 🍴14 Lift 15 Dec–15 Nov B82–109 M40–66 Pn147 Sea

★*Ostrea* ☎527323 rm12 1 Apr–20 Sep Sea

Trois-Épis (Les) 68 (Haut-Rhin) (☎89) Map **11** B2

★★★★**Grand** ☎498065 tx880229 rm48 ⇌44 🍴4 Lift B133–306 Màlc Pn205–275 Pool

★★★*Marchal* LE ☎498161 rm45 ⇌31 🍴5 G Lift 15 Jan–15 Dec

Trouville 14 (Calvados) 6,700 (☎31) Map **8** D4

★★★★**Bellvue** 1 pl MI-Foch ☎881485 rm100 ⇌90 🍴2 G Lift 15 Mar–15 Nov B84–248 Màlc Pn155–230 St15%

★★★**Flaubert** r G-Flaubert ☎883723 rm45 ⇌17 🍴7 Lift 15 Feb–15 Nov LD Beach Sea

★★★**Résidence** (n rest) r de la Plage ☎880466 rm50 ⇌40 🍴7 G Lift 1 Apr–1 Oct B74–173 St15% Sea

★*Dunes* 3 r de la Plage ☎881649 rm23 (A) ⇌16 🍴3

🛏🚗*Chantecler* 113 av du GI-de-Gaulle N🛏 ☎880040 BL G

Troyes† 10 (Aube) 75,550 (☎25) Map **10** C3

★★★**Grand** av MI-Joffre (opp Station) ☎439284 rm102 ⇌55 🍴25 Lift B66–125 Màlc St15%

★★★**Royal** 22 bd Carnot ☎436801 rm41 ⇌20 🍴10 Lift LD B64–104 M30 Pn120–160

★★**France** 18 quai Dampierre ☎433830 rm61 ⇌26 🍴18 Lift B39–113 M25–35 St15%

★★**Paris** (n rest) 56 r Salengro ☎433715 tx Chamco840809 rm30 ⇌1 🍴10 G 10 Jan–22 Dec B41–87

🛏🚗24 **Contant** 15 bd Danton ☎434819 Ren

🛏🚗*M Roy* 6 r P-Gillon ☎438293 N🛏 Hon/Lnc

At **Breviandes** (4km)

★★*Bonne Fermière* ☎162543 rm15 🍴14 G

At **Pont-Ste-Marie** (3km E)

🛏🚗*14 Juillet* r R-Salengro ☎811245 N🛏 Frd

At **St-Julien-les-Villas** (2km SE)

🛏🚗*Pourille* 43 bd de Dijon ☎435684 N🛏

🛏🚗*Selection-Auto* 43 bd de Dijon ☎435684 N🛏 G5

Troyes Airport

At **Barberey** (6km NW on N19)

☆☆☆ **Novotel Troyes Aéroport** rte de Paris ☎721214 tx840759 rm60 ⇌60 Lift B120–140 Pool

Tulle† 19 (Corrèze) 21,650 (☎55) Map **16** C3

★★**Toque Blanche** 29 r J-Jaurès & pl Brigouleix ☎267541 rm11 ⇌11 B47–114 M22 Pn90–95

Uriage-les-Bains 38 (Isère) (☎76) Map **27** B3

★★**Alpes** Grand allee ☎891028 rm42 ⇌10 G 1 May–30 Sep B40–116 M32–40 Pn85–110

★★**Manoir** LE ☎891088 rm19 ⇌2 🍴4 Dec–Oct B43–89 M32

Ury See **Fontainebleau**

Uzerche 19 (Corrèze) 3,250 (☎55) Map **16** C3

★★**Ambroise** ☎731008 rm20 ⇌5 🍴15 G · 16 Dec–14 Nov B43.50–62.50 M16–22

★★**Teyssier** r Pont-Turgot ☎731005 rm25 (A8) ⇌10 G

🛏🚗*Pomme* pl A-Bover ☎731228 G30

Uzès 30 (Gard) 7,400 (☎66) Map **27** A2

★*Hostellerie Provençale* 3 r Grande Bourgade ☎221106 rm10 ⇌1 🍴3 Jan–Oct B32–52 M17–37

Vaison-la-Romaine 84 (Vaucluse) 5,250 (☎90) Map **27** B2

France

★★**Beffroi** (n rest) r de l'Eveche ☎9360471
rm20 (A10) ⇌4 ▥5 Etr–Oct B37–108

Val-André (Le) 22 (Côtes-du-Nord) (☎96)
Map **7** B3

★★**Grand du Val André** 80 r Al-Charner
☎722056 rm45 ⇌6 ▥11 G Apr–Sept LD
B34–96 M35–60 Pn75–125 Beach Sea

★**Bains** pl Gl-de-Gaulle ☎722011 rm26 ⇌3
▥4 Etr–20 Sep LD B33–77 M27–80
Pn70–85 Sea

Valdahon 25 (Doubs), 3,600 (☎81)
Map **11** A1

★★**Franche Comte** ☎592318 rm20 ⇌20 G
15 Jan–15 Dec B83–96(double) M25
Pn110–130

Val-d'Isère 73 (Savoie), 1,350 (☎79)
Map **28** C4

★★★**Aiglon** ☎060405 rm27 ⇌18 ▥8 G
25 Nov–10 May 1 Jul–31 Aug

★★★**Bellier** ☎060377 rm20 ⇌14 ▥4
5 May–5 Dec

★★★**Christiania** ☎060825 txCo/32077 Offitour
Valdi rm44 ⇌38 ▥4 Lift 1 Dec–30 Apr LD
B165–276 M50 St15%

★★**Savoie** ☎060371 tx32077 rm35 ⇌19
▥12 Lift 1 Dec–1 May Pool

★**Edelweiss** ☎060379 rm21 ⇌4 ▥3
20 Dec–1 May

Valencay 36 (Indre) 3,200 (☎54)
Map **9** A3

★★★**Espagne** 8 r du Château ☎400002
rm19 ⇌15 ▥12 15 Dec–20 Dec

★**Lion d'Or** ⓁⒺ pl Marché ☎000087 rm15
⇌15 G B40–78 M23–48 Pn75–85

Valence-d'Agen 82 (Tarn et Garonne)
4,450 (☎63) Map **16** C2

★★**Tout-Va-Bien** ⓁⒺ 35 r de la République
☎395483 rm29 ⇌20 ▥7 G B40–66 M25–65
Pn75–95

Valence-sur-Rhône†26 (Drôme) 70,350
(☎75) Map **27** B3

☆☆☆**Novotel Valence Sud** av de Provence
(N7) ☎422015 tx345823 rm107 ⇌107 Lift
B120–140 Pool

★★**Pic** 285 av V-Hugo ☎431532 rm10 ⇌10
1 Sep–31 Jul (closed Wed) G

★**Lyon** (n rest) 23 av P-Sémard ☎440063
rm47 ⇌6 ▥5 G B28–64

⬥⭒♢**Molière** 164 av V-Hugo ☎441137 N♨ M/c
BL/Jag/Por/Rov/Tri

Valenciennes†59 (Nord) 43,250 (☎20)
Map **3** B1

☆☆☆**Motellerie** ☎461626 tx11864F rm67
⇌30 ▥37 Pool

☆☆☆ **Novotel Valenciennes-Ouest** ☎442080
tx120970 rm80 ⇌80 Lift B120–140 Pool

★★**Modern** (n rest) r de Lille ☎462070
rm30 ⇌10 ▥4 G B38–91

⬥⭒♢**Marceau** 27 pl de l'Esplanade ☎466072
N♨ Frd

Valloire 73 (Savoie) 950 (☎79) Map **28** C3

★★**Grand Valloire & Galibier** ⓁⒺ ☎001 rm43
⇌26 ▥10 G Lift 15 Jun–15 Sep B66–152
M30–60 Pn85–155

Valognes 50 (Manche) 6,100 (☎33)
Map **8** C4

★**Louvre** 28 r Religieuses ☎400007 rm19 ⇌4
▥2 G 1 Jan–10 Dec B33–77 M17–26 Pn60–68

Val-Suzon 21 (Côte-d'Or) 150 (☎80)
Map **10** C2

★★★**Val-Suzon** ☎316015 rm19 (A12) ⇌5
▥14 G 15 Feb–4 Jan B40–144 M45–75

Vannes†56 (Morbihan) 43,550 (☎97)
Map **7** B2

★★★**Marebandière** 4 r A-Briand ☎663429
rm40 ⇌15 ▥23 Lift 4 Jan–15 Dec LD B89–95
(double) M26 Pn89–92

★★**Richemont** 28 av Fravel-&-Lincy
☎661295 rm45 ⇌17 G

★**Ste-Anne** 8 pl Libération ☎632736 rm19
⇌15 ▥7 (closed Oct 15–30) LD B38–86
M30–60

★**Marée Bleue** 8 pl B-Hakeim ☎662429
rm16 ▥4 4 Jan–15 Dec LD B44–60(double)
M26–85 Pn66–73

★**Relais Nantais** (n rest) 38 r A-Briand
☎661585 rm14 ⇌1 ▥1

Autorep 41 r du Vincin ☎662617 (closed
weekends) Frd

⬥⭒♢**Lambert & Dupré** 95 av E-Herriot
☎542070 N♨ Ren

⬥⭢24 **Maheo** 48 av V-Hugo ☎661156 Opl

⭒♢**Ouest** 5 av du Prés-Roosevelt ☎662720
N♨ G10

Varces 38 (Isère) (☎76) Map **27** B3

★**Escale** ☎978019 rm7 (A2) ⇌7 G 15 Feb–
15 Jan LD B120–180(double) M62–178

Varengeville-sur-Mer 76 (Seine-Maritime)
1,000 (☎35) Map **9** A4

★★**Terrasse** ⓁⒺ ☎851254 rm28 ⇌8 G
15 Mar–30 Sep ♨ Sea

Varetz See **Brive-la-Gaillard**

Vars (Col de) 05 (Hautes-Alpes) 800
(☎92) Map **28** C3
At **Ste-Marie** (8km N on N202)

★★★**Ste-Marie** ☎455002 rm18 ⇌18 ▥18
15 Dec–15 Apr 15 Jul–15 Sep B99–178 M46
Pn130–195

Vatan 36 (Indre) 2,300 (☎54) Map **9** B2

★★**France** 16 pl de la République ☎497411
rm12 ⇌2 ▥2 G Mar–Jan

Vence 06 (Alpes-Maritimes), 11,700 (☎93)
Map **28** C2

★★★★**Domaine St-Martin** rte de Coursegoules
☎580202 tx470282 rm28 (A8) ⇌28 G 1 Feb–
1 Dec LD B320–490 M120 St15.5% ♨ Pool
Sea

★★**Diana** (n rest) av Poilus ☎582856 rm25
⇌25 G Lift B85–115

★★**Régina** av Alliés ☎580334 rm25 ⇌6
▥7 10 Dec–15 Oct

★★**Seigneurs** pl Frêne ☎580424 rm10 ▥10
15 Nov–15 Oct

★**Fleurs** 8 rte de Grasse ☎580307 rm7 ⇌3 ▥3
LD Pn120 St10%

Vendôme†41 (Loir-et-Cher) 18,550 (☎39)
Map **9** A2

★★**Grand St-Georges** 14 r Poterie ☎772542
rm35 ⇌30 Lift B50–125 M28

★**Vendôme** ⓁⒺ 15 fbg Chartrain ☎770288 rm20
⇌7 ▥8 G Lift B47–122 M22–45

⬥⭢24 **Motoculture** 45 rte de Paris
☎770943 N♨770853 Opl/Vau G100

⬥⭒♢**R Garcia** 68 fbg Chartrain ☎770938 N♨
Frd

Venthon See **Albertville**

Verdun†55 (Meuse) 26,950 (☎28)
Map **10** D3

★★★**Bellevue** rond-point-de-Lattre-de-
Tassigny ☎860424 tx86464 rm82 ⇌60 G
Lift 1 Mar–31 Jan

★★**Bourguignonne** rte Ciel ☎495145 rm16
(A6) ⇌10 ▥1 1 Feb–Dec

Veretz 37 (Indre-et-Loire), 1,350 (☎47)
Map **9** A2

★**St-Honoré** ☎553006 rm10 ⇌3 ▥1
1 Mar–15 Nov LD B48–83(double) M26–48
Pn73–90

Vernet (Le) 31 (Haute-Garonne), 1,300
(☎61) Map **16** C1

★**Platanes** N20 ☎085013 rm23 ⇄4 ⋔4
16 Oct–14 Sep LD B43–78 M20–36

Vernet-les-Bains 66 (Pyrénées-Orientales)
1,350 (☎68) Map **22** D4
★★*Alexandra* rm35 ⇄23 G

Verneuil-sur-Avre 27 (Eure) 6,900 (☎32)
Map **9** A3
★★*Clos* 4 r Ferté-Vidame ☎322181 rm10 (A)
⇄4 ⋔8 15 Jan–15 Dec

Verniaz (La) See **Evian-les-Bains**

Versailles† 78 (Yvelines) 97,150 (☎1)
Map **9** B3
★★★★**Trianon Palace** 1 bd de la Reine
☎9503412 tx698863 rm130 ⇄100 ⋔30 Lift
B153–246 M62 St15%
★★**Clagny** (n rest) 5 Impasse Clagny
☎9501809 rm19 ⋔9 G Lift B71–156
★★**St-Louis** (n rest) 28 r St-Louis ☎9502355
rm25 ⇄10 ⋔6 B54–96(double)
★**Cheval Rouge** 18 r A-Chernier (off r de la
Paroise) ☎9500303 rm41 ⇄11 ⋔11 10 Jan–
20 Dec LD B47–124 M41.50
⌂&◎**M P Augereau** 67 av St Cloud ☎9501120
N✦ AR
⌂&◎**Deschamps** 5 r St-Simon ☎9500397 N✦
MB/Toy

Vervins 02 (Aisne) 3,300 (☎23) Map **10** C4
★★**Tour du Roy** ☎980011 rm13 ⇄10 ⋔3
15 Feb–15 Jan B60–140 M50–100 Pn150

Vesoul 70 (Haute-Saône) 20,100 (☎84)
Map **11** A2
★★**Nord** 7 r Aigle Noir ☎750256 rm36
⇄25 ⋔7 G Lift B55–107 M21–55
★**Relais N19** rte de Paris ☎753656 rm26
⇄13 ⋔5 G 20 Jan–22 Dec LD B75–148
M28–70
⌂&◎*Central* 1 r L-Jobad ☎751229 (closed
weekends) Frd
⌂&◎*Euro-Garage-Paillotel* 69 av A-Briand
☎752133 N☎755507 BL G8
⌂&◎*Larue* 90 bd des Alliés ☎753403 N✦ Peu
G20
⌂&◎**Motte** 12 r Fleurier ☎753115 N✦ Fia G10

Veyrier-du-Lac 74 (Haute-Savoie) 1,720
(☎50) Map **28** C4
★★*Acacias* ☎458160 rm23 ⇄7 1 Mar–31 Oct
★★*La Chaumière* ☎448006 rm35 ⇄15 ⋔2 G
★**Col-Vert** Ⓔ ☎448023 rm12 ⇄12 15 Feb–
15 Nov B79–93(double) M37 &àlc Pn106–117
(double) Lake

Vichy† 03 (Allier) 32,300 (☎70) Map **27** A4
★★★★**Pavillon Sévigné** 10 pl Sévigné (off av
A-Briand) ☎985542 tx39064 rm55 ⇄35 ⋔9
Lift 1 May–30 Sep
★★★**Albert-1er** (n rest) av P-Doumer
☎987293 rm35 ⇄25 ⋔7 Lift B71–156
★★★**Ambassadeurs** 1 r du Parc ☎982526
tx Covieta 990246 rm94 ⇄64 ⋔3 Lift
May–25 Sep B62–278 M46 ⌘ Pool Golf
★★★*Russie & Mediterranée* 12 av A-Briand
☎987685 rm80 ⇄20 ⋔13 G Lift 15 May–30 Sep
★★*Amirauté* 27 r Prés-Wilson ☎986422
rm82 ⇄28 ⋔5 Lift 2 May–30 Sep
⌂&◎*Excelsior* 12 av Victoria ☎985556
N☎988109 Chy G200
⌂&◎**Nimes** 102 av Poincaré ☎983432 N✦ Ren
⌂&◎**Perfect** 2 r de Lisbonne ☎983243 N✦
Lnc/MB
⌂&◎**St-Blaise** 11 r d'Allier ☎986371 N✦
BL/Jag/Rov/Tri G50

Vic-sur-Aisne 02 (Aisne) 1,600 (☎23)
Map **9** B4
★**Lion d'Or** pl Gl-de-Gaulle ☎555020 rm17
⋔6 Jan–July Sep–Dec LD B35–90 M28–70

Vic-sur-Cère 15 (Cantal) 2,050 (☎71)
Map **16** D2

At **Col de Curebourse** (6km SE on D54)
★**Auberge des Monts** ☎475171 (A4) rm27
⇄20 Etr–1 Oct LD B61–78 M22–30&àlc
Pn64–71

Vienne† 38 (Isère) 28,800 (☎74) Map **27** B4
☆☆**KM500** (8km S on N7) ☎598144
tx380343 rm44 ⇄10 G B108–140(double)
M29–55 Pool
★★**Nord** 9 pl Miremont ☎850196 rm43 ⇄10
⋔14 G Lift 16 Jun–15 Sep
⌂&◎*Gévaudan & Dumond* 7 pl C-Jouffroy
☎850607 G6

At **Pont-Evêque** (3km E on N502)
★*Midi* pl Eglise ☎852011 rm30 (A) ⇄9 ⋔10

Vierzon† 18 (Cher) 36,550 (☎36) Map **9** B2
★**Boulevard** 3 r Dr P-Roux ☎753982 rm23
⇄1 ⋔9 G 1 Mar–31 Jan
★★**Continental** (n rest) 104 av E-Vaillant
☎753522 rm36 ⇄15 ⋔18 G Lift
⌂&◎**Perchaud** 58 av J-Jaurès ☎753757 N✦ Frd

Villefranche-sur-Mer 06 (Alpes-Maritimes)
7,300 (☎93) Map **28** C2
★★★★**Versailles** r Ml-Foch ☎808956 rm49
⇄43 ⋔6 Lift 20 Dec–20 Oct B110–170
M56&àlc Pn173–185 Pool Sea
★★★**Provençal** r Ml-Joffre ☎807142 rm45
⇄30 ⋔13 Lift Pn80–105 Sea
★★★**Welcome** quai Courbet ☎808881 rm35
⇄30 ⋔1 G Lift 20 Dec–1 Nov LD B68–176
M45 Pn100–154 Sea
★**Coq-Hardi** bd Corne d'Or ☎807106 rm11
(A11) ⇄6 1 Dec–31 Oct B35–80 M28
Pn68–75 Sea

Villefranche-sur-Saône† 69 (Rhône)
30,700 (☎74) Map **27** B4
★★★**Plaisance** 96 av Liberation ☎653352
rm61 (A5) ⇄29 ⋔33 G Lift 30 Dec–23 Dec
B72–108
★**Ecu de France** (n rest) 35 r d'Anse
☎683448 rm26 B36–99
⌂&◎*Caladoise* 87 r P-Berthier ☎1863 N✦
⌂◎*Europe* 1000 r Ampère ☎655059 N✦
Aud/VW
⌂&◎*Gambetta* 28 bd Gambetta ☎650406 N✦
Frd G10

Villeneuve-de-Marsan 40 (Landes)
2,150 (☎57) Map **15** B2
★**Europe** pl Foirail ☎582008 rm26 ⇄/⋔26
LD B47–94 M22–70 Pn70–100 Pool

Villeneuve de Rivière See **St-Gaudens**

Villeneuve-lès-Avignon 30 (Gard) 9,000
(☎90) Map **27** B2
★★★**Prieuré** pl Chapitre ☎251820 tx431042
rm30 (A17) ⇄30 Lift 1 Mar–30 Oct B145–330
Màlc ⌘ Pool
★★**Magnaneraie** 37 r Camp de Bataille
☎251111 tx201/431033 rm21 ⇄17 ⋔4 G
1 Mar–15 Jan B66–179 M35–70 Pn165–178
⌘ Pool

Villeneuve Loubet See **Cagnes-sur-Mer**

Villeneuve-sur-Lot 47 (Lot-et-Garonne)
23,050 (☎58) Map **16** C2
★★★**Parc** Ⓔ 13 bd de la Marine ☎700168
rm42 ⇄15 ⋔27 G Lift B79–140 Pn108–158
★**Prune d'Or** Ⓔ pl Gare ☎700118 rm18
⇄2 ⋔4 G Mar–Jan B37–94 M26–60
Pn85–95
⌂➤◎24 **Lompech** 29 bd Voltaire ☎702461
BMW/Opl

Villeneuve-sur-Yonne 89 (Yonne) 4,850
(☎86) Map **10** C2
★**Boursine** ☎660185 rm8 G Nov–Sep
★**Dauphin** r Carnot ☎871855 rm9 ⇄2 G LD
B29–67 M30–44&àlc Peu

Villers-les-Pots See **Auxonne**

Villers-Semeuse See **Charleville-Mézières**

France

Villerville 14 (Calvados) 750 (☎31)
Map **9** A4
★*Bellevue* Ⓔ r Clemenceau ☎872022 rm20
⇆9 ▥3 G 1 Feb–17 Feb

Vincennes See **Paris**

Vire 14 (Calvados) 14,400 (☎31) Map **8** C3
★★*Cheval Blanc* Ⓔ 2 pl du 6 Juin 1944
☎680021 tx170428 rm22 ⇆11 ▥1
29 Jan–2 Jan B56–91 M33 Pn100–165

Vironvay See **Louviers**

Vitrac 24 (Dordogne) 650 (☎53) Map **16** C2
★*Plaisance* Ⓔ au Port ☎293304 rm20 ⇆1 ▥4
G 1 Feb–30 Nov

Vitré 35 (Ille-et-Vilaine) 12,900 (☎99)
Map **8** C3
★*Chêne Vert* 2 pl de la Gare ☎750058 rm22
⇆4 ▥4 G 1 Jan–30 Sep 31 Oct–31 Dec B32–93
M20–40&àlc

Vitrolles 13 (Bouches-du-Rhône) Map **27** B2
See also **Marseille Airport**
🛢☸*Kennings* 15 4ème av ☎890699 N☸
BL/Jag/Rov/Tri

Vitry-le-Francois 51 (Marne) 20,100
(☎26) Map **10** C3
★★*Poste* pl R-Collard ☎740265 rm30 ⇆12
▥16 Lift
★*Bon Séjour* rte de St-Dizier ☎740236 rm25
(A12) ⇆2 G 1 Mar–31 Jan LD B33–68
M18–30 Pn60
★*Cloche* 34 r A-Briand ☎740384 rm24 (A10)
⇆6 ▥4 G B41–87 M22–35
★*L'Etoile* 4 fbg Châlons ☎741256 rm22 (A3)
⇆1 ▥7 G Bfr57 M17–42 Pn56
🛢☸24 *François 1er* 3 r du Vieux Port
☎740438 N☸741794 N☸ Frd
🛢☸24 *Perthois* 22 r Domine de Verzet
☎741851 N☸741794 N☸ Ren

Vittel 88 (Vosges) 6,800 (☎29) Map **11** A2
🛢☸*Letterme* av de Châtillon ☎080709 Ren
G50

Vizille 38 (Isère) 7,300 (☎76) Map **27** B3
★*Parc* Ⓔ 5 av A-Briand ☎680301 rm29 ⇆6
▥4 LD B45–75 M23–38 Pn70–90

Vogelgrun See **Neuf-Brisach**

Voreppe See **Grenoble**

Vouvray 37 (Indre-et-Loire) 2,750 (☎47)
Map **9** A2
★*Grand-Vatel* av Brûlé ☎561032 rm12 (A4)
⇆2 30 Nov–5 Jan 20 Jan–15 Nov
🛢☸*Sports* av Brûlé ☎561044 G4

Vouziers 08 (Ardennes) 5,500 (☎24)
Map **10** C4
★★*Rennes* 12 r Chanzy ☎308403 rm23 ⇆6
▥2 G

Vrine (La) 25 (Doubs) (☎81) Map **11** A1
★*Hostellerie de la Vrine* Ⓔ ☎382004 rm36
⇆36 G B38–96 M25–40 Pn80

Wimereux 62 (Pas-de-Calais) 6,750 (☎21)
Map **3** A1
★★*Atlantic* Digue de Mer ☎324101 rm10 ⇆6
▥4 Lift LD B59–122 M50–80 St15% Beach Sea
★*Centre* 78 r Carnot ☎324108 rm18 ⇆1 G
25 Jan–15 Dec B34–73 M23 Pn68

Wissant 62 (Pas-de-Calais) 5,241 Map **3** A1
★*Normandy* ☎359011 rm33 ⇆4 ▥7
1 Mar–1 Nov LD B48–159 Pn66–80 Sea

Yenne 73 (Savoie) 2,200 Map **27** B4
★*Logis Savoyard* pl C-Dullin ☎367038 rm13
(A4) 15 Sep–15 Nov B28–30 M20 Pn46

Yvetot 76 (Seine-Maritime) 10,750 (☎35)
Map **9** A4
🛢☸*Roussel Automobiles* N13 bis ☎950088
Ren

Yvoire 74 (Haute-Savoie) 350 (☎50)
Map **11** A1
★*Flots Bleus* Ⓔ r du Port ☎8 rm20
15 May–15 Sep

Monaco/hotels and garages

Monte-Carlo 24,650 (☎93) Map **28** C2
★★★★*Hermitage* Sq Beaumarchais ☎306731
tx47432 rm215 ⇆215 Lift ⚓ Golf Pool Beach
★★★★*Métropole* av Grande-Bretagne
☎505741 tx469936 rm150 ⇆130 Lift
B83–316 M70&àlc Pn180–400 St15% Pool Sea
★★★*Alexandra* (n rest) 35 bd Princesse-
Charlotte ☎506313 rm55 ⇆37 ▥8 Lift
B59.50–151 Sea
★★★*Helder* 2 av de la Madone ☎306307
rm42 ⇆22 ▥10 Lift
★★*Europe* 6 av Citronniers ☎308365
tx47668 rm50 ⇆20 ▥20 Sea

★★*Reserve & Suisse* 7 av Princesse-Grace
☎308244 rm40 ⇆9 ▥23 Lift Sea
🛢☸*British Motors* 4 Impasse des Carrières
☎302485 N☸ BL/RR
☸*Frontière* 1 bd Charles-III ☎304905 N☸
MB
🛢☸*Monaco Motors* 11 r Princesse-Florestine
☎302722 N☸ Hon/Rov G10
🛢☸*Riviera* 6 r Genets ☎306326 G400
☸*Vulca Pneus* 9 bd Charles-III ☎304312 N☸
M/c
At **Monte-Carlo Beach**
★★★★*Old Beach* ☎350471 tx479432 rm46
(A6) ⇆46 Lift May–Sep B188–316 Màlc St15%
⚓ Pool Beach Golf Sea

GERMANY

Population 62,101,400 **Area (Federal Republic)** 95,980 sq miles
Maps 4, 5, 11, 12 & 13

How to get there If you use one of the short-crossing Channel ferries and travel via Belgium, West Germany is just within a day's drive. The distance from Calais to Cologne is just under 260 miles.

By driving through northern France and entering Germany near Strasbourg, the journey usually takes two days. This entry point is also used if travelling by the longer Channel crossings: Cherbourg, Dieppe, or Le Havre to southern Germany. The distance from Le Havre to Strasbourg is just over 400 miles, a journey which will take at least one or two days. The longer-crossing car ferries operating across the North Sea to Holland can be an advantage if visiting northern Germany. Alternatively, it is possible to use the ferries operating between Harwich and Bremerhaven or Hamburg.

Travel information

AA agents
Port agent (PA)

2800 Bremen 1 (PA) The General Steam Navigation Co MBH, Am Wall 102, POB 10.55.09 ☎310011; ta Glyconic-Bremen; tx 0244585.

2850 Bremerhaven (PA) The General Steam Navigation Co MBH, Containerterminal, Bremerhaven (Gatehouse 1), POB 2003 ☎0471-46954; ta Glyconic-Bremerhaven.

2000 Hamburg 11 (PA) The General Steam Navigation Co MBH Katharinenfleet 5 ☎362721; ta Glyconic-Hamburg; tx 0212500.

Accidents In large towns dial 110 for **fire, police** and **ambulance**. For other areas, see the telephone directory.

You are generally required to call the police when individuals have been injured or considerable damage has been caused. Not to give aid to anyone injured will render you liable to a fine. Expert opinion should be sought to ascertain liability, when damage exceeds £150. This advice, however, will have to be paid for.

Accommodation There is a good selection of hotels, most of which are listed in the Hotel Guide. This is distributed free by the Tourist Office in London, which can also provide details of accommodation in castles and stately homes. Regional and local tourist organisations also have details of inns and boarding houses.

Germany

For a nominal charge, tourist information offices will usually assist in finding hotel accommodation (see page 163). Enquiries by post should be accompanied by an international reply coupon (obtainable from the post office).

There is also a reservations service operated by the ADZ (Allgemeine Deutsche Zimmerreservierung). This organisation will make instantly confirmed bookings at a number of hotels in major cities. Full information about this service, including details of the hotels concerned, may be obtained from ADZ, Untermainanlage 6, 6000 Frankfurt/Main 1 ☎(0611) 234444; tx 04-16666. Prices indicated normally include a service charge (10–15%) and VAT (11%). Reduced prices apply to children under ten years of age sharing a room with their parents.

Reservations are not normally held after 18.00hrs.

Berlin

Documents required for travel through the German Democratic Republic to West Berlin.

Be sure you have a valid, standard passport (children over 16 years of age must have a separate passport), transit visa, national driving licence and registration book. The Green Card is now accepted, but make sure that it covers you for the GDR before you depart from the United Kingdom. Third party insurance can be arranged at the border crossings. Visas for journeys to West Berlin can be obtained at the frontier crossings at a cost of DM10.

Note Application for visas can be made to the Consular Section of the Embassy of the German Democratic Republic, 34 Belgrave Square, London SW1X 8QB ☎01-235 4465. Tourists travelling directly between West Germany and West Berlin are exempt from paying road tax, but must pay a visa charge.

Customs crossings

The main frontier Customs houses officially open for transit to West Berlin are listed below. The names printed in italics are within the GDR, the others outside it.

Frankfurt	*Wartha*; Herleshausen
Hamburg	*Horst*; Lauenburg
Hannover	*Marienborn*; Helmstedt
Munich	*Hirschberg* Saalebrücke; Rudolphstein

Hours Crossings are open day and night.

West Berlin Entry is possible at Drewitz/Dreilinden on the routes from Frankfurt, Hannover and Munich, and at Staaken on the route from Hamburg.

East Berlin Entry for day visits from West Berlin is at Checkpoint Charlie on Friedrichstrasse/Aimmerstrasse. There are no restrictions for tourists of non-German nationality who wish to make a day trip from West to East Berlin, but make sure this is mentioned on the insurance policy.

BAOR

Service personnel should consult their Standing Orders or Commanding Officer before taking a car to Germany or using it there. Although enjoying some privilege they will be regarded to some extent as residents in the country and tourist regulations (as outlined in this section) may not apply. For example, a tourist can use a warning triangle not strictly to the German regulations, but a service man will break local regulations unless his conforms.

Breakdowns

If your car breaks down, try to move it to the verge of the road so that it does not obstruct traffic flow. A warning triangle must be placed to the rear of the vehicle and flashing warning lights, if fitted to the vehicle, must be used.

The ADAC operates a breakdown service, similar to that run by the AA, called the *Strassenwacht*. By courtesy of the ADAC, patrols will assist AA members upon production of their *5-Star Travel Booklet*. Patrol cars operate on motorways, on the more important roads and in urban areas. On motorways, patrols are notified by the Motorway Authorities whom you can contact by using the emergency telephones. The direction of the nearest telephone is indicated by the point of the black triangle on posts alongside the motorways. If you break down on a road not equipped with emergency telephones or not covered by the *Strassenwacht* or if you need breakdown assistance in big cities, please call the nearest ADAC office, the telephone number of which is given on the cover of the official telephone directory. If there is nobody at the office, the automatic answering service will advise you of the nearest assistance point. Operating times on the main tourist routes are at least from 08.00 to 19.00hrs in summer and from 08.00 to 18.00hrs in winter, whereas in certain densely-populated urban areas there is a 24-hr service.

Germany

The following ADAC area centres can be called day and night:

Berlin	(030) 868686
Bremen	(0421) 446262
Dortmund	(0231) 523052
Düsseldorf	(0211) 434949
Frankfurt	(0611) 772222
Hamburg	(040) 28999
Hannover	(0511) 8500222
München	(089) 767676
Nurnberg	(0911) 551414
Stuttgart	(0711) 233333

In addition, the Deutscher Touring Automobile Club (DTC), with which the AA is allied, has recently introduced a patrol service which provides a free daytime 30-minute repair service. The Automobile Club of Germany (AvD) and the Auto Club Europa (ACE) also operate a patrol service. The AA is not associated with these clubs and details are not available.

British Consulates   108 Berlin GDR, 32–34 Unter den Linden ☎220-2431
1 Berlin 12, Uhlandstrasse 7–8 ☎3095293 3095146
53 Bonn, Friedrich-Ebert-Allee 77 ☎234061
2850 Bremerhaven-F (Ost Seite) Eiswerkestrasse ☎(010-49) 471-7 1084
4 Dusseldorf, Nordsternhaus, 14 Georg-Glockstrasse ☎434281/5, 434481/4
6 Frankfurt (Main) Bockenheimer Landstrasse 51/53 ☎720406/9
2 Hamburg 13, Harvestehurderweg 8A ☎451351/5
3 Hannover, Uhlemeyerstrasse 9–11 ☎237641/5
8 Munich 40, Amalienstrasse 62 ☎394015/9
7 Stuttgart 1, Kriegsbergstrasse 28 ☎293216/8

Crash helmets   It is obligatory for all drivers and passengers of motorcycles which can exceed 40km (25mph) to wear crash helmets.

Currency and banking   The unit of currency is the Deutschmark, which is divided into 100 pfennigs.

Sterling travellers' cheques can be exchanged at all banks, savings banks, exchange offices at frontiers, main railway stations, and airports. There is no limit to the sum of money which may be imported or exported, either in German or in foreign currency.

Banking hours   Most banks are open from Monday to Wednesday and Friday 08.30–12.30hrs and 13.45–15.45hrs, and Thursday 08.30–12.30hrs and 13.45–17.30hrs; closed on Saturdays. Exchange offices of the Deutsche-Verkehrs-Kredit-Bank are located at most railway stations, and road and rail frontier crossing points. Generally they are open from early morning until late at night.

Dimensions   Private cars and trailers are restricted to the following dimensions:
Cars   height   4 metres;
             width   2.5 metres;
Car/trailer combination 18 metres.

Drinking and driving   If there is a definite suspicion that a driver is under the influence of alcohol, the police can compel him to undergo a blood test. However, no one can be made to undergo a breath test (breathalyser). A driver is considered incapable of driving with an alcohol content in the blood of 0.8% but even a lower alcohol content can be considered to make a driver relatively incapable. A convicted driver is always punished by imprisonment, fine or suspension of driving licence if the blood-alcohol level is 1.3% or more.

A visiting motorist who is convicted will not be allowed to drive in Germany, and this will be noted on his driving licence.

Ferries (internal)   **Cuxhaven–Brunsbüttelkoog** *Map 5 A4/B4*
River Elbe   ☎Cuxhaven (04721) 36026: Brunsbüttel (04852) 1270
Service Departures from either port at 08.00, 10.00, 12.00, 14.00, 16.00 and 18.00hrs with additional services at 06.00 and 20.00hrs in July and August.
Duration 75 minutes depending on tide

Germany

Charges

Vehicles	cars	DM11.00–18.00
	caravans	DM4 per metre
	motorcycles	DM5
	motorcycles with sidecar	DM7.50
Passengers		DM9.50

Glückstadt–Wischhafen *Map 5 B4*
☎ Glückstadt (04124) 2430
Service Departures from Glückstadt November to March:
every 20mins 06.15–19.15hrs and at 20.15, 21.45, 23.15,
02.00, 03.30, and 05.00hrs; April to October: every 20mins
05.00–21.00hrs and at 22.20, 23.40, 02.00 and 03.30hrs.
Departures from Wischhafen November to March: every
30mins 06.00–19.30hrs and at 21.00, 22.30, 24.00, 02.45
and 04.15hrs; April to October: every 20mins 05.00–20.40hrs
and at 21.40, 23.00, 00.20, 02.45 and 04.15hrs.
Duration 35 minutes
Charges

Vehicles	cars	DM5–8
	motorcycles	DM1.50
	motorcycles with sidecar	DM3.00
Passengers		DM1.20

iver Weser

Bremerhaven–Nordenham/Blexen *Map 5 A4*
☎ (0471) 21693
Service Departures from Bremerhaven every 30mins
08.30–19.30hrs, also at 20.30, 21.30, 22.30, 23.30, 01.30,
04.30, 05.30, 06.30, and 07.30hrs. Departures from
Nordenham/Blexen every 30mins 08.30–20.00hrs, also at
21.00, 22.00, 23.00, 24.00, 02.00 and 04.00hrs.
Duration 10 minutes
Charges

Vehicles	cars	DM2–6
	motorcycles	DM0.60
	motorcycles with sidecar	DM1–2
Passengers		DM1.10

Reductions are available for return journeys.

hine

Cars are not carried on boats passing through the Rhine Gorge
between Bonn and Mainz. One suggested method for
incorporating a river trip is to take a day-return excursion from
Koblenz.
Rhine cruises: for further information apply to the Köln-
Düsseldorf Steamship Company, 5 Köln 1, Frankenwerft 15.
Cross-river services Unless otherwise stated, departures are
at frequent intervals between the times given below:

1   Bad Godesberg–Nieder Dollendorf *Map 4 D1*
Service All year round 05.45–22.00hrs, except Sunday and
public holidays: 07.45–22.00hrs.
Charges

Vehicles	cars	DM1.50–2.50
	motorcycles	DM1.50
Passengers		DM0.60

2   Königswinter–Mehlem *Map 4 D1*
Service All year round 05.45–22.50hrs, except Sunday and
public holidays: 07.45–22.50hrs.
Charges as for No. 1

3   Bad Honnef–Rolandseck *Map 4 D1*
Service March to November: 06.30–22.00hrs; December to
February: 06.30–21.00hrs.
Charges as for No. 1

4   Linz–Bad Kripp *Map 4 D1*
Service 06.00–24.00hrs all year round
Charges as for No. 1

Germany

5   Boppard–Filsen *Map 5 A1*
Service on demand

Jan–Mar	07.00–20.00hrs	Sun 08.00–20.00hrs
Apr–May	06.30–21.00hrs	Sun 08.00–21.00hrs
Jun–Aug	06.30–22.00hrs	Sun 07.30–22.00hrs
Sep	06.30–21.00hrs	Sun 08.00–21.00hrs
Oct–Dec	07.00–20.00hrs	Sun 08.00–20.00hrs

Charges as for No. 8

6   St Goar–St Goarshausen *Map 11 B4*
Service

Jan–Feb	06.00–20.00hrs
Mar–Apr	06.00–21.00hrs
May–Sep	06.00–22.00hrs
Oct–Nov	06.00–21.00hrs
Dec	06.00–20.00hrs

On Sundays services commence 1 hour later.
Charges as for No. 8

7   Lorch–Nieder Heimbach *Map 11 B4*
Service on demand

Apr–Sep	05.15–20.00hrs	Sun 07.00–20.00hrs
Oct–Mar	05.15–18.00hrs	Sun 07.30–20.00hrs

Charges as for No. 8

8   Rüdesheim–Bingen *Map 11 B4*
Service

Apr–Sep	05.45–22.15hrs
Oct–Mar	05.50–21.45hrs

Charges

Vehicles	cars	DM2–3
	motorcycles	DM1.50
	motorcycles with sidecar	DM2
Passengers	adults	DM0.80
	children (up to ten years)	DM0.30

9   Greffern–Drusenheim (France) *Map 11 B3*
See No. 11

10   Kappel–Rhinau (France) *Map 23 B3*
See No. 11

11   Plittersdorf–Seltz (France) *Map 11 B3*
Services 9–11

Mar–Oct Mon to Fri	06.30–20.00hrs
Sat, Sun and public holidays	06.30–22.00hrs
Nov–Feb Mon to Fri	06.30–19.00hrs
Sat, Sun and public holidays	07.00–19.00hrs

Charges Free

12   Weil–Hüningen (France) *Map 11 B2*
Service departures from Weil every 15mins during greater
part of day 05.45–20.00hrs; half-hourly service early
morning, midday and evening. On Saturdays, Sundays and
public holidays additional services are provided at 20.30hrs,
with a further service at 21.30hrs during the summer months.
Departures from Hüningen every 15mins during greater part
of day 05.55–20.10hrs; half-hourly service early morning,
midday and evening; on public holidays there are additional
services at 20.35 and 21.35hrs.
Charges Free

**Bodensee
(Lake Constance)**

Konstanz–Meersburg *Map 12 C2*
Service 24-hour service every 15mins from early morning to
late evening; hourly at night.
Duration 20 minutes
Charges

Vehicles	cars	DM4–8.50
	motorcycles	DM1.60
	motorcycles with sidecar	DM2
Passengers	adults	DM1.20

Germany

Friedrichshafen–Romanshorn (Switzerland) *Map 12 C2*
Service departures from Friedrichshafen every 2hrs between
07.00–19.00hrs;
departures from Romanshorn every 2hrs between
10.00–20.00hrs.
Duration 50 minutes
Charges

Vehicles	cars	DM12.00–15.20 (according to length, up to 4.10 metres and over)
	motorcycles	DM8.80
	motorcycles with sidecar	DM9.20
	caravans	DM12.00
Passengers		DM2.80 (drivers free)

The vehicle charges above are 'high season rates' applicable
from July to September. At other times the charges are
reduced by DM1.60 for a motorcycle, DM2.40 for a large car.

Island of Sylt

Niebüll–Westerland *Map 1 A1*
No road exists between the mainland and the Island of Sylt,
but there is a railway over the Hindenburg Dam to Westerland.
Cars are loaded by ramp onto the trains. Vehicles must be
alongside 20mins before each departure.
Service There are 8–13 trains daily in each direction.

06.02–19.45   from Niebüll
06.10–22.35   from Westerland
Duration approx half-hourly
Charges

Vehicles	cars up to 1,100kg (1ton 1cwt 73lb)	DM35.00
	cars over 1,100kg	DM40.00
	motorcycles (solo)	DM3.60–7.50 according to weight
	moped	DM3.20
Passengers accompanying cars		free

Holidays and events   Holidays based on religious festivals are not always fixed on
the calendar but any current diary will give actual dates. The
Whit period (a religious holiday) should not be confused with the British Spring Holiday.

Fixed holidays

1 January	New Year's Day
6 January	Epiphany*
1 May	Labour Day
17 June	National Day
15 August	Assumption***
1 November	All Saints' Day** (not Hesse)
25/26 December	Christmas

Moveable holidays

Good Friday
Easter Monday
Ascension Day
Whit Monday
Corpus Christi**
Day of Prayer
(usually mid November)

The holidays marked with asterisks are holidays of the Roman Catholic faith and are only
observed in the Catholic areas as follows:

*   Baden-Württemberg and Bavaria
**   Baden-Württemberg, Saarland, North Rhine-Westphalia, Rhineland, Palatinate
Hesse and Bavaria.
***   Saarland and Catholic areas of Bavaria.

Annual events

January	**Berlin** Agricultural Show
Garmisch–Partenkirchen International winter sports
February	**Frankfurt am Main** International Spring Fair

Germany

March	**Wiesbaden** International Sports Goods Fair
April	**Harz Mountains** Walpurgis Night celebrations **Marburg** May Market with singing in the market place **Saarbrücken** International Saar Fair
May	**Dülmen** Round-up of wild horses in Merfelder Bruch **Friedrichshafen** International Lake Constance Fair **Weingarten** Ancient equestrian procession of the Holy Blood **Wiesbaden** International May Festival
June	**Berlin** International Film Festival **Hamburg** German Derby **Hamelin** Pied Piper plays (June/September) **Heidelberg Castle** Illumination and gala firework display **Kiel** Regatta Week **Koblenz** Operetta on the Rhine (June/September) **Recklinghausen** Ruhr Festival **Würzburg** Mozart Festival
July	**Bayreuth** Richard Wagner Festival **Hamburg** Show Jumping Derby Week **Munich** Opera Festival **Ravensburg** Birch Festival
August	**Baden-Baden** Horseracing (week) **Nürburgring** German Grand Prix **Mosel District** Wine festivals
September	**Berlin** Festival weeks: opera, ballet, theatre (September/October) **Frankfurt am Main** International Motor Show **Munich** Oktoberfest Beer Festival (September/October) **Southern & Western Germany** Wine harvest festivities (September/October)
October	**Mannheim** International Film Week

A more comprehensive list of events can be obtained from the German National Tourist Office (see page 163).

Insurance   This is compulsory; see page 11.

Lights   Driving on sidelights only is prohibited.

When fog, falling snow, or rain substantially affect driving conditions, dipped headlights or foglamps should be used even during daylight. The use of two foglamps together with dipped headlamps in such conditions is required by law. Motorcycles without sidecars may use foglights.

Rear foglights may only be used if, because of fog, the visibility is less than 50 metres.

Medical treatment   The provision of medical benefits in Germany is administered by local sickness insurance offices *(Allgemeine Orskrankenkassen* – known as ADK), normally open Monday to Friday mornings only. Their address can be obtained by local enquiry, at the town hall, post offices etc.

You should first present form E111 (see page 13) to the local sickness insurance office, which will provide you with a sickness document *(Krankenschein)* and a list of names of doctors or dentists who operate within the sickness insurance scheme. The document should then be taken to the doctor or dentist you choose, who will treat you without

Germany

charge. Any medicine prescribed by the doctor will be supplied by the chemist, but you will normally have to pay a small fixed charge for each item. This charge is not recoverable. If you or your dependants need hospital treatment, you should first obtain a certificate to this effect from a doctor, which you should then present with form E111 to the local sickness insurance office. A further certificate *(Kostenübernahmeschein)* entitling you to free hospital treatment (third class) will then be issued to you to take to the hospital authorities.

If you enter hospital urgently, and are thus unable to contact the local sickness insurance office beforehand, you should present form E111 to the hospital authorities, and ask them to obtain from the local sickness insurance office the further certificate *(Kostenübernahmeschein)*.

Motoring clubs

The principal German motoring clubs are the ADAC **(Allgemeiner Deutscher Automobil Club)** and the DTC **(Deutscher Touring Automobil Club)** who have offices at all major frontier crossings and larger towns. They will assist all foreign motorists in difficulties but may charge for their major services. AA members should produce their *5-Star Travel Booklet* when requesting service.

All telephone directories in Germany contain information on how to call the ADAC road patrols and assistance. The ADAC also maintains a 24-hour emergency service at Munich on telephone number (089) 22 22 22.

Parking

Parking is forbidden in the following places: on a main road or one carrying fast-moving traffic; on or near tram lines; within 15 metres (49ft) of a bus or tram stop; 5 metres (16ft) before or after an intersection, road junction or pedestrian crossing; within 10 metres (32ft) of traffic lights and 'give way' signs if the lights or the signs would be obscured by the parked vehicle; at taxi ranks; above manhole covers; on the left-hand side of the road (unless the road is one-way). A vehicle is considered to be parked if the driver has left it so that it cannot be immediately removed, if required. When stopping is prohibited under all circumstances, this is indicated by an international sign. Parking meters and special areas where parking discs are used, are indicated by signs which also show the permitted duration of parking. Disabled drivers may be granted special parking concessions; application should be made to the local traffic authority. Spending the night on the roadside in a vehicle or trailer is permitted for one night, provided that the vehicle is lit and parked in a lay-by. The sign showing an eagle in a green triangle prohibits both stopping and parking.

Passengers

Children under twelve years old are not allowed to travel on the front seats of cars.

Petrol

Popular brands of petrol are available and there are many filling stations. Average prices are about DM0.93 for super grade (97.99 octane) and DM0.88 for normal grade (9/92 octane). Petrol will cost more on motorways.

Pilot service

In Munich there is a pilot service *(Lotsendienst)*; pilots may be hired to guide motorists either to a place in the city or through to an exit road. These pilots are licensed drivers covered by adequate insurance, and will drive the vehicle if requested.

Charges for this service are:

per hour	pilot	DM18
	pilot-driver	DM20
per 90min	guide	DM35

Rates are considerably reduced if the hire extends over several hours. Pilot stations are open daily from 08.00–20.00hrs in summer, and 08.30–19.00hrs in winter. They are located on the following main radial roads leading into Munich:

autobahn from Stuttgart–Obermenzing Station ☎8112412
autobahn from Nürnberg–Freimann Station ☎325417
autobahn from Salzburg–Ramersdorf Station ☎672755
autobahn from Garmisch–Unterdill Station ☎756330
federal road B13 from Holzkirchen–Harlaching Station ☎6909666

Pilot service stations will also supply tourist information and, for a fee, will make arrangements for accommodation.

Police fines

The police are empowered to impose and collect fines of up to DM40 on the spot in cases of violation of traffic regulations. If a road user considers he is innocent of the alleged offence he can refuse to pay the

161

Germany

fine and request his case be tried in court. You are advised to ask for a receipt if the fine is paid on the spot.

Postal and telephone charges

Rates for post to the United Kingdom are:

Air mail and surface mail	DM
Postcards	0.50
Letters up to 20gm	0.70
20–50gm	1.20
50–100gm	1.50

Telephone and charges

The German telephone system is efficient and provides a dialling system to most European countries including the UK (for which the code is 0044). Charges are based on units of time which vary according to the distance and the time of day. Many hotels and garages provide, as a service, direct line telephones but charges are likely to be up to double the public rate. The cost per unit for a local call from post offices etc is DM0.23.

Priority

On pedestrian crossings (zebra crossings) pedestrians have the right of way over all vehicles except trams. Buses have priority when leaving public bus stops and other vehicles must give way to a bus driver who has signalled his intention to leave the kerb.

Roads

The road system is dominated by a comprehensive network of motorways *(Autobahnen)*, which carry most of the long-distance traffic. The *Bundesstrassen* or state roads – marked by black-numbered yellow boards – vary in quality. In the north and in the touring grounds of the Rhine Valley, Black Forest, and Bavaria, the roads are good and well graded.

Holiday traffic

Traffic at weekends increases considerably during the school holidays which are from July to mid September. In order to ease congestion, heavy lorries are prohibited on all roads at summer weekends, and on all Sundays and public holidays.

Motorways

There are about 4,270 miles of toll-free motorways *(Autobahnen)* open and more are under construction, or in preparation. The excellent system stretches in an unbroken line from the Belgian frontier to Berlin; from the Dutch frontier to Munich via Cologne, Frankfurt, Stuttgart, or Nürnberg; from Lübeck to Basle via Hamburg and Hannover. Nearly all motorways are part of the European international network. In general, motorways are two-lane dual carriageways, but in hilly areas there is an extra lane for lorries; these are sometimes signposted *Kriechspuren* (crawling lanes).

On certain hilly sections with only two lanes, lorries, coaches, and cars towing caravans are forbidden to overtake.

To join a motorway, follow the blue and white signposts; exits are indicated by an arrow-shaped sign bearing the word *Ausfahrt* in white letters on a blue background. The regulations are usually similar to those in Great Britain. Vehicles incapable of exceeding 60kph (37mph) are prohibited. See Speed limits page 163.

A well-planned chain of petrol stations and roadhouses is available in addition to many well-situated parking places. The usual distance between petrol stations is between 12 and 15 miles, but it is sometimes much farther; signposts give adequate warning of the distance to the next petrol station. Signs used are R for *Rasthaus* (roadhouse), T for *Tanken* (petrol station), and P for parking. Most motorways carry heavy traffic in the summer, particularly at weekends. Delays are likely on the Cologne–Frankfurt–Karlsruhe, and Frankfurt–Nürnberg–Munich sections, and at the Salzburg and Kufstein frontiers leading into Austria.

Motorway telephone

Emergency telephone posts are placed at intervals of 2km ($1\frac{1}{4}$ miles) along motorways. Black arrows on white safety posts show the direction to the nearest post. When you lift the flap covering the voice tube, you are automatically connected with the motorway police. After you give details of the service required, the police will inform the ADAC patrol service. You should ask for *ADAC Strassenwachthilfe* (road patrol assitance). There is no charge for calls.

Winter conditions

In normal weather, roads are seldom obstructed, although from November to March it is advisable to avoid the heights of the Black Forest, Southern Bavaria, and the Harz region. In the north, conditions can be severe in times of ice and snow. The motorways are all kept clear.

Germany

Road signs

Translations of some written signs are given below:

Anfang	Beginning
Ausfahrt	Exit
Baustofflagerung	Road works material
Durchfahrt verboten	No through traffic
Einbahnstrasse	One–way street
Einfahrt freihalten	Leave entrance free
Ende	End
Fahrbahnwechsel	Change traffic lane
Fahrt frei	Cancellation of previous restrictions
Freie Fahrt	No speed limit
Frostschäden	Frost damage
Gegenverkehr	Oncoming traffic
Glatteisgefahr	Ice on road
Haltestelle	Public transport stopping place
Landschafts-Schutzgebie	Nature reserve
Langsam fahren	Drive slowly
Radweg kreuzt	Cycle-track crossing
Rollsplit	Loose grit
Sackgasse } Sackstrasse }	Cul-de-sac
Schlechte Wegstrecke	Bad surface
Seitenstreifen nicht befahrbar	Use of verge not advised
Starkes Gefälle	Steep down gradient
Strassenschäden	Road damaged
Taxenstand	Taxi rank
Umleitung	Diversion
Vorsicht beim Überholen	Overtake with caution

Seat belts

If your vehicle is fitted with seat belts it is compulsory to wear them.

Shopping hours

Generally these are: *foodshops* from Monday to Friday 08.30–18.30hrs, Saturdays 07.30–13.00hrs; *department stores* from Monday to Friday 09.00–18.30hrs, Saturdays 09.00–14.00hrs (first Saturday each month 09.00–18.00hrs). Some shops close for lunch between 13.00 and 15.00hrs.

Speed

The speed limit in built-up areas is 50kph (31mph) unless otherwise indicated by signs. Outside built-up areas the limit for private cars is 100kph (62mph) unless signposted 120kph (75mph). Motorways *(Autobahnen)*, dual carriageways and roads with at least two marked lanes in each direction, which are not specifically signposted 130kph (81mph) have a recommended speed limit of 130kph. Vehicles towing a caravan or trailer are limited to 80kph (49mph) even on the *Autobahnen*. All lower limits must be adhered to. Anyone driving so slowly that a line of vehicles has formed behind him must permit the following vehicles to pass. If necessary he must stop at a suitable place to allow this.

Distance

Outside built-up areas, motor vehicles to which a special speed limit applies, as well as vehicles with trailers with a combined length of more than 7 metres (23ft), must keep sufficient distance from the preceding vehicle so that an overtaking vehicle may pull in.

Motorways

Motorways *(Autobahnen)* and highways (indicated by a blue sign with white car) may be used only by those vehicles which are capable of exceeding 60kph (37mph) on the level. On motorways there is a recommended speed limit of 130kph (80mph). Motorway traffic may exceed 50kph (31mph) within built-up areas.

Signs

A blue rectangular sign showing upper and lower speeds in white (*eg* 70–110km) is used to promote a steady flow of traffic.

Tourist information offices

The UK office of the German National Tourist Board is in London at 61 Conduit Street, W1R 0EN. Their telephone number is 01-734 2600. In the Federal Republic there are regional tourist associations – (DFV) whilst in most towns these are local tourist offices, usually situated near the railway station or town hall. Any of these organisations will be pleased to help tourists with information and hotel and other accommodation. The offices are usually open from 08.30 to 18.00hrs but in larger towns until 20.00hrs.

Germany

Traffic lights   At some intersections with several lanes going in different directions, there are lights for each lane; watch the light for your lane.

Tyres   The legal requirement for tyres in Germany is a minimum tread depth of 1mm over the whole surface or whole width of the tyre.

Wheel chains   These must not be used on some free roads. In winter months the ADAC hires out chains, either special or the Kantenspur type, for cars and caravans. The construction of some vehicles allows only the use of the special chains. Chains can only be returned to ADAC offices and only during the hours of opening. On production of a valid AA membership card, chains may be hired at the following reduced charges.

Deposit	*members (DM)*	*non-members (DM)*
special	60	90
Kantenspur	120	180

Hire charge per day (days of collection and return are both counted as whole days)

	members (DM)	*non-members (DM)*
special (used)	1.50	3.00
Kantenspur (used)	3.00	4.50
special (unused)	0.75	1.50
Kantenspur (unused)	1.50	2.25

In addition, there is a basic fee of DM7.50 to members, DM15 to non-members.

If chain(s) are lost or damaged, or their wear exceeds the normal, the following amounts will be charged:

Special chains badly worn or damaged	up to DM15
Kantenspur chains badly worn or damaged up to	DM30
Packaging, badly soiled or torn	DM2
Fitting clamp missing	DM1
Fitting stretcher missing	DM1.50

Chains are sold in pairs and if one chain is lost, half the selling price will be charged; for loss of two chains, full selling price is charged.

If the deposit receipt is lost, the chains can be returned only to the station from which they were hired.

Chains are considered to have been used if the seal on the packaging has been removed in which case the hire charge is calculated on the basis of the fees for used chains for the whole period of hire, irrespective of the actual number of days in use. The maximum period for hire is 40 days. Reservations are not possible and the ADAC does not dispatch the chains by post.

Chains are available in several sizes, but, as foreign-made tyres may be different, it is not guaranteed that the appropriate size will be available; in this case alternative arrangements must be made. Further details may be obtained from the ADAC Head Office, Department 'Strassendienste Schneeckettenverleih', 8 München 70, Baumgartnerstr 53 ☎(089) 76761. (No wheel chains are actually hired out from head office).

Also see Road and winter conditions, page 40.

Visitors' registration   A visitor staying overnight should report to the police, but this is usually done by the hotel or campsite management who complete the registration form. If staying with friends at a private address, the host should notify the authorities within seven days.

Warning triangles   Triangles are compulsory for all vehicles. They must be placed about 100 metres (109yd) behind a vehicle (or fallen object or load) on an ordinary road, and 200 metres (219yd) behind a vehicle on a motorway. Vehicles over 2,500kg (2tons 9cwt 24lb) must also carry a yellow flashing light.

Although the warning triangle sold by the AA does not correspond exactly to the type prescribed for Germany, it is legally acceptable for use by bona fide tourists.

Germany/hotels and garages

Prices are in deutschmarks

A tax of 11% is payable on all accounts. You will usually find that this is added as a separate item on garage accounts but it is included in the hotel charges quoted in this gazetteer. You are advised to check at the time of booking.

Abbreviations:
Pl   Platz
Str   Strasse

Aachen (Aix-la-Chapelle) Nordrhein-Westfalen 242,010 (☎0241) Map **4** D1
★★★★**Quellenhof** Monheimsallee 52 ☎48161 tx0832864 rm140 ⊸110 ▥10 G Lift B52–158 Pool
★★**Benelux** (n rest) Franzstr 21 ☎22343 rm24 ⊸9 ▥13 G Lift B44–100
★★**Berliner Hof** (n rest) Bahnhofstr 4 ☎33757 rm65 ⊸10 ▥10 G Lift
★★**Brabant** Stolberger Str 42 ☎500025 rm24 ▥8 G Lift B30–60
★★**Buschhausen** Adenauerallee 215 ☎63071 rm75 (A15) ⊸75 G Lift Pool
★**Braun** Lütticherstr 517 ☎74535 rm13 ⊸4 ▥4 G B29–58 M6–25
★**Drei Türme** Ludwigsallee 25 ☎35219 rm10 G B30–60 M7.85–14.50 Pn42.50–45
★**Hindenberg** Jülicher Str 31 ☎16093 rm40 ⊸4 ▥11 G Lift 1 Jan–20 Dec B36–102 M8.80–18
★**Lousberg** (n rest) Saarstr 108 ☎20332 rm26 ▥8 G Lift B28–68
▨⇙**Cockerill** Herzogstr13 ☎503870 N☷ M/c Toy G10
▨⇙**T Dreis** Kamperstr 22 ☎73092 N☷ BL/Jag/Peu/Rov/Tri
▨⇙**24 Kuckhartz** Viktoriastr 74 ☎503083 N☎20011 Ren G5
▨⇙**Scharenberg & Jessen** Roermonderstr 62 ☎31142 N☷ Frd

Achern Baden-Württemberg 20,610 (☎07841) Map **11** B3
★★★**Seehotel** ☎3011 tx0752240 rm43 ⊸42 Lift B42–104 M16.50–28 Pn65–75 Pool Lake
★**Götz Sonne Eintracht** Hauptstr 112 ☎5055 rm33 ⊸9 ▥20 G Lift B36.50–105 M12–25 Pool

Adelsried Bayern 1,510 (☎08294) Map **12** D3
★**Schmid** Augsburger Str 28 ☎891 rm100 (A35) ⊸10 ▥40 G Lift B27–62 M7–18 Pn45–60 Pool

Adenau Rheinland-Pfalz 3,210 (☎02691) Map **4** D1
★**Wilden Schwein** Hauptstr 117 ☎2055 rm7 ⊸2 G 27 Dec–25 Nov LD B28–75 M8.50–25

Ahlhorn Niedersachsen 3,600 (☎04435) Map **5** A3
☆**Motel Nadermann** (on B213) ☎302 rm10 ⊸2 B19–55 M4–15
▨⇙**Auto Riemann** Wildeshauser Str ☎882 Aud/VW G5

Ahrweiler Rheinland-Pfalz 10,000 (☎02641) Map **4** D1
★**Stern** Marktpl 9 ☎34738 rm15 ▥3 G LD 15 Jan–15 Dec B29–81 M10–20 Pn42–56

Aibling (Bad) Bayern 9,310 (☎08061) Map **13** A2
★★**Schuhbräu** ☎5831 rm45 (A9) ⊸12 ▥8 26 Dec–25 Nov G Lift B30–76 M7–15 Pn46–52
★**Lindner** Marienpl 5 ☎5295 rm27 ⊸7 ▥7 G B30–86 M5.50 Pn43–53

Alpirsbach Baden-Württemberg 7,050 (☎07444) Map **11** B3
⇙**24 K Jautz** Hauptstr 29 ☎23454 N☷ M/c Frd
At **Ehlenbogen** (4km N)

★★**Adler** Hauptstr 1 ☎2215 rm22 ▥7 G closed 1 Dec–9 & 16 Jan–14 Feb B26–62 M8–15 Pn32–36

Alsfeld Hessen 17,815 (☎06631) Map **5** B1
☆☆**Autobahn Roadhouse** ☎759 tx49415 rm74 ⊸18 ▥20 G Lift
★**Zum Schwalbennest** Pfarrwiesenweg 14 ☎2964 rm16 ▥16 G
▨►24 E Hartmann Hersfelder Str 81 ☎835 Opl
▨►24 W Klöss Grünbergerstr 72 ☎707 M/c Frd G10

Altena Nordrhein-Westfalen 28,015 (☎02352) Map **5** A2
⇙**K Lienkamper** Rahmedestr 141 ☎50430 N☷ AR/BL/Jag/Rov/Tri G

Altenahr Rheinland-Pfalz 2,210 (☎02643) Map **4** D1
★★**Lochmuhle** (near Mayschloss) ☎345 rm70 (A8) ⊸40 ▥30 G Lift B37.50–119 M14.50–30 Pn96.50–185 Lake Pool
★★**Post** Brückenstr 2 ☎208 rm46 ⊸31 G Lift B33.50–102 M8–18 Pn46.50–64 Pool

Amberg Bayern 50,010 (☎09621) Map **13** A4
★**Goldenes Lamm** Rathausstr 6 ☎12153 rm24 ▥5 G B19–40 M6–16

Andernach Rheinland-Pfalz 29,015 (☎02632) Map **4** D1
★★**Rhein** Rhein prom ☎42240 rm25 ⊸5 ▥9 G Lift 15 Mar–1 Nov B24–62 M8.50–17 Pn30–36
★**Anker** K-Adenauer Allee 21 ☎42907 rm32 ⊸3 ▥8 G 15 Mar–15 Nov B26.50–59 M7.50 Pn33–35
⇙**Altenhofen** Koblenzer Str 73 ☎44447 N☷ AR G200
▨⇙**E Kirsch** Fullscheuenveg 36 ☎42424 N☷ Ren G20
i►24 P Krämer Koblenzer Str 27 ☎42969 Cit G20

Arnsberg Nordrhein-Westfalen 82,010 (☎02931) Map **5** A2
★★**Goldener Stern** Alter Markt 6 ☎3662 rm25 ▥4 G B29–62 M5–18 Pn42–45

Aschaffenburg Bayern 55,550 (☎06021) Map **12** C4
★★★**Aschaffenburger Hof** Frohsinnstr 11 ☎21441 tx04188736 rm70 ⊸18 ▥42 G Lift B33–99 M10–18 Pn45–58
★★★**Romantik-Hotel-Post** Goldbacher Str 19 ☎21333 ta Post-Hotel tx04188736 rm75 ⊸50 ▥25 G Lift B48–100 M12–38 Pn78–112 Pool
▨►24 Amberg Würzburger Str 67 ☎21418 N☎22776 N☷ AR/BL/Fia/Jag/Rov/Tri G
▨►24 Auto-Haus Pappelweg 8, Nilkheim ☎8588 Ren G5

Assmannshausen Hessen 3,015 (☎06722) Map **11** B4
★★**Anker** Rheinstr 5 ☎2912 rm48 (A18) ⊸3 ▥2 Apr–Oct B30–74 M9.50–21
★★**Krone** Rheinstr 10 ☎2236 rm86 (A52) ⊸48 G Lift 15 Mar–15 Nov B38–141 Màlc Pool

Attendorn Nordrhein-Westfalen 23,159 (☎02722) Map **5** A2
★★**Burg Schnellenberg** (3·5km W) ☎4081 rm38 ⊸29 ▥9 G closed 15 Jan–10 Feb B30–90 Pn58–78 ⇙

Germany

Augsburg Bayern 260,025 (☎0821)
Map **12** D3

☆☆☆☆ **Holiday Inn – Turmhotel** Wittelsbacher Park ☎57051 tx533225 rm185 ⇄185 G Lift B86–126 Pn82–110 M15 Pool

★★★ **Drei Mohren** Maximilianstr 40 ☎510031 tx053710 rm109 ⇄85 🍴16 G Lift LD B62–135 M21–27 Pn83–112

★★ **Ost** Fuggerstr 4 ☎33088 tx053576 rm66 ⇄6 🍴28 Lift B29–74

★★ **Weisses Lamm** Ludwigstr 36 ☎35021 rm66 (A) ⇄17 🍴17 Lift ⨼

★ **Post** Fuggerstr 7 ☎36044 rm50 🍴25 G Lift B29–72 M12 Pn50–60

🚗 **Listle** Kriegshaberstr 58 ☎403055 N🅿 Ren

🚗 **R Stolber** Lange Gasse 20 ☎24878 N🅿 BL/Jag/Rov/Tri G5

Aurich (Ostfriesland) Niedersachsen 34,020 (☎04941) Map **5** A4
★ **Piquerhof** Bahnhofstr 1 ☎4118 rm48 ⇄5 G

Bad Each placename beginning with Bad is listed under the name that follows it.

Bacharach Rheinland-Pfalz 2,941 (☎06743) Map **11** B4
★★ **Altkölnischer Hof** Blüchers 2 ☎1339 rm45 ⇄2 🍴14 G Lift 25 Mar–1 Nov B28.50–79 M8.50–17 Pn40–52

★★ **Engelsburg** (3km N) ☎(06744) 243 rm12 ⇄5 🍴1 G 15 May–10 Oct B29–70 M9–15

Baden-Baden Baden-Württemberg 48,015 (☎07221) Map **11** B3
🚗🚗🚗🚗 **Bellevue** Lichtentaler Allee ☎23721 rm97 ⇄68 🍴18 Lift 25 Mar–31 Oct B48–180 M25–27 Pn92–160 Pool

🚗🚗🚗🚗 **Selighof** Fremersbergstr 125 ☎23385 rm58 ⇄51 🍴3 G Lift Etr–26 Oct B50–152 M20–28 Pn110–127 ⨼ Pool

🚗🚗🚗🚗 **Speigenbarger Bad Hotel Badischer Hof** ☎22827 tx781121 rm90 ⇄70 G Lift B43–120 M22 Pn75–119

★★★ **Europäischer Hof** Kaiserallee 2 ☎23561 ta Europe tx784388 rm150 ⇄132 G Lift

★★★ **Waldhotel Fischkultur** Gaisbach 91 ☎71051 ta Forellenhof rm29 (A14) ⇄19 🍴4 G Lift B51.50–137 M34 Pn39–205

★★★ **Golf** Fremersbergstr 113 (2km SW) ☎23691 rm85 ⇄65 🍴20 G Lift 1 Apr–31 Oct B55–160 M25–35 Pn40–125 Pool

★★★ **Zum Hirsch** Hirschstr 1 ☎23896 rm107 (A28) ⇄63 🍴17 G Lift LD B38.50–140 M23–27 S%

★★ **Bären** Hauptstr 36 ☎71046 rm80 ⇄50 🍴10 G Lift B35–105 M18 Pn59–84

★★ **Müller** Lange Str 34 ☎23211 rm32 ⇄20 Lift LD B32–90

★ **Bischoff** (n rest) Römerpl 2 ☎22378 rm27 🍴1 G 1 Feb–30 Nov B22–55

★ **Römerhof** (n rest) Sofienstr 25 ☎23415 rm27 🍴16 G Lift 1 Feb–15 Dec B22–70

🚗 **H P Nagel** Lange Str 104 ☎22672 N🅿 BL/Jag/Rov/Tri

🚗 **Nippon** Aumattstr 8 ☎63527 N🅿 Dat/Hon/Maz G10

🚗 **E Scheibel** Hubertusstr 19 ☎62005 N🅿

Badenweiler Baden-Württemberg 4,016 (☎07632) Map **11** B2
★★★★ **Römerbad** Schlosspl 1 ☎701 tx772933 rm114 ⇄100 G Lift 1 Mar–6 Jan B50–160 M30–40 Pn90–150 ⨼ Pool

★★★ **Park** E-Eisenlohr Str 15 ☎5091 rm87 ⇄75 🍴3 G Lift 1 Mar–10 Nov B35–160 M13–25 Pn75–135 Pool

Bamberg Bayern 74,019 (☎0951) Map **12** D4
★★★ **Bamberger Hof Bellevue** Schönleinspl 4 ☎27474 tx0662867 rm45 ⇄30 🍴3 G Lift

★★ **Straub** Ludwigstr 31 ☎25838 rm37 ⇄5 🍴2 G B28–72 M8–14 Pn48–62

🚗 **Schüberth** Siechenstr 87 ☎62253 N🅿 M/c Ren

Bardowick Niedersachsen (☎04131) Map **5** B4
🚗 **R Rech** Bahnhofstr 8 ☎121128 N🅿 AR/BL/Rov G

Bayreuth Bayern 67,019 (☎0921) Map **12** D4
★★★ **Bayerischer Hof** Bahnhofstr 14 ☎23061 tx642737 rm48 ⇄24 🍴3 G Lift

★★ **Goldener Hirsch** Bahnhofstr 13 ☎23046 rm45 ⇄15 🍴3 G Lift

★★ **Post** (n rest) Bahnhofstr 21 ☎5010 rm52 ⇄12 🍴6 G Lift

🚗 **R Keil** Markgrafenallee 28 ☎22622 N🅿 BL/Fia/Vlo

🚗 **L Münch** Rathenaustr 3 ☎66001 N🅿 BL/Fia/Vlo

Bayrischzell Bayern 1,715 (☎08023) Map **13** A2
★★ **Alpenrose** Schliersee Str 100 ☎620 rm35 ⇄5 🍴25 G B30–90 M10–20 Pn38–60 Pool

★ **Maria-Theresia** Tannermühlweg 358 ☎424 rm18 ⇄8 🍴2 15 Dec–15 Oct B26–82 M10–18

Berchtesgaden Bayern 24,450 (☎08652) Map **13** B2
★★★ **Geiger** Berchtesgadener Str III ☎5555 rm55 ⇄45 Lift B44–168 M20–30 Pn65–117 Pool

🚗🚗24 **H Buckwinkler** Bahnhofstr 21 ☎2364 N🅿4437 Aud/Por/VW

🚗🚗24 **G Köppl** Hindenburg Allee 1 ☎2615 N🅿477 M/c Aud/VW G10

At Königssee
★★ **Königssee** ☎2343 tx56212 rm115 ⇄35 G Pool

★★ **Schiffmeister** ☎3022 rm44 (A) ⇄12 G Lift 20 Dec–10 Oct ⨼ Pool Lake

Berg Bayern 6,311 (☎Starnberg 08151) Map **12** D2
★★ **Schloss Berg** Seestr 17 ☎5621 rm25 ⇄8 🍴1 ⨼ Pool Lake

Bergen Niedersachsen 13,110 (☎05051) Map **5** B3
★ **Kohlmann** Lubenstr 6 ☎2012 rm16 (A9) ⇄7 🍴7 G B20–65 M7–32 Pn36–49.50

Bergzabern (Bad) Rheinland-Pfalz 6,015 (☎06343) Map **11** B3
★★★ **Park** Kurtalstr 83 ☎2415 rm40 (A6) ⇄16 🍴11 G Lift 1 Jan–15 Nov 15 Dec–31 Dec LD B39–131 M12–20 Pn47–100 Pool

Berlin 2,050,010 (☎030) Map **6** D3
★★★★★ **Berlin Hilton** 30 Budapester Str 2 ☎261081 tx184380 rm343 ⇄301 🍴18 Lift

★★★★★ **Kempinski Berlin** 15 Kurfürstendamm 27 ☎881091 tx0183553 rm333 ⇄333 Lift Pool

★★★★ **Ambassador** 30 Bayreuther Str 42 ☎240101 tx184259 rm118 ⇄118 G Lift B103.50–177 M10.50–12.50 Pn139.50–159.50 Pool

★★★★ **Berlin** 30 Kurfürstenstr 62 ☎269291 tx0184332 rm260 ⇄185 🍴75 Lift B68–110 M15 Pn102–112

★★★★ **Europaischer Hof** Messedamm 10 ☎302011 tx0182882 rm179 ⇄110 🍴69 G Lift B50–94 M13 Pn72

★★★★ **Franke** 31 A-Achilles Str 57 ☎8921097 tx0184857 rm69 ⇄69 G Lift B50–89 M14–18 Pn78–112

★★★★ **Park Zellermayer** 15 Meinekestr 15 ☎882051 tx184200 rm140 ⇄140 G Lift B72–134 Màlc

Germany

★★★★*Plaza* 15 Knesebeckstr 63 ☎882081
tx184181 rm135 (A) ⇄121 ⋒11 G Lift
★★★★*Savoy* 12 Fasanenstr 9 Charlottenberg
☎310654 tx184292 rm115 ⇄85 ⋒30 Lift
B65–140 M16–20 Pn97–117
★★★★*Schweizerhof* 30 Budapester Str 21
☎26961 tx185501 rm361 ⇄271 ⋒84 G Lift
Pool
★★★*Kurfürstendamm* 31 Eisenzahnstr 1
☎8854025 tx183522 rm112 ⇄45 ⋒67 G Lift
★★★*Lichtburg* 15 Paderborner Str 10
☎8918041 tx0184208 rm54 ⇄54 G Lift
B45–82 M12–15 Pn77–92
★★★*Zoo* 15 Kurfürstendamm 25 ☎883091
tx0183835 rm144 ⇄103 ⋒1 G Lift B40–138
M16 Pn72–114
★★*Astrid* (n rest) 12 Bleibtreustr 20
Charlottenburg ☎8815959 rm11 ⋒2 Lift
B30.75–55.50
★★*Sachsenhof* 30 Motzstr 7 ☎2162074
rm61 ⇄13 ⋒1 Lift
★★*Stephanie* (n rest) 12 Bleibtreustr 38
Charlottenburg ☎8818073 tx0184216 rm50
⇄8 ⋒6 Lift B44–98
★*Charlottenburger Hof* (n rest) 12
Stuttgarterpl 14 ☎3244819 rm34 (A26) B25–56
⊟*Austin-Service* Naumannstr 79 ☎7843051
N☎ BL/Rov/Tri
⊟*H Butenuth* Forckenbeckstr 94 ☎3341051 Frd
⊟♨*H Richtzenhain* Kantstr 126 ☎3124391
BL/Rov/Tri G10
⊟♨*Uhland* Uhlandstr 187, Kurfürstendamm
☎8834378 G90
⊟*F Wacha* Stettiner Str 10 ☎4938967
N☎3534925 N☎ BL/Chy/Jag/Rov/Tri G20

Bernkastel-Kues Rheinland-Pfalz 7,814
(☎06531) Map **11** A/B4
★★*Burg-Landshut* Gestade 11 ☎3019 rm35
⇄4 ⋒7 Apr–Nov LD B28.50–86 M7.50–18
Pn46–52.50
★★*Drei Könige* (n rest) Bahnhofstr 1 ☎2327
rm40 ⇄9 ⋒15 G Lift 15 Mar–15 Nov B28–90
★★*Post* Gestade 17 ☎300 rm17 (A7) ⇄4
⋒1 G Feb–Dec LD B18.50–54

Biberach an der Riss Baden-
Württemberg 28,920 (☎07531) Map **12** C2
★★★*Reith* (n rest) Ulmer Str 7 ☎7828 rm43
⋒28 G Lift B24–62
★★*Goldenes Rad* Radgasse 7 ☎7969 rm40
⇄2 ⋒12 G Lift B27–60 Màlc Pn45–50
Schwaben Bleicherstr 26 ☎7878 N☎ M/c Frd
G5

Bielefeld Nordrhein-Westfalen 322,023
(☎0521) Map **5** A2
★★*Bielefelder Hospiz* (n rest) Altstädter
Kirchpl 3 ☎64585 rm40 ⇄6 ⋒18 G Lift
B31.50–45
★★*Brand's Busch* Furtwaengler Str 52
☎22236 rm41 (A4) ⇄5 ⋒31 G Lift B26–74
M7.50–19.50 Pn40–65
★★*Kaiserhof* Düppelstr 20 ☎65066
tx0932656 rm145 ⇄40 ⋒20 G Lift
⊟♨24 *Handels* Herforder Str 241 ☎35084
N☎ BL/BMW/Peu G10

Biersdorf See **Bitburg**

Bingen Rheinland-Pfalz 26,940 (☎06721)
Map **11** B4
★★*Starkenburger Hof* (n rest) Rheinkai 1
☎14341 ta Rheinhotel rm30 ⇄8 ⋒8 G
1 Feb–22 Dec B23–85
⊟♨*L Honrath* Mainzer Str 71 ☎13131
Aud/Por/VW
⊟♨*Pieroth* Mainzerstr 439 ☎17355 Frd

Bitburg Rheinland-Pfalz 12,019 (☎06561)
Map **11** A4
★*Mosella* Karenweg 11 ☎3147 rm16 ⇄3 ⋒3
G B20–44 Pn31–35

H Hamdorf Daunerstr 2 ☎2810 N☎ M/c G3
♨24 *Jegen* Saarstr ☎3860 N☎ Ren G5
C Metzger Mötscherstr 49 ☎3462 N☎
AR/BL/Jag/Rov/Tri
At **Biersdorf** (12km NW)
★★★*Dorint Sporthotel Sudeifel* am Stausee
☎(06569)841 tx47/29607 rm240 ⋒240 Lift
B50–104 Pn82–107

Blankenheim Nordrhein-Westfalen 8,110
(☎02449) Map **4** D1
★★*Schlossblick* Nonnenbacher Weg 2 ☎238
rm35 ⋒20 G LD B20–59 M11–19 Pool Lake

Bocholt Nordrhein-Westfalen 49,990
(☎02871) Map **4** D2
⊟♨*Schmitz* Uhlandstr 27 ☎6025 N☎
♨♨*Schreiber* Munsterstr 11 ☎8348 N☎42573
BL G10

Bochum Nordrhein-Westfalen 433,623
(☎0234) Map **4** D2
★★★*Parkhotel Haus Bochum* Bergstr 141
☎16091 rm17 G
⊟*Reuter* Harpener Hellweg 7 ☎59881 N☎ Frd

Bonn Nordrhein-Westfalen 287,015
(☎02221) Map **4** D1
★★★★*Konigshof* Adenauerallee 9 ☎631831
ta Royalhotel tx886535 rm82 ⇄82 G Lift
B70–130 Màlc Pn105–125
☆☆☆*Motel Bonn* Reichsstrl Rottgen ☎251021
rm34 ⇄35 closed 24 Dec–2 Jan B48.75–77
M6–18 Pn55.50
★★★*Stern* Markt 8 ☎654455 tx886508
rm65 ⇄32 ⋒24 Lift B41–110 Màlc Pn71–96
★★★*Beethoven* Rheingasse 26 ☎631411
tx886467 rm60 ⇄9 ⋒29 G Lift B33–92
M12–24 Pn98–132
★★*Bergischer Hof* Münsterpl 23 ☎633441
rm28 ⇄5 ⋒6 Lift B35–98 Pn53–58
★★*Eden* Hofgarten 6 ☎638071 rm33
★★*Savoy* (n rest) Berliner Freiheit 17
☎651356 rm25 ⇄6 ⋒2 Lift
♨24 *J Bachem* Vorgebirgstr 100 ☎631151
N☎614343 (closed weekends) GM
Germania Martinstr 66 ☎281 rm8 ⇄1 ⋒3
B20–55 M7.50–18.50 Pn36–46
♨♨*J Knüfker* Lievelingsweg 4 ☎670444 N☎
Chy/Sim G
⊟*J Kümpel* Bonner Talweg 321 ☎232061 N☎
BL/Jag/Rov/Tri G50
⊟*Mahlberg* k-Frowein Str 2 ☎636656 N☎
BL/Jag G5
At **Röttgen**
☆☆☆*Bonn* Reichsstr 1 ☎251021 rm34 ⇄34

Bonndorf Baden-Württemberg 5,213
(☎07703) Map **11** B2
★★*Schwarzwald* Rothausstr 7 ☎421 rm67
⇄27 ⋒5 G Lift B29–82 M8–18 Pn43–56 Pool
Germania Martinstr 66 ☎281 rm8 ⇄1 ⋒3
B20–55 M7.50–18.50 Pn36–46

Boppard Rheinland-Pfalz 9,613 (☎06742)
Map **5** A1
★★★*Bellevue* Rheinallee 42 ☎2081
tx426310 rm84 (A84) ⇄40 ⋒44 G Lift B40–110
M15–25&àlc Pn65–95 Pool
☆☆*Ebertor* Heerstr (B9) ☎2085 tx426310
rm48 (A32) ⋒48 G Etr–1 Nov B39–59 M12–20
Pn57–71
★★*Günther* (n rest) Rheinallee 40 ☎2335
rm20 ⇄17 ⋒2 Lift 15 Jan–30 Nov B20–58
★★*Rheinlust* Rheinallee 29 ☎3001
tx426319 rm82 (A40) ⇄9 ⋒30 G Lift
1 May–31 Oct B22–78 M9.50 Pn42–60
★★*Spiegel* Rheinallee 34 ☎2971 rm31 ⇄14
⋒10 G Lift B31–92 M10–18 Pn50–80 Lake
★*Hünsrückerhof* Steinstr 26 ☎2433 rm26
B22.50–27.50 M7.50–16 Pn27.50–30.50

Braubach Rheinland-Pfalz 4,210 (☎02627)
Map **5** A1

Germany

★**Hammer** Untermarkstr 15 ☎336 rm12
⇄1 ▥4 G B20–48 M6.50–14 Pn38–45

🛇🕪24 **J Siemon** Brunnenstr 28 ☎636 N☏ Ren G

Braunlage Niedersachsen 8,020 (☎05520)
Map **5** B2

★★★★**Maritim Kongers & Sport**
Am Pfaffenstieg ☎3051 tx096261 rm275
⇄275 G Lift B71–184 M16 Pn90 🍽 Pool

★★★**Weidmannsheil** Obere Bergstr 8 ☎3081
rm88 ⇄30 ▥16 G Lift B45–140 M17–25
Pn76–102 Pool

Braunschweig (Brunswick)
Niedersachsen 270,005 (☎0531) Map **5** B3

★★★★**Atrium** Berliner Pl 3 ☎73001 tx0952576
rm130 ⇄100 ▥30 G Lift B65–180 M11

★★★**Forsthaus** Hamburger Str 72 ☎32801
rm49 ⇄4 ▥24 G Lift

★★**Frühlings** Bankpl 7 ☎49317 rm63 ⇄12
▥18 G Lift B31–76 M12–15

★**Touring** Celler Heerstr 174 ☎53098 rm22
⇄2 ▥2 G

M Gottschling Ackerstr 34 ☎74546 N☏
BL/Jag/Rov/Tri

🛇**Könnecke** Gifhorner Str 150 ☎311124 N☏
Cit/Peu/Ren G100

🛇🕪24 **Opel-Dürkop** Helmstedterstr 60
☎7031 Bed/Opl G4

🛇🕪🛆 **Sitte** Kurzestr 7 ☎76102 N☏ G5

Braunsfeld See **Köln (Cologne)**

Breisig (Bad) Rheinland-Pfalz 6,315
(☎02633) Map **4** D1

★**Rheineck** Brunnenstr 8 ☎9180 rm31 (A14)
⇄3 ▥1 G

★**Vater und Sohn** Zehnerstr 78 ☎9148 rm8
⇄1 ▥2 G B25–72 M7–17 Pn30–39

Bremen Bremen 572,050 (☎0421) Map **5** A3

AA agents; see page 154

★★★★**Park** in the Bürgerpark ☎340031
tx0244343 rm150 ⇄115 ▥35 G Lift B78–228
M18–26

★★★**Columbus** Bahnhofspl 5 ☎314161
tx0244688 rm136 ⇄93 ▥28 Lift B50.50–104
Màlc

☆☆☆ **EuroCrest** A-Bebel Allee 4 ☎230041
tx244560 rm144 ⇄60 ▥84 Lift B87–111
M13–15 Pn74.50

★★**Schaper-Siedenburg** Bahnhofstr 8
☎310106 rm80 ⇄7 ▥18 Lift B30–80 Màlc

🛇🛆**Dienst** In der Vahr 66a ☎469033 N☏
AR/Peu

🛇🕪24 **H Harms** Hastedter Heerstr 303
☎492074 N☏ Chy

🛇**H Baecker** A-Nobel Str 18 ☎490016 N☏ BL/Jag/Tri

🛇🛆**C Pollmann** Stresemannstr 9 ☎444131
N☏ Frd G

At **Brinkum** (4km S)
☆**Atlas** G-Daimler Str 3 ☎874037 rm30 ▥30
G 10 Jan–20 Dec

Bremerhaven Bremen 150,020 (☎0471)
Map **5** A4

AA agents; see page 154

★★★**Nordsee–Naber** T-Heuss Pl ☎47001
tx2-38881 rm125 ⇄55 ▥55 G Lift B43–130
M12–25

★★**Haverkamp-Seiffert** Schleswigerstr 27
☎45031 tx238679 rm90 ⇄20 ▥30 G Lift
B31–90 M10.50–17.50

H Baecker Reuterdamm 11 ☎53081 N☏
Bed/BL/Vau

🛇🛆**H Jobus** Langener Landstr 184 ☎84382
N☏ Ren G20

Brinkum See **Bremen**

Brodenbach Rheinland-Pfalz 610
(☎02605) Map **4** D1

★★**Post** Dorfstr 35 ☎348 rm30 (A11) ⇄5 ▥4
G 1 Apr–15 Nov B18–54 M9–18 Pn30–40 Lake

Bruchsal Baden-Württemberg 40,025
(☎07251) Map **11** B3

★★**Friedrichshof** Bahnhofspl 7 ☎2692 rm65
⇄6 ▥8 G Lift B20.50–60 M9.50–18.50

W Hetzel Murgstr 12 ☎2283 N☏ M/c
BL/Jag/Rov/Tri G20

Brunswick See **Braunschweig**

Büdelsdorf See **Rendsburg**

Bühlertal Baden-Württemberg 8,215
(☎07223) Map **11** B3

★**Rebstock** Hauptstr 110 ☎73118 rm50 ⇄2
▥40 G 15 Dec–15 Nov

Camberg Hessen 5,300 (☎06434)
Map **5** A1

★**Elephant** Limburger Str 24 ☎7572 rm10 G
B21–38 M6.50–12

Celle Niedersachsen 80,021 (☎05141)
Map **5** B3

★★**Celler Hof** Stechbahn 11 ☎28061
tx925117 rm50 ⇄15 ▥25 G Lift B36–112
M9.50–22.50 Pn55–88

★★**Hannover** Wittinger Str 56 ☎34870 rm20
⇄5 ▥20 G B32–94 M4–19

Von Maltzan & Trebeljahr Hohe Wende 3
☎3921 N☏ Frd

Cham Bayern 12,515 (☎09971) Map **13** B4

★★**Randsberger Hof** Randsberger Hofstr 15
☎1916 rm65 ⇄12 ▥30 G Lift B26–76
M6–15 Pn38–46

Coblence See **Koblenz**

Coburg Bayern 46,713 (☎09561) Map **6** C1

★★**Der Festungshof** Festungshof 1 ☎7781
rm20 ⇄5 ▥5 G B31–85 M10–25

Cochem Rheinland-Pfalz 8,213 (☎02671)
Map **11** B4

★★**Alte Thorschenke** Brückenstr 3 ☎7059
rm55 ⇄25 ▥2 G Lift 10 Mar–5 Jan B31–120
M14–30 Pn54–84

★★**Am Hafen** Uferstr ☎490 rm16 ⇄1 ▥8 G
B32.50–71 M5.50–20 Pn39.50–52

★★**Germania** Moselprom 1 ☎262
tx0869422 rm31 ⇄18 ▥3 G 1 Mar–31 Dec

🛇🛆**Cochem** Sehler Anlagen 53 ☎626 N☏ Opl
G3

🛇🕪24 **M J Schneider** Moselprom 54 ☎7487
M/c G6

Cölbe See **Marburg an der Lahn**

Cologne See **Köln**

Constance See **Konstanz**

Crailsheim Baden-Württemberg 25,024
(☎07951) Map **12** C3

★★**Post-Faber** Langue Str 2-4 ☎8038 rm60
⇄20 ▥14 G Lift B26–78 M9–16 Pn38–58

Crefeld See **Krefeld**

Creglingen Baden-Württemberg 5,915
(☎07933) Map **12** C4

★★**Krone** Hauptstr 12 ☎558 rm30 (A10)
⇄1 ▥5 G 20 Jan–20 Dec B18.50–60 M6–15
Pn30–38

★★**Lamm** Hauptstr 31 ☎501 rm18 G
B19.50–56 M3–15 Pn26–32

Cuxhaven Niedersachsen 63,010 (☎04721)
Map **5** A4

★★★**Donners** Seedeich 2 ☎35018 rm85
⇄18 ▥67 G Lift LD B36–54 M9–30 Pn49–82
Pool Sea

Darmstadt Hessen 138,024 (☎06151)
Map **11** B4

★★**Weinmichel** Schleiermacherstr 8–10
☎26822 tx419275 rm74 ⇄25 ▥34 Lift
B36–98 M10–20

🛇🕪**Darmstadt** Kasinastr 62 ☎86061 Opl

ⓘ♨24 J Wiest Riedstr 5 ☎8641 Aud/Por/VW

Daun Rheinland-Pfalz 7,021 (☎06592) Map **4** D1
★★ **Hommes** Wirichstr 9 ☎538 rm41 ⇄41 G Lift 20 Dec–15 Nov B35–43 M13–24 Pn52–60 Pool

ⓘ♨24 M Gessner Abt-Richard Str 3 (B257) ☎2405 N♨3293 Aud/VW

Dechsendorf See **Erlangen**

Delmenhorst Niedersachsen 70,015 (☎04221) Map **5** A3
☆☆ **Annenriede** Annenheider Damm 129 ☎6871 rm33 (A2) ⇄2 ⋒31 G B28–60 M7.50–12.50
★★ **Central** Bahnhofstr 16 ☎19010 rm36 ⇄8 ⋒5 G B24–71 M from 7
ⓘ C Duna Bremer Str 157 ☎70061 N♨ Ren
ⓘ♨A Jannarelli Düsternortstr 136 ☎19156 N♨ Cit G10

Detmold Nordrhein-Westfalen 65,013 (☎05231) Map **5** A2
★★ **Detmolder Hof** Lange Str 19 ☎28244 rm30 ⇄2 ⋒8 G B33–72 M8.75–18
★ **Friedrichshöhe** Paderbornerstr 6 (4km SE) ☎47053 rm15 ⇄8 ⋒8 G B22–37 M6–15 Pn36–40
⅏ Bergmann Lagesche Str 19 ☎25396 Frd
⅏ H Budde Marienstr 18 ☎22227 N♨ BL/Rov/Tri G6
ⓘ♨S Wagner Grünstr 34 ☎27252 N♨ Ren G

Diez/Lahn Rheinland-Pfalz 11,050 (☎06432) Map **5** A1
★ **Imperial** Rosenstr 42 ☎2131 rm17 ⋒7 G B20–46 M8–18 Pn28–31
At **Schaumberg** (4.5km SW)
★ **Waldecker Hof** ☎2076 rm34 G Lake

Dinkelsbühl Bayern 10,510 (☎09851) Map **12** C3
★★ **Deutsches Haus** Weinmarkt 3 ☎2346 rm11 ⇄3 ⋒5 G 1 Mar–30 Nov B25–74 M8–18 Pn38–52
★★ **Goldene Kanne** Segringer Str 8 ☎2363 rm24 ⇄5 ⋒6 G 15 Dec–15 Nov
★★ **Goldene Rose** Marktpl 4 ☎2276 rm20 ⇄5 ⋒5 G 15 Mar–15 Nov 20 Dec–7 Jan B26.50–72 M10.50 Pn43–53
ⓘ♨24 A Seiferlein Augsburger Str 1 ☎2243 Opl

Dobel Baden-Württemberg 1,605 (6km E of **Bad Herrenalb**) (☎07083) Map **11** B3
★★★ **Mönchs Waldhotel** Neuenburger Str 49 ☎8888 rm42 ⇄5 ⋒22 G B27–48 Pn58–71
★★ **Funk** Hauptstr ☎2077 rm30 (A7) ⇄3 ⋒5 G 20 Dec–6 Nov B29.50–83 M9.50–25 Pn53–65

Donaueschingen Baden-Württemberg 18,215 (☎0771) Map **11** B2
ⓘ⅏A Zimmermann F-Ebert Str 76 ☎2246 N♨ Sim G10

Donauwörth Bayern 17,020 (☎0906) Map **12** D3
★★ **Zur Traube** Kapellstr 14 ☎3142 rm33 (A21) ⇄2 ⋒10 G Lift B25–87 M5–14 Pn40–65
★ **Schwarzer Adler** Hindenburg Str 29 ☎825 rm15 G

Dortmund Nordrhein-Westfalen 640,050 (☎0231) Map **5** A2
★★★★ **Römischer Kaiser** Olpestr 2 ☎528331 tx822441 rm130 ⇄90 ⋒20 G Lift B75–100 M18–24
★★ **Westfalenhalle** Rheinlanddamm 200 ☎125063 tx822321 rm109 ⇄6 ⋒46 Lift ⅏
★★ **Wittekindshof** Westfalendamm 270 ☎594049 tx822414 rm24 ⇄3 ⋒8 G
ⓘ♨Niestendiedrich Ruhrallee 29 ☎126570 N♨ AR/Peu/Vlo G4
Peters Arminiusstr 51 ☎17845 N♨ Frd

Duisburg Nordrhein-Westfalen 602,040 (☎0203) Map **4** D2
★★★ **Steigenburger Duisburger Hof** Neckarstr 2 ☎331021 tx855750 rm146 ⇄60 ⋒40 G Lift B49–130
★★ **Prinzregent** Universitätsstr 1 ☎20956 tx0855457 rm76 ⇄24 Lift
24 I Schwenke Bahnhofstr 123 ☎445555 M/c Rov G40
ⓘ O Weber Koloniestr 80 ☎371048 N♨

Düren Nordrhein-Westfalen 88,915 (☎02421) Map **4** D1
★★★ **Germania** J-Schregal Str 20 ☎15005 rm58 ⇄8 ⋒32 G Lift B24–83
★ **Nachtwächter** Kölner Landstr 12 ☎74031 rm40 (A10) ⋒36 9 Jan–20 Dec B25.50–58 M6–16

Durlach See **Karlsruhe**

Dürrheim (Bad) Baden-Württemberg 10,511 (☎07726) Map **11** B2
★★★ **Kreuz** Friedrichstr 2 ☎8044 tx7921312 rm59 (A9) ⇄26 ⋒11 G Lift B33–74 M10–22 Pn59–62 Pool

Düsseldorf Nordrhein-Westfalen 680,009 (☎0211) Map **4** D2
★★★★ **Park** Corneliuspl 1 ☎8651 tx8582331 rm160 ⇄160 Lift B108–180 Màlc Pn19–38
★★★ **Börsen** (n rest) Kreuzstr 19a ☎363071 tx08587323 rm80 ⇄80 Lift B48–140
★★★ **Savoy** Breite Str 4 ☎320541 tx08587324 rm80 (A10) ⇄52 ⋒13 Lift
★★ **Vossen Am Karlplatz** Bilker Str 2 ☎325010 rm43 ⇄8 ⋒10 G Lift B41–92
ⓘ♨A Brüggemann Harffstr 53 ☎78181 N♨ BL/Jag/Rov/Tri
ⓘ H Dülpers Volmerstwerther Str 27 ☎391321 N♨ Ren G
ⓘ♨C Weber Himmelgeister Str 45 ☎330101 N♨ Frd G20

Eberbach am Neckar Baden-Württemberg 15,715 (☎06271) Map **12** C4
★★ **Krone-Post** Hauptstr 1 ☎2310 rm45 (A10) ⇄13 ⋒2 1 Dec–31 Oct LD B26–65 M10–18 Pn40–80 Sea
★ **Ochsen** Bahnhofstr 27 ☎2283 rm20 ⋒10 G Lift 1 Feb–20 Dec B25–70 M10–25

Ebernburg See **Kreuznach (Bad)**

Ebrach Bayern 2,410 (☎09553) Map **12** D4
★ **Klosterbräu** Marktpl 4 ☎212 rm23 (A6) ⋒15 G B23–55.20 M8–12 Pn32–38

Echterdingen See **Stuttgart**

Ehlenbogen See **Alpirsbach**

Elfershausen Bayern 2,210 (☎09704) Map **17** B1
★★★ **Gastehaus Ullrich** ☎281 rm40 (A5) ⇄22 ⋒14 G Lift B26.80–79.60 M7.80–22 Pn45.80–65 Pool

Elten Nordrhein-Westfalen 3,600 (☎02828) Map **4** D2
★★ **Kur** Lindenallee 10 ☎2091 rm19 ⇄8 ⋒2 G LD B28–60 Pn40–45 Lake

Eltville am Rhein Hessen 15,050 (☎06123) Map **11** B4
★ **Rosenhof** am Marktpl ☎3360 rm6 ⇄2 ⋒2 B25–59
At **Erbach im Rheingau** (2km SW)
★★★★ **Schloss Reinhartshausen** Hauptstr 35 ☎4081 rm42 (A) ⇄26 ⋒6 Lift 15 Mar–15 Nov

Emden Niedersachsen 53,920 (☎04921) Map **4** D4
★ **Deutsches Haus** Neuer Markt 7 ☎22048 rm27 ⇄4 ⋒5 G B26–45
★ **Goldener Adler** Neutorstr 5 ☎24055 rm22 ⇄5 ⋒10 G B28–70 Pn55–65

Germany

&N Westermann Auricherstr 227 ☎42051
N♨ Frd G20

Emmendingen Baden-Württemberg
24,914 (☎07641) Map **11** B2
★★Park (n rest) Markgrafenstr 9 ☎8639
rm23 ⇔2 ∭2 G B19–47.50 ♨

Emmerich Nordrhein-Westfalen 29,011
(☎02822) Map **4** D2
★★Zimmermann Bahnhofstr 30 ☎70617
rm24 ⇔3 ∭12 G B31–76 M7.50–26 Pn32–70

Ems (Bad) Rheinland-Pfalz 18,009
(☎02603) Map **5** A1
★★★Balzer Villenprom 1 ☎2915 rm80 (A25)
⇔42 ∭20 G Lift 1 Apr–15 Oct B25–60
M10–14 Pn40–50 Pool
★★★Kurhaus Römerstr 3 ☎731 rm110 ⇔45
Lift B40–123 M7.20–20
★★Russischer Hof Römerstr 23 ☎4462
rm25 ⇔12 Lift Feb–Nov B33–80 M10–20
Pn46–64

Ennepetal Nordrhein-Westfalen 38,104
(☎02333) Map **4** D2
★★Burgmann ☎71517 rm12 ∭8 G
15 Jan–15 Dec B30–66 Pn55 Sea

Erbach im Rheingau See **Eltville**

Erlangen Bayern 100,020 (☎09131)
Map **12** D4
★★★★Transmar Kongress Beethovenstr 3
☎87091 tx629750 rm138 ⇔138 G Lift LD
B69–129 M5–25 Pool
★★★Grille Bunsenstrasse 35 ☎6136 rm66
⇔25 ∭37 G Lift B40.50–112 M20
★★Luise (n rest) Pfälzer Str 15 ☎32835 rm68
⇔41 ∭7 G Lift B27–80 Pool
&N24 Lehner G-Scharowsky Str 11
☎33058 N♨65206 M/c BL/Jag/Rov/Tri G50
At **Dechsendorf** (5km NW)
★Rasthaus Am Heusteg Heustteg 13
☎41225 rm18 ∭3 G B18–44 M6–20

Eschweiler Nordrhein-Westfalen 50,000
(☎02403) Map **4** D1
★Park Parkstr 16 ☎6188 rm18 ⇔4 ∭6
B28–58 M7–20

Essen Nordrhein-Westfalen 685,024
(☎0201) Map **4** D2
★★Touring (n rest) Frankenstr 379 ☎45054
rm53 ⇔24 ∭2 G
&Fischer Altenessener Str 289 ☎352041 N♨
Frd
At **Essen-Rüttenscheid**
★★★Arosa Rüttenscheider Str 149 ☎795451
tx857354 rm68 ⇔32 ∭34 Lift B76–197 M20

Ettlingen Baden-Württemberg 36,015
(☎07243) Map **11** B3
★★★Erbprinz Rheinstr 1 ☎12071 tx0782848
rm49 ⇔45 ∭4 G Lift B74–180 Màlc
★Rebstock Leopoldstr 13 ☎2281 rm14 G
&N24 Walz & Zimmermann Schleinkoferstr 2
☎16708 BL/Jag/Rov/Tri G

Fallingbostel Niedersachsen 11,019
(☎05162) Map **5** B3
★★Berlin Dueshornerstr 7 ☎532 rm10 ⇔10
G 25 Dec–15 Dec B32–74 M6–18 Pn43–50.50
F Kallbach Michelsenstr 9 ☎578 N♨ Chy/Cit/Vau

Feldafing Bayern 4,110 (☎08157) Map **12** D2
★★★Kaiserin Elizabeth Tutzinger Str 2
☎1213 tx526408 rm70 (A25) ⇔35 G Lift
B26–120 M16–20 Pn58–102 ♨ Lake

Feldberg im Schwarzwald Baden-
Württemberg 1,814 (☎07655) Map **11** B2
★★Albquelle ☎213 rm19 B25–58 M6–14
Pn40–42

Flensburg Schleswig-Holstein 93,110
(☎0461) Map **1** A1

★★Europa Rathausstr 1 ☎17522 rm70 ⇔20
B20–65 M9–18
★★Flensburger Hof Süderhofenden 38
☎17320 rm28 ∭23 G Lift B50–85
&N H & M Patersen Gutenbergstr 11
☎17851 N♨ BL/Cit/Jag/Peu/Rov/Tri G25
At **Kupfermühle** (9km N)
★★An der Grenze Europastr 3 ☎4098 rm45
⇔45 G Lift ♨ Pool Lake

Forbach Baden-Württemberg 3,610
(☎07228) Map **11** B3
★★Friedrichshof Landstr 1 ☎2333 rm24
⇔1 ∭7 G 1 Dec–30 Sep

Frankfurt am Main Hessen 642,819
(☎0611) Map **5** A1
★★★★★Intercontinental W-Leuschner Str 43
☎230561 tx413639 rm814 ⇔814 G Lift
B89–198 Pool
★★★★Frankfurter Hof Kaiserpl (off
Bethmannstr) ☎20251 tx411806 fraho d
rm400 ⇔400 G Lift B99–170 M22–30
★★★★Hessischer Hof F-Ebert-Anlage 40
☎740251 tx0411776 rm108 (A28) ⇔100 G
Lift B46–140 M25
★★★★Park Wiesenhüttenpl 28 ☎230571
tx0412808 rm270 ⇔242 ∭16 G Lift B60–155
M25
★★★★Savigny Savignystr 14 ☎740481
tx412061 rm92 ⇔45 ∭37 B65–128
☆☆☆EuroCrest Isenburger Schneise 40
☎678051 tx416717 rm312 ⇔186 ∭126 Lift
B84–125 M16–40
★★★Monopol Metropole Mannheimer Str 11
☎230191 rm93 ⇔63 ∭3 G Lift B41–96 M12
Pn111 Pool
★★★National Baseler Str 50 ☎234841
tx0412570 rm95 ⇔45 ∭40 G Lift B52–132
M18–20
&Deutsche Renault Hanauer Landstr 344
☎417021 N♨ Ren
&B Kneifel Praunheimer Landstr 21 ☎785079
N♨ BL/Jag/Rov/Tri
&N24 G Von Opel Mainzer Landstr 330
☎75031 N♨ GM/Opl
&N K H Steiger Fritzlarer Str 18 ☎703041 N♨
Chy/Sim

Freiburg im Breisgau Baden-
Württemberg 180,005 (☎0761) Map **11** B2
★★★★Colombi Rottecking 16 ☎31415
tx772750 rm84 ⇔58 ∭15 G Lift
★★★Rappen Münsterpl 13 ☎277231 rm17
⇔6 ∭7 Lift Mar–Jan
★★★Victoria Eisenbahn Str 54 ☎33211
rm52 ⇔14 ∭13 G Lift B44–110 M14–24
★★Falken Rathausgasse 32 ☎36984 rm15
⇔8 24 Aug–26 Jul B34.80–91.60 M13–30
Pn52–62
★★Park Post (n rest) Eisenbahn Str 35
☎36077 rm60 ∭8 G Lift 15 Jan–15 Dec
★Schlossbergblick (n rest) Ludwigstr 36
☎36927 rm48 (A) ⇔15 ∭10 G Lift
6 Jan–20 Dec
★★Schotzky (n rest) Werderring 8 ☎33171
rm45 ⇔6 ∭2 10 Jan–20 Dec B28–70
★★Zum Roten Bären Oberlinden 12
am Schwabentor ☎36969 rm24 ⇔7 ∭5 G
B25–72 M12–20
&N24 F Speck Habsburger Str 99 ☎31131
BL/Jag/Rov/Tri G3

Freising Bayern 32,010 (☎08161)
Map **13** A3
★★Bayerischer Hof Untere Hauptstr 3
☎3125 rm70 ⇔19 ∭18 G Lift B25.80–59.60
M8–15

Freudenstadt Baden-Württemberg 19,515
(☎07441) Map **11** B3
★★★Rappen Strassburger Str 16 ☎3503
rm96 (A35) ⇔52 ∭1 G Lift

Germany

★★★**Waldeck** Strassburger Str 60 ☎2441
rm68 ⇌33 ▥15 G Lift LD B33–107 M18
Pn49–75
★★★**Waldlust** Lauterbadstr 92 ☎2051
tx764268 rm100 ⇌60 G Lift 15 Dec–1 Nov
⅏ ∩
★★**Dreikönig** M-Luther Str 3 ☎3333 rm23
⇌7 ▥1 G
★★**Krone** Marktpl 29 ☎2007 rm30 ▥3 G
★★**Post** Stuttgarter Str 5 ☎2421 rm55 (A)
⇌25 ▥15 G Lift
★★**Stokinger** ☎2187 rm45 (A35) ⇌9 ▥9 G
15 Dec–31 Oct B28–114 M16–36 Pn44–75
Pool
★★**Württemberger Hof** Lauterbadstr 10
☎2075 tx764388 rm22 ⇌2 ▥11 G Lift
B37–97 M8+12 Pn55–76 ⅏ Pool
★**Park** Lauterbadstr 103 ☎2318 rm26 ▥5 G ⅏
★**Zum See** Forststr 17 ☎2688 rm10 (A4) G
B25–56 M8–20 Pn30–34
▯⍾▸**24 Hornberger & Schilling** Stuttgarter
Str 45 ☎2429 Opl
▯⍾▸**Oberndorfer & Knauf** Murgtalstr 35
☎2278 N⅏ Frd

Friedberg Hessen 24,924 (☎06031)
Map **5** A1
▯⍾▸**G Von Opel** Frankfurter Str 9 ☎5548 N⅏
Opl

Friedrichshafen Baden-Württemberg
53,011 (☎07541) Map **12** C2
★★**Buchhorner Hof** Friedrichstr 33 ☎21011
rm56 ⇌14 ▥2 G B24–78 Pn53–76
▯⍾▸**Frank** Meistershofenerstr 9 ☎21617 N⅏
M/c Frd

Fulda Hessen 60,019 (☎0661) Map **5** B1
★★★**Lenz** Leipziger Str 122 ☎77067 tx49733
rm60 (A7) ⇌7 ▥42 B27–101 M12–29
Pn47–68
▯⍾▸**F Bohl** Weichselstr 48 ☎78088 M/c Dat
G10
▯**W Fahr** Langebrücke-Andreasberg 4 ☎79078
Opl
▯⍾▸**Friedrich & Maier** Dr Raabe Str 1 ☎6036
N⅏ BL/Jag/Rov/Tri

Fürstenfeldbrück Bayern 26,811
(☎08141) Map **12** D3
★**Post** Hauptstr 7 ☎9701 rm42 (A9) ⇌25
▥5 G Lift B30–70 M6–18
⍾▸**Rössig** Augsburger Str 5 ☎12219 N⅏ Peu
G5

Füssen Bayern 11,505 (☎08362) Map **12** D2
▯⍾▸**G Gerhager** Oberleitnerstr 14 ☎7562 N⅏

Garmisch-Partenkirchen Bayern
27,525 (☎08821) Map **12** D2
★★★**Wittelsbach** Von Brug Str 24 ☎53096
rm60 ⇌45 ▥15 G Lift 20 Dec–15 Oct
B46–98 M15–22 Pn57–82 Pool
★★**Drei Mohren** Mohrenpl 7 ☎2030 rm59
⇌23 G 15 Dec–31 Oct
★★**Flora** Hauptstr 85 ☎4393 rm40 ⇌15 ▥1
G Lift 20 Dec–30 Oct B33–78 M11–30
Pn41–54
★★**Garmischer Hof** (n rest) Bahnhofstr 51
☎51091 rm40 ⇌10 ▥7 Lift B26–82
★★**Partenkirchner-Hof** Bahnhofstr 15
☎58025 rm75 (A21) ⇌75 G Lift
15 Dec–15 Nov B46–112 M16–19 Pn65–95
Pool
▯**Maier** Burgstr 12a ☎3776 N⅏ Peu
M Paulus Zugspitzstr 30 ☎54041 N⅏
Simson Hauptstr 18 ☎53977 N⅏ Ren

Gelsenkirchen Nordrhein-Westfalen
328,014 (☎0209) Map **4** D2
★★★★**Maritim** Am Stadtgarten 1 ☎15951
tx0824636 rm250 ⇌250 G Lift B71–141 Pool
★★**Post** Bahnhofsvorpl 1 ☎21645 rm60 ⇌12
▥18 Lift B28–69 Pn35–45

▯⍾▸**E Heilmann** T-Otto Str 150, Hauptstr 50
Buer ☎54066 N⅏ Opl G10

Gernsbach Baden-Württemberg 14,808
(☎07224) Map **11** B3
★**Ratsstuben** Hauptstr 34 ☎2141 rm12
▥12 15 Nov–15 Oct B19–42 M8–16 Pn28–30

Giessen Hessen 78,607 (☎0641) Map **5** A1
★★**Kuebel** Bahnhofstr 47 ☎77070 rm53 ⇌11
▥29 B44–90 M15àlc
☆**An Der Lahn** Lahnstr 21 ☎73516 rm14 ▥4
G B24–67 M6–9
▯⍾▸**24 Mohr** Grunberger Str 85 ☎35051
AR/Peu G20

Godesberg (Bad) Nordrhein-Westfalen
72,000 (☎02229) Map **4** D1
★★★**Dreesen** Rheinaustr 1 ☎364001
tx0885417 rm84 ⇌46 ▥20 G Lift B37–122
Màlc
★★★**Godesburg** ☎363008 tx885503 rm14
⇌1 ▥13 B70–165 M16–22
★★★**Insel** Theaterpl 5 ☎364082 tx885592
rm70 ⇌30 ▥35 Lift B38–90 M8–19
★★★**Park** Kaiserstr 1 ☎363081 tx885463
rm57 ⇌25 ▥11 G Lift
★★**Eden** Kaiserstr 5a ☎356034 tx885440
rm38 ⇌28 Lift
★★**Rheinland** Rheinallee 17 ☎366071 rm32
(A12) ⇌7 ▥6 G LD B26.50–95 M10–18
Pn70–120 St11%
★**Sonnenhang** Mainzer Str 275 ☎346820
rm11 ⇌1 ▥5 G B21–58 M5–11 Pn31–44
▯⍾▸**A Köhler** Koblenzerstr 123 ☎352167 N⅏
M/c Hon G5

Göppingen Baden-Württemberg 55,004
(☎07161) Map **12** C3
★★**Hohenstaufen** Obere Freihofstr 64
☎73484 rm52 (A10) ⇌6 ▥22 G B21.50–79.50
M9.50–37
★**Apostel** (n rest) Marktstr 7 ☎73462 rm28
▥10 G 7 Jan–23 Dec B24–58

Goslar Niedersachsen 52,014 (☎05321)
Map **5** B2
★★★**Achtermann** Rosenortstr 20 ☎21001
tx0953847 rm92 ⇌34 ▥58 G Lift
★★**Haus Riechenberg** am Grauhof-Brunnen
☎81081 rm30 (A 10) ▥21 G Lift B25–78 M12
Pn48–75

Göttingen Niedersachsen 122,511
(☎0551) Map **5** B2
★★★**Gebhards** Goethe Allee 22 ☎56133
rm61 ⇌15 ▥24 Lift Pool
★★**Bojana** Jüdenstr 3 ☎46046 rm59 ⇌3 ▥6 G
★★**Kronprinz** (n rest) Groner Tor Str 3 ☎44028
rm56 ⇌4 ▥4 G B27–77
★★**Sonne** Paulinerstr 10 ☎56738 rm74 (A18)
⇌45 ▥20 G Lift 5 Jan–20 Dec B30–75 M8–16
Pn50–62
⍾▸**24 G Müller** Burgstr 6 ☎57587 N⅏ M/c
⍾▸**E Münstermann** Weender Landstr 29
☎54058 N⅏ Fia G120
▸▸**24 W Richter** Benzstr 4 ☎73037
N☎77777 M/c Cit/Peu/Ren G30
▯▸▸**24 Rothe** Am Lutteranger 8 ☎34304 N⅏
BL/Rov/Tri G20

Gräfelfing Bayern 13,520 (☎089)
Map **12** D2
At **Lochham** (1km NE)
★★**Würmtaler** Rottenbucher Str 55
☎851281 rm40 (A) ▥10 G

Grafenau Bayern 5,011 (☎08552)
Map **3** B3
At **Schlag** (1km S)
★★**Sonnenberg** ☎203337 rm25 ⇌12 ▥4 G
May–Oct 12 Dec–Feb Pool

Grainau Bayern 3,209 (☎08821) Map **12** D2
★★★**Badersee** ☎8686 rm41 ⇌20 ▥6 G Lift
Dec–31 Oct Lake

Germany

★★Post Postgasse 10 ☎8853 rm35 ⇆8 🅟9 G
19 Dec—23 Oct B30—98 M15 Pn50—65

Grimlinghausen See
Neuss-Grimlinghausen

Grossenbrode Schleswig-Holstein 2,000
(☎04367) Map **1** B1
★★Baltic (E4) ☎371 rm80 ⇆8 🅟65 G Lift Pool
Beach Sea

Gross-Gerau Hessen 13,000 (☎06152)
Map **11** B4
★Adler Frankfurter Str 11 ☎2286 rm83 ⇆5
🅟12 G ✿

Günzburg Bayern 13,511 (☎08221)
Map **12** C3
★★Hirsch Marktpl 18 ☎5610 rm21 (A10)
⇆1 🅟12 G

Hagen Nordrhein-Westfalen 243,324
(☎02331) Map **5** A2
★★Deutsches Haus Bahnhofstr 35 ☎21051
tx0823640 rm41 ⇆4 🅟31 G Lift B39—104
M16—24

Hagnau Baden-Württemberg 1,321
(☎07532) Map **12** C2
★Messmer (n rest) Meersburger Str 12
☎6227 rm14 ⇆5 🅟3 B28—80 Lake

Haltingen Baden-Württemberg 5,300
(☎07621) Map **11** B2
★Rebstock Grosse Gasse 30 ☎62257 rm14
(A4) 🅟5 G B20—55 M8—20
🅑**L Luhr** Basler Str 65 ☎62195 N☙ AR G10

Hamburg Hamburg 1,800,007 (☎040)
Map **4** B4

AA agents; see page 154

★★★★★Vier Jahreszeiten Neuer
Jungfernstieg 9—14 ☎34941 tx0211629 rm200
⇆200 G Lift B124.50—244 Màlc Lake
★★★★Atlantic An der Alster 72 ☎248001
tx2163297 rm320 ⇆320 G Lift B119—218
M19 Pool Lake
★★★Berlin Borgfelder Str 1 ☎257221
tx0213939 rm96 ⇆96 G Lift B83.50—136
M25àlc Pn115.50
★★★Central-Smolka Isestr 98 ☎475057
tx215275 rm40 ⇆20 🅟16 G Lift B54.50—120
Màlc
☆☆☆**EuroCrest** Mexikoring 1 ☎6305051
tx2174155 rm125 ⇆67 🅟58 G Lift
★★★Europäischer-Hof Kirchenallee 45
☎248171 tx2162493 rm300 ⇆120 🅟180 G
B92—140 M13.50 Pn80—90 ✿
★★★Parkhochhaus Drehbahn 15 ☎341656
ta Hochpark tx0212475 rm107 ⇆50 🅟57 G
Lift B74—117 M14 Pn76—133
★★★Reichshof Kirchenallee 34 (off
Steindamm) ☎248191 tx02163396 rm400
⇆150 🅟200 G Lift B55—140 M17—20
★★Schümann (n rest) Langenhorner-Chaussee
157 ☎520825 rm22 ⇆16 🅟6 G B44—69
☆**Hamburg** (n rest) Hoheluftchaussee 119
☎473067 tx211645 rm37 ⇆12 G B41.50—93
★Pacific Neuer Pferdemarkt 30 ☎4395051
rm59 ⇆4 🅟8 Lift
🅑**A Dannmeyer** Grosslohering 66 ☎6724569
N☙ BL/Rov/Tri
🅑➤**24 Hertzel** Eppendorfer Landstr 51
☎4603061 N☙540211 Peu
🅑**International** Stresemannallee 54 ☎563579
N☙
🅑☙**Motor-Company** Ruhrstr 63 ☎855011
N☙ Frd
🅑**L Nemeth** Koppel 65 ☎244840 N☙
BL/Jag/Peu/Rov/RR/Tri
☙🅟**P Nitzschke** Steinbecker Hauptstr 84
☎7128459 N☙ BL/Rov/Tri G3

☙🅟**Touren & Sportwagen** Goldbekpl 3
☎271121 N☙ AR/BL/Jag/Rov/Tri
🅑☙🅟**Vidal** Angerstr 22 ☎257901 N☙ Jag/Ren/
Rov

Hameln Niedersachsen 66,704 (☎05151)
Map **5** B3
🅑☙🅟**F Krüger** Hastenbecker Weg 29 ☎12821
BL/Jag/Rov/Tri
K Reissdorf Wallbaumstr 6, Berliner pl ☎3764
N☙ M/c Chy/Vlo G

Hanau am Main Hessen 90,022
(☎06181) Map **12** C4
🅑☙🅟**Schäfer** E-Kaiserstr 5 ☎24621 N☙ Opl
G150

Hannover Niedersachsen 575,030
(☎0511) Map **5** B3
☆☆☆**EuroCrest** Tiergartenstr 117 ☎523092
tx922748 rm110 ⇆110 G Lift B78—93 M17—40
★★★Europäischer Hof Luisenstr 4 ☎17644
ta Rummelshotel rm56 ⇆17 🅟8 Lift
★★★Kastens Luisen Hof Luisenstr 1 ☎16151
ta Kasteniüs tx0922325 rm220 (A35) ⇆120
🅟26 G Lift B49—168 M17 Pn83—133
☆☆☆**Park Kronsberg** opp Hannover-Messe
☎861086 tx923448 rm105 ⇆31 🅟62 G Lift
B37—100 M11—25 Pn62—100
★★Central Kaiserhof E-August pl 4
☎327811 tx922810 rm55 ⇆25 🅟30 G Lift
B53—105 M12—26 Pn70—86
☆☆**Treffpunkt** Hannoversche Str 109
☎61721 rm56 ⇆4 🅟8 G B30—90 M8—16
🅑☙**Diesterstrasse** Diesterstr 33 ☎444016
N☙ Frd
🅑☙**Euro-Auto** Leisewitzstr 43 ☎851088 N☙
G7
🅑**E Gross** Davenstedter Str 101 ☎451071
N☙ BL/Jag/Rov/Tri
🅑**Heidorn** Viktoriastr 8 ☎441167 N☙ Rov
🅑**Jaguar-Automobile** Am Listholze 70
☎691150 N☙ Jag
🅑**W Rudhart** Am Klagesmarkt 3 ☎16531 N☙ Opl

Hannover Airport
☆☆☆**Holiday Inn** am Flughafen ☎730171
tx09/24030 rm150 ⇆150 Lift B84—113
M15àlc Pool

Harzburg (Bad) Niedersachsen 27,010
(☎05322) Map **5** B2
★★★Bodes Stadtpark 48 ☎2041 rm90 (A22)
⇆38 🅟40 G Lift B36—117 M15—22 Pn53—78
★★Braunschweiger Hof H-Wilhelm Str 2
☎7035 rm39 (A23) ⇆5 🅟23 G Lift
B26—72 M10—36
★Goldener Schlüssel ☎81313 rm7 🅟7 G
B30—52 M8 Pn48—50

Hattenheim Hessen 1,950 (☎06723)
Map **11** B4
★★Ress Hauptstr 25 ☎3013 ta Weinress rm26
⇆4 🅟2 G 15 Feb—15 Dec LD B23—70 M10
Pn48—56

Heide Schleswig-Holstein 23,500 (☎0481)
Map **1** A1
🅑☙**W Leinweber** Hamburger Str 115 ☎3022
Opl G20

Heidelberg Baden-Württemberg 130,025
(☎06221) Map **11** B4
★★★★★Europäischer Hof F-Ebert-Anlage 1a
☎27101 ta Europahotel tx461840 rm125
⇆115 G Lift B49—200 M23.50—30
★★★Alt Heidelberg (n rest) Rohrbacher Str 29
☎25575 rm30 ⇆20 🅟8 Lift B36—90
☆☆☆**EuroCrest** Pleikartsförster Str ☎71021
tx461650 rm68 ⇆39 🅟29 G
★★Bayrischer Hof Bismarckpl ☎24646 rm46
⇆11 🅟9 Lift 10 Jan—22 Dec B28—74
★★Neckar (n rest) Bismarckstr 19 ☎23260
rm35 ⇆9 🅟14 Lift 2 Jan—24 Dec B36—90

Germany

★★Schwarzes Schiff Neuenheimer Landstr 5
☎46071 rm44 ⇨10 ▥21 G Lift B35–70
M10–15 Pn55–70

★★Stiftsmühle In der Neckarhalle 129
☎80555 tx0461848 rm35 (A5) ⇨16 Lift
B23–84 Màlc Pn52–72

★Kohler (n rest) Goethestr 2 ☎24360 rm43
⇨4 ▥19 Lift 8 Jan–16 Dec B24–68

★Vier Jahreszeiten Haspelgasse 2 ☎24164
rm25 (A3) ⇨9 ▥3 15 Jan–20 Dec
B33.50–92

i➤24 Center H-Lanz Str 6 ☎28683 M/c Hon/
Sab G25

Bosch-Dienst K-Benz Str 2 ☎22171 N✿ M/c
(Lucas Agent)

☖Leyland Am Taubenfeld 39 ☎81091 N✿ BL/
Jag/Rov/Tri G

i☖J Pfotzer Speyerer Str 11 ☎27191 N✿ Opl

➤24 Raichle & Baur Hebelstr 12 ☎24954
N☎71155 BL/Peu/Rov/Tri

Heilbronn Baden-Württemberg 117,015
(☎07131) Map **12** C3

★★★Insel F-Ebert-Brücke ☎88931 tx728777
rm120 ⇨100 ▥10 G Lift LD B38–108 M16
Pn78–88

★★Kronprinz Bahnhofstr 29 ☎83941
tx728561 rm35 ⇨4 ▥12 G Lift LD
B34.50–80 M9–17

☖➤24 Autohaus Fend Karlstr 49 ☎81081 N✿
BL/Jag/Rov/Tri G10

Hellern See Osnabrück

Helmstedt Niedersachsen 29,017
(☎05351) Map **6** C3

★★Petzold Schöninger Str 1 ☎6001 rm28 ⇨4
▥9 G B22–62 M9–18

☖☖Wagner Grosser Stern 3 ☎3607 N✿ Aud/
VW G10

Heppenheim an der Bergstrasse
Hessen 24,041 (☎06252) Map **11** B4

★Goldenen Engel Grosser Markt 2 ☎2563
rm36 (A12) ⇨3 ▥13 B24–70 M5.50–16.50

Herford Nordrhein-Westfalen 70,011
(☎05221) Map **5** A3

★Twachtman Bügelstr 4 ☎2283 rm45 G Lift

☖☖Holzapfel-Auto Johannisstr 2 ☎3318 N✿
Cit G5

Herrenalb (Bad) Baden-Württemberg
4,720 (☎07083) Map **11** B3

★★★★Mönchs Post Dobler Str ☎2002
tx07245123 rm50 ⇨30 ▥15 G Lift B44–110
M18–22 Pn73–98 Pool Golf

Herrenberg Baden-Württemberg 24,010
(☎07032) Map **12** C3

★Neue Post Wilhelmstr 48 ☎5156 rm7 ▥2
10 Jan–23 Dec B23.50–59 M5–14

Hersbruck Bayern 9,014 (☎09151)
Map **12** D4

★Schwarzer Adler M-Luther Str 26 ☎2231
rm30 G 10 Jul–20 Jun

Hersfeld (Bad) Hessen 30,025 (☎06621)
Map **5** B1

★★Parkhotel Rose am Kurpark 9 ☎4454
ta Rosehotel rm25 ⇨10 ▥11 G Lift
15 Jan–20 Dec B30–85 M10–26 Pn58–108

☖☖Friedrich M-Becker Str 3 ☎72001 N✿
Aud/VW G50

Hilchenbach Nordrhein-Westfalen 16,029
(☎02733) Map **5** A1

★★Deutscher Hof Dammstr 10 ☎4339 rm25
⇨5 ▥5 G B28–70 M7–18 Pn42–50

Hildesheim Niedersachsen 107,405
(☎05121) Map **5** B3

★★★★Rose Markt 7 ☎1955 tx927126 rm50
⇨28 ▥9 Lift B43.50–85 M13.50–25

R Krumrey Siemensstr 20 ☎57041 N✿ Cit/Peu G

☖☖Schwalenberg Senkingstr 11 ☎53434/
52163 N✿ G

☖Touren & Sportwagen Hildebrandtstr 27
☎56148 N✿ BL/Jag/Rov/Tri G50

Hilpoltstein Bayern 9,515 (☎09174)
Map **12** D3

★Post Marktstr 8 ☎207 rm15 ⇨15 G

☖➤24 Auto-Sebesic Heidecker Str 40 ☎500
Aud/VW G20

Hindelang Bayern, 5,056 (☎08324)

★★Luitpoldbad A-Gross Weg ☎325 rm110
⇨80 ▥14 G Lift 1 Jan–5 Nov B25–106
M14–18 Pn55–97 ✎ Pool

Hinterzarten Baden-Württemberg 2,220
(☎07652) Map **11** B2

★★★★Adler ☎711 tx07-72692 rm71 (A6)
⇨54 ▥8 G Lift B62.50–215 M18–30 Pn97–142
✎ Pool ○

★★Weisses Rössle Freiburger Str 38 ☎1411
rm72 (A28) ⇨33 ▥9 G Lift B34–175 M12–48
Pn64–115 ✎ Pool

★Linde Rathausstr 2 ☎315 rm22 ⇨4 ▥4 G
20 Dec–10 Nov

Hockenheim Baden-Württemberg 17,017
(☎06205) Map **11** B4

★★Luxhof An der Speyerer Brücke ☎32333
rm45 (A25) ⇨29 ▥2 G B27–90 M10–16 Pool
Lake

Höchenschwand Baden-Württemberg
2,014 (☎St-Blasien 07672) Map **11** B2

★★★Kurhaus ☎354 tx7721212 rm54 ⇨22
▥22 G Lift LD B36–102 M18 Pn60–80 ✎ Pool

Hof Bayern 56,029 (☎09281) Map **6** C1

★★Strauss Bismarckstr 31 ☎2066 rm63 (A)
⇨6 ▥5 G Lift

☖➤24 Autoveri C-Benz Str 4 ☎9067 M/c Frd

Hoheleye See Langewiese

Hohenschwangau Bayern 2,900
(☎08362) Map **12** D2

★★Haus Müller Alpseestr 14 ☎9256 rm30
(A) ⇨10 ▥1 G

★★Lisl Und Jagerhaus Neuschwansteinstr 1
☎9106 rm44 (A16) ⇨23 ▥5 G 15 Dec–30 Oct
B32–130 M10 Pn55–86

Holzminden Niedersachsen 24,008
(☎05531) Map **5** B2

☖☖Kujath Allersheimerstr 34 ☎2030 N✿ Opl

Homburg vor der Höhe (Bad) Hessen
53,030 (☎06172) Map **5** A1

★★★★Ritter's Park prom 69 ☎20044
tx415143 rm150 ⇨120 Lift

☖☖Recht Heuchelheimerstr 8 ☎31555 N✿ G4

Honnef am Rhein (Bad) Nordrhein-
Westfalen 23,500 (☎02224) Map **4** D1
At **Windhagen** (8km SE)

★★★Waldbrunnen ☎(02645)3111 tx8579443
rm16 ⇨16 G B50–110 M11–23 ✎ ○ Pool

Hornberg Baden-Württemberg 5,021
(☎07833) Map **11** B2

★★★Bären Hauptstr 85 ☎504 rm45 ⇨21 ▥9
G Lift

Horstmar Nordrhein-Westfalen 6,411
(☎02558) Map **4** D2

★Crins ☎7370 rm9 G B23–46 M6.50–9.50
Pn24

Husum Schleswig-Holstein 25,021
(☎04841) Map **1** A1

★★★Park Thordsen Erichsensweg 23 ☎61061
tx28526 rm66 ⇨30 ▥30 G Lift ✎

☖➤24 Auto Poggenburgstr 3 ☎2046
N☎3183 Aud/Por/VW G15

Idar-Oberstein Rheinland-Pfalz 40,032
(☎06781) Map **11** B4

24 **Barth & Frey** Tiefensteinerstr 153 ☎31015 Opl
H P Steuer Nahbollenbacher Str 90 ☎(06784)565 N M/c AR/Hon

Ingolstadt Bayern 90,005 (☎0841) Map **12** D3
★★***Rappensberger*** Harderstr 3 ☎2307 rm93 (A48) 23 38 G Lift
★**Adler** (n rest) Theresienstr 22 ☎2707 rm50 4 14 6 Jan–23 Dec B22–33
★**Auwaldsee** ☎68484 rm12 1 1 G Mar–Nov B20–50 M7.50 Lake
Bacher Goethestr 56 ☎56061 (closed weekends) Frd G5
24 ***E Willner*** Goethestr 61 ☎56005 Opl
At **Gaimersheim** (☎08458) on B13 7km W
★★**Heidehof** Ingolstaedter Str 121 ☎711 rm18 2 16 G Lift B52–91 M13–18àlc Pool

Iserlohn Nordrhein-Westfalen 100,050 (☎02371) Map **5** A2
★★**Deutsches Haus** Bahnhofstr 2 ☎23722 rm31 6 21 B27.50–75 M10–30
★★**Korth** In der Calle 6 ☎40410 rm24 (A9) 4 1 G B28–84 Pool
24 **Sportcar Centre** Baarstr 119 ☎40878 AR/BL/Jag/Rov/Tri G10

Isny Baden-Württemberg 12,541 (☎07562) Map **12** C2
★★**Hirsch** Bergtorstr 2 ☎543 rm16 (A9) 1 1 G Dec–Oct B26–59 M5–15 Pn34–45
★★**Hohe-Linde** Lindauer Str 75 ☎2401 rm30 5 14 G B29.50–75 M10–20 Pn42–52 Pool
Gruber Maierhofer Str 6 ☎2357 N Frd

Jülich Nordrhein-Westfalen 32,290 (☎02461) Map **4** D1
★★**Kratz** Kölnstr 5 ☎2408 tx5170 rm23 5 4 G B30–80 M9–20
Schüsseler Römerstr 9 ☎2539 N BL/Jag/Rov/Tri G20

Kaiserslautern Rheinland-Pfalz 103,015 (☎0631) Map **11** B4
★★★***President*** Mühlstr 14 ☎73061 tx045708 rm60 60 G Lift
24 ***Hübner*** Mainzer Str 83 ☎42058 N Opl G15
Schicht Kaiserstr 74 ☎58233 N BL/BMW/Rov/Tri G10

Karlsruhe Baden-Württemberg 285,021 (☎0721) Map **11** B3
★★★**Berliner Hof** (n rest) Douglasstr 7 ☎22242 rm41 2 26 Lift B30–69
★★★**Kaiserhof** Marktpl ☎26615 rm40 14 21 Lift B40–111 M8–21
★★★**Parkhotel** Ettlinger Str 23 ☎60461 tx07825443 rm126 126 Lift B82–125
★★★**Schloss** Bahnhofpl 2 ☎31805 tx7826746 rm100 30 10 Lift B38–118 M10–20 Pn68–168
★★**Am Markt** (n rest) Kaiserstr 76 ☎27777 rm32 4 6 Lift B35–79
★★**Eden** Bahnhofstr 19 ☎28718 rm58 (A3) 14 22 G Lift B43.50–140 M12.50
★★**Hasen** Gerwigstr 47 ☎695070 rm37 34 G Lift B34.50–78 M8–20
★**Kübler** (n rest) Bismarckstr 39 ☎26849 rm67 3 36 G Lift B33–78
Badenia Liststr 18 ☎590070 N Peu/Sim G10
24 **Böhler** Ottostr 6 ☎404051 Vlo G
Olm Kussmaulstr 15 ☎751099 N BL/Jag/Rov/Tri G60
F Opel H-Billing Str 8 ☎27931 N Opl
Zentral Blumenstr 4 ☎27141 N Chy/Sim
At **Durlach** (6km E)
★★★**Maison Suisse** Hildebrandstr 24 ☎406049 rm15 5 6 G 17 Jan–23 Dec B25–65 M15–21

Kassel Hessen 206,009 (☎0561) Map **5** B2
★★★★***Wilhelmshöhe*** Schlosspark 2 ☎30061 ta Schlosshotel tx992261 rm65 46 8 G Lift
★★★**Park-Hotel-Hessenland** Obere Königsstr 2 ☎14974 ta Parkhotel tx099773 rm149 40 50 G Lift B28–115 M12–18 Pn53–93
★★★**Reis** W-Hilpert Str 24 ☎16203 tx099740 rm101 78 G Lift B36.50–103 Màlc
24 ***F Lindemann*** Leipziger Str 35 ☎54056 AR/BL/Peu
F Richter Schillerstr 46 ☎16464 N Frd

Kehl Baden-Württemberg 30,011 (☎07851) Map **11** B3
R Geiger Strassburge Str 11 ☎5046 N Aud/Por/VW
Zipperer Königsberger Str 10 ☎8077 N

Kelheim Bayern 12,617 (☎09441) Map **13** A3
★★**Ehrnthaller** Donaustr 22 ☎3333 rm71 29 13 G Lift B25–74 M7.50–16.50 Pn39–44

Kettwig Nordrhein-Westfalen 18,000 (☎02144) Map **4** D2
★★★★***Hugenpoet*** A-Thyssen Str 51 ☎6054 rm23 18 1 G Lift

Kiel Schleswig-Holstein 265,033 (☎0431) Map **1** B1
★★★***Conti-Hansa*** Schlossgarten 7 ☎40901 tx0292813 rm59 49 10 G Lift
★★***Flensburger Hof*** Grosser Kuhberg 9 ☎91114 rm78 15 14 G Lift
Herold Zum Brook 1 ☎74066 N Cit/Fia/Lnc

Kirchheim Hessen 4,015 (☎06625) Map **5** B1
☆☆☆**Center** ☎631 ta Moki tx4-93337 rm140 108 32 G B47–85 M9–18 Pool

Kirchheim unter Teck Baden-Württemberg 32,540 (☎07021) Map **12** C3
★★**Park Henzler** Eichendorffstr 99 ☎54900 rm80 10 20 Lift B47–88 M8.50–12
K Ramsperger Hindenburgstr 45 ☎54026 Aud/Por/VW

Kissingen (Bad) Bayern 22,528 (☎0971) Map **5** B1
★★★**Bristol** Bismarckstr 8 ☎4031 rm90 45 35 G Lift Mar–Nov B41–132 M16–20 Pn53–85 Pool
★★**Fuerst Bismark** Bismarckstr 90 ☎3119 rm40 (A2) 2 26 G Lift 20 Jan–20 Dec B35–95 M9–15 Pn53–56 Pool
K H Fürsch Kapellenstr 35 ☎61413 N BL/Toy

Kleve Nordrhein-Westfalen 45,719 (☎02821) Map **4** D3
★★***Parkhotel Robbers*** Tiergartenstr 45 ☎23406 rm18 (A3) 3 4 G 1 Jan–23 Dec Pool
★***König von Preussen*** (n rest) Bahnhofstr 1 ☎24449 rm18
24 ***W Könen*** Kalkarerstr 11 ☎22081 Opl G10

Klosterreichenbach Baden-Württemberg (☎07442) Map **11** B3
★★**Sonne-Post** ☎2277 rm30 12 7 G 20 Dec–1 Dec B32.50–96 M11–27 Pn46–60

Kniebis Baden-Württemberg (☎07442) Map **11** B3
★★★**Lamm** ☎2077 rm72 (A42) 36 10 G Lift LD B23–108 M17–25 Pn45–77 Pool

Koblenz (Coblence) Rheinland-Pfalz 119,023 (☎0261) Map **5** A1
★★★***Diehls*** Ehrenbreitstein ☎72010 rm63 (A) 25 20 G Lift
★★★**Kleiner Riesen** Rheinanlagen 18 ☎32077 rm22 10 G B30–93

Germany

★★**Hohenstaufen** E-Schüller Str 41 ☎35051 rm68 ⇌6 🅿7 G Lift

★**Scholz** Moselweisser Str 121 ☎42488 rm28 ♨10 15 Jan–15 Dec B29.50–66 M8–18 Pn42–46

&⊘ **G Schilling** Andernacher Str 232 ☎85003 N♨ M/c Ren G50

🗋 **P Wirtz** Bonner Andernacher Str ☎83028 N♨ Bed/Opl G50

At **Stolzenfels** (8km S)

★**Cron** Rhenser Str 3 ☎37736 rm34 ⇌2 G 1 Apr–10 Oct

Kochel am See Bayern 3,515 (☎08851) Map **12** D2

★★★**Schmied von Kochel** Schlehdorfer Str 6 ☎216 rm34 ⇌12 ♨12 G Lift Lake

Köln (Cologne) Nordrhein-Westfalen 985,050 (☎0221) Map **4** D1 **See Plan**

★★★★★**Excelsior-Ernst** Dompl ☎2701 Plan **1** tx8882645 rm146 ⇌146 G Lift

★★★**Augustinerplatz** (n rest) Hohe Str 30 ☎236717 Plan **3** tx8882923 rm58 ⇌58 G Lift B40–135

★★★**Dom** Domkloster 2a ☎233751 Plan **5** tx8882919 rm150 ⇌120 G Lift B79–220.50 M18–32

★★★**Lyskirchen** Filzengraben 28 ☎234242 Plan **6** rm64 ⇌13 ♨36 G Lift B50–118 M10–24 Pool

★★★**Rheingold** (n rest) Engelbertstr 33 Plan **8** ☎248031 tx8882923 rm60 ⇌10 ♨40 G Lift

★★**Adria** (n rest) Hohe Pforte 19 ☎236033 Plan **9** rm70 ⇌15 ♨4 G Lift

★★**Berlin** Domstr 10 ☎123051 Plan **10** tx8885123 rm90 ⇌44 ♨44 G Lift 4 Jan–15 Dec B33.50–86.50 Pn52–58

★★**Continental** Brüsseler Str 40 ☎212926 Plan **12** rm445 ⇌25 G Lift 5 Jan–20 Dec B38–110

🗋&⊘ **F J Kempen** Marktstr 37 ☎374981 N♨ BL/Jag/Rov/Tri G40

🗋&⊘ **Kierdorf** Universitäts 91 ☎448061 N♨ Frd

Kirschbaum Aachener Str 90 ☎514342 N♨ G10

🗋 **B P Raderthal** Brülerstr 274 ☎381062 G3

At **Köln Braunsfeld**

★★★★**Regent** Melatengürtel 15 ☎54991 Plan **2** tx8881824 rm160 ⇌15 ♨119 G Lift

At **Köln Lindenthal**

☆☆☆**EuroCrest** Dürener Str 287 ☎435966 Plan **4** tx8882516 rm153 ⇌77 ♨76 G Lift B75–108 Màlc

★★**Bremer** Dürener Str 225 ☎445033 Plan **11** tx8882063 rm70 (A15) ⇌70 G Lift B59–95 M25 Pool

At **Köln Mülheim**

★★★**Kaiser** Genovevastr 10 ☎623057 Plan **7** tx8873546 rm80 ⇌80 G Lift B40–130

Königssee See **Berchtesgaden**

Königsfeld im Schwarzwald Baden-Württemberg 5,721 (☎07725) Map **11** B2

★★★**Schwarzwald** H-Voland Str 10 ☎7091 rm55 ⇌14 ♨28 G Lift B42.50–73 M12.50–24 Pn58–79 Pool

Königstein im Taunus Hessen 16,211 (☎06174) Map **5** A1

★★★**Sonnenhof** Falkensteiner Str 7 ☎5033 tx041036 rm47 (A25) ⇌34 ♨5 G B50–120 M14–35 Pn78.50–111 Pool

★★**Parkhotel Berder** Frankfurter Str 1 ☎7105 rm40 ⇌6 ♨10 G B31–97 M8–50 Pn40–65

Königswinter Nordrhein-Westfalen 36,434 (☎02223) Map **5** A1

★★★**Düsseldorfer Hof** Rheinallee 14 ☎22011 tx885235 rm54 ⇌20 ♨18 G Lift

★**Siebengebirge** Hauptstr 342 ☎21359 rm10

(A2) ♨2 G 1 Feb–15 Dec B26–65 M10–15 Pn39–48

Konstanz (Constance) Baden-Württemberg 71,050 (☎07531) Map **12** C2

★★★★**Steigenberger Insel** auf der Insel 1 ☎25011 tx733276 rm106 ⇌103 Lift B29–138 Pn91–121 Lake

★★**Deutsches Haus** (n rest) Marktstätte 15 ☎27065 rm42 ⇌6 ♨20 G Lift B32–98

★★**Krone** Marktstätte 6 ☎23093 rm46 ⇌10 ♨2 G Lift

🗋🏍**24 L Vendrame** Radolfzeller Str 65 ☎79098 M/c BL/Jag/Rov/Tri G10

Krefeld (Crefeld) Nordrhein-Westfalen 23,270 (☎02151) Map **4** D3

★★★**Park Krefelder Hof** Uerdinger Str 245 ☎59291 tx0853748 rm150 ⇌90 ♨60 G Lift B75–140 M19.50–27 Pool Golf

🏍**24 E Preckel** Virchowstr 139 ☎36033 Ren

i&⊘**Zimpel** Weeserweg 25 ☎771011 N♨64074 BL/Fia/Jag/Rov/Tri G20

Kreuznach (Bad) Rheinland-Pfalz 44,010 (☎0671) Map **11** B4

🗋&⊘ **Holzhäuser** Mannheimer Str 185 ☎30031 N♨ Frd

At **Ebernburg** (6km S)

★★**Schloss & Reichsgräfin von Sickingen** ☎2207 rm10 ⇌2 G

Kreuzwertheim See **Wertheim**

Kronberg/Taunus Hessen 17,513 (☎06173) Map **5** A1

★★★★**Schloss** Hainstr 25 ☎5033 tx415424 rm53 ⇌51 Lift B95–190 Golf

Kulmbach Bayern 26,050 (☎09221) Map **6** C1

★★★**Hansa Hönsch** (n rest) Weltrichstr 2 ☎7995 rm29 ⇌15 ♨11 G Lift B30–70

🗋🏍**24 A Dippold** Kronacher Str 2 ☎2017 Aud/Por/VW G

Kupfermühle See **Flensburg**

Laasphe Nordrhein-Westfalen 6,100 (☎02752) Map **5** A1

★★★**Fasanerie** Lahnstr 55 ☎333 rm33 ♨6 G ≛

Lahnstein Rheinland-Pfalz 22,014 (☎02621) Map **5** A1

★★★**Dorint Rhein-Lahn** im Kurzentrum ☎151 tx0869827 rm210 ⇌210 G Lift B68–104 M16 Pn80–84 ≛ Pool

Lahr Baden-Württemberg 40,008 (☎07821) Map **11** B3

★**Schulz** Alte Bahnhofstr 6 ☎22674 rm22 ⇌2 ♨16 G B20–54 M9.50–21

🏍**24 Link** Lotzbeckstr 2 ☎24021 Aud/Por/VW G15

Landau in der Pfalz Rheinland-Pfalz 39,516 (☎06341) Map **11** B3

★★**Körber** Reiterstr 11 ☎4050 rm40 ⇌10 ♨10 G 15 Jan–15 Dec B30–70 M15–25 Pn50–70

🗋🏍**24 R Kruppenbacher** A-Croissant Str 3 ☎5054 Frd G5

Landsberg am Lech Bayern 16,010 (☎08191) Map **12** D2

🗋🏍**24 A Popp** Münchner Str 34 ☎2288 Opl G10

Strobl Schongauer Str 15 ☎2433 N♨

Landshut Bayern 56,021 (☎0871) Map **13** A3

🗋 **K Meusel** Ottostr 15 ☎72048 N♨ Frd

Langenargen Baden-Württemberg 5,815 (☎07543) Map **12** C2

★★**Schiff** Marktpl 1 ☎2407 rm42 ⇌5 ♨19 Lift Mar–Oct B24–82 Pn40–98 Lake

Langenisarhofen Bayern (☎09938) Map **13** B3

Germany

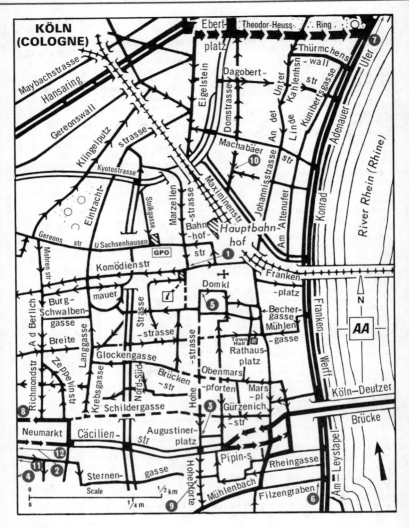

KÖLN
(COLOGNE)

Maybachstrasse
Hansaring
Gereonswall
Klingelputz
Kyotostrasse
Eintracht-
Gereons str
U Sachsenhausen
GPO
Komödien str
Burg-
Schwalben-
gasse
Breite
Langgasse
Glockengasse
Schildergasse
Neumarkt
Cäcilien-
Sternen-
gasse

Ebert
platz
Theodor-Heuss-
Ring
Thürmchens
wall
Eigelstein
Dagobert-
Domstrasse
Unter
Kahlenhsn
str
Kunibertsgasse
An der
Linde
Machabäer
Johannisstrasse
str
Maximinenstr
Marzellen
-strasse
Stolkgasse
Bahn-
hof-
Hauptbahn-
hof
Am
Altenufer
str
Franken
-platz
Domkl
Frankenwerft
Becher-
gasse
Mühlen
-gasse
Town
Hall
Rathaus-
platz
Brücken-
str
Obenmars
-pforten
Mars
-pl
Gürzenich
-str
Augustiner-
platz
Pipin-s
Rheingasse
Köln-Deutzer
Brücke
Am Leystapel
Mühlenbach
Filzengraben
Hohepforte

Richmondstr
A d Berlich
Mohren str
Zeppelinstr
Krebsgasse
Nord-Süd-
Hohe -strasse

River Rhein (Rhine)
Adenauer
Ufer
Konrad

N
AA

Scale
0   ½ km
0   ¼ m

Köln (Cologne)

1	★★★★★	Excelsior-Ernst
2	★★★★	Regent (Köln-Braunsfeld)
3	★★★	Augustinerplatz
4	☆☆☆	Crest (Köln-Lindenthal)
5	★★★	Dom
6	★★★	Lyskirchen

7	★★★	Kaiser (Köln-Mülheim)
8	★★★	Rheingold
9	★★	Adria
10	★★	Berlin
11	★★	Bremer (Köln-Lindenthal)
12	★★	Continental

Germany

★**Buhmann** ☎277 rm19 (A11) ⇥1 G
20 Jan–24 Dec LD B23.50–46 M4.50–12
Pn25.50–27.50
Langewiese Nordrhein-Westfalen 400
(☎02758) Map **5** A2
At **Hoheleye** (3km SW)
★**Hochsauerland** ☎313 tx875629 rm60
(A30) ⇥30 ▥30 G Lift LD B45.50–105
M10.50 Pn69–86 Pool
Lautenbach Baden-Württemberg 1,922
(☎07802) Map **11** B3
★**Sternen** Hauptstr 47 ☎3538 rm37 ⇥10
▥18 G Lift 1 Dec–31 Oct B28.50–81 M8–16
Pn35–42
Lengfeld See **Würzburg**
Leonberg Baden-Württemberg 35,910
(☎07152) Map **12** C3
★★★**Eiss** nr the Autobahn ☎43021
tx0724141 rm120 (A15) ⇥30 ▥20 G Lift
LD B35–85 M7.50
★★**Sonne** Stuttgarter Str 1 ☎27626 rm40
(A20) ⇥15 ▥10 G B25–75 M8–15
Lichtenfels Bayern 14,023 (☎09571)
Map **6** C1
▯✇24 Szymansky Bamberger Str 43 ☎3654
M/c BL/Cit G5
Liebenzell (Bad) Baden-Württemberg 6,210
(☎07052) Map **11** B3
★★★**Krone** Badweg 7 ☎2081 rm42 ⇥24
▥18 G Lift
★★**Kurhotel Helenbad** (n rest) ☎2091 rm39
⇥1 ▥2 G Apr–31 Oct
Lieser Rheinland-Pfalz 1,419 (☎06531)
Map **11** A4
★★**Mehn** Moselstr 2 ☎3011 rm27 ⇥11 ▥8 G
1 Feb–15 Dec B24–58 M6–20 Pn37–44
Limburg an der Lahn Hessen 29,026
(☎06431) Map **5** A1
★★**Dom** Grabenstr 7 ☎6249 rm53 ⇥10 ▥37
G Lift B29–78 M9–19 Pn59–63
★★**Zimmermann** Blumenröderstr 1 ☎42030
rm23 (A2) ⇥4 ▥6 G B27–75 M5–15
★**Huss** Bahnhofspl 3 ☎6638 tx0484839 rm38
⇥5 ▥11 G Lift B31.50–89 M8.50–17 Pn44–62
▯✇24 W Möbus Grabenstr 18 ☎22007 N▧
Opl
Lindau im Bodensee Bayern 25,542
(☎08382) Map **12** C2
★★★**Bayerischer Hof** Seeprom ☎5055
tx054340 rm87 ⇥69 ▥3 G Lift Etr–Oct
B41–179 M19.50–24 Pn77–125.50 Pool Lake
★★★**Reutemann** Seeprom ☎5055 tx054340
rm40 ⇥27 ▥4 G Lift B38–126 M18.50–22.50
Pn71–101 Pool Lake
★★**Kellner** (n rest) Alwindstr 7 ☎5686 rm12
⇥3 ▥3 G Etr–Oct B20–32
★★**Seegarten** Seeprom ☎5055 tx054340
rm39 ⇥4 ▥11 G Lift Mar–Oct B27–98
M15.50 Pn56–84 Pool Lake
★**Lindauer Hof** Seehafen (harbour) ☎4064
rm35 ⇥35 Lift Lake
Lindenfels Hessen 4,609 (☎06255)
Map **12** C4
★★**Hessisches Haus** Kurgarten ☎2405 rm30
⇥1 ▥12 G Lift 1 Apr–30 Sep B26–68 M7–16
Pn36–48 Pool
Lindenthal See **Köln (Cologne)**
Lingen Niedersachsen 46,307 (☎0591)
Map **4** D3
★**Nave** Marienstr 29 ☎4188 rm28 ⇥4 ▥4 G
Lippstadt Nordrhein-Westfalen 67,050
(☎02941) Map **5** A2
★★★**Koppelmann** Lange Str 30 ☎3045 rm38
⇥10 ▥6 G Lift
▯✇H Jathe Erwitter Str 119 ☎12485 M/c
BL/Sab G20

▯H W Lenzke Rixbecker Str 44 ☎4646 N▧
Lochham See **Gräfelfing**
Lörrach Baden-Württemberg 45,020
(☎07621) Map **11** B2
★★★**Binoth am Markt** Baslerstr 169 ☎2673
rm40 ⇥8 ▥10 G Lift B22–68
▯✇**Büche & Tröndle** Tumringer Str 290
☎8502 N▧ Aud/Por/VW
Lübeck Schleswig-Holstein 234,033
(☎0451) Map **5** B4
★★★**Lysia** Holstentorpl 7 ☎71077 tx26707
rm72 ⇥17 ▥55 G Lift B59–122 M16.50–18
Pn89–105
★★**Mühlenteich** (n rest) Mühlenbrücke 6
☎77171 rm11 ▥5 Lift B26–59 Lake
★**Kaiserhof** Kronsforder Allee 13 ☎791011
rm45 ⇥8 ▥26 Lift B36–92 M6–12.50
★**Lindenhof** Lindenstr 1a ☎84015 rm40 ⇥5
▥2 G B29–75 M8–20
▯✇**Jäckel** Travemünder Allee 15 ☎33088 N▧
Ren
✇**Laismann & Kühl** Geniner Str 66 ☎54031
N▧ Rov G3
At **Ratekau** (10km N) (☎04504)
☆**Waldklause** (on E4) ☎1603 rm18 (A1)
▥11 G
Ludwigsburg Baden-Württemberg 80,022
(☎07141) Map **12** C3
At **Monrepos (Schloss)** (5km NW)
★★★★**Monrepos** ☎30101 tx7264720 rm83
⇥40 ▥43 G Lift B75–135 Màlc
Ludwigshafen am Rhein Rheinland-Pfalz
182,050 (☎0621) Map **11** B4
★★★★**Europa** Ludwigspl 6 ☎519011
tx04–64701 rm90 ⇥90 G Lift
Mainz Rheinland-Pfalz 190,009 (☎06131)
Map **11** B4
★★★**Central** Bahnhofspl 8 ☎674001
tx04/187794 rm72 ⇥33 ▥18 Lift
★★★**Europa** Kaiserstr 7 ☎63095
tx04187702 rm55 ⇥22 Lift
★★★**Mainzer Hof** Kaiserstr 98 ☎28471
tx04187787 rm75 ⇥40 ▥35 G Lift B72–105
M15 Pn72–87
i Reichert Saarstr 1 ☎24578 Opl
Mallersdorf Bayern 5,031 (☎08772)
Map **13** A3
★**Ohne Sorge** (n rest) Hofmark 5 ☎272 rm8
⇥1 B15–36
Manderscheid Rheinland-Pfalz 1,310
(☎06572) Map **11** A4
★★**Zens** Kurfürsten Str 35 ☎769 rm46 ⇥11
▥12 G Lift 20 Dec–5 Nov LD B30–90 M14–18
Pn48–68 Pool
Mannheim Baden-Württemberg 320,048
(☎0621) Map **11** B4
★★★★**Mannheimer Hof** A-Anlage 4 ☎45021
tx462245 rm200 ⇥144 ▥3 Lift B46–140
M17–22 Pn88–119
★★★**Augusta** A-Anlage 45 ☎408001
tx0462395 rm110 (A41) ⇥34 ▥54 G Lift
B37–104 M16–20 Pn60–70
★★★**Park** (n rest) Friedrichspl 2 ☎23841
rm56 ⇥20 ▥36 Lift
★★**Bundesbahn** Hauptbahnhof ☎22926 rm45
⇥6 ▥35 Lift B34.50–67 M8 Pn44.50–58.50
★★**Mack** (n rest) Mozartstr 14 ☎23888
tx0462116 rm75 (A9) ⇥14 ▥17 G Lift
10 Jan–16 Dec B33–72
▯✇24 K R Bayer Neckarauerstr 99 ☎852297
N▧409602 Ska/Vau G2
✇**Kannenberg** Fahrlachstr 90 ☎408021 N▧
GM G10
▯✇**H Kohlhoff** Obere Riedstr 117 ☎735083
N▧ Frd
▯✇**Schwind** ☎22614 N▧ Ren

Germany

👁24 H Sebastian Sekenheim Autobahn Tankstelle ☎475122 M/c G100

At **Sandhofen** (10km N)
☆**Weber** ☎771222 rm29 ⇄4 ⋔10 G Lift B24–62

Marburg an der Lahn Hessen 70,040 (☎06421) Map **5** A1
★★★**Ortenberg** G-Voigt Str 21 ☎61049 rm43 (A10) ⇄12 ⋔12 G LD B27–86 M12–22 Pn38–50
★★**Europäischer Hof** (n rest) Elisabethstr 12 ☎60006 rm66 ⇄11 ⋔40 G Lift B29.50–99
🛢♨**Autodienst H Gnau** Neue Kasseler Str 11 ☎61017 N♨ Ren

At **Cölbe** (7km N)
★★**Orthwein** Kasselerstr 48 an der B3 ☎82594 rm26 ⋔23 G B19–42 M5.50–13

Maria Laach Rheinland-Pfalz (☎02652) Map **4** D1
★★**See** ☎251 rm76 ⇄7 ⋔16 G Lift B21–85 Pn45–74 Pool Lake

Marienberg (Bad) Rheinland-Pfalz 5,313 (☎02661) Map **5** A1
★★★**Kneipp-Kurhotel Wildpark** ☎269 rm40 ⇄20 ⋔20 Lift 20 Dec–20 Nov B32–95 M10–30 Pn51–72 Pool

Marktheidenfeld Bayern 9,111 (☎09391) Map **12** C4
★**Anker** Obertorstr 6 ☎3420 rm30 ⇄15 G Lift B22–65 M10
★**Schöne Aussicht** Brückenstr 8 ☎455 rm30 ⇄1 ⋔20 G Lift

Marktoberdorf Bayern 14,330 (☎08342) Map **12** D2
★**Sepp** Bahnhofstr 13 ☎2414 rm42 (A8) ⇄30 ⋔12 G B25–60 M9–12 Pn34–38
🛢👁24 **P Schmid** Hauptstr 33 ☎2837 BL G

Mayen Rheinland-Pfalz 21,406 (☎02651) Map **4** D1
🛢♨**Kiesselbach & Sürth** Markt 32 ☎2086 Opl G5

Meersburg Baden-Württemberg 5,013 (☎07532) Map **12** C2
★★★**Weisshaar** St-Lochner Str 24 ☎9006 rm22 ⇄18 ⋔4 G 1 Dec–31 Oct Lake
★★**Brandners 3 Stuben** Winzergasse 1 ☎6019 rm13 (A9) ⇄2 ⋔11 G 15 Feb–20 Dec B40–80 M15 Pn45–66
★★**Weinstube-Löwen** Marktpl 2 ☎6013 rm16 ⋔16 Feb–15 Dec B31.50–68 M12.50–15
★**Zum Bären** Marktpl 11 ☎6044 rm14 ⋔2 G 1 Mar–15 Nov B22–50 M10–16

Memmingen Bayern 36,014 (☎08331) Map **12** C2
★★★**Adler** Maximilianstr 3 ☎87015 rm45 ⇄13 ⋔12 G Lift B34.50–71 M10–35 Pn40–60
🛢**Draxler** Birkenweg 1 ☎4717 N♨ BL/Jag/Rov/Tri G3
🛢**C Schenk** Donaustr 29 ☎86048 Opl

Mergentheim (Bad) Baden-Württemberg 20,220 (☎07931) Map **12** C4
★★★★**Victoria** Poststr 2 ☎7036 tx074224 rm100 ⇄75 ⋔7 G Lift B35–105 M13–18 Pn55–75 Pool

Merklingen Baden-Württemberg 1,402 (☎07337) Map **12** C3
★**Ochsen** Hauptstr 12 ☎483 rm13 ⋔12 G

Meschede Nordrhein-Westfalen 33,030 (☎0291) Map **5** A2
★★★**Hennesse** ☎7102 rm50 ⇄50 G

Mindelheim Bayern 11,243 (☎08261) Map **12** D2
★★**Post** Maximilianstr 39 ☎203 rm60 ⇄6 ⋔10 G Lift 10 Jan–20 Dec

🛢E Schragl Landsberger Str 20 ☎1468 N♨ Aud/VW

Minden Nordrhein-Westfalen 84,011 (☎0571) Map **5** A3
★★**Silke** (n rest) Fischerglacis 21 ☎23736 rm26 (A8) ⇄20 G B35–80 Pool

Mittenwald Bayern 8,323 (☎08823) Map **12** D2
★★**Post** Obermarkt 9 ☎1094 rm78 ⇄24 ⋔16 G B25–95 M9.50–25 Pn45–80 ♨
★**Jagdhaus Drachenburg** Elmauerweg 20 ☎1249 rm14 ⇄3 ⋔6 18 Dec–25 Apr 15 May–20 Oct B23–62 M17–21 Pn38–49
★**Zerhoch** (n rest) H-Barth Weg 7 ☎1508 rm19 ⇄12 ⋔3 G 15 Dec–3 Nov B29–85
🛢👁24 **Biller** Partenkirchner Str 62 ☎1497 BL/BMW/Rov/Tri G30

Mogendorf Rheinland-Pfalz 1,111 (☎02623) Map **5** A1
★**Eiser** Hauptstr 11 ☎2410 rm10 ⇄10 G

Möhringen See **Stuttgart**

Monchengladbach Nordrhein-Westfalen 265,050 (☎02161) Map **4** D2
★★★★**Dorint Park** Hohenzollernstr 5 ☎23054 tx0852656 rm102 ⇄69 ⋔33 Lift B60–96 M16 Pn32 ♨ Pool
☆☆☆**Holiday Inn** am Geroplatz ☎31131 tx852363 rm128 ⇄128 Lift B74–98 M15àlc Pn95–107 ♨ Pool
★★**Coenen** Giesenkirchener Str 41 ☎(02166) 40171 rm50 ⇄50 G B56–94 M10–18.75
🛢♨**Issels** Rheydter Str 225 ☎13045 N♨ Ren
W Kremer Laden Str 20 N♨ BL/Lnc/Rov G15
🛢♨**J Massier** Künkelstr 125 ☎22116 N♨ BL/Rov/Tri G25
🛢👁24 **E Menke** Erkelenzer Str 8 ☎8991 Fia/Vau G5
H Orth Erzberger Str 173 ☎44141 N♨ Frd

Monrepos (Schloss) See **Ludwigsburg**

Monschau Nordrhein-Westfalen 11,813 (☎02472) Map **4** D1
★★**Horchem** Kurstr 14 ☎490 rm14 ⇄7 ⋔4 G 15 Mar–20 Feb LD B25–61 M12–18 Pn36–40
★**Herrlichkeit** (n rest) Haagweg 3a ☎3190 rm7 ⋔6 G B22–48

Montabaur Rheinland-Pfalz 11,010 (☎02602) Map **5** A1
★★★**Montabaur** ☎5005 rm39 (A6) ⇄3 ⋔19 B27–145 M15–25 Pn56
☆☆**Heiligenroth** (n rest) 4,5km NE on autobahn ☎5045 rm28 ⋔28 Lift B38–58.80
★**Post** Bahnhofstr 30 ☎3361 rm34 ⇄2 ⋔9 G Lift 12 Jan–21 Dec B21–52 M5–15
★**Schlemmer** Kirchstr 18 ☎5022 rm30 ⇄8 ⋔8 G 10 Jan–16 Dec B23–60 Pn35–45
Montabaur Alleestr 8, Unterwesterwald ☎4058 N♨ Frd G15

Mülheim an der Mosel Rheinland-Pfalz 1,002 (☎06534) Map **11** A4
★★**Moselhaus Selzer** Moselstr 7 ☎707 rm12 ⇄3 ⋔5 G 1 Mar–15 Nov B24.50–80 M7.50–20 Pn37–50

Mülheim an der Ruhr Nordrhein-Westfalen 189,010 (☎02133) Map **4** D2
★★★**Noy** Schlossstr 28 ☎44671 rm50 ⇄12 ⋔22 G Lift B46.50–148 M12–20

Müllheim Baden-Württemberg 12,515 (☎07631) Map **11** B2
☆☆☆**Euro** Bundesstr 3 ☎5522 tx772916 rm57 ⇄6 ⋔45 G B23–75 M14–16

München (Munich) Bayern 1,300,055 (☎0811) Map **13** A3 See Plan
★★★★**Bayerischer Hof** Promenadepl 6 ☎228871 Plan **1** tx523406 rm400 ⇄359 ⋔41 G Lift B57–194 M23–24 Pn111–176 Pool

Germany

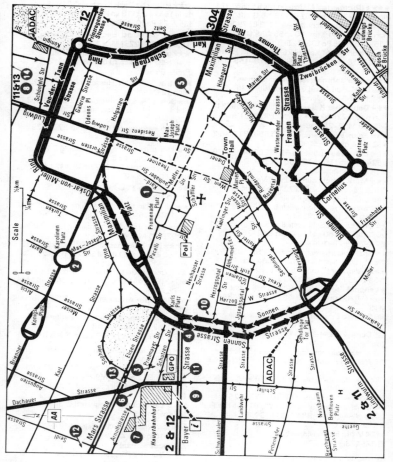

München (Munich)

1	★★★★Bayerischer Hof	8	☆☆☆EuroCrest
2	★★★★Continental	9	★★★Mark
3	★★★★Excelsior	10	★★Daniel
4	★★★★Königshof	11	★★Drei Löwen
5	★★★★Vier Jahreszeiten	12	★★Edelweiss
6	★★★Deutscher Kaiser	13	★★Feldhütter
7	★★★Eden-Wolff	14	★Leopold

Germany

★★★★ **Continental** M-Joseph Str 5 ☎557971
Plan **2** tx522603 rm151 ⇦119 🛏6 G Lift
★★★★ **Excelsior** Schützenstr 11 ☎557906
Plan **3** tx0522419 rm110 ⇦55 🛏55 G Lift
B65–135 Màlc Pn105–125
★★★★ **Königshof** Karlspl 26 ☎558412 Plan **4**
tx0523616 rm120 ⇦120 G Lift B70–155 Màlc
Pn110–135
★★★★ **Vier Jahreszeiten** Maximillianstr 17
☎228821 Plan **5** tx523859 rm365 ⇦365 G
Lift B100.50–271 Màlc
★★★ **Deutscher Kaiser** Arnulfstr 2 ☎558321
Plan **6** tx0522650 rm180 ⇦90 🛏20 G Lift
B42–98 M22–25 Pn85–93
★★★ **Eden-Wolff** Arnulfstr 4 ☎558281 Plan **7**
tx523564 rm214 ⇦130 G Lift
☆☆☆ **EuroCrest** Effinerstr 99 ☎982541 Plan **8**
tx524757 rm155 ⇦70 🛏85 G Lift B70–93
M15–30 Pn100–105
★★★ **Mark** Senefelderstr 12 (off Vaverstr)
☎592801 Plan **9** tx0522721 rm105 ⇦42
🛏45 G Lift B36–82 M14& àlc Pn64–76
★★ **Daniel** (n rest) Sonnenstr 5 ☎554945
Plan **10** rm81 ⇦35 🛏28 Lift B33–54
★★ **Drei Löwen** Schillerstr 8 ☎595521 Plan **11**
tx052367 rm160 ⇦110 G Lift B42–96
M16–20 Pn78–104
★★ **Edelweiss** (n rest) Menzinger str 103
☎8111001 Plan **12** rm28 ⇦9 🛏12 G B35–78
★★ **Feldhütter** Elisenstr 5 (off Luisenstr)
☎594126 Plan **13** tx523113 rm58 ⇦8 🛏4 Lift
★ **Leopold** Leopoldstr 119 ☎367061 Plan **14**
tx05215160 rm83 ⇦23 🛏33 G Lift B37–83
M13
🛢🔊 **Behnke** Brenner Str 54 ☎521729 N🔧
Peu/Tri
🛢🔊 **Corsa** Zielstattstr 63 ☎786087 N🔧
Lot/Peu
🛢🔊 **H Hanauer** Hiblestr 20 ☎183051 N🔧 Ren
🛢🔊 **Helbig** Friedenstr 30 ☎400277 N🔧08106
N🔧 BMW/Toy
🛢 **Konig** Eggenfeldener Str 100 ☎934022 N🔧
AR/Jag/Rov/RR
🔊 **Lotus** A Rosshaupter Str 104 ☎3592574
🛢🚗24 **München** Geyerstr 34 ☎767781 N🔧 Frd
🛢 **Oppel** Amalienstr 38 ☎281178 N🔧
AR/Chy/Jag G20
🚗24 **Wilhelm** Freisinger Landstr 11
☎325423 BL/Jag/Rov/Tri

Munich See **München**

Münster/Westfalen Nordrhein-Westfalen
260,050 (☎0251) Map **5** A2
★★★ **Kaiserhof** (n rest) Bahnhofstr 14 ☎40059
tx892141 rm100 ⇦30 🛏50 G Lift B39–140
★★★ **Schloss Wilkinghege** Steinfurter Str 374
(4km NW) ☎213045 rm37 (A17) ⇦17 🛏20
G B47–160 Pn75
★★ **Mauritzhof** Eisenbahnstr 17 ☎42366 rm26
⇦4 🛏9
★ **Conti** Berliner Pl 2a ☎40444 rm59 ⇦6 🛏41
Lift B47.50–120
🛢 **J Berghoff** Wolbecker Str 44 ☎60308 N🔧
Ren
🛢 **Ing W Brandes** Altenberger Str 32
☎(02533)521 N🔧 BL/Rov/Tri G10

Murnau Bayern 8,040 (☎08841) Map **12** D2
★★★ **Alpenhof** Ramsechstrasse 8 ☎1045 rm52
⇦52 G Lift B52–180 M18.50–32
Pn90.50–106.50 Pool

Nagold Baden-Württemberg 19,231
(☎07452) Map **11** B3
★★ **Post** Bahnhofstr 2 ☎4048 rm42 (A16)
⇦16 🛏6 G Lift B25.50–76 M10–25
Pn51.50–69.50

Nauheim (Bad) Hessen 25,049 (☎06032)
Map **5** A1

★★★ **Hilbert's Park** Kurstr 2 ☎31945
tx0415514 rm118 ⇦118 Lift B43–129
M17–25 Pn70–149

Neckargemünd Baden-Württemberg
13,015 (☎06223) Map **12** C4
★★ **Zum Ritter** Neckarstr 40 ☎7035
tx461837 rm30 ⇦30 G B38–72 M12–24
Pn55–65

Neckarsteinach Hessen 4,212 (☎06229)
Map **12** C4
★★ **Schiff** Neckargemünderstr 2 ☎324 rm38
⇦4 🛏6 Lift 15 Jan–15 Dec B28–68 M8–18
Pn35–40
★★ **Schwalbennest** Bahnhofstr 27 ☎479
rm20 🛏5 G

Neresheim Baden-Württemberg 6,707
(☎07326) Map **12** C3
★ **Klosterhospiz** ☎6282 rm45 🛏13 Lift
B18–50 Pn26–35

Neubeuern Bayern 2,511 (☎08035)
Map **13** A2
★★ **Burg** Marktpl 23 ☎2456 rm17 ⇦1 🛏15 G
Lift 1 Mar–15 Jan B40–70 M12–20 Pn45–55

Neuenahr (Bad) Rheinland-Pfalz 28,034
(☎02641) Map **4** D1
★★★★ **Kur** Kurgartenstr 1 ☎2291 tx861812
rm230 ⇦145 🛏7 Lift B45–120 M12–25
Pn79–117 Pool
★★★ **Dorint** Am Dahliengarten ☎2325
tx0861805 rm112 ⇦112 G Lift B60–96 M16
⚓ Pool
★★ **Goldener Anker** Mittelstr 18 ☎2386 rm68
⇦18 🛏40 G Lift B33–86 M14 Pn45–62.50
★★ **Hamburger Hof** (n rest) Jesuitenstr 11
☎26017 rm33 ⇦10 🛏13 G
🛢🔊 **H Eich** Heerstr 35 ☎2224 N🔧 G10

Neumünster Schleswig-Holstein 91,510
(☎04321) Map **1** B1
★★ **Wappenklause** Gasstr 12 ☎45071 rm22
⇦16 🛏1 B22.50–72 M9–24àlc
🛢🔊 **H Fröhling** Kieler Str 239 ☎32031 N🔧
Frd G10
🛢🔊 **E Landschoof** Rungerstr 5 ☎31921 N🔧
BL/Rov/Tri G5

Neuss Nordrhein-Westfalen 118,027
(☎02101) Map **4** D2
At **Neuss-Erfttal**
☆☆☆ **Novotel Düsseldorf-Neuss**
am Derikurner Hof ☎17081 tx8517634 rm120
⇦120 Lift B120–140 ⚓ Pool
At **Neuss-Grimlinghausen** (4.5km SW on B5)
★ **Minnesänger & Kaisersaal** Bonner Str 71
☎19115 rm30 (A18) 🛏30 G

Neustadt an der Aisch Bayern 10,506
(☎09161) Map **12** D4
★★ **Römerhof** R-Wagner Str 1 ☎2498 rm38
⇦1 🛏9 G 15 Jan–15 Dec B25–70 M12–20

Neustadt an der Weinstrasse
Rheinland-Pfalz 52,543 (☎06321) Map **11** B2
Naumer A-Kolping-Str 71 ☎13038 N🔧 Frd
At **Schöntal** (3km W)
★ **Königsmühle** Schöntalstr 10 ☎2487 rm24
(A4) ⇦1 🛏7 B27–72 M10–20

Neustadt Im Schwarzwald Baden-
Württemberg 11,500 (☎07651) Map **11** B4
★★★★ **Adler Post** Hauptstr 16 ☎5066 rm37
⇦25 G B37–104 M12–20 Pn50–80 Pool

Neuwied Rheinland-Pfalz 63,013 (☎02631)
Map **5** A1
P Wirtz Allensteiner Str 15 ☎5195 N🔧 Opl G30

Niefern Baden-Württemberg 9,710
(☎07233) Map **12** C3
★★ **Decker** Pforzheimer Str ☎875 rm46 ⇦13
🛏17 G

Nierstein Rheinland-Pfalz 6,613 (☎06133) Map **11** B4
★**Rhein** Mainzer Str 16 ☎5161 rm15 ⇆4 ⋔11 G 10 Jan–20 Dec B29–79 M9–30 Sea

Nonnenhorn Bayern 1,605 (☎08382) Map **12** C2
★★★**Strand** Wasserburger Str ☎8223 rm28 ⇆20 ⋔5 G Apr–Oct LD B36–140 M15–18 Pn50–82 Pool Lake

Norden Niedersachsen 24,208 (☎04931) Map **4** D4
★**Deutsches Haus** Neuer Weg 26 ☎4271 rm45 ⇆8 ⋔16 G Lift 15 Jan–Dec B27–76 M9.50–26 Pn50–62

Nordhorn Niedersachsen 50,051 (☎05921) Map **4** D3
★**Euregio** Dortmunderstr 20 ☎5077 rm26 ⋔24 G B30–67 M8–16 Pn45
i *Veddeler* Neuenhäuser Str 83 ☎4045

Nördlingen Bayern 17,511 (☎08931) Map **12** D3
★★**Sonne** Marktpl ☎5067 tx051749 rm40 ⇆10 ⋔10 G B26–80 M8.80–16 Pool Lake
⛽⚙ *Bruckschlegl* Augsburgerstr 12 ☎3352 N✦ Ren G20

Northeim Niedersachsen 34,025 (☎05551) Map **5** B2
★★**Sonne** Breite Str 59 ☎4071 rm34 ⇆6 ⋔6 G

Notschrei Baden-Württemberg (☎07602) Map **11** B2
★★**Wald** ☎219 rm40 ⇆6 ⋔12 G Lift Pool

Nürburg Rheinland-Pfalz 324 (☎02691) Map **4** D1
At **Nürburgring** (1km SW)
★★**Sport Tribune** ☎2035 tx0863919 rm50 (A21) ⇆4 ⋔23 G B18–74 M9.50–24 Pn35–51

Nürnberg (Nuremberg) Bayern 515,047 (☎0911) Map **12** D4
★★★★★**Grand** Bahnhofstr 1 ☎203621 tx0622010 rm163 ⇆122 ⋔21 G Lift B50–220 M22–25 Pn90–138
★★★★**Carlton** Eilgutstr 13 ☎203535 tx0622329 rm117 ⇆90 ⋔27 Lift B64–160 Pn129
✩✩✩**EuroCrest** Münchner Str 283 ☎49441 ta Crestotel tx622930 rm94 ⇆70 ⋔24 Lift B75–102 M15–30 Pn109
★★★**Sterntor** Tafelhofstr 8 ☎203101 tx0622632 rm120 ⇆60 G Lift B35–100 M11–18 Pn53–89
★★★*Victoria* Königstr 80 ☎203801 rm63 ⇆24 ⋔5 Lift
★★**Drei Linden** Aussere Sulzbacher Str 1 ☎533620 rm30 ⇆12 ⋔11 G B30–85 M10–25
★★**Kaiserhof** Königstr 39 ☎203686 tx0626012 rm66 ⇆16 ⋔5 G Lift B30–105 M6
i➤24 *W Kussberger* Adam Klein Str 150 ☎203333 N✦ M/c Ren G
⛽⚙ *Motus* Sandreuth Str 26 ☎42001 N✦ M/c Bd/Jag/Rov/Tri G10

Neuser Röthensteig 2 ☎37378 N✦ AR G30

Oberammergau Bayern 4,910 (☎08822) Map **12** D2
★★**Alte Post** Dorfstr 19 ☎517 rm60 ⇆16 ⋔8 G
★★**Bold** König Ludwigstr 10 ☎520 rm49 ⇆27 ⋔5 G B26–80
★★**Friedenshöhe** König Ludwig Str 31 ☎598 rm11 ⇆4 ⋔7 G 25 Dec–31 Oct B34–63 M8–18 Pn50–58
★★**Schilcherhof** Bahnhofstr 17 ☎4740 rm25 (A7) ⇆3 ⋔6 G 25 Dec–3 Nov B17–56 M10–13 Pn30–41
★**Daheim** (n rest) Theaterstr 2 ☎529 rm15 closed 20 Oct–20 Dec B23–48

Oberhausen Nordrhein-Westfalen 248,052 (☎02132) Map **4** D2

★★★**Ruhrland** Berlinerpl 2 ☎805031 tx0856900 rm60 ⇆25 ⋔25 G Lift B36–112 M13–20
⛽⚙ *Kupka* Duisburgerstr 188 ☎21824 N✦ Opl G10

Oberkirch Baden-Württemberg 17,023 (☎07802) Map **11** B3
★★**Obere Linde** Hauptstr 25 ☎3038 rm30 ⇆6 ⋔12 G Mar–Dec B28–82 M11–18 ⚓
⛽➤24 *L Müller* Appenweiererstr 11 ☎3356 Opl
At **Ödsbach** (3km S)
★★**Grüner Baum** Almstr 33 ☎2801 tx0752627 rm50 (A8) ⇆10 ⋔35 G B27–72 M10–30 Pn47–60 ⚓ Pool

Oberstaufen Bayern 6,410 (☎08386) Map **12** C2
★★**Kurhotel Hirsch** (n rest) Kalzhöfer Str 4 ☎2032 rm27 ⇆8 ⋔10 G B34–82

Oberstdorf Bayern 11,746 (☎08322) Map **12** C2
★★★*Wittelsbacher Hof* Prinzenstr 24 ☎1018 rm78 ⇆35 ⋔37 G Lift 18 Dec–10 Apr 20 May–10 Oct Pool
⛽➤ *Nebelhorn* Nebelhornstr 59 ☎4669 Fia G40

Oberwesel Rheinland-Pfalz 5,050 (☎06744) Map **11** B4
★★**Auf Schönburg** ☎8198 rm10 ⇆8 1 Mar–30 Nov B75–98 (double) M18–36
★**Goldner Pfropfenzieher** ☎207 rm19 (A2) ⇆5 ⋔3 G B19–56 M6–9 Pn36–43
⛽24 *Becker* Liebfrauenstr 46 ☎386 M/c Opl G12

Ochsenfurt Bayern 11,400 (☎09331) Map **12** C4
★**Bären** Haupt Str 74 ☎2282 rm30 ⇆2 ⋔14 G 15 Jan–10 Dec B17–65 M10–18

Ödsbach See **Oberkirch**

Oestrich Hessen 9,210 (☎06723) Map **11** B4
★★★**Schwan** Rheinallee 5 ☎3001 tx42146 rm60 (A25) ⇆30 ⋔26 G Lift 15 Feb–30 Nov B45–100 M20àlc Pn70

Oeynhausen (Bad) Nordrhein-Westfalen 45,045 (☎5731) Map **5** A3
★★**Hahnenkamp** (2·5km NE) Alte Reichsstr 4 ☎5041 tx9724836 rm25 ⇆7 ⋔13 G B26–85 M10–25 Pn52–70 Pool

Offenbach Hessen 121,017 (☎0611) Map **11** B4
★★**Graf** Schlosstr 19 ☎811702 rm28 (A2) ⇆4 ⋔11 G B40–72 M6.50–16.50 Pn61–66

Offenburg Baden-Württemberg 55,052 (☎0781) Map **11** B3
★★★**Palmengarten** Okenstr 13 ☎5031 tx752849 rm76 ⇆28 ⋔16 G Lift B30–120 Pn65–85
★★**Park Waldhorn** (n rest) F-Volk Str 11 ☎24517 rm34 ⇆6 ⋔8 G
★**Sonne** Hauptstr 94 ☎71039 rm39 (A14) ⇆6 ⋔11 G B32.50–79 M5.50–18
Fandrich Auto C-Benz Str 6 ☎5200 N✦ BL/Jag/Rov/Tri
⛽⚙ *A Linck* Freiburger Str 26 ☎5005 N✦ Opl
At **Ortenberg** (4km SE)
★**Glattfelder** ☎6219 rm17 ⋔6 G B16–42

Olpe Nordrhein-Westfalen 23,032 (☎02761) Map **4** A1
★★**Tillmann** Kölner Str 15 ☎5252 rm17 ⇆2 ⋔8 G B28.75–76.50 M8–24 Pn39.50–43

Oppenheim Rheinland-Pfalz 6,025 (☎06133) Map **11** B4
★★**Kurpfalz** Wormserstr 2 ☎2291 rm19 ⇆12 ⋔7 G 10 Jan–20 Dec B22–69 M8–30

Ortenberg See **Offenburg**

Osnabrück Niedersachsen 159,513 (☎0541) Map **5** A3

181

Germany

***Hohenzollern** H-Heine Str 17 (nr main
rly sta) ☎27292 ta Hozo Osnabrück
tx094776 rm100 ⇌28 ⑰17 Lift B38–130
M15–26 Pn60–116 Pool
🍴&🚗 **H van Beers** Bahlweg 16 ☎73596 N🚗
M/c AR/Rov/Tri
🍴 **G Ciupka** Pferdstr 2 ☎572629 N🚗 BL/Tri G
🍴&🚗 **Heiter** Hansastr 33 ☎64077 Frd
🍴&🚗 **Schiermeier** Pagenstecherstr 61,
Frankenstr 25 ☎63033 N🚗 Opl
At **Hellern** (4km SW)
🍴&🚗24 **W Düing** Lengericher Landstr 2
☎42381 N🚗 Chy G8

Ottobeuren Bayern 7,015 (☎08332)
Map **12** C/D2
★★Hirsch Marktpl 12 ☎552 tx54504 rm67
⇌19 ⑩10 G Lift Pool

Paderborn Nordrhein-Westfalen 104,047
(☎05251) Map **4** A2
🍴&🚗24 **F Kleine** Bahnhofstr 36 ☎24444 N🚗
Frd
🍴&🚗 **R Sprenger** Detmolder Str 44 ☎56119
N🚗 AR/BL/Fia

Passau Bayern 50,024 (☎0851) Map **13** B3
★★Schloss Ort Dreiflusseck ☎4211 rm34
⇌8 ⑩10 G Lift 15 Jan–20 Dec
★★Weisser Hase Ludwigstr 23 ☎4066 rm94
⇌12 ⑩12 G Lift B33–95 M20–20
🍴&🚗 **O Hausmann** Theresienstr 27 ☎2998
N🚗 BL/Peu
🍴&🚗24 **F Hofbauer** Neuburgerstr 141 ☎6017
Opl

Pfaffenhafen Bayern (☎08441) Map **4** D1
🍴&🚗 **F X Stiglmayr** Scheyerer Str 70 ☎894
N🚗 BMW/Sim G3

Pforzheim Baden-Württemberg 110,033
(☎07231) Map **11** B3
★★★Ruf Bahnhofspl 5 ☎16011 tx783843
rm41 ⇌25 ⑩3 Lift LD B45.50–120 M16àlc
★★Schwarzwald an Schossgatter 7 ☎32818
rm26 ⇌3 ⑩7 Lift B27.50–77 M10–16
🍴 **K Bossert** Frankstr 15 ☎12413 N🚗 BL/Rov
G10
🍴&🚗 **Brenk & Linkenheil** Karlsruher Str 22
☎17033 N🚗 M/c Frd

Pirmasens Rheinland-Pfalz 60,410
(☎06331) Map **11** B3
🍴&🚗24 **W Schütz** Winzler Str 207 ☎75199 N🚗
M/c BMW/Fia G5

Prien am Chiemsee Bayern 7,213
(☎08051) Map **13** A2
★★Bayerischer Hof Bernauer Str 3 ☎1095
rm50 ⇌40 ⑩3 G Lift B30.50–80 Pn44–55

Prüm Rheinland-Pfalz 5,621 (☎06551)
Map **4** D1
★Gebauer Hahnpl 6 ☎2346 rm9 G B7.50–15
M7–16
🍴&🚗 **Schönhofen** Tiergartenstr 90 ☎2523

Puttgarden Schleswig-Holstein 510
(☎04371) Map **1** B1
★Dänia am Fährbahnhof ☎3016 tx29814
rm66 ⑩66 Lift Mar–Oct B45–85 Sea

Quickborn Schleswig-Holstein 11,014
(☎04106) Map **5** B4
★Jagdhaus Waldfrieden Bundesstr ☎3771
rm11 ⇌1 ⑩10 B32.50–79 M15–35 Pn60

Rastatt Baden-Württemberg 41,031
(☎07222) Map **11** B3
★★Blume Kaiserstr 38 ☎3222 rm35 (A16)
⇌5 ⑩9 G Lift BD M26.50–81 M7.50–18
★★Schwert Herrenstr 3a ☎32740 rm22 ⇌4
⑩11 G B22–60 M9–19 Pn42–54
★Katzenberger's Adler Josefstr 7 ☎32103
rm7 ⑩1 G 1 Nov–30 Sep

Ratekau See Lübeck

Ratingen Nordrhein-Westfalen 87,000
(☎02102) Map **4** D2
★★★Krummenweg ☎17619 rm20 ⇌15 G
10 Jan–12 Dec Pool

Ravensburg Baden-Württemberg 43,018
(☎0751) Map **12** C3
★★Europa Goethepl ☎23963 rm41 ⇌7 ⑩13
G Lift
★★Waldhorn Marienpl 15 ☎23017 rm25
⇌6 ⑩15 G B25–70 M14–28

Regensburg Bayern 133,542 (☎0941)
Map **13** A3
★★★Avia Frankenstr 1 ☎4093 tx065703
rm94 (A45) ⇌15 ⑩49 G Lift B25–85 M12.50
Pn50–90
★★Karmeliten Dachaupl 1 ☎54308
tx06/5170 rm80 ⇌12 ⑩26 Lift 7 Jan–20 Dec
B28–80 M12–16
★★Straubinger Hof A-Schmetzer Str 33
☎54462 rm68 ⇌2 ⑩35 G Lift B26–64
M8–15 Pn37–52
🍴 **N Boeckh** Wöhrdstr 31a ☎53366 N🚗 Opl
🍴&🚗 **Kellnberger** Kirchmeierstr 24 ☎25160 G10
&🚗 **O Seitz** Alte Straubinger Str 19 ☎52872
N🚗 BL/Jag/Rov/Tri G4

Reichenhall (Bad) Bayern 14,516
(☎08651) Map **13** B2
★★★Axelmannstein Salzburger Str 4 ☎4001
tx56112 rm156 (A30) ⇌134 G Lift B43–148
M21–23 Pn71–125 🏊 Pool
★★★Kurhotel Luisenbad Ludwigstr 33
☎5081 tx056131 rm86 ⇌35 ⑰17 G Lift
B45–174 M20–24 Pn72–194 Golf ◯ Pool
🍴 **Prechter** Innsbrucker Str Angerl 6 ☎2078
N🚗 Frd

Reit im Winkl Bayern 2,618 (☎08640)
Map **13** A2
★★Unterwirt ☎8811 rm65 ⇌29 G Lift Pool

Remagen Rheinland-Pfalz 14,516 (☎02642)
Map **4** D1
★Anker ☎24477 rm11 ⑩2 G LD B25–56
M10 Pool
★Central Bahnhofstr 4 ☎24636 rm22 ⑩3 G
★Fassbender Markt Str 78 ☎24572 rm21 (A7)
G B21–46 M8.60–16
★Pinger ☎22582 rm62 (A15) ⇌36 ⑩4 G Lift
B22–60 M9–14 Pn36–40

Remscheid Nordrhein-Westfalen 137,049
(☎02123) Map **4** D2
★★★Leyer Bismarckstr 45 (at main rly sta)
☎48027 rm27 ⇌1 ⑩16 G

Rendsburg Schleswig-Holstein 34,511
(☎04331) Map **1** B1
★Germania Paradepl 3 ☎22997 rm16 G
B33–66 M7–18
At **Büdelsdorf**
🍴&🚗 **J Suhr** Hollerstr 9 ☎3406 N🚗 Frd

Rengsdorf bei Neuwied Rheinland-Pfalz
2,505 (☎02634) Map **5** A1
★★Stern Hauptstr 56 ☎204 rm50 ⇌7 ⑩3
G 1 Apr–15 Oct

Reutlingen Baden-Württemberg 96,038
(☎07121) Map **12** C3
★★Ernst Leonhardspl ☎44081 tx729898
rm76 ⇌12 ⑩51 G Lift LD B35–103 M8.50–15
Pool
★★Reutlinger Hof (n rest) Kaiserstr 33
☎17075 rm45 (A12) ⇌3 ⑩18 G Lift B20–65
Pool
🍴 **Specht** Bühlweg 2 Ohmenhausen ☎54775
N🚗 BL/Cit/Rov/Tri

Rheinzabern Rheinland-Pfalz 3,400
(☎06341) Map **11** B3
★Goldenes Lamm Hauptstr 53 ☎2377 rm20
(A4) ⑩4 G 10 Jan–20 Dec B15–40 M8–15

Germany

Rheydt Nordrhein-Westfalen (☎02166)
Map **4** D2
★★*Dorint Park* H Junkers Str 2 ☎44011
tx852371 rm33 ⇆6 ⋔27 G Lift

Riedlingen Baden-Württemberg 8,814
(☎07371) Map **12** C2
★★**Brücke** Hindenburgstr 4 ☎2449 rm17
⇆17 G Dec–Oct B17–45 M6.50–18 Pn22–36
⋔⋗24 *M Schlegel* Neu Unlinger Str 20
☎500 N⋗8266 Opl

Rosenheim Bayern 38,527 (☎08031)
Map **13** A2
★★★**Goldener Hirsch** Münchner Str 40
☎12029 rm40 (A7) ⇆7 ⋔4 G Lift B29–80
Pn40–60
⋔⋗*Fink* ☎37439 N⋗ BL/Jag/Rov/Tri
⋔*E Hatje* Mayerbachstr 7 ☎6300 N⋗ Ren
G Rupp Innstr 34 ☎13970 N⋗ M/c BL
⋗⋗24 *A Schierghofer* Oberaustr 10b ☎1047
N⋗ 4773 N⋗ M/c AR G15

Rotenburg Niedersachsen 19,532
(☎04261) Map **5** B3
★*Deutsches Haus* Grosse Str 51 ☎3300
rm10 1 Aug–15 Jul B25–50 Pn40
⋔⋗*K Lengen* Harburgerstr 67 ☎809 G6

Rothenburg ob der Tauber Bayern
12,550 (☎09861) Map **12** C4
★★★★*Eisenhut* Herrngasse 3 ☎2041
tx61367 rm85 ⇆65 G Lift 1 Mar–7 Jan
★★★★**Goldener Hirsch** Untere Schmiedgasse
16 ☎2051 tx061372 rm80 (A20) ⇆50 ⋔16 G
Lift 15 Jan–15 Dec LD B32–130 M12–28
★★★**Burg** (n rest) Klostergasse 1 ☎2252
rm20 ⇆15 G Mar–Dec B27–79 Pool
★★**Markusturm** Rödergasse 1 ☎2370 rm30
⇆11 ⋔16 G B28–90
★★**Reichs-Küchenmeister** Kirchpl 8 ☎3406
rm33 ⇆9 ⋔9 G Lift B27–70 M7–20 Pn45–60
★★**Tilman Riemenschneider** Georgengasse 11
☎4606 tx61384 rm54 ⇆38 ⋔6 G Lift B27–87
M4.50–18 Pn49–76
★★**Gasthof zur Glocke** Plönlein 1 ☎3025
rm30 (A12) ⇆8 ⋔12 G Lift B23–76 M7.50–20
⋔⋗**Central** Schützenstr 11 ☎3088 N⋗
MB G15
⋔⋗24 *H Döhler* Ansbacher Str 35 ☎2084
M/c Bed/Opl G

Rottach-Egern Bayern 6,333 (☎08022)
Map **13** A2
★★★★*Bachmair* Seestr 47 ☎6444 rm220
⇆220 G Lift B103–366 M20–35 Pool Lake

Rottenburg Baden-Württemberg 30,053
(☎07472) Map **12** C3
★★*Martinshof* E-Bolzpl 5 ☎8081 rm30 ⇆4
⋔14 G Lift

Röttgen See **Bonn**

Rottweil Baden-Württemberg 24,015
(☎0741) Map **11** B2/3
★*Johanniterbad* Johannsergasse 8 ☎6083
rm28 ⇆8 ⋔10 Lift
★*Lamm* Hauptstr 45 ☎45015 rm20 ⇆1 G
⋔⋗24 *J Rieble* Nägelesgrabenstr 22 ☎7065
M/c Hon/Opl G100

Rüdesheim Hessen 7,007 (☎06722)
Map **11** B4
★★★*Deutscher Hof* Rheinstr 21 ☎3016
ta Parkhotel tx42122 rm95 (A) ⇆35 ⋔25 G Lift
★★★*Jagdschloss Niederwald* (6·5km W)
☎2367 rm46 ⇆30 ⋔13 G 15 Nov–15 Dec
B40–95 M15–18.50 Lake
★★*Darmstädter Hof* Rheinstr 29 ☎2485
rm50 ⇆3 ⋔7 G Apr–Nov B33–92 M11–30
Pn46–65
⋔*Corvers* Landstr 2 ☎2345 N⋗5157 N⋗
Ren G20

Rheingau Geisenheimerstr 59 ☎3117 N⋗
Aud/VW
⋔*Rüdesheim* Geisenheimer Str 18 ☎2542
Opl G20

Saarbrücken Saarland 230,051 (☎0681)
Map **11** A3
★★★★**Berlin** Faktoreistr ☎33030 tx04421409
rm63 ⇆42 ⋔14 G Lift B51–113 M9–54
☆☆☆*Novotel* Zinzinger Str ☎51071
tx4428836 rm100 Lift B120–140 Pool
★★**Christine** Gersweiler Str 39 ☎55081
tx4428736 rm65 ⇆33 ⋔7 G Lift closed
24–31 Dec B29–98 M15–70 Pool
★★**Wien** Gutenberg Str 29 ☎55088 rm27
⋔20 G Lift B23–56 Màlc
Dechent Mainzer Str 168 ☎815011 Bed/Opl
A Häfner Dudweiler Str 73 ☎30481 N⋗ Rov
⋔⋗*Industrie Gmbh* H-Böcking Str 16
☎64011 Frd G300
Ritz Sulzbacherstr 33 ☎36529 N⋗ BL/Jag/Rov/
Tri G
⋔*Saar-Auto* U-Sulzbachstr ☎33001 Sim

Säckingen Baden-Württemberg 14,822
(☎07761) Map **11** B2
★*Kater Hiddigeigei* Tanzenpl 1 ☎2818 rm21
(A5) ⇆5 ⋔2 G B24–67 M6–15 Pn33–43

Sand Baden-Württemberg 900 (☎07226)
Map **11** B3
★★*Plättig* ☎227 rm75 ⇆30 ⋔20 G Lift
B20–94 Pn45–73 ⇌ Pool

Sandhofen See **Mannheim**

St Georgen Baden-Württemberg 15,012
(☎07724) Map **11** B2
★★**Hirsch** Bahnhofstr 70 ☎7125 rm22 ⇆7
⋔15 G B42.50–81 Màlc Pn47–48

St Goar Rheinland-Pfalz 3,530 (☎06741)
Map **11** B4
★★**Goldenen Löwen** Heerstr 1 ☎274 rm11
⇆3 ⋔5 B27.50–75 M9–26 Pn47.50–65
★★**Hauser** Heerstr 160 ☎333 rm15 ⇆2 ⋔4
G 1 Feb–15 Dec B25–58 M8 Pn40–46
★*Schneider* Heerstr ☎289 rm17 ⋔7
Mar–Jan B28.50–87 M7.50–20 Pn42–55
⋔*Landsknecht* ☎278 Frd G30

St Goarshausen Rheinland-Pfalz 2,512
(☎06771) Map **5** A1
★★**Erholung** Nastätter Str 161 ☎684 rm95
⇆16 ⋔14 G B25.50–69 M8.50–17 Pn36–44

St Märgen Baden-Württemberg 1,613
(☎07669) Map **11** B2
★★*Hirschen* Feldberger Str 9 ☎201 rm42
⇆11 ⋔24 G

Saulgau Baden-Württemberg 15,614
(☎07581) Map **12** C2
★★**Kleber-Post** Hauptstr 100 ☎3051 rm50
⇆10 ⋔20 G B28.50–73 Màlc

Schackendorf See **Segeberg (Bad)**

Schaumburg See **Diez/Lahn**

Schlag See **Grafenau**

Schlangenbad Hessen 5,218 (☎06129)
Map **11** B4
★★**Staatliches Kurhaus** Rheingauer Str 47
☎411 rm100 ⇆48 ⋔46 G Lift B44–131
M16.50–21.50 Pn77–123

Schleswig Schleswig-Holstein 32,532
(☎04621) Map **1** A1
★★*Stadt Hamburg* Lollfuss 108 ☎7058
rm50 ⇆8 ⋔3
★★**Strandhalle** am Jachthafen ☎22021 rm28
⇆18 ⋔6 G B28–82 M9–22 Pn49–66 Lake
★★**Zum Weissen Schwan** Gottortstr 1
☎32712 rm19 (A4) ⇆2 ⋔4 G B30.50–69
M10–16 Sea
⋔*J Lorenzen* Flensburger Str 43 ☎23085
N⋗25555 Opl G50

🏠♉**A Wriedt** Flensburger Str 8 . ☎23387 N♻
Ren G8

Schluchsee Baden-Württemberg 2,109
(☎07656) Map **11** B2
★**Schiff** ☎252 rm32 ⇌4 ⋔2 1 Dec–1 Nov
B20–30 Màlc Pool

Schmiden See **Stuttgart**

Schönberg See **Seelbach**

Schönmünzach Baden-Württemberg 950
(☎07447) Map **11** B3
★★**Post** Murgtalstr 635 ☎313 rm60 ⇌26 ⋔10
Lift 10 Dec–10 Nov B26–88 M14–78
Pn24–64

Schöntal See **Neustadt an der
Weinstrasse**

Schriesheim Baden-Württemberg 11,840
(☎06203) Map **11** B4
★★**Luisenhöhe** Eichenweg ☎65617 rm28
(A10) ⇌2 ⋔20 G B26–82 M8–12

Schwabach Bayern 33,630 (☎09122)
Map **12** D4
🏠♉24 **Feser** Limbacher Str 26 ☎85035
Aud/VW G20

Schwäbisch Hall Baden-Württemberg
31,333 (☎0791) Map **12** C3
★★**Goldener Adler** Markt 11 ☎6364 rm18
⇌4 G 15 Jan–22 Dec

Schwalenberg Nordrhein-Westfalen 1,700
(☎05284) Map **4** B2
★★**Schloss Burg Schwalenberg** ☎167 rm9
⋔7 G

Schwarzenfeld Bayern 6,213 (☎09435)
Map **13** A4
★**Brauerei-Bauer** Hauptstr 30 ☎205
rm25 ⋔6 G B15–37 M5.80–11.50

Schweinfurt Bayern 57,038 (☎09721)
Map **12** C4
★★**Central** (n rest) Zehntstr 20 ☎1325 rm36
⇌20 ⋔10 G Lift B26–62

Schwelm Nordrhein-Westfalen 34,523
(☎02125) Map **4** D2
★★**Prinz von Preussen** Altmarkt 8 ☎13444
rm22 ⋔14 B23.50–70.50 M7.50–23.50

Seelbach Baden-Württemberg 4,410
(☎07823) Map **11** B3

At **Schönberg** (6km NE)
★★**Geroldseck** ☎2044 rm29 (A3) ⇌4 ⋔15 G
B29–82 M11–20 Pn46–58 Pool

Seesen Niedersachsen 25,030 (☎05381)
Map **5** B2
★★**Goldener Löwe** Jacobsonstr 20 ☎1202
tx0957316 rm30 ⇌6 ⋔10 G B20–63 M9–18
Pn40–65
Hoffmann Autobahnzubringerstr ☎1215 N♻
Frd G

Segeberg (Bad) Schleswig-Holstein
14,013 (☎04551) Map **5** B4
At **Schackendorf** (5km NW on B404)
★★**Stefanie** ☎3600 rm35 (A20) ⇌11 ⋔11 G
B19.50–50 M7–15 Pn36–45

Siegburg Nordrhein-Westfalen 37,240
(☎02241) Map **4** D1
★★**Stern** Marktpl 14 ☎60021 rm35 ⇌14 ⋔12
G Lift 15 Jan–15 Dec B26–78
★**Kaiserhof** Kaiserstr 80 ☎50071 rm48 ⇌2
G Lift B30–86 M10–18
🏠**M Bässgen** Frankfurter Str 1 ☎66001 N♻
Opl
🏠**H Gerards** Hauptstr 140 ☎65496 N♻ Cit G15
🏠♉**J Odenthal** Luisenstr 88 ☎61001 N♻

Siegen Nordrhein-Westfalen 121,550
(☎0271) Map **5** A1

★★★**Johanneshöhe** Wallhausenstr 1
☎335079 rm26 ⇌4 ⋔20 G B29.50–100
M10–20 Pn56.50–77
🏠♉24 **M Hoppmann** Eiserfelder Str 196
☎31091 N♻ Opl G20

Sigmaringen Baden-Württemberg 15,425
(☎07571) Map **12** C2
🏠♉**J Zimmermann** Joungnaur Str 2A ☎1696
N♻ Opl

Sindelfingen Baden-Württemberg 56,048
(☎07031) Map **12** C3
☆☆☆**Eurocrest** W-Haspel Str 101 ☎81088
tx7265778 rm145 ⇌57 ⋔88 Lift B82–112
M14–25 Pn105–109

Soest Nordrhein-Westfalen 43,019
(☎02921) Map **5** A2
★★**Andernach zur Börse** Thomästr 31 ☎3227
rm24 ⇌1 ⋔10 4 Jan–9 Jul 3 Aug–30 Dec B11–
22 M.12.50–20
🏠**H Siedler** Riga Ring 15 ☎73051 Frd

Solingen Nordrhein-Westfalen 180,032
(☎02122) Map **4** D2
🏠♉**Witte** Bismarckstr 41 ☎23574 N♻

Speyer Rheinland-Pfalz 45,024 (☎06232)
Map **11** B4
★**Goldener Engel** Mühlturm Str ☎76732 rm34
⇌9 ⋔15 Lift B28.90–58.90
Galant Tullastr 1 ☎33235 BL/Rov/Tri

Steinweiler Rheinland-Pfalz (☎06349)
Map **11** B3
★**Zum Schwanen** ☎8369 rm10 ⇌1 ⋔1 G
B15–39 M6–15 Pn28–31

Stolzenfels See **Koblenz**

Straubing Bayern 44,520 (☎09421)
Map **13** A3
★★**Seethaler** Theresienpl 25 ☎8022 rm30
⇌13 ⋔13 G B35–65 Màlc
★★**Wittelsbach** Stadtgraben 25 ☎5017 rm53
⇌5 ⋔10 G Lift B24–60 M7.50–12.50
🏠**J Griesbeck** Heerstr 7 ☎4001 N♻

Stuttgart Baden-Württemberg 600,055
(☎0711) Map **12** C3
★★★★**Schlossgarten** Schillerstr 23 ☎299911
tx0722936 rm125 ⇌80 ⋔37 G Lift
★★★★**Steigenberger Graf Zeppelin**
A-Klettpl 7 ☎299881 tx722418 rm280
⇌260 ⋔10 G Lift B55–150 M20 Pool
★★★**Park** Villastr 21 (off Neckarstr) ☎280161
tx0723405 rm81 ⇌40 ⋔28 G Lift B40–120
M18–25
★★★**Reichsbahn** Bahnhofpl 2 ☎299801
tx723543 rm108 ⇌45 ⋔34 Lift
★★★**Rieker** (n rest) Friedrichstr 3 ☎221311
rm63 ⇌63 G Lift B49–88
★★**Ketterer** Marienstr 3 ☎294151 tx722340
rm75 ⇌20 ⋔20 G Lift B40–97 M9–16
Pn52–72.50
🏠**AVG Verkaufs** Chemnitzer Str 7 ☎722094
BL/Jag/Peu/Rov/Tri G10
W & M Krauss Hauptstätter Str 12
☎602769 N♻ M/c (Lucas Agent) G
Paulinen Stotzstr 8 ☎854551 N♻
BL/Jag/Rov/Sim/Tri
🏠♉24 **Staiger** Nordbahnhofstr 25 ☎20801
N♻☎20802 N♻ GM G
At **Echterdingen** (11km S)
★★★**Flughafen** ☎790211 tx07245677
rm128 ⇌128 G Lift B86–126 M18
★★**Graf Zeppelin** (n rest) Stuttgarter Str 51
☎793433 rm39 ⇌39 G 15 Jan–20 Dec B30–
75 Pool
At **Möhringen** (7km S on rd 27)
🏠♉**Schwaben** Vaihinger Str 131 ☎713005
N♻ Frd
At **Schmiden** (9km NE)

Germany

&D**24 Ceslik** Kanalstr 14 ☎511560 N❸
Jag/Rov/Tri G4
At **Vaihingen** (6km SW)
&D *Schwabengarage* ☎713005 (closed
weekends) Frd

Tegernsee Bayern 4,515 (☎08022)
Map **13** A2
★★★*Eybhof* Schwaighofstr 53 ☎3141 rm25
⇘14 ▥1 G 16 Dec–31 Oct B26–85 Lake

Tettnang Baden-Württemberg 14,042
(☎07542) Map **12** C2
★★*Rad* Lindauer Str 2 ☎6001 rm45 (A)
⇘10 ▥6 G

Timmendorfer Strand
Schleswig-Holstein 10,520 (☎04503)
Map **1** B1
★★*Villa Frieda* (n rest) Höppnerweg 1 ☎2304
rm15 ⇘7 1 Apr–30 Sep B38.50–42.50 Pool

Titisee Baden-Württemberg 12,008
☎07651 Map **11** D2
★★★*Brugger* ☎8239 tx7722332 rm60
⇘26 ▥5 G Lift Pool Golf ○ Lake
★★★*Schwarzwald* Seestr 12 ☎8111
tx7722341 rm94 ⇘82 G Lift 19 Dec–5 Nov
B46–172 M19–24 Pn75–105 ◢ Pool Lake
★★*Seehof* (n rest) ☎18314 rm22 ⇘11 ▥5 G
Lift Apr–Oct B27–80 Lake
★★*Waldlust* Neustädter Str 41 ☎8256 rm42
(A22) ⇘23 ▥4 G 1 Jan–31 Oct B28–92
M12–20 Pn42–60
☆ *Rauchfang* Bärenhofweg 2 ☎8255 rm15
⇘7 ▥8 G B26–78 M6.50–14 Pool
★*Seerose* (n rest) Seestr 21 ☎8274 rm20
(A9) ⇘2 20 Dec–15 Oct B16–43

Todtmoos Baden-Württemberg 2,220
(☎07674) Map **12** B2
★★*Löwen* Hauptstr ☎105 rm37 (A) ⇘3 ▥14
G 20 Dec–2 Nov

Tölz (Bad) Bayern 13,019 (☎08041)
Map **13** A2
★★★*Jodquellenhof* Ludwigstr 13 ☎891
rm70 ⇘40 ▥4 G Lift Pool
★*Gaissacher* Umgehungsstr ☎9583 rm29
(A10) ⇘13 ▥1 G 1 Dec–30 Nov B26.50–73
M7–17 Pn40–50
★*Kolberbräu* Marktstr 29 ☎9158 rm39
(A20) ⇘20 G Lift B26–92 M16–30 Pn40–53
&D*O Fussel* Ludwigstr 31 ☎3351 G7

Traben–Trarbach Rheinland-Pfalz 7,012
(☎06541) Map **11** B4
★★*Clauss-Feist* on the Moselufer ☎6431
rm27 (A3) ⇘9 ▥3 G Lift 1 Apr–31 Oct B22–64
M9.50 Pn37–51
&D**H Zündorf** Rissbacher Str ☎9266 N❸ Aud/
VW

Traunstein Bayern 14,118 (☎0861)
Map **13** B2
★★*Parkhotel Traunsteiner Hof* Bahnhofstr 11
☎3623 rm65 ⇘10 ▥18 G Lift B30–77 M8–75
i&D**24 K Schaffler** Wasserburger Str 64 ☎3552

Travemünde Schleswig-Holstein 12,490
(☎04502) Map **5** B4
★★★*Golf* Helldahl 12 ☎4041 tx0261434
rm60 (A32) ⇘53 ▥7 Lift B40–132 Màlc
Pn68–113 Pool Sea

Tremsbüttel Schleswig-Holstein 1,210
(☎04532) Map **4** B4
★★★*Schloss* ☎6544 rm18 ⇘12 ▥1 G
B41.50–173 M17–38 ◢

Trendelburg Hessen 6,021 (☎05675)
Map **5** B2
★★*Burg* ☎312 rm21 (A5) ⇘7 ▥14 Feb–Nov
B45–85 Pn80

Triberg Baden-Württemberg 7,007
(☎07722) Map **11** B2

★★★★*Parkhotel Wehrle* ☎4081 rm60 (A24)
⇘48 ▥2 G LD B32–112 M18–36 Pn53–84
Pool

Trier Rheinland-Pfalz 101,043 (☎0651)
Map **11** A4
★★★*Dorint Porta Nigra* Porta Nigra pl
☎78161 tx72895 rm67 ⇘67 G Lift
★★*Park Bürgerverein* Viehmarktpl 14
☎43043 rm80 ▥22 G Lift
★*Dom* (n rest) Hauptmarkt 18 ☎74710 rm22
▥6 B26–66
&D*J Arweiler* Am Verteilerring ☎74577 N❸ GM
C Metzger im Siebenborn ☎87063
(closed weekends) AR/BL/Jag/Rov/Sab/Tri

Trittenheim Rheinland-Pfalz 1,504
(☎06507) Map **11** A4
★*Moselperle* Moselweinstr 67 ☎2221 rm13
⇘3 ▥3 G 10 Jan–20 Dec B20–46
M5.50–16 Pn30–37 Pool

Tübingen Baden-Württemberg 73,633
(☎07122) Map **12** C3
☆ *Stadt Tübingen* Stuttgarter Str 97 ☎31071
rm39 ▥27 G B32.50–90

Tuttlingen Baden-Württemberg 33,035
(☎07461) Map **12** C2
★*Ritter* Königstr 12 ☎8855 rm18 (A12) ▥5
G B20–56 M7.50–24

Überlingen Baden-Württemberg 17,515
(☎07551) Map **12** C2
★★*Bad* Christophstr 2 ☎63477 tx733909
rm55 (A) ⇘25 ▥5 G Lift Mar–Nov Pool Lake
★★*St Leonhard* St-Leonhard Str 83 ☎61041
ta Parkhotel rm43 ⇘8 ▥20 G Lift B34–124
M14–29 Pn51–72 ◢ Pool Lake
★★*Seegarten* Seeprom 7 ☎63498 rm28 ⇘10
▥14 G Lift 1 Feb–30 Nov LD B33.50–123
M12–18 Pn51–79 Lake

Uffenheim Bayern 5,116 (☎09842)
Map **12** C4
★*Traube* am Marktpl 3 ☎8288 rm16 (A10)
⇘1 ▥2 G Jan–Nov LD B15–32 M5–10.50

Ulm Baden-Württemberg 98,314 (☎0731)
Map **12** C3
★★*Bundesbahn* Bahnhofspl ☎65151 ta
Bubaho tx0712871 rm118 ⇘100 G Lift B25–
105 M8
★★*Goldenes Rad* (n rest) Neuer Str 65
☎62422 rm22 ⇘3 ▥10 Lift B28–80
★★*Neutor-Hospiz* Neuer Graben 23 ☎61191
tx712401 rm93 ⇘27 ▥49 G Lift LD
B36–97 M16
★*Garni am Münster* (n rest) Münsterpl 14
☎64162 rm30 ⇘5 ▥10
★*Roter Löwen* Ulmer Gasse 8 ☎64355 rm27
⇘2 ▥15 G Lift B32–67
★*Schlossbräustüble* Hintere Rebengasse 2
☎63839 rm20 G 1 Jun–31 Dec
&D**24 Schwaben** Marchtaler Str 23 ☎61121
N❸65549 N❸ M/c Frd/Hon

Ürzig/Mosel Rheinland-Pfalz 1,400
(☎06532) Map **11** A4
★*Moselschild* Hauptstr 12–14 ☎2106
tx04721542 rm17 ⇘4 ▥15 Feb–15 Jan G
B36–92 M12–30 Pn50–65
★*Rotschwänzchen* ☎2183 rm10 ⇘7 ▥3 G
B28–60 M10–20 Pn36–42

Vaihingen See **Stuttgart**

Vaihingen an der Enz Baden-
Württemberg 22,027 (☎07042) Map **12** C3
★*Post* (n rest) Franckstr 23 ☎4071 rm29 ⇘2
▥11 G Lift 12 Jan–20 Dec B24.50–61

Villingen Baden-Württemberg 83,046
(☎07721) Map **11** B2
★★*Ketterer* Brigachstr 1 ☎52095 tx792554
rm36 ⇘4 ▥16 G Lift

185

Germany

Wahlscheid Nordrhein-Westfalen 5,200
(☎02206) Map **4** D1
★★★*Schloss Auel* (1.5km NE) ☎2041
tx887510 rm26 (A) ⇌15 ⋔2 G ✒ Pool
Walchensee Bayern 650 (☎08858)
Map **12** D2
★★*Post* Seestr 52 ☎238 rm68 ⇌5 ⋔5 G ✒
Lake
Walldorf Baden-Württemberg 13,526
(☎06227) Map **11** B4
☆☆☆☆ **Holiday Inn** 1.5km SW near
autobahn exit ☎62051 tx466009 rm127 ⇌127
Lift LD B77–108 M14 Pn105–129 Pool
★★*Vorfelder* Bahnhofstr ☎2085 tx466016
rm40 ⇌30 ⋔4 G Lift
Wangen im Allgäu Baden-Württemberg
23,333 (☎07522) Map **12** C2
★★*Alte Post* Postpl 2 ☎21019 rm42 ⇌12
⋔4 G LD B22–34 M12–27 Pn35–46
★*Gasthof Taube* Bindstr 47 ☎21338 rm14
⋔5 G B18–48 M7–14 Pn34–39
🖪🛇*Dreher* Leutkircher Str 5 ☎3019 N🛇 Opl
Wasserburg am Inn Bayern 7,014
(☎08071) Map **13** A2
★★*Fletzinger* Fletzingergasse 1 ☎3876 rm30
⇌14 ⋔1 G 7 Jan–20 Dec B24–60 M7–14
Pn42–46
Weiden in der Oberpfalz Bayern 42,844
(☎0961) Map **13** A4
★★*Schmid* Obere Bachgasse 8 ☎42231
rm18 (A3) ⇌4 ⋔6 G B23–54 M8–12
�'t24 *Auto Friedrich* Bahnhofstr 17 ☎44843
N🛇 BL/Peu/Rov/Tri
🖪🛇*Stegmann* Ohmstr 1 ☎43055 N🛇 Aud/VW
Weinheim an der Bergstrasse
Baden-Württemberg 42,015 (☎06201)
Map **11** B4
★★*Fuchs'sche Mühle* Birkenauer Tal Str 10
(2km NE) ☎61031 rm26 ⇌17 ⋔5 G Lift
LD B30–60 M10–20 Pool
Weissenburg in Bayern Bayern 16,520
(☎09141) Map **12** D3
🛇*Kellner* Augsburger Str 48 ☎2638 N🛇
BL/Cit G2
Wertheim Baden-Württemberg 21,526
(☎09342) Map **12** C4
★★*Schwan* Mainpl 3 ☎1278 rm30 ⇌3 ⋔15
G 1 Feb–23 Dec B29.50–74 M9–18 Pn35–49
★*Badischer Hof* by the Tauberbrücke ☎1288
rm17 ⇌1 ⋔3 G
At **Kreuzwertheim**
★*Herrnwiesen* Herrnwiesen 4 ☎7725 rm17
⇌2 ⋔12 G B24–56
Wertingen Bayern 4,218 (☎08272)
Map **12** D3
★*Hirsch* Schulstr 7 ☎2083 rm30 (A17) ⇌3
⋔3 G B21–49 M6–8 Pn34
Wesel Nordrhein-Westfalen 60,040
(☎0281) Map **4** D2
★★★*Kaiserhof* F-Etzel Pl 1 ☎21972 rm37
⇌5 ⋔16 G Lift
🚍24 *Herzog* Schermbecker Landstr 18
☎5405 N🛇(02858)529 N🛇 Frd G10
Westerland auf Sylt Schleswig-Holstein
11,111 (☎04651) Map **1** A1
★★★*Stadt Hamburg* Strandstr 2 ☎7058
rm80 ⇌25 ⋔39 Lift B32–180 M18.50–23.50
Pn63–132
Wetzlar Hessen 35,046 (☎06441)
Map **5** A1
★★*Eulerhaus* (n rest) Buderus Pl 1 ☎43549
rm31 ⇌10 ⋔5 Lift B27.50–69
Wiedenbrück Nordrhein-Westfalen 16,100
(☎05242) Map **5** A2
☆ **Wiedenbrück** Gütersloherstr 143 ☎8782
rm52 (A21) ⇌3 ⋔21 G B21.50–63.50

Wiesbaden Hessen 253,456 (☎06121)
Map **11** B4
★★★★★*Nassauer Hof* Kaiser-Friedrich Pl 3
☎39681 tx4186847 rm160 ⇌160 G Lift
B115–195 M25
★★★★★*Schwarzer Bock* Krauzpl 12 ☎3821
tx04186640 rm170 ⇌130 ⋔40 Lift B71–184
M20–40 Pn104–141 Pool
★★★*Blum* Wilhelmstr 44 ☎39611
tx04186692 rm90 ⇌58 ⋔13 Lift B36–132
M10–15
★★*Central* Bahnhofstr 65 ☎372001
tx4186604 CHWID rm70 ⇌27 ⋔5 G Lift
B30–83 M10.75–66
★*Oranien* Platter Str 2 ☎301058 tx4186217
rm94 ⇌18 ⋔33 G Lift B29–78 M12 Pn47–60
Nerotal Mainzer Str 141 ☎79780 N🛇 AR/Peu
G5
🖪*W Rauch* Waldstr 134 ☎86594 N🛇 Ren
🖪🛇*Wiesbaden* Stresemannring (nr main rly stn)
☎39401 Opl
At **Wiesbaden-Dotzheim**
🖪*H Heil* Stegerwaldstr 35 ☎420222 N🛇
BL/Jag/Rov/Tri
At **Wiesbaden-Sonnenberg**
★*Köhler* König Adolf Str 6 ☎540804 rm12
B22.50–45 M5–12 Pn36
Wildbad im Schwarzwald Baden-
Württemberg 12,227 (☎07081) Map **11** B3
★★★★*Sommerberg* (2.5km SW)
Heermannsweg 5 ☎644 tx724015 rm100
⇌100 G Lift B65–200 Màlc Pn90–130 ✒ Pool
Wildungen (Bad) Hessen 16,723
(☎05621) Map **5** B2
★★★*Staatliches Badehotel* Dr-Marc Str
☎4061 tx0994612 rm59 ⇌6 ⋔35 G Lift Golf
Pool
🖪🛇*Mette* Berliner Str 7 ☎4004
Wilhelmshaven Niedersachsen 107,051
(☎04421) Map **5** A4
★★*Loheyde* Ebertstr 104 ☎43048 rm75 (A18)
⇌11 ⋔11 G B25–80 M4.50
🖪🛇*A Hillmann* Rheinstr 202, Banter Weg 5
☎26474 N🛇 M/c
🚍24 *R Reuter* Bismarckstr 231 ☎26171
N🛇 M/c Hon G3
Wimpfen (Bad) Baden-Württemberg 6,009
(☎07063) Map **12** C3
★★*Weinmann* Marktpl 3 ☎8582 rm20 ⇌4 ⋔6
G Lift
Wolfach Baden-Württemberg 6,511
(☎07834) Map **11** B3
★★*Krone* Marktpl 33 ☎350 rm23 (A9) ⇌3
⋔10 G B28.50–83 M12.50–25 Pn38–50 ✒
Golf ○
★*Hecht* Hauptstr 51 ☎538 rm13 ⋔4 G
Wolfenbüttel Niedersachsen 54,034
(☎05331) Map **5** B3
★*Stadtschenke* Grosse Kirchstr 9 ☎2359
rm25 ⇌3 ⋔3 G LD B23–62 M5–18
🖪🛇*24 M Horter* Adersheimerstr 62 ☎43046
N🛇 Frd G10
Wolfratshausen Bayern 11,022 (☎08171)
Map **13** A2
★★*Haderbräu* Untermarkt 17 ☎1315 rm28
⇌2 ⋔1 G
Worms Rheinland-Pfalz 77,044 (☎06241)
Map **11** B4
★★★*Dom* Obermarkt 10 ☎6277 rm60 ⇌22
⋔35 G Lift B31.50–74 Màlc Pn48–60
★★*Europäischer-Hof* (n rest) Bahnhofstr 28
☎6333 rm25 ⇌4 G Lift
★*Central* (n rest) Kämmererstr 5 ☎4718 rm25
⇌3 ⋔6 G Lift
🖪🛇*Berkenkamp* Speyerer Str 88 ☎6343
N🛇 Frd G100

ⓘ❤*E K Will* Karolingerstr 1 ☎23332 N❤
BL/BMW G5

Wuppertal–Barmen Nordrhein-Westfalen
(☎0202) Map **4** D2
ⓘ❤*H Wilke* Stennert 8 ☎666517 N❤
RL/Rov/Tri G3

Wuppertal–Elberfeld Nordrhein-Westfalen
(☎0202) Map **4** D2
★★★★*Kaiserhof* (n rest) ☎450516 tx8591405
rm84 ⇤84 Lift
★★*Post* (n rest) Poststr 4 ☎450131 rm56 ⇤3
🍴39 Lift 2 Jan–23 Dec B40–84
★★*Rathaus* Wilhelmstr 7 ☎450148 rm30
⇤6 🍴24 G Lift

Wuppertal–Langerfeld Nordrhein-
Westfalen (☎0202) Map **4** D2
★*Neuenhof* Schwelmer Str 246 ☎602536
rm18 ⇤7 🍴2 G B31–100 M7.50–18.50

Würzburg Bayern 112,454 (☎0931)
Map **12** C4
★★★*Excelsior* Haugerring 2 ☎50484 rm54
⇤35 G Lift B31–96 Màlc
★★★*Rebstock* Neubaustr 7 ☎50075
tx06/8684 rm81 ⇤29 🍴52 Lift B48–98
M13.50àlc
★★*Central* (n rest) Koellikerstr 1 ☎56952
rm21 🍴9 G Lift B32–75
★★*Franziskaner* Franziskaner Pl 2 ☎50360
rm47 ⇤4 🍴19 Lift B31.50–79 M7.50–15.50

★★*Walfisch* Am Pleidenturm 5 ☎52960
rm44 ⇤30 🍴5 G Lift B30–85 M12–19.50
Pn54–69
ⓘ*W Heinsen* Mainaustr 45, Mergentheimer
Str 31 ☎42046 N❤ Frd
ⓘ*Körber* Sanderstr 31 ☎54646 N❤ Aud/VW
At **Lengfeld**
ⓘ❤*Stoy* Industrierstr ☎271721 N❤ Chy/Sim

Zell an der Mosel Rheinland-Pfalz 5,515
(☎06542) Map **11** B4
★★*Schloss* ☎4084 rm11 ⇤2 🍴9
20 Jan–5 Dec LD B46–134 M15–30
★*Marienburg* ☎2382 rm11 ⇤1 🍴5
1 Mar–31 Oct LD B20–48 Pn31.50–37

Zusmarshausen Bayern 2,213 (☎08291)
Map **12** D3
★★*Post* Augsburger Str ☎302 rm30 (A1) ⇤6
🍴5 G 1 Jan–30 Oct 25 Nov–31 Dec LD
B26–72 M7–16 Pool

Zweibrücken Rheinland-Pfalz 38,439
(☎06332) Map **11** B3
★★*Rosen* (n rest) Von Rosen Str 2 ☎3109
rm44 ⇤8 🍴20 G Lift B22–60
ⓘ❤*Carbon* Zweibrückerstr 4 ☎3570 N❤ Frd
G30

Zwischenahn (Bad) Niedersachsen 21,829
(☎04403) Map **5** A4
☆*Ferien* (on B75 2km E) Am Schlart ☎2005
rm27 ⇤22 G B26–77 M8–23 Pool

ITALY & SAN MARINO

Population 54,683,136 Area 131,000 sq miles Maps 28–34

How to get there   Although there are several ways of getting to Italy, entry will most probably be by way of France or Switzerland. The major passes, which are closed in winter, are served by road or rail tunnels. The distance to Milan from the Channel ports is approximately 650–700 miles, requiring one or two night stops. Rome is 360 miles further south. Car-sleeper services operate during the summer from Boulogne, Brussels or Paris to Milan.

Travel information

AA Port agents   *Note* Mail sent to these addresses from outside Italy should have the postal code prefixed with the letter I.

16124 Genova (Genoa) Gastaldi & CSpA, Via Cairoli 1, PO Box 1855
☎283891 (16 lines)
57100 Livorno (Leghorn) Gastaldi & CSpA, Via Grande 164, PO Box 751
☎(0586)39021/2
98100 Messina (Sicily) Gastaldi & CSpA, 201 Garibaldi Via, ☎(090)55110
80133 Napoli (Naples) Gastaldi & CSpA, Piazza Municipio 81/84 ☎(081) 323001, 324846
90139 Palermo (Sicily) Gastaldi & CSpA, Via Mariano Stabile 2 ☎(091) 589844
96100 Siracusa (Syracuse) (Sicily) Luigi Mazzone & Figli, Via Dei Mille 12 ☎20086

Accidents   **Fire, police, ambulance** (Public emergency service) ☎113.

The recommendations on page 21 apply.

No particular procedure is required following an accident, excepting that a report must be made to the insurance company within three days.
If the accident involves personal injury it is obligatory that medical assistance is sought for the injured party, and that the incident is reported to the police. On some *autostrade* there are emergency telephones as well as emergency push-button call boxes (see page 193).

Italy

Accommodation
Hotels are classified into categories from *4* to *de luxe,* and there are three categories of pensions. All charges must be agreed by the Provincial Tourist Board *(Ente Provinciali per il Turismo).* The Italian State Tourist Office publishes every year the official list of all Italian Hotels and Pensions *(Annuario Alberghi)* which can be consulted at its London office or major travel agents.

Good accommodation is provided by the Jolly Hotels, of which there are over forty. These are standardised establishments, most of which are included in the gazetteer in the three-star and four-star categories.

Breakdowns
Try to move the car to the verge of the road, and place a warning triangle on the road at least 50m to the rear of the vehicle to warn following traffic of an obstruction. The Soccorso Stradale Gratuito ACI (Soccorso Autostradale SAS on motorways) is a breakdown service operated by the Automobile Club d'Italia (ACI). This service, which is not available for caravans, can be obtained from public telephones by dialling 116 and from emergency telephones or radio telephones on motorways. In an emergency to call the police, fire or ambulance or to report the theft of a car, dial 113.

To obtain assistance when the breakdown vehicle arrives, you will be asked for your *Carta Carburante* (a fuel and breakdown card obtainable at the frontier or Italian State Tourist offices abroad), which contains two special breakdown coupons.

Although the road service is free, provided a *Carta Carburante* is held, a calling fee will be levied at the following rates:
between 06.00–22.00hrs, lire 3,500;
between 22.00–06.00hrs, lire 4,500.

Each breakdown coupon entitles you to:
1 Free assistance for up to half an hour (except for calling fee) on the spot from a mechanic, but you must pay for spare parts, petrol and oil.
2 Towage to the nearest ACI workshop. Towage is free up to 40km (24 miles) and a fee of L2,000 is charged for every 10 kilometres (or part thereof) beyond 40km. You must pay for the work carried out in repair shops.

Alternatively, requests for assistance on the motorways can be made to the *Servizio Assistenza Vacanze.* This is a service operated by FIAT in conjunction with the ACI and operates during the last two weekends in June and the first two Sundays in September, and daily in July and August. Assistance is free but a call fee, as quoted in the previous paragraph, must be paid. If the repairs take longer than 30mins, the mechanic will call the previous mentioned breakdown service to undertake the repairs.

AA members who have a Continental *5-Star Travel Booklet* may use their Credit Vouchers to settle emergency accounts, in which case the charge would be repayable to the AA by the member on his return home.

British Consulates
Note Mail sent to these addresses from outside Italy should have the postal code, prefixed with the letter I before the town name.
09100 Cagliari (Sardinia), Via San Lucifero 87 ☎62755
50123 Florence, Palazzo Castelbarco, Lungarno Corsini 2 ☎212594 and 284133
16121 Genoa, Via XII Ottobre 2, (13-Piano) ☎564833/6
98100 Messina, Corso Garibaldi 267/A ☎46977
20121 Milan. Via San Paolo 7 ☎803442/6
80122 Naples, Via Francesco Crispi 122 ☎682482
90143 Palermo, Via Marchese di Villabianca 9 ☎253364/6
00187 Roma, Via XX Settembre 80A, ☎4755441/5
34132 Trieste, Via Rossini 2 ☎69135
10125 Turin, Corso Vittorio Emanuele 1 ☎657676/7
30100 Venice, Accademia 1051 (PO Box 679) ☎27207

Currency and banking
The unit of currency is the Italian lira. The import of Italian lira bank notes is limited to L35,000 – other currency is not restricted. Export of currency is restricted to Italian bank notes up to L35,000 and other currency up to L200,000. To export currency in excess of this amount it must have been declared on form V2 on entry.

Banking hours
Most banks are open from Monday to Friday 08.30 to 13.30hrs.

Dimensions and weight
Private cars and trailers are restricted to the following dimensions and weights:

Italy

restrictions	cars	height	4 metres,
		width	2.5 metres;
	caravans	length	6 metres;
		weight	The maximum permitted gross weight is that stated by the manufacturers, or 80% of the gross weight of the towing vehicle – whichever is the lighter.

Drinking and driving
Any driver found to be driving under the influence of alcohol may be sentenced to a term of imprisonment of up to six months and fined from L25,000 to L100,000.

Driving licence
A valid British driving licence, if accompanied by an official Italian translation, will be accepted in Italy.

Ferries (Internal)
All details are subject to alteration.

Lake Como
Cadenabbia–Bellagio
Cadenabbia–Varenna
Bellagio–Varenna
Service frequent daily services between 07.00–20.30hrs approx.
Duration 10 minutes Cadenabbia to Bellagio; 30 minutes Cadenabbia to Varenna; 15 minutes Bellagio to Varenna.
Charges

Vehicles	cars	L1,500–L3,200	*charges include*
		(according to length)	*drivers only*
	motorcycles	L1,100–L1,300	
Passengers		L700–L800	

Lake Maggiore
Intra-Laveno
Service about every half hour between 05.00–23.40hrs.
Duration 20 minutes
Charges

Vehicles	cars	L1,650–L3,100	*charges include*
		(according to length)	*drivers only*
	motorcycles	L1,100	
Passengers		L550	

Lake Garda
Torri del Benaco–Maderno
Service 7–11 sailings daily
Duration 30 minutes
Charges

Vehicles	cars	L1,500–L2,500	*charges include*
		(according to length)	*drivers only*
	motorcycles	L1,000	
Passengers		L700	

Holidays and events
Holidays based on religious festivals are not always fixed on the calendar but any current diary will give the actual dates. The Whit holiday should not be confused with the British Spring Holiday.

Fixed holidays

1 January	New Year's Day
6 January	Epiphany
19 March	St Joseph's Day
25 April	Liberation Day
1 May	Labour Day
1st Sun in June	Republic Day
15 August	Assumption of the Virgin Mary
1 November	All Saints' Day
1st Sun in November	National Unity Day
8 December	Immaculate Conception
25 December	Christmas Day
26 December	St Stephen's Day

Italy

Moveable holidays	Easter Monday
	Ascension Day
	Corpus Christi
	Feast of St Peter & St Paul

Annual events

February	**Agrigento** Almond Blossom Festival, folklore gathering
	San Remo Song Festival
April	**L'Aquila** Good Friday Procession
	Taranto Procession of The Mysteries, strange religious rites
May	**Cagliari** Feast of Sant' Efisio, celebrated since 1657
	Sassari Costume Cavalcade (Cavalcata Sarda)
June	**Florence** Football match in 16th-century costume
	Pisa 'Battle of the Bridge' 'fought' in medieval dress
	Brindisi Corpus Christi Festival
July	**Siena** The Palio Festival, famous for its horse race
	Venice The Feast of the Redeemer, celebrated on the Lagoon
August	**Venice** Organ concerts in St Mark's Basilica
	Ascoli Piceno Historical Pageant and Jousting
September	**Naples** The Piedgrotta Festival, song contests and procession
	Arezzo Joust dating from the 13th century
	Venice Regatta dating from 1300
	Viterbo The procession of the 'Santa Rosa' Tower
October	**Treviso** Autumn Musical Celebration

A more comprehensive list can be obtained from The Italian State Tourist Office (see page 196).

Horn, use of

In built-up areas the use of the horn is prohibited except in cases of immediate danger. At night flashing headlights may be used instead of the horn.

Outside built-up areas it is compulsory to use the horn when warning of approach is necessary.

Insurance

This is compulsory; see page 11.

Third-party insurance is also compulsory for certain boats and engines in Italian waters.

Frontier insurance Short-term third-party insurance can be obtained at the frontier; approximate rates in lire are as follows:

	15 days	*30 days*	*45 days*
cars	14,000	21,000	28,000
motorcycles	7,000	10,500	14,000
trailers	11,200	16,800	22,400
caravans	11,200	16,800	22,400

Frontier insurance for motorboats is carried out by the representatives at each port. Charges are as follows:

	15 days	*30 days*	*45 days*
up to 80hp	3,000	6,000	9,000
80hp to 120hp	5,000	10,000	15,000

These prices should be used only as a guide.

Italy

Lights
Full-beam headlights can be used only outside cities and towns. Dipped headlights are compulsory in tunnels and bridges even if they are well lit. Foglights may be used only in pairs and in fog or snow when visibility is restricted.

Medical treatment
Medical benefits in Italy are administered by the National Institute for Sickness Insurance (*Istituto Nazionale per l'Assicurazione Contro le Malattie* known as INAM) which has main offices in each provincial capital, and sub-offices in almost every district. Addresses may be obtained by enquiry at the local post office, town hall or found in the telephone directory.

To obtain medical and dental treatment take form E111 (see page 13) to the INAM office. You will be given a certificate of entitlement and a list of sickness insurance scheme doctors and dentists. Take the certificate to any doctor or dentist on the list and you will be treated free of charge. Without the certificate you will have to pay for treatment and may have difficulty in getting a refund afterwards. If you need prescribed medicines, show the certificate of entitlement to the chemist. Some medicines are free but a small charge is made for others.

If hospital treatment is needed, the doctor will give you a certificate (*proposta di ricovero*) which entitles you to free treatment in certain hospitals. A list of hospitals can be obtained from an INAM office. In an emergency, if you cannot contact the INAM, show form E111 to the hospital authorities and ask them to contact INAM immediately.

Motoring clubs

There are two motoring organisations in Italy. The Touring Club Italiano (TCI) which has its head office at 10 Corso Italia, 20122 Milano, and the Automobile Club d'Italia (ACI) whose head office is at 8 Via Marsala, 00185 Rome. Both clubs have branch offices in most leading cities and towns. They will assist motoring tourists on touring matters, road and traffic conditions and AA members should produce their *5-Star Travel Booklet* when requesting service. For Breakdown assistance see page 22.

The hours of opening of the TCI are usually between 09.00 and 19.00hrs although some open earlier and close later. A few are closed all day on Mondays or Saturdays. However, all close for three hours for lunch between 12.00 and 16.00hrs.

The ACI offices open between 08.30 and 13.30hrs Monday to Friday. A 24-hour information service is in operation although the interpreters are on duty only between 09.00 and 17.00hrs. The telephone number is (06)4212.

Museum card
This card entitles you to visit all the Italian state museums, art galleries, and archaeological sites without payment of the normal entrance fees. A list of establishments is provided with the card. This card can be purchased from any AA service centre.

Nationality plates
It is compulsory for foreign registered vehicles to display a distinctive sign at the rear of the vehicle. Failure to comply with this regulation will incur an on-the-spot-fine of 10,000 lire.

Parking
Parking is forbidden within 5 metres (16½ft) of cross-roads or road intersections, on a main road or one carrying fast-moving traffic, on or near tram lines, opposite another stationary vehicle, on or within 12 metres (39½ft) of a bus or tram stop. Violators of parking regulations are subject to heavy fines. There is a blue zone (*zona disco*) in most cities; in such areas parked vehicles must display a disc on the windscreen.
Discs are set at the time of parking, and show when parking time expires according to the limit in the area concerned. Disc parking operates 08.00–20.00hrs on working days. Discs can be obtained from petrol stations and automobile organisations. There are also green zones (*zona verde*) where parking is absolutely prohibited 08.00–09.30hrs and 14.30–16.00hrs. Vehicles will be towed away at the owner's expense even if they are not causing an obstruction.

Passengers
No vehicle may carry more passengers than the number for which it was constructed. Passengers must always allow drivers free movement.

Petrol
The approximate price of petrol per litre is: super (98–100 octane) L500; normal (84–87 octane) L485.

Italy

Petrol coupons, which give an appreciable discount on pump prices, are available for tourists. These are obtainable from the AA, the National Tourist Office, and at most major Italian frontiers (with currency other than Lire), but are not sold inside Italy. They are available only on personal application. Each tourist may purchase coupons for up to 400 litres of petrol for a car, 200 litres for a motorcycle of 125cc or more, or 100 litres for a motorcycle under 125cc. Unused coupons are reimbursed by the issuing office.

During the winter, between October and April the opening hours of petrol filling stations are from 07.00–12.30hrs and from 15.00–19.00hrs. On Sundays and holidays service is further restricted because 75% of filling stations are closed. During the summer, opening hours are longer but many stations will be closed during the lunch time. As a general rule you should keep your tank topped up.

See Petrol, page 39.

Police fines   The police are authorised to impose and collect fines on the spot for violation of traffic regulations. The police must hand over a receipt for the amount of the fine paid.

Postal and telephone charges   Rates for mail to the UK are:

Surface mail

Letters	first 20gm	L200
	20–50gm	L350
	50–100gm	L480
	100–250gm	L950
Postcards	up to five words	L70
	fully written	L130
Express surcharge		L400
Registration surcharge		L400

The *poste restante (Fermo posta)* address in Rome is Posta e Telegrafo, Piazza San Silvestro, 00187 Roma.

Telephone rates   Telephone communication with the UK is good; the charge is L2,130 for the first three minutes and L710 each further minute. If dialled direct the charge is twelve tokens every minute. There are plenty of public telephones operated by a 50-lire token *(gettone)*; these are available from all tobacco shops, bars and news-stands. Internal trunk calls, although subject to delay, can be dialled direct by using the area code number.

Priority   Traffic on State highways *(Strade Statali)*, which are all numbered and indicated by signs, has right of way, as do public service vehicles and, on postal routes, buses belonging to the service. These bus routes are indicated by a special sign.

If two vehicles are travelling in opposite directions and the driver of each vehicle wants to turn left, they must pass in front of each other (not drive round as in the UK).

Roads   Motorways reach to most parts of the country. Other main roads are generally good, and there is an exceptional number of bypasses; secondary roads are often poor. Mountain roads are usually well engineered; details of the main passes are given on pages 28–35.

Italy's motorways *(autostrada)* were the first in Europe. There are about 3,884 miles of them, and more are under construction. To join a motorway, follow the green signposts; vehicles which cannot exceed 40kph (24mph) and motorcycles under 150cc are prohibited.

Tolls are charged on all motorways except the A3 from Salerno to Reggio, the A19 and A29 in Sicily, the A28 from Portogruaro to Pordenone, and on the Raccordo Autostradale from Ferrara to Porto Garibaldi, Florence to Siena, Val di Chiana to Perugia, Rome to Fiumicino Airport, Rome to Lido di Ostia, Avellino to Salerno, and from Scalo Sicignano (A3) to Potenza.

Motorway telephones   On the *Autostrade* A1 (Milan–Florence–Rome), A8/9 (Milan–the Lakes–Chiasso), and A11 (Florence–Pisa N), there are radio panels at 1850m (1¼-mile) intervals; each has two buttons, one to call an ambulance and one to call a breakdown vehicle. A light appears on the lower part of the panel when the call is received. If the breakdown occurs between panels, either walk to the nearest panel or wait for a police patrol – you *must not* stop a passing vehicle.

The *Autostrade* A6 (Fossano–Savona) and A10 (Savona–Ventimiglia) have telephone boxes at 2km (1¼-mile) and ½km (⅓-mile) intervals respectively. As soon as the door of the box is opened, you are in contact with the operator who will take action on any message.

On the *Autostrade* A7 (Serravalle–Milan) telephone boxes are also available, but to get help you have to press a button to contact the operator.

Tolls   The methods of calculating tolls vary; they are based either on the Italian horsepower, the wheelbase, or the cubic capacity of the vehicle, and the distance covered. There is no simple uniform ratio between engine capacity and the Italian rating of horsepower. If there is any doubt, a reference book giving the horsepower of all makes of car is available at each toll station. The rates are given in lire for small (under 10hp Italian), medium – including minis (10–15hp Italian), and large cars (over 15hp Italian).

Toll payment On the majority of the toll motorways a travel ticket is issued on entry, and the toll is paid on leaving the motorway. The travel ticket gives all relevant information about the toll charges, including the toll category of the vehicle. At the exit, the ticket is handed in.

On some motorways – notably A8, A9, A11, A14 (Pescara–Lanciano) and A12 (Rome–Civitavecchia) – the toll is paid at intermediate toll stations for each section of the motorway used.

On a few motorways the destination must be declared and the toll paid on entering the motorway. There is no refund on break of journey.

	cars small	medium	large	motor- cycles
*A1 Milan–Bologna	1,850	2,850	4,150	1,550
*A1 Milan–Florence (Nord)	2,650	4,150	6,250	2,250
*A1 Milan–Rome	5,050	7,950	11,750	4,250
*A2 Rome–Naples	1,750	2,800	4,100	1,450
A3 Naples–Salerno	300	550	700	250
A4 Turin–Milan	750	1,100	1,650	450
A4 Milan–Mestre (Venice)	2,100	3,050	4,350	1,650
A4 Mestre (Venice)–Trieste	750	1,150	1,600	650
A4/5 Milan–Aosta	1,300	2,300	2,900	950
A5 Turin–Aosta	950	1,850	2,200	800
A6 Turin–Savona	1,050	1,650	2,400	800
A7 Milan–Genoa	1,200	1,700	2,550	1,000
A8 Milan–Sesto/Varese	400	700	900	300
A8/9 Milan–Como	500	900	1,100	400
A10 Genoa–Savona	500	750	1,150	400
A10 Savona–Ventimiglia (Menton)	1,850	2,900	4,000	1,100
A11 Florence–Pisa	750	1,350	1,650	600
A12 Genoa–Livorno	1,650	2,950	3,800	1,400
A12 Rome–Civitavecchia	600	1,100	1,300	500
*A13 Bologna–Padua	1,050	1,700	2,500	900
*A14 Bologna–Rimini (Sud)	1,000	1,550	2,300	850
*A14 Bologna–Pescara	3,200	5,000	7,400	2,700
*A14 Pescara–Bari	3,100	4,950	7,200	2,500
*A14 Bari–Taranto	550	900	1,350	450
*A15 Parma–La Spezia	900	1,500	2,200	750
*A16/14 Naples–Bari	2,300	3,700	5,500	2,000
A18 Messina–Catania (Nord)	900	1,300	1,400	550
A20 Messina–Patti	800	1,200	1,800	650
A20 Cefalu–Buonfornello	150	250	400	150
A21 Turin–Piacenza	1,150	1,700	2,500	1,000
A21 Piacenza–Brescia	500	800	1,150	400
A22 Brenner Pass–Modena	2,800	4,400	6,500	2,400
A23 Palmanova–Udine	100	150	250	100
A24 Rome–L'Aquila	1,000	1,950	2,300	850
A25 Rome–Avezzano	900	1,700	2,000	750
A25 Popoli–Pescara	300	550	650	250
A27 Mestre (Venice)–Vittorio Veneto	700	1,000	1,450	600
*A30 Caserta–Salerno	550	850	1,250	450
A31 Vicenza–Piovene Rocchette	350	500	750	300

All prices should be used only as a guide.

*A special tariff reduction has been introduced enabling tourists to pay the lowest tariff *ie* the motorcycle tariff, when travelling on the following motorways: A1 Milan–Rome, A2 Rome–Naples, A13 Bologna–Padua, A14 Bologna–Pescara–Bari–Taranto, A15

Italy

Parma–La Spezia, A16/14 Naples–Bari, A30 Caserta–Salerno. To claim the reduced toll tariff make sure you inform the attendant, before he issues a ticket when you enter the motorway, that you are driving a foreign registered vehicle. You will then be issued with a ticket which should be marked with 1 (one) in the box marked *classe*. You must complete the ticket with your name and surname, the registration number of the vehicle and your signature before arriving at the exit booth to leave the motorway.

Caravans There are varying additional charges, but generally the charge for a caravan is the same as for a medium-to-large-sized car.

Winter conditions   It is possible to approach northern Italy, Milan, and Turin by road or rail tunnels. See Passes and tunnels, pages 28–39, and Tyres, page 196.

From Switzerland via the Simplon or St Gotthard rail tunnels;
via the Grand St Bernard road tunnel;
via the San Bernardino road tunnel;
also via the Julier and Maloja passes.

From France via the Mont Blanc road tunnel;
via the Fréjus rail tunnel when the Mont Cenis pass is closed.
In favourable weather, via the Lautaret and Montgenèvre passes.
Also via the French Riviera coast, entering at Ventimiglia.

From Austria via the Resia and Brenner passes; wheel chains may be necessary in severe weather.

The Plöcken pass is closed in winter, but the roads entering Italy at Dobbiaco and Tarvisio are normally free from obstruction.

Roads within the country, apart from those in the Dolomites, are not seriously affected in winter, although during January and February certain highways across the Apennines may be obstructed. Touring in the Dolomites is generally confined to the period from early May to mid October.

Road signs   Signposting is good on most main roads, although signs tend to point across the roads indicated.
Translations of some written signs are given below:

Banchina non transitabile	Shoulder of road not to be driven on
Banchina cedevole	Shoulder of road too soft or sinking under the vehicle wheels
Divieto di accesso	No entry
Entrata	Entrance or turn-in
Crocevia	Cross-roads
Lavori in corso	Road works ahead
Parcheggio	Parking
Passaggio a livello	Level crossing
Rallentare	Reduce speed
Semafori sincronizzati	Synchronised traffic lights (see Traffic lights)
Senso unico	One-way street
Sosta autorizzata/regolamentata	Parking permitted (time in minutes usually indicated)
Sosta vietata	Parking forbidden
Sosta vietata Rimozione Forzata	Parking forbidden. The vehicle will be towed away
Strada dissestata	Ruined or in very bad condition
Svolta	Bend
Uscita	Exit or turn-out
Vietato ingresso veicoli	No entry for vehicles
Vietato transito autocarri	Closed to heavy vehicles
Zona disco	Blue zone

Shopping hours   Most shops are usually open Monday to Saturday; *food shops* from 08.30–13.00hrs and 16.00–20.00hrs, closed from 13.00hrs on Mondays; *other shops* from 09.00–12.30hrs and 15.30–19.30 hrs.

Speed   The maximum speed limit in built-up areas, unless otherwise indicated, is 50kph (31mph). Mopeds are restricted to 40kph (24mph) on all roads unless there is a lower limit. On normal roads limits are 80kph to 110kph; motorways 90kph to 140kph depending on the cc of the vehicle's engine. Limits are signposted. Any infringement of speed regulations can result in punitive fines of up to £400 or imprisonment, and these penalties have been enforced. See Traffic lights page 196.

Italy

Tourist information offices
The Italian State Tourist organisation (ENIT) has an office in London at 201 Regent Street, W1R 8AY ☎01-439 2311. It will be pleased to assist you with any information regarding tourism. In Italy there are three organisations: the *Ente Nazionale Italiano per il Turismo* (ENIT) with offices at frontiers and ports; the *Assessorati Regionali per il Turismo* (ART) and the *Enti Provinciali per il Turismo* (EPT) who will assist tourists through their regional and provincial offices. The *Aziende Autonomedi Cura Soggiorno e Turismo* (AACST) have offices in places of recognised tourist interest and concern themselves exclusively with matters of local interest.

Traffic lights
In some places synchronised traffic signals are used; these are preceded by a sign bearing the words *Semafori sincronizzati per velocita.......km/ora;* vehicles travelling at the speed shown (.......kph) will not have to stop or slow down at the lights.

Tyres
Snow tyres These may be used on roads where wheel chains are compulsory, provided that they are used on all four wheels.

Spiked or studded tyres Vehicles with spiked tyres may be used provided that:
1 they are used between 15 November and 15 March
2 they do not exceed 120kph (74mph) on motorways, and 90kph (56mph) on other roads.
All signed lower limits must not be exceeded.
3 they must not exceed a total weight of 3,500kg.
4 they are fitted to all wheels, including those of a trailer (if any).
Visitors are also advised to have mud flaps fitted behind the rear wheels.

Wheel chains Roads where these are compulsory are marked by a national sign. Chains cannot be hired in Italy, but can be purchased at garages or vehicle accessory shops everywhere. Approximate prices per pair are as follows: iron, L10,000–20,000; steel/iron, L20,000–30,000. Drivers of vehicles proceeding without wheel chains on roads where they are compulsory, are liable to prosecution.

See also Road and winter conditions, page 40.

Visitors' registration
Police registration is required within three days of entering Italy. If staying at a hotel the management will attend to the formality, but the visitor is responsible for checking that this has been carried out. Your permit of stay will last three months as a tourist. Should you wish to stay for a longer period, an extension must be obtained from the police. In Rome there is a special police information office for assistance to tourists; interpreters can be provided. ☎461950 and 486609.

Warning triangles
These are compulsory for all vehicles except motorcycles. They must be placed on the road 50 metres (55yd) behind the vehicle (or a fallen object or load) and must be visible to following traffic from 100 metres (109yd).

Triangles may be hired or purchased at the Italian frontier. A charge of L1,500 is made, for which a receipt is given. On leaving Italy, the motorist must return the triangle and the receipt in order to obtain a refund of L1,200.

San Marino

Map 30 C2
A small Republic with an area of 23 sq miles and a population of 19,000. Situated in the hills of Italy near Rimini. The official information office in the UK is the Italian State Tourist Office at 201 Regent Street, London W1R 8AY. The chief attraction is the city of San Marino on the slopes of Monte Titano. Its laws, motoring regulations and emergency telephone numbers are the same as Italy and the latter will be found on pages 188–196.

Italy/hotels and garages

Prices are in Italian lire

Abbreviations:
pza   piazza

Abano Terme Padova 14,880 (☎049)
Map **30** C4
★★★★**Bristol Buja** via Monteortone 2
☎669390 tx43210 rm157 ⇌140 G Lift
B13900–30800 M8000 Pn16800–25800
⤸ Pool
★★★★**Trieste & Victoria** viale delle Terme
☎669101 tx43250 rm100 ⇌80 Lift 20 Mar–
5 Nov LD B23500–40000 M8000 Pn22000–
31000 ⤸ Pool Golf
★★★**Milano** viale delle Terme 133 ☎669661
rm98 ⇌47 G Lift 1 Apr–11 Nov
🛇⚡**Colombo** via Martiri d'Ungheria 3
☎669627 N🛇 BMW/Frd
🛇⚡**Euganea** via F-Busonera 59 ☎669134
Fia G50

Acquapendente Viterbo 6,000 (☎0763)
Map **31** B2
★★**Milano** via Cassia 29 ☎74110 rm25 ▥6
G LD B4500–13000 M6000–9000
Pn16000–20000
★**Roma** viale del Fiore 13 ☎74016 rm26 ⇌7
▥4 G B4500–10100 M4150 Pn8850–10150 ⤸

Acqui Terme Alessandria 22,800 (☎0144)
Map **28** D3
★★★**Nuove Terme** pza Italia ☎2106 rm70
⇌42 ▥7 Lift
🛇**Carrara** corso Divisione Acqui 7 ☎53735
Aud/VW G25

Agognate Novara (☎0321) Map **28** D4
★★**Meridiana** Autostrade Torino ☎23156
rm17 ⇌17 G Lift ⤸ Pool

Alassio Savona 14,050 (☎0182) Map **28** D2
★★★★**Diana** via Garibaldi 104 ☎42701
tx27655 rm84 ⇌42 G Lift 15 Mar–20 Oct
B14300–36600 M7500 Pool Beach Sea
★★★★**Mediteranée** via Roma 63 ☎42564
rm82 ⇌70 G Lift 1 Apr–Oct B16000–38000
M10000 Pn22000–32000 Beach Sea
★★★**Cesio Residence** via Milite Ignosto 41
☎40269 rm44 ⇌44 G Lift Beach Sea
★★★**Curtis-Centrale** corso Europa 16 ☎42437
rm44 ⇌44 G Pn10000–14500
★★★**Flora** Lungomare Cadorna 22 ☎40336
rm50 ⇌25 ▥6 Lift LD Beach Sea
★★★**Ideale** corso Dante 18 ☎40376 rm70
⇌20 Lift 1 May–20 Sep LD
★★★**Majestic** via L-da Vinci 300 ☎42721
rm72 ⇌52 ▥20 G Lift May–10 Oct
B8500–22000 M4000–6000 Pn12000–18000
Beach Sea
★★★**Regina** via Garibaldi 108 ☎40215 rm39
⇌17 ▥20 G Lift 1 Apr–25 Oct Beach Sea
★★**Aida** via F Gioia ☎44085 rm42 (A10) ⇌42
Lift Nov–mid Oct LD B10500–15000 M4500
Pn8000–13500
★★**Badano Residence Sur Mer** via
Gramsci 30 ☎40964 rm18 ⇌3 ▥15 Lift
15 Jan–20 Oct B11500–13500(double)
★★**Bellevue** via A-Vespucci 11a ☎42013
rm34 (A4) ⇌4 ▥12 Lift 15 Mar–10 Oct Beach
Sea
★★**Londra** via Roma 41 ☎40380 rm30 ⇌30
G Lift LD B9000–18000 M5000 Pn16800
Beach Sea
★★**Mare** via Boselli 1 ☎40635 rm47 ⇌36 Lift
18 Dec–30 Oct B7200–16400 M4500
Pn7000–14000 Beach Sea
★★**Martini** via V-Veneto 31 ☎40436 rm37
⇌19 Lift 1 Apr–25 Oct
★★**Mirafiori** via L-da Vinci 90 ☎40756 rm30
⇌10 Lift B5200–16400 M4000 Pn8000–14000

★★**Toscana** via L-da Vinci ☎40657 rm70
⇌40 ▥7 Lift
★★**Villa Carlotta** via Adelasia 11 ☎40463
rm17 ⇌8 ▥2 G B4500–12000 M3000–4000
Pn6000–9000 Beach Sea
★**Bel Sit** via Don Boselli 28 ☎40395 rm48
⇌48 Lift 15 Mar–20 Oct Beach Sea
★**Rendez-Vous** via Milano 8 ☎40421 rm32
⇌10 ▥4 G Lift Beach Sea

Alba Cuneo 30,450 (☎0173) Map **28** D3
★★**Savona** pza Savona ☎2381 rm120 ⇌120 G
Lift B7200–18000 M5000 Pn15000–18000

Albisola Marina Savona 6,300 (☎019)
Map **28** D3
★★★**Corallo** ☎41784 rm24 ⇌13 ▥7 G
15 Mar–31 Oct B6600–15200 M5000
Pn9500–13500 Sea

Alessandria Alessandria 103,000 (☎0131)
Map **28** D3
★★**Europa** corso V-Marini ☎2219 rm34 ⇌4
▥26 G Lift B11100–21600 M6000–8000
Pn19000–20000 St15%
🛇⚡**24 Marenco di Arona** via Verona 14
☎2212 G100
🛇**Rolandi** corso Galilei ☎63439 N🛇 M/c BL/
BMW/Jag/Rov/Tri

Amalfi Salerno 6,400 (☎089) Map **33** B3
★★★★**Santa Caterina** via Statale ☎871012
rm62 (A9) ⇌59 G Lift B11700–25800
M8500 Pn17150–26300 Pool Beach Sea
★★★**Aurora** pza Matteotti ☎871209 rm33 ⇌33
G Lift 1 Apr–31 Oct B10500–21600
M4000–4500 Pn15000–18000 Beach Sea
★★★**Luna** Lungomare ☎871002 rm45 ⇌45
G Lift B10000–26000 M6000 Pn17000–23000
Pool Beach Sea
★★★**Miramalfi** ☎871247 rm44 ⇌30 ▥14 Lift
B8200–19200 M5000 Pn14500–17500
Pool Beach Sea
★★**Bellevue** ☎871846 rm23 ⇌12 ▥11 G
B9000–13500 M3500 Pn8000–12500 Beach
Sea
★★**Marina Riviera** via F-Gioia 22 ☎871104
rm18 ⇌9 ▥9 G 15 Mar–31 Oct B5500–12900
M4000 Pn10000–13000 Beach Sea
At **Lone** (2.5km NE)
★★★**Caleidoscopio** ☎871220 rm35 ⇌15
▥8 G Pool Beach Sea
At **Minori** (3km E)
★★**Caporal** ☎877408 rm25 ⇌25 G LD
B5500–9500 M5000 Pn8000–12000 Beach
Sea
★★**Santa Lucia** via Nazionale 44 ☎877142
rm26 ⇌9 ▥11 1 Jan–1 Dec Beach Sea

Anacapri See **Capri (Isola di)**

Ancona Ancona 107,150 (☎071)
Map **30** D2
☆☆☆**AGIP** SS 16 Adriatica km 293 ☎508241
rm51 ▥51 Lift B9000–18800
★★★**Jolly** via XXIX Settembre 14 ☎201171
tx56343 Jolly Anrm89 ⇌89 Lift B14400–
22600 M5800 Pn24200
★★★**Passetto** via Thaon di Revel 1
☎28932 rm45 ⇌18 ▥27 G Lift Sea
🛇**SAMET** via de Gasperi 80 ☎31548 N🛇
M/c Frd

Anguillara Sabazia Roma 5,350 (☎06)
Map **31** B3
★★**Gli Etruschi** via Vigna di Valle ☎9028154
rm11 ⇌5 ▥6 Lake

Aosta Aosta 39,000 (☎0165) Map **28** C4
★★★**Ambassador** via Duca degli Abruzzi
☎42230 rm45 ⇌19 ▥26 G
☆☆☆**Motelalp** ☎40007 rm52 ⇌52
B13500–22000 M5000 Pn20000
★★★**Valle d'Aosta** corso Ivrea 174 ☎41845
rm102 ⇌102 G Lift

197

Italy

★★*Miravalle* (n rest) Porossan (2km N)
☎44310 rm24 ⇌20 G
★★Rayon de Soleil Strada Gran St-Bernardo
(2km N) ☎2247 tx0165 rm32 ⇌32 G Lift
15 Mar–30 Oct LD B8300–18600 M4800
Pn12000–17000
★★*Turin* via Torino 14 ☎44593 rm50 ⇌50 G
Lift
★*Cavallo Bianco* via E-Aubert 15 ☎2214 rm12
i⅍*Fabris-Ford* pza Zerbion ☎2619
N☎2379 M/c Frd G30
F Gal via Monte Emilius 9 ☎2353 BL/Rov
⅍**SICAV** corso Battaglione 83 ☎40146 Fia
G2000
At **Peroulaz** (13km S)
★★*Jolie Bergère* ☎4912 rm42 ⇌4 ⋒9 G

Arabba Belluno (☎0436) Map **13** A1
★Posta ☎79105 rm25 ⇌6 ⋒4 G Closed May
Oct Nov B4500–1300 M4500–5000
Pn8000–10000

Arenzano Genova 10,500 (☎010)
Map **28** D3
★★*Roma* (n rest) ☎917314 rm47 ⇌8 ⋒1 Lift
B8100–17600 Sea
★*Europa* (Pensione) ☎917384 rm15 ⇌3 G
30 Apr–30 Oct LD B5000–9500 M3500–4500
Pn8500–9500 Sea

Arezzo Arezzo 90,200 (☎0575) Map **30** C2
★★★Continentale pza G-Monaco 7 ☎20251
rm80 ⇌45 ⋒15 Lift B8500–20000 M5000
Pn20000
⅍**Magi Ezio di Piero & Corrado Magi** via
M-Perennio 24/1 ☎21264 N⅍ BL

Argegno Como 800 (☎031) Map **29** A4
★*Belvedere* ☎821116 rm17 ⇌4 ⋒2 G
Mar–10 Nov B5800–15500 M5000
Pn10000–14000 St9% Lake

Arma di Taggia Imperia (☎0184)
Map **28** D2
★★★★*Vittoria Grattacielo* via Lungomare
☎43495 rm77 ⇌77 G Lift 20 Dec–28 Feb
15 May–15 Oct ⅋ Pool Beach Sea
★★Europa via Stazione 137 ☎43797 rm30
⇌30 G B4600–9500 M4200 Pn12000

Arona Novara 16,600 (☎0322) Map **28** D4
At **Fornaci**
★★Clipper via Sempione 18 ☎3364 rm12
⇌4 G Lake

Arzachena See **Sardegna (Isola) Sardinia**

Ascoli Piceno Ascoli Piceno 56,350
(☎0736) Map **32** C3
★★★*Gioli* viale A-de Gaspari ☎4450 rm38
⇌8 ⋒12 G

Assisi Perugia 24,400 (☎075) Map **31** B3
★★★Giotto via Fontebella 41 ☎812209 rm72
⇌45 ⋒14 G Lift B8700–19700 M6500
Pn21700–22850
★★★Subasio via Frate Elia 2 ☎812206 rm70
⇌70 G Lift B8500–19200 M6000
Pn18000–21000
★★★Windsor Savoia Porta San Francisco
☎812210 rm33 ⇌33 ⋒33 G Lift LD B7400–
17500 M6000 Pn17000–19000
★★Umbra via Degli Archi 2 ☎812240 rm27
⇌18 B7500–17200 M6000–7000
Pn19000–23000

Asti Asti 79,900 (☎0141) Map **28** D3
★★★Salera via del Fortino ☎211815 rm54
⇌54 G Lift LD B14500–23000 M6000
Pn25000
i⅍24 G Vignetti via Ticino 1 ☎55016 M/c
G30

Avellino Avellino 56,800 (☎0825) Map **33** B3
★★★Jolly via Tuoro Cappuccini 97a ☎32191
rm74 ⇌57 Lift B10000–26000 M6000
Pn20200–25700

i⅍C Medici via Tagliamento 82 e/o ☎38133
M/c Frd G10

Barbarano See **Gardone Riviera**

Bardolino Verona 5,800 (☎045) Map **29** B4
★★★Vela d'Oro ☎623067 tx48444 rm60
(A10) ⋒52 May–Sep LD B10500–18000
M5500 Pn19000 ⅋ Pool Lake

Bardonecchia Torino 3,250 (☎0122)
Map **28** C3
★★★Genys-Splendid viale Bramafam 41
☎9001 rm60 ⇌30 ⋒6 Lift 20 Dec–31 Mar
1 Jul–30 Aug

Bari Bari 374,550 (☎080) Map **34** C4
★★★★Palace via Lombardi 13 ☎216551
tx81111 Palaceba rm154 ⇌102 ⋒50 G Lift
★★★Jolly via G Petroni 15 ☎364366
tx81274 Jolly BA 2 rm164 ⇌164 G Lift
B19200–33700 M6500 Pn30400
★★★Nazioni Lungomare Nazario Sauro 7
☎331188 rm132 ⇌88 Lift Sea
★★Grand Moderno via Crisanzio 80 ☎213313
rm51 ⇌21 G Lift B6000–18000
i⅍24 L F Tray 65 Japigia 48 ☎330158 Frd G7
At **Torre a Mare** (12km)
☆☆☆**AGIP** ☎300001 rm95 ⋒95 Lift
B7600–17550

Baveno Novara 4,300 (☎0323) Map **28** D4
★★Beau Rivage via della Vittoria 36 ☎2534
rm80 (A7) ⇌25 G Lift Apr–Oct LD
B6650–17300 M6300 Pn12000–15500
★★Nazionale San Gottardo via Nazionale 7
☎2529 rm25 ⇌8 Lift Apr–Oct Lake
★★Simplon ☎2112 tx20217 rm100 ⇌100 G
Lift 20 Mar–30 Oct LD B10800–26400
M5000–7000 Pn12000–20000 ⅋ Pool Lake
★★Splendid via Sempione 12 ☎2583 tx20217
rm100 ⇌100 G Lift 18 Mar–30 Oct LD
B11200–29800 M6500–7500
Pn12000–24000 ⅋ Pool Golf Lake
★*Ripa* via Sempione ☎2589 rm10 G
Apr–Sep Lake
At **Feriolo** (3km SW)
★★*Carillon* ☎2915 rm20 ⇌2 ⋒15 G
1 Apr–15 Oct

Belgirate Novara 550 (☎0322) Map **28** D4
★★★Milano via Sempione 2 ☎7495 rm65
⇌40 G Lift LD B10200–20400 M4000–7000
Pn12000–18000 St9% Lake
★★*Villa Carlotta* ☎7487 rm112 ⇌83 ⋒9 G
Lift LD Pool Lake

Bellagio Como 3,400 (☎031) Map **29** A4
★★★★★*Serbelloni* via Roma 1 ☎950216
ta Grandhotel rm115 ⇌110 G Lift Apr–Oct
⅋ Pool Lake
★★★Lac pza Mazzini ☎950320 rm48 ⇌41
⋒3 Lift Etr–Sep B7500–19800 M5500–6000
Pn12000–16800 St9% Lake
★★*Belvedere* ☎950410 rm41 ⇌10 ⋒7 G Lift
Apr–10 Oct Pool Lake
★★Firenze pza Mazzini ☎950342 rm52 ⇌25
⋒4 Lift May–Sep B10000–25000 M6000
Pn16000–20000 Lake
★★Metropole pza Mazzini 5 ☎950409 rm58
⇌50 G Lift Apr–Oct B7500–26000 M7000
Pn20000–25000 St% Pool Lake

Bellano Como 3,700 (☎0341) Map **29** A4
★★Meridiana ☎821126 rm29 ⇌29 G Lift LD
B6500–19000 M4500 Pn14000 St9% Lake

Bellaria Igea Marina Forli 11,800 (☎0541)
Map **30** C2
At **Bellaria**
★*Levante* via C-Colombo 1 ☎44223 rm32
⋒32 Lift 1 May–30 Sep B9000–18000
M4500–5000 Pn10000–13500 Sea
At **Igea Marina**

Italy

★★★**Touring Spiaggia** (2km S) Lungomare
Pinzon 217 ☎630419 rm39 ⇆9 ⋔30 Lift
27 May–17 Sep B8800–16000
M4000–6000 Pn10000–14000 Pool Beach Sea

Belluno Belluno 36,100 (☎0437) Map **30** C4
⬙**Bianchet Moretti** via T-Vecellio ☎25789
N⬙ AR

Eucar via T-Vecellio 79 ☎24776 N⬙ Frd

Bergamo Bergamo 129,950 (☎035) Map **29** A
★★★**Excelsior San Marco** (n rest) pza
Repubblica 6 ☎232132 rm101 ⇆46 ⋔35 G Lift
★★★**Moderno** viale P Giovanni XXIII 106
☎233033 rm96 ⇆32 ⋔37 Lift B9000–24000
M6000 Pnfr14000
★★*Agnello d'Oro* via Gombito 22 ☎249883
rm25 ⇆5 ⋔20 Lift B7000–11000
M6000–8000 Pn16000
⬙*T Masserini* via Borgo Palazzo 193
☎237326 N⬙ BL/Rov/Tri
⬙⬙*Universal* via Suardi 40 ☎234500
GM G100

Biella Vercelli 56,000 (☎015) Map **28** D4
★★★**Astoria** (n rest) viale Roma 9 ☎20545
rm50 ⇆50 G Lift B20500–33000
⬙*GI-Emme* via Losana 6 ☎33907 N⬙ M/c
GM G70

Bivigliano Firenze (☎055) Map **29** B2
★★**Giotto Park** ☎409608 rm38 (A21) ⇆21
B7200–21600 M5000–5500 Pn12500–19500
⬙

Bologna Bologna 492,725 (☎051) Map **29** B3
★★★★★**Royal Carlton** via Montebello 8
☎554141 tx51356 rm254 ⇆254 G Lift
B33000–48000 Màlc
★★★★**Jolly de la Gare** pza XX Settembre 2
☎264405 tx51076 rm172 ⇆172 Lift
B21500–34000 M7500 Pn34500
★★★★*Milano* via Pietramellara 51 ☎239442
tx51213 rm86 G Lift
☆☆☆**AGIP** via M-E-Lepido 203 ☎401131
rm60 ⋔60 Lift B9550–20250
☆☆☆ **Euro Crest** pza della Constitutione
☎372172 tx51676 rm164 ⇆159 ⋔5 G Lift
B17500–40000 M7000 Pn33000–40000 Pool
★★★*Metropolitan* (n rest) via dell'Orso 4
☎272801 rm40 ⇆30 ⋔10 G Lift
ⓘ⬙**24** *Centercar* via Fruili Venezia Guilia 5
☎491006 BMW G50
Cisa via A-di-Vincenzo 6 ☎370434 N⬙ BL
C Cesari via della Grada 9 ☎554554 N⬙
BL/Rov/Tri/VW
⬙⬙*F Stracciari* via Bovi Campeggi 3
☎551555 N⬙ M/c Ren

Bolsena Viterbo 3,950 (☎0761) Map **31** B3
★★**Columbus** ☎98009 rm48 (A40) ⇆40 G
B6200–16000 M5000 Pn16900–18000 Lake
★★**Lido** via Cassia ☎98026 rm12 (A12) ⇆12
G LD B13300(double) M5000 Pn17200 Lake

Bolzano-Bozen 107,100 (☎0471) Map **12** D1
★★★★**Alpi** via Alto Adige 35 ☎26671 tx40156
rm112 ⇆95 G Lift B14000–32600 M5500
Pn24500–28500
☆☆☆**AGIP** Ponte Roma ☎33364 rm18 ⋔18
B3750–6600
★★★**Grifone** pza Walther 7 ☎27057
tx40081 rm130 ⇆70 ⋔20 Lift LD B16100–
40200 M6600 Pn28000–33200 Pool
★★★**Laurin** via Laurin 2 ☎47500 tx40081
rm120 ⇆74 G Lift Pool
★★*Cita di Bolzano* pza Walther 21 ☎21240
rm97 ⇆50 Lift
★★**Figl** pza Grano 9 ☎21412 rm24 ⇆6 Lift
★★**Luna** via Bottai 25 ☎21429 rm80 ⇆62
⋔25 G Lift B11000–29000 M5000
Pn20000–24000 ⬙
★★**Scala** via Brennero 11 ☎41111 rm65 ⇆65
G Lift LD B12000–26000 Pn20000–22000 Pool

⬙**Bolzano** via Roma 98 ☎36265 N⬙ BL
⬙**Mich** via Galilei 6 ☎41119 N⬙ M/c BL/Rov/Tri
ⓘ⬙**24 1000 Miglia** via Macello 13 ☎26340
N⬙21000 GM
ⓘ⬙**SAS Motor** via Macello 53 ☎25373 N⬙
BMW
E Tasini via Roma 61b ☎916118 N⬙ Frd

Bonassola La Spezia 1,200 (☎0187)
Map **29** A2
★★**Lungomare** ☎813632 rm44 ⋔12
1 Apr–30 Sep B5350–9700 M4500
Pn9500–11000

Borca di Cadore Belluno 750 Map **13** A1
At **Corte di Cadore** (2km E)
★★★*Boite* ☎82001 rm84 ⋔84 Lift
20 Dec–30 Mar 1 Jun–30 Sep ⬙

Bordighera Imperia 11,900 (☎0184)
Map **28** D2
★★★★*Grand del Mare* via Aurelia ☎22201
rm105 ⇆105 G Lift 20 Dec–30 Sep Pool
Beach Sea
★★★★*Jolanda* Corso Italia 85 ☎21325 rm45
⇆40 Lift Dec–Oct B11800–23300 M7800
Pn19000–21000 Sea
★★★*Belvedere* via Romana 56 ☎21408 rm76
⇆33 Lift 23 Dec–30 Sep Sea
★★**Elisa** via Romana 70 ☎21313 rm35 (A5)
⇆25 ⋔2 G Lift 15 Dec–15 Oct B7000–17000
M6500 Pn11000–16000 Sea
★★**Excelsior** via GI-Biamonti 30 ☎21488
rm42 ⇆20 ⋔10 Lift B6500–19000
M5500–6500 Pn12000–21500
⬙*G Renalto* via Ferrara 8 ☎22908 N⬙ Frd

Bormio Sondrio 4,050 (☎0342) Map **12** D1
★★*Funivia* ☎91341 ta Funitel rm41 ⇆19 G
Lift 1 Nov–30 Sep
★★**Posta** via Roma 66 ☎901106 rm58 ⇆28
⋔13 Lift LD Dec 15–Apr 15–Jun–Sep
B8200–17400 M6000 Pn19800–22000

Brescia Brescia 213,130 (☎030) Map **29** A/B4
☆☆☆**AGIP** viale Bornata 42 ☎361654 rm42
⋔42 Lift B4300–9750
⬙*Astra-Motor* via F-Boario 16 ☎57561 N⬙ Frd
Brescia Motori via L-Apollonia 17A ☎50051
N⬙ BL/Rov/Tri

Bressanone-Brixen Bolzano 16,150
(☎0472) Map **13** A1
★★★**Elefante** Rio Bianco 4 ☎22288 tx40491
rm48 (A16) ⇆48 G Mar–Oct B17500–35000
M5500 Pn23000 St%
★★★**Gasser** via Giardini 19 ☎22105 rm30
⇆27 G 20 Mar–22 Oct B8000–28000
M4500–5500 Pn14500–22000
ⓘ⬙**24 Lanz** via Stazione 32 ☎22226 M/c
Aud/VW G30

Breuil See **Cervinia-Breuil**

Brindisi Brindisi 85,100 (☎0831) Map **34** B2
★★★**Internazionale** Lungomare Regina
Margherita ☎23475 rm87 ⇆87 G Lift
B12500–21000 M6000 Pn23000 Sea
★★★**Jolly** corso Umberto 149 ☎22941
tx86078 Jolly Br rm77 ⇆54 Lift
B10700–25000 M6000 Pn20000–24900
★★**Rosetta** via San Dionisio 2 ☎23423 rm34
⇆1 ⋔17 G
Giovine Biagio via Cappuccini 70 ☎23037
N⬙ M/c Opl
ⓘ⬙**Tullio Marino** via Appia 340 ☎81888
M/c Frd G10

Brunico-Bruneck Bolzano 10,800 (☎0474)
Map **13** A1
★★★**Posta** Greben 9 ☎85127 rm64 ⇆34 ⋔8
Lift B12000–28000 M4000–6000
Pn17000–23000
⬙**24 F Crepaz** via A-Hofer 5 ☎85173 Opl

Cadenabbia Como (☎0344) Map **29** A4

Italy

★**Beau-Rivage** via Regina 87 ☎40426 rm20
⇦3 ⋔2 1 Apr–30 Oct B6000–17200 M5000
Pn8500–14000 St9% Lake

Cagliari See **Sardegna (Sardinia)**

Caltagirone See **Sicilia (Sicily)**

Camaiore (Lido di) Lucca 4,041 (☎0584)
Map 29 B2
★★★**Grand & Riviera** pza Matteotti 64
☎64571 rm80 ⇦50 ⋔10 G Lift 15 Apr–15 Oct
B6000–25000 M10000 Pn23000–30000
★★*Pineta Mare* viale C-Colombo 195 ☎64623
rm33 ⇦33 Lift Sea
❀L **Galletti** via Brancola 2 ☎64059 Jag/Vlo
Camogli Genova 7,050 (☎0185) Map 29 A3
★★★★**Cenobio Dei Dogi** via Cuneo 34
☎770041 rm74 ⇦44 ⋔30 Lift ❧ Pool Beach
Sea
★★*Casmona* via Garibaldi 103 ☎770015
rm34 (A15) ⋔11 Sea
Campione d'Italia See page 296
(Italian enclave in Switzerland)
Campobasso Campobasso 44,050 (☎0874)
Map 33 B4
P Vitale via XXIV Maggio 95 ☎61069 N❦
Aud/MB/Por/VW

Campo Nell'Elba See **Elba (Isola d')**

Canazei Trento 1,500 (☎0462) Map 13 A1
★★**Croce Bianca** via Roma 3 ☎61111 rm30
⇦30 G 1 Jun–30 Sep 20 Dec–15 Apr
B6300–20000 M5500–6400 Pn13500–20500
Candeli See **Firenze**
Cannero Riviera Novara 1,450 (☎0323)
Map 28 D4
★★**Cannero** Lungo Lago ☎78046 rm32 ⇦32
G Lift B9000–20000 M7000
Pn14000–16000 Lake
Caorle Venezia 11,100 (☎0421) Map 30 C4
★★**Excelsior** via Vespucci ☎81515 rm55
⇦55 Lift 15 May–30 Sep B1100–18500
M5500 Pn10500–14000 St9% Beach Sea
★★**Parigi** ☎81430 rm51 ⇦45 Lift
20 May–20 Sep B6400–14950 M4500
Pn 9700–10800 Sea
❦❦**24 G Cecotto** via Strada Nuova 64
☎81315 M/c

Capo Boi See **Villasimius** under
Sardegna (Sardinia)

Capri (Isola di) Napoli 12,350 (☎081)
Map 32 D1
★★★★★**Quisisana** via Carmerelle 2
☎8370788 tx71520 rm130 ⇦130 Lift
B30200–46600 M14000 Pn51400–57600
❧ Pool Sea
★★★★**Tiberio Palace** via Croce 13
☎8370100 ta Avinitiberio rm96 ⇦85 ⋔11 Lift
25 Mar–31 Oct B17500–33100 M8000
Pn25500–32600 St9% Sea
★★*Manfredi Pagano* viale Campi 15
☎837202 ta Manfredi rm30 ⇦12 ⋔2 Sea
At **Anacapri**
★★★**San Michele** ☎8371427 rm50 ⇦35
⋔10 G Lift 1 Mar–15 Nov LD B8000–20500
M6000 Pn13000–18000 Pool Sea
Carbonin di Dobbiaco See
Cortina d'Ampezzo
Carrara (Marina di) Massa Carrara
7,920 (☎0585) Map 29 A2
★★**Mediterraneo** via Genova 2 bis ☎57397
rm50 ⇦5 ⋔15 Lift B6300–18500
M5500–7450 Lift Pn13000–19500 Sea
★★*Paradiso* viale Litoraneo 121 ☎5115
rm24 ⇦5 15 May–30 Sep Beach Sea
Casale Monferrato Alessandria 43,700
(☎0142) Map 28 D3
❦❦**Casalese** Corso Indipendenza 16
☎2130 N❦ Opl/Vau

Caserta Caserta 65,500 (☎0823)
Map 33 A3
★★★**Jolly** via V-Veneto 9 ☎25222
tx71548 Jolly C E rm92 ⇦92 Lift
B14500–24700 M6500 Pn25700
❦❦**24 Colombo** via Colombo 56 ☎25268
Cit/Lnc/MB/Ren G90
❦❦❦*M Masullo* via Roma 92 ☎26441
N❦ BL/Rov/Tri
Cassino Frosinone 28,300 (☎0776)
Map 32 C2
★★**Florida** pza Diaz 14 ☎22041 rm30
⇦10 ⋔4 G B3700–9400 M3500
Pn10000–12000
Castellina in Chianti Siena 2,900
(☎0577) Map 29 B2
★★**Villa Casalecchi** ☎740240 rm15 ⇦9
⋔6 Apr–Oct LD B15350–22750 M9900
Pn26300 Pool
At **Ricavo** (4km N)
★★★**Tenuta di Ricavo** ☎740221 rm25 ⇦25
1 Apr–31 Oct LD **Pn** 21000–28000 St9% Pool

Castelvetrano See **Sicilia (Sicily)**

Castiglioncello Livorno 3,433 (☎0586)
Map 29 B2
★★★**Miramare** via Marconi 8 ☎752435
rm64 ⇦24 ⋔18 G 25 Apr–25 Sep LD
B10000–21600 M7000–8000
Pn17000–24000 ❧ Pool Golf ◯
★★**Guerrini** via Roma 12 ☎752047 rm29
⇦2 ⋔11 B6300–14450 M4200
Pn9500–15750

Catania See **Sicilia (Sicily)**

Catanzaro Catanzaro 89,700 (☎0961)
Map 34 C2
☆☆☆**AGIP** exit Strada due Mari ☎51791 rm76
⋔76 Lift B8800–20000
Autosabin via Nuora Bellavista 35–39
☎41522 N❦ Frd

Cattolica Forli 15,850 (☎0541) Map 30 C2
★★★★**Victoria Palace** via Carducci 24
☎962921 rm92 ⇦92 Lift 1 May–30 Sep LD
B9800–28600 M6000–6500 Pn16000–25000
Beach Sea
★★★**Caravelle** ☎962417 rm45 ⇦45 G Lift
Apr–31 Oct Beach Sea
★★★**Diplomat** via del Turismo ☎962200
rm80 ⇦80 G Lift 25 May–15 Sep
B9000–22000 M5000 Pn15000–20000 ❧
Beach Sea
★★★*Europa-Monetti* via Curiel 33
☎961159 rm84 ⇦70 Lift Beach
★★★**Gambrinus Mare** viale Oriani ☎961347
rm42 ⇦33 Lift 1 May–15 Oct
B6000–14000 M4000 Pn9000–13000
Beach Sea
★★★**Moderno Majestic** viale d'Annunzio 13
☎961169 rm60 ⇦60 Lift 20 May–20 Sep LD
B5000–10000 M4000 Pn10000–16500
Beach Sea
★★★**Rosa** via Carducci 80 ☎963275 rm53
⇦23 ⋔30 Lift 20 May–20 Sep
B5500–11200 M3500–4000
Pn10300–14500 Sea
★★*Maxim* via Facchini 7 ☎962137 rm55
⇦4 ⋔51 May–Sep
★★*Nord-Est* via Carducci 60 ☎961293
rm72 ⇦16 Lift 30 Apr–20 Oct Beach Sea
★★**Senior** viale del Prete ☎963443 rm46 (A)
⇦16 ⋔30 G Lift 1 May–30 Sep B9000–11500
M3000 Pn12000–14000 Pool
★**Bellariva** via Fiume 10 ☎961609 rm26
(A15) ⇦6 ⋔6 May–Sep B4100–10300
M3500–5000 Pn 9900–12500
❦❦*A Fernando* via del Prete 4 ☎961055 M/c
Aud/VW G20

Cava de'Tirenni Salerno 48,350 (☎089)
Map **33** B3
★★**Victoria** corso Mazzini 4 ☎841064 rm42
⇥10 🅿27 G Lift B6900–15300 M4000–4200
Pn11800–13900 ⚓

Cavaglia' Vercelli 3,100 (☎0161)
Map **28** D4
★★**Prateria** ☎96115 rm32 ⇥25 G
⌐1 Feb–30 Nov B9500–18000 M6000 Pn16000

Cavi See Lavagna

Celle Ligure Savona 4,800 (☎019)
Map **28** D3
★★★**San Michele** Piani ☎990017 rm57
⇥57 G Lift 1 Jun–30 Sep LD B12500–23000
M6000–7000 Pn14000–17000 Pool Beach Sea

Ceriale Savona 4,210 (☎0182) Map **28** D2
★★**Torelli** Lungomare ☎90040 rm60 ⇥23
Lift 23 Dec–1 Nov Beach Sea

Cernobbio Como 8,250 (☎031) Map **29** A4
★★★★★**Villa d'Este** ☎511471 tx38025
rm160 ⇥150 🅿10 G Lift Apr–31 Oct
⚓ Pool Golf Lake
★★★**Regina Olga** ☎510171 rm70 ⇥70 🅿15
G Lift LD B16000–28000 M6000–6500
Pn23000–25000 St9% Pool Lake
★**Asnigo** pza San-Stefano ☎510062 rm23
🅿10 16 Mar–15 Oct B8500–18000 M5000
Lake

Cervia Ravenna 24,150 (☎0544)
Map **30** C3
★★**Buenos Aires** Lungomare G Deledda 130
☎71948 rm58 ⇥2 🅿56 Lift 1 Apr–30 Sep
B8800–17100 M5500–6000 Pn10000–14300
Beach Sea
★★**K2** viale del Mille 98 ☎71025 rm37 ⇥1
🅿36 20 May–20 Sep Beach Sea
🕭⚓**Opel Cervia** via Oriani 57 ☎91390 Opl
At **Milano Marittima** (3km N)
★★★★**Aurelia** viale 2 Giugno 31 ☎972082
rm113 (A) ⇥113 Lift 1 May–30 Sep ⚓ Pool
Beach Sea
★★★★**Mare & Pineta** viale Dante ☎972262
rm200 ⇥200 G Lift 20 May–20 Sep ⚓
Beach ∩ Sea
🕭⚓**Europa** viale 2 Giugno 15 ☎92276 Fia
G80

Cervinia–Breuil Aosta 2,050 (☎0166)
Map **28** D4
★★★★**Cervinia** ☎94028 rm78 ⇥74 🅿4 G
Lift 1 Dec–30 Apr
★★**Valdôtain** Lago Bleu ☎94428 rm27 🅿27
G 30 Nov–5 May 28 Jun–24 Sep

Cesenatico Forli 19,500 (☎0547)
Map **30** C2
★★★**Britannia** viale Carducci 129 ☎80041
rm44 ⇥44 G Lift 27 May–15 Sep
B9000–20000 M5000–7000
Pn12000–19000 Pool Beach Sea
★★★**Grand** pza Costa ☎80012 rm120 ⇥57
G Lift 1 Jun–20 Sep ⚓ Beach Sea
★★★**Internazionale** via Ferrara 7 ☎80231
rm52 ⇥32 🅿20 Lift 1 Jun–20 Sep
⚓ Pool Beach Sea
★★★**Torino** viale Carducci 55 ☎80044 rm48
🅿48 Lift 20 May–20 Sep B5600–12600
M4000–6000 Pn11000–15000 Sea
🕭⚓**Internazionale** viale Carducci 95
☎81418
🕭⚓**Luciano** via A-Saffi 91 ☎81347 BMW/
Lnc/MB

Chiavari Genova 31,900 (☎0185)
Map **29** A2/3
★★**Mignon** via Tripoli 5 ☎309420 tx0185
rm32 ⇥20 Lift
★★**Santa Maria** via T-Groppo ☎309621
rm36 ⇥8 G Lift B5500–14200 M4300–5900
Pn 9000–14500 Sea

Tigullio Rocks (on SS1) ☎318193 rm11
⇥7 🅿11 Lift B5500–14900 Pool Beach Sea
i Cantero corso Dante 90 ☎307018 G525
🕭**24 G Ughini** corso de Michiel 125
☎308278 N🕭390549 Aud/MB/VW

Chiavenna Sondrio 7,450 (☎0343)
Map **12** C1
★★★**Conradi** ☎32300 rm34 ⇥6 🅿6 G Lift
★★**Nazionale** pza Bertacchi ☎32303 rm17
⇥1 🅿2

Chioggia Venezia 52,100 (☎041)
Map **30** C3
★★**Grande Italia** pza Vigo ☎400515 rm61
⇥20 Lift 15 Dec–6 Nov B8300–22100 Sea
🕭**Autolagunare** via Orti Est 31 ☎401110
Fia

Chiusa-Klausen Bolzano 4,050 (☎0472)
Map **13** A1
★**Posta** ☎47514 rm61 ⇥19 🅿5 G Lift
B6500–19000 M4000–6000 Pn12000–15000
Pool

Chivasso Torino 26,300 (☎011)
Map **28** D3
★**Moro** (n rest) via Roma 17 ☎9102191
rm39 ⇥7 G

Cirella Cosenza 1,207 (☎0985) Map **34** C2
☆**Autostello** ☎86055 rm82 (A51) ⇥41 🅿70
B13800–22600 M5000 Pn12000–19000 St%
Beach Sea

Citta 'della Pieve Perugia 6,500 (☎0578)
Map **31** B3
★★**Barzanti** via Santa Lucia ☎28010 rm30
⇥26 🅿12 G B7500–12000 M4000
Pn13500–14500 ⚓ Pool Golf

Civitavecchia Roma 46,150 (☎0766)
Map **31** B3
SAC Lungomare Garibaldi 42 ☎21830 N🕭 BL

Claviere Torino 200 (☎0122) Map **28** C3
★★**Bes** ☎8805 rm19 (A) ⇥12 G
1 Dec–15 Apr 15 Jun–15 Sep

Colico Como 5,250 (☎0341) Map **29** A4
★★**Isola Bella** via Nazionale 6 ☎940101
rm46 ⇥26 🅿4 G
★**Gigi** ☎940268 rm18 ⇥4 G B5500–12500
M5000 Pn11000–12500 St%
★**Risi** pza Cavour 1 ☎940123 rm71 (A21)
⇥50 G Lift LD B6000–18000 M4000
Pn14000 Lake

Como Como 98,550 (☎031) Map **29** A4
★★★**Flori** (n rest) via per Cernobbio 12
☎557642 rm49 ⇥41 🅿7 G Lift 1 Apr–30 Nov
B10500–29800 Lake
★★**Engadina** (n rest) viale Rosselli 22
☎550415 rm21 ⇥9 🅿12 Lift B7000–17000
St9%
★★**Firenze** pza Volta 16 ☎272001 rm34 ⇥7
🅿4 Lift LD
★★**Park** (n rest) viale Rosselli 20 ☎556782
tx031 rm42 ⇥15 🅿15 Lift Mar–Nov
★★**San Gottardo** pza Volta ☎263531 rm56
⇥20 🅿2 G Lift
★★**Tre Re** ☎265374 rm33 ⇥13 G LD
B7500–16000 M5000 Pn14000–15000
i 🕭Autorimessa Dante via Dante 59
☎272545 Ren G120
Grassi & Airoldi via Napoleona 50 ☎266027
N🕭 BL/Rov/Tri
At **Lipomo** (4km S)
★**MEC** (n rest) via Provinciale per Lecco
☎269227 rm35 🅿29 ⚓

Conca dei Marini Salerno 750 (☎089)
Map **33** B3
★★★**Belvedere** ☎871266 rm33 ⇥30 🅿3 Lift
1 Apr–30 Oct B7650–21800 M6400
Pn18650–20850 Pool Beach Sea

Italy

Corte di Cadore See **Borca di Cadore**
Cortina d'Ampezzo Belluno 8,650 (☎0436)
Map **13** A1
★★★★ **Corona** corso C-Battisti ☎3251
tx44004HCR rm56 (A10) ⇨40 🅿2 G Lift
20 Jun–10 Sep 20 Dec–31 Mar B12500–32000
M8000 Pn16000–27000
★★★★ **Cristallo Palace** via R-Menardi
☎4281 rm100 ⇨100 G Lift Jun–Sep Dec–Mar
Pn36000–53000 ⤴ Pool Sea
★★★★ **Miramonti-Majestic** ☎4201 rm143
⇨113 🅿30 G Lift 20 Dec–31 Mar
10 Jun–10 Sep ⤴ Pool Golf
★★★★ **Savoia** via Roma 62 ☎3201
tx44004SAV rm145 ⇨145 C Lift
20 Dec–30 Mar 28 Jun–10 Sep ⤴ Pool
☆☆☆ **AGIP** via Roma 70 ☎839101 rm28 🅿28
Lift B7000–18000
★★★ **Ampezzo** via 29 Maggio 15 ☎4241
rm78 ⇨53 🅿8 Lift 20 Dec–30 Mar
15 May–30 Sep LD B15000–35000
M7000–10000 Pn18000–28000
★★★ **Ancora** corso Italia 72 ☎3261 rm88 (A)
⇨57 🅿7 G Lift 5 Dec–5 Oct
★★★ **Concordia** corso Italia 28 ☎4251 rm78
(A) ⇨40 G Lift 20 Jun–10 Sep
★★★ **Cortina** corso Italia 94 ☎4221 rm55 ⇨55
Lift 20 Dec–15 Apr 20 Jun–20 Sep
B 15000–37000 M7000–10000
Pn18000–29500
★★★ **Europa** corso Italia 207 ☎3221
tx44004 Azientur for Europa rm52 ⇨43 🅿9 Lift
B17500–37000 M7000–9000
Pn21500–28500
★★★ **Poste** pza Roma 14 ☎4271 tx44044
rm82 ⇨82 G Lift 20 Dec–10 Oct
B 14000–43200 M8000–12000
Pn21000–38000
★★ **Alpes** via Verra 4 ☎2021 rm37 ⇨4
20 Dec–30 Mar 25 Jun–25 Sep
B 16500–24000 M4000–5000
Pn17000–20000
★★ **Menardi** Majon 114 ☎2400 rm40 ⇨35
G Dec–Mar Jun–Sep
★ **Tiziano** Campo di Sotto 26 ☎2504 rm41
⇨21 15 Jun–15 Sep 20 Dec–30 Mar
🛏 🕭 **Dolomiti** corso Italia 182 ☎61077 N⏀
Fia/Lnc
At **Carbonin di Dobbiaco** (17km NE)
★★ **Ploner** ☎72240 rm103 (A) ⇨15 🅿5 G
20 Dec–30 Sep ⤴ ☊

Cosenza Cosenza 102,550 (☎0984)
Map **34** C2
★★★ **Jolly** Lungo Crati De Seta 2b ☎24489
rm64 ⇨48 Lift B13800–23000 M5500
Pn23000
At **Rende** (6km NW)
☆☆☆ **AGIP** Castiglione Cosentino Scalo
☎839101 rm65 🅿65 Lift B8900–20500
🛏 🕭 **AMC** via S Pellico ☎39598 N⏀ M/c BMW

Costalunga (Passo di) Trento Map **13** A4
★★ **Passo di Carezza** ☎61023 rm43 ⇨10 G
15 Jun–1 Oct
★★ **Savoy** Carezza al Lago ☎61824 rm45
⇨15 🅿15 Lift ⤴

Courmayeur Aosta 2,550 (☎0165)
Map **28** C4
★★★★★ **Royal** ☎83621 rm80 ⇨80 G Lift
22 Dec–Mar 27 Jun–10 Sep Pool
★★★★ **Pavillon** ☎82420 rm40 ⇨40 G Lift
1 Jun–10 Oct 1 Dec–30 Apr LD
B15500–41000 M8000 Pn25000–36000 Pool
★★★ **Alpes** ☎89981 rm56 ⇨56 G Lift
6 Dec–28 Sep

Cremona Cremona 82,650 (☎0372)
Map **29** A3

★★★ **Continental** pza Libertà 27 ☎430209
rm51 ⇨51 G Lift LD B8800–19000 M5000
Pn17500–19000
General Cars via Castelleone 77 ☎20343 N⏀
GM

Cuneo Cuneo 56,050 (☎0171) Map **28** C/D3
★★★ **Augustus Minerva** corso Giolitti 1
☎65934 rm67 ⇨47 🅿10 Lift
★★ **Royal Superga** via Pascal 3 ☎3223 rm48
⇨29 G
🛏 🕭 **Cunicar** via Torino ☎66442 N⏀ BL/Rov/Tri

Desenzano del Garda Brescia 18,750
(☎030) Map **29** B4
★★★ **Mayer & Splendid** pza del Porto
☎9141409 rm56 ⇨12 🅿23 G 1 Mar–10 Nov
B5300–12600 M5000–6000
Pn10000–12500 Lake
★★★ **Ramazzotti** viale Dal Molin 78 ☎9141808
rm22 ⇨10 G B7500–15000 Lake
★★ **Barchetta** pza Matteoti 27 ☎9141006
rm36 ⇨8 🅿2 Lake
★★ **Eden** Lungolago C-Battisti 27 ☎9141416
rm30 (A12) ⇨10 🅿4 B5000–13200
M4500–5000 Pn10200–13000 Lake
★★ **Vittorio** Portovecchio 18 ☎9141504
rm35 ⇨20 🅿5 B6000–13000 M4500
Pn12500 Lake

Diano Marina Imperia 6,950 (☎0183)
Map **28** D2
★★★★ **Diana Majestic** via degli Oleandri 15
☎45445 rm80 ⇨80 G Lift 15 Mar–20 Oct LD
B19000–33000 M9000–11500
Pn48000–70000 Pool Beach Sea
★★ **Florida** via St-Elmo 21 ☎45226 rm88
⇨15 🅿73 Lift 15 May–30 Sep Beach Sea
★★ **Riviera** (Pensione) viale Torino 6 ☎45147
rm32 🅿32 Lift Beach Sea
★★ **Teresa** viale Torino 34 ☎45007 rm138 (A)
⇨52 🅿6 Lift May–30 Sep Beach Sea
🏍 **G Ghiradi** via Gl-Ardoino 131 ☎45334 AR G

Elba (Isola d') Livorno 28.250 (☎0565)

Lacona 140 Map **31** A3
★★★ **Capo Sud** (Hotel & Bungalows)
☎964021 rm34 ⇨2 🅿32 G 15 May–30 Sep
LD B6300–17900 M5000–7000
Pn10800–18400 ⤴ Beach Sea

Marciana-Marina 1,830 Map **31** A3
★★★ **Primula** ☎99010 rm63 ⇨40 🅿23 G
1 Apr–30 Oct Pool
At **Procchio** (7km SE)
★★★★ **Golfo** ☎907523 rm95 ⇨40 🅿55 G
15 May–15 Oct ⤴ Pool Beach Sea
At **Spartaia** (5.5km SE)
★★★ **Désirée** ☎907502 rm72 ⇨20 🅿52
15 Apr–15 Oct LD **Pn**14200–26000 ⤴ Beach
Sea

Marina di Campo 4,308 Map **31** A3
★★★★ **Iselba** ☎97096 rm45 (A3) ⇨21 🅿22
15 May–15 Oct LD B22600–44600 M9000
Pn34000–40000 Beach Sea

Porto Azzurro 2,940 Map **31** A3
★★★ **Elba International** ☎968611 tx68279
rm242 ⇨242 Lift 1 Apr–10 Oct ⤴ Pool Beach
Sea
★ **Belmare** ☎95012 rm55 (A30) LD
B6000–11350 M4500–5500 Pn11000–12600
Sea

Portoferraio 10,950 Map **31** A3
★★★ **Darsena** ☎92661 rm55 ⇨45 Lift Sea
★★★ **Garden** ☎98043 rm55 ⇨50
22 Apr–7 Oct Beach Sea
★★★ **Hermitage** ☎93932 rm90 ⇨80 🅿10
Lift 15 May–15 Oct ⤴ Pool Beach Sea
🛏 🕭 **Bardi Emilia** viale Elba 157 ☎93583 N⏀
Frd

Italy

Empoli Firenze 45,500 (☎0571) Map **29** B2
★★**Tazza d'Oro** via del Papa 46 ☎72129
rm56 ⇌49 G Lift B6300–15600 M4800
Pn12000

Erice See **Sicilia (Sicily)**

Fano Pesaro & Urbino 50,650 (☎0721)
Map **30** C2
★★**Astoria** viale Cairoli ☎82474 rm42
⇌32 1 May–1 Oct B4700–11400
M3500–4000 Pn7000–12000 Beach Sea
★★**Excelsior** Lungomare Simonetti 17
☎82558 rm30 ₪19 May–Sep Beach Sea
🛏🏷**24 L Eusebi** via C-Pisacane 50 ☎84300
Aud/VW

Fasano del Garda See **Gardone Riviera**

Ferentino Frosinone 16,370 (☎0775)
Map **32** C2
★★**Bassetto** via Casilina Sud ☎394931 rm72
⇌72 G Lift

Feriolo See **Baveno**

Ferrara Ferrara 155,500 (☎0532) Map **29** B3
★★★**Astra** viale Cavour 55 ☎26234 rm82
⇌33 ₪19 G Lift B9300–20900 M5300
Pn18300–22800 St9%
★★★**Europa** (n rest) corso Giovecca 49
☎33460 rm46 ⇌12 ₪7 G Lift
★★★**San Giorgio** (n rest) via Garibaldi 93
☎33141 rm85 ⇌11 ₪31 G Lift
🛏🏷**SIRA** via Bologna 306 ☎93375 N🏷 M/c
Frd

Fiesole Firenze 14,600 (☎055) Map **29** B2
★★★★**Villa San Michele** via Doccia 4 ☎59451
rm32 ⇌32 B41650–63400 M17500
Pn68050 St14%
★★**Aurora** pza Mino 39 ☎59100 rm22 ⇌20
B9300–28600 M7000 Pn24000–27000
At **San Domenico** (2.5km S)
★★**Bencista** ☎59163 rm35 (A1) ⇌9 ₪1 G
21 Mar–31 Oct

Finale Ligure Savona 14,250 (☎019)
Map **28** D2
★★★**Moroni** viale delle Palme 20 ☎63333
rm113 ⇌80 ₪33 G Lift 10 May–10 Oct
B16000–26000 M7000 Pn23000 Beach Sea
★★★**Tritzo** viale Torino 127 ☎63279 rm50
⇌27 ₪4 Lift 1 Dec–15 Oct Beach Sea
★**Principe** pza Oberdan 8 ☎63330 rm30
⇌24 15 Mar–15 Oct Beach Sea
At **Varigotti** (5km E)
★★★**Nik-Mehari** via Aurelia 104 ☎698030
rm30 ⇌30 G Lift Beach Sea
★★**Nazionale** via Aurelia 183 ☎698012 rm26
⇌8 B6000–21000 M6500 Pn8000–16500
Beach Sea

Fiore (on Lake Arvo) See **Lorica**

Firenze (Florence) Firenze 464,900 (☎055)
Map **29** B2 **See Plan**
★★★★★**Excelsior** pza Ognissanti 3 (off
Lungarno A-Vespucci) ☎294301 Plan **1**
tx57022 rm220 ⇌210 ₪10 G Lift
★★★★★**Grand** pza Ognissanti 1 (off Lungarno
A-Vespucci) ☎294401 Plan **2** tx57055 rm151
⇌151 G Lift
★★★★★**Savoy** pza della Repubblica 7
☎283313 Plan **3** tx57220 rm96 ⇌96 Lift
B31700–60400 M11500
★★★★★**Villa Medici** via il Prato 42 ☎261331
Plan **4** tx57179 rm105 ⇌105 G Lift
B27700–68100 Valk Pool
★★★★**Aerhotel Baglioni** pza Unità Italiana 6
☎218441 Plan **5** rm193 ⇌193 Lift
B21000–45700 Valk
★★★★**Jolly** pza V-Veneto 4 ☎2770 Plan **6**
tx57191 Jolly Fl rm145 ⇌145 Lift
B24900–49000 M8500 Pn39500–39900 Pool

★★★★**Londra** via Jacopo da Diacceto 20
☎262791 Plan **7** tx58152 rm105 ⇌105 G Lift
B22300–43600 M9000
★★★★**Minerva** pza Santa M-Novella 16
☎284555 Plan **8** tx57414 rm108 ⇌93 ₪15 G
Lift B19300–44300 M8500 Pool
★★★**Adriatico** via Maso Finiguerra ☎261781
Plan **10** rm106 ⇌70 ₪36 Lift B15000–26500
M6000 Pn24000
☆☆☆**AGIP** Raccardo Firenze-Mare Autostrada
del Sole (12km NW) ☎440081 Plan **21** rm109
₪109 Lift B10000–27000
★★★**Belvedere** (n rest) via B-Castelli 3
☎222501 Plan **11** rm27 ⇌27 Lift
1 May–30 Nov B15300–29500 St9% 🍽 Pool
★★★**Berchielli** (n rest) Lungarno Acciaioli 14
☎211530 Plan **12** rm78 ⇌28 ₪7 Lift
★★★**Croce di Malta** via della Scala 7
☎282600 Plan **14** tx Richiesto rm120 ⇌120 G
Lift
★★★**Embassy** via Nazionale 23 ☎260806
Plan **15** rm25 ⇌13 ₪4 G Lift
☆☆☆**EuroCrest** viale Europa 205 ☎686841
Plan **13** tx57376 rm92 ⇌92 Lift
B22000–33000 M8000 Pn34700–40200 Pool
★★★**Hermitage** (Pensione) vicolo Marzio 1
☎287216 Plan **16** rm16 ⇌12
★★★**Kraft** via Solferino 2 ☎284273 Plan **17**
rm66 ⇌62 Lift B16600–37550 M7500
Pn27400–32800 Pool
★★★**Regency** pza d'Azeglio 3 ☎577728
Plan **32** rm31 ⇌19 ₪12 B17500–32000
M6500 St9%
★★★**Roma** (n rest) pza Santa M-Novella 8
☎270366 Plan **18** rm61 ⇌25 ₪7 B12100–
31400
★★★**Villa Park San Domenico** via della
Piazzola ☎576697 Plan **20** rm19 ⇌19 G Lift
B16400–28500 M10000 Pn26400
★★**Autostrada** via L-Giori ☎371925 Plan **22**
rm45 ⇌30 ₪10 G Lift Pool
★★**Basilea** via Guelfa 41 ☎214587 Plan **23**
rm49 ⇌39 G Lift B8150–18700
★★**David** (n rest) via Michelangelo 1
☎675867 Plan **24** rm26 ⇌6 ₪5
★★**Franchi** (n rest) via Sgambati 28 ☎372425
Plan **32** rm35 ₪35 G Lift
★**Jenning's Riccioli** (n rest) Lungarno delle
Grazie 2 ☎23724 Plan **25** rm65 ⇌60 Lift
15 Mar–30 Nov
★★**Liana** (n rest) via V-Alfieri 18 ☎587608
Plan **26** rm22 (A13) ⇌9 ₪9 G B4750–18200
★★**Rapallo** via Santa C-d'Alessandria
☎472412 Plan **27** tx57273 rm40 ⇌15 ₪10
G Lift B10400–22200 M6200 Pn18500–
20700
★★**Rigatti** (Pensione) Lungarno Diaz 2
☎23022 Plan **28** rm25 ⇌7 Lift 15 Mar–30 Nov
★**Losanna** via Alfieri 9 ☎587516 Plan **30**
rm9 ⇌1 G Lift B4700–9000 M2500
Pn8000–9000 St%
★**Morandi** (n rest) pza S S Annunziata 3
☎212687 Plan **31** rm30 ⇌8 ₪4 Lift B6700–
14570
🛏🏷**24 Europa** Borgognissanti 96 ☎260846
GM G700
🛏🏷**M Ronchi** via Crimea 8 ☎489855 N🏷
🛏🏷**Scala** Lungarno del Tempio 44 ☎677740
N🏷 BMW G20
🛏**Zaniratti** viale Fratelli Rosselli 55 ☎471465
N🏷 BL/Rov/Tri
At **Candeli** (6km SE on road to **Bagno a
Ripoli**)
★★★★**Villa Massa** ☎630051 Plan **9** rm37
(A11) ⇌37 G Lift Pool Lake
At **Sesto Fiorentino** (9km NE)
★★**Villa Villoresi** ☎4489032 Plan **29** rm30
⇌20 ₪10 LD B10800–24050 M7600
Pn23000–27000 Pool

Italy

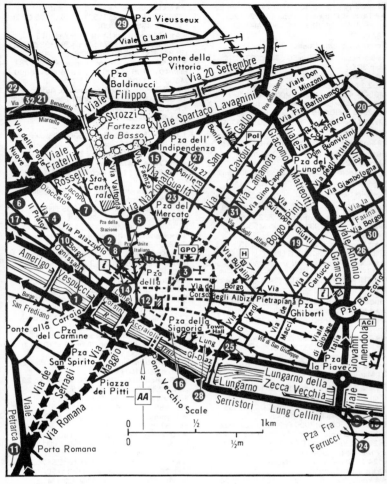

Firenze (Florence)

1	★★★★★Excelsior	17	★★★Kraft
2	★★★★★Grand	18	★★★Roma
3	★★★★★Savoy	19	★★★Regency
4	★★★★★Villa Medici	20	★★★Villa Park San Domenico
5	★★★★Aerhotel Baglioni	21	☆☆☆AGIP
6	★★★★Jolly	22	★★Autostrada
7	★★★★Londra	23	★★Basilea
8	★★★★Minerva	24	★★David
9	★★★★Villa Massa (at Candeli 6km SE on road to Bagno a Ripoli)	25	★★Jenning's Riccioli
		26	★★Liana
10	★★★Adriatico	27	★★Rapallo
11	★★★Belvedere	28	★★Rigatti
12	★★★Berchielli	29	★★Villa Villoresi (at Sesto Fiorentino 9km NE)
13	★★★EuroCrest		
14	★★★Croce di Malta	30	★Losanna
15	★★★Embassy	31	★Morandi
16	★★★Hermitage	32	★★Franchi

Florence See **Firenze**

Foligno Perugia 51,500 (☎0742)
Map **31** B3
★★★ **Umbria** via C-Battisti 1 ☎52821 rm47
⇄36 ▥6 G Lift B6500–19200 M4500–6000
Pn16000–19000

🏂⊘ *O Barnocchi* viale Firenze 77 ☎53501 N🏂
Frd

Edilferro viale Firenze 77 ☎50177 N🏂 AU/
Aud/VW

Forio See **Ischia (Isola d')**

Forli Forli 108,600 (☎0543) Map **30** C2
🏂⊘ *Automec* viale Ridolfi 7 ☎28280 N🏂
AR G50

Fornaci See **Arona**

Forte dei Marmi Lucca 10,400 (☎0584)
Map **29** B2
★★★ **Alcione** viale Morin 137 ☎89952 rm43
⇄32 ▥6 G Lift 1 Jun–30 Sep B8000–25000
M9000 Pn14000–26000 Beach Sea
★★★ **Astoria Garden** via L-da Vinci 110
☎80754 rm50 ⇄50 G Lift 15 May–15 Oct
LD B10800–31600 M7000 Pn19000–24000
🏊 Beach Sea
★★★ **Byron** viale Morin 46 ☎80087 rm37
(A6) ⇄30 ▥1 1 Jun–30 Sep B17500–40000
M9000 Pn18000–31000
★★★ **Raffaelli Park** via Mazzini 37 ☎81494
tx59239 ⇄34 (A5) ⇄5 ▥2 Lift LD
B17000–39000 M9000 Pn28000–38000
St9% 🏊 Pool Beach Sea
★★★ **Raffaelli Villa Angela** via G-Mazzini 64
☎80652 tx59239 rm60 (A20) ⇄50 ▥10
1 Mar–30 Oct LD B13000–24000 M8500
Pn15000–27000 St9% 🏊 Pool Beach Sea
★★ **Adams Villa Maria** Lungomare 110
☎80901 rm44 (A8) ⇄36 Lift 1 Jun–30 Sep
B8000–31000 St% Sea

Fregene Roma 1,210 (☎06) Map **31** B2
★★ *Fiorita* (Pensione) via Castellammare
☎6460435 rm40 ⇄40 G Sea

Frosinone Frosinone 43,425 (☎0775)
Map **32** C2
★★ **Palace Hasser** via Brighindi ☎852747
rm60 ⇄60 G Lift B8000–17500 M4500
Pn15000
★ *Garibaldi* via Plebliscito 48 ☎20051 rm15
▥1 LD
🏂⊘ *SICA* via Marittima 1 ☎20042 Frd

Gabicce Mare Pesaro & Urbino 5,450
(☎0541) Map **30** C2
★★★ *Adriatica* pza Mateotti 1 ☎61304
ta Fronzoni rm71 ⇄8 ▥42 G Lift 1 Apr–15 Oct
Beach Sea
★★ **Club de Bona** via Panoramica 33
☎962622 rm40 ⇄6 ▥34 G Lift 1 May–30 Sep
LD B7500–17000 M6000 Pn12000–16000
Pool Beach Sea
★★ **Excelsior** via V-Veneto 76 ☎961789 rm46
⇄46 G Lift 1 May–30 Sep B8500–11000
M3000–4000 Pn8500–11500 Sea
★★ *Valbruna* Redipuglia 1 ☎961843 rm45
⇄5 ▥5 G Lift 20 May–30 Sep Beach Sea

Gaeta Latina 23,650 (☎0771) Map **32** C2
★★★ *Serapo* Spiaggia di Serapo ☎40092
rm72 ⇄24 ▥39 G Lift Beach Sea

Garda Verona 3,400 (☎045) Map **29** B4
★★★★ **Eurotel** via Gardesana 18 ☎624107
tx48444 Europlan att Eurotel rm218 (A89) ⇄90
▥128 G Lift B10000–33000 M7000
Pn21000–27500 🏊 Pool Lake
★★★ **Regina Adelaide Palace** via 20
Settembre ☎624013 rm53 ⇄6 ▥47 Lift LD
B12500–23000 M6500 Pn20000 Lake
★★ **Tre Corone** via Lungolago 44 ☎624033
rm26 ⇄22 Lift 15 Feb–4 Nov B7000–18000

M5000–6000 Pn13000–14000 Lake

Gardone Riviera Brescia 2,650 (☎0365)
Map **29** B4
★★★★ **Grande Albergo** ☎20261 tx30254
rm202 ⇄153 ▥19 Lift Etr–Oct B12000–39000
M9000 Pn18000–34000 Pool Lake
★★★ **Eurotel** via Vittoriale 11 ☎21161 rm69
⇄48 ▥21 G Lift 16 Feb–15 Sep
B10000–30000 M5500 Pn21000–25000
🏊 Pool Lake
★★★ **Lac** corso Repubblica 58 ☎20124
rm30 ⇄17 Lift 1 Mar–30 Oct B9000–23000
M6000 Pn10000–19000 Lake
★★ **Bellevue** via Zanardelli 44 ☎20235 rm34
⇄3 ▥15 G 1 Apr–10 Oct B6200–12400
M4800 Pn9000–12600 Lake
★ *Garda & Suisse* ☎20150 rm19 G
1 Apr–1 Oct Lake
At **Barbarano** (1km E)
★★★ *Astoria* ☎20761 rm96 ⇄80 G Lift
Pool Lake
★★ *Barbarano Galeazzi* ☎20256 rm76 (A)
⇄20
At **Fasano del Garda** (1.5km NE)
★★ *Riccio* ☎21987 rm27 (A7) ⇄27 Lift

Gela See **Sicilia (Sicily)**

Genova (Genoa) Genova 807,150 (☎010)
Map **29** A3

| AA | agents; see page 188 |

★★★★ **Corvetto Plaza** via M Piaggio 11
☎893642 rm100 ⇄62 ▥38 G Lift
B18300–39600 M8000 Pn30000–32000
★★★★ *Savoia Majestic* Stazione Centrale
Principe ☎261641 tx27426 rm120 ⇄120 Lift
★ *Principessa* (Pensione) via Roccatagliata 4
☎580909 rm23 ⇄2 Lift 🏊 Sea
🏂⊘ *ARA* via Marsilio de Padova 6 ☎317388 N🏂
Chy/Sim
i🏂⊘24 *Augusto* via Erzelli Ge Cornigliano 3
☎412190 G10
🏂⊘ *Dilia* viale C&M Rosselli 18r ☎361689 N🏂
Frd
Italpiave via Piave 1 ☎308501 N🏂
🏂⊘ *B Koelliker* via S Piox 79 ☎315306 N🏂
BL/Jag
🏂⊘ *Oram* via G-Bandi 10 Ge Quarto ☎384653
N🏂 Jag/Vlo
▯ *XX-Settembre* via Corso Sardegna 6/ZR
☎511941 N🏂 Cit G80

Genzano di Roma Roma 16,250 (☎06)
Map **31** B2
★★ **Villa Robinia** viale Frattelli-Rosselli 19
☎9396409 rm30 ⇄30 Lift B6000–10800
M4500 Pn12500

Ghiffa Novara 2,150 (☎0323) Map **28** D4
★★ *Castello di Frino* ☎59181 rm13 (A6) ⇄6
▥4 1 Apr–30 Sep 🏊 Pool Lake
★★ **Ghiffa** via Belvedere 66 ☎59285 rm26
⇄15 G Lift Etr–30 Sep LD B6900–21800
M6500 Pn13500–18800 Lake

Gioia del Colle Bari 27,850 (☎080)
Map **34** C3
★★★ *Artu* via Circonvaliazione Statale 100
☎830009 rm23 ⇄10 Lift 🏊 Pool
▯🏂⊘24 *Carrozzeria* via Santeramo 120
☎830417 M/c AR/Aud/Fia/VW G20

Gioia Tauro Reggio di Calabria 15,725
(☎0966) Map **34** C1
★★★ *Park* via Nazionale ☎51159 rm44
⇄33 Lift
🏂🏂 *Calabria* via Nazionale 111 ☎51965 Ren

Giulianova Lido Teramo 21,550 (☎085)
Map **32** C3
▯ *Ubaldo & Forlini* via G-Galilei 180
☎862747 N🏂 GM

Golfo Aranci See **Sardegna (Sardinia)**

Italy

Gorizia Gorizia 43,625 (☎0481) Map **30** D4
★★*Transalpina* via Caprin 30 ☎2008 rm55
⇆55 G Lift 5 Sep–16 Aug

Grado Gorizia 10,300 (☎0431) Map **30** D4
★★*Hungaria* via Carducci 13 ☎80183 rm48
⇆4 🗎20 Lift 1 Apr–30 Sep B6600–15200
M4000 Pn11500–14000

Gravedona Como 2,850 (☎0344)
Map **29** A4
★*Turismo* ☎85227 rm14 ⇆7 G
1 Mar–30 Nov LD B6100–12600 M4500
Pn10000–12500 St9% Lake

Gravellona-Toce Novara 7,350
(☎0323) Map **28** D4
★*Helios* ☎84096 rm19 ⇆11 B4700–11000
M4500 Pn10000–12000

Grignano Trieste (☎040) Map **30** D4
★★★★*Adriatico* ☎224241 rm102 ⇆70 🗎30 G
Lift 15 Mar–30 Oct B21000–36000 M8000
Pn29000–32000 ❧ Pool Beach Sea

Grosseto Grosseto 66,850 (☎0564)
Map **31** A3
✰✰✰*AGIP* exit Roma ☎24100 rm32 🗎32 G
Lift B4000–10400
★★★*Lorena* via Trieste 3 ☎25501 rm60
⇆12 🗎36 G Lift B15500–27000 M6000
Pn 25500
🖩❧24 O Biagini via Senese 55 ☎23054
N❧ VW
🖩❧ Morelli via Privata dei Curiazi 13
☎23000 N❧ BL/Rov/Tri/Vlo

Guardistallo Pisa 1,050 (☎0586)
Map **29** C2
★★*Villa Elena* ☎655035 rm30 (A10) ⇆28
🗎2 G B8100–14600 M5000 Pn13500
❧ Pool Sea

Igea Marina See**Bellaria Igea Marina**

Iglesias See**Sardegna (Sardinia)**

Imperia Imperia 41,550 (☎0183) Map **28** D2
❧ *Riviera Motori* via Mattectti 175
☎20297/20701 N❧ BL

Ischia (Isola d') Napoli 41,350 (☎081)
Map **32** C1

Forio 8,230
★*Splendid* (1km NE) ☎997165 rm40 ⇆40
1 Apr–30 Oct B7600–14400 M5200
Pn12300–15800 ❧ Pool Sea

Ischia 15,450
★★★★*Jolly* via A-de Luca ☎991744
ta Termhotel tx71267 Jolly GAT rm220 ⇆220
Lift B22800–40600 M10500 Pn39000 Pool
★★★*Grand & Parco Aurora* Lungomare
C-Columbo ☎991722 rm65 (A15) ⇆25 🗎40
G Lift 1 Apr–31 Oct B13600–25200 M6500
Pn17500–22500 Pool Beach Sea

Lacco Ameno 3,300
★★★★*Reginella* ☎994304 rm50 ⇆26 🗎24
G Lift ❧ Pool

Ivrea Torino 29,400 (☎0125) Map **28** D4
★★★*Sirio* via Lago Sirio 47 ☎3646 rm35
⇆14 🗎21 G Lift Lake
★★*Eden* (n rest) corso Massimo d'Azeglio 67
☎49190 rm36 ⇆4 🗎32 G Lift B8000–12500
🖩❧ M Peroni via San Lorenzo 10 ☎422002
N❧ Aud/VW

Jesolo (Lido di) Venezia 21,900
(☎0421) Map **30** C4
★★★★*Las Vegas* via Mascagni 3 ☎91200
tx41443 rm110 ⇆110 Lift 1 May–30 Sep LD
B16500–34000 M6000 Pn16000–24000
★★★*Excelsior* via Zara 2 ☎90284 tx0421
rm80 ⇆30 🗎50 Lift 10 May–20 Sep Beach
★★★*London* via Dalmazia 508 ☎90988
rm84 ⇆76 Lift May–Sep B7500–17600
M4500–5000 Pn8300–13000 Beach Sea

★★★*Oxford* via Zara 25 ☎91320 rm60 ⇆30
🗎30 G Lift 1 May–10 Oct Beach Sea
★★★*Ritz* via Zanella 2 ☎90861 rm48 🗎48
Lift May–30 Sep Beach Sea
★★*Brezza* via Altinate ☎91932 rm40 ⇆34
🗎36 G Lift 20 May–30 Sep LD B11000–18000
M5000 Pn9000–15000 Pool Beach Sea
★★*Palace & Principe* pza Mazzini 38
☎90341 rm133 ⇆83 Lift 28 May–30 Sep
★★*Regina* via Bafile 115 ☎90383 rm60
⇆60 G Lift 1 Apr–30 Sep B8300–16000
M4000 Pn12000–15000
★★*Termini* via Altinate ☎90488 tx41433
rm45 ⇆45 Lift 10 Apr–30 Sep B8000–16400
M5500 Pn 6500–14000 St9% Pool Beach Sea
Brusa pza Mazzini ☎91344 N❧ Frd

At **Jesolo Pineta** (6km E)
★★*Danmark* via Oriente 170 ☎961013
tx41433 rm58 ⇆32 🗎14 1 May–30 Sep
B7200–13800 M4000 Pn7000–12800
Pool Beach Sea

La Each placename beginning with La is listed
under the name which follows it.

Lacco Ameno See**Ischia (Isola d')**

Lacona See**Elba (Isola d')**

Laigueglia Savona 2,600 (☎0182)
Map **28** D2
★★★*Aquilia* via Asti 1 ☎49040 rm40 ⇆40 G
Lift 20 Dec–20 Oct LD B9500–15000
M5000–6000 Pn8000–13500 Beach Sea
★★★*Laigueglia* Liberta 14 ☎49002
ta Sighel rm55 ⇆55 G Lift Apr–Oct Beach Sea
★★★*Royal* via Roma 176 ☎49283 rm30
⇆30 G Lift Sea
★★*Mariolina* via Concezione 15 ☎49029
rm23 🗎16 B7000–12000 M4000
Pn8500–11500 Beach Golf ◯ Sea
★★*San Giorgio* via Dante 190 ☎49166
rm43 ⇆20 🗎13 1 May–30 Sep Beach Sea
★★*Splendid* pza Badaro 4 ☎49325 rm46
⇆27 🗎19 Lift B10000–28000 M8000
Pn15000–24000 Pool Beach
★★ *Villa Ida* via Roma 90 ☎49042 rm40
⇆16 🗎4 15 May–30 Sep
★★*Windsor* pza 25 Aprile 7 ☎49000 rm50
⇆30 🗎20 Lift 25 Apr–25 Oct B9500–16000
M4000 Pn10000–13000 Beach Sea
★*Astoria* via Torino 25 ☎49062 rm27 ⇆18 G
20 May–30 Sep LD B5000–13000 M4000
Pn 7500–10000 Beach Sea

Lainate Milano 16,460 (☎02) Map **29** A4
✰*Italmotel* via Manzoni 43 ☎9370869
rm34 ⇆34 B22200 (double) M5950 Pn23000
❧ Pool

Lavagna Genova 14,000 (☎0185)
Map **29** A2/3
★★*Tigullio* via Matteotti 3 ☎307623 rm42
⇆14 🗎6 G Lift 15 Mar–15 Nov B4900–15100
M4300–6300 Pn1000–13500 Sea
🖩❧*A Ghiorsi* via C-Battisti ☎309987 N❧
Aud/Por/VW

At **Cavi** (3km SE)
★*Scogliera* (n rest) ☎390072 rm21 ⇆21 G
May–Sep B7600–14400 (double) Beach Sea

Lecce Lecce 86,400 (☎0832) Map **39** B1
★★★*Astor* ☎26911 rm66 ⇆46 🗎10 G Lift
B15000–26000 M6000 Pn22000
Auto Motor via Oberdan 7 ☎54836 N❧
BL/Rov/Tri

Leghorn See**Livorno**

Lenno Como 1,600 (☎0344) Map **29** A4
★★*San Giorgio* ☎40415 rm35 ⇆12 G Lift
15 Apr–15 Oct B9500–22500 M7000
Pn15500–18500 St9% ❧ Lake

Lerici La Spezia 14,500 (☎0187)
Map **29** A2

Italy

★★★**Doria** via A-Doria ☎967124 rm42 ⇆15
🏠15 Lift LD B9200–18200 M5500
Pn16000–17900
★★**Venere Azzurra** (n rest) Lungomare
Biaggini 33 ☎967210 rm22 ⇆1 🏠14 G
1 Mar–31 Oct Sea

Lesa Novara 2,550 (☎0322) Map **28** D4
★★**Giardino** ☎7283 rm40 (A4) ⇆2 🏠8 LD
B6650–13350 M4350 Pn10000–12500 Lake

Levanto La Spezia 6,750 (☎0187)
Map **29** A2
★★★**Crystal** via Vallesanta ☎808261 rm16
(A9) ⇆1 🏠16 1 May –30 Sep Sea
★★**Nazionale** ☎808102 rm23 ⇆6 🏠5
1 Apr–31 Oct Sea
★**Garden** (Pensione) corso Italia 6 ☎808173
rm15 Lift 1 Apr–30 Sep B4600–9300 M4000
Pn10000 Sea

Levico Terme Trento 5,610 (☎0461)
Map **29** B4
★★★**Bellavista** via V-Emanuele 2 ☎71136
rm77 ⇆77 🏠9 G Lift 25 May–30 Sep
B7000–21000 M7000 Pn13000–20000
Pool Lake

Lido di Camaiore See **Camaiore (Lido di)**

Lido di Jesolo See **Jesolo (Lido di)**

Lignano Sabbiadoro Udine 5,100
(☎0431) Map **30** C4
At **Lignano Pineta** (5km SW)
★★★**Medusa Splendid** Arco dello Scirocco
13 ☎72211 rm56 ⇆8 🏠48 Lift
1 May–30 Sep Beach Sea
At **Lignano Riviera** (7km SW)
★★★**Eurotel** calle Mendelssohn 9 ☎729992
rm59 ⇆59 Lift 15 May–20 Sep B9500–24000
M6500 Pn21500–27000 Pool Beach Sea

Limone sul Garda Brescia 1,000 (☎0365)
Map **29** B4
★★**Azzurro** ☎94000 rm32 1 Apr–30 Oct
Lake

Lipomo See **Como**

Livorno (Leghorn) Livorno 177,550
(☎0586) Map **29** B2
AA agents; see page **188**
★★★**Giappone** (n rest) via Grande 65
☎24751 rm58 ⇆28 🏠16 Lift B9400–19800
🏠&D**G Malloggi** via Prov Pisma 631 ☎422230
MB
🚗24 **G Scotti** via della Cinta Esterna 36
☎24007 N🅰 M/c
At **Stagno** (5km N on SS1)
☆☆☆**AGIP** ☎93067 rm49 🏠49 Lift
B6000–16000

Loano Savona 13,250 (☎019) Map **28** D2
★★★**Garden Lido** Lungomare N-Sauro 9
☎669666 rm88 ⇆48 🏠40 G Lift
20 Dec–30 Sep Pool Beach Sea
★★**San Marco** (n rest) via Private Mazza 9a
☎668094 rm23 ⇆1 🏠4 Lift 1 May–5 Oct
1 Dec–15 Mar Sea
★**Aurelia** via Mazza 2 ☎668264 rm13 ⇆1
Lift Sea

Lone See **Amalfi**

Macerata Macerata 44,250 (☎0733)
Map **30** D2
☆☆☆**AGIP** via Roma 31 ☎31146 rm51 🏠51 Lift
B6000–12000
🏠**Pettinella** via dei Velini 147 ☎31628 N🅰 Frd

Macomer See **Sardegna (Sardinia)**

Macugnaga Novara 800 (☎0324) Map **28** D4
★★**Lagger** Frazione-Pecetto ☎65139 rm21
⇆17 B5500–14600 M6000 Pn12000–15000

Maderno Brescia 6,327 (☎0365) Map **29** B4
★★**Milano** Lungolago 12 ☎641223 rm40
⇆12 Etr–30 Sep Lake

Madonna di Campiglio Trento (☎0465)
Map **29** B4
★★★★**Alpes** ☎41002 rm91 ⇆91 Lift
15 Jul–30 Aug
★★★**Savoia** ☎41004 rm57 ⇆47 🏠10 G Lift
B15000–36000 M9000 Pn26300–32300

Maiori Salerno 6,200 (☎089) Map **33** B3
★★★**Reginna Palace** via Lungomare ☎877183
rm73 ⇆63 🏠10 G Lift 1 Apr–15 Oct LD
B11500–26000 M6000 Pn19000–22000
St9% 🏊 Pool Beach Sea
★★★**San Francesco** via S-Tecla 54 ☎877070
rm44 ⇆44 G Lift B7000–13000 M3500
Pn10000–13000 Beach Sea

Malcesine Verona 3,600 (☎045) Map **29** B4
★★★**Malcesine** pza Pallone 1 ☎600173
rm43 ⇆17 🏠11 G Lift Apr–Oct Lake
★★**Bellevue San Lorenzo** Val di Sogno
☎600088 rm25 ⇆7 🏠8 1 Apr–30 Oct Pool
Lake
★★**Vega** ☎600151 rm20 ⇆20 Lift
1 Apr–31 Oct

Mantova Mantova 66,600 (☎0376)
Map **29** B3
🏠**Filippini** via Curtatone e Montanara 58
☎29696 N🅰 Aud/Por/VW
🏠&D**A Giovanazza** via G-Acerbi 37 ☎27254
N🅰 Ren

Maratea Potenza 4,900 (☎0973) Map **33** B3
★★★★**Santavenere** ☎76160 rm44 (A) ⇆40
🏠4 Etr–10 Oct Beach Golf Sea

Marciana Marina See **Elba (Isola d')**

Marghera See **Mestre**

Marina di Carrara See **Carrara (Marina di)**

Marina di Massa See **Massa (Marina di)**

Marina di Pietrasanta See **Pietrasanta
(Marina di)**

Marina Equa See **Vico Equense**

Marsala See **Sicilia (Sicily)**

Massa (Marina di) Massa Carrara 8,820
(☎0585) Map **29** A2
★★★★**Tirreno** via Mazzini 22 ☎20016 rm45
⇆33 🏠1 May–Sep G Beach Sea
★★★**Marina** viale Magliano 3 ☎20192
rm32 ⇆32 May–Oct B9800–20600 M4500
Pn14000–22000 Beach
★**Internazionale** (Pensione) via Siena 1
☎29243 rm14 G 15 May–30 Sep LD Sea

Matelica Macerata 8,750 (☎0737) Map **30** C2
☆☆☆**AGIP** SS256 km29 ☎8381 rm16 🏠16
B6000–12000

Mazzaro See **Taormina** under **Sicilia (Sicily)**

Meina Novara 2,250 (☎0322) Map **28** D4
★**Bel Sit** via Sempione 86 ☎6483 rm12 ⇆3
🏠9 G LD B7500–8500 M4500
Pn7500–8500 Lake

Menaggio Como 3,350 (☎0344) Map **29** A4
★★★**Bellavista** via IV Novembre 9 ☎32136
rm39 ⇆18 🏠8 Lift 1 Apr–15 Oct B7000–19000
M5000 Pn11000–16000 Lake
★★★**Victoria** via al Lago 7 ☎32003 rm98
⇆58 🏠17 G Lift Apr–Oct B12000–32000
M10000–11000 Pn19000–28000 🏊 Pool Lake
★★**Loveno** via N Sauro 5 ☎32110 rm13 (A5)
⇆7 G 15 Mar–30 Oct B6500–18000
M5000–7000 Pn11000–16000 Lake
At **Nobialto** (1km N)
★★**Miralago** ☎32363 rm28 ⇆8 🏠18 G
15 Mar–15 Oct

Mendola (Passo della) Trento e Bolzano
(☎0471) Map **12** D1
★★**Caldaro** ☎63124 rm24 ⇆2 G 🏊 Pool

Merano–Meran Bolzano 34,600 (☎0473)
Map **12** D1

207

★★★★★*Bristol* via O-Huber 14 ☎23361
rm150 ⇆150 1 Apr–31 Oct G Lift Pool
★★★*Augusta* via O-Huber 2 ☎30331 rm25
⇆25 G Lift 1 Mar–31 Oct B14500–29000
M5500 Pn20000–24000
☆☆☆*Eurotel* via Garibaldi 5 ☎24316 tx40471
rm130 ⇆70 ⑪60 G Lift B11500–26000
M5000 Pn26000–43000
☆☆☆*Eurotel Astoria* (n rest) via Winkel 21
☎25442 rm90 ⇆84 ⑪6 G Lift 10 Mar–15 Nov
B13000–35000 Pool Golf
★★★*Mirabella* via Mirabella 1 ☎26112 rm30
⇆16 ⑪14 Lift 1 Mar–1 Nov B11800–27600
M5000–7000 Pn17000–23000 Pool
★★★*Palace* via Cavour 4 ☎23791 tx40256
rm102 ⇆102 Lift B17000–46000 M9000
Pn22000–34000 St9% Pool
★★★*Savoy* via Rezia 1 ☎22228 rm50 ⇆50
Lift 1 Apr–31 Oct LD B14500–37000 M6500
Pn19000–27000 Pool
★★*Adria* via Gilm 2 ☎26183 rm51 (A10) ⇆43
Lift 1 Mar–15 Nov LD B10500–23000 M5500
Pn16000–21000 St9% Pool
★★*Irma* via Belvedere 7 ☎30124 rm60 ⇆36
⑪21 Lift 20 Feb–6 Nov B10000–32000
M6000 Pn16000–25000 Pool
★★*Mendola* via Winkel 35 ☎22330 rm40 ⇆8
⑪26 Lift Mar–Oct Pool
★★*Regina* via Cavour 101 ☎33432 rm75
⇆30 ⑪39 G Lift 15 Mar–31 Oct B9500–27000
M6000 Pn12500–21500
★*Livonia* Christomannos Strada 31 ☎24126
rm20 ⇆3 ⑪12 Pool
★*Westend* ☎22054 rm22 ⇆4 ⑪6
15 Mar–10 Nov LD B8500–21000
M4000–4800 Pn13500–15500
Merano via Roma 288 ☎32074 Opl/Ren
Messina See **Sicilia (Sicily)**

Mestre Venezia (☎041) Map **30** C4
★★★*Bologna & Stazione* pza Stazione
☎931000 rm133 ⇆23 ⑪89 Lift B10000–22000
M6500 Pn18000–20000
★★★*Plaza* via Stazione ☎929388 rm220
⇆130 ⑪85 Lift B14200–24400 M7000
Pn21500–22500
★★★*Sirio* via Circonvallazione 109 ☎51728
rm110 ⇆2 ⑪78 G Lift
★★★*Tritone* pza Stazione 16 ☎930955 rm67
⇆24 ⑪30 Lift B12500–22000 M6500
Pn24000
★★*Aurora* (n rest) pza G-Bruno 15 ☎989832
rm33 ⇆15 ⑪14 Lift B6800–17100
★★*Venezia* pza XXVII Ottobre ☎972400
rm100 ⇆60 G Lift
Autolambro corso del Popolo 7 ☎986255
N☎56094 N☎ M/c BL/Rov/Tri G50
☎☊*Damiani & Giorgio* via Torino 40 ☎932844
N☎ M/c Frd
☎☊*S Lorenzo* via Giustizia 27 ☎926722 N☎
GM G10
☊*Roma* via Piave 182 ☎929611 N☎ Fia
At **Marghera** (1km S)
★★*Vienna* via Rizzardi 54 ☎921979 rm76
⇆15 ⑪15 Lift 15 Mar–30 Oct B7700–15900
M4000 Pool
☎☊*Sartori* piazzale Autostrada 12 ☎920444
N☎
Milano (Milan) Milano 1,732,500 (☎02)
Map **29** A4 **See plan**

| AA | agents; see page 188 |

★★★★★*Duomo* via San Raffaele 1 ☎8833
Plan **1** tx33086 rm160 ⇆160 Lift
B32500–45000 M8500 St9%
★★★★★*Excelsior-Gallia* pza Duca d'Aosta 9
☎6277 Plan **2** tx32160 Galliaot rm280 ⇆280
G Lift B27500–50000 M10000 St14%
★★★★★*Palace* pza della Repubblica 20
☎6336 Plan **3** tx32026 rm208 G Lift

★★★★★*Principe & Savoia* pza della
Repubblica 17 ☎6230 Plan **4** ta Principal
tx31052 rm358 (A60) ⇆358 G Lift
B35000–56600 Màlc St12%
★★★★*Jolly President* Largo Augusto
☎7746 Plan **5** tx33054 Jolly Mi rm201
⇆201 G Lift B35000–47000 M8500
Pn49500
★★★★*Manin* via Manin 7 ☎667251 Plan **6**
tx34385 rm106 ⇆100 ⑪6 Lift B29110–40230
M8720 Pn43720–68450
★★★★*Select* via Baracchini 12 (off via A
Albricci) ☎8843 Plan **7** tx33256 rm140 ⇆86
⑪54 Lift B27500–55000
★★★★*Touring* via Tarchetti 2 (off via Manin)
☎665653 Plan **9** tx24118 rm277 ⇆241 ⑪36
G Lift B32500–46000 M8000 Pn48500
☆☆☆*AGIP* Milano Tangenziale Ovest ☎8465246
Plan **11** rm180 ⑪180 Lift B10050–23550
★★★*American* via Finocchiaro Aprile 2
☎666441 Plan **8** tx33150 Amerotel rm306
⇆25 ⑪281 G Lift B12500–20150 M4000
Pn17500–20000 St9%
★★*Adriatico* (n rest) via Conca del Naviglio 20
☎8324141 Plan **10** ta Adriaotel rm105 ⇆7
⑪98 G Lift
☆☆*Dei Fiori* (n rest) Ingresso Autostrada A7
Genova ☎8436441 Plan **13** rm56 ⇆53 Lift
B11000–18000
☆☆*Fini* (n rest) via del Mare 93 ☎8464041
Plan **15** rm78 ⇆78 G Lift
★★*Gamma* (n rest) via Valassori Peroni 85
(off via Porpora) ☎292602 Plan **16** rm55 ⇆10
⑪45 G Lift
★★*Terminus* viale V-Veneto 32 ☎664917
Plan **17** rm68 ⇆25 ⑪4 G Lift
☊☎*ACAM* via Masolino da Panicale 4
☎391326 N☎ M/c Ren
☊☎*Bellaviti & Pirona* via Boccaglione 4
☎564034 Ren G100
☊☎*Forlanini* via Mecenate 84 ☎5060340 N☎
Fia
☊*Lambromotori* viale Fulvio Testi ☎2479660
M/c BL/Rov/Tri
di Tarchini SVAI via Durini 14 ☎701240 N☎
At **San Donato Milanese** (8km SE on road
No. 9)
☆☆☆*AGIP* Ingresso Autostrada del Sole
☎512941 Plan **12** rm275 ⑪275 Lift
B9650–22600
At **San Giuliano Milanese** (12km SE)
☊☎*Autosprint* via F-Baracca 1 ☎9846871
N☎

Milano Marittima See **Cervia**

Minori See **Amalfi**

Misurina Belluno (☎0436) Map **13** A1
★★*Sorapiss* ☎8209 rm22 ⑪9 1 Jun–30 Sep
20 Dec–30 Apr B8000–15000 M5000
Pn13000–15000 Lake

Modena Modena 176,800 (☎059)
Map **29** B3
★★★★*Canalgrande* corso Canalgrande 6
☎217160 tx51480 rm78 ⇆78 G Lift
★★★★*Fini* via E-Est 441 ☎238091 tx21286
rm100 ⇆100 G Lift B28500–43000 Màlc
★★★★*Palace* via E-Est 65 ☎236091 rm64
⇆54 G Lift
☆☆☆*AGIP* via E-Est 1014 ☎361249 rm17
⑪17 B4900–10900
☆☆☆*AGIP* (n rest) Raccordo Autostrada
Brennero-Modena (Autostrata del Sole)
☎338221 rm184 ⑪184 Lift B13500–26000
★★*Geminiano* ☎231303 rm23 ⇆11 Lift
☊☎➤24 *Barbieri* v Emilia Est 1040 ☎360260
Rov G800
☊*W Bellei* via E-Est 1127 ☎366271
N☎ Frd

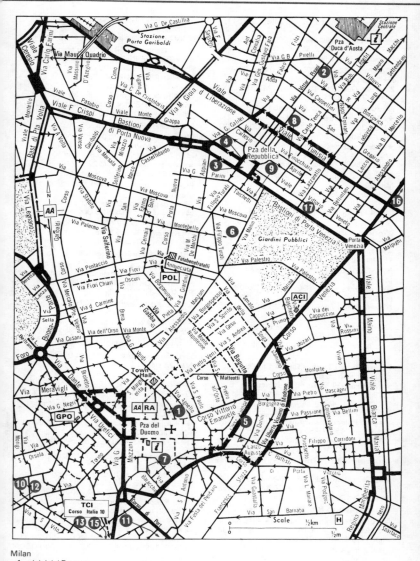

Milan

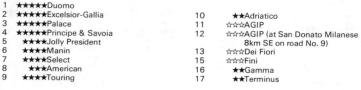

1	★★★★★Duomo		
2	★★★★★Excelsior-Gallia	10	★★Adriatico
3	★★★★★Palace	11	☆☆☆AGIP
4	★★★★★Principe & Savoia	12	☆☆☆AGIP (at San Donato Milanese
5	★★★★Jolly President		8km SE on road No. 9)
6	★★★★Manin	13	☆☆☆Dei Fiori
7	★★★★Select	15	☆☆☆Fini
8	★★★American	16	★★Gamma
9	★★★★Touring	17	★★Terminus

Italy

Mogliano Veneto Treviso 21,650 (☎041) Map **30** C4
★★★★**Villa Condulmer** ☎450001 rm33
⇨33 B16000–34000 M8000–10000
Pn29000–32000 🍴 Pool Golf ∩

Moltrasio Como 2,800 (☎031) Map **29** A4
★★**Caramazza** ☎290050 rm19 ⇨12 G Lift
2 Apr–25 Oct LD B7400–17300 M5300
Pn14500–15800 Lake

Molveno Trento 1,000 (☎0461) Map **29** B4
★★**Miralago** ☎58935 rm54 ⇨54 Lift
1 May–30 Sep 20 Dec–31 Mar B5000–13000
M4000–5000 Pn9000–15000 Pool Lake
★**Cima Tosa** via Scuole 3 ☎58928 rm32
⇨8 ⋔9 Jun–Sep B5500–12400
M4000–5000 Pn8000–12000 Lake

Mondovi' Cuneo 21,950 (☎0174)
Map **28** D3
★★★**Park** via del Vecchio 2 ☎3550 rm60
⇨3 ⋔57 Lift
🗑🏧24 **Franco Govone** via Piave 6 ☎43111
N ☎40355 Cit

Moneglia Genova 2,850 (☎0185)
Map **29** A2
★★**Mondial** ☎49339 rm36 ⇨4 ⋔32 G Lift
15 Mar–15 Oct

Monfalcone Gorizia 30,850 (☎0481)
Map **30** D4
★★**Lussino** via Duca d'Aosta 37 ☎72409
rm23 ⇨3 ⋔2
Novati & Mio via C-Columbo 13 ☎72765 N☒
Frd

Montalto di Castro Viterbo 6,250
(☎0766) Map **31** B3
☆☆☆**AGIP** via Aurelia ☎89090 rm32 ⋔32
B5400–11100

Montecatini Terme Pistoia 21,400
(☎0572) Map **29** B2
★★★★**Croce di Malta** via IV-Novembre 18
☎79381 rm110 ⇨110 G Lift 1 Apr–15 Nov
B18000–36000 M8500–10000
Pn30000–35000 Pool
★★**Lido Franco Risorgimento** via IV-
Novembre 14 ☎70731 rm56 ⇨44 Lift
1 Apr–30 Oct B6000–14500 M6000
Pn9000–14000

Montegrotto Terme Padova 8,400 (☎049)
Map **30** C4
★★★**Terme Zurigo** via Neronianal ☎793555
rm84 ⇨8 ⋔76 Lift B10900–16500 M6000
Pn15000–18000 Pool

Montesilvano Marina See **Pescara**

Muccia Macerata 900 (☎0737) Map **32** C4
☆☆☆**AGIP** Bivio Maddalena (SS 77) ☎43138
rm38 ⋔38 B6000–12000

Napoli (Naples) Napoli 1,224,300
(☎081) Map **32** D2

AA agents; see page 188

★★★★★**Excelsior** via Partenope 48
☎417111 tx71043 rm160 ⇨160 G Lift
B29500–57000 M14000 Pn46500–56000
St14% Sea
★★★★★**Vesuvio** via Partenope 45 ☎391523
tx71127 rm180 ⇨180 G Lift Sea
★★★★**Mediterraneo** Ponte di Tappia
☎312240 rm221 ⇨221 G Lift B17400–26800
Màlc Sea
★★★★**Royal** via Partenope 38 ☎400244
tx71167 rm316 ⇨316 G Lift B21850–35700
Màlc Pool Sea
★★★**Parker's** corso V-Emanuele 135
☎684866 tx71578 rm86 ⇨53 ⋔12 G Lift
B12200–32400 M9000 Pn34000–49000 Sea
Gallo & Bacialli pza Piedigrotta 3
☎680514 N☒ Lnc G100

☒**S Luigi** via Gl-Francesco Pinto 59
☎514865 N☒ Ren
☒**SVAI** via S-Veniero 20 ☎611122 N☒ Frd

Nervi Genova 19,147 (☎010) Map **29** A3
★★★**Giardino Riviera** Passeggiata a Mare
☎378581 rm35 ⇨22 ⋔2 G Lift
B11500–25000 M6000–7000
Pn13000–22000 Beach Sea
☆☆**Milano** via Somma Donato 39 ☎378292
rm50 (A19) ⇨30 ⋔4 G Lift B9000–19000
M6000 Pn14000–16000 Sea

Nobiallo See **Menaggio**

Noli Savona 3,100 (☎019) Map **28** D2
★★★**Capo Noli** via Aurelia ☎748945 rm52
⇨20 ⋔32 Lift 15 May–30 Sep Sea
★★**Monique** via Collegio 22 ☎748930 rm32
⇨4 ⋔16 Lift 28 May–30 Sep Beach Sea

Nova Levante Bolzano 1,600 (☎0471)
Map **13** A1
★★★**Posta** Strada Dolomiti ☎61113 rm70
⇨28 ⋔7 G Lift 18 Dec–20 Oct 🍴 Pool

Numana Ancona 2,650 (☎071) Map **32** C4
★★**Numana Palace** ☎950156 rm110 ⇨3
⋔90 1 May–30 Sep Pool

Nuoro See **Sardegna (Sardinia)**

Ora Bolzano 2,450 (☎0471) Map **25** A1
★★**Elefant** via Nazionale ☎80129 rm32
⇨4 ⋔15 G Lift B8000–17000 M5000
Pn14000–17000

Orbetello Grosseto 14,150 (☎0564)
Map **31** A3
★★**Nazionale** (n rest) corso Italia 48
☎867062 rm33 ⇨10 ⋔1 G

Oristano See **Sardegna (Sardinia)**

Orta San Giulio Novara 1,250 (☎0322)
Map **28** D4
★★★**San Rocco** via Gippini 12 ☎90191
rm42 ⇨42 G Lift LD B16500–30000 M9000
Pn32000 Beach Lake

Ortisei-St Ulrich Bolzano 4,050 (☎0471)
Map **13** A1
★★★**Aquila** via Rezia 7 ☎76203 rm96 (A15)
⇨70 G Lift 1 Dec–1 Oct 🍴
★★★**Gardena** ☎76315 rm50 ⇨46 G Lift

Ospedaletti Imperia 3,300 (☎0184)
Map **28** D2
★★★**Floreal** corso Regina Margherita 83
☎59638 rm26 ⇨12 ⋔6 Lift 1 Dec–30 Sep
B6500–13000 M4500 Pn12000–14500 Sea
★★★**Rocce del Capo** Lungomare C-Colombo
☎59733 ta Capotel rm26 ⇨5 ⋔21 Lift
Pool Beach Sea
★**Petit Royal** via Regina Margherita 86
☎59026 rm30 ⇨9 ⋔6 Lift 15 Dec–30 Sep LD
B6600–18000 M5500–8000 Pn11500–15000
Sea

Padova (Padua) Padova 239,275 (☎049)
Map **30** C4
★★★★**Park Villa Altichiero** strada Altichiero 2
☎615111 rm70 ⇨70 Lift B 12500–20300
M7000–8000 Pn23000–25000 Pool
★★★**Biri** piazzale Stanga (Autostrada
terminal) ☎42442 rm63 ⇨10 ⋔53 G Lift
★★★**Europa** Largo Europa 3 ☎661200 rm57
⇨24 ⋔33 Lift B14500–24500 M7000
Pn26000
★**Maritan** via Gattamelata 8 ☎50118 rm23
⇨15 ⋔11 Lift
☒**C Meneghini** via N-Tommaseo 80
☎27272 N☒ Frd
☒☒**Superauto** via N-Tommaseo 76
☎45143 N☒ Por/VW

Paestum Salerno 1,457 (☎0828)
Map **33** B3

★★Calypso Zona Pineta ☎811031 rm40
(A35) ⊷40 G 1 Jun–30 Sep B8500–14600
M3000–6000 Pn14000–16000 St10%
Beach Sea
★★Mec ☎843073 rm40 ⊷16 ⬚24 Lift
1 Apr–30 Sep

Palermo See**Sicilia (Sicily)**

Pallanza Novara 8,958 (☎0323) Map **28** D4
★★★Majestic via V-Veneto 32 ☎42453
tx20393 rm100 ⊷95 ⬚5 G Lift 1 Apr–15 Oct
B14000–32000 M7000 Pn20000–30000
⧓ Pool Lake
★★Belvedere pza IV-Novembre 10 ☎41122
ta Bellevue rm90 (A40) ⊷43 ⬚36 Lift
Apr–Oct B8200–21850 M6000
Pn13100–19600
★★San Gottardo viale delle Magnolie
☎42119 rm40 ⬚23 G Lift 1 Apr–10 Oct
B7000–18000 M4800 Pn11500–15500
St9% Lake

Parma Parma 176,650 (☎0521) Map **29** B3
★★Button (n rest) via S Vitale 7 ☎22317
rm44 ⊷27 ⬚17 G Lift LD B7800–17300
★★Milano viale Ponte Bottego 9 ☎35877
rm47 ⊷12 ⬚14 G Lift
★★Principe (n rest) via E-Est 46 ☎40996
rm43 ⊷43 G Lift
🏚**Bottesini** via Golese 30 ☎24219
N⧓ M/c Hon/Vlo
🏚**Mattioli** via F-Tanara 11 ☎33458 N⧓
BL/Rov/Tri
🏚**P Torelli** via E-Lepido 44 ☎403412 N⧓
M/c GM

Pedraces Bolzano 433 (☎0471) Map **13** A1
★★Sporthotel Teresa (1km S) ☎85023
rm58 ⊷52 G Lift Pool

Pegli Genova 21,047 (☎010) Map **28** D3
★★★Mediterraneo (n rest) Lungomare 69
☎480185 rm73 ⊷73 Lift B13500–21000 Sea

Peroulaz See**Aosta**

Perugia Perugia 134,400 (☎075)
Map **31** B3
★★★Brufani Palace pza Italia 12 ☎20741
rm117 ⊷97 ⬚11 G Lift
★★★Rosetta pza Italia 19 ☎20841 rm108
(A88) ⊷47 ⬚26 G Lift B7950–18200
M5500 Pn16500–20000
🏚**Negri & Ricci** via Romana 35 ☎30676
M/c BMW

Pesaro Pesaro e Urbino 88,550 (☎0721)
Map **30** C2
★★★Mediterraneo viale Trieste 199 ☎31556
rm54 (A12) ⊷54 Lift B7500–13900
M4500–5000 Pn10000–14000
★★Atlantic viale Trieste 365 ☎61911 rm40
⊷25 ⬚15 Lift 10 May–30 Sep Beach Sea
★★Touring viale Trieste 203 ☎31093 rm33
⊷33 Lift Beach Sea
🏚**A Gabellini** Strada Romagna 119 ☎39124
N⧓ Aud/Por/VW

Paole del Monte via Porta Rimini ☎32919
N⧓ BL

Pescara Pescara 131,800 (☎085) Map **32** C3
☆☆☆**AGIP** Autostrada Adriatica ☎968221
rm85 ⬚85 Lift LD B7100–15050
★★★Carlton viale Riviera 35 ☎26373 rm71
⊷20 ⬚51 Lift B12200–22400 M6000
Pn17500–21000 Beach Sea
🏚**MADA** via Tiburtina Valeria ☎51342 N⧓ Frd
At **Montesilvano Marina** (8km N)
★★★★Grand Montesilvana via Riviera 28
☎838330 rm150 ⊷150 G Lift 1 Jun–30 Sep
LD B10000–18000 M6500 Pn18000 Beach Sea
★★★Serena Majestic tx68279 rm216 ⊷84
⬚128 G Lift 18 Apr–31 Oct ⧓ Pool Beach

Piacenza Piacenza 108,800 (☎0523)
Map **29** A3
★★★Croce Bianca Largo Matteoti 16
☎21231 rm85 ⊷30 ⬚25
★★Cappello via Mentano 8 ☎25721 rm58
⊷13 ⬚9 G Lift
☆☆**K2** via Emilia Parmense 133 ☎25381
rm48 ⊷26 ⬚8 G Lift B5200–11400
M3500 Pn12900–13500
Agosti & Lunardi via Perletti 5 ☎28920 N⧓
BL/Jag/Toy
Mirani & Toscani via E-Parmense 6 ☎62744
N⧓ Frd

Piano di Sorrento Napoli 10,050 (☎081)
Map **33** A3
★★★Nastro Azzurro (3km S) ☎8786818
rm55 ⊷27 ⬚28 G Lift 1 Apr–31 Oct
B9250–19000 M8000 Pn18000–19600
St9% ⧓ Pool Sea

Piazza Armerina See**Sicilia (Sicily)**

Pietra Ligure Savona 9,525 (☎019)
Map **28** D2
★★★★Royal via delle Palme 129 ☎67192
rm105 ⊷80 ⬚25 G Lift 15 Jan–31 Oct ⧓
Pool Beach Sea

Pietrasanta (Marina di) Lucca (☎0584)
Map **29** B2
★★★Lombardi Fiumetto ☎20431 rm40
⊷30 ⬚3 Lift May–Sep B11000–33000
M7000–8000 Pn19500–28500 ⧓ Pool Beach
Sea
★★Battelli Motrone ☎20010 rm42 (A16)
⊷35 G Lift 1 Jun–19 May B5000–14000
M8000 Pn14000–20000 St9% ⧓ Beach Sea
★★Esplanade viale Roma 235 ☎21151
rm36 ⊷36 Lift B9200–20600 M6000–8000
Pn15000–22000 Sea
★★Pinamar via Catalani 74 ☎20277 rm20
⊷16 15 May–30 Sep
★★Venezia (n rest) via Firenze 48 ☎20731
rm34 ⊷34 G Lift 1 Jun–30 Sep
B12500–23500 Sea

Pineta See**Lignano Pineta**

Piombino Livorno 40,500 (☎0565)
Map **31** A3
★★Centrale pza G Verdi 2 ☎32581 rm44
⊷15 G Lift
🏚**24 E Bianchetti** pza Costituzione 54
☎33017 Frd

Pisa Pisa 103,400 (☎050) Map **29** B2
★★★★Cavalieri pza Stazione ☎43290
rm102 ⊷54 ⬚48 G Lift
☆☆**California** via Aurelia ☎890726 rm74
⬚74 B9000–18200 M6500 Pn17500–20900
Pool
★★Kinzica pza Arcivescovado ☎22300 rm33
⊷23 B8400–18450 Màlc
★★Touring (n rest) via G-Puccini 6 ☎46374
rm40 ⊷20 Lift
🏚**G Finocchi** via Galcesana ☎86147 N⧓
Aud/VW
🏚**del Seppia** pza Don Minzoni 5 ☎29598 N⧓
M/c BL/Rov/Tri

Pisticci Matera 16,850 (☎0835) Map **34** C3
☆☆☆**AGIP** SS 407 Basentana km 137 & 400
☎632007 rm64 ⬚64 Lift B7500–16800

Polignano a Mare Bari 13.900 (☎080)
Map **34** B2
★Grotta Palazzese via Narciso 59 ☎740261
rm14 ⊷10 Sea

Pordenone Pordenone 51,025 (☎0434)
Map **30** C4
★★★Moderno pza XX-Settembre ☎22565
rm134 ⊷22 ⬚55 G Lift
🏚**Automobile** viale Grigoletti ☎32591 N⧓
BL/Jag/Rov/Tri

Italy

🏨➤ Cossetti & Vatta viale Venezia ☎31474 Ren

Port'Ercole Grosseto (☎0564) Map **31** A3
★**Don Pedro** ☎833914 rm44 G Lift
Apr–Oct B10750–23000 M5000–8000
Pn20000–23000 Sea

Porto Azzurro See Elba (Isola d')

Porto Ferraio See Elba (Isola d')

Portofino Genova 850 (☎0185) Map **29** A2/3
★★★★**Splendido** ☎69195 rm70 ⇄53 ▥7 G
Lift 26 Mar–19 Oct ⍥ Sea
★★**Piccolo** ☎69015 rm26 ⇄6 ▥8
15 Mar–15 Oct Sea

Porto San Giorgio Ascoli Piceno 14,900 (☎0734) Map **32** C4
★**Terazza** via A-Costa ☎4244 rm37 ▥17 G Lift
B4300–13500 M5000–7000
Pn7000–13000
🏨➤ **Petracci** via Nazionale Àdriatica 235
☎4248 N➤

Positano Salerno 3,350 (☎089) Map **33** A3
★★★**Montemare** via Pasitea 58 ☎875010
rm36 ⇄36 Sea
★★★**Savoia** via C Colombo 29 ☎875003
rm46 ⇄30 ▥14 Lift 1 Apr–15 Oct
★★**Buca di Bacco** ☎875004 rm31 ▥8 Lift
Jan–Oct B9600–21300 Màlc Pn18300–21300 Sea
★★**Maresca** ☎875140 rm19 (A5) ⇄12 ▥5 G
LD B4900–10200 M3000 Pn8500–13500 Sea
★★**Margherita** via G Marconi 31 ☎875188
rm14 ⇄9 G 15 Mar–30 Oct B5300–13400
M3500–4000 Pn10000–13000 Sea
★★**Poseidon** ☎875014 rm54 ⇄48 ▥6 G Lift
Etr–15 Oct B13500–25000 M6000 Pn20000 Pool Sea

Potenza Potenza 60,750 (☎0971) Map **33** B3
🏨➤ **L Olita** via del Gallitello ☎29823 GM

Pozzuoli Napoli 60,990 (☎081) Map **32** D1
Pelli via Scarfoglio ☎7605322 N➤ GM

Praiano Salerno 1,700 (☎089) Map **33** A/B3
★★**Grand Tritone** ☎874005 rm75 ⇄40 ▥35
Lift Etr–15 Oct LD B10500–25000 M6000
Pn1900–22000 Pool Beach Sea
★★**Tramonto d'Oro** ☎871608 rm39 ⇄39 G Lift

Procchio See Marciana-Marina under Elba

Pugnochiuso Foggia (☎0884) Map **34** C4
★★★**Faro** ☎79011 rm191 ⇄191 Lift

Ragusa See Sicilia (Sicily)

Rapallo Genova 28,600 (☎0185) Map **29** A3
★★★★**Savoia** pza III Novembre ☎50492 rm63
⇄37 G Lift Beach Sea
★★★**Bel Soggiorno** via Gramsci 10 ☎54527
rm24 ⇄12 Lift
★★★**Eurotel** via Aurelia Ponente 22 ☎60981
rm65 ⇄52 ▥13 G Lift B17000–32000
M7500–9000 Pn24000–32000 Pool
★★★**Grande Italia** Lungomare Italia 1
☎50492 rm64 (A12) ⇄40 ▥10 G Lift
B7400–26800 M6000–7650 Pn18550–26150 Beach Sea
★★★**Marsala** Lungomare V-Veneto ☎50348
rm36 ⇄20 ▥8 Lift B7800–19600 M6000
Pn14000–17800 Sea
★★★**Miramare** Lungomare V-Veneto 27
☎50293 rm24 ⇄10 Lift B8100–21000
M7000–8000 Pn19000–22000 Sea
★★★**Moderno & Reale** via Gramsci 6
☎50601 rm49 ⇄35 ▥5 Lift LD B11500–23000
M6500–7500 Pn16000–25000 Sea
★★★**Riviera** via Gramsci 2 ☎50248 rm26
⇄25 ▥1 Lift 20 Dec–6 Nov LD B15300–28000
M7000–8000 Pn20000–25000 Sea

★★**Piccolo** via Dante 6 ☎54975 rm10 ⇄10
Lift 20 Dec–30 Sep Sea
★**Bandoni** (Pensione) via Marsala 24 ☎50423
rm16 ⇄7 ▥1 Lift B4800–12600 M2800
Pn8500–10800 Sea
★**Elvezia** (Pensione) via Ferraretto 12
☎50564 rm11 ⇄2 LD B5850–11600
M3800 Pn8500–8700 Sea
🏨➤ **E Massa** via G-Mameli 182 ☎50689 BL

Ravello Salerno 2,450 (☎089) Map **33** B3
★★★**Caruso Belvedere** via Toro 52 ☎871527
rm26 ⇄19 ▥1 G Sea
★★★**Palumbo** via Toro 34 ☎857244 rm47
(A15) ⇄30 ▥1 G 1 Apr–15 Nov B10700–24400
M7000 Pn22000–26000 Sea
★★**Parsifal** pza Fontana ☎857144 rm19 ⇄14
G 1 Apr–30 Sep B5500–13000 M5500
Pn7500–14000 Sea

Ravenna Ravenna 137,050 (☎0544)
Map **30** C3
★★★★**Jolly Mameli** pza Mameli 1 ☎35762
rm75 ⇄75 G Lift B19000–31000 M7000
Pn31000
★★★**Bisanzio** (n rest) via Salara 30 ☎27111
rm40 ▥6 Lift B14300–35500
★★★**Centrale Byron** (n rest) via IV-Novembre 14
☎22225 rm57 ⇄12 ▥21 Lift B7300–16600
★★**Nuovo San Marco** (n rest) via XIII-Giugno
14 ☎24307 rm30 ⇄12
☆**Romea** via Romea 1 ☎61247 rm39 ⇄38 G
Lift B10000–17000 M5000 Pn18000
🏨➤ **Emiliana-Motor** via Faentina 74 ☎460068
N➤ Frd
🏨➤24 Ravennate via M-Perilli 40 ☎39079
N➤28061 Fia/Ren G10

Reggio Di Calabria Reggio Di Calabria
174,500 (☎0965) Map **34** C1
C Mazzone via San Caterina 12 ☎48600 N➤
M/c Aud/Por/VW

Reggio Nell'Emilia Reggio Nell'Emilia
129,800 (☎0522) Map **29** B3
★★★★**Astoria** viale Nobili 4 ☎35245 rm81
⇄61 ▥20 G Lift
★★★**Posta** (n rest) pza C-Battisti 4 ☎32944
rm56 ⇄14 ▥24 G Lift 25 Aug–31 Jul
B7800–25000
🏨➤ Reggem Motors viale Montefiorino 1
☎22259 N➤ Frd

Rende See Cosenza

Ricavo See Castellina in Chianti

Riccione Forli 30,100 (☎0541) Map **30** C2
★★★★**Atlantic** viale Milano 11 ☎601155
tx55192 rm60 ⇄30 ▥30 G Lift 20 May–20 Sep
B16000–36000 M6000–9000
Pn18000–30000 Pool Beach Sea
★★★★**Beaurivage** viale d'Annunzio 132
☎41703 rm55 ⇄23 ▥32 Lift 15 May–15 Sep
B12600–23200 M6000–7000 ⍥
★★★★**Saviolo Spiaggia** viale d'Annunzio 2
☎43252 rm70 ⇄70 Lift 10 May–30 Sep
Pool Beach Sea
★★★**Abner's** Lungomare Repubblica ☎600601
tx55153 rm50 ⇄50 Lift B16500–33000
M5000–10000 Pn18000–28000 St% ⍥
Beach Sea
★★★**Arizona** viale d'Annunzio 22 ☎48520
rm70 ⇄70 Lift 10 May–30 Sep LD
B10000–27000 M8000–9000
Pn15000–20000 Beach Sea
★★★**Lungomare** viale Milano 7 ☎41601
rm58 ⇄58 G Lift 20 May–20 Sep
B9500–19000 M5000–8000 Pn10000–19000
Sea
★★★**Vienna & Touring** viale Gramsci 79
☎41041 tx55153 rm94 ⇄94 G Lift
15 May–30 Sep LD B13500–29000
M5000–9000 Pn16000–24500 ⍥ Beach Sea

★★**Alexandra** viale Torino 61 ☎615344
tx55153 Fashotel rm55 ⇆55 Lift Etr–30 Sep
B12500–24000 M5000–9000
Pn15000–22500 St% ✇ Beach Sea
★★**Nevada** via Milano 46 ☎601245 rm48
⇆48 G Lift 1 May–10 Oct B9500–13000
M6000 Pn11000–18000 Beach Sea
★★**Santo Stefano** via Tassoni 5 ☎42391
rm49 ⇆38 ⋔4 Lift May–Sep B5500–15000
M4500 Pn6500–10800 Sea
★**Sarti** viale Torino 1 ☎42264 tx55192 rm54
⇆54 Lift 1 May–30 Sep Sea
⏚**Dante** via Zandonai 29 ☎41516 GM
⏚**Morelli & Muccioli** via R-Molari 26
☎41436 N✇ Aud/VW G40
Rimini Forli 123,300 (☎0541) Map **30** C2
★★★**Ambasciatori** viale A-Vespucci 22
☎27642 tx55132 rm70 ⇆70 G Lift
B14500–45000 M9000 Pn22000–35000
✇ Pool Beach Sea
★★★**Fantasy** viale Regina Elena 93 ☎24922
rm65 ⋔65 G Lift 1 May–30 Sep Beach Sea
★★★**France** viale Regina Margherita 48
☎32237 rm71 ⇆21 ⋔50 Lift 1 May–5 Oct
Pool Beach Sea
★★★**President** via Tripoli 270 ☎25741
rm50 ⇆20 G Lift 1 May–30 Sep B9000–16900
M4500–6000 Pn9500–14800 Sea
★★**Alpen** (Pensione) viale Regina Elena 203
☎80662 rm56 ⇆4 ⋔38 Lift 1 May–30 Sep LD
B5500–13000 M3500 Pn6400–10600 Sea
★★**Constellation** viale Regina Elena 73
☎55071 rm35 ⇆35 G Lift 1 May–30 Sep Sea
★★**Gran Bretagna** viale Carducci 2 ☎22613
rm29 ⋔12 25 May–20 Sep
⏚**Grattacielo** viale P-Amedeo 11 ☎24610
N✇ Opl G100
⏚**24 F Masini** via XXIII Settembre 6
☎234668 N✇ Chy/Sim/Vlo
Ruggeri via Nuova Circonvallazione ☎771071
N✇ Chy/Sim
⏚**E Sartini** viale P-Amedeo 13 ☎27548 N✇
Fia G70
⏚**F Sartini** via Nuova Circonvallazione 22
☎770311 N✇ Fia
⏚**A Terenzi** viale Tiberio 30 ☎24297 N✇ Frd
At **Rivazzurra** (4km SE)
★★★**Grand Meeting** viale Regina Margherita
46 ☎32123 rm48 ⇆30 ⋔18 G Lift
1 May–30 Sep B6000–12000 Pn9500–15000
Beach Sea
★★★**Little** via Gubbio 16 ☎33258 rm45 ⋔27
G Lift 15 May–30 Sep
Rivazzurra See **Rimini**
Riva del Garda Trento 12,700 (☎0464)
Map **29** B4
★★★**Grand Riva** pza Garibaldi 10 ☎52340
tx40278 rm140 ⇆80 Lift 10 Apr–10 Oct Lake
★★★**Lac & Parc** viale Rovereto 28 ☎52122
tx40258 rm170 ⇆130 Lift ✇ Pool Lake
★★★**Marina** ☎52736 rm30 ⇆3 ⋔15 Lift
Apr–Sep Pool Lake
★★**Bellavista** ☎52334 rm28 ⇆6 G Lift
1 May–15 Oct Lake
★★**Centrale** pza III-Novembre 27 ☎52344
rm70 ⇆12 Lift Etr–5 Oct
Roccaraso L'Aquila 1,600 (☎0864)
Map **32** C2
☆☆☆**AGIP** SS17 dell'Appennino Abruzzese
☎62443 G Lift B5500–14000
Rolle (Passo di) Trento (☎0439) Map **13** A1
★**Passo di Rolle** ☎68216 rm27 ⇆4 LD
B3700–12000 M5000 Pn11000–15000
Roma (Rome) Roma 2,856,350 (☎06)
Map **31** B2 **See Plan**
★★★★★**Bernini-Bristol** pza Barberini 23
☎463051 Plan **1** tx61554 Bernbris rm116
⇆116 G Lift B24500–49500 Màlc St14%

★★★★★**Grand Flora** via V-Veneto 191
☎462151 Plan **2** rm177 ⇆151 ⋔26 G Lift
★★★★★**Hassler-Villa Medici** Trinita dei
Monti 6 ☎6792651 Plan **3** tx61208 rm100
⇆100 G Lift
★★★★**Boston** via Lombardia 47 ☎4751569
Plan **4** rm120 ⇆120 Lift
★★★★**Commodore** (n rest) via Torino 1
☎4751515 tx63170 Plan **6** rm65 ⇆40 ⋔25
G Lift B16550–25800 M6500
★★★★**Eliseo** via de Porta Pinciana 30
☎460556 Plan **7** tx61693 rm60 ⇆60 Lift
LD B22000–33500 M7500
★★★★**Jolly** corso d'Italia 1 ☎8495 Plan **8**
tx60134 rm200 ⇆200 G Lift B34500–50150
M8500 Pn49000
★★★★**Lord Byron** via de Notaris 5 ☎3609541
Plan **9** tx62217 rm55 ⇆45 ⋔10 G Lift
B27500–38600 M8500 St9%
★★★★**Quirinale** via Nazionale 7 ☎489101
Plan **10** tx61332 rm200 ⇆180 G Lift
B25500–48000 M7500 Pn40500–44500
★★★★**Ville** via Sistina 69 ☎688941 Plan **11**
rm189 ⇆189 G Lift LD B28200–44800 M6400
☆☆☆**AGIP** via Aurelia (8km W road No. 1)
☎626843 Plan **21** rm222 ⋔222 Lift
B10200–23950
★★★**Britannia** (n rest) via Napoli 64
☎482104 Plan **12** tx62292 rm32 ⇆32 G Lift
B18500–28900
★★★**Columbus** via delle Conciliazione 33
☎6564874 Plan **13** tx64010 ⇆110 ⋔80 Lift
B12500–27500 M6000 Pn42000–47500
St9%
★★★**Continental** (n rest) via Cavour 5
☎462141 Plan **14** tx61421 rm260 ⇆132
⋔105 G Lift
★★★**Dinesen** (n rest) via de Porta Pinciana 18
☎471410 Plan **15** rm50 ⇆25 Lift
★★★**Nord–Nuova** via G-Amendola 3
☎465441 Plan **16** tx61556 rm160 ⇆160 G
Lift LD B19900–34800 M6400 Pn28000
★★★**Park** via A-Morelli 5 ☎870184
Plan **18** tx61693 rm35 ⇆35 Lift B16300–23300
M5000
★★★**Regina Carlton** via V-Veneto 72
☎4758841 Plan **19** tx59142 rm134 ⇆124 ⋔10
G Lift B35450–51300 M9400 Pn51250
★★★**Rivoli** (n rest) via Taramelli 7 (off viale
B-Buozzi) ☎878140 Plan **20** rm50 ⇆46 Lift
★★**Alba** (n rest) via Leonina 12 ☎484471
Plan **22** rm22 ⇆17 B8700–15200
★★**Ariston** (n rest) via Turati 16 ☎7310341
Plan **23** rm110 ⇆90 Lift B8000–18000
★★**Astrid** (Pensione) (n rest) Largo A-Sarti 4
☎390818 Plan **24** rm20 Lift 1 Dec–30 Oct
B9500–17000
★★**Nordland** via Alciato 14 ☎6231841
Plan **25** rm125 ⋔95 Lift B7500–17000
M6000–7000 Pn13000–15000
★**Margutta** (n rest) via Laurina 34 ☎688440
Plan **28** rm25 ⇆25 Lift B10300–15200
★**Scalinata di Spagna** (Pensione) pza Trinita
dei Monte 17 ☎6793006 Plan **29** rm14 ⇆6
⋔6 G Lift B8000–17000 St9%
⏚**Bellancauto** pza Villa Carpegna 52
☎6223359 N✇ Chy/Sim
⏚**24 Cirilcar** via G-Martucci 1 ☎8310047 N✇
M/c
⏚**Marche Orlando** Circonvallazione Trionfale
133 ☎3599893 N✇ M/c Jag/Ska/Toy
⏚**Pandolfi** via Collatina 52 ☎2580710
N☎2581509 N✇ M/c Ska G150
At **Storta (La)**
☆**Bela** via Cassia 1801 ☎6990232 Plan **5**
rm44 ⇆44 B13200–17300 M3800
Pn14700–19600 St10% ✇ Pool
Rovereto Trento 31,200 (☎0464) Map **29** B4
⏚**24 Roverauto** corso Verona ☎23970 N✇ GM

Italy

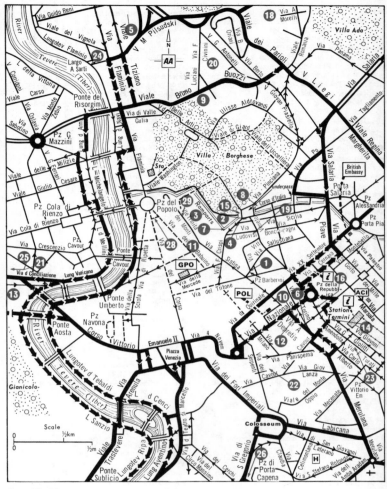

Roma (Rome)
1   ★★★★★Bernini-Bristol
2   ★★★★★Grand Flora
3   ★★★★★Hassler Villa Medici
4   ★★★★Boston
5   ☆Bela (at La Storta 17km NW
     on road No. 2)
6   ★★★★Commodore
7   ★★★★Eliseo
8   ★★★★Jolly
9   ★★★★Lord Byron
10   ★★★★Quirinale
11   ★★★★Ville
12   ★★★Britannia
13   ★★★Columbus

14   ★★★Continental
15   ★★★Dinesen
16   ★★★Nord-Nuova
18   ★★★Park
19   ★★★Regina Carlton
20   ★★★Rivoli
21   ☆☆☆AGIP
22   ★★Alba
23   ★★Ariston
24   ★★Astrid
25   ★★Nordland
28   ★Margutta
29   ★Scalinata di Spagna

Italy

Rovigo Rovigo 51,250 (☎0425) Map **30** C3
★★**Bologna** viale Regina-Margherita 6
☎22406 rm16 ⇆4 B6700–13900 M4000
Pn13600–14700

Saint-Vincent Aosta 4,750 (☎0166)
Map **28** D4
★★★★*Billia* viale Piemonte ☎3446 rm134
⇆134 G Lift ‰ Pool
📽**24 Ford di Fabris** pza Zerbion ☎2619
Frd G20

Salerno Salerno 159,300 (☎089)
Map **33** B3
★★★★**Jolly delle Palme** Lungomare Trieste 1
☎225222 tx77050 rm106 ⇆98 Lift
B16500–27000 M7000 Pn28500
📽 **G Jannone** via Picenza 12 ☎351229 N‰
BL/Jag/Rov/Tri
At **Vietri Sul Mare** (3km W)
★★★★**Lloyd's Baia** via dei Marinis ☎210145
tx77043 rm120 (A8) ⇆110 🍴10 G Lift
B14300–30800 M8000 Pn21700–32300 Pool
Beach Sea

Salo' Brescia 10,650 (☎0365) Map **29** B4
★★★**Duomo** via Duomo 18 ☎21026 rm28 ⇆25
Lift B9300–19000 M5000–6000
Pn11000–15000 Lake
★**Ideal** via Pietro de Salò 11 ☎20873 rm28
(A8) ⇆18 🍴4 G Apr–Oct LD B6500–16000
M5000 Pn12500–15000 Lake

Salsomaggiore Terme Parma 17,900
(☎0524) Map **29** A3
★★★★**Porro** viale Porro 10 ☎78221 rm85
⇆38 🍴41 Lift B14400–31700 M9000
& àlc Pn29500–31500 Pool

San Bartolomeo al Mare Imperia 2,500
(☎0183) Map **28** D2
★*Mayola* ☎44239 rm80 ⇆60 Lift
20 Apr–10 Oct Beach Sea

San Benedetto del Tronto Ascoli
Piceno 44,600 (☎0735) Map **32** C3
★★**Pierrot** Lungomare Rinascimento 15
☎65386 rm45 🍴45 1 May–31 Sep Pool
Beach Sea
★**Arlecchino** viale Trieste 24 ☎2959 rm24
⇆24 G B6800–14700 M10000 Pn12000–
17000 Pool Beach ∩ Sea
E Montevidoni d Fil corso Mazzini 241 ☎2691
N‰
📽**G E Tommassini** corso Mazzini 249 ☎5608
N‰ Aud/VW

San Candido-Innichen Bolzano 3,000
(☎0474) Map **13** A1
★★*Park Sole Paradiso* ☎73120 rm50 ⇆50
G20 Dec–4 Apr 1 Jun–30 Sep

San Domenico See **Fiesole**

San Donato Milanese See **Milano**
(Milan)

San Gimignano Siena 7,600 (☎0577)
Map **29** B2
★★**Cisterna** pza della Cisterna 23 ☎940328
rm47 ⇆16 🍴18 Lift B7900–17700 M4500
Pn16000–19500

San Mamete See **Valsolda**

San Martino di Castrozza Trento 328
(☎0439) Map **13** A1
★★★*San Martino* ☎68011 rm46 ⇆42 G
12 Dec–4 Apr 20 Jun–9 Sep
★★★*Savoia* ☎68094 rm73 ⇆73 G Lift
1 Jul–10 Sep 20 Dec–10 Apr LD B13000–
16000 M7000 Pn20000–24000
★*Belvedere* ☎68000 rm30 ⇆14 🍴12 G Lift
25 Jun–10 Sep 20 Dec–10 Apr B9800–22600
M5000 Pn13500–18000

San Menaio Foggia 493 (☎0884)
Map **33** B4

☆**Sole** (1km E) ☎91153 rm38 (A18) ⇆32 LD
Pn13000–20000 Beach Sea

San Remo Imperia 64,800 (☎0184)
Map **28** D2
★★★★★**Royal** corso Imperatrice ☎84321
tx27511 rm141 ⇆132 🍴9 G Lift 20 Dec–30 Sep
B20500–55000 M10500 Pn27000–46000
‰ Pool Sea
★★★★*Miramare* corso Matuzia 9 ☎882381
rm80 (A7) ⇆64 🍴8 Dec–Oct LD B11000–
27000 M8000 Pn18000–23000 Pool Sea
★★★★*Savoy* via Nuvoloni 40 ☎84921
rm160 (A) ⇆140 G Lift 20 Dec–30 Sep Pool
Sea
★★★**Astoria** corso Matuzia 8 ☎70791 rm96
⇆77 Lift B10000–32000 M7000 Pn19000–
28000 Sea
★★★**Europa & Pace** corso Imperatrice 27
☎70605 rm80 ⇆40 G Lift B8600–28200
M8000 Pn18000–28000 Sea
★★★*Grand Londra* corso Matuzia 2
☎79961 rm140 ⇆130 G Lift Pool Beach Sea
★★★*Parco* corso Mazzini 109 ☎85305 rm30
⇆17 🍴13 G Lift 15 Dec–31 Oct LD
B9500–20250 M6500 Pn17000–18500 Pool
Sea
★★★**Residence Principe** via Asquasciati 48
☎83565 rm60 ⇆60 G Lift B11200–23700
M6500 Pn19000–20400 ‰
★★**Beau Rivage** corso Trieste 49 ☎85146
rm30 ⇆1 🍴30 Lift LD B8000–15000 M4500
Pn15000 Sea
☆☆**Bobby** corso Marconi 146 ☎60256
rm74 (A10) ⇆20 🍴54 G Lift B14500–28000
M7000 Pn22500 Pool Sea
★★**King** corso Cavalotti 92 ☎86054 rm28 ⇆24
10 Dec–10 Oct B7800–19600 M6000
Pn14000–16000 Beach Sea
★★**Morandi** corso Matuzia 25 ☎85275 rm34
⇆28 🍴11 G Lift B6500–20400 M5000–6000
Pn13000–18800 Beach Sea
★★**Paradiso** corso Imperatrice ☎85112
rm40 ⇆21 🍴17 G Lift B10000–20400 M6000
Pn15300–18800 Sea
📽**Toselli** corso Matuzia 51 ☎85572 N‰
GM/MB G90

Santa Caterina Valfurva Sondrio
(☎0342) Map **12** D1
★★**Sobretta** ☎935505 rm27 ⇆12 🍴8 G
28 Jun–20 Sep 1 Dec–1 May LD
B4700–12400 M5000 Pn9000–14000

Santa Cristina val Gardena Bolzano
1,600 (☎0471) Map **13** A1
★★*Posta* ☎76678 rm60 ⇆30 G (closed Nov)
Lift ‰ Pool

Santa Margherita Ligure Genova
12,900 (☎0185) Map **29** A3
★★★★★*Imperial-Palace* via Pagana 19
☎88991 rm105 ⇆105 Lift 20 Dec–30 Oct
Pool Beach Sea
★★★★*Miramare* via Milite Ignoto 30
☎87014 rm73 ⇆73 G Lift Pool Beach Sea
★★★**Continentale** via Pagana 8 ☎86512
rm61 ⇆61 LD B14000–37900 M10000
Pn18000–34000 ‰ Pool Sea
★★★**Laurin** corso Marconi 3 ☎89971 rm41
⇆41 Lift 21 Dec–20 Nov B20400–43000
M10000 Pn29250–39000 Beach Sea
★★★**Mediterraneo** via Vittoria 18a
☎86881 rm25 ⇆23 Lift B9900–22900
M8000 Pn16500–21000
★★★**Metropole** via Pagana 2 ☎86134 rm50
(A12) ⇆44 G Lift 20 Dec–6 Nov
B15000–31500 M8000 Pn20000–29000
Beach Sea
★★★*Park Suisse* via Favale 31 ☎89571
rm75 ⇆68 G Lift 1 Mar–15 Nov LD Pool Sea

Italy

★★★ **Regina Elena** Lungomare Milite Ignoto 44 ☎87004 tx28563 rm64 ⇌56 ⋔8 G Lift B19600–48200 M12000 Pn25500–43500 Beach Sea
★★★ **Tigullio** (n rest) corso E-Rainusso 3 ☎87455 rm40 ⇌40 Lift ⚓ Pool Golf
★★ **Villa Anita** viale Minerva ☎86543 rm20 (A5) ⇌3 ⋔7 G B9000–14500 M5500 Pn10000–13000 Sea
★ **Europa** via Trento 5 ☎87187 rm16 ⇌2 G

Sapri Salerno 7,580 (☎0973) Map **33** B3
★★ **Tirreno** corso Italia ☎31157 rm56 ⇌7 ⋔19 G Lift LD B4700–11700 M4200 Pn9300–13000 St15% Sea
i⚫24 Comisso via Pisacane 22 ☎31370 N☎31356 M/c Frd G2Q

Sardagna See **Trento**

Sardegna (Isola) (Sardinia) 135,750 Map **31** Inset

Arzachena Sassari 6,340 (☎0789)
On the *Costa Smeralda*
★★★★ **Romazzino** ☎96020 ta Rankotel Portocervo tx79059 rm100 ⇌100 May–Oct Lift Pool Beach Sea

Cagliari Cagliari 225,900 (☎070)
★★★★ **Jolly Regina Margherita** viale Regina Margherita 44 ☎651971 tx79050 rm130 ⇌104 Lift B11800–30700 M6500 Pn22800–26350
☆☆☆ **AGIP** Circonvallazione Nuova ☎494003 rm57 ⋔57 Lift B7500–14800
⚫ **SIMAUTO** via Tasso 13 ☎487671 N☎ BL/Jag/Rov/Tri

Golfo Aranci Sassari (☎0789)
★★ **Margherita** ☎46906 rm25 ⇌4 ⋔7 LD B7500–17000 M5000 Pn13000–16500 St9% Beach Sea

Iglesias Cagliari 29,000 (☎0781)
★★★ **Artu** pza Q-Sella 12 ☎2492 rm22 ⇌4 ⋔5 G

Macomer Nuoro 10,350 (☎0785)
☆☆ **AGIP** SS131 di Carlo Felice km 145 rm30 ⋔30 B6050–12450

Nuoro Nuoro 33,850 (☎0784)
☆☆ **AGIP** via Trieste ☎34071 rm57 ⋔57 Lift B6050–12450
i A Sanna viale della Republica 40 ☎33124 M/c

Oristano Cagliari 27,950 (☎0783)
i⚫24 U&C Annis via Liguria 6 ☎2370 N☎3270 MB G25
⚫24 D A Leoni Palazzo Corrias ☎2097 N☎ M/c Ren

Sassari Sassari 112,800 (☎079)
★★★★ **Jolly Grazia Deledda** viale Dante 47 ☎271235 tx79056 SAS rm140 ⇌140 Lift B19500–34000 M7000 Pn31500 Pool
☆☆☆ **AGIP** Loc Serra Secca ☎271440 rm57 ⋔57 Lift B9500–22000
★★ **Jolly** (n rest) via Mancini 2 ☎35001 rm59 ⇌22 G Lift B9600–21850

Villasimius Cagliari 2,150 (☎070)
★★★ **Timi-Ama** ☎79228 rm64 ⇌64 15 May–30 Sep ⚓ Beach Sea
At **Capo Boi** (6km W)
★★★ **Grand Capo Boi** ☎79225 tx79266 rm103 ⇌67 ⋔34 Lift 1 May–20 Oct LD Pn 19500–38000 ⚓ Pool Beach Sea

Sarzana La Spezia 19,200 (☎0187) Map **29** A2
☆☆☆ **AGIP** Nuova Circonvallazione ☎61491 rm51 ⋔51 Lift

Sassari See **Sardegna (Sardinia)**

Savona Savona 80,380 (☎019) Map **28** D3

☆☆☆ **AGIP** via Nizza-loc Zinola ☎801961 rm60 ⋔60 Lift B8800–20000
★★★ **Miramare** via Giordano 5 ☎803333 rm22 ⇌22 G Lift B17000–28000 M6000 Pn23000 Beach Sea
★★★ **Riviera-Suisse** via Paleocapa ☎20683 rm54 ⋔36 G Lift B7300–24400
C M Spirito corso Viglienzoni 8f ☎806860 N☎ Chy/Sim

Sciacca See **Sicilia (Sicily)**

Selva di Val Gardena Bolzano 2,250 (☎0471) Map **13** A1
★★ **Solaia** ☎75104 rm30 (A30) ⇌24 ⋔6 1 Dec–10 Apr 20 Jun–30 Sep B13500–39000 M6500–7500 Pool

Senigallia Ancona 39,650 (☎071) Map **30** D2
★★★ **Ritz** Lungomare Dante Alighieri 142 ☎63563 tx56358 rm150 ⋔150 Lift 15 May–15 Oct B11000–22200 M5000 Pn15900–21000 Pool Beach Sea
★★ **Excelsior** Lungomare Dante Alighieri 148 ☎61491 rm94 ⋔90 Lift 1 May–30 Sep Sea
i⚫24 G E Luzi via Podesti 156 ☎62035 N☎62677 Aud/Por/VW

Sessa Aurunca Caserta 29,475 (☎0823) Map **32** C2
☆☆☆ **AGIP** Bivio Appia- Domiziana (SS7) ☎930230 rm45 ⋔45 Lift B5000–15500

Sesto Calende Varese 10,550 (☎0331) Map **28** D4
★★ **Tre Re** pza Garibaldi 25 ☎91229 rm25 ⇌14 ⋔13 Lift 10 Mar–10 Dec Lake

Sesto Fiorentino See **Firenze**

Sestriere Torino 700 (☎0122) Map **28** C3
★★★ **Duchi d'Aosta** colle del Sestriere ☎7123 ta Duchihotel rm173 ⇌99 Lift 5 Dec–15 Apr
★ **Torre** colle del Sestriere ☎7041 rm150 Lift 3 Dec–9 Apr

Sestri Levante Genova 21,650 (☎0185) Map **29** A2
★★★★ **Villa Balbi** viale Rimembranze 1 ☎42941 rm90 (A70) ⇌60 ⋔30 G Lift 14 May–11 Sep B10000–29000 M8000 Pn18000–29500 Pool Beach Sea
★★★ **Miramare & Europa** via Cappellini 3 ☎41055 rm37 ⇌23 ⋔10 Lift Apr–Oct Beach Sea
★★★ **Vis a Vis** via della Chiusa 28 ☎42661 rm47 ⇌29 ⋔18 G Lift ⚓ Sea
★★ **Eden** viale delle Parme ☎41792 rm25 ⇌20 ⋔15 1 Mar–10 Oct
★★ **Helvita** via Cappuccini 17 ☎41175 rm28 ⋔28 Lift 15 Mar–30 Sep B15200(double) M6000–Pn15100
★★ **Mimosa** via Antica Romans Occidentale ☎41449 rm25 ⇌22 Pool
★ **Daria** via le Rimembranze 46 ☎41139 rm23 ⇌5 ⋔11 Lift B7200–14400 M4500 Pn9500–13000 Sea

Settimo See **Torino**

Sicilia (Sicily) 4,819,000 Map **33** Inset
AA agents; see page 188

Agrigento Agrigento 49,150 (☎0922)
★★★ **Jolly dei Templi** contrada Angeli ☎25622 tx91086 Jolly AG rm146 ⇌146 Lift B15000–25000 M6500 Pn26200 Pool
⚫P Capizzi viale della Vittoria 115 ☎26854 N☎ M/c BL

Caltagirone Catania 38,780 (☎0933)
★★ **Artu** pza San Luigi ☎22360 rm23 ⇌4 ⋔5 G

Castelvetrano Trapani 30,650 (☎0924)
★★★ **Zeus** via le V-Veneto ☎41389 rm50 ⇌36 G Lift

Catania Catania 399,650 (☎095)
☆☆**AGIP** Ognina (SS114) ☎424003 rm45
🛏45 Lift B9000–22000
★★★**Jolly Trinacria** pza Trento 13 ☎228960
tx97080 rm159 ⇌159 Lift B22500–33000
M6500 Pn33500
🏠🕿**24 D A Bottaro** via Conte di Torino 29d
☎222543 N🚗328940 M/c Aud/Fia/MB/VW G

Erice Trapani 28,350 (☎0923)
★★★**Ermione** ☎24900 rm45 ⇌45 Lift LD
B10950–21950 M6000 Pn22500 Sea

Gela Caltanissetta 71,725 (☎0933)
☆☆**AGIP** Giardinelli (SS117 bis) ☎933032
rm91 🛏91 Lift B6250–12050
☆**Motel delle Mimose** via Indipendeza 11
☎30232 rm7 🛏7 G

Marsala Trapani 81,750 (☎0923)
☆☆☆**AGIP** exit Mazara del Vallo (SS115)
☎951611 rm32 🛏32 B4500–9300

Messina Messina 259,900 (☎090)
★★★★**Jolly Della Stretto** via Garibaldi 126
☎43401 tx98074 Jolly ME rm99⇌99 Lift
B15000–27000 M7000 Pn27000 Sea
🏠🕿**A Rossitto** via N-Fabrizi 13 ☎33143
N🚗 Opl

Palermo Palermo 661,250 (☎091)
★★★★**Jolly del Foro Italico** ☎235842
tx91076 Jolly P-A rm290 ⇌290 G Lift
B20000–30000 M7500 Pn33000 Pool Sea
★★★**Delle Palme** via Roma 398 ☎215570
rm180 ⇌180 G Lift
☆☆☆**AGIP** via della Regione Siciliana
☎403102 rm100 🛏100 Lift B7000–18500
RAF viale Michelangelo 2040 ☎400900 N🚗
Frd
🏠🕿**RICREA** via Catania 14 ☎240817 N🚗
Bed/Vau
🛑🕿**24 SIA** via G-Leopardi 90 ☎297200 N🚗
Ren

Piazza Armerina Enna 22,200 (☎0935)
★★★**Jolly** via Altacura ☎81446 rm58 ⇌53
Lift B10200–21450 M6000 Pn22200–24300

Ragusa Ragusa 63,550 (☎0932)
★★★**Jonio** Strada Nazionale 115 ☎24322
rm49 ⇌6 🛏10 G
🚗**CAI** via R-Morandi 1–15 ☎24047 Cit

Sciacca Agrigento 33,600 (☎0925)
☆☆☆**AGIP** via Figuli (SS115) ☎21978 rm38
🛏38 B6500–16000

Siracusa (Syracuse) Siracusa 116,750
(☎0931)
★★★★**Grand Villa Politi** via M Politi Laudien 3
☎32100 rm93 ⇌93 Lift B18530–26340
M9810 Pn26160–29430 🏖 Pool Sea
☆☆☆**AGIP** viale Teracati 30 ☎66944
rm76 🛏76 Lift B9000–21300
★★★**Jolly** corso Gelone 43 ☎64744
tx97108 Jolly SR rm102 ⇌102 Lift
B20500–31300 M7000 Pn32500
🏠🕿**V Liistro** viale Teracati ☎24600 N🚗 Frd

Taormina Messina 9,950 (☎0942)
★★★★**San Domenico Palace** pza San
Domenico 5 ☎23701 tx98013 Domhotel
rm101 ⇌101 G Lift 🏖 Pool Beach Sea
★★★★**Mazzarò Sea Palace** N16 ☎24004
tx98041 rm77 ⇌50 🛏27 G Lift 1 Mar–15 Nov
★★★**Jolly Diodoro** via Bagnoli Croce 75
☎23312 tx98028 Jolly TAO rm103 ⇌103
Lift B18900–36400 M9000 Pn33900 Pool Sea
★★★**San Pancrazio** (Pensione) (n rest)
via L Pirandello 22 ☎23252 rm17 ⇌7 🛏5
B5700–13500 Sea
★★**Villa Paradiso** via Roma 6 ☎23922
tx98062 rm33 ⇌28 🛏5 Lift LD B12250–23100
M8500 Pn21000–23000 Sea
At **Mazzarò** (5.5km E)

★★★★**Sant' Andrea** via Nazionale 137
☎23125 ta Santandrea tx98062 rm34 (A10)
⇌29 🛏5 Etr–31 Oct B15650–29700 M10150
Pn25800–33500 Beach Sea

Siena Siena 65,500 (☎0577) Map **29** A2
★★★★**Park** via Marciano 16 ☎44803 rm52
⇌52 G Lift
★★★**Moderno** via Baldassare Peruzzi 19
☎42453 rm72 ⇌10 🛏23 G Lift
★★**Palazzo Ravizza** Pian dei Mantellini 34
☎280462 rm27 ⇌11 🛏1 Lift B8300–18300
M4500
★★**Albergo Senese** (n rest) via Camollia 86
☎48324 rm30 ⇌3 Lift B7000–17000

Siracusa (Syracuse) See **Sicilia (Sicily)**

Sirmione Brescia 3,550 (☎030) Map **29** B4
★★★**Cortina Palace** via Grotte 12 ☎916021
tx30395 rm54 ⇌40 🛏14 Lift 6 Apr–20 Oct Pool
Lake
★★★**Florida** via Colombare ☎919018 rm28
⇌20 Pool Lake
★★★**Sirmione** pza Castello ☎916331 rm82
⇌70 Lift 1 Apr–6 Nov B10000–25200 M8000
Pn17500–23500 St9% Pool Lake
★★★**Terme** viale Marconi ☎916261 rm68
⇌49 🛏4 Lift 7 Apr–Oct **Pn** 19000–32000 St9%
Pool Lake
★★**Lac** via Colombare 54 ☎916026 rm29
⇌19 🛏4 Mar–Oct LD B6700–14600 M6000
Pn15000–16500 Lake

Solda Bolzano (☎0473) Map **12** D1
★★**Grand** ☎75422 rm110 ⇌23 G
Dec–Apr Jun–Sep 🏖
★**Posta Ortler** ☎75424 rm42 (A22) ⇌4 🛏5 G
20 Dec–20 Apr 20 Jun–20 Sep B6500–16000
M4500–5500 Pn10000–17000

Sondrio Sondrio 23,450 (☎0342)
Map **29** A4
★★★**Posta** pza Garibaldi 19 ☎22734 rm37
⇌12 🛏13 G Lift

Sori Genova 4,813 (☎0185) Map **29** A3
★★**Rondini** via Crispi 33 ☎78944 rm15 ⇌7
🛏1 Etr–15 Oct Beach Sea

Sorrento Napoli 16,150 (☎081) Map **33** A3
★★★★**Europa Palace** via Correale 34
☎8781501 rm71 (A10) ⇌58 🛏13 G Lift LD
B8600–17200 M5500 Pn17450–19600
Beach Sea
★★★★**Excelsior Vittoria** pza Tasso 34
☎8781900 tx71127 Vesuvio rm184 ⇌184 G
Lift 16 Mar–31 Oct B16150–30000 M8500
Pn25500–31500 St9% Pool Beach Sea
★★★★**Imperial Tramonto** via V-Veneto
☎8781940 tx71345 rm104 ⇌75 🛏29 Lift
B10200–29400 M7600–8700 Pn22200–
29500 Pool Beach Sea
★★★**Aminta Grand** via Nastro Verde 7
☎8781821 rm73 ⇌63 🛏10 G Lift 1 Apr–31 Oct
B11650–24800 M7000 Pn19000–21500
Pool Sea
★★★**Bellevue Syrene** pza della Vittoria 2
☎8781024 rm51 ⇌27 🛏15 G Lift Beach Sea
★★★**Cocumella** via Cocumella 7 ☎8781660
rm60 ⇌35 🛏14 Lift Mar–Oct B9350–25100
M6500–7600 Pn18500–21000 🏖 Pool
Beach Sea
★★★**Eden** via Correale 25 ☎8781909 rm60
⇌20 🛏40 Lift Mar–Nov Pool Beach Sea
★★★**Vesuvio** corso Italia 248 ☎8781804
tx71493 rm37 ⇌22 🛏12 G Lift B6800–21360
M6000 Pn12500–17500 Beach Sea
🏠🕿**Porto** via L-de-Maio ☎8781036

Spartaia See **Marciana-Marina** under **Elba**

Spezia (La) La Spezia 122,800 (☎0187)
Map **29** A2

Italy

★★★★**Jolly Del Golfo** via XX Settembre 2
☎27200 tx37047 Jolly SP rm110 ⇌110 Lift
B21000–36000 M6500 Pn32000
🐾**Cozzani & Rossi** pza Caduti per la Liberta 6
☎25386 N🅰 BL
🛢🐾**L'Auto per Tutti** via Manzoni 31 ☎501324
N🅰 Frd

Spoleto Perugia 37,000 (☎0743)
Map **31** B3
☆☆☆**AGIP** via Flamina (SS3) ☎49368 rm57
🏢57 Lift B5000–10200

Spotorno Savona 4,460'(☎019) Map **28** D2
★★★**Royal** Lungomare Kennedy ☎745074
rm100 ⇌100 G Lift May–Oct B13500–31000
M8500 Pn15000–22000 St9% Beach Sea
★★**Palace & Grand** ☎745112 rm100 ⇌65
Lift 25 May–31 Jul Beach Sea
★**Villa Teresina** via Imperia ☎745160 rm26
1 Apr–30 Sep B6000–11000 M3500
Pn7500–9000

Stagno See Livorno

Storta (La) See Roma (Rome)

Stresa Novara 5,100 (☎0323) Map **28** D4
★★★★★**Grand des Iles Borromées**
Lungolago ☎30431 rm145 ⇌116 🏢7 Lift
B13000–47000 M13000 Pn40000–51000
St4% 🏊 Pool Lake
★★★★**Bristol** via Nazionale del Sempione 73
☎30409 tx20217 rm200 ⇌200 G Lift
15 Mar–30 Oct B11200–29800 M7000–8000
Pn12000–25000 🏊 Pool Lake
★★★**Regina Palazzo** Lungolago 27
☎30171 tx20381 rm130 ⇌130 G Lift Apr–Oct
B23900–39800 M9250 Pn25000–34000 🏊
Pool Golf ⌂ Lake
★★★**Astoria** Lungolago ☎30259 rm98 ⇌65
🏢33 G Lift Pool Lake
★★★**Palma** Lungolago ☎30266 rm125
⇌111 🏢14 G Lift Mar–Nov B11700–29400
M8000 Pn15000–25000 🏊 Pool Lake
★★**Italia** Lungolago ☎30540 rm36 ⇌13 🏢3
Lift Lake
★★**Lido la Perla Nera** Piazzale Stazione
Funivia ☎30384 rm27 ⇌20 🏢1 Mar–Oct
LD B8300–20600 M6000 Pn13000–17500
St9% Lake
★★**Milano & Speranza au Lac** pza Imbarcadero
☎31190 rm171 (A87) ⇌103 🏢54 G Lift Mar–
Oct B10600–25200 M7000–8000
Pn16000–22000 🏊 Lake
★★**Parco** via Gignous 1 ☎30335 rm41 (A18)
⇌41 G Lift Apr–Sep LD B7800–20100
M5300 Pn13500–19000 St% Lake
★★**Royal** via Nazionale del Sempione
☎30471 rm43 ⇌32 🏢8 Apr–Oct LD B7800–
19600 M6000 Pn12000–16000 St9% Lake
★**Elena** (n rest) pza Cadorna ☎31043 rm14
⇌3 G Lift
★**Flora** via Nazionale del Sempione 30
☎30524 rm23 ⇌11 G Apr–Oct LD
B6500–16000 M5000 Pn10000–15500 Lake

Suna See Verbania

Susa Torino 7,356 (☎0122) Map **28** C3
★★**Napoleon** ☎2704 rm46 ⇌46 G Lift LD
B8500–15000 M5500 Pn16000

Syracuse See Siracusa under Sicilia
(Sicily)

Taormina See Sicilia (Sicily)

Taranto Taranto 238,750 (☎099)
Map **34** B1
★★★★**Jolly Mar Grande** viale Virgilio 90
☎30861 tx86079 Jolly TA rm97 ⇌82 Lift
B12200–29600 M6500 Pn23400–28700 Pool

Terni Terni 111,050 (☎0744) Map **31** B3
G Belli via Lungonera 53 ☎409191 N🅰 BL

Terracina Latina 35,350 (☎0733) Map **32** C2

★★**Palace** Lungomare Matteotti ☎727285
rm72 ⇌72 G Lift LD B6200–13400 M4000
Pn11500–14000 Beach Sea

Tirano Sondrio 8,750 (☎0342) Map **29** A4
★**Posta & Stelvio** via Lungo Aeda
4 Novembre N1 ☎702555 rm34 ⇌3 🏢9 G Lift

Tolmezzo Udine 10,340 (☎0433)
Map **13** B1
🐾**CAT** via Paluzza 3 ☎2151 N🅰 Fia

Tonale (Passo del) Brescia (☎0364)
Map **12** D1
★★**Redivalle** ☎91349 rm56 ⇌50 G 1 Dec–
1 May 15 Jun–15 Sep B8500–22000 M5500
Pn10000–17000

Torbole Trento 802 (☎0464) Map **29** B4
★★**Casa Beust** via Benaco 21 ☎55111 rm28
⇌9 1 May–30 Sep
★★**Ifigenia** via Lungolago Verona 39
☎55134 rm46 ⇌32 Lift 1 Apr–10 Oct LD
B4700–17000 M4800 Pn7000–14500 Lake
★★**Lago di Garda** ☎55135 ta Gianflippi
rm38 ⇌10 Lift Etr–Oct Lake

Torino (Turin) Torino 1,202,850 (☎011)
Map **28** D3
★★★★★**Jolly Principi di Piemonte** via
P-Gobetti 15 (off via Roma) ☎519693 tx23120
Jolly PR rm103 ⇌103 Lift B38000–54000
M10000 Pn55500 Pool
★★★★**Jolly Ambasciatori** corso V-Emanuele
104 ☎5752 tx23296 Jolly TO rm197 ⇌197
G Lift B30800–45000 M9000 Pn46800
★★★★**Palace** (n rest) via Sacchi 8 ☎548585
tx23411 rm125 ⇌125 G Lift B31000–45000
★★★**Patria** (n rest) via Cernaia 42 ☎519903
rm109 ⇌83 🏢6 G Lift B10950–24400
🐾**CAR** corso P-Oddone 30 ☎480294 N🅰
Ren
G Garrone corso Casale 466 ☎890079 N🅰
Vlo
🛢**B Koelliker** via Barletta 133–135 ☎353632
N🅰 BL/Jag/Rov/Tri
At **Settimo** (8km NE on Autostrade to Ivrea)
☆☆☆**AGIP** ☎8001855 rm100 🏢100 Lift
B5000–10200

Torre a Mare See Bari

Torri del Benaco Verona 2,500 (☎045)
Map **29** B4
★★**Continental** ☎626195 rm33 ⇌33 G
25 Mar–10 Oct B6500–14000 M5000
Pn12000–15000 Lake

Tremezzo Como 1,400 (☎0344) Map **29** A4
★★★**Grand Tremezzo** Grande Parco
☎40446 rm104 ⇌80 G Lift Apr–Oct 🏊 Pool
Beach Sea
★★**Bazzoni** via Regina ☎40403 rm150
⇌75 🏢15 Lift Lake

Trento Trento 95,850 (☎0461) Map **29** B4
★★★**Grand** via Alfieri 21 ☎26297 rm95 ⇌15
🏢73 Lift
★★**Venezia** pza Duomo 45 ☎26335 rm80
⇌40 🏢18 G Lift B5500–15000 M5000
Pn10500–14000
🛢🐾**Bolghera** via Bolghera 45 ☎26859 N🅰 Fia
G20
E Franceschi via Brennero 264 ☎80110 N🅰 GM
Mille Miglia via Muredei 8 ☎21986 N🅰 Frd
At **Sardagna** (4km)
☆☆☆**AGIP** via Brennero 168 (SS12) ☎81117
rm45 🏢45 Lift B11000–23000

Treviso Treviso 91,450 (☎0422) Map **30** C4
★★★**Continental** (n rest) via Roma ☎57216
rm86 ⇌30 🏢56 G Lift
🐾**Bobbo** via della Repubblica 270 ☎62396
Peu/Vlo
🛢🐾**Sile Motori** viale della Repubblica 278
☎62743 N🅰 BL/Rov/Tri

🏨&🕎 **SOCAART** viale della Repubblica 19
☎63725 N🍴 M/c Frd

🏨 **Trevisauto** viale Felissent 19a ☎63265 GM

Tricesimo Udine 6,450 (☎0432) Map **30** C4

★★ *Boschetti* pza Mazzini 9 ☎851230 rm32
⇌20 🛏12 Lift

Trieste Trieste 271,550 (☎040) Map **30** D4

★★★ **Jolly Cavour** corso Cavour 7 ☎7694
tx46139 Jolly TS rm179 ⇌165 G Lift B12000–
32000 M7500 Pn25000–33000

☆☆☆ **AGIP** (Autostrada A4) Area di Servizio
Duino Sud ☎208273 rm80 🛏80 Lift
B8800–20000

☆☆☆ *Valrosandra* ☎226221 rm76 ⇌76 G
Pool

★★ **Colombia** (n rest) via Geppa 18 ☎69434
rm40 ⇌11 🛏29 B11400–23800

★ *Citta di Parenzo* (n rest) via degli Artisti 8
☎30119 rm46 ⇌5 🛏4 Lift

Antonucci via Villan de Bacchino 2 ☎414396
N🍴 Fia

Filotecnica Giuliana via F-Severo 42
☎764248 N🍴 BL/Rov/Tri/Vlo

🏨 **A Grandi** viale Flavia 120 ☎817201 N🍴 Fia

🏨&🕎 **Regina** via Raffineria 6 ☎725345 M/c
BMW/GM G300

Turin See **Torino**

Udine Udine 103,500 (☎0432) Map **30** C4

☆☆☆ **AGIP** viale Ledra 24 (SS13) ☎63841
rm105 🛏105 Lift B6000–14950

★★★ **Astoria** pza XX-Settembre 10 ☎207091
tx45120 rm80 ⇌80 G Lift B15900–27200
M7000 Pn27500

★★★ **Cristallo** pza G-d'Annunzio ☎205951
rm81 ⇌36 🛏45 G Lift B8800–14100
M5000 Pn16300

🕎 *Autofriulana* viale Europa Unita 33
☎56330 N🍴 BL/Rov/Tri G100

Edera via dello Cisterna 18 ☎205358 N🍴
Chv/Sim

🏨&🕎 **24 Furgiuele & Baldelli** viale Venezia 383
☎54350 N🍴 M/c Frd G20

🕎 *Nord* viale L-da Vinci ☎55669 N🍴 Ren

Valsolda Como 2,500 (☎0344) Map **29** A4
At **San Mamete**

★★ **Stella d'Italia** ☎68139 rm38 ⇌24 G
Lift 15 Apr–15 Oct B8250–21000 M7000
Pn11000–15000 Lake

Valtournanche Aosta 2,025 (☎0166)
Map **28** D4

★★ **Tourist** ☎92070 1 Dec–30 Apr
15 Jun–15 Sep LD **Pn**9000–13000

Varallo Vercelli 7,950 (☎0163) Map **28** D4

☆☆☆ **AGIP** d'Alagna (SS299) ☎52447 rm38
🛏38 Lift B5600–13000

Varazze Savona 15,200 (☎019) Map **28** D3

★★ **Delfino** via Colombo 48 ☎97073 rm26
(A15) ⇌14 🛏3 G Lift B6400–15000
M4000–5000 Pn8500–14000 Beach Sea

★★ **Europa** via Garibaldi 10 ☎96683 rm36
⇌19 🛏17 B5000–11000 M4500–5500
Pn6000–10000

Varenna Como 800 (☎0341) Map **29** A4

★★ **Olivedo** ☎830115 rm25 (A4) ⇌6 LD
B8000–18000 M5300 Pn12000–14000
St9% Lake

★★ *Royal* pza San Giorgio 5 ☎83102 rm65 (A)
⇌12 G 1 May–10 Oct Lake

Varese Varese 87,950 (☎0332) Map **28** D4

★★★ **Palace** via L-Manara 11 ☎230120
tx38163 rm100 ⇌60 🛏30 Lift Mar–Nov
B15000–31000 M7000 Pn22000–28000 🍴
Lake

🏨&🕎 *C F Buzio* viale Belforte 2 ☎282716 N🍴
M/c BL/Rov/Tri

Varigotti See **Finale Ligure**

Vasto Chieti 26,490 (☎0873) Map **33** A4

★★★ **Panoramic** via G-Smargiassi ☎2152
rm47 ⇌19 🛏28 G Lift B9000–18300
M4500 Pn12400–16200 Sea

Venezia (Venice) Venezia 365,450
(☎041) Map **30** C4

See also **Mestre** and **Marghera**

No road communications in city. Vehicles may
be left in garages in Piazzale Roma at end of
causeway from mainland or at open parking
places on the mainland approaches. Garages
will not accept advance bookings. Transport to
hotels by waterbus, etc, for which there are fixed
charges for fares and porterage. Hotel rooms
overlooking the Grand Canal normally have a
surcharge.

★★★★★ **Europa & Britannia** Canal Grande-
San Marco 2159 ☎700477 tx41123 rm140
⇌130 🛏10 Lift B31500–57000 M13000
Pn46000–58000 St9% 🍴 Pool Beach Golf Sea

★★★★★ **Gritti Palace** Canal Grande ☎26044
tx41125 rm92 ⇌92 Lift B40500–69000
Màlc St12%

★★★★★ **Royal Danieli** Riva degli Schiavoni
☎26480 tx41077 rm245 ⇌245 Lift
B43500–72000 M17000 Pn74000–133000

★★★★ *Gabrielli-Sandwirth* Riva degli Schiavoni
☎31580 tx41228 rm123 ⇌96 Lift 16 Mar–
31 Oct

★★★★ **Luna** pza San Marco ☎89840 tx41236
rm122 ⇌111 Lift

★★★★ *Monaco* Canal Grande-San Marco 1325
☎700211 rm82 ⇌66 🛏9 Lift

★★★★ **Regina & Roma** Canal Grande-
San Marco 2205 ☎700544 tx41123 rm65
⇌65 Lift B29500–51000 M13000
Pn44000–56000 St9% 🍴 Pool Beach Golf Sea

★★★ **Cavalletto** San Marco 1107 ☎700955
tx41684 rm81 ⇌54 🛏27 Lift 15 Mar–30 Nov
B14000–30400 M6700 St9% Sea

★★★ **Concordia** c larga San Marco 367
☎706866 tx41340 rm60 ⇌54 🛏6 Lift
B27000–37000 M9000

★★★ **Saturnia & International** via XXIII Marzo
San Marco 2399 ☎708377 tx41355 Saturnia
rm96 🛏96 Lift B27000–47000 M9500
Pn36000–56000

★★★ *Savoia e Jolanda* Riva degli Schiavoni
4187 ☎24130 rm91 ⇌52 🛏6 Lift

★★ *Antico Panada* c larga San Marco 656
☎25824 tx41340 rm47 ⇌25 B7600–22000
M5000–6000 Pn18000–24700

★★ *Calcina* (Pensione) Zattere 780 ☎27045
rm30 🛏8 B8800–19500 M6000 St9% Sea

★★ *Flora* (n rest) via XXII Marzo 2283a
☎700337 rm45 🛏13 Lift 15 Feb–15 Nov
B16000–30000

★★ *Giorgione* Santi Apostoli 4,587 ☎25810
rm58 ⇌46 🛏6 Lift B13000–33000
M7000–7500 Pn22000–29000

★★ **Metropole** riva degli Schiavoni 4149
☎705044 tx41340 rm64 ⇌52 🛏12 Lift
B37000–48800 M11000 Sea

★★ *San Marco* pza San Marco 877 ☎22447
rm60 ⇌7

🏨&🕎 **24 San Marco** piazzale Roma ☎32213
N🍴 Fia G1000

Venezia Lido Venezia 13,296 (☎041)
Map **30** C4

There is a car ferry service from Venice
(Piazzala Roma)

★★★★★ *Excelsior* Lungomare Marconi
☎60201 tx41023 rm272 ⇌272 G Lift

★★★★ *Bains* Lungomare Marconi 17 ☎65921
tx41142 Des Bains rm293 ⇌233 🛏60 Lift
May–Sep LD 🍴 Pool Beach Sea

★★★ *Adria Urania & Villa Nora* viale Dandolo
29 ☎760120 ta Biasutti rm100 (A15) ⇌88
🛏28 Lift Apr–Oct B20000–50000

Italy

★★Buon Pesce (n rest) San Nicolo 50
☎760533 rm29 (A5) ⇄15 G 1 Apr–15 Oct
B10500–23000 Sea
★★Centrale via M-Bragadin 30 ☎760052
rm38 ⇄24 Lift 1 Apr–30 Sep LD
B10500–30000 M7500 Pn18000–25000
St9%
★Villa Pannonia (n rest) via Doge Michiel 48
☎760162 rm28 ▥12 1 Apr–30 Oct

Ventimiglia Imperia 26,950 (☎0184)
Map **28** D2
★★Posta via Cavour 56 ☎31218 rm21 ⇄3
▥15 1 Dec–4 Nov B7000–11500 M5000
Pn15000
★★Terminus Svizzero pza Stazione 20
☎31138 rm28 ⇄5 ▥6 G
⏚**G Revelli** via Tenda 156, via Nervia ☎32459
N⬧ BMW/Sim

Verbania Novara 34,700 (☎0323) Map **28** D4
At **Suna** (1.5km N)
★★Pesced'Oro ☎502330 rm24 ⇄6 ▥2
Etr–Sep LD B5200–12400 M4200
Pn10000–11500 Lake

Vercelli Vercelli 56,500 (☎0161) Map **28** D3
★★★Viotti via Marsala 7 ☎61602 rm56 ⇄22
▥34 Lift B9500–21000 M5000–7000
Pn18000–20000
★Savoia viale Garibaldi 14 ☎65047 tx8500
rm38 ⇄3 ▥1

Verona Verona 270,850 (☎045) Map **29** B4
★★★★Colomba d'Oro via C-Cattaneo
10 ☎21510 rm60 ⇄57 ▥14 G Lift
B14400–36800
★★★★Due Torri pza Sant' Anastasia 4
☎34130 tx48524 rm100 ⇄70 ▥30 G Lift
B30100–48850 M10100
★★★Accademia via Scala 12 ☎21643 rm90
⇄90 G Lift
☆☆☆**AGIP** via Unita d'Italia 346 ☎521271
rm68 ▥68 Lift B7500–13900
★★★San Pietro via Santa Teresa 1 ☎582600
tx48523 rm58 ⇄58 G Lift B14100–23800
★★Italia via G-Mameli 54 ☎48028 rm40 ⇄3
G Lift
★Capuleti via del Pontiere 26 ☎32970 rm36
⇄20 Lift B7000–15000 M5000
Pn15000–16000
⏚⬧**l'Autocommercio** via F Torbido 6
☎521526 Chy/Sim
⏚⬧**Auto-Motor** Stradone Santa Lucia 21
☎500344 N⬧ Aud/Por/VW
⏚⬧**SVAE** via Torricelli ZAI ☎508088 N⬧ Frd

Viareggio Lucca 57,800 (☎0584) Map **29** B2

★★★★Palace via F-Gioia 2 ☎46134 rm76
⇄58 ▥18 Lift B17500–41000 M8000–9000
Pn28000–33000 Sea
★★★Continental Esplanade pza Puccini 18
☎50228 rm128 ⇄70 ▥10 G Lift May–Oct LD
★★Excelsior viale Carducci 88 ☎50726
rm106 ⇄63 Lift 1 May–30 Sep LD Beach Sea
★★Garden ☎44025 rm43 ⇄20 ▥20 Lift
B6500–22000 M5000–7000 Pn14000–19000
ℹ⬧**24 Autosalone Lupori** via Galvani 9
☎42266 M/c Cit/Peu G50
⏚⬧**Felice** viale M-Buonarroti 67 ☎42580 N⬧
Opl/Vau G80
⏚⬧**l Pecchia** viale del Tigli 8 ☎43312 Cit G10

Vicenza Vicenza 119,650 (☎0444) Map **29** B4
☆☆☆**AGIP** via degli Scaligerri ☎45155 rm66
▥66 Lift B9000–20500
★★★Jolly Campo Marzio viale Roma 21
☎24560 rm41 ⇄24 Lift B11500–26000
M6500 Pn23000–29000
★★Jolly Stazione (n rest) viale Milano 92
☎22209 rm74 ⇄38 Lift B8200–19400
⏚⬧**Americana** viale San Lazzaro 15 ☎31866
N⬧ M/c GM
Sabema viale della Pace 250 ☎500348
M/c BMW G5

Vico Equense Napoli 15,960 (☎081)
Map **33** B3
★★Oriente ☎8798143 rm33 ⇄30
1 Apr–30 Oct B5500–12000 M4000
Pn10000–11000 Sea
At **Marina Equa** (2.5km S)
★★★★Axidie ☎8798181 rm30 ⇄15 ▥15
Apr–Oct B10750–27300 M7000
Pn13000–24000 St9% ⬧ Pool Beach Sea

Vieste Foggia 12,044 (☎0884) Map **34** C4
★★★Degli Ulivi ☎79061 rm202 ▥202 Lift

Vietri sul Mare See **Salerno**

Villasimius See **Sardegna (Sardinia)**

Vipiteno-Sterzing Bolzano 4,900 (☎0472)
Map **12** D1
★★Aquila Nera pza Città 1 ☎65120 rm35 (A)
⇄3 ▥6 G Pool
★★Corona-Krone Città Vecchia 139 ☎65210
rm43 (A) ⇄19 G

Viterbo Viterbo 56,600 (☎0761) Map **31** B3
★★Leon d'Oro via della Cava 36 ☎31012
rm48 ⇄8 ▥22 G Lift 10 Jan–20 Dec
B5300–11900 M4000–4500
Pn12800–15400
⏚⬧**Tedeschi** pza del Caduti 12 ☎38767
N⬧ Frd G20

San Marino/hotels

Prices are in Italian lire

★★★Grand via Lungomonte 28 Luglio
☎992400 rm54 ⇄54 G Lift Mar–Nov
B13500–21000 M4500–10000
Pn19500–22000
★★★Titano via Marzo 25 ☎991007 rm66
⇄24 ▥20 G Lift

★★Excelsior via J-Istriani ☎991163 rm25
⇄3 ▥15 G
★Tre Penne via G-di Simone delle Penne
☎992437 rm12 (A7) ⇄4 ▥5 1 Mar–30 Nov
LD B6200–14400 M3560–7000
Pn12500–14500 St15%

LUXEMBOURG

Population 357,300 **Area** 1,000 sq miles **Map** 10 D4, 11 A4

How to get there   Luxembourg is easily approached through either Belgium or France. Luxembourg City is just over 200 miles from Ostende, about 250 miles from Boulogne or Calais, and is therefore within a day's drive of the Channel coast.

Travel information

Accidents   **Fire, police, ambulance** ☎012 – Civil Defence emergency service *(Secours d'urgence)*.

There are no firm rules to adopt following an accident. However, in most cases the recommendations on page 21 are advisable.

Accommodation   A national guide to hotels, inns, restaurants, and boarding houses in the Grand Duchy can be obtained free of charge from the National Tourist Office.

Details of holiday flats and chalets are also available from this source.

Breakdowns   Try to move the vehicle to the verge of the road and place a warning triangle to warn following traffic. The Automobile Club du Grand-Duché de Luxembourg (ACL) operates a 24-hour road assistance service which can be utilised by AA members: ☎311031 at any time. This service operates throughout the whole country. The service permits up to half-an-hour's on-the-spot breakdown assistance free to AA members upon production of the Continental *5-Star Travel Booklet*.

The vehicles of the ACL are yellow in colour and bear a black inscription *'Automobile Club, Service Routier'*. This service should not be confused with the *Secours Automobile Luxembourg* which is a commercial enterprise whose representatives will charge for all services rendered and will not accept Credit Vouchers. This enterprise is not connected with the AA or any other motoring organisation.

British Consulate   Luxembourg, 28 boulevard Royal ☎29864/5/6

Currency and banking   The unit of currency is the Luxembourg franc, divided into 100 centimes. There are no restrictions on the amount of

Luxembourg

foreign or local currency which can be taken into or out of the country, but because of the limited market for Luxembourg notes in other countries, it is advisable to change them before leaving. Belgian currency is also used in Luxembourg.

Banking hours

From Monday to Friday 09.00–12.00hrs and 13.30–16.30hrs. Banks are usually closed on Saturdays.

Dimensions and weight restrictions

Private cars and trailers are restricted to the following dimensions:

cars   height 4 metres;
                     width 2.50 metres;
car and trailer overall length 18 metres;
caravan   weight 75% of towing vehicle.

Drinking and driving

A person suspected of driving while under the influence of alcohol may have to undergo a breath test. A driver, if convicted, faces severe penalties including heavy fines and/or imprisonment.

Holidays and events

Holidays based on religious festivals are not always fixed on the calendar but any current diary will give actual dates. The Whit period (a religious holiday) should not be confused with the British Spring Holiday.

Fixed holidays

1 January	New Year's Day
1 May	May Day
23 June	National Day
15 August	Assumption
1 November	All Saints' Day
25 December	Christmas Day
26 December	St Stephen's Day

In addition, banks, shops, and public administration close on certain other days which are not public holidays.

25 February	Carnival Monday
2 November	All Souls' Day

Moveable holidays

Easter Monday
Ascension Day
Whit Monday
Shrove Monday
Local Luxembourg City Holiday

Annual events

March
: **Luxembourg** 'Europleinair' Camping Fair

April
: **Grevenmacher** Easter Exhibition
Luxembourg 'Emaischen' traditional festival
Grevenmacher Wine Fair

May
: **Luxembourg and Diekirch** Procession of the Octave of Our Lady of Luxembourg
Luxembourg International Fair
Wiltz Broom Festival with folklore procession
Echternach Dancing procession
Wormeldange Wine Fair

June
: **Luxembourg** National Day (23 June)
Luxembourg 'Tour de Luxembourg' International Cycle Race

July
: **Nationwide** concerts, folklore events, gymnastic shows and exhibitions (July–August)
Wiltz Open Theatre Festival
Nospelt 'Fortnight of Pottery and Ceramics' (July–August)

Luxembourg

August	**Rosport** Procession of the Holy Virgin **Luxembourg** The 'Schobermesse' Fair and Market (August/September)
September	**Schwebsingen** Wine Festival **Grevenmacher** Wine and Grape Festival with folklore procession

A more comprehensive list can be obtained from the
Luxembourg National Tourist Office (see page 224).

Horn, use of

In built-up areas it is prohibited to use the horn except to avoid an accident.

Outside built-up areas use the horn instead of the lights, during the day, to warn of approach.

Insurance

This is compulsory; see page 11.

Lights

It is prohibited to drive on sidelights only. At night and also during the day when necessary, vehicles parked on a public road must have their sidelights on if the public lighting does not enable them to be seen from a sufficient distance. Vehicles equipped with a side parking light may use this instead of sidelights. Should fog or snow reduce visibility to less than 100 metres, vehicles stopped or parked outside a built-up area must be illuminated by dipped headlights or foglights. Two foglights may be used at the same time as sidelights but headlights together with fog- or spot lights may not be used at the same time. Outside built-up areas at night it is compulsory to flash one's headlights before overtaking another vehicle, at places where visibility is restricted, and whenever road safety requires it.

Medical treatment

Medical benefits in Luxembourg are administered by the National Sickness Insurance Office, 10 rue de Strasbourg, Luxembourg, which has agencies throughout the Grand Duchy. To obtain medical treatment form E111 (see page 13) should be presented to the local Sickness Insurance Office, which will provide the necessary document to be taken to any doctor or dentist. The medical practitioner will charge a fee (a receipt should be obtained) which is generally refunded by the local Sickness Insurance Office. Similarly you will have to pay initially for any medicines that are prescribed; a proportion of the cost may be refunded. Hospital treatment normally will be free after a certificate provided by the doctor is presented with form E111 to the local Sickness Insurance Office. In emergencies admission to hospital can be made without prior authorisation.

Motoring club

The **Automobile Club du Grand–Duché de Luxembourg** (ACL) has its head office at 13 Route de Longwy, Helfenterbruck/Bertrange, Luxembourg ☎311031. AA members should produce their *5-Star Travel Booklet* when seeking assistance.

ACL office hours are 08.30–12.00hrs and 13.30–18.00hrs from Monday to Friday; closed Saturday and Sunday.

Overtaking

Outside built-up areas at night it is compulsory to flash one's headlights before overtaking another vehicle. During the day use the horn instead of lights.

Parking

Spending the night in a vehicle or trailer on the roadside is prohibited. Parking is forbidden on or near tramlines, opposite another stationary vehicle, and within 12 metres (39½ft) of a bus or tram stop. In the city of Luxembourg (in the centre and the railway station area), Esch-sur-Alzette, Dudelange, and Wiltz, there are short-term parking areas known as blue zones. In these areas parked vehicles must display a disc on the windscreen; discs are set at the time of parking and show when parking time expires according to the limit in the area concerned. Discs are available free of charge from the ACL, the Luxembourg Communal Administration, principal banks, petrol companies, and other firms. Discs of other countries may be used if they conform; Parisian ones do, those used in the United Kingdom do not. In special parking zones a vehicle must be moved at least 150 metres before re-parking. Park on the right-hand side of the road in the direction of the traffic flow unless parking is prohibited on this side.

A disabled driver may obtain special concessions for parking if he applies to the Administration Communale or police station.

Luxembourg

Petrol
The approximate price of petrol per litre is: super (98 octane) Fr12.34, normal (90 octane) Fr11.94.

Police fines
The police are authorised to impose and collect on-the-spot fines from any motorist infringing traffic regulations. The officer collecting the fine should issue an official receipt. Refusal to pay results in court proceedings and non-residents may be arrested or detained.

Postal and telephone charges
Rates for post to the United Kingdom are:

Air mail and surface mail		Fr
Postcards		5
Letters	up to 20gm	8
	20–50gm	14
	50–100gm	18
	100–250gm	40

Telephone rates
The charge for a 3-minute telephone call to the UK is Fr56.25; for each additional minute Fr18.75. A local call costs Fr3.

The address of the *poste restante* office in Luxembourg is 38 place de la Gare.

Roads
There is a comprehensive system of good main and secondary roads.

Motorways
Only short sections are at present open, 7km between Luxembourg and the airport, 14km between Luxembourg and Esch-sur-Alzette, and 4km of the Luxembourg by-pass, but a future network of 160km is planned.

Seat belts
If your vehicle is fitted with seat belts it is compulsory to wear them.

Shopping hours
While some shops are closed Monday mornings, the usual hours of opening are: from Monday to Saturday 08.30–12.00hrs, 14.00–18.30hrs.

Speed
The placename indicates the beginning and end of a built-up area. The following speed limits for cars are in force if there are no special signs:

built-up areas 60kph (37mph)
main roads without any signs 90kph (56mph)
main roads indicated by signs 120kph (74mph)
motorways 120kph (74mph)

All lower signposted speed limits must be adhered to.

Tourist information offices
Office National du Tourisme (National Tourist Office), local authorities, and tourist information societies *(Syndicats d'Initiatives)* organise information offices at the following addresses:

	Telephone
Luxembourg Air Terminal, place de la Gare	481199
Luxembourg, place d'Armes (Cercle)	22809
Echternach, Porte St Willibrod	72230
Diekirch, place Guillaume	83023
Ettelbruck, Town Hall	82068
Clervaux, 93 Grand rue	92072
Larochette	87676
Viaden, Victor Hugo House	84257
Wiltz, Castle	96199
Mondort-les-Bains, Casino	67018 or 67575
Grevenmacher, Town Hall	75311
Esch-sur-Alzette, Town Hall	52101
Beaufort	86081

Tyres
Spiked tyres The use of spiked tyres is prohibited.

Visitors' registration
Visitors staying up to three months are required to enter their names in the hotel or campsite register. Visitors staying with private persons are required to notify the Administration Communale within 48 hours of their arrival.

Warning triangles
These are compulsory for all vehicles (except motorcycles). They must be placed about 30 metres (33yd) behind the vehicle, fallen object or load on the road.

Luxembourg/hotels and garages

Prices are in Belgian francs

Abbreviations:
av   avenue
pl   place
r   rue
rte   route

Beaufort 900 Map **11** A4
★★*Meyer* ☎86262 rm50 ⇌25 ▥4 G Lift

Berdorf 950 Map **11** A4
★★*Ermitage* ☎79184 rm16 (A9) ⇌8 G
Etr–1 Oct

Clervaux 1,550 Map **11** A4
★★*Abbaye* r Principale ☎91049 rm50 (A5)
⇌12 ▥8 G Lift 1 Apr–15 Oct & 20–30 Dec LD
B435–1200 M190–400 Pn590–960
★★*Claravallis* av de la Gare 33 ☎91034
rm21 ⇌7 ▥2 G B485–1150 M200–560
Pn700–900
★★*Grand Central* pl du Château ☎91105
rm32 ⇌24 ▥3 Lift 1 Jan–15 Nov B590–1180
M360–500 Pn800–950
★★*Koner* Grand r 14 ☎91002 rm24 ⇌6 ▥4
G 1 Mar–31 Dec LD B540–1380 M450–900
Pn900–1250
★★*Parc* ☎91068 rm12 ⇌3 ▥2 G

Diekirch 5,600 Map **11** A4
★*Beau-Séjour* Esplanade 12 ☎83403 rm38
⇌4 ▥4 15 Nov–15 Oct B445–780
M250–600 Pn575–725
★*Hiertz* r Clairefontaine 1 ☎83562 rm7 ⇌4

Dommeldange Map **11** A4
☆☆☆ *Novotel-Luxembourg* rte d'Echternach
☎435643 tx1418 rm121 Lift B120–140
≈ ○ Pool

Echternach 4,200 Map **11** A4
★★★*Bel-Air* rte de Berdorf ☎729383 tx2640
rm44 ⇌44 G Lift 15 Dec–15 Nov B950–2000
M500–1000 Pn1400–1650
★★*Commerce* du Marché 16 ☎72301
rm50 (A10) ⇌8 ▥1 G Lift B450–1100
Pn740–995
★★*Parc* r Hôpital 9 ☎729481 rm35
⇌25 ▥5 G Lift Mar–Nov 15 B500–1300
M325 Pool
★*Marmann* r de Luxembourg 7 ☎72188
rm25 ⇌2 G
★*Universal et Cheval Blanc* ☎72142 rm33
⇌20 1 Mar–31 Oct B580–1060 M350
Pn680–850

Ehnen 410 Map **11** A4
★★*Simmer* ☎76030 rm23 ⇌19 ▥4 G 1 Mar–15 Jan
★*Moselle* r du Vin 131 ☎76022
rm22 ⇌6 ▥7 G Lift 17 Jan–31 Nov B450–1200
Màlc Pn700–1100

Esch-sur-Alzette 27,800 Map **11** A4
⊛○ *Grand du Centre* r de la Libération 42
☎53937 N⊛ Opl G
⊛○ *J Rech* r de Luxembourg 32 ☎52929 N⊛ Ren

Esch-sur-Sûre 300 Map **10** D4
★*Moulin* ☎89107 rm33 ▥31 1 Mar–31 Dec
B500–650 Pn650–700

Ettelbruck 6,050 Map **11** A4
★★*Central* r de Bastogne 25 ☎819351 rm28
⇌4 ▥8 G Lift 15 Jan–15 Dec LD
B530–1060 M260–800 Pn800–1000
⊛○ *P Wengler* av des Alliés 36 ☎82157 N⊛
Frd G30

Findel Airport See Luxembourg

Grevenmacher 3,050 Map **11** A4
★*Poste* (n rest) r de Trèves 28 ☎75136 rm12
⇌1 G Etr–Sep B380–840

Grundhof Map **11** A4
★★*Brimer* ☎86251 rm23 ⇌18 ▥5 G Lift
2 Feb–15 Nov B700–1500 M350 Pn1200
★*Ferring* rte Mullertal 33 ☎86015 rm25
▥16 G Lift 20 Mar–20 Nov LD
B600–1000 M300–500 Pn930–980

Haller 170 Map **11** A4
★★*Hallerbach* ☎86151 rm25 (A) ⇌14 ▥1 G

Heinerscheid 1,000 Map **11** A4
★*Wagener* ☎98503 rm14 G

Hespérange See **Luxembourg**

Kautenbach 250 Map **11** A4
★*Hatz* ☎96561 rm11 1 Nov–30 Sept

Larochette 1,450 Map **11** A4
★★*Château* r Medernach 1 ☎87598 rm45
▥3 G Lift 5 Feb–10 Jan LD B480–1440
M350–400 Pn790–1180
★★*Poste* ☎87006 rm40 ⇌15 ▥2 1 Feb–31 Dec
LD B550–1325 M450–800 Pn975–1200

Luxembourg 78,825 Map **11** A4
★★★★*Kons* pl de la Gare ☎486021
tx2306 rm137 ⇌57 ▥39 Lift B650–1500
★★★*Central Molitor* av de la Liberté 28
☎489911 tx2613 rm36 ⇌36 Lift B900–1300
M280–395
★★★*Dauphin* (n rest) av de la Gare 42
☎488282 rm37 ⇌20 ▥17 Lift
★★★*Rix* bd Royal 20 ☎27545 rm20 ⇌9 ▥6
Lift B700–1550
★★*Continental* Grande r 86 ☎23616 rm43
(A37) ⇌14 ▥4 G Lift B620–1340
M125–450 Pn940–1090
★★*Empire* pl de la Gare 34 ☎485252 rm45
⇌5 ▥15 Lift
★★*Graas* (n rest) av de la Liberté 76 ☎484445
rm32 ⇌2 Lift B350–830
★*Francais* (n rest) pl d'Armes 14
☎23009 rm21 (A4) ⇌2 Lift B750–980
★*Wellington* (n rest) r M-Rodange 1
☎488235 rm16
▥ *Hubert-Frères* rte d'Esch 106 ☎24998
N⊛ Lnc
▥⊛○ *Grand de Luxembourg* rte d'Arlon 293
☎471061 N⊛ Chy/Sim
Grand de la Pétrusse r des Jardiniers 13
☎22664 N⊛ BL/Jag/Rov/Tri
▥⊛○ *P Lentz* rte d'Arlon 257 ☎20925 N⊛ Vau
⊛○ *Mackel & Pirsch* rte de Thionville 208
☎482008 N▥470953 Maz G4
At **Findel Airport** (6km E on N2 & E42)
★*Airfield* rte Trèves 6 ☎431934 rm7 ⇌7 G
At **Hespérange** (5km SE)
▥⊛○ *J P Engel* rte de Thionville 326 ☎36179
N⊛ Chy/Sim G10
At **Strassen** (2km W on N9)
★★*Dany* rte d'Arlon 72 ☎318062 rm17 ⇌6
▥11 G B610–1200 M200 Pn850–1250

Martelange 135 Map **10** D4
★*Maison Rouge* rte d'Arlon ☎64006 rm12
G 1 Nov–31 Sep LD B400–645 Màlc Pn850

Mersch 4,400 Map **11** A4
★*7 Châteaux* r d'Arlon 3 ☎32093 rm16 G
★*Marisca* pl Etoile 1 ☎328456 rm19 ⇌2 ▥7 G
1 Nov–30 Sep LD B540–1130 M220–500
Pn950–1050

Mondorf-les-Bains 2,450 Map **11** A4
★★★*Grand Chef* av des Bains 36 ☎68012
rm46 ⇌27 ▥9 G Lift Etr–15 Oct
★★★*Terminus Golf* av des Bains 21 ☎68017
rm40 ⇌20 ▥1 G Lift Etr–Oct B530–1340
Pn950–1100

Strassen See **Luxembourg**

Vianden 1,500 Map **11** A4
★★*Heintz* Grande r 55 ☎84155 rm30 ⇌25
G Lift 1 Mar–5 Nov Pool
★*Orianienburg* Grande r 126 ☎84153 rm55
(A5) ⇌20 ▥5 G Lift 1 Feb–31 Dec LD
B390–930 M350–800 Pn800–950

Wiltz 4,050 Map **10** D4
★★*Vieux Château* Grande r 1 ☎96018 rm13 (A2)
⇌3 ▥5 LD B685–1470 M375–650
Pn850–1150

NETHERLANDS

Population 13,077,000 **Area** 14,400 sq miles **Maps** 3 & 4

How to get there There are direct ferry services to the Netherlands. Services operate from Harwich to the Hook of Holland, Hull to Rotterdam (Europoort), Felixstowe to Rotterdam (Europoort), Great Yarmouth to Scheveningen (The Hague) and Sheerness to Flushing (Vlissingen); the sea journey can take between 7 and 14hrs depending upon the port of departure. Alternatively one of the short Channel crossings can be used, and then the Netherlands can be easily reached by driving through France and Belgium. The distance from Calais to The Hague is just over 220 miles and is within a day's drive.

Travel information

AA agents All representatives are under appointment by Koninklijke Nederlandsche Toeristenbond, ANWB.

Hague (The) ANWB, Wassenaarseweg 220 ☎(070) 264426.

Accidents **Fire, police, ambulance** Amsterdam and The Hague ☎222222, Rotterdam ☎94. Numbers for other towns are in the front of the local telephone directories. If necessary, contact the State Police Emergency Centre ☎(03438) 4321.

In the event of a serious or complicated accident, especially when personal injury has been sustained, the police should be called before the vehicles are moved.

Accommodation The official hotel guide includes details of the most important hotels in the Netherlands. Information on other types of accommodation such as guesthouses, furnished rooms, and bungalows can be obtained from tourist information offices (VVV) (see Tourist information offices page 230).

Hotels are officially classified and the category is exhibited outside each. Room prices must by law be indicated in hotel reception and in each bedroom but they are not subject to official control. The service charge amounts to 15%, and it is usual for this to be included in the charges as well as the value added tax.

The National Reservation Centre will secure accommodation free of charge. Application may be made direct, by post, telephone or telex to NRC Amsterdam, PO Box 3387, Hoofdpostkantor, NZ Voorburgwal 182, Amsterdam 1001 ☎020 211 211, tx 15754.

Netherlands

Applications for reservations may also be made to one of the VVV offices, which will book a room for a small charge.

Breakdowns If your car breaks down, try to move it to the verge of the road so that it obstructs the traffic flow as little as possible, and place a warning triangle behind the vehicle to warn following traffic of the obstruction (see page 230).

Patrol services The Royal Dutch Touring Club ANWB, maintains a nationwide road patrol service called *Wegenwacht* (the watch on the road), similar to AA Road Patrol Service. The service operates on main roads between 07.00 and 23.00hrs, and on less important roads if circumstances permit.

For assistance, stop a passing patrol car during the above hours, or telephone the ANWB Head Office which has an Emergency Centre ☎ (070) 264426 operating a 24-hour service.

AA members should produce their *5-Star Travel Booklet* if they call upon this service.

British Consulates Amsterdam OZ, Johannes Vermeerstraat 7 ☎ 736128
Rotterdam 2, Parklaan 18 ☎ 361555

Crash helmets It is obligatory for drivers and passengers of motorcycles to wear crash helmets.

Currency and banking The unit of currency is the gulden (Fl), which is also known as the guilder and is divided into 100 cents. There are no restrictions limiting the import of currency. All imported currency may be freely exported, as well as any currency exchanged in, or drawn on an account established in, the Netherlands.

Banking hours In all cities and towns, banks are open from Monday to Friday 09.00–15.00hrs, but closed on Saturday. At all ANWB offices, money can be exchanged from Monday to Friday 08.45–16.45hrs, and on Saturdays 08.45–12.00hrs; there are also exchange offices at the principal railway stations (*eg* Amsterdam, Arnhem, Eindhoven, The Hague, Hook of Holland, Maastricht, Rosendaal, Rotterdam, Utrecht, and Venlo).

Dimensions Private cars are restricted to the following dimensions:

cars	height including load 4 metres width 2.20 metres on 'B' roads, 2.50 metres on 'A' roads;
cars and trailers	overall length 18 metres

Drinking and driving Drivers suspected of having consumed alcohol may be required to undergo a blood test. Penalties for persons found guilty of driving under the influence of alcohol include a term of imprisonment and a driving ban of up to five years.

Ferries (internal) All particulars are subject to alterations. In many cases sailings are augmented to meet traffic demands.

Vlissingen (Flushing)–Breskens *Map 3 B2*
There is a frequent daily service. Last sailings:
From Vlissingen – 23.10hrs *Duration* 20 minutes
From Breskens – 23.25hrs

Charges (single journey)	15 May–15 Sep	16 Sep–14 May
Vehicles	Fl	Fl
Car (including driver)	5.75	4.00
Passengers	1.00	1.00
Children (4–10 years)	0.50	0.50
Children (under 4)	free	free

Kruiningen–Perkpolder *Map 3 B2*
There is a frequent daily service. Last sailings:
Duration 15–20 minutes

From Kruiningen –	23.05hrs Monday–Friday
	22.25hrs Saturday–Sunday
From Perkpolder –	23.25hrs Monday–Friday
	22.45hrs Saturday–Sunday

Charges as for Vlissingen (Flushing)–Breskens above

Netherlands

Den Helder–Texel *Map 4 C3*
There is a regular daily service in both directions until 21.05hrs.
Duration 15 minutes

Charges (return journey)	
Vehicles	Fl
Car	16.50
Motorcycles	2.50
Passengers	3.50
Children (4–9 years)	1.75
Children (under 4)	free

Further internal services operate as follows:

Zijpe–Anna Jacoba *Map 3 B2*
Frequent sailings in each direction until 23.00hrs
Duration 7 minutes

Maassluis–Rozenburg *Map 4 C2*
Regular service until 00.30hrs
Duration 15 minutes

Firearms   The Dutch laws concerning the possession of firearms are the most stringent in Europe. Any person crossing the frontier with any type of firearm will be arrested. The law applies also to any object which, on superficial inspection, shows any resemblance to real firearms (*eg* plastic imitations, etc). If you wish to carry firearms, real or imitation, of any description into the Netherlands, seek the advice of the Netherlands Consulate.

Holidays and events   Holidays based on religious festivals are not always fixed on the calendar but any current diary will give actual dates. The Whit period (a religious holiday) should not be confused with the British Spring Holiday.

Fixed holidays	1 January	New Year's Day
	25, 26 December	Christmas

Moveable holidays	Good Friday
	Easter Monday
	Ascension Day
	Whit Monday

Annual events	**May**	**Scheveningen** Opening of the Herring Season
		Alkmaar Cheese Market, Fridays (May/Sep)
		Gouda Cheese Market, Thursdays (May/Sep)
	June	**Amsterdam, The Hague, Rotterdam** Holland Festival
		Assen International TT Motorcycle Races
	July	**Kinderkijk** Windmill Open Days (July/Aug)
	August	**Laren** International Jazz Festival
		Zandvoort Dutch Grand Prix (Formula 1)

A comprehensive list of events can be obtained from the National Tourist Office (see page 230).

Insurance   This is compulsory. See page 11.

Lights   Dipped headlights must be used at all times in built-up areas and outside built-up areas when meeting oncoming traffic. In fog or falling snow, foglights may be used in pairs in conjunction with sidelights only. Headlights should be flashed as a warning of approach at night provided that they do not inconvenience other traffic.

Medical treatment   As a member of the EEC, the Netherlands provides medical benefits to persons of affiliated countries. Most doctors and dentists are affiliated to the Sickness Fund (ANOZ) and will provide free treatment on production of form E111 (see page 13). Drugs are also free if they are supplied by a doctor or by an approved chemist to which you have taken the doctor's prescription. Urgent hospital treatment is usually provided free on production of E111; ask the

Netherlands

authorities to obtain the necessary authority from the ANOZ in Utrecht within two days. The medical benefits are administered by the Netherlands General Sickness Insurance Fund, *Algemeen Nederlands Onderling Ziekenhuis* (ANOZ), Kaap Hoorndreef 24–28, Utrecht ☎030-317541.

Motoring club

The **Koninklijke Nederlandsche Toeristenbond (ANWB)** has its headquarters at Wassenaarseweg 220, The Hague, and offices in numerous provincial towns. They will assist motoring tourists generally and supply road and touring information. AA members should produce their *5-Star Travel Booklet* when requesting service. Offices are usually open between 08.45 and 16.45hrs Monday to Friday, and 08.45 and 12.00hrs on Saturdays. Traffic information may be obtained by telephoning (070) 264455 and the ANWB Emergency Centre in Amsterdam is open 24hrs a day, seven days a week ☎(070) 264426.

Parking

Vehicles must not stop where there are signs reading *Stopverbod* (no waiting). You can stop elsewhere provided that you keep to the extreme right of the road and do not interfere with other traffic. You are allowed to stop to let passengers in and out at bus stops. Parking meters and/or parking discs are used in many towns. Discs can be obtained from police stations and must be displayed on the windscreen.

They must be set at the time of parking and show when parking time lapses according to the limit in the area concerned. Failure to observe zonal regulations could result in a fine or the vehicle being towed away. Regulations about parking lights at night are given under Lights, page 228.

Spending the night in a vehicle or trailer on the roadside is not permitted.

Passengers

Children under six years must not be carried on the front seats. Children 6–12 years may occupy the front seats provided they wear a safety belt.

Petrol

The approximate price of petrol per litre is: super (97.99 octane) Fl 1.086; normal (96 octane) Fl 1.07.

Police fines

In some districts the police are empowered to impose and collect on-the-spot fines from motorists infringing local traffic regulations.

Postal and telephone charges

Air mail rates to the UK are:

Postcards		Fl 0.45
Letters up to	20gm	Fl 0.75
	20 to 50gm	Fl 1.30
	50 to 100gm	Fl 2.75

The address of the *poste restante* office in Amsterdam is Hoofdpostkantoor, NZ Voorburgwal.

Telephone rates

STD calls can be made to all the major cities in the UK; the cost is Fl0.85 for each minute. Calls can be made from all main post offices. There is an English-speaking instruction service available by dialling 008. All internal calls can be made automatically, and many calls to Belgium, Luxembourg, and West Germany can be made automatically from most parts of the country. Local calls cost 25 cents.

Priority

Regulations in the Netherlands take account of the very large numbers of cyclists for whom special tracks are provided on a number of roads. Motor vehicles generally have priority over this slower moving traffic except when controlled by the appropriate road signs. However, cyclists proceeding straight ahead at intersections have priority over all turning traffic. Visitors should be particularly alert.

Roads

There is a network of motorways carrying most inter-city and long-distance traffic. Other main roads usually have only two lanes but are well surfaced. Signposting is good; in some places there are special by-way tours signposted by the ANWB. The best way to see the countryside is to tour along minor roads, often alongside canals, with the aid of large-scale maps.

Netherlands

Motorways
There are about 950 miles of motorway open and more are being built; a very comprehensive network of 1,864 miles is planned. No tolls are charged (but see Toll Bridges). Nearly all the motorways are part of the European international network.

Toll bridges

		car	car/ caravan
Zeeland (Oosterschelde) bridge		Fl 3.50	Fl 5.00
Grevelingen dam (no toll)			
Haringvliet bridge (no toll)			

These three major constructions form the first part of the Delta plan designed to harness the waters of the Rhine Delta. Other dams are being built nearer the coast but the whole scheme will not be completed until 1978. *Waalbrug* (near Tiel) car Fl1.75–2.50.

Toll tunnel
Benelux Tunnel (Vlaardingen near Rotterdam) car Fl 1.00 car/caravan Fl 2.50

All toll charges should be used only as a guide.

Road signs
Translations of some written signs to be seen on the road are given below:

Bushalte	Bus stop
Doorgaand rijverkeer gestremd	No through way
Doorgaand verkeer	Through traffic
Een file	Single lane
Fietspad	Cycle path – motor vehicles prohibited
Langzaam rijden	Slow down
Opspattend grind	Loose grit
Pas op; filevorming	Attention; single-lane traffic ahead
Rijwielpad	Cycle path – motor vehicles prohibited
Tegenliggers	Two-way traffic
Voetpad	Footpath – vehicles prohibited
Wegomlegging	Detour
Werk in uitovering	Roadworks

Seat belts
If your car is fitted with seat belts it is compulsory to wear them.

Shopping hours
Stores Monday 13.00–17.30hrs, Tuesday–Saturday 09.00–17.30hrs; *Food shops* 08.00–18.00hrs.
Most *food shops* close for one half day per week. This varies according to location.

Speed
The placename indicates the beginning and end of a built-up area. The following speed limits for cars are in force if there are no special signs. Built-up areas 50kph (31mph). Outside built-up areas it is 100kph (62mph) on motorways and 80kph (49mph) on other roads. Car/trailer combinations are limited to 80kph (49mph).

Tourist information offices

The Netherlands National Tourist Office (NBT), Savory & Moore House, 143 New Bond Street, London W1Y 0QS ☎01-499 9367 will be pleased to assist you with any information regarding tourism and it has branch offices (VVV) in all towns and large villages in the Netherlands. They can be recognised by the sign illustrated on the left (blue with white lettering).

There are three types of these branch offices: Travel Offices giving detailed information about the whole of the Netherlands; Information Offices giving general information about the Netherlands and detailed information about their own region, and Local Information Offices giving detailed information about that locality.

Tyres
Although residents are not permitted to use spiked tyres, visitors may do so provided that they do not exceed 80kph (49mph).

Visitors' registration
Visitors staying less than eight days need not register.

Warning triangles
These are compulsory for all vehicles except motorcycles; they must be used at night if a stopped vehicle's lighting system fails, and by day if a vehicle is not readily visible.

230

Netherlands/hotels and garages

Prices are in florins (guilden)

Abbreviations:
bd   boulevard

Aalsmeer Noord-Holland 20,800 (☎02977)
Map **4** C3
★**Drie Kolommen** Stationsweg 19 ☎24528
rm17 ⇄4
🛏🅿**Boom** Oosteinderweg 220 ☎25667 N🚗
BL/Rov/Tri G250

Alkmaar Noord-Holland 65,200 (☎072)
Map **4** C3
☆☆☆**Alkmaar** Arcadialaan 2 ☎120744
ta Pehatel rm93 (A) 🛆93 B39.50–69.50 M12.50
🛏🅿**Klaver** Helderseweg 29 ☎27033 N🚗
BL/Jag/Rov/Tri G100
🛏🅿**W Schmidt** Nassauplein 1 ☎13545 N🚗
Frd

Almelo Overijssel 62,650 (☎05490)
Map **4** D3
☆☆☆**Postiljon** Aalderinkssingel 2 ☎15261
tx44817 rm50 ⇄2 🛆48 B49–83 M12.50
★★**Bagatelle** Grotestr 3 ☎14644 rm24 ⇄1
🛆22
🛏🅿**Almelo** Wierdensestr 107 ☎12472 N🚗 Frd
🛏🅿**Konink** H-R-Holst Laan 1 ☎11064 N🚗
Aud/Por/VW

Amersfoort Utrecht 87,800 (☎033)
Map **4** C3
★★**Berg** Utrechtseweg 225 ☎16110 rm22
🛆13 G B38–75 M40
★★**Witte** Utrechtseweg 2 ☎14142 rm17 ⇄10
🛆5 B53.50–112 M40
🛏🅿**Lips** Kapelweg 12 ☎14841 N🚗 Ren
🛏🅿**J J Molenaar's** Barchman Wuytierslaan 2
☎30304 N🚗 BL/Jag/Rov/Tri G65

Amsterdam Noord-Holland 751,200
(☎020) Map **4** C3 **See Plan**
★★★★★**Amstel** Prof-Tulpplein 1 ☎226060
Plan **1** tx12545 rm118 ⇄118 G Lift B115–255
M42.50
★★★★★**Hilton** Apollolaan 138 ☎780780
Plan **2** tx11025 rm276 ⇄276 Lift
B120.50–206.50
★★★★**Adda Park** Stadhouderskade 25
☎717474 Plan **3** tx11412 rm180 ⇄180 🛆4
G Lift B96–142.50 M20 Pn136
★★★★**American** Leidsekade 97 ☎245322
Plan **4** tx11379 rm185 ⇄183 🛆12 Lift
★★★★**Apollo** Apollolaan 2 ☎735922
ta Apollogies Plan **5** tx14084 rm225 ⇄225 Lift
B155–211 Màlc
★★★★**Caransa** Rembrandtsplein 19 ☎229455
Plan **6** tx13342 rm66 ⇄66 Lift B106–149
Pn160
★★★★**Carlton** (n rest) Vijzelstr 2 ☎222266
Plan **7** tx11670 rm144 ⇄144 G Lift B115–165
★★★★**Doelen** Nieuwe Doelenstr 24 ☎221727
Plan **8** tx14399 rm92 ⇄92 Lift B106–149 M23
Pn116.50
☆☆☆☆**EuroCrest** De Boelelaan 2 ☎429855
Plan **9** tx13647 rm260 ⇄260 Lift B105–135
Màlc
★★★★**Krasnapolsky** Dam 9 ☎263163
Plan **10** tx12262 rm300 ⇄244 G Lift
B65–165 M25 Pn104–204
★★★★**Pulitzer** Prinsengracht 315 ☎228333
Plan **11** tx16508 rm175 ⇄175 Lift
B125–189 M10–22 Pn175
★★★**Amster Centre** Herengracht 255
☎221724 Plan **12** tx15424 rm110 ⇄110 Lift
★★★**Centraal** Stadhouderskade 7 ☎185765
Plan **13** ta Hocentra tx12601 rm119 ⇄104
Lift B52–137 Màlc
☆☆☆**Euro E9** J-Muyskensweg 10 ☎946000
Plan **15** tx13382 rm140 🛆128 B54–85

★★★**Port van Cleve** Nieuw Zyds Voorburgwal
178 ☎244860 Plan **14** tx13129 rm110 ⇄110
G Lift B85–150 M15–30 Pn95–125
★★★**Schiller** Rembrandtsplein 26 ☎231660
Plan **17** tx14058 rm92 ⇄87 Lift B74–128 M15
Pn91–102
★★**Ams Hotel Terdam** Tesselschadestr 23
☎126876 Plan **19** rm60 (A40) ⇄35 🛆5 Lift
B52–120 M16–20 Pn64–90
★★**Delphi** (n rest) Apollolaan 101 ☎795152
Plan **26** tx16659 rm47 ⇄16 🛆22 Lift B45–110
☆☆**Euro Amsterdam** Sloterweg 535 (7km on
rd to The Hague) ☎158455 Plan **18**
ta Moteldam tx15524 rm80 ⇄80 G B49–70
★★**Piet Hein** (n rest) Vossiusstr 53 ☎727205
Plan **20** rm31 (A10) 🛆22 Mar–Dec B55–110
★★**Roode Leeuw** Damrak 93 ☎240396
Plan **21** rm80 ⇄48 🛆3 Lift B48–96 M17.50
Pn74.50–84.50
★**De Amstel** (n rest) Weesperzijde 28
☎946407 Plan **24** rm22 🛆12 G B28–75
★**Gerstekorrel** Damstr 22 ☎241367 Plan **22**
rm39 (A4) 🛆7 2 Jan–23 Dec B26–70
★**Leijdsche Hof** (n rest) Leidsegracht 14
☎232148 Plan **25** rm14 🛆3 B25–60
🅿**AEM** Overtoom 399 ☎181234 N🚗 Vau G60
🛏🅿**J C Doorn** Vuurwerkweg 5 ☎273030 N🚗
Chy/Sim
🛏🅿**Nassaukade** Nassaukade 380 ☎128333
N🚗 Toy
🛏🅿**Sieberg** Stadhouderskade 93 ☎717944
N🚗

Apeldoorn Gelderland 134,100 (☎055)
Map **4** C3
★★★**Keizerskroon** Koningstr 7 ☎217744
rm24 ⇄24 B47–160 M8.50–30
★★**Bloemink** Loolaan 56 ☎214141
tx49253 Bloap rm33 ⇄11 🛆15 B30–75 M20
★**Suisse** Stationplein 15 ☎212040 rm12
🛏🅿**Bakker** Gazellestr 21 ☎214208 N🚗 Ren
G130
🛏🅿**H Gerritsen** Asselsestr 238 ☎253222 Frd
G60
🛏🅿**B Van der Heuvel** Stationsplein 7
☎212163 N🚗 BL/Rov/Tri G65
🛏🅿**J J T Veer** Molenstr 78 ☎212809
M/c Dat

Arcen en Velden Limburg 7,650
(☎04703) Map **4** D2
★**Maas** Schansstr 18 ☎1556 rm24 ⇄2 🛆7 G

Arnhem Gelderland 126,100 (☎085)
Map **4** D2
★★★**Groot Warnsborn** Bakensbergseweg 277
☎455751 tx45596 rm29 (A14) ⇄14 🛆15 G
★★★**Haarhuis** Stationsplein 1 ☎427441
tx45357 rm98 ⇄45 🛆53 G Lift B52.50–85
M12.50–17.50
☆☆☆**Postiljon** Europaweg 25 ☎453741
tx45028 rm30 🛆28 B50–78 Màlc
★★★**Rijn** Onderlangs 10 ☎434642 tx45982
rm27 ⇄13 🛆12 G B70–130 M12.50–20
★★**Bosch** Apeldoornsestr 4 ☎435150 rm50
⇄12 🛆12 B35–85 M15
★**Leeren Doedel** Amsterdamseweg 467
☎332344 rm11 ⇄3 🛆3 B35.50–86
M7.50–40 Pn55–60
★**Riche** (n rest) Willemsplein 35 ☎424466
rm17 G
★**Rijnzicht** (n rest) Utrechtseweg 123
☎420865 rm12 🛆3 1 Mar–31 Oct B29–94
🛏🚙**Hendriks & Zeuner** Sperwerstr 2
☎422912 Maz G10
🛏🅿**Moll's** Velperweg 33 ☎452971 BL/Jag/
Rov/Tri
🛏🅿**J Reymes** Amsterdamseweg 5a ☎423204
N🚗 G50
🛏🅿**Rosier & Meijer** Velperweg 10 ☎629033
N🚗 Frd

231

Netherlands

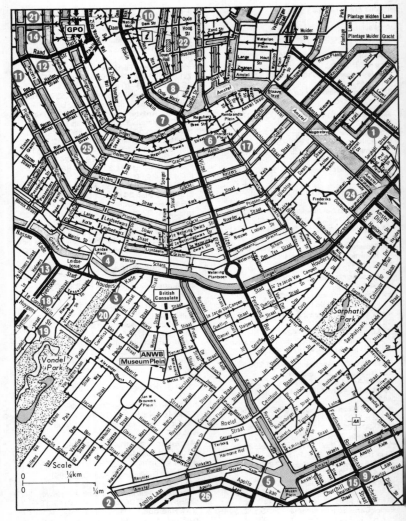

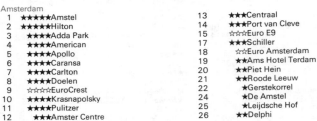

Amsterdam

1	★★★★★Amstel
2	★★★★★Hilton
3	★★★★Adda Park
4	★★★★American
5	★★★★Apollo
6	★★★★Caransa
7	★★★★Carlton
8	★★★★Doelen
9	☆☆☆☆☆EuroCrest
10	★★★★Krasnapolsky
11	★★★★Pulitzer
12	★★★Amster Centre
13	★★★Centraal
14	★★★Port van Cleve
15	☆☆☆Euro E9
17	★★★Schiller
18	☆☆Euro Amsterdam
19	★★Ams Hotel Terdam
20	★★Piet Hein
21	★★Roode Leeuw
22	★Gerstekorrel
24	★De Amstel
25	★Leijdsche Hof
26	★★Delphi

Assen Drenthe 43,800 (☎05920) Map **4** D3
i∌AZA Beilerstr 17 ☎15249 M/c MB G60

Baarn Utrecht 25,050 (☎02154) Map **4** C3
★★★★★ *Kasteel Hooge Vuursche*
Hilversumsestraatweg 14 ☎12541 tx14110
rm27 ⊷22 🗋5 Lift
★ *Promenade* Amalialaan 1 ☎2913 rm17 ⊷2
🖰🏧 **M Koog** Eemnesser 57A ☎12619 N🌢
Chy/Sim G2

Beek Limburg 12,650 (☎04402) Map **4** C2
☆☆ *Euromotel Limburg* E9 Beek–Maastricht
☎2462 tx56059 rm62 ⊷20 🗋42 B51.50–86
M15 Pn79.50–86

Bergen Noord-Holland 14,350 (☎02208)
Map **4** C3
★★ *De Boschhoek* Studler van Surcklaan 14
☎2134 rm23 (A) ⊷5 🗋5

Bergen aan Zee Noord-Holland 350
(☎02208) Map **4** C3
★★ *Nassau-Bergen* Van de Wijckplein 4
☎2345 rm32 ⊷8 🗋10 B59–127 M32
Pn80–110 Pool Sea
★ *Monsmarem* Zeeweg 31 ☎2335 rm42 🗋18
Apr–Sep LD B25–70 M15 Pn48–58
★ *Prins Maurits* Van Hasselstr 7 ☎2364 rm24
⊷12 🗋3 G 1 Mar–1 Nov B45–75 (double) M15

Berg en Dal Gelderland 2,000 (☎08895)
Map **4** C/D2
★★ *Park 'Val Monte'* Oude Holleweg 5
☎1704 tx48428 rm92 ⊷53 🗋37 B44–118
M17.50–22.50 Pn70–115

Bergen–op Zoom Noord-Brabant 40,800
(☎01640) Map **4** C2
★★ *Gouden-Leeuw* Fortuinstr 14 ☎35000
rm22 ⊷5 🗋17 G B46–113 M20
★ *Draak* Grote Markt 37 ☎33661 rm27 ⊷4
★ *Schelde* Antwerpsestr 56 ☎33390 rm18
🗋3 B25–60 M15–50 Pn40
🖰🏧 **Difoga** Bredasestr 25 ☎35910 N🌢 Frd
🖰🏧 **Swagemakens** Korenbeursplein 1b
☎36285 N🌢 AR
🖰🏧 **24 Vos** Ravelstr 10 ☎42050 Cit G5

Beverwijk Noord-Holland 37,551 (☎02510)
Map **4** C3
🖰🏧 **Admiral & Zn** Laan der Nederlanden 1
☎36050 N🌢 Cit G5
🖰🏧 **Wijkeroog** Bullerlaan 6 ☎39129 N🌢
BL/Rov/Tri G

Bilthoven Utrecht 16,050 (☎030)
Map **4** C3
★★ *Heidepark* J-Steenlaan 22 ☎782477 rm20
⊷8 🗋8

Blaricum Noord-Holland 8,150 (☎02153)
Map **4** C3
★ *Vita Nova* Naarderweg 49 ☎3750 rm10

Bloemendaal Noord-Holland 17,950
(☎023) Map **4** C3
★★ *Iepenhove* Hartenlustlann 4 ☎258301
rm44 ⊷6 🗋25 G Lift B46.50–99 M17.50–30
Pn64–70 Lake
🖰🏧 **24 Van Loon's** Korte Kleverlaan 30
☎259311 Lnc/Ren/Sab G20

Born Limburg 7,350 (☎04498) Map **4** C1
☆☆☆ *EuroCrest* Julianaweg 6 ☎1666
tx56248 rm49 ⊷17 🗋32 B55–86

Boskoop Zuid-Holland 13,000 (☎01727)
Map **4** C2
★ *Florida* A-P-Van Neslaan 1 ☎2282 rm9 ⊷7 G
🖰🏧 **Erste Boskoops e Autogarage Kok en
Co** Plankier 2-4-6 ☎2110 N🌢4150 M/c
MB/Opl G70

Breda Noord-Brabant 118,100 (☎01600)
Map **4** C2
☆☆ *Euromotel Brabant* Heerbaan 4 ☎149754
tx54263 rm82 ⊷22 🗋60 Lift B55–80 M25

★★ *Oranje* Stationsplein 7 ☎131851 rm48 (A)
⊷10 🗋4 G
☆ *Euromotel Breda* Roskam 20 (4km S)
☎122177 tx54126 rm80 (A47) 🗋56
🖰🏧 **R Van Nunen** Haagweg 442 ☎134223
N🌢 BL/Rov/Tri
🖰🏧 **24 P Otten** Beverweg 4 ☎122533
🖰🏧 **Tigchelaar** Boeimeersingel 6 ☎124400
Frd
At **Ginneken** (2km S)
★★★ *Mastbosch* Burgemeester Kerstenslaan 20
☎650050 tx54406 rm47 ⊷43 🗋4 Lift

Breskens Zeeland 4,200 (☎01172)
Map **3** B2
★ *Wapen van Breskens* Grote Kade 33
☎1401 ta Valk rm21 (A3) 🗋6 G LD
B22.50–95 M4–30 Pn35–55 Sea
🖰🏧 **Vroon's** Mercuriusstr 11 ☎1729 N🌢 Frd G10

Bunnik See **Utrecht**

Burg (Den) Texel (☎02220) Map **4** C3
🖰🏧 **J Rey** Waalderstr 5 ☎2345 N🌢 BMW G30

Bussum Noord-Holland 37,850 (☎02159)
Map **4** C3
★★★ *Jan Tabak* Amersfoortsestraatweg 27
☎42753 rm34 ⊷34 🗋
★ *Gooiland* Stationsweg 16 ☎43724
rm14 🗋2 G B33.50–85 M10.50 Pn45–52
🖰🏧 **Eurocar** Huizerweg 14 ☎31007 BL/Tri
🖰🏧 **Van Meurs** Huizerweg 84 ☎34047 G10

Delden Overijssel 6,350 (☎05407)
Map **4** D3
★ *Zwaan* Langestr 2 ☎1206 rm19 (A6) ⊷2 🗋7
G B33–85 M19.50–25 Pool

Delft Zuid-Holland 86,150 (☎015) Map **4** C2
★ *Central* Wijnhaven 6 ☎123442 rm15 🗋10
★ *Zwaantje* (n rest) Koningsplein 5 ☎120492
rm8 🗋11 15 Apr–15 Oct
🖰🏧 **A M Bakker** Houttuinen 22 ☎143960 N🌢
Ren
🖰🏧 **P H Blansjaar** H-de Grootstr 51 ☎120751
N🌢 Aud/Chy/VW G5
🖰🏧 **Kinesis** Vulcanusweg 281 ☎569202 N🌢
Frd

Den Haag See **Haag (Den)**

Den Helder Noord-Holland 60,421
(☎02230) Map **4** C3
🖰🏧 **Ceres** Baljuwstraat 139 ☎30000 Peu G

Deventer Overijssel 65,600 (☎05700)
Map **4** D3
★★★ *Postiljon* Deventerweg 121 ☎24022
tx49028 rm48 ⊷48 Lift B50–79 M16 Pn67.50
🖰🏧 **Hardonk's** Gl-Gibsonsstr 6 ☎13945 Bed/
MB/Vau

Doetinchem Gelderland 34,950 (☎08340)
Map **4** D2
🖰🏧 **Gelderse-Auto** Keppelseweg 10
☎33250 N🌢 Frd G100

Domburg Zeeland 3,900 (☎01188)
Map **3** B2
★★ *Bad* Domburgseweg 3 ☎1241 rm65 (A20)
⊷25 🗋2 G 10 May–5 Sep LD Pn63.25–88.75

Dordrecht Zuid-Holland 101,850 (☎078)
Map **4** C2
★★ *Bellevue-Groothoofdspoort* Boomstr 37
☎37900 rm20 ⊷10 🗋10 B45–95
🖰🏧 **24 Ames** J-de Wittstr 162 Brouwersdijk 30
☎43322 Aud/VW G50
🖰🏧 **A V D Ban** Dubbelsteynlaan 51 ☎61600
N🌢 BL/Rov/Tri G10
🖰🏧 **H W Van Gorp & Zonen** A-Cuypsingel 296
☎42044 N🌢 Bed/Vau
🖰🏧 **Kern's** Copernicusweg 1 ☎71633 Ren

Drachten Friesland 33,950 (☎05120)
Map **4** C/D3
🖰🏧 **Siton** de Knobben 25 ☎14455 N🌢 Opl

Netherlands

Dronten Gelderland 16,550 (☎03210)
Map **4** C3
⌂🏠 **Visser** De Ketting 1 ☎3114 N🏠 GM

Edam Noord-Holland 21,550 (☎02993)
Map **4** C3
★**Dam** Keizersgracht 1 ☎1766 rm11

⌂🏠**24 Griep & Frikkee** Schepenmakersdijk 4
☎1602 N☎1772 Ren

Ede Gelderland 79,900 (☎08380) Map **4** C2
★**De Witte Hinde** Stationsweg 132 ☎13951
rm21 ⊲1 🏠1
⌂🏠**24 Van der Kolk** Klaphekweg 30 ☎19112
Frd G100
⌂🏠**G Van Silfhout** Proosdijweg 1 ☎14041
N🏠 Ren G4
⌂🏠**Vonk** Veenderweg 31 ☎10397 N🏠 Cit G15

Eemnes See **Laren**

Eernewoude Friesland 300 (☎05117)
Map **4** D3
★★**Princenhof** Piet Miedemaweg 15 ☎9206
rm47 (A3) ⊲23 🏠16 1 Apr–10 Oct
B42.50–180 M22–28 Pn49.50–100 Lake

Egmond aan Zee Noord-Holland 5,750
(☎02206) Map **4** C3
★**Bellevue** Strandboulevard A7 ☎1387
rm41 (A5) ⊲30 🏠2 Lift 2 Jan–27 Dec
B40.50–116 M7.50–35 Pn45–65 Sea
⌂🏠**J A Karels** Trompstr 17 ☎1250 BL

Eindhoven Noord-Brabant 192,600 (☎040)
Map **4** C2
★★★★**Cocagne** Vestdijk 47 ☎444755
tx51245 rm205 ⊲205 G Lift B90–179 M15
☆☆☆☆**Holiday Inn** ☎433222 tx51775 rm200
⊲200 Lift B98–146 Pn127 Pool
⌂🏠**Van Laarhoven's** Bruggelaan 10 ☎413615
N🏠 BL/Jag/Rov/Tri G20
⌂**J Van der Meulen** Kanaaldijk-Zuid 7g
☎116110 Opl G
🍴🏠**Van der Meulen-Ansems** Vestdijk 27
☎444550 N🏠 Frd
⌂🏠**T Vlemmings** Stratumsedijk 23 ☎116336
N🏠 Bed/Sab/Vau

Emmeloord Overijssel 13,550 (☎05270)
Map **4** C3
⌂🏠 **Gorter** Kampwal 50 ☎3541 N🏠 GM G

Emmen Drenthe 86,725 (☎05910)
Map **4** D3
⌂🏠 **Van Boven** P-Foggstr 10 ☎11277
N🏠 Bed/Vau G200
⌂🏠 **Hesselink** Noordbargerstr 11 ☎12741 N🏠
Ren G40
⌂🏠**24 Jong** Statenweg 5 ☎22330 Cit G
⌂🏠 **Misker** Odoornerweg 4 ☎11190 N🏠 BL/
Jag/Tri G5

Enkhuizen Noord-Holland 13,450
(☎02280) Map **4** C3
★**Port van Cleve** Dijk 74 ☎2510 rm10 ⊲1
🏠6 G B35–80 Màlc
⌂🏠**Watses** Westerstr 273 ☎2708 N🏠 Frd G10

Enschede Overijssel 141,600 (☎053)
Map **4** D3
★★★**Memphis** Tromplaan 55 ☎318244 rm37
⊲35 Lift
★★**Park** Hengelosestr 200 ☎353855 rm18
🏠2 G LD 19.50–33 M22.50 Pn50
⌂🏠**A M T** Burg M-van Veenlaan 7 ☎27165
Bed/Vau G100
⌂🏠 **Fischer** Oldenzaalsestr 137 ☎354555 N🏠
Frd
⌂🏠**24 C Jassies** Hengelosestr 74 ☎327025
N☎842000 N🏠 BL/Jag/Rov/Tri G10

Flushing See **Vlissingen**

Ginneken See **Breda**

Goes Zeeland 28,550 (☎01100) Map **3** B2

234

★★★**Korenbeurs** Grote Markt 17 ☎27110
rm30 ⊲5 🏠7
★**Het Wapen van Zeeland** rm13 🏠2
★**Ockenburgh** van de Spiegelstr 104 ☎16303
rm12 (A) 🏠1 G
⌂🏠 **Adria** Marconistr 1 ☎20440 N🏠 Frd
⌂🏠 **Van Fraassen** Voorstad 79 ☎27353 N🏠
Cit
🏠**V Oeveren** Couwerverstr 51 ☎16100 N🏠
BL/MB/Rov/Tri
⌂🏠**Van Strien** van de Spiegelstr 92 ☎14840
N🏠 Aud/VW G

Gorinchem Zuid-Holland 28,350 (☎01830)
Map **4** C2
☆☆☆**Gorinchem** van Hogendorpweg 10
☎22400 rm15 ⊲15 B55–83 M15
☆☆**Romeyn & Van Zanten** Concordiaweg 33
☎244455 Frd G50
⌂**24 Van Mill** Banneweg 1 ☎32344 GM

Gouda Zuid-Holland 56,450 (☎01820)
Map **4** C2
★**Zalm** Markt 36 ☎12344 rm25 🏠1 B45–65
M20–50
⌂🏠**J L Hulleman** Parrallelweg 2 ☎12977 N🏠
Frd G5
⌂🏠**Noordegraaf's** Raam 184 ☎17795 N🏠 Cit

Groesbeek Gelderland 18,100 (☎08891)
Map **4** C2
★**Wolfsberg** Mooksebaan 12 ☎1327 rm19
⊲1 🏠13 G

Groningen Groningen 163,400 (☎050)
Map **4** D4
☆☆☆**Euromotel** Expostielaan ☎258400
tx53795 rm109 ⊲109 Lift B52.50–82 M16
Pn80.50
☆☆**Clingendael** Donderslaan 156 ☎252040
rm59 ⊲10 🏠49 G B52.50–95 Màlc
★★**Grand Frigge** Heerestr 72 ☎136342 rm86
(A) ⊲20 🏠40 Lift
⌂🏠**'A–Z'** Friesestraatweg 22 ☎120012 N🏠
Hon G100
⌂🏠**A V Eerden** Korreweg 51 ☎128416 N🏠
⌂🏠 **Geba** Flemingstr 1 ☎250015 N🏠 BL/Rov/Tri
⌂🏠**24 Gronam** Rijksweg 130 ☎411552
N☎344996 Frd
⌂🏠**Van der Molen** Oosterhamrikkade 114
☎771811 N🏠 Opl
⌂🏠**J K Oosterhuis** Westerkade 11 ☎120246
N🏠 Toy
⌂**F Pekelder** Nieuwe Boteringestr 65
☎126304 N🏠 Maz G4

Gulpen Limburg 4,450 (☎04450) Map **4** C1
At **Wittem** (1·5km E)
★★**Kasteel Wittem** Wittemerallee 3 ☎1208
rm8 ⊲8 B80 (double) Pn70

Haag (Den) (Hague, The) Zuid-Holland
479,400 (☎070) Map **4** C2

| **AA** | agents; see page 226 |

★★★★**Bel Air** J-de Wittlaan 30 ☎572011
tx31444 rm350 ⊲350 Lift B89–126 M30
Pn110–144 Pool
★★★★**Grand Central** Lange Poten 6
☎469414 tx32000 rm137 ⊲123 🏠14 Lift
B75–126 M14.50–16.50 Pn89–106
★★★**Parkhotel de Zalm** (n rest) Molenstr 53
(off Noordeinde) ☎624371 tx33005 rm132
⊲88 🏠21 G Lift B38–115
⌂🏠**Case** Pletterijstr 6 ☎858780 N🏠 Chy
⌂🏠**Centraal** Prinses Margrietplantsoen 10
☎814131 N🏠 Frd
⌂🏠**Gemex** Reinkenstr 51 ☎603588 N🏠 G100
⌂🏠**Haag** Calandplein 2 ☎889255 N🏠 Ren
⌂🏠**Internationale** Scheldestr 15 ☎850300
N🏠 Hon/Sab/Ska/Vlo

🛏🕽*F Van der Valk* 2e Schuytstr 290 ☎325860 N🍴

🛏🕽*Zoet* Koninginnegracht 1b ☎185165 N🍴 Chy

At **Rijswijk** (3km SE)

☆☆*Hoornwijck* J-Thijssenweg 2 ☎903130 tx32538 rm74 ⇆30 ⋔44 G

At **Scheveningen** (☎070)

★★★★*Europa* Zwolsestr 2 ☎512651 tx33138 rm183 ⇆98 ⋔85 G Lift B70–120 M30 Pn60 ♎ Sea

★★★*Eurotel* Gevers Deijnootweg 63 ☎512821, tx32799 rm84 ⇆59 ⋔25 Lift B63–110 M20 Pn78

★★*Badhotel* Gevers Deijnootweg 15 ☎512221 rm96 ⇆20 ⋔76 Lift B45–100 M15 Pn65–85

★*Bali* Badhuisweg 1 ☎514371 rm34 (A12) ⇆8 ⋔2 B27.50–70 M25

Haarlem Noord-Holland 164,700 (☎023) Map **4** C3

★★*Lion d'Or* Kruisweg 34 ☎321750 rm35 ⇆6 ⋔16 Lift B52–113 M21.50

🛏🕽*Haarlemsche-Autocentrale* Jansweg 9 ☎319265 Frd

🛏🕽*E Kimman* Zijlweg 35 ☎326555 BL/Jag/ Rov/Tri

Harde 't (Elburg) Gelderland (☎05255) Map **4** C3

★★*Vale Ouwe* Eperweg 94 ☎1341 rm12 ⇆3 ⋔4 G B74.50–99 M22.50 Pn55–60

Hague (The) See **Haag (Den)**

Harderwijk Gelderland 28,550 (☎03410) Map **4** C3

★★*Baars* Smeepoortstr 52 ☎12007 rm18 ⋔4 G B40–100 M13.50–22.50 Pn52.50–62.50

🛏🕽*Van der Ploeg* Schimmelstr 1 ☎14106 N🍴 BL/Rov/Tri

Haren Groningen 18,700 (☎050) Map **4** D4

☆☆☆*Postiljon* Emmalaan 33 ☎347041 tx53688 rm57 ⇆24 ⋔33

Harlingen Friesland 14,550 (☎05178) Map **4** C3/4

★*Zeezicht* Zuiderhaven 1 ☎2536 rm10 B25–50 M3–29 Pn50 Sea

🛏🕽*W Molenaar* Heiligeweg 54 ☎2925 N🍴 Frd G40

Heelsum Gelderland (☎08373) Map **4** C2

★★*Klein Zwitserland* Klein Zwitserlandlaan 5 ☎9104 tx45627 rm62 ⇆33 ⋔29 Lift B67.50–145 M35 ✍ Pool

Heemstede Noord-Holland 27,400 (☎023) Map **4** C3

🛏🕽*Barnhoorn* Roemer Visscherplein 21 ☎242250 N🍴 Toy

Heerenveen Friesland 34,950 (☎05130) Map **4** C3

☆☆☆*Postiljon* Schans 65 ☎24041 rm44 (A) ⇆4 ⋔40 G

🛏🕽*Vriesema* Schans 1 ☎22581 N🍴 M/c BL/Rov/Tri G5

Heerlen Limburg 71,500 (☎045) Map **4** C/D1

★★*Grand* Wilhelminaplein 17 ☎713846 rm62 ⇆5 ⋔30 G Lift B35–125 M19–21

🛏🚧24 *Canton-Reiss* Valkenburgerweg 34 ☎718040 GM

🛏🕽*Sondagh* Looierstr 19 ☎711399 N🍴 Cit G20

🛏🕽*Van Haaren* Schandelerboord 25 ☎711152 Frd

🛏🕽*Heynen* Frankenlaan 1 ☎713600 N🍴 Ren

🛏🕽*Zuid* Heesbergstr 60 ☎412641

Helmond Noord-Brabant 59,250 (☎04920) Map **4** C2

★★★*West-Ende* Steenweg 1 ☎24151 rm36 ⇆12 ⋔12 Lift 2 Jan–24 Dec B28.50–35 M12.50–14.50

🛏🕽*Alards* Gerwenseweg 31 ☎22608 N🍴 BL/Rov G100

🛏🕽*J Gorp* Engelseweg 220 ☎39670 N🍴 Cit

🛏🕽*Van de Heuvels'* Kamerlingh Onnesstr 5 ☎36888 N🍴 Ren G15

Hengelo Overijssel 72,300 (☎05400) Map **4** D3

★★★*'t Lansink* Storkstr 18 ☎10066 rm22 ⇆8 ⋔14 G 2 Jan–24 Dec

★*Kroon* Deldenerstr 62 ☎12872 rm32 ⋔13 G

🛏🕽*G Ter Haar* Breemarsweg 140 ☎13901 N🍴 BL/Tri

🛏🕽*Van Laar & Feijten* Enschedesestr 127 ☎22966 Vlo G10

🛏🕽*W Noordegraaf* Oldenzaalsestr 19 ☎14444 M/c Frd

's-Hertogenbosch Noord-Brabant 86,200 (☎073) Map **4** C2

★★*Royal* Visstr 26 ☎131551 rm14 ⇆1 ⋔5

🛏🕽*Lautenslager* Havenstr 7 ☎130636 N🍴 Ska/Toy

Hilversum Noord-Holland 94,050 (☎02150) Map **4** C3

★★*Hof van Holland* Kerkbrink 1 ☎46141 tx43399 rm30 ⇆16 ⋔14 Lift B66–119 M17–25

🛏🕽*De Graaf's* Bosdrift 140 ☎44255 Ren

🛏🕽*F J Kroymans* Soestdijkerstraatweg 66 ☎55151 N🍴 BL/Jag/Rov/Tri

🛏🕽*J K Poll* Zeverijnstr 2 ☎47841 N🍴 Frd

Hoek van Holland (Hook, The) Zuid-Holland 7,750 (☎01747) Map **3** B2 **See Plan**

★*Witte Huis* D-Van den Burgweg 69 ☎2385 Plan **1** rm11 ⇆1 ⋔6 G 1 Mar–31 Oct

Holten Overijssel 8,850 (☎05483) Map **4** D3

★*Hoog Holten* Holterberg 25 ☎1306 rm27 ⋔8 B31–55 M10–30 Pn44.50–55 ✍

★*Lösse Hoes* Holterberg 46 ☎1353 rm22 ⇆9 ⋔13 G LD B35.50–105 M10–62.50 Pn55–67.50 Pool

Hoogerheide Noord-Brabant 6,300 (☎01646) Map **4** C2

★*Pannenhuis* Antwerpsestraatweg 100 ☎2540 rm24 ⋔9 G 2 Jan–24 Dec B32.50–85 M14 Pn37.50

🛏🕽*P J Wils* Raadhuisstr 88 ☎2530 N🍴 BL/Tri

Hook (The) See **Hoek van Holland**

Hoorn Noord-Holland 24,650 (☎02290) Map **4** C3

★*Keizerskroon* Breed 31 ☎14401 rm26 G

🛏🚧24 *Koopmans* Dampten 5 ☎16912 N☎17393 M/c Hon/Ska

🛏🕽*Van der Linden & Van Sprankhuizen* Berkhouterweg 11 ☎12910 N🍴 Fia/GM G

Kampen Overijssel 29,500 (☎05202) Map **4** C3

★★★*Stadsherberg* IJsselkade 48 ☎2645 rm16 ⇆6 ⋔10 Lift B47.50–105 M25–50 Pn65–70

★★*Van Dijk* (n rest) IJsselkade 30 ☎14925 rm28 (A6) ⇆8 ⋔1 B27.50–65

🛏🚧24 *J H R Van Noort* Oudestr 33 ☎2241 Frd

🛏🕽*Westerhof* IJsseldijk 2 ☎3386 N🍴 Sim G8

Katwijk aan Zee Zuid-Holland 37,450 (☎01718) Map **4** C3

🛏🕽*Modern* W-Sluiterstr 31 ☎13941 Cit G25

Koewacht Zeeland (☎01146) Map **3** B2

🛏🕽*Hako* Eikenlaan 37 ☎228 N🍴 Vlo

Koog (De) Texel (☎02228) Map **4** C3

★★*Opduin* Minister Ruyslaan 22 ☎445 rm54 (A10) ⋔33 G Lift B43–134 M27.50–67.50 Pn56.50–74.50 Pool

Laren Noord-Holland 13,650 (☎02153) Map **4** C3

Netherlands

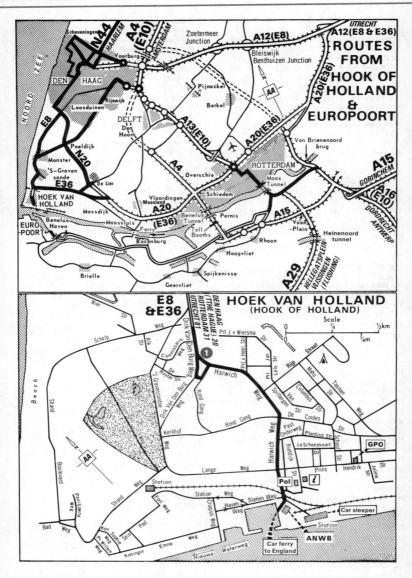

ROUTES FROM HOOK OF HOLLAND & EUROPOORT

HOEK VAN HOLLAND (HOOK OF HOLLAND)

Hoek van Holland (Hook of Holland)
1   ★Witte Huis

Netherlands

🏚🕪 *Laren's* Ruiterweg 10 ☎86500 N🍴 Cit

At **Eemnes** (2km S)
☆☆ **Witte Bergen** Rijksweg 2 ☎86754 rm62
⇆62 🛗 B41.50–68 M10–55
Leeuwarden Friesland 85,100 (☎05100)
Map **4** C4
★★★ **Oranje** Stationsweg 4 ☎26241 rm54
(A6) ⇆8 🛗28 G Lift B35–100 M18.50
Pn63–78
🏚🕪**24 Molenaar** Keidam 2 ☎61115
N☎81441 BL/Jag/Rov/Tri
🏚🕪 **Nagelhout** Brandemeer 2 ☎63633 N🍴 Toy
🏚🕪 **Rosier's** Spanjaardslaan 162 ☎20043 N🍴
Ren
🏚🕪**Zeeuw** Leeuwerikstr 119 ☎29988 N🍴 Frd
Leiden Zuid-Holland 99,900 (☎071)
Map **4** C3
☆☆☆ **Holiday Inn** Haagse Schouwweg 10
☎769310 tx32541 rm190 ⇆190 Lift
B82.50–120 M25 Pn127.50 🏊 Pool
★**t' Karrewiel** Steenstr 55 ☎122509 rm11 🛗3
🏚🕪 **LAG** van Oldenbarneveldtstr 37 ☎151683
N🍴 BL/Tri
🏚🕪 **Poot** Lammenschansweg 132 ☎764800 N🍴
BL/Rov/Tri
Leusden Utrecht (☎033) Map **4** C2/3
★★★ **Treek** Trekerweg 23 ☎1425 rm16 ⇆2
🛗7 G Lift
Leuvenum Gelderland 150 (☎05770)
Map **4** C3
★★ **Roode Koper** van Sandbergweg 82
☎7393 rm26 (A) ⇆7 🛗9
Lochem Gelderland 17,300 (☎05730)
Map **4** D3
🏚🕪 **Van de Straat** Tramstr 36 ☎1652 M/c BL/
Tri G20
Loosdrecht Utrecht 7,850 (☎02158)
Map **4** C3
★ **Driesprong** Veendijk 1 ☎3230 rm6
B27.50–55 Màlc Lake
Maarsbergen Utrecht 1,525 (☎03433)
Map **4** C2
☆ **Maarsbergen** Woudenbergseweg 44 ☎341
tx47986 rm17 🛗12 G B46.50–63
M12.50–42.50
Maastricht Limburg 111,050 (☎043)
Map **4** C1
★★★ **Casque** Vrijthof 52 ☎14343 tx56657
rm40 ⇆20 🛗14 G Lift B52.50–113
M17.50–47.50 Pn85–110
★★★ **Derlon** O-L-Vrouweplein 6 ☎12542
tx56256 rm30 ⇆15 🛗4 G Lift B57–131.50
M20–35 Pn67.50–152.50
★★ **Dominicain** (n rest) Helmstr 16 ☎14656
rm16 ⇆4 🛗1
🏚🕪 **Bollen** Calvariestr 22 ☎18923 N🍴 BMW
🏚🕪 **Cartigny** T-Van der Schuerlaan122
☎36000 Bed/Opl/Vau
🏚🕪 **J J Molenaar's** Dr Bakstr 82 ☎30084
BL/Rov/Tri
Middelburg Zeeland 36,400 (☎01180)
Map **3** B2
★★ **Nieuwe Doelen** Loskade 3 ☎12121 rm30
🛗12 Lift LD B40–110 M20–35
★ **Commerce** Loskade 1 ☎36051 rm33 ⇆9
🛗16 Lift B34–85
★ **De Huifkar** Markt 19 ☎12298 rm9 ⇆4 🛗4
B41.50–83 M15 Pn70–80
🏚🕪 **Louisse** Gortstr 60 ☎25851 N🍴 Opl
Middelharnis Zuid-Holland 14,250
(☎01870) Map **3** B2
🏚🕪 **Auto Service** Kastanjelaan 41 ☎3094 N🍴
Chy/Sim

🏚🕪 **Knöps** Langeweg 113 ☎2222 GM
Mook-en-Middelaar Limburg 5,800
(☎08896) Map **4** C2
★★★ **Plasmolen** Rijksweg 170 ☎1444
rm32 ⇆17 🛗6 G B27.50–95 M15 Pn53.50–
121.50 🏊 Lake
★ **Schans** Rijksweg 95 ☎1209 rm12 ⇆1 🛗5 G
Naarden Noord-Holland 17,350 (☎02159)
Map **4** C3
☆☆☆ **Euro** Amersfoortsestraatweg 92 ☎44641
tx43465 rm50 (A12) 🛗50 B50–70 Pn82.50
Nijmegen Gelderland 148,500 (☎080)
Map **4** C2
🏚🕪 **Jansen & Ederveen** ☎224800 N🍴 Ren
🏚🕪 **Neerbosch** Schependomlaan 88 ☎773044
N🍴 M/c Ren G
🏚🕪 **Vossen** Molenweg 119 ☎770144 N🍴
BL/Rov/Tri
🏚🕪 **T Wolf's** Waalkade 8 ☎225111 N🍴 Frd
Nijverdal Overijssel 18,925 (☎05486)
Map **4** D3
🏚🕪 **Blokken** Bergleidingweg 27 ☎12959 N🍴
BL/Tri
🏚🕪 **H Valk** Boomcateweg 19 ☎12487 🍴 Bed/
Vau
Noordgouwe Zeeland (☎01112) Map **3** B2
🏚🕪 **Akkerdaas** Kloosterweg 2 ☎347 N🍴 GM G
Noordwijk aan Zee Zuid-Holland 22,400
(☎01719) Map **4** C3
★★★ **Palace** Koningin-Wilhelmina bd 3
☎19231 tx32010 rm94 ⇆32 🛗40 Lift Sea
★★ **Clarenwijck** Koningin-Astrid bd 46
☎12727 rm25 ⇆18 LD B40–105 M20
Pn50–65 Sea
★★ **Huis ter Duin** Koningin-Astrid bd 5
☎19220 tx31713 rm89 ⇆89 G Lift
1 Jan–11 Sep LD B80–185 M30&àlc Pn115 🏊
Beach Golf Sea
★★ **Noordzee** Koningin Wilhelmina bd 8
☎19205 tx32504 rm84 (A10) ⇆26 🛗5 G Lift
Sea
★★ **Zinger** bd Zeereep 1 ☎19330 rm46 ⇆13
🛗27 G B37.50–123 M15–25 Sea
★ **Duinlust** Koepelweg 1 ☎12916 rm25
1 Apr–1 Oct B33–76 M15
🏚🕪 **Rijnland** Beeklaan 5 ☎14300
Oisterwijk Noord-Brabant 16,300
(☎04242) Map **4** C2
🏚🕪 **Dungen** Dorpstr 9 ☎2486
Oldenzaal Overijssel 26,650 (☎05410)
Map **4** D3
🏚🕪 **Olde Monnikhof** Vos de Waelstr 20
☎4461 Opl
🏚🕪 **Munsterhuis** Ollemolenstr 4 ☎5661 Ren
G100
Ommen Overijssel 16,150 (☎05291)
Map **4** D3
★★ **Zon aan de Vecht** Voorbrug 1 ☎1141 rm20
⇆2 🛗5 G O
🏚🕪 **Leerentveld** Hammerueg 1 ☎2500
N☎1475 Chy/Sim
Oostburg Zeeland 18,500 (☎01170)
Map **3** B2
★ **Commerce** Burchtstr 20 ☎2912 rm22 G
Oosterbeek Gelderland 13,800 (☎085)
Map **4** C2
★★★ **Bilderberg** Utrechtseweg 261 ☎333060
rm55 ⇆40 G Lift
★ **Dreyeroord** Graaf Van Rechterenweg 12
☎333169 rm35 (A7) ⇆7 🛗12 Lift
B33.50–99 M15–79 Pn41–59
★ **Strijland** Stationsweg 6 ☎332126 tx75085
rm31 (A10) ⇆30 B31–81 M9.50–17
Pn55.50–59.50
🏚🕪 **Hoog en Laag** Utrechtseweg 84 ☎334751
N🍴 Toy
Oss Noord-Brabant 45,650 (☎04120)
Map **4** C2

Netherlands

★★Alem Molenstr 81 ☎22114 rm19
B30–58 M18 Pn45–48
🛏&◑**J Putters** Hertogensingel 36 ☎23600 N🅟
AR/MB G6
🛏&◑**Uyting & Smits** Oude Molenstraat 27
☎26925 N🅟 GM G15

Overveen Noord-Holland (☎023) Map **4** C3
★Roozendaal Bloemendaalseweg 260
☎324517 rm13 ⇆2 🏠11 B37.50–100 M17.50 ·
Pn72–110

Papendrecht Zuid-Holland 24,200 (☎078)
Map **4** C2
☆☆☆**Staatse Schans** Lange Tiendweg 2
☎52099 tx23631 rm33 ⇆26 🏠7 Lift
B74.50–119 M from 13

Poeldijk Zuid-Holland 4,150 (☎01749)
Map **4** C2
★★Verburgh Julianastr 2 ☎5209 rm16 🏠10
B40.50–71 M5–19.50 Pn59.50

Renkum Gelderland 34,550 (☎08373)
Map **4** C2
★★Nol in't Bosch Hartenseweg 60 ☎9101
rm30 ⇆8 🏠14

Rijswijk See **Haag (Den)**

Roermond Limburg 36,700 (☎04750)
Map **4** D2
🛏&◑**Nedam** Oranjelaan 802 ☎23351 Opl/Vau
🛏&◑**Opheij** W II Singel 29 ☎12125 N🅟
Lnc/Hon G293

Roosendaal Noord-Brabant 51,700
(☎01650) Map **4** C2
★Central Stationsplein 9 ☎35650 rm19 ⇆11
🏠4 G
🛏&◑**Hennekam** Adm-Lonckestr 1 ☎36924 Frd
🛏&◑**Van Poppel** Van Beethovenlaan 9
☎45350 N🅟☎37001 N🅟 BL

Rotterdam Zuid-Holland 614,800 (☎010)
Map **4** C2
★★★★Park Westersingel 70 ☎363611
tx22020 rm96 🏠96 Lift B83.75–177.50 M30
★★★Atlanta A-Van Nesstr 4 ☎110420
tx21595 rm185 ⇆100 🏠85 G Lift B79–124
M30 Pn104–140
★★★Central Kruiskade 12 ☎140744 tx24040
rm75 ⇆35 🏠40 Lift B60–100 M25–29
Pn110–135
★★★Regina (n rest) Spoorsingel 75 ☎656500
rm66 ⇆38 🏠10 Lift
★★★Rijn Schouwburgplein 1 ☎132900
tx21640 rm140 ⇆20 🏠120 Lift B55–140
M25–100
★★★Savoy (n rest) Hoogstr 81 ☎139280
tx21525 rm96 ⇆14 🏠82 Lift
★★Baan (n rest) Rochussenstraat 345
☎770555 rm14 🏠7 B25–70
★★'s-Gravenburg 's-Gravendijkwal 100
☎365174 ta Sgrabu rm32 ⇆8 🏠2 G
☆☆**Skyway Euromotel** Vliegveldweg 61
☎158000 tx22064 rm94 (A40) ⇆54 🏠40 Lift
B57–82 M13–15 Pn85
★Holland (n rest) Provenierssingel 7
☎653100 rm25 🏠2 B32.50–52.50
★Pax (n rest) Schiekade 110 ☎653107 rm48
(A14) 🏠16 Lift B35–75
★Witte Paard Groenezoom 245 ☎192020
rm9 ⇆2 🏠1 G B40–90 Màlc
🛏&◑**Dunant** Dunanstr 22 ☎760166 N🅟 Toy
Excelsior Boezemsingel 12 ☎144644 N🅟
BL/Jag/Rov/Tri
🛏&◑**24 G A M** Smirnoffweg 21–23 ☎298211
N🅟 MB G30
🛏&◑**Hoogenboom** Geijssendorfferweg 9
☎298844 N🅟 Aud/VW
🛏&◑**Rotterdamsche Auto Centrale** Westplein
3 ☎115555 N🅟 Chy G8
🛏&◑**M Speelman** Struitenweg 15 ☎293061
N🅟 Maz
At **Schiedam** (5km W)

🛏&◑**H W Van Gorp** Nieuwlandplein 15
☎708222 N🅟 Bed

Rozendaal Gelderland (☎08302) Map **4** D2
★★Roosendael Beekhuizensweg 1 ☎629213
rm17 ⇆17 G B65.50–171 M35 Pn85

Sassenheim Zuid-Holland 12,734
(☎02522) Map **4** C3
★Bruine Paard Hoofdstr 241 ☎11151 rm10
B32.50–65 M15 Pn45–50
🛏&◑**Bakker's** Hoofdstr 133 ☎11427 N🅟 Cit G

Scherpenzeel Gelderland 7,750 (☎03497)
Map **4** C2
★★Witte Holevoet Holevoetplein 282 ☎1336
rm9 ⇆4 🏠1 B37.50–80 M25

Scheveningen See **Haag (Den)**

Schiedam See **Rotterdam**

Schoondijke Zeeland 1,950 (☎01173)
Map **3** B2
☆**West** Westr 9 ☎1389 rm12 (A6) ⇆1 🏠11
B31.50–63 M13–18 Pn45

Sittard Limburg 34,300 (☎04490) Map **4** C1
🛏&◑**Cartigny** Rijksweg Zuid 208 ☎5900 N🅟 Sim

Sluis Zeeland 3,150 (☎01178) Map **3** B2
★Korenbeurs Kade 1 ☎1402 rm14 ⇆3 🏠3
★Sanders de Paauw Kade 42 ☎1224 rm10
⇆1 🏠5 G LD B66–90 (double) M10–50
Pn50–60

Sneek Friesland 28,150 (☎05150) Map **4** C3
★★Wijnberg Marktstr 23 ☎12421 rm27 (A)
⇆6
★Bonnema Stationstr 64 ☎13175 rm24 🏠2
B32.50–85 M4–35 Pn42.50–47.50
&◑**Bakker** Oosterkade 4 ☎13262 BL/Tri
🛏&◑**Fritsmas** Oude Koemarkt 16b ☎12030 M/c
Opl G20
🛏&◑**F Ozinga's** Parkstr 16 ☎13344 Frd
🛏🚙**H de Vries** Gedempte Pol 32 ☎13291
N🅟13092 Ren G40

Tegelen Limburg 18,400 (☎077) Map **4** D2
🛏🚙**Linssen** Roermondseweg 139 ☎31421
Chy/Sab G

Terneuzen Zeeland 33,750 (☎01150)
Map **3** B2
🛏&◑**R R Visser** Parkeerterrein ☎7900 Bed/Vau

Tilburg Noord-Brabant 151,550 (☎013)
Map **4** C2
★★Postelse Hoeve Dr Deelenlaan 10
☎671977 rm19 🏠7 B30–60 Pn50–58 Lake
🛏&◑**H J de Groot** Lage Witsiebaan 78
☎681916 Bed/Vau
🛏🚙**W A Holland** Hart Van Brabantlaan 100
☎422600 N🅟 BL/Jag/Rov/Tri G50
🛏🚙**Knegtel** Spoorlaan 175 ☎424100 Frd G

Utrecht Utrecht 250,900 (☎030) Map **4** C2
☆☆☆☆**Holiday Inn** Jaarsbeursplein 24
☎910555 tx47745 rm235 ⇆235 G Lift
B100–135 Pool
★★★Pays Bas Janskerkhof 10 ☎333321
tx47485 rm46 ⇆12 🏠9 Lift B52.50–112.50
★★Hes Maliestr 2 ☎316424 rm20 ⇆10 🏠10
Lift B72.50–115 M22
🛏&◑**Arijjansen** M-Pololaan 71 ☎883520 N🅟
BL/Sab/Tri
🛏&◑**Hartog** Lange Nieuwstr 79 ☎332261
N🅟 BL/Tri
🛏&◑**Van Meeuwen's** Weerdsingel OZ 42
☎719111 N🅟 Bed/Vau
🛏🚙**24 Renault** Maliebaan 71 ☎333435 N🅟
Ren G100
🛏&◑**Stichtse** Leidseweg 128 ☎931744 Frd
At **Bunnik** (8km SE) (☎03405)
☆☆☆**Postiljon** Motorestoweg 8 ☎2744 rm19
⇆4 🏠15 B42–65

Valkenburg Limburg 12,800 (☎04406)
Map **4** C1

★★★*Grand Voncken* Walramplein 1 ☎12841
rm54 (A) ⇄35 ▥3 Lift
★★★*Prinses Juliana* Broekhem 11 ☎12244
rm45 (A13) ⇄13 ▥12 G Lift B60–160
M42.50
★★*Bouwes Vossen* Nieuweweg 7 ☎15341
rm28 ▥5 1 May–1 Oct
★★*Oranje Nassau* Broekhem 19 ☎13548
rm37 (A4) ⇄8 ▥10 G Lift Etr–Nov Pool
ᵇ*Auto-Caubo* Oud-Valkenburger Weg 25
☎15041 G7
ᵇ☒*Corbey* Wilhelminalaan 29 ☎12514 Ren
G15
ᵇ*Poot* Hoofdstr 104 ☎16947 N☒ BL/Rov/Tri
G25

Veendam Groningen 26,200 (☎05987)
Map **4** D3
ᵇ☒*Bakker* Kerkstr 55b ☎2288 N☒ Bed/Vau
G20

Veenendaal Utrecht 35,850 (☎08385)
(13km SW of Ede) Map **4** C2
ᵇ☒24 *Lagendijk* Buurtlaan Oost 81 ☎11500
N☒14397 M/c Bed/Vau G5

Veere Zeeland 4,300 (☎01181) Map **3** B2
★*Campveerse Toren* Kade 2 ☎291 rm8 (A)

Velp Gelderland 21,280 (☎08302) Map **4** D2
☆☆*EuroCrest* Prés Kennedylaan 102
☎629210 tx45527 rm74 ⇄38 ▥36 Lift
B76–98 M20–55
★★*Beekhuizen* Beekhuizenseweg 70
☎619591 rm24 ⇄24 Lift B52.50–80 M25–35
Pn70–80
ᵇ☒24 *Van Kampen* Hoofdstr 73 ☎6655
N☒612522 N☒ Ren

Venlo Limburg 61,700 (☎077) Map **4** D2
★★★*Bovenste Molen* Bovenste Molenweg 12
☎41045 tx58393 rm65 ⇄85 Lift
B72.50–154 M12.50–35 Pn85 ≥ Pool
★★*Willhelmina* Kaldenkerkerweg 1 ☎16251
rm44 ⇄5 ▥5
★*Deckers* Mgr Nolensplein 44 ☎16858 rm10
ᵇ☒*AML* Wezelseweg 53E ☎96666 N☒ MB
G200
ᵇ☒*Brauckmann* Kaldenkerkerweg 97
☎17575 Opl
ᵇ☒*EVA* Tegelseweg 41 ☎13251 N☒ Bed/Vau
G10
ᵇ☒*Vanden Hombergh* Straelseweg 18
☎11441 N☒ Frd
ᵇ☒*Nefkens & Zonen* Straelseweg 52
☎12474 Peu
ᵇ☒24 *K Peters* Burg Bloemartsstr 30 ☎10455
N☒10990 N☒ Vlo

Venray Limburg 31,550 (☎04780) Map **4** C2
ᵇ☒*Van Haren* Maasheeseweg 24 ☎5300 Frd
G80

Vierhouten Gelderland 900 (☎05771)
Map **4** C3
★★★*Mallejan* Nunspeterweg 70 ☎241 rm42
⇄42 G Lift B55–110 M15–45 Pn95–100 ≥ ◯

Vlaardingen Zuid-Holland 78,350 (☎010)
Map **4** C2
★★★*Delta* Maasbd 15 ☎345477 tx23154
rm24 ⇄24 Lift B80–140 Màlc Pool
ᵇ☒*EVAG* Boslaan 6 ☎344144 N☒ Frd

Vlissingen (Flushing) Zeeland 43,850
(☎01184) Map **3** B2
★★★*Britannia* bd Evertsen 44 ☎13255 rm35
⇄35 Lift B75–115 M15–27.50
Pn117.50–137.50 Sea
★★*Strand* bd Evertsen 4 ☎12297 rm36 ⇄10
▥26 Lift B51–105 Pn69.50–142 Sea
ᵇ☒*P Kruger* Pres-Roosveltlaan 754 ☎12008
N☒ M/c
ᵇ☒*Centrum Zeeland* Coosje Buskenstr 127
☎12866 N☒ Bed/Vau

ᵇ☒*Muynck's* P-Krugerstr 237 ☎19010 N☒
M/c BL/Tri

Volendam Noord-Holland 13,950
(☎02993) Map **4** C3
★★*Van Diepen* Haven 35 ☎3705 rm18 ▥10 G
B65–75 (double) M10–22.50 Sea

Voorschoten Zuid-Holland 21,350 (☎01717)
Map **4** C2/3
ᵇ☒*Karand* Hofweg 39 ☎69307 N☒ G350

Wageningen Gelderland 26,466 (☎08370)
Map **4** C2
ᵢ☒24 *Van der Kolk* Stationstr 21 ☎19155
Frd G100

Warnsveld Gelderland 7,100 (☎05750)
Map **4** C3
★★★*Kap* Rijksstraatweg 166 ☎14323 rm22
⇄5 ▥7 G 2 Jan–28 Dec B25–67 M16.50
Pn45.50–106

Wassenaar Zuid-Holland 28,250 (☎01751)
Map **4** C3
★★*Bianca* Gravestr 1 ☎19206 rm14 (A4) ▥10
LD B57.50–90 M17.50.Pn70–75
★★*Duinoord* Wassenaarse Slag 26 ☎12961
rm20 ⇄5 ▥4 B29–95 M25–40
☒*A Blankespoor* Oostdorperweg 29 ☎12405
N☒ BL/Jag/Rov/Tri
ᵇ☒*Jansen* Rijksstraatweg 773 ☎79940
Aud/VW

Wittem See Gulpen

Zaandam Noord-Holland 69,300 (☎075)
Map **4** C3
☒*Kraanedbijf Hoogwout* Hoffemastrad 16
☎162337 G5
ᵇ☒*Verenigde* ☎172751 N☒ Frd

Zandvoort Noord-Holland 16,300 (☎02507)
Map **4** C3
★★★*Bouwes* Badhuisplein 7 ☎5041 tx41096
rm59 ▥59 Lift LD B55–110 M22.50 Pn81 Sea
★★*Bernsen* (n rest) Hogeweg 70 ☎2202 rm13
▥6 Apr–6 Sep B19.50–50
★★*Hoogland* Westerparkstr 5 ☎5541 rm26
⇄1 ▥23 Feb–Dec B39.50–64

Zeist Utrecht 58,650 (☎03404) Map **4** C2
★★*'t Kerckebosch* Arnhemse Bovenweg 31
☎14772 tx40827 rm31 ⇄13 ▥13
B42.50–110 Màlc
ᵇ☒*J J Molenaar's* 2e Hogeweg 109 ☎18041
N☒ BL/Jag/Rov/Tri G5
ᵇ☒*A F Philippo* Laan Van Cattenbroeck 23
☎14529 N☒ Toy

Zutphen Gelderland 28,200 (☎05750)
Map **4** D3
★★*'s-Gravenhof* Kuiperstr 11 ☎13917 rm12
⇄3 ▥5
ᵇ☒*H Nijendijk* Spittaalstr 34 ☎15257 N☒ BL
ᵢ☒24 *Zutphen* Stationsplein 25 ☎10711 N☒
Frd G10

Zwolle Overijssel 77,850 (☎05200) Map **4** D3
☆☆*Postiljon* Hertsenbergweg 1 ☎160131
tx42180 rm72 ⇄72 B62–92
★★★*Wientjes* Stationsweg 7 ☎11200 rm28
⇄17 B54–134 M22
★★*Gytenbeek* Stationsplein 13 ☎10910 rm39
⇄10 ▥5
ᵢ☒24 *All-Round* Ceintuurbaan 7 ☎42300
Lnc/Maz
ᵇ☒*Autobedrijf Smit* Ceintuurbaan 3 ☎32555
Opl
ᵇ☒*Spaay* Assendorperdijk 44 ☎13183 N☒
BL/Jag/Rov/Tri
ᵇ☒*Vapro* Katwolderweg 28 ☎14909 N☒
Bed/Dat/Vau

PORTUGAL

Population 8,545,120 Area 34,500 sq miles Maps 17, 18, 23 & 24

How to get there   The usual approach to Portugal is via France and Spain, entering Spain on the Biarritz to San Sebastián road at the western end of the Pyrenees. The distance from the Channel ports to Lisbon, the capital, is nearly 1,300 miles, a distance which will require three or four night stops. The driving distance can be shortened by using one of the car/sleeper services from Boulogne or Paris to Biarritz.

Travel information

AA Port agents   **Lisbon 2** Sociedade Comercial Garland, Laidley SARL, Travessa do Corpo Santo, 10–20, PO Box 2127 ☎363191/5

Oporto Sociedade Comercial Garland, Laidley SARL, 131 rua Infante D Henrique, ☎27091/27095

Accidents   **Fire, police,** and **ambulance** Public emergency service ☎115. There are no firm rules of procedure after an accident, however, the recommendations on page 21 are advised.

Accommodation   A list of hotels is available from the Tourist Office in London. Hotels are officially approved and classified by the office of the Secretary of State for Information and Tourism. Details of officially authorised charges must be exhibited in the reception area, and in every bedroom. There is normally a 10% service charge, and at resorts an extra charge of 3.1% is payable. The cost of meals served in bedrooms, other than breakfast, is subject to an increase of 10%. Children under eight years of age are granted a discount of 50% on prices of meals.

While commendations and complaints about hotels are an important source of information to us, members may also like to know that an official complaints book, which must be kept in all establishments, enables guests to record their comments.

Complaints may also be made in writing to local Tourism Delegations and Boards or to the State Tourism Department, Palácio Foz, Praça dos Restauradores, Lisbon. The Government has encouraged the building of well-equipped hotels, particularly in the Algarve region. Tourist inns known as *pousadas* and *estalagems* are controlled by the

Portugal

Direcção General de Turismo, the official Portuguese tourist organisation; details of most of these are included in the gazetteer.

Pousadas are Government-owned but privately run. They have been specially built or converted, and are often located in the more remote touring areas where there is a lack of other hotels. Visitors may not usually stay more than five nights.

Estalagems are small, well-equipped wayside inns (although there are some in towns), privately-owned and run, and normally in the one- or two-star category.

Breakdowns
If your car breaks down, try to move it to the verge of the road so that it obstructs the traffic flow as little as possible and place a warning triangle. Should you break down or need assistance on the Ponte Abril 25 (on the southern approach to Lisbon), keep the vehicle as near to the right-hand side of the bridge as possible, remain in the vehicle and hang a white handkerchief out of the window. You must wait inside the vehicle until the road patrol arrives. Vehicles must not be towed, except by purpose-built vehicles, or pushed by hand on the bridge. If you run out of petrol you can buy 10 litres (2gal 1½pt) at a cost of Esc 200 from the bridge authorities.

If you require roadside assistance you should telephone the nearest breakdown centre operated by the *Automóvel Club de Portugal* (ACP) who will help you but will charge for their services. AA members should produce their *5-Star Travel Booklet.* The ACP operates a 24-hour breakdown service in the following locations: Lisbon ☎777354 & 775475, Coimbra ☎(0039) 26813 and Oporto ☎(02) 29273.

British Consulates
Figueira da Foz Qunita de Santa Maria, Estrada da Tavarede ☎22235

Lisbon rua São Domingos à Lapa 35/39 ☎661191, 661122, 661147

Portimão rua Santa Isabel 21–1° Esq ☎(0082) 23071

Vila Real de Santo Antonio rua General Humberto Delgado 4 ☎29

Crash helmets
It is compulsory for all riders of motorcycles to wear crash helmets.

Currency and banking
The unit of currency is the escudo, which is divided into 100 centavos; 1,000 escudos are known as 1 conto.

It is prohibited to import or export more than Esc1,000 in Portuguese currency. There is no restriction on the importation of foreign currencies or travellers' cheques, which must be declared at the Customs on entry if it exceeds Esc20,000. Amounts in excess of this figure may only be exported if they tally with the amount declared on entry.

Banking hours
Banks are usually open from Monday to Friday 09.00–12.00hrs and 14.00–15.30hrs.

Dimensions and weight restrictions
Private cars and trailers are restricted to the following dimensions and weights:

Cars
height 4 metres;
width 2.5 metres;

Trailers
length 12 metres;
weights (unladen) 750kg (14cwt 85lb)

if the towing vehicle's engine is 2,500cc or less; 1,500kg (1 ton 9cwt 59lb) for vehicles with an engine capacity in excess of 2,500cc but under 3,500cc.

Vehicle/trailer combination length 18 metres.

Ferries
All details are subject to alteration.

Vila Real de Santo Antonio—Ayamonte (Spain)
Map 23 B2 **(across River Guadiana)**

Service
There is an hourly service from 09.00 to 20.00hrs, or when at least two cars have cleared Customs.

Additional services are available on request (double fare payable).
Duration 15 minutes

Charges

Vehicles	cars	Esc60–190	or the equivalent
Passengers		Esc9	in Spanish currency

Small river ferry boats are used, and the loading of caravans may be difficult and complicated. Only small numbers of vehicles can be carried on each service.

Portugal

Holidays and events	Holidays based on religious festivals are not always fixed on the calendar but any current diary will give actual dates. The Whit period (a religious holiday) should not be confused with the British Spring Holiday.	

Fixed holidays

1 January	New Year's Day
25 April	Portugal's Day
1 May	Labour Day
10 June	National Day
13 June	St Anthony's Day (Lisbon only)
24 June	St John's Day (Oporto only)
15 August	Assumption
5 October	Republic Day
1 November	All Saints' Day
1 December	Independence Day
8 December	Immaculate Conception
24, 25 December	Christmas

Moveable holidays

Shrove Tuesday
Good Friday
Corpus Christi

Annual events

March — **Braga** Grand religious ceremonies and processions for Holy Week

April — **Loule** Fair of Our Lady of Piety

May — **Sesimbra** Procession of Our Lord Jesus of the Wounds

June — **Santarém** Great Annual Fair at Ribatejo
Evora Annual Fair of St John
Lisbon Festival of Popular Saints
Sintra Fair of St Peter and San Pedro of Penaferrim

July — **Vila Franca de Xira** Great Festival of Red Waistcoat
Faro Fair of Our Lady of Carmo
Covilhã Fair and Festival of St James

August — **Guimarães** Great Festival and Fair of St Walter
Rio Caldo (Terras do Bouro) Pilgrimage of St Benedict of the Open Door

September — **Lamego** Pilgrimage of Our Lady of the Needy
Nazaré Great Annual Festival of Our Lady of Nazaré

November — **Golegã** St Martin's Annual Fair (horse show)

A more comprehensive list of events can be obtained from the National Tourist Office (see page 244).

Insurance

Third Party insurance is not compulsory. See page 11.

Lights

Parking lights must be used in badly-lit areas and when visibility is poor. The use of full headlights is prohibited in built-up areas.

Medical treatment

There is no free medical treatment for visitors.

Motoring club

The Autómovel Club de Portugal (ACP) which has its headquarters at rua Rosa Araújo 24–26, Lisbon has offices in a number of provincial towns. They will assist motoring tourists generally and supply information on touring and other matters. Some of their more specialised services may have to be paid for but if you are an AA member you should produce your *5-Star Travel Booklet*.

Portugal

ACP offices are normally open 09.30—12.45 and 14.30—17.00hrs Monday to Friday; English and French are spoken. Offices are closed on Saturday and Sunday but the ACP operates a 24-hour breakdown service in and around Lisbon, Coimbra and Oporto (see Breakdowns).

Nationality plate The penalty for failure to display a nationality plate, or for displaying one of the wrong size or type, is a fine of Esc200.

Overtaking Vehicles more than 2 metres wide must stop, if need be, to facilitate passing.

Parking Parking is forbidden in the following places: within 20 metres (66ft) of a junction, bend, or rise with limited visibility, on a main road outside a built-up area, and within 5 metres (16½ft) of any other cross-roads or road intersection; on a main road or one carrying fast-moving traffic; on or near tram lines; opposite another stationary vehicle; within 15 metres (48½ft) of a bus stop and 3 metres (10ft) off a tram stop. At night parking is prohibited on all roads outside built-up areas.

Vehicles parked on the side of the road must be left facing in the direction of the traffic flow, except where regulations decree otherwise or where parking is allowed on only one side of the road.
Spending the night in a vehicle by the roadside is prohibited.

There are short-term parking areas known as blue zones in some towns; in these areas, parked cars must display a disc on the windscreen. Discs are set at the time of parking, and show when parking time expires according to the limit in the area concerned. They are obtainable free of charge from the local police or the motoring club. Failure to observe zonal regulations could result in a fine or the vehicle being towed away. There are a few parking meters in Oporto.

Petrol The approximate price of petrol per litre is: super (98 octane) Esc21; normal (85 octane) Esc18.

Police fines Police are empowered to impose on-the-spot fines of up to Esc1,000. The officer collecting the fine should issue an official receipt.

Postal and telephone charges Rates for mail to the United Kingdom are:

Airmail and surface mail	Esc
Postcards	6.00
Letters 5—20gm	8.50
20—50gm	15.00
50—100gm	20.00

Post offices are open 24 hours in Lisbon at Praça dos Restauradores and at the airport, and in Oporto at the Município.

The address of the *poste restante* office in Lisbon is Praça do Comércio.

Telephone rates The cost of a 3-minute call to the UK is Esc90. A local call costs Esc1.50. Trunk services are available and there are English-speaking operators for international calls. In Lisbon and Oporto there is an automatic dialling system in use. Public call boxes are red.

Roads Main roads and most of the important secondary roads are good, as are the mountain roads of the north-east.

Motorways There are about 43 miles of motorway (*auto estrada*) open; more sections are under construction and 200 miles of toll motorways are planned for completion by 1981. Most of the motorways are part of the European international network. The main stretches open to traffic are:

E3   Lisbon—Vila Franca de Xira—Carregado
     (toll: Esc5 for cars)
E4   Lisbon—Ponte Abril 25†—Fogueteiro (for Setúbal)
     (toll: see below)
E50 Porto (Oporto) bypass

†**Ponte Abril 25** Pedestrians, bicycles, and bicycles with auxiliary motors of less than 50cc, are prohibited. Drivers must maintain a speed of 30—60kph (18—37mph) on the bridge. Speed is checked by radar. Heavy vehicles must keep at least 20 metres (66ft) behind the preceding vehicle.

Portugal

Toll bridges

River Tagus bridges *Map 23 A4*

Ponte Abril 25

	Esc
Cars	
up to 3.30 metres	10
3.30–4.70 metres	20
over 4.70 metres	25
Caravans/trailers	*plus* 15
Motorcycles – over 50cc	10
under 50cc not permitted	

Ponte Setembro 28

Cars
7.50 Single
12.50 Return

Winter conditions

The winter months in the northern provinces are usually rainy, but snow is rare except in the Estrela mountains.

Shopping hours

Shops are usually open Monday to Friday 09.00–13.00hrs and 15.00–19.00hrs and Saturday 09.00–13.00hrs. Markets are open Monday to Saturday 07.00–13.00hrs.

Speed

The beginning of a built-up area is indicated by a sign bearing the placename; there are no signs showing the end – the only indication is the sign for the beginning of the area (on the other side of the road) for motorists coming from the other direction. In built-up areas the limit is 60kph (37mph), or 50kph (31mph) for vehicles towing trailers. Outside built-up areas private vehicles must not exceed 120kph (74mph) on motorways and 90kph (56mph) on other roads. Vehicles towing trailers must not exceed 70kph (43mph) outside built-up areas. There is a minimum speed limit of 40kph (24mph) on motorways, except where otherwise signposted.

Leaflets giving details in English are handed to visitors at entry points. Also see Motorways, above.

Tourist information centres

The Portuguese National Tourist Office, 1/5 New Bond Street, London W1Y 9PE ☎01-493 3873, will be pleased to assist you with information regarding tourism. Within Portugal an office of the Direcção General de Turismo is in Lisbon at Palacio Foz, Praça dos Restauradores ☎367031 and local information offices will be found in most provincial towns under this name or one of the following: Comissão Municipal de Tourismo, Junta de Turismo or Câmara Municipal.

Visitors' registration

A visitor staying overnight should report to the police, but this is often done by the hotel or campsite management who complete the registration form. If you are staying with friends the host should notify the authorities.

Warning triangles

Triangles are compulsory for all vehicles except motorcycles, mopeds, and scooters. They must be placed 30 metres (33yd) behind the obstacle and must be visible to following traffic from 100 metres (109yd).

Prices are in escudos

Abbreviations:

av	avenida
Capt	Captain
Cdt	Commandant
espl	esplanade
r	rua

Abrantes Santarém 9,050 Map **23** B4
★★★***Turismo*** Largo de Santo António ☎256 rm24 ⇌24 G 🎾 Pool Lake
J dos Santos Bioucas Estrada Nacional 2 ☎160 N✱ Aud/BL/MB G15

Albergaria a Velha Aveiro 3,620 (☎0034) Map **17** A2
☆**Alameda** (n rest) Estrada Nacional ☎52409 Map **17** A2 rm18 ⇌18 G B180–410

Albufeira Faro 7,480 Map **23** A2
★★★★**Balaia** Praia M-Luisa ☎52681 rm186 ⇌186 Lift B890–1320 M260 Pn1390–1500 🎾 Pool Beach Sea
★★★***Sole e Mar*** ☎52121 tx8217 Gong 1 P rm74 ⇌74 Lift
★★***Estalagem do Cerro*** ☎52191 rm50 ⇌33 Lift Sea
★★***Estalagem Mar à Vista*** Cerro da Piedade ☎52154 rm42 ⇌32 ⋒6 Lift

Alcácer do Sal Setúbal 13,190 Map **23** A3
★★***Estalagem da Barrosinha*** Estrada Nacional 5 ☎62363 rm15 (A) ⇌12

Alcobaça Leiria 4,800 (☎0044) Map **23** A4
Assessor Quinta da Roda ☎43032 N✱
CIVEAI Quinta da Roda ☎42302 N✱

Alijó Vila Real 2,200 (☎0099) Map **17** B2
★***Pousada Barão de Forrester*** ☎62215 rm12 ⇌3 ⋒3 G

Aljubarrota Leiria 5,795 Map **17** A1
★***Estalagem do Cruzeiro*** ☎42112 rm13 (A4) ⇌6 ⋒2 G

Alpedrinha Castelo Branco 1,410 Map **17** B1
★**Estalagem São Jorge** ☎57154 rm10 ⇌4 ⋒4 (closed Sep) B340–485(double) M140 Pn450–780 St%

Amarante Porto 4,000 (☎0025) Map **17** B2
At **Serra do Marão** (25km E on N15 to Vila Real)
★★**Pousada de São Gonçalo** Serra do Marão ☎46113 rm18 ⇌14 G B250–450 M130–160 Pn510–710

Areias de Pêra Faro (3km E of **Armacão de Pêra**) Map **23** A2
★★***Estalagem São Jorge*** ☎Armaçao de Pera 55204 rm25 (A) ⇌19 ⋒5 G

Armacão de Pêra Faro 1,790 (☎0082) Map **23** A2
★★★***Estalagem Algar*** av Beira-Mar ☎55353 rm18 ⇌18 1 Mar–31 Oct
★★★***Garbe*** ☎55187 tx18285 rm104 ⇌85 Lift Pool

Aveiro Aveiro 19,460 (☎0034) Map **17** A2
★★**Arcada** (n rest) r Viana do Castelo 4 ☎23001 rm55 ⇌38 Lift B210–520
M dos Santos Gamelas av 5 de Outubro 18 ☎22031 M/c BL/Tri G10
Agencia Commercial Ria r Conselheiro L Magalhães 15 ☎23011 MB
Stand Justino Largo L-de Camões 2 ☎23593 N✱ GM

Azeitão Setúbal Map **23** A3
★**Estalagem Quintas das Torres** ☎2080001 rm12 (A2) ⇌10 B330–500

Barcelos Braga 4,150 (☎0023) Map **17** A2
Avenida ☎82019 Cit/Ren G30
Castro r F-Borges ☎82008 BL/MB G20

Beja Beja 19,190 (☎0079) Map **23** B3
Cameirinha Terreiro dos Valentes 5 ☎23192 N✱ MB/Peu/Ren G20
Costa & Silva r de Lisboa ☎24161 Bed/Opl/Vau G15
Mabor av M-Fernandes 27 ☎22191 N✱ BL/BMW
Stand Castilho r G-Palma 21 ☎22591 N✱ BL G10

Braga Braga 37,630 (☎0023) Map **17** A2
Ranhada & Teixeira av MI G-da Costa 20 ☎22913 N☎22912 Frd G20

Bragança Bragança 10,970 Map **18** C2
★★**Pousada de São Bartolomeu** Estrada de Turismo ☎22493 rm15 (A5) ⇌10 ⋒2 G B280–510 M160 Pn670–770

Bucaco (Bussaco) Aveiro 3,696 Map **17** A1
★★★★***Palace*** ☎Mealhada 93101 rm93 ⇌93 G Lift

Caldas de Rainha Leiria 15,010 (☎0012) Map **23** A4
★**Central** Largo do Dr J-Barbosa 22 ☎22078 rm40 ⇌7 ⋒4 B182–480 Màlc
Auto Mecanica r Tenente Cl-Santos Costa 22 ☎22947 BL/Cit/MB
A Flóres r Heróís da Grande Guerra 104 ☎23011 AR/Hon/Peu/Ren G4
Leira r Capt F-de Sousa ☎22561 N✱ Frd
UNICAL Estrada da Tornada ☎22383 M/c Aud/Chy/Sim/VW

Canas de Senhorim Viseu 2,075 (☎0032) Map **17** B1
At **Urgeiriça** (1km NE on N234)
★★★**Urgeiriça** ☎67267 rm76 (A17) ⇌5 B220–580 M140 Pn430–500 🎾 Pool

Caramulo Viseu (☎0032) Map **17** A1
★***Estalagem de São Jeronimo*** ☎86291 rm6 ⇌6 G

Carcavelos Lisboa 7,300 Map **23** A4
★★***Estalagem Rota do Sol*** r Jorge V ☎2470152 rm15 ⇌6 ⋒6

Cascais Lisboa 20,540 Map **23** A4
★★★★**Estoril Sol** ☎282831 tx12624 rm404 ⇌404 G Lift LD B480–1100 M200 Pn700–800 Pool Beach Golf Sea
★★★***Baia*** Estrada Marginal ☎281033 rm59 ⇌59 G Lift Sea
★★★***Estalagem Albatroz*** r F-Aronca 100 ☎282821 rm16 ⇌16 Lift
★★★***Nau*** r Dr-I-Doyle Lote 14 ☎282861 rm34 ⇌34 G Lift Sea
★★***Estalagem Solar D-Carlos*** r Latino Coelho 8 ☎280961 rm9 ⇌6
Rali av J-F-Ulrich ☎280531 Frd
Reparadora de Cascais r das Amendoeiras ☎289045 N✱ BL
At **Praia do Guincho** (4km W)
★★★★***Guincho*** ☎289325 rm36 ⇌36 G Lift 🎾 Beach Sea
★★***Estalagem do Forte*** (Muchaxo) ☎2850342 rm24 ⇌24 Pool Beach Sea
★★**Estalagem Mar do Guincho** ☎2850251 rm13 ⇌13 B180–500 M140 Pn460–610 Sea

Castelo Branco Castelo Branco 21,730 Map **17** B1
Avenida av MI-Carmona 75 ☎421 N✱ M/c BL/Mor G40
Da Biera r de Santo António 1 ☎190 Dat G10
24 Mocambicana estrada da Cruz de Montalvao ☎1310 Chy/Sim G20

Castelo do Bode See **Tomar**

Castelo do Vide Portalegre 3,420 (☎0045) Map **23** B4
★★***Estalagem de São Paulo*** ☎111 rm43 ⇌43 G

Chaves Vila Real 11,470 Map **17** B2

Portugal

★★Estalagem Santiago (n rest) r do Olival
☎22545 rm31 ⇆31 B230–564

🏠 **Auto-Mecanica** r do Sarugueiro
☎22485 M/c G50

🏠 **Moderna** Largo do Tabolado ☎257 M/c
BL G10

Coimbra Coimbra 24,350 (☎0039)
Map **17** A1
★★★Bragança Largo das Ameias 10
☎22171 ta Brazanzotel rm83 ⇆57 🏠26 Lift
🏠 **Carvalho & Sobrinho** r M-Almeida e
Sousa ☎27071 N🕭 Ren
🏠 **Coimbra** Largo das Ameias 11 ☎22038
Frd G30
🏠 **Industrial** av F-de Magalhães ☎27123
GM G25
🏠 **S José** av F-de Magalhães 216 ☎25578
BL/Tri G20

Colares Sintra 5,500 Map **23** A4
★Estalagem do Conde Quinta do Conde
☎2991652 rm11 ⇆11 1 Feb–31 Oct
B335–620 M150 Sea
At **Praia das Macãs** (4km NW by N375)
★★★Miramonte ☎2991230 rm92 ⇆92
B330–440(double) M140 Pn500 Pool

Costa da Caparica Setúbal 2,660
Map **23** A4
★★Estalagem Colobri ☎3200776 rm25
⇆25 🏠25 Lift
★★Estalagem Rosa dos Ventos r Dr-C-Freire
☎2400303 ta Rosaventos rm27 ⇆20 🏠7
May–Oct

Covilhã Castelo Branco 25,280 (☎0059)
Map **17** B1
🏠 **Valente & Irmãos** r Rui Faleira 37
☎22746 N🕭 Frd G20

Curia Aveiro 2,810 (☎0031) Map **17** A1
★★★Palace ☎Mealhada 52131 rm225 ⇆90
G Lift 1 May–15 Oct 🏊 Pool

Elvas Portalegre 14,550 Map **23** B3
★★Estalagem D Sancho II 20 Praça
D-Sancho II ☎2127 rm24 Lift
★Pousada de Santa Luzia (outside the walls
of Elvas on the main road from Borba to
Badajoz) ☎194 rm11 ⇆9
🏠 **Autunes & Guerra** av Badajoz ☎22341
M/c GM G15
At **Praia de Faro** (8km SW)
★★Estalagem Aeromar ☎23542 rm18 ⇆18
Lift Sea

Ericeira Lisboa 2,570 Map **22** A4
★★Estalagem Morais r M-Bombarda 3
☎54611 rm40 ⇆21 🏠19 Lift Pool Sea

Espinho Aveiro 11,640 (☎02) Map **17** A2
★★★Praia Golfe ☎920630 rm119 ⇆119 G Lift
B415–600 M170 Pn755 Pool Golf Sea

Esposende Braga 1,530 (☎0023)
Map **17** A2
★★Estalagem do Zende Estrada Nacional
☎89333 rm14 ⇆14 🏊
★★Suave Mar av E-Duarte Pacheco
☎89445 rm46 (A2) ⇆37 🏠9 B240–560
M110–150 Pn380–400 🏊 Pool

Estoril Lisboa 15,740 Map **23** A4
★★★★★Palacio ☎260400 tx12757 rm170
⇆170 Lift B1020–1485 M250 Pn1159 Pool
Golf Sea
★★★★Cibra Estrada Marginal ☎261811 rm89
(A11) ⇆89 Lift Sea
★★★Estalagem Claridade r Mouzinho de
Albuquerque 14 ☎263434 rm12 ⇆12
B215–570 M140 Pn420–740 Sea
★★★Estalagem Lennox Country Club
r Infante de Sagres 5 ☎260424 ta Lennox
Estoril rm17 (A7) ⇆17 Lift LD B625–1260
M175 Pool Lake Sea

246

★★The Founder's Inn r A-Henriques 11
☎262221 rm12 ⇆12 B175–250 Màlc
At **Monte-Estoril**
★★★Atlântico Estrada Marginal ☎260270
rm101 (A) ⇆101 G Lift Pool Sea
★★★Grande av Sabóia ☎264609 rm73 ⇆67
🏠6 Lift 🏊 Pool Sea
★★★Miramar r do Pinheiro 1 ☎264050 rm49
⇆47 🏠4 Lift B210–520 M140 Pn280–610
Pool Sea
🏠 **Gomes** Largo de Ostende 4 ☎260021 N🕭 BL

Estremoz Évora 9,570 Map **23** B3
★★★Pousada da Rainha Santa Isabel
Castelo de Estremoz ☎648 rm23 ⇆23 Lift

Évora Évora 35,410 (☎0069) Map **23** B3
★★★★Pousada Dos Lóios ☎24051 rm29
⇆28 B460–600 M150–180
★★★Planicie r M-Bombarda 40 ☎24026
rm33 ⇆33 Lift B335–545 M160 Pn745–779 Sea
🏠 **Lagril** r Dr A-Jose de Almeida 5 ☎22083
N🕭 Chy/Sim

Faro Faro 21,580 (☎0089) Map **23** A/B2
★★★★Eva av de República ☎24054 tx18224
rm150 ⇆124 🏠26 Lift LD B380–840 M190
Pn675–725 Pool Sea
★★★Faro Praça D-F-Gomes 2 ☎22076 rm52
⇆52 Lift B275–720 M170 Pn477–615
★★Albacor (n rest) r Brites de Almeida 25
☎22093 rm39 ⇆39 🏠2 Lift
🏠24 **Farauto** Largo do Mercado 51
☎23032 N🕭 23033 M/c GM
🏠 **Gharb** r do Alportel 121a ☎23071 N🕭 Cit
🏠 **Monumental** r D-Joao de Castro 4–6
☎26406 Chy/Sim G20
🏠 **H D Santos** r dos Bombeiros Portugueses
13 ☎24330 N🕭 BL/Tri
🏠 **UTIC** r Dr Francisco de Sousa Vaz
☎24936 N🕭 Ren
At **Praia de Faro** (8km SW)
★★Estalagem Aeromar ☎23542 rm20
⇆20 Feb–Nov B435–670 M140

Fátima Santarém 6,430 (☎0049) Map **17** A1
★★★Fátima ☎97251 rm76 ⇆76 Lift
★★Estalagem Os Três Pastorinhas Cova da
Iria ☎97229 rm92 ⇆92 G Lift

Figueira da Foz Coimbra 14,560 (☎0033)
Map **17** B1
★★★★Figueira av Dr O-Salazar ☎22146
rm110 ⇆54 🏠56 Lift Sea
★★Portugal (n rest) r da Liberdade 41
☎22176 rm50 ⇆15 🏠15 G Jul–Sep
🏠 **Carvalho e Sobrinho** r Dr L-Carriço 20
☎24473 N🕭 Ren

Foz do Arelho Leiria 650 (☎0012)
Map **23** A4
★★Facho ☎97110 rm45 ⇆25 G Lake

Fundão Castelo Branco 5,080 (☎0059)
Map **17** B1
★★Estalagem da Neve r de São Sebastião
☎52215 rm12 ⇆9
🏠 **Maful** r A-Pinto ☎52372 BL/Toy G

Guarda Guarda 14,590 Map **17** B1
★★★De Turismo Largo de São Francisco
☎206 rm96 ⇆96 G Lift B235–500 M170
Pn545 Pool
★★Aliança r V-da Gama ☎22135 rm6 (A10)
⇆16 B200–320
★★Filipe r V-da Gama 9 ☎659 rm32 ⇆7
🏠 **J Carvalho dos Santos** Largo Serpa
Pinto 13 ☎121 N🕭 M/c BMW/VW G10
🏠 **Graca Morais** r Vasco da Gama ☎22259
N🕭 Chy/Hon/Maz/Ren/Sim G20
🏠 **Neofor** r D-Luis I 20 ☎57 Frd G5

Lagos Faro 10,360 (☎0082) Map **23** A2
★★★Meia Praia ☎62001 tx18289 rm65 ⇆65
Lift LD B270–880 M170 Pn365–720 🏊 Pool
Beach 🌊 Sea

★★★ *São Cristóvão* Rossio de São João
☎63051 rm80 ⇌80 Lift Lake
★★ *Mar Azul* (n rest) ☎62181 rm18 ⇌14 🏠1
B150—365 Sea
★★ *Pensão Dona Ana* Praia de Dona Ana
☎62322 rm11 ⇌5 Apr—Oct

Lamego Viseu 10,350 (☎0032) Map **17** B2
★ *Estalagem de Lamego* (n rest) ☎62162
rm7 ⇌5 G
🛏🕭 *Calauto* R D J de Silva Campos Neves
☎62445 N🖢 BL G

Leca do Balio Porto Map **17** A2
★★★ *Estalagem Via Norte* Estrada via Norte
☎9480294 rm12 ⇌12 G B395—940 M170
Pn690—890 Pool

Leiria Leiria 10,290 (☎0044) Map **17** A1
★★★ *Euro-Sol* r Dr J-Alves da Silva ☎24101
rm54 ⇌54 G Lift Pool
★★ *Estalagem Claras* av Heróis de Angola
☎22373 rm11 ⇌11 B285—470 Pn510
★ *Central* r V-da Gama 5 ☎22442 rm41 ⇌41
🛏🕭 *Industrial* r Capt Mouzinho de
Albuquerque ☎24061 N🖢 GM G20
🛏🕭 *Industriauto* r de Tomar ☎22643 BL/Tri
G20
🛏🕭 *F H da Rocha Marquês* Largo Cónego
Maia 314 ☎23882 MB/MG/Mor

Lisboa (Lisbon) Lisboa 782,270 Map **23** A4
See Plan

| AA | agents; see page 240 |

★★★★★ *Ritz* r R-da Fonseca ☎684131 Plan **1**
tx12589 rm306 ⇌306 G Lift B1083—1411 Sea
★★★★ *Avenida Palace* r de Dezembro 123
☎30154 Plan **2** tx1815 Palace P rm95 ⇌95
Lift
★★★★ *Eduardo VII* av Fontes Pereira de
Mello 5 ☎530141 Plan **3** ta Eduardotel rm100
⇌100 Lift
★★★★ *Fénix* Praça Marquês de Pombal 8
☎535121 Plan **4** ta Husa tx1170 Husa rm125
⇌125 Lift
★★★★ *Flórida* Duque de Palmela 32
☎576145 Plan **5** tx12256 rm120 ⇌120 G Lift
B587—960 M195 Pn780
★★★★ *Mundial* r D-Duarte 4 ☎863101 Plan **6**
tx12308 rm146 ⇌146 Lift B507—721 M195
Pn800
★★★★ *Plaza* Travessa do Salitre 7 ☎363922
Plan **7** tx16402 rm100 ⇌100 Lift
B465—1050 M150
★★★★ *Tivoli* av da Liberdade 185 ☎530181
Plan **8** tx12588 rm344 ⇌344 G Lift
B705—1010 M200 Pn1060—1110
★★★ *Flamingo* r Castilho 41 ☎532191 Plan **9**
rm35 ⇌35 G Lift B375—590 M170&àlc Pn590
★★★ *Torre* r dos Jeronimos 8 ☎636262
Plan **10** rm52 ⇌52 Lift B360—580 M135
Pn545—720
★★ *Borges* r Garrett 108 ☎361952 Plan **12**
rm105 ⇌55 🏠50 Lift B335—580 M110—140
Pn395—470
★★ *Jorge V* r Mouzinho da Silveira 3
☎562525 Plan **13** rm49 ⇌49 Lift
★★ *Miraparque* av Sidonio Pais 12 ☎554181
Plan **14** tx16745 Mitel-P rm100 ⇌100 Lift
B380—590 M140 Pn540
★★ *Principe* av Duque de Avila 199 ☎536151
Plan **15** rm54 ⇌54 Lift
★ *Estalagem do Cavalo Branco* av A-Gago
Continho 146 ☎726121 Plan **16** rm24 (A) ⇌24
🛏🕭 *A M Almeida* r A-da Silva ☎2100787 N🖢
BL/Rov
🛏🕭 *Angolana* r Visconde Seabria 10A
☎770425 M/c G200
🛏🕭 *Conde Barão* av 24 de Julho 62 ☎671011
M/c (Lucas Agent) G5

🛏🕭 *J J Gonçalves* r A-Patricio 11e ☎767095
N🖢 BL/Jag/Tri
🛏🕭 *J J Gonçalves* r das Laranjeiras 12
☎782071 N🖢 & r Marquês sã da Bandeira 120
☎774773 BL
🛏🕭 *J J Gonçalves* r R-Sampaio 30 BL G40
🛏🕭 *Industrial* r A Herculano 66 ☎682041
Bed/Vau G20
🛏🕭 *Martins & Almeida* av Visconte Valmor 70a
☎773671 N🖢 Jag
🛏🕭 *J Mendes Coelho* r G-Freire 5a/f
☎539801 N🖢 Frd
🛏🕭 *Palma Morgado* av Visconde Valmor 68b
☎770584 N🖢 Lot
🛏🕭 *Rali* r C-Mardel 12 ☎562061 N🖢 Frd
🛏🕭 *Sovendo* av Infante Santo 13a ☎607116
N🖢 Cit

Luso Aveiro 2,480 (☎0031) Map **17** A1
★★★★ *Termas* ☎93450 ta Banhos rm157
⇌157 Lift 1 Jun—15 Oct B220—500 M170
Pn530—1120 🏊 Pool
★★ *Lusitano* r Costa Simões ☎93258 rm82
⇌9 G 1 Jun—30 Sep
★ *Estalagem do Luso* r Dr L-Pais Almoches
☎93114 rm8 ⇌8 🏊

Macedo de Cavaleiros Bragança 3,240‾
Map **17** B2
★ *Estalagem Caçador* Largo Pinto de Azevedo
☎56 rm22 ⇌6

Mangualde Viseu 4,840 (☎0032) Map **17** B1
★★ *Estalagem Cruz de Mata* Estrada
Nacional ☎62556 rm12 ⇌12

Matosinhos Porto (☎02) Map **17** A2
🛏🕭 *Brito* r Dr-A-Cordeiro 536 ☎933482 N🖢
Ren G40

Monte Estoril See **Estoril**

Monte Gordo Faro Map **23** B2
★★★ *Das Caravelas* ☎458 ta Caravelotel
tx18220 rm87 ⇌87 Lift LD B225—590 M170
Pn450—590 🏊 Pool Beach Sea
★★★ *Dos Navegadores* r Goncalso Velho
☎2490 tx18254 rm104 ⇌104 Lift
Last dinner 8pm 🏊 Pool
★★★ *Vasco da Gama* ☎321 tx18220 rm180
⇌180 Lift B225—375 M170 Pn450—590 🏊
Pool Beach Sea

Montes de Alvor See **Portimão**

Nazaré Leiria 8,550 Map **17** A1
★★★ *Dom Fuas* Estrada da Foz ☎46351
rm42 ⇌37 Apr—Oct LD B480(double) M140
Lift Sea
★★★ *Nazare* Largo Afonso Zupquete ☎46311
ta Hotedazare rm50 ⇌50 Lift B390—580
M165 Pn595 Sea
★★★ *Praia* av Vieira Guimaraes 39 ☎46423
rm40 ⇌40 Lift Sea

Óbidos Leiria 4,720 (☎0012) Map **23** A4
★★ *Estalagem do Covento* r Dr-J-de Ornelas
☎95217 rm13 ⇌13
★ *Pousada do Castelo* (on the Caldas da
Rainha-Torres Vedras-Lisbon road) ☎95105
rm6 ⇌3 B220—450 M130—160 Pn480—680

Oeiras Lisboa 14,880 Map **23** A4
☆☆ *Continental* Marine Drive ☎2431186
tx12669 rm140 ⇌140 G Pool Beach Sea

Ofir Braga (☎0023) Map **17** A2
★★★ *Estalagem do Parque do Rio* ☎89521
ta Riotur rm36 ⇌30 🏠6 Lift Apr—Oct B445—690
M150 Pn550 🏊 Pool
★★★ *Pinhal* Estrado do Mar ☎89473 rm100
⇌100 Lift 🏊 Pool Lake

Olhão Faro 10,830 (☎0089) Map **23** B2
★ *Caique* r Dr-O-Salazar 37 ☎72167 rm40
⇌40 G
🛏🕭 *C Santos* Estrada Nacional-Brancanes
☎72071 N🖢 BL/MB/Rov G200

247

Portugal

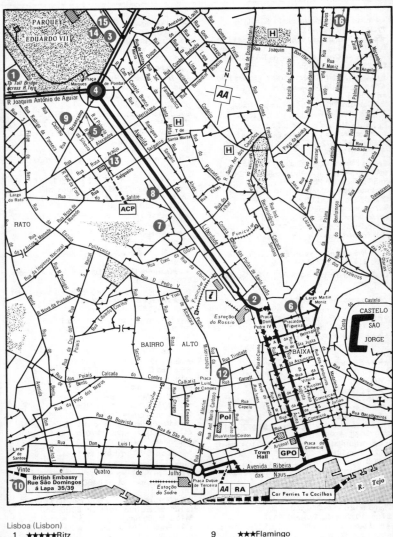

Lisboa (Lisbon)

1	★★★★★Ritz	9	★★★Flamingo
2	★★★★Avenida Palace	10	★★★Torre
3	★★★★Eduardo VII	12	★★Borges
4	★★★★Fénix	13	★★Jorge V
5	★★★★Flórida	14	★★Miraparque
6	★★★★Mundial	15	★★Principe
7	★★★★Plaza	16	★Estalagem do Cavalo Branco
8	★★★★Tivoli		

Oliveira de Azeméis Aveiro 7,600
Map **17** A2
i✿♨Justino av Dr-A-J-de Almeida ☎62061
GM G10

Oliveira do Hospital Coimbra 2,260
Map **17** B1
★★**Pousada Santa Barbara** ☎52252 rm17
⇌17 G B320–450 M130–160 Pn670–770

Oporto See **Porto**

Paredes Porto Map **17** A2
✿♨**Ružo Estacão de Servico e Sorcar** ☎22164
N♨ BL/Fia/Sim G10

Penafiel Porto Map **17** B2
♨✿♨ **Central de Penafiel** av de J-Júlio 213
☎22071 Aud/VW G8
✿♨ **Sameiro** r da Vista Alegre ☎22241 BL G10

Peniche Leiria 12,500 Map **23** A4
♨✿♨ **Patricio** av Dr-A-O-Salazar 14 ☎99233 BL
G52

Portalegre Portalegre 13,140 Map **23** B4
★**Alto Alenetejo** r 19 de Junho 59 ☎330 rm23
(A8) ⇌4 ▥4
i✿♨Portalegre r 1 de Maio 94 ☎167 M/c Frd G4
♨✿♨ **Rodrigues & Figueira** av Frei Amador
Arrais ☎1072 N♨ Opl

Portimão Faro 18,210 (☎0082) Map **23** A2
★★★★**Alvor Praia** Praia dos tres Irmaos
(5km SW) ☎24020 ta Salvor hotel tx18299
rm241 ⇌241 G Lift B620–1440 M280
Pn942.50–1220 ⚓ Pool Sea
★★**Estalagem Miradoiro** r Machado Santos
☎23011 rm30 ⇌30
★**Estalagem Mira-Foia** r V-Vaz das Vacas 33
☎22011 rm25 ⇌13 Lift
♨✿♨ **Anibal** Avenida 3 ☎22337 N♨ Ren G6
♨➤✿24 **Farauto** r D-Carlos 1 ☎23083 N♨
Cit/GM
♨✿♨**Pardal & Antónia** r D Carlos 1 ☎23227
N♨ Chy/Sim G10
✿♨ **Porti** av D Alfonso Henriques ☎22228 N♨
Aud/Cit/VW G50
At **Montes de Alvor** (5km W on N125)
★★★★**Penina-Golf** ☎22051 tx18207 rm200
⇌200 Lift G B675–1100 M270 Pn1185 ⚓
Pool Beach Golf Lake

Porto (Oporto) Porto 310,440 (☎02)
Map **17** A2

AA agents; see page 240

★★★★**Infante de Sagres** Praça Filipa de
Lancastre 62 (off av dos Aliados) ☎28101
tx22378 rm84 ⇌84 Lift B645–855 M280
Pn1145
★★★**Batalha** Praça de Batalha 116 ☎20571
tx25131 Hotbat rm147 ⇌70 ▥72 Lift
B375–650 M180 Pn685
★★★**Grande** r de Santa Catarina 197
☎28176 ta Grandotel rm100 ⇌95 ▥5 G Lift
★★★**Império** Praça de Batalha 130 (off r São
Ildefonso) ☎26861 rm95 ⇌95 Lift
♨✿♨**A M Almeida** r Costa Cabral 954
☎495045 N♨ BL/Rov
♨✿♨**M A de Freitas** r do Heróismo 291
☎54155 N♨ Frd
♨✿♨**J J Gonçalves** r do Heróismo 333
☎53179 N♨ BL/Jag/Tri
♨✿♨ **Moto Meca** r M-Pinto de Azevedo 574
☎63066 GM
i➤24 Palhinhas Camp Lindo 328 ☎485185
Cit G12
✿♨**Queiroz** r R-Ivens 749 ☎933199 N♨ M/c
G10
i✿♨ C Santos via Rápida ☎64165 BL/Rov
♨✿♨ **Stock** r de Sta Catarina 1891-1899
☎488785 N♨ Lnc/Maz

Praia da Rocha Faro 2,085 (☎0082)
Map **23** A2
★★★★★**Algarve** ☎24001 tx18247 rm200
⇌200 Lift B850–1390 M285 Pn1275–1530
⚓ Pool Sea
★★★**Estalagem Mira Sol** ☎24046 rm38 (A)
⇌38
★★**Bela Vista** ☎24055 rm27 ⇌27 Lift
★★**Estalagem Alcala** ☎24062 rm20 ⇌20
Sea
★★**Estalagem São José** ☎24037 rm25
(A14) ⇌22 ▥3 B315–720 M140 Pn490–700
Sea

Praia da Salema Faro (☎0082)
Map **23** A2
★★**Estalagem Infante do Mar** ☎65137
rm30 ⇌30 Pool

Praia das Macãs See **Colares**

Praia de Faro See **Faro**

Praia de Santa Cruz Lisboa (☎0011)
Map **23** A4
★★**Estalagem de Santa Cruz** r J-P-Lopes
☎8 rm32 ⇌32 Lift Sea

Praia do Guincho See **Cascais**

Riba de Ave Braga 2,800 Map **17** A2
★**Estalagem de São Pedro** ☎38 rm9 ⇌1

Rio de Mouro Lisboa 10,410 Map **23** A4
★★**Estalagem Gruta do Rio** av Gago
Coutinho 1 ☎2960535 rm6 ⇌3 ▥3 G Lake

Sagres Faro 1,200 (☎0082) Map **23** A2
★★★**Baleeira** ☎64212 tx18267 rm114
⇌114 LD B630–1230 M170 Pool Sea
★★**Estalagem Descobertas** Estrada Marginal
☎64251 rm17 ⇌17 1 Jan–31 Dec
★★**Pousada do Infante** Ponta da Atalaia
☎64222 rm15 ⇌15 G B410–510(double)
M130–160 Pn610–710 Sea

Santa Clara-a-Velha Beja 2,570
Map **23** A2
★★**Pousada de Santa Clara** Barragem
Marcello Caetrano ☎52250 rm6 ⇌6
B350–450(double) M130–160 Lake

Santa Luzia See **Viana do Castelo**

Santarém Santarém 20,030 (☎0043)
Map **23** A4
★★**Abidis** r Guilherme de Azevedo 4
☎22017 rm28 ⇌6

Santiago do Cacém Setúbal 5,890
(☎0017) Map **23** A3
★**Pousada de Santiago** (on the main road on
the descent into Santiago do Cacém) ☎22459
rm7 (A3) ⇌4 B280–510 M160 Pn350–890
Pool

São Bras de Alportel Faro 7,600
Map **23** B2
★**Pousada de São Bras** (in the Serra do
Caldeirão on the main road 5km N) ☎42305
rm17 (A) ⇌7 G

Serém Aveiro 1,108 Map **17** A2
★★**Pousada de Santo Antonio** Mourisca do
Vouga ☎52230 rm12 ⇌12 G B410–510
(double) M130–160 Pool

Serpa Beja 7,990 (☎0079) Map **23** B3
★★**Pousada de São Gens** ☎52327 rm18 (A)
⇌12 G

Serra do Marão See **Amarante**

Sesimbra Setúbal 16,610 Map **23** A3
★★★★**Do Mar** ☎2233326 rm119 ⇌119 Lift
B580–1500 M190 Pn750–1040 Pool Sea
★★★★**Espadarte** espl do Atlantico ☎2233189
rm80 ⇌80 Lift B380–680 M140 Pn500
★★**Nautico** (n rest) r Bairro Infante D-Henrique
☎2233233 rm15 (A3) ⇌15 Sea

Setúbal Setúbal 58,580 (☎04) Map **23** A3

Portugal

★★★★ Esperancea av L-Todi 220 ☎25151 rm76 ⇌54 ⋔23 Lift Sea
★★ Estalagem de São Filipo ☎23844 rm15 ⇌15 Sea
ⅰ☜ Bocage av Portela 43 ☎23169 BL
☖☜ Gemorauto av de Goa 30 ☎29012 GM
☖☜ A Marquês dos Santos av Combatentes da Grande Guerra 81 ☎23131 Frd

Sines Setúbal 7,000 (☎0017) Map **23** A3
★★★ Malhada r do Farol ☎62105 rm37 ⇌37

Sintra Lisboa 15,990 Map **23** A4
★★★★ Palacia de Seteais ☎2933200 rm18 ⇌18 G Lift B705–1110 M250 Pn1130 Sea
★★ Estalagem da Raposa (n rest) r Dr A-Costa 3 ☎2930465 rm8 ⇌6

Tavira Faro 10,260 (☎0081) Map **23** B2
★★★ Eurotel Quinta das Oliveiras ☎22041 tx12546 rm80 ⇌80 Lift B285–630 M150 ☜ Pool ∩ Sea

Tomar Santarém 16,470 (☎0049) Map **23** B4
★★ Estalagem de Santa Iria Parque do Mouchão ☎32427 rm10 ⇌7

At **Castelo do Bode**
★★ Pousada San Pedro ☎38159 rm17 ⇌17 Pool ∩ Lake

Torres Vedras Lisboa 14,830 (☎0011) Map **23** A4
☖☜ Agular & Oliveira r dos Polomos ☎23910 Cit G40
☖☜ Atlântica r Santos Bernardes 21 ☎22155 Aud/BL/MB/VW G10
☖☜ Fonsecas av 5 de Outubro 47 ☎23082 N☜ Opl
ⅰ☜ Foroeste Parque do Choupal ☎23115 Frd G10
ⅰ☜ Torrense Praca do Imperio ☎22021 M/c Chy/Sim G20

Ugeiriça See **Canas de Senhorim**
Vale do Lobos Faro (18km W of **Faro**) (☎0089) Map **23** B2
★★★★ Dona Filipa ☎94141 tx18248 rm129 ⇌129 Lift B750–1875 M240–260 ☜ Pool Beach Golf Sea

Valença Viano do Castelo 1,810 (☎0021) Map **17** A3
★★ Pousada de São Teotónia ☎22252 rm16 ⇌16 G B410–510 (double) M130–160
ⅰ☜ N I T A ☎22307 M/c BL G8

Viana do Castelo Viana do Castelo 13,780 (☎0028) Map **17** A3
★★★★ Do Parque Azenhas do D Prior ☎24151 rm120 ⇌120 Lift B550–815 M190 Pn670–700 ☜ Pool Sea

★★ Alianca ☎23002 rm40 (A) ⇌15 Sea
★★ Rali av Alfonso III ☎22176 rm39 ⇌39 Lift ☜ Pool ∩
☖☜ SA r de Aveiro 156 ☎22749 N☜ BL/Tri G10
☖☜ Vianense ☎22092 N☜ Aud/VW

At **Santa Luzia** (2km NW; also funicular connection)
★★★★ Santa Luzia ☎22192 rm48 ⇌48 G Lift ☜ Pool Sea

Vila de Feira Aveiro (15km NW of **Oliveira de Azeméis**) 5,220 (☎0026) Map **17** A2
★★ Estalagem de Santa Maria r dos Condes de Feijo ☎96130 rm18 ⇌8 Lake

Vila do Conde Porto 15,870 (☎0022) Map **17** A2
★★ Estalagem do Brasão r J M de Melo ☎64016 rm24 ⇌24
☖☜ Ferreira & Barreto r 5 Outubro 284 ☎63157 BL/Dat G10

Vila Franca de Xira Lisboa 16,280 (☎0013) Map **23** A4
★ Estalagem de Gado Bravo Estrada do Cabo ☎324 rm8 ⇌3
★ Estalagem da Leziria r Palha Blanco ☎129 rm20 (A) ⇌6 Lake
☖☜ G Cunha Praceta da Justica 19 ☎22529 N☜ BL

Vila Meã Viseu (☎0032) Map **17** B1/2
★★ Estalagem Viriato ☎93125 rm12 ⇌12 B290–500(double) M140 Pool

Vila Real Vila Real 13,250 (☎0099) Map **17** B2
★★ Tocaio av Carvalho Araujo 45 ☎23106 rm52 ⇌52 G Lift
☖ Correira, Silva & Pureza Timpeira ☎23108 Chy/Sim
ⅰ☜ Moreira de Carvalho & Botelho r MI-Teixeira Rebelo 17 ☎23007 GM
☖☜ C Sousa & Camilo Praça Diogo Cao ☎23035 N☜ Cit/Fia

Viseu Viseu 19,530 (☎0032) Map **17** B2
★★★ Grao Vasco ☎23511 rm90 ⇌90 Lift B380–750 Málc Pool
Guedes & Filhos r 5 de Outubro 79 ☎23905 N☜ M/c Chy/Sim G30
ⅰ☜ Infante de Sagres av Capt-S-Pereira 139 ☎23583 BL/Rov/Tri
ⅰ☜ Lopes r da Paz 21 ☎23561 Frd G80
ⅰ☜ Lopes & Figueiredo av da Belgica ☎25151 M/c BL/Fia/Tri/Tri G20

SPAIN & ANDORRA

Population 34,032,801 Area 196,700 sq miles Maps 17–26

How to get there   From the Channel ports, Spain is approached via France. The two main routes are at either end of the Pyrenees Mountains, the Biarritz to San Sebastián road at the western end for central and southern Spain or the Perpignan to Barcelona road at the eastern end for the Costa Brava. The distance from Calais to Madrid is over 970 miles and usually requires two or three night stops. It is possible to shorten the road journey by using the car sleeper services between Boulogne or Paris and Biarritz or Narbonne.

Travel information

AA Port agents   **Bilbao** Viajes Ecuador SA, Luchana 1 (Head Office), Bilbao 8 ☎234567, 246715 & 231270. Office hours: Monday–Saturday 09.00–13.30hrs; 16.00–19.30hrs (19.00hrs Saturday)

Accidents   **Fire, police, ambulance.** In Madrid and Barcelona dial 091 for **police**, and 2323232 for **fire** service; in other towns call the operator.

Ambulance   There is an assistance service for the victims of traffic accidents which is run by the Central Traffic Department. At the moment the service operates day and night on the NI Madrid–Irún road, on the NII road in the province of Lerida, on some roads in the provinces of Valencia (NIII, N340, N332, and N430) and Vizcaya (N625, N634, N240, C639, C6211, C6315, C6318, and C6322).
There is an SOS telephone network on these roads; motorists in need of help should ask for *auxilio en carretera* (road assistance). The special ambulances used are in radio contact with the hospitals participating in the scheme.
There are no firm rules of procedure after an accident; however, in most cases, the recommendations on page 21 are advisable.

Accommodation   Spain has some of the most attractively furnished hotels in Europe – especially luxury hotels converted from former monasteries or palaces. Provincial hotels are pleasantly old-fashioned; usually the plumbing and lavatories are just about adequate, and do not compare with those in

251

Spain

modern hotels in coastal resorts. Hotels are officially classified, and the category exhibited outside each. Charges must be approved by the State Tourism Department (*Ministerio de Informacion y Turismo*). While commendations or complaints about hotels are an important source of information to us. AA members may also like to know that Spanish hotels must keep an official complaints book. During the past ten years, the government has undertaken the building of state hotels, including *albergues, paradores,* and *refugios,* details of which are given in the gazetteer.

Albergues are modern inns catering for the passing motorist, and are classified as motels. Accommodation is limited, and you cannot usually stay for more than one night. There are facilities for garaging, minor repairs, and refuelling.

Paradores are fully-appointed tourist hotels, usually on the outskirts of towns or in the country. Some are newly built, but others are converted country houses, palaces, or Moorish castles. They offer very good value for money.

Refugio are designed to provide adequate shelter in remote or mountainous districts.

Breakdowns

If your car breaks down, try to move it to the verge of the road so that it obstructs the traffic flow as little as possible and place a warning triangle 30 metres behind the vehicle to warn following traffic. A 24-hour breakdown service is run by the Spanish Motoring Club (RACE) in collaboration with a private firm (ADA) in the Madrid area only. This service is available to touring motorists and AA members should produce their *5-Star Travel Booklet* when seeking assistance. To obtain assistance telephone 4554646, 4554787, 2340300 or 2534353. Elsewhere in Spain there is no road patrol service and if you need help you must make your own arrangements with a garage. If you wish to use *5-Star Travel Service* credit vouchers ensure that the garage will accept them in payment before allowing any work to be undertaken.

British Consulates

Note A number with a ° following the numeral (eg 2°) is the floor number of the building.

Algeciras, Avenida Francisco Franco 11 ☎661600
Alicante, Canalejas 1 ☎209018
Almeria, Calle Gerona 32 ☎214403/215982
Barcelona 11, Edificio Torre de Barcelona, Avenida Generalisimo Franco 477 (13°)
Apartado de Correos 12111 ☎2591601/2391300
Bilbao 8, Alameda de Urquijo 2–8 ☎4157600
Cádiz, Avenida Ramon de Carranza 26–27 (5°B) ☎211124
Ibiza, Avenida Bartolone Rosello 24 (9°) ☎301818
Jerez de la Frontera, Nuno Decanas 1 ☎334600
Madrid 4, Calle de Fernando el Santo 16 ☎4190200 (12 lines)
Málaga, Edificio Duquesa, Calle Duquesa de Parcent 4 ☎217571
Palma (Mallorca), Jaime III 5 (1°) ☎212085
Seville, Plaza Nueva 8 ☎228875
Tarragona, Santian 4 ☎201246
Vigo, Plaza de Compostela 23 (6°), PO Box 49 ☎211450

Currency and banking

The unit of currency is the peseta, which is divided into 100 centimos.

There are no restrictions on importing or exporting foreign currencies, travellers' cheques, etc, if a declaration is made to the Customs on entry. Travellers' cheques, etc, may be changed only at banks, authorised travel agencies, or hotels. Spanish bank notes to a maximum value of 50,000 pesetas may be imported, but not more than 3,000 pesetas in bank notes may be exported.

Banking hours

Banks are usually open 09.00–14.00hrs Monday to Saturday. There are exchange offices at travel agents which are open 09.00–13.00hrs and 16.00–19.00hrs from Monday to Friday, and 09.00–13.00hrs on Saturday.

Customs

Tourists should be warned that it is likely that the Spanish Customs authorities will demand a heavy deposit against duty and taxes on portable articles of high value such as musical instruments, portable radios and television sets, cassette recorders etc. Such an outlay may not be budgeted for and may cause inconvenience particularly since any deposit placed may not be readily available for refund when leaving the country.

Dimensions

Private cars and trailers are restricted to the following dimensions:

cars	height 4 metres; width 2.5 metres;
vehicle/trailer combinations	length 18 metres.

Spain

Drinking and driving

A driver suspected of driving while under the influence of alcohol may be required to undergo a breath test. If the test indicates a level in excess of 0.8% the driver will be considered to be under the influence of alcohol. A heavy fine, together with the withdrawal of the driving licence, will be imposed on a person found guilty.

Driving licence

A British driving licence is not acceptable in Spain and an International Driving Permit (IDP) must be obtained prior to departure from the UK.

Ferries

Ayamonte–Vila Real de Santo António (Portugal) across the River Guadiana. See Portugal page 241.

Holidays and events

Holidays based on religious festivals are not always fixed on the calendar but any current diary will give actual dates. The Whit period (a religious holiday) should not be confused with the British Spring Holiday.

Fixed holidays

1 January	New Year's Day
6 January	Epiphany
19 March	St Joseph's Day
1 May	St Joseph the Worker
18 July	National Day
25 July	St James of Spain
15 August	Feast of the Assumption
12 October	Our Lady of El Pilar
1 November	All Saints' Day
8 December	Immaculate Conception
25 December	Christmas Day

Moveable holidays

Maundy Thursday
Good Friday
Corpus Christi

Annual events

February	**Bocairente (Valencia)** Moors and Christians festivals
March	**Valencia** San José Fallas
April	**Vich (Barcelona)** Mercat del Ram
May	**Jerez de la Frontera (Cádiz)** Horse Fair
June	**Calella (Barcelona)** Aplec de la Sardana Festival
July	**Pamplona (Navarra)** San Fermin Festival (including running bulls)
	Anguiano (Logroño) Dance of the Stilts
August	**Elche (Alicante)** Mystery of Elche
	Betanzos (La Coruña) San Roque Festivals
September	**Logroño** Riojana Wine Harvest Festival
	Barcelona Festival of Our Lady of Mercy

Insurance

This is compulsory. See page 11.
Frontier insurance If you do not hold insurance cover, you must take out a short-term insurance policy which is issued by offices of the Guarantee Syndicate for Special Automobile Risks, by tourist offices, and by Customs offices.

Bail bond

An accident in Spain can have very serious consequences, including the impounding of the car, and property, and the detention of the driver pending trial. A bail bond can often facilitate release of person and property, and you are advised to obtain one of these from your insurer, for a nominal premium, together with your Green Card. A bail bond is a written guarantee that a cash deposit of usually up to £1,000 will be paid to the Spanish Court as surety for bail, and as security for any fine which may be imposed, although in such an event you will have to reimburse any amount paid by your insurers. In very serious cases the Court will not allow bail and it has been known for a minor Spanish court to refuse to accept bail bonds, and to insist on cash being paid by the driver. Nevertheless, motorists are strongly advised to obtain a bail bond and to ensure that documentary evidence of this (in Spanish) is attached to the Green Card.

Lights

Passing lights (dipped headlights) are compulsory on motorways and fast dual carriageways even if they are well lit. The use of full headlights in built-up areas is prohibited but it is also an offence to travel with faulty sidelights. You are advised to carry an adequate supply of spare bulbs.

Spain

Medical treatment

There is no free treatment for visitors.

Motoring club

The **Real Autómovil Club de España** (RACE) which has its headquarters at General Sanjurjo 10, Madrid 3 ☎4473200 is associated with local clubs in a number of provincial towns. These clubs will assist motoring tourists generally and supply road and touring information. AA members should produce their *5-Star Travel Booklet* when requesting service. Motoring club offices are normally open from 09.00–13.00hrs only and are closed on Sundays and public holidays. For RACE road assistance, see Breakdowns.

Nationality plate

The penalty for failure to display a nationality plate, or for displaying one of the wrong size or type, is a fine of approx Pta500.

Overtaking

Both at night and during the day, drivers who are about to be overtaken must operate their right-hand indicator light to show the driver following that his intention to overtake has been understood. Outside built-up areas drivers about to overtake must sound their horn during the day and flash their lights at night. Stationary trams must not be overtaken while passengers are boarding or alighting.

Parking

Parking is forbidden in the following places: within 5 metres (16½ft) of cross-roads or an intersection; near a level crossing; on or near a pedestrian crossing; within 5 metres of the entrance to a public building; on a main road or one carrying fast-moving traffic; on or near tram lines; within 7 metres (23ft) of a tram or bus stop. You must not park on a two-way road if it is not wide enough for three vehicles. In one-way streets, vehicles are parked alongside buildings with even numbers on even dates and on the opposite side on odd dates; any alteration to this system is announced by signs or notices in the press.

Drivers may stop their vehicles alongside another parked vehicle if there is no space free nearby and the flow of traffic is not obstructed, but only long enough to let passengers in or out or to load or unload goods.

In some cities, there are short-term parking areas known as blue zones indicated by signs. In these areas parked cars must display a disc on the windscreen; discs are set at the time of parking, and show when parking time expires according to the limit in the area concerned. The maximum parking period is 1½hrs during the day; there is no parking limit 21.00–08.00hrs. Parking discs are available from town halls and some hotels, travel agencies, etc. Foreign parking discs are recognised if they carry the same indications as Spanish discs.

It is forbidden to park facing oncoming traffic. Vehicles wrongly parked may be towed away.

Madrid

You may not park for more than 90mins in central Madrid, except after 21.00hrs. The police supply parking discs for use in the Madrid blue zone; discs must be displayed on the inside of the windscreen on the side nearest the pavement. Except on Sundays and bank holidays (when shops are closed) there is a limited parking period, as shown on the disc, from 08.00hrs to 21.00hrs. After 21.00hrs parking is allowed until 10.00hrs next day; the disc must still be displayed, and must show the exact time of arrival unless the vehicle is to be collected before 08.00hrs.

If the authorised period is exceeded, the police can tow the vehicle away. A driver whose vehicle has been towed away should contact the Municipal Office, Avenida de Valladolid 6 ☎2472635. Failure to comply with the regulations can result in a fine of up to 500 pesetas, which includes towing costs.

Motorcycles, scooters, and mopeds need not use discs if they are parked in special parking places. Vehicles weighing more than 2,000kg (1ton 19cwt 41lb) are not allowed in the zone between 09.00 and 14.00hrs, and 16.00 and 22.00hrs.

Passengers

It is recommended that children under the age of fourteen travel in the rear seat of a vehicle.

Petrol

The approximate price of petrol per litre is: super (98 octane) Pta33; normal (85 octane) Pta25.50.

Police fines

The police are authorised to impose on-the-spot fines on any motorist infringing the local traffic regulations. The officer collecting the fine should issue an official receipt. Visiting motorists must pay their

Spain

fines immediately (which gives a reduction of 20% in most cases), unless they give the name of a person or corporation in Spain which will guarantee payment of the fine. If not, the vehicle will be held until the fine is paid.

A fine may be levied on a motorist who does not carry his driving licence and IDP. Fines for all motoring offences range from Pta250 to Pta5,000.

Postal and telephone charges		Pta
Rates to the UK are:		
Postcards		7.00
Letters up to 20gm		20.00
Letters up to 5gm		25.00

The address of the *poste restante* office in Madrid is Edificio de Correos y Telegrafos, Lista de Correos, Plaza de Cibeles, Madrid 14.

Telephone rates
An automatic call to the UK, or one through the operator, costs approximately Pta243 for the first three minutes and Pta78 for each additional minute. The internal telephone system connects all principal towns, but long delays on trunk calls are not unusual. Local calls are covered by a flat rate of Pta5; hotels, restaurants, etc, usually make an additional charge.

Roads
The surfaces of the main roads vary, but on the whole are good; traffic is light. The roads are winding in many places and at times it is not advisable to exceed 30–35mph. Secondary roads are often rough, winding, and encumbered by slow, horse-drawn traffic. All main roads are prefixed N; six of those radiating from Madrid are numbered in roman numerals. Secondary roads are prefixed C.

Holiday traffic
Holiday traffic, particularly on the coast road to Barcelona and Tarragona and in the San Sebastián area, causes congestion which may be severe at weekends.

Motorways
There are approximately 815 miles of motorway (*autopista*) open, and more are under construction; a network of about 1,800 miles of toll *autopista* is planned. Apart from a few stretches of toll-free motorways in the Madrid and Barcelona areas, tolls are charged on most of the other sections. The main toll motorways are as follows:

A1	**Irún–San Sebastián**	toll: cars Pta35, car and caravan Pta90
A1/A68	**San Sebastián–Bilbao**	toll: cars Pta210, car and caravan Pta415
A2	**Barcelona–Lérida**	toll: cars Pta265, car and caravan Pta325
A2	**Lérida–Zaragoza**	toll: cars Pta225, car and caravan Pta225
A2/A7	**Barcelona–Tarragona**	toll: cars Pta150, car and caravan Pta275
A4	**Cádiz–Seville**	toll: payable in three stages, and includes Puente Carranza, cars Pta190, car and caravan Pta445
A6	**Villalba–Guadarrama** Tunnel	toll: cars Pta275, car and caravan Pta440
A7	**Tarragona–Peniscola**	toll: cars Pta195, car and caravan Pta390
A7	**Castellón–Valencia**	toll: cars Pta115, car and caravan Pta200
A7	**Silla–Gandia**	toll: cars Pta125, car and caravan Pta210

Spain

A7	**Altea–Alicante**	toll: cars Pta105, car and caravan Pta150
A17	**Barcelona–La Junquera (Frontier)**	toll: payable in two stages, cars Pta125, car and caravan Pta380
A19	**Barcelona–Mongat–Maturó**	toll: cars Pta45, car and caravan Pta70
A68	*****Bilbao–Amézaga**	

Note The toll charges for this section are not available at the time of going to press.

Winter conditions   Most roads across the Pyrenees are either closed or affected by winter weather, but the roads to Biarritz and Perpignan in France avoid the mountains. The main routes into Portugal are unaffected.

Within the country, motoring is not severely restricted although certain roads may be temporarily blocked, particularly in January and February. The most important roads likely to be affected are San Sebastián–Burgos–Madrid and Granada–Murcia, but these are swept immediately there is a snowfall. On the Villacastín–Madrid road there is a tunnel under the Guadarrama Pass.
Roads likely to be affected by heavy snowfall are:

Pass	Road
Pajares	León–Gijon
Reinosa	Santander–Palencia
Escudo	Santander–Burgos
Somosierra	Burgos–Madrid
Orduña	Bilbao–Burgos
Barazar	Bilbao–Vitoria
Piqueras	Logroño–Madrid
Navacerrada	Madrid–La Granja

The Real Automóvil Club de España will give you up-to-date information about road conditions. See also Passes and tunnels, page 28.

Road signs   Translations of some written signs to be seen on the road are given below:

Aduana	Customs
Al paso	Drive slowly
Atencion a la Senalizacion	Watch out for road signs
Camineros	Roadman's hut
Cañada	Beware of cattle
Cedo el paso	Give way
Cuidado (or, Precaución)	Caution
Despacio	Slow
Desvio	Diversion
Direccion unica	One-way street
Estacionamiento de automoviles	Car park
Estacionamiento prohibido	Parking prohibited
Llevar la derecha (la izquierda)	Drive on the right (the left)
Obras	Workmen
Paso prohibido	No thoroughfare
Peligro	Danger
Curva peligroso	Dangerous bend
Vuelta permitida	Turning permitted

Seat belts   It is compulsory to wear seat belts if they are fitted to the vehicle.

Shopping hours   Shops are open Monday to Saturday: *foodshops* 09.00–13.00hrs and 17.00–21.00hrs; *stores* 09.30–13.30hrs and 16.30–20.00hrs (17.00–20.30hrs from June to September).

Speed   In built-up areas vehicles are limited to 60kph (37mph) except where signs indicate a lower limit. Outside built-up areas cars are limited to 100kph (62mph) on motorways, roads with two or more lanes in each direction or roads with an additional lane for slow vehicles and 90kph (56mph) on other

Spain

roads. Vehicles towing a caravan or trailer are limited to 50kph (31mph) inside built-up areas, and 80kph (49mph) outside built-up areas if the weight of the caravan exceeds half the unladen weight of the towing vehicle.

Tourist information offices
The Spanish National Tourist Office, Metro House, St. James' Street, London SW1 ☎01-499 0901, will be pleased to assist you with information regarding tourism and there are branch offices in most of the leading Spanish cities, towns and resorts. Local offices are normally closed at lunchtime.

Traffic lights
In some cases the green light remains on with the amber light when changing from green to red. Two red lights, one above the other, mean 'no entry'. Usually, lights on each side of cross-roads operate independently and must be obeyed independently.

A policeman with a whistle may over-ride the traffic lights, and he must be obeyed.

Turning
Unless there is a 'turning permitted' sign, three-point turns and reversing into side streets are prohibited in towns.

Tyres
Spiked tyres Spikes on tyres must be 10mm in diameter and not more than 2mm in length.

Visitors' registration
There are no police formalities for a stay of less than three months.

Warning triangles
Vehicles weighing more than 3,500kg (3tons 8cwt 100lb) and passenger vehicles with more than nine seats (including the driver's) must be equipped with two warning triangles. A triangle must be placed 30 metres (33yd) in front of and behind the obstacle. Both must be visible from a distance of at least 100 metres (109yd).

Andorra

Maps 20 & 22
Andorra is an independent Republic covering 180 sq miles with a population of 25,000. It is situated high in the Pyrenees between France and Spain and jointly administered by these two countries. French and Spanish are both spoken and the currency of either country is accepted. General regulations for France and Spain apply to Andorra with the following exceptions:

Accidents
Fire and **ambulance** ☎18 **police** ☎21222

Breakdowns
The Automobile Club d'Andorra ☎20890 will offer advice and assistance in the event of a breakdown. However, owing to many unnecessary journeys made in the past, the motorist is now asked to go to the garage and personally accompany the mechanic or breakdown vehicle to his car.

British Consulate
Andorra comes within the Consular District of the British Consul-General at Barcelona — see Spain page 253.

Medical treatment
There is no free medical treatment for visitors.

Spain/hotels and garages

Prices are in pesetas

Abbreviations:
av   avenida
c   calle
Cdt   Commandant
ctra   carretera
Gl   Generalissimo
pl   plaza
ps   paseo

Aguadulce See **Almería**

Aigua-Blava See **Bagur**

Alarcón Cuenca 400 Map **25** B4
★★★*Parador Marques de Villena* ☎1 rm11
⊐11 G Lift

Albacete Albacete 93,230 (☎967)
Map **25** B3
★★★*Llanos* av Rodrigues Acosta 9
☎223750 rm102 ⊐97 ▥5 G Lift B1015–1555
M500 Pn1552

Albufereta (La) See **Alicante**

Alcanar Tarragona 7,070 Map **21** B2
★★*Biarritz* (n rest) ☎737025 rm24 ⊐24 G
Jun–Sep B300–770 ➤ Pool Beach Sea

Alcañiz Teruel 10,820 (☎974) Map **21** B2
★★★*Parador Nacional de la Concordia*
☎130400 ta Paral rm12 ⊐12 Lift
B1185–1560 (double) M480
▥◐ *Aguiló* av B-Esteban 28 ☎130823 N☕
BL/MB G10

Algeciras Cádiz 81,660 (☎956) Map **24** C1
★★★★*Reina Cristina* Paseo de las
Conferencias ☎671390 tx78057 rm114 ⊐114
G Lift B1148–2140 Màlc ➤ Pool Sea
★★*Alarde* (n rest) Alfonso XI-4 ☎660408
ta Hotelsa tx78009-ARDE rm68 ⊐68 Lift
B680–1240
☆*Solimar* (Bungalows) Málaga road (3km N
road No. 340) ☎660650 rm14 ⊐14
1 Mar–1 Nov Sea
▥◐24 *M G Gaggero* c Zorrilla 34
☎673769 N☕ M/c
▥◐*Mecanicos* ctra Cádiz-Málaga 21
☎660950 N☕ BL/Rov

Alhama de Aragón Zaragoza 1,590
Map **19** B1/2
★★★*Termas y Parque* Gl-Franco 20 ☎1
rm149 G Lift 9 Apr–15 Oct Pool

Alicante Alicante 184,720 (☎965)
Map **26** C2
★★★★*Meliá* Playa de El Postiguet ☎205000
tx66131 rm580 ⊐580 G Lift B1170–2460
M650 Pool Sea
★★★*Gran* Navas 41 ☎214401 rm72 ⊐72 G
Lift
★★★*Palas* c de Cervantes 5 ☎209309 rm60
⊐60 Lift LD B620–1320 M500–600
Pn1770–1950 ➤ Pool Sea
★★*Benacantil* (n rest) San Telmo 7
☎215618 rm47 ⊐12 ▥35 Lift Sea
★★*Cabo* Playa de San Juan ☎650100
rm35 ⊐35 Lift 15 Jun–15 Sep B480–560
★★*Gran Sol* (n rest) Mendez Nuñez 3
☎203000 rm150 ⊐150 Lift B1120–2640 Sea
★★*Pastor* San Fernando 42 ☎224941 rm26
⊐14 Lift
▥◐24 *Levante* av Orihuela 117 ☎221947
N☕ BL G10
◐▥ *V M Llavador* c Reyes Catolicos 41
☎221109 N☕ BL
▥◐24 *Nuevo* T-Aznar Domenech 7
☎221427 N☕
At **Albufereta (La)** (3km N)
★★★*Villa Linda* ☎262208 rm34 ⊐29 ▥5 G
LD B360–870 M350 Pn850 Pool

Almería Almería 114,510 (☎951)
Map **25** B1
★★★*Costacabana* (4km E near airport)
☎222063 rm102 ⊐102 Lift ➤ Pool Beach Sea
★★★*Costasol* (n rest) Generalísimo 58
☎234011 ta Solhotel rm55 ⊐55 Lift
B715–975
★★★*Perla* pl del Carmen 7 ☎238877 rm44
⊐44 B333–736
▥◐24 *J Artes de Arcos* c Altamira ☎221400
G20
▥◐*Automecanica Almeriense* Paraje Los
Callejones ☎237033 N☕ G10
◐24 *Salinas & Alcazar* ctra Granada 2°
Tramo 6 ☎234202 N☕ Cit G
At **Aguadulce** (11km W)
★★*Novotel-Aguadulce* ctra N340 ☎36 rm80
⊐80 Lift ➤ Pool Beach Sea

Almuñécar Granada 13,250 (☎958)
Map **25** A1
★★★*Portamar* Playa Puerta del Mar ☎210
rm72 ⊐72 G Lift Beach Sea

Almunia de Doña Godina (La)
Zaragoza 4,910 (☎976) Map **21** A3
★*Patio* av del Generalísimo 6 ☎600608
rm11 ⊐5 G B215–485 M200–375

Almuradiel Cuidad Real Map **25** A3
★★★*Podencos* ctra NIV-K232
☎363738 rm80 ⊐68 ▥3 G

Alquería del Niño Perdido See
Villarreal de los Infantes

Alsasua Navarra 7,050 (☎948) Map **19** B3
★★*Alaska* ctra Madrid-Irun (7km) 402
☎560100 rm30 (A15) ⊐30 G 1 Mar–1 Nov
B554–1028 M400 Pn1000–1300 Pool
▥◐◐ *P Celaya Urrestarazu* ctra Gl-Irun-
Madrid ☎560233 M/c Cit G8
▥◐*J Oraa* Venta Abajo ☎560153
N☕ Ren G20
At **Ciordia** (6.4km SW on N1)
★★*Alzania* ☎8 rm36 ⊐36 G Lift

Andraitx See **Mallorca** under **Baleares
(Islas de)**

Antequera Málaga 40,910 (☎952)
Map **24** D1
☆☆*Albergue Nacional* Parque M-Cristina
☎841740 ta Paral rm17 ⊐14 B285–785
M375 Pn1020
★★*Vergara* Infante D-Fernando 59
☎841940 rm19 ⊐9 ▥10

Aranda de Duero Burgos 18,370 (☎947)
Map **19** A2
☆☆☆ *Bronces* ctra Madrid-Irun ☎500850
rm30 ⊐27 ▥3 G B475–1185 M350 Pn650
☆☆*Albergue Nacional* ☎50050 ta Paral
rm21 ⊐21 G
▥◐ *Electro-Sanz* ctra Madrid-Irun km 160,
av C-Miralles 61 ☎501134 N☕ BL G

Aranjuez Madrid 29,550 (☎91) Map **25** A4
▥ *L Checa* ctra Andalucia 26 ☎8910207 N☕
▥◐*Infantas* ctra Andolucia km44 ☎2940929
Cit G150

Arcaute See **Vitoria**

Arcos de la Frontera Cádiz 25,970
Map **24** C1
★★★*Parador Nacional Casa de Corregidor*
pl d'España ☎362 rm21 ⊐21

Arenas de Cabrales Oviedo Map **18** D4
★*Naranjo de Bulnes* rm20 ⊐6

Arenys de Mar Barcelona 8,330 (☎93)
Map **22** D3
★★*Floris* Playa Cassá 80 ☎3920384 rm32
(A19) ⊐25 ▥26
★*Residencia Impala* (n rest) Apartado 20
☎7921504 rm52 ⊐14 ▥38 Jun–Sep
B365–876 Pool Sea

261

Spain

Astorga León 11,790 (☎987) Map **18** C3
★**Cantabrico** (n rest) pl de la Aduana 1
☎615250 rm30 ⇆6 ⋔6 G B205–435 M250
Pn600–645
i≉24 M Alonso ctra Madrid Coruña 60
☎615259 N☎616056 M/c BL G

Ávila Ávila 1,131 (☎918) Map **18** D1
★★★★**Palacio Valderrábanos** pl Catedral 6
☎211025 rm73 ⇆73 G Lift B1085–1900
M500 Pn1775
★★★**Parador Nacional Raimundo de
Borgoña** ☎211340 rm27 ⇆27 Lift
B695–1540 M400 Pn1360–1510
★★**Cuatro Postes** ☎212944 rm36 ⇆36
Lift B270–771 M310 Pn860
★★**Reina Isabel** av J-Antonio 17 ☎220200
rm44 ⇆11 ⋔2 B349–763 M310 Pn795–890
Ayamonte Huelva 13,100 Map **23** B2
★★★**Parador Nacional Costa de la Luz**
☎125 ta Paral rm20 ⇆20 Pool Sea
Badajoz Badajoz 101,710 (☎924) Map **23** B3
★★★**Zurbaran** ps Castelar ☎223741 rm215
⇆215 G Lift B810–1120 M450 Pn1550–1750
⅋ Pool Lake
⅋☎**24 Inbasa** ctra Sevilla ☎224547 G40
Bagur Gerona 2,230 (☎972) Map **22** D3
★★**Sa Riera** Playa de sa Riera ☎623000 rm37
⇆16 ⋔21 B315–700 M300 Pn765–820 Sea
At **Aigua-Blava** (2km SE)
★★★**Aigua-Blava** Playa de Fornells ☎622058
rm85 (A39) ⇆85 1 Apr–20 Oct B705–1620
M475 Pn1050–1400(double) ⅋ Pool Sea
★★★**Parador Nacional de la Costa Brava**
☎312162 ta Paral rm40 ⇆40 Lift
At **Playa d'Aiguafreda** (5km NE)
★★★★★**Cap sa Sal** ☎312100 rm230 ⇆230 G
Lift 1 Jun–30 Sep Pool Sea
Bailén Jaén 13,230 Map **25** A2
✩✩✩**Albergue Nacional** (1km S) ☎372
rm40 ⇆40
Balaguer Lérida 11,680 (☎973) Map **22** C3
★★★**Conde Jaime de Urgel** c Urgel 2
☎445604 rm60 ⇆57 ⋔3 G Lift B710–1520
M440 Pool
Baleares (Islas de)

Ibiza Map **22** Inset

Santa Eulalia del Rio 9,300 (☎971)
★★★★**S'argamassa** ☎330051 rm217 ⇆217
G Lift 1 May–30 Sep ⅋ Beach Sea
Mallorca (Majorca)

Andraitx 3,800 Map **22** D1
At **Camp de Mar** (5km S)
★★★**Camp de Mar** ☎671000 rm75 ⇆75 G
Lift Apr–Oct B765–1430 M425 Pn1300 ⅋
Pool Sea

Cala Ratjada (☎971) Map **22** D1
★★★**Son Moll** Playa Son Moll ☎563100
rm118 ⇆118 Lift 1 Apr–31 Oct B534–950
M300 Pn800 Pool Sea

Formentor Map **22** D1
★★★★★**Formentor** ☎531300 tx68523
HFORM E rm132 ⇆132 G B1675–2650
M750 Pn2500 ⅋ Pool Beach ⌂ Sea

Magaluf (☎971) Map **22** D1
★★★★**Meliá** ☎681050 rm271 ⇆271 Lift
1 Apr–31 Oct B1620(double) M495 Pn1645
⅋ Sea

Paguera 90 (☎971) Map **22** D1
★★★★**Villamil** ☎686050 rm100 ⇆100 Lift
(closed 15 Nov–15 Dec) B1530–2760 M430
Pn1925 ⅋ Pool Beach Sea
★★★**Bahia** ☎686100 rm54 ⇆54 ⅋ Pool Sea

Palma de Mallorca 234,100 (☎971)
Map **22** D1

★★★★★**Meliá** c de Monseñor Palmer
☎233740 tx68538 rm240 ⇆240 Lift
B1170–2015 M620 Pool
★★★★★**Son Vida** ☎232340 tx68651
rm169 ⇆169 Lift B1975–3350
Pn2900–3100 ⅋ Pool ⌂ Golf Sea
★★★★★**Victoria** av Calvo Sotelo 21 ☎232542
tx68558 rm172 ⇆172 Lift B1450–2900
M660 Pn2485 Pool Sea
★★★★**Alcina** ps Maritimo 26 ☎231140
tx68792 rm90 ⇆90 Lift B420–1028 M370
Pn960–1050
★★★★**Maricel** C'as Catalá Beach ☎231240
rm55 (A8) ⇆55 G Lift B600–1460 M425
Pn1200–1400 ⅋ Pool Sea
★★★**Paso** c Alvaro de Bazán 3 ☎237602
tx68652 rm254 ⇆254 Lift B425–690 M250
Pn700 Pool
⅋☎**Oliver** c G L Labres 12 ☎273581 N☎ GM
⅋☎**Talleres Minaco** Aragón 27 ☎463540 N☎
Peu/Rov
At **Playa de Palma (Ca'n Pastilla)**
★★★**Acapulco** ☎261800 rm100 ⇆93 ⋔7
Lift B506–877 M325 Pn1025 Pool Sea
★★**Oasis** ☎260150 rm110 ⇆110 G Lift
B465–920 M225 Pn835–945 Pool Beach Sea
At **Playa de Palma Nova** (16km SW)
★★★**Hawaii** ☎681150 rm204 ⇆204 Lift
B515–800 M260 Pn800 Pool Beach Sea
Pollensa 9,960 Map **22** D1
At **Cala San Vicente**
★★★★**Molins** ☎530200 rm100 ⇆100 G Lift
B795–1210 M425 Pn1250 ⅋ Pool Sea
At **Puerto de Pollensa** (6km NE)
★★★**Capri** ps Anglada Camarasa ☎531600
rm33 ⇆33 G Lift 1 Apr–30 Oct LD B528–866
M340 Pn940–1050 Beach Sea
★★★**Miramar** ps Anglada Camarasa ☎531400
rm70 ⇆70 G Lift 1 Mar–31 Oct B385–770
M325 Pn860–1000 ⅋ Beach Sea
★★★**Uyal** ps de la Gola ☎43 rm83 ⇆83 Lift
1 Apr–30 Oct Beach Sea
Menorca (Minorca) Map **22** Inset
Mahón 19,280 (☎971)
At **Villacarlos** (3km W)
★★★★**Agamenon** Fontanillas ☎362150
rm75 ⇆75 Lift 1 Apr–31 Oct B540–1060
M390 Pn1055–1145 Pool Sea
★★★**Rey Carlos III** Miranda de Cala Corp
☎363100 rm87 ⇆87 G Lift Apr–Oct
B610–1320 M400 Pool Sea
Bañeza (La) León 8,840 Map **18** C3
✩**Albergue Nacional** (1km NW) ☎641850
rm12 ⇆4 G B285–800 M360
Bañolas Gerona 10,020 (☎972) Map **22** D3
★★**Lago** ☎341 rm19 ⇆19 G Lake
★★**Mundial** pl de España 23 ☎25 rm38 ⇆8 G
Baños de Montemayor Caceres 1,020
Map **18** C1
★★**Balneario** Calvo Sotelo 24 ☎579 rm100
⇆40 G Lift 1 Jun–30 Sep
Barajas See **Madrid**
Barcelona Barcelona 1,745,140 (☎93)
Map **22** C3 **See Plan**
AA agents; see page 252
★★★★★**Avenida Palace** av J-Antonio 605
☎3019600 Plan **1** tx54734 Aptel rm225
⇆225 Lift B2035–2535 M650
★★★★★**Ritz** av J-Antonio 668 ☎3185200
Plan **2** tx52739 rm185 ⇆185 Lift B1950–3300
M850 Pn2900
★★★★★**Rotonda** ps de San Gervasio 53
☎2470400 Plan **3** rm100 ⇆100 G Lift
★★★★**Condado** Aribau 201 ☎2172500 Plan **4**
ta Hocon rm90 ⇆90 Lift
★★★★**Christina** (n rest) av Gl-Franco 458
☎2176800 Plan **5** rm125 ⇆125 G Lift

Spain

Barcelona
1 ★★★★★Avenida Palace
2 ★★★★★Ritz
3 ★★★★★Rotonda
4 ★★★★Condado
5 ★★★★Cristina
6 ★★★★Diplomatic
7 ★★★★Majestic
8 ★★★★Manila
9 ★★★★Presidente

10 ★★★★Regente
11 ★★★Astoria
12 ★★★Dante
13 ★★★Derby
14 ★★★Florida (at Mont-Tibidabo 12km NW)
15 ★★★Meson Castilla
16 ★★★Regina

Spain

★★★★**Diplomatic** vía Layetana 122 ☎3173100
Plan **6** tx54701 rm215 ⇄215 G Lift
B2175–4300 M800 Pool
★★★★**Majestic** ps de Gracia 70 ☎2154512
Plan **7** tx52211 rm350 ⇄350 G Lift
B1150–2410 M625 Pn2175–4460 Pool
★★★★**Manila** Rambla de los Estudios 111
☎3186200 Plan **8** tx54634 rm250 ⇄250 G
Lift B1940–3890 M600
★★★★**Presidente** av del Generalísimo 570
☎2273141 Plan **9** ta Husa tx52180 rm161
⇄161 G Lift B2655–3475 M740 Pn2903 Pool
★★★★**Princesa Sofia** (not on plan)
tx51032 (not on plan) rm511 ⇄511 G Lift
B3400–4400 M900 Pn3640
★★★★**Regente** Rambla de Cataluña 76
☎2152570 Plan **10** rm66 ⇄66 Lift Pool
★★★**Astoria** (n rest) c Paris 203 (off c de Urgel)
☎2185600 Plan **11** rm108 ⇄108 G Lift
B750–1600
★★★**Dante** (n rest) c Mallorca 181 ☎2540300
Plan **12** tx52588 rm81 ⇄81 G Lift
★★★**Derby** Loreto 21 ☎2393007 Plan **13**
rm116 ⇄116 G Lift
★★★**Meson Castilla** (n rest) Valldoncella 5
☎3182182 Plan **15** rm55 ⇄55 G Lift
★★★**Regina** (n rest) c Vergara 4 (off pl de
Cataluña) ☎3013232 Plan **16** rm102 ⇄102
Lift B750–1470
🛏**M Aguilar** c Mallorca 27 ☎2397275 N🖢 GM
🛏🖢**Benedicto** Córcega 418 ☎2587405 N🖢
BL G6
🛏🕭**California** Mallorca 419 ☎2363545 N🖢
M/c G250
🛏🖢24 **Layetana** Travesera de Gracia 17
☎3212327 Frd
🛏🕭**F Roca** Diputación 43 ☎3251550 N🖢 M/c
Chy/Jag/Rov/RR/Sim
🛏🕭**Romagosa** c Bolivia 243 ☎3071957
(closed Fri & weekends) Peu/Rov
🛏🕭**Ryvesa** Aragón 179 ☎2531600 N🖢 BL
🛏🕭🖢**G Salamanca** c Laforja 75 ☎2284496 N🖢
M/c Hon G50
At **Mont-Tibidabo** (12km NW)
★★★**Florida** (n rest) ☎2475000 Plan **14**
rm52 ⇄52 Lift 1 Jun–1 Sep

Bayona Pontevedra 7,890 Map **17** A3
★★★**Parador Nacional Del Conde de
Gondomer** ☎142 ta Paral rm66 ⇄66 G ✈
Pool Beach Sea

Benajarafe See Torre del Mar

Benalmadena Málaga (☎952) Map **24** D1
★★★**Siroco** ☎441075 tx77135 rm252 ⇄252
Lift B585–920 M400 Pn1075–1200 ✈ Pool
Sea
★★**Delfin** ctra de Cádiz ☎441640 rm78 ⇄78
Lift B470–840 M300 Pn750–800 Pool Sea
Benavente Zamora 11,780 (☎988)
Map **18** C2
★**Martin** ctra Madrid ☎858 rm30 ⇄8 🛏8 G
Benicarló Castellón 12,830 (☎964)
Map **21** B2
☆☆☆**Albergue Nacional** ctra de Peniscola
☎470100 ta Paral rm108 ⇄108 B910–1560
M480 Pn1710–1915 ✈ Pool Sea
★★**Sol** av Magallanes 90 ☎471349 rm16 (A8)
⇄16 G 1 Jun–30 Sep Sea
Benicasim Castellón 2,920 (☎964)
Map **21** B2
★★★★**Azor** ps Maritimo ☎300350 tx65503
GIMEN rm88 ⇄88 Lift Mar–Oct B635–1135
M440 Pn1173–1450 ✈ Pool ○
★★★**Voramar** ☎300150 rm55 ⇄55 G Lift
Etr–10 Oct B554–966 M340–375 Pn975–1085
Beach Sea
Benidorm Alicante 12,120 (☎965)
Map **26** D2

★★★★**Gran Delfin** playa de Poniente
☎853400 rm99 ⇄99 G Lift 1 Apr–1 Oct
B1360–2510 M595 Pn2055–2300 ✈ Pool Sea
★★★**Europa** Rincón de Loix ☎360800 rm48
(A) ⇄43 🛏5 Lift 15 Mar–30 Nov Pool Sea
★★★**Planesia** pl de San Jaime 2 ☎360303
rm36 ⇄36 Lift Apr–Oct Sea
☆☆**Marola** La Cala ☎360932 rm20 ⇄20 G
Apr–Oct Sea
★★**Presidente** av Filipinas ☎853950
rm228 ⇄228 Lift B265–600 M210 Pn580–615
Pool Sea
🛏🖢24 **Autonautica** ctra Alicante-Valencia
☎853562 BL/Frd

Bielsa Huesca 620 Map **21** B4
★★**Parador Monte Perdido** Valle de Pineta
☎23 rm16 ⇄16 G Lift

Bilbao Vizcaya 410,490 (☎944) Map **19** B3
See Plan
★★★★**Aranzazu** R-Arias 66 ☎4413100 Plan **1**
tx32164 (Cahar E) rm171 ⇄171 G Lift
B1300–1950 M360
★★★★**Avenida** av H-de Saracho ☎4334000
Plan **2** tx31040 ta Hotare rm116 ⇄116 Lift
B1075–1750 M360
★★★★**Carlton** (n rest) pl F-Moyúa 2 ☎4162200
Plan **3** tx32233 rm146 ⇄146 Lift B1495–2950
★★★★**Ercilla** Ercilla 37 ☎4438800 Plan **4**
tx43449 rm585 ⇄585 G Lift B1500–2500
🛏🕭**Rotarduy** Alameda de Urquijo 85 ☎419900
N🖢 Peu

Blanes Gerona 16,020 (☎972) Map **22** D3
★★★★**Park** ☎330250 rm131 ⇄126 🛏5 G Lift
1 May–10 Oct ✈ Pool Beach ○ Sea
★★★**Pop Coronat** ps de la Maestranza 97
☎330050 ta Popostal rm34 ⇄22 🛏12 Lift Sea
★★**Horitzo** ps Maritimo 11 ☎330400 rm122
⇄95 🛏27 G Lift B405–750 M275 Pn750 Sea
★★**San Francisco** ☎330477 rm32 ⇄32 Lift
May–Oct B310–620 M245 Pn580–612 Sea

Burgos Burgos 119,920 (☎947) Map **19** A3
★★★★**Almirante Bonifaz** Vitoria 22
☎206943 ta Albotel tx39430 rm76 ⇄76 Lift
B590–1780 M500 Pn1375–1725
★★★★**Landa Palace** Madrid road 2km
☎206343 rm33 ⇄33 G Lift
★★★**Condestable** Vitoria 8 ☎200644 rm77
⇄77 G Lift
★★**El Cid** ctra de Francia ☎221900 rm38 (A11)
⇄29 🛏9 G B615–1200 M475 Pn1235–1310
🛏🕭**J Barrios** c de Vitoria 113 ☎224900 N🖢
Fia
🛏🕭**Mecanico 'Suizo'** San Agustin 5 ☎202364
N🖢 M/c Aud/VW
🛏🖢24 **Pedro** av Vitoria 105 ☎224528
N☎223031 BL
🛏🖢24 **T Port y Hortigueira** ctra Vitoria 245
☎226410 N☎224920
🛏🖢24 **Turismo** Vitoria 29 ☎208848 BL G100

Burriana Castellón 22,650 (☎964) Map **26** D4
★★★**Aloha** (Playa 2.5km W) ☎510104 rm30
⇄30 Lift 15 Mar–Sep B470–890 M320
Pn900–975 Pool Sea

Cabrera (La) Madrid 701 (☎91) Map **19** A1
★★**Mavi** ctra Madrid-Irun 58 ☎8688000
rm43 ⇄14 🛏29 B294–667 M264
Pn756–786

Cáceres Cáceres 55,060 (☎927) Map **24** C4
★★★**Alcantara** av Virgen de Guadalupe 14
☎221700 rm67 ⇄67 Lift B515–725 M240
🛏🕭**M Sanchez** av H-Cortes 22 ☎225200 N🖢
Ren

Cadaques Gerona 1,270 (☎972) Map **22** D3

Spain

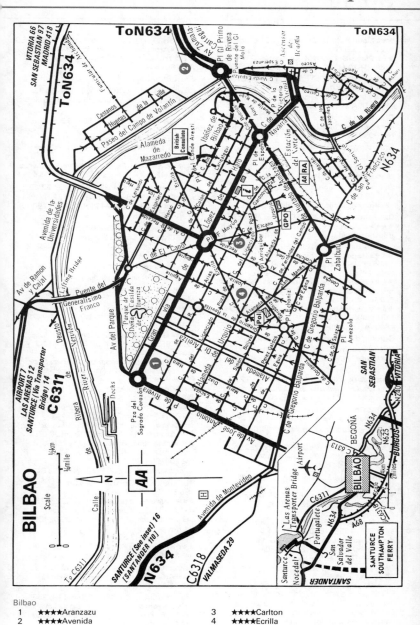

Bilbao

1	★★★★Aranzazu	3	★★★★Carlton
2	★★★★Avenida	4	★★★★Ecrilla

Spain

★★★**Llané Petit** Dr Bartomens 36 ☎258050
rm35 ⇆35 G Lift 1 Apr–30 Sep B493–1016
★★★**Playa-Sol** 258100 rm49 ⇆49 G Lift
B595–1515 M250–400 Pool Sea

Cádiz Cádiz 135,740 (☎956) Map **24** C1
★★★★**Atlantico** Parque Genovés ☎212301
rm141 (A) ⇆133 Lift Pool Sea
⌂⚫**SAINA** av del Puente ☎231604 N⚫ Ren

Calafell Tarragona 3,360 (☎977) Map **22** C2/3
★★★**Miramar** San Juan de Dios 107 ☎690101
rm100 ⇆80 ⍟20 G Lift 1 Apr–15 Oct

Cala Ratjada See **Mallorca** under **Baleares
(Islas de)**

Cala San Vicente See **Pollensa** under
Mallorca under Baleares (Islas de)

Calatayud Zaragoza 17,220 (☎976)
Map **19** B1/2
⌂⚫**Vicor** A-Simón 3 ☎881863 Fia

Caldetas Barcelona 1,050 (☎93) Map **22** D3
★★★★**Colon** ps 16 ☎7910351 rm83 ⇆83 Lift
B690–1530 M400 Pn1425 Pool Beach Golf Sea

Calella Barcelona 9,700 (☎93) Map **22** D3
★★★★**Vegas** ☎7690850 rm115 (A15) ⇆60
⍟55 Lift May–Oct LD B350–750 M275
Pn600–825 Pool Sea
★★★★**Mont-Rosa** ps de las Rocas ☎7690508
rm120 ⇆120 Lift May–Oct B440–880 M310
Pn955–1045 Pool Sea
★★★**Velamar** Bruguera 49 ☎7690509 rm74
(A39) ⇆33 ⍟41 3 May–10 Oct Pool
⌂**Misse** San Jaime 299 ☎7690851 N⚫ Cit

Calella de Palafrugell See **Palafrugell**

Calpe Alicante 3,400 (☎965) Map **26** D3
★★**Venta la Chata** (4km N) ☎830308 rm17
⇆17 G ⚓ Sea

Cambados Pontevedra 10,640 Map **17** A3
★★**Parador Nacional del Albariño** ps de
Cervantes ☎1 ta Paral rm8 ⇆8

Camp de Mar See **Andraitx** under
Mallorca under **Baleares (Islas de)**

Carolina (La) Jaén 15,770 (☎953)
Map **25** A2/3
★★★**Perdiz** ctra N IV ☎660300 tx27578
rm89 (A55) ⇆89 G B1100–1650 M480
Pn2210(suites) Pool

Castelldefels Barcelona 13,220 (☎93)
Map **22** C3
★★★**Catite** ps Garbi 134 ☎6651700 rm31
⇆25 ⍟6 May–Sep B395–825 M345
Pn830–938 Pool Sea
★★★**Neptuno** ☎6651400 rm42 (A3) ⇆25 ⍟17
Lift B595–1355 M520 Pn1375–1775 ⚓ Pool Sea
★★★**Rancho** ps de la Marina 212 ☎6651900
rm60 ⇆60 Lift B670–1320 M450
Pn1070–1250 ⚓ Pool Sea

Castellón de la Plana Castellón 93,970
(☎964) Map **21** B1
★★★**Mindoro** Moyano 4 ☎222300 rm101
⇆101 G Lift B770–1410 M410 Pn1520(double)
⌂⚫**Levante** Gl-Moscardo 4 ☎213035 N⚫
▮⚫**24 Tagerbaf** Hnos Vilataña ☎216653 G40
At **Grao de Castellón** (5km E)
★★★★**Golf** Playa del Pinar ☎221950
ta Golfazahar rm65 ⇆65 G Lift ⚓ Pool Beach
Golf Sea
★★★**Turcosa** av Buenavista ☎222150 rm70
⇆70 Lift B570–1115 M390 Pn1185–1310 Sea

Castro Urdiales Santander 12,400 (☎944)
Map **19** A3/4
★★**Rocas** av de la Playa ☎860400 rm61
⇆61 G Lift Sea

Cazorla Jaén 9,370 Map **25** A2
★★**Parador Nacional el Adelantado** ☎295
ta Paral rm30 (A8) ⇆16 G B470–1165 M400
Pn1230 ∩

Cestona Guipúzcoa 4,380 (☎943) Map **19** B3
★★★★**Arocena** ☎867040 rm109 ⇆91 ⍟18
G Lift 15 Jun–15 Oct B555–1110 M425
Pn1180 ⚓ Pool

Ciordia See **Alsasua**

Ciudad Real 42,000 (☎926) Map **25** A3
⌂⚫**Calatrave** ctra Carrion km 242 ☎220315
N⚫ MB

Ciudad Rodrigo Salamanca 13,320
(☎923) Map **18** C1
★★★**Parador Nacional Enrique II** pl del
Castillo 1 ☎460150 ta Paral rm34 ⇆24
B335–835 M400
⌂⚫**F M Rubio** av España 20 & ctra Salamanca
☎460943 N⚫

Comarruga Tarragona (☎977) Map **22** C2
★★★**Europa** ☎661850 rm162 ⇆162 G Lift
Apr–Oct B580–1250 M435 Pn1540–1790
⚓ Pool Beach Sea

Comillas Santander 2,410 Map **19** A4
★★★**Casal del Castro** San Jeronimo ☎89
rm45 ⇆45 Lift 1 Jun–30 Sep B660–1290
M450 Pn1260–1400 ⚓

Condado de San Jorge See **Playa de Aro**

Contreras See **Minglanilla**

Córdoba Córdoba 235,630 (☎957)
Map **24** D2
★★★★★**Meliá Cordoba** Jardines de la Victoria
☎226380 rm106 ⇆106 G Lift B1200–2220
M650 Pool
★★★★**Gran Capitan** av America 3–5
☎221955 rm99 ⇆99 G Lift B1260–1650
M500 Pn1605
★★★★**Parador Nacional de la Arruzafa** av
de la Arruzafa ☎226240 ta Paral rm56 ⇆56
Lift ⚓ Pool
★★★**Cordobes** Medina Azahara 7
☎235500 rm103 ⇆103 Lift
★★**Marisa** (n rest) Cardenal Herrero 10
☎226317 rm16 ⇆4 ⍟12 B351–544
★★**Zahira** Conde del Robledo 1 (off av del
Gran Capitan) ☎226260 rm100 ⇆100 Lift
★**Brillante** ctra el Brillante 91 ☎275800
rm32 ⇆9 ⍟12 LD B270–615 M250
Pn670–708
⌂**Contarini** av Cádiz 58 ☎234303 M/c BL

Coruña (La) (Corunna) La Coruña
189,650 (☎981) Map **17** B4
★★★★**Finisterre** ps del Parrote ☎223075
rm135 ⇆135 Lift Jul–Sep ⚓ Pool Sea
⌂⚫**L R Amada** Gl-Sanjurjo 117 ☎283400
Cit/Rov
At **Santa Cruz** (7.5km SE)
★★★**Porto Cobo** Playa de Santa Cruz ☎56
rm58 ⇆58 Lift Pool Beach Sea

Covarrubias Burgos 980 Map **19** A2
★★★**Arlanza** pl de D-Urracas ☎28 rm31
⇆29 ⍟2 Lift

Cuenca Cuença 34,490 (☎966) Map **25** B4
★★★**Torremangana** San Ignacio de Loyola 9
☎223351 rm112 ⇆112 G Lift B700–950 M775
Pn1495–1645

Cullera Valencia 15,740 (☎963) Map **26** D3
★★★**Sicania** ctra El Faro ☎223 rm115 ⇆115
G Lift 1 Dec–31 Oct ⚓ Sea
⌂⚫**V Ausina** Sevilla 2 ☎522220 N⚫ Cit

Daroca Zaragoza 2,900 Map **19** B1
★★**Daroca** Mayor 34 ☎253 rm20 ⇆20 Lift

Denia Alicante 16,500 (☎965) Map **26** D3
At **Playa de las Marinas** (4km N)
★★**Angeles** ☎780458 rm59 ⇆59
30 May–1 Oct B430–920 M275–400 Pn775
⚓ Beach Sea

Deva Guipúzcoa 4,490 (☎943) Map **19** B3

★★**Miramar** J-J Aztiria 36 ☎601144 rm60 ⇌60 G Lift LD B495–1095 M425 Pn1167–1250 Sea

El A placename beginning with **El** is listed under the name which follows it.

Escala (La) Gerona 3,120 (☎972) Map **22** D3

★★★*Barca* E-Serra 25 ☎770162 rm26 ⇌26 May–Sep Sea

★★★*Bonaire–Juvines* ps L-Albert 4 ☎770068 rm80 ⇌80 Lift B380–985 M290–327 Pn850–1027 Pool Beach Sea

★★★*Nieves Mar* ps Maritimo ☎310300 rm80 ⇌80 Lift 15 Jan–15 Nov ✇ Pool Sea

★★★*Voramar* ps L-Albert 2 ☎310108 rm42 ⇌40 Lift 25 Mar–2 Oct Pool Beach Sea

★★*Marquesado* (n rest) ps L-Albert 2 ☎310150 rm32 ⇌32 G 1 Jun–30 Sep Pool Sea

Escorial (El) See **San Lorenzo de El Escorial**

Estartit Gerona (☎972) Map **22** D3

★*Vila* Santa Ana 34 ☎758113 rm58 (A20) ⇌6 ⌷28 May–Sep B228–680 M245 Pn600–685

Estella Navarra 10,370 (☎948) Map **19** B3

★★*Residencia Tatan* (n rest) ps de las Llanos ☎550025 rm19 ⇌8 ⌷8

Estepona Málaga 21,160 (☎952) Map **24** C1

★★★★★*Atalaya Park* ☎811644 tx77210 rm500 ⇌500 Lift B1535–2450 M600 Pn2010–2450 ✇ Pool Beach Golf ◯ Sea

★★★*Santa Marta* Apartado 2 ☎811340 ta Martotel rm38 ⇌32 ⌷6 G 1 Apr–31 Oct ✇ Pool Beach Sea

★*Buenavista* Gl-Franco 119 ☎800137 rm45 ⇌20 ⌷2 G Lift LD B200–515 M220 Pn645–660 Sea

Ferrol del Caudillo (El) La Coruña 87,740 (☎981) Map **17** B4

★★★*Parador Almirante* Vierna 1 ☎353400 ta Paral rm27 ⇌23 ⌷4 G

⏛◐*Castelos* av Generalísimo 336 ☎313406 N◈ Frd

Figueras Gerona 22,090 (☎972) Map **22** D3

★★★★*President* ctra N II de Madrid a Francia ☎501700 rm75 ⇌56 ⌷19 G Lift B665–1295 M345 Pn1057

☆☆☆*Ampurdan* ctra Madrid Francia ☎500592 rm48 ⇌48 G Lift

★★★*Duran* c Lasauca 5 ☎501250 rm60 ⇌60 G Lift B330–915 M320 Pn775–975

★★★*Rallye* Cruce ctra Francia ☎501330 rm15 ⇌15 G Lift

★★*Trave* ctra de Olot ☎500591 rm59 (A25) ⇌38 ⌷21 G LD B365–430 M250 Pn700

H J Bordas pl Alcazar 6 N◈

⏛◐**Central** Caamaño 16 ☎500667 N◈ BL/Opl/Peu

⏛◐**Victoria** pl de la Victoria 12 ☎500293 N◈ Rov

Formentor See **Mallorca** under **Baleares (Islas de)**

Fornells de la Selva Gerona Map **22** D3

★★★*Fornells Park* ☎209925 rm37 ⇌37 LD Pool

Fuengirola Málaga 20,600 (☎952) Map **24** D1

★★★★*Mare Nostrum* ctra de Cadiz ☎462140 ta Hispanotel rm246 ⇌246 G Lift 1 May–31 Oct B690–1560 M425 Pn1300 ✇ Pool Beach Sea

★★★*Florida* Playa Florida ☎461847 rm116 ⇌107 ⌷9 Lift B365–730 M300 Pn850 Beach Sea

⏛◐*Pauli* ☎462058 Aud/Fia/MB/Opl/Tri/VW G40

Fuente Dé Santander Map **18** D3

★★*Parador Nacional del Rio Deva* ☎Camaleño 7 ta Parel rm10 ⇌10

Fuenterrabía Guipúzcoa 10,470 (☎943) Map **19** B3

★★*Guadalupe* Puntal de España ☎641650 rm35 ⇌22 ⌷13 15 May–30 Sep B501–1012 M395 Pn988–1050 Pool Sea

★★*Parador Nacional el Emperador* pl de Armas del Castillo ☎641873 ta Paral rm16 ⇌16 At **Jaizkibel** (8km SW)

★★★*Jaizkibel* Monte Jaizkibel ☎641100 rm13 ⇌6 G Sea

Gandía Valencia 36,340 (☎963) Map **26** D3 At **Playa de Gandía** (4km E)

★★★★*Bayren* de Neptuno ☎2840300 rm164 ⇌164 G Lift LD B695–1540 M550 Pn1490–1635 Pool Beach ✇ Sea

Gelida Barcelona 2,680 Map **22** C3

★*San Jorge* Cuartel Oeste ☎10 rm30 G Pool

Gerona Gerona 50,340 (☎972) Map **22** D3

★★★*Ultonia* (n rest) av Jaime 22 ☎203850 rm45 ⇌43 ⌷2 Lift B420–910

★★*Europa* (n rest) garreta Julio 23 ☎202750 rm26 ⇌12 ⌷14 Lift B425–835

★★*Peninsular* (n rest) Gl-Primo de Rivera 1 ☎203800 rm68 ⇌22 Lift B317–714 M300

⏛◐*J Andreu* ctra Barcelona 204 ☎206808 N◈ Cit G

⏛◐**24 Blanch** ronda San Antonio Maria Claret 10 ☎204381 N☎202824 BL

⏛◐*Santiago Juando* c Ultonia 9 ☎200169 N☎202589 Ren

Getafe See **Madrid**

Gijón Oviedo 187,610 (☎985) Map **18** D4

★★★★*Hernan Cortés* F-Vallin 5 ☎346000 ta Cortesotel rm109 ⇌92 ⌷17 Lift Sea

★★*Parador Nacional Molino Viejo* Parque de Isabel la Catolica 19 ☎354945 rm6 ⇌6

⏛◐**24 Norte Motor** Mariano Pola 10 ☎322150 Ren

Granada Granada 190,430 (☎958) Map **25** A1

★★★★★*Meliá* Ganivet 5 ☎227400 tx78429 rm221 ⇌221 Lift B1530–2380 M700

★★★★*Alhambra* Penapartida 2 ☎221468 tx78400 rm133 ⇌120 ⌷13 Lift B910–2020 M550 Pn1800–1850 Pool

★★★★*Brasilia* Recogidas 7 ☎227448 rm60 ⇌60 Lift

★★★*Guadalupe* av de los Alijares ☎223423 rm90 ⇌90 Lift B685–1150 M375

★★★*Kenia* Molinos 65 ☎227507 rm19 ⇌18 ⌷1

★★★*Parador Nacional de San Francisco* in the Alhambra ☎221462 ta Paral rm26 ⇌26 B1250–1695 M500

★★*Inglaterra* (n rest) Cetti Merien 4 (off Gran via de Colon) ☎221558 rm50 ⇌45 ⌷5 Lift B445–785

★*America* Real Alhambra 53 ☎227471 rm14 ⇌5 ⌷3 1 Mar–9 Nov LD B257–684 M305 Pn680–760

⏛◐*Autiberia* ps de Ronda 103 ☎235448 N◈

⏛◐*Colon* Calvo Sotelo 75 ☎234207 N◈ Cit G100

⏛◐*Servicio Union* c Cisne 5 ☎233100 N◈ M/c Fia/Peu

At **Sierra Nevada** (40km SE)

★★★*Sol & Nieve* ☎480300 ta Skiotel rm70 ⇌33 ⌷37 G Lift ✇ Pool

Grao de Castellón See **Castellón de la Plana**

Gredos Avila Map **18** C/D1

267

Spain

★★**Parador Nacional** ☎El Barco de Ávila 550
ta Paral rm68 ⇹68 Lift B800–1700 M500
Pn1635–1735

Guadalajara Guadalajara 31,920 (☎911)
Map **19** A1
★★★**Pax** ctra Madrid-Barcelona ☎221800
rm61 ⇹61 G Lift ⏵ Pool
★**Reloj** Dr Mayoral 11 ☎1525 rm14
⛽🍴**24 Taberné** Ingeniero Mariño 27 ☎211038
M/c
ℹ🍴**24 Taberné** ctra Nacional Madrid-
Barcelona km51400 ☎212447 N☎213066

Guadalupe Cáceres 3,070 Map **24** D4
Hospederia del Monasterio (Monastery
where accommodation is provided by the
monks) ☎36700 rm38 ⇹19 🛁13 B375–765
M320 Pn875–1055
★★**Parador Nacional de Zurbaran** Marqués
de la Romana 10 ☎75 ta Paral rm20 ⇹20 G
Lift B745–1005 M400 Pn760

Huelva Huelva 96,690 (☎955) Map **23** B2
★★★**Tartessos** (n rest) Gran Via 13
☎216700 rm82 ⇹82 Lift
ℹ🅿**City** ps de las Palmeras 25 ☎251903 N☎
BL

Huesca Huesca 33,190 (☎974) Map **20** C2
★★★**Pedro I de Aragón** ps de Gl-Franco 34
☎220300 rm52 ⇹52 Lift B486–987 M445
Pn1115
🅿**Autoloto** Alcampel ☎211113 N☎ BL
ℹ🍴**24 Commercial Niagara** Ramón y Cajal 73
☎222414 N☎223861 G150

Igualada Barcelona 27,940 (☎93)
Map **22** C3
★★★**America** ctra N11 ☎8031000 rm52
⇹52 G Lift B560–1225 M445 Pn1317–1357
Pool

Irún Guipúzcoa 45,060 (☎943) Map **19** B3
★★**Lizaso** (n rest) Martires de Guadalupe 5
☎611600 rm20 ⇹3 🛁4 B255–680
★**Paris** (n rest) ☎616545 rm22 ⇹1 🛁6
1 Apr–10 Nov B285–630

Jaca Huesca 11,130 (☎974) Map **20** C3
★★★**Gran** ps Generalísimo 1 ☎360900 ta
Jacotel rm80 (A30) ⇹80 G Lift B488–1236
M475 Pn1100–1200 ⏵ Pool

Jaén Jaén 78,160 (☎953) Map **25** A2
★★**Nervión** (n rest) Madre Soledad Torres
Acosta 3 ☎234688 rm42 ⇹24 🛁18 Lift
★★**Rey Fernando** pl Coca de la Piñera 7
☎211840 ta Horefer rm36 ⇹29 🛁7 G Lift
ℹ🅿**Lopez** av de Madrid 54 ☎220132 N☎
Opl/Peu/Ska
🍴**24 San Cristobal y Ada** av Generalisimo
Franco 14 ☎223635 M/c

Jaizkibel See **Fuenterrabía**

Jarandilla de la Vera Cáceres 3,040
Map **18** C1
★★★★**Parador Nacional de Carlos V** ☎98
ta Paral rm23 ⇹23

Jávea Alicante 7,130 Map **26** D3
★★★★**Parador Nacional Costa Blanca**
☎790200 ta Paral rm60 ⇹60 G Lift B910–1560
M480 Pn1770–1985 Pool Sea
ℹ🅿**Javea** av de Ondara 11 ☎790178 N☎
BL/Frd/Ren G20

Jerez de la Frontera Cádiz 149,870
(☎956) Map **24** C1
★★★★**Cisnes** (n rest) J-Antonio Primo de
Rivera 25 ☎343541 rm63 ⇹52 🛁8 Lift
★★**Aloha** ☎332500 rm30 ⇹30 Pool

Junquera (La) Gerona 1,960 (☎972)
Map **22** D4
★★★**Puerta de España** ctra N 11 ☎540120
rm26 ⇹26

★★**Mercé Park** ctra N11 (4km S) ☎502704
rm50 ⇹50 Lift B345–845 M315 Pn825–940

La A placename beginning with **La** is listed
under the name which follows it.

Laredo Santander 10,260 (☎942)
Map **19** A4
★**Ramona** av J-Antonio 4 ☎605336 rm28
(A15) ⇹17 LD B205–560 M265 Pn635–725
ℹ🍴**J Emeterio** ☎605145

Lecumberri Navarra 650 (☎948)
Map **19** B3
★★**Ayestaran** ctra 64 ☎7 rm120 ⇹42 🛁15
G ⏵

León León 105,240 (☎987) Map **18** C/D3
★★★★**Conde Luna** Independencia ☎216700
rm150 ⇹150 G Lift Pool
★★★★**San Marcos** ☎237300 tx89809 rm258
⇹258 Lift B1325–2750 M650
★★★**Oliden** (n rest) Playa de Santo Domingo
4 ☎227500 rm50 ⇹45 🛁5 Lift
★★★**Riosol** av de Palencia 3 ☎223650
rm142 ⇹142 Lift B358–750 M300 Pn845
ℹ🍴**24 Iban** c Burgo Nuevo 4 ☎212304 Ren

Lérida Lérida 90,880 (☎973) Map **21** B3
★★★**Condes de Urgel** av de Barcelona
☎202300 rm105 ⇹105 Lift B1020–1740
★★**Principal** (n rest) pl Paheria 8 ☎240900
rm45 ⇹12 🛁33 Lift B373–646
ℹ🅿**Moncasi** av de las Garrigas 38 ☎201650
N☎ Peu G200

Llafranch See **Palafrugell**

Llanes Oviedo 15,510 Map **18** D4
★★**Penablanca** (n rest) Pidal 1 ☎400166 rm40
⇹20 🛁20 15 Jun–16 Sep B430–895 Sea

Llansá Gerona 2,680 (☎972) Map **22** D3
At **Puerto de Llansa** (2km NE)
★★★**Mendisol** Playa de Grifeu ☎380100
rm35 ⇹35 G 1 Jun–20 Sep B375–882 M330
Pn900–1000 Sea
★★**Berna** ☎380150 rm38 ⇹23 15 May–15
Sep B313–741 M285 Pn835 Sea
★**Miramar** ps Maritimo 2 rm31 1 Apr–30 Sep

Lloret de Mar Gerona 7,060 (☎972)
Map **22** D3
★★★★**Monterrey** ctra de Tossa ☎364050
rm234 ⇹187 🛁47 G Lift May–Oct LD ⏵ Pool
Sea
★★★★**Rigat Park** Playa de Fanals ☎365200
rm110 ⇹110 G Lift 1 May–30 Sep ⏵ Beach Sea
★★★★**Santa Marta** Playa de Santa Christina
☎364904 rm78 A18 ⇹74 🛁4 G Lift Mar–Oct
B1040–2140 M725 Pn1925–2105 ⏵ Pool
Beach Sea
★★★**Solterra Playa** pl de España ☎364462
rm53 ⇹52 🛁1 Lift
★★**Excelsior** ps M-J-Verdaguer 16 ☎364137
rm45 ⇹45 Lift May–Oct LD B300–773 M290
Pn750–820 Sea
★★**Fanals** ctra de Barcelona ☎364112
rm80 ⇹51 🛁29 G Lift Etr–Oct ⏵ Pool Sea
★★**Mañana** ctra Tossa ☎364180 rm14 ⇹9
Jun–Sep
★★**Santa Rosa** Senia del Barral ☎364362
rm136 ⇹136 Lift 1 Jun–15 Sep Pool
ℹ🍴**24 El Celler** San Pedro 102 ☎365397 BL
ℹ🍴**24 Estacion Servico** ctra de Blanes
☎365470 Cit G50
ℹ🍴**Fanals** ctra de Blanes ☎335864 Fia

Logroño Logroño 84,460 (☎941)
Map **19** B3
★★★★**Carlton Rioja** av Rey J-Carlos I 5
☎222600 rm120 ⇹120 Lift B1650–2550
M615 Pn2195
★★**Gran** Gl-Vara de Rey 5 ☎212100 rm84
⇹84 G Lift

Los A placename beginning with **Los** is listed under the name which follows it.

Luarca Oviedo 19,600 (☎985) Map **18** C4
★**Gayoso Tres Estrellas** Parque ☎640050 rm27 ⇄27 Lift B586–1027 M300 Pn1160

Madrid Madrid 3,146,070 (☎91) Map **19** A1 **See Plan**

AA agents; see page 252

★★★★★**Meliá Castilla** Capt Haya 37 ☎2708000 Plan **1** tx23142 rm1000 ⇄1000 G Lift B2810 M780 Pool
★★★★★**Meliá** Princesa 27 ☎2418200 Plan **2** tx22537 rm250 ⇄250 G Lift B2275–3700 M920
★★★★★**Palace** pl de las Cortes 7 ☎2326300 Plan **3** tx27704 rm525 ⇄525 G Lift B2395–3770 M850 Pn4095–4610
★★★★★**Plaza** pl de España 8 ☎2471200 Plan **4** tx27383 rm420 ⇄420 Lift Pool
★★★★★**Ritz** pl de la Lealtad 5 ☎2212857 Plan **5** tx22272 RIPAL rm168 ⇄168 G Lift B3200–4900 Màlc
★★★★★**Washington** av J-Antonio 72 ☎2470200 Plan **6** ta Washotel rm125 ⇄125 Lift
★★★★★**Wellington** Velázquez8 ☎2754400 Plan **7** tx22700 rm325 ⇄325 G Lift B1810–3320 M800 Pn2000–3000 Pool
★★★★**Castellana** ps Castellana 57 ☎4100200 Plan **8** ta Grand Met tx27686 GRAM-E rm278 ⇄278 G Lift B1705–2980 M610 Pn2475–3300
★★★★**Emperador** av J-Antonio 53 ☎2472800 Plan **9** rm230 ⇄230 Lift B1250–2100 M550 Pn1900(double) 2100(single) Pool
★★★★**Emperatriz** López de Hoyos 4 ☎2761910 Plan **10** rm170 ⇄170 Lift
★★★★**Gran Via** av J-Antonio 25 ☎2221121 Plan **11** rm162 ⇄162 Lift
★★★★**Sanvy** c Goya 3 ☎2760800 Plan **12** rm109 ⇄109 G Lift Pool
★★★**Balboa** Núnez de Balboa 112 ☎2625440 Plan **13** tx27578 rm110 ⇄110 G Lift
★★★**Carlos-V** (n rest) c Maestro Victoria 5 (off c de la Arenal) ☎2314100 Plan **14** rm67 ⇄67 Lift B1012–1340
★★★**Carlton** ps de las Delicias 26 ☎2397100 Plan **15** rm150 ⇄150 Lift B440(double) Pn840(double)
★★★**Lope de Vega** (n rest) av J-Antonio 59 ☎2477000 Plan **16** rm50 ⇄50 Lift
★★★**Madrid** (n rest) Carretás 10 (off Puerto del Sol) ☎2216520 Plan **17** rm71 ⇄71 Lift B660–1160
★★★**Nacional** ps del Prado 48 ☎2273010 Plan **18** rm189 ⇄146 ▥43 G Lift
★★★**Principe Pio** ps de Onésimo Redondo 16 ☎2470800 Plan **19** rm200 ⇄190 ▥10 Lift
★★★**Tirol** (n rest) Marqués de Urquljo 4 ☎2481900 Plan **20** rm92 ⇄84 G Lift B745–1100
★★**Mercator** (n rest) Atocha 123 ☎2392600 Plan **22** rm90 ⇄90 G Lift
⛽24 **Pardal** F-de la-Hoz 50 ☎4198201 Chy/Rov
⛽ **Ram** P-Santa M de la Cabeza 92 ☎4683251 N☜ Rov
⛽24 **Simca Española** Ayala 89 ☎4012050 Chy/Sim
⛽ **Standard** A-Lopez 88 ☎2698806 N☜ BL/Tri G40
⛽24 **Unidos** c J-Picon 4 ☎2461164 & c Villafranca 7 ☎2566649 N☜ G30
At **Barajas** (15km N)

★★★★★**Barajas** ☎2054296 Plan **23** tx22255 Madas E rm230 ⇄230 Lift Pool
☆☆**Olivos** ctra N IV ☎6956700 rm100 ⇄100 G B779–1013 (double) M360 Pool

Magaluf See **Mallorca** under **Baleares** (Islas de)

Mahon See **Menorca** under **Baleares** (Islas de)

Málaga Málaga 374,450 (☎952) Map **24** D1
★★★★**Málaga Palacio** av Cortina del Muelle ☎211571 tx77021 rm235 ⇄235 Lift Pool Sea
★★★**Gaviota** ps de Salvador Rueda ☎250150 rm25 ⇄25 G Lift Pool Sea
★★★**Nar Anjos** ps Sancha 29 ☎224316 tx77061 Trion E rm38 ⇄35 ▥3 G Lift Sea
★★**Parador Nacional de Gibralfaro** ☎221902 ta Paral rm12 ⇄12
★★**Niza** Marqués de Larios 2 ☎217761 rm53 ⇄30 Lift
★★**Penón** Marqués de Larios 4 ☎213602 rm29 ⇄10 ▥12 Lift
⛽**Taillefer** ctra la Union ☎222940 N☜
At **Rincon de Victoria** (13km E)
★★★**Elimar 2** Quiepo de Llano ☎401200 rm80 ⇄80 G Lift B455–960 M320 Pn890–980 (double)

Mallorca See **Baleares** (Islas de)

Manzanares Ciudad Real 15,690 (☎926) Map **25** A3
☆☆**Albergue Nacional** (2km S) ☎610400 rm42 ⇄37 B465–1610 M485 Pn1400–1515
★**Cruce** ctra Madrid-Cádiz km 173 ☎611900 rm40 ⇄36 ▥4 LD B551–1327 M480 Pn1966 Pool
⛽24 **J Serrano Calvillo** ctra Madrid-Cádiz km 171 ☎611192 BL G100

Maqueda Toledo 510 Map **25** A4
★★★**Cazador** ctra de Madrid-Badajoz ☎20 rm30 (A15) ⇄30 G B485–830 M325 Pn605 Pool

Marbella Málaga 33,200 (☎952) Map **24** D1
★★★★★**Meliá Don Pepe** ctra de Cádiz ☎770300 tx77055 rm226 ⇄226 G Lift B2200–4240 M1000 ☞ Pool Golf Sea
★★★★★**Monteros** ☎771700 tx77059 rm168 ⇄168 Lift LD B2700–4600 Pn4250–8000 ☞ Pool Beach ∩ Golf Sea
★★★★**Chapas** Route de Málaga km 198 ☎831375 tx77057 Luzma e rm117 ⇄117 Apr–Oct B715–1700 M450 Pn1370–1500 ☞ Pool ∩ Béach Sea
★★★★**Golf Guadalmina** ☎811744 tx77058 rm80 ⇄80 ☞ Pool Beach Golf Sea
★★★★**Guadalpin** ctra Cádiz-Málaga ☎771100 ta Pinotel rm103 ⇄103 B575–900 M350 Pn1000 Pool
★★★**Artola** ctra de Cádiz ☎831390 rm43 ⇄43 G Lift B680–935 M350 ☞ Pool Beach Golf Sea
★★★**Fuerte**-Castillo de San Luis ☎771500 ta Forotel rm110 ⇄110 G Lift LD B715–1390 M525 Pn1315–1365 ☞ Pool Beach Sea
★★★**San Cristobal** (n rest) Ramón y Cajal 16 ☎771250 ta Resimar rm109 ⇄109 Lift Sea
⛽24 **Auto Servicios Andaluces** ctra de Cádiz km 188,800 ☎771896 BL/Peu G5

Mataró Barcelona 73,130 (☎93) Map **22** D3
★★★**Castell de Mato** N II ☎7901681 rm52 ⇄52 Lift B735–1290 M450 Pn2300–2600 (double)

Mazagón Huelva Map **23** B2

Spain

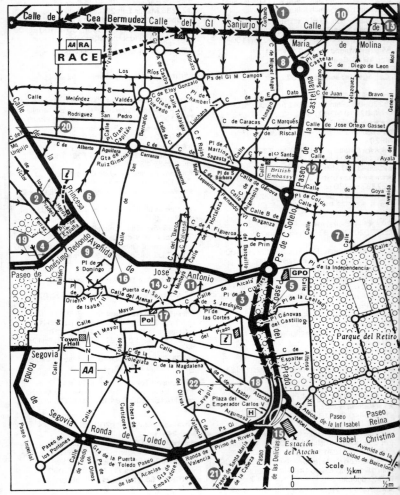

Madrid

1	★★★★★Meliá Castilla		13	★★★Balboa
2	★★★★★Meliá		14	★★★Carlos-V
3	★★★★★Palace		15	★★★Carlton
4	★★★★★Plaza		16	★★★Lope de Vega
5	★★★★★Ritz		17	★★★Madrid
6	★★★★★Washington		18	★★★National
7	★★★★★Wellington		19	★★★Principe Pio
8	★★★★Castellana		20	★★★Tirol
9	★★★★Emperador		21	★★★Olivos (at Getafe 12.5km S)
10	★★★★Emperatriz		22	★★Mercator
11	★★★★Gran Via		23	★★★★★Barajas (at Barajas 15km N)
12	★★★★Sanvy			

★★★ Parador Nacional Cristobal Cólon
☎303 ta Paral rm20 (A10) ⇆20 B910–1530
M480 Pn905 Pool Sea

Medinaceli Soria 1,440 Map **19** B1
★★ Duque de Medinaceli N11 ☎58 rm13
⇆2 ₥3 G LD Pool
♨24 Vicente Martinez Medina ctra Madrid-
Zaragoza km 150 ☎17 G25

Menorca See **Baleares (Islas de)**

Mérida Badajoz 40,060 (☎924) Map **24** C3
★★★ Emperatriz pl España 19 ☎302640
rm43 ⇆43 B625–1200 M400–500
Pn1400–1600

★★★ Parador Nacional via la Plata pl de
Queipo de Llano 3 ☎301540 ta Paral rm45
⇆45 G B1185–1560 M375

Mieres Oviedo Map **18** C/D4
δ♨ **Tunon** E-Cangas 3 ☎472144

Mijas Málaga 9,320 Map **24** D1
★★★ Mijas ☎463940 rm106 (A15) ⇆106
B500–1095 M440 Pn1445 ⇆ Pool Sea

Minglanilla Cuenca 2,950 Map **26** C3
At **Contreras**
★★ Contreras (10km E on Madrid-Valencia
road) ☎Villagordo del Cabriel 10 rm9 (A3)
⇆3 ₥4 G Mar-Nov G B275–820 M200
Pn700–800 Pool Lake
δ♨24 **Marco** ctra Madrid-Valencia ☎36
N♨80 Chy G20

Mojácar Almería 1,812 Map **25** B1
★★★ Moresco ☎478025 rm147 ⇆147 Lift
1 Apr–31 Oct B655–1145 M385 Pn1255–1395
Pool Sea

Molar (El) Madrid Map **19** A1
δ♨ **M Sato** ctra de Francia km 42 ☎32 M/c
Ren G20

Monachil Granada Map **25** A1
★★★ Parador Nacional Sierra Nevada
☎480200 rm32 ⇆32 G B684–1468 M426
Pn798–1448

Montblanch Tarragona 5,020 Map **22** C3
★★ Ducal av Gl-Mola ☎860025 rm40 ⇆20
₥20 G
δ♨ **D J Palliso Porta** ctra de Reus ☎860864
N♨ Ren

Montseny Barcelona 310 Map **22** D3
★★★ San Bernat ☎8670651 rm18 ⇆18 G ∩

Montserrat Barcelona 730 Map **22** C3
★★★ Abat Cisneros pl del Monasterio 10
☎16 rm41 ⇆31 ₥10 Lift

Mont-Tibidabo See **Barcelona**

Motilla del Palancar Cuenca 4,270
Map **25** B4
★★★ Sol ctra Madrid-Valencia 11 ☎331025
rm37 ⇆19 ₥18 G B270–595 M290 Pn790–800

Motril Granada 31,720 (☎958) Map **25** A1
★★★ Costa Nevada ctra de Granada ☎600500
rm65 ⇆65 ⇆ Pool
δ♨24 **Litoral** R-Acosta 11 ☎601296 Chy/Rov

Murcia Murcia 243,760 (☎968) Map **26** C2
★★★ Reina Victoria pl de M-Tornel 1
☎212269 rm75 ⇆40 ₥10 G Lift B340–656
M250 Pn692–841
★★★ 7 Coronas Meliá Ronda de Garay 3
☎217771 rm124 ⇆124 G Lift B1020–1690
M500
δ♨ **T Guillen Guillen** ctra de Alicante 119
☎241212 N♨ Peu G50

Navalmoral de la Mata Cáceres 9,710
Map **24** D4
★ Moya ☎530500 rm40 ⇆15 ₥5 G
B219–558 M245 Pn575–690
δ♨ **Moya** ctra Madrid-Lisboa km 180 ☎530500
N♨ Ren G10

Nerja Málaga 8,570 (☎952) Map **25** A1
★★★★ Parador Nacional ☎520050 ta Paral
rm40 ⇆40 G Lift B910–1695 M375–500
Pn940 ⇆ Pool Beach Sea
★★★ Portofino Puerta del Mar 2 ☎520150
rm12 ⇆12 20 Mar–Oct

Ojén Málaga Map **24** D1
★ Refugio Nacional de Cazadores de Juana
☎826140 ta Paral rm9 ⇆9 G

Olite Navarra 2,920 (☎948) Map **19** B3
★★★ Parador Principe de Viana ☎740000
ta Paral rm34 ⇆10

Olot Gerona 21,240 (☎972) Map **22** D3
★★★ Montsacopa c Mulleras ☎260762 ta
Mocopa rm72 ⇆34 ₥1 G Lift
♨24 Maso av Gerona 7 ☎261575 Aud/Rov/
VW G10
δ♨24 **Ferran** Jose Ayats 9 ☎261546

Orense Orense 73,380 (☎988) Map **17** B3
★★ Barcelona av Pontevedra 13 ☎220800
rm47 ⇆10 ₥10 Lift LD B299–693 M305
★★ Residencia Parque (n rest) Parque de San
Lázaro 24 ☎213200 rm50 ⇆14 ₥22 Lift
B235–650
δ♨ **Renault** ctra de Vigo (km 556) ☎216147
N♨ Ren

Oropesa Toledo 3,580 Map **24** D4
★★★ Parador Nacional de Virrey Toledo
pl del Palacio 1 ☎21 ta Paraloro rm47 ⇆47 Lift
B910–1560 M480

Oviedo Oviedo 154,120 (☎985) Map **18** C4
★★ España (n rest) Jovellanos 2 ☎222345
rm100 ⇆100 G Lift B1235–2095
★★ Principado San Francisco 8 ☎217792
rm63
★ Pasaje Palacio Valdés 1 ☎214580 rm36
⇆6 ₥1 Lift

Paguera See **Mallorca** under **Baleares
(Islas de)**

Pajares Oviedo 1,360 Map **18** C3
At **Puerto de Pajares** (5km S by N630)
★★ Parador Nacional de Pajares ☎490100
ta Paral rm29 ⇆7 ₥3 G B355–1005 M400
Pn1910–2335 (double)

Palafrugell Gerona 12,260 (☎972)
Map **33** D3
★★★ Cavallers (n rest) c Callavers 1 ☎300362
rm17 ⇆15 ₥2 1 Jun–30 Sep
δ♨ **J M Suquet** Bagur 19 ☎300248 N♨ Cit G50
At **Calella de Palafrugell** (5km SE) 4,000
★★★★ Alga ☎300058 ta Algotel rm54 ⇆54
Lift B1080–1920 M600 Pn1440–1800 ⇆
Pool Sea
★★★ Garbi Mirto ☎300100 rm36 (A6) ⇆34
Lift 1 Apr–30 Sep B433–871 Pool Sea
★★★ Mestral ☎300258 rm59 ⇆59 Lift
1 May–30 Sep ⇆ Pool Sea
★★ Mediterráneo Playa Baños ☎300150
rm38 ⇆20 ₥18 Lift 10 May–30 Sep LD
B290–740 Pn750–830 Sea
★★ Torre Canadell ☎300300 rm58 (A) ⇆38
1 May–15 Oct Sea
At **Llafranch** (6km E)
★★★ Paraiso ☎300450 rm55 ⇆55 G Lift
20 May–20 Sep LD B650 M265 Pn800–1100
⇆ Pool
★★★ Terramar ☎300200 rm56 ⇆51 ₥5 G
Lift Apr–Oct B680–1700 M400
Pn1100–1375 (double) Sea
★★ Llafranch ps Cypsele 35 ☎300208 rm28
⇆24 Sea
★ Levante San Francisco de Blanes ☎300366
rm20 ⇆8 ₥12 (closed 2 Nov–2 Dec) LD
B380–960 M350 Pn775–1000 Sea

Spain

At **Tamariu** (4km SE)
★★★**Hostalillo** Bellavista 11 ☎300158 rm72
⇆72 G Lift 20 May–20 Sep LD B700–1200
M425 Pn950–1256 Sea
★★★**Tamariu** ps del Mar 3 ☎300108 rm48
(A23) ⇆40 ▥8 G 15 Apr–30 Sep LD B335–800
M325–400 Pn775–900 Sea

Palamós Gerona 10,090 (☎972) Map **22** D3
★★★**Trias** ps del Mar 16 ☎314100 rm77
⇆67 ▥10 G Lift Mar–Oct Pool Sea
★★**Marina** av de Generalísimo 48 ☎314250
rm62 ⇆34 ▥28 Lift LD B305–740 M315
Pn750–865 Sea
★★**San Juan** c Mayor de San Juan 30
☎314208 rm31 ⇆23 ▥8 B500–1040
M285 Pn790–955 Pool Sea
★★**Vostra Llar** av J-Antonio 16 ☎314262
rm30 1 Jun–30 Sep
♨**Central** ctra a San Feliú 6 ☎314466 Fia
At **San Antonio de Calonge** (2.5km S)
★★★**Lys** ctra de San Feliú ☎314150 rm29
(A5) ⇆16 ▥11 20 May–25 Sep LD B280–535
M215–265 Pn690–715
★★★**Rosa dels Vents** ps del Mar ☎314216
ta Rosavents rm70 ⇆70 G Lift 19 May–30 Sep
LD B478–1296 M410 Pn900–1400 Beach ∩
Sea
★★★**Rosamar** ps del Mar 33 ☎314165 rm68
⇆68 G Lift 1 Apr–10 Oct LD Beach Sea
★★**Petit** c Progreso 10 ☎314062 rm25 ⇆25
May–Sep B271–582 M230 Pn595–645
▯♨24 **F Palli Marena** ctra de Palamos a San
Feliú 2 ☎314330 Chy/Sim G200

Palma de Mallorca See **Mallorca** under
Baleares (Islas de)

Pamplona Navarra 147,170 (☎948)
Map **19** B3
★★★★**Tres Reyes** Jardines de la Taconera
☎226600 tx36720 rm180 ⇆180 G Lift
B1670–2900 M660 Pn2765–3145 Pool
★★★**Toro** ☎Ainzoain 85 tx27578 rm77 ⇆77 G
★★**Yoldi** av San Ignacio 11 ☎224800 rm50
★**Hostal Valerio** av de Zaragoza 5 ☎212416
rm16 ⇆1 Lift Jan–Dec
▶♨24 **Redin** Arrieta 9 ☎246848 N▯245122
BL G10

Pancorbo Burgos 750 Map **19** A3
★★★**El Molino** ctra G-Madrid-Irún km 305
☎18 rm48 ⇆48 G Pool

Peniscola Castellón 2,720 Map **21** B2
★★★**Hosteria del Mar** ctra Benicarlo ☎480600
rm85 ⇆85 Lift LD B975–1840 M425
Pn1350–1475 ♨ Pool Beach Sea

Piedra (Monastery of) Zaragoza Map **19** B1
★★★**Monasterio** ☎Nuévalos 2 rm61 ⇆61
Apr–31 Oct B549–898 M360 Pn1020 ♨ Pool

Pineda de Mar Barcelona 7,780 (☎93)
Map **22** D3
★★**Mont Palau** c Mayor 21 ☎7623387 rm99
(A17) ⇆80 ▥10 Lift Mar–Nov B275–630
M200–265 Pn620–680
★★**Taurus Park** ps Maritimo rm400 ⇆340

Plasencia Cáceres 27,170 (☎927) Map **18** C1
★★★**Alfonso VIII** c Alfonso-VIII 32 ☎410250
rm56 ⇆56 Lift B561–1212 Pn1226
i F Sanchez Alvarez c Alfonso-VIII ☎412392
N▯412143 Cit G80

Playa d'Aiguafreda See **Bagur**

Playa de Aro Gerona 493 (☎972) Map **22** D3
★★★**Cliper** ☎817000 rm40 ⇆40
1 May–15 Oct LD B360–850 M250–300
Pn750–800 Sea
★★★**Cosmopolita** ps del Mar ☎817350
rm91 ⇆91 ▥7 Lift Etr–Nov Beach Sea
★★★**Miramar** ☎817150 rm45 ⇆45 G Lift
May–Oct B340–735 Beach Sea

★★★**Rosamar** pl del los Martires ☎817304
rm61 ⇆54 ▥17 Lift 15 May–30 Sep LD
B313–806 M340 Pn965
★★★**Xaloc** ☎817300 rm43 ⇆43
15 May–Sep B250–590 M250 Beach Sea
★★**Bell Repos** Virgen del Carmen ☎81700
rm40 ⇆27 ▥2 G 20 May–20 Oct Sea
★★**Pins** ☎817219 rm60 ⇆60 Lift
★★**Japet** ctra de Palamos ☎817366 rm48
⇆26 ▥22 closed 10 Dec–15 Oct B305–710
M310 Pn815–910
At **Condado de San Jorge** (2km NE)
★★★**Cap Roig** ☎315351 tx57204 rm160
⇆160 G Lift Mar–20 Nov B605–1510 M540 ♨
Pool Sea
★★★**Park San Jorge** ☎327316 rm85 ⇆80
▥5 Lift 27 May–20 Oct ♨ Beach Sea

Playa de Gandía See **Gandía**

Playa de las Marinas See **Denia**

Playa de Palma (Ca'n Pastilla) See
Palma de Mallorca under **Mallorca** under
Baleares (Islas de)

Playa de Palma Nova See **Palma de
Mallorca** under **Mallorca** under **Baleares
(Islas de)**

Pobla-de-Segur Lérida 500 Map **22** C3
▯▶24 **San Cristóbal** av Estación 2 ☎680524
N▯680360 G

Pollensa See **Mallorca** under **Baleares
(Islas de)**

Ponferrada León 45,260 (☎987) Map **18** C3
★★**Madrid** J-Antonio 50 ☎411550 rm54
⇆54 Lift
★**Maran** (n rest) A-Lopez Pelaez 29 ☎411800
rm24 ⇆2 ▥15 B220–500

Pontevedra Pontevedra 52,450 (☎986)
Map **17** A3
★★★**Parador Nacional Casa del Baron**
Maceda 21 ☎852195 ta Paral rm27 ⇆27
▯♨◐ **C Abreu Antas** av de Lugo-Mourente
☎851353 N♨ Cit
▯ **S Varela Pasarin** c Benito Corbal 36
☎850735 N♨

Port-Bou Gerona 2,360 (☎972) Map **22** D4
★**Costa Brava** J-Antonio 26 ☎390386 rm34
Apr–Sep LD B202–490 M250–325 Pn570–640

Potes Santander 1,210 Map **18** D3
★★**Parador Nacional** ☎7 de Camaleño rm10
⇆13

Premiá de Mar Barcelona 11,280 (☎93)
Map **22** D3
★★**Premiá** c San Miguel 46 ☎7510997 rm23
⇆23 B305–525

Puebla de Sanabria Zamora 1,590 (☎988)
Map **18** C3
☆☆**Albergue Nacional** ☎620001 rm24 ⇆18 G

Puerto de Llansá See **Llansá**

Puerto de Pajares See **Pajares**

Puerto de Pollensa See **Pollensa** under
Mallorca under **Baleares (Islas de)**

Puerto de Santa María (El) Cadiz 42,150
(☎956) Map **24** C1
☆☆☆☆**Meliá el Caballo Blanco** ☎863745
rm89 ⇆89 Lift B1330–1860 M550 Pn2250
♨ Sea
★★★**Fuentebravia** ctra de Rota ☎862727
rm90 ⇆90 Lift Pool Beach Sea
▯♨◐ **Guadalete** c F-Zamacola 13 ☎864692 N♨
BL

Puerto Lapice Ciudad Real 1,300 Map **25** A3
★★**Puerto** ctra Madrid-Cádiz ☎576000 rm37
▥5 G B360–655 M300

Puerto Lumbreras Murcia 7,990 (☎968)
Map **24** B2

☆☆*Albergue Nacional* ☎27 ta Paral rm19 ⇌11 G Jan–Dec

Puertomarin Lugo 2,960 Map **17** B3
★★★*Parador Nacional* ☎20 ta Paral rm10 ⇌10 Lake

Puigcerda Gerona 5,530 (☎972) Map **22** C4
★★*Maria Victoria* Florenza 9 ☎880300 rm50 ⇌21 ⑪16 G Lift B530–855 M330 Pn947 Lake
★★*Martinez* ctra de Llivia ☎880250 rm15 ⇌15 LD B840–980

Reinosa Santander 10,900 Map **19** A3
i☎24 **Hermanos Hidalgo** Pozo Pozmeo ☎751883 G4

Reus Tarragona 59,100 (☎977) Map **22** C2
⑧⑩*Rull* av 15 de Enero 25 ☎302269 N☻ Peu

Ribadeo Lugo 8,970 (☎982) Map **18** C4
☆☆*Albergue Nacional* ☎110825 ta Paral rm49 ⇌49 G Lift Sea
★★*Eo* (n rest) av de Astunias ☎110750 rm20 ⇌20 1 Apr–1 Oct B595–800 Pool Sea
⑧*D A Justo Rivas* San Roque 56 ☎110029 N☻ Ren G8

Ribadesella Oviedo 7,110 Map **18** D4
★★★*Gran de Sella* ☎860150 rm73 ⇌73 Lift Mar–Oct LD B1010–2095 M525 Pn1730–1917 ✇ Pool Sea

Ribas de Freser Gerona 3,130 (☎972) Map **22** C/D3
★★*Cataluna* (n rest) San Quintin 37 ☎727017 ta Hocata rm26 ⇌4 ⑪12 G Pool
★★*Montagut* Aguas de Ribas ☎727021 rm100 ⇌32 ⑪16 G 1 Jul–15 Sep ✇ Pool
★★*Prats* San Quintin 20 ☎727001 rm25 ⇌20 ⑪3 LD B335–610 M310 Pn705–770

Ronda Málaga 30,080 (☎952) Map **24** C1
★★★*Reina Victoria* c Jerez 39 ☎871240 rm73 ⇌62 ⑪11 Lift Pool

Rosas Gerona 6,190 (☎972) Map **22** D3
★★★*Coral Playa* ctra playa ☎256250 rm125 ⇌110 ⑪15 Lift 1 Apr–10 Oct
★★★*Vistabella* Cala Cañyellos Petites ☎256200 rm43 ⇌43 Etr–1 Oct B625–1075 M385 Pn1135(double) Beach Sea
★★*Terraza* ☎256154 rm85 ⇌62 ⑪13 G Lift 15 Mar–30 Oct ✇ Pool Beach Sea
★*Goya* Riera Ginjolers ☎256123 rm68 ⇌38 ⑪30 15 May–30 Sep LD B325–670 M375 Pn760 ✇ Pool

Rubena Burgos 190 Map **19** A3
★★*Fuente de Ray* ctra Madrid-Francia ☎1 rm11 ⇌2

Sabiñánigo Huesca 8,610 (☎974) Map **21** B4
★★*Pardina* ☎480975 rm64 ⇌64 Lift B600–1070 M390 Pn700 Pool Lake
i☎24 **Arranz** Zaragoza 9 ☎480043 BL

S'agaro Gerona 160 (☎972) Map **22** D3
★★★★★*Gavina* ☎321100 tx57132 rm74 ⇌74 Lift B2620–5240 M1200 Pn2650–3900 ✇ Pool Beach Sea
★★★*Caleta Park* playa de St Pol ☎320012 rm105 ⇌105 G Lift Mar–Oct LD B650–1700 M475 Pn1300–1500 Pool Sea

Sagunto Valencia 47,030 (☎963) Map **26** D4
⑧⑩*Segui Sánchez* ctra Barcelona km 24 ☎461900 BL G10

Salamanca Salamanca 125,220 (☎923) Map **18** C2
★★★*Gran* (n rest) pl Poeta Iglesias 3 ☎213500 rm94 ⇌94 G Lift
★★★*Monterrey* J-Antonio 73 ☎4400 rm98 ⇌84 Lift Pool
★★*Clavero* Consuelo 15 ☎218108 rm39 ⇌19 ⑪6
i☎24 *M N Bermejo* av Italia 11 ☎223539 M/c Aus/Chy G400

i☎24 *La Paz* av Pérez Almeida 69 ☎220546 N☎227852 G10
⑧⑩*Moneo* c Ramón y Cajal 11 ☎214106 N☻ Fia

At **Santa Marta de Tormes** (4km E)
★★★*Jardin Regio* ☎6 rm108 ⇌108 G Lift ✇ Pool

Saler (El) See **Valencia**

Salou Tarragona 4,700 (☎977) Map **22** C2
★★★*Picnic* ctra Salou-Reus ☎380158 rm43 ⇌43 Pool
★★★*Salou Park* ☎380208 rm102 ⇌102 Lift 1 May–30 Sep B940–1680 M600 Pn1200–1600 Pool Sea
★★*Gaviotas* ☎380362 rm18 ⇌18 1 Feb–20 Dec LD B335–820 M355 Pn1030 Sea
★★*Planas* pl Bonet 2 ☎380108 rm100 ⇌67 ⑪33 Lift 1 Apr–30 Oct B309–863 M310 Pn813–893 Sea
⑧⑩*International* c P-Martell ☎380614 N☻ M/c G18

San Antonio de Calonge See **Palamós**

San Feliú de Guixols Gerona 12,510 (☎972) Map **22** D3
★★★★*Murla Park* ps Generalísimo 21 ☎320450 rm89 ⇌79 ⑪10 Lift LD B515–1330 M350–450 Pn1025–1325 Pool Sea
★★★★*Reina Elisenda* (n rest) ps Generalísimo 6 ☎320700 rm70 ⇌70 Lift 1 May–30 Sep ✇ Pool
★★★*Montecarlo* Montaña de San Elmo ☎320000 rm60 ⇌60 Lift 1 Jun–30 Sep Sea
★★★*Montjoi* San Elmo ☎320300 tx57139 rm64 ⇌64 G Lift Apr-Sep LD B415–1080 M400 Pn700–1150 Pool Sea
★★★*Murla* Gl-Mola 48 ☎320450 rm92 ⇌81 ⑪11 Lift Pool Sea
★★*Rex* Rambla J-Antonio 18 ☎320762 rm74 ⇌48 ⑪26 1 Apr–30 Oct Sea
★★*Ideal* c Especieros 6 ☎320612 rm24 ⇌24 May–Oct
★★*Jecsalis* ctra Gerona 9 ☎320258 rm63 ⇌20 ⑪43 G Lift Jun–Sep B425–1050 M360–375 Pn950–1000
★★*Nautilus* pl San Pedro 5 ☎320516 rm22 ⇌18 ⑪4 Lift May–Oct
★★*Noies* Rambla J-Antonio 10 ☎320400 rm50 ⇌50 Apr–Sep Lift B480–960 M300 Pn800–900(double) ✇ Sea
★★*Turist* San Ramón 39 ☎320841 rm23 ⇌10 G Lift Apr–Oct B210–555 M260 Pn527–667
⑧⑩*Central* av Gl-Mola 45 ☎320092 N☻ Chy/Sim
⑧⑩*Metropol* ctra Gerona 7 ☎320982 N☻ Ren

San Lorenzo de El Escorial Madrid 7,450 (☎91) Map **18** D1
★★★★★*Felipe II* Cerro de las Damas ☎2961400 rm110 ⇌110 G Lift Pool
★★★★*Victoria* Juan de Toledo 4 ☎2961200 rm90 ⇌90 G Lift Pool
★★★*Miranda & Suizo* Floridablanca 20 ☎2960000 rm50 ⇌50 Lift

San Pedro de Alcantara Málaga (☎952) Map **24** C1
★★★*Cortijo Blanco* ☎811440 rm119 ⇌86 ⑪33 1 Apr–1 Nov B521–947 M415 Pn1072 ✇ Pool

San Pol de Mar Barcelona 2,040 (☎93) Map **22** D3
★★★*Gran Sol* ctra de Francia ☎7600051 rm41 ⇌41 Lift LD B555–1110 M390 Pn1000–1160 ✇ Pool Beach Sea
★★*Torre Martina* ctra Madrid-Francia km 670 ☎8905125 rm35 (A) ⇌35 May–10 Oct Sea

San Roque Cádiz 17,730 (☎956) Map **24** C1
★★★*Rio Grande* ctra Cádiz-Málaga ☎868 rm22 ⇌22

Spain

San Sebastián Guipúzcoa 165,830 (☎943)
Map **19** B3
★★★★*Londres & Inglaterra* Zubieta 2
☎444133 rm153 ⇄153 Lift Sea
★★★*Gudamendi* (4km W) ☎214000 rm20
⇄20 Sea
★★★*Monte Igueldo* Monte Igueldo ☎210211
rm121 ⇄121 G Lift B1550–2020 M500
Pn1835 Pool Sea
★★*Niza* Zubieta 56 ☎444170 rm41 ⇄36 ⋔5
Lift B615–1230 Sea
★*Juaristi* Sanchez Toca 1 ☎467533 rm20
⋔10 Apr–Oct B255–595
🛏❀*Amara* c Amara ☎422239 Frd
🚗24 *Gruas España* av Isabel 11–15
☎458352 G
🛏❀*Izaguirre* av de Tolosa Infierno ctra de
Madrid km 4 ☎214160 N❀ Cit

Santa Cristina de Aro Gerona 980
Map **22** D3
★★★*Costa Brava Golf* ☎837052 tx57252
CB6H E rm91 ⇄91 Lift Mar–Oct B1100–2500
M500 Pn1300–1850 ⛱ Pool Golf
★★*Riu d'Or* (n rest) Taulera 2 rm16 ⇄16 G
1 Jun–30 Sep ⛱ Pool

Santa Cruz See **Coruña (La)**

Santa Cruz de Mudela Ciudad Real
Map **19** A3
🛏🚗24 *Izquierdo* ☎342022 N❀ Cit G

Santa Eulalia del Rio See **Ibiza** under
Baleares (Islas de)

Santa María de Huerta Soria 1,010
Map **19** B1
★★★*Albergue Nacional* ☎2520 ta Paral
Sta Ma Huerta rm40 ⇄40 G

Santa Marta de Tormes See **Salamanca**

Santander Santander 149,700 (☎942)
Map **19** A4
★★★★*Bahia* av Alfonso-XIII 5 ☎221700
tx35859 rm181 ⇄162 ⋔19 Lift Sea
★★*Cólon* pl de las Brisas ☎272300 rm43 ⇄6
20 Jun–9 Sep Sea
🛏❀*Gallo* Magallanes 19 ☎232237 N❀ Vlo
G10
🛏❀*Sancho* c Castilla 62 ☎370017 N❀ Frd/MB
🛏❀*Setién Herrá* av Parayas, c del Miera
☎239001 N❀ M/c MB/VW G
🚗❀*J Vidal de la Pena* ps de Pereda ☎239805
Ren/Rov

Santiago de Compostela La Coruña
70,890 (☎981) Map **17** B4
★★★★★*Reyes Catolicos* pl de España 1
☎582200 ta Hostal tx86004 rm157 ⇄105 ⋔52
G Lift B1325–2750 M650&àlc Pn1950–2450
★★★*Peregrino* av R-de Castro ☎591850
rm148 ⇄148 Lift B671–1702 M405
Pn1260–1400 Pool

Santillana del Mar Santander 3,920
Map **19** A4
★★★*Parador Nacional de Gil Blas* ☎1
rm45 (A21) ⇄24 G B445–1150 M400
Pn1060–1240
★★*Altamira* Canton 1 ☎2 rm27 ⇄16
Apr–Oct LD B265–675 M280 Pn700–778

Santo Domingo de la Calzada
Logroño 5,640 Map **19** A3
★★*Parador Nacional* ☎340300 ta Paral rm27
⇄27 B495–1030 M400 Pn1160–1260

Segovia Segovia 41,880 (☎911) Map **18** D1
★★★*Sirenas* J-Bravo 30 ☎411897 rm52
⇄48 ⋔4 G Lift B506–1182 M455
Pn1105–1230 ⛱ Pool

Seo de Urgel Lérida 8,010 (☎973)
Map **22** C4

★*Andria* av J-Antonio 1 ☎350300 rm25
⇄12 ⋔1 G B223–621 M275 Pn660–770
★*Avenida* av Gl-Franco 18 ☎350104 rm40
⇄7 ⋔23 Lift B217–574 M245 Pn605–755
🛏🚗24 *Carrillo* av Guillermo 5 ☎350570 BL

Sevilla (Seville) Sevilla 548,070 (☎954)
Map **24** C2
★★★★★*Alfonso XIII* San Fernando 2
☎222850 tx72191 rm300 ⇄300 G Lift Pool
★★★★*Cólon* J-Canalejas 1 ☎222900 rm260
⇄260 Lift
★★★*Inglaterra* pl Nueva 7 ☎224970
tx72244 rm120 ⇄120 G Lift B1000–1950
M500&àlc Pn1775
★★★*Luz Sevilla* Martin Villa 2 ☎222991
tx72112 rm150 ⇄150 G Lift B1740–2880
M675 Pn2570(double)
★★★*Acuarium* ☎258207 rm44 ⇄44 Lift
★★★*Fleming* Sierra Nevada 3 ☎361900
rm90 (A6) ⇄90 Lift B525–1240 M415
Pn1130–1240
★*Doña María* (n rest) don Remondo 19
☎224990 ta Maryhotel rm61 ⇄61 Lift
B1000–1950 Pool
★*Simon* Garcia de Vineusa 19 (off av Quiepo
de Llano) ☎226660 rm48 ⇄20 LD B300–640
M260 Pn600–720
🛏❀*R Falcon* Almaden de la Plata 19 ☎352284
GM G10
🚗❀*Quiles* ctra de Carmon 53 ☎351882 Maz

Sierra Nevada See **Granada**

Sitges Barcelona 11,450 (☎93) Map **22** C2/3
★★★*Antemare* ☎8940600 ta Aladin rm72
⇄72 Lift B874–1528 M500 Pn1250–1575
Pool Sea
★★★*Platjador* ps Ribera 35 ☎8940312
rm44 ⇄44 Lift 19 Mar–Oct LD B475–1030
M285 Pn870–955 Sea
★★★*Terramar* ps Calvo Sotelo ☎8940050
rm209 ⇄209 Lift May–Sep B1000–2250
Màlc ⛱ Pool Beach Golf Sea
★★*Arcadia* c Socias ☎8940900 ta Aladin
rm38 ⇄38 G Lift Jun–Sep B528–906 Sea
★★*Luna Playa* Puerto Alegre 51 ☎8940430
rm11 ⇄11 G Lift B453–936 Sea
★*Sitges* San Gaudencio 5 ☎8940072
rm52 ⇄11 ⋔17 Lift May–Oct B239–668
★*Romantic* San Isidro 23 ☎8940643 rm55
⇄40 May–Oct B275–550 M225 Pn525–600

Somosierra Madrid 150 Map **19** A1
★★*Mora* ☎6 rm19 ⇄19 G

Soria Soria 25,030 (☎975) Map **19** B2
★★★*Meson Leonor* ☎220250 rm60 (A19)
⇄60 G
★★*Parador Nacional Antonio Machado*
☎213540 rm14 ⇄14 G
G Ruiz Pedroviejo c Sorovega 8 ☎213243

Suances–Playa Santander 5,050 Map **19** A4
★*Lumar* ctra de Tagle ☎214 rm31 ⇄3 ⋔23
15 Jun–15 Sep Sea

Talavera de la Reina Toledo 45,330
(☎925) Map **24** D4
★★*Auto Estación* av Toledo 1 ☎800300
rm40 (A31) ⇄31 ⋔9 G B310–520 M210
Pn605–655
★★*Talavera* av G-Ruiz 1 ☎800200 rm80
(A17) ⇄80 Lift B295–630 M220 Pn660–720

Tamariu See **Palafrugell**

Tarifa Cádiz 15,830 (☎956) Map **24** C1
★★★*Meson de Sancho* ctra Cádiz-Málaga
☎684900 rm39 (A18) ⇄39 LD B698–925
M350 Pn1258–2045 ⛱ Pool Sea
☆☆*Balcón de España* ☎684326 rm40 ⇄40
G Apr–Oct B470–940 M450 Pn970–1070
Pool ⋒

★★Dos Mares ctra Cádiz–Málaga ☎684117 rm19 ⇋19 G Apr–Nov B423–821 M325 Pn785–912 ♨ Beach ○ Sea

Tarragona Tarragona 78,240 (☎977) Map **22** C2

★★★★★Imperial Terrace Rambla de San Carlos ☎203040 tx56441 Hitsa E rm170 ⇋170 G Lift B920–1880 M525 Pn1650–1820 ♨ Pool Sea

★★★★Lauria Rambla Generalísimo 20 ☎203740 ta Reslau rm72 ⇋72 Lift B690–1165 M415 Pn1195 Pool Sea

★★Astari via Augusta 97 ☎203840 rm83 ⇋55 ⋔28 G Lift 1 Mar–30 Oct Pool Sea

★★Nuria via Augusta 217 ☎202840 rm61 ⇋51 G Lift LD 15 Mar–Oct B290–615 M280 Pn673–713(double) Sea

🛏🚗24 **Minicar** Cdt Rivadulla 40 ☎211865 G30

🛏🚗**Tarrauto** Ramon y Cajal 40 ☎211315 N�***☎*** Chy G50

Teruel Teruel 21,600 Map **26** C4

★★★Parador Nacional ctra de Zaragoza ☎602553 ta Paral rm41 (A11) ⇋40 G Lift

★★Civera av de Sagunto 23 ☎602300 rm45 ⇋45 Lift

🛏**B Z Coll** Ronda 18 de Julio 5 ☎601235 N☎

🛏🚗**J Z Coll** av da Sagunto 15 ☎601061 N☎ BL/Frd

Toja (Isla de La) Pontevedra 8,100 (☎986) Map **17** A3

★★★★Gran ☎303 rm214 ⇋204 ⋔10 G Lift 1 Jul–31 Aug ♨ Pool Beach Golf Sea

Toledo Toledo 44,380 (☎925) Map **25** A4

★★★Parador Conde de Orgaz ☎221850 rm20 ⇋20

Tordesillas Valladolid 6,600 Map **18** D2

★★★Montico (5km E on N122) ☎770551 rm34 ⇋34 G B765–1125 M440 Pn1395 ♨ Pool

Torre del Mar Málaga (☎952) Map **24** D1 At **Benajarafe** (9km W)

★★España ☎20 Benajarafe rm20 (A) ⇋20 G

Torredembarra Tarragona 3,750 Map **22** C2

★★★Costa Fina av Virgen de Montserrat ☎71 rm48 ⇋48 G Lift 1 Apr–1 Oct ♨ Sea

Torrelavega Santander 42,950 (☎942) Map **19** A4

🛏🚗**Renault** c Ceferino Calderon 12 ☎882216 N☎

Torremolinos Málaga 5,000 (☎952) Map **24** D1

★★★★Carihuela Palace av de Montemar ☎380200 ta Caritel tx77124-Carit rm107 ⇋107 Lift ♨ Pool Beach Sea

★★★★Meliá av de Montemar ☎380500 tx77060 rm284 ⇋284 G Lift B1145–2270 M400–500 ♨ Pool Sea

★★★★Pez Espada ☎380300 ta Pespada tx77047 rm149 ⇋149 G Lift LD B1250–2740 M550–700 Pn2150–3000 ♨ Pool Beach Sea

★★★★Pinar ctra de Cádiz 134 ☎382644 rm73 ⇋73 ♨ Pool

★★★Edén ☎384600 rm100 ⇋100 Lift Pool Beach Sea

★★★Isabel Playa del Lido ☎381744 rm40 ⇋40 Lift 20 Dec–15 Nov B468–1046 M250 Pool Beach Sea

★★★Mercedes los Tajos ☎380100 tx77004 rm95 ⇋95 Lift Pool Sea

★★★Nidos (Bungalows) c los Nidos ☎380400 tx77151 Amgua E rm70 ⇋70 Jun–Oct B403–816 M275 Pn845–915 ♨ Pool Beach Sea

★★★Parador Nacional Del Golf ☎381255 rm40 ⇋40 B1185–1560 M500 Pool Beach Golf Sea

★★★Santa Monica ctra de Cádiz ☎880347 rm31 ⇋29 ⋔2 Lift Sea

★★★Tropicana ☎386600 tx77107-Tropi-E rm86 ⇋86 Lift closed Nov–Feb B750–1830 M400 Pn1175–1500(double) Pool Beach Sea

★★Panorama c Mercedes 14 ☎386277 rm53 ⇋52 ⋔1 G Lift Mar–Nov B430–650 M250 Pn725 Pool Sea

🛏🚗**Salamanca** av C-Alessandri 27 ☎381151 N☎ M/c Ben/Opl/RR

🛈🚗24 **Unidos** c Borbollon ☎382875 M/c

Tortosa Tarragona 46,380 (☎977) Map **21** B2

🛈🚗24 **Moderno** Ronda Docks 22 ☎441238 N☎411081 M/c

Tossa de Mar Gerona 2,520 (☎972) Map **22** D3

★★★Alexandra av de la Palma ☎340150 rm76 ⇋72 ⋔4 Lift 1 Apr–15 Oct Pool Sea

★★★Ancora av de la Palma ☎340299 rm60 ⇋30 ⋔30 G Jun–Sep LD B330–790 M325 Pn865–985 ♨ Beach ○ Sea

★★★Florida av de la Palma 21 ☎340308 rm45 ⇋45 Lift May–10 Oct B395–840 M300 Pn815–895 ♨

★★★Mar Menuda Playa de Mar Menuda ☎341000 ta Immsa rm40 ⇋40 Lift May–Sep B500–1390 M430–450 Pn1235–1430 ♨ Pool Beach Sea

★★★Terranova c Givarola ☎340289 rm113 ⇋113 Lift 1 Jun–30 Sep Pool Sea

★★★Voramar (n rest) av de la Palma ☎340354 rm63 ⇋63 1 May–10 Oct Sea

★★Corisco J-Antonio 8 ☎340174 rm28 ⇋19 ⋔9 Lift Apr–Oct B345–895 M325 Pn780–895 (**Pn** only Jul & Aug) Sea

★★Hacienda ☎340216 rm16 ⇋16 May–Sep LD B500–640(double)

★★Suizo (n rest) ☎341014 rm24 ⇋24

★★Villa Romana (n rest) ☎340258 rm28 ⇋16 ⋔12 G 15 May–10 Oct

★Cap d'Or ps del Mar ☎340081 rm12 ⇋8 ⋔4 Apr–Oct B310–640 M250 Pn720 Sea

★San Francisco ☎340149 rm22 ⇋6 ⋔16 May–Sep LD 15 May–20 Oct

🛏🚗**Nautica** ctra San Felíu ☎340377 Fia

Trujillo Cáceres 10,590 (☎927) Map **24** C4

★Madrid–Lisboa ctra Madrid–Portugal ☎48258 ta Madrillisboa rm23 ⇋5 ⋔11 G

Tudela Navarra 20,940 (☎948) Map **19** B2

★★Morase ☎821700 rm26 ⇋21 ⋔5 G Lift

★Tudela ctra de Zaragoza ☎820558 rm16 ⇋12 ⋔4 LD B298–636 M325 Pn630–920 **Navascues** av del Instituto ☎820209 N☎ BL

Úbeda Jaén 30,190 (☎953) Map **25** A2

★★★Parador Nacional Condestable Dávalos pl Váquez de Molina 1 ☎750345 ta Paral rm25 ⇋25 G

Valdepeñas Ciudad Real 24,400 (☎926) Map **25** A3

☆☆☆**Hidalgo** (7km N) ctra Andalucia ☎311640 rm54 ⇋54 G Lift B1385(double) M530 Pn1505–1555 Pool

★Vista Alegre ctra Madrid–Cádiz ☎312040 rm17 ⇋17 B620–735 Màlc

Valencia Valencia 653,690 (☎963) Map **26** C/D3

★★★★Reina Victoria c de las Barcas 4 ☎3211360 rm100 ⇋100 Lift B1465–2330 M575 Pn2100–2350

★★★Alhambra c del Convento de San Francisco (nr pl de Caudillo) ☎3217250 ta Alhambrotel rm52 ⇋52 Lift B1008–1395 M450 Pn1507

Spain

★★★ Excelsíor (n rest) Hermanas Chabás 5 (off pl de Caudillo) ☎3213040 rm65 ⇄65 Lift B710–1410
★★ Bristol (n rest) Abadia de San Martin 3 (off c San Vicente) ☎3224895 rm40 ⇄20 ⋔20 Lift Jan–Dec B525–845
🏨⇔*Elektron* Dr Sumsi 38 ☎274715 N☢ G
🏨⇔*Montalt* c San Vincente 118 ☎3343739 Frd
🏨⇔*F Rodriguez* Al Cadarso 15 ☎278437 G100
At **El Saler** (12km S)
★★★ Parador Nacional Luis Vives ☎3236850 ta Paral rm40 ⇄40 B1230–1560 M480 Pn1985–3160 Pool Beach Golf Sea

Valladolid Valladolid 236,340 (☎983) Map **18** D2
★★★★ Olid Melia pl San Miguel 10 ☎254204 tx26312 metel e rm237 ⇄237 G Lift B1090–1825 M540
★★★ Conde Ansurez (n rest) Maria de Molina 9 ☎222277 ta Anzurezco rm76 ⇄76 Lift B994–1618
🏨⇔*Willi* av Gijon ☎271875 N☢ Peu/Vlo
Verín Orense 8,870 (☎988) Map **17** B3
★★★ Parador Nacional de Monterrey ☎410075 rm23 ⇄23 G B570–1025 M400 Pn1092–1178 Pool

Vich Barcelona 25,910 (☎93) Map **22** D3
★★★ Parador Nacional (16km NE) ☎309 rm31 ⇄31 G Lift Lake
★★ Cólon ps J-Antonio 1 ☎8891917 rm40 ⇄30 ⋔3 G 210–620 M230 Pn650–700

Viella Lerida 2,140 (☎973) Map **22** C4
★★★ Parador Nacional de Aran ☎640100 ta Paral rm135 ⇄135 G Lift B740–1600 M500 Pn1635(double) Pool

Vigo Pontevedra 197,140 (☎986) Map **17** A3
★★★★ Bahia De Vigo av Cánovas del Castillo 5 ☎226700 tx83014 rm107 ⇄107 G Lift B840–1990 M550 Pn1735–1910(double) Sea

Vilafranca del Penedés Barcelona 17,700 ☎93 Map **22** C3
🏨⇔24 **S Romeu** av Barcelona 2 ☎8920910 G15

Villacarlos See **Menorca** under **Baleares (Islas de)**

Villacastin Segovia 1,730 Map **18** D1
☆☆☆ *Albergue Nacional* ☎41 rm20 ⇄13 G

Villafranca del Bierzo León 6,120 (☎987) Map **18** C3
☆☆☆ **Parador Nacional Villafranca del Bierzo** ☎540175 ta Paral rm40 (A12) ⇄40 G LD B565–1165 M400 Pn1235–1355

Villajoyosa Alicante 16,260 (☎965) Map **26** C/D2
★★★★ Montiboli ☎890250 rm49 (A18) ⇄49 G Lift B850–2200 M630 Pn1840–2150 Pool Beach Sea

Villalba Lugo 17,300 Map **17** B4
★★ Parador Nacional Condes ☎510011 rm6 ⇄6 Lift B815–1095 M400
🏨⇔24 *Pita* av Generalísimo 74 ☎6201865 N☢

Villanueva y Geltrú Barcelona 35,710 (☎93) Map **22** C2
★ Solvi 70 ps Ferrer Pl 1 ☎8933243 rm31 ⇄31 G B280–560 M250 Pn600–620 Sea
🏨⇔*Nautisport* Gas 11 ☎8931516 G30

Villarreal de los Infantes Castellón
33,220 (☎964) Map **26** D4
At **Alqueria del Niño Perdido** (4km S on
N340)
☆☆☆ *Ticasa* ☎510200 rm26 ⇿26 ‰ Pool

Vinaroz Castellón 13,730 (☎964)
Map **21** B2
★★ *Duc de Vendôme* (1.5km on N340)
☎450944 rm12 ⇿12 G Sea
★★ *Roca* ctra Valencia Barcelona ☎450350
rm36 ⇿36 G B425–710 M290 Pn845 ‰ Sea
🛏🕭 *Aragon* San Agustin 11 ☎450893
N☎450265 N🛢 Cit G15
🛏🚗24 *J Verdera* San Francisco 131
☎450304 N☎451911 N🛢 G50

Vitoria Alava 136,870 (☎973) Map **19** B3
★★★★ *Canciller Ayala* Ramon y Cajal 6
☎220800 ta Cancillerotel tx32471 YALA-E
rm185 ⇿161 🏠24 G Lift B1200–1800
★★ *Fronton* (n rest) San Prudencio 7
☎211400 rm36 ⇿8 🏠28 Lift
At **Arcaute** (4km)
★ *Iradier* N1 ☎217100 rm27 ⇿20 🏠7 G
1 Feb–30 Oct

Zafra Badajoz 11,980 (☎924) Map **24** C3
★★★ *Parador Nacional Hernan Cortes* pl d
M-Cristina ☎550200 rm26 ⇿21 🏠5
🛏🕭 *D C Dominguez* ctra de los Santos 2a
☎550489

Zamora Zamora 49,030 (☎988) Map **18** C2
★★ *Cuatro Naciones* av J-Antonio 7 ☎512275
rm40 ⇿30 🏠10 Lift B334–798 M305

★★ *Parador Nacional Condes de Alba &
Aliste* ☎514497 ta Paral rm19 ⇿19 G LD
B695–1515 M425 Pn1335–1467 Pool

Zaragoza Zaragoza 479,850 (☎976)
Map **20** C2
★★★★★ *Corona de Aragon* via Imperial
☎224945 tx58067-Hocaz rm237 ⇿237 G Lift
B1625–2750 M650 Pn2700 Pool
★★★★ *Gran* c Costa 5 ☎221901 tx58010-
Ghoza-E rm 169 ⇿169 Lift
★★★ *Goya* Requeté Aragonés 6 (off ps de la
Independencia) ☎229331 rm150 ⇿150 G Lift
B810–1420 M500
★ *Conde Blanco* (n rest) Predicadores 84
☎238600 rm83 ⇿83 Lift B320–720
On **NII Madrid** road (8km SW)
★★ *Cisne* ☎332000 rm61 ⇿47 🏠4
B329–1028 Màlc Pool

Zarauz Guipúzcoa 11,640 (☎943)
Map **19** B3
★★★★ *Gran* Alameda de Madoz 7 ☎830400
rm74 ⇿56 🏠18 G Lift 1 Jun–30 Sep B730–
1425 M490 Pn1585 ‰ Sea
★★★ *Nautico-Playa* (n rest) Vizconde Zolina 11
☎841303 rm74 ⇿74 Lift May–Sep Sea
★★★ *Zarauz* av de Navarra 4 ☎830200 rm82
⇿82 Lift Jun–15 Sep LD B780–1700 M500
Pn1480–1600 Sea
★★ *Alameda* Travesia Alameda ☎830143
rm26 🏠4 May–3 Sep LD B254–523 M330
Pn750

Andorra/hotels and garages

Prices are in Spanish pesetas

Abbreviations:

av   avenida
c   calle
pl   placa

Andorra la Vella 2,463 Map **22** C4
★★★ *Andorra Palace* Prat de la Creu
☎21072 tx And 208 rm140 ⇿140 G Lift ‰
Pool
★★★ *Park* ☎20979 tx203 rm96 ⇿96 LD
B1721–2907 M688–860 Pn2615–2890 ‰
Pool
★★ *Internacional* Mossen Tremosa 2 ☎21422
rm50 ⇿30 🏠20 Lift
★★ *Mirador* c de la Vall ☎20920 rm65 ⇿30
🏠5
★★ *Pyrénées* ☎20508 tx Pyreflor And 209
rm81 ⇿32 🏠20 Lift B465–930 M330
Pn770–990
★★ *Riberpuig 'la Truita'* ☎20773 tx And 208
rm120 ⇿60 Lift Pool
🛏🚗 *Motorauto* av Santa Coloma 52 ☎20423
GM
🛏🕭 *Sud-América* av Meritxell 90 ☎20626 N🛢
AR Por

Encamp 806 Map **22** C4
★★★ *Oros* pl de Encamp ☎31222 rm54 ⇿14
🏠40 G Lift

Escaldes (Les) 2,300 Map **22** C4
★★★ *Catalunya* ☎21315 rm50 (A44) ⇿24
🏠20
★★★ *Roc Blanc* pl dels Co-Princeps 5 ☎21486
tx224 rm100 ⇿100 Lift B1450–2800 M595
Pn2300 ‰ Pool
★★★ *Tudel* pl dels Co-Princeps ☎20563 rm60
⇿12 🏠40 G Lift
★★ *Lina Pla Pujol* (n rest) ☎20934 rm15 🏠6
★★ *Pla* ☎21432 rm34 ⇿15 Lift 15 May–
1 Sep LD B335–720 M200–300 Pn600–700
★★ *El Refugi* (n rest) av Carlemany 36
☎21435 rm54 ⇿10 G Lift B250–550
★★ *Valira* ☎20565 rm50 ⇿45 🏠3 Lift
🛏🕭 *Central* av Carlemany 34 bis ☎20501
BL/Cit G250
🛏🚗 *Internacional* av Carlemany 65 ☎21492
Peu

Pas de la Casa Map **22** C4
★ *Vendaval* ☎51142 rm16 ⇿1 🏠6

Santa Coloma (3.5km SW of **Andorra la
Vella**) Map **22** C4
★★★ *La Roureda* av d'Enclar 18 ☎20681 rm56
⇿36 1 May–30 Sep LD B535–955 M335
Pn980

Sant Julià de Lòria 1,392 Map **22** C4
★★★ *Co Princeps* ☎41002 rm80 ⇿80 Lift
15 May–30 Sep B640–1020 M340 Pn1070
★★ *Sardane* pl Major ☎41018 rm25 (A3)
⇿22 Mar–Sep LD B826 Pn1400–1721

SWITZERLAND & LIECHTENSTEIN

Population 6,385,000 **Area** 15,950 sq miles **Maps** 11, 12, 27, 28, 29.

How to get there From Great Britain, Switzerland is usually approached via France. The distance from the Channel ports to Bern, the capital is approximately 470 miles, a distance which will normally require only one night stop. Car-sleeper services operate during the summer between Calais and Lyss.

Travel information

AA agents The AA has no agent in Switzerland but is allied to the Touring Club Suisse whose head office is at 9 rue Pierre Fatio, Geneva 3 ☎357611.

Accidents **Fire** ☎118 **Police, ambulance** ☎117 except in the following departments – Rapperswil (055) and Sargans (085) – where the number is 17 or 18. The three-digit number system is being extended to all areas of the country. In provincial areas ☎111 (11); this connects you with the postal services, who will then connect you with the police giving you precedence over other callers. If you have no change to put in a telephone slot, ☎112 (12) to call the post office line-fault department, who will immediately inform the police.

The most important principle is that all persons involved in an accident should ensure, as far as is possible, that the traffic flow is maintained. Should the accident have caused bodily injuries, the police must be called immediately. Those injured should be assisted by the persons at the scene of the accident until the arrival of medical help. It is not necessary to call the police if the accident has only caused material damage, although the party at fault should immediately report the damage and exchange particulars. If this is not possible, he must advise the police.

Accommodation Hotels are not officially classified but the Guide to Swiss Hotels, published annually by the Swiss Hotel Association, groups hotels according to prices. The guide, which also contains details of spas and facilities for sports, is available from the Swiss National Tourist Office in London and local tourist offices which issue hotel guides on a regional basis.

Switzerland

Prices generally include service and taxes. Provided that children do not occupy separate rooms, reductions of up to 50% are granted for children up to six years of age, and up to 30% for those over six and up to twelve years. The electronic hotel-reservations panels at the Tourist Office, Zürich, Kloten Airport, open daily from 06.30 to 23.30hrs, and at Zürich's main railway station, enable passengers to see at a glance which hotels have rooms available and to make immediate contact with the hotel selected in order to make a reservation.

Breakdowns   The major motoring club, the Touring Club Suisse, operates a patrol service and a day and night breakdown service but it is likely that you will be charged for any service. The service *(Touring Secours)* operates from several centres throughout the country and can be summoned by telephone. The number is being standardised to 140 and it is as well to try this number first, (except in the Chur zone) but if the call is not successful proceed as follows:

note the first three figures (two in the Zürich zone) on the instrument from which you are making your call. Find the corresponding number in the places on the map below and ring the centre indicated by the arrow.

When calling, give the operator the password *Touring Secours, Touring Club Suisse,* and state your location and if possible the nature of the trouble. The operator will state within a short time whether it will be a black and yellow patrol car or garage assistance, and how soon help can be expected.

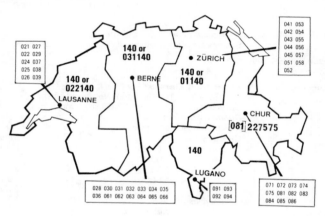

British Consulates   4001 Basel, Rittergasse 35 ☎(061) 235843
3005 Berne, Thunstrasse 50 ☎(031) 445021/8
1211 Geneva, 37–39 rue de Vermont ☎(022) 343800 and 332385
6900 Lugano, Via Maraini 14A, Loreto ☎(091) 545444
1842 Territet-Montreux, 15 Bourg Dessous, 1814 Latour de Peliz Vaud ☎(021) 541207
8008 Zürich, Bellerivestrasse 5 ☎(01) 471520/26

Currency and banking   The unit of currency is the Swiss franc, divided into 100 centimes. There are no restrictions on the import or export of currency.

Banking hours   Basel 08.15–16.30hrs (Wednesday 18.30)
Berne 08.00–16.30hrs (Thursday 18.00)
Geneva 08.30–16.30hrs (Wednesday 17.30)
Lausanne 08.30–12.30, 13.30–16.30hrs (Friday 17.30)
Lugano 08.30–12.30, 13.30–16.00hrs
Zürich 08.30–16.30hrs (Monday 18.00)

There are exchange offices in nearly all TCS offices open during office hours. At railway stations in large towns, and at airports, exchange offices are open 08.00–20.00hrs (these hours may vary from place to place). Banks are closed on Saturdays and Sundays.

Switzerland

Dimensions   Private cars and trailers are restricted to the following dimensions:

cars	height	4 metres;
	width	2.30 metres;
caravans	length	6 metres including tow bar;
	width	2.10 metres.

Luggage trailers may not be wider than the towing vehicle. Special regulations apply to four-wheel-drive vehicles towing trailers.

The Swiss Customs Officials can authorise slightly larger limits for foreign caravans for direct journeys to their destination and back, *eg*

width	maximum 2.20 metres (7ft 2in);
length	maximum 6.50 metres (21ft 4in) if Alpine passes are used;
	maximum 7.00 metres (23ft) if no Alpine passes are used.

A charge of Fr5 is made for these special permits.

It is dangerous to use a vehicle towing a trailer on some mountain roads; motorists should ensure that roads on which they are about to travel are suitable for the conveyance of car/trailer combinations.

Drinking and driving   A blood test may be required if there is definite suspicion that the driver is under the influence of alcohol. A driver is considered to be intoxicated if the amount of alcohol in his blood exceeds 0.8%. The penalty is either a fine or a prison sentence, and the withdrawal of the offender's driving licence for a period of at least two months.

Ferries (internal)   *All particulars are subject to alteration*
Sailings are often augmented to meet traffic demands.

Bodensee See Germany, page 158.
(Lake Constance)

Lake Lucerne   **Beckenried–Gersau** *Map 11 B1*
(Available from 15 March to 9 November only)
Service about 12 sailings 07.00–19.00hrs.
Duration 15 minutes
Maximum weight 10 tons

Charges		Single	Return
Cars not over	600kg	Fr8	Fr14
	1,000kg	9	16
	1,300kg	10	17
	1,500kg	11	19
	2,000kg	12	21
Motorcycles –	solo	6	10
	with sidecars	8	14
Passengers		2	3
Children		1	2

Charges include drivers' fares.

Lake Zürich   **Horgen–Meilen** *Map 11 B2/12 C2*
Service sailings every half hour 06.15–19.45hrs.
Duration 10 minutes
Charges *Vehicles* – cars (including drivers) Fr5 single
motorcycles (not including drivers) Fr2;
Passengers – Fr1.00 single.

Hazard warning lights   The use of hazard warning lights is permissible but they should supplement, and not take the place of, a warning triangle which must always be used to give advance warning of an obstruction.

Holidays and events   Public holidays based on religious festivals are not always fixed on the calendar but any current diary will give actual dates. The Whit period (a religious holiday) should not be confused with the British Spring Holiday.

Switzerland has a long list of public holidays varying from canton to canton, even from town to town depending upon the predominant religious aspects of the area. The following list is therefore not complete but it is representative and qualified generally.

Fixed holidays	1 January	New Year's Day
	2 January	Bank Holiday
	1 May	Labour Day (not all cantons)

Switzerland

	1 August	National Day (not a full day in all cantons)
	1 November	All Saints' Day (Roman Catholic areas)
	25 December	Christmas
	26 December	Boxing Day (not in all cantons)
Movable holidays	Good Friday	(except Tessin)
	Easter Monday	(except Obwald)
	Ascension Day	
	Whit Monday	
	Corpus Christi	(Roman Catholic areas)
Annual events	February	**Basel** Carnival
	March	**Geneva** International Motor Show
	April	**Basel** Swiss Industries Fair **Montreux** 'Golden Rose of Montreux' International TV Festival
	June	**Berne** Arts Week **Geneva** Rose weeks **Zürich** June festival weeks (opera, plays, concerts, exhibitions, etc) **Mürren** International High Alpine Ballooning weeks
	July	**Locarno** International Film Festival **Interlaken** William Tell Festival, plays (July/August)
	August/ September	**Lucerne** International Festival of Music
	August	**Geneva** Geneva Festival **Gstaad** Yehudi Menuhin Festival
	September	**Lausanne** National Autumn Trade Fair **Montreux-Vevey** International Music Festival
	October	**Geneva** Exhibition of Watches and Jewellery
	November	**Lausanne** West Swiss Antiques Fair
	December	**Arth, Küssnacht a R** Festival of St Nicholas processions

A comprehensive list of annual events can be obtained from the Swiss National Tourist Office (see page 284).

Insurance

This is compulsory; see page 11.

Frontier insurance If you do not hold insurance cover, frontier insurance (blue certificate) should be effected at the Customs border house.

Lights

Driving on sidelights only is prohibited. Spotlights are forbidden. Foglights can be used only in pairs of identical shape, brilliance, and colour, dipped headlights must be used in cities, and towns. Dipped headlights must be used at all times in tunnels, whether they are lit or not, and failure to observe this regulation can lead to a fine. Switzerland has a 'tunnel' road sign (a red triangle showing a tunnel entrance in the centre) which serves to remind drivers to turn on their dipped headlights. In open country, headlights must be dipped at least 200 metres (220yd) in front of any pedestrian or oncoming vehicle (including trains parallel to the road), when requested to do so by the driver of an oncoming vehicle flashing his lights, or when reversing, travelling in lines of traffic or stopping. Dipped headlights must be used when waiting at level crossings, traffic signals, or near roadworks. Dipped headlights must be used in badly-lit areas when visibility is poor.

Drivers of motorcycles and mopeds must use dipped headlights even during good daylight.

Switzerland

Medical treatment
There is no free medical treatment for visitors.

Motoring club

The **Touring Club Suisse** has branch offices in all important towns and has its head office in 1211 Geneva 3, at 9 rue Pierre-Fatio. The telephone number is (022) 357611. The TCS will extend a courtesy service to all motorists but their major services will have to be paid for. The club is affiliated with the AA whose members should produce their *5-Star Travel Booklet* when requesting service.

TCS offices are usually open from 08.30 to 12.00hrs and 13.30 to 17.00hrs, during the week and between 08.00 and 11.30hrs on Saturday mornings (summer only). They are not open on Sunday. The club maintains a 24-hour, seven-day a week emergency centre at their head office which can be contacted by telephone (022) 358000.

Parking
Parking restrictions are indicated by international signs or by broken yellow lines or crosses at the side of the road, or yellow markings on pavements or poles. Parking is forbidden where it would obstruct traffic or view on a main road or one carrying fast-moving traffic, and on or within 1.5 metres (5ft) of tram lines. Stopping is forbidden, even for passengers to get in or out of a vehicle or for unloading goods, in places marked by a continuous yellow line at the side of the road or red markings on pavements or poles. When parked on a slope or incline, use the handbrake and place chocks or wedges under the wheels. If you have to stop in a tunnel you must immediately switch off your engine. You cannot spend the night in a vehicle or trailer on the roadside in the canton of Tessin.

Blue zones
In some large towns, there are short-term parking areas known as blue zones. In these areas parked vehicles must display a disc on the windscreens; discs are set at the time of parking, and show when parking time expires. Restrictions apply 08.00–19.00hrs on weekdays throughout the year. Discs can be obtained free of charge from the TCS, the police, some large shops, or tobacconists' shops. Failure to observe zonal regulations could result in a fine or the vehicle being towed away.

Red zone
In Lausanne, a red zone system is in operation; for this, adjustable discs entitling up to 15 hours' parking are available free from the local TCS office, the tourist information office, or the parking attendant. These discs may be used for either red or blue zones, one side of the disc to be used for the blue zone and the other for the red zone. Failure to observe zonal regulations could result in a fine or in the vehicle being towed away.

Passengers
Children under twelve years of age are not allowed to travel in the front seats of a vehicle.

Petrol
The approximate price of petrol per litre is: super (98/100 octane) Fr0.99; normal (90/93 octane) Fr0.95. It is an offence to run out of petrol – even if you carry a reserve – on a motorway. A fine of Fr30 can be imposed.

Police fines
The police are empowered to impose on-the-spot fines on any motorists contravening the local traffic regulations; for more serious infringements, the case would be taken to court. The officer collecting the fine should issue an official receipt. Fines are extended to include other regulations; *eg* displaying an L sign when the learner driver is not at the wheel; having an illegible number plate; not carrying a driving licence.

Postal and telephone charges

		Fr
Surface mail	Postcards	0.70
	Letters 5–20gm	0.80
	20–50gm	1.60
Air mail	Enquire at local post offices.	
	The address of the *poste restante* in Bern is Postlagernd, Schanzenpost, Bern 1.	

Hours of opening
Post offices in towns are open from Monday to Friday 07.30–12.00hrs and 13.45–18.00hrs. On Saturdays they generally close at 11.00hrs.

Telephone rates
The telephone service is an extremely good one with subscriber dialling available throughout the country and for

Switzerland

calls to many foreign countries. A 3-minute call to Britain costs Fr6.00 and Fr2.00 for each additional minute. A local call costs 40cts and there are reductions at certain hours during the day and at weekends.

Priority
When the road is too narrow for two vehicles to pass, vehicles towing trailers have priority over other vehicles; heavy vehicles over light vehicles. If two vehicles of the same category cannot pass, the vehicle nearest to the most convenient stopping point or lay-by must reverse. On mountain roads if there is no room to pass, the descending vehicle must manoeuvre to give way to the ascending vehicle – unless the ascending vehicle is obviously nearer a lay-by. If two vehicles are travelling in opposite directions and the driver of each vehicle wants to turn left, they must pass in front of each other (not drive round). Drivers turning left may pass in front of traffic islands in the centre of an intersection. Lanes reserved for buses have been introduced; these are marked with either a continuous or broken yellow line and the word 'bus'. Bus lanes may be supplemented with the sign 'Bus lane only – Voie reservee aux bus' (a circular blue sign with the white silhouette of a bus superimposed on it). Only the broken yellow line may be crossed, either at a junction when turning or to enter the premises of a company.

Roads
The road surfaces are generally good, but many main roads are narrow. A network of motorways is being built (see below). There is ample scope for touring and it is quite easy to negotiate the popular passes in summer; of these the St Gotthard, Simplon, and Susten, which provide good routes to the south, are outstanding. See pages 28–35 for details of mountain passes and pages 36–39 for road and rail tunnels; note also Priority, above.

Signposting is excellent and warnings of any obstructed roads are prominently displayed. Main roads are numbered. Near towns and on some mountain circuits, traffic congestion may be severe at weekends. At the beginning and end of the German school holidays (see page 162) traffic increases considerably.

Alpine postal roads
On any stretch of mountain road, the driver of a private car may be asked by the driver of a postal bus, which is painted yellow, to reverse, or otherwise manoeuvre to allow the postal bus to pass.

If postal buses run in convoys, then each one except the last carries a red circular sign with a white diagonal bar. These vehicles are often driven at high speed, although by very experienced drivers, and other road users must take great care. Postal bus drivers often sound a distinctive three-note horn and no other vehicles may use this type of horn in Switzerland.

Motorways
There are approximately 563 miles of toll-free motorway (Autobahn or autoroute) and more are under construction; a network of 1,143 miles is planned.

Motorways are numbered N (national road) and are divided into classes 1, 2 and 3; they vary from the usual two-lane dual carriageway to 25ft-wide two-lane roads with limited access points. To join a motorway, follow the green and white signposts, or signposts with the motorway symbol. Vehicles unable to exceed 60kph (37mph) and motorcycles under 50cc are forbidden. The only speed restrictions are for vehicles towing trailers (see Speed, overleaf) but, as an experiment, certain sections have a recommended maximum limit.

Motorway telephones
These are placed 2km (1¼ miles) apart along all motorways, and give an automatic connection with the motorway control police. Ask for TCS patrol assistance. A patrol will normally be sent, but if one is not available, help will be sent from a TCS affiliated office.

Weather services
The Touring Club Suisse operates a weather service to give up-to-the-minute conditions of mountain passes. The information appears on notices placed at strategic points along the roads leading up to the passes. When the weather is exceptional, special bulletins are issued by the TCS through the press and broadcasting services. By dialling 163 on the national telephone system, you can also get road/weather reports in French, German, or Italian, according to the canton from which the call is made.

Winter conditions
Entry from France and Germany: the main entries are seldom affected, although the Faucille pass on the Dijon–Geneva road, and also minor routes through the Jura, Vosges, and Black Forest may be obstructed.

Switzerland

To Italy: from western Switzerland — during the winter months this is via the Grand St Bernard road tunnel or the Simplon or St Gotthard rail tunnels (see pages 36, 37); wheel chains are sometimes necessary on the approach to the Grand St Bernard road tunnel. From eastern Switzerland, the San Bernardino road tunnel (see page 36) or the Julier or Maloja passes can be used.

To Austria: the route across northern Switzerland via Liechtenstein is open all the year.

Within the country: the main highways linking Basel, Zürich, Lucerne, Berne, Lausanne, and Geneva are unaffected. The high passes are usually closed in the winter months but it is generally possible to drive within reasonable distance of all winter sports resorts. According to weather conditions, wheel chains or snow tyres may be necessary.

Seat belts   It is compulsory to wear seat belts.

Shopping hours   Shops are open in general 08.30–18.30hrs from Monday to Friday, and 08.30–16.00hrs on Saturdays with the exception of *food stores* which close at 17.30hrs.

Speed   Because the country is mountainous with many narrow and twisting roads, it is not safe to maintain a high speed. Built-up areas are indicated by signs bearing the placename: in these areas the limit is 60kph (37mph) for all vehicles.
Outside built-up areas the limit is 100kph (62mph) except on motorways where vehicles are subject to a limit of 130kph (80mph). Car/caravan or luggage trailer combinations are restricted to 80kph (49mph) on all roads outside built-up areas. These limits do not apply if another limit is indicated by signs or if the vehicle is subject to a lower general speed limit.

Tourist information offices   The Swiss government maintains an excellent information service in London at the Swiss National Tourist Office, Swiss Centre, 1 New Coventry Street, W1V 3H6, ☎01-734 1921. In all provincial towns and resorts throughout the country there are tourist information offices who are pleased to help tourists with local information and advice.

Tyres   Spiked or studded tyres. These may be used on light motor vehicles and on trailers drawn by such vehicles from 1

284

Switzerland

November to 31 March provided they are fitted to all four wheels and a speed of 80kph (49mph) is not exceeded. They are prohibited on motorways and fast motor roads. Spiked or studded tyres may not be substituted for wheel chains when these are compulsory. On-the-spot fines of Fr30 are imposed for the use of spiked or studded tyres after 31 March.

Wheel chains These are generally necessary on journeys to places at high altitudes. Roads with a sign 'chains compulsory' (a tyre with chains on it drawn on a white board which also includes the name of the road) are closed to cars without wheel chains. It is a punishable offence to drive without this equipment. On other roads (indicated by a rectangular sign with the words *Chains a neige ou pneus a neige* — Wheel chains or snow tyres) drivers of cars not fitted with them may be accused of breaking the law if they hold up traffic.

Visitors' registration A visitor staying overnight should report to the police, but this is often done by the hotel or campsite management who complete the registration form. If staying with a friend or relative at a private address, the host should notify the authorities.

Warning triangles It is compulsory to use a warning triangle to give advance warning of an obstruction and one should be used if a vehicle is stopped on the road for any reason. It should be placed on the roadside at least 50 metres (55yd) behind the stopped vehicle or obstruction but on motorways the distance should be increased to 150 metres (164yd).

If vehicles are fitted with hazard warning lights these may also be used in conjunction with a triangle but their use in no way effects the obligation to place a triangle in position.

Liechtenstein

Map 12 D1/2 The principality of Liechtenstein has a population of 23,000 and an area of 65 sq miles. Although it is an independent state it is represented in diplomatic and other matters by Switzerland. Vaduz is the capital.

Traffic regulations, insurance laws, and the monetary unit are the same as for Switzerland and prices are adjusted to match those in the major country.

Switzerland/hotels and garages

Prices are in Swiss francs

Abbreviations:
pl   place, Platz
pza   piazza
r   rue
rte   route
Str   Strasse

Aarau Aargau 17,045 (☎064) Map **11** B2
★**Goldenen Löwen** Rathauspl ☎221531
rm10
🛏🚗 **F Brack** Buchserstr 19 ☎221851 N🚗 Frd
G10
🛏🚗 **Hohglass** Entfelderstr 8 ☎221332 N🚗
Dat/GM
🛏🚗 **Rebmann** Buchserstr 66 ☎221444 N🚗
Cit G6

Adelboden Bern 2,900 (☎033) Map **11** B1
★★★★**Nevada Palace** ☎732131 tx32384
rm80 ⇌45 🛁8 G Lift 15 Dec–15 Apr
15 Jun–15 Sep B41–112 M30–35
Pn65–135 🏊 Pool
★★**Park Bellevue** ☎731621 rm46 ⇌20 🛁3
G Lift 18 Dec–18 Apr 1 Jun–15 Oct B36–152
M15–25 Pn45–95 Pool
★**Alpenrose** ☎731161 rm35 (A4) ⇌8 🛁3 G
18 Dec–20 Apr 10 Jun–25 Sep B26–108
M14–20 Pn40–75
★**Bären** ☎732151 rm12
★**Edelweiss** ☎732241 rm32 Lift 20 Dec–15
Apr 15 Jun–30 Sep B30–78 M15–30

Adliswil See Zürich

Aigle Vaud 4,300 (☎025) Map **11** A1
★★**Nord** pl du Centre ☎21055 rm18 ⇌4 🛁4
Lift B30.50–91 M15–25

Airolo Ticino 1,880 (☎094) Map **11** B1
★★★**Alpes** ☎881722 rm25 ⇌7 🛁3 Lift B23–86
M5–27 Pn55–70
★★**Motta & Poste** ☎881917 rm24 ⇌3 🛁8
Lift B35–85 M15–22 Pn40–65
🛏🚗 **Airolo** ☎881765 AR/BL/Cit
🛏🚗 **E Brasi** ☎881177 Toy G6
🛏🚗24 **Wolfisberg** via San Gottardo
☎881055 N🚗881195 M/c G

Altdorf Uri 6,600 (☎044) Map **11** B1
★**Schwarzer Löwen** Gotthardstr ☎21007
rm19 ⇌2 🛁4 G Lift B25–70 M13 Pn52–62
★**Wilhelm Tell** Gotthardstr ☎21020 rm20
🛁1
🛏🚗 **Central** Gotthardstr 54 ☎22355 Cit/Dat/
Vlo

Alterswil Fribourg Map **11** B1
🛏🚗24 **Piller** Hofmatt ☎441237 BL

Ambri-Piotta Ticino 400 (☎094)
Map **12** C1
★★**Poste** rte Internatinale du St-Gotthard
☎891221 rm45 (A) ⇌3 🛁3 G Lift 1 Apr–31 Oct

Amsteg Uri 600 (☎044) Map **11** B1
★★★**Stern & Post** Gotthardstr ☎64190
tx78445 rm40 ⇌20 G Lift B22–108 M10–20
Pn35–90

Andermatt Uri 1,300 (☎044) Map **11** B1
★★★**Badus** ☎67286 rm23 ⇌11 🛁9 G Lift
B28–90 M9–19 Pn39–55
★★★**Schweizerhof** ☎67189 rm28 ⇌15 G
★★**Alpenhof** ☎67239 rm30 G
Dec–31 Mar Jun–16 Oct B29–72 M16–20
Pn48–55
★★**Helvetia** ☎67515 rm30 ⇌18 🛁10 Lift
B41–82 M9–18 Pn47–57
★★**Krone** ☎67206 tx78446 rm52 ⇌14 🛁12
Lift B30–90 M12–20 Pn120–180

★★**Monopol Metropol** ☎67575 tx78443 rm31
⇌22 🛁2 G Lift Dec–Oct B28–108 M12–28
Pn48–90 Pool
★★**St Gotthard** ☎67204 rm27 (A) ⇌9 G
Dec–Apr May–Oct
★**Löwen** ☎67223 rm21 15 May–15 Oct
★**Schlüssel** Gotthardstr ☎67198 rm25 G
🛏🚗24 L **Loretz** ☎67243 Ren G8
At **Hospental** (2km SW)
★★**Meyerhof** ☎67207 rm30 ⇌4 G
1 Jun–1 Oct 15 Dec–Apr B25–70 M15–20
Pn40–60

Appenzell Appenzell 5,000 (☎071)
Map **12** C2
★★**Hecht** ☎871025 rm35 ⇌10 Lift B37–59
M15–25 Pn48–65
★★**Santis** ☎872644 rm34 ⇌14 🛁8 G Lift
1 Feb–8 Jan B37–124 M16–28 Pn60–70
🛏🚗 **W Baumann** Weissbadstr ☎871466
Dat/Fia/Peu

Arbon Thurgau (☎071) Map **12** C2
★★★**Metropole** Bahnhofstr 49 ☎463535
tx77247 rm40 ⇌15 🛁21 Lift 15 Jan–15 Dec
Pool Lake
★**Frohsinn** ☎461046 rm7 15 Oct–15 Sep
B26.50–59 M9–12 Lake
★**Rotes Kreuz** ☎461914 rm24 ⇌2 🛁7
B29–74 M5–18.50 Pn40–50 Lake

Arlesheim Basel (☎061) Map **11** B2
★**Ochsen** ☎725225 rm15 🛁1 13 Jul–26 Jun
(closed Thursdays)

Arolla Valais (☎027) Map **28** C4
★★**Grand & Kurhaus** ☎831161 rm70 ⇌29
Lift Xmas–Etr Jul–Aug B34.50–99 M15–25
Pn52–76

Arosa Graubünden 2,600 (☎081) Map **12** C1
★★★★**Kulm** ☎310131 tx74279 rm150
⇌120 🛁30 Lift 26 Nov–17 Apr 25 Jun–15 Oct
B40–75 M30 Pn65–100 🏊 Pool
★★★**Alexandra-Palace** ☎310111 tx74261
rm160 ⇌160 G Lift 2 Apr LD
B120–180 M25–28 Pn117–177 Pool Lake
★★★**Cristallo** ☎312261 tx74270 rm40 ⇌28
🛁8 Lift Jun–Sep Dec–Apr Lake
★★★**Post & Sport** ☎311361 rm75 ⇌45 Lake
★★★**Seehof** ☎311541 tx74277 rm78 ⇌40
G Lift 17 Dec–mid Apr LD B41–152 M22–28
Pn60–130 Lake
★★★**Sport Valsana** ☎310275 tx74232
rm100 ⇌53 🛁10 Lift Dec–Apr Jun–Oct
B41–152 M14 Pn45–95 🏊 Pool Lake
🛏🚗24 **Grand Dosch** ☎312222 AR/MB/Opl
G40

Arth-am-See Schwyz 6,300 (☎041)
Map **11** B1
🛏🚗24 **Rigi** Zugerstr ☎821223 Chy/Sim G2

Ascona Ticino 3,000 (☎093) Map **28** D4
★★★★**Acapulco** Lago Maggiore ☎354521
tx79399 rm44 ⇌35 🛁4 Lift 28 Feb–31 Oct
B59–177 Màlc Pn87–145 Pool Lake
★★★★**Ascona** ☎351135 rm56 ⇌56 G Lift
Mar–Dec B45–200 M25 Pool Lake
★★★**Schweizerhof** via Locarno ☎351214
rm70 ⇌11 🛁4 G Lift 1 Mar–31 Oct B37–124
M17–22 Pn55–88 Pool
★★★**Tamaro au Lac** ☎353939 tx79379
rm57 (A7) ⇌21 🛁7 G Lift 12 Feb–15 Nov
B25–60 Pn45–80 Lake
★**Piazza au Lac** ☎351181 rm20 (A5) ⇌5
1 Mar–31 Oct B30–90 M18 Lake
🛏🚗 **Buzzini** via Cantonale 124 ☎352414 N🚗
Aud/VW G4
🛏🚗 **Cristallina** via Circonvallazione ☎351320
N🚗 AR/BL/Jag/Rov G40
🛏🚗 **Storelli** via Cantonale ☎352196 N🚗 Toy

Avenches Vaud (☎037) Map **11** A1

Switzerland

⌂᪥*J P Divorne* rte de Berne 6 ☎751263 Opl G2

Baar Zug 7,000 (☎042) Map **11** B2
★★Lindenhof Dorfstr ☎311220 rm8 ⇆3
🅟2 Lift B27–57 M14–25

Baden Aargau 14,000 (☎056) Map **11** B2
★★Verenahof Kurpl ☎225251 rm106 (A24)
⇆39 🅟7 G Lift B41–191 M20–30 Pn50–150 Pool
★Bären Bäderstr 36 ☎225178 rm60 ⇆10 🅟20
G Lift B33–150 M18–28 Pn45–90 Pool
★Park Haselstr 9 ☎225353 rm14 ⇆2 🅟8 Lift B35–85
᪥***Diebold*** Mellingerstr 18 ☎27785 Frd

Bad Ragaz–Pfafers See Ragaz–Pfafers (Bad)

Bâle See Basel

Balsthal Solothurn 5,200 (☎062)
Map **11** B2
★Kreuz Hauptstr ☎713412 rm18 ⇆3 🅟7 G Lift B22–60 Màlc
★Rössli ☎715858 rm9

Basel (Bâle) Basel 238,500 (☎065)
Map **11** B2 **See Plan**
★★★★★Drei Könige Blumenrain 8 ☎255252
Plan **1** ta Troisrois Basel tx62937 rm82
⇆80 G Lift B60–220 M16 Pn92–157
★★★★★Euler Centralbahnpl 14 ☎234500
Plan **2** tx62215 rm70 ⇆70 G Lift
★★★★Bernina Innere Margarethenstr 14
☎237300 Plan **3** tx63813 rm35 ⇆20 🅟12 Lift
★★★★International Steinentorstr 25
☎221870 Plan **4** tx62370 rm160 ⇆148 🅟12
G Lift B70–180 M15–30 Pn102–162 Pool
★★★★Schweizerhof Centralbahnpl 1
☎222833 Plan **5** tx62373 rm75 ⇆70 Lift B86–130
★★★Cavalier Reiterstr 1 ☎392262 Plan **6**
rm27 ⇆27 Lift B32–82
★★★Drachen Aeschenvorstadt 24
☎239090 Plan **7** tx62346 rm43 ⇆17 🅟19
G Lift B38–107 Màlc
★★★Europe Clarastr 35–43 ☎268080 Plan **8**
tx64103 rm173 ⇆32 🅟141 G Lift B65–120 M7.60–30
★★★Excelsior Aeschengraben 13 ☎225300
Plan **9** tx62303 rm50 ⇆50 G Lift
★★★Touring & Red Ox Ochsengasse 2
☎329393 Plan **10** tx62480 rm104 ⇆40 🅟20
G Lift
★★★Greub Centralbahnstr 11 ☎231840
rm56 ⇆8 🅟1 Lift B24–96 M10–20
★★Jura Centralbahnpl 11 ☎231800 Plan **12**
rm65 ⇆7 🅟21 Lift B30.50–107 M3–20 àlc
★★Krafft Obere Rheingasse 12 ☎268877 Plan
13 rm52 ⇆8 G Lift B29–96 Màlc Pn65–84
★★Merkur Theaterstr 24 ☎233740 Plan **14**
rm25 ⇆4 🅟3 B33–75 M12.50–15.50 Pn50–60
★★St-Gotthard-Terminus Centralbahnstr 13
☎225250 Plan **15** rm34 ⇆9 🅟4 Lift B28–82
★★Victoria am Bahnhof (n rest)
Centralbahnpl 3 ☎225566 Plan **16** tx62362
rm109 ⇆18 🅟44 Lift B41–112 M14
★Blaukreuzhaus Petersgraben 23 ☎258140
Plan **17** rm64 (A20) ⇆7 🅟10 G Lift B24–54
★Bristol Centralbahnstr 15 ☎223822
Plan **18** rm30 ⇆4 🅟1 Lift B28–90 M6.50–18 Pn34–56
★Helvetia Küchengasse 13 ☎230688 Plan **20**
rm25 🅟5 B35–60
★Hospiz Engelhof (n rest) Nadelberg Stifts-
gasse 1 ☎252244 Plan **21** rm62 ⇆4 Lift B22–68
★Steinbock Centralbahnstr 16 ☎225844
Plan **22** rm27 🅟4 Lift B36–76 M 9–19 àlc
᪥***24 AAA*** Brüglingerstr 2 ☎342233
Bed/Dat/Vau
⌂᪥***Autavia*** Hardstr 14 ☎427878 Frd

᪥***Delta*** St-Johanns Ring 30 ☎449910
N᪥ Hon/Sab
᪥**Dreispitz** Reinacherstr 28 ☎345555 N᪥ BL
᪥***Dufour*** Dufourstr 36 ☎231214 N᪥ BL
᪥***Grosspeter*** Grosspeterstr 12 ☎356070
N᪥ Opl
᪥***St-Johann*** Ryffstr 16 ☎438450 N᪥ BL/Fia
ɪ C Scholotterbeck Viaduktstr 40 ☎220050
Cit/Jag/RR
᪥**₦24 Settelen** Türkheimerstr 17 ☎383800
N☎222210 Toy/Tri
᪥**G Uecker** Näfelserstr 19 ☎385076 N᪥ Chy/Sim

Beatenberg Bern 1,323 (☎036) Map **11** B1
★Beauregard ☎411341 rm22 🅟6 20 Dec–25
Apr 15 May–31 Oct B31–88 M14.50 Pn40–65 Lake
★Jungfrаublick ☎411581 ta Zahler rm20 Lake

Beckenried Nidwalden 2,000 (☎041)
Map **11** B1
★★Edelweiss ☎641252 rm30 ⇆6 🅟4 G
B29–74 M13–16 Pn36–55 Lake
★Mond ☎641204 rm50 Lift Lake
★Nidwaldnerhof ☎641484 rm56
May–Oct B24–70 M13–20 Pn42–60 Lake
★Sonne ☎641205 rm25 G Apr–Oct
B26.50–58 M12–15 Pn36–40 Lake

Bellinzona Ticino 13,400 (☎092)
Map **29** A4
★★★Unione via Gl Guisan ☎255577
tx73474 rm34 ⇆21 🅟3 Lift LD B24–74
M17–20 Pn56–76
᪥***G Ferrari*** via Lugano 31 ☎251668 N᪥
Toy G5
᪥***Gottardo*** viale Portone 6 ☎252818 N᪥
BL/Tri

Belvédère See Furka Pass

Bergün Graubünden 608 (☎081) Map **12** C1
★Weisses Kreuz ☎731161 rm34 ⇆8 🅟20
15 Dec–10 Apr 5 Jun–30 Oct B33–63 M16–20

Berlingen Thurgau (☎054) Map **12** C2
★Seestern ☎82404 rm9 (A) 🅟1 Feb–25 Dec
Lake

Bern (Berne) Bern 164,800 (☎031)
Map **11** B1
★★★★★Bellevue Palace Kochergasse 3
☎224581 tx32124 rm143 ⇆115 G Lift B50–200
★★★★★Schweizerhof Bahnhofpl 11 (nr Sta)
☎224501 tx32188 rm110 ⇆95 G Lift B50–230
M25–30 &àlc
★★★★Savoy Neuengasse 26 ☎224405
tx32445 rm77 ⇆25 🅟18 Lift B50–108
M18.50 Pn111–135
★★★Bären Schauplatzgasse 4 ☎223367
tx33199 rm57 ⇆23 🅟34 Lift B55–108
M18–25 Pn96–101
★★★Bristol (n rest) Schauplatzgasse 10 (off
Bärenpl) ☎220101 tx33199 rm90 ⇆19 🅟39
Lift B35–98
★★★Touring Eigerpl ☎458666 tx33356
rm56 ⇆16 🅟31 Lift
★★Continental (n rest) Zeughausgasse 27
(off Weisenhauspl) ☎222626 rm38 ⇆14 Lift
★Goldener Schlüssel Rathausgasse 72
☎220216 rm30 B31–60 M7–20 Pn45–47
★Stamm Bernastr 6 ☎430684 rm13 B23–50
★Volkshaus Zeughausgasse 9 ☎222976
rm66 Lift
᪥**Egghölzli** Egghölzlistr 1 ☎446366 N᪥
Bed/Hon/Peu/Vau G10
᪥**Marti** Eigerpl 2 ☎451515 N᪥ BMW
᪥**Rodtmatt** Rodtmattstr 103 ☎423330 N᪥
BL/Maz/Sab/Tri
⌂᪥**C Scholotterbeck Elite** Freiburgstr 447
☎553311 N᪥ Jag/Lnc/Sab G10
᪥**₦24 Willy** Freiburgerstr 443 ☎552511 Frd G20

Switzerland

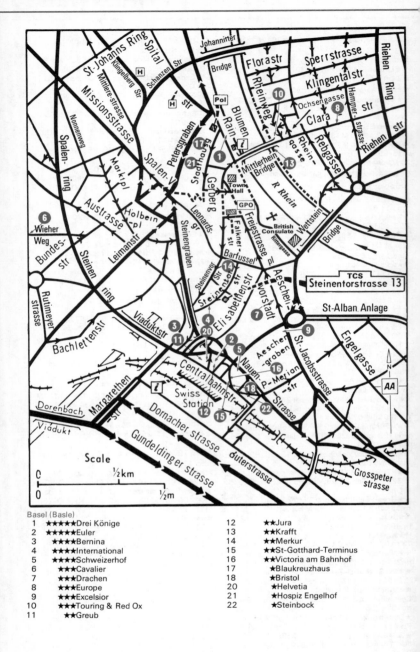

Basel (Basle)

1	★★★★★Drei Könige	12	★★Jura
2	★★★★★Euler	13	★★Krafft
3	★★★★Bernina	14	★★Merkur
4	★★★★International	15	★★St-Gotthard-Terminus
5	★★★★Schweizerhof	16	★★Victoria am Bahnhof
6	★★★Cavalier	17	★Blaukreuzhaus
7	★★★Drachen	18	★Bristol
8	★★★Europe	20	★Helvetia
9	★★★Excelsior	21	★Hospiz Engelhof
10	★★★Touring & Red Ox	22	★Steinbock
11	★★Greub		

At **Gümligen** (6km E)
🛏♨ *Schwarz* ☎523636 N♨ Vlo G20
At **Muri** (3km SE on N6)
☆☆ **Krone** ☎521666 rm12 ⇆12 G B55–102 M12–25 ♨
🛏♨ *Muri* Thunstr 25 ☎521600 N♨ BL G10
At **Wabern** (2km S)
🛏♨ **Wabern** Seftigenstr 198 ☎542622 N♨ M/c BL/Jag/Rov/Tri G10

Bevaix Neuchâtel (☎038) Map **11** A1
☆ *Bevaix* ☎461464 rm23 ♨23 Lake

Bex-les-Bains Vaud 4,800 (☎025) Map **28** C4
★★ *Salines* ☎52453 rm100 (A) ⇆12 G Lift 1 May–15 Oct ♨ Pool
☆ **St-Christophe** ☎36777 rm15 ♨10 B30.50–101 M14
🛏♨ **Rallye** r Servannaz ☎51225 N♨ Sab/Toy

Biasca Ticino (☎092) Map **12** C1
★★ *Poste* via Stazione ☎722121 rm10 ⇆2 ♨2 G B26.50–65 M16–30 Pn48–52
🛏♨ *Maggetti* via San Gottardo ☎721266 Chy/Sim

Biel (Bienne) Bern 59,200 (☎032) Map **11** B1/2
★★★★ **Elite** pl Gl-Guisan ☎225441 tx34101 rm50 ⇆50 G Lift B56–110 Màlc Pn96–118
★★★ **Continental** r d'Aarberg 29 ☎223255 tx34440 rm65 ⇆65 G Lift B55–96 M8–22 Pn79–84 Lake
★★ *Bären* Nidaugasse 22 ☎24573 rm17 ⇆8 G Lift
🛏♨ **City** Oberer quai 32 ☎236388 N♨ BL/Chy/Rov/Sim G5
🛏♨ **Giro** Solothurnstr 126 ☎421542 N♨ BL/Maz
🛏♨ **Mühle** Heilmannstr 16 ☎222201 N♨ BL/Ren/Tri G10
🛏♨ **Progress** Portstr 32 ☎259666 AR/Bed/Vau
At **Bözingen** (3km)
🛏♨ **Grand du Jura** Gouffistr 18 & Renferstr 1 ☎419333 Frd G20

Bissone Ticino (☎091) Map **29** A4
★★★ *Ring* Lago di Lugano ☎688591 tx79378 rm108 ⇆108 G Lift ♨ Pool Lake

Bivio Graubünden 190 (☎081) Map **12** C1
★★★ *Post* ☎751275 rm45 (A12) ⇆16 ♨2 G 1 Dec–20 Oct B26–106 M18–24 Pn40–60

Blonay-sur-Vevey Vaud (8km N of **Montreux**) 1,360 (☎021) Map **11** A1
★★ *Bahyse* ☎531322 rm20 (A) ⇆2 G
★ *Beaumont* ☎531244 rm38 (A) G 20 Dec–15 Oct Lake

Bollingen St-Gallen (☎055) Map **12** C2
☆☆ *Schiff* am oberen Zürichsee ☎271813 rm12 G B33–60 M6.50–19.50 Lake

Bönigen Bern 1,750 (☎036) Map **11** B1
★★ **Seiler au Lac** ☎223021 rm50 ⇆15 ♨8 G Lift 20 Dec–15 Oct LD B33–119 M15–22 Pn46–85 Lake

Bözingen See **Biel (Bienne)**

Brè See **Lugano**

Brestenberg Aargau 1,450 (☎064) Map **11** B2
★★ *Schloss* ☎541131 rm23 ⇆5 ♨5 Lift B35–100 M20 Pn67–85 ♨ Lake

Brienz Bern 2,900 (☎036) Map **11** B1
★★ *Bären* ☎512412 rm33 (A) ⇆4 ♨6 G Lift Pool
★★ *Gare* ☎512712 rm12 ⇆3 B27–70 M7–19 Lake
★★ *Schönegg* (n rest) ☎511113 rm16 (A6) ⇆7 15 Dec–31 Oct B26–92 Lake
★ *Weisses Kreuz* Tachstr ☎511781 rm55 (A) Lake
🛏♨ *Kienholz* ☎512165 Dat/Frd

Brig (Brigue) Valais 3,900 (☎028) Map **11** B1
★★★ *Europe* (n rest) ☎31323 rm25 ⇆5 ♨4 Lift
★★★ *Sporting* (n rest) ☎32363 rm33 ⇆6 ♨15 G Lift B24–66
★★ *Brigerhof* Rhônesandstr 18 ☎31607 rm29 ⇆5 ♨24 G Lift 1 Apr–30 Nov
★★ *Müller* Kantonstr ☎32295 rm60 ⇆12 ♨5 G Lift 1 Apr–1 Nov
★★ *Victoria-Terminus* ☎31503 rm47 ⇆19 ♨16 G Lift 10 Dec–10 Nov B33–95 M16–20 Pn51–70
At **Glis** (2km E)
🛏♨ *Saltina* ☎32562 M/c Toy G4

Brissago Ticino 1,940 (☎093) Map **28** D4
★★ *Mirto & Belvédère* ☎651328 rm29 ⇆12 ♨10 G Lift 1 Mar–1 Nov LD B31–134 M14–20 Pn44–110 Lake

Brugg Aargau 5,508 (☎056) Map **11** B2
★★★ *Rotes Haus* Hauptstr 7 ☎411479 tx Rohot 53084 rm21 ⇆5 ♨9 Lift

Brunnen Schwyz 1,850 (☎043) Map **11** B1
★★ *Bellevue* ☎311318 rm50 ⇆14 ♨9 G Lift Mar–Oct Lake
★★ *Elite* ☎311024 rm75 (A25) ⇆35 ♨12 G Lift Mar–Oct LD B30–94 M16–22 Pn50–65 Lake
★★ *Metropole* ☎311039 rm12 ⇆1 ♨8 G Lift Mar–Nov Lake
★★ *Schmid* ☎311882 rm24 ⇆8 Lift 1 Apr–30 Oct
★★ *Waldstätterhof* ☎331133 tx78378 rm99 ⇆93 ♨6 G Lift B45–160 M20–24 Pn65–120 ♨ Lake
★★ *Weisses Kreuz* ☎311736 rm30 ♨3 B26–78 M10–16 Pn32–44 Lake
★★ *Weisses Rössli* ☎311022 rm30 ⇆4 G B26–51 M14–18
★ *Alpina* ☎311813 rm22 ⇆2 ♨2 B29–90 M12 Pn36–55
♦ *Wolfsprung* ☎311173 rm10 ⇆3 G Etr–31 Oct Lake
🛏♨ *Inderbitzin* Gersauerstr 17 ☎311313 MB G3
🛏♨ *J Strübli* Schwyzerstr 11 ☎311304 Frd

Buchs St-Gallen 5,300 (☎085) Map **12** C2
★★ *Chez Fritz Bahnhof* ☎61377 rm15 ⇆1 G B30.50–79 M15–20
🛏♨ *Sulser* St-Gallerstr 19 ☎61414 N♨ Opl

Bulle Fribourg 5,300 (☎029) Map **11** A1
★★★ *Alpes* ☎29292 rm30 ⇆5 ♨25 Lift B35–80 M7–26 & àlc
★★ *Rallye* rte de Riaz ☎28498 rm20 (A4) ♨20 G Lift B24–45 M8 Pn42
🛏♨ *Moderne* r de la Poterne 3 ☎26363 N♨ Cit/Dat

Burgdorf Bern (☎034) Map **11** B1
🛏♨ *Central* ☎223406 N♨ Cit/Vau G6

Bürgenstock Nidwalden (☎041) Map **11** B1
★ *Waldheim* ☎641306 rm54 ⇆6 ♨5 G Lift Pool

Bussigny See **Lausanne**

Campione d'Italia See **Lugano**

Carouge See **Genève (Geneva)**

Cassarate See **Lugano**

Castagnola See **Lugano**

Celerina Graubünden 713 (☎082) Map **12** C1
★★★ *Cresta Palace* ☎33564 tx74461 rm110 ⇆71 ♨16 G Lift 18 Jun–20 Sep 26 Nov–Etr B36–127 M22–35 Pn55–150 ♨ Pool
★★ *Cresta Kulm* ☎33373 rm50 (A5) ⇆35 ♨15 G Lift 15 Dec–15 Apr 15 Jun–15 Sep LD B35–110 M16–20 Pn45–96

Cham Zug (☎042) Map **11** B2
♨ *Ettmüller* Steinhauserstr ☎365370 N♨ Cit

Champéry Valais 861 (☎025) Map **28** C4

Switzerland

★★★**Champéry** ☎84245 rm55 ⇌25 ⋔10 G
mid Jun—mid Sep mid Dec—Etr B37—150
M22 Pn50—85
★★**Alpes** ☎84222 rm24 ⇌10 ⋔10
15 Dec—30 Apr Jun—Sep B31—90 M17—24
Pn45—65
★★**Beau-Séjour** ☎84343 rm28 ⇌6 ⋔1
12 Apr—6 Sep B31—122 M14—20 Pn45—75
★★**Parc** ☎84235 rm40 (A6) ⇌4 ⋔12
Dec—Sep B31—60 M16—25 Pn50—65

Champex Valais 73 (☎026) Map **28** C4
★★★**Alpes & Lac** ☎41151 rm65 ⇌45 ⋔2 G
Lift 15 Jun—15 Sep LD B30—120 M20—25
Pn48—90 ✿ Pool Lake

Château-d'Oex Vaud (☎029) Map **11** B1
★★★*Beau-Séjour* ☎47423 rm48 ⇌20 ⋔4 G
Lift Dec—Oct
★★★**Chalet du Bon Accueil** ☎46320 rm17
⇌10 G Dec—Oct LD B30—110 M15—25
Pn55—80
★★★*Victoria* ☎46434 rm18 ⇌15 ⋔3 G Lift
20 Dec—Etr Jun—Sep Pool
★★*Ermitage* ☎46003 rm27 ⇌8 Dec—Oct
🛏◆24 **Burnand** ☎47539 BL/Cit/Vlo G5
🛈◆24 **Pont** Petit Pré ☎46173 M/c GM G10

Chaumont See Neuchâtel

Chaux-de-Fonds (La) Neuchâtel 38,900
(☎039) Map **11** A1
★★★*Club* r du Parc 71 ☎235300 tx35548
rm40 ⇌40 Lift B35—85
🛈◆24 **Étoile** r F-Courvoisier 28 ☎231362
Chy/Sim
🛏◆24 **Metropole** r du Locle 64 ☎269595
AR/BL/Jag
🛏◆*J Rieder* ☎235404 N✿ Cit G3
🛏◆24 *Trois Rois* bd des Eplatures 8 ☎268181
Frd/Lnc

Chernex See Montreux

Chexbres Vaud 1,343 (☎021) Map **11** A1
★★★**Bellevue** ☎561481 rm18 ⇌12 Lift
B31—82 M23 Lake
★★★**Signal** ☎562525 rm82 ⇌64 ⋔18 G Lift
Mar—Nov LD B38—130 M18—26 Pn64—100
✿ Pool Lake
★★*Cécil* ☎561292 rm24 ⇌9 ⋔2 G Lift
B31—87 M18—21 Pn55—72 Pool Lake

Chur (Coire) Graubünden 24,800 (☎081)
Map **12** C1
★★★*City* Martinspl 4 ☎225444 tx74583
rm75 ⇌45 ⋔25 Lift
★★★**Duc de Rohan** Masanserstr 44 ☎221022
tx74161 rm35 ⇌32 ⋔1 G Lift B34—99 Màlc
Pool
★★**A B C** (n rest) Bahnhofpl ☎226033 rm38
⇌8 ⋔20 G Lift B36—108 Màlc
★★**Drei Könige** Reichsgasse 18 ☎221725
rm40 ⇌9 G Lift B27—80 M13—24 Pn44—72
☆☆**Sommerau** Emserstr ☎225545 tx74172
rm45 ⇌21 ⋔24 B40—74 Màlc
★★**Stern** Reichsgasse 11 ☎223555 tx74198
rm55 ⇌6 ⋔34 G Lift B30—84 M13—18
Pn68—82
★★**Weisses Kreuz** Vazerolgasse 19 ☎223112
rm22 ⇌4
🛏◆*Autocenter Tribolet* Rossbodenstr 14 N✿
🛏◆*F Bayer* Emserstr 2 ☎222604 Ren G4
🛏◆*Calanda* Kasernenstr 30 ☎221414 Fia/Lnc
🛏◆*Comminto* Rossbodenstr 24 ☎223737 N✿
Peu/Rov G10
🛏◆*Grand Dosch* Kasernenstr ☎215171 N✿
G30
🛈◆24 *Lidoc* St-Margrethenstr 9 ☎221313
AR/MB G

Claro Ticino (☎092) Map **29** A4
☆ *San Gottardo* ☎63566 rm35 ⋔28

Collonge-Bellerive Genève Map **28** C4

★★**Bellerive** ☎521282 rm7 ⇌6 1 Feb—20 Dec
B35—60 M8—22 Pn40—45 Lake
Coppet Vaud (☎022) Map **11** A1
🛏◆*Port* rte de Suisse ☎761212 N✿
BL/Jag/Rov G10
Cornaredo See Lugano
Cossonay Vaud Map **11** A1
🛏◆*A Meystre* Grande r ☎871170 N✿ Cit
Couvet Neuchâtel (☎038) Map **11** A1
★*Aigle* Grande r 27 ☎632644 rm16

Crans-sur-Sierre Valais 1,750 (☎027)
Map **28** C4
★★★★**Alpina & Savoy** ☎412142 tx38134
rm66 ⇌56 ⋔1 G Lift 15 Dec—15 Apr
6 Jun—15 Sep
★★★**Elite** ☎414301 rm30 ⇌30 Lift Jun—Oct
15 Dec—15 Apr LD B36—111 M15—18 Pn50—85
Pool Lake
★★★**Robinson** ☎411353 rm15 ⇌11 ⋔4 Lift
B41—102 M15—20 Pn55—80
★★★**Royal** ☎413931 tx38227 rm70 ⇌62 ⋔8
Lift 10 Dec—15 Apr 10 May—10 Sep B15—80
M20 Pn55—120
★★★**Splendide** ☎412056 rm32 ⇌28 ⋔2 G
Lift Jun—Oct Dec—Apr B59—88 M18 Pn65—80

Cully See Lausanne

Därligen Bern 361 (☎036) Map **11** B1
★*Strandbad* ☎227544 rm40 ⇌2 ⋔6
B22—84 M14—18 Pn43—68 Lake
Davos Graubünden 7,378 (☎083) Map **12** C1
At **Dorf**
★★★**Meierhof** promenade ☎61285 tx74363
rm44 ⇌19 G Lift LD B36.50—75 M22—28
Pn68—118
At **Laret** (8km NE)
★*Tischiery's im Landhaus* ☎52121 rm50
(A12) ⇌6 G 10 Jun—10 Oct 1 Dec—15 Apr
B33—100 M15—25
At **Platz**
★★★**Morosani Sport** promenade ☎35821
tx74350 rm104 (A59) ⇌68 G Lift Dec—Oct
B36—202 M18—26 Pool
★★★**Schweizerhof** promenade ☎36221
tx74324 rm105 ⇌90 G Lift 3 Dec—15 Apr
20 May—30 Sep B36—122 M18—22 Pn58—88
Pool
★**Belmont** (n rest) Tanzbühlstr 2 ☎35032
rm25 20 Jun—20 Sep 1 Dec—4 Apr B25—80
Délémont Bern 7,500 (☎066) Map **11** B2
★**Bonne Auberge** Grande r 32 ☎221758
rm9 ⇌2 ⋔4 G Mar—Dec B30—74
M17.50—25&àlc Pn50—66
★*Central* Grande r 10 ☎223363 rm10 Lift
🛈◆24 **Mercay** Maltière 20 ☎221745 BMW/Fia
🛏◆*Stand* r du Stand ☎222424 N✿ MB/Lnc
G10
🛈◆24 **Willemin** rte de Moutier ☎222461 Ren
Disentis Graubünden (☎086) Map **12** C1
★★**Cristallina** ☎75656 tx74302 rm14 ⇌10
⋔2 G B28—70 M9.50—17.50 Pn58—63
Dürrenast See Thun (Thoune)
Ebikon See Luzern (Lucerne)
Ebligen Bern (☎036) Map **11** B1
★*Hirschen* ☎511515 14rm (A5) ⇌3 ⋔5 Lift
Apr—Nov B33—82 M12—14 Lake
Echallens Vaud (☎021) Map **11** A1
At **Villars-le-Terroir**
☆☆*Beauregard* ☎811917 rm20 ⇌20 G
Eclepens Vaud (☎021) Map **11** A1
★*Auberge Communale* ☎877193 rm8 ⇌1
⋔3 G B23—55 M12&àlc Pn47—50
Egerkingen/Olten Solothurn (☎062)
Map **11** B2
☆☆*AGIP* (junction N1/N2) ☎612121
tx68644 rm80 ⇌40 ⋔30 G B30—69 M6—22

i♠24 Reinhart ☎611250 Frd/Toy G6

Einigen Bern (☎033) Map **11** B1
☆ **Hirschen** ☎543272 rm23 ♨20 G B31–59
M8–12 Lake

Einsiedeln Schwyz (☎055) Map **12** C1
★★★ **Drei Könige** ☎532441 rm52 ⇆14 ⋒37
G Lift B40–76 M15–20 Pn62

Emmenbrücke See **Luzern (Lucerne)**

Engelberg Obwalden 2,600 (☎041)
Map **11** B1
★★★ **Bellevue** ☎941213 tx78555 rm90 ⇆45
G Lift May–Oct Dec–Apr ⋗
★★ **Hess** ☎941366 rm80 ⋒31 Lift Dec–Nov
★ **Engelberg** Dorfstr 14 ☎941168 rm30 ⇆6 ⋒8
î♠24 **Grand Epper** Dorfstr ☎942424 N⋗
Aud/VW G60

Entlebuch Luzern (☎041) Map **11** B1
★★ **Drei Könige** ☎721227 rm13 ⇆3 ⋒1 G

Estavayer-le-Lac Fribourg (☎037)
Map **11** A1
★ **Lac** ☎631343 rm18 ⇆6 ⋒2 1 Feb–31 Dec
Pool Lake

Etoy-Buchillon Vaud (☎021) Map **11** A1
☆☆ **Péchers** rte du Lac Genève-Lausanne
☎763277 rm14 ⇆2 ⋒12 G 1 Feb–31 Dec
B35.50–62 M7–15 Pool Lake

Evolène Valais 1,300 (☎027) Map **28** C4
★ **Hermitage** ☎831232 rm22 ⇆12 G
1 Jun–16 Sep 25 Dec–1 Jan
★ **Dent-Blanche** ☎831105 rm40 (A) G
20 Dec–15 Apr 1 Jun–30 Sep
★ **Eden** ☎831112 rm18 G Dec–Oct
★ **Evolène** ☎831202 rm43 ⇆14 ⋒3 G
B22.50–41 M13–18 Pn36–55 ⋗ Pool

Faido Ticino 1,200 (☎094) Map **12** C1
★★ **Faido** ☎381555 rm17 ⇆2 G Lift
★★ **Milan** ☎381307 rm41 ⇆21 G Lift
1 Apr–31 Oct B31–66 M16–20 Pn51–66

Faulensee Bern 262 (☎033) Map **11** B1
★★ **Bellerive** ☎543774 rm27 ⇆11 ⋒6 G
1 Dec–28 Feb 1 Apr–31 Oct Pool Lake
☆☆ **Marti** ☎542888 rm18 ⇆2 ⋒14
1 May–1 Oct Lake
★ **Sternen** ☎541306 rm14 ⇆1 ⋒8 G B30–84
M10–25 ⋗ Pool Lake

Fiesch Valais 520 (☎028) Map **11** B1
★ **Glacier & Poste** ☎81102 rm40 ⇆6 G Lift

Filzbach Glarus 393 (☎058) (2km W of
Obstalden) Map **12** C1
★ **Rössli** Kerenzerbergstr ☎321818 rm15
★ **Seeblick** ☎321455 rm10 B18–20 Lake

Fleurier Neuchâtel 3,413 (☎038) Map **11** A1
★ **Commerce** ☎611733 rm26 G Lift
î♠ **L Duthé** r de Temple 34 ☎611637 N⋗
Aud/Ren/VW G3
î♠24 **Hotz** r de l'Industrie 19 ☎612922 N⋗
BMW/Chy/Cit G8

Flims-Waldhaus Graubünden (☎081)
Map **12** C1
★★★★ **Park Waldhaus** ☎391181 tx74125
rm206 ⇆145 G Lift Jun–Sep mid Dec–mid Mar
LD B50–210 M32–35 Pn70–160 ⋗ Pool ⃝
★★★ **Schloss** ☎391245 rm40 (A18) ⇆14 ⋒10
G Lift Dec–Apr Jun–Sep B30–48 M13–19
Pn54–80
★★★ **Segnes** ☎391281 tx74125 rm80 ⇆45
⋒10 Lift 15 Dec–15 Apr 25 May–15 Oct LD
B40–128 M22.50–28.50 Pn52–102 ⋗
★★★ **Alpes** Hauptstr ☎390101 rm90 ⇆90 G
Lift Dec–15 Apr Jun–15 Oct B50–120
M15–25 Pn70–90 Pool
★★ **National** ☎391224 rm24 ⇆6 ⋒6 Lift
18 Dec–10 Apr 27 May–15 Oct LD B33–60
M12–20 Pn53–78

Flüela-Pass Graubünden (☎083) Map **12** C1

★ **Flüela-Hospiz** ☎36864 rm10 G 1 May–31 Oct Lake

Flüelen Uri 1,700 (☎044) Map **11** B1
★★ **Hirschen** Axenstr ☎21201 rm30 G LD
B25–52 M6–20 Lake
★ **Weisses Kreuz** ☎21717 rm40 ⇆1 G
May–31 Oct B20–60 Màlc Pn38–42 Lake
î♠24 **Sigrist** ☎21260 Fia/Ren G5

Founex Vaud (☎022) Map **11** A1
☆☆ **Founex** ☎762535 tx23623 rm124 ⇆48
⋒76 Lift B44–76 Pool Lake
î♠⋗ **H Loosli** Bidon 5 ☎761425 Aud/VW

Frauenfeld Thurgau 14,700 (☎054) Map **12** C2
î♠⋗ **Lüthi** Zürcherstr 332 ☎76221 BL/Chy/Dat/
Jag/Rov/Sim

Fribourg Fribourg 29,000 (☎037) Map **11** B1
★★ **Fribourg** r Perolles 1 ☎222522 tx36303
hofri rm35 ⇆11 ⋒19 Lift
î♠⋗ **Central** r de l'Industrie 7 ☎223505 N⋗ Frd
î♠24 **Gendre** rte de Villars 105 ☎240331
Aud/Por/VW
At **Marly** (3km S)
î♠24 **Sarine** ☎461431 BL/BMW/Jag/Rov/Tri

Frick Aargau (☎064) Map **11** B2
★ **Engel** ☎611314 rm22 ⋒8 G

Frutigen Bern 5,700 (☎033) Map **11** B1
★ **Simplon** ☎711041 rm35 ⇆1 B22.50–57
M8–20 Pn36–46
î♠24 **Bahnhof** ☎711414 Aud/Frd/VW G12
î♠24 **Widi** ☎711053 Opl G20

Fürigen Nidwalden (☎041) (5km N of **Stans**)
Map **11** B1
★★ **Fürigen & Bellevue** ☎611254 rm96 ⇆80
G Lift ⋗ Lake

Furka Pass Uri (☎044) Map **11** B1
★ **Furkablick** ☎67297 rm20 G 1 Jul–16 Oct
B28–62 M16
At **Belvédère**
★★ **Seiler's Belvédère** ☎82530 rm40 ⇆10
15 Jun–25 Sep

Gandria See **Lugano**

Genève (Geneva) 170,000 (☎022)
Map **28** C4 **See Plan**

AA	**agents; see page 278**

★★★★★ **Des Bergues** quai-des-Bergues 33
☎315050 Plan **1** tx23383 rm130 ⇆111 ⋒19
Lift B110–240 M40 Pn190–220 Lake
★★★★★ **Président** quai Wilson 47 ☎311000
Plan **2** tx22780 rm270 ⇆270 G Lift B170–229
M48 Lake
★★★★★ **Rhône** quai Turrettini 3 ☎319831
Plan **3** tx22213 rm350 ⇆290 ⋒60 G Lift
B90–190 M32–35
★★★★ **Richemond** Jardin Brunswick
☎311400 Plan **4** tx22598 rm130 ⇆110 ⋒20
Lift B98–247 M33 Lake
★★★★ **Beau Rivage** quai-du-Mont-Blanc 13
☎310221 Plan **5** tx23362 rm120 ⇆120 Lift
B110–215 Màlc
★★★★ **Paix** quai-du-Mont-Blanc 11 ☎326150
Plan **6** tx22552 rm109 ⇆83 ⋒26 Lift Lake
★★★ **Ambassador** quai des Bergues 21
☎317200 Plan **7** tx23231 rm92 ⇆92 ⋒92 G
Lift B60–120 Pn98–113 Lake
★★★ **Angleterre** quai-du-Mont-Blanc 17
☎328180 Plan **8** tx22668 rm64 ⇆64 Lift Lake
★★★ **Berne** r de Berne 26 ☎316000 Plan **9**
tx22764 rm80 ⇆80 Lift B55–110 M20–30
Pn95–110
★★★ **Century** (n rest) av de Frontenex 24
☎368095 Plan **10** tx23223 rm140 ⇆105 ⋒15 Lift
★★★ **Cornavin** (n rest) bd J-Fazy 33 ☎322100
Plan **11** tx22853 rm125 ⇆65 ⋒50 G B70–120
★★★ **Eden** r de Lausanne 135 ☎326540
Plan **12** tx23962 rm54 ⇆30 ⋒24 G Lift
B55–90 M18 Pn71–81 Lake

Switzerland

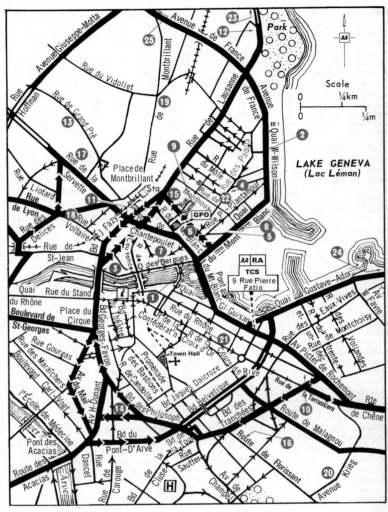

★★★Grand-Pré (n rest) r du Grand-Pré 35
☎339150 Plan **13** tx23284 rm100 ⇆50 ⋔50
G Lift B60–110

★★★Lutetia r de Carouge 12 ☎204222
Plan **14** tx28845 Aspan CH rm42 ⇆42 Lift

★★★Méditerranée r de Lausanne 14
☎316250 Plan **15** tx23630 rm165 ⇆165 G
Lift B75–150 M6–9 ⚓ Pool Golf ◯ Lake

★★★Résidence rte de Florissant 11 ☎461833
Plan **16** tx28526 rm125 ⇆100 ⋔10 Lift
B44–130 Màlc ⚓

★★Ariana (n rest) r J-R Chouet 7 ☎339950
Plan **17** rm51 ⇆16 ⋔26 Lift B38–90 Lake

★★Epoque r Voltaire 10 ☎452550 Plan **18**
tx22940 rm54 ⇆18 ⋔18 G Lift

★★Montbrillant r Montbrillant 2 ☎337784
Plan **19** rm34 ⇆6 ⋔6 Lift B30–58

★★Parc av Krieg 42 ☎479041 Plan **20** rm63
⇆24 ⋔21 G Lift Pool

★★Touring Balance pl Longemalle 13
☎287122 Plan **21** tx23630 rm58 ⇆26 ⋔13
Lift B35–95 M18–20 Pn62–100 Lake

★Adris (n rest) r Gevray 6 ☎315225 Plan **22**
rm23 ⇆7 Lift B30–75

⋔⅋⚬**Acacias-Motors** r Boissonnas 11
☎433600 N⚓ Chy/Sim G5

⋔⅋⚬**Athénée** rte de Meyrin 122 ☎960044
Ben/RR/Sab G50

⋔⅋⚬**Autobritt** r de l'Ancien Port 4 ☎320010
N⚓ AR/BL/Rov/Tri

⚑⅋⚬**Badan** r de Lausanne 20 ☎325500 Rov

⋔⅋⚬**Blanc & Paiche** bd des Tranchées 50
☎468911 N⚓ Maz

⋔⅋⚬**Bouchet** rte de Meyrin 54 ☎968900 BL/Peu

⚑⅋⚬24 **E Frey** 23 rte des Acacias ☎421010
BL/MB/Toy

⋔⅋⚬**Import** r Viguet 1 ☎425804 N⚓ BMW G10

⚑⅋⚬**Metropole** rte du Pont-Butin ☎921322 N⚓
Frd

⋔⅋⚬**Nouveau** r Pré Jérome 21 ☎202111 N⚓
M/c BL/BMW

At **Carouge** (2km S)

⚑⅋⚬24 **Claparede Val d'Arve** rte de Veyrier 90
☎429950 N☎431710 BL/Fia/Jag G

At **Mies** (10km N on N01)

☆**Buna** (n rest) ☎551535 rm6 ⋔6

At **Vésenaz** (6km NE on No37)

★Tourelle (n rest) rte d'Hermance 26 ☎521628
rm24 (A2)⇆10 ⋔8 15 Jan–15 Dec B30–90 M15

Genève Airport (7km N)

At **Fernay Voltaire** (in France, 4km from airport)

☆☆☆**Novotel Genève Aeróport** rte le Meyrin
☎(023) 415011 from CH, (50) 415011 from F
tx300615F rm79 ⇆79 G Lift B120–140(French
francs) Pool

Gersau Schwyz 1,890 (☎041) Map **11** B1

★★Beau Rivage ☎841223 rm33 ⇆4 ⋔17 Lift
Apr–Oct B30.50–101 M5–14 Pn40–65 Pool

★★Bellevue (n rest) ☎841120 rm23 ⇆5
B25–70 Pool Lake

★★Müller am Vierwaldstättersee ☎841212
tx78641 rm75 ⇆30 G Lift Apr–Oct ⚓ Lake

★Seehof du Lac ☎841245 ta Dulac rm24
30 Apr–1 Oct

Giessbach Bern (☎036) Map **11** B1

★Park ☎511515 rm80 G Lift 15 May–30 Sep
⚓ Pool Lake

Giswil Obwalden 2,700 (☎041) Map **11** B1

★Krone Brünigstr ☎681151 rm97 ⇆16 ⋔24 G

Glarus Glarus 5,800 (☎058) Map **12** C1

★★Glarnerhof Bahnhofstr 2 ☎614106 rm32
⇆16 G Lift B39–100 M14–20 Pn55–75

⋔⅋⚬**Central** Landsgemeindepl ☎611834 N⚓
GM/Rov G10

⚑⅋⚬24 **K Enz** Schweizerhofstr 7 ☎611770 Cit/Frd

Glattbrugg See **Zürich Airport**

Gletsch Valais (☎028) Map **11** B1

★★Glacier du Rhône ☎731515 ⸱rm110 (A25)
⇆15 G 15 Jun–30 Sep B38–122 M19–22

Glion See **Montreux**

Glis See **Brig (Brigue)**

Goldswil Bern 610 (☎036) (2km E of
Interlaken) Map **11** B1

★Park ☎222942 rm60 ⇆4 20 Mar–30 Sep

⚑⅋⚬**Burgseeli** Hauptstr ☎221043 N⚓ Toy/Vau

Göschenen Uri (☎044) Map **11** B1

★St-Gotthard ☎65263 rm22 ⇆2 G

Grächen Valais (☎028) Map **28** D4

★★Beausite ☎562656 rm42 ⇆6 ⋔3 G Lift
Dec–Oct B24.50–40 M12–14 Pn35–50 Pool

★Grächerhof & Schönegg ☎40172 rm35

Greppen Luzem 349 (☎041) Map **11** B1

★St-Wendelin ☎811016 rm14 G Mar–Nov
B28–67 M8–21 Pn42–48 Lake

Grindelwald Bern 3,100 (☎036) Map **11** B1

★★★★Regina ☎531515 tx32663 rm100 ⇆80
⋔20 G Lift 15 Dec–15 Oct ⚓ Pool Lake

★★★Belvédère ☎531818 tx32217 rm60 ⇆36
G Lift 18 May–2 Oct B52–144 M18–24 Pool

★★★Park Schönegg ☎531853 tx33645
rm70 ⇆45 ⋔4 G Lift 20 May–5 Oct
19 Dec–5 Apr Pool

★★★Schweizerhof ☎532202 rm45 ⇆39 ⋔3
Lift 18 Dec–15 Apr 25 May–30 Sep B48–146
M18–22 Pn70–93 Pool Lake

★★★Sunstar ☎545417 tx32530 rm168 (A33)
⇆143 ⋔25 G Lift 17 Dec–9 Apr 1 Jun–15 Oct
B62–98 M18–25 Pn74–113 ⚓ Pool

★★Derby ☎545461 tx32897 rm78 (A32)
⇆34 ⋔27 G Lift (closed 15 Nov–1 Dec)
B36–121 M15 Pn55–80 ⚓

☆☆**Grindelwald** ☎532131 tx3818 rm18 ⇆18
G Dec–Oct B45–102 M12–16

★★Hirschen ☎532777 rm36 (A12) ⇆8 ⋔5 G
Lift B31–102 M6.50–24 Pn40–78

★Alpenblick ☎531105 rm16 G B22–52

⚑⅋⚬**Rothenegg** Rotheneggstr ☎531507 M/c
Aud/Rov/VW

Grosshöchstetten Bern 1,700 (☎031)
Map **11** B1

★Löwen Dorfstr ☎920210 rm6 ⋔6 G Lift
B19–38 M12 ⚓ Pool Golf ◯ Lake

Gruyères Fribourg (☎029) Map **11** A1

★★Gruyerotel (n rest) ☎61933 rm34 ⇆34
Lift Dec–Oct B35–80

★★Hostellerie St-Georges ☎62246 rm14
Mar–Oct

Gstaad Bern 1,700 (☎030) Map **11** B1

★★★Bellevue ☎43264 tx33632 rm56 ⇆48
⋔8 G Lift Dec–Apr Jun–Oct B45–200 M15
Pn75–130 ⚓ Pool

★★National Rialto Hauptstr ☎43474 rm50
⇆25 ⋔6 Lift B29–130 M15–25 Pn45–72 ⚓

★★Olden ☎43444 rm18 (A5) ⇆12 ⋔2 G
B32–162 M15–30 Pn50–75

★Rössli ☎43412 rm29 (A5) ⇆11 ⋔3 G

Gsteig (Le Châtelet) Bern 740 (☎030)
Map **11** B1

★Viktoria ☎51034 rm12 ⇆4 ⋔6 G LD
B25–70 M10–18 St%

Gstein-Gabi Valais (☎028) Map **28** D4

★★Weissmies Simplonstr ☎291116 rm17 (A2
⇆2 ⋔2 G LD B18–60 M13–19 Pn36–56

Gümligen See **Bern**

Gunten Bern 323 (☎033) Map **11** B1

★★Hirschen ☎512244 rm67 ⇆67 G Lift
14 May–30 Sep B37–68 M18–22 Pn60–72
Lake

★★Lac ☎511421 rm62 ⇆12 ⋔6 G Lift
15 May–30 Sep Lake

★Bellevue ☎511121 rm33 G 1 Mar–30 Nov
Lake

Switzerland

Gurtnellen Uri (☎044) Map **11** B1
★**Gotthard** ☎65110 rm15 ⇌1 ▥2 G LD
B19–73 M10–25 Pn38–55

Guttannen Bern 557 (☎036) Map **11** B1
★**Bären** ☎731261 rm40 G B22.50–47.50
M8–16 Pn35–40

Gwatt Bern (☎033) Map **11** B1
★**Lamm** ☎362233 rm16 B25–50 M8–22

Handegg Bern (☎036) Map **11** B1
★★**Handeck** ☎731131 rm44 (A22) ⇌9 ▥4 G
May–Oct B31–78 M8–17 Pn42–50

Heiden Appenzell 3,100 (☎071) Map **12** C2
★★★**Heiden** ☎911115 rm60 ⇌12 ▥30 G Lift
LD **Pn**75–85 Pool Lake
★★**Krone** Dorfpl ☎911127 tx71101 rm35 (A)
⇌16 ▥6 G Mar–Oct Pool Lake

Hergiswil Nidwalden 2,900 (☎041)
Map **11** B1
★★★**Pilatus** ☎951555 tx72527 rm74 ⇌26
▥14 Lift B27–110 M14–19 Pn60–90 Pool Lake
★★★**Belvédère** ☎951185 tx78444 rm59 ⇌10
▥8 Apr–30 Oct Pool Lake
★★**Friedheim** Kantonstr ☎951282 rm35 ⇌3
G Lift Pool Lake

Hertenstein Luzern 38 (☎041)
(2km W of **Weggis**) Map **11** B1
★★★**Hertenstein** ☎931444 tx72284 rm80
⇌40 ▥4 G Lift 15 Mar–15 Nov Pool Lake

Hilterfingen Bern 2,500 (☎033) Map **11** B1
★**Schönbühl** ☎432143 rm23 ⇌1 ▥3
Mar–Nov LD B27–74 M8–16 Pn36–55 Lake

Horw Luzern 4,700 (☎041) Map **11** B1
★★**Waldhaus** ☎421154 rm29 ⇌6 ▥2 G Pool
◯ Lake
🛢🔧**E Frey** ☎414949 N🚗 Frd G12
🛢🔧**W Liniger** ☎413274 N🚗 Bed/Dat/Vau

Hospental See Andermatt

Ilanz Graubünden 1,590 (☎086) Map **12** C1
★**Casutt** ☎21131 rm15 ▥5 G B26–75
M7–15 Pn34–45
🛢🗭24 **Spescha** ☎21424 Cit/Frd G25

Immensee am Zugersee Schwyz 1,380
(☎041) Map **11** B1
★★**Rigi–Royal** ☎811161 rm90 (A24) ⇌24
▥24 LD B28–87 M10–16 Pn40–55 Lake

Innertkirchen Bern 1,194 (☎036)
Map **11** B1
★**Hof & Post** ☎711951 rm25 G

Interlaken Bern 4,368 (☎036) Map **11** B1
★★★★**Beau-Rivage** Höheweg 211 ☎224621
tx32827 rm113 (A4) ⇌87 G Lift Apr–Oct
B42–85 Pool
★★★★**Victoria-Jungfrau** Höheweg 41
☎212171 tx32602 rm240 ⇌169 G Lift
30 Apr–15 Oct Pool
★★★**Bellevue Garden** Marktgasse 59
☎224431 rm60 ⇌25 Lift 1 May–30 Sep Lift
LD B28–110 M20–22 Pn50–80
★★★**Bernerhof** Bahnhofstr 16 ☎223131
tx32338 rm36 ⇌18 ▥18 G Lift B56.50–123
M16
★★★**Carlton** Höheweg 92 ☎223821 tx33655
rm50 ⇌30 G Lift 1 May–30 Sep B28–100
M15–19 Pn44–70
★★★**Eurotel** (n rest) Rugenparkstr 13
☎226233 rm40 ⇌21 ▥11 Lift 20 Dec–20 Oct
B35–96
★★★**Goldey** (n rest) Goldey 85 ☎224445 rm39
⇌18 ▥21 Lift May–mid Oct LD B50–140 Lake
★★★**Jura** Bahnhofpl 45 ☎228812 rm80 ⇌14
Lift
★★★**Krebs** Bahnhofstr 4 ☎227161 rm55 ⇌40
G Lift 1 May–10 Oct B35–110 M19–24
Pn60–84 Golf

★★★**Lac** Höheweg 225 ☎222922 tx33773
rm46 ⇌31 ▥3 G Lift B36–132 M17–20
Pn44–84
★★★**Royal St-Georges** Höheweg 139
☎227575 tx33975 rm115 ⇌64 ▥12 G Lift
1 Apr–31 Oct B28–126 M16–20 Pn50–90
★★**Beau Site** Seestr 16 ☎228181 tx33977
rm56 ⇌24 G Lift B27–104 M14–21àlc
Pn40–73
★★**Belvédère** Höheweg 95 ☎223221 rm48
⇌25 G Lift 15 Apr–15 Oct B33–126 M18–25
★★**Interlaken** Höheweg 74 ☎222012 rm75
⇌12 G Lift 1 May–1 Oct
☆☆**Marti** Brünigstr ☎222602 rm26 (A5) ▥21
Etr–31 Oct
★★**National** Jungfraustr 46 ☎223621 rm47
⇌21 ▥9 Lift 15 Apr–15 Oct B30–112 M17–20
Pn50–80
★★**Neuhaus** Seestr 121 ☎228282 rm50 ▥40
Apr–Oct B32–114 M12 Pn51–152 Lake
★★**Nord** Höheweg 70 ☎222631 rm68 ⇌22
▥8 G Lift B27–104 M15–19 Pn38–73
★★**Oberland** Postgasse 1 ☎229431 rm68
⇌7 ▥8 Lift B32.50–115 M12–19 Pn40–73
★★**Splendid** Höheweg 33 ☎227612 rm40
⇌7 ▥1 G Lift B27–84 M12–20 àlc Pn52–64
★★**Weisses Kreuz** Höheweg 2 ☎225951
rm73 ⇌25 ▥9 Lift B27–104 M15–20 Pn38–73
★**Anker** Marktgasse 57 ☎221672 rm19
B31–67 M8–9 Pn38–42 Lake
★**Harder-Minerva** Harderstr 15 ☎222361
rm25 ⇌2 ▥10 G B29–110 M12–25 Pn34–66
★**Merkur** Bahnhofpl 35 ☎226655 tx32953
rm36 ⇌16 ▥20 Lift B35–104 M14–18
Pn46–73
🛢🔧**Bohren & Urfer** Rugenparkstr 34
☎223231 N🚗 Cit/Fia G10
🛢🗭24 **Harder** Harderstr 25 ☎223651
N☎222333 Frd/MB
🛢🗭24 **National** Centralstr 34 ☎222143
Chy/Sim/Tri G10
🛢🔧24 **Touring** Seestr 109 ☎221515
N☎222333 N🚗 Toy/Vlo
🛢🗭**Waldegg** Waldeggstr 34a ☎221939 BL

Kandersteg Bern 913 (☎033) Map **11** B1
★★★★★**Royal Bellevue** ☎751212 tx32332
rm32 ⇌32 G Lift 20 May–20 Oct
20 Dec–20 Apr B65–180 M9–45 🍴 Pool ◯
★★★**Park Gemmi** ☎751117 tx32771 rm40
⇌15 G Lift 12 Apr–6 Oct B31–100 M15–22
Pn46–85
★★★**Schweizerhof** ☎751241 rm53 ⇌14 ▥6
G Lift 15 Dec–31 Mar 1 Jun–30 Sep
B33.50–111 M15–23 Pn40–70 🍴
★★**Adler** ☎751121 rm20 ⇌9 ▥3
1 Dec–31 Oct LD B35.50–95 M12–15
Pn50–65
★★**Alpenrose** ☎751170 rm35 ⇌3 ▥6
Dec–Sep B26–80 M15–17 Pn47–58
★★**Bernerhof** Hauptstr ☎751142 rm45 ⇌10
▥8 G Lift 15 Dec–15 Apr 15 May–Oct
★**Doldenhorn** ☎751251 rm22 (A) Dec–30 Sep

Kerzers Fribourg (☎031) Map **11** B1
★**Löwen** ☎955117 rm15 ⇌1 ▥2 B16–48
M10–14 Pn26–41

Klosters Graubünden 3,000 (☎083)
Map **12** C1
★★★★**Grand Vereina** ☎41161 tx74359
rm105 ⇌80 ▥2 G Lift 18 Dec–30 Mar
20 Jun–4 Sep B52.50–205 M18–25
Pn60–130 🍴 Pool
★★★**Alpina** ☎41233 rm30 ⇌12 G Lift
★★★**Silvretta** ☎41353 tx74336 rm120 ⇌90
▥6 Lift 10 Dec–15 Apr B40–240 M24–32
Pn65–150
★**Sport-Hof** ☎41460 rm14 ⇌4 ▥3 G
Dec–Apr

Krattigen bei Spiez Bern (☎033)
Map **11** B1
★★**Bellevue-Bären** ☎543929 rm30 (A5) ⇌2 ⋒1 G Lift B29–84 M9–20 Pn38–58 Lake
★**Seeblick** ☎542969 rm20 15 Mar–15 Oct B28–60 M12–18 Pn36–41 Lake

Kreuzlingen Thurgau 12,600 (☎072)
Map **12** C2
Central Hauptstr 118 ☎84222 Aud/VW

Kriens See **Luzern (Lucerne)**

Küsnacht See **Zürich**

Kussnacht am Rigi Schwyz 5,700 (☎041)
Map **11** B1
★★**Hirschen** ☎811027 rm35 ⇌12 ⋒12 G Lift B30–87 M12–17 Pn37–60 Lake
☆***Picnic*** ☎811555 rm12 ⇌2 ⋒1 G 1 Mar–15 Dec Lake
★***Tell's Hohle Gasse*** ☎811429 rm30 (A) ⇌2 G
24 Aebi Hürtelstr ☎811050 M/c Aud/RR/VW

La Each placename beginning with La is listed under the name which follows it.

Lachen Schwyz 3,458 (☎055) Map **12** C2
★★**Bären** ☎631602 rm16 ⇌3 ⋒1 G Lift LD B29.50–81 M10–17 Pn56–75 Lake

Langenbruck Basel (☎062) Map **11** B2
★**Baren** ☎601414 rm13 (A4) ⇌5 G 1 Aug–30 Jun B26–88 M7.50–28

Laret See **Davos**

Lausanne Vaud (☎021) Map **11** A1
At **Bussigny**
☆☆☆**Novotel Lausanne Ouest** ☎892871 tx25752 rm100 ⇌100 G Lift B120–140 Pool
At **Cully** (8.5km SE)
☆☆**Intereurop** ☎992091 tx25973 rm60 ⇌60 G Lift B45–80 M7 Pn54–59 Lake
At **Ouchy**
★★★★★**Beau Rivage** chemin-de-Beau-Rivage ☎263831 tx24341 rm240 ⇌240 G Lift B106–192 M40 Pn160–190 Lake
★★★★★**Palace** Grand Chêne 7 ☎203711 tx24171 rm200 ⇌200 Lift B65–350 M35 Pn125–190 Lake
★★★★**Continental** pl de la Gare 2 ☎201551 tx24500 rm116 ⇌97 ⋒19 Lift B56–109 Màlc
★★★★**Royal Savoy** av d'Ouchy 40 ☎264201 tx24640 rm120 ⇌108 ⋒10 G Lift B30–180 M30 Pn90–146 Pool ∩ Lake
★★★**Carlton** av de Cour 4 ☎263235 tx24800 rm55 ⇌46 ⋒9 Lift B60–120 M28–30 Pn80–115 Lake
★★★**City** r Caroline 5 ☎202141 tx24400 rm65 ⇌17 ⋒4 Lift LD B32–92 M15–25 Pn69–107
★★★**Jan** av de Beaulieu 8 ☎361161 tx24485 rm60 ⇌34 ⋒9 G Lift B35–110 M18 Pn71–101
★★★**Mirabeau** av de la Gare 31 ☎206231 tx25030 rm72 ⇌29 ⋒9 G Lift B35–130 Màlc Lake
★★★***Paix*** av B-Constant 5 ☎207171 tx24080 rm130 ⇌100 G Lift
☆☆☆**Parking** av du Rond-Point 9 ☎271211 tx25300 rm100 ⇌100 G Lift LD B64–109 M15–28 Pn79–124
★★★***Terminus*** av de la Gare 52 ☎204501 tx24454 rm80 ⇌50 ⋒30 G Lift
★★★**Victoria** (n rest) av de la Gare 46 ☎205771 rm65 ⇌50 G Lift B40–120 M15–20
★**Angleterre** pl du Port 9 ☎264145 rm36 ⇌13 ⋒6 B32–85 M9–33 Lake
★**France** (n rest) r de Mauborget 1 ☎233131 rm50 Lift B29.50–66
Autonor rte A-Fauquez 91 ☎373960 N BL G15
24 City rte de Geneve 60 ☎242600 N☎203071 BL/BMW
Edelweiss av de Morges 139 ☎253131 N Bed/Opl G10
24 Gare av de la Gare 45 ☎203761 N☎203071 BL/BMW/Jag/Tri G80
Jan Petit Rocher 6 ☎361921 N M/c Toy G20
Occidental av de Morges 7 ☎258225 N
Red Star av du Léman 2 ☎207231
24 Tivoli av de Tivoli 3 ☎203071 BL/BMW/Jag/Tri
At **Pully**
★★★***Montillier*** av de Lavaux 35 ☎287585 rm53 ⇌21 Lift Lake
At **Renens**
Etoile rte de Cossonay 101 ☎349691 N Fia/Lnc/MB G20
At **St-Sulpice**
☆**Pierrettes** ☎254215 rm21 ⋒21 B58–65(double) Màlc Pool Lake

Lauterbrunnen Bern 2,880 (☎036)
Map **11** B1
★★**Jungfrau** ☎551223 rm26 (A4) ⇌6 ⋒6 G 15 Dec–30 Oct B40–104 M15–25 Pn45–66 Pool
★★**Silberhorn** ☎551471 rm26 ⇌9 ⋒7 G B30.50–101 M12–22 Pn45–68
★★**Staubbach** ☎551381 tx33755 rm34 ⇌19 ⋒4 G Lift B37–109 M17–25 Pn50–75
★**Oberland** ☎551241 rm38 (A6) ⇌8 ⋒2 Lift LD B26–91 Pn45–70
★***Trümmelbach*** (n rest) ☎553232 rm10 ⇌2 G May–Sep

Leissigen Bern (☎036) Map **11** B1
★**Kreuz** ☎471231 rm30 ⇌10 ⋒20 Lift B45–84 M12–28 Lake

Lenk Bern 1,871 (☎030) Map **11** B1
★★★***Park Bellevue*** ☎31761 rm78 (A) ⇌29 ⋒2 G Lift 31 May–30 Sep 20 Dec–31 Mar Pool
★★★***Wildstrubel*** ☎31506 rm52 ⇌28 ⋒3 Lift 1 Jun–28 Sep 20 Dec–Etr Pool

Lenzerheide Graubünden 183 (☎081)
Map **12** C1
★★★***Park*** ☎341525 rm37 ⇌8 ⋒14 G Lift Jun–Sep Dec–Apr Pool
★★★***Post*** ☎341160 rm26 ⇌8
At **Valbella**
★★***Waldhaus*** ☎341109 rm45 ⇌4 ⋒4 Lake

Leysin Vaud (☎025) Map **11** A1
★★★***Grand*** ☎62471 tx24483 rm149 ⇌34 ⋒68 Lift 20 Dec–30 Apr 20 May–30 Oct Pool
★***Mont-Riant*** ☎62235 rm21 Lift Dec–Apr Jun–Sep

Liestal Basel 10,300 (☎061) Map **11** B2
★★★***Engel*** Kasernenstr 10 ☎912511 tx62086 rm36 (A12) ⇌12 ⋒15 G
★**Bahnhof** Bahnhofpl 14 ☎910072 rm15 G B30–60 M20
★**Radackerhof** Rheinstr 93 ☎943222 rm32 (A14) ⋒8 G B31–75 M6–20
Blank Tiergartenstr 1 ☎913838 N Bed/Vau
Peter Gasstr 11 ☎919140 N Frd
Rhein Buser Rheinstr 95 ☎945025 N Cit/Vlo G3

Locarno Ticino 10,200 (☎093) Map **28** D4
★★★★★**Palma** Lungolago Motta ☎336771 tx79322 rm119 ⇌81 ⋒12 G Lift B35–100 M30–35 Pool Lake
★★★★***Reber au Lac*** via Verbano (off via San Gottardo) ☎336723 tx79024 rm93 ⇌55 ⋒8 G Lift Pool Lake
★★★**Lac** pza Grande ☎312921 tx73098 rm33 ⇌31 Lift B36–101 M15–25 Pn70 Lake
★★★**Park** via Gottardo 8 ☎334554 ta Paloc tx79773 rm85 ⇌51 ⋒4 G Lift 1 Apr–25 Oct B35–158 M28–34 Pn66–116 Pool Lake

★★★ **Quisisana** via del Sole 17 ☎336141 rm74 ⌁47 ▥8 Lift B35–80 M20–30 Pn50–110 Pool Lake

★★ **Belvédère** via al Sasso ☎311154 rm50 ⌁15 G Lift 15 Mar–31 Oct B27–90 M18–25 Pn50–70 Lake

★★ **Montaldi** pza Stazione ☎336633 rm65 (A15) ⌁22 Lift B24.50–105 Màlc

▯☼◊ **5 Vie** pza 5 Vie ☎311616 N❧ Cit

▯☼◊ **St-Antonio** via Vallemaggia 16 ☎311665 Opl G20

At **Muralto** (1km W)

▯☼◊ **G Franzoni** via Gottardo ☎357158 N❧

▯☼◊ **Starnini** via Sempione 11 ☎333355 N❧ M/c BL/Rov G10

Locle (Le) Neuchâtel (☎039) Map **11** A1

▯❧24 **Trois Rois** r de France 51 ☎312431 N☎268181 Lnc

Lucerne See **Luzern**

Lugano Ticino 21,000 (☎091) Map **29** A4

★★★★ **Arizona** via Massagno 20 ☎29343 tx79087 rm56 ⌁56 G Lift Pool Lake

★★★★ **Excelsior** Riva V-Vela ☎228661 tx79151 rm81 ⌁81 ▥10 Lift B63–140 Lake

★★★★ **Splendide-Royal** riva A-Caccia 7 ☎542001 tx73032 rm73 (A10) ⌁66 G Lift Pool

★★★ **Bellevue au Lac** riva A-Caccia 10 ☎543333 tx79440 rm72 ⌁60 ▥12 G Lift Apr–Oct B58–130 M22–30 Pn73–90 Pool Lake

★★★ **Gotthard-Terminus** via Cl Maraini 1 ☎27777 tx73761 rm45 ⌁12 ▥13 G Lift B35–110 M15–18 Pn45–70 Lake

★★★ **International** via Nassa 68 ☎227541 rm80 ⌁55 ▥12 G Lift Mar–Oct B30–122 M17–18 Pn51–90 Lake

★★ **Continental-Beauregard** Basilea 28 ☎561112 tx79222 rm80 (A20) ⌁30 ▥2 G Lift 15 Mar–15 Nov B34–58 M14 Pn40–65 Lake

★★ **Everest** (n rest) via Ginevra 7 ☎229555 rm45 ⌁12 ▥12 G Lift B35–120

★★ **Walter** pza R-Rezzonico 7 ☎27425 rm40 ⌁19 ▥5 Lift LD B39–91 M13–24 Pn57–68 Lake

▯☼◊ **Cencini** via Ceresio 2 ☎512826 N❧ BMW/Jag G10

▯☼◊ **Centro Mercedes Descagni** via Cantonale 24 ☎220732 N❧ MB G10

▯☼◊ **N Crescionini** via Franscini 8 ☎28343 Opl

▯☼◊ **Stazione** via San Gottardo 13 ☎22465 N❧ Bed/Vau G20

At **Brè** (5km E)

★ **Brè** ☎514761 rm20 ⌁5 G Mar–Nov B30–80 M10–15

At **Campione d'Italia** (10km S)

(Italian enclave; prices in Swiss francs)

★★★ **Grand** ☎687031 ta Grandhotel Campione rm45 ⌁17 ▥28 G Lift B69–146 Lake

At **Cassarate**

★★★★ **Castagnola** ☎512213 rm76 ⌁56 ▥11 G Lift 15 Dec–15 Nov B35–170 M20–25 Pn50–100 ☙ Pool Lake

★ **Atlantic** (n rest) via Concordia 12 ☎512921 rm25 ⌁4 ▥4 Lift B31–78

▯☼◊ **Vismara** via Concordia 2 ☎512614 N❧ Frd

At **Castagnola** (2km E)

★★★ **Belmonte** ☎514033 tx79517 rm43 ⌁15 ▥16 G Lift Mar–Oct B36–152 M18–25 Pn50–90 Pool Lake

★★ **Carlton** ☎513812 rm60 ⌁12 ▥30 G Lift 15 Mar–25 Oct LD B32–103 M15–22 Pn46–72 Pool Lake

★★ **Helvetia** (n rest) ☎514121 rm37 ⌁4 G Lift Mar–Nov Lake

At **Cornaredo**

▯☼◊ **R Camenisch** Pista del Ghiaccio ☎519725 N❧ BL/Maz/Tri

At **Gandria** (5km E)

★ **Moosmann** ☎517261 rm30 ⌁17 20 Mar–31 Oct Lake

At **Maroggia-Melano** (10km S)

☆☆ **Lido** ☎687971 rm27 ⌁3 ▥24 Mar–Oct Pool Lake

At **Melide** (6km S)

★★ **Riviera** ☎687912 rm21 ⌁21 Lift B45–120 M5–10 Pool Lake

At **Paradiso**

★★★★ **Admiral** via Geretta 15 ☎542324 tx73177 rm92 ⌁81 ▥11 G Lift Pool

★★★★ **Eden** Riva Paradiso 7 ☎542612 tx79156 rm75 ⌁75 G Lift B88–216 M30–35 Pn250–290 Pool Lake

★★★ **Beau Rivage** ☎542912 rm90 ⌁70 Lift Etr–Oct B41–122 M14–20 Pn55–80 Pool Lake

★★★ **Conca d'Ora** ☎543131 rm35 ⌁18 Lift 15 Mar–Oct B36–102 M18–20 Pn50–72 Lake

★★★ **Flamingo** viale Funicolare San Salvatore ☎541321 rm20 ⌁12 Lift Mar–Nov B47–68 M16–18 Pn46–56

★★★ **Lac Seehof** ☎541921 tx79555 rm54 ⌁30 ▥24 Lift Apr–20 Oct B66–87 M78–100 Pn78–100 Pool Lake

★★★ **Meister** viale Funicolare II ☎541412 tx79365 rm82 ⌁51 G Lift Apr–Oct LD B40–80 M20–25 Pn55–100 Pool Lake

★★★ **Paix** via Cattori 18 ☎542331 rm87 ⌁48 ▥25 Lift Etr–31 Oct Pool Lake

★★ **Primerose** Riva Paradiso 6 ☎542841 rm27 (A3) ⌁14 ▥6 G Lift Apr–Oct B30–82 M16–18 Pn48–62 Lake

★★ **Victoria** ☎542031 rm35 ⌁6 Lift Etr–20 Oct Lake

▯☼◊ **Autocentro** Riva Paradiso 26 ☎543412 N❧ Lnc/RR G6

At **Vezia** (3km NW)

☆ **Vezia** ☎563631 rm75 ▥25 G 1 Feb–30 Nov B29–88 M9.50–17 Pool

Lungern am See Obwalden (☎041) Map **11** B1

★ **Rössli** ☎691171 rm18 ⌁2 B18–53 M10–15 Pn32–44 Lake

Luzern (Lucerne) Luzern 67,500 (☎041) Map **11** B1 See Plan

★★★★★ **Carlton-Tivoli** Haldenstr 57 ☎232333 Plan **1** tx72456 rm100 ⌁100 G Lift Apr–Oct B68.50–177 M25 Pn99–126 ☙ Lake

★★★★★ **Grand National** Haldenstr 4 ☎243322 Plan **2** tx78130 rm210 ⌁166 G Lift Apr–3 Oct B65–210 M30–35 Pn117–166 Lake

★★★★★ **Palace** Haldenstr 10 ☎221901 Plan **3** tx78155 rm168 ⌁165 ▥3 G Lift B60–205 M28–35 Pn101–163 Lake

★★★★★ **Schweizerhof** Schweizerhofquai 3 ☎225801 Plan **4** tx78277 rm185 (A3) ⌁125 Lift B44–196 M26 Pn91–154 Lake

★★★★ **Astoria** Pilatusstr 29 ☎235323 Plan **5** tx78220 rm95 ⌁60 ▥35 Lift B53–130 M15

★★★★ **Balances & Bellevue** Weinmarkt 7 ☎231833 Plan **6** tx78183 rm80 ⌁80 Lift 30 Apr–31 Oct B57–160 Màlc Lake

★★★★ **Montana** Adligenswilerstr 22 ☎225791 Plan **7** tx78591 rm70 ⌁55 ▥7 G Lift Apr–Oct B52–156 M22–25 Pn66–96 Lake

★★★ **Château Gütsch** Kanonenstr ☎233883 Plan **8** tx78233 rm40 ⌁37 Lift Pool Lake

★★ **Luzernerhof** Alpenstr 3 ☎224444 Plan **10** rm85 ⌁45 ▥26 Lift B45–139 M16–25 Pn75–100

★★★ **Royal** Rigistr 22 ☎231233 Plan **11** rm56 ⌁37 Lift Apr–Oct B30–54 Pn45–72 Lake

★★★ **Rütli** Hirschengraben 38 ☎224162 Plan **12** rm70 ⌁36 ▥20 Lift

★★★ **Schiller** Sempacherstr 4 ☎224821 Plan **13** tx78621 rm80 ⌁26 ▥26 G Lift B31–98 M13–17 Pn46–76

★★★ **Union** Löwenstr 16 ☎220212 Plan **14** tx78163 rm120 ⌁68 Lift B30–109 M16–18 Pn50–65

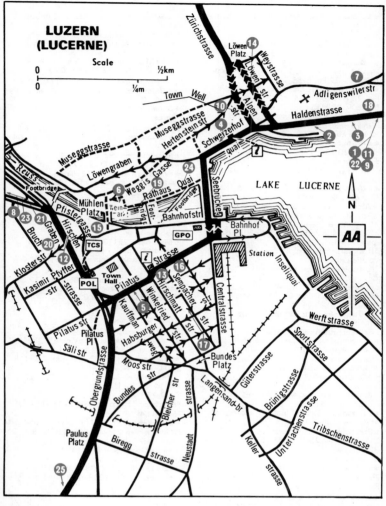

LUZERN (LUCERNE)

Switzerland

★★★**Wilden Mann** Bahnhofstr 30 ☎231666
Plan **15** tx78233 rm55 ⇹40 ⋔3 Lift B31–126
M17–19 Pn50–87
★★**Continental** Morgartenstr 4 ☎237566
Plan **16** tx78553 rm38 ⇹4 ⋔8 Lift
★★**Diana** Sempacherstr 16 ☎221635
Plan **17** rm40 ⇹10 ⋔30 Lift 1 Apr–31 Oct B43–
102 M13–17 Pn55–68
★★**Eden au Lac** Haldenstr 47 ☎220806
Plan **18** tx78160 rm46 ⇹23 G Lift Apr–Oct
B34.50–103 M16 Pn50–72 Lake
★★**Raben am See** Kornmarkt 5 ☎220734
Plan **19** rm36 ⇹15 ⋔3 G Lift 15 Feb–23 Jan
B24–76 M6–50 Pn38–55
★★**Rothaus** Klosterstr 4 ☎235015 Plan **20**
rm50 ⇹20 ⋔30 Lift B29.50–89 M12 Pn42–68
★★**Seeburg** ☎311922 Plan **22** tx78270 rm126
⇹93 ⋔3 G Lift B41–129 M19–26 Pn54–88
Lake
★★**Untergrund** (n rest) Baselstr 57 ☎224751
Plan **23** rm80 ⇹50 ⋔1 Lift
★**Alpes** Rathausquai 5 ☎225825 Plan **24**
tx78293 rm41 (A41) ⇹4 ⋔19 Lift B30–88
M15 Pn53–69
⛽**City-Parking** Zürichstr 35 ☎365151 G400
(petrol only)
☖⛽**E Epper** Horwerstr 81 ☎411122
Jag/Peu/Rov
☖⛽**Koch Panorama** Löwenstr 18 ☎226666
Chy/Fia/Sim
☖⛽**Letzi** Hirschengraben 48 ☎238022 Opl G5
i☖⛽**Macchi** Maihofstr 61 ☎363344
BL/Maz/Rov/Sab/Tri
☖⛽**Ottiger** Spitalstr 8 ☎365555 N⊛
AR/Fia/MB
⛽**Schwerzmann** Habsburgerstr 29,
Kaufmannweg 24 ☎228181 N⊛ BL/Rov/Tri
At **Ebikon** (4.5km NE)
☖⛽**Zai** Luzernerstr 57 ☎367500 Dat/MB
At **Emmenbrücke** (1km N)
★★**St-Christoph** ☎531308 rm14 ⇹3 LD
B23–54 M8
★**Emmenbaum** Gerliswilstr 8 ☎552960
(not on plan) rm15 ⇹4
★**Landhaus** ☎531737 (not on plan) rm25 G
At **Kriens** (5km SW)
☆**Süd Kriens** Autobahn Luzern-Süd
☎413546 Plan **25** rm38 ⋔38 G Jan–Nov
B20(double)
At **Seeburg** (2km E)
★★★**Hermitage** Seeburgstr 72 ☎313737
Plan **9** rm34 ⇹7 ⋔14 G Lift B37–102 M16–30
Pn57–77 Lake

Lyss Bern (☎032) Map **11** B1
☖⇥**Aebi** Bernstr 40 ☎844994 N☎841172
M/c Cit G10
☖⇥**Autobahngarage** Bielstr 98 ☎843838
Dat G20

Maloja Graubünden 100 (☎082) Map **12** C1 .
★★**Kulm** ☎43105 rm30 ⇹9 ⋔7 G Lift
15 Dec–20 Oct B30.50–103 M12–25 Pn34–70
★**Sport** ☎43126 rm20 ⇹6 May–Oct
Dec–Apr
☖⇥**24 Kulm** ☎43151 Maz G12

Marly See **Fribourg**

Maroggia-Melano See **Lugano**

Martigny Valais 7,000 (☎026) Map **28** C4
★★★★**Rhône** ☎21717 tx38341 rm42 ⇹13
⋔29 G Lift B35–80
★★★**Central** pl Centrale ☎21184 tx38341
rm30 ⇹21 G Lift B26–80
★★★**Forclaz** av du Léman 15 ☎22701 rm36
⋔22 G Lift 1 May–30 Oct
★★★**Poste** ☎21444 rm32 ⇹22 ⋔7 G Lift
B29–68
★★**Kluser** ☎22641 rm38 ⇹15
★★**St-Bernard** ☎22612 rm35 ⇹7 ⋔1 G

★★**Suisse** av de la Gare ☎21572 rm30 ⋔10
G Lift
☆**Sports** ☎22078 rm21 ⋔21 G
☖⛽**Central** r M Morand 11 ☎22294 N⊛
Aud/VW
i⇥**24 Mont-Blanc** av du Grand St-Bernard
☎21181 N☎23318 M/c Ren G20

Meggen Luzern 2,200 (☎041) Map **11** B1
★★**Balm** ☎371135 rm20 ⇹5 20 Jan–20 Dec
B31–81 Pool
★**Splendid** ☎372625 rm22 (A) ⇹4 Mar–Nov
Pool Lake

Meiringen Bern 3,700 (☎036) Map **11** B1
★★**Löwen** ☎711407 rm20 ⇹3 ⋔6 B24–54
M12–16
★**Baer** Hauptstr ☎712112 rm33
★**Post** Hauptstr ☎711221 rm27
★**Weisses Kreuz** ☎711216 rm32
i⇥**24 Ch & E Boss** ☎711631 M/c Frd/MB G10

Melide See **Lugano**

Merligen Bern 454 (☎033) Map **11** B1
★★★★**Beatus** ☎512121 tx32447 rm78
⇹53 ⋔25 G Lift Apr–Nov B81–238 M26–30
Pn95–150 Lake
☆**Mon Abri** ☎511399 rm38 (A10) ⋔38
B29–68 M9.50–17 Pn35–42 Lake
☖⇥**24 K Wittwer** Thunersee ☎512222 Cit/
Jag/Sab G10

Mettendorf Thurgau (☎054) Map **12** C2
⇥**24 W Debrunner** Hauptstr 90 ☎99119
N☎99696 Opl/Toy/Vau G3

Meyriez See **Murten**

Mies See **Genève**

Minusio Ticino (☎093) Map **28** D4
★★★★**Esplanade** via delle Vigme ☎332121
tx79470 rm86 ⇹40 G Lift Pool Lake
★★**Remorino** (n rest) ☎331033 rm25 ⇹15
⋔10 Lift Mar–Nov B22–55 Lake
★**Navegna-au-Lac** via la Riva ☎332222 rm18
(A4) ⇹16 ⋔1 G LD B37–122 M16–18
Pn50–65 Lake

Montana-Vermala Valais 1,750 (☎027)
Map **28** C4
★★★**Mirabeau** ☎413912 tx38365 rm54 ⇹46
G Lift Jun–Sep Dec–Apr B25–120 M25
Pn60–115
★★★**St-Georges** ☎412414 rm52 ⇹29 ⋔8
G Lift Dec–Apr Jun–Oct
★★**Bellavista** ☎414133 rm30 ⇹15
★★**Eldorado** ☎411333 rm28 (A) ⇹15 Lift
Dec–Oct Lake
★★**Lac** ☎413414 rm35 ⇹1 Jun–Oct Dec–Apr
G Lake
☖⇥**24 A Bagnoud** M/c Maz G10
☖⇥**24 Lac** ☎411818 AR/Ren G50

Montreux Vaud 12,300 (☎021) Map **11** A1
★★★★★**Eurotel** ☎622951 tx24666 rm150
⇹120 ⋔30 G Lift B58–186 M22–28
Pn91–126 Pool Lake
★★★★**Excelsior** r Bon Port 21 ☎613305
tx24720 rm85 ⇹75 ⋔11 G Lift Pool Lake
★★★★**Palace** av des Alpes ☎613231
tx24235 rm210 ⇹145 G ⛽ Pool
★★★**Bonivard** r Bonivard 1 ☎613358 rm76
⇹40 G Lake
★★★**Eden** r du Théâtre 11 ☎612602
tx25200 rm105 ⇹105 G Lift LD B60–170
M25–28 Pn90–125 Pool Lake
★★★**Golf** r Bon Port 35 ☎614133 rm60 ⇹60
G Lift B59–142 M20 Pn62–90 ⛽ Pool
★★★**Lorius** Grande Rue 89 ☎613404 rm65
⇹15 Lift ⛽ Pool Lake
★★★**National** chemin du National 2 ☎622511
tx24650 rm40 ⇹40 Lift ⛽ Pool Lake
★★★**Suisse & Majestic** av des Alpes 43
☎612331 tx24674 rm155 ⇹125 Lift
B40–150 M15–17 Lake

★★Bon Accueil Grande Rue 80 ☎620551
tx25250 rm39 ⇌24 ⋒15 G Lift B33–132 Lake
★★Europe av des Alpes ☎614622 rm102 ⇌36
⋒36 G Lift Mar–Oct B30–78 M16–22
Pn40–80 Lake
★★Palmiers r Stravinsky 2 ☎612242 rm32
⇌8 ⋒5 G Lift Lake
★★Parc & Lac Grande Rue 38 ☎623738
rm65 ⇌24 ⋒4 Lift Mar–Oct B25–80 M16
Pn45–70 Lake
★★Terminus r de la Gare 22 ☎612563 rm60
⇌14 Lift Lake
🛏🖈**Belmont** av Belmont 40 ☎613511 N🖈 Cit
🛏🖈**24 Central** Grande Rue 106 ☎612246
Opl/Vau
🛏🖈**L Mettraux** av du Théâtre 7 ☎613463
N🖈 Frd/Jag/Rov
At **Chernex** (2km NE)
★Iris ☎624252 rm23 ⇌4 ⋒4 G Lake
At **Glion** (3km E)
★★★Victoria ☎625121 rm66 ⇌31 ⋒10 G Lift
Pn65–150 Pool Lake
At **Rennaz** (12km S)
☆**Rennaz-Montreux** ☎601541 rm20 ⋒20
At **Villeneuve** (4km S)
★Byron ☎601061 rm48 ⇌18 ⋒7 Lift B30–120
Pn55–85 🍴 Lake

Morcote Ticino 600 (☎091) Map **28** D4
★Rivabella ☎691314 rm11 (A) ⇌4 ⋒1 G
Apr–Oct Lake

Morges Vaud 6,500 (☎021) Map **11** A1
★★Lac St-Jean ☎716371 tx25265 rm25
⇌8 ⋒7 Lift 25 Jan–22 Dec B75–135 M25–36
Pn86–118 🍴 Lake

Morgins Valais (☎025) Map **28** C4
★Beau-Site ☎83138 rm15

Morschach Schwyz 600 (☎043) Map **11** B1
★Fronalp ☎311122 rm75 G LD B24–52
M12–15 Pn38

Münchenbuchsee Bern (☎031) Map **11** B1
☆☆**Bern-Biel** ☎860199 tx3053 rm30 ⇌30
G B29–42

Münsingen Bern (☎031) Map **11** B1
☆**Münsingen** (n rest) ☎920422 rm32 (A10)
⋒32 B35–65

Münster Valais (☎028) Map **11** B1
🛏🖈**24 Grimsel** ☎82350 M/c Cit/Frd G30

Muralto See **Locarno**

Muri See **Bern**

Mürren Bern 318 (☎036) Map **11** B1
No road connection: take funicular from
Lauterbrunnen or **Stechelberg**
★★★Eiger ☎551331 tx32966 rm50 ⇌30 Lift
11 Jun–17 Sep 15 Dec–15 Apr B35–75
M15–19 Pn40–100

Murten (Morat) Fribourg 2,800 (☎37)
Map **11** A/B1
★★Bâteau ☎712644 ta Schiffhotel rm15
⇌1 1 Mar–31 Oct Lake
★★Weisses Kreuz Rathausgasse ☎712641
rm30 (A) ⇌8 Lift Feb–Dec
At **Meyriez** (1km N)
★★★★Vieux Manoir ☎711283 rm24 ⇌12
Lift Mar–Jan Lake

Mustair Graubünden 800 (☎082)
Map **12** D1
★★Münsterhof ☎85541 rm19 ⇌1 ⋒1 G
B22–56 M9.50–17.50 Pn39–48

Näfels Glarus (☎058) Map **12** C1
★★Schwert ☎341722 rm10 ⇌3 ⋒3 G Lift
B28–65
🛏🖈**J Felber** Hauptstr ☎341031 Frd

Neuchâtel Neuchâtel 33,500 (☎038)
Map **11** A1

★★★Beau Lac quai L-Robert 2 ☎258822
tx35122 rm52 ⇌18 ⋒23 Lift B34–114
M11.50–28.50 Lake
★★★Touring ☎255501 rm50 ⇌40 Lift
B25–75 M8–16 Lake
★Central Treille 9 ☎241313 rm31 ⇌15
⋒16 Lift Lake
★★City pl Piaget 12 ☎255412 rm35 ⇌3 Lift
🛏🖈**Cote** r de Neuchâtel 15 ☎317573 N🖈
BL/Rov/Tri
🛏🖈**M Faccinetti** av Portes-Rouges 1
☎242133 (closed weekends) Bed/Fia
🛏🖈**1er Mars** Pà-Mazel 1 ☎244424
BMW/Toy
🛏🖈**24 Trois Rois** P-A-Mazel 11 ☎258301
Frd/Lnc
At **Chaumont**
★★Chaumont & Golf ☎334141 rm32 ⇌9
Lift 20 Mar–31 Oct

Neuhausen am Rheinfall Schaffhausen
10,300 (☎053) Map **11** B2
★★Bellevue ☎22121 rm27 ⇌13 ⋒7 G Lift
B28–96 M17
🛏🖈**24 Central** Centralstr 121 ☎21621 N🖈
AR/Frd

Neuveville (La) Bern 2,800 (☎038)
Map **23** A1
★Fauçon Grande r ☎513125 rm20 ⇌1 ⋒1 G
B23–50 M7–20 Pn36–40
☆**Neuveville** ☎512060 rm21 ⋒18 G 1 Mar–
31 Jan B26.50–57 M7–12 Lake

Niederurnen Glarus 3,000 (☎058)
Map **12** C1
★Mineralbad Badstr ☎211703 rm7 G

Nyon Vaud 6,100 (☎022) Map **11** A1
★★★Beau-Rivage r de Rive 49 ☎613232
tx27439 rm46 ⇌23 ⋒6 G Lift 1 Feb–31 Dec
Lake
★★★Clos de Sadex rte de Lausanne
☎612831 rm18 ⇌14 B42–150 M28
Pn88–125 Lake
★★★Nyon r de Rive 15 ☎611931 tx23591
rm22 ⇌5 ⋒7 Lift Dec–Oct B26–90 M9–30
🍴 Pool Lake
🛏🖈**L Jaques** rte de Lausanne ☎612902
N🖈 Aud/VW
🛏**Quai** quai des Alpes ☎614133 N🖈 Chy/Sim

Oberhofen Bern 1,500 (☎033) Map **11** B1
★★Montana ☎431661 rm30 ⇌2 G Lift
1 Apr–10 Oct
★★Moy Staatstr ☎431514 rm60 ⇌11 G Lift
15 May–30 Sep B26–93 M18–30 Pn58–70
Pool Lake
★Kreuz Hauptstr ☎431448 rm30 ⇌4 ⋒4 G
Lift Mar–Dec B27–80 M12–20 Pn41–52 Lake
★Landte ☎431553 rm20 ⇌2 ⋒5 Feb–Nov
B26–78 M15–20 Pn42–57 Lake

Oerlikon See **Zürich**

Olten Solothurn 20,000 (☎062) Map **11** B2
★★★Schweizerhof Bahnhofquai 18 ☎214571
tx68313 rm45 ⇌13 ⋒4 G Lift B30–68
★★Glockenhof Mühlegasse 6 ☎222186 rm30
⇌8 G Lift
🛏🖈**City** Baslerstr 90 ☎212333 N🖈 AR/Aus
G10
🛏🖈**Moser** Baslerstr 47 ☎214280 Chy/Sim
At **Starrkirch** (2km)
🛏🖈**Elite** Aarauerstr 235 ☎221212 N🖈 Frd

Ouchy See **Lausanne**

Paradiso See **Lugano**

Parpan Graubünden 89 (☎081) Map **12** C1
★Alpina Hauptstr ☎351184 rm45 ⇌12 ⋒14
G Lift 15 Dec–30 Apr 1 Jun–31 Oct B27–98
M15–20 Pn40–76

Payerne Vaud (☎037) Map **11** A1
🛏🖈**Promenade** pl du Gl-Guisan 1 ☎612505 Frd

Perly Genève Map **28** C4
☐*Touring* rte St Julien 266 (☎712540

Pfäffikon Schwyz 1,900 (☎055) Map **12** C2
★*Höfe* rm7 ▥4
★*Sternen* ☎481291 rm24 (A9) ⇄1 G
B24–48 M9–18

Pompaples Vaud (☎021) Map **11** A1
★*Milieu du Monde* ☎877205 rm8 B21–42

Ponte Tresa Ticino 473 (☎091) Map **28** D4
★★★*Zita* ☎96825 rm34 (A) ⇄8 ▥15 Pool Lake
☆*Ponte Tresa* ☎96544 rm29 ▥11 Pool Lake

Pontresina Graubünden 774 (☎082)
Map **12** C1
★★★*Kronenhof Bellavista* ☎66333 tx74488
rm150 ⇄73 G Lift 15 Dec–15 Apr
15 Jun–15 Sep ✆ Pool
★★★*Müller* ☎66341 rm51 (A11) ⇄20 ▥10 G
Lift Jan–30 Sep LD B35–110 M15–18 Pn55–86
★★★*Schweizerhof* Berninastr ☎66412
tx74442 rm92 ⇄45 ▥20 G Lift 4 Jun–15 Oct
15 Dec–15 Apr B47–80 M17–22
★★*Park* ☎66231 rm72 ⇄25 ▥8 G Lift
15 Dec–31 Mar 11 Jun–18 Sep LD B41–160
M16–22 Pn54–100
★★*Steinbock* ☎66371 rm26 ⇄4 ▥1 G LD ✆
☐*Roseg* ☎66120 N✆ BMW

Porrentruy Bern 6,500 (☎066) Map **11** A2
★★*Cheval-Blanc* r Traversière 15 ☎661141
rm32 ⇄7 ▥3 Lift
☐✆24 *Gare* r Cuenin 21 ☎661408 Ren G10
☐✆24 *Ponts* Sur les Ponts 5 ☎661206 GM
G26
☐✆*St-Germain* r du Jura 5 ☎661913
N☎665448 M/c Frd G10

Porto-Ronco Ticino (☎093) Map **28** D4
★*Eden* ☎355142 rm16 ▥2 Mar–Oct LD
Pn34–53 Lake

Poschiavo Graubünden 4,304 (☎082)
Map **12** C1
At **Prese (Le)** (4.5km S)
★★★*Prese* ☎50333 rm28 ⇄22 Lift
14 May–17 Oct B36–132 M15–25 Pn59–89
✆ Pool Lake

Pully See **Lausanne**

Ragaz-Pfäfers (Bad) St-Gallen 2,600
(☎085) Map **12** C1
★★★★*Quellenhof* ☎90111 tx74197 rm135
⇄80 ▥21 G Lift Apr–30 Oct B61–232 M38
Pn85–180 ✆ Pool Golf
☆☆*Touring Mot* ☎92355 rm62 ⇄6 Motel
Units B24–45 M16–25 ✆ Pool
★*Park* ☎92244 rm60 (A20) ▥2 G
Apr–Oct B25–33 M14–20 Pn40–60

Rapperswil St-Gallen 5,600 (☎055)
Map **12** C2
☐✆*Helbling* Rütistr 2 ☎272323 N✆ Frd

Raron Valais (☎028) Map **11** B1
☆*Simplonblick* ☎51274 tx38661 rm19 ▥19
B24–52 Màlc Pool

Reiden Luzern (☎062) Map **11** B2
★★★*Sonne* ☎812121 rm32 ⇄15 ▥10 G Lift
B22–48 M5–19 Pn34–36

Renens See **Lausanne**

Rennez See **Montreux**

Rheinfelden Aargau 4,600 (☎061)
Map **11** B2
★★*Schwanen* Kaiserstr 8 ☎875344 rm70
⇄25 G Lift 1 Mar–15 Nov
★*Ochsen* ☎875101 rm30 ▥3 G Mar–Nov
★*Storchen* Marktgasse 61 ☎875322 rm30
▥12 Lift
☐✆*Grell* Kaiserstr 30 ☎875051 Frd G10

Ringenberg Bern 1,800 (☎036)
(4km NE of **Interlaken**) Map **11** B1

Alpina ☎222031 rm19 ▥10 Dec–Oct Lake
★★**Rolle** Vaud (☎021) Map **11** A1
★★*Tête Noire* ☎752251 rm20 ⇄15 Lake

Romanshorn Thurgau 6,650 (☎071)
Map **12** C2
☐*Bodan* ☎631502 rm60 ▥60 Lake
☐✆*Schmiedstube* Bahnhofstr 39 ☎631111
N✆ BL/Cit/Sab

Rorschach St-Gallen 12,800 (☎071)
Map **12** C2
★★★*Anker* Hauptstr 71 ☎414243 tx77454
(anko) rm33 ⇄10 ▥11 G Lift Lake
☐✆24 *Central* ☎412222 N☎412312
Aud/VW G5

Rüschlikon Zürich 3,400 (☎01) Map **11** B2
★*Belvoir* Säumerstr 37 ☎7241808 rm14 Lake

Saanenmoser Pass Bern 200 (☎030)
Map **11** B1
★★★*Golf & Sport* ☎43222 rm54 ⇄26 ▥4 G
Lift 1 Jul–15 Sep 15 Dec–15 Apr LD B36–151
M20–28 Pn72–110 ✆ Lake

Saas-Fee Valais 600 (☎028) Map **28** D4
★★*Beau Site* ☎48102 tx38284 rm80 ⇄15
Lift 15 Dec–20 Apr 15 Jun–20 Sep Lift
★*Bergfreude* ☎48137 rm25 ⇄5 ▥8 LD
B24–45 M11–16 Pn42–58

Sachseln am Sarnersee Obwalden 2,500
(☎041) (3km S of **Sarnen**) Map **11** B1
☆☆☆*Kreuz* ☎661466 rm71 ⇄19 ▥26 G Lift
B30–120 M8–24 Pn48–75

St-Blaise Neuchâtel 1,900 (☎038) Map **11** A1
★*Cheval Blanc* Grande r 18 ☎333007 rm12
⇄4 ▥8 G B22.50–77 M8.50–25 Pn30–55
☐✆*Lac* ☎332188 N✆ Cit G10

St-Gallen St-Gallen 76,300 (☎071)
Map **12** C2
★★★★*Walhalla* Poststr ☎222922 tx77160
rm57 ⇄57 G Lift B68–126 M20
★★★*Hecht* am Bohl 1 ☎226502 tx77173
rm58 ⇄17 ▥11 Lift B47–112 M17 Pn74–90
★★★*Im Portner* Bankgasse 12 ☎229744
rm18 ⇄12 ▥6 Lift B61–146 M15–25
☐✆*Capitol* Rorschacherstr 239 ☎242218 N✆
BL/Tri
☐✆24 *Central* Unterer Graben 21 ☎206191
GM/Opl G1
☐✆24 *City* Lerchenfeld ☎291131 Aud/Chy/
NSU/VW G500
☐*H Erb* Fürstenlandstr 149 ☎273333 N✆
Bed/Vau
☐✆*Lutz* Fürstenlandstr 25 ☎282121 N✆
Chy/Cit/Dat
☐✆*Lutz* Vadianstr 57 ☎232382 N✆ Chy/Cit/
Dat G50

St-Gotthard Pass Ticino (☎094) Map **11** B1
★*Monte Prosa* ☎881235 tx CH-78446 rm22
G 15 May–20 Oct Lake

St-Luc Valais 240 (☎027) Map **28** D4
★★*Bella Tola* ☎651444 rm40 ⇄13 ▥8 G Lift
Jun–Sep LD B27–78 M15–22 Pn55–67
★★*Cervin* ☎651393 rm66 ⇄12 12 Apr–6 Sep ✆

St-Maurice Valais 2,700 (☎025) Map **28** C4
★*Alpes* ☎36223 rm12
★*Ecu du Valais* ☎36386 rm25 ⇄10

St-Moritz-Bad See **St-Moritz**

St-Moritz-Champfér See **St-Moritz**

St-Moritz Graubünden 2,600 (☎082)
Map **12** C1
★★★★★*Crystal* ☎21165 tx74449 rm110
⇄110 Lift Dec–Oct Pool
★★★★★*Kulm* ☎21151 tx74472 rm215
⇄215 G Lift 24 Nov–7 Apr 29 Jun–7 Sep
B80–360 M30–35 Pn115–235 ✆ Pool Lake
★★★★*Carlton* ☎21141 tx74454 rm130
⇄130 G Lift 21 Jun–1 Sep 29 Nov–29 Mar
✆ Pool Lake

★★★★**Suvretta-House** ☎21121 tx74491 rm239 ⇌187 G Lift Dec–Mar Jun–Sep Pn85–195 ✦ Pool Lake
★★★**Bellevue** ☎22161 tx74428 rm42 ⇌10 ▥30 G Lift Lake
★★★**Belvédère** ☎33905 tx74435 rm70 ⇌55 ▥10 Lift Dec–Apr Jul–25 Sep B40–160 Màlc ✦ Pool Lake
★★★**Calonder** (n rest) ☎33651 tx74435 rm54 ⇌25 Lift 30 Jun–15 Sep 1 Dec–15 Apr ✦
★★★**Casper Badrutt** ☎34012 rm63 ⇌30 G Lift 5 Dec–Etr 1 Jul–1 Sep Lake
★★★**Neues Post** ☎22121 tx74430 rm84 ⇌45 ▥12 Lift B30–90 M16–19 Lake
★★**Bären** Hauptstr ☎33656 rm90 ⇌50 G Lift Pool
★★**Margna** Bahnhofstr ☎22141 tx74402 rm71 ⇌27 ▥15 G Lift 5 Dec–1 Sep Lake
►◀24 M Conrad ☎33788 BL/Fia/Lnc G2
▦⬕Grand Dosch ☎81200 AR/MB/Opl G150
At **St-Moritz-Bad** (1km S)
★**National** ☎33274 rm30 ▥30 Lift 15 Jun–30 Sep 1 Dec–30 Apr LD B25–70 M10–15 Pn45–55 Lake
At **St-Moritz-Champfèr** (3km SW)
★★★★**Eurotel** ☎21175 tx74458 rm150 ⇌112 ▥26 G Lift 11 Jun–25 Sep 29 Oct–24 Apr B43–286 M24 Pn82–182 ✦ Pool
★★**Chesa Guardalej** ☎34781 rm36 ⇌33 ▥3 Lift Jun–Apr Lake

St-Sulpice See **Lausanne**

Ste-Croix Vaud (☎024) Map **11** A1
★**Jura** r du Jura ☎612145 rm12 ⇌3 ▥3 G B22–52 M16–25 Pn42–48 ◖

Samedan Graubünden 1,700 (☎082) Map **12** C1
★★★**Bernina** Hauptstr ☎65421 tx74486 rm80 ⇌40 ▥20 G Lift 15 Jun–10 Oct B35.50–127 M18–24 Pn54–90 ✦
▦⬕24 Palü Hauptstr ☎65331 N✿ BL/Jag/MB/Toy/Tri G10
▦⬕Pfister ☎65666 Frd/Sim/Vlo G12

Santa Maria Graubünden 400 (☎082) Map **12** D1
★**Schweizerhof** Hauptstr ☎85124 rm30 ⇌4 ▥9 G Lift 1 May–31 Oct LD B30–85 M17 Pn44–65

Sargans St-Gallen 2,100 (☎085) Map **12** C1
★★**Post** ☎21214 rm14 (A11) ⇌8 ▥5 G LD B20–50 M8–22 Pn40–43 Lake

Sarnen Obwalden (☎041) Map **11** B1
At **Wilen**
★★**Wilerbad am Sarnersee** ☎661292 rm87 ⇌20 ▥8 G Lift Pool

Schaffhausen Schaffhausen 31,000 (☎053) Map **11** B2
★★**Bahnhof** Bahnhofstr 46 ☎54001 rm42 ⇌25 ▥9 Lift B25–90 Pn41–66
★★**Kronenhof** Kirchhofpl 7 (off Vordergasse) ☎56631 rm30 ⇌8 ▥18 Lift
★★**Park Villa** Parkstr 18 ☎52737 rm39 (A8) ⇌20 B35–110 M12–20&àlc Pn56–70
★**Kreuz** Mühlenstr 88 ☎51982 rm17 ⇌3 ▥1
▦⬕Turm Grabenstr 10 ☎56223 N✿ BL/Jag/Tri

Schoenried Bern 243 (☎030) (4km NE of **Saanen**) Map **11** B1
★★★**Ermitage & Golf** ☎42727 rm30 ⇌16 ▥6 G Dec–Mar Jun–Sep LD B30.50–151 M14.50–25 Pn55–95 ✦ Lake

Schwanden Glarus (☎058) Map **12** C1
★**Adler** ☎811171 rm11 ⇌1 15 Jan–28 Dec
▦►◀24 O R Müller Thermastr 22 ☎811535 N✿ Ren/Tri

Seeburg See **Luzern (Lucerne)**

Servion Vaud (☎021) Map **11** A1
☆☆**Fleurs** ☎932054 rm32 ▥14 G B30–55 M8 Pn46–50

Sierre (Siders) Valais 7,200 (☎027) Map **28** C4
★★**Arnold** rte du Simplon ☎551721 rm32 ⇌3 ▥6 G Lift
★★**Atlantic** ☎552535 rm37 ⇌25 ▥12 Lift Pool
★**Victoria** rte de Sion 5 ☎551007 rm15 ⇌2 B23–77 M13–18
▦⬕24 International av M-Hubert 20 ☎551436 N✿ Chy/Sim
▦⬕Parc rte du Simplon 22 ☎551509 BL/MB
▦►◀24 Rawyl rte du Simplon ☎550308 Frd G5

Sigriswil Bern 3,920 (☎033) (3km NE of **Gunten**) Map **11** B1
★**Adler** ☎512424 rm27 ⇌11 ▥10 G Lift B30–80 M14–20 Pn38–68 Pool

Sihlbrugg Zürich 82 (☎01) Map **11** B2
☆☆**Sihlbrugg** ☎7299600 rm18 ⇌8 ▥10 G B30–53

Sils-Maria Graubünden 118 (☎082) Map **12** C1
★★★★**Waldhaus** ☎45331 tx74444 rm150 ⇌85 ▥4 G Lift 15 Dec–15 Apr 1 Jun–15 Oct B36–220 M27–36 Pn62–145 ✦ Pool Lake
★★★**Alpenrose** ☎45321 rm70 ⇌24 G Lift 1 Jun–30 Sep ✦ Lake
★★**Maria** Hauptstr ☎45317 rm40 (A) ⇌11 ▥2 G
At **Sils-Baseglia**
★★★**Margna** ☎45306 tx74496 rm75 ⇌48 ▥6 15 Jun–15 Oct 15 Dec–15 Apr ✦
★**Privata** ☎45247 rm20 20 Dec–15 Apr 1 Jun–20 Oct
★**Seraina** ta Sils rm40 ⇌10 ▥2 Jun–Nov Dec–May

Silvaplana Graubünden 333 (☎082) Map **12** C1
★★**Sonne** ☎48152 rm57 ⇌26 ▥11 Lift Lake
★**Corvatsch** (n rest) ☎48162 rm16 Nov–Apr Jun–Oct B25–37 M8–20 Lake
▦⬕Corvatsch ☎48114 Cit/Ren G8

Simplon-Dorf Valais (☎028) Map **28** D4
★**Poste** ☎59121 rm24 (A12) ⇌5 ▥2 G B17–40 M12–20 Pn30–38 ◖

Simplon-Kulm Valais (☎028) Map **28** D4
★★**Bellevue** ☎59331 rm45 ⇌3 G 1 Mar–1 Nov

Sion (Sitten) Valais 16,000 (☎027) Map **28** C4
★★★**Rhône** r du Scex 10 ☎228291 tx38104 rm44 ⇌44 G Lift
★★★**France** pl de la Gare ☎25051 rm40 ⇌15 ▥15 G Lift ✦
★★**Continental** rte de Lausanne ☎24641 rm24 ⇌12
★★**Touring** av de la Gare ☎231551 rm27 ⇌23 G Lift
▦⬕Aviation rte Cantonale Corbassières ☎223924 N✿ Maz/Vlo G10
▦⬕Hediger batassé ☎220131 N✿ Chy/Sim
▦►◀24 Kaspar rte de Tunnel 22 ☎221271 N☎231919 Frd
▦►◀24 Nord av Ritz 35 ☎223413 N☎231919 N✿ Ren G10
▦⬕Tourbillon 23 av de Tourbillon ☎222077 Peu

Sisikon Uri (☎044) (7km S of **Brunnen**) Map **11** B1
★★★**Tellsplatte** ☎21612 rm40 ⇌8 ▥30 G Lift 1 Apr–31 Oct B24–72 Màlc Lake

Solothurn (Soleure) Solothurn 18,400 (☎065) Map **11** B2
★★★**Krone** Hauptgasse 64 ☎24438 rm35 ⇌16 G
▦⬕AVAG Baselstr 30 ☎20481 Aud/VW
▦⬕O Howald Engistr 13 ☎223718 N✿ AR/Ren

Spiez Bern 6,600 (☎033) Map **11** B1

Switzerland

★★★**Eden** Seestr ☎541154 rm60 (A4) ⇄23
G Lift 1 May–30 Sep B30–130 M18–28
Pn50–85 🛥 Pool Lake
★★**Alpes** Seestr 38 ☎543354 rm40 ⇄8 🏚10
G Lift B28–92 M18 Pn46–70 🛥 Pool Lake
★★**Erica** (n rest) ☎541735 rm26 ⇄4
1 Apr–30 Sep B24–88 Lake
★★**Terminus** Bahnhofpl ☎543121 rm60 ⇄28
Lift B30–108 M16–24 Pn44–75 Lake
★**Krone** Seestr 28 ☎544131 rm14 G Lake
🏚⊕**Schönegg** Oberlandstr 54 ☎542158 N🖷 Frd

Stans Nidwalden 4,000 (☎041) Map **11** B1
★★**Stanserhof** Stansstaderstr 20 ☎614122
rm23 ⇄10 🏚1 G Lift B24–60 M7–18 Pn38–44

Stansstad Nidwalden 1,400 (☎041)
(11km S of **Luzern**) Map **11** B1
★★★**Freienhof** ☎613531 rm50 ⇄30 G Lift
B25–90 M6.50–18 Pn42–65 🛥 Pool Lake
★★**Schützen** Stanserstr 23 ☎611355 rm50
⇄25 🏚3 G Lift
★★**Winkelried** ☎612622 rm46 ⇄15 🏚20 Lift
Lake

Starrkirch See Olten

Steckborn Thurgau (☎054) Map **12** C2
🏚⊕24 **Bürgi's Erben** Bahnhofstr ☎82251 N🖷
BL/Dat/Sab G5

Sursee Luzern 4,300 (☎045) Map **11** B2
★★**Hirschen** Oberstadt 10 ☎211048 rm13
⇄2 🏚4 G Lift
★**Bellevue** Mariazell ☎211844 rm16 🏚1 Pool
Lake
★**Brauerei** ☎211083 rm9 B25–41 M7–25
Pn44–49
🏚⊕**A Burkhardt** Münsterstr ☎212555
BMW/Fia G5
🏚⊕**Central** Luzernstr 18 ☎211144 N🖷 Frd
🏚⊕**Estumag** Baslerstr 1 ☎213143 N🖷

Tafers Fribourg (☎037) Map **11** B1
🏚⊕24 **Touring** ☎441750 M/c Opl

Tarasp-Vulpera See Vulpera (Tarasp)

Tegna Ticino (☎093) Map **28** D4
☆☆**Betulla** ☎811851 rm20 B50–100 Pool

Teufen Appenzell 4,400 (☎071) (6km S of
St-Gallen) Map **12** C2
★**Linde** ☎331419 rm14 G
★**Ochsen** ☎332188 rm14

Thalwil Zürich 11,500 (☎01) Map **11** B2
★★**Thalwilerhof** Bahnhofstr 16 ☎7200603
rm30 (A5) ⇄3 🏚5 G Lift B26–80 M8–20 Lake

Thielle Neuchâtel (☎038) Map **11** A1
☆☆☆**Novotel Neuchâtel Est** rte de Berne
☎335757 tx35402 rm60 ⇄60 Lift Pool

Thun (Thoune) Bern 29,100 (☎033)
Map **11** B1
★★★★**Elite** Bernstr 1 ☎232823 rm39 ⇄14
⇄25 Lift B34–90 M12 Pn56–71
★★★**Falken** Bälliz 46 rm30 ⇄8 🏚12 Lift
25 Jan–22 Dec
★★★**Freienhof** Freienhofgasse 3 ☎224672
rm65 ⇄32 🏚32 G Lift LD B44–86 M17–18
Pn58–62
★★**Beau-Rivage** ☎222236 rm36 ⇄18 G Lift
Mar–Oct B34–112 M20 Pn48–85 Pool Lake
★★**Bellevue** Hofstettenstr 25 ☎225301 rm40
⇄8 Lift 1 May–30 Sep Pool Lake
★**Metzgern** Rathauspl ☎222141 rm8
B24–48 Pn45
🏚⊕**City** Kyburgstr ☎229577 N🖷 Cit/Lnc/Maz
🏚⊕**Hürzeler** Allmendstr 38 ☎223300
BL/Fia/Jag/Rov
🏚⊕24 **Moser** Gwattstr 24 ☎341515
Aud/Chy/Por/Vlo/VW
🏚⊕**Oberland** Bernstr 14 ☎264633 Bed/Vau
G3
🏚⊕**Stucki** Bernstr 47 ☎375222 Frd

🏚⊕**P Sutter** Burgstr 2 N☎542738 Chy/Sim
G25
🏚⊕24 **Touring** Schlossmattstr 10 ☎224455
N☎341515 MB/Toy
At **Dürrenast** (2km S)
★★★**Holiday** Gwattstr 1 ☎365757 rm55
⇄6 🏚49 Lift B44–108 M12 Lake

Thusis Graubünden 1,600 (☎081) Map **12** C1
★★**Post & Viamala** ☎811412 rm31 ⇄8 🏚3 G
B22–32 M8–10
☆**Viamala** Hauptstr ☎811822 Frd/Opl G12

Tiefencastel Graubünden 327 (☎081)
Map **12** C1
★★**Posthotel Julier** Julierstr ☎711415
rm50 (20) ⇄19 🏚11 G Lift B25–70 M14
Pn38–48
★**Albula** ☎711121 rm25 (A15) ⇄5 🏚15
B25–32 M12–18 Pn40–47
🏚⊕24 **S Gruber's** ☎711144 Frd G40

Travers Neuchâtel (☎038) Map **11** A1
★**Cret** ☎631178 rm6 Mar–Jan B20–46
M10–25 Pn38–45

Tschiertschen Graubünden 174 (☎081)
Map **12** C1
★**Bruesch** ☎321130 rm25 15 Dec–30 Apr
15 Jun–30 Sep

Unterwasser St-Gallen 670 (☎074)
Map **12** C2
★★★**Sternen** ☎52424 rm80 ⇄25 G Lift
B25–104 M10–28 Pn50–80 🛥 Pool

Valbella See Lenzerheide

Vallorbe Vaud 3,900 (☎021) Map **11** A1
★**France** ☎831022 rm16
☆**Jurats** ☎831991 rm16 🏚16 B30–66
🏚⊕24 **Relais Mont d'Or** La Frontière
☎831488 Fia/Opl

Verbier Valais (☎026) Map **28** C4
★★★**Grand Combin** ☎71515 ta Grancombin
rm35 ⇄25 🏚5 Lift 12 Apr–6 Sep B35–134
M20–30 Pn70–90 Lake
🏚⊕24 **Verbier** ☎71777 M/c G100

Vernayaz Valais (☎026) Map **28** C4
★**Victoria** ☎81416 rm20 G B20–41 M4–12

Verrieres (Les) Neuchâtel 1,200 (☎038)
Map **11** A1
★**Gare** pl de la Gare ☎661633 rm6 G LD
B25.50–55 M10–16

Versoix Genève (☎022) Map **28** C4
★**Pavillon** rte de Lausanne 66 ☎551032
rm17 (A4) Lake

Vesenaz See Genève

Vevey Vaud 16,300 (☎021) Map **11** A1
★★★★**Trois Couronnes** r d'Italie 49 ☎513005
tx25270 rm90 ⇄90 Lift B60–200 M35–40
Pn110–150 Lake
★★★**Comte** av des Alpes ☎541441 tx38195
rm45 ⇄25 Lift Mar–Nov Lake
★★★**Lac** ☎511041 tx25577 rm60 ⇄48 G Lift
B25–160 M25–35 Pn60–120 Lake
★**Famille** ☎513931 rm62 ⇄16 🏚21 G Lift
B29–70 M8–9 Pn30–45

Vezia See Lugano

Villars-le-Terroir See Echallens

Villars-sur-Ollon Vaud (☎025) Map **28** C4
★★**Montesano et Régina** ☎32551 tx24727
rm85 (A) ⇄24 🏚18 Lift Dec–Apr Jun–Sep

Villeneuve See Montreux

Villmergen Schwyz (☎057) Map **11** B2
🏚**R Huber** Hauptstr ☎61379 N☎68857 N🖷
Aud/MB/Rov G4

Vira-Gambarogno Ticino (☎093)
(13.5km SE of **Locarno**) Map **29** A4
☆☆☆**Bellavista** ☎611116 rm62 ⇄16 🏚46 Lift
1 Apr–15 Nov B41–61 Màlc Pool Lake

Switzerland

Vira-Mezzovico Ticino (☎091) Map **29** A4
☆☆**Mezzovico** ☎98364 rm89 ⇄24 ▥18 Pool

Visp Valais 2,300 (☎028) Map **28** D4
★★★**Touring** (n rest) pl de la Gare ☎62626
rm55 ⇄16 ▥11 G Lift
🛏🚗**Albrecht** ☎62123 Frd G70
🛏🚗**Touring** Kantonstr ☎462562 Aud/Por/VW
G200

Vitznau Luzern 1,000 (☎041) Map **11** B1
★★★★**Park** ☎831322 tx78340 rm90 ⇄70 G
Lift Apr–Oct B45–180 M25–30 Pn95–140 ⚓
Pool Golf Lake
★★★**Vitznauerhof** ☎831315 tx72241 rm61
⇄46 G Lift Apr–Oct LD B37.50–137 M17–26
Pn55–98 ⚓ Lake
★★**Terrasse Terminus** ☎831303 rm30 ⇄6
▥6 Lift

Vulpera (Tarasp) Graubünden 300 (☎084)
Map **12** D1
★★★**Schweizerhof** ☎91331 tx74427 rm80
⇄50 G Lift Dec–Apr Jun–Sep **Pn**90–114 ⚓
Pool Golf Lake
★★★**Waldhaus** ☎91112 tx74427 rm120
⇄90 G Lift May–Oct **Pn**105–129 ⚓ Pool
Golf Lake

Wabern See **Bern**

Wädenswil Zürich 11,700 (☎01) Map **11** B2
★★★**Lac** ☎7800031 rm23 ⇄5 ▥9 Lift B33–79
M7.50 Lake
★**Engel** Engelstr 2 ☎750011 rm10 Lake
🛏🚗**Zentrum** Seestr 114 ☎7808080
BL/BMW/GM G3

Wassen Uri 900 (☎044) Map **11** B1
★★**Krone** Gotthardstr ☎65334 rm15 (A7)
⇄3 ▥5 G 1 Mar–31 Oct B33.50–86
M9.50–22 Pn42–56
★★**Post** (n rest) ☎65231 rm25 ⇄2 Apr–Oct
★**Alpes** ☎65233 rm15 ⇄6 B31–71 M4–24
Pn42–55
🛏🚗**24 J Mattli** ☎65233 G4

Wattwil St-Gallen 6,400 (☎074) Map **12** C2
★**Toggenburg** Dorfpl 2 ☎71242 rm10

Weesen St-Gallen 1,300 (☎058) Map **12** C1
🛏🚗**24 P Jörg** Hauptstr ☎431130 Bed/Dat/Vau
G10

Weggis Luzern 2,300 (☎041) Map **11** B1
★★★**Albana** ☎932141 tx78637 rm75 ⇄60 G
Lift 1 Apr–31 Oct B35–110 M16–24 Pn50–88
⚓ Lake
★★★**Beau Rivage** Gotthardstr ☎931422
tx72525 rm42 ⇄24 ▥15 G Lift 15 Mar–15 Oct
B40–120 M20–23 Pn65–90 Pool Lake
★★★**Park** ☎931313 rm66 ⇄40 G Lift
25 Apr–30 Sep B30–120 M18–23 Pn45–90
⚓ Lake
★★★**Waldstätten** ☎931341 tx72428 rm41
⇄41 Lift B40–106 M15 Pn60–80 Lake
★★**Belvédère** Luzernerstr ☎931384 rm17
⇄2 ▥2 G 1 May–1 Oct Lake
★★**Bühlegg** ☎932123 rm20 ▥10 G Lift
Apr–Oct LD B30–98 M14–18 Pn35–62 Lake
★★**Central** ☎931317 rm50 ⇄11 ▥7 G Lift
1 Feb–30 Nov B28–104 M15–20 Pn37–74 Pool
Lake
★★**Post Terminus** ☎931251 rm84 (A) ⇄4
Lift 1 May–30 Sep Lake
★★**Rigi** Seestr ☎932151 rm45 (A30) ⇄2
May–Oct B28–90 M14–20 Pn34–62 Lake
★**Felsberg** ☎931136 rm20 ▥9 May–Sep
B30–90 M14–20 Pn34–62 Lake
★**Frohburg** (n rest) ☎931022 rm20 ⇄18
Mar–Oct B28–120 Lake
★**National** Seestr ☎931225 rm39 ⇄33 ▥4 G
Lift Mar–Oct B35–52 M8–10 Pn48–70 Lake
★**Rössli** Seestr ☎931106 rm25 ▥6 G Lift
1 Apr–20 Oct LD B30–78 M12–18 Pn38–54
Lake

★**Seehotel du Lac** ☎931151 rm40 ⇄30 ▥1
Lift Apr–Oct B35.50–115 M14–20 Pn42–72
Lake

Wengen Bern 1,230 (☎036) Map **11** B1
No road connection; take train from
Lauterbrunnen
★★★**Palace National** ☎552612 tx32702
(Palwe ch) rm140 ⇄65 Lift 18 Dec–Etr
20 Jun–10 Sep ⚓
★★★**Waldrand** ☎552855 tx32340 rm49 ⇄34
▥3 Lift 1 Dec–10 Apr 25 May–26 Sep B35–110
M16–18 Pn50–84

Wengernalp Bern (☎036) Map **11** B1
No road connection; take train from
Lauterbrunnen
★★**Jungfrau** ☎551622 ta Wengernalphotel
rm25 ⇄16 Nov–Apr

Wil St-Gallen 11,000 (☎073) Map **12** C2
★★★**Derby Bahnhof** Bahnhof pl 1 ☎222626
tx77252 rm28 ⇄13 ▥4 G
🛏🚗**24 Bahnhofgarage Wil** untere Bahnhofstr 9
☎221112 BL/Ren/Tri
🛏🚗**Toggenburg** Toggenburgerstr 76 ☎221818
N⚓ BL/BMW

Wilderswil Bern 1,700 (☎036)
(2km S of **Interlaken**) Map **11** B1
★★**Bären** ☎223521 rm60 (A39) ⇄6 ▥2 G
Lift 1 Dec–31 Oct B31.50–91 M12–16
Pn44–58 Lake
☆☆**Luna** ☎228414 rm16 ⇄8 ▥8
★**Alpenrose** ☎221024 rm40 (A8) ⇄5 ▥6
Apr–Oct B30–84 M12–18 Pn38–54
★**Viktoria** ☎221670 rm15 B19–38 M8–12
Pn33–35 St6%

Wildhaus St-Gallen 1,200 (☎074) Map **12** C2
★★★**Acker Montana** ☎52221 tx71208
rm110 (A50) ⇄55 ▥35 G Lift B35–130
M17–27 Pn40–95 Pool
★★**Hirschen** ☎52252 rm80 (A20) ⇄20 ▥40
G Lift B28–90 M7.50–20 Pn45–65 Pool

Wilen See **Sarnen**

Winterthur Zürich 80,400 (☎052) Map **12** C2
★★★★**Garten** Stadthausstr 4 ☎232231
tx76201 rm60 ⇄60 G Lift
★★★**Krone** Marktgasse 49 ☎232521 rm37
⇄17 ▥15 G Lift LD B40–75 M10–20
🛏🚗**Eulach** Technikumstr 67 ☎222333
Bed/Opl
🛏🚗**Riedbach** Frauenfeldstr 9 ☎272222 N⚓
BL/BMW/Ren G5
🛏🚗**A Siegenthaler** Frauenfelderstr 44
☎272900 N⚓ Chy/Sim

Wohlen Zürich 8,000 (☎057) Map **11** B2
🛏🚗**E Geissmann** Villmergerstr 20 ☎65644
BMW/Frd G20

Yverdon Vaud 16,400 (☎024) Map **11** A1
★★**Prairie** av des Bains 9 ☎211919 rm35
⇄14 ▥8 Lift B42–92 M18–30 Pn66–76 ⚓
🛏🚗**Belair** av des Sports 13 ☎213381 Frd
🛏🚗**Croisée** rte de Lausanne ☎24850 N⚓
Ren G5
🛏🚗**Remparts** Champs Lovat 1 ☎213535
Peu/Vau

Zermatt Valais 1,400 (☎028) Map **28** D4
No road connection; take train from **Täsch**
or **Visp**
★★★★**Mont Cervin** ☎77150 tx38329
rm135 (A20) ⇄95 ▥20 Lift 1 Dec–20 Apr
1 Jun–15 Oct LD B45–194 M28–32
Pn75–130 Pool
★★★**Beau-Site** ☎77201 tx38361 rm110
⇄110 Lift Dec–Apr May–Sep LD **Pn**55–110
Pool
★★★**National Bellevue** ☎77161 tx38201
rm93 ⇄56 ▥14 Lift Dec–Sep **Pn**57–106 ⚓
★★★**Schweizerhof** ☎77521 tx38201 rm48
⇄38 Lift Dec–Apr Jun–Oct **Pn**57–101 ⚓

Switzerland

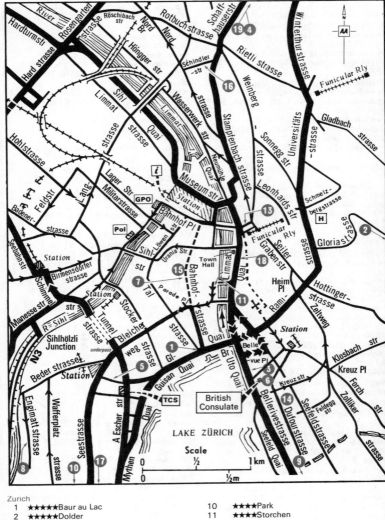

1 ★★★★★Baur au Lac
2 ★★★★★Dolder
3 ★★★★★Eden au Lac
4 ★★★★Airport (at Glattbrugg 8km
      NE on N4)
5 ★★★★Ascot
6 ★★★★Bellerive au Lac
7 ★★★★Carlton Elite
8 ★★★★Engematthof
9 ★★★★Ermitage au Lac (at Küsnacht
      12km S on N17)

10 ★★★★Park
11 ★★★★Storchen
13 ★★★Central
14 ★★★Excelsior
15 ★★★Glockenhof
16 ★★Burma
17 ★★Jolie Ville Motor Inn (at
      Adliswil 4km SE on N4)
18 ★★Krone
19 ★★Sternen (at Oerlikon 4km N)

★★★**Zermatterhof** ☎78040 tx38275 rm102
(A7) ⇆66 🅼3 Lift 26 Nov–15 Oct B52–114
M26–32 Pn60–155 🍴
★★**Dom** ☎77223 rm43 ⇆31 🅼4 Lift
10 Dec–30 Sep B20–100 M12–18 Pn48–75

Zernez Graubünden 740 (☎082) Map **12** C1
★★**Baer & Post** Curtinstr ☎81141 rm19 (A12)
⇆5 🅼14 G Dec–Oct LD B25–70 M14
Pn48–70 Pool

Zug Zug 19,800 (☎042) Map **11** B2
★★★**City Ochsen** Kolinpl ☎213232 rm35
⇆25 Lift B36–116 M20
★**Guggital** Zugerbergstr ☎212821 tx65134
rm33 ⇆23 🅼9 G Lift B45–104 Lake
★**Rössli** Vorstadtstr 8 ☎210394 rm18 🅼10
Lift (closed 20 Dec–15 Jan) B27–60 M9–25
Lake
ℹ️🚙24 *Kaiser* Baarerstr 50 ☎212424
BL/MB/Tri
🅖🚙*C Keiser* Grabenstr 18 ☎211818 Ren G10
🅖*Spatz* Chamerstr 75 ☎212818 N☎212851
Fia/Maz G5

Zuoz Graubünden 780 (☎082) Map **12** C1
★★**Engiadina** Hauptstr ☎71355 rm40 ⇆12
🅼3 G Lift

Zürich Zürich 440,200 (☎01) Map **11** B2
See Plan
★★★★★**Baur au Lac** Talstr 1 ☎2211650
Plan **1** tx53567 rm163 ⇆163 G Lift B100–240
M35–38 Lake
★★★★★**Dolder** Kurhausstr 65 ☎326231
Plan **2** tx53449 rm194 (A64) ⇆194 G Lift 🍴
Pool Golf Lake
★★★★★**Eden au Lac** Utoquai 45 ☎479404
Plan **3** tx52440 rm50 ⇆41 🅼9 Lift B100–200
Màlc Pn170–195 Lake
★★★★**Ascot** Lavaterstr 15 ☎2011800
Plan **5** tx52783 rm60 ⇆60 Lift B72–150
M7.50&àlc Pn104–142
★★★★**Bellerive au Lac** Utoquai 40 ☎327010
Plan **6** tx53272 rm60 ⇆50 🅼8 Lift B80–145
M25 ∩ Lake
★★★★**Carlton Elite** Bahnhofstr 41 ☎2116560
Plan **7** tx52781 rm72 ⇆72 Lift B90–212 Màlc
★★★★**Engematthof** Engimattstr 14
☎2012504 Plan **8** tx56327 rm82 ⇆24 🅼58 G
Lift B45–100 🍴
★★★★**Park** Kappelistr 41 ☎2016565 Plan **10**
tx56909 rm565 ⇆135 🅼180 Lift Lake
★★★★**Zum Storchen** Weinpl 2 ☎2115510
Plan **11** tx53354 rm77 ⇆55 🅼22 Lift B90–210
Màlc

★★★**Central** Centralpl ☎326820 Plan **13**
tx54909 rm64 ⇆40 🅼18 Lift B40–130 M6–30
★★★**Excelsior** (n rest) Dufourstr 24
☎342500 Plan **14** tx59295 rm40 ⇆21 🅼13
Lift B54–122
★★★**Glockenhof** Sihlstr 31 ☎2115650 Plan **15**
tx52466 rm104 ⇆92 🅼12 Lift B74–119 M8–25
★★**Burma** Schindlerstr 26 ☎261008 Plan **16**
rm23 ⇆3 Lift B34–73 M6–10
★★**Krone** Limmatquai 88 ☎324222 Plan **18**
rm40 ⇆4 Lift
🅖🚙*ABC* Seefeldstr 7 ☎340404 N🚙 Fia G10
🅖*Auto Benz* Seefeldstr 214 ☎552222 N🚙
BL/Rov/Tri/Vlo
🚙*Canonica* Albisriederstr 401 ☎549824 N🚙
BL
🅖🚙*E Frey* Badenerstr 600 ☎545700 N🚙
Bl/Jag/Rov/Tri G10
🅖🚙*Grand Günthardt* Austr 40 (off
Manessestr) ☎352233 N🚙 Chy/Sim G50
🅖🚙*J H Keller* Vulkanstr 120 ☎642410 N🚙
Hon
🅖🚙24 *Riesbach* Dufourstr 182 ☎552211
N☎322503 Frd G245
🅖🚙*Ruwa* Winterthurerstr 281 ☎480115 N🚙
BL/Tri
🅖*Schmohl* Mühlebachstr 26 ☎322716
N🚙 Lnc/RR
🅖🚙*Titan* Badenerstr 527 ☎524455 N🚙
Sab

At **Adliswil** (4km SE on N4)
★★**Jolie Ville Motor Inn** ☎7108585 Plan **17**
tx52507 rm70 (A35) ⇆35 🅼35 B46–98 M8–25
&àlc

At **Küsnacht** (12km S on N17)
★★★★**Ermitage au Lac** Seestr 80 ☎9105222
Plan **9** rm25 ⇆25 Lift 15 Feb–15 Dec Pool Lake

At **Oerlikon** (4km N)
★★**Sternen** Schaffhauserstr 335 ☎467777
Plan **19** tx56999 rm52 ⇆14 🅼18 G Lift
B34–76 M10–25

Zürich Airport
At **Glattbrugg** (8km NE on N4)
★★★★**Airport** Oberhauserstr 30 ☎8104444
Plan **4** tx53287 rm47 ⇆27 🅼20 G Lift
B65–100 M18 Pn101–106 Pool
🅖🚙*Barbieri* Glatthofstr 3 ☎8106601 N🚙

Zweisimmen Bern 1,500 (☎300)
Map **11** B1
★★**Bristol** Bahnhofstr ☎21208 rm32 ⇆1 G
★★**Krone** Lenkstr ☎22626 rm40 ⇆30 🅼6 G
Lift
☆*Sport* Saanenstr ☎21431 rm20 ⇆20

Liechtenstein/hotels & garages

Prices are given in Swiss francs

Bendern (☎075) Map **12** C2
🅖🚙*Auto Center* Landstr 755 ☎32070 N🚙
Maz G10

Schaan 2,300 (☎075) Map **12** C2
★★**Linde** Lindenpl ☎21704 rm25 ⇆5 🅼1
B25–76 M7.50–18
🅖🚙*Fanal* Feldkircherstr 52 ☎24604 N🚙
Chy/Sim

Triesenberg 1,400 (☎075) (5km SE of
Vaduz) Map **12** C1/2
★*Masescha* ☎22337 rm12 G B22–50
M9–20

Vaduz 3,000 (☎075) Map **12** C1/2

☆☆☆*Triesen* ☎22666 rm33 ⇆8 🅼25 G
Apr–Oct
★★**Real** ☎22222 tx77809 rm10 ⇆10 Lift
B60–95 M25–40
★★**Sonnenhof** Marestr ☎21192 rm31 (A12)
⇆31 G Lift 5 Feb–5 Jan B70–185 Pn105–115
Pool
★*Engel* ☎21057 rm19 ⇆9 🅼6 Lift B38–80
Màlc
★*Löwen* Herrengasse ☎21408 rm12 ⇆1🅼1
B24–70 M8.50–20 Pn48–60
🅖🚙24 *Muhlehol 3* Hauptstr 584 ☎21668
AR/Ren G10

Useful words and phrases

This is not meant to be a comprehensive vocabulary and has been compiled specifically for the non-linguist. The AA publication 'Car Components Guide' written in twelve languages, will also prove useful.

English	French	German	Italian	Spanish

Essential information

English	French	German	Italian	Spanish
Please where is the toilet?	S'il vous plaît, où sont les toilettes?	Bitte, wo ist die Toilette?	Per favore, dove sono i gabinetti?	¿Por favor, donde està el WC?
Male	Messieurs Hommes	Herren	Signori Uomini	Caballeros
Female	Dames Femmes	Damen	Signore Donne	Señoras

Route directions

English	French	German	Italian	Spanish
motorway	autoroute	Autobahn	auotostrada	autopista
street; road	rue	Strasse	strada	calle
main road				carretera
left	gauche	links	sinistra	izquierda
right	droite	rechts	destra	derecha
fork; branch; bear	talonnement	Abzweigung	forca di strada	bifurcación
turn	tourner	ein-, abbeigen	voltare	volver; girar; dar la vuelta
forward	tout droit	geradeaus	diretta	todo sequida
crossroads	croisement	Kreuzung	incrocio; croce	cruce; encrucijada
roundabout	sens giratoire	Rondell; Kreisverkehr	giro	giratoria
bridge	pont	Bruecke	ponte	puente
church	église	Kirche	chiesa	iglesia
public house	café; taverne	Gasthaus	osteria	fonda; café; hostería
level crossing	passage à niveau	Bahnuebergang	passaggio a livello	paso a nivel

Greetings

English	French	German	Italian	Spanish
Good morning (afternoon), Sir	Bonjour, monsieur	Guten Morgen, (Guten Tag) (Herr X)	Buon giorno, Signore	Buenos dias, señor
Good evening, Madam	Bonsoir, madame	Guten Abend, (Frau X)	Buona sera, Signora	Buenas noches, señora
Good-bye, Miss X	Au revoir, mademoiselle	Auf Wiedersehen, (Fräulein X)	Arrivederci, Signorina	Hasta la vista, Señorita
Excuse me	Excusez-moi	Entschuldigen Sie	Mi scusi	Dispénseme Vd
If you please	S'il vous plaît	Bitte	Per favore	Hágame Vd el favor
Thank you	Merci	Danke	Grazie	Gracias
Yes. No	Oui. Non	Ja. Nein	Si. No	Si. No

Speaking the language

English	French	German	Italian	Spanish
Do you speak . . . ?	Parlez-vous . . . ?	Sprechen Sie . . . ?	Parla . . . ?	¿Habla Vd . . . ?
I speak . . .	Je parle . . .	Ich spreche . . .	Io parlo . . .	Yo hablo . . .
I do not speak . . .	Je ne parle pas . . .	Ich spreche nicht . . .	Io non parlo . . .	Yo no hablo . . .
French	français	französisch	francese	francés
English	anglais	englisch	inglese	inglés
Spanish	espagnol	spanisch	spagnolo	español
Portuguese	portugais	portugiesisch	portoghese	portugués
German	allemand	deutsch	tedesco	aleman
Italian	italien	italienisch	italiano	italiano
Dutch	hollandais	holländisch	olandese	holandés
Do you understand . . . ?	Comprenez-vous . . . ?	Verstehen Sie . . . ?	Capisce . . . ?	Comprende Vd . . . ?
I do not understand . . .	Je ne comprends pas . . .	Ich verstehe nicht . . .	Non capisce . . .	No comprendo . . .
Speak slowly	Parlez lentement	Sprechen Sie langsam	Parli adagio	Hable Vd despacio
Could you repeat it?	Répétez	Wiederholen Sie	Ripeta	Repita

English	French	German	Italian	Spanish
At the shops				
How much?	Combien?	Wieviel?	Quanto?	¿Cuánto cuesta?
Cheaper	Meilleur marché	Billiger, preiswerter	A miglior prezzo	Lo más barato
Too dear	Trop cher	Zu teuer	Troppo caro	Demasiado caro
One, two, three, four, five, six, seven, eight, nine, ten, eleven, twelve, thirteen, fourteen, fifteen, sixteen, seventeen, eighteen, nineteen, twenty.	Un, deux, trois, quatre, cinq, six, sept, huit, neuf, dix, onz, douze, treize, quatorze, quinze, seize, dix-sept, dix-huit, dix-neuf, vingt.	Eins, zwei, drei, vier, fünf, sechs, sieben, acht, neun, zehn, elf, zwölf, dreizehn, vierzehn, fünfzehn, sechzehn, siebzehn, achtzehn, neunzehn, zwanzig.	Uno, due, tre, quattro, cinque, sei sette, otto, nove, dieci, undici, dodici, tredici, quattordici, quindici, sedici, diciassette, diciotto, diciannove, venti.	Uno, dos, tres, cuatro, cinco, seis, siete, ocho, nueve, diez, once, doce, trece, catorce, quince, diez y seis, diez y siete, diez y ocho, dize y nueve, veinte.

Telling the time

English	French	German	Italian	Spanish
Yesterday	Hier	Gestern	Ieri	Ayer
Yesterday evening	Hier soir	Gestern Abend	Ieri sera	Ayer tarde
Tonight	Cette nuit	Heute Nacht	Questa notte	Esta noche
This morning	Ce matin	Heute Morgen	Questa mattina	Esta mañana
Today	Aujourd'hui	Heute	Oggi	Hoy
This afternoon	Cet après-midi	Heute Nachmittag	Questo pomeriggio	Esta tarde
At noon	A midi	Mittags	A mezzogiorno	A mediodía
At midnight	A minuit	Um Mitternacht	A mezzanotte	A medianoche
This evening	Ce soir	Heute Abend	Questa sera	Esta noche
Tomorrow	Demain	Morgen	Domani	Mañana
Tomorrow morning	Demain matin	Morgen früh	Domani mattina	Mañana por la mañana
Tomorrow evening	Demain soir	Morgen Abend	Domani sera	Mañana por la tarde
The day after tomorrow	Après-demain	Übermorgen	Dopo domani	Pasado mañana
Early. Late	Tôt. Tard	Früh. Spät	Presto. Tardi	Temprano. Tarde
At once	Tout de suite	Sofort	Subito	En seguida
Second (in time)	Seconde	Sekunde	Secondo	Segundo
Minute (in time)	Minute	Minute	Minuto	Minuto
Hour	Heure	Stunde	Ora	Hora
What time is it?	Quelle heure est-il?	Wieviel Uhr ist es?	Che ore sono?	¿Qué hora es?
Monday	Lundi	Montag	Lunedì	Lunes
Tuesday	Mardi	Dienstag	Martedì	Martes
Wednesday	Mercredi	Mittwoch	Mercoledì	Miércoles
Thursday	Jeudi	Donnerstag	Giovedì	Jueves
Friday	Vendredi	Freitag	Venerdì	Viernes
Saturday	Samedi	Samstag	Sabato	Sábado
Sunday	Dimanche	Sonntag	Domenica	Domingo

Dining out

English	French	German	Italian	Spanish
Please show me . . . a good restaurant	Indiquez-moi un bon restaurant	Wollen Sie mir . . . nennen (angeben) ein gutes Restaurant	Mi indichi un buon ristorante	Indíqueme un buen restaurant
What time is . . .	A quelle heure est . . .	Um wieviel Uhr servieren Sie (gibt es)	A che ora é . . . ?	¿A qué hora se sirve . . . ?
breakfast	le petit déjeuner	das Frühstück	la prima colazione	el desayuno
lunch	le déjeuner	das Mittagessen	la colazione	el almuerzo
dinner	le dîner	das Abendessen	il pranzo	la comida
Can you serve me quickly?	pouvez-vous me préparer rapidement à manger?	Können Sie mir schnell etwas zu essen zubereiten?	Può prepararmi presto da mangiare?	¿Puede servirme de prisa?
How much is the meal?	Quel est le prix du repas?	Was kostet die Mahlzeit?	Qual è il prezzo del pasto?	¿Cuánto cuesta el cubierto?
Is the price of drink included?	Boisson comrise?	Ist das Getränk inbegriffen?	Bevanda compresa?	¿Está incluida la bebida?
Show me the menu	Montez-moi le menu?	Zeigen Sie mir das Menü	Mi faccia vedere la lista delle vivande	Muéstreme el menú

308

English	French	German	Italian	Spanish
Give me the wine list	Donnez-moi la carte des vins	Geben Sie mir die Weinkarte	Mi dia la lista dei vini	Déme Vd la lista de vinos
What is the special dish of the region?	Quelle est la spécialité du pays?	Welches ist die hiesige Spezialität?	Qual'è la specialità del paese?	¿ Cuál es el plato especial de la región?

Something to eat

English	French	German	Italian	Spanish
I should like . . .	Je voudrais . . .	Ich möchte . . .	Vorrei . . .	Yo quería . . .
some soup	de la soupe	Suppe	della zuppa, della minestra	Sopa
some clear soup	du bouillon	Fleischbrühe	del brodo	caldo o consomé
some fish	du poisson	Fisch	del pesce	pescado
fried fish	une friture de poisson	Gebratenen Fisch	una frittura di pesce	pescado frito
a lobster	du homard	Hummer	dei gamberi	langosta
some meat	de la viande	Fleisch	della carne	carne
a chop or a cutlet	une côtelette	ein Kotelett	una cotoletta	una chuleta
some veal	du veau	Kalbfleisch	del vitello	ternera
some beef	du boeuf	Rindfleisch	del manzo	vaca
some lamb	du mouton	Hammelfleisch Schafffleisch	dell'agnello	cordero
some pork	du porc	Schweinefleisch	.del maiale	cerdo
some ham	du jambon	Schinken	del prosciutto	jamón
some chicken	du poulet	Huhn	del pollo	pollo
some beefsteak	du beefsteak	Beefsteak	una bistecca	bistek . . .
. . . underdone,	. . . saignant	. . . blutig (englisch)	. . . al sangue	. . . poco pasado
. . . well done	. . . cuit	. . . durch durchgebraten, gar	. . . ben cotta	. . . bien pasado
. . . medium done	. . . à point	. . . halbenglisch	. . . cotta a puntino	. . . a punto
some bread	du pain	Brot	del pane	pan
some butter	du beurre	Butter	del burro	mantequilla
an omelette	une omelette	eine Orhelette	una frittata	una tortilla
a ham omelette	. . . au jambon	eine Schinken- omelette	. . . col prosciutto	. . . con jamón
a mushroom omelette	. . . aux champignons	eine Omelette mit Champignons	. . . coi funghi	de setas
a savoury omelette	. . . aux fines herbes	eine Omelette mit	. . . con verdura	de finas hierbas
a salad	une salade	Salat	. . . una insalata	ensalada
some vegetables	des légumes	Gemüse	dei legumi	legumbres
tomatoes	des tomates	Tomaten	dei pomodori	tomates
some potatoes	des pommes de terre	Kartoffeln	delle patate	patatas
Cabbage	du chou	Kohl	cavolo	coles
Cauliflower	du chou-fleur	Blumenkohl	cavolfiori	coliflores
Green peas	des petits pois	Grüne Erbsen	dei pisellini	guisantes
Beans	des haricots	Bohnen	dei fagiuoli	habichuelas, judías
some salt and pepper	du sel et du poivre	Salz und Pfeffer	del sale e del pepe	sal y pimienta
some oil and vinegar	de l'huile et du vinaigre	Öl und Essig	dell'olio e dell'aceto	aceite y vinagre
some mustard	de la moutarde	Senf, Mostrich	della senape	mostaza
(with) no garlic please	(avec) sans ail, s'il vous plait	(mit) ohne Knob- lauch bitte	per favore (con) senza aglio	por favor (con) sin ajo
Cheeses	Fromages	Käse	Formaggio	Queso
Fruits	Fruits	Früchte	Frutta	Frutas
Biscuits	Biscuits	Biskuits, Kekse	Biscotti	Bizcochos
Tart	Tarte	Torte	Torta	Tarta
Pastries	Pâtisseries	Feines Gebäck	Pasticceria	Pastelería
Chocolate	Du chocolat	Schokolade	Della cioccolata	Chocolate
Ice creams	Glaces	Eis	Gelato	Helados
Lemon	Un citron	Eine Zitrone	Un limone	Un limón
An orange	Une orange	Eine Orange	Un'arancia	Una naranja
Grapes	Du raisin	Weintraube	Dell'uva	Uvas
An apple	Une pomme	Ein Apfel	Una mela	Una manzana
A pear	Une poire	Eine Birne	Una pera	Una pera
A banana	Une banane	Eine Banane	Una banana	Un plátano
Strawberries	des fraises	Erdbeeren	Delle fragole	fresas
Raspberries	des framboises	Himbeeren	Dei lamponi	frambuesas
Cherries	des cerises	Kirschen	Delle ciliegie	cerezas

Something to drink

English	French	German	Italian	Spanish
A bottle	Une bouteille	Eine Flasche	Una bottiglia	Una botella
Half a bottle	Une demi- bouteille	Eine halbe Flasche	Una mezza bottiglia	Media botella
Water	De l'eau	Wasser . . .	Dell'acqua	Aqua
Iced water	. . . glacée	geeistes Wasser	. . . ghiacciata	. . . helada

English	French	German	Italian	Spanish
Hot water	. . . chaude	warmes Wasser	. . . calda	. . . caliente
White wine	Du vin blanc	Weisswein	Del vino bianco	Vino blanco
Red wine	Du vin rouge	Rotwein	Del vino rosso	Vino tinto
Cider	Du cidre	Obstwein, Most	Del sidro	Sidra
Orangeade	De l'orangeade	Orangeade	Una aranciata	Naranjada
Lemonade	De la citronnade	Zitronensaft	Una limonata	Limonada
Beer	De la bière	Bier	Della birra	Cerveza
Mineral water	De l'eau minérale	Mineralwasser	Dell'acqua minerale	Agua mineral
Liqueurs	Des liqueurs	Liköre	Dei liquori	Licores
Coffee	Du café	Kaffee	Del caffè	Café
Tea	Du thé	Tee	Del tè	Té
Milk	Du lait	Milch	Del latte	Leche
Sugar	Du sucre	Zucker	Dello zucchero	Azúcar
Jam	De la confiture	Konfitüre	Della marmellata	Dulce
Cream	De la crème	Sahne	Della panna	Crema

The finale

English	French	German	Italian	Spanish
Waiter! the bill	Garçon! l'addition	Kellner! die Rechnung	Cameriere! Il conto	¿Camarero! la cuenta
Are tips included?	Pourboire compris?	Ist das Trinkgeld inbegriffen?	Mancia compresa?	¿Está incluída la propina?

At the garage

English	French	German	Italian	Spanish
Fill up the tank, please . . .	Faites le plein s'il vous plaît . . .	Füllen Sie den Tank . . .	Mi faccia il pieno . . .	Sírvase llenar el depósito . . .
with petrol	d'essence	mit Benzin	di benzina	de gasolina
with oil	d'huile	mit Öl	d'olio	de aceite
Give me five, ten, twenty, thirty litres of petrol	Mettez-moi cinq, dix, vingt, trente litres d'essence	Geben Sie mir fünf, zehn, zwanzig, dreissig Liter Benzin	Mi metta cinque, dieci, venti, trenta litri di benzina	Póngame cinco, diez, veinte, treinta litros de gasolina
Check the water	Vérifiez l'eau	Sehen Sie bitte das Wasser nach	Verifichi l'acqua	Compruebe el agua
Fill the radiator	Remplissez le radiateur	Füllen Sie den Kühler auf	Riempia il radiatore	Llene el radiador
Have you a can with some water?	Avez-vous un arrosoir avec de l'eau?	Haben Sie eine Kanne mit Wasser?	Avete un innaffiatoio con acqua?	¿Tiene usted una regadera con agua?
Check the tyre-pressure	Vérifiez les pneus	Sehen Sie die Reifen nach	Verifichi le gomme	Compruebe los neumáticos
Wash the windscreen	Lavez le parebrise	Waschen Sie die Windschutzscheibe	Lavi il parabrezza	Lave Vd el parabrisas
I wish to garage my car here; what is the charge per night?	Je désire garer ma voiture ici; quel est le prix par nuit?	Ich möchte meinen Wagen hier einstellen; was kostet das pro Nacht?	Vorrei lasciare qui la mia automobile; quanto costa per notte?	Deseo dejar mi automóvil aquí; ¿cuánto me cobrará por una noche?
Upper cylinder lubricant	Superlubrifiant	Obenschmiermittel	Olio additivo da rodaggio	Superlubricante
I have a puncture; please mend it	J'ai crevé un pneu; veuillez le réparer	Ein Pneu ist geplatzt; bitte reparieren Sie ihn	Ho bucato una gomma; me la ripari	He reventado un neumático; sírvase repararlo
I want . . .	Je désire . . .	Ich wünsche . . .	Vorrei . . .	Deseo . . .
a tyre	un pneu	einen Reifen	una gomma	un neumático
an inner tube	une chambre à air	einen Schlauch	una camera d'aria	una cámara de aire
a sparking plug	une bougie	eine Kerze	una candela	una bujía
Please check (test) the battery	Veuillez vérifier la batterie	Wollen Sie bitte die Batterie nachsehen	Verifichi la batteria	Haga el favor de comprobar la batería
Will you please adjust . . .	Veuillez régler . . .	Wollen Sie bitte . . . einstellen	Regoli . . .	Quiere Vd reglar . . .
the brakes	les freins	die Bremsen	i freni	los frenos
the ignition	l'allumage	die Zündung	l'accensione	el encendido
the steering	la direction	die Steuerung	lo sterzo	la dirección

310

English	French	German	Italian	Spanish
Something is wrong with . . . my car	Quelque chose ne va pas . . . à ma voiture	Es funktioniert etwas nicht . . . an meinem Wagen	Qualche cosa non va . . . alla mia automobile	Hay algo que no va bien . . . en mi coche,
my engine	dans mon moteur	an meinem Motor	nel motore	en mi motor
the clutch	dans le débrayage	an meiner Kupplung	nella frizione (nel disinnesto)	en el embrague
My car won't start	Ma voiture ne démarre pas	Mein Wagen fährt nicht an	La mia automobile non si mette in moto	Mi coche no arranca
The self-starter is faulty	Le démarreur est détraqué	Der Anlasser funktioniert nicht	La messa in moto è guasta	El motor de arranque de mi automóvil está averiado
The windscreen wiper does not work	L'essuie-glace ne fonctionne plus	Der Scheibenwischer funktioniert nicht mehr	Il tergicristallo non funziona più	El limpia-parabrisa no funciona
The carburettor wants adjusting	Le carburateur a besoin d'un réglage	Der Vergaser muss eingestellt werden	Il carburatore deve essere regolato	El carburador precisa un reglaje
The radiator leaking; it must be soldered	Le radiateur a une fuite; il faudrait le ressouder	Der Kühler hat ein Leck (ist undicht) und muss gelötet werden	Il radiatore perde; bisognerebbe saldarlo	El radiador pierde y hay que volverlo a soldar
My engine knocks; will you please look at it?	Mon moteur cogne; veuillez l'examiner	Mein Motor klopft; würden Sie ihn nachsehen?	Il motore batte; lo guardi	Mi motor golpea; sírvase examinarlo
My engine has seized up; will you please repair it	Mon moteur est grippé; réparez-le, s'il vous plaît	Mein Motor sitzt fest; reparieren Sie ihn, bitte	Il mio motore è guasto; lo ripari, per favore	Mi motor está agarrotado; quiere Vd proceder a repararlo
The clutch does not work	L'embrayage ne fonctionne plus	Die Kupplung funktioniert nicht mehr	La frizione non funziona più	El embrague no funciona
The fuses are blown	Les fusibles ont sauté	Die Sicherungen sind durchgebrannt	Le valvole sono saltate	Los fusibles se han quemado
I want some new bulbs	Il me faut des ampoules neuves	Ich brauche neue Birnen	Mi occorrono delle nuove lampadine	Me hacen falta lámparas nuevas
How long will this repair take?	Combien de temps prendra cette réparation?	Wie lange wird diese Reparatur dauern?	Quanto tempo occorre per questa riparazione?	¿Quánto tiempo durará esta reparación?
How much will it cost?	Combien coûtera-t-elle?	Wieviel kostet sie?	Quanto costerà?	¿Cuánto costará?
I wish to hire a car	Je désire louer une automobile . . .	Ich möchte ein Auto . . . mieten	Vorrei noleggiare un'automobile	Deseo alquilar un automóvil
with a driver	avec chauffeur	mit Chauffeur	con autista	con conductor
without a driver	sans chauffeur	ohne Chauffeur	senza autista	sin conductor

At the chemist's

English	French	German	Italian	Spanish
Please make up this prescription	Veuillez préparer cette ordonnance	Wollen Sie bitte dieses Rezept zubereiten	Mi prepari, per favore, questa ricetta	Sírvase prepararme esta receta
How much?	Quel en est le prix?	Was kostet es?	Quanto costa?	¿Cuánto cuesta?
Have you a remedy for . . .	Avez-vous un médicament . . .	Haben Sie eine Arznei . . .	Ha una medicina . . .	¿Tiene Vd un medicamento . . .
a cough?	contre la toux?	gegen Husten	contro la tosse?	para la tos?
a toothache?	contre les maux de dents?	gegen Zahnschmerzen	contro il mal di denti?	para el dolor de muelas?
a headache?	contre les maux de tête?	gegen Kopfschmerzen	contro il mal di testa?	para el dolor de cabeza?
insomnia?	contre l'insomnie?	gegen Schlaflosigkeit	contro l'insonnia?	para el insomnio?
sea-sickness?	contre le mal de mer?	gegen Seekrankheit	contro il mal di mare?	para el mareo?
indigestion?	contre les troubles digestifs?	gegen Verdauungsstörungen,	contro i disturbi digestivi?	para el dolor de estómago?
diarrhoea?	contre les coliques?	gegen Kolik?	contro la colica?	para los cólicos?

English	French	German	Italian	Spanish
I want . . .	J'aimerais . . .	Ich möchte . . .	Vorrei . . .	Desearía . . .
a laxative	un laxatif	ein Abführmittel	un lassativo,	un laxante
a packet of cotton wool	un paquet d'ouate	ein Paket Watte	un pacchetto di ovatta	un paquete de algodón
sanitary towels	des serviettes hygiéniques	Monatsbinden	degli assorbenti igienici	vendas higiénicas
toilet paper	du papier hygiénique	Toilettenpapier	della carta igienica	papel higiénico
razor blades	des lames de rasoir	Rasierklingen	delle lamette da rasoio	hojos de afeitar
sun lotion	un produit anti-solaire	ein Sonnenschutz-mittel	un prodotto anti-solare	un producto antisolar

Metric conversion tables

To convert miles to kilometres, read the appropriate number in the central column as the measurement in miles, and its equivalent in kilometres opposite in the left-hand column. To convert kilometres to miles, read the appropriate number in the central column as the measurement in kilometres, and its equivalent in miles opposite in the right-hand column. Use the tables in similar fashion for other conversions.

Kilometres		Miles	Metres		Feet	Kilograms		Pounds
1.609	1	0.621	0.305	1	3.281	0.454	1	2.205
3.219	2	1.243	0.610	2	6.562	0.907	2	4.409
4.828	3	1.864	0.914	3	9.843	1.361	3	6.614
6.437	4	2.486	1.219	4	13.123	1.814	4	8.818
8.047	5	3.107	1.524	5	16.404	2.268	5	11.023
9.656	6	3.728	1.829	6	19.685	2.722	6	13.228
11.265	7	4.350	2.134	7	22.966	3.175	7	15.432
12.875	8	4.971	2.438	8	26.247	3.629	8	17.637
14.484	9	5.592	2.743	9	29.528	4.082	9	19.842
16.093	10	6.214	3.048	10	32.808	4.536	10	22.046
32.187	20	12.427	6.096	20	65.617	9.072	20	44.092
48.280	30	18.641	9.144	30	98.425	13.608	30	66.139
64.374	40	24.855	12.192	40	131.233	18.144	40	88.185
80.467	50	31.069	15.240	50	164.042	22.680	50	110.231
96.561	60	37.282	18.288	60	196.850	27.216	60	132.277
112.654	70	43.496	21.336	70	229.658	31.751	70	154.324
128.748	80	49.710	24.384	80	262.467	36.287	80	176.370
144.841	90	55.923	27.432	90	295.275	40.823	90	198.416

Kilograms per sq cm		Pounds per sq in	Litres		Gallons	Litres		Pints
0.070	1	14.224	4.546	1	0.220	0.568	1	1.76
0.141	2	28.447	9.092	2	0.440	1.136	2	3.52
0.211	3	42.671	13.638	3	0.660	1.705	3	5.28
0.281	4	56.894	18.184	4	0.880	2.273	4	7.04
0.352	5	71.118	22.730	5	1.100	2.841	5	8.80
0.422	6	85.341	27.276	6	1.320	3.410	6	10.56
0.492	7	99.565	31.822	7	1.540	3.978	7	12.32
0.562	8	113.788	36.368	8	1.760	4.546	8	14.08
0.633	9	128.012	40.914	9	1.980			
0.703	10	142.235	45.460	10	2.200			

Index

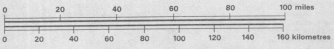

AA Guide to Motoring on the Continent

```
0        20        40        60        80      100 miles
|---------|---------|---------|---------|---------|
0    20    40    60    80    100   120   140   160 kilometres
|-----|-----|-----|-----|-----|-----|-----|-----|
```

SCALE OF ATLAS: 33 MILES TO ONE INCH (APPROX)

Map Legend

Motorway and junction	
Toll motorway	
Motorway under construction	= = = = =
Transit route (GDR)	
Single carriage motorway	
Principal route	
Main road	
Other road	
Mountain road tunnel	}::::::::::::{
Mountain pass	
Mountain railway tunnel connection	+++++++++++++
Road snowbound during winter	
Road number	E4
Distance in kilometres	22
Frontier	
Place with AA hotels, sometimes garages	●
Place with AA listed garage only	◉
Town	○
Hovercraft ferry	Ⓗ
Vehicle ferry	— — Ⓥ OSLO
River and lake	Drava
Canal	
Mountain/Volcano	▲
Overlaps and numbers of continuing pages	6

LONDON

LE HAVRE

BREST

PARI

3

7   8   9

NANTES   CHATEAUR

BORDEAUX

15   16

TOULOUSE

LA CORUNA

BILBAO

17   18   19   20

OPORTO   VALLADOLID   ZARAGOZA

21   22

BARCEL

MADRID

LISBOA

VALENCIA

PALMA

Balearic Is

23   24   25   28

SEVILLA   GRANADA

MALAGA

© The Automobile Association

Key to atlas pages

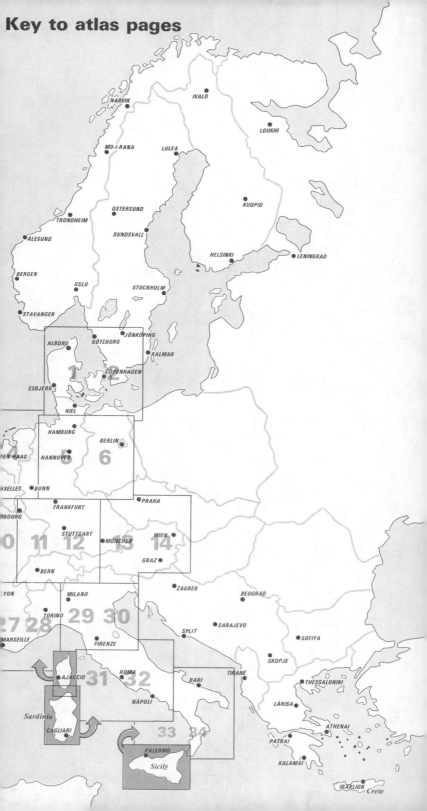

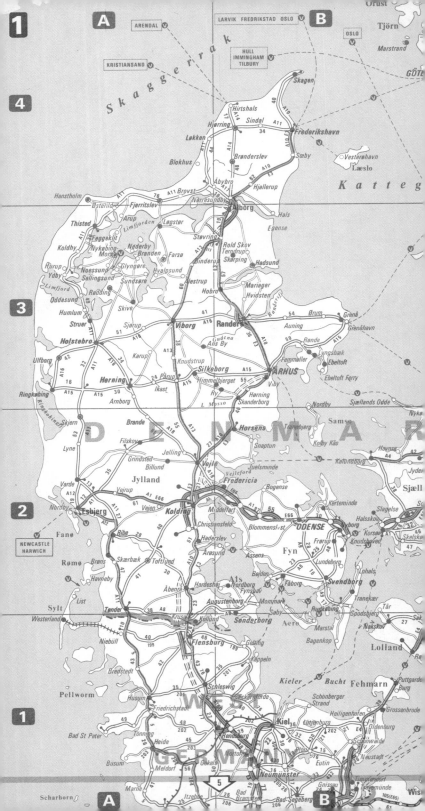

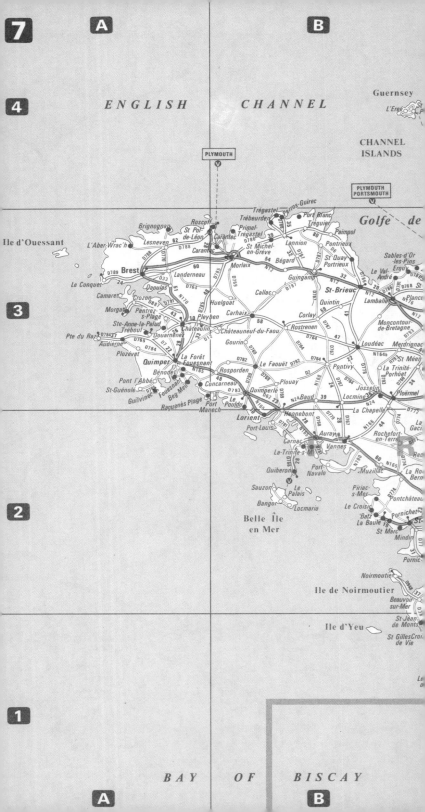

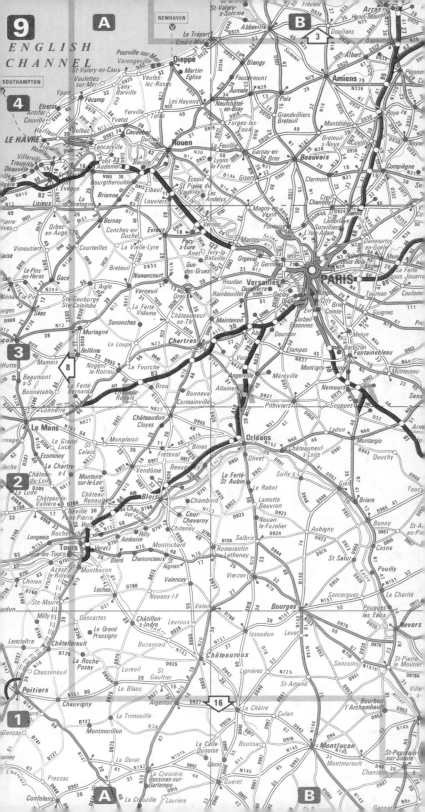

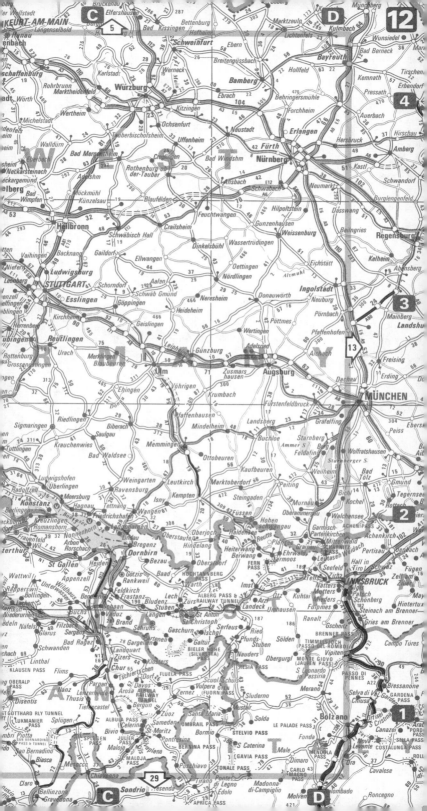

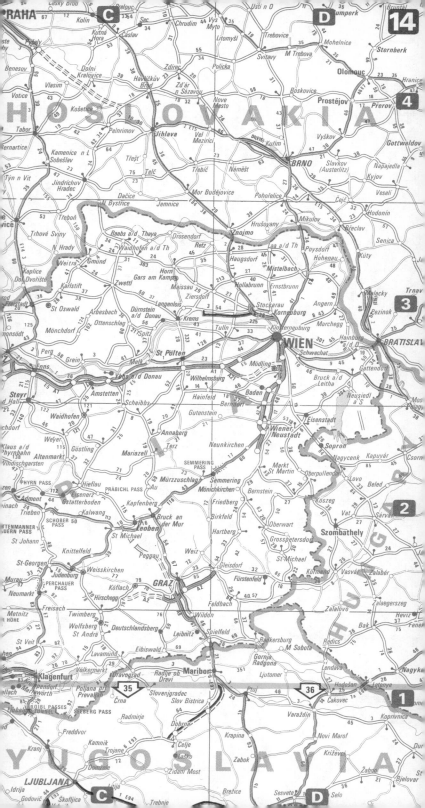

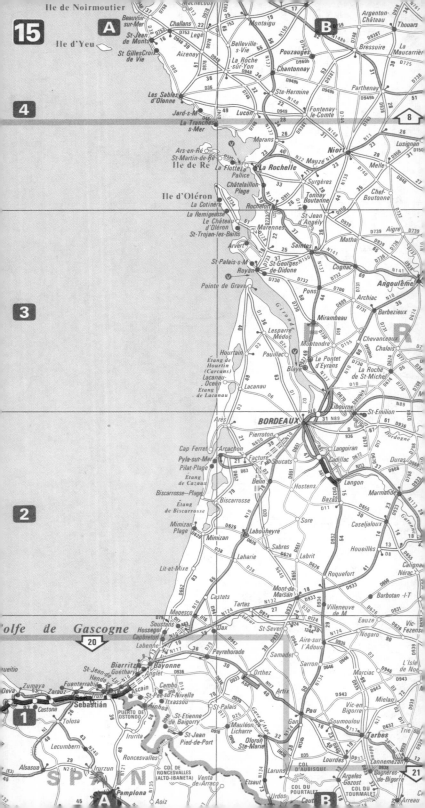

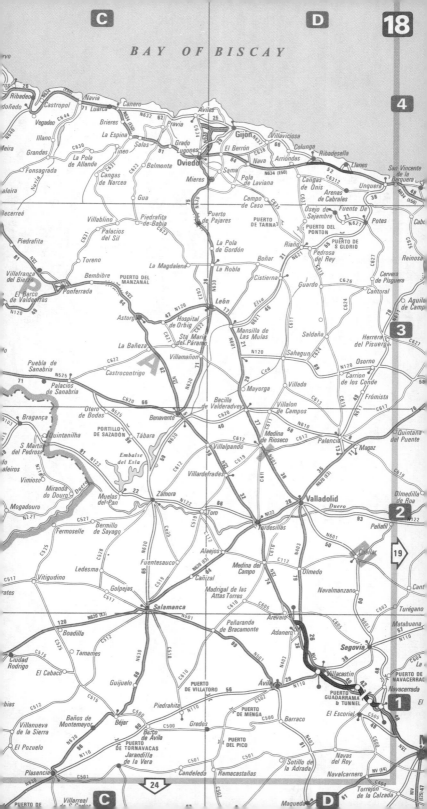

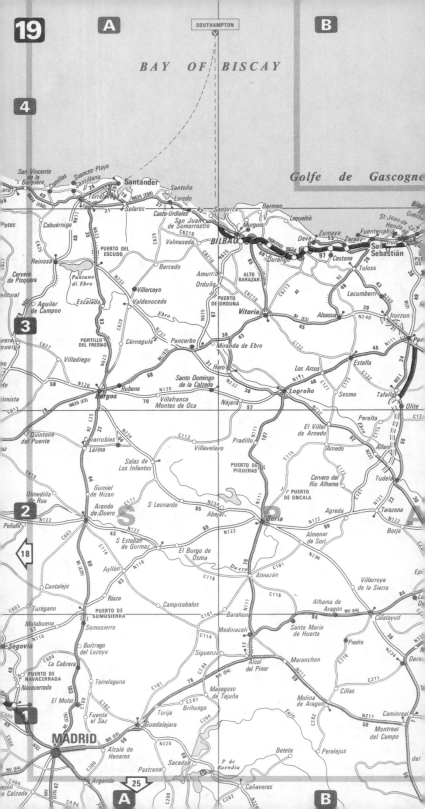

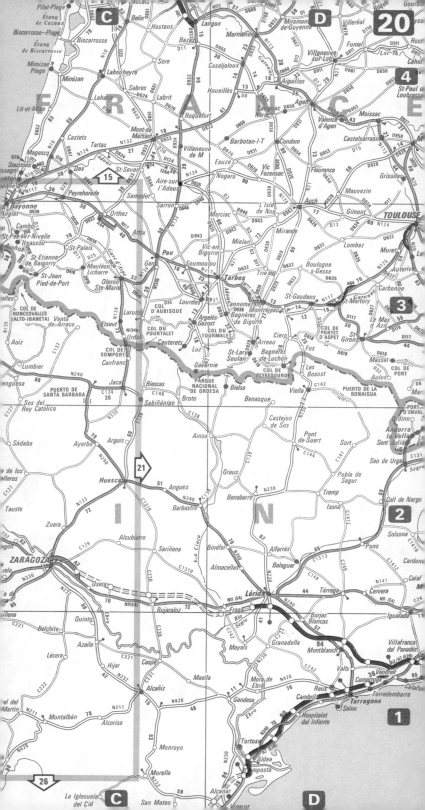

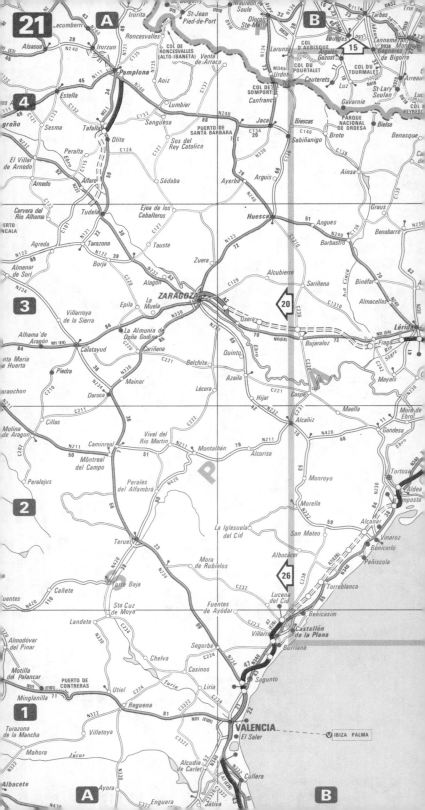

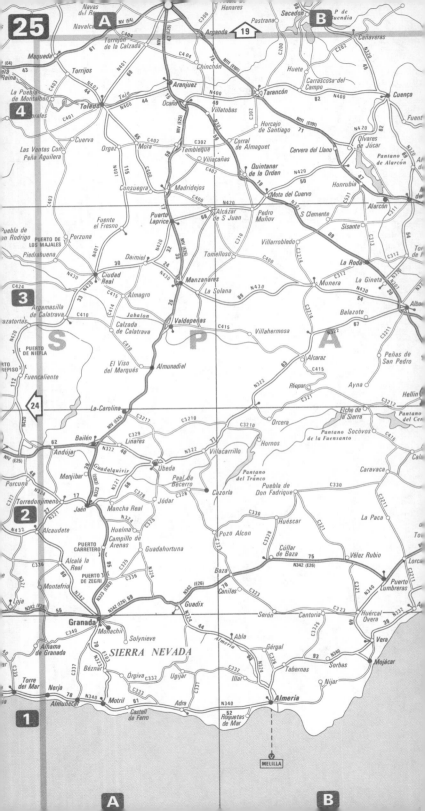

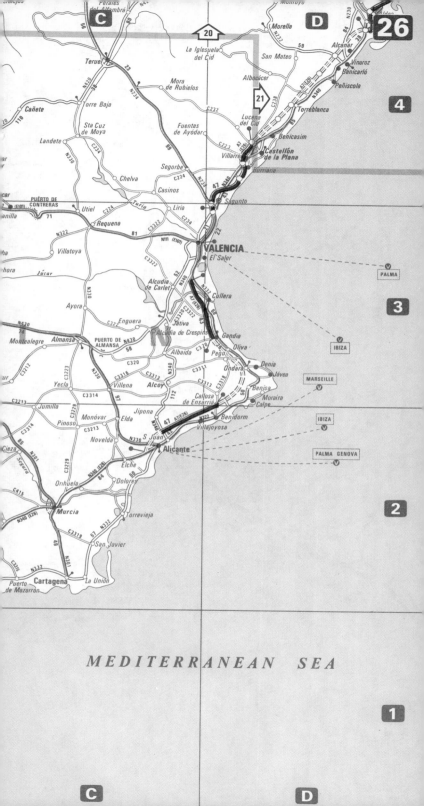

C   20   D   26

La Iglesuela
del Cid
Peñíscola

4

3

PALMA

IBIZA

MARSEILLE

IBIZA

PALMA GENOVA

2

MEDITERRANEAN SEA

1

C   D

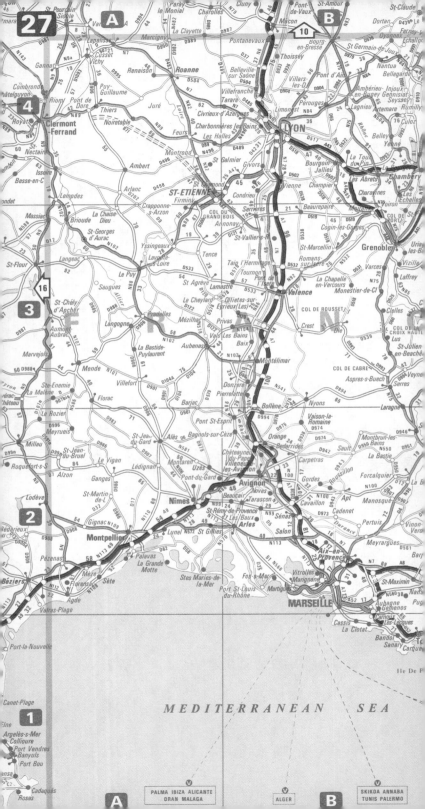

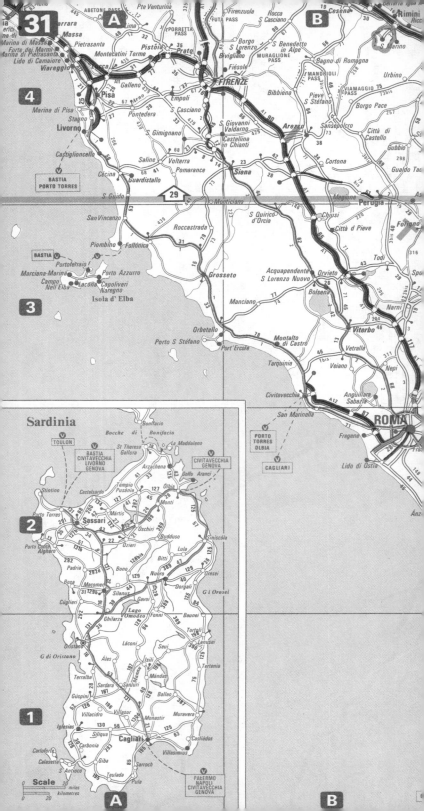

Accommodation report (confidential)

to The Automobile Association,
Hotel & Information Services, Fanum House, Basingstoke,
Hants RG21 2EA.

town, country, hotel

your star rating   location   date of stay

food   rooms

service   sanitary arrangements   value for money

general remarks

town, country, hotel

your star rating   location   date of stay

food   rooms

service   sanitary arrangements   value for money

general remarks

town, country, hotel

your star rating   location   date of stay

food   rooms

service   sanitary arrangements   value for money

general remarks

name (block letters)

address (block letters)

	for office use only
membership no.	acknowledged	recorded

350

Garage report (confidential)

cut along dotted rule

to   The Automobile Association,
Hotel & Information Services, Fanum House, Basingstoke,
Hants RG21 2EA.

town, country, garage

address

telephone no.

agents for   were AIT vouchers   recommended
used for payment

remarks

town, country, garage

address

telephone no.

agents for   were AIT vouchers   recommended
used for payment

remarks

town, country, garage

address

telephone no.

agents for   were AIT vouchers   recommended
used for payment

remarks

name (block letters)

address (block letters)

membership no.	for office use only	
	acknowledged	recorded

351

Road report

to   The Automobile Association,
Overseas Routes,
Fanum House, Basingstoke,
Hants RG21 2EA.

section of road

from   to

passing through   road no.

names shown on signposts

remarks: *ie* surface, width, estimated gradient, description of landscape

section of road

from   to

passing through   road no.

names shown on signposts

remarks: *ie* surface, width, estimated gradient, description of landscape

vehicle used   date of journey

name (block letters)

address (block letters)

| membership no. | for office use only |
| | acknowledged   recorded |